A History of
Modern Europe

A HISTORY OF
MODERN EUROPE

Third Edition
From the Renaissance to the Present

JOHN MERRIMAN
Yale University

W. W. NORTON & COMPANY
New York · London

For Laura Merriman and
Christopher Merriman

Copyright © 2010, 2004, 1996 by John Merriman

All rights reserved
Printed in the United States of America

Editor: Steve Forman
Project editor: Kate Feighery
Production manager, College: Eric Pier-Hocking
Composition: Westchester Book Group
Manufacturing: Courier Companies—Westford division

Library of Congress Cataloging-in-Publication Data

Merriman, John M.
   A history of modern Europe : from the Renaissance to the present / John
Merriman.—3rd ed.
      p. cm.
   Includes bibliographical references and index.
   ISBN: 978-0-393-93433-5 (pbk.)
   1. Europe—History—1492–   I. Title.

D228.M485   2009
940.2'1—dc22   2009027982

W. W. Norton & Company has been independent since its founding in 1923,
when William Warder Norton and Mary D. Herter Norton first published lectures delivered at the People's Institute, the adult education division of New York
City's Cooper Union. The firm soon expanded its program beyond the Institute,
publishing books by celebrated academics from America and abroad. By mid-
century, the two major pillars of Norton's publishing program—trade books and
college texts—were firmly established. In the 1950s, the Norton family transferred control of the company to its employees, and today—with a staff of four
hundred and a comparable number of trade, college, and professional titles published each year—W. W. Norton & Company stands as the largest and oldest
publishing house owned wholly by its employees.

W. W. Norton & Company, Inc., 500 Fifth Avenue, New York, N.Y. 10110
                              www.wwnorton.com

W. W. Norton & Company Ltd., Castle House, 75/76 Wells Street, London
W1T 3QT

   4 5 6 7 8 9 0

CONTENTS

PART THREE NEW CULTURAL AND POLITICAL HORIZONS

PART FIVE THE AGE OF MASS POLITICS

PART SIX CATACLYSM

MAPS

PREFACE

Caught as we are in a global economic crisis, the interconnections of economies, nations, and societies around the world could not be clearer. The ongoing social and cultural turmoil of immigrant communities excluded from the mainstream by the former imperial powers demonstrates that history does not go away: the effects of Europe's imperial ambitions and vast empires, although they no longer exist, remain with us. The relatively recent disappearance in 1989–1992 of a more recent empire, that of the Soviet Union, has also had an enormous impact on Europe, and indeed much of the world, transforming international relations while presenting imposing challenges. Russia, to be sure, remains a major power, but it is commonplace now to consider the United States as the one remaining superpower, with an informal empire stretching across the globe through its great economic, political, and military influence.

Empires have greatly shaped European history since the Renaissance. Trade with Africa, Asia, and the Americas led to colonization and empire. Within Europe, rivalries between empires—such as those of England and Spain in the sixteenth and seventeenth centuries, the Ottoman Turkish Empire and the Austrian Habsburg and Russian Empires, and Britain and France in the eighteenth century—reflected both the consolidation and expansion of state power and also shaped the evolution of warfare. During the first fifteen years of the nineteenth century, Napoleon's empire extended through much of the European continent and led to conquests as far as Egypt.

The rise and fall of empires—Portuguese, Spanish, Dutch, Ottoman, British, French, and that of the Soviet Union—is a major theme developed in the third edition of *A History of Modern Europe*. More than ever, the history of Europe cannot be understood without attention to Europe's interaction with cultures in the rest of the world. Europeans, to be sure, have for centuries learned from Muslim, Asian, African, and American cultures. The influence of the Ottoman Empire in Eastern Europe and the Balkans commands additional attention in this volume. At the same time, through commercial contact, conquest, and intellectual, religious, and political influence, as well as, finally, decolonization, the European powers and cultures have affected the histories of non-Western peoples. The construction of stronger and more efficient states facilitated the development of national identities—consider, for example, the role of the British Empire in the emergence in the eighteenth and nineteenth centuries of the sense of being British, and of the wrenching bewilderment among many Britons when the empire ended after World War II. At the same time, national identities developed in the newly independent states that were once colonies. Reflecting recent scholarship, this third edition describes in greater detail the end of the British Empire in Africa, specifically the bloody story of decolonialization in Kenya.

The third edition emphasizes the dynamism of European trade, settlement, and conquest and their great impact not only on Asia, Africa, and the Americas, but also on the history of European peoples. Comparisons are made between the Spanish Empire in Latin America and the English colonies in the Americas. Unlike the Spanish Empire, trade was the basis of the burgeoning English Empire. The Spanish Empire reflected the combination of the absolutism of the Spanish monarchy and the determination to convert—by force if necessary—the indigenous populations to Catholicism. In sharp contrast, many settlers came to the North American English colonies in search of religious freedom. And, again in contrast to the building of the Spanish Empire a century earlier, the English colonists sought not to convert the indigenous peoples to Christianity, but rather to push them out of colonial areas of settlement. While the Spanish colonies reflected state centralization, their English counterparts evolved in a pattern of decentralization that would culminate in the federalist structure of the United States. British rule in India, particularly interesting because of the cultural interaction that took place there, receives more well-deserved attention. And so does the expansion of Dutch rule in Southeast Asia and the response of China and Japan to the Western powers.

Many of the chapters have been usefully reduced in size. There are other changes, as well. The section on the middle classes has been moved to Chapter 14, "The Industrial Revolution," so that "Liberal Challenges to Restoration Europe" stands alone as Chapter 15. In the twentieth century, Joseph Stalin and Stalinism have been moved from the chapter on "Revolutionary Russia and the Soviet Union" (Chapter 23) to the discussion of the Europe of dictators (Chapter 25). I have amplified the discussion of the National Socialism of the Nazis and fascism as a European-wide phenomenon during the inter-war period. The post–World War II chapters have been reorganized and streamlined. Decolonialization and the Cold War, certainly two of the major occurrences in the decades that followed the war, have been combined in Chapter 28. The final chapter has been shortened and brought up to date.

We move away from the traditional textbook strategy of continually contrasting Western and Eastern Europe. For example, the third edition of *A History of Modern Europe* places the emergence of the concept of political sovereignty not only in early modern England and the Dutch Republic, but also in the Polish-Lithuanian Commonwealth during the early modern period. We offer expanded coverage of the heroic rising of the Jews of the Warsaw ghetto against the Nazis in 1943, and of the Warsaw Uprising little more than a year later. We explore the roots of the economic and political problems that continue to beset Western and Eastern Europe, for example by demonstrating how the simmering ethnic tensions that burst into bloody civil war in Bosnia after the disintegration of Yugoslavia echoed the quarrels that eroded the stately Habsburg monarchy a century earlier.

The third edition draws on exciting studies in the social history of ideas, approaches that stand at the intersection of intellectual, social, and cultural history. Volume 1 explains how artistic patronage during the Renaissance and the Golden Age of Dutch culture reveals some of the social foundations of art. Recent studies on the family economy, village and neighborhood life, and the changing structure of work have all enriched this book's account of the transformation of European society from an overwhelmingly peasant society into an increasingly urban and industrial world. The account of the emergence of mass politics in the nineteenth century draws on recent studies of popular culture and the symbolism and power of language.

We retain a narrative framework with the goals of both analyzing the central themes of the European experience and telling a story. Each chapter can be read as part of a larger, interconnected story. Moreover, this book stresses the dynamics of economic, social, political, and cultural change, but within the context of the amazing diversity of Europe. The history of modern Europe and its influence in the world presents extraordinary characters, well known and little known. The text brings the past to life, presenting portraits of men and women who have played major roles in European history: religious reformers such as Martin Luther and Jean Calvin; Queen Elizabeth I, who solidified the English throne, and Maria Theresa, who preserved the Habsburg monarchy; King Louis XIV of France and Tsar Peter the Great, two monarchs whose reigns exemplified the absolute state; great thinkers like Kepler and Voltaire; Napoleon, heir to the French Revolution, but also in some ways a despot in the tradition of absolute rulers, and perhaps even an originator of total war. Inevitably, we discuss the monstrous Adolf Hitler, examining the sources of his growing popularity in Germany in the wake of World War I, and Joseph Stalin, discussing his Communist state and murderous purges. But ordinary men and women have also played a significant role in Europe's story, making their own histories. This book thus evokes the lives of both leaders and ordinary people in periods of rapid economic and political change, revolution, and war.

The growth of strong, centralized states helped shape modern Europe. Medieval Europe was a maze of overlapping political and judicial authorities. In 1500, virtually all Europeans defined themselves in terms of family, village, town, neighborhood, and religious solidarities. Over the next three centuries, dynastic states consolidated and extended their territories while increasing the reach of their effective authority over their own people. Portugal, Spain, England (and later as Great Britain), France, the Netherlands, and Russia built vast empires that reached into other continents. The European Great Powers emerged. With the rise of nationalism in the wake of the French Revolution and the Napoleonic era, demands of ethnic groups for national states encouraged the unification of Italy and Germany and stirred unrest among Croats, Hungarians, and Romanians, who were anxious for their own national states. Ordinary people demanded freedom and political sovereignty, with revolution both a reflection of and a motor for political change. The emergence of liberalism in the nineteenth century and the quest for democratic political structures and mass politics have transformed Europe, beginning in Western Europe. Even the autocracies of Russia and Central and Eastern Europe were not immune to change, and there the quest for democracy still continues.

While discussing dynastic rivalries and nationalism, the book also considers how wars themselves have often generated political and social change. French financial and military contributions to the American War of Independence further accentuated the financial crisis of the monarchy of France, helping to spark the French Revolution. French armies of military conscripts that replaced the professional armies of the age of aristocracy contributed to the emergence of nationalism in Britain and France in the eighteenth century. The defeat of the Russian army by the Japanese in 1905 brought political concessions that helped prepare the way for the Russian Revolution of 1917. The German, Austro-Hungarian, Ottoman, and Russian Empires disappeared in the wake of World War I and World War II; the economic and social impact of these wars generated political instability, facilitating the emergence of fascism and communism. World War I and the role played by colonized peoples gave impetus to movements for independence within the British, French, and Dutch Empires that would ultimately be successful, transforming the world in which we live.

Like politics, religion has also been a significant factor in the lives of Europeans and, at times, in the quest for freedom in the modern world. Catholicism was a unifying force in the Middle Ages; for centuries European popular culture was based on religious belief. Imperial missionaries carried their religions into Africa and Asia in the aggressive quest for converts. Spanish conquerors forced indigenous populations in the Americas to convert to Christianity. Religion has also been a frequently divisive force in modern European history; after the Reformation in the sixteenth century, states extended their authority over religion, while religious minorities demanded the right to practice their own religion. Religious (as well as racial and cultural) intolerance has scarred the European experience, ranging from the expulsion of Jews and Muslims from Spain at the end of the fifteenth century, to Louis XIV's abrogation of religious toleration for Protestants during the seventeenth century, to the horror of the Nazi Holocaust during World War II. Religious conflict in Northern Ireland and the bloody civil war and atrocities perpetuated in Bosnia in the 1990s recall the ravaging of Central Europe during the Thirty Years' War.

The causes and effects of economic change are another thread that weaves through the history of modern Europe. The expansion of commerce in the early modern period, which owed much to the development of the means of raising investment capital and obtaining credit, transformed life in both Western and Eastern Europe, and directly led to the European empires that followed. The Industrial Revolution, which began in England in the eighteenth century and spread to continental Europe in the nineteenth, depended on a rise in population and thus of agricultural production, but also manifested significant continuities with the past. As important as were inventions, the Industrial Revolution also drew on technology that had been in place for centuries. It ultimately changed the ways Europeans worked and lived. Here, too, European empires are an important, fascinating part of the story.

European history remains crucial to understanding the contemporary world. The political, religious, economic, and global concerns that affect Europe and the world today can best be addressed by examining their roots and development. Globalization has carried movement between the continents to new levels. For centuries, Europe sent waves of emigrants to other parts of the world, particularly North and South America. Now the pattern has been reversed. The arrival of millions of migrants from other continents, particularly Africa and Asia, has posed challenges to European states and Europeans. Moreover, the poverty of some of the states of Eastern Europe and the Balkans, and the tragic events in Bosnia in the 1990s, have increased immigration into Western European countries. Immigrants have added to the religious and cultural complexity of European states. As globalization continues to transform Europe and the world, it becomes even more important and exciting to study the continent's history. With the initiation of a new single currency within most of the member states of the European Union and the continued expansion of that organization, Europe has entered a new era, even as a daunting global economic crisis and the threat of terror in the post-9/11 world present some unprecedented challenges. This third edition enhances our understanding of Europe and the world today, as we contemplate not only the distressing failures and appalling tragedies of the past, but also the exhilarating triumphs that have been part of the European experience.

ACKNOWLEDGMENTS

Charles Tilly died during the time I was working on the third edition of *A History of Modern Europe*. His friends, colleagues, and former students—I am all three—miss him very much. He taught me that it is better not to see history as a series of bins that one opens and then shuts before getting on to the next topic, but rather to look for the big news, the major themes, that have been the dynamics of change and provide revealing continuities, even amid astonishing change. At the same time, he believed in keeping ordinary people fully in view by analyzing, describing, and evoking their histories.

I remain indebted to many colleagues and friends who shared their knowledge, expertise, and suggestions with me, including David Underdown, Laura King, Richard Brodhead, Daniel Orlovsky, Mark Steinberg, John Lynn, Mark Micale, Linda Colley, Roberto González-Echevarria, Ivo Banac, Vincent Moncrief, Laura Engelstein, Geoffrey Parker, David Marshall, David Bell, and my late friend Robin Winks. I also want to thank Jeffrey Burds, Harold Selesky, Leslie Page Moch, Richard Stites, David Cannadine, Jim Boyden, Paul Hanson, Michael Burns, Ivan Marcus, Thomas Kaiser, Christopher Johnson, Louise Tilly, Paul Monod, Judy Coffin, Mark Lawrence, John Sweets, Harold Nelson, Kathleen Nilan, Henry Hyder, Jim McClain, Alan Forrest, Martin Ultee, George Behlmer, Mary O'Neal, Mary Jo Maynes, Thomas Head, Jonathan Dewald, Johan Åhr, Margaret McLane, Jan Albers, Martha Hoffman-Strock, Tom Maulucci, Michael Levin, Daryl Lee, Max Oberfus, and my dear friend Peter McPhee. I am particularly grateful to Joel Mokyr for his many helpful suggestions. Special thanks also to Jeffrey Brooks, Eric Jennings, Christopher Reid, and Aristotle Kallis. I also greatly appreciate suggestions given by Doron Ben-Atar, Robert Brown, Alexander Ganse, Bradley Woodworth, David Goldfrank, Adel Allouche, Leon Plantagna, Michael Sibalis, James McMillan, Steven Wheatcroft, Rachel Fuchs, Kenneth Loiselle, and Maya Jasanoff.

For the third edition, my thanks to Elinor Accampo (University of Southern California), Paul Freedman (Yale University), Wayne te Brake (Purchase College), Timothy Snyder (Yale University), Anders Winroth (Yale University),

Andrew Devenney (Central Michigan University), Nicholas Murray (Adirondack Community College), Paul Deslandes (University of Vermont), Alex Porter, Zech Jonathan, Anne Riegert (Université de Rouen), Sven Wanegffelen (Université de Rouen), Steven Pincus (Yale University), Carol Merriman, Lindsay O'Neill (University of Southern California), Charles Beem (Michigan State University), Brian McClure (Michigan State University), Charles Keith (Michigan State University), Valerie Hansen (Yale University), Paul Bushkovitch (Yale University), Charles-Édouard Levillain (University de Lille), Robert Schwartz (Mount Holyoke College), Jay Winter (Yale University), Sarah Cameron (Yale University), Keith Wrightson (Yale University), Francesca Trivellato (Yale University), Steve Sawyer (American University of Paris), Steven Englund (American University of Paris), Michael Driedger (Brock University), Charles Lansing (University of Connecticut), Brian Peterson (Union College), Michael Mahoney (Yale University), Chuck Walton (Yale University), David Large (Montana State University), Frank Snowden (Yale University), Daniel Brückenhaus (Yale University), Jonathan Sperber (University of Missouri), and especially to Piotr Wandycz (Yale University), Victoria Johnson (University of Michigan), Christine Brouwer (Yale University), Michael Galgano (James Madison University), Bruno Cabanes (Yale University), and Gary Shanafelt (McMurry University). The third edition benefited greatly from conferences organized by the Civic Space Institute at the Larzowski School of Law and Commerce in Warsaw. Thanks to my colleagues and friends Andrzej Kaminski (Georgetown University and the Larzowski School of Law and Commerce), Jim Collins (Georgetown University), Wojciech Falkowski (University of Warsaw), Krzysztof Lazarski (Larzowski School of Law and Commerce), Daria Nałęcz (Larzowski School of Law and Commerce), Randy Roberts (Purdue University), Gabor Agoston (Georgetown University), Ashley Dodge, and Ted Weeks (University of Southern Illinois).

I have the greatest admiration for W. W. Norton, which remains a very special independent publisher. My friend Donald Lamm, former chairman of the board and former president of Norton, has always embodied the best in publishing. He and Steve Forman, a wonderful editor and valued friend, first proposed this project to me. Alan Cameron in London's Norton office has long provided support. Sandy Lifland's deft and patient work as developmental editor contributed greatly to the first edition. Sarah England, then Steve's assistant and now an editor at Norton, was extremely helpful throughout the preparation of the second edition, and Kate Feighery and JoAnn Simony were for the third edition. A special thanks to Carol Merriman, who has patiently lived with and encouraged this and other projects for many wonderful years.

The third edition of A History of Modern Europe is dedicated to Laura Merriman and to Christopher Merriman, with much love.

Balazuc (Ardèche),
March 5, 2009

A History of
Modern Europe

PART ONE

FOUNDATIONS

As Europe emerged from the Middle Ages, a dynamic era of trade, statebuilding, and global discovery began that would for centuries affect the lives of rich and poor alike, not only in Europe but across the oceans as well. Spanish and Portuguese conquerors and merchants expanding their trade routes laid the foundations for the first transoceanic European empires. During the Italian Renaissance, which lasted from about 1330 to 1530, humanists rediscovered texts from classical Greece and Rome. Renaissance artists and scholars celebrated the beauty of nature and the dignity of mankind, helping shape the intellectual and cultural history of the modern world. Moreover, after a period when almost all of Western Europe adhered to Roman Catholicism, abuses in the Church would lead to cries for reform that would not be stilled until most of Europe was divided between Protestants and Catholics. By 1540, the Reformation had carved out large zones of Protestant allegiance in central and northern Europe, as well as in England and parts of France. Religious conflict and wars would tear Europe apart, leading to reform in the Church but leaving permanent religious divisions where once there had been near-uniformity of belief and worship.

CHAPTER 1

MEDIEVAL LEGACIES AND TRANSFORMING DISCOVERIES

Jacob Fugger (1455–1525) was one of the sons of a weaver who settled in the southern German town of Augsburg. At age fourteen, he joined his brothers as a trader in spices, silks, and woolen goods. He traded, above all, with the Adriatic port of Venice, where he learned double-entry book-keeping (keeping track of business credits and debits), which was then unknown in the German states. Jacob Fugger amassed a vast fortune, and he began to loan sizable sums to various rulers in Central Europe. Fugger's name soon became known "in every kingdom and every region, even among the heathens. Emperors, kings, princes, and lords sent emissaries to him; the pope hailed him and embraced him as his own dear son; the cardinals stood up when he appeared." When asked if he wanted to retire, Jacob Fugger replied that he intended to go on making money until he dropped dead.

The family history of the Fuggers intersected with economic growth and statemaking in Central Europe. The Fuggers emerged as the wealthiest and most influential of the international banking families that financed warring states, answering the call of the highest bidder. In 1519, the Fuggers helped Charles V become Holy Roman emperor by providing funds with which the scheming Habsburg could bribe the princes who were electors to vote for him. The Fuggers raised and transported the money that made possible imperial foreign policy. Loaning money to ambitious rulers, as well as to popes and military entrepreneurs, the Fugger family rose to princely status and facilitated the consolidation of territorial states and the emergence of a dynamic economy not only in the Mediterranean region but also in the German states and northwestern Europe by helping merchants and manufacturers find credit for their enterprises.

The growth of trade and manufacturing ultimately changed the face of Europe. The expanding economy contributed to a sense that many Europeans

3

(*Left*) Jacob Fugger, merchant-banker and creditor of rulers and popes, traded with the port of Seville (*right*), a stepping-off point for colonization of the New World.

had in 1500 of living in a period of rebirth and revitalization. In Italy, the cultural movement we know as the Renaissance was still in bloom, and it was spreading along trade routes across the Alps into northern Europe (see Chapter 2). The by-products of trade and exploration were an increasing exchange of ideas and a growing interconnectedness among European states.

Although famine, disease, and war (the horsemen of the apocalypse) still trampled their victims across Europe, significant improvements in the standard of living occurred. The European population rose in the late fifteenth century and continued to rise throughout the sixteenth century. Europe's population stood at about 70 million in 1500 and around 90 million in 1600 (well less than a third of that today). These gains overcame the horrific loss of one-third of the European population to the Black Death (the bubonic plague) in the mid-fourteenth century. The expansion of the population revived European commerce, particularly in the Mediterranean region and in England and northwestern Europe, where the Fuggers and other merchant-bankers were financing new industry and trade. Towns multiplied and their merchants grew more prosperous, building elegant houses near markets.

The pace of change was quickened by several inventions that would help shape the emergence of the modern world. Gunpowder, first used in China and adopted by Europeans in the fourteenth century, made warfare more deadly, gradually eliminating the heavily armed knight. The invention of the printing press in the mid-fifteenth century engendered a cultural revolution first felt in religious life, with the Bible and other religious texts now more widely available to be read, discussed, and debated. The compass, first used to determine direction by Chinese and Mediterranean navigators in the eleventh or twelfth century, now helped guide European exploration across the oceans.

Spanish and Portuguese conquerors and merchants seeking riches in the New World established the first European transoceanic empires. Population growth; the growth of trade and manufacturing, which facilitated the exchange of ideas and gradually increased the standard of living; the use of gunpowder and the compass; and the development of printing all stimulated and facilitated the establishment of colonies across the oceans by the European powers.

MEDIEVAL CONTINUITIES

England and France emerged as sovereign states, standing as exceptions amid the territorial fragmentation that characterized medieval Europe. Smaller territories also began to coalesce into larger units and rulers consolidated and extended their authority. European society took on the shape it would have for centuries, with three orders—clergy, nobles, and peasants—standing in relationships of mutual obligation to each other. Material well-being remained at a subsistence level for most peasants but nonetheless improved overall as commercial trade across greater distances began to rise in the eleventh century. Moreover, small-scale textile manufacturing developed as towns grew, particularly in Italy and northwestern Europe during the twelfth and thirteenth centuries.

The Fragmentation of Europe

With the end of the Roman Empire in the fifth century, Europe experienced an influx of new peoples. From the east came the Magyars (Hungarians), who settled in Central Europe, where they were converted to Christianity. From Scandinavia came the so-called Northmen (Norse or Vikings), who reached Ukraine, and who for the most part became Christians. Arabs invaded Europe in the eighth century, subsequently expanding their influence into North Africa, as well as Spain. Mongols poured into what is now Russia and Ukraine, sacking Kiev in the 1230s, before their empire began to collapse in the fifteenth century. The princely state of Muscovy, which had been one of their tributaries, gradually expanded in size, reaching the southern Ural Mountains and the Caspian Sea and emerging as a dynastic state. This multitude of influences contributed to both the political and cultural fragmentation of Europe.

In 1500, Europe was a maze of about 1,500 fragmented states. Economic, political, and judicial institutions were overwhelmingly local. Territories and cities were subject to a confused array of overlapping jurisdictions. The city-states of Italy and the trading towns of northern Germany managed to preserve their independence from territorial rulers. The town walls that protected residents against bandits and disease (during times of plague and epidemics) stood also as symbols of urban privileges. Paris, for example, was dotted with enclaves of ecclesiastical authority.

Part of Europe's fragmentation was due to its three systems of law: civil, canon, and customary. The legal concepts, principles, and procedures of civil law evolved from Roman law, which was based on the rational interpretation of written law applied to human affairs. Civil laws were decreed and thereby sanctioned by rulers, whose authority stemmed in part from their right to make or impose laws. The development of civil law, then, was conducive to the development of sovereign states by closely associating the power of rulers of states with the force of law. Canon law, established by the pope for the Western Church, codified in Latin the canons of Church councils and the revealed authorities of the Bible and Church fathers. As with civil law, canon law helped affirm, at least in principle, the authority of spiritual rulers—the popes, cardinals, and bishops—by closely linking the law to the authority of the rulers in general, whose subjects owed them personal allegiance.

Yet, to be sure, in the late Middle Ages, cross-cutting allegiances—the most common being to both secular and ecclesiastical authorities—were often the norm. Subjects of competing authorities used the system to exploit jurisdictional conflicts to their own ends, whenever possible. This sometimes served to reinforce the influence of multiple authorities. Thus, the effective authority of rulers could end up being rather distant.

Customary, or common law, was a codification of established custom, implying a constant reference to decisions taken earlier by judges. It was the usual mode of law in all areas where Roman law was not used. In Western Europe, customary law developed out of the customs of feudalism (see below), a set of reciprocal economic, social, and political relationships that encouraged decentralized power structures.

In England, where common law unified the customary law for the whole land, laws were overseen by local courts, which contributed to the decentralization of English royal authority. Unlike Roman law, which helped shape the sense that the ruler was a sovereign lawgiver who could override custom, customary law helped corporate groups (such as guilds, which were craft associations) or individuals assert their interests and rights by establishing precedents that, at least in principle, could override the ruler's intervention in the legal process.

Europe's political fragmentation was accompanied by cultural fragmentation, reinforced by the many languages spoken. Latin, the language of culture, was still spoken in university towns—thus the "Latin Quarter" in Paris. Distances and difficulties in travel and communication were also imposing. It sometimes took months for mail to arrive. The shortest time to travel from Madrid to Venice was twenty-two days, and the longest, in bad weather, was four times that.

At the Crossroads of Cultures

Europe stood at the crossroads between civilizations and religions (see Map 1.1). After the collapse of the Roman Empire, Christendom had been split between the Roman Catholic Church and the Eastern Orthodox Church following the Great Schism between the two churches in 1054. The claim by the bishop of Rome—the pope—to authority over all Eastern Christians (as well as a festering doctrinal dispute over the nature of the Holy Trinity) led to the break, culminating in the pope's excommunication of the patriarch of Constantinople. By 1500, the Eastern Orthodox Church held the allegiance of most of the people in Russia and the Balkans. The Roman Catholic and Orthodox worlds met in the eastern part of Central Europe, with Poland, Bohemia, and Hungary looking to the West.

Christianity, as an alternate source of allegiance and power claiming to be a universal state (with its own language, Latin), presented a potential impediment to state authority. It also provided a common culture that engulfed much of Europe. As both the Church and the monarchies became more centralized, conflict between them became inevitable. The Church itself had been a centralized religious authority since the end of the Roman Empire, which left the papacy in Rome independent of secular rule. After the middle of the eleventh century, the popes were elected by the Church cardinals, each of whom had been appointed by a previous pope. Bishops and abbots pledged obedience to the pope in return for tenure over abbey lands and ecclesiastical revenues.

In the Ottoman Empire, religious and political sovereignty rested in the same person, the sultan. In contrast, rulers of territorial states in Europe had succeeded in making themselves largely autonomous from Church authority. Although the Church was wealthy and powerful (owning about 25 percent of the land of Catalonia and Castile and perhaps 65 percent in southern Italy), princes were unwilling to let the Church interfere with their authority, even though ecclesiastical leaders in many cases had crowned them. During the fourteenth and fifteenth centuries, rulers refused to allow ecclesiastical courts in their territories. The pope commanded his bishops and other clergy to be loyal to the rulers of secular states.

During the medieval period, Western Christians attempted to win back lands conquered by Muslims, especially seeking to recapture Jerusalem. The first of eight "Crusades" that lasted to 1270 began in 1095. In 1204, believing the Eastern Orthodox religion to be heresy, the Crusaders conquered the Eastern Orthodox Byzantine Empire, which had extended from eastern Italy to the Black Sea's eastern end. In the mid-fourteenth century, the Ottoman Turks conquered two-thirds of Anatolia, much of the Balkan Peninsula, and Greece. By 1400, Islam stretched from southern Spain and North Africa all the way to northern India and beyond to islands in Southeast Asia. During the fourteenth and early fifteenth centuries, the Byzantine Empire (which was Greek in culture and Eastern Orthodox Christian in religion) was

MAP 1.1 THE OTTOMAN EMPIRE, c. 1500

AUSTRIA

HUNGARY

MOLDAVIA

WALLACHIA

BOSNA

SERBIA

RUMELI

NAPLES

SICILY

ADRIATIC SEA

SEA OF AZOV

BLACK SEA

AEGEAN SEA

CRETE

MEDITERRANEAN SEA

ANADOLU

Constantinople

KARAMAN

DULKADIR

PERSIA

EGYPT

CYPRUS

Ottoman Empire, 1503

0

0

250 miles

250 kilometers

reduced to a small area straddling the straits between Asia and Europe, which included its capital, Constantinople (modern Istanbul). Finally, the Ottoman Turks captured Constantinople after a lengthy siege in 1453, the final act of the decline of the Byzantine Empire. During the next four decades, the Ottomans doubled their European territory, conquering Serbia in 1459, Bosnia in 1463, Albania in 1479, and Herzogovina in 1483. The addition of Hungary extended the Ottoman Empire to the Danube River.

The Ottoman Turks possessed a large army—much of it recruited from converts to Islam, notably the infantry (the janissaries)—and a strong navy. Effective diplomacy complemented military strength. During the first half of the sixteenth century, the Ottomans also absorbed Egypt and moved into Iran, reaching Baghdad in what is now Iraq in 1534, and then the Persian Gulf. This was the apogee of the Ottoman Empire, which made use of loyal elites at the local level to bring in the revenues that financed the state. For the next several centuries, Roman Catholic Europe would view Islam as a perpetual threat to its religion and culture. Yet a sizable majority of the myriad populations the Ottoman Turks ruled remained Christian and were allowed to continue to practice their religion. Despite the existence of a common Islamic high culture, the Islamic Ottoman Turks accepted non-Muslims in their empire, and the latter always represented a significant majority of the population. In contrast, Christian states systematically persecuted and expelled Muslims. For centuries, Western writers outdid each other in describing the Ottoman Turks as "the scourge of God," barbaric, despotic, and cruel. However, the Russian Orthodox Church (which was greatly influenced by its Byzantine heritage), Greek Orthodox Church (also an Eastern Orthodox Church), Roman Catholic Church, and the Islamic religion coexisted remarkably well in the Balkans under Ottoman Turkish rule. The Ottomans established the *millet* system, which allowed autonomy for religious minorities, with leaders of religious communities appointed by the sultan.

Much of Europe thus confronted a huge semicircle of states under direct or indirect Turkish control. The Western powers, which had launched Christian crusades against the Muslims, now were forced into a series of defensive wars against Islam, which to the West was embodied by the Ottoman Empire. To aid in their defense, the Venetians constructed a series of fortifications along the Adriatic coast.

The Structure of Society

Medieval society was roughly divided into three social groups: the clergy, who prayed and cared for souls; nobles, who governed and fought; and peasants, who labored in the fields. Burghers, town residents whose entrepreneurial activity made possible the economic dynamism of medieval Europe between 1000 and 1350, were, despite their increasing importance, outside this classical typology.

The clergy had many roles, serving as priests, teachers, judges, nurses, landlords, and chaplains. But they could only be tried in ecclesiastical courts, and, in the evolution of the modern state, their status as a group apart would come into question. The secular clergy (that is, priests who did not belong to a specific religious order) ministered to the population as a whole. Most of the secular clergy were as poor as their parishioners, but bishops generally were from noble families. The regular clergy included hundreds of thousands of monks and nuns living in monasteries and convents according to strict religious rules, cut off from the outside world by their vows (and in some places legally considered dead).

Nobles owned most of the land, with their status and income stemming from this, as well as from their military functions. Noble titles connoted superiority of birth, and noble families usually intermarried. Nobles were not supposed to work but were to stand ready to defend their monarch and the interests and honor of their families.

Peasants, who made up about 85 percent of the population of Europe in 1500, lived in villages or in small settlements on the lands of nobles, dependent on the latter for protection in exchange for labor. Peasants had no legal status, with the exception of those (for the most part in Western Europe) who owned land. In some places, they were considered barely better than animals by the lords who oppressed them and the clergy who told them their lot in life was to suffer in anticipation of heavenly rewards.

Villages or, within towns, parishes formed the universe of most Europeans. Local solidarities took precedence over those to the rulers of states, whose effective reach in many places remained quite limited. Many villages were, for all intents and purposes, virtually self-governing; village councils decided which crops would be planted on common land and set the date

The poor man, the artisan, and the lord in the late fifteenth century. Note the subservient role of women and children in each family.

plowing was to begin. Such councils coexisted with the seigneurial authority of lords.

At least a fifth of the European population lived in dire poverty. For ordinary laborers, three-quarters of their earnings went to purchase food. Towns and cities were crowded with poor people struggling to get by. A pope complained of vagrants in Rome "who fill with their groans and cries not only public places and private houses but the churches themselves; they provoke alarms and incidents; they roam like brute beasts with no other care than the search for food." The poor wandered everywhere their feet could carry them, finding work where they could, sometimes begging, sometimes stealing. Acts of charity, encouraged by the Catholic Church, which viewed such acts as essential for salvation, helped many poor people survive. But while poor beggars from within communities were tolerated and sometimes given assistance, townspeople and villagers alike feared the poor outsider, particularly gypsies. Banditry was pervasive most everywhere, for example, between Venetian and Turkish territory, between the Papal States and the Kingdom of Naples, and in the Pyrenees Mountains. The story of Robin Hood, the thirteenth-century English bandit and popular hero alleged to have stolen from the rich to give to the poor, had its continental counterparts.

Feudalism

Feudalism developed during the ninth and tenth centuries in response to the collapse of the authority of territorial rulers. Between about A.D. 980 and 1030, law and order broke down in much of Europe, and violence became the norm. This unstable period was characterized by warfare between clans and between territorial lords, attended by retinues of armed men, as well as the ravages of predatory bands. The power structure (king, lords, vassals, and peasants) that emerged in feudal times was a reaction against the anarchy and instability of earlier years. Feudalism also should be seen in the context of an overwhelmingly agricultural economy, where rulers and lords retained great estates.

Despite an increase in the power of great lords, there remained a crucial difference between a king and a lord. Kings were anointed by the ecclesiastical authority in a sacred rite, and therefore claimed to rule "by the grace of God" even when they were incapable of coercing the great lords and their families. The mighty lords imposed obligations of loyalty and military service on "vassals." Their vassals received, in exchange, protection and the use of lands (called fiefs) to which, at least in principle, the lords retained rights. The heirs of vassals would inherit the same conditions, although a vassal had to pay the lord a fee upon inheriting an estate. Vassals agreed to fight for their lord for a certain number of days a year and to ransom the lord if he were captured. For their part, lords adjudicated disputes between vassals. Vassals could join together to oppose a king who failed to meet his

In this Italian miniature from 1492, a vassal kneels to formally certify his allegiance to his lord and cement their mutual obligations to each other.

obligations; likewise, a king or lord could punish a vassal who neglected his obligations to his lord. Elaborate ceremonies featuring solemn oaths, sworn before God and blessed by churchmen, specified the mutual obligations of lord and vassal. "You are mine," a powerful lord in Aquitaine in what is now southwestern France reminded a vassal, "to do my will." Thus, feudalism was a system in which the more powerful extracted revenue or services from the less powerful, with the peasantry, at the bottom of social hierarchy, the weakest of them all.

Feudalism finally waned in the monarchical states in the late fourteenth century with the emergence of stronger state structures, as well as the reimposition of the authority of the Roman Catholic Church in much of Europe. Thus, feudal relationships dissolved as the strength of rulers increased and the independence of nobles declined in stronger states. Royal courts gradually usurped the judicial authority of nobles (although in some places not entirely). Furthermore, the development of a money economy (payment in gold or silver, or in coins minted by rulers) increasingly made feudal relationships obsolete. One sign of this was the shift to cash payment by peasants to lords, instead of payment in services, crops, or animals.

The Black Death of the mid-fourteenth century also helped sound the death knell of feudalism in Western Europe by killing off one-third to one-half of the population (see "A Rising Population," p. 19). As wages rose because of a shortage of labor, peasants were able to improve their legal status. The plague had also killed many lords. When lords tried to reimpose feudal relationships, some spectacular rebellions occurred. Resentment against royal troops (along with the imposition of new taxes) contributed to peasant rebellions in Flanders (1323–1328), northern France (the Jacquerie of 1358), and the Peasants' Revolt in England in 1381. There was also unrest among the urban poor, as ordinary people resisted attempts to return to the way things were before. States took advantage of the chaos by assessing new taxes, such as the hearth tax (a tax on households). By increasing their authority, the monarchies of Western Europe gradually brought the feudal era to a close.

A Subsistence Economy

Agriculture lay at the base of the European economy, in which the ownership of land was the principal determinant of status. Peasants were constantly engaged in a protracted and, more often than not, losing battle against nature. Much land was of poor quality, including hilly and rocky terrain or marshland that could not be farmed. In most of Europe, small plots, poor and exhausted soil, and traditional farming techniques limited yields. Steep slopes had to be cleared and terraced by hand. Peasants plowed with hand "swing" plows. Furthermore, villages held some land in common, originally granted by lords. This was economically wasteful, but for centuries common land offered the landless poor a necessary resource for survival. And under the best of circumstances, peasants had to save about one-fifth to one-eighth of their seed for replanting the following year.

Peasants owed their lords most of what they produced. Peasants also had to pay part of what meager benefits they managed to extract from the land to lords, by virtue of the latter's status and ownership of land. Lords increasingly found it more advantageous to rent out plots of land, and gradually many commuted labor services to cash, which they spent on goods, including luxuries, available at expanding markets and fairs. These included silk, cotton, and some spices that traders brought from the Levant (countries bordering on the eastern Mediterranean). Peasants (like other social groups) also had to tithe (give 10 percent of their revenue) to the Church. These tithes had traditionally been in-kind, but they were increasingly monetized during the late Middle Ages. In a fundamentally subsistence economy, this left the rural poor—that is, most families—with little on which to get by.

Yet even with the rise in population, lords in the thirteenth century had faced frequent shortages of labor and were forced to grant favorable terms to peasants. Many peasants in Western Europe succeeded in purchasing their freedom, transforming their obligations into rents paid to the lords. Nonetheless, even free peasants still had to pay feudal dues to lords and fees for the right to mill grain, brew beer, or bake bread, monopolies that the lords retained.

Serfdom began to disappear in France and southern England in the twelfth century. Rulers had reason to encourage the movement toward a free peasantry in Western Europe, because free peasants could be taxed, whereas serfs—who were legally attached to the land they worked—were entirely dependent on the lords who owned the land. In Western Europe, the free peasantry reflected the growth in the authority of rulers and a relative decline in that of nobles. In the West, most peasant holdings were increasingly protected by civic law or by custom.

Pieter Bruegel the Elder: *The Peasants' Wedding* (1568). On that special day, they would probably eat as well as they ever would.

In contrast to the emergence of a free peasantry in the West, most peasants in Eastern and Central Europe lost their freedom during the sixteenth century, forced to become serfs as landowners sought to assure themselves of a stable labor supply. This in itself was a sign that nobles there were carving out territorial domination virtually independent from that of kings and other rulers, as in Poland.

Many people were constantly on the move in Europe. Free peasants moved toward the frontiers of Europe in search of land, which they brought under cultivation. Peddlers, artisans, and agricultural laborers traveled great distances in search of work. Shepherds led their sheep from the plains to summer pastures at higher elevations, and then back down in the fall (transhumance). Hundreds of thousands of rural people also migrated seasonally from the Pyrenees, Alps, and other mountainous regions to undertake construction work in towns, or to follow the harvests. Roads were also full of vagabonds and beggars.

Most poor families survived by eating bread and not much else. For peasants, meat was something that lords and burghers ate, fruit was rare, and vegetables were poor; rye bread, soup, and perhaps peas, cabbage, and beans were the staples of the peasant's diet, depending on the region. In southern France, grain made from chestnuts served as the bread of the poor. The Mediterranean lands produced olives and wine, as well as wheat.

Beer was limited to northern Europe, particularly the German states, England, and Scandinavia.

Agricultural growth, which had been steady until the beginning of the fourteenth century, slowed down until the mid-fifteenth century in the wake of the Black Death. But once the population began to grow again, plots that had been abandoned were plowed once more. In regions of relatively fertile land, the "three-field system" became more common. This left about a third of all land fallow (unplanted) in order to replenish its fertility during the growing season. This mode of agricultural production necessitated relatively sizable landholdings, and thus could not be used on small peasant plots. But over the long run it increased agricultural yields. Yet this did not necessarily aid the peasant family, because dependency on a seigneur could force them to give more attention to cultivation in the interest of the lord, leaving less time to supplement the family economy by hunting, fishing, or looking after livestock. Overall, however, farming techniques and tools improved during the fifteenth century. Innovations such as the use of mills and metal harvesting implements were introduced, although not adopted in some places until much later. These methods would remain basically the same until the nineteenth century.

Free peasants contributed to the rise in agricultural production. Not all peasants were desperately poor. Many could survive (and a minority did quite well) when famine, disease, and war left them alone, selling in the nearest market what produce they had left over after replanting and obligations to lords and the Church had been paid up for that year.

The medieval innovation of the three-field system allowed for the renewal of one field by leaving it fallow for a season.

The growth in the European population during the medieval period depended on these modest increases in agricultural yields. Some lords became market-oriented farmers in response to increased population. This in itself increased agricultural production. In England, Flanders, northern France, and Sicily (as well as North Africa), grain was intensively cultivated for the market. Urban growth encouraged cash-crop farming, enriching nearby landlords, merchants, and wealthy peasants. Prosperous agriculture was to be found in the rich valley of the Po River in central Italy, the plains of Valencia in Spain, and the Beauce, between the Loire River and Paris. Landowners brought more land under cultivation, cleared forests, drained marshes and swamps, and where possible, irrigated arid fields.

Religion and Popular Culture

Religion played an enormous part in the lives of Europeans in the Middle Ages. Christianity shaped a general system of belief and values that defined the way most people viewed themselves and the world in which they lived. The Church, its faith and learning preserved during the so-called Dark Ages before the medieval period, viewed itself as a unifying force in Europe. This gave the clergy great prestige and moral authority as distributors of the sacraments (above all, penance, the forgiveness of sins), without which Christians believed that salvation could not be achieved. When preachers passed through villages, the faithful waited long into the night to have their confessions heard. One of Europe's most traveled routes took pilgrims from many countries to the shrine of Santiago de Compostela in northwestern Castile (Spain). The Church blessed oaths of fealty (loyalty) sworn by vassals to lords and rulers, and it took an important role in the rites of passage (birth, marriage, death). The Italian Renaissance (see Chapter 2), to be sure, would rediscover the dignity of humanity, but did so within the context of Christian belief.

Religious themes and subjects permeated virtually all medieval art and music. In the twelfth century, magnificent Gothic cathedrals began to be built. The construction of these colossal churches often lasted as long as a century, absorbing enormous resources, and paid for by gifts, large and small, from people of all walks of life. Church bells tolled the hours (clocks would remain novelties until the end of the sixteenth century) and called people to Mass.

Western Christendom was interlocked with Western civilization, although Muslim and Jewish heritages remained strong in Spain and Turkish-controlled areas. Jews remained outcasts, although in general they did not live apart from the Christian population until the fifteenth century, when they were forced to do so by civil and ecclesiastical authorities. The popes forced Jews in Rome to wear distinctive badges; Venice established the first Jewish "ghetto" in 1516. Many Jews, forbidden to enter certain trades, were forced to wander in search of towns where they could live in relative peace.

Storytellers, both amateur and professional, kept oral traditions of popular culture alive at a time when most people were illiterate. Accomplished storytellers passed on their tales during evening gatherings, when villagers, principally women, gathered together to mend garments, tell stories, and keep warm. Many of these stories and tales reflected the fatalism of societies in which most people died relatively young.

Most people believed in magic and the presence of the supernatural on earth. By such views, sorcerers or saints could intervene between people and the bad luck that might befall them. Primitive healers were believed to stand between disease and survival. People believed that rubbing certain saints' images could bring good fortune. When the wine harvest failed in some parts of France, villagers whipped statues of the saints that had failed them. Superstitions abounded. In some places it was believed that it was a good sign to encounter a wolf, deer, or bear, that a stork landing on a house assured its occupants of wealth and longevity, that meeting a white-robed monk in the morning was a bad omen and a black-robed one a good one, that a crow cawing over the house of someone sick meant death was on its way, and that a magpie announced a cure. In the Balkans, garlic was believed to ward off evil. Such beliefs helped peasants cope with a world in which droughts, harvest failures, accidents, and myriad fatal illnesses could bring personal and family catastrophe. "Cunning folk" and witches were believed by many to determine earthly events. A "cunning man" might discover the identity of a thief by placing papers with names inside little clay balls; the guilty party's name would be the first to unravel inside a bucket of water.

A village festival.

Religious holidays and festivals interspersed the calendar year, still governed by the agricultural calendar. At the beginning of Lent in some places in Western Europe, frolicking young men carried torches of blazing straw through the village to ensure agricultural and sexual fertility. Carnival was the highlight of the year for most people in early modern Europe. People ate and drank as at no other time, tossing flour, eggs, and fruit at each other and playing games. Carnival also stood the world on its head, if only briefly. The poor acted out the misdeeds of the wealthy in elaborate plays. Ordinary people could poke fun at the powerful in elaborately staged farces and parades by spoofing the behavior of judges, nobles, and clergymen.

The Emergence of Early Modern Europe

The late Middle Ages brought significant economic, social, and political changes that shaped the emergence of early modern Europe. Following the devastation of the Black Death in the fourteenth century, Europe's population slowly revived and then grew. More land was brought into cultivation, providing a greater supply of food. Yet the balance between life and death remained precarious; famine, disease, and war still intervened frequently to check population growth.

However, the continent's trade and manufacturing developed rapidly, particularly in the Mediterranean region (especially the Italian city-states) and in northwestern Europe. Prosperous banking families provided capital for traders and manufacturers, as they did for states, and basic mechanisms for the transfer of credit evolved. Trade with Asia and the Middle East developed at a rapid pace, catching up with the amount of trade Europeans carried out with the Muslim world. Towns grew in size, and their merchants became more prosperous, reflecting the importance of trade and textile manufacturing on urban growth. As they grew richer, some merchant families purchased land and noble titles. Merchants became important figures in every state. Many nobles resented the new status of these commoners, believing the old saying, "The king could make a nobleman, but not a gentleman." The growing prosperity of the entrepreneurial elite of many towns in Western Europe reflected their relative independence from territorial rulers. One of the characteristics of this independent status was the proliferation of guilds and other organizations that reflected a more dynamic economy.

Yet some aspects of the modern state system were already in place. During the period from 1350 to 1450, the rulers of France, Spain, England, Scotland, Denmark, Norway, Sweden, and Hungary consolidated and extended their authority over their territories, eroding the domains of feudal lords and ecclesiastical authorities. The Iberian Peninsula was divided between Castile and Aragon—joined through the marriage of Queen Isabella and King Ferdinand in 1469, forming contemporary Spain—and Portugal, the borders of which have not changed since the late Middle Ages. The basic layout of three Scandinavian states already existed. And important states of East Central and Central Europe (Hungary, Bohemia, and Poland-Lithuania, a confederation created in 1386 and which early in the sixteenth century extended from the Baltic to the Black Sea), were already reasonably well defined. Even the Swiss cantonal federation had emerged. Most of the small territorial fragments lay in the German states or Italy.

A Rising Population

Europe's population had almost doubled between 1000 and 1300, rising from about 40 million to about 75 million people. But early in the fourteenth century, the population began to decline, probably because of rampant disease. Then, in the middle of the century, the Black Death ravaged Europe, killing between a third and half of the European population. Spread by fleas carried by rats, the bubonic plague reached Constantinople from Asia in 1347. Within three years, it had torn through Europe. Victims died horrible deaths, some in a few days, others lingering in agony. Some villages were completely abandoned, as people tried to flee the path of the scourge. In vain, states and cities tried frantically to prevent the arrival of travelers, fearful that they carried plague with them.

For the next century, births and deaths remained balanced (with higher mortality rates in cities wiping out increased births in the countryside). Europe only began to recover during the second half of the fifteenth century, thanks to a lull in epidemics and the absence of destructive wars. However, the population did not reach the level it had been at in 1300 until about 1550, when it began to rise rapidly, particularly in northern Europe (see Table 1.1).

Europeans remained perpetually vulnerable to disease and disaster. The bubonic plague was the worst of epidemics, but influenza, typhus, malaria, typhoid, and smallpox also carried off many people, particularly the poor, who invariably suffered from inadequate nutrition. Moreover, Europeans looked to the heavens not only in prayer but also to watch for the bad weather that could ruin harvests, including storms that brought flooding. Famine still devastated regularly, a natural disaster that checked population growth, killing off infants, children, and old people in the greatest numbers. "Nothing new here," a Roman wrote in the mid-sixteenth century, "except that people are dying of hunger."

Life for most people was short. Life expectancy, once one had made it out of infancy and childhood alive, was about forty years. Women lived longer than men, but many of them died during childbirth. About a fifth of all babies born died before they reached their first birthday. Of 100 children born, less than half lived to age twenty and only about a fifth celebrated a fortieth birthday. Christ, who died at age thirty-three, was not considered to have died young.

TABLE 1.1 THE EUROPEAN POPULATION IN THE SIXTEENTH AND
SEVENTEENTH CENTURIES (IN MILLIONS)

	1500	1600
Spain and Portugal	9.3	11.3
Italian states	10.5	13.3
France	16.4	18.5
Low Countries*	1.9	2.9
British Isles	4.4	6.8
Scandinavia	1.5	2.4
German states	12.0	15.0
Switzerland	0.8	1.0
Balkans	7.0	8.0
Poland	3.5	5.0
Russia	9.0	15.5

*Currently Belgium, the Netherlands, and Luxembourg.
Source: Richard Mackenney, *Sixteenth-Century Europe: Expansion and Conflict* (New York: Macmillan, 1993), p. 51.

The balance between life and death was precarious. In most towns, deaths outnumbered births almost every year. Prosperous families had more children than the poor (the opposite pattern of today). The exposure and abandonment of newly born infants was common. Furthermore, couples may have limited births through sexual abstinence. The fact that one partner often died prematurely also served as a check on population. So too did relatively late marriage. Most English men married at between twenty-six and twenty-nine years of age, women between twenty-four and twenty-six years.

The choice of a marriage partner was important for economic reasons (although in parts of Western Europe, up to a fifth of women never married). Marriages were often arranged—parents played a major and often determining role in choosing partners for their children. For families of means, particularly nobles, the promise of a sizable dowry counted for much. Yet some evidence suggests that by the end of the sixteenth century, at least in England, the inclinations of the bride and groom were sometimes difficult to ignore. For the poor, marriage could offer the chance of improving one's situation. Thus, a young woman whose family could provide a dowry, however modest, or who had a skill, was an attractive prospective spouse, as was a young man with a trade.

Wives remained legally subservient to their husbands, although in the "economy of makeshifts" in the poor household their role as managers of income and as workers gave them some minimal degree of equality. Sexual infidelity, while common, ran against the grain of a popular sense of justice, which placed a premium on loyalty and mutual obligation between marriage partners. Such liaisons might also jeopardize the system of inheritance and the protection of family property by leading to the appearance of unanticipated offspring, in an age when contraceptive techniques were rudimentary and not well known. Still, about a fifth of English brides were pregnant at the time of their wedding, as sexual relations between couples expecting to marry were very common.

Kinship and village solidarities defined the lives of ordinary people. In some places, extended families were common; that is, parents and sometimes other relatives lived with couples. In some places, such as England, the nuclear family (a couple and their children) was the most common household. When children of the lower classes began their working lives—usually at the age of fourteen or fifteen, or earlier for some apprentices—their obligations to their parents did not end. Often, however, they left home in search of work, rarely, if ever, to return. The poor turned to family and neighbors for help in bad times, as well as for help with harvests, if they owned land.

An Expanding Economy

One of the hallmarks of medieval society had been the marked expansion of trade and manufacture that began in the eleventh century. During the twelfth and thirteenth centuries, merchants greatly increased the amount of products carried on land routes and in the low galley-ships that hugged the Mediterranean coastline, more confident than ever before that their goods would find purchasers. In the markets of Flanders and northern France, olive oil, fruit, and wine from the Mediterranean region were exchanged for timber, cereals, and salted herring.

With the expansion in commercial activity, a money economy slowly developed. Yet trade and barter remained important, particularly for peasants, most of whom were part of a subsistence economy. Currency still did not penetrate some mountainous regions.

Yet overall, the late Middle Ages brought a significant rise in the availability of credit to states and entrepreneurs. Banking families in Venice and other Italian city-states were already well-established in the thirteenth century. Some merchants were no longer itinerant travelers, but rather sedentary entrepreneurs able to raise capital, such as from borrowing from banking families or other merchants or moneylenders, and extend and obtain credit. They also developed bills of exchange (see Chapter 5), which were orders drawn upon an agent to pay another merchant money at a future date, perhaps in another country and in another currency. Here and there, merchants began to work on a commission basis, and some specialized in transporting goods. They began to keep registers of profits and losses, using double-entry bookkeeping. All these changes facilitated a commercial boom in the sixteenth century, even if the multiplicity of states and the tolls between and within them hindered commerce.

The sixteenth century also brought a marked increase in basic manufacturing, which in some regions may have multiplied by 500 percent. The

Bankers sitting behind their *banco* (counter) doing
business.

extraction of iron, copper, and silver quadrupled, for example, in Central
Europe. Large-scale production, however, was limited to mining and textiles, as well as to arms manufacturing and shipbuilding.

The production of textiles, whether for distant markets or local consumption, dominated the manufacturing economy. Techniques for the production of silk had been imported from China into Europe by Arabs in the
tenth century. First centered in the Italian states, production spread during the second half of the fifteenth century across the Alps to the German
states, France, and Spain, which no longer depended on imported silk
from Persia and Asia.

The manufacture of cloth developed in Tuscany, northern France, Flanders, and the Netherlands. The woolens industry of Flanders, which had
begun during the medieval period, boomed, centered in the towns of Ypres,
Ghent, and Bruges. England, which continued to export wool to the continent, became a major producer of woolen goods in the fourteenth century.
Antwerp emerged as Europe's first important center of international trade.

Urban merchants and artisans were organized into guilds, which regulated production and distribution, thus protecting, at least in principle, guild
members and consumers. The structure of craft production was organized
hierarchically. Apprentices who learned their craft became journeymen and,
if all went well, could eventually become masters, joining a masters' guild
and employing journeymen and training apprentices. Most cloth was finished in towns by craft artisans. Through the guilds, masters could preserve
the quality of work within their particular trades and, at the same time, the
reputations of their town. During the fourteenth and fifteenth centuries, it
became increasingly difficult for journeymen to become independent master
craftsmen. Early in the sixteenth century, some German journeymen refused
to work for masters who paid them less than they desired or had been used
to receiving.

In the cottage (domestic) industry, merchant-capitalists put out spinning, weaving, and other work into the countryside. Here a woman is spinning in her home.

Some craftsmen worked outside the walls of cities or in the countryside to avoid guild monopolies and specifications on wages and piece rates. Likewise, merchant-capitalists who owned raw materials put out spinning, weaving (sometimes renting out looms), and other work into the country-side, where labor was cheaper. Rural production spread rapidly in northern Italy, the Netherlands, northern France, and England between 1450 and 1550. Hundreds of thousands of peasants produced woolen or linen yarn or wove it into cloth; then urban workers dyed, bleached, or shrunk the cloth, which merchants then sold. This "cottage industry" (also sometimes called "domestic industry") would remain an important part of the manu-facturing process well into the nineteenth century.

The Growth of Towns

During the twelfth and thirteenth centuries, European towns grew rapidly in both number and size, reflecting economic development and increased security in medieval Europe. Fortified stone ramparts, gates, and towers gave towns unique visible characteristics. Towns were the residence of most courts (including municipal courts), hospitals, and fraternal associations, such as religious confraternities and guilds. Town halls and churches were the cornerstones of the medieval towns. In addition to the "bourgeois" or "burghers" (townspeople), most towns had a relatively large number of clergy living within their walls, ministering to the needs of the population or living a cloistered existence in convents and monasteries.

Most major towns in Europe were founded before 1300. In Poland, about 200 new towns were created between 1450 and 1550, adding to the 450 already in existence. Northern Italy and the Low Countries had the densest networks of towns. However, even there town dwellers remained a relatively small minority of the population, no more than about 15 percent. In 1500 only about 6 percent of Europeans resided in towns of more than 10,000 people. In the German states, about 200 of 3,000 towns had more than 10,000 residents. Only Constantinople, Naples, Milan, Paris, and Venice had more than 100,000 inhabitants.

In Italy, Venice, Florence, Genoa, Milan, and Pisa became independent city-states in about 1100, establishing control over surrounding smaller towns and villages. The decline of the Byzantine Empire and the inability of the Holy Roman Empire to establish its authority throughout Italy prevented the development of large territorial states on the peninsula. The prosperity of the city-states, too, impeded the creation of a single state, or even two or three major ones. Freed of feudal overlords, the dynamism of these city-states underlay the Renaissance (see Chapter 2). Venetian and Genoese merchants sent trading fleets carrying goods to and from the Levant and beyond, as well as along the spice routes to Central Asia, India, and China (visited by the Italian adventurer Marco Polo during his long voyage from 1275 to 1292).

In northern Europe, as well, the growth of cities and towns was linked to the expansion of long-distance trade and commerce. In northern Germany, independent trading towns were enriched by the Baltic grain trade, as Polish landowners, like their Hungarian and Bohemian counterparts, exported grain to the Netherlands and other Western countries. Lübeck and Hamburg with other northern German trading cities formed the Hanseatic League, which at first was a federation established to defend against banditry. These towns began to thrive in the mid-twelfth century, establishing networks of trade that reached from London all the way to Novgorod in northwestern Russia. The Polish Baltic port of Gdańsk had its own currency, fleet, army, and diplomats. Likewise, towns in southern Germany formed leagues to resist territorial lords and to protect trade routes. The fairs held outside the towns of Champagne in northern France, as well as in Lyon and Beaucaire farther south on the Rhône, served as trading points between northern Europe and Mediterranean merchants. The market function of trading towns swelled their populations. Landowners, particularly in regions of commercialized agriculture, sold their produce in the town markets.

Medieval Europe boasted major urban centers of learning. Paris (theology), Montpellier (medicine), and Bologna (Roman law) were major university centers. Oxford and Cambridge Universities were founded in the thirteenth century. Universities existed not in the sense that we know them today. Rather, the term referred to a corporately organized body of students or masters in one town. By 1500, dozens of towns had universities. And, in turn, literacy (limited to a small proportion of the population) rose faster in towns than in the countryside, as the equivalent of secondary education—limited to a privileged few—shifted from rural monasteries to town church or grammar schools.

Town governments were dominated by oligarchies of rich merchants, guild masters, and property owners (in Italian towns, nobles were part of these oligarchies). Despite the fact that many peasants still lived in towns, working fields outside town walls during the day and returning home before the gates slammed shut at nightfall, town and country seemed in some ways worlds apart.

Municipal Liberties

In feudal Europe, towns stood as zones of freedom, because their residents were not, in most cases, bound by service obligations to lords. Contemporaries held that "town air makes [one] free." No town person in Western Europe could be a serf. Urban freedoms had to be obtained from lords, however. Towns purchased charters of exemption from taxes in exchange for payments. Urban oligarchs jealously guarded this municipal independence against nobles and rulers eager to attain revenue and political consolidation. In some cases, rulers actively sought alliances with towns against nobles. Towns could also loan money to kings waging war against recalcitrant vassals or other rulers, including popes. Where territorial rulers were weak, as in Italy and the German states, towns obtained the greatest degree of freedom. Towns developed less rapidly in areas where rulers and nobles exercised strong authority.

Traditions of municipal liberties would leave a significant heritage in Western Europe, ultimately shaping the emergence of constitutional forms of government. Whereas social relationships in the countryside were largely defined by personal obligations, in towns these were replaced by collective rights through guilds and other associations. In England, northern France, the Netherlands, Flanders, and Switzerland, urban medieval confraternities struggled to maintain their independence from rulers and rural nobles. Lacking the associational infrastructure of many towns in Western Europe, however, Eastern European towns were not able to stem the tide of the increasing power of nobles and, in the case of Russia, the tsars. As the Muscovite state expanded its authority, the tsars ran roughshod over urban pretensions. Most towns in the East enjoyed none of the special charters of rights that characterized towns in the West. Russian rulers considered towns their personal property, and Russian lords demanded the service and allegiance of townspeople.

The Emergence of Sovereign States

Although the term "state" was not yet being used to denote a political entity, by 1500 the largest monarchical kingdoms (see Map 1.2) were taking on some of the characteristics of the modern state. During the late fifteenth century, France, Spain, and England evolved into "new monarchies." What was "new" about them was their growing reach, an evolution begun

MAP 1.2 EUROPE IN 1500 Europe in 1500 was a maze of fragmented realms although sovereign monarchical states were beginning to emerge.

in the late medieval era. While monarchies grew stronger in Western Europe, however, they were actually weakened in Eastern and East Central Europe during the late Middle Ages. Struggles for power, civil war, and the growing domination of lords hindered the emergence of strong states there at least until the late sixteenth century.

Sovereign states emerged in Western Europe during the medieval period as rulers moved toward greater authority and independence. Yet, to be sure, these states were not "nation-states" in the modern sense, in which citizens feel that they belong to a nation by being, for example, Spanish, French, or Italian. Such national states, defined by ethnic bonds and cultural and linguistic traditions, would only develop beginning in the mid-eighteenth century and, above all, the nineteenth century. Medieval rulers governed a complex hodgepodge of territories, semi-independent towns, feudal vassals, and corporate institutions such as guilds that were largely independent of the crown, exchanging personal and/or corporate privileges for loyalty.

Between the tenth and fifteenth centuries, the kingdoms of France, England, and Spain grew into sovereign states as their rulers consolidated their territories by establishing their primacy over rivals. These rulers made laws and imposed administrative unity to a degree that was unprecedented. They asserted their authority, but not domination, over the nobles of the territories they claimed. Royal authority directly touched more subjects than ever before. Monarchs could raise and command armies, mint money, impose taxes, summon advisers, and appoint officials to represent and enforce their will.

The French kings, their territories clustered around Paris, had little real power during the medieval period. Until the mid-fifteenth century, the kings of England held Normandy, Brittany, Maine, Anjou, and Aquitaine, and the counts of Flanders held wealthy lands in what is now northern France and southern Belgium. During the Hundred Years' War (1337–1453), French kings raised the funds and armies necessary to expel the English from France (with the exception of the Channel port of Calais). During the last half of the fifteenth century, the French kings ended the *de facto* independence of large, prosperous provinces that were technically fiefs of the crown. In 1482, France absorbed Burgundy, whose powerful dukes were related to the kings of France, and a decade later the regent for Charles VIII (ruled 1483–1498) invaded Brittany, adding it to France. Through timely royal marriages and warfare, the French monarchs established the foundations for a stronger, more centralized monarchy.

England, too, emerged as a stronger monarchical state during the late medieval period, but with significant differences from its continental counterparts. The vassals of King John (ruled 1199–1216) and the people of London rebelled against more taxes he imposed to finance his attempt to recover continental territories lost to France. In 1215, the king was forced to sign the Magna Carta, the "great Charter of Liberties." John agreed to

The seal of King John (1215) on the Magna Carta, a cornerstone of English common and constitutional law.

impose major taxes only with the permission of a "great council" that represented the barons and to cease hiring mercenaries when his barons refused to fight. Later in the century, King Edward I (ruled 1272–1307) summoned barons, bishops, and representatives from England's major towns in the hope of obtaining their agreement to provide funds for another war against the king of France. From that "parley," or "parliament," came the tradition in England of consultation with leading subjects and the origins of an English constitutional government that constrained royal authority. The division of Parliament into two houses, the House of Lords and the House of Commons, which consisted of landed nobles and representatives of towns, developed during the reign of Edward III (ruled 1327–1377). Parliament's role as a representative institution increased as the king required new taxes to fight the Hundred Years' War against France. Parliament approved these levies.

In Central Europe, the Holy Roman Empire was not really a sovereign state. It dated from A.D. 962, the year when German nobles elected a ruler. By the end of the thirteenth century, the principle that the Holy Roman emperor would be elected, and not designated by heredity, had been established. Considering themselves the successors of the Roman Empire, the Holy Roman emperors saw themselves as the protectors of the papacy and of all Christendom. This involved the emperor in the stormy world of Italian politics.

The Holy Roman Empire encompassed about 300 semi-autonomous states, ranging from several large territories to a whole host of smaller states, principalities, and free cities that carried out their own foreign policy and fought wars. The emperor, selected by seven princes, could not consolidate his authority, levy taxes, raise armies or, increasingly, enforce his will outside of his own hereditary estates.

The Austrian Habsburgs, the ruling house in the German Alpine hereditary lands, had gradually extended their territories in the fourteenth and fifteenth centuries between the Danube River, the Adriatic Sea, and the Little Carpathian Mountains in Eastern Europe. Beginning in 1438, when the first Habsburg was elected Holy Roman emperor, until 1740 (when the male line was extinguished), only Habsburgs held the title of Holy Roman emperor. Smaller states, such as the thirteen cantons of Switzerland, struggled to maintain their autonomy against rising Habsburg power.

Developing State Structures

The growth in the number of royal officials helped rulers consolidate more effective power. Rulers had always had some kind of advisory council, but the importance of their advisers grew in the fourteenth and fifteenth centuries. Chanceries, treasuries, and courts of law represented an early stage of bureaucratization. Serving as royal officials, some humble men of talent began to reach positions of influence within states.

Rulers still earned revenue from their own lands. But in order to meet the expenses of their states, they drew income from taxation, the sale of offices (posts in the service of the monarch that were often both prestigious and lucrative) and government bonds, and the confiscation of land from recalcitrant nobles. Like other rulers, popes also centralized administration and finances, selling posts. Rulers imposed taxes on salt, wine, and other goods, impositions from which nobles and clergy were generally exempt. States in the sixteenth century became the great collectors and distributors of revenue. Moreover, the gradual growth of public debt was another sign of the increased authority of monarchical states. Royal dependency on the loans of merchant-bankers enriched the latter, providing more capital for their ventures. Rulers, surrounded by courtiers and councils, lived in a grander fashion. As they worked to consolidate their authority and territories, thrones became increasingly hereditary. As even wealthy people were apt to die young, such succession arrangements, which varied throughout Europe, mattered considerably.

With the strengthening of sovereign states in the fifteenth century, which entailed the loss of the right to have armies of retainers, nobles depended more on monarchies for the sanction of their power and honor. More of them came to court and served as royal officials. The sale of royal offices, especially in France and Spain, encouraged loyalty to the throne. Royal courts now adjudicated property disputes, gradually eroding noble jurisdiction over the king's subjects, although in France and many of the German states nobles retained rights of justice over peasants.

In the fifteenth century, regular channels for diplomacy emerged among the states of Europe. The Italian city-states were the first to exchange permanent resident ambassadors. By the middle of the century, Florence, Milan, Venice, and the kingdom of Naples all routinely exchanged ambassadors, who provided news and other information, while representing the interests of their states.

Limits to State Authority

Significant constraints, however, still limited the authority of rulers. We have seen that the privileges of towns, established through the purchase of royal charters of financial immunity, tempered royal power. Some regions (for example, Navarre in Spain), nominally incorporated into realms, maintained autonomy through representative institutions. And, to be sure, distance and physical impediments such as mountains and vast plains also prevented the effective extension of royal authority.

Even more important was the tradition that assemblies of notable subjects had rights, including that of being consulted, as in the case of England cited above. In the thirteenth century, rulers had convoked assemblies of notable subjects to explain their policies and to ask for help. Because they depended on those whom they assembled to provide military assistance when they required it, they also heard grievances. From this, parliaments, assemblies, diets, and Estates developed, representing (depending on the place) nobles, clergy, towns, and, in several cases, commoners.

Early in the sixteenth century, an Italian exile told the king of France what the monarch would need to attack the duchy of Milan: "Three things are necessary: money; more money; and still more money." The most powerful states—France, Habsburg Austria, and Spain—could raise sizable armies with relative ease. But, to meet the extraordinary expenses of wartime, they increasingly borrowed money from wealthy banking families. Rulers also utilized subsidies from friendly powers, imposed special taxes and forced loans, and sold offices. Sixteenth-century inflation would make wars even more expensive.

Royal levies to finance warfare through direct taxation could only be imposed with the consent of those taxed, except peasants, who had limited rights. The dialogue between rulers and assemblies, and the strength and weakness of such representative bodies, over the centuries would define the emergence and nature of modern government in European states.

The princes of the German states had to ask assemblies of nobles for the right to collect excise taxes. In Poland-Lithuania and Hungary, noble assemblies were more important than royal authority. In Bohemia, the rights of towns partially balanced noble prerogatives. Rulers could suspend decisions of those "sovereign" bodies, yet such assemblies could not be completely ignored because rulers needed their support, or at least compliance, particularly in time of war.

The prerogatives of nobles and churchmen also impeded royal authority. They invariably resisted royal taxes, which fell on the poor—the vast majority of the population—whom no one represented. Nobles still had to be convinced or coerced to provide armies. Kings became, at least in principle, supreme judges (though not for the clergy, as ecclesiastics were generally tried in Church courts), with royal courts offering litigants and petitioners a final appeal.

The struggle between rulers and the popes dated to the late eleventh century, when the popes and Holy Roman emperors had struggled for primacy. During the "lay investiture crisis," which began in 1060, the popes had contested the right of lay rulers to appoint bishops and invest them with signs of spiritual authority, normally a staff and a ring. (The dispute ended in 1122 when Emperor Henry V relinquished the imperial claim to the power to

Theodore Galle's *Nova reperta* ("New discoveries") celebrates the discovery of the New World and forms of the new technology (gunpowder, the compass, the clock, the saddle with stirrups).

invest bishops with spiritual authority, and the pope recognized the emperor's right to give fiefs to the bishops once they had been consecrated, which left them with the status of vassals recognizing the lay authority of the emperor.) The clergy generally taught obedience to secular as well as ecclesiastical rulers. Furthermore, in the late medieval period, kings were able to further consolidate their power when popes granted the rulers of France, Spain, and some German towns certain rights over the clergy, including that of naming bishops.

Transforming Discoveries

In the late Middle Ages, stunning developments in warfare and exploration transformed Europe and its relationship with the rest of the world. Moreover, the invention of printing created a culture of books, facilitating the spread of knowledge, ideas, and debate, at a time when exploration led to developing trade networks across the oceans, conquest, and empires.

Gunpowder, Warfare, and Armies

Warfare became more pervasive in the early modern period because of dynastic quarrels between rulers as they sought to consolidate or increase their territories. Although kings still depended on nobles to raise armies and to command on the battlefield, the face of battle was revolutionized in the late medieval period. Invented in China, gunpowder was brought to Europe in the thirteenth century by the Arabs. Gunpowder moved warfare from "chiefly a matter of violent housekeeping" between lords and vassals to sometimes massive struggles between dynastic rivals. First used in battle in the early fourteenth century, gunpowder could propel arrows and, increasingly, lead bullets. Gunpowder soon became the explosive for early versions of rifles, or muskets, which could be standardized in caliber and ammunition and for which clockmakers could produce spring-driven wheel locks that functioned as firing mechanisms.

Gradually replacing the lance, sword, crossbow, and longbow in battle, the rifle eroded the role of the noble as a privileged warrior since heavily armored knights could now be more easily shot off their horses by guns than unseated by lances or brought down by arrows. This reduced the role of cavalry in battle. Cavalrymen now wore light armor, and, while they might well carry a lance, they also sometimes were armed with pistols. Pikemen, however, remained essential to any army; their thirteen-foot-long weapons, made of a long wooden pole topped by a sharp iron point, protected the infantry while soldiers reloaded. The furious attack of pikemen could tear apart the rows of riflemen as they knelt to reload.

Now exploding artillery shells could wound or kill many combatants at once. At the Battle of Novara (1513) in northern Italy, where Swiss soldiers defeated a French army, artillery fire killed 700 men in three minutes. Deadly bombardments during battles had a devastating effect on the morale of the enemy. Naval battles grew fiercer as cannon replaced rams on warships. The sleek galleys that raced along the coast of the Mediterranean during the warm summer months gave way to ships large enough to transport heavy cannon. The threat from enemy artillery forced the construction of massive fortifications around towns, which left the defense with a solid advantage in warfare. Sieges lasted longer than ever before. Victorious armies, frustrated by lengthy sieges, sometimes slaughtered the surviving civilian population.

Although frontier garrisons, artillery units, and the king's household guards were virtually the only true standing armies, their size increased during the wars of the late fifteenth and the sixteenth centuries. During the Hundred Years' War (1337–1453), major battles were fought with between 7,000 and 15,000 soldiers on each side. During the struggles between the Austrian Habsburg and French Valois dynasties on the Italian peninsula in the fifteenth and sixteenth centuries, armies reached 25,000 men in size. Some nobles still had private armies but served their kings as commanders and cavalrymen.

Mercenaries, the original "free lances," increasingly replaced feudal levies (and urban militias, where they existed) in armies mobilized by rulers to defend or expand their territorial interests. These might include Albanians, Englishmen, Scots, Greeks, Poles, and Swiss pikemen. Mercenaries received modest, though irregular, pay and expected acceptable rations and the opportunity to pillage the towns they conquered. Assuming these conditions were met, they seem to have deserted far less frequently than soldiers recruited by states from their own populations.

Yet most states had some kind of conscription, whether a formalized draft of men between the ages of fifteen and sixty or a hasty roundup when war approached. Loyal nobles, royal officials, and paid recruiters provided soldiers. Peasants made up more than three-quarters of armies, as they did the European population. Criminals also ended up in armies, often as the price of their release from prison or from execution, though they might well carry with them forever a branded letter as part of their sentence (such as the letter "V" for the French word *voleur*—thief).

Conditions of military service were difficult at best. In addition to barely adequate lodging and food, infractions of rules were dealt with harshly, including the infamous and often fatal "running the gauntlet" through troops lined up on both sides, dispensing blows with sticks or swords. Officers dispensed justice without trial or appeal, and sentences were carried out immediately. The severed heads of deserters or other serious offenders were impaled on pikes for several days at the entrance to a camp, sending a clear message.

Except for royal guards, artillery units, and other specialized forces, uniforms were rare in any army, although most soldiers sported some type of identification, such as an armband or a tunic bearing a national or regional symbol like the English red cross, the barred cross of Lorraine, or the lion of Lyon.

Epidemics and disease—dysentery and typhoid, among others—carried off far more than did wounds received in battle. But casualty figures were also alarming, however inaccurately kept. The wounded often died from inadequate—even for the time—medical treatment and from neglect.

The Printing Press and the Power of the Printed Word

The advent of printing in Europe in the fifteenth century in some ways marked the end of the medieval period. The invention of woodblock printing and paper had occurred in China in the eighth century; both reached Europe from the Arab world via Spain in the thirteenth century. Before the arrival of these technologies, monks and scribes had copied books on parchment sheets; a single copy of the Bible required about 170 calfskins or 300 sheepskins. Because it was much cheaper than parchment, paper more readily accommodated scholars, officials, and merchants. But the process of copying itself remained slow. Cosimo de' Medici, the Florentine banker and patron of Renaissance art, hired 200 scribes to copy 200 volumes in two years' time.

All this changed in the fifteenth century when Flemish craftsmen invented a kind of oil-based ink. This and the innovation of a wooden hand press made possible the invention of movable metal type in the German cathedral town of Mainz in about 1450 by, among several others, Johannes Gutenberg (c. 1395–1468). His stunningly beautiful Latin Bibles are treasured today. Printing shops soon started up in the Italian states, Bohemia, France, and the Netherlands, and in Spain and England by the 1470s (see Map 1.3). By 1500, about 35,000 books were published each year in Europe, and a century later the number had jumped to between 150,000 and 200,000 books.

Books provided scholars with identical ancient and medieval texts to discuss and critique. Accounts of discoveries and adventures in the New World filtered across Europe from Spain, England, and France. The number of scholarly libraries—which were really just private collections—grew rapidly. New professions developed: librarians, booksellers, publishers, typesetters,

MAP 1.3 SPREAD OF PRINTING THROUGH EUROPE, 1450–1508   Towns and dates at which printing shops were established throughout Europe.

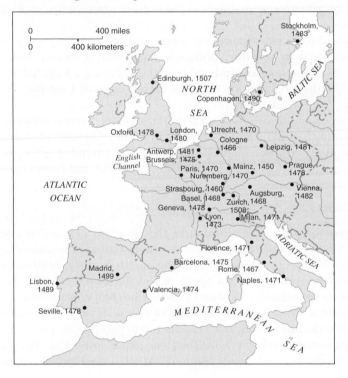

and editors. Moreover, with the greater dissemination of knowledge came an increase in the number of universities, rising from twenty in 1300 to about seventy in 1500.

More people learned how to read, although literate individuals remained far in the minority. In Florence and other prosperous cities, the rate of literacy may have been relatively high, although in the Italian city-states as a whole it is unlikely that more than 1 percent of workers and peasants could read and write. The literate population of the German states in 1500 was about 3 or 4 percent. But among the upper classes many more people developed the habit of reading.

Not all that was published pleased lay and ecclesiastic leaders, and printing made censorship considerably more difficult. No longer could the destruction of one or two manuscripts hope to root out an idea. Thus, Pope Alexander VI warned in a bull in 1501: "The art of printing is very useful insofar as it furthers the circulation of useful and tested books; but it can be very harmful if it is permitted to widen the influence of pernicious works. It will therefore be necessary to maintain full control over the printers."

Exploration and Conquest in the New World:
The Origins of European Empire

By the last decade of the fifteenth century, the inhabitants of the Iberian Peninsula already had several centuries of navigational and sailing accomplishments behind them. The Portuguese, who had the advantage of the magnificent port of Lisbon, had captured a foothold on the Moroccan coast in 1415, beginning two centuries of expansion. Early in the fifteenth century, they began to explore the west coast of Africa and had taken Madeira and the Azores islands in the Atlantic. Their goal was to break Muslim and Venetian control of European access to Asian spices and silk.

King Ferdinand and Queen Isabella of Spain initially rejected the request of the Genoese cartographer and merchant Christopher Columbus (1451–1506), who sought financial backing for an ocean voyage to reach the Indies. In 1492, however, fearing that Portuguese vessels might be the first to reach the wealth of Asia by sea, the royal couple consented to support the expedition.

Late in 1492, Columbus set sail with three ships. He believed the earth was a perfect sphere, and since Africa stood in the way of a voyage sailing to the east, he thought it possible to reach the Orient by sailing west across the Atlantic Ocean, which he believed to be narrow. After more than nine weeks on the open seas, the small fleet reached not Asia but rather the small Caribbean island of San Salvador in the Americas. He then came ashore in Cuba and finally Hispaniola (now the Dominican Republic and Haiti). "What on earth have you come seeking so far away?" he was asked. "Christians and spices," he replied. But he also probably believed that he would find gold, and asked the Indians he encountered on the shore in sign language if they knew where some could be found. Columbus was impressed with the beauty of Hispaniola (although he remained convinced that he had discovered islands near India) and the "docility" of the indigenous people. Yet, in the absence of gold, he suggested that the Spanish crown could make Hispaniola profitable by selling its people as slaves, a looming tragedy. Columbus, whose greatest contribution was to find a way across the sea using the trade winds, made three subsequent voyages of discovery, the last beginning in 1502, after which he gave up his search for a passage to Asia.

Portugal, a much poorer state than Spain, struggled to defend its trade routes against Spanish encroachments. In 1487 Bartholomew Dias (c. 1450–1500) first rounded the Cape of Good Hope, the southern tip of Africa, reaching the Indian Ocean, and then Calcutta on the southwest coast of India. The cargo of spices the Portuguese explorer Vasco da Gama (c. 1460–1524) brought back to Lisbon from India in 1498 paid for his costly expedition sixty times over. The Portuguese established fortified bases along the Indian Ocean, including at Goa. The maritime route across the Indian Ocean to the South China Sea could now compete with the overland spice and silk routes that had long linked Europe to the markets of the East. However, the Portuguese found that a thriving maritime trade network

Portuguese, wearing Western attire, meeting robed Japanese upon disembarking in 1542.

already existed between China, Japan, Southeast Asia, India, the Persian Gulf, and East Africa. The European trading presence was new. An Indonesian ruler remarked of the Portuguese adventurers, "The fact that these people journey so far from home to conquer territory indicates clearly that there must be very little justice and a great deal of greed among them." This had made them "fly all over the waters in order to acquire possessions that God did not give them."

In 1493, Pope Alexander VI divided the non-Christian world into zones for Spanish and Portuguese exploration and exploitation (see Map 1.4). His proclamation seemed to justify conquests, as well as the conversion of indigenous peoples. He awarded Portugal all of sub-Saharan Africa and Asia; Spain, the pope's ally, received most of the Americas. Portugal claimed Brazil, which became the largest colony in the Americas, established in the second half of the sixteenth century.

Soon more and more Spanish explorers reached the Americas. Vasco Núñez de Balboa (c. 1475–1519) established Spanish sovereignty over what is now Panama. Cuba, in turn, fell, and then served as a staging point for the conquest of Mexico by Hernando Cortés (1485–1547), which opened a new chapter in European expansion. Cortés, who first crossed the Atlantic in 1506 to Hispaniola, landed on the coast of Mexico in 1519. He went to see the Aztec ruler, Montezuma. The Aztec capital of Tenochtitlán (present-day Mexico City) was then larger than any other European city except Constantinople. Montezuma sent him away, although he later sent him gifts of gold and silver. Despite the fact that he had been ordered to limit his expedition to exploration and trade, Cortés was determined to conquer Mexico in the name of Emperor Charles V. The interests of the Spanish crown would remain paramount in the construction of Spain's overseas empire. Cortés formed alliances with Montezuma's non-Aztec peoples, who naively hoped that Cortés might help them achieve independence. The Spanish adventurer then conquered Mexico with no more than sixteen horses and six hundred soldiers, with the help of his Native American allies.

Farther south, Francisco Pizarro (c. 1476–1541) led his men in the conquest of the Inca Empire in Peru. Although the Incas were a people rich in precious metals and culture, they had never seen iron or steel weapons before, nor did they have draft animals. When Pizarro's horses lost their shoes in Peru and there was no iron available to replace them, he had them shod in silver. In the 1540s more silver was discovered in Mexico, and also in the Andes Mountains, completely transforming the economy of Spanish conquest. Imported silver enhanced the integration of the Spanish Empire into the expanding trade of Europe.

The victory of the conquistadors (conquerors) was the victory of steel-bladed swords over stone-bladed swords. Moreover, the surprise element of cannon contributed to the Spanish victory in the Americas and of the Portuguese in Southeast Asia. A witness to a Portuguese attack in 1511

Map 1.4 Exploration and Conquest, 1492–1542   Pope Alexander VI divided the non-Christian world into zones for Spanish and Portuguese exploration and exploitation. Portuguese, Spanish, French, and English explorers set out to find new routes to Asia, the New World, and around the world.

Aztec emissaries agreeing to a treaty with Cortés, who is seated with his interpreter standing to his left.

remembered, "the noise of the cannon was as the noise of thunder in the heavens and the flashes of fire of their guns were like flashes of lightning in the sky: and the noise of their matchlocks was like that of ground-nuts popping in the frying-pan."

Steeped in tales of crusading chivalry and conquest, the conquerors set out looking for adventure and wealth. Cortés, for example, was of a modest Castilian noble family; his father had fought against the Moors in southern Spain, and thus was himself a veteran of another imperial conquest, the Reconquista, which had expelled the Moors from the Iberian Peninsula. "We came here to serve God and the king," said one Spaniard in the Americas, "but also to get rich." Most died young, far from home, their dreams of wealth shattered by the harsh realities of life in what seemed to them a strange and often inhospitable world. Ferdinand Magellan (c. 1480–1521), the Portuguese-born explorer, was killed by angry islanders on a Pacific beach. His crew nonetheless circumnavigated the globe, having proven that a southwest passage to India did exist, returning to Spain in 1522.

Many of the conquistadors, and many of the later settlers (mostly men) who were attracted by tales of gold and silver, died in the New World; during the first ten years of Spanish settlement of Hispaniola, as much as two-thirds of the European population perished. However, many times more of the native people they encountered perished as a result of contact with the newcomers. The smallpox the Spanish brought with them wiped out people who had no immunity to diseases brought from Europe. The indigenous population of Mexico fell from about 25 million—or more—in 1520 to perhaps as few as 1 million in 1600. The native population of Peru fell from about 7 million in 1500 to half a million in 1600. Other European diseases, including measles, typhus, and bubonic plague, decimated the native population. In Guatemala, a Mayan Indian kept a chronicle of the ravages of European disease among his people: "Great was the stench of the dead. After our fathers and grandfathers succumbed, half of the people fled to the fields. The dogs and vultures devoured the bodies. . . . We were born to die." In turn, the Indians gave the Spanish syphilis, which then spread in Europe.

The exchange of diseases was a tragic consequence of the meeting between the Old and New Worlds, but there were beneficial exchanges as well. Before the arrival of Europeans, there were no domesticated animals larger than the llama and alpaca in the Americas, and little animal protein in the Indian diet. Spaniards brought horses and cattle with them. Sheep had accompanied Columbus on his second journey. The 350 pigs brought to Cuba by Columbus had multiplied to over 30,000 by 1514. They provided manure for farming but ate their way through forest land and eroded the indigenous agricultural terrace system, upsetting the ecological balance of conquered lands.

Every year the Spanish galleons returned with tobacco, potatoes, new varieties of beans, cacao, chili peppers, and tomatoes. These crops contributed to an increase in the European population. Maize fed European farm animals. In turn, the Spaniards planted wheat, barley, rice, and oats in their colonies.

In 1565, a Spanish galleon completed a voyage of global trade by sailing across the Pacific Ocean from Manila to unload cinnamon on the coast of Mexico. Spanish ships returned with silver, which could purchase silks, porcelain, spices, jade, and mother-of-pearl brought by Chinese junks to the Philippines. Shipping routes led from Seville to the Caribbean and to the ports of Veracruz in Mexico and Cartagena in Colombia. They returned with Mexican and Peruvian silver that replenished the coffers of European princes and merchants. All five continents—Europe, Asia, Africa, North America, and South America—thus moved closer together in reciprocal economic relationships that represented the beginnings of a globalization of trade.

The Spanish sought not only trade with the Americas but also empire. Spanish legal documents affecting the new colonies declared that Indians would keep all lands they already held, but that all other territories henceforth belonged either to the crowns of Spain or were to be divided up among the conquerors as booty. The Spanish proclaimed the *requerim-*

iento, which required that Indians accept both Spanish rule and Christianity. The conquistadors built new towns, placing the church, town hall, and prison around a central marketplace (*plaza*), as towns developed on a rectangular grid plan.

In return for the pope's blessing of the colonial enterprise, missionaries began to arrive in the Americas, hoping to convert the Indians to Christianity. The harsh reality of the colonial experience for the natives, however, was largely untempered by the good intentions of some, but not all, of the missionaries. "For this kind of people," snapped a Portuguese priest in Brazil in 1563, "there is no better way of preaching than the sword and the rod of iron." A Spanish judge in Mexico said of his people that they "compelled [the Indians] to give whatever they asked, and inflicted unheard-of cruelties and tortures upon them."

Spaniards, Portuguese, and other Europeans sought to impose their culture on the peoples they conquered, although Christian teaching made only limited headway in India and virtually none in China. Unlike its view of Muslims, the Church did not consider Indians infidels, but rather as innocents who could be taught Christian beliefs. "Are these Indians not men?" asked a Dominican priest in Santo Domingo in a sermon to shocked colonists in 1511, "Do they not have rational souls? Are you not obliged to love them as you love yourselves?" A papal pronouncement depicted the Indians as "true men . . . capable not only of understanding the Catholic faith, but also, according to our information, desirous of receiving it." The Spaniards already had experience in dealing with the diversity of language and culture on the Iberian Peninsula, although nothing like what they found in the Americas. In the 1590s, a Franciscan friar boasted that he had built over 200 churches and baptized more than 70,000 Indians. In Latin America, Christian belief sometimes merged with local religious deities, customs, and shrines to create a distinctive form of Christianity.

Obligatory labor service, brutally enforced, first formed the relationship between rulers and the ruled. The crown of Castile established a system of encomienda, by which Spanish settlers would hold Indians "in trust," but not their lands. They could exact tribute in kind or labor. The system gradually ended and a wage system—not much better—came into place. Moreover, repartimiento allowed royal officials to force Indians to work for specific periods. In Central America, Spanish colonists invoked the medieval Christian concept of a "just war" against "heathens" as a justification for enslavement.

The Church and the crown periodically tried to protect the Indians against the harsh treatment accorded them by many of their Spanish countrymen in the name of profit. Bishop Bartolomé de Las Casas (1474–1566), whose father had accompanied Columbus on his second voyage to the Americas and who had himself been a conquistador before becoming a priest, spoke out against the treatment of Indians. He saluted the "marvelous government, laws, and good customs" of the Mayas of Central America, whom he wanted placed under the authority of the Church. Charles V ordered a pause in Spanish conquests until such moral issues could be considered, but the Spanish destruction of what they considered pagan temples and idols continued and the empire continued to expand.

As the Indian population was depleted through disease, overwork, and brutality, the Spanish looked for new sources of labor. Domestic slavery still existed in Italy, Spain, and Muscovy in the sixteenth century, as well as in the Arab world, and some Indians in the New World also had slaves. By the fifteenth century, Portuguese traders along the coast of West Africa had begun to make profits selling Africans as servants in Lisbon or as sugar plantation workers in the Portuguese Atlantic islands. Portugal soon dominated the African network of slave-trading, which depended on chieftains and traders in African kingdoms, merchants in Seville and Lisbon, settlers in Mexico and Peru, and Brazilian sugar growers. The Spaniards believed that Africans could best survive the brutally difficult work and hot climate of America. Between 1595 and 1640 about 300,000 slaves were transported to the Spanish colonies in the Americas, and five times that many would be shipped during the next century.

Gradually, more Spanish settlers arrived to populate the American colonies, including small traders, shoemakers, blacksmiths, and masons. (In Paraguay, the governor asked that no lawyers be allowed to emigrate, "because in newly settled countries they encourage dissension and litigation.") By the mid-sixteenth century about 150,000 Spaniards had crossed to America, and by the end of the century about 240,000 Spaniards had emigrated there. Most never returned to Spain.

In 1552, a Spanish official wrote King Charles V (ruled 1516–1556, Holy Roman emperor 1519–1558) that the discovery of the East and West Indies was "the greatest event since the creation of the world, apart from the incarnation and death of Him who created it." But Michel de Montaigne (1533–1592), a French writer who had met Indians brought back from Brazil, offered another view in 1588, when he observed that "so many goodly cities [were] ransacked and razed; so many nations destroyed and made desolate; so infinite millions of harmless peoples of all sexes, states, and ages, massacred, ravaged and put to the sword . . . ruined and defaced for the traffic of pearls and pepper."

Conclusion

The economic and political structures of early modern Europe drew on the dynamism of the medieval period. Demographic vitality finally overcame the catastrophic losses brought by the Black Death. Within Europe, commerce and manufacturing expanded. Mediterranean traders roamed as far as the Middle East and even Asia. And although much of Central Europe and the Italian peninsula remained a hodgepodge of small states, rulers in

France, England, and Spain had consolidated their authority, and sovereign monarchical states began to emerge.

Above all, three salient movements of change brought the Middle Ages to an end. The first was the Renaissance, or cultural rebirth, which began in the mid-fourteenth century in the Italian city-states (see Chapter 2). The commercial prosperity of Florence, above all, but also of Venice and other independent city-states made possible this period of extraordinary accomplishment in literature and painting. The invention of printing began to transform one culture after another. Second, the exploration and colonization of the New World would ultimately help end the Mediterranean Sea's role as the center of European prosperity and would lead to Spain's emergence as a world power, along with England and the Netherlands (see Chapters 5 and 6). Colonization brought the establishment of European empires abroad; between 1500 and the late eighteenth century, more than 1.5 million Europeans crossed the ocean to live in the New World. Third, the Reformation (see Chapter 3), which began in the second decade of the sixteenth century, challenged the unity of the Roman Catholic Church and its dominance in much of Europe.

CHAPTER 2

THE RENAISSANCE

～⁓～

In 1508, Pope Julius II summoned Michelangelo from Florence to the papal city of Rome. He commissioned the artist to paint frescoes (paintings on plaster) on the ceiling of the new Sistine Chapel, a ceremonial chapel next to the papal residence in the Vatican. With some reluctance (since he considered himself primarily a sculptor), Michelangelo agreed to undertake the project. He signed a contract that stipulated a payment of 3,000 ducats and began work that very day in May.

During the long, difficult years of intense creativity, Michelangelo often lay on his back, staring at the ceiling (still the best position from which to study his masterpiece), before climbing up the scaffolding to work. His frescoes, depicting Creation, Original Sin, the Flood, and the ancestors of Christ, are a triumph of religious painting. However, Pope Julius II, offended by the nude figures in the *Last Judgment* frescoes, ordered painters to cover the nudes with fig leaves. As a result, Michelangelo left Rome in disgust. He left behind what is arguably the most beautiful pictorial ensemble in Western painting.

Michelangelo's work represents the epitome of art during the Renaissance, a time of cultural rebirth. From about 1330 to 1530, the city-states of the Italian peninsula emerged as the intellectual and artistic centers of Europe. It was a period during which classical texts were rediscovered, thereby reviving the ideas, architecture, arts, and values of ancient Greece and Rome. By celebrating the beauty of nature and the dignity of mankind, Renaissance artists and scholars helped shape the intellectual and cultural history of the modern world. During the fifteenth century, Michelangelo, as well as Leonardo da Vinci and many other Renaissance sculptors and painters, enjoyed the patronage of wealthy families and produced some of the immortal works of the European experience. From about 1490 to 1530, Rome, too, was the center of a final period of artistic innovation, the High Renaissance, during which time the popes, including Julius II, commissioned paintings, sculptures, and churches.

Yet, weakened by internal political turmoil, the Italian city-states were ravaged by foreign invaders beginning in 1494. Unable to resist French invasion and then Spanish domination, after 1530 the city-states were no longer able to support artistic glories, and the Renaissance ended in a mood of discouragement, in striking contrast to the contagious optimism that had characterized its greatest moments.

THE CITY-STATES OF THE ITALIAN PENINSULA

The city-states were the fundamental political unit of the Italian peninsula, the most urbanized part of the Western world, even though the vast majority of the population of the Italian peninsula still lived in the countryside. In 1200, there were several hundred independent city-states on the Italian peninsula; gradually, however, that number was reduced, as many were absorbed as subject territories by more powerful city-states. A century later, at least twenty-three cities in the northern and central parts of the peninsula had populations of more than 20,000. It was within these city-states that the achievements of the Renaissance took place.

The city-states of Renaissance Italy were the most urbanized part of the Western world. Pictured here is the Loggia dei Lanzi, the principal gathering place in Florence. In the foreground, one can see priests and nuns praying while Florentine citizens go on about their day.

Thriving Economies

The economic prosperity and social dynamism of the city-states made the cultural achievements of the Renaissance possible. The city-states had become independent and prosperous because of the expansion of commerce during the eleventh and twelfth centuries. The Italian peninsula formed a natural point of exchange between East and West.

Intensively studied in the twelfth and thirteenth centuries, Roman law provided a framework for order and the development of political life within the Italian city-states. The Roman Empire had depended on a network of largely autonomous cities and towns, particularly in the plains of the northern part of the peninsula. These had been linked by a system of roads, unrivaled in Europe, all of which, as the saying goes, eventually led to Rome.

The people of the Italian peninsula had suffered the ravages of the Black Death and the other epidemics of the fourteenth century, but the ensuing economic recession, which led to declines in manufacturing and population in the central Italian region of Tuscany, did not affect much of the northern part of the peninsula, which still prospered. Drawing wool from England and Spain, Florence's textile industry employed about 30,000 workers. The finished Florentine cloth and woolen goods were then traded throughout the Mediterranean, and to Burgundy, Flanders, England, and as far as Asia. Agriculture thrived in the broad river valleys of Tuscany and Lombardy. The production of grains, vegetables, and wine, aided by the drainage of swamps and marshes and by irrigation, not only fed the urban population but also provided an agricultural surplus that could be invested in commerce and manufacturing. The proximity of Mediterranean trade routes bolstered international trade and small-scale manufacturing and brought prosperity to ambitious Italian merchants.

The development of banking during the early fourteenth century helped finance internal trade and international commerce. By the beginning of the fifteenth century, the Church's condemnation of usury no longer was taken to apply to banking, as long as the rates of interest were not considered excessive. Florence's gold florin became a standard currency in European trading centers. The bankers of that city, with agents in Avignon and many other cities throughout its trading network, were central to European commerce and monarchical and papal finances. Unlike traders elsewhere in Europe, Florentine merchants had broad experience with bills of exchange and deposit, which provided credit to purchasers. There were, however, risks to such loans. In the fifteenth century, the king of England forced Florentine merchants to loan him money, or face expulsion from the realm and lose all their assets there. But he defaulted on the loans after his invasion of France failed during the Hundred Years' War, and several major Florentine merchant companies went into bankruptcy.

Venice and Genoa were also major trading and banking cities, as well as centers of shipbuilding and insurance. Each city had long traded with the

This miniature depicts the Piazzetta of the Republic of Venice, with all the activity of a major Adriatic port.

East Indies and the Far East. Venice, in particular, had been a major center of trade and transcultural exchange between the Christian West and Muslim East since the eighth century. Venice linked sea routes with the long overland routes to Constantinople through the desolate mountains of the Balkans. Merchants hedged their bets on whether their shipments would fall victim to the sudden Mediterranean storms, to roving pirates, or to some other mishap on the overland route through Central Asia. The merchants carried fine woolens and linen from the Italian peninsula and northern Europe, as well as metals, to the East. They returned with cotton, silk, and, above all, spices, including pepper, cinnamon, nutmeg, ginger, and sugar, which arrived via Alexandria or Constantinople from the East Indies, luxury goods to awaken the palates of wealthy Europeans. Merchants from both East and West used towns in Crimea, a peninsula extending into the northern Black Sea, as intermediary points for trade from Muscovy, Persia, India, and China (see Map 2.1).

Merchant capitalism eroded the power of the nobility by expanding the ranks and influence of townsmen. The wealth and status of urban merchants—although nobles also engaged in trade—allowed them to

MAP 2.1 REACH OF TRADE DURING THE FIFTEENTH CENTURY Major trade routes, both by land and sea, led from the Italian city-states of Venice, Genoa, and Florence, as well as from northern Europe and the Baltic regions. The Italian city-states formed a natural point of exchange between East and West. Products that were traded are shown at their source.

dominate the oligarchies that ruled the city-states. Prosperity increased the strong sense of municipal identity and pride; the Florentine political theorist Niccolò Machiavelli insisted, "I love my native city more than my own soul."

Social Structure

The social structure of the Italian city-states resembled that of other urban centers of trade and manufacturing in England, France, Flanders, and Holland. In the city-states, the *pòpolo grasso,* or "fat people," were the elite, including nobles, wealthy merchants, and manufacturers. The *mediòcri* were the middling sort, including smaller merchants and master artisans. The *pòpolo minuto,* or "little people," made up the bulk of the urban population. In cities, artisans and laborers were burdened by high taxes on consumption. Urban elites owned much of the richest land of the hinterland, which was worked by tenant farmers, sharecroppers, and agricultural laborers, as well as by peasant landowners. In the northern and central part of the Italian peninsula, most peasants were free to be miserably poor, while in the southern part many still owed obligations to their lords.

The "fat people" of the city-states comprised no more than 5 percent of the population. The great patricians assumed the status of princes of their cities, whether as dukes, cardinals, or, in the case of Rome, as the pope himself. Although social differences remained sharp in Italian city-states, as everywhere, commercial wealth made possible some degree of social mobility, above all in Florence, the wealthiest city. New families, enriched by commerce, rose into the ruling elite, although opportunities to do so declined noticeably by the end of the fifteenth century.

An elaborate and highly ritualized etiquette based upon mutual flattery maintained social distance. The wealthiest families became even richer despite the recession that extended throughout much of the fourteenth and fifteenth centuries; their prosperity made them even more eager not to be taken for anyone of more modest station. Thus, one of the powerful dukes of Milan insisted that his wife be called *Illustrissima* ("Illustrious One"). Flattery and subservience could be found in every greeting, and in every letter penned to a prince: "Nothing in the world pleases me more than your commands," and the ominous "I live only insofar as I am in your excellency's graces," which was sometimes true enough.

Urban patriarchs dominated their cities through power and patronage. They dispensed titles, privileges, and cash as they pleased. The duke of Ferrara affirmed his power by going door to door once a year to "beg" on behalf of the poor, an inversion of reality that served to define his authority and the subordination of everyone else. But princes and patriarchs also ruled through intimidation, occasionally eliminating enemies with astonishing cruelty.

Renaissance Political Life

The originality of the Italian city-states during the Renaissance lay not only in their remarkable artistic accomplishments but also in their precociously innovative forms of political structure. The organization of some of the city-states into constitutional republics was closely linked to the cultural achievements of the Renaissance. Nonetheless, there was nothing democratic about the city-states of Renaissance Italy, for the elites had brutally crushed the popular uprisings of artisans and shopkeepers that occurred in Siena and other towns during the fourteenth century.

Fourteenth- and fifteenth-century republics were constitutional oligarchies dominated by the most powerful families who filled the executive bodies, legislative or advisory councils, and special commissions that governed each city-state. The percentage of male citizens enjoying the right to vote ranged from about 2 percent in fifteenth-century Venice to 12 percent in fourteenth-century Bologna, the former percentage seeming most representative of the restricted nature of political rights in Renaissance Italy. Venice, Siena, Lucca, and Florence (at least until the waning days of domination by the powerful Medici family) were the most stable oligarchic republics of Renaissance Italy; Genoa, Bologna, and Perugia went back and forth between republican and despotic governments (see Map 2.2).

Some of the other city-states became outright hereditary despotisms (*signori*) run by a single family. Milan, a despotism under the control of the Visconti family, had grown prosperous from metallurgy and textile manufacturing. Francesco Sforza, a *condottieri* (mercenary of common origins), who had married the illegitimate daughter of the last Visconti duke in 1447, helped overthrow the republic less than three years later. Sforza imposed his family's rule with the support of Milanese nobles. The Sforza family thereafter skillfully played off rivalries between other powerful families, sometimes implementing their will with sheer force. The duke of Milan tolerated a council of 900 men drawn from the city's leading citizens, but he appointed magistrates and officials—and in general ruled—as he pleased. Likewise, princely families, such as the Este family of Ferrara and the Gonzaga family of Mantua, ran the smaller city-states.

By contrast, Venice, an energetic, prosperous Adriatic port city of lagoons and canals built on a number of small islands, remained in principle a republic. Its constitution offered a balance of political interests: the *doge*, an official elected for life by the Senate, served as an executive authority whose prerogatives were not that far from those of a monarch. The Great Council, consisting of about 2,500 enfranchised patricians, elected the Senate, which represented the nobility, an increasing number of whom were ennobled merchants living in elegantly decorated houses facing the canals. No one represented the poor, more than half the population of Venice.

Like the monarchies beyond the Alps, the Italian city-states developed small, efficient state bureaucracies, as the despots or oligarchs (a few men

MAP 2.2 CITY-STATES IN RENAISSANCE ITALY, 1494   The city-state was the fundamental political unit of the Italian peninsula; the number of city-states was reduced as many of them were absorbed by the more powerful city-states.

or families running the government) of each city improved the effectiveness of state administration. Thus, Florence and Venice had special committees responsible for foreign affairs and commerce. Many offices were sold or filled by members of the leading families linked by marriages. Personal relations between powerful families, for example, between the Medicis and the Sforza, facilitated diplomacy. The Medici engaged financial specialists for the management of the fiscal policies of their city and their family, although the latter, to the detriment of Florence, almost

Portrait of Francesco Sforza, one of the elite *pòpolo grasso.*

always took precedence. ("Better a city ruined," said Cosimo de' Medici, "than lost.")

The *condottieri* were central to the political and military situation in Italy. A military ethos permeated the courts of the Italian princes. A young prince learned military exercises, including jousting (horseback combat with long lances that could occasionally be deadly), and he began to hunt, sometimes using falcons. Some dukes hired themselves and their private armies out to the highest bidders, such as powerful Italian princes, the king of France, or the Holy Roman emperor.

Renaissance princes and oligarchs surrounded themselves with an imposing retinue of attendants. The court of Urbino, not particularly wealthy compared to some of the others, employed a staff of 355 people. This number included 45 counts of the duchy, 17 noblemen of various pedigrees, 22 pages, 5 secretaries, 19 chamber grooms, 5 cooks, 19 waiters, 50 stable hands, and 125 servants and jacks-of-all-trades, including the *galoppini,* who galloped around on a variety of errands.

Florence, Milan, Venice, Naples, and the Papal States were as aggressive as France and the other monarchies beyond the Alps. They dominated their weaker neighbors through force, intimidation, and alliances, picking them off one by one, as in chess. When they were not battling each other, Florence and Venice combined to limit Milanese control to Lombardy, while establishing their own authority over their respective regions. Venice controlled territory from the Alps to the Po River. Genoa, bitterly divided between merchant factions and nobles living in the hills above the Mediterranean port, struggled to maintain its autonomy because it lay physically exposed to more powerful Milan, as well as to the kingdom of France.

The Papal States, which bordered Tuscany east of the Apennines and to their south, functioned like any other city-state. The pope, too, was a temporal, as well as a spiritual, prince. He was elected for life by cardinals, the highest bishops of the Church, who were, in turn, appointed by the pope. Like monarchs and urban oligarchs, popes had to contend with the ambitious nobles of the Papal States. They, too, conspired with and sought alliances against other city-states. The eternal city was only the peninsula's eighth largest city in the late fourteenth century, ruled by a beleaguered papacy amid distant echoes of past glories. The city-states were increasingly freed from the authority and interference of the papacy. This began with the "Babylonian Captivity" (1309–1378), when the popes lived in Avignon under the direct influence of the king of France and, for a time, a rival pontiff claimed authority from Rome (see Chapter 3). The declining role of the papacy in temporal Italian affairs further aided the rise of Florence, Milan, and Venice.

Florence: Anatomy of a Renaissance City

Florence was the cradle of the Italian Renaissance, fulfilling the prediction of the Tuscan poet Dante Alighieri (1265–1321) that a new civilization would arise on the Italian peninsula. Indeed, early in the Renaissance, the language of the region, Tuscan, emerged as the "courtly language" used by an increasing number of educated Italians beyond Tuscany.

The walled city dominated its rich hinterland of gentle hills and prosperous plains. The Arno River, which flows through Florence, was navigable from the Mediterranean port of Pisa except during the summer months. In 1406, Florence conquered Pisa, another center of textile production, once a worthy challenger of Genoa for maritime trade but now divided into quarreling factions. This window on the sea aided Florentine commerce, enabling the city to become a maritime power.

Several other factors contributed to Florence's becoming the center of the revival of classical learning. Roman law and Latin had long been the foundation of training of Florentine ecclesiastics, lawyers, and notaries. Although the influence of the Church remained strong, the Medici rulers encouraged a cultural movement that had strong secular elements. Both Christian and secular traditions, then, infused Florentine civic life.

The combination of a dynamic craft tradition and an economy closely tied to the production of luxury goods made Florence receptive to artistic innovation. The city honored the accomplishments of its citizens—including cultural achievements. Lastly, Florence's reputation as a relatively educated city helped attract talented newcomers from rural Tuscany and other regions. It had many schools, including a university, and boasted a rate of literacy unmatched in Europe. In the fifteenth century, at least 8,000 children in a population of 100,000 attended church and civic schools, as well as private academies. It was said that even laborers could recite Dante's verses by heart.

The bell tower of the Palazzo Vecchio, the government building completed early in the fourteenth century, watched over the dynamic center of international banking, commerce, and the manufacture of cloth, woolens, silk, and jewelry. By the middle of the fourteenth century, Florence had become the fifth largest city in Europe. Before the plagues of the 1340s, about 100,000 people lived there. After falling by half, Florence's population revived during the next half-century, equaling that of London and

A Florentine council in session.

Seville, but not Venice and Naples, each of which then had at least 100,000 inhabitants.

Wealthy merchants, the *grandi*, governed Florence with the support of merchants, lawyers, and craftsmen of more modest means. Organized into seven major guilds, the merchants and manufacturers, particularly the cloth merchants, kept the fourteen lesser guilds (whose members included artisans and shopkeepers) in a subordinate position. The guilds elected the nine members of government, the *Signoria*, which administered the city. The Signoria proposed laws and conducted foreign affairs. Its members led the processions through the narrow streets during the various religious holidays. Two assemblies, the Council of the People and the Council of the Commune, served as a legislature. Citizens wealthy enough to pay taxes elected the 600 to 700 members of these councils, which met as needed to approve the decisions of the Signoria.

During the fifteenth century, the business of government went on in the palaces of the wealthiest citizens of Florence. The elite feared that the poor would revolt as they had in 1378 in the uprising known as the Ciompi, or "the wooden shoes," so named because many of the laborers could only afford such footwear. Suffering from economic hardship and aided by disgruntled members of the lower guilds, the cloth workers had risen up in a bloody insurrection in the hope of expanding the guild system already in power. The possibility of another uprising of the poor thereafter remained in the memory of the "fat people," causing them to keep the workers in a position of resentful subservience.

The renewal, then, of the Florentine elite with new families provided change within continuity, despite no small degree of political turbulence in the fifteenth century. The crowning cultural achievements of the Renaissance were not only rooted in Florence's prosperity but also in the relative social and political stability within that innovative city-state.

In 1434, Cosimo de' Medici (1389–1464) and his family seized control of Florentine political life. The family drew its great wealth from banking and the manufacture and commerce of textiles. Supported by a few patrician families, Cosimo banished prominent members of the most powerful rival clans. The Medici now controlled the offices of government. They manipulated the electoral process masterfully, using their wealth to curry support. Cosimo reflected the marketplace toughness of his family.

Florentine nobles generally accepted Medici rule because stability contributed to prosperity. Wealthy families continued to conspire against each other, even as Florence warred against Venice, but the powerful families remained staunchly patriotic, devoted to their city. Nonetheless, some Florentine nobles continued to oppose the Medici. In the Pazzi conspiracy of 1479, Lorenzo the Magnificent (1449–1492), Cosimo's grandson, survived an assassination attempt during Mass. Several hours later, four of the enemies of the Medici were hanging upside down from a government building, including the archbishop of Pisa. Lorenzo composed verses to be placed under their heads and commissioned Sandro Botticelli (c. 1445–1510) to paint them as they swung. Renaissance culture and the often violent political world of the city-states here converged.

The establishment of a Council of Seventy, which elected committees assigned responsibility for domestic and foreign affairs, helped the Medici tighten their grip on the reins of the Florentine republic. Lorenzo extended the family's banking interests and its influence with the pope in Rome. Among the many honors bestowed on the Medici family, Lorenzo considered the papal nomination of his thirteen-year-old son to the rank of Church cardinal "the greatest achievement of our house."

A DYNAMIC CULTURE

Economically and intellectually dynamic, Florence emerged as the center of the Renaissance. As Florence solidified its leading position on the Italian peninsula, its people rediscovered and celebrated classical learning. While glorifying antiquity, Renaissance poetry, prose, and painting emphasized the dignity of the individual, made in the image of God. It gradually moved concepts like beauty and virtue away from theological constraints.

The Rediscovery of Classical Learning

The Tuscan poet Petrarch (Francesco Petrarca, 1304–1374) was among the earliest and most influential of those who rediscovered and celebrated the classics of Latin antiquity. Petrarch, the son of a Florentine notary, learned Latin from a monk who inspired the boy to pursue his fascination with the classical world, which he came to view as a lost age. As a young man, Petrarch lived in Avignon, among an international community of lawyers and churchmen at the papal court during the "Avignon Papacy" (1309–1378), when the popes were subject to the influence of the kings of France. There he copied ancient works from manuscripts and books. Petrarch and his friends searched far and wide for more classical manuscripts. They uncovered the *Letters to Athens* of the Roman orator and moralist Marcus Tullius Cicero (106–43 B.C.), among other texts, stored in the cathedral of Verona. The study of Cicero led Petrarch to see in classical philosophy a guide to life based on experience.

Petrarch's successors found and copied other classical manuscripts. Among them were classical literary commentaries, which provided humanists with a body of information about the authors in whom they were interested. Scholars brought works of classical Greek authors, including the playwright Sophocles, from Constantinople and from the libraries of Mount Athos, an important center of learning in the Eastern Orthodox Church. Knowledge of Greek texts (as well as certain Arabic and Hebrew texts) spread slowly through Italy after the arrival of Greek teachers from Constantinople.

The development of printing (see Chapter 1) permitted the diffusion of a variety of histories, treatises, biographies, autobiographies, and poems. Printing spread knowledge of classical texts and the development of textual criticism itself. Many Renaissance scholars considered Cicero to represent the model of the purest classical prose (although others considered him too long-winded), and by 1500 more than 200 editions of his works had been printed in Italy, including his influential *On Oratory* and his letters. Libraries were established in many of the Italian city-states, including Florence, Naples, and Venice, and provided scholars with common texts for study.

From Scholasticism to Humanism

The Romans had used the concept of *humanitas* to describe the combination of wisdom and virtue that they revered. The term came to refer to studies that were intellectually liberating, the seven liberal arts of antiquity: grammar, logic, arithmetic, geometry, music, astronomy, and rhetoric (the art of expressive and persuasive speech or discourse). Medieval scholasticism was a system of thought in which clerics applied reason to philosophical and theological questions. Those teachers and students who shifted their

A humanist educator and his charges.

focus from the scholastic curriculum—law, medicine, and theology—to the curriculum of Latin grammar, rhetoric, and metaphysics became known as "humanists." They considered the study of the "humanities" to be essential for educating a good citizen.

Renaissance humanists believed that they were reviving the glory of the classical age. They considered their era greater than any since the Roman Empire. They also believed the Italian peninsula, although divided by political units, dialects, and by the Apennine Mountains, shared a common, distinct culture.

Venerating classical civilization, the humanists turned their backs on medieval scholasticism, which they believed was composed of irrelevant theological debates and encouraged ascetic withdrawal from the world. Scholastics celebrated the authority of Church texts and revered the saint, the monk, and the knight. Petrarch rejected idle philosophic speculation or even knowledge that seemed irrelevant to mankind. He mocked scholastics, remarking that they can tell you "how many hairs there are in the lion's mane . . . with how many arms the squid binds a shipwrecked sailor. . . . What is the use, I pray you, of knowing the nature of beasts, birds, fishes and serpents, and not knowing, or spurning the nature of man, to what end we are born, and from where and whither we pilgrimage."

The humanists proclaimed the writers of antiquity to be heroes worthy of emulation. Although virtually all humanists accepted Christianity, and clerical religious culture persisted intact, humanism stood as an alternative approach to knowledge and culture. Humanists believed that a knowledge of the humanities could civilize mankind, teaching the "art of living." Petrarch insisted that the study of classical poetry and rhetoric could infuse daily life with ethical values.

Unlike the scholastics, humanists believed that it was not enough to withdraw into philosophy. Petrarch rediscovered the classical ideal that the philosopher, or humanist, was a wise man who could govern. Cicero had written that what made an individual great was not the gifts of good fortune, but the use to which he put them. The active life, including participation in public affairs, had formed part of his definition of true wisdom. From the literature of the Greek and Roman past, humanists looked for guides to public life in their own city-states. The first half of the fifteenth century is often referred to as the period of "civic humanism" because of the influence of humanists and artists on the city-states themselves. Like the classic writers of ancient Rome, Renaissance writers were concerned with wisdom, virtue, and morality within the context of the political community. Humanists wrote boastful histories of the city-states, philosophical essays, stirring orations, and flattering biographies, as well as poetry, eagerly imitating classical styles.

The Renaissance and Religion

While rediscovering classic texts and motifs, the Renaissance remained closely linked to religion. Dante's *Divine Comedy* (1321), an allegorical poem, provides the quintessential expression of medieval thought by its demonstration of the extraordinary power that both Latin classical learning and Christian theology exerted on educated thought and literature. In his voyage through Hell, Purgatory, and Heaven, Dante encounters historical figures suffering terrible agonies for their sins, waiting expectantly for admission into Heaven, or already reaping the benefits of having lived a good life. Renaissance humanists could reject medieval scholasticism without turning their backs on the Church. Indeed, they claimed that they were searching for the origins of Christianity in the classical world from which it had emerged.

Although not the first to do so, humanists took classic texts, which were pagan, and ascribed to them meanings prophetic of Christianity. For example, the *Aeneid,* the long epic written by Virgil (70–19 B.C.), had been commissioned by the Roman emperor Augustus in the hope that it would offer the most favorable image of himself and of the empire, that is, of Rome bringing peace and civilization to the world. The hero of the *Aeneid,* Aeneas, personifies the ideal qualities of a Roman citizen, wanting to fulfill his patriotic duties, seeking glory for the empire but never for himself. The humanists transformed Aeneas's journey into an allegory for the itinerary of the Christian soul, appropriating antiquity into theology by viewing it as a foreshadowing of the true religion.

The place of the Church in Italian life remained strong during the Renaissance, the relative decline in the papacy's temporal power notwithstanding. There was thus considerable continuity between the medieval period and the Renaissance in matters of religion. There were at least 264 bishops in Italy, as many as in the rest of the Christian world. In 1427, Florence had more than 1,400 clerics out of a population of 38,000 living in ecclesiastical institutions. Religious festivals dotted the calendar. The colorful Venetian water processions of elaborately decorated gondolas, jousting, boat races, and the annual horse race (*palio*) sponsored by rival neighborhoods in Siena still bear witness to the playful but intense festivity of the Renaissance city-states, a festivity that gave ritualized religious expression to civic and political life.

The Renaissance Man and Woman

Renaissance literature and poetry, preoccupied with nature, beauty, and reason, placed the individual at the forefront of attention. Renaissance writers praised mankind as "heroic" and "divine," rational and prudent, rather than intrinsically unworthy by virtue of being stained by original sin, as Church theologians held. This, too, represented a revival of the classic vision of the moral greatness of the individual and his or her ability to discover truth and wisdom.

By this view, the lay person could interpret morality through the ancient texts themselves, without the assistance of the clergy. Once someone had learned to read Latin and Greek, neither ecclesiastical guidance nor formalized school settings were necessary for the accumulation of wisdom. Universities in general remained under the influence of the theological debates of scholasticism, although the universities of Florence, Bologna, and Padua gradually added humanist subjects to their curricula. Relatively few humanists emerged from the universities, which remained training grounds for jurists, doctors, and clerics.

"These studies are called liberal because they make man free," a humanist wrote; they are humane "because they perfect man . . . those studies by which we attain and practice virtue and wisdom; that education which calls forth, trains and develops those highest gifts of body and of mind, which ennoble man." The young Giovanni Pico della Mirandola (1463–1494) exclaimed, "O highest and most marvelous felicity of man! To him it is granted to have whatever he chooses, to be whatever he wills." Pico described the individual as an independent and autonomous being who could make his own moral choices and become, within the context of Christianity, "the molder and sculptor of himself."

The political theorist Niccolò Machiavelli (1469–1527), too, found personal fulfillment in the study of the classics. He had been employed in the Florentine chancery, serving as a diplomat. Purged when the Medici overthrew the republic in 1512, he took up residence in the countryside. Machiavelli complained that his days consisted of mundane exchanges with rustics. But "when evening comes I return home and go into my study. On the threshold I strip off my muddy, sweaty, workday clothes, and put on the robes of court and palace, and in this graver dress I enter the antique courts of the ancients and am welcomed by them, and there again I taste the food that alone is mine, and for which I was born. And I make bold to speak to them and ask the motives of their actions, and they, in their humanity, reply to me. And for the space of four hours I forget the world, remember no vexation, fear poverty no more, tremble no more at death: I pass indeed into their world." Machiavelli evoked the exhilaration of the individual discovering the joys of antiquity.

The development of the autobiography in literature reflected the celebration of the individual, however much the genre was limited to public people and the image that they sought to present of themselves, revealing virtually nothing of private life. In the first half of the fifteenth century, the portrait and the self-portrait emerged as artistic genres; princes, oligarchs, courtiers, and other people of wealth joined Christ, the Virgin Mary, and popular saints as subjects of painting.

A growing sense of what it meant to be "civilized" arose in the Italian city-states and highlighted the place of the individual in society. The Italian patrician may have been cleaner and more perfumed than people elsewhere in Europe. Books on good conduct and manners emerged. The writer Baldassare Castiglione (1478–1529) urged the person of taste to show that "whatever is said or done has been done without pains and virtually without thought" as if correct behavior had become part of his or her very being. Women, he contended, should obtain a "knowledge of letters, of music, of painting, and . . . how to dance and be festive."

A drawing by Leonardo da Vinci that illustrates his understanding and appreciation of human anatomy.

Castiglione's *The Courtier* (1528) described the ideal courtier, or attendant at a court, as someone who had mastered the classics and several languages, and who could paint, sing, write poetry, advise and console his prince, as well as run, jump, swim, and wrestle. This idea of a "universal person," or "Renaissance man," had existed for some time, although, of course, not everyone had the leisure or resources to study so many subjects.

Although he was not a humanist and could not read Latin, Leonardo da Vinci (1452–1519)—painter, sculptor, scientist, architect, military engineer, inventor, and philosopher— became the epitome of the "Renaissance man." The illegitimate son of a notary from a Tuscan village, he was apprenticed to a Florentine painter at the age of twelve. Following acceptance into the master's guild in Florence, he remained in the workshop of his master until moving in 1482 to Milan, where he enjoyed the patronage of the Sforza family. Taking the title "Painter and Engineer of the Duke of Milan," Leonardo taught students in his workshop and undertook scientific studies of human and animal anatomy. His drawings were the first modern scientific illustrations. Leonardo began compiling his prodigious notebooks, in which he jotted down his ideas, perceptions, and experiences. He also sculpted an equestrian monument, designed costumes for theatrical performances, worked as a military engineer, and decorated palaces. In 1500, Leonardo returned to Florence, then went back to Milan six years later, beckoned by the governor of Francis I, king of France. When the Milanese freed themselves from French hegemony, he went south to Rome, where Pope Leo X (pope 1513–1521) provided him with a salary. In 1516, the French king brought Leonardo to his château on the Loire River at Amboise, where he sketched court festivals, and served as something of a Renaissance jack-of-all-trades before his death in 1519.

If the Renaissance is often said to have "discovered" mankind in general, this meant, for the most part, men. The Church considered women to be sinful daughters of Eve. Legally, women remained subordinate to men; they could own property and make their wills, but they could not sell property without their husbands' permission. Both rich and poor families continued to value boys more than girls; poor families were far more likely to abandon female babies or to place them in the care of a distant wet nurse. Many families viewed girls as a liability because of the necessity of providing a dowry, however large or small, for their marriage. Some families of means sent daughters off into convents. Because of the strict gender division within the Church, women there could aspire not only to holiness and sainthood, but also to leadership in a world of women. Life in a convent left them free to study.

Some patricians, however, educated their girls as well as their boys in the humanities. These girls studied letters, orations, and poems with tutors. A small number of women went on to write because they could not enter learned professions. Isotta Nogarola (1418–1466), a fifteenth-century humanist from Verona, abandoned secular life for quiet religious contemplation and scholarship. In her discussion of the fall of mankind in the Garden of Eden, she apologized for the weakness of women's nature, and she lamented that she fell short of "the whole and perfect virtue that men attain." Several women, however, managed to become publishers, booksellers, and printers, including several nuns who set the type for works by Petrarch. The achievement of such status required literacy and family connections to the trade—for example, being the widow or daughter of a printer and thus having family links to a guild. It was rare for a female printer to sign her name to her work, and her status was viewed as provisional—until, for example, a male heir came of age.

Overall, the Renaissance did not bring about any significant loosening in the restrictions placed on women, and women's social and personal options may even have been reduced. In the Italian city-states, women had less of a role in public life than they had enjoyed in the courts of medieval Europe. They presided over social gatherings, but for the most part in a ritualized, decorative role. Although Renaissance authors idealized love and women, the role of women continued to be to serve their fathers, husbands, or, in some cases, their lovers. When the education of young women clashed with a father's plans for his daughter to marry, marriage won out without discussion. Men's feelings were the focus of considerable attention by Renaissance writers; women's feelings and opinions usually were assumed to be unimportant. To be sure, women in large, powerful families like the Sforza, Este, and Gonzaga exerted influence and were patrons to artists. Yet the subjects they commissioned artists and sculptors to portray were essentially the same as those of their male counterparts, and, in patriarchal households, their husbands made the decisions.

RENAISSANCE ART

When the German painter Albrecht Dürer (1471–1528) visited Venice on one of his two trips to the northern Italian peninsula, he was surprised and delighted by the fact that artists there enjoyed considerably more status than in his native Nuremburg: "Here," he wrote, "I am a gentleman, at home a sponger."

The prestige and support given to the Renaissance artist created a nurturing environment for the remarkable artistic accomplishments that characterize that special period's place in history. Great works of Renaissance architecture, painting, and sculpture are still studied by specialists and appreciated by millions of people each year.

Architecture

Despite the Renaissance concept of the "ideal city" of architectural harmony, reflected in the first treatises on architecture, Florence, Siena, Perugia, and other Italian cities retained their medieval cores, which contained their markets and their public buildings, such as the town hall. But during the fifteenth century, the narrow streets and alleys of many Italian cities became interspersed with splendid buildings and dotted with works of art commissioned by wealthy families.

Florence underwent a building boom during the fifteenth century. Construction of its elegant residences stimulated the economy, providing employment to day laborers, skilled artisans—brick- and tilemakers, masons, roofers, carpenters, cabinetmakers, and joiners—and decorative artists, including goldsmiths, sculptors, and painters. Renaissance architecture emphasized elegant simplicity, an expansion of the simple rustic fronts that had characterized medieval building. Renaissance architects combined plain white walls with colorful, intricate arches, doors, and window frames. In the fifteenth century, expensive palaces of monumental proportions with columns, arches, and magnificent stairways were considered sensible investments, because they could later be sold at a profit.

Like writers and painters, Renaissance architects looked to antiquity for models. Filippo Brunelleschi (1377–1446) first applied theories of classical architecture to the Foundling Hospital in Florence, the earliest building constructed in Renaissance style. Fourteenth-century architects planned churches in the form of a circle, the shape they thought was in the image of God, with no beginning and no end. But they may also have drawn on Rome's Pantheon, a round classical temple. After going to the papal city to study the ruins of classical architecture, Brunelleschi solved daunting technical problems to construct the vast dome, or cupola, of that city's cathedral (Duomo). The magnificent structure, completed in 1413 after work lasting more than a century, reflects the architect's rejection of the northern Gothic architectural style, with its pointed arches, vaulting, and flying buttresses. Inspired by excavations of classical ruins and the rebuilding of Rome in the late fifteenth century, architects began to copy classical styles closely, adding ornate Corinthian columns and great sweeping arches.

Patronage and the Arts

Renaissance art could not have flourished without the patronage of wealthy, powerful families, though commissions by guilds and religious confraternities were not uncommon. Artists, as well as poets and musicians, were eager, like Leonardo, to be invited into a patrician's household, where there were few or no expenses, and time to work. Lesser artists painted coats of arms, tapestries, and even portraits of the prince's pets—dogs and falcons.

Some humanists not fortunate enough to be given the run of a powerful patrician's place found posts as state secretaries, because they could draft impressive official correspondence. They tutored the children of patrician families, and a few worked as papal courtiers. Such humanists penned orations, scrupulously imitating Cicero, for formal state receptions, clamorous festivals, and funerals. Pope Leo X, a Medici who composed and played music himself, brought to his court a number of distinguished artists, in addition to Leonardo da Vinci, and musicians, as well as humanists whom he employed as officials and envoys. At the same time, the genres of wit and satire developed and became part of the ribald and "sharp-tongued" life of the political and social world of the city-state. Her well-heeled friends winked and joined in the laughter when Isabella of Mantua dressed one of her dwarfs as a bishop to greet a visiting dignitary. The biting satires and lampoons of Pietro Aretino (1492–1556), who enjoyed in succession

Pope Leo X, here presented by Raphael with two cardinals, brought artists and musicians to his court.

the patronage of a banker, a cardinal, the duke of Mantua, the Medici of Florence, and a Venetian doge and nobleman, spared neither secular nor ecclesiastical leaders from mocking jokes and rhymes. Aretino attacked social climbers and the venality of offices in the city-states with particular venom. He spared the one person he referred to as divine—himself.

Because the classical texts suggested that the active life included playing a salutary role in one's community, humanist families of means believed that they should demonstrate wisdom by making good use of their riches. Commissioning works of art seemed to confirm moral leadership, and therefore the right to govern. Wealthy families also used art to reflect the image that they wished to give of themselves, for example, commissioning portraits to impress the family of a prospective spouse.

The Medici of Florence, the greatest of the secular patrons of the arts, commissioned buildings, paid for the elaborate decoration of chapels and altarpieces, and restored monasteries. Although wags suggested that he may have been more interested in the expensive bindings of the books he purchased than in their contents, Cosimo de' Medici collected manuscripts and even read some of them. The wealthy banker oversaw the construction of fine palaces and churches. Michelangelo (1475–1564), who designed the Medici tomb in the church of Saint Lorenzo in Florence, was but one sculptor who enjoyed the favor of the Medici.

The long economic recession of the fifteenth century may have actually contributed to the arts. Finding insufficient profits in commerce and manufacturing for their money, patrician families spent considerable sums on paintings and sculpture. This may, in turn, have accentuated the recession by turning productive capital away from economic investments. At the same time, so the argument goes, the recession offered families of means more time to devote to culture.

Masaccio's *Adoration of the Magi* (1426).

Patrons of the arts often specified not only the subject of the work they were commissioning but certain details as well, requiring, for example, that specific saints be depicted. The size of the work of art and its price were also specified, of course, including the cost of blue pigment or gold for paintings and bronze or marble for sculptures. Cherubs cost more. Although one of the dukes of Ferrara paid for his paintings by their size, increasingly patrons paid the artist for his time—and thus his skill—as well as for the materials he used. The contract for a work of art might specify whether it was to be completed by the artist himself, or if assistants from the master's workshop could be employed for certain parts. Patrons sometimes appeared on the canvas, as in the case of *The Adoration of the Magi* (1426) by Tommaso di Giovanni Masaccio (1401–1428), which includes portraits of the notary who commissioned the painting and his son. Conversely, patricians occasionally commissioned artists to humiliate their enemies, as when a painter in Verona was paid to sneak up to the walls of a rival palace and paint obscene pictures.

Renaissance Artists

Because of its basis in the craft tradition, in the medieval world painting was considered a "mechanical" art. This made the status of the artist ambiguous, because he sold his own works and lacked the humanist's education. Michelangelo's father tried to discourage his son from becoming a sculptor, an art that he identified with stone cutting. Michelangelo himself sometimes signed his paintings "Michelangelo, sculptor," as if to differentiate himself from a mere painter. Yet, in his treatise on painting (1435), the humanist Leon Battista Alberti, irritated by contemporary insistence that painting was a "mechanical art," insisted that the artist was no longer a craftsman but a practitioner of a "high art."

Of the artists whose social origins are known, the majority had fathers who were urban shopkeepers or artisans, most often in the luxury trades.

Next in number—surprisingly—came the sons of nobles, perhaps reflecting the relative decline in noble fortunes during the Renaissance. Then came the children of merchants and educated professionals such as notaries, lawyers, and officials. A few painters, like Raphael (1483–1520), were sons of artists. Only a handful were the sons of peasants.

The contemporary association between craftsmen and painters was appropriate, because, like the former, artists entered a period of apprenticeship. Architects and composers lacked such formal training. The painters' guild of Venice required five years of apprenticeship, followed by two years of journeyman status, requirements similar to those by which silversmiths, shoemakers, cabinetmakers, and other craftsmen were trained. Some masters had sizable workshops, where apprentices trained and often lived together, sometimes working on the same paintings (which is one reason it is difficult to authenticate some canvases). Because women could neither become apprentices nor attend universities, there were no prominent female Renaissance artists until well into the sixteenth century.

Indeed, artists claimed that they deserved more esteem than a craftsman. Leonardo praised the painter, who sits "at his easel in front of his work, dressed as he pleases, and moves his light brush with the beautiful colors . . . often accompanied by musicians or readers of various beautiful works." The artist's quest for the humanist ideals of beauty and God helps explain the rise of some artists of the Renaissance period from practitioners of a "mechanical art," to the description of Michelangelo offered by a Portuguese painter: "In Italy, one does not care for the renown of great princes: it's a painter only that they call divine." Not all painters ascended to such heights, of course, but in general the status of the artist rose during the Renaissance. Michelangelo, Leonardo, Raphael, and Titian (Tiziano Vecellio, c. 1490–1576) lived as gentlemen, the last knighted by Holy Roman Emperor Charles V. Some artists and writers were crowned with laurels—thus the designation of "poet laureate"—by their adoring city-states.

Painting and Sculpture

The rediscovery of antiquity, nature, and mankind transformed European painting. Renaissance artists reflected the influence of the neo-Platonists. In the late fifteenth and early sixteenth centuries, the neo-Platonists appropriated Plato's belief that eternal ideas—such as beauty, truth, and goodness—existed beyond the realm of everyday life. Humanists believed that the mind could transcend human nature and come to understand these eternal ideas. The artist could reproduce the beauty of the soul through imagination and, in doing so, reach out to God. To Dante, art was "the grandchild of God." For Michelangelo, beauty "lifts to heaven hearts that truly know."

Artists sought to achieve the representation of beauty in a realistic way by using the proportions created by God in the universe. It was the

Stories of Saint John the Evangelist: Vision on the Island of Patmos, fresco by Giotti, Peruzzi Chapel in the Basilica of Santa Croce in Florence.

supreme compliment to say of a Renaissance painter that his work had surpassed nature in beauty. Leonardo put it this way: "Painting . . . compels the mind of the painter to transform itself into the mind of nature itself and to translate between nature and art." During the Renaissance, nature ceased to be mere background. Painters now faithfully depicted the beauty of mountains, rocks, and gardens for their own sake.

Objects of everyday life increasingly appeared in paintings, reflecting a greater preoccupation with realistic depiction. Take, for example, Raphael's painting of the pudgy Pope Leo X, staring off into space while fiddling with a magnifying glass with which he has been examining a book (see p. 64).

Beauty could be portrayed with extraordinary richness. The memorable figures of the frescoes of Giotto di Bondone (c. 1266–1337) in the chapels of Holy Cross Church in Florence, particularly their facial expressions, reflect humanity, deeply personal emotion, and naturalism, unseen since the classical age. The fame of Giotto, who is usually considered the first great painter of the Renaissance, spread rapidly throughout much of Italy, and his style greatly influenced his successors. Raphael, who admired and learned from Michelangelo, eight years his senior, wrote of trying to paint a beautiful woman, "I use as my guide a certain idea of the beautiful that I carry in my mind." Raphael's figures reflect a softness and inner beauty

Masaccio's *The Expulsion of Adam and Eve from Eden* (c. 1427).

that contrast with the powerful, stirring subjects of the tempestuous Michelangelo. Reflecting neo-Platonist influence, Titian early in the sixteenth century strove to bring the viewers of his paintings closer to the idea of the eternal form of female beauty that he sought to represent with his depictions of Venus.

The Greeks and Romans believed that the painter and sculptor understood and portrayed the soul when they reproduced the human face. Leonardo's famous *Mona Lisa* (1503–1507), with its mysterious, confident half-smile, is a compelling illustration of this undertaking. "Movements of the soul," wrote Alberti early in the fifteenth century, "are recognized in movements of the body." The artist had to be able to reveal the emotions and passions of the figures he depicted.

Renaissance artists used a large repertoire of stylized portrayals of emotion, the meanings of which were immediately recognized by virtually all viewers of their paintings. The Florentine Masaccio intended his extraordinary fresco *The Expulsion of Adam and Eve from Eden* (c. 1427) to represent the tortured souls, as well as bodies, of those biblical figures. Masaccio's Adam covers his eyes with his fingers in anguish in this truly gripping depiction of Adam and Eve's crushing grief as they leave the Garden of Eden. Although Renaissance artists generally avoided many of the routine associations of the medieval period (gold for piety, for example), certain colors were used for symbolic purposes. Violet was often a color of reverence, white that of charity, red of fire, and gray of earth. Clear colors, intense light, and ideal proportions were combined in representations of Christ. Deep coloring, more subtle and natural than the blues and golds of medieval painting, enriched the canvas.

Medieval and Byzantine artists typically painted rigid images on a flat space, thus their work often appeared two-dimensional and lifeless; linear forms were arranged in order of importance, accompanied by symbols easily identifiable to the viewer. The Renaissance development of perspective theory, in which parallel lines recede from the surface and seem to converge on the vanishing point, facilitated the realistic presentation of figures and movement. Renaissance artists believed that naturalism could only be achieved through the use of perspective. Masaccio first applied the mathematical laws of perspective to painting in his revolutionary *Trinity* (1425), which makes a two-dimensional surface seem to be three-dimensional. The mastery of light

Andrea Mantegna's *The Dead Christ* (c. 1506), an example of Renaissance treatment of perspective.

also contributed to innovative uses of space; for example, through the technique of foreshortening, artists proportionally contracted depth so as to give the viewer the illusion of projection or extension into space. In his realistic *The Dead Christ* (c. 1506), Andrea Mantegna (c. 1430–1506) utilized this technique, which had been pioneered by Masaccio. This shortcut allowed the artist to create the visual impression of a three-dimensional body on a flat surface. Florentine artists, in particular, used perspective to develop high relief and silhouette, presenting rounded figures on the canvas surface by effective use of tones and shades.

This mastery of perspective by the naturalist painter Masaccio and, above all, the sculptor Donatello (c. 1386–1466) helped Renaissance painters choose difficult, complicated themes and treat them with a more complex realism. Donatello utilized perspective to achieve dramatic action through gradations of relief. In *The Feast of Herod* (c. 1417), sculpted in bronze for the stone basin in the Siena Baptistery, Donatello captures the shocked reaction of the king and guests as John the Baptist's head is presented to Herod. In Leonardo's painting *The Last Supper* (c. 1495–1498), Christ's disciples crowd around the table. The viewer's eye is drawn along the lines of perspective of the ceiling to the central figure of Christ, whose image stands out because it is framed by a large window. Leonardo identifies Judas, the betrayer of Christ, not by leaving him without a halo nor by placing him alone on the other side of the table from Christ, but by painting him as the only figure in shadow.

To Leonardo, painting was the highest form of science, based on "what has passed through our senses." He believed that "the scientific and true principles of painting first determine" the components of painting: "darkness, light, color, body, figure, position, distance, nearness, motion, and rest." The work of Michelangelo reflects a mastery of mathematics, anatomy, and optics. Animals, birds, and inanimate objects also took on a lifelike quality based upon artists' discovery of proper proportions.

The quest for the natural representation of beauty led some artists to depict the human body in nude form, which some took to be a more natural and expressive form borrowed from classical paganism. Michelangelo believed that the depiction of the human body in sculpture was the ultimate expression of mankind as a divine creation, made in God's image. In his sculptures and paintings of the nude figure, the muscles and sinews of the body are infused with the emotions and passions of humanity.

Religious, public, and private life overlapped, as the people of Renaissance Italy sought religious meanings in everything they saw. Art with religious subjects also served a teaching function for the Church. In many patrician houses, a religious image could be found in every room. Devotional images, known as *ex votos*, were often erected in public spaces to fulfill a vow made to a saint in times of danger or illness. Patricians commissioned paintings with religious themes to realize similar vows. Moreover, the splendid tombs sculpted for patricians and popes may have reflected a preoccupation with glorifying the individual, but they nonetheless also emphasized eternal salvation.

Religious themes continued to dominate painting, accounting for perhaps nine of every ten paintings; the Virgin Mary was the most popular figure, followed by Christ and the saints (above all, Saint John the Baptist, the patron saint of Florence). The visualization of certain episodes in the life of Christ or of the martyrdom of Saint Sebastian were intended to stimulate piety and encourage morality. Thus, artists took on a role similar to preachers, whose orations evoked a powerful emotional response.

Classical symbolism abounded in Renaissance painting and influenced the depiction of religious themes, incorporating images drawn from pagan Rome. Artists used details about history or mythology that patrons insisted grace their canvases. Some of the classical gods stood as Renaissance symbols of moral or physical qualities. Michelangelo modeled his Christ in *The Last Judgment* (1536–1541) on a classical portrayal of the god Apollo.

Yet, along with scenes from classical mythology, paintings with secular themes increased in number, notably portraits of famous men or of wealthy patricians, but also of more ordinary people as well. Aretino, who criticized everything, found fault with the democratization of the portrait, despite the fact that he was the son of a shoemaker, insisting, "It is the disgrace of our age that it tolerates the portraits even of tailors and butchers."

A section of Michelangelo's fresco, *The Creation of Man*, on the ceiling of the Sistine Chapel, the Vatican, showing God banishing Adam and Eve from the Garden of Eden.

High Renaissance Style

During the period of the High Renaissance (1490–1530), the city-states of Italy lost much of their economic and political vitality, confronting French invasion and then Spanish domination. In the midst of economic decline as well as internecine political warfare, artists no longer enjoyed the lavish patronage of wealthy patrician families. Instead, the Church became their patron.

The papacy inspired the monumentalism of the High Renaissance. Besieged in the first two decades of the sixteenth century by denunciations of the sale of indulgences—the purchase of the remission of some punishment in Purgatory for one's sins or for those of some family member—the papacy sought to assert its authority and image (see Chapter 3). Papal commissions in Rome were one attempt to recover public confidence and made possible the artistic achievements of the High Renaissance. Following excavations beginning in the 1470s that heightened interest in the ancient Roman Empire, Raphael himself oversaw the reconstruction of Rome and personally supervised excavations of the Roman Forum. Influenced by and more dependent on the Church, the canvases of the painters of the High Renaissance became even larger as they became less concerned with rational order and more with achieving a powerful visual response in their viewers.

Some humanists now began to claim that the papacy was the heir to the glories of classical Rome. Popes took names that echoed the Roman Empire. Julius II (pope 1503–1513) ordered a medal struck that read

Leonardo da Vinci's *The Last Supper* (c. 1495–1498).

"Julius Caeser Pont[ifex]. II," a term that meant "high priest" in classical Rome. Wide boulevards and spaces were forged to accommodate waves of pilgrims descending upon the city.

Leonardo's *The Last Supper* is perhaps the first example of the style of the High Renaissance, or what is sometimes called the Grand Manner. Mannerism (a term from the Italian word for style), which particularly characterized the 1520s, is marked by heightened scale, exaggerated drama, and the submersion of detail to a total emotional effect. Donato Bramante (1444–1514), who constructed St. Peter's Basilica in Rome in the "grand manner" of the High Renaissance, designed its grand Byzantine dome, which was completed by Michelangelo and a successor.

Painters of the High Renaissance increasingly presented large, ambitious, complex, and sometimes even bizarre canvases. Mannerism's imaginative distortions and sense of restlessness offered an unsettling vision in tune with new uncertainties. Mannerism marked something of a reaction against the Renaissance ideal of attaining classical perfection. Thus, some painters ignored the rules of perspective; emotionalism, as well as mysticism and illusionism, won out over classicism. Toward the end of his career, Michelangelo's work reflected this influence. His majestic marble *Moses* (1515), sculpted for the tomb of Pope Julius II, has an immensely prominent head, with an exaggerated facial expression. It reflects Michelangelo's tragic vision of human limitations, including his own. Raphael and Titian presented human figures who seem almost empowered by divine attributes but who nonetheless retain their humanity.

THE END OF THE RENAISSANCE

Late in the fifteenth century, the Italian city-states entered a period of economic and political decline, making the peninsula more vulnerable to foreign invasion. Subsequently, some of the battles between Spain and France,
Europe's two dominant powers, were fought on the Italian peninsula. The
exploration and gradual colonization of the Americas, first by Spain, and the
increase in trade and manufacturing in northwestern Europe, helped move
economic and cultural vigor toward the Atlantic Ocean, to Spain and northwestern Europe, most notably, England, France, and the Dutch Netherlands, and to the New World (see Chapter 5).

Economic Decline

The economic decline of the northern Italian city-states during the second
half of the fifteenth century undermined the material base of Renaissance
prosperity, indeed the economic primacy of the Mediterranean region. The
Italian city-states lost most of their trading routes with Asia. The Turks conquered Genoese trading posts in the Black Sea, the traditional merchant
route to Asia, and in the Aegean Sea. Turkish domination reduced Genoa's
once mighty commercial network to trade centered on the Aegean island of
Chios. Of the Italian city-states, Venice alone continued to prosper. After
the Ottoman conquest of Constantinople in 1453, merchants in Venice concluded a deal with the Turks by which they received a monopoly on trade
with the East, leaving the other city-states without access to their traditional
Asian markets. Venice's economy soon diversified with small-scale manufacturing, however, particularly as the Turkish threat to its interests mounted in
the eastern Mediterranean and Venetian galleys no longer could venture
into the Black Sea.

Merchants of the Italian city-states sought alternatives. The Genoese
established a trading post in the Muslim city of Málaga on the southern
coast of Spain, although this made them dependent on local Muslim middlemen. Portuguese fleets began to monopolize the spice trade with India
and beyond.

The Florentine silk and woolen industries, long prosperous, now faced
stiff competition from French and Dutch producers and merchants in northwestern Europe. The dazzling prosperity of the great Italian merchant families ebbed. The economy of Europe—and even of world commerce
itself—was changing. Portuguese, Spanish, English, and Dutch traders
looked to the New World for new products and significant profits (see Chapter 1). The rapid growth of Portuguese and then Spanish trade accentuated
the rise of the Atlantic economy. Competition from the larger sailing ships of
England, Holland, and Portugal overwhelmed Florence and Genoa and then,
more gradually, Venice.

Foreign Invasion

As long as the Italian peninsula remained free from the intervention of France and Spain or other powers, the city-states could continue to prosper while fighting each other and casting wary glances toward the Ottoman Empire as it expanded its influence in the Mediterranean. But the city-states, divided by economic interests and with a long tradition of quarreling among themselves, became increasingly vulnerable to the expansion of French interests.

France had adhered to an alliance of Milan and Florence against Venice, signed in 1451. But the three city-states recognized the threat the aggressive French monarchy posed to the peninsula. Furthermore, following the capture of Constantinople in 1453, Turkish ships now appeared more frequently in the Adriatic Sea. It seemed imperative to end the struggles between the city-states. The Peace of Lodi (1454), signed by Florence, Milan, and Venice, established a new political order. Helping discourage Turkish or French aggrandizement, the treaty brought four decades of relative peace, which saw some of the crowning artistic glories of the Renaissance.

The establishment of this Italian League formalized this balance of power—it was already called that—between the strongest city-states. Whenever one or two of the states became aggressive—as when Venice and the Papal States attacked Ferrara—the others joined together to restore the status quo. Such wars were fought for the most part by mercenaries, imported and organized by *condottieri* paid for the task. For the moment, Milan's strong army served as a barricade against French invasion.

Perhaps accentuated by the ebbing of prosperity, political life within the city-states deteriorated. In Florence, the Medici despotism faced opposition from republicans. In the 1480s, Perugia had become a warring camp, torn between two rival families. In 1491, 130 members of one faction were executed on a main square and hanged from poles for all to see. Then, in repentance, the oligarchs erected thirty-five altars on that same square, and ordered priests to say Mass for three days in atonement. In a number of the city-states, some patrician families tried to outdo each other in their violence, crushing their opponents with brutality, then praying over the bodies. The leading Florentine families faithfully attended church, even as they undertook murders of vengeance in defense of family honor. Considerable tension, then, remained between two parallel codes of conduct, one religious, the other defined by family loyalties.

The Italian peninsula then became a battleground for the dynastic ambitions and rivalries of the French kings and the Holy Roman emperors, powerful rulers who could mobilize considerably larger armies than those of the city-states. The absorption of the wealthy and strategically important duchy of Burgundy into the Holy Roman Empire accentuated the struggle between the Habsburg dynasty and Charles VIII (ruled 1483–1498) of

France. The latter decided to press his dubious claim to the throne of Naples, encouraged by the Sforza family of Milan, the enemy of Naples. In response, Naples allied with Florence and Pope Alexander VI (pope 1492–1503), himself a Florentine member of the Borgia family, against Milan.

In 1494, Charles VIII invaded the Italian peninsula with an army of 30,000 men. His French cavalry, Swiss mercenary infantry, and Scottish bowmen tore through northern Italy. In Florence, the Medici ruler handed over Pisa to France in exchange for leaving. This angered Florentine republicans. When the French army entered Florence, the Florentines drove the Medici from power (after sixty years of rule). The new Florentine government, establishing the Great Council as a legislative assembly, contributed to the city's artistic splendors by commissioning works of art that symbolized republican independence and ideals. Leonardo and Michelangelo painted scenes of Florentine military victories for the meeting hall of the Great Council. Seven years later, the city government commissioned Michelangelo's great statue *David*. Michelangelo's conscious imitation of a Donatello bust of the same name from early in the fifteenth century referred back to the republic's successful resistance to challenges at that time.

In the meantime, the army of Charles VIII moved toward Naples, devastating everything in its path. It marched into the city to cheers from Neapolitans who opposed the harsh taxes that had been levied by their rulers. But an anti-French coalition that included King Ferdinand of Aragon—whose dynastic territories included Sicily, Venice, and the Papal States—and the Holy Roman emperor rallied to defeat the French forces. Although the French army left the Italian peninsula, the city-states' troubles had only just begun.

In Florence, Girolamo Savonarola (1452–1498), a charismatic Dominican monk who had predicted the French invasion, opposed both the Medici in Florence and the papacy on the grounds that both were worldly and corrupt. He had welcomed Charles VIII of France as "an instrument in the hands of the Lord who has sent you to cure the ills of Italy," including the sinfulness of the Florentines. With the Medici driven from power, Savonarola took virtual control of the Florentine republic. His denunciation of abuses within the Church led to his excommunication by Pope Alexander VI. Savonarola also incurred the enmity of patrician families by appealing for support to all ranks of Florentine society. With the pope's blessing, Savonarola's enemies first hanged and then burned him—the penalty for heresy—in 1498.

The next year, Louis XII (ruled 1498–1515), the new king of France, invaded the Italian peninsula, intent on making good his claim on the duchy of Milan. He did so with the support of the corrupt Pope Alexander VI, who wanted French assistance as he tried to solidify papal territorial claims, as well as to look after the extended interests of his children. To encourage the French king, the pope annulled Louis's marriage, so that he could marry his

Girolamo Savonarola being burned at the stake in Florence, sixteenth-century painting.

predecessor's widow, thereby keeping Brittany within his domains. When Julius II, who had been a bitter enemy of Alexander VI, became pope in 1503, he drove the powerful Borgia family from Rome. Then the dissolute pope set about trying to restore territorial holdings taken from the Papal States by Venice and its allies, constructing an alliance against the Venetians and becoming the last pope to lead his troops into the field of battle. That year the Spanish army defeated the French army and the Habsburgs absorbed the kingdom of Naples. Milan remained a fief of Louis XII until French forces were driven from the city in 1512, the same year that a Spanish army defeated the Florentines and the Medici overthrew the republic. Three years later, French troops overwhelmed Swiss mercenaries and recaptured Milan. After the intervention of Emperor Charles V in 1522 and French defeats, the Lombardy city became a Spanish possession in 1535.

Machiavelli

A mood of vulnerability and insecurity spread through the Italian peninsula as the city-states battled each other. Peasants, crushed by taxes and hunger, ever more deeply resented the rich. In turn, wealthy people were increasingly suspicious of the poor, viewing them as dangerous monsters capable of threatening social order.

The devoted Florentine Niccolò Machiavelli was among those seeking to understand why the once proud and independent city-states of Italy now seemed virtually helpless before the invasion of foreign powers. Machiavelli's view of politics reflects his experience living in Florence during these tumultuous decades. The turmoil in Florence led him to write his *Histories* in 1494, which described the decline of

The pensive Niccolò Machiavelli.

the city-states. Influenced by his experience in government, Machiavelli, who had served as a Florentine diplomat at the court of the king of France and in Rome, believed himself to be a realist. He considered war a natural outlet for human aggression. But he also preferred the resolution of disputes by diplomacy. He believed that the absence of "civic virtue" accounted for the factionalism within and rivalries between the city-states. By civic virtue, Machiavelli meant the effective use of military force.

In 1512, the Medici overthrew the Florentine Republic, returning to power with the help of the papal army and that of Spain. Following the discovery of a plot, of which he was innocent, against the Medici patriarchs, Machiavelli was forced into exile on his country estate outside of the city. Florence had changed. A Medici supporter wrote one of the family heads: "Your forefathers, in maintaining their rule, employed skill rather than force; you must use force rather than skill."

A year later, Machiavelli wrote *The Prince* (1513). In it he reflected on the recent history of the Italian peninsula and offered a pessimistic assessment of human nature, marked by his belief that a strong leader—the prince—could arise out of strife. By making his subjects afraid of him, the prince could end political instability and bring about a moral regeneration that Machiavelli believed had characterized antiquity. Drawing on Cicero, he studied the cities of the Roman Republic and the Roman Empire. Machiavelli can be considered the first political scientist, because his works reflect a systematic attempt to draw general, realistic conclusions from his understanding of the recent history of the Italian city-states. This preoccupation with the past in itself reveals the influence of the Renaissance.

Machiavelli put his faith in political leadership. Regardless of whether the form was monarchical or republican, he believed that the goal of government should be to bring stability to the city. A sense of civic responsibility could only be reestablished through "good laws and institutions," but these, for Machiavelli, depended completely on military strength. He called on the Medici to drive away the new barbarians. Machiavelli's *The Art of War* (1521) expressed hope that the brutish mercenaries who had devastated the Italian peninsula would give way to soldier-citizens who would restore virtue. But for the Italian city-states, it was too late.

Machiavelli's invocation of "reasons of state" as sufficient justification for political action and as a political principle in itself, and his open admiration of ruthless rulers, would leave a chilling legacy, reflected by his belief that the "ends justify the means." While it is unlikely that Machiavelli had a sense of the state in the impersonal, modern sense of the term, he held that "good arms make good laws."

The Decline of the City-States

For much of the first thirty years of the sixteenth century, in Italy foreign armies fought against each other and against alliances formed by the city-states. The army of France in Italy reached 32,000 men by 1525, that of Spain 100,000 soldiers. Only Venice could resist the two great powers. In 1521, the first war broke out between Holy Roman Emperor Charles V (King Charles I of Spain) and King Francis I of France, who became the first Western ruler to ally with the Ottoman Turkish sultan. Charles V's armies decimated the French at Pavia, Italy, in 1525, carting the French king off to Madrid, where he remained until his family paid a ransom. In 1527, Charles V's mercenary army, angry over lack of pay, sacked Rome. By the Peace of Cambrai (1529), France gave up claims to Naples and Milan. But with the exception of Venice, the Italian city-states were now in one way or another dependent upon Charles V, the Holy Roman emperor, as the Spanish army repulsed new French invasions. In Rome, where Spanish merchants already had a significant presence, the pope increasingly depended on the Holy Roman emperor for defense against the Turks, as Charles added to his resources by taxing ecclesiastical revenues.

The long wars drained the city-states of financial resources and men, devastating some of the countryside. Nobles, whose political power had been diminished by the wealthy merchants of the fourteenth and fifteenth centuries, took advantage of the chaos to return to prominence in some cities. Patrician families struggled to maintain their authority against newcomers, including wealthy merchants who had married into poorer noble lines and who began to ape the styles of nobles. The Medici, after having once again been expelled by republicans, reconquered their city in 1530 after a siege of ten months. But in Florence, too, the Renaissance was over.

Artistic styles had already begun to reflect the loss of Renaissance self-confidence that accompanied the devastating impact of the French invasion. Botticelli seemed to abandon the serenity and cheerful optimism that characterized the Renaissance. To his painting *Mystical Nativity*, Botticelli added an anxious inscription: "I Sandro painted this picture at the end of the year 1500 in the troubles of Italy." Botticelli thereafter became preoccupied with suffering and the Passion of Christ, reflecting the fact that the High Renaissance was more closely tied to ecclesiastical influence. The deteriorating political situation, combined with the expansion of Spanish influence after 1530, made it more difficult for artists to find patronage in the Italian city-states.

Soon in Italy only Venice, the city of Titian, remained a center of artistic life. Machiavelli, who died in 1527, the year Charles V's troops pillaged Rome, sensed that the humiliation of the Italian city-states by foreign armies brought to a close a truly unique period in not only the history of Italy but in Western civilization. Of the great figures of the High Renaissance, only Michelangelo and Titian lived past 1530.

Impulses Elsewhere

The cultural glories of the Renaissance ebbed even as different kinds of discoveries by Europeans opened up new possibilities for mankind. Columbus's transatlantic voyages were signs that the economic and cultural vitality of Europe was shifting away from the Mediterranean to Spain and, to a lesser extent, England. The economic interests of these states would increasingly be across the Atlantic Ocean. The mood of optimism associated with the Renaissance seemed to have moved to central and northern Europe as Italy lapsed into a considerably less happy period. Many humanists and artists began to emigrate north of the Alps to lands considered by most cultured Italians to have been barbarian only a century earlier. Now new universities in northern Europe beckoned them.

Other dramatic changes had already begun to occur across the Alps. Relentless calls for reform of the Catholic Church led to a schism within Christendom: the Reformation. In northern Europe, the Dutch monk and humanist Erasmus expressed the exhilaration many men of learning felt when he wrote, "The world is coming to its senses as if awakening out of a deep Sleep."

CHAPTER 3

THE TWO
REFORMATIONS

After paying a handsome sum to Pope Leo X in 1515, Albert of Hohenzollern received a papal dispensation (exemption from canon law) that enabled him to become archbishop of Mainz, a lucrative and prestigious ecclesiastical post. Otherwise, under canon law, the twenty-three-year-old Albert would have been ineligible due to his age (archbishops were supposed to be at least thirty years old) and because he already drew income from two other ecclesiastical posts. As part of his payment to the pope and in order to repay the large sum of money loaned to him by the Fugger banking family, the new archbishop authorized the sale of the St. Peter's indulgence, which would release a sinner from punishment for his sins. Johann Tetzel, a Dominican friar who was in charge of the sale of papal indulgences in the archbishopric of Mainz, was commissioned to preach the indulgence. Half of the proceeds were to go to the papacy, and half to Albert and the Fuggers. In his tour of parishes, Tetzel emotionally depicted the wailing of dead parents in Purgatory, pleading with their children to put coins in the box so that they could be released from their suffering.

The sale of indulgences, particularly their commercial use to allow clergymen to obtain multiple posts, had drawn increasing criticism in some of the German states. Indeed, no other ecclesiastical financial abuse drew as much passionate opposition as did indulgences. More than this, the Roman papacy itself faced considerable opposition in the German states, as the pope had appointed foreigners to many key ecclesiastical posts and had attempted to force the German states to provide him with money for a war against the Turks. The young German monk Martin Luther was among those denouncing Tetzel, the sale of indulgences, and the role of the Roman papacy in the German states.

This opposition to the papacy created a schism that would tear Christendom apart beginning in the second decade of the sixteenth century. Origi-

(*Left*) The young Martin Luther by Lucas Cranach. (*Right*) The pope selling indulgences.

nating in the German states and Switzerland, a movement for religious reform began to spread across much of Europe, in part reflecting the influence of Renaissance humanism in northern Europe. Reformers rejected the pope's authority and some Church doctrine itself. The movement for reform, or of "protest," came to be called the "Reformation." It led to the establishment of many Protestant denominations within Christianity. The followers of the German priest Martin Luther became Lutherans, while those of the Frenchman Jean Calvin in Switzerland became known as Calvinists. King Henry VIII established the Church of England (Anglican Church). Under attack from many sides, the Roman Catholic Church undertook a Counter-Reformation, or Catholic Reformation, which sought to reform some aspects of ecclesiastic life, while reaffirming the basic tenets of Catholic theology and belief in the authority of the pope.

By 1600, the pattern of Christian religious adherence had largely been established in Europe. Catholicism remained the religion of the vast majority of people living in Spain, France, Austria, Poland, the Italian states, Bavaria, and other parts of the southern German states. Protestants dominated England and much of Switzerland, the Dutch Netherlands, Scandinavia, and the northern German states. Wars fought in the name of religion broke out within and between European states, beginning in the late sixteenth century and culminating in the Thirty Years' War (1618–1648). These conflicts shaped the next century of European history, with religious divisions affecting the lives of millions of people.

The Northern Renaissance

Until the middle of the fifteenth century, the Renaissance had been limited to the Italian peninsula. Northern Europe enjoyed very little of the economic and cultural vitality of the Italian city-states, where wealthy merchant and banking families patronized humanists and artists. The country estates of noble families were rarely centers of learning. The future Pope Pius II claimed in the mid-fifteenth century that "literature flourishes in Italy and princes there are not ashamed to listen to, and themselves to know, poetry. But in Germany princes pay more attention to horses and dogs than to poets—and thus neglecting the arts they die unremembered like their own beasts."

In about 1460, Renaissance humanism began to influence scholars in northern Europe. As in Italy, humanism changed the way many people thought about the world. Humanists were interested in morality and ethics, as well as in subjecting texts to critical scrutiny. Therefore, debates over religion, and the Bible itself, attracted their attention. Humanists began to criticize Church venality and corruption, and the seeming idleness of monastic life. They also called into question scholasticism and its influence on religious theology, as well as criticizing parts of religious practice that they considered illogical and therefore superstitious. The spread of humanism in northern Europe was gradual, first influencing isolated scholars. In the beginning, it posed no immediate threat to the Church; humanists could not imagine organized religion beyond Roman Catholicism. But the cumulative effect of the Northern Renaissance, and humanism in particular, helped engender a critical spirit that by the first decades of the sixteenth century directly began to challenge Church practices and then doctrine.

Northern Art and Humanism

The Northern Renaissance that began in the late fifteenth century reflected considerable Italian influence. Italian ambassadors, envoys, and humanists brought Renaissance art and humanistic thought to northern Europe. Many of the Italian envoys to northern Europe had studied the classics. They carried on diplomacy with oratorical and writing skills learned by reading Cicero and other Roman authors. Yet, much of the artistic creativity in northern Europe, particularly Flanders, emerged independent of Italian influence. Like the Italian city-states, in the Dutch Netherlands, which had a well-developed network of trading towns, wealthy urban families patronized the arts. Lacking the patronage of the Church, which so benefited Florentine and other Italian painters, Flemish painters did few church frescoes (which, in any case, a wet climate also discouraged). They emphasized decorative detail, such as that found in illuminated manuscripts, more than the spatial harmonies of Italian art. Dutch and Flemish painters favored realism more than Italian Renaissance idealism in their portrayal of the human body. They broke away from religious subject matter and Gothic use of dark, gloomy colors and tones. In contrast to Italian painting, intense religiosity remained an important element in Flemish and German painting, and it was relatively rare to see a depiction of nudes.

Albrecht Dürer's visits to Italy reflect the dissemination and influence of the Italian Renaissance beyond the Alps. The son of a Nuremberg goldsmith, Dürer was apprenticed to a book engraver. As a young man, he seemed irresistibly drawn to Italy as he wrestled with how to depict the human form. During two visits to Venice—in

Albrecht Dürer's *Self-Portrait* (1500).

1494 and 1505–1506—he sought out Italian painters, studying their use of mathematics in determining and representing proportion.

Literary societies, academies, and universities contributed to the diffusion of Renaissance ideals in northern Europe. Francis I established the Collège de France in 1530 in Paris, which soon had chairs in Greek, Hebrew, and classical Latin. Northern universities became centers of humanistic study, gradually taking over the role royal and noble households had played in the diffusion of education. In Poland, the University of Krakow, which had its first printing press in 1476, emerged as a center of humanism in the late fifteenth and early sixteenth centuries. But some universities were quite slow to include humanists; only one humanist taught at the University of Cambridge in the early sixteenth century.

Some nobles now sent their children to humanist schools or employed humanists as tutors, as did a number of wealthy urban bourgeois. Some Italian artists and scholars found employment in northern courts. Leonardo da Vinci, Renaissance artist and scientist, was employed by King Francis I of France. Kings and princes also hired humanists to serve as secretaries and diplomats.

Latin gradually became the language of scholarship beyond the Alps. German, French, Spanish, and English historians borrowed from the style of the Roman historians to celebrate their own medieval past. Unlike Italian historians, they viewed the medieval period not as a sad interlude between two glorious epochs but as a time when their own political institutions and customs had been established.

In England at the end of the sixteenth century, Latin remained the language of high culture. There Machiavelli's *The Prince* was widely read and debated in Latin. When continental scholars traveled to England, they could discuss common texts with their English counterparts. Sir Thomas More (1478–1535), English lawyer and statesman, reflected the influence of Renaissance humanism, writing poetry in Latin. In his *Utopia* (1516), a satire of contemporary political and social life, More asked readers to consider their own values in the context of their expanding knowledge of other societies, including those of the New World.

The spread of the cultural values of Renaissance humanism across the Alps into the German states and northern Europe helped prepare the way for the Reformation. Like the Renaissance, the Reformation was in some ways the work of humanists moving beyond what they considered to be the constraints of Church theology. Humanists, who had always been concerned with ethics, attacked not only the failings of some clerics but also some of the Church's teachings, especially its claim to be immune to criticism. They also condemned superstition in the guise of religiosity. Northern Renaissance humanists were the sworn enemies of scholasticism, the medieval system of ecclesiastical inquiry in which Church scholars used reason to prove the tenets of Christian doctrine within the context of assumed theological truths. By suggesting that individuals who were not priests could interpret the Bible for themselves, they threatened the monopoly of Church theologians over biblical interpretation.

Erasmus's Humanistic Critique of the Church

An energetic Dutch cleric contributed more than any other person to the growth of Renaissance humanism in northern Europe. Born to unmarried parents and orphaned in Rotterdam, Desiderius Erasmus (c. 1469–1536) spent seven years in a monastery. Ordained a priest in 1492, he taught at the universities of Cambridge and Louvain, and then worked as a tutor in Paris and in Italy. As a young man, Erasmus may have suffered some sort of trauma—perhaps a romantic attachment that was either unreciprocated or inopportunely discovered. Thereafter compulsively obsessed with cleanliness, he was determined to infuse the Church with a new moral purity influenced by the Renaissance.

The patronage of Holy Roman Emperor Charles V and several other statesmen permitted Erasmus to apply the scholarly techniques of humanism to biblical study. Erasmus's *In Praise of Folly* (1509) was a satirical survey of the world as he saw it but also a clear call for a pure Christian morality shorn of the corruption he beheld in the monastic system. Thus, he wrote that priests claimed "that they've properly performed their duty if they reel off perfunctorily their feeble prayers which I'd be greatly surprised if any god could hear or understand." He believed that the scholastics of the Middle Ages had, like the barbarians, overwhelmed the Church with empty, lifeless theology.

Erasmus's attacks on those who believed in the curing power of relics (remains of saints venerated by the faithful) reflected his Renaissance sense of the dignity of the individual. His *Handbook of the Christian Soldier* (1503), which called for a theology that de-emphasized the sacraments, provided a guide to living a moral life. The little book went through twenty Latin editions and was translated into ten other languages. Erasmus wrote at length on how a prince ought to be educated and how children should be raised. The most well-known intellectual figure of his time in Europe, Erasmus greatly expanded the knowledge and appreciation of the classics in northern Europe.

Portrait of Desiderius Erasmus by Hans Holbein the Younger.

He and other major Northern Renaissance figures forged a Christian humanism focused on the early Christian past. Following his lead, northern humanists turned their skills in editing texts in Greek and Latin to the large body of early Christian writings.

THE ROOTS OF THE REFORMATION

In principle, the pope governed the Church in all of Western Christendom. But in reality, the emergence of the monarchical states of France, England, and the kingdoms of Spain in the late Middle Ages had eroded papal authority. Gradually these rulers assumed more prerogatives over the Church in their states. This expansion of monarchical authority itself provided the impetus toward the development of churches that gradually took on a national character as monarchs bargained for authority over religious appointments and worked to bring ecclesiastical property under their fiscal control by imposing taxation.

In the Italian and German states and in Switzerland, where many smaller, independent states ruled by princes, urban oligarchs, or even bishops survived, the very complexity of territorial political arrangements served to limit the direct authority of the pope. For in these smaller states, too, the ability of the pope and his appointees to manage their own affairs depended on the cooperation of lay rulers. Furthermore, the territorial expanse of Western

Christendom and daunting problems of transportation and communication made it difficult for the papal bureaucracy to reform blatant financial abuses. That the papacy itself increasingly appeared to condone or even encourage corruption added to the calls for reform.

Yet Erasmus and other northern humanists, while sharply criticizing the Church, were unwilling to challenge papal authority. The papacy, however, had other, more vociferous critics. First, the monarchs of France, Spain, and England had repudiated the interference of the pope in temporal affairs, creating what were, for all intents and purposes, national churches. Second, religious movements deemed heretical by the Church rejected papal authority. Some people sought refuge from the turmoil in spiritualism. Others based their idea of religion on personal study of the Bible, turning away from not only papal authority but also the entire formal hierarchy of the Church. Third, within the Church, a reform movement known as conciliarism sought to subject the authority of the popes to councils of cardinals and other Church leaders. More and more calls echoed for the reform of clerical abuses. As the Church seemed determined to protect its authority, to critics it also seemed more venal, even corrupt, than ever before. By questioning fundamental Church doctrine and the nature of religious faith, the resulting reform movement, culminating in the Reformation, shattered the unity of Western Christendom.

The Great Schism (1378–1417)

In the fourteenth century, the struggle between the king of France and the pope put the authority of the papacy in jeopardy. The French and English kings had imposed taxes on ecclesiastical property. In response, Pope Boniface VIII's bull *Unam Sanctam* (1302) threw down the gauntlet to lay rulers, asserting that "it is absolutely necessary for salvation for everyone to be subject to the Roman pontiff." King Philip IV of France ordered Boniface's arrest, and the pope died a year later, shortly after his release from captivity. Philip then arranged the election of a pliant pope, Clement V (pope 1305–1314). In 1309, he installed him in the papal enclave of Avignon, a town on the Rhône River. During the "Avignon Papacy" (1309–1378), the popes remained under the direct influence of the kings of France. At the same time, the popes continued to build up their bureaucracies and, like the monarchs whose authority they sometimes contested, to extract ever greater revenues from the faithful.

In 1377, Pope Gregory XI (pope 1370–1378) returned to Rome, in the hope that his presence there might calm the political situation in the Italian states. When Gregory XI died a year later, a group of cardinals in Rome, most of whom were French, elected Pope Urban VI (pope 1378–1389), popularly believed to be faithful to the Avignon Papacy. After a Roman mob invaded the proceedings, the cardinals fled. Upon their return several months later, a smaller group of thirteen cardinals was vexed by the new pope's denunciation of their wealth and privileges. Furthermore, they now viewed him as temperamentally unstable, unfit to be pope. They elected another pope, Clement VII, who claimed to be pope between 1378 and 1394. He returned to set up shop in Avignon, leaving his rival, Urban VI, in Rome. The Great Schism (1378–1417) began with two men now claiming authority over the Church.

The two popes and their successors thereafter sought to win the allegiance of rulers. The Avignon popes, like their pre-Schism predecessors, were under the close scrutiny of the king of France, and the Roman pope was caught up in the morass of Italian and Roman politics. France, Castile, Navarre, and Scotland supported the Avignon popes; most of the Italian states, Portugal, the Holy Roman Empire, and England obeyed the Roman popes. In 1409, Church dignitaries gathered at the Council of Pisa to resolve the conflict, and they elected a third pope. However, neither of the other two would agree to resign. And, in the meantime, secular rulers forced the popes to make agreements that increased the authority of the former over the Church in their states. The Great Schism enabled lay rulers to construct virtual national churches at the expense of papal power.

Heretical and Spiritual Movements

The chaos of two and then three popes claiming authority over the Church, along with the ruthlessness and greed of the claimants, greatly increased dissatisfaction with the organization of the Church. From time to time, heresies (movements based on beliefs deemed contrary to the teaching of the Church) had denied the authority of the papacy and demanded reform. In the twelfth century, the Waldensians in the Alps and the Albigensians in the south of France had defied the papacy by withdrawing into strictly organized communities that, unlike monasteries and convents, recognized neither Church doctrine nor authority.

An undercurrent of mysticism persisted in Europe, based on a belief in the supremacy of individual piety in the quest for knowledge of God and eternal salvation. William of Occam (c. 1290–1349), an English monk and another critic of the papacy, rejected scholastic rationalism. Scholasticism had become increasingly linked to the theology of Thomas Aquinas (1225–1274), who had deduced the existence of God from what he considered rational proofs that moved from one premise to the next. Occam, in contrast, posited that the gulf between God and man was so great that scholastic proofs of God's existence, such as those of Aquinas, were pointless because mankind could not understand God through reason. "Nominalists," as Occam and his followers were known, believed that individual piety should be the cornerstone of religious life. Nominalists rejected papal authority and the hierarchical structure of the Church. Their views reflected and accentuated the turn of more clergy and laymen toward the Scriptures as a guide for the individual's relationship with God, emphasizing the importance of leading a good, simple life. The Great Schism may have increased the yearning for spirituality as well as for the institutional reform of the Church.

The English cleric and scholar John Wyclif (c. 1328–1384) also questioned the pope's authority and claimed that an unworthy pope did not have to be obeyed, views that drew papal censorship. For Wyclif, the Church consisted of the body of those God had chosen to be saved, and no more. Stressing the role of faith in reaching eternal salvation, he insisted that reading the Scriptures formed the basis of faith and the individual's relationship with God. Wyclif also put himself at odds with Church theology by rejecting transubstantiation (the doctrine that holds that during Mass the priest transforms ordinary bread and wine into the body and blood of Christ).

Wyclif's de-emphasis of rituals and his advocacy of a religion based on faith suggested the significantly reduced importance of the Church as intermediary between man and God. Wyclif, who had powerful English noble and clerical protectors, called for Church reform. But the Peasants' Revolt of 1381 in England, in which wealthy churchmen were targets of popular wrath, gave even Wyclif's powerful protectors pause by raising the specter of future social unrest. An English Church synod condemned Wyclif, but he was allowed to live out his remaining years in a monastery. Some of his English followers, poor folk known as the Lollards, carried on Wyclif's work after his death. They criticized the Church's landed wealth and espoused a simpler religion. Led by gentry known as "Lollard knights," the Lollards rose up in rebellion in 1414, but were brutally crushed by King Henry V.

In Bohemia in Central Europe, Jan Hus (c. 1369–1415), a theologian, had learned of Wyclif's teaching. He, too, loudly criticized the worldliness of some clerics, and called for a return to a more unadorned religion. Rejecting the authority of the papacy and denouncing popes as "antiChrists," Hus held that ordinary people could reform the Church.

The Challenge of Conciliarism to Papal Authority

The doctrine of conciliarism arose not only in response to the Great Schism but also to growing demands from many churchmen that the Church must undertake reform. The Council of Constance (1414–1418) was called to resolve the Great Schism and to undertake a reform of the Church. Many of the ecclesiastical dignitaries who attended also wanted to limit and define the authority of the papacy.

There were at least four significant parties to conciliarism: the popes themselves; bishops who supported councils as a way of resolving Church problems; secular rulers, particularly French kings, but also Holy Roman emperors, intervening in the Great Schism; and heretics condemned at Constance, who were far more radical than the mainstream conciliarists in their challenge to papal authority.

The Council of Constance first turned its attention to Jan Hus. Holding a safe-conduct pass given to him by the king of Bohemia, Hus travelled to the Council of Constance in 1414 but was arrested and put on trial for heresy. Hus refused to recant Wyclif's views, defending his own belief that the faithful, like the priest saying Mass, ought to be able to receive communion, the Church's rite of unity, in the two forms of bread and wine. The council condemned Hus, turning him over to the Holy Roman emperor, who ordered him burned at the stake as a heretic. The Hussites, the only major fifteenth-century dissidents within the Church, fought off several papal armies. They finally won special papal dispensation for the faithful to take communion in both bread and wine; their "Utraquist" ("in both kinds") church lasted until 1620.

The Council of Constance resolved the ongoing conflicting claims to papal authority by deposing two of the claimants and accepting the resignation of the third. In 1417, the council elected Martin V (pope 1417–1431). But the Great Schism, with its multiple papal claimants, by delaying any serious attempts at reform, had reinforced the insistence of some prelates that councils of Church bishops ought to have more authority than the pope.

Convoked by the pope, at least in principle, councils brought together leading ecclesiastical dignitaries from throughout Europe. These councils deliberated on matters of faith, as well as on the organization of the Church. But some councils began to come together in defiance of papal authority. Those holding a "conciliar" view of the Church conceived of it as

Jan Hus being burned at the stake as a heretic.

a corporation of cardinals that could override the pope. William of Occam had argued a century earlier that, when confronted by a heretical pope, a general council of the Church could stand as the repository of truth and authority. Some reformers wanted to impose a written constitution on the Church. At the Council of Basel, which began in 1431, exponents of unlimited papal authority and their counterparts favoring conciliarist positions both presented their views. In 1437, the pope ordered the council moved to Ferrara, and then the next year to Florence. Some participants, mostly conciliarists, continued to meet in Basel until 1445, although the pope declared that council schismatic. Fifteen years later, Pope Pius II (pope 1458–1464) declared the conciliar movement to be a heresy.

Clerical Abuses and Indulgences

The assertion by some churchmen that councils had authority over the papacy merged easily with those who called for the reform of blatant abuses within the Church. Some monasteries were mocked as hypocritical institutions no more saintly than the supposedly profane world monks and nuns sought to leave behind. Several new religious orders had been founded at least partially out of impatience with, if not disgust with, ecclesiastical worldliness.

Critics of the papacy attacked with particular energy ecclesiastical financial and moral abuses. They claimed that the papacy had become an investment trust run by the priests who administered the papacy's temporal affairs. No clerical financial abuse was more attacked than indulgences, which were based on the idea of transferable merit. Through granting indulgences, the Church supposedly reduced the time a soul would have to suffer punishment in Purgatory (that halfway house between Hell and Heaven that had emerged in Church belief early in the Middle Ages) for sins committed on earth. The practice of selling indulgences began during the Crusades as a means of raising revenue for churches and hospitals. Those seeking the salvation of their souls did not purchase God's forgiveness (which could only be received in the confessional) but rather cancelled or reduced the temporal punishment (such as the obligation to undertake pilgrimages, or give charity, or say so many prayers) required to atone for their sins. In 1457, the pope had announced that indulgences could be applied to the souls of family members or friends suffering in Purgatory. Some people had the impression that purchasing indulgences rather than offering real repentance brought immediate entry to Heaven for oneself or one's relatives. "The moment the money tinkles in the collecting box, a soul flies out of Purgatory," went one ditty. The implication was that wealthy families had a greater chance of opening the doors of Heaven for their loved ones than poor people. One papal critic interpreted all of this to mean that "the Lord desireth not the death of a sinner but rather that he may live and pay."

Another clerical practice that was much criticized was that of the sale of Church offices, known as simony. More than ever before, those who participated in—and benefited from—this practice were Italian clerics. Most popes appointed Italians as cardinals, many of whom lived in Rome while accumulating great wealth from ecclesiastical sees (areas of a bishops' jurisdiction) they rarely if ever visited. Some prominent families looked to the Church to provide lucrative sinecures—offices that generated income but that required little or no work—for their children. Reformers decried the appointment of unqualified bishops who had purchased their offices.

Many priests charged exorbitant fees for burial. Resentment also mounted, particularly in the German states, because clerics were immune from civil justice and paid no taxes. Indulgences and pardons, swapped for gold or services, had since 1300 become a papal monopoly. Commenting on Leo's death in 1521, one wag remarked, "His last moments come, he couldn't even have the [Last] Sacrament. By God, he's sold it!"

The papacy also came under attack for moral abuses. In the diocese of Trent in the early sixteenth century, about a fifth of all priests kept concubines. Nepotism, the awarding of posts to relatives or friends, seemed to reign supreme. In the fifteenth century, Pope Paul II was mocked as the "happy father," not revered as the Holy Father. Alexander VI (pope 1492–1503) looked after his own children with the care of any other father. Paul III (pope 1534–1549) made two of his grandsons cardinals, their expensive hats far bigger than the young heads upon which they rested.

The sacrament of penance also generated popular resentment against the clergy. Since 1215, the faithful were required to confess their sins at least once a year to a priest. This sacrament originated in the context of instruction to encourage good behavior. But for many people, penance had become the priest's interrogation of the faithful in the confessional, during which the confessor sought out details of misdeeds in order to determine one of the sixteen stated degrees of transgression. The Church's call for sinners to repent seemed particularly ironic in view of popularly perceived ecclesiastical abuses.

Given a boost by the conciliar movement, calls for reform echoed louder and louder. The representatives of the clergy who had gathered at the Estates-General of France in 1484 criticized the sale of Church offices. In 1510, the Augsburg Diet, an imperial institution of the Holy Roman Empire, refused to grant money to the pope for war against the Turks unless he first ordered an end to financial abuses. The imperial representative Assembly (Reichstag) had increasingly served as a forum for denunciations against the papacy. In 1511, King Louis XII of France, whose armies had backed up his territorial ambitions in northern Italy, called a council with the goal of reasserting the conciliar doctrine and ordered reforms in the monastic houses of his realm. The Fifth Lateran Council, which met from 1512 to 1517, urged more education for the clergy, sought to end some monastic financial abuses, and insisted that occupants of religious houses uphold their vows of chastity. The council also suggested missions to carry the Church's influence into the Americas. Pope Leo X, however, emphatically insisted that he alone could convoke Church councils, and the Fifth Lateran Council itself forbade sermons denouncing the moral state of the Church.

Martin Luther

Martin Luther (1483–1546) was born in the small town of Eisleben in central Germany. He was the son of a miner whose family had been prosperous peasants. His peasant background could be seen in the coarseness of his language, song, and humor. The stocky, pious, and determined Luther began his studies in 1501 at the University of Erfurt, where he took courses in philosophy and then began the study of law.

In July 1505, Luther was engulfed in a violent storm as he returned to Erfurt after a visit home. As a bolt of lightning struck not far from where he stood in terror, the young student cried out to the patron saint of travelers, "Help me, Saint Anne, I will become a monk." Returning safely to Erfurt, he gathered his friends together and told them, "Today you see me, henceforth, never more." They escorted him to the nearby monastery of the Augustinian monks, which he entered against his father's wishes. Luther prayed, fasted, and, outside the monastery, begged for charity. In 1507, he was ordained a priest and soon became a doctor of theology, administrator of eleven Augustinian monasteries, and dean of the theological seminary in the town of Wittenberg.

Luther had, for some time, been wracked with gnawing doubt concerning his personal unworthiness. Was he not a sinner? He had been saved from the storm, but would he be saved from damnation on Judgment Day? Was there really any connection between good works effected on earth and salvation? If mankind was so corrupted by sin, how could charity, fasting, or constant prayer and self-flagellation in the monastery earn one entry to Heaven? He later recalled, "I tried hard . . . to be contrite, and make a list of my sins. I confessed them again and again. I scrupulously carried out the penances that were allotted to me. And yet my conscience kept telling me: 'You fell short there.' 'You were not sorry enough.' 'You left that sin off your list.' I was trying to cure the doubts and scruples of the conscience with human remedies. . . . The more I tried these remedies, the more troubled and uneasy my conscience grew."

Luther's lonely study of theology in the tower library of the monastery did not resolve his doubts. Like other Augustinians, he had been influenced by the nominalism of William of Occam, which emphasized individual piety. This led Luther closer to his contention that faith, not good works, was the key to salvation. Indeed, the teachings of Saint Augustine himself also suggested to him that each person could be saved by faith alone through the grace of God. Believing man is saved "not by pieces, but in a heap," Luther became obsessed with a phrase from the Bible (Romans 1:17), "The just shall live by faith." Such a conclusion broke with the accepted teachings of the Church as defined by medieval scholasticism. But more than faith was troubling Luther. He was also especially troubled by the abuse of the ecclesiastical sale of indulgences.

On October 31, 1517, Luther tacked up on the door of the castle church of Wittenberg "Ninety-five Theses or Disputations on the Power and Efficacy of Indulgences." He denounced the theoretical underpinnings of the papal granting of indulgences out of the "treasury of merits" accumulated by Christ and the saints. He then had his theses printed and distributed in the region and invited those who might want to dispute his theses to present themselves to debate with him, as was the custom. In February 1518, Pope Leo X demanded that Luther's monastic superior order him to cease his small crusade. Luther refused, citing his right as a professor of theology to dispute formally the charges now leveled against him. And he found a protector, Frederick III, elector of Saxony, a religious ruler who turned to the Bible as he mulled over matters of state.

In April, as denunciations against Luther poured into Rome, he successfully defended his theses before his Augustinian superiors. Pope Leo was

An allegorical painting of the dream of Frederick the Wise wherein Martin Luther uses an enormous quill to tack his Ninety-Five Theses to the door of the castle church at Wittenberg.

trying to remain on good terms with Frederick III, a strong candidate for election as Holy Roman emperor. Instead of immediately summoning Luther to Rome, he therefore proposed that a papal legate travel to Augsburg to hear Luther out. At their meeting, the legate warned Luther to desist or face the consequences. Luther's friends, suspecting that the pope had ordered his arrest, whisked him away to safety.

Luther sought a negotiated solution. He agreed to write a treatise calling on the German people to honor the Church, and promised neither to preach nor publish anything else if his opponents would also keep silent. At this point Luther did not seek to create a new church, but merely to reform the old one. A papal representative sent to meet with Luther in Leipzig in June 1519 accused him of being a Hussite, that is, of denying the pope's authority. Luther admitted that he did not believe the pope to be infallible.

Luther crossed his Rubicon, but unlike Caesar moved not toward Rome but away from it. "Farewell, unhappy, hopeless, blasphemous Rome! The wrath of God come upon thee, as you deserve," he wrote a friend, "We have cared for Babylon and she is not healed; let us then leave her. . . ." Luther would not be silenced. "I am hot-blooded by temperament and my pen gets irritated easily," he proclaimed.

Three treatises published in 1520 marked Luther's final break with Rome. Here Luther developed his theology of reform, one that went far beyond the prohibition of indulgences and the sale of ecclesiastical offices. He argued his view that faith alone could bring salvation, that good works follow faith but do not in themselves save the soul. Nor, he argued, does the absence of good works condemn man to eternal damnation. Upon reading one of these tracts, Erasmus, loyal critic of the Church, stated emphatically, "The breach is irreparable."

Developing the theological concept of "freedom of a Christian," Luther's immediate goal was to free German communities from the strictures of religious beliefs and institutions that seemed increasingly foreign to their faith. He called on the princes of the German states to reform the Church in their states. In doing so, he argued that the Scriptures declared the Church itself to be a priestly body that was not subject to the pope's interpretation. Luther acknowledged only two of the seven sacraments, those instituted by Christ, not the papacy: baptism and communion. After first retaining penance, he dropped it, arguing that faith was sufficient to bring about a sinner's reconciliation with God. If this was true, the monastic life no longer seemed to Luther to provide any advantage in the quest for salvation. And he rejected what he called the "unnatural" demands of poverty, chastity, and obedience.

On June 15, 1520, Pope Leo X excommunicated Luther from the Church, accusing him of forty-one heresies. The papal bull of excommunication called Luther "the wild boar who has invaded the Lord's vineyard." In Wittenberg, a crowd burned papal bulls and documents. Luther defiantly tossed the writ of excommunication into the flames.

Charles V had been elected Holy Roman emperor following his father's death in 1519. He had promised before his election that no one would be excommunicated within the empire without a proper hearing. Through the influence of Frederick III of Saxony, Charles summoned Luther to the German town of Worms in April 1521 to confront the imperial Diet (assembly).

Before the Diet, Luther was asked if he had written the imposing number of treatises and books placed on the table. Acknowledging them all, Luther replied: "I am bound by the Scriptures I have quoted and my conscience is captive to the Word of God. I cannot and I will not retract anything, since it is neither safe nor right to go against conscience. I cannot do otherwise, here I stand, may God help me. Amen." The Diet condemned Luther's beliefs. Charles V, in agreement with the pope, signed the Edict of Worms in May 1521, placing Luther under the "ban of the empire." This forbade him from preaching and declared him a heretic. Several men loyal to Frederick III, Luther's protector, escorted him to safety.

By declaring Luther an outlaw and forbidding any changes in religion in the Holy Roman Empire, the Edict of Worms made religious reform an issue of state. But Luther could not have survived the ban of the empire if his influence had not already spread, convincing many that through Luther they had now discovered the true Gospel.

SOCIAL BACKGROUND OF THE REFORMATION IN THE GERMAN STATES

Challenging the ways people in Central Europe had thought about religion for centuries, the movement for reform, spread by preachers, found converts in the German states. During the early 1520s, the proponents of Martin Luther's reform convinced many clergy and lay people to reconsider their religious beliefs and to restructure their communities. Social and political unrest, perhaps encouraged by the quest for religious reform, began to stir in the central and southern German states as peasants rose up against their lords. This uprising, although roundly condemned by Luther, left no doubt that the Reformation would shake the foundations of the German states.

Urban Centers of Reform

At first the Reformation was overwhelmingly an urban phenomenon in the German states and then Switzerland. The decentralized political structure of the Holy Roman Empire and traditions of popular participation in urban government aided the movement for reform, for example in the free cities in the northern German states like the powerful Baltic trading city of Lübeck, leader of the Hanseatic League, and self-governing towns in the southern German states. Each German town had its own elite of prosperous burghers. Reformers found these communities fertile ground for Luther's ideas. Complaining of incompetent or lazy priests, members of some towns had endowed posts for preachers in order to attract vigorous, effective priests, a good many of whom now followed Luther.

German towns also had a particularly well-developed sense of civic solidarity that included a belief that all citizens of the town shared a common fate in the material world—vulnerability to bad times, and a certain degree of prosperity in good times—and that salvation itself was something of a group enterprise. Erasmus had asked, "What else is the city but a great monastery?" Luther sought to spark a more personal religion that would make people not only better Christians, but better citizens of their communities as well. In many towns, urban leaders and ordinary people may have accepted reform because it appeared more promising than unreformed Catholicism for the maintenance of local order.

Yet no simple formula could predict how the Reformation would fare in German towns. In the southern German states, urban nobles, merchants, and bankers remained staunchly Catholic. These property-owning groups were more conservative by instinct. Here the role of personality and the configuration of local social and political life came into play; so did pure chance, including such factors as whether preachers and reform literature arrived, how both were received, and by whom.

The Process of Reform

Social and political factors thus helped shape religious outcomes. While the embrace of the Reformation did not constitute a social revolution, in many cases clergy supporting religious reform were drawn from the middle and lower middle classes, groups with some possibility of social mobility. The "middling sort," in turn, brought reform to the lower classes. This process might be marked by the spontaneous singing of Lutheran hymns by those sitting in Mass, or by some other signs of a turn to reform. While archbishops and bishops in general opposed Luther, the lower clergy, particularly those of recent ordination, became influential converts in their towns. Communities accepted reformers by consensus, as local governments began to bow to the wishes of townspeople.

Thus, a crowd cheered in Basel when a priest carried the Bible instead of the communion host during the feast of Corpus Christi. Priests began to wear simpler clothes instead of rich robes. For the first time some of the Mass was said in German. Some reformed priests began to give the faithful both bread and wine during communion. Some crowds mocked Church rituals in angry ways: ringing cow bells to disrupt Mass; heckling priests trying to deliver sermons; smashing stained-glass windows, crucifixes, statues, and other images of the saints; and even destroying relics considered sacred. Such largely spontaneous actions bewildered Luther, who remained in most ways a very conservative man.

Luther and his followers denied the special status of the clergy as a group marked off from the rest of the population. In the early days of the Reformation, some reformers undertook expeditions to "rescue" nuns from convents. A number of former priests began to take wives, which at first shocked Luther, since this represented the end of clerical celibacy, which the Church had proclaimed in the eleventh century. Luther asserted in 1521, "Good Lord! Will our people at Wittenberg give wives even to monks? They will not push a wife on me!" But by 1525 he changed his mind, and married a former nun. The marriage of clerics further broke down the barrier between the priest and the people, symbolizing the "priesthood of all believers" by eliminating the clerical distinction of celibacy. Nonetheless, Luther limited the task of interpreting the Scriptures to professors of theology.

The Peasants' Revolt

In the southern German states, some burghers worried that law and order would collapse, and that the poor might rise up. Some lords and burghers expressed concern that the villagers might "turn Swiss," referring to the Swiss towns that lived without lords and were self-governing and independent. News of several strange and alarming prophecies circulated.

In 1524–1525, peasants rose up against their lords in parts of the central and southern German states (see Map 3.1). They demanded the return of rights (such as to hunt freely and to pasture their animals on the common lands) that lords had usurped. They also asked for the abolition of serfdom and the tithe, which they declared to be against God's will. Bands of poor people burned castles and monasteries.

The peasants' revolt spread into Austria and Carinthia, and up into Thuringia and Saxony. Pamphlets called for social as well as religious reform. Thomas Münzer (c. 1491–1525), a priest and theologian, merged religious reform with social revolution. He preached against the Church and Luther with equal fury, for he believed that both the Church and Luther had humbled themselves to lay authorities. Münzer led a peasant army in Thuringia, where Luther's reform movement had made many converts.

In the northwestern German states, also in 1525, some towns that had been won over to religious reform rose up against Catholic princes. Swabian peasants promulgated twelve articles against their lords, princes, and bishops, demanding that communities have the right to choose their own pastors. But here, too, the demands of the rebels had a social content. They asked for an end to double taxation by both lay and ecclesiastical lords and the "death tax" by which heirs had to give up the deceased's finest horse, cow, or garment. They demanded the end of serfdom, the return of common lands to their use, and free access to forests and streams.

Luther had some sympathy with the plight of the poor. Some of his followers began to see in his teaching a means of resistance against the powerful. But Luther rejected the idea that his central theological idea of

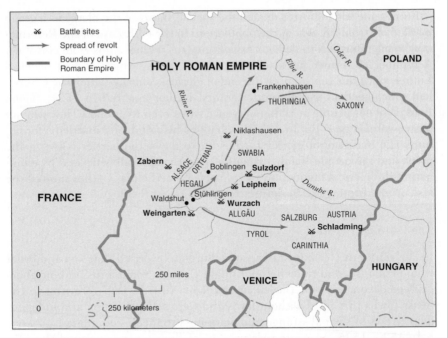

MAP 3.1 THE PEASANTS' REVOLT, 1525–1526   Sites of peasant uprisings in parts of the central and southern German states. The revolt began in Waldshut and Stühlingen in the southern German states and spread east to the Tyrol and Salzburg in Austria, and north to Thuringia and Saxony.

"Christian freedom," which he believed applied only to the spiritual realm, could be extended into the relationship between lord and peasant. Luther asked lords to "act rationally" and "try kindness" when confronted by peasant demands. As nobles and churchmen began to accuse him of fomenting insurrection, he denounced the peasants in extravagant language. In *Against the Murdering, Thieving Hordes of Peasants,* he advised the German princes to "brandish their swords. . . . You cannot meet a rebel with reason. Your best answer is to punch him in the face until he has a bloody nose." Catholic and reformed princes put aside their differences to crush the revolt, in which more than 100,000 peasants perished. Münzer was defeated, captured, tortured, and beheaded.

THE SPREAD OF THE REFORMATION

Because of the intertwining of religion and politics, what began as a movement for Church reform became entangled in princely rivalries in the German states. As the breach between Catholic and reformed princes widened, religion became a source of division rather than of unity.

Although Luther had never intended to bring about a permanent division within Christianity, his followers gradually created a new church in many of the German states. The Reformation then spread beyond the German states.

Divisions within Christendom

The Augsburg Confession, a summary of beliefs presented by Luther's friends to the Diet that gathered in that city in 1530, became the doctrinal basis of the Lutheran Church. It was implemented by princes and prelates in the reformed states and towns, and in some places by a council, known as a Consistory, of ministers and lawyers.

Some humanists influenced by the Renaissance were attracted by Luther's writing. In the tradition of their predecessors who had rediscovered the classics, they admired Luther's return to the Scriptures as an original source of knowledge. One of Luther's converts later wrote that his own excitement at the new teaching was so great that he studied the Bible at night with sand in his mouth so that he would not fall asleep. Humanists transformed some monasteries into schools. The first reformed university began in Marburg in 1527.

But as the gap between reformers and the Church grew larger, Erasmus was caught in the middle. His own criticism of ecclesiastical abuses did not go far enough for reformers, but it went too far for churchmen. Erasmus remained loyal to Church doctrine. Similarly, Luther and the humanists parted ways by 1525. For the latter, humanistic knowledge was an end in

The Augsburg Confession read before Charles V in 1530.

itself; for the reformers, rhetoric was a method for teaching the Scriptures and for arguing in favor of ecclesiastical reform. Many reformers were less committed than humanists to the belief that man is a rational and autonomous being. Luther himself did not share the humanists' Renaissance optimism about mankind. He was not interested in rediscovering mankind but was instead preoccupied with an individual's relationship to God. Furthermore, Luther opposed attempts by philosophers to intrude in theological questions. Nonetheless, a humanist curriculum continued to influence the training of reform ministers.

Luther's followers gained their first martyrs in 1523, when two former monks were executed in Brussels for their beliefs. German princes requested from Holy Roman Emperor Charles V that a "free general council or at least a national council" consider the growing religious division within the Holy Roman Empire. The Diet of Speyer (1526) proclaimed that each German prince was "to live, govern, and bear himself as he hopes and trusts to answer to God and his imperial majesty." This truce gave reformers time to win even more converts. In 1529, German princes again gathered in Speyer. Some of them prepared a "protest" against the policies of Charles V and the Catholic princes, who had declared themselves against Luther. The followers of Luther thus became known as "Protestants."

Luther's writings, translated into Latin, then spread beyond the German states, following trade routes east and west. The reformers easily revived the anti-papal Hussite traditions of Bohemia and Moravia and that of the Waldensians in the southwestern Alps. German merchants carried reform to the Baltic states and Scandinavia. In Denmark, King Christian II adopted Lutheranism for his state. When Lutheranism was declared its official religion in 1527, Sweden and its territory of Finland had the first national reformed church.

Charles V and the Protestants

Holy Roman Emperor Charles V, the pope's most powerful potential advocate, was a pious man who first denounced Luther with passion. But extensive Habsburg imperial interests kept him fighting a war in Western Europe against King Francis I of France, which prevented him from acting against those who supported Luther. The French king, for his part, was pleased that religion was dividing the German princes, thereby weakening the imperial crown that he had coveted. Charles V was away from his German states between 1521 and 1530, for the most part in Italy, crucial years during which the Reformation spread within the Holy Roman Empire. In 1524, the first Protestant leagues were formed between states. Protestant governments dissolved convents and monasteries, turning them to secular uses, such as hospices or schools.

The Christian crusade against the Turks in Eastern Europe and the Mediterranean preoccupied Charles and other Catholic princes as well. In

1526, the Turks defeated the Hungarian king at Mohács in Hungary. This left Lutheran missionaries an open field there, although Muslim Turks did not care about which version of Christianity their non-Muslim subjects practiced. A subsequent Turkish advance forced Charles to offer concessions to Lutheran princes in exchange for assistance against the Turks. (Luther's hymn "A Mighty Fortress Is Our God" began as a martial song to inspire soldiers against the Ottoman forces.)

To be sure, not all political and religious leaders and their followers were intolerant of other religions. But in a time of sharp religious contention, too few shared the toleration of a French traveler to Turkey in 1652, who reported, "There are many in Christendom who believe that the Turks are great devils, barbarians, and people without faith, but those who have known them and who have talked with them have quite a different opinion, since it is certain that the Turks are good people who follow very well the commandment given us by nature, only to do to others what we would have done to us."

For a time, Charles V held out hope for conciliation with the Protestants. In 1531, however, the princes of Hesse, Saxony, and other states and cities that had adopted religious reform formed the Schmalkaldic League. Although first and foremost a defensive alliance, the princes intended that the league would replace the Holy Roman Empire as the source of their political allegiance. Up until this time, Charles had accepted temporary truces, and thus toleration of Protestants. He had suspended the Edict of Worms (which had condemned Luther as a heretic) until a general council of the Church could be held. When the pope announced that it would be held in the Alpine town of Trent (see p. 116), the stage was set for confrontation with the Protestants. Meanwhile, however, Charles was still preoccupied by hostilities with Francis I of France, who shocked many Christians by allying with the Turks against the Habsburgs. After Charles forced an end to the wars by launching an invasion of France from the Netherlands, he was finally ready to move against Protestants, routing the Schmalkaldic League in battle in 1547. He then forced reconversion on the people in about thirty German cities. By that time, however, Protestantism had established itself definitively in much of Central Europe.

The Peace of Augsburg

Charles V now tried to bring more of the German princes and their people back into the Catholic fold. He tried without success to impose moderate Catholic reform in Central Europe to answer some of the criticism of the reformers. But several of the Catholic princes took up arms against him in a short war in 1551. The political complexity of the myriad German states militated against a general settlement. The Holy Roman emperor gave up the idea of restoring Catholicism in all of the German states.

MAP 3.2 THE RELIGIOUS SITUATION IN EUROPE AFTER THE PEACE OF AUGSBURG, 1555   The Peace of Augsburg stipulated that the religion of the ruler of each of the Holy Roman Empire's states would be the religion of the state. The map indicates areas that were Roman Catholic, Anglican, Calvinist/Zwinglian, Lutheran, Eastern Orthodox, and Anabaptist.

The Peace of Augsburg of 1555 was a compromise. It was agreed upon by the imperial representative assembly after Charles, worn down by the complexity of imperial politics, refused to participate. It stipulated that the religion of the ruler of each of the empire's states would be the religion of the state (*cuius regio, eius religio*) (see Map 3.2). Protestants living in states with a Catholic ruler were free to emigrate, as were Catholics in the same situation. The Peace of Augsburg thus recognized that the institutions of the Holy Roman Empire could not provide a solution to what now appeared to be permanent religious divisions in Central Europe. It acknowledged that the Reformation in the German states was an accomplished fact. Thus, what had begun as a "squabble among monks" shaped the territorial and political history of Germany. Through the compromise that allowed each prince to determine the religion of his state, the Peace of Augsburg reaffirmed German particularism, the existence of many independent German states.

THE REFORMATION IN SWITZERLAND AND FRANCE

The next stage of the Reformation occurred in Switzerland, land of rugged peasants, craftsmen, and mercenary soldiers. The thirteen sparsely populated, independent cantons of Switzerland (then about a million people) were loosely joined in a federal Diet, closer in organization and in spirit to the Italian city-states than to the German states. Unlike the German states, where the conversion of a powerful prince could sway an entire state, there were no such territorial rulers in Switzerland. The Swiss reformers, then, would be even more closely tied to privileged residents of towns of relatively small size. Their movement would also soon spread to parts of France.

Zwingli and Reform

In Zurich, then a town of about 6,000, Huldrych Zwingli (1484–1531) preached salvation through faith alone. In 1522, several citizens of Zurich publicly munched sausages during Lent in defiance of the Lenten ban on eating meat. Zwingli published two tracts on their behalf in which he insisted that the Scriptures alone should be the basis of religious practice, and that as there was nothing in the Bible about sausages, they could be eaten at any time. This scriptural test also led Zwingli and his followers to iconoclasm, the stripping of images and altar decorations from churches because nothing about them could be found in the Bible. The Zurich municipal council then embraced reform. It ordered the canton's priests to preach only from the Bible, and two years later it forbade the saying of Mass. Zwingli convinced the town's magistrates that tithes should be used to aid the poor, whom he believed represented the real image of God.

A doctrinal conflict among reformers helped define the character of the Swiss Reformation. Luther maintained that communion represented the physical presence of Christ. In this he had not diverged far from the Catholic Church, which insisted that through the miracle of transubstantiation (which the pope formulated in 1215), the priest transformed bread and wine into the actual body and blood of Christ, the sacrament of the Holy Eucharist. But to Luther, who condemned Catholic worship of the Eucharist, the bodily presence of Christ in the Eucharist came from the fact that Christ and God were universally present. Zwingli, by contrast, believed that communion was only a symbol of Christ's real presence in the Eucharist and that Luther's refusal to abandon this idea demonstrated that he still stood with one foot in Rome. The "Sacramentarian Controversy" emerged as the first major doctrinal dispute among Protestants. The Augsburg Confession of 1530 sealed the rift by excluding reformers who rejected Lutheranism, such as Zwingli and his followers.

Between 1525 and 1530, some German-speaking parts of Switzerland and regions of the southern German states accepted Zwingli's reforms. In 1531, Catholic forces attacked Protestant cantons because Zwingli was actively espousing his version of reform there. Zwingli, carrying a sword and a Bible, led the Protestant forces into the Battle of Kappel and was killed in the fighting. Both Catholics and Lutherans claimed Zwingli's death to be divine judgment against his religious positions. The peace that followed, however, specified that each canton could choose its own religion.

(*Left*) Woodcut of Huldrych Zwingli. (*Right*) Burning church ornaments and religious statues in Zurich.

MAP 3.3 RADICAL RELIGIOUS MOVEMENTS   Areas in which there were Hussites, Utraquists, Anabaptists, and Mennonites.

Radical Reformers

The reforms of Zwingli were not the only kind spreading in southern Germany and Switzerland in the 1520s. Some groups had even more radical ideas in mind for changing religious morality and communal life. Radicals shared an impatience with the plans of more moderate reformers, although they sometimes had very different visions of what this would constitute. Some were Anti-Trinitarians who rejected the orthodox Christian teaching that God consisted of the Father, the Son, and the Holy Spirit. Many radicals believed that they had been called to form the communities in which they sought to implement "godly living" (see Map 3.3).

Most radical reformers in the 1520s held apocalyptic beliefs, convinced that the world would soon end with a victory of God's true faithful over the forces of evil, in which they included those who did not agree with them or tolerate their views. Some radical reformers who had broken with Zwingli in Zurich became known as Anabaptists—"anabaptism" means rebaptism in Greek. Believing that neither Luther nor Zwingli had sufficiently transformed religious morality and community life, they sought to implement "godly" living on the model of the New Testament. Because they could find no reference to infant baptism in the Bible, they began baptizing adults in 1525 against Zwingli's advice. They believed that only adults could manifest true faith and therefore be worthy of baptism.

Anabaptist groups sprung up in areas influenced by Protestant reform, including Zurich, the Netherlands, parts of Italy, and Poland. Anabaptists were a very diverse group. Many Anabaptists advocated a congregational form of organization, because for them membership was through free will or voluntary self-selection, rather than through territorial organization of churches as was true for Catholics, Lutherans, and Zwinglians. Yet there were major differences between groups. Some Anabaptists in Switzerland and southern Germany formed communities of believers seeking isolation— "separation from iniquity," as they put it—from the struggles and temptations of the sinful secular world. These Anabaptists did not accept temporal government and refused to take civil oaths, pay taxes, hold public office, or serve in armies. However, other Anabaptists did seek alliances with local rulers and sought to be loyal subjects.

Catholic and Protestant states moved to crush these communities of radicals, seeing them as seditious rebels against God-given authority in church and state. At the Diet of Speyer in 1529, Charles V, along with Catholic and Protestant rulers in the empire, declared Anabaptism a crime punishable by death, usually by—with intentional irony—drowning, "the third baptism." Some of these radical reformers sought refuge in the mountains of the Tyrol and Moravia, and in the Netherlands, while others accepted a martyr's death or spoke out against authorities who persecuted them.

In 1534, a radical group of Anabaptists led by a local preacher took over the town government of Münster by election. Those not sympathetic to Anabaptism left town willingly or were expelled. Soon several thousand Anabaptists from as far away as the Netherlands arrived in Münster, believing it to be the "New Jerusalem," where God's chosen people would be protected. The Anabaptists established a council of twelve that expropriated Catholic Church property, abolished private property, banned the use of money, and established communally held property and a system of barter.

Münster's territorial ruler and his allies laid siege to the town. Inside Münster, John of Leiden, a Dutchman, gained influence as a leader and prophet. He convinced the ministers and elders of Münster to abolish private property, which they justified on biblical grounds—upon Christ's return, believers would not need possessions. Moreover, sharing possessions helped them ration goods during the siege. They also began to practice polygamy, in part because there were four times as many women than men in town. John of Leiden, who became king of Münster, led the way by taking sixteen wives. He also ordered the burning of all books in Münster except the Bible. Forces sent by Lutheran and Catholic princes stormed the town in June 1535 and tortured to death John of Leiden and other lesser leaders, placing their mutilated corpses in iron cages that still hang in a church steeple in Münster.

After the fall of Münster, Dutch Anabaptists led by a former Catholic priest named Menno Simons (1496–1561) tried to save adult baptism by preaching disciplined, godly living and Christian pacifism. They became known as Mennonites, and some of them left for the Americas more than a century later in search of religious toleration. Other descendants of such radical reformers include the adult-baptizing Hutterites of Moravia, the forebears of a group who settled in the American Midwest and the Canadian prairies. Likewise, the Unitarian religion has roots in this period, deriving from the Anti-Trinitarian views of God as being one, not the trinity of Father, Son, and Holy Spirit.

Jean Calvin and Reform

France, too, provided fertile ground for reform. The French monarchy had traditionally maintained a stubborn independence from Rome. Pope Leo X had signed the Concordat of Bologna (1516) with King Francis I, giving the king the right to appoint bishops and abbots in France. Initially the Valois ruler was far more preoccupied with his wars against Charles V and the Habsburgs than with the stormy tracts of an obscure German monk. The threat of heresy, however, convinced him in 1521 to order Luther's writings confiscated and burned. Yet Protestant propaganda arrived in France from Germany. In 1534, reformers affixed placards in Paris denouncing the Mass and on the king's bedroom door in his château at Amboise. The "affair of the placards" convinced the king to combat reform in earnest.

Jean Calvin (1509–1564) embodied the second major current of the Reformation. He was born in the small town of Noyon in northern France, where his father worked as a secretary to the local bishop. Calvin's mother died when he was about five years old, and his father sent him to Paris to be trained as a priest. He then decided that his son should become a lawyer, because he might earn more money.

Late-Renaissance humanism and particularly the teachings of Erasmus helped stimulate in the pious young Calvin an interest in religious reform during his legal studies. In 1534, the Catholic hierarchy and the king himself moved to crush this movement. Finding exile in the Swiss town of Basel, Calvin probably still considered himself a follower of Erasmus within the Catholic Church. In Basel, he penned tracts denouncing the papacy and calling on the king of France to end religious persecution.

Throughout his life, Calvin was overwhelmed by anxiety and self-doubt, compounded by his virtual abandonment by his father and his forced exile. He was also terror-struck by the power of nature and, in particular, by storms as manifestations of God's power—rather like Luther. Humanity seemed to Calvin to be poised before an abyss, a metaphor he frequently used. He feared that oceans might rise and sweep humankind away. Around him Calvin saw only the absence of order.

Like other thinkers of the early sixteenth century, Calvin believed that he lived in a time of extraordinary moral crisis: "Luxury increases daily, lawless passions are inflamed, and human beings continue in their crimes and profligacy more shameless than ever." It seemed to Calvin that the sense of religious community that ought to bind people together was dissolving.

Calvin argued that the Catholic Church had made the faithful anxious by emphasizing the necessity of good works in achieving salvation. The anxiety of never knowing how many good works were enough had, Calvin insisted, turned Catholics to seek the intercession of saints. He attacked the sacrament of penance with particular vehemence: "The souls of those who have been affected with some awareness of God are most cruelly torn by this butchery . . . the sky and sea were on every side, there was no port of anchorage." Calvin also rejected the increasingly human-like images given God and Christ over the previous century. Unlike Luther, Calvin emphasized not reconciliation with God through faith, but rather obedience to his will. He sought to provide a doctrine that would reassure the faithful of God's grace and of their own salvation. There was hope in Calvin's thought, faith that the labyrinth—another of his frequent images—of life could be successfully navigated. The imposition of order, based upon the mo-

(*Left*) Jean Calvin. (*Right*) A Calvinist service. Note the austerity of the church.

rality dictated by the Bible, would put an end to some of life's haunting uncertainties.

With this in mind, Calvin developed in his *Institutes of the Christian Religion* (1536–1559) the doctrine of election or predestination: "God's eternal decree. . . . For all are not created in equal condition; rather, eternal life is foreordained for some, eternal damnation for others." The belief in predestination called into question the efficacy of good works. If one's fate were predestined and if good works in themselves (as the Catholic Church claimed) did not bring eternal salvation, why lead a righteous life? Calvin believed that good works were signs of having been chosen by God for eternal salvation, though they did not in themselves guarantee Heaven.

Whereas medieval theologians had condemned lending money for profit, Calvin, unlike Luther, distinguished between usury and productive loans that would raise capital and increase the well-being of the entire community. Replacing penance as a means of imposing individual discipline, Calvin preached collective, communal discipline in the pursuit of holiness. Validating economic activity, later Calvinists came to view prosperity, along with "sober living," as a sign of election by God. In the late nineteenth century, this came to be known as the "Protestant ethic."

Late in 1536, Calvin went to the Swiss lakeside city of Geneva, a town of about 13,000 people. With the first successes of the Reformation, word of which had originally been carried there by German merchants, Geneva broke away from the domination of the Catholic House of Savoy. Earlier that year, troops of the Swiss canton of Bern, which had embraced Zwinglian reform, occupied the city. Bern established a protectorate, with Geneva retaining its nominal independence. Citizens elected magistrates and members of two representative councils.

In 1537, Calvin persuaded the smaller and most powerful of the two councils to adopt a Confession of Faith, swearing that the people of Geneva "live according to the holy evangelical law and the Word of God." Residency in Geneva would be contingent on formal adherence to the document. The Mass was banned, and priests were informed that they had to convert to reformed religion or leave the city.

Calvin hoped to impose Christian discipline and asceticism on the city in order to construct a righteous society. His "Ecclesiastical Ordinances" would provide for the organization of religious life in reformed Geneva, but they threatened the powers of the councils. Calvin insisted that the Consistory, the judiciary of the reformed church made up of lay elders (called presbyters), would have the right to discipline all citizens and to dispense harsh penalties against those who transgressed Geneva's religious laws. These penalties would include excommunication from the church, exile, imprisonment, and even execution. Calvin wanted municipal supervisors to monitor the religious behavior of the people, but the councils hesitated to surrender their authority to Calvin, who was French, or to assume such a supervisory role. In 1538, the councils told Calvin to leave Geneva.

In 1540, the majority of citizens of Geneva, believing that the town's ties to Bern limited its sovereignty, elected new magistrates, who executed the leaders of the pro-Bern faction. The two councils then invited Calvin to return to oversee reform in Geneva, and they adopted his Ecclesiastical Ordinances. Calvin returned to the city he had called "a place so grossly immoral."

To John Knox, a Scottish reformer, Geneva seemed "the most perfect school of Christ that ever was on earth since the days of the Apostles." But many citizens of Geneva resisted the close scrutiny of the Consistory. One man named his dog "Calvin" in protest. Always on the alert for the "many ambushes and clandestine intrigues Satan daily directs against us," Calvin forced another man who had publicly criticized him to wear a hair shirt (a shirt made of coarse animal hair) and walk slowly through town, stopping at street corners to pray and acknowledge Calvin's authority. Calvin took it upon himself to decide whether future bridegrooms were free from venereal disease and could marry in Geneva. He determined the punishment of merchants who cheated their clients. Drinking establishments were permitted (indeed part of Calvin's salary was paid in barrels of wine) if no lewd songs were sung or cards played, a Bible was always available, and grace said before meals. The Consistory imposed penalties for laughing during a sermon, having one's fortune told, or praising the pope. Calvin's death in 1564 was brought on by a variety of illnesses that were probably compounded by his chronic state of exhaustion and his fretful anxiety about the possibility of reforming a fallen and sinful world.

Calvinist Conversions

Calvinism proved the most aggressive version of the reformed religions, finding converts in places as diverse as France, the Netherlands, a number of German states, Hungary, Transylvania, Poland, and Scotland, where, following the efforts of the fiery reformer John Knox, the Scottish Parliament accepted Calvinism in 1560 as the national religion. In France, Calvinism made some inroads among all social classes during the 1530s, following the flow of reform literature coming from Switzerland and the German states. People who could not read could nonetheless listen to the Bible being read aloud.

Henry II, who came to the throne of France in 1547, denounced the "common malady of this contagious pestilence which has infected many noble towns." The Parlement of Paris created a special chamber to hear heresy cases—"the Burning Chamber"—and tried about 500 people. The sadistic king attended many of the executions himself. A magistrate from Bordeaux described the courage of the Protestant martyrs:

> Fires were being kindled everywhere . . . the stubborn resolution of those who were carried off to the gallows . . . stupefied many people.

They saw innocent, weak women submit to torture so as to bear witness to their faith . . . men exulting upon seeing the dreadful and
frightful preparations for and implements of death that were readied
for them . . . half charred and roasted, they looked down from the
stakes with invincible courage . . . they died smiling.

The judicial system could not keep up with the rapid pace of conversion,
including the conversion of many nobles. By 1560, there were more than
2,000 Protestant, or Huguenot (so named after a leading French reformer
in Geneva, Besançon Hugues), congregations in France.

Calvinism became the dominant religion of reform in the Netherlands. To
root out Protestants there, Philip II of Spain expanded the Inquisition (which
had been set up by the Spanish crown after the expulsion of the Moors and
Jews from Spain in 1492 and later extended to the Spanish Empire in the
Americas). When the Dutch declared independence from Spain in 1581,
Calvinism quickly became part of the Dutch national movement during the
long war of independence that followed (see Chapter 5).

THE ENGLISH REFORMATION

Unlike continental reform, the English Reformation began with a struggle between the king and the Church. But this dispute must also be
placed in the context of discontentment with ecclesiastical venality, and
the distant rule of Rome. Lollard influence persisted among the middle
and lower classes, which resented the wealth of the high clergy and
papal authority. Merchants and travelers returned to England from the
continent with Lutheran tracts. Among Luther's small group of followers
at the University of Cambridge was William Tyndale, who published the
first English translation of the New Testament. Burned at the stake as a
heretic in 1536, his last words were "Lord, open the eyes of the king of
England."

Henry VIII and the Break with Rome

King Henry VIII of England (ruled 1509–1547) was a religious conservative
who published a book in 1521 defending the Catholic view of the sacraments against Martin Luther, prompting the pope to grant him the title of
"defender of the faith." The Catholic Church in England already enjoyed
considerable autonomy, granted by the pope in the fourteenth century, and
the king could appoint bishops.

The issue of royal divorce led to the English break with Rome. Henry's
wife, Catherine of Aragon (1485–1536), had given birth five times, but
only an extremely frail girl, Mary Tudor, survived. Henry not only urgently

(*Left*) Henry VIII. (*Right*) Anne Boleyn.

desired a male heir for the prestige of the dynasty but he also desired Anne Boleyn (1507–1536), a lady-in-waiting with long black hair and flashing eyes.

Henry had obtained a special papal dispensation to marry Catherine, who was his brother's widow, and now sought the annulment of this same marriage. Obtaining an annulment—which meant, from the point of view of the Church, that the marriage had never taken place—was not uncommon in sixteenth-century Europe, providing an escape clause for those of great wealth. Henry justified his efforts by invoking an Old Testament passage that placed the curse of childlessness on any man who married his brother's widow. He furthermore claimed that English ecclesiastical authorities, not the pope, had the authority to grant an annulment. Pope Clement VII (pope 1523–1534) was at this time a prisoner of Charles V, the Holy Roman emperor, whose armies had occupied Rome, and who happened to be Catherine of Aragon's nephew. In addition to these political circumstances, the pope opposed the annulment as a matter of conscience. At Henry's insistence, Lord Chancellor Thomas Wolsey (1475–1530), in his capacity as cardinal-legate, opened a formal church proceeding in London in 1529 to hear the king's case. But Pope Clement ordered the case transferred to Rome, where the English king had no chance of winning.

Furious, Henry blamed Wolsey for this defeat. Stripped of his post, Wolsey died a shattered man in 1530 on the way to his trial for treason and certain execution. The king had named Thomas More to be his lord chancellor in

1529. But More, a lawyer and a humanist, was a vigorous opponent of the reform movement. Although a layman, each Friday More whipped himself in memory of Christ's suffering. More balked at Henry's plan to have his marriage to Catherine of Aragon annulled. In 1533, Henry secretly married the pregnant Anne Boleyn. He then convoked Parliament, which dutifully passed a series of acts that cut the ties between the English church and Rome. The Act in Restraint of Appeals (1533) denied the pope's authority. Thomas Cranmer (1489–1556), archbishop of Canterbury, showed himself a loyal servant of the throne by simply declaring Henry's marriage to Catherine, who was sent to a convent, annulled. The Act of Succession in 1534 required all of the king's subjects to take an oath of loyalty to the king as head of the Church of England. Thomas More refused to do so, and Henry ordered his execution. When Pope Clement named another cleric languishing in the Tower of London a cardinal, Henry scoffed, "Let the pope send him a [cardinal's] hat when he will, but I will provide that whensoever it cometh, he shall wear it on his shoulders, for his head he shall have none to set it on."

Sir Thomas More, painted by Hans Holbein the Younger. More, who is here shown as lord chancellor, was later executed for his beliefs.

The Act of Supremacy, also passed in 1534, proclaimed the king "supreme head of the Church of England." Another law made possible the execution of anyone who denied the king's authority over the clergy, or who supported "the bishop of Rome or his pretended power." Parliament limited fees that the clergy could assess for burials and forbade bishops of the Church of England from living away from their sees. Reforms brought the clergy under civil law. The lack of resistance to Henry's usurpation of ecclesiastical authority reflected the pope's unpopularity, as well as the growing strength of the English monarchy.

After the Break with Rome

Henry VIII's nascent Church of England remained doctrinally conservative in contrast to some of the continental reform churches. Several dozen people were burned at the stake for heresy in the 1530s after Henry broke with Rome, including twenty-five Anabaptists. In 1536, in the Church of England's first doctrinal pronouncement, Ten Articles affirmed the essential tenets of Lutheran reform: salvation by faith alone (although good works were still advised), three sacraments, and rejection of the concept of Purgatory and the cult of saints. However, six more articles promulgated two years later reaffirmed some aspects of orthodox Catholic doctrine, including transubstantiation and clerical celibacy.

Thomas Cromwell (1485–1540), Wolsey's ambitious protégé, oversaw the dissolution of England's 600 monasteries, completed in 1538 despite a northern insurrection (the "Pilgrimage of Grace") in defense of the Roman Catholic Church. Two-thirds of the monasteries were sold within ten years, the largest transfer of land in England since the Norman Conquest of 1066. The appropriation of Church lands doubled royal revenue, allowing the construction of forts along the troublesome border with Scotland and on the Channel coast, and financing the purchase of new ships of war. Nobles, particularly those living in the more prosperous south, were the chief purchasers of monastic lands. Many turned their acquisitions into pastureland for sheep, or undertook more intensive agricultural production.

A few months after she married Henry, Anne Boleyn gave birth to a daughter, Elizabeth, a future queen of England. But Henry then had Anne tried on charges of adultery with one of his courtiers, claiming that she had coyly dropped her handkerchief in order to attract him. Anne was executed in 1536, insisting to the end that "a gentler nor a more merciful prince [than Henry] was there never." Next the king married Jane Seymour, who died shortly after giving birth to a son. Another Anne, this one from a small German state, was next in line, as Henry sought allies against Spain and the other Catholic powers. But this Anne did not please Henry—he claimed he had never consummated his marriage to this woman he disparaged as a "Flemish mare." He divorced her, too. Catherine Howard became Henry's fifth wife, but in 1542 he ordered her dispatched for "treasonable unchastity." Henry's sixth wife, a pious older woman named Catherine Parr, could have been excused for entering the marriage with considerable trepidation, but managed to outlive her husband.

THE CATHOLIC REFORMATION

The Catholic Church responded to the schism within Christendom by reasserting the pope's authority and strengthening its own organization. The Catholic Reformation (sometimes called the Counter-Reformation) was both a defensive response by the Church to the success of Protestantism and an aggressive attempt to undertake reform within the limits determined by Catholic theology.

Retreat to Dogmatism

In 1536, Pope Paul III (pope 1534–1549) designated a commission to report on possible reforms in the Church. This commission documented the lack of education of many clergy and the scandalous cases of bishops and priests earning benefices from sees and parishes they never visited. But the papacy held firm on matters of Catholic Church doctrine. Paul III rejected a last-ditch attempt in 1541 by one of his cardinals and several German bishops to reach agreement on the thorny theological issue of salvation by faith alone. Luther, too, vehemently refused to accept compromise. The papacy then went on the offensive. The next year, the pope ordered Cardinal Gian Pietro Carafa to establish an Inquisition in Rome to root out Protestantism in Italy.

Carafa became Pope Paul IV (pope 1555–1559) despite the opposition of Holy Roman Emperor Charles V. He once declared, "If our own father were a heretic, we would gladly carry the wood to burn him!" The new pope retreated into doctrinal orthodoxy and aggressive repression. He formalized pre-publication censorship, establishing a list—the Index—of forbidden books in 1559. Censors ordered other books altered, and refused to authorize the printing of publications they deemed controversial.

As part of the Catholic Reformation's efforts to combat, contain, and eliminate "error" in all forms, Paul IV invented the "ghetto," ordering Jews living in the Papal States to reside in specific neighborhoods, which they could leave only at certain times. In a 1555 bull, he stated that the Jews were guilty of killing Christ, and therefore ought to be slaves. In much of Catholic Europe, Jews had to wear yellow caps to identify themselves, could not own land, and were excluded from most professions.

Ignatius of Loyola and the Jesuits

Ignatius of Loyola (1491–1556), a dashing Basque noble, became one of the leading figures of the Catholic Reformation. While recovering from a grave injury suffered in battle, Loyola read an account of the life of Christ and a book on the lives of saints. He vowed to help rekindle Catholic orthodoxy throughout Europe. Loyola made a pilgrimage to a Spanish monastery, left his sword in a chapel, gave his rich robe to a poor man, put on a sackcloth, and traveled through Spain and Italy. Gradually Loyola attracted followers. The Inquisition came to suspect him because his claims to help people through "spiritual conversion" seemed dangerously close to heresy. He defended himself ably, however, receiving only a short prison sentence.

Loyola wanted to establish a new order that could inculcate the same kind of intense religious experience that he had undergone while lying wounded. He traveled to Rome, offered his services to the pope, and organized the Society of Jesus, which was officially approved by the pope in 1540. Under

Loyola's military-style leadership, the Jesuits, as the order's members became known, grew rapidly in number and influence as aggressive crusaders for the Catholic Reformation.

The Jesuit order provided a model for Church organization, orthodoxy, and discipline. Jesuits underwent a program of rigorous training and took a special oath of allegiance to the pope. They combined the study of Thomas à Kempis's mystical *Imitation of Christ* (1418) and Loyola's own intense devotional reflections.

When Loyola died in 1556, there were more than a thousand Jesuits. Counselors to kings and princes and educators of the Catholic elite, the Jesuit religious order contributed greatly to the success of the Catholic Reformation in Austria, Bavaria, and the Rhineland. Jesuits also contributed to the Church's reconquest of Poland, where religious toleration had been proclaimed in 1573 and some landowners had converted to Calvinism. In the service of the Catholic Reformation, Jesuits began to travel to North America, Latin America, and Asia, eventually establishing a presence even in the court of the Chinese emperors. They led "missions," delivering fire-and-brimstone sermons, which were aimed at rekindling loyalty to the Church.

The Council of Trent

In 1545, at the insistence of Holy Roman Emperor Charles V, Pope Paul III convoked the Council of Trent (1545–1563) to assess the condition of the Catholic Church and to define its doctrines. While such an internal reckoning had seemed inevitable for some time, the papacy had long viewed conciliarism as a potential threat to its authority and invoked every possible reason for delay. Once convened, the Council of Trent, which met off and on for eighteen years, made the split within Western Christendom irreparable. Most of the prelates who came to the Alpine town of Trent believed the central goal of the council was a blanket condemnation of what the Church viewed as heresy, as well as the reaffirmation of theological doctrine. Although the pope himself never went to Trent, the Italian delegates dominated the proceedings, coughing and sneezing during speeches with which they disagreed.

The council rejected point after point of reformed doctrine, declaring such positions "to be anathema." It reaffirmed the authority of the pope and of the bishops, the seven sacraments, and the presence of Christ in the Eucharist. It also unequivocally opposed the marriage of clerics and reaffirmed belief in Purgatory and in the redeeming power of indulgences, although the practice of selling them was abolished.

In 1562, Pope Pius IV (pope 1559–1565) convoked the last session of the Council of Trent. The council ordained the creation of seminaries in each diocese to increase the number and quality of priests. The priests were henceforth to keep parish registers listing the births, baptisms, and deaths of the faithful, which in recent times have provided historians with extraordinarily useful demographic information. Some monastic houses undertook reforms. The infusion of better educated clergy in the southern German states and Austria aided the Church's efforts to maintain its influence there.

The papacy emerged from the Council of Trent much more centralized, better organized and administered, and more aggressive, like the most powerful European states themselves. Gradually a series of more able popes helped restore the prestige of the papacy within the Church.

Putting Its House in Order

"The best way," one churchman advised, "to fight the heretics is not to deserve their criticisms." Some leaders within the Catholic Church reasoned that the Church should put its own house in order and seek to reconvert people who had joined the reformed religions. Pius V (pope 1566–1572) declared war on venality, luxury, and ostentation in Rome. But abuses still seemed rampant. In 1569, the Venetian ambassador to France reported that the French "deal in bishoprics and abbeys as merchants trade in pepper and cinnamon." Pius V sent some bishops living in Roman luxury packing to their sees, putting those who refused to leave in prison.

Reformers wanted to bring order and discipline to members of religious orders and the secular clergy. "No wonder the Church is as it is, when the religious live as they do [in monasteries and convents]," Teresa of Avila (1515–1582) exclaimed in response to the demeaning battles between religious houses in Spain, struggles that she tried to end. Some churchmen, however, now rejected monastic life as irrelevant to the activist missionary tasks of the Church, another sign of the influence of Protestant reform. New orders, such as the Capuchins—an offshoot of the Franciscans—and the female order of the Ursulines, worked to bring faith to the poor and the sick. The missionary work of Vincent de Paul (1581–1660) also helped restore faith among the poor. Seeing the success Reformation preachers had with mass-produced pamphlets, the Catholic Church also produced catechisms that spread Church teachings, along with accounts of the lives of the saints. The Catholic Reformation encouraged other new devotional confraternities (religious brotherhoods of people who heard Mass together), some bringing together laymen of various social classes. The cult of the Virgin Mary became more popular. The Protestant Reformation had emphasized the religious life of the individual and the development of his or her personal piety through Bible study and personal reflection. The Catholic Reformation, too, now encouraged individual forms of devotion and spirituality.

Culture during the Two Reformations

The Protestant Reformation began as a religious reaction against abuses within the Church. But it also reflected profound changes in European society. The Reformation followed not only the discovery of the printing press but also the expansion of commerce, the arteries of which became the conduits of reform. Both the Protestant and Catholic Reformations affected art, architecture, print culture, education, popular culture, and family life at a time when religious belief and practice had an enormous impact on daily life.

Print Culture

The printing press did not cause the Reformation, but it certainly helped expand it. A rapid expansion in the publication of pamphlets, books, and other printed material occurred at a time when reformers were challenging Church doctrine and papal authority. The printing of Luther's works facilitated their rapid diffusion, with perhaps a million copies circulating through the German states by the mid-1520s. The German reformer called the printing press "God's highest and ultimate gift of grace by which He would have His Gospel carried forward." Luther's Wartburg translation of the Bible went through fifty printings in two years. He wrote 450 treatises and delivered more than 3,000 sermons; his collected works fill more than 100 volumes and 60,000 pages. Luther also published a hymnal containing many hymns that are sung today. He directed many of his dialogues, poems, and sermons to ordinary Germans, and even to children, adopting popular religious themes and images.

Since about 1480, the diffusion of printing had contributed to the expansion of a lay culture in the German states. Much of what was printed was published in the vernacular, that is, German, as opposed to Latin. Although religious literature was the greatest output of early printing presses, other favored themes of books and pamphlets included nature, the discoveries of the explorers, the acquisition of technical skills (such as medical skills from self-help medical handbooks), manuals of self-instruction (such as how to

Private devotion: an old woman reading the Bible.

defend oneself in court, or how to make beer and wine), and everyday morality. Visual, often satirical images such as woodcut illustrations and broadsheets, directed at those who could not read, probably reached far more people than did printed tracts, however. Caricatures portrayed Luther as Hercules, as an evangelical saint doing battle with wretched animals representing the Church, as a new Moses, as a miracle worker, and, in one popular legend, as the inventor of bratwurst sausage.

Lay Education and Reading

The Reformation, drawing on printing, also profited from increased educational opportunities for laypeople in Europe, which engendered a critical spirit among students and scholars. The number of universities rose steadily during the last half of the fifteenth century. More people could read than ever before—although in most places no more than 5 to 10 percent of the population. Lutherans and Calvinists stressed the importance of education as essential to individual and critical study of the Scriptures, and de-emphasized the clergy's role in religious instruction.

During the Reformation, princes and ecclesiastical leaders intensified their efforts to secure religious conformity by controlling what people read. The "blue library" (so called because small books or pamphlets were wrapped in blue paper) helped diffuse pamphlets deemed acceptable and sold at a low price by itinerant peddlers. Each Western European country had such a "literature of bits and pieces." Didactic stories were meant to instruct people about religious events, saints, and ideals approved by the Church, and to distance them from the "superstitions" of popular culture. Yet many people living in England probably still knew far more about Robin Hood than they did about the Bible. A chapbook (a small book of popular literature) published in Augsburg in 1621 told the story of Saint George slaying the dragon. The Catholic hierarchy removed the dragon from the story, while Protestants left out Saint George.

Popular Rituals and Festivals

Protestant ministers, like their Catholic counterparts, tried to root out such rituals as baptizing a child by dunking her three times for good luck. Songs rife with pagan imagery had survived virtually unchanged since medieval times. Religion and magic remained closely intertwined; the Catholic Church had been unable to eradicate the difference in the popular mind between prayer and good luck charms, for example.

Many a village became the site of an elaborate tug-of-war between state and ecclesiastical authorities and ordinary people. The clergy, often previously active participants in festive occasions, were caught in the middle and moved away from what they considered "profane" amusements. The Catholic hierarchy tried to suppress some popular festivals and rein in

Pieter Brueghel the Elder's *Combat between Carnival and Lent* (1559). Note the contrast between the church on the left with the somewhat more pious-looking people near it, and the drinking place on the other side of the square. Revelry seems to be winning out.

others, returning them to the control of the clergy by imposing a religious purpose that seemed to have been lost in all the fun. A dance known as the "twirl" in southern France was banned in 1666 because boys tossed girls into the air "in such an infamous manner that what shame obliges us to hide most of all is uncovered naked to the eyes of those taking part and those passing by." Ecclesiastical and lay hierarchies, Catholic and Protestant, came to view popular festivity as immoral, or at least licentious. *Combat between Carnival and Lent* (1559), a painting by Pieter Brueghel the Elder (see above), depicts Carnival as a fat man and Lent as a thin woman. Under the twin assault of absolutism and ecclesiastic hierarchy, Lent won. The clergy also began a long and often unsuccessful struggle for control over lay confraternities, which had their origins in religious devotion, but they now were often fiercely independent and more like festive clubs, especially during Carnival. Carnival was largely eradicated in Protestant countries, but it survived in some Catholic ones, although often much transformed.

Social and political elites contrasted the "civility" of their beliefs, conduct, and manners with the "barbarity" or "savagery" of popular beliefs and customs. Didactic literature stressing polite comportment and etiquette became popular among people of wealth, further separating them from the poor. The Church tried to impose strict sexual mores on ordinary people, while encouraging gestures of deference toward social superiors.

The Role of Women

Although convents and nunneries were almost always abolished in a Protestant state, reformers nonetheless encouraged women to take an active role in the religious process of being saved. Protestant women, like men, were encouraged to read the Bible themselves, or, as most could not read, to have it read to them. In the case of Anabaptists, women appear to have made decisions about not baptizing their children; most Anabaptist martyrs were female. More women than men seem to have converted to Calvinism in France, perhaps attracted by special catechism classes, or by the fact that in Calvinist services, men and women sang psalms together.

Yet Protestant reformers still believed women were subordinate to men. Although a few women published religious pamphlets in the early 1520s and others undertook devotional writing and publishing later, women could not be ministers nor could they hold offices within the new churches. Calvin believed that the subjugation of women to their husbands was crucial for the maintenance of moral order. Protestant denominations provided a domestic vision of women, emphasizing their role in the Christian household.

The fact that a Protestant minister could now marry, however, reflected a more positive view not only of women but of the family as a foundation of organized religion. One pamphleteer admonished husbands that their wives were "no dish-clouts . . . nor no drudges, but fellow-heirs with them of everlasting life, and so dear to God as the men."

Because they no longer considered marriage a sacrament, Protestants also reluctantly accepted divorce in limited cases. Luther viewed adultery, impotence, and abandonment as reasons for divorce, but he condemned Henry VIII's effort to divorce Catherine of Aragon. Divorce remained quite rare and occurred only after a long, expensive legal process only the rich could afford.

In Catholic areas, women could still rise to positions of importance in convents, or in the new charitable religious orders. But the Council of Trent reaffirmed the Catholic Church's ideal of female chastity, reinforced by the widespread cult of the Virgin Mary. The chapbooks of the Catholic Reformation still taught that the female body was a source of sin, and therefore had to be controlled.

Witches came to reflect superstitious aspects of popular religion. Catholic and Protestant churchmen identified and persecuted witches as part of the campaign to acculturate the masses with "acceptable" beliefs. Witch hunts peaked during the first half of the seventeenth century. In the southwestern states of the Holy Roman Empire alone, more than 300 witch trials resulted in the execution of 2,500 people between 1570 and

1630, almost all women (in itself not surprising, as Church authorities and priests were all male).

Theologians and judges sought to demonstrate that accused witches embodied the kingdom of the devil. To some extent, the Catholic Reformation wanted to create the idea of a satanic realm of evil on earth with which to juxtapose orthodoxy. "Witches," identified by common reputation, sometimes stood accused of saying Latin prayers backward or performing "black Masses" while standing facing their "congregations," instead of facing the altar, defiantly inverting the kingdom of God. One woman was accused of "consuming" several husbands. Often "witches" were blamed for evil that had befallen villagers: a fire, the unexplained death of a cow, or a male suddenly smitten with impotence.

Most of those accused of being witches were rural, poor, and single women who were victims of other villagers, particularly small town officials and wealthy peasants (it was the opposite in 1692 in Salem, Massachusetts, where many of the women accused of witchcraft had just inherited property, and therefore were resented by the community). Some "witches" confessed under pain of torture, such as one woman in southern France, who was "scorched like a pig" and cooked alive, having been accused of spreading an "evil powder" while committing crimes.

Women stood out as targets because they were transmitters of the collective memory of popular culture. They were genealogists, storytellers, and healers, but almost always without formal education. Women were in many ways the guardians of tradition, although also regarded by the Catholic hierarchy as the source of sin. The social exclusion or even execution of women had a social value for those in power, affirming authorities' position and role as interpreters of beliefs and customs deemed appropriate.

After the persecution of witches ebbed, some lay authorities then turned their attention to outcasts, the socially marginal. In the Austrian Netherlands, a sign "useless to the world" was hung above the head of a beggar. Monarchies increasingly demonstrated their authority in carrying out sentences of royal justice and, therefore, the justice of God. Those found guilty of capital crimes—at least those of the lower classes—were tortured and then executed in public, their mutilated bodies exhibited for all to see.

The Baroque Style

The monumentalism, flamboyance, and theatrical religiosity of the baroque style complemented the Catholic Reformation. "Baroque" refers to a style of extravagant and irregularly shaped ornamentation (the term itself comes from Old French for "irregularly shaped pear"). As an architectural, artistic, and decorative style, the baroque triumphed in southern Germany, Austria, Flanders, Spain, and other Catholic regions during the first decades of the seventeenth century (but was also popular in Protestant England, where it merged with the classical style).

As in the Renaissance, in Rome the Church remained a major patron of the arts, expressing religious themes through visual representation. Its goal was to impress—indeed, to overwhelm—the emotions through awe-inspiring dimensions, opulence, movement, and, in painting, lurid color. The Baroque style sought to express the experience of the soul. Baroque palaces and churches featured exuberant curves and ornate decoration and were cluttered with lustrous marble altars, ornate statues, golden cherubs, and intensely colorful murals and ceiling paintings. The baroque merged easily with neoclassicism—the revival of an architectural design dominated by Greek and Roman forms. The

Gianlorenzo Bernini's *The Ecstasy of Saint Theresa* (1645–1652).

Gesú Church of the Jesuits in Rome is a masterpiece of baroque style. With its vast ceilings and enormous paintings of the ascension of Christ and the assumption of the Virgin Mary, it symbolizes the spirit of the Catholic Reformation. The baroque style used optical illusions such as Gesú's false cupola to achieve the impression that the viewer is reaching for Heaven.

The monumental fountains in Rome of the Venetian sculptor Gian-lorenzo Bernini (1598–1680) best represent the period of high baroque of the Catholic Reformation. He also sculpted the magnificent canopy over the high altar of St. Peter's. Bernini sought to communicate the intensity of religious experience. In the altarpiece *The Ecstasy of Saint Theresa* (1645–1652), Bernini depicted the saint's convulsions of joy when an angel stabs her with a spear as beams of sunlight engulf the scene. Bernini wrote, "It pleased the Lord that I should see this angel in [this] way. . . . In his hands I saw a long golden spear and at the end of the iron tip I seemed to see a point of fire. With this he seemed to pierce my heart several times so that it penetrated to my entrails." This highly sexual description stands in marked contrast with the puritanical impulse that had seen Renaissance popes order the painting of fig leaves on nudes.

THE LEGACY OF THE TWO REFORMATIONS

In 1600, more than half of Europe remained primarily Catholic, including Spain, France, and Habsburg Austria, three of the four most powerful states in Europe. The fourth was England, and it was overwhelmingly Protestant. The Dutch Netherlands, at war with its Spanish overlords, was largely Protestant as well. Unlike the case of the German states, where the religion of the princes determined the religion of the state, the Reformations in France, the Netherlands, and Scotland were to a great extent movements from below. The Reformation generated a strong missionary impulse among Protestants and Catholics alike. With the gradual opening up of the world to European commerce and colonization, the Jesuits, particularly, ranged far and wide. In the burgeoning Spanish Empire, conquest and the quest for religious conversion, which was remarkably successful, went hand in hand. More than a few missionaries, however, found martyrdom, for example in Asia.

In Central Europe, the complexity of the state system facilitated reform. The Peace of Augsburg of 1555, as we have seen, reinforced German particularism, the persistence of small, independent states. In contrast, the larger, centralized, and more powerful states like Spain and France most successfully resisted the reform movement, despite the wars of religion that lay ahead in the latter. Yet, in both states, the Catholic Church remained subordinate to the monarchy, with both the French and Spanish kings retaining considerable authority over ecclesiastical appointments.

Protestant reformers accepted a separation of functions within the community, what Luther called the "realm of the spirit" and the "realm of the world." Henceforth, the political institutions of the Protestant states remained relatively secularized. In the German states and in Scandinavia, Lutheranism was introduced as a state church, in part because reformers originally needed the protection of princes against Catholic rulers, notably Charles V, the Holy Roman emperor. In England, Anglicanism also took on the status of a state religion. Both Lutheran and Anglican reforms rigorously subordinated the church to the state, separating the spiritual and temporal realms. Whereas Zwingli had called for the complete fusion of church and state, Calvinism alone provided for the institutional separation of both; after Calvin's death the magistrates of Geneva restricted the church's autonomy. Anabaptist sectarians, in contrast, wanted their communities to have nothing at all to do with the state.

The Lutheran and Calvinist states were not necessarily any more tolerant of religious dissent than those that remained Catholic. Following the Peace of Augsburg, German princes used their control of the reformed churches to consolidate their political authority. Lutheranism remained wedded to a patriarchal structure of society, which appealed to property owners at all social levels.

In an attempt to obtain religious adherence, some princes declared that church attendance would be mandatory and those who were absent would be punished. Nonetheless, compelling people to attend Sunday services did not guarantee what or even if they believed. One can never know how typical were the thoughts of one girl who related that the sermon she had just sat through was "such a deale of bible babble that I am weary to heare yt and I can then sitt downe in my seat and take a good napp." In one English parish in 1547, it was reported that "when the vicar goeth into the pulpit to read what [he] himself hath written, then the multitude of the parish goeth straight out of the church, home to drink."

In some places, to be sure, ordinary Protestants and Catholics coexisted and even shared churches. In Saxony, Catholics heard Mass in the lavishly decorated front part of a church and Lutherans used the end of the nave, which had little adornment, for their own services, by common accord. The division of the church was marked by a painting of the Last Supper, the importance of which both sides agreed upon. In some towns in the Netherlands in the late sixteenth century, dissenters from the Dutch Reformed religion, including Catholics, could worship in churches that were deliberately hidden from public view. Ordinary people thus greatly contributed to the religious peace that emerged in the immediate post-Reformation period, sometimes defying tyrannical rulers who insisted on religious orthodoxy.

The Peace of Augsburg and the Council of Trent did not end the rivalry between Catholics and Protestants, nor, for that matter, the rivalry between different Protestant denominations. Religious intolerance and conflict would, to a great extent, help define the first half of the seventeenth century, the age of the wars of religion.

CHAPTER **4**

THE WARS OF RELIGION

 $\mathcal{O}$ n May 23, 1618, a crowd of protesters carried a petition to Prague's Hradcany Palace, where representatives of the royal government of Bohemia were gathered. The crowd stormed into the council chamber, engaged Catholic officials in a heated debate, organized an impromptu trial, and hurled two royal delegates from the window. The crowd below roared its approval of this "defenestration" (an elegant term for throwing someone out a window), angered only that neither man was killed by the fall. Catholic partisans construed their good fortune as a miracle, as the rumor spread that guardian angels had swooped down to pluck the falling dignitaries from the air. Protestants liked to claim that the men had been saved because they fell on large dung heaps in the moat below.

The different reactions to the Defenestration of Prague illustrate how the Reformation left some of Europe, particularly the German states, a veritable patchwork of religious allegiances. Religious affiliation, like ethnicity, frequently did not correspond to the borders of states. The Peace of Augsburg in 1555 ended the fighting between German Protestant and Catholic princes. It stated that the religion of each state would henceforth be that of its ruler. Hundreds of thousands of families left home and crossed frontiers in order to relocate to a state where the prince was of their religious denomination.

The German states entered a period of relative religious peace, but in France in 1572, the Huguenots (the popular name for the French Protestants) rebelled against Catholic domination, setting off a civil war. Moreover, after years of mounting religious and political tension, Dutch Protestants led the revolt against Spanish Catholic authority in 1572, beginning a bitter struggle that lasted until the middle of the next century.

Then in 1618, religious wars broke out again in the German states with unparalleled intensity. The Thirty Years' War (1618–1648) devastated Central Europe, bringing into the conflict, in one way or another, almost all of the powers of Europe. Armies reached unprecedented size, and fought with a cruelty that may also have been unprecedented.

The wars of religion in France and the Thirty Years' War began because of religious antagonisms, but the dynastic ambitions of French princes lay not far behind the rivalry between Protestants and Catholics. In the Thirty Years' War, the dynastic rivalry between the Bourbons of France and the Habsburgs of Austria—both Catholic dynasties—came to the fore, eventually dominating religious considerations.

The wars of religion resulted in the strengthening of the monarchies of France, Austria, and the smaller German states as well. Kings and princes further extended their administrative, judicial, and fiscal reach over their subjects in the interest of maintaining control over their populations and waging war. In France, a stronger monarchy emerged out of the trauma of religious struggles and competing claimants to the throne. Germany, in contrast, remained divided into several strong states and many smaller ones. Competing religious allegiances reinforced German particularism, that is, the multiplicity of independent German states.

THE WARS OF RELIGION IN SIXTEENTH-CENTURY FRANCE

Early in the sixteenth century, France was divided by law, customs, languages, and traditions. Under King Francis I (ruled 1515–1547), the Valois monarchy effectively extended its authority. Of Francis I, it was said, "If the king endures bodily fatigues unflinchingly, he finds mental preoccupations more difficult to bear." Yet, the French monarch ruled with an authority unequaled in Europe, however much he was still dependent on the good will of nobles. When the king sought loans to continue a war, a Parisian noble assured him that "we do not wish to dispute or minimize your power; that would be a sacrilege, and we know very well that you are above the law."

When the Reformation reached France in the 1540s and 1550s, Calvinism won many converts (see Chapter 3). At a time when nobles were resisting the expansion of the king's judicial prerogatives and the proliferation of his officials, religious division precipitated a crisis of the French state and brought civil war.

A Strengthened Monarchy

Francis I and his successors became more insistent on their authority to assess taxes on the towns of the kingdom, many of which had held privileged exemptions granted in exchange for loyalty. Raising an army or royal revenue depended on the willingness of the most powerful nobles to answer the king's call. The monarchs had justified such requests with an appeal to the common good in tactful language that also held out the possibility of the use of force. Now the French king wished to tax the towns even when there was no war.

Francis reduced the authority of the Catholic Church in France. The Concordat of Bologna (1516), signed between Francis and Pope Leo X, despite

King Francis I of France, looking very regal and proud of his increased authority, despite not being painted wearing his crown.

the resistance of the French clergy, established royal control over ecclesiastical appointments. Many more royal officials now represented and enforced the royal will in the provinces than ever before. One sign of the growing power of the monarchy was that nobles lost some privileges of local jurisdiction to the royal law courts. Francis confirmed and enhanced Paris's identity as the seat and emerging symbol of royal power. The sale of offices originated in the king's desire for the allegiance of nobles and for the revenue they could provide the monarchy. His successors would depend increasingly on the sale of offices and titles for raising revenue. Finding nobles unwilling to provide all the funds the king desired, the monarchy, in turn, put the squeeze on peasants, extracting more resources through taxation.

The political and religious crises in the middle decades of the sixteenth century threatened monarchical stability in France. They pushed the country into a period of chaos brought by the lengthy, savage war of religion during which the four Valois kings who succeeded Francis I proved unable to rule effectively.

Economic Crisis

The end of a period of economic expansion provided a backdrop for the political and religious struggles of the French monarchy. The population of France had risen rapidly between the late fifteenth century and about 1570, reversing the decline in population resulting from plagues and natural disasters in the fourteenth and fifteenth centuries. Land under cultivation increased, particularly near the Mediterranean, where landowners planted olive trees on hills and terraces. But by 1570, the increase in cultivable land slowed down in much of France. The European population, which had risen to about 100 million people during the sixteenth century, outstripped available resources. Prices rose rapidly in France, as in most of Europe, pushed upward relentlessly by population increase. Beginning in the late 1550s, the purchasing power of the laborer declined dramatically, whereas that of landowners remained stable, fed by high prices. As agricultural income fell, nobles demanded vexing services from peasants, such as repairing roads and paths on their estates. Many wealthy nobles rented out land to tenant farmers, then took the proceeds back to their luxurious urban residences. Nobles of lesser means, however, did not do as well as the owners of great estates, because the rents they drew from their land failed to keep pace with rising prices.

As the price of profitable land soared, peasant families tried to protect their children by subdividing land among male offspring. Many peasants with small parcels of land became sharecroppers at highly disadvantageous terms—working someone else's land for a return of roughly half of what was produced. Both trends worked against increased agricultural efficiency, reducing land yields. Landless laborers were barely able to sustain themselves.

Taxes and tithes (payments owed the Catholic Church—in principle, 10 percent of income) weighed heavily on the poor. Peasants, particularly in the southwest, sporadically revolted against taxes, and against their landlords, during the period from 1560 to 1660. The popular nicknames of some of the groups of rebels reflect their abject poverty and desperation: the "poor wretches," who rose up against the nobles in central and southern France in 1594–1595, and the "bare feet." Many of the rebels espoused the popular belief that their violence might restore an imagined world of social justice in which wise rulers looked after the needs of their people.

French Calvinists and the Crisis of the French State

Followers of John Calvin arriving in France from nearby Geneva attracted converts in the 1540s and 1550s. Henry II (ruled 1547–1559), who succeeded his father Francis I, began a religious repression that created Calvinist martyrs, perhaps further encouraging Protestant dissent. The spread of Calvinism led the king to sign the Treaty of Cateau-Cambrésis in 1559, ending the protracted struggle between France and Spain. After decades of reckless invasions, Henry II agreed to respect Habsburg primacy in Italy and control over Flanders. King Philip II (ruled 1556–1598) of Spain, in return, promised that Spain would desist in its attempts to weaken the Valois kings. These two most powerful kings in Europe ended their struggle for supremacy not only because their resources were nearly exhausted, but also because as Catholic rulers they viewed with alarm the spread of Calvinism in Western Europe, both within the Netherlands (a rich territory of the Spanish Habsburgs) and within France itself. After signing the treaty, Henry II and Philip II could now turn their attention to combating Protestantism.

Some nobles in France, wary of the extending reach of the Valois monarchy and tired of providing funds for wars, resisted the monarchy. The conflict between the monarchy and the nobility compounded growing religious division in the last half of the sixteenth century. Perhaps as many as 40 percent of French nobles converted to Calvinism, some of them nobles of relatively modest means squeezed by economic setbacks.

In 1559, King Henry II was accidentally killed by an errant lance during a jousting tournament celebrating peace with Spain. He was succeeded by his fifteen-year-old son, who became Francis II (ruled 1559–1560). Catherine de' Medici (1519–1589), Henry II's talented, manipulative, and domineering widow, served as regent to the first of her three sickly and incapable sons. Catherine was reviled as a "shopkeeper's daughter," as her Florentine ancestors had been merchants, bankers, and money changers, all things incompatible with the French concept of nobility (but not with the Italian one). That she was the daughter of the man to whom Machiavelli had dedicated *The Prince* added to the "legend of the wicked Italian queen" in France.

The throne immediately faced challenges to its authority by three powerful noble families, each dominating large parts of France. Religious differences sharpened the rivalry between them. The Catholic Guise family, the strongest, concentrated its influence in northern and eastern France. In the south, the Catholic Montmorency family, one of the oldest and wealthiest in the kingdom, held through marriage alliances the allegiance of some of the population there. The influence of the Huguenot Bourbon family extended into central France and also reached the far southwestern corner.

In 1560, Louis, prince of Condé (1530–1569), a member of the Huguenot Bourbon family, conspired to kidnap Francis II and remove him from the clutches of the House of Guise, who were related to Francis's wife,

Catherine de' Medici, widow of Henry II, served as regent to Francis II.

Mary Stuart, queen of Scotland. The Guise clan, who discovered the plot, killed some of the Bourbon conspirators. Francis died after a stormy reign of only eighteen months, succeeded by his ten-year-old brother Charles IX (ruled 1560–1574), under the regency of their mother.

The rivalry between the Guise, Montmorency, and Bourbon families undermined royal authority. Henry II's lengthy war with Spain had drained the royal coffers, and the economic downturn made it extremely difficult to fill them again. Catherine's efforts to bring some of the nobles who had converted to Protestantism to the royal court and to bring about a rapprochement between the two denominations failed utterly. Such attempts only infuriated the House of Guise, several of whose members held important positions within the Catholic Church hierarchy. For their part, Philip II of Spain and the Jesuit religious order backed the Guise family. The political crisis of France, then, became increasingly tied to the struggle of the Church with Protestants.

Taking advantage of the confusion surrounding the throne, French Calvinists became bolder in practicing their religion. Religious festivals occasioned brawls between Catholics and Huguenots. Calvinists seized control of Lyon in 1562, forcing the rest of the population to attend their services. Where they were a majority, Calvinists desecrated Catholic cemeteries, smashed ornate stained-glass windows, shattered altar rails of churches, and covered statues of saints with mud. Catholics replied by slaughtering Calvinists, more than once forcing them to wear crowns of thorns, like Christ, to their death. Both sides burned the "heretical" books of the other denomination. The violence of a holy war was accentuated by rumors that the Huguenots indulged in orgies, while Protestants accused Catholics of idolatry and of doing the devil's work.

Yet in France—as in other parts of Europe where the Reformation had taken hold—some brave souls urged religion toleration. For example, an abbot warned in 1561:

> I am well aware of the fact that many think it wrong to tolerate two religions in one kingdom, and in truth it could be wished that there were only one, provided it were the true religion. . . . there is indeed no sense in wanting to use force in matters of conscience and religion, because conscience is like the palm of the hand, the more it is pressed, the more it resists, and lets itself be ordered only by reason and good advice.

In 1562, the first full-scale religious war broke out in France. It began when Francis, the duke of Guise (1519–1563), ordered the execution of Huguenots who had been found worshipping on his land. In the southwestern town of Toulouse, more than 3,000 people were killed in the fighting; the bodies of Protestants were tossed into the river, and their neighborhoods were burned as part of a "purification." Members of the Catholic lay confraternities took oaths to protect France against "heresy" and erected crosses in public places as a sign of religious commitment. Catholics won back control of several major cities.

This first stage of the war, during which a Huguenot assassinated Francis, the duke of Guise, ended in 1563. A royal edict granted Huguenots the right to worship in one designated town in each region, as well as in places where Calvinist congregations had already been established. Intensifying the eagerness of the powerful quarreling noble families to impose their will on the monarchy was the fact that Francis had died childless and young King Charles IX and his younger brother had no sons. There was no clear heir to the throne of France.

In 1567, war between French Protestants and Catholics broke out again. It dragged on to an inconclusive halt three years later in a peace settlement that pleased neither side. In 1572, Charles and Catherine, though Catholics, at first agreed to provide military support to the Dutch Protestants, who had rebelled against Spanish authority. The goal was to help weaken France's principal rival. But pressured by his mother and fearful of upsetting the more radical Catholics, as well as the pope, Charles soon renounced assistance to the Dutch and agreed to accept instead the guidance of the Catholic House of Guise. With or without the king's knowledge or connivance, the Guise family tried but failed to assassinate the Protestant leader Admiral Gaspard de Coligny (1519–1572), a Montmorency who had converted to Protestantism and whom they blamed for the earlier murder of the Catholic Francis, duke of Guise.

The marriage between Charles's sister, Margaret, a Catholic Valois, and Henry of Navarre, a Bourbon Huguenot, was to be, in principle, one of religious reconciliation. The negotiations for the wedding had specified that the Huguenots in Paris come to the wedding unarmed. But the king's Guise advisers, and perhaps his mother as well, convinced him that the only way of preventing a Protestant uprising against the throne was to strike brutally against the Huguenots. Therefore, early in the morning on August 24, 1572, Catholic assassins hunted down and murdered Huguenot leaders. During what became known as the Saint Bartholomew's Day Massacre, the (new) duke of Guise killed Admiral Gaspard de Coligny, whose battered corpse was thrown through a window, castrated, and then dragged through the dusty streets of Paris by children. For six days Catholic mobs stormed through the streets, killing more than 2,000 Protestants. Outside of Paris, another 10,000 Protestants perished. The Parlement of Toulouse, one of the twelve judicial courts of medieval origin that combined judicial and administrative functions, made it legal to kill any "heretic." The pope had a special Mass sung in celebration of the slaughter. Thousands of Huguenots emigrated or moved to safer places, including fortified towns they still held in the southwest.

Charles IX died in 1574 and was succeeded by his ailing brother, Henry III (ruled 1574–1589). At his coronation, the crown twice slipped from Henry's head, a bad omen in a superstitious age. The new king was a picture of contradictions. He seemed pious, undertook religious pilgrimages, and hoped to bring about a revival of faith in his kingdom. He also spent money with abandon and enjoyed dressing up as a woman, while lavishing every attention on the handsome young men he gathered around him.

Henry III also had to confront a worsening fiscal crisis compounded by a series of meager harvests. But when he asked the provincial Estates (regional assemblies dominated by nobles) for more taxes, the king found that his promises of financial reform and of an end to fiscal abuses by royal revenue

The Saint Bartholomew's Day Massacre, 1572, in which more than 2,000 Huguenots perished in Paris.

agents were not enough to bring forth more revenue. The Estates deeply resented the influence of Italian financiers at court, the luxurious life of the court itself, and the nobles who had bought royal favor.

The Catholic forces around the king were not themselves united. A group of moderate Catholics, known as the *politiques,* pushed for conciliation. Tired of anarchy and bloodshed, they were ready to put politics ahead of religion. The *politiques* therefore sought to win the support of the moderate Huguenots, and thereby to bring religious toleration and peace to France.

In 1576, Henry III signed an agreement that liberalized the conditions under which Protestants could practice their religion. Concessions, however, only further infuriated the intransigent Catholics, who became known as the "fanatics" (*dévots*). Angered by these concessions to Huguenots, a nobleman in the northern province of Picardy organized a Catholic League, which because of its size posed a threat not only to Huguenots but also to the monarchy. It was led by the dashing Henry, duke of Guise (1550–1588), who was subsidized by Philip II of Spain, and vowed to fight until Protestantism was completely driven from France. But another military campaign against Protestants led to nothing more than a restatement of the conditions under which they could worship.

Henry III's reconciliation with the House of Guise did not last long. The death of the last of the king's brothers, Francis, duke of Anjou, in 1584 made Henry of Navarre, a Protestant, heir to the throne. This was the Catholics' worst nightmare. The Catholic League threw its full support behind the aged, ambitious Catholic Cardinal de Bourbon, who was next in line after Henry of Navarre.

Henry of Navarre

Henry of Navarre (1553–1610) was born in the town of Pau on the edge of the Pyrenees Mountains in southwestern France. The son of Antoine of Bourbon, patriarch of the powerful Bourbon family, and Jeanne d'Albret, Henry inherited the keen intelligence of his mother and his father's indecisiveness. His mother was a committed Huguenot and raised Henry in that faith. When his father, who was notoriously unfaithful to his wife, sent her back to the southwest in 1562, Henry converted to Catholicism, his father's religion. After his father's death in battle, Henry reembraced Protestantism. Taken to the royal court as a hostage by Catherine de' Medici, he was permitted to have Huguenot tutors. Among his friends at court were the future Henry III and Henry, duke of Guise. It was after Henry of Navarre's wedding in Paris in August 1572 to Margaret, Catherine de' Medici's daughter, that the Saint Bartholomew's Day Massacre occurred. Henry then was given the choice of embracing Catholicism or being executed. He chose the former. When the fighting temporarily ended, Henry had more time for his favorite pursuits—pursuing women and hunting.

The Huguenots had every reason to be wary of a young man who seemed to change faiths with such ease. Furthermore, he seemed to have reconciled himself to the Saint Bartholomew's Day Massacre, still counted the duke of Guise among his friends, had accompanied the Catholic army, albeit under guard, and had written the pope begging forgiveness for past misdeeds.

But having left Paris and the watchful eye of the Catholic dukes, Henry then formally abjured Catholicism and took up residence as royal governor in the southwest, where Protestantism was strong. There he tried to steer a path between militant Catholics and Huguenots. His endorsement of mutual religious toleration won wide approval. After Henry of Navarre became heir to the throne in 1584, the Catholic League rallied its forces, drawing its muscle from the artisans of Paris and other northern towns. In defiance of the king, it forced the Parlement of Paris to withdraw the toleration afforded the Huguenots. The Catholic League's goal was to put the Cardinal de Bourbon on the throne, although the duke of Guise wanted it for himself.

The struggle between the "three Henrys" now began in earnest. Henry (Valois) III first allied with Henry (Bourbon) of Navarre and with the duke of Montmorency against Henry, duke of Guise. The Guise family provocatively accused the king in 1585 of destroying the kingdom through inept rule and called for a rebellion that would bring the duke of Guise to the throne and drive Protestantism from the kingdom.

Henry III then switched partners, joining the duke of Guise against Henry of Navarre. The Treaty of Nemours (1585) between Catherine de' Medici and Henry, duke of Guise, abrogated all edicts of religious toleration and turned over a number of towns to the Catholic League. Now the odd man out, Henry of Navarre prepared for a new war. He denounced Spanish meddling and in a quintessentially *politique* statement, called on soldiers "to rally around me . . . all true Frenchmen without regard to religion." Although he increasingly depended on German and Swiss mercenaries for his army and benefited from the intervention of a German Protestant force, Henry's denunciation of foreign influence was a shrewd piece of political propaganda aimed at moderate Catholics—the *politiques*—and the Catholic clergy.

In 1587, Henry of Navarre defeated the combined forces of the king and the Catholic League at Coutras, near Bordeaux. Here his defensive position and use of artillery and cavalry proved decisive. But instead of following up his surprising victory by pursuing the Catholic army, Henry went back to hunting and making love. As a contemporary put it, "All the advantage of so famous a victory floated away like smoke in the wind."

That year, 1587, Queen Elizabeth I of England put to death Mary Stuart, the Catholic queen of Scots and the niece of the duke of Guise (see Chapter 5). Angered by Henry III's inability to prevent the execution of his niece, Guise, at the urging of the king of Spain, marched the next year to Paris, where he and the Catholic League enjoyed support. The Spanish king hoped to keep the French king from contemplating any possible assistance to England as the Spanish Armada sailed toward the English Channel. When Henry III sent troops to Paris to oppose the duke of Guise, the Parisian population rose in rebellion on May 12, 1588, stretching barricades throughout the city center. The king ordered his troops to withdraw. The "Day of Barricades" marked the victory of a council led by clergymen known as the Sixteen, then the number of neighborhoods in Paris.

For several years, the Sixteen had been energetically supporting the League, while denouncing the king, the Catholic *politiques,* and Huguenots with equal fervor. The hostility of the population of Paris convinced the king to accept Cardinal de Bourbon (1523–1590) as his heir, the duke of Guise as his lieutenant-general, and to convoke the Estates-General (representatives of the provincial Estates, which the monarch could summon in times of great crisis).

Then in 1588, the delegates to the Estates-General, many of them members of the Catholic League, gathered in the Loire Valley town of Blois. Scathing written grievances were submitted to the delegation, including one from Paris that denounced the king as a "cancer . . . filled with filth and infectious putrefaction" and called for "all heretics, whatever their quality, condition or estate, [to] be imprisoned and punished by being burned alive." By now, however, the English fleet had defeated Philip II's Armada in the Channel (see Chapter 5), and the nobles found Henry III

Assassination of Henry, duke of Guise.

less intimidated than they had anticipated. When the duke of Guise heard a rumor that the king was planning his assassination, he replied, "He does not dare." But Henry III's bodyguards murdered Henry, duke of Guise, shortly before Christmas 1588 in the Château of Blois, as Catherine de' Medici lay dying in a room beneath the bloody struggle. The Valois king had the Cardinal de Bourbon and other prominent members of the Catholic League arrested.

The duke of Guise's assassination drove the Catholic League to full-fledged revolt against Henry III. More than 300 towns, most of them in the north, now joined the "Holy Union" against the king. As Catholics prepared to fight Catholics, Henry of Navarre (again Protestant) appealed for peace: "We have been mad, senseless and furious for four years. Is that not enough?"

Henry III was then forced to make an alliance of convenience with Henry of Navarre against the Catholic League. As their combined armies besieged Paris, a monk assassinated Henry III in August 1589. The king's Swiss guards, who had not done a terribly good job protecting their king, threw themselves at the feet of Henry of Navarre, telling him, "Sire, you are now our king and master."

The Catholic League, however, had proclaimed five years earlier that Cardinal de Bourbon would become king upon Henry III's death. Henry imprisoned his potential rival. Henry of Navarre's forces defeated Catholic League armies twice in Normandy, in 1589 and in 1590. But once again

Henry failed to take advantage of the situation his shrewd generalship had made possible. He dawdled before finally laying siege to starving Paris.

The arrival of a Spanish army from Flanders to provision Paris helped win Henry further support from moderate Catholics, who resented Spanish intervention that might prolong the siege. Fatigue began to overcome religious conviction. Henry also played on resentment at the involvement of the pope in French affairs (Henry had been excommunicated in 1585 and, for good measure, a second time six years later). As Henry's army besieged Paris, Spanish troops defeated forces loyal to him in several provinces. The death of Cardinal de Bourbon in 1590 led Philip II to proclaim the candidacy of the late Henry II's Spanish granddaughter as heir to the throne of France, and then to suggest that he might claim it himself. In the meantime, Henry's continued successes on the battlefield and conciliatory proclamations furthered his popularity.

Henry of Navarre, a man of changing colors, had another major surprise up his sleeve. In 1593, he astonished friend and foe alike by announcing that he would now again renounce Protestantism. This move, however, reflected his shrewd sense of politics. Paris, as he put it, was worth a Mass, the price of the capital's obedience. Following his coronation as Henry IV at Chartres the following year, Paris surrendered after very little fighting. Henry's entry into his capital was a carefully orchestrated series of ceremonies that included the "cure" of hundreds of people afflicted with scrofula (a tuberculous condition) by the royal touch, a monarchical tradition in France and England that went back centuries. Henry nodded enthusiastically to the women who came to their windows to catch a glimpse of the first Bourbon king of France.

Catholic League forces gradually dispersed, one town after another pledging its loyalty to Henry, usually in return for payments. Henry's declaration of war on Spain in 1595 helped rally people to the monarchy. The pope lifted Henry's excommunication from the Church. Henry invaded Philip's territory of Burgundy, defeating his army. In 1598, the last Catholic League soldiers capitulated. Henry, having secured the frontiers of his kingdom, signed the Treaty of Vervins with Philip II to end the war that neither side could afford to continue. However, bringing stability to France would be no easy matter. The wars of religion had worsened the plight of the poor. Disastrous harvests and epidemics in the 1590s compounded the misery. The wars of the Catholic League caused great damage and dislocated the economy in many parts of France. The indiscriminate minting of coins by both sides worsened inflation.

Henry's emissaries gradually restored order by promising that "the Well-Loved," as the king became known, would end injustices and provide "a chicken in every pot." He did slightly reduce the direct tax, of which the peasants bore the brunt. Henry also rooted out some of the corruption in the farming of taxes, whereby government officials allowed ambitious middlemen to collect taxes in exchange for a share. But, in all, even more of the tax burden fell upon the poor.

Gradually Henry succeeded in putting the finances of the monarchy on a firmer footing. In 1596, he convinced an Assembly of Notables to approve a supplementary tax. A new imposition (the *paulette*) permitted officeholders, through an annual payment to the throne, to assure that their office would remain in the hands of their heirs. The *paulette* gave the wealthiest nobles of the realm a greater stake in the monarchy. But while increasing royal revenue, it intensified the phenomenon of the venality of office: the purchase of offices and the noble titles that went with them.

Henry could rarely rest at ease. In 1602 and again two years later, he uncovered plots against him by nobles in connivance with the Spanish monarchy. He survived nine assassination attempts. Indeed, Jesuit pamphleteers called for his assassination. Small wonder that he carried two loaded pistols in his belt and that some nervous soul tasted his food and drink before he did.

In 1598, Henry's Edict of Nantes made Catholicism the official religion of France. But it also granted the nation's 2 million Protestants (in a population of about 18.5 million) the right to worship at home, hold religious services and establish schools in specified towns—almost all in the southwest and west—and to maintain a number of fortified towns. The Edict of Nantes also established chambers in the provincial parlements, or law courts dominated by nobles, to judge the cases of Protestants (see Map 4.1).

But careful to placate powerful sources of Catholic opposition, a series of secret decrees also promised Paris, Toulouse, and other staunchly Catholic towns that Protestant worship would be forbidden within their walls. The Edict of Nantes thus left the Protestants as something of a separate estate with specified privileges and rights, but still on the margin of French life. "What I have done is for the sake of peace," Henry stated emphatically. Yet former Catholic Leaguers howled in protest. By registering royal edicts, the parlements gave them the status of law. In this case, they only gradually and grudgingly registered the edict, which provided the Huguenots with arguably more secure status than any other religious minority in Europe.

Henry's foreign policy, which appeared pro-Protestant, supporting the Dutch rebels against Spain and certain German states against the Catholic Habsburgs, was based on dynastic interests. This support of Protestant rebels and princes made it impossible for Henry to consider further concessions to the Huguenots.

At the same time, the Catholic Reformation bore fruit in France. The Church benefited from a revival in organizational zeal and popularity. Henry allowed the Jesuits to return to France in 1604, a sign that religious tensions were ebbing, and he admitted several Italian religious orders.

With various would-be assassins lurking, Henry had to think about an heir. He sought a papal annulment of his marriage to Margaret of Valois, whom he had not seen in eighteen years. While waiting, he prepared to marry one of his mistresses, but she died miscarrying their child. With the

MAP 4.1 WARS OF RELIGION IN FRANCE IN THE SIXTEENTH
CENTURY   France at the time of the Edict of Nantes, 1598.
The map indicates neutral provinces, Huguenot provinces,
and Catholic League provinces during the wars of religion, as
well as Huguenot and Catholic League towns and battle sites
during the wars.

blessing of the Church, he then arranged to marry Marie de' Medici (1573–
1642), a distant relative of Catherine de' Medici. This second marriage of
convenience brought a sizable dowry that Henry used, in part, to pay off
more international debts.

Intelligent and well organized, Henry kept abreast of events throughout
his vast kingdom. But he had little sense of protocol, often rushing out of the
Louvre palace by himself as his guards scurried to catch up. His wit was well
known: when formally welcomed by a long-winded representative of the
town of Amiens, who began "O most benign, greatest and most clement of
kings," Henry interjected, "Add as well, the most tired of kings!" When a
second spokesman began his official greeting, "Agesilaus, king of Sparta,
Sire," Henry cut him short, "I too have heard of that Agesilaus, but he had
eaten, and I have not."

Henry had a charismatic and somewhat contradictory personality. In contrast to the portraits he encouraged depicting him as Hercules or Apollo, or arrayed in a splendid white plume and a warrior's helmet, the king of France was extremely slovenly, sometimes wearing torn or ragged clothes. He became renowned for his physical vigor on the battlefield and gambled large sums, with a notorious lack of success. Marie de' Medici bore the constant burden of her husband's various infidelities and occasional bouts of gonorrhea. Henry produced six illegitimate children by three mistresses, along with the three born to the queen. His nine offspring made up what he proudly referred to as his "herd."

Although he knew nothing of music or poetry, and regularly fell asleep at the theater, Henry IV nonetheless was a patron of new architectural projects that added to the beauty of the city of Paris and imprinted his rule upon it. He ordered the construction of four quays facilitating the docking of boats along the Seine River, and had built the splendid Place Dauphine, ringed by elegant buildings on the western end of the island of Cité, where his equestrian statue now stands. And he orchestrated the construction of the Place Royale, with pavilions of symmetrical arcades, brick construction, and steeply inclining roofs in the northern architectural style.

Statemaking

Restoring monarchical prestige and authority in France, Henry IV laid the foundations for what would become the strongest power in seventeenth-

The Place Dauphine, seen here from Pont-Neuf, was one of Henry IV's grand architectural projects.

century Europe. His reign was an exercise in early modern European statemaking as he reimposed royal authority throughout the realm. Henry was suspicious of any representative institutions, which he believed threatened the exercise of royal authority: he never convoked the Estates-General, and he ignored the provincial parlements.

Henry IV made the monarchy more powerful by dispensing privilege, favors, and, above all, money with judiciousness that earned loyalty. The difficulties of extracting resources were complicated by the division of the provinces into more peripheral "state provinces" like Languedoc, Burgundy, and Provence, which had been recently added to the realm and retained some of their traditional privileges, and the "election provinces." In the former, the noble Estates assessed and collected taxation; in the latter, royal officials assumed these functions. Provincial governors represented the interests of the monarchy in the face of the privileges and resistance to taxes maintained by the provincial parlements and Estates. Conciliatory royal language began to disappear when it came to asking for money. The governors strengthened the monarchy at the expense of towns that prided themselves on their ancient privileges, further eroding their fiscal independence.

The royal privy council, some of whose members were chosen, like Sully, from the ranks of lesser nobles known for their competence and dedication, strengthened the effectiveness of state administration and foreign relations. The king personally oversaw this council, excluding troublesome nobles. Henry monitored the activities of his ambassadors and his court, whose 1,500 residents included the purveyors of perfume, of which he might have made greater use.

Much of Henry's success in achieving the political reconstruction of France can be credited to his arrogant minister of finance, Maximilien de Béthune, the baron and, as of 1604, the duke of Sully (1560–1641). Sully was the son of a prosperous Protestant family whose great wealth had earned ennoblement. He established budgets and systematic bookkeeping, which helped eliminate some needless expenses.

The monarchy gradually began to pay off some international debts, including those owed to the English crown, and the Swiss cantons, whose good will Henry needed to counter Spanish influence in the Alps. These repayments allowed Henry to contrast his honor in the realm of finances with that of the Spanish monarchy, whose periodic declarations of bankruptcy left creditors grasping at air.

Meanwhile, the nobles reaffirmed their own economic and social domination over their provinces. In 1609, Charles Loyseau, a lawyer, published a *Treatise on Orders and Plain Dignities* that portrayed French society as a hierarchy of orders, or three estates: the clergy, the nobility, and everyone else. He portrayed the king as the guarantor of this organic society. Henry restored the hierarchy of social orders based upon rank and privilege. But the boundaries between and within these estates were fairly fluid. A few

A FAUT ESPERER Q'EU SE JEU LA FINIRA BENTOT

At the time of the Estates-General in 1789, an image of an impoverished, elderly peasant carrying on his back a noble and a priest while scratching out a living from the soil.

newcomers ascended into the highest rank of dukes and peers who stood above even the "nobles of the sword," the oldest and most powerful nobles traditionally called on by the monarchy to provide military support. The "nobles of the robe," while not a coherent or self-conscious group, were men who claimed noble status on the basis of high administrative and judicial office, for example, in the parlements. Henry strengthened the social hierarchy by bolstering established institutions, including the parlements, the treasury, the universities, and, ultimately, the Catholic Church.

Henry also took an interest in encouraging French manufacturing, particularly silk and the production of tapestries. To promote internal trade, he encouraged investment in the construction of several canals linking navigable rivers. He was the first king to take an active interest in supporting a permanent French settlement in the New World, thereby increasing the prospects of French fishermen and trappers following Jacques Cartier's exploration of the St. Lawrence River in 1534. Samuel de Champlain founded the colony of Quebec in 1608. Two years later, the first two French Jesuit missionaries arrived in what became known as New France.

On May 14, 1610, Henry's carriage became ensnared in traffic in central Paris. When some of his guards dashed forward to try to clear the way, a crazed monk named François Ravaillac jumped up to take revenge for the king's protection of Protestants. He stabbed the king three times, fatally.

Louis XIII and the Origins of Absolute Rule

Henry's sudden death left Marie de' Medici, his widow, as regent for his young son, Louis XIII (ruled 1610–1643), who was eight years old at the time. Neither Philip III (ruled 1598–1621) of Spain nor James I of England, nor any of the princes of the German states, were in a position to try to intervene in France on behalf of either Huguenots or Catholics. Marie put aside Henry's planned campaign against the Habsburgs and adopted a policy that considered Catholic powers to be friends.

Marie foiled several nobles' plots against her in 1614–1616. The convocation of the Estates-General in 1614 accentuated the eagerness of noble rivals to gain influence with the young king. One of them convinced Louis to impose his own rule. The king ordered the murder of one of his mother's confidants; Louis then exiled his unpopular mother, hoping to restore calm. When a group of nobles took this as occasion to raise the standard of revolt, the young king's army defeated them at Ponts-de-Cé near Angers in 1620. The royal army then defeated a revolt by Huguenot nobles in the southwest and west.

Emotionally, the stubborn and high-strung boy-king Louis XIII never really grew up. Throughout his life, he demonstrated the psychological burdens of having been regularly whipped as punishment on his father's orders. His father's murder when he was young also marked him. Louis XIII's marriage to an Austrian princess began with a wedding-night fiasco that, whatever happened between the precocious young couple, led to a six-month period in which they did not even share a meal. Finally, things went better. After suffering several miscarriages, the queen produced an heir in 1638, but the royal couple was otherwise unhappy.

Louis XIII was intelligent and liked to sketch and listen to music, the latter calming him when he fell into a rage. He enjoyed hunting and winning at chess, once hurling the offending pieces at the head of a courtier who had the bad grace to checkmate him. Louis was a pious man who attended church every day. But he was also invariably willful, ruthless, and cruel, lashing out savagely at his enemies; indeed, no other ruler of France ordered as many executions as Louis XIII. Among those executed were a number of nobles convicted of dueling, a practice that the king detested because it represented to him the possibility that nobles could raise private armies against the throne.

During Louis XIII's reign, Cardinal Armand Jean du Plessis de Richelieu (1585–1642) expanded the administrative authority and fiscal reach of the crown, dramatically increasing tax revenues. Richelieu's family, solidly entrenched in the west of France, had long served the monarchy in court, army, and church. The gaunt, clever Richelieu staked his future on and won the patronage of the queen mother. He perfected the art of political survival during the court struggles of the next few years. Richelieu was a realist. His foreign and domestic policies reflected his *politique* approach to both.

In 1629, Richelieu prepared a long memorandum for his king. "If the King wants to make himself the most powerful monarch and the most highly esteemed prince in the world," he advised that "[The Estates and the parlements] which oppose the welfare of the kingdom by their pretended sovereignty must be humbled and disciplined. Absolute obedience to the King must be enforced upon great and small alike." Richelieu divided France into thirty-two districts (*généralités*), organizing and extending the king's authority. Officials called intendants governed each district, overseen by the king's council and ultimately responsible to the king himself.

In order to enhance the authority of the monarchy and the Church, Richelieu turned his attention to the Huguenots. After forcing the surrender of insurgent Protestant forces at La Rochelle in 1628, he ordered the destruction of the Huguenot fortresses in the south and southwest, as well as the châteaux of other nobles whose loyalty he had reason to doubt.

During the Thirty Years' War (1618–1648, see p. 145), Louis XIII, influenced by Richelieu, reversed his mother's pro-Spanish foreign policy, returning to the traditional French position of opposition to the Habsburgs. The dynastic rivalry between the two powers proved greater than the fact that both kings were Catholic. Louis XIII thus surprised and outraged the Spanish king by joining England and the Dutch Republic, both Protestant powers, against the powerful Catholic Austrian Habsburgs during the Thirty Years' War. And in 1635, France declared war against Spain itself.

Richelieu's successes, however, did not stand well with his resentful enemies within France. His toleration of Huguenot worship drew the wrath of some Catholic nobles, as did continuing costly wars against the Catholic Habsburgs, which led to French subsidies to Protestant Sweden. Revolts occurred in Dijon and Aix, both seats of provincial parlements, where local notables resented having to bow to the authority of royal officials.

One of the most conservative Catholic nobles, a royal minister, briefly turned the king against Richelieu. Marie de' Medici, returned from brief disgrace, tried to convince her son to dismiss the cagey cardinal. The "Day of Dupes" (November 10, 1630) followed, which amounted to little more than a high-stakes family shouting match between Marie de' Medici, Louis XIII, and Richelieu. Marie left thinking she had won the day, but awoke the next morning to find that the king had ordered her exile. The king's own brother led a second plot against Richelieu from 1641 to 1642, backed by the king of Spain.

After decades of religious wars, the assassination of Henry IV, and a fragile, temperamental young monarch around whom plots swirled, the monarchy of France had nonetheless been greatly strengthened, building upon the accomplishments of his predecessor. Louis XIII's sometimes decisive and brutal actions enhanced the reputation of the king who was known to many of his subjects as "The Just," whether fitting or not. A hypochondriac whose health was even worse than he feared, Louis XIII died of tuberculosis in 1643 at the age

Philippe de Champagne's portrait of the sad-eyed Louis XIII.

of forty-two. But the man-child monarch had, with Richelieu, laid the foundations for absolute monarchical rule in France.

THE THIRTY YEARS' WAR (1618–1648)

In Central Europe, religious divisions and intolerance led to the Thirty Years' War, a brutal conflict during which the largely mercenary armies of Catholic and Protestant states laid waste to the German states. Dynastic rivalries were never far from the stage, bringing the continental Great Powers into the fray. When the war finally ended, the Treaty of Westphalia (1648) established a territorial and religious settlement that lasted until the French Revolution.

Factionalism in the Holy Roman Empire

The Holy Roman Empire was a loose confederation of approximately 1,000 German autonomous or semi-autonomous states. These states ranged in size from powerful Habsburg Austria to Hamburg, Lübeck, and other free cities in the north, and even smaller territories no more than a few square kilometers in size run by bishops. It would have been almost impossible for a traveler to determine where one state stopped and another began had it not been for the frequent toll stations, which provided revenue for each. The southwestern German state of Swabia, for example, was divided among sixty-eight secular and forty ecclesiastical lords and included thirty-two free cities.

Geographic factors further complicated the political life of the German states. A few of the largest states included territories that were not contiguous. The Upper Palatinate lay squeezed between Bohemia and Bavaria; the Lower Palatinate lay far away in the Rhineland. The former was predominantly Lutheran, the latter Calvinist.

Since 1356, when the constitutional law of the Holy Roman Empire had been established, seven electors (four electoral princes and three archbishops) selected each new Holy Roman emperor. The empire's loose federal structure had a chancery to carry out foreign policy and negotiations with the various German princes. But only in confronting the threat of the Turks from the southeast did the German princes mount a consistent and relatively unified foreign policy.

Other institutions of the Holy Roman Empire also reflected the political complexity of Central Europe. An imperial Diet brought princes, nobles, and representatives of the towns together when the emperor summoned them. An Imperial Court of Justice ruled on matters of importance to the empire. The Holy Roman Empire, once the most powerful force in Europe, had been weakened by its battles with the papacy in the thirteenth century. Yet for some states the empire offered a balance between the desire for a figure of authority who could maintain law and order and their continued political independence.

The Peace of Augsburg (1555), which ended the war between the Holy Roman Emperor Charles V and the Protestant German states, had stated that, with the exception of ecclesiastical states and the free cities, the religion of the ruler would be the religion of the land (*cuius regio, eius religio*) (see Chapter 3). This formula, however, did not end religious rivalries or the demands of religious minorities that rulers tolerate their beliefs. The Peace of Augsburg, in fact, reinforced German particularism. It also helped secularize the institutions of the Holy Roman emperor by recognizing the right of the German princes to determine the religion of their states. This also served to end the hope of Charles V to establish an empire that would bring together all of the Habsburg territories in the German states, Spain, and the Netherlands.

The Origins of the Thirty Years' War

Rudolf II (1557–1612), king of Bohemia and Holy Roman emperor (he succeeded his father Maximilian II as Holy Roman emperor in 1576), wanted to launch a religious crusade against Protestantism. He closed Lutheran churches in 1578, reneging on an earlier promise to Bohemian nobles that he would tolerate the religion to which a good many of them had converted.

Moreover, Rudolf's cousin Archduke Ferdinand II (1578–1637) withdrew the religious toleration Maximilian II had granted in Inner Austria.

Rudolf's imperial army, which had been fighting the Turks on and off since 1593, had annexed Transylvania. The emperor moved against Protestants both there and in Hungary. But in 1605, when Rudolf's army undertook a campaign against the Turks in the Balkans, Protestants rebelled in both places. A Protestant army invaded Moravia, which lies east of Bohemia and north of Austria, close to the Habsburg capital of Vienna. In the meantime, Emperor Rudolf, only marginally competent on his best days (he was subject to depression and later to fits of insanity), lived as a recluse in his castle in Prague. His family convinced his brother Matthias (1557–1619) to act on Rudolf's behalf by making peace with the Hungarian and Transylvanian Protestants, and with the Turks. This Peace of Vienna (1606) guaranteed religious freedom in Hungary. Matthias was then recognized as head of the Habsburgs and Rudolf's heir.

Most everyone seemed pleased with the peace except Rudolf, who concluded that a plague that was ravaging Bohemia was proof that God was displeased with the concessions he had granted Protestants. He denounced Matthias and Ferdinand for their accommodation with the Protestants and with the Turkish "infidels." Matthias allied with the Protestant Hungarian noble Estates and marched against Rudolf, who surrendered. Rudolf ceded Hungary, Austria, and Moravia to Matthias in 1608, and Bohemia in 1611. Rudolf was forced to sign a "Letter of Majesty" in 1609 that granted Bohemians the right to choose between Catholicism, Lutheranism, or one of two groups of Hussites (see Chapter 3). Protestant churches, schools, and cemeteries were to be tolerated.

The decline in the effective authority of the Holy Roman emperor contributed to the end of a period of relative peace in the German states. In the last decades of the sixteenth century, these states had become increasingly quarrelsome and militarized. "The dear old Holy Roman Empire," went one song, "How does it stay together?" Rulers of some member states began to undermine imperial political institutions by refusing to accept rulings by the Imperial Supreme Court and even to attend the occasional convocations of the Diet. "Imperial Military Circles," which were inter-state alliances responsible for defense of a number of states within the empire, had become moribund because of religious antagonisms between the member states.

For a time, the Catholic Reformation profited from acrimonious debates and even small wars between Lutherans and Calvinists. But increasingly Protestants put aside their differences, however substantial, in the face of the continued determination of some Catholic rulers to win back territories lost to Protestantism.

Acts of intolerance heated up religious rivalries. In 1606, in Donauwörth, a southern German imperial free city in which Lutherans held the upper hand and Catholics enjoyed toleration, a riot began when Lutherans tried to prevent Catholics from holding a procession. The following year, Duke Maximilian of Bavaria sent troops to assure Catholic domination. This angered Calvinist princes in the region, as well as some Lutheran sovereigns. The imperial Diet, convoked two years later, broke up in chaos when Holy Roman Emperor Rudolf II refused to increase Protestant representation in the Diet. The political crisis now spread further when some of the German Catholic states sought Spanish intervention in a dispute over princely succession in the small northern Rhineland Catholic territories of Cleves-Jülich, which Henry IV of France threatened to invade. In 1609, Catholic German princes organized a Catholic League, headed by Maximilian of Bavaria. Six Protestant princes then signed a defensive alliance, the Protestant Union, against the Catholic League.

Matthias, who had been elected Holy Roman emperor in 1612, wanted to make the Catholic League an institution of Habsburg will. He also hoped to woo Lutherans from the Protestant Union, which was dominated by the Calvinists. But Matthias's obsession with Habsburg dynastic ambitions, his history of having fought with the Protestant Dutch rebels against Spain (see Chapter 5), and his opportunistic toleration of Lutheranism cost him the confidence of some Catholic princes. Archduke Ferdinand, ruler of Inner Austria, waited in the wings to lead a Catholic crusade against Protestantism. Ferdinand, who had inherited the throne of Hungary in 1617 and that of Bohemia the following year, became Holy Roman emperor upon his uncle Matthias's death in 1619. Ferdinand was a pious man whose confessor convinced him that he could only save his soul by launching a war of religion. In the meantime, Protestant resistance in Bohemia mobilized, seeking Protestant assistance from Transylvania and the Palatinate.

Conflict in Bohemia

In Bohemia, Ferdinand imposed significant limitations on Protestant worship. In Prague, Calvinists and Lutherans began to look outside of Bohemia for potential support from Protestant princes. Protestant leaders convoked

FERDINAND II PAR LA GRACE DE DIEU EMPERVR DES ROMAINS.

Ferdinand II, Holy Roman Emperor and King of Bohemia.

MAP 4.2 THE THIRTY YEARS' WAR, 1618–1648   Protestant and Catholic armies clashed in battles that ranged back and forth across Europe.

an assembly of the Estates of Bohemia, citing rights specified by Rudolf's "Letter of Majesty" of 1609. Ferdinand ordered the assembly to disband.

Following the Defenestration of Prague in 1618, Protestant leaders established a provisional government in Bohemia. "This business of Bohemia is likely to put all Christendom in combustion," predicted the English ambassador to the Dutch capital of Amsterdam. Indeed it began a destructive war between Catholic and Protestant forces that would last thirty years, lay waste to many of the German states, and finally bring a religious and territorial settlement that would last for two centuries.

Bohemia rose in full revolt against not only the Church but the Habsburg dynasty as well. With almost no assistance from the nobles, the rebels turned to the Protestant Union, promising the Bohemian crown to Frederick, the young Calvinist elector of the Palatinate and the most important

Protestant prince in Central Europe. In 1619, the Estates offered Frederick the crown, and he accepted.

The Protestant cause, like that of the Catholics, became increasingly internationalized and tied to dynastic considerations (see Map 4.2). Now Holy Roman Emperor Ferdinand II learned that Protestant rebels had refused to recognize his authority in Bohemia and had offered his throne to Frederick. Even more determined to drive Protestants from his realm but lacking an army, Ferdinand turned to outside help. The Catholic king of Spain agreed to send troops he could ill afford; the price of his intervention was the promise of the cession of the Rhineland state of the Lower Palatinate to Spain. The Catholic Maximilian I of Bavaria also sent an army, expecting to be rewarded for his trouble with the Upper Palatinate and with Frederick's title of elector in the Holy Roman Empire.

The Expansion of the Conflict

Protestant armies besieged Vienna, the Habsburg capital, until the arrival of Catholic armies in 1619. The Dutch could not provide assistance to the Protestants, as they were fighting for independence from Spain. Several of the German Protestant states also declined, fearing Catholic rebellions in their own lands. However, with Spanish armies and monies already on the way, the internationalization of the Bohemian crisis had reached the point of no return.

In 1620 the Catholic League raised a largely Bavarian army of 30,000 troops. Count Johannes von Tilly (1559–1632) commanded the Catholic forces. The depressed, indecisive count from Flanders managed to subdue Upper Austria and then defeated the main Protestant Union army at the Battle of White Mountain, near Prague, in November. With the Catholic forces now holding Bohemia, Tilly's army then overran Silesia, Moravia, Austria, and part of the Upper Palatinate. The extent of the Catholic victory expanded the war, increasing the determination of the Catholic League to crush all Protestant resistance and, at the same time, of the Protestant forces to resist at all costs.

Frederick's Protestant forces fought on, counting on help from France and other states who had reason to fear an expansion of Habsburg power in Central Europe. Frederick also hoped to convince James I of England that a victory of the Catholic League would threaten Protestantism. But the English king had placed his hopes on the marriage of his son, Charles, to the sister of Philip IV of Spain (see Chapter 5). Again dynastic rivalries outweighed those of religion.

The war went on, and Tilly's army won a series of small victories. In 1622, the Spanish army defeated Dutch forces at Jülich in the Rhineland, eliminating any possibility of English armed assistance to Frederick through Holland. For the moment, Frederick's only effective force was a plundering mercenary horde in northeastern Germany. Tilly's victory over a Protestant army in 1623 and conquest of most of the Palatinate forced Frederick to abandon his claims to Bohemia's throne after having been king for all of one winter. But encouraged by the renewed possibility of English assistance after James's plans for the marriage of his son to the Spanish princess fell through, Frederick turned north to Scandinavia for assistance.

The Danish Period

Christian IV (ruled 1588–1648), the Protestant king of Denmark, had ambition and money, but not a great deal of sense. Also duke of the northern German state of Holstein, the gambling, hard-drinking Dane wanted to extend his influence and perhaps even add territories in the northern German states. Frederick's difficulties seemed to offer the Danish sovereign the opportunity of a lifetime. In 1625, he led his troops into the northern German states, assuming that the English and the Dutch, and perhaps the French as well, would rush to follow his leadership against the Habsburgs.

But King James I of England had died and was succeeded by Charles I, whose provocative policies generated increasing opposition from Parliament (see Chapter 6), leaving him little time to consider intervening on behalf of the Protestant cause on the continent. England and the Netherlands sent only some money and a few thousand soldiers to help the Danish king. Moreover, Louis XIII of France, who was besieging Protestants at La Rochelle, provided the Danes with only a modest subsidy to aid the fight against the Habsburgs. Christian, essentially left to his own devices, was unaware of the approach of a large imperial army commanded by one of the most intriguing figures in the age of religious wars.

Albrecht Wallenstein (1583–1634) was a Bohemian noble who, after marrying a wealthy widow, had risen to even greater fortune as a supplier of armies. Raised a Lutheran, he converted to Catholicism at age twenty and became the most powerful of the Catholic generals. The fact that a convert could rise to such a powerful position again reveals how a religious war evolved into not only a dynastic struggle between the rulers of France, Spain, and Austria, as well as Sweden and Denmark, but also into an unprincipled free-for-all in which mercenary soldiers of fortune played a major part. Wallenstein, an ardent student of astrology, was ambitious, ruthless, and possessed a violent temper. His abhorrence of noise was obsessive—and odd, for a military person. Because he detested the sound of barking or meowing, he sometimes ordered all dogs and cats killed upon arriving in a town, and forbade the townspeople and his soldiers from wearing heavy boots or spurs or anything else that would make noise. He alternated between extreme generosity and horrible cruelty, and was always accompanied by an executioner awaiting his master's command. Wallenstein, entrusted by Ferdinand with raising and commanding an army drawn from states for the Catholic cause, marched north with 30,000 men.

The Catholic army defeated the Danes in 1626, and then marched to the Baltic coast, crossed into Denmark, and devastated the peninsula of Jutland. But Wallenstein's successes engendered nervous opposition within the Catholic states. Furthermore, his troops devastated the lands of friend and foe alike, extracting money and food, plundering, and selling military leadership positions to any buyer, including criminals.

Christian, who had bankrupted his kingdom during this ill-fated excursion, signed the Treaty of Lübeck in 1629, whereby he withdrew from the war and gave up his claims in northern Germany. The treaty was less draconian than it might have been because the seemingly endless war was wearing heavily on some of the Catholic German states. They feared an expansion of Habsburg power, and some of them did not want to add Protestants to their domains.

Ferdinand II now implemented measures against Protestants without convoking the imperial Diet. He expelled from Bohemia Calvinist and Lutheran ministers and nobles who refused to convert to Catholicism and ennobled new men, including foreigners, as a means of assuring Catholic domination. He confiscated the property of nobles suspected of participating in any phase of the Protestant rebellion. With Frederick's electorship now transferred to Maximilian I of Bavaria, the Habsburgs could count on the fact that a majority of the electors were Catholic princes. Captured Habsburg dispatches in 1628 made clear that Ferdinand sought to destroy the freedom of the Protestant German cities of the Hanseatic League in the north in the interest of expanding the Habsburg domains. These revelations alarmed Louis XIII of France.

Ferdinand found that it was not easy to impose Catholicism in territories where it had not been practiced for decades. In the Upper Palatinate, the first priests who came to celebrate Mass there were unable to find a chalice. Half of the parishes in Bohemia were without clergy. Italian priests brought to Upper Austria could not be understood by their parishioners. The Edict of Restitution (1629) allowed Lutherans—but not Calvinists, who were few in number in the German states except in the Palatinate—to practice their religion in certain cities, but ordered them to return to the Catholic Church all monasteries and convents acquired since 1552, when signatories of the Peace of Augsburg had first gathered. Because the Edict of Restitution also gave rulers the right to enforce the practice of their religion within their territories, the war went on.

The Swedish Interlude

In the meantime, England, the Dutch Republic, the northern German state of Brandenburg, and the Palatinate asked the Lutheran king Gustavus Adolphus (ruled 1611–1632) of Sweden to intervene on the Protestant side. The possibility of expanding Swedish territory, a kingdom of

King Gustavus Adolphus of Sweden in battle.

barely a million inhabitants, was more than Gustavus, with an adventurer's disposition, could resist.

Gustavus, the "Lion of the North," who survived a shipwreck at the age of five, had been tutored in the art of war by mercenary soldiers. He also played the flute, composed poetry, and conversed in ten languages. Gustavus retained, as did a disproportionate number of rulers in his century, a violent temper. Once, coming upon two stolen cows outside an officer's tent, he dragged the thief by the ear to the executioner. His courage was legendary—he barely paused as cannonballs exploded nearby and as his horses were shot out from under him or fell through the ice.

Gustavus, influenced by an appreciation of Roman military tactics, formed his battle lines thinner—about six men deep—than those of rival commanders. This allowed his lines to be more widely spread out. Gustavus organized his army into brigades of four squadrons with nine cannon to protect them, sending the unit into battle in an arrow-shaped formation. Superior artillery served his cause well, hurling larger shot farther and more accurately than the cannon of his enemies.

The dashing young Swedish king subdued Catholic Poland with his army of about 70,000 men. Swedish intervention and the continuing woes of Spain, now at war in the Alps, Italy, and the Netherlands, gave Protestants reason for hope. After defeating a combined Polish and Habsburg army in 1629, Swedish troops occupied Pomerania along the Baltic Sea.

In 1630, sure of a Catholic majority, Emperor Ferdinand convoked the imperial electors to recognize his son as his heir. He also wanted them to support his promise to aid Spain against the Dutch in exchange for Spanish assistance against the Protestant armies. But the Protestant electors of Saxony and Brandenburg refused even to attend the gathering. Catholic electors demanded that the powerful Wallenstein be dismissed; even the king of Spain feared the general's powerful ragtag army. Ferdinand thereby dismissed the one man whose accomplishments and influence might have enabled the Habsburg monarchy to master all of the German states.

Despite a sizable subsidy from the king of France, Gustavus Adolphus enjoyed the support of only several tiny Protestant states. Some Lutheran German states still hoped to receive territorial concessions from the Habsburgs. The Catholic dynasty preferred Lutherans to Calvinists, viewing the latter as more radical reformers. Ferdinand now sent Tilly to stop the invading Swedes. He besieged the Protestant city of Magdeburg in Brandenburg, forcing its surrender in 1631. The subsequent massacre of the population and accompanying pillage had an effect similar to that of the Defenestration of Prague; the story of the atrocities spread across Protestant Europe. Brandenburg and Saxony now allied with Sweden. The combined Protestant forces under Gustavus Adolphus defeated Tilly's imperial Catholic army at Breitenfeld near Leipzig. The Swedish army, swollen by German mercenaries, then marched through the northern German states, easily reversing Habsburg gains over the previous twelve years.

The expansion of Swedish power generated anxiety among both Protestant and Catholic states, including France, although Louis XIII had helped finance Gustavus Adolphus. In Bavaria, the Swedes defeated Tilly, who was killed in battle in 1632. The rout of the Catholic imperial forces seemed complete. Spain, its interests spread too far afield in Europe and the Americas, could not then afford to help. The plague prevented another Catholic army from being raised in Italy; even the pope begged off a request for help by complaining that the eruption of Mount Vesuvius was preventing the collection of taxes.

In April 1632, Ferdinand turned once again to Wallenstein to save the Catholic cause, the latter agreeing to raise a new imperial army in return for almost unlimited authority over it. Wallenstein reconquered Silesia and Bohemia. Against him, Gustavus led the largest army (175,000) that had ever been under a single command in Europe. Although reason dictated that the Swedish army should dig in for the winter of 1632, Gustavus took a chance by attacking Wallenstein in the fog at Lützen in Saxony in November. The two sides fought to a bloody draw, but a draw amounted to a Catholic victory. Gustavus Adolphus fell dead in the battle, facedown in the mud.

Wallenstein's days were also numbered. His new army was now living off the land in Central Europe, engendering peasant resistance. Furthermore, Wallenstein, who was ill, demanded command of a Spanish army that had subsequently arrived to help the Catholic forces. In the meantime, it became known that Wallenstein had considered joining Gustavus after the Battle of Breitenfeld in 1631, and that he was offering his services to both France and the German Protestants. Ferdinand dismissed Wallenstein for the final time, and then ordered his murder. In February 1634, an Irish mercenary crept into Wallenstein's room, and killed him with a spear.

With the aid of the remnants of Wallenstein's forces, the Spanish army defeated the combined Swedish and German Protestant army in 1634 in Swabia. The elector of Saxony abandoned the Protestant struggle, making peace in 1635 with Ferdinand. One by one, other Protestant princes also left the war. The Catholic forces now held the upper hand.

The Armies of the Thirty Years' War

The Thirty Years' War was certainly one of the cruelest episodes in the history of warfare. A contemporary described the horror of the seemingly endless brutalities that afflicted Central Europe:

> [The soldiers] stretched out a hired man flat on the ground, stuck a wooden wedge in his mouth to keep it open, and emptied a milk bucket full of stinking manure droppings down his throat—they called it a Swedish cocktail. . . . Then they used thumb-screws . . . to torture the peasants. . . . They put one of the captured bumpkins in the bakeoven and lighted a fire in it. . . . I can't say much about the captured wives, hired girls, and daughters because the soldiers did not let me watch their doings. But I do remember hearing pitiful screams in various dark corners.

Several factors may have contributed to the barbarity of soldiers during the Thirty Years' War. Mercenaries and volunteers were usually fighting far

Soldiers pillaging a farmhouse during the Thirty Years' War, some torturing the farmer over his hearth while others rape the women and steal the food.

from home, living off the land to survive. Strident propaganda against other religions may have contributed to the brutality. In response, however, Gustavus Adolphus and other leaders imposed harsh penalties, including execution, for atrocities, not wanting to so frighten the local population that ordinary channels of provisioning the army would disappear.

During the Thirty Years' War, at least a million men took arms. The armies were enormous for the time. Even Sweden, where there was no fighting, felt the impact of the death of at least 50,000 soldiers between 1621 and 1632 from battle wounds and, more often, disease. Yet, considering the number of troops engaged in the long war, relatively few soldiers perished in battle, particularly when compared to those who succumbed to illness and to civilians who died at the hands of marauding troops. Armies rampaged through the German states, Catholic and Protestant, speaking many languages, taking what they wanted, burning and looting. Marburg was occupied eleven different times. Atrocity followed atrocity.

The armies themselves remained ragtag forces, lacking discipline and accompanied by, in some cases, the families of soldiers. The presence of large numbers of women (including many prostitutes) and children as camp followers may have contributed to the length of the war, making life in the army seem more normal for soldiers.

Soldiers, for the most part, wore what they could find. Some, if they were lucky, had leather clothes, carried rain cloaks against the damp German climate, and wore felt hats. Some Habsburg troops sported uniforms of pale gray, at least at the beginning of a campaign. As the months passed and uniforms disintegrated, soldiers were forced to disrobe the dead, friend and foe alike, or to steal from civilians. At best, soldiers wore symbols indicating their regiment and fought behind banners bearing the colors of the army— thus the expression "show your colors." The Swedes wore a yellow band around their hats. The imperial forces placed red symbols in their hats, plumes, or sashes if they could find them.

Most armies also lacked a common language. The Habsburg army included Saxons, Bavarians, Westphalians, and Austrians; Maximilian's Bavarian army counted various other Germans, Italians, Poles, Slovenes, Croats, Greeks, Hungarians, Burgundians, French, Czechs, Spaniards, Scots, Irish, and Turks.

Some soldiers may have joined regiments because they were searching for adventure; others joined out of religious conviction. Yet a multitude of soldiers fought against armies of their own religion, changing sides when a better opportunity arose. Army recruiters gave religion not the slightest thought in their search for soldiers to fill quotas for which they were being handsomely paid. In any case, recruits on both sides were attracted by the strong possibility that they would be better clothed and fed—bread, meat, lots of beer, and occasionally some butter and cheese—than they were when they joined up.

The Wars of Religion and Dynastic Struggles (1635–1648)

Between 1635 and 1648, what had begun as a religious war became a dynastic struggle between two Catholic states, France and Habsburg Austria, the former allied with Sweden, the latter with Spain. France declared war on Philip IV of Spain in 1635. Richelieu hoped to force Habsburg armies away from the borders of France. He took as a pretext the Spanish arrest of a French ally, the elector of Trier. Alliances with the Dutch Republic and Sweden had prepared the way, as did reassurances given by neighboring Savoy and Lorraine, and by French protectorates in Alsace.

The French incursions into the Netherlands and the southern German states did not go well. Louis XIII's army was short on capable commanders and battle-experienced troops, largely because France was already fighting in Italy, the Pyrenees, and the northern German states. But France's involvement, like that of Sweden before it, did provide the Protestant states with some breathing room. French forces joined the Swedish army, helping defeat the imperial army in Saxony.

The wars went on. When the pope called for representatives of the Catholic and Protestant states to assemble in Cologne for a peace congress in 1636, no one showed up. Four years later, another combined French and Swedish force defeated the Habsburg army. Maximilian I of Bavaria then sought a separate peace with France. Devastating Spanish defeats in northern France in 1643, as well as in the Netherlands and the Pyrenees, and the outbreak of rebellions inside Spain, left the Austrian Habsburgs with no choice but to make peace.

At the same time, unrest in France, including plots against Richelieu, and the English Civil War, which began in 1642, served to warn other rulers of the dangers that continued instability could bring. The Swedish population was tiring of distant battles that brought home nothing but news of casualties. In the German states, calls for peace echoed in music and plays. Lutheran ministers inveighed against the war from the pulpit. Among the rulers of the great powers, only Louis XIII wanted the war to go on, at the expense of the Austrian Habsburgs. He helped subsidize an invasion of Hungary by Transylvanian Protestants in 1644. As Swedish and Transylvanian forces prepared to besiege the imperial capital of Vienna, Holy Roman Emperor Ferdinand III (ruled 1637–1657), who had succeeded his father, concluded a peace treaty with the prince of Transylvania, promising to tolerate Protestantism in Hungary. After Habsburg armies suffered further defeats in 1645, Ferdinand III realized that he had to make peace, and offered an amnesty to princes within the empire who had fought against him.

The preliminaries for a general peace agreement had begun in 1643 and dragged on even as a Franco-Swedish army drove the imperial army out of the Rhineland and Bavaria in 1647. Following another French victory early in 1648, only the outbreak of the Fronde, a rebellion of nobles against the king's authority in France (see Chapter 7), forced the young Louis XIV to seek peace.

The Treaty of Westphalia (1648)

The Treaty of Westphalia was unlike any previous peace settlement in history, which had invariably been between two or three states, rarely more. Its framers believed that they could restore international stability and diplomatic process in a Europe torn by anarchy by eliminating religious divisions as a cause of conflict. The treaty proved almost as complicated as the Thirty Years' War itself. Two hundred rulers converged on Westphalia. Thousands of diplomats and other officials shuttled back and forth between two towns. Letters took ten to twelve days to reach the courts of Paris and Vienna, at least twenty to Stockholm, and a month to arrive in Madrid. In the meantime, the French tried to delay any treaty, hoping to force Spain to surrender. In the summer of 1648, the Swedes reoccupied Bohemia, hoping to win a larger indemnity and toleration for the Lutherans. When, by the separate Treaty of Münster, Spain finally formally recognized the *fait accompli* of Dutch independence, the Spanish Army of Flanders fought against France in a last-ditch effort to help Ferdinand III. In August 1648, the French defeated a Spanish force a month after the Swedes had captured part of Prague. His back to the wall, Ferdinand signed the peace treaty, finally concluded on October 24, 1648.

The Treaty of Westphalia redrew the map of Europe, confirming the existence of the Dutch United Provinces and Switzerland. The treaty did not end the war between Spain and France, but it did end the wars of the German states and in doing so put an end to one of the most brutal, ghastly periods in European history. Sweden absorbed West Pomerania and the bishoprics of Verden and Bremen on the North Sea (see Map 4.3). France, by an agreement signed two years earlier, annexed the frontier towns of Metz, Toul, and Verdun, and parts of Alsace. Maximilian I of Bavaria kept the Upper Palatinate, and therefore the status of elector. Frederick's Protestant son ended up with the Lower, or Rhine Palatinate. With this addition of an elector, eight votes would now be necessary to elect the Holy Roman emperor.

With minor exceptions, the territorial settlement reached in Westphalia remained in place until the French Revolution of 1789. For the most part, the treaty ended wars of religion in early modern Europe. It encouraged religious toleration, finally rewarding those people who had worked for and advocated religious toleration, or suffered intolerance and repression, during the long, bloody conflicts. The philosopher Baruch Spinoza (1632–1677), who had been forced to flee intolerance in Portugal, undoubtedly spoke for many when he wrote, "As for rebellions which are aroused under the pretext of religion . . . opinions are regarded as wicked and condemned

MAP 4.3 EUROPE AFTER THE TREATY OF WESTPHALIA, 1648   The treaty ended the Thirty Years' War.

as crimes, and their defenders and followers sacrificed. Not to the public well-being, but only to the hate and barbarism of their opponents."

The Treaty of Westphalia reinforced the strong autonomous traditions of the German states, which emerged from the long nightmare of war with more independence from the considerably weakened Holy Roman Empire. Member states thereafter could carry out their own foreign policy, though they could not form alliances against the empire. The Habsburg dynasty's dream of forging a centralized empire of states fully obedient to the emperor's will had failed. Bohemia lost its independence. Bohemian Protestant landowners recovered neither their lands nor their religious freedom.

By the Treaty of Westphalia, German Calvinists gained the same rights as those previously granted to Lutherans. The settlement granted religious toleration where it had existed in 1624. But it also confirmed the Peace of Augsburg's establishment of territorial churches—Catholic, Lutheran, or Calvinist—still to be determined by the religion of the ruler. Dissident groups were often forbidden, and their followers were persecuted. Generally speaking, Lutheranism remained dominant in the northern half of the Holy Roman Empire, Catholicism in the southern half, with Calvinists in the Rhineland.

Before his death in battle, Gustavus Adolphus noted "all the wars of Europe are now blended into one." More than 200 states of varying sizes had fought in the war. The devastation brought by thirty years of war is simply incalculable. Catholic Mainz, occupied by the Swedes, lost 25 percent of its buildings and 40 percent of its population. In four years, the predominantly Protestant duchy of Württemberg lost three-quarters of its population while occupied by imperial troops. Almost 90 percent of the farms of Mecklenburg were abandoned during the course of the war. Many villages in Central Europe were now uninhabited. Although devastation varied from region to region during the Thirty Years' War, German cities lost a third of their population, and the rural population declined by 40 percent. Central Europe, like the rest of the continent, may have already been suffering from the economic and social crisis that had begun in the 1590s. But the wars contributed to the huge decline of the population of the states of the Holy Roman Empire from about 20 million to 16 million people.

A year before the Treaty of Westphalia, a Swabian wrote in the family Bible: "They say that the terrible war is now over. But there is still no sign of peace. Everywhere there is envy, hatred and greed; that's what the war has taught us. . . . We live like animals, eating bark and grass. No one could have imagined that anything like this would happen to us. Many people say there is no God . . . but we still believe that God has not abandoned us."

War was not alone in taking lives: epidemics, the worst of which was the bubonic plague, and diseases, including influenza and typhus, also took fearsome tolls. Towns were clogged with starving, vulnerable refugees from the fighting and marauding. The flight of peasants from their lands reduced agricultural productivity. It would be decades before the German states recovered from the Thirty Years' War.

Although much of the religious settlement of the Treaty of Westphalia would endure, dynastic rivalries still raged. France had emerged from its religious wars with a stronger monarchy; Louis XIII had made his state more centralized and powerful. France's rivals, too, would extend their authority within their own states. In the mid-seventeenth century, Europe would enter the era of monarchical absolutism. The most powerful European states— above all, Louis XIV's France—would enter a period of aggressive territorial expansion. Dynastic wars would help shape the European experience from the mid-seventeenth century to the French Revolution of 1789.

PART TWO

STATEMAKING

During the last half of the fifteenth century, the balance of economic and political power in Europe began to shift away from the Mediterranean region and the Italian city-states. The discovery and then colonization of the Americas contributed greatly to the development of the Atlantic economy, adding to the strength of Spain and then, beginning a century later, of England, transporting their rivalry across the Atlantic Ocean. The surprising English naval victory over the Spanish Armada in 1588 symbolized the subsequent shift in power from southern to northern Europe, even if Spain remained militarily stronger until the 1630s.

In the seventeenth century, when aggressive European monarchs were running roughshod over noble prerogatives and town privileges, England and the Dutch Republic both maintained their representative governments. The English Civil War led to the defeat and execution of the king in 1649, the fall of the monarchy, and in 1688, to the "Glorious Revolution," which affirmed the civil liberties of the English people and the rights of Parliament. In the largely Protestant Netherlands, which earned its independence after a protracted struggle against Catholic Spain, the prosperous merchants retained a republican form of government and helped generate the golden age of Dutch culture. In contrast, many European rulers relentlessly extended their power between 1650 and 1750, becoming absolute rulers. In principle, they were above all challenge from within the state itself, affecting the lives of more people than ever before through taxation, military service, and the royal quest for religious orthodoxy as Europe entered the era of absolutism.

CHAPTER 5

THE RISE OF THE ATLANTIC ECONOMY: SPAIN AND ENGLAND

~~~

In 1585, Protestant England went to war with Catholic Spain. On July 30, 1588, English observers on the cliffs above the English Channel first caught sight of the supposedly invincible Spanish Armada, a force of 130 ships. On the night of August 7, the English fleet attacked King Philip II's Armada along the English coast. After the Armada anchored near Calais, the English sent ships set on fire against the Armada, which caused the Spanish ships to break their tight tactical formation. With the help of strong winds, the English then pinned the Spanish ships against the shore, and destroyed six of them, in the longest and most intense naval artillery battle, much of it at such close range that the sailors could hurl insults at each other. Superior English cannon, shot, and gunners took their toll on the Armada. More than 1,000 Spaniards died during the long battle that day. The captain of one Spanish ship that had failed to answer the flagship's call for help was hanged from a yardarm, his body hauled from ship to ship to reestablish discipline.

The English ships failed to follow up their advantage, however, letting the Spanish galleons escape. The rough winds of the Channel carried the Spanish ships away from the dangerous Flemish shoals toward the North Sea and then on a long, northern voyage up to the straits between the Orkney and Shetland Islands. This was decidedly the long way to reach the safety of Spanish ports. More than thirty Spanish ships sank in gales off the western coasts of Scotland and Ireland. When some of the ships of the Armada limped into port in Spain, the fleet's captain wrote King Philip II, "I am unable to describe to Your Majesty the misfortunes and miseries that have befallen us, because they are the worst that have been known on any voyage; and some of the ships that put into this port have spent the last fourteen days without a single drop of water." Of the 130 ships that had sailed against

English vessels attack the Spanish Armada off Calais in the English Channel in 1588.

England, only 60 could now be accounted for. At least a third had been sunk or wrecked, and many others were severely damaged.

Victory over the Spanish Armada accentuated England's rise to international dominance. English armies then crushed an Irish rebellion in 1603, ending fears of an effective Irish alliance with Catholic Spain. Despite the defeat of the Spanish Armada, however, Philip did not make peace with England, and the war between the two nations dragged on until 1604.

Economic Expansion

The rise of Spain, England, and the Netherlands must be seen in the context of the sixteenth-century expansion of the European economy. By 1450, the European population had begun to recover slowly from the Black Death, the disastrous plague that had swept the continent a century earlier. In general, the population continued to rise until the mid-seventeenth century, when religious and dynastic wars and new plagues led to such devastation that the period has become known as "the age of crisis." These cataclysms particularly struck Central Europe. But the Mediterranean region, too, suffered population decline, and the European population of the Turkish Ottoman Empire remained extremely sparse, about half that of France and Italy in 1600.

During the sixteenth century, the commercial and manufacturing center of Europe shifted from the Mediterranean to northwestern Europe. England and France established colonies in North America, and English and

Dutch traders ventured beyond the coast of India to the East Indies. By 1700, Venice—which, alone among the Italian city-states, had managed to retain significant trade links with Asia—had become a virtual backwater because it had failed to adapt to the global economy that was expanding across the Atlantic Ocean to the Americas. Spain, France, England, and the Dutch United Provinces emerged as burgeoning colonial powers in the late sixteenth century, developing trade routes to Asia and gradually establishing empires.

Spain's preeminence did not survive the end of the seventeenth-century economic crisis. Its merchants lacked the flexibility shown by the English and Dutch to adjust to the varying demand for colonial products and to create new trading opportunities. The extraction and importation of silver dominated their efforts. Furthermore, merchants in Amsterdam and London, not those in the Spanish city of Seville, expanded trade by using innovative commercial techniques. Spanish merchants proved less able than their northern rivals to lower costs of transportation from the New World. In contrast, English textile merchants found new markets in Spain and the Mediterranean for their cloth.

Increased Agricultural Productivity

Populations cannot grow unless the rural economy can produce enough additional food to feed more people. During the sixteenth century, farmers brought more land into cultivation at the expense of forests and fens (marsh lands). Dutch reclamation of land from the sea in the Netherlands in the sixteenth and seventeenth centuries provides the most spectacular example of the expansion of farm land; the Dutch reclaimed more than 36,000 acres between 1590 and 1615 alone. Modest agricultural progress was, however, limited to Western Europe, in villages with access to urban merchants, markets, and trade routes. In Russia and Eastern Europe, hundreds of thousands of serfs who were legally bound to the land labored to produce enough grain to feed the population and to generate a surplus that their lords could sell to Western European traders.

Population growth generated an expansion of small-scale manufacturing, particularly handicrafts, textiles, and metallurgy in England, Flanders, parts of northern Italy, the southwestern German states, and in parts of Spain. Only iron smelting and mining required marshaling a significant amount of capital. Rural industry was an intrinsic part of the expansion of industry. Woolens and textile manufacturers, in particular, utilized rural cottage (domestic) production, which took advantage of cheap and plentiful rural labor. Members of poor peasant families spun or wove cloth and linens at home for scant remuneration in an attempt to supplement meager family income.

Expansion of Trade

Extended trading networks developed the European economy. Improved banking and other financial services contributed to the expansion of trade. By the middle of the sixteenth century, financiers and traders commonly accepted bills of exchange in place of gold or silver or other goods. Bills of exchange, which had their origins in medieval Italy, were promissory notes that could be sold to third parties, and in this way they provided credit. At mid-century, an Antwerp financier only slightly exaggerated when he claimed, "One can no more trade without bills of exchange than sail without water." Merchants no longer had to carry gold and silver over long, dangerous journeys, nor did they have to identify and assess the approximate value of a variety of coins issued by mints here and there. Thus, an Amsterdam merchant purchasing soap from a counterpart in Marseille could go to an exchanger and pay him the equivalent sum in guilders, the Dutch currency. The exchanger would then send a bill of exchange to a colleague in Marseille, authorizing him to pay the Marseille merchant in his own currency after the actual exchange of goods had taken place. Bills of exchange contributed to the development of banking, as exchangers began to provide loans, profiting from the interest attached to them.

The rapid expansion in international trade increased the role of merchant capitalists, particularly in northern Europe, in the emerging global economy. The infusion of capital stemmed largely from gold and silver brought by

The money changer's office.

Spanish vessels from the Americas. This capital financed the production of goods, storage, trade, and even credit across Europe and overseas. Moreover, an increased credit supply was generated by investments and loans by bankers and wealthy merchants to states and by joint-stock partnerships, an English innovation (the first major company began in 1600). Unlike short-term financial cooperation between investors for a single commercial under-taking, joint-stock companies provided capital by drawing on the investments of merchants and other investors who purchased shares in the company.

Amsterdam and then London emerged as the banking and trading cen-ters of Europe. (Not until the eighteenth century, however, did the Bank of Amsterdam and the Bank of England begin to provide capital for business investment.) Merchant towns in Castile, Catalonia, Italy, Holland, and England, as well as the Hanseatic cities of northern Germany, each had their own merchant dynasties.

The Global Economy

Trade with the Americas and Asia provided new outlets for European goods. It also brought from the New World products such as tomatoes, corn, bell peppers, rum, and spices to those who could afford them. The construction of larger ships, weighing as much as eighty tons, a size that would not be sur-passed until the middle of the nineteenth century, facilitated oceangoing trade. From seaports, trade followed the major rivers—principally the Rhine, which flows from Switzerland to the North Sea; the Danube, which flows from Central Europe to the Black Sea; the Seine, which links Paris to the English Channel; and the Rhône, which carries boat traffic from Lyon to the Mediterranean. The Scheldt River estuary led from the North Sea to the powerful trading and manufacturing city of Antwerp, which already had a population of more than 100,000 people. There, vast quantities of English and Flemish goods and, increasingly, colonial products were traded for goods from the German and Italian states. Land trade routes also remained important—for example, the route from Marseille to northern France and the Netherlands, that from Valencia on the Mediterranean to Madrid and Toledo in the heart of Castile, and that from Piedmont to the western Ger-man states and the Netherlands.

Specially chartered East Indian trading companies helped mobilize investment capital in England and the Netherlands and, enjoying monopo-lies issued to them by each state, set out to make money. When Hugo Grotius published his treatise on the freedom of the seas in 1609, he subti-tled it *The Right which Belongs to the Dutch to Take Part in the East India Trade*. Although officially independent of each government, trade companies represented the interests of the state. Above all, in England colonial trade played a major role in the development of the national economy, principally because England's manufactured goods increasingly found markets in its developing settlement colonies in North America.

Overseas trading remained a risky business, however; storms, wars, and pirates all posed considerable risks. England, Spain, Portugal, and France spent fortunes maintaining fortresses and trading ports in colonies and along trading routes. Funds available to finance global treks could quickly disappear in times of political crisis or international conflict, and distant markets for European goods, never very certain, could quickly dry up. Appropriately enough, the first English company to receive royal authorization for a monopoly on colonial trade was called the London Merchant Adventurers. Spanish kings, in particular, were notorious for declaring bankruptcy and thus repudiating all debts after borrowing money from wealthy subjects based on the expectation—sometimes in vain—of the arrival of valued colonial goods or bullion.

The major European powers had only limited means of exerting authority over their merchants and other subjects in distant places. Trading strategies followed negotiations and, often, angry confrontations between royal officials and aggressive trading lobbies. This, in addition to the daunting problems of distance, discouraged early attempts to establish the kind of full-fledged colonies in Asia and Africa that Spain and then England had in the Americas. Moreover, diseases indigenous to regions to which Europeans traveled as well as those they carried with them made life not only dangerous but often short, particularly in tropical climates.

Price Revolution and Depression

The rise in population and the economic boom of the sixteenth century brought a considerable rise in prices, particularly during the last few decades of the century. It seemed to one Spaniard that "a pound of mutton now costs as much as a whole sheep used to." Between 1500 and 1600, the price of wheat rose by 425 percent in England, 650 percent in France, and 400 percent in Poland. Prices rose dramatically even before the arrival of silver from Latin America, a cause of continued inflation during the second half of the century. The cost of living far outdistanced wage increases as real income fell for ordinary people. Among those who suffered were small landholders in England, relatively poor nobles in France and Italy whose tenants had long-term leases, and landless laborers and wage earners in city and country alike.

Those affected adversely by the price revolution were quick to blame rapacious landlords, greedy merchants, hoarders of grain, selfish masters in the crafts, usurers, and the spirit of acquisition engendered, some believed, by the Reformation. Basic long-term causes included the infusion of gold and particularly silver brought principally by the Spanish from the Americas, currency debasement undertaken by monarchs to help finance wars, and the population increase itself, which placed more pressure on scarce resources.

A long depression followed the economic expansion of the sixteenth century. This in itself reflected the relative decline of Mediterranean trade, symbolized by the end of Venetian supremacy by 1600. The Thirty Years' War (1618–1648) also disrupted trade and manufacturing. International trade fell off dramatically. Furthermore, Spaniards had begun to exhaust the gold and silver mines of Latin America, disrupting the money supply. A leveling off of the population probably compounded the saturation of European markets. Urban growth slowed, and many of Europe's old ecclesiastical, administrative, and commercial centers stagnated. In sharp contrast, ports such as Amsterdam, Hamburg, and Liverpool grew with the expansion of the Atlantic trading system.

THE RISE OF SPAIN

Sixteenth-century Spain, the most powerful state of its time, was not one kingdom but two: Castile and Aragon. Castile was by far the larger and wealthier; its vast stretch of mountainous land across much of the center of the Iberian Peninsula contained a population of about six million

MAP 5.1 SPAIN IN THE LATE FIFTEENTH CENTURY

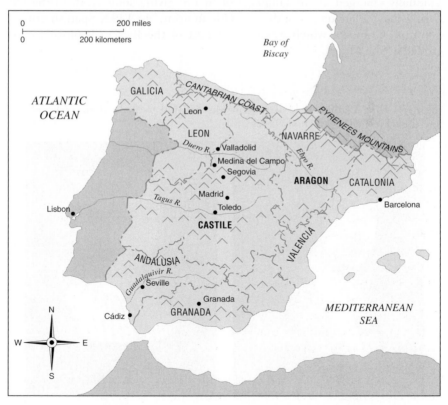

people, five-sixths of the population of Spain as a whole. Aragon, lying in northern Spain, had prospered during the Middle Ages because of its flourishing Mediterranean trade. It became a federation of dominions, including Catalonia and Valencia, greatly influenced by Mediterranean peoples and cultures (see Map 5.1). In contrast, Portugal was a relatively poor Atlantic state of mariners lying on the western edge of Iberia, despite its precocious development of trade routes along the West African coast and as far as the Indian Ocean and beyond. It had a population of about 1 million people (roughly equivalent to that of Aragon). Following the death of the Portuguese king without a male heir, Philip II of Spain claimed the Portuguese throne by virtue of being the only son of Isabella of Portugal, daughter of King Manuel I. Portugal was merged into the Spanish kingdom in 1580. (Portugal did not regain its independence until 1640.)

Centralization and the Spanish Monarchy

In 1469, Isabella of Castile (1451–1504) married Ferdinand (1452–1516), heir to the throne of Aragon. Castilian policies were successfully implemented to create a relatively centralized monarchy. The Castilian dialect gradually emerged as the language of Spain, giving some truth to the old saying that "a language is a dialect with an army." In 1492, Spanish armies captured Granada, which was the last part of the Iberian Peninsula controlled by the Moors.

(*Left*) King Ferdinand II of Aragon was devoted to the Catholic Church. (*Right*) Isabella, Queen of Castile.

Ferdinand and Isabella and their successors were known as the Catholic monarchs because of their devotion to the Church. But like other monarchs, they brought the Church, its privileges, and some of its income from tithes and the sale of indulgences under royal control. While the Reformation shook the foundations of the Church in much of Europe, it barely challenged Spanish religious orthodoxy. The Spanish Inquisition, whose original purpose had been to enforce the conversion of Islamic Moors and Jews in the late fifteenth century, served the Catholic Reformation in the late sixteenth century. The tribunal of the Inquisition interrogated and punished those accused of questioning Church doctrine. Housed in Castile, the Inquisition became a respected agent of royal as well as Church authority in some parts of Spain. Elsewhere—in Sicily and the Dutch Netherlands, above all—local people resisted the Inquisition, seeing it as another aspect of Spanish domination.

In Castile, Ferdinand and Isabella centralized the system of justice and made towns more subservient to the royal will. They stripped the Castilian nobles of some of their privileges while dispensing titles and positions. In Catalonia and Valencia, on the other hand, nobles resisted, maintaining most of their noble prerogatives. Nonetheless, because they feared a revolt of the lower classes, the Catalan and Valencian nobles became willing allies with the crown in maintaining social hierarchy and order.

Parliamentary traditions in the Spanish principalities to some extent limited the reach of the Castilian monarchy. The rulers of Spain were not able to tamper with Catalonia's traditionally less centralized constitutional traditions, which dated from the late thirteenth and fourteenth centuries, when Catalonia itself had been a Mediterranean power. Thus, the territories of Catalonia and Valencia maintained their political institutions, principally their *Cortes* (assembly), which continued to limit the authority of the monarchy and which had to be consulted in order to achieve compliance with royal edicts. The Spanish monarchy therefore was less a "new monarchy"—at least outside of Castile—than that of France, because particularly strong institutional limits on its effective authority remained.

In Castile, disagreements between the monarchy and the Cortes there were frequent during the middle decades of the sixteenth century. The Cortes excluded nobles and included only representatives from the eighteen most important cities and towns of Castile. The Castilian Cortes, which maintained the right to approve special taxes, refused taxes to subsidize the monarchy for thirty-five years (1541–1575), obviously hampering the royal fiscal apparatus. The long reign of Philip II began (1556) and ended (1598) with a declaration of royal bankruptcy.

The Spanish Economy

Although income from its colonies never accounted for more than about 10 percent of the crown's total income, Spain's colonial empire in the Americas contributed to its expanding economy. During the first years of the Spanish colonial period, Mexican gold helped finance the next wave of conquests. In 1545, Spaniards discovered the rich silver mines of Potosí (then in Peru, now in Bolivia), and a year later they uncovered more deposits in Mexico. A new refining process helped Spain triple the silver resources of Europe to its own profit. Mules carried silver extracted at Potosí on a fifteen-day journey down 12,000 feet and many miles to the port of Arica in northern Chile; then the sea voyage of several months by convoy began. Among other things, the silver paid for slaves brought from the coast of Africa. The Spanish Empire contributed considerably to the sixteenth-century European trading boom. Spain shipped colonial products and Spanish woolens to France and the Italian city-states. Spanish ships also supplied the colonies with wine, oil, European grain, shoes, and clothing.

The Castilian economy developed rapidly. The mountain ranges and central plateaus of Castile were divided between land for agricultural production and for raising sheep. The wool trade formed the basis of the Castilian export economy. The mining of silver, lead, iron, and mercury also developed in sixteenth-century Castile. Agricultural production was closely linked to manufacturing, as were sheep to the production of woolen goods. Nonetheless, 85 percent of the land of Spain could not be plowed because it was too mountainous or rocky, or could not be irrigated because of the high elevation.

Spanish royal revenue came from peasant obligations owed on royal domains as well as from taxes on commerce and manufacturing, import and export taxes, levies assessed for moving sheep through specific mountain passes, and payment from the Church for collecting tithes (the ecclesiastical tax of 10 percent of revenue). The crown imposed protectionist measures against foreign goods, banned the export of gold and silver, and attracted Italian and Flemish craftsmen to Spain.

In northern Spain, the mountains and valleys of the rainy Cantabrian coast were populated by farmers and fishermen. To the south, the Castilian provinces of Andalusia and Granada produced wheat, olives, and wine. Castilian farmers expanded production by terracing hillsides and planting them in perennials, including grapevines and olive trees. Demand for textiles increased, and farmers planted flax and hemp. Farm towns built irrigation works and processing facilities such as wine and olive presses, flax-soaking ponds, and grist and fulling mills to turn these crops into market commodities.

Spanish nobles incurred no social stigma by engaging in wholesale or international commerce until the eighteenth century. Many nobles capitalized on their revenues from farm products by building facilities to store and process the products—including flour mills, tanneries, and wine cellars, which often doubled as taverns. Several wealthy dukes became shipping magnates. They owned the tuna fishing rights on Castile's Mediterranean shore, exporting fish preserved in salt or olive oil all over Europe.

The Expansion of the Spanish Empire

Through marriage and inheritance, Spain's territorial interests reached far and wide. The Spanish throne passed to the Austrian branch of the Habsburg dynasty in 1496, with Ferdinand and Isabella's daughter, Princess Joanna, marrying Philip the Fair, the Habsburg duke of Burgundy, the son of Maximilian, the Holy Roman emperor. A year after Isabella's death in 1504, Ferdinand, hoping to produce an heir to the Spanish throne, married a niece of King Louis XII of France. But their infant son died three years later—royal families were also subject to the harsh demographic realities of the age. In 1516, the Flanders-born son of Joanna and Philip the Fair inherited the throne of Castile and Aragon as Charles I of Spain. In

Charles V was the grandson of Ferdinand and Isabella. This portrait is by Titian (1548).

1519, he became Holy Roman Emperor Charles V (ruled 1519–1558) upon the death of his grandfather, Maximilian I. Along with Spain's American territories, he inherited Aragon's Italian possessions. The emperor only briefly resided in Catalonia and rarely visited Castile. But with far-flung dynastic interests, he demanded extraordinary taxes from his Spanish subjects to pay for his wars abroad, including the defense of the Spanish-Italian possessions of Naples, Sicily, and Sardinia against France during the 1520s.

The king's departure from Spain in 1520 was followed by open revolt against royal taxation. The revolt of the *Comuneros* (urban communities) began in Toledo and spread to other towns in northern Castile. Bourgeois and artisans opposed the royal officials Charles had imported from Flanders, but the revolt was also directed against Castilian nobles. After royal forces burned the arsenal and town of Medina del Campo in north-central Castile in August 1520, the young king suddenly switched tactics. He suspended supplementary tax collections and agreed not to appoint any more foreigners to office in Spain. When uprisings continued, Charles's army gradually restored order, brutally executing the leaders of the rebellion.

With an eye toward his succession, Charles V arranged the marriage of his son, Philip, to the English princess Mary Tudor of England in 1554. Charles

MAP 5.2 HABSBURG LANDS AT THE ABDICATION OF CHARLES V, 1558   The division of the Habsburg lands between Philip II (who had already begun to rule Spain in 1556) and Ferdinand I.

formally abdicated as Holy Roman emperor in 1558, dividing the Habsburg domains between his son Philip and his brother Ferdinand (see Map 5.2). Philip II (ruled 1556–1598) inherited Spain, the Netherlands, the Spanish colonies in the Americas, and parts of Italy. Ferdinand I (ruled 1558–1564), who was elected Holy Roman emperor, inherited the Habsburg ancestral domains, including Austria. This ended the period when one ruler held all Habsburg territories and also eliminated any possibility that a single Catholic monarch would rule all of Europe. It did not, however, end the cooperation and strong family ties between the two branches of the Habsburg dynasty. Mary Tudor's death in 1558 eliminated the intriguing prospect that England might have become part of the Spanish Empire.

Philip II inherited the problem of ruling a vast empire. Like its rivals France and England, the Spanish state developed a large, centralized bureaucracy, including royal councils, essential to the operations of the empire. The council of state and the council of war offered the king advice on matters of internal and colonial policy. Royal secretaries handled correspondence and busied themselves with the operations of the royal household. Most such officials were commoners, for whom such positions provided financial and social advantages.

The Council of the Indies oversaw the administration of Spain's vast empire, sending viceroys and other officials to enforce the royal will and assure the extraction of precious metals for the royal coffers. The monarchy sent officials, many trained in law, to the Americas. It could take two years for administrative instructions or correspondence to reach distant officials in Latin America and for their response to arrive in Spain. One official awaiting instructions put it this way, "If death came from Madrid, we should all live to a very old age."

The Age of Philip II

Spanish power peaked during the reign of Philip II. Madrid, in the center of Castile, became a capital city of nobles and bureaucrats, many of whom, in one way or another, lived off the court. The city grew from a town of about 30,000 people in the 1540s to well over 150,000 inhabitants in the 1620s. Madrid survived through a "command economy"; royal commissioners paid government-fixed prices for what they wanted from the capital's hinterland. As Spain's capital grew, it had to import supplies, which were transported from distant regions by countless mule trains that traversed rough mountain ranges and deep valleys.

Philip decided that he needed a permanent royal residence that would provide an elegant symbol of his power. Outside of Madrid, Philip built the magnificent Escorial Palace. Virtually the king's only public appearances after he became crippled by gout were elaborate religious ceremonies at the palace, carefully orchestrated to uphold the sanctity of the throne. Rituals of court etiquette affirmed a sense of authority, social hierarchy, and order that were supposed to radiate from the Escorial through Spain and to the far reaches of the empire.

Philip II led a tragic life marred by the premature deaths of four wives and a number of children. Perhaps because of sadness, he wore only black. The king himself may have contributed to the misfortunes of his offspring. In 1568, he ordered Don Carlos, his bad-tempered and irresponsible twenty-three-year-old son by his first marriage, placed under lock and key. Don Carlos seemed unfit to rule; furthermore, detesting

Philip II of Spain ruled during the height of Spanish power.

SOLIMANVS·IMPERATOR
TVRCHARVM, 1526.

The Ottoman Empire of Suleiman the Magnificent threatened Spanish rule during the sixteenth century.

his father, he may have even entered into contact with Dutch leaders who had begun to denounce Spanish policies in their land. Don Carlos's death six months later haunted Philip, inevitably generating stories that he had ordered him murdered. The introverted king thereafter lived among the whispers of intrigue and storms of aristocratic rivalries of the noble families and factions.

With Habsburg domination of Italy secured by the 1559 Peace of Cateau-Cambrésis with France, Philip turned his attention to fighting the Turks. The Ottoman Empire had expanded into Europe following the conquest of Constantinople in 1453 (see Chapter 1), taking advantage of dynastic and religious wars between its European rivals. Suleiman the Magnificent (ruled 1520–1566) expanded his territories in the Balkans, where some of the Ottoman cultural heritage endures today, and into the rich plains of Hungary. The Turks also became bolder in their attacks on Spanish ships in the central and western Mediterranean. When the Turks took the Venetian island of Cyprus in 1571, the pope helped initiate the Holy League, in which Venice and Spain allied. The long naval war against the Ottoman Empire lasted from 1559 to 1577. With southern Spain virtually undefended and with the Moriscos (Moors who had been forced to convert to Christianity) rebelling (1568–1570) against taxes, the Turks might well have captured Granada. But a Spanish-Austrian Habsburg fleet defeated the sultan's larger navy in the Adriatic Sea at the Battle of Lepanto (1571), a monumental struggle in which more than 200 galleys fought, taking the lives of thousands of combatants. The Turkish threat in the western Mediterranean ended, although the possibility of the further expansion of the Ottoman Empire in southeastern and central Europe remained. In the meantime, overexpansion had already planted the seeds of Spanish imperial decline.

THE RISE OF ENGLAND

The consolidation and then the extension of the authority of the Tudor monarchy facilitated England's emergence as a power late in the sixteenth century. From the reign of Henry VII to that of Elizabeth I, the Tudor monarchs held in check the great landed magnates, putting down rebellions and extending the reach and prestige of royal government. During the same period, the English state expanded its control over Wales and Ireland while holding at bay Scottish threats to the Tudor dynasty.

The House of Tudor

Victorious in the long War of the Roses between the Lancaster and York families, Henry Tudor, the last claimant to the throne of the Lancasters, became the first Tudor monarch as Henry VII (ruled 1485–1509). Like Isabella of Castile and Ferdinand of Aragon, the ambitious Henry VII set out to make the Tudor state so powerful that it could resist any challenge from noble factions and "overmighty subjects."

Thomas Wolsey, who was archbishop of York and adviser to the king, brought to the King's Council loyal officials drawn from the ranks of the nobility and high clergy. These men met in a room known as the Star Chamber because its blue ceiling, like the night sky, was spangled with stars. The Star Chamber became one of the highest courts in the land.

Henry VII strengthened royal authority in England. He imposed tariffs protecting the cloth and wool industries, decreed acts unifying weights and measures, and put forth edicts punishing vagabondage and begging. He reduced expenses by disbanding his army, while filling royal coffers by selling monopolies (the exclusive right to import and market foodstuffs or commodities). Monopolies were extremely unpopular, however, among the middle and lower classes because they kept the prices of some products artificially high.

The king won the loyalty of most nobles. When selling offices failed as a means of assuring compliance, he resorted to the sheer coercive power of the throne. The Star Chamber enforced compliance, exacting fines and sometimes arresting the recalcitrant for real or imagined offenses. Henry obtained from Parliament writs of attainder and forfeiture, by which he could declare anyone guilty of treason, order their execution, and seize their property.

Henry VII depended not only upon the personal loyalty of local elites but also on the efficiency and prestige of about 600 unpaid justices of the peace. These men, largely drawn from prosperous landed families, dispensed justice, collected taxes, enforced troop levies, and maintained order. Their judicial authority covered every criminal offense except treason. While maintaining a strong tradition of decentralized government in England, the justices of the peace also strengthened the efficiency and prestige of the monarchy. Gradually, the royal Assize Courts took responsibility for felony cases. Charged with enforcing parliamentary statutes and the orders of the Privy Council, which administered the Tudor state, the Assize Courts also helped extend the state's effective authority.

Henry VIII became king upon his father's death in 1509 and married Catherine of Aragon, who was Ferdinand and Isabella's daughter, as well as his brother's widow. Beneath Henry's proud and impetuous character lay a deep-seated inferiority complex that he tried to overcome with grand deeds. The single-minded Henry dreamed of standing at the head of an empire. The new king spent vast sums fighting against France for more than a decade, beginning in 1512. Cardinal Wolsey, who had been his father's trusted adviser, sought to restrain Henry's ambition. But when the House of Commons refused to provide the king with more funds, Henry simply debased the currency, giving the state more spending power at the cost of higher inflation.

Foreign wars devastated royal finances. To raise money, the spendthrift monarch heaped more financial obligations on the backs of the poor. Wolsey utilized the cynically named "amicable grant," a royal assessment first imposed in 1525 on lay and ecclesiastical revenues. Peasants in southeastern England rebelled against these new levies. They were sometimes led by rural "gentlemen." Henry responded to the threat by forcing landowners to loan money to the crown, imprisoning some of the wealthiest and confiscating their estates, and further debasing the currency, adding to inflation.

To make his monarchy more efficient, Henry shifted royal government, including control of the state's finances, from the royal household of the king's servants to a small but able bureaucracy of officials, who were loyal to both the king and Parliament. He reduced the size of the king's advisory council and formalized its structure. The Privy Council assumed oversight functions and routinely communicated with the local justices of the peace. The king appointed new administrative officials and established new revenue courts. At the same time, the general acceptance of the "king's law"—common law—gradually helped generate a sense of national unity.

Henry extended the power of his monarchy by breaking with Rome in the 1530s over his divorce of Catherine of Aragon. He established the Church of England (see Chapter 3), which kept some of the ritual and doctrine of the Catholic Church. Henry became head of the Church of England, dissolving monasteries and confiscating and selling ecclesiastical lands. Henry planted the seeds for future conflicts between Protestants and Catholics in England.

Fearing that the Welsh or Irish might assist Holy Roman Emperor Charles V in an attempt to invade England to restore Catholicism, Henry established English domination over Wales and direct rule over Ireland. Since the late twelfth century, English lords had gradually increased their military colonization of Ireland, pushing back the Gaelic tribes and claiming the finest land by virtue of ancient titles. The English kings delegated authority to

English nobles. Yet effective English authority remained fragile in Ireland as long as the crown's continental interests took precedence. After the English Reformation, the crown selected English Protestants for all posts in Ireland. And after a minor rebellion against royal authority, which was put down with great cruelty, in 1541 Henry proclaimed himself king of Ireland and head of the Irish Church. In exchange for the Gaelic chieftains' recognition of Henry as their king and acceptance of English law, the crown recognized them as Irish lords. Thereafter, however, the costs of administering Ireland increased rapidly, requiring more troops, as the Irish chafed at English rule. Queen Elizabeth's policy of English settlement in Ulster during the 1590s generated Gaelic resistance in the Nine Years' War (1594–1603). Resistance was led by Hugh O'Neill (1540–1616), Earl of Tyrone. English forces defeated a combined Irish and Spanish force at the Battle of Kinsale in 1601. This completed the English conquest of Gaelic Ireland. O'Neill left Ireland and ended up in Rome, where he was welcomed by the pope. Religious persecution frequently forced Catholics to hear Masses in secret in the countryside, with priests using rock slabs as altars, or "Mass rocks."

Scotland also proved to be a thorny problem for England. Although in 1503 the Scottish King James IV had married Henry VII's daughter, Margaret Tudor, relations between Scotland and England deteriorated when Henry VIII became king. When James invaded England in 1513 in support of France, Henry VIII undertook a major military campaign against the Scots. This ended with a bloody English victory at the Battle of Flodden, where James IV was killed. Nonetheless, Catholic Scotland remained an ally of Catholic France. In 1542, an English army again invaded Scotland, defeating the Scots at Solway Moss. Following James V's sudden death a month after the battle, Mary Stuart (James's six-day-old daughter) became queen of the Scots. In 1546, after Henry's war with France dragged to a halt, another English army laid waste to Scotland, sacking the capital and university town of Edinburgh.

Henry VIII died in 1547. On his deathbed, the king, whose insistence on divorce began the English Reformation, hedged his bets, leaving money to pay for Catholic Masses to be said for the eternal repose of his soul. The nine-year-old son of Henry and Jane Seymour became King Edward VI (ruled 1547–1553), governing under the tutelage of his uncle, the duke of Somerset, who served as Lord Protector. While seeking accommodation with Protestant dissenters, the young Edward undertook an aggressive campaign on behalf of the Reformed Church of England.

Wars against Catholic Scotland and France continued. The Lord Protector was intent on destroying Catholicism in Scotland. After English troops defeated a French force sent to help the Catholic cause there, the young Catholic queen of Scots, Mary Stuart (1542–1587), fled to safety, marrying Francis, the son of Henry II, the king of France. Tensions between Protestants and Catholics worsened in England. Moreover, landowners resisted

Mary Tudor, later queen of England.

paying more taxes to finance new wars. Allied with fearful Catholic nobles, the earl of Warwick overthrew Somerset in 1549. Warwick assumed the role of Lord Protector and took the title of duke of Northumberland.

Northumberland quickly betrayed the Catholic lords who had supported him. He tightened the crown's control over the Church of England and undertook a repressive campaign against Catholicism. Northumberland's influence over the sickly young king whetted his desire for power. He plotted for Lady Jane Grey (1537–1554; Henry VIII's niece and third in line to the monarchy) to ascend the throne after she married his son. After Edward's death, Northumberland proclaimed his daughter-in-law queen of England. But most nobles rallied to the cause of Mary Tudor (ruled 1553–1558), the daughter of Henry VIII and Catherine of Aragon. She seemed to them the rightful heir to the throne, despite the fact that she was Catholic.

Mary Tudor succeeded her half brother and attempted to return England to Catholicism. She restored all rituals and doctrines of the Catholic Church and she acknowledged the primacy of the pope over the Church of England. The queen abrogated Henry VIII's reforms and began to persecute Protestants, some of whom fled to France. "Bloody Mary" embellished the macabre heritage of the Tower of London with the heads of Northumberland, his son, and Lady Jane Grey, who had ruled for only nine days. Mary married Philip II, who ascended the Spanish throne in 1556. England joined Spain in its war against France, which had long rivaled the Habsburgs in Italy. Calais, the last English outpost in France, was soon lost. Sparked by widespread opposition to her Catholicism, which was popularly identified with France and Spain, a rebellion broke out against the queen. When Mary died in 1558, few in England grieved.

Elizabeth I (ruled 1558–1603), Anne Boleyn's daughter, restored Protestant rule to England when she became queen at age twenty-five, succeeding Mary, her half sister. Elizabeth's throne was threatened by religious division, which was compounded by the antagonism of Catholic France and Spain. Not many people could have expected the young queen to succeed.

Elizabeth was a woman of intelligence, vanity, sporadic fickleness, and an occasional flash of temper. She enjoyed music, dancing, hunting, and the company of men. Tall, with reddish hair and an olive complexion, she was cautious, even suspicious, having been raised in a world of conspiracy. The queen preferred to wait out many pressing problems in the hope that they would just go away. Educated in the tradition of Italian humanism, Elizabeth learned French, German, and Italian, as well as Latin, and enjoyed translating texts from these languages into English.

Elizabeth never married. It was not uncommon for women to remain unmarried in early modern Europe—in England, about 10 percent of all women remained single throughout their lives—but it was unusual for a monarch not to marry. The question of whether Elizabeth would ever take a husband preoccupied the other rulers of Europe, as well as her subjects.

In response to a parliamentary petition that she marry and produce a direct heir, Elizabeth responded that she trusted God to ensure that "the realm shall not remain destitute of an heir." As for her, it would be enough that at the end of her life "a marble stone shall declare that a queen, having reigned such a time, lived and died a virgin." Elizabeth rejected one continental hopeful after another, beginning with the handsome but dull Philip II of Spain, Catholic widower of Mary Tudor. Nor was marriage the outcome of a two-year romance with the handsome Lord Robert Dudley, the death of whose wife in 1560 from a suspicious fall down a flight of stairs understandably fueled rumors for some years.

Queen Elizabeth dancing with Robert Dudley.

Religious Settlement and Conflict under Elizabeth I

Elizabeth was determined to find a means to resolve religious conflict within England, which might one day threaten her reign. Elizabeth had been raised a Protestant, but she did not hold particularly strong religious convictions and rarely attended church. Although she was thought to favor some Catholic rituals, when she first encountered a procession of monks with candles and incense at Westminster Abbey, she cried out, "Away with these torches, we see very well." She dismissed many Catholic advisers.

In 1559, Parliament passed the Act of Uniformity and the Act of Supremacy, which established the lasting foundations of the Church of England, reorganizing it to have Protestant dogma but essentially Catholic structure. The Uniformity Bill imposed the *Book of Common Prayer* (1550) on religious services of the Church of England and required attendance at public worship and imposed fines for not attending services. The bill barely passed the House of Lords (which was primarily composed of Catholics), and probably would not have passed at all had two bishops not been imprisoned in the Tower of London and thus been unable to vote. The Act of Supremacy required all officials, clergy, and candidates for university degrees to take an oath acknowledging the queen as "governor" of the English Church. This title replaced that of "head" of the Church and suggested that the queen would not interfere in matters of doctrine. The Thirty-Nine Articles, enacted in 1563, provided an institutional framework for subsequent relations between state and church in England. The landed elite, strengthening its control of Parliament during Elizabeth's reign, generally supported the Church of England.

Some English Protestants wanted to carry the reforms farther than Elizabeth's religious settlement. They sought to eliminate from the Church of England what some members considered vestiges of elaborate Catholic ceremonies, such as baptismal crosses, altar rails before which the faithful knelt while receiving communion, elaborate priestly garb, and stained-glass windows.

Puritanism, the English version of Calvinism, first emerged in the late 1550s as a dissident force within the Church of England. Puritans were drawn primarily from the middle and lower classes. They insisted on a simplified but more intense religion based on individual conscience, the direct authority of the Holy Scriptures, and a community of belief in which preaching played a preeminent role. Although a few Puritans served as bishops in the Church of England, others wanted the Church of England to be separate from the English monarchy. The Tudor monarchy, on the other hand, wanted to make the Church serve its secular goals of national glory, prosperity, and public order.

A modest Catholic revival, aided by the arrival of Catholic Jesuit missionaries from the continent, accentuated religious divisions in England. Royal religious policies became harsher. Dissident Protestants suffered persecution along with Catholics. A Jesuit missionary was tortured to death on the rack in 1581, and six years later the first Puritan was executed for having spoken in Parliament on behalf of free speech in the name of his religion.

Since Elizabeth had no heirs, the Catholic Mary Stuart stood next in line for succession to the English throne. After her husband King Francis II of France died in 1560, Mary returned to her native Scotland to assume the power that her mother wielded as regent until her death that same year. The Scottish Reformation had begun in earnest when the theologian John Knox (c. 1505–1572) returned home from Geneva to preach reform. Soon after coming to the throne of England, Eliza-

Mary, Queen of Scots.

beth had made peace with Scotland and France. But Elizabeth and Protestants worried that if Mary became queen of England, she would restore Catholicism to England. When Protestants forced Mary to abdicate the Scottish throne in 1568, she fled to England. Elizabeth kept her potential rival under virtual house arrest.

In 1569, Catholics in the moors and bogs of the isolated English north rebelled in the hope of putting Mary Stuart on the English throne, precipitating Elizabeth's order for her rival's imprisonment. The Catholic force marched southward, but hastily retreated upon learning that sizable English forces loyal to Elizabeth awaited them. English troops defeated a second Scottish army near the border between the two countries. Elizabeth ordered the execution of over 500 of the rebels. This "Northern Rising" ended in complete failure, and the Catholic Church's hopes for a successful Counter-Reformation in England were finally dashed. Pope Pius V excommunicated Elizabeth in 1570 from the Church to which she did not wish to belong, removing the queen's Catholic subjects from the obligation of obedience to her and encouraging several more plots against her. Two years later, French Catholics undertook the Saint Bartholomew's Day Massacre of Protestants in Paris (see Chapter 4), the horror of which firmed Elizabeth's resolve to resist Mary's claims to the throne at all costs. She then vowed to support the Dutch, most of whom were Protestant, in their rebellion against Catholic Spain. In 1583, she foiled a plot, which involved the Spanish and French embassies, to depose her in favor of Mary Stuart.

Four years later, under pressure from Parliament, Elizabeth ordered Mary Stuart's execution.

Elizabeth's Statemaking

The reach and efficiency of the English state increased under Elizabeth's guidance. Lords and other wealthy gentlemen served on the Privy Council, which consisted of between twelve and eighteen members drawn from the nobility, landed elite, and officers in the royal household. It oversaw the lord-lieutenants, a new office that gave noblemen control of local militia. England's queen, like her predecessors, used patronage to foster loyalty to the crown. The most desirable posts were at court, including those in the royal household. Some of these carried life tenures and a few were hereditary. In Elizabethan England, unlike France, churchmen did not serve in the highest offices of the realm. The most powerful officials at court, such as the Lord Chancellor, dispensed patronage by selecting officials and filling local positions in the counties. Closely tied to the satisfaction of the private interests of the landed elite, the office of the Exchequer resembled similar offices created by continental monarchs who did not have to contend with a representative body as powerful as the English Parliament, divided into the House of Lords and the House of Commons. Although it met during only three of the forty-five years of Elizabeth's reign, Parliament retained an important role in government because the crown needed its assent for new laws and new taxes.

Upon ascending the throne, Elizabeth found the crown's financial situation bleak. Revenues raised through taxation and customs dues were inadequate to finance the war against Spain and campaigns in Ireland. The sale of some royal lands, forced loans, the occasional seizure of a Spanish ship laden with silver or gold, and purveyance (the right of agents of the monarchy to buy food at below-market prices) could only be temporary expedients. The collection of "ship money" (a tax on ports, which the crown with dubious logic extended to inland towns as well) was extremely unpopular and generated resistance during the hard times of the 1590s. But by exercising frugality in the expenses of government and increasing taxation, the crown managed to replenish its coffers, another sign of a stronger and more efficient state, despite a decade and a half of expensive warfare against Spain. The English monarchy in the Elizabethan Age was relatively more efficient than that of Spain or France.

English nobles by the 1590s no longer had full-fledged private armies that could threaten the throne's monopoly on force. This contrasted with the situation in France during the same period, when the Guise and Bourbon families, among others, maintained their own armies in the wars of religion.

Foreign wars also served to increase the reach of central government in England. The second half of the sixteenth century brought regular training for the militia, which provided the bulk of troops as needed, along with gentlemen volunteers and cavalrymen still recruited by summons. During the last eighteen years of Elizabeth's reign, more than 100,000 soldiers were impressed into service for wars on the continent and to maintain English hegemony in Ireland. Lord-lieutenants assumed responsibility for troop levies in the counties. The vast majority who were conscripted as soldiers were the poorest of the poor—unfortunate men who happened to be at the wrong place at the wrong time when the press-gangs turned up to roll them out of taverns or even out of church and into the queen's service.

The monarchy imposed English law on northern England, Wales (which Henry VIII had absorbed into England), and Ireland. The emergence of a national market economy increasingly linked to London also played an important part in the nationalization of English political institutions. Within England, the sense of belonging to a nationality was certainly more advanced than anywhere on the continent. With the exception of part of Cornwall in southwestern England (where the Cornish language was spoken), the people of England spoke English, however great the variation in dialect and accents. A somewhat Anglicized Welsh elite began to send their sons to Oxford and Cambridge Universities.

The fact that Britain is an island may have made the English more xenophobic and precociously nationalistic than their continental counterparts. Strong traditions of local government and loyalties persisted in England, however, fueled by social differences and the overwhelming influence of wealthy local landed families. The county and parish remained the economic, social, and political universe of most people in England. The state still remained an abstraction until the tax collector or the press-gang arrived.

Demographic and Economic Expansion

In the last half of the sixteenth century, England emerged as a commercial and manufacturing power. The population of England and Wales grew rapidly, from about 2.5 million in the 1520s to more than 3.5 million in 1580, reaching about 4.5 million in 1610. Reduced mortality rates and increased fertility, the latter probably generated by expanding work opportunities in manufacturing and farming (leading to earlier marriage and more children), help explain this rapid rise in population. While epidemics and plague occasionally took their toll, the people in England still suffered them less often than did those on the continent. Furthermore, despite the wrenching effects of the English Reformation, the country had been spared the protracted wars of religion that occurred in France and Central Europe.

English towns grew as migrants arrived in sufficient numbers to overcome high mortality rates caused by catastrophic health conditions stemming from poor sanitation. London became the second largest city in the world, its population rising from about 50,000 in the 1520s to 200,000 in 1600, and jumping its walls to 375,000 in 1650 (only Edo [Tokyo] was larger). The next biggest towns in England lagged far behind: Norwich, Newcastle, and

Bristol boasted only about 25,000 people each. About 8 percent of the population of England lived in London by the mid-seventeenth century.

England provides the primary example of the expansion of agricultural production well before the "agricultural revolution" of the eighteenth and nineteenth centuries. A larger population stimulated increased demand for food, as well as for manufactured goods. Through crop specialization, English agriculture became more efficient and market oriented than almost anywhere on the continent. Between 1450 and 1650, the yield of grain per acre increased by at least 30 percent. In sharp contrast with farming in Spain, English landowners brought more dense marshes and woodlands into cultivation.

The great estates of the English nobility largely remained intact, and many wealthy landowners aggressively increased the size of their holdings. Timely marriages also increased the size of landed estates. Primogeniture (the full inheritance of land by the eldest son) helped keep land from being subdivided. Younger sons of independent landowners left behind the family land to find other respectable occupations, often in the church or in urban trades. Larger farms were conducive to more commercialized farming at a time when an expanding population pushed up demand and prices. Some landowners turned a part of their land into pastureland for sheep in order to supply the developing woolens trade.

Some of the great landlords, as well as yeomen (farmers whose holdings and security of land tenure guaranteed their prosperity and status), reorganized their holdings in the interest of efficiency. Open-field farmers selected crops in response to the growing London market. Between 1580 and 1620, in a quest for greater profits, landlords raised rents and altered conditions of land tenure in their favor, preferring shorter leases and forcing tenants to pay an "entry fee" before they would agree to rent them land. They evicted those who could not afford their new, more onerous terms. They also pushed tenants toward more productive farming methods, including crop rotation. During hard years, the peasants might be forced to sell their land, while wealthy neighbors could survive with relative ease.

Many landowners utilized "enclosure" to expand their holdings. Parliamentary acts of enclosure aided landowners by allowing them to buy wastelands, consolidate arable strips of land, and divide up common lands and pasture areas. The enclosure of common lands, sold by villages to the highest bidders, over the long run would spell the end of the common rights of villagers to use the land, and the removal of tenants in order to consolidate estates marked a push toward "agrarian individualism." Enclosure drew considerable resistance, for it left many of the rural poor fenced out of common land on which they had depended for firewood, gleaning, and pasturing. Thomas More's *Utopia* (1516), which describes an imaginary island where all people live in peace and harmony, blamed England's economic inequities on enclosure. Riots against enclosure were widespread in the

In this seventeenth-century woodcut, a country wife engages in domestic industry, part of the expansion of textile manufacturing that transformed England's economy.

1590s, a decade in which popular tax rebellions shook France, Spain, Austria, and Ukraine, among other places, and again in the 1620s and 1630s.

England's exceptional economic development drew upon the country's natural resources, including iron, timber, and, above all, coal, extracted in far greater quantities than anywhere on the continent. New industrial methods expanded the production of iron, brass, and pewter in and around Birmingham. But, primarily, textile manufacturing developed the English economy. Woolens (which accounted for about 80 percent of exports), worsteds (sturdy yarn spun from combed wool fibers), and cloth found eager buyers in England as well as on the continent. Moreover, late in the sixteenth century, as English merchants began making forays across the Atlantic, these textiles were also sold in the New World. Cloth manufacturers undercut production by urban craftsmen by "putting out" work to the villages and farms of the countryside. In such domestic industry, poor rural women and girls could do spinning and carding (combing fibers in preparation for spinning) of wool in their homes.

The English textile trade was closely tied to Antwerp, where workers dyed English cloth. Sir Thomas Gresham, a sixteenth-century entrepreneur, became England's representative in the bustling river port. Wining and dining the city's merchants and serving as a royal ambassador, he so enhanced the reputation of English merchants that they could operate on credit, no small achievement in the sixteenth century. At home, he convinced the government to end special privileges accorded the Hanseatic cities of northern Germany and to authorize lucrative English trading monopolies. Gresham's shrewd sense of finance saved the relatively meager royal coffers from bankruptcy on several occasions through the negotiation of timely loans.

Gresham advised the crown to explore the economic possibilities of the Americas. This led to the first concerted English efforts at colonization. Far more than Spanish colonialism, English overseas ventures were undertaken with commercial profits in mind. When the Spanish, hoping to crush the Dutch rebellion that began against their rule in 1566, closed the Scheldt River, English merchants responded by seeking new, more distant outlets for trade across the oceans. From 1577 to 1580, Sir Francis Drake (1540–1596), an explorer and privateer, sailed around Cape Horn in his search for a passage that would permit commercial ties with Asia. Sir Walter Raleigh (1554–1618), a Renaissance scholar, poet, historian, and explorer, said of Drake, "A single purpose animates all his exploits and the chart of his movements is like a cord laced and knotted round the throat of the Spanish monarchy."

English Society in the Tudor Period

English society under the Tudors reflected what a churchman writing in 1577 called "degrees of people," that is, sharply defined social groups. Contemporaries sometimes simplified English social structure by dividing people into the ranks of "gentlemen," "the middling sort," and "the poor." Ownership of land in the form of estates—inherited or acquired—conferred status, or "gentility," in England. All nobles (that is, with a noble title passed on by inheritance) were gentry, but the vast majority of gentry were not titled nobles or peers in the House of Lords. Gentry status came from the ownership of land, and gentry dominated the House of Commons. In exchange for military service, the crown granted titles that were inherited by the eldest son.

The nobility and gentry dominated England for more than the next three centuries from their country manors that commanded the surrounding countryside. Ordinary people addressed the nobleman as "your lordship" and the wealthy gentleman as "sir"; poor women curtsied to them as a mark of respect. Village bells were rung in their honor when they passed through. Wealthy landowners mediated in village disputes and provided some charity in exchange for deference. (One man of means chatted with "his people" in the street: "I asked a poor woman how many children she had. She answered 'Six.' 'Here,' I said, 'is a sixpence for them.' 'No, sir,' she said proudly, not realizing the gentleman was offering a gift, 'I will not sell my children.'") The education of gentlemen at Oxford and Cambridge Universities or through private tutoring helped shape common cultural values and social homogeneity among what was increasingly becoming a national elite.

An Elizabethan country house, late sixteenth century.

Yeomen stood beneath the gentry on the social ladder, but they could move up if they were able to purchase and maintain large estates, and they could vote in parliamentary elections.

Within the upper reaches of the "middling sort" were men considered "of sufficiency," even if they were not lords or gentlemen. They were believed by virtue of steady income to be worthy of assuming some kind of public responsibility. England's precocious economic boom in the sixteenth century increased the wealth and status of merchants and manufacturers. Wealthy merchants and artisans from the guilds served on town councils, perpetuating their influence from generation to generation.

Lower on the social scale were smallholders, farmers who owned just enough land to get by ("husbandmen"), poor clergymen depending for survival upon small fees rendered for their services, and ordinary craftsmen. The majority of the population owned neither land nor skills, and thus lay at the bottom of the social hierarchy. Most laboring families lived in rented one-room cottages. Cottagers, employed as farmhands but also often employed as spinners, weavers, carders, or nail makers, lived on bread, cheese, lard, soup, beer, and garden greens, occasionally supplemented by harvest-time feasts provided by their employers. Farm servants lived in Spartan accommodations. In London and smaller towns, the urban poor struggled to survive as common laborers, porters, and sweepers, or in other menial occupations, living in squalor in whatever pitiful lodgings they could afford, or, for many, living without shelter.

During the sixteenth century, the rich got richer—and lived that way, dressing and eating differently from the poor. Responding to complaints that "a Babylon of confusion" might blur class lines because anyone with money could purchase the most elegant clothing, Parliament had earlier in the century decreed that only dukes, earls, and barons could wear sable cloth woven of gold and embroidered with gold and silver. Ben Jonson (1572–1637), author of scurrilous satires on London life, wrote that to become recognized as a gentleman, a man had to go to London, "where at your first appearance 'twere good you turned four or five hundred acres of your best land into two or three trunks of apparel."

Cardinal Wolsey had earlier attempted to moderate the dietary excesses of wealthy people, including the high clergy. Copying sumptuary regulations that could be found throughout Europe since the Middle Ages, he specified the number of separate dinner courses that people of various ranks might consume, with the largest number—nine—reserved for cardinals like himself. The poor, however, ate no such meals. Soaring food and lodging prices sapped the meager earnings of craftsmen, landless cottagers, rural laborers, and unskilled workers.

There was, to be sure, some degree of social mobility in Tudor England as new economic opportunities brought greater prosperity to gentry, yeomen, merchants, and manufacturers. Some yeomen achieved gentry status. The interests and lifestyles of the middling sort gradually moved closer to those of gentlemen and their families. Some apprentices became independent masters within their trades. But social advancement remained relatively rare among the poor, whose numbers were rapidly expanding along with their impoverishment.

The Quest for Public Order

After almost a century of inflation accentuated by a rising population, harvest failures in the 1590s brought the period of economic expansion to an abrupt halt in England. Never had there seemed to be so many poor and hungry people on the roads, dressed in rags, sleeping in fields, searching for wild berries or edible roots, and begging, just trying to get by. "They lie in the streets," one man of means observed, "and are permitted to die like dogs or beasts without any mercy or compassion showed them at all."

Ordinary people sometimes took matters into their own hands. Food riots spread throughout much of England, as the poor seized grain and sold it at what they considered a reasonable price. Women usually made up the majority of participants in the food riots because it fell to them to try to make ends meet at the market. Such disturbances increased the resolve of the state to maintain order at all costs.

Punishing a man by exposing him at a pillory, sixteenth-century England.

The prosecution of serious crimes increased rapidly during Elizabeth's reign, peaking between 1590 and 1620. Vagrancy was the most prevalent of these offenses, as people took to the road in search of food. Vagrants were arrested and placed in stocks for three days, before being sent home. Thefts rose in number and audacity. A contemporary estimated that there were twenty-three different categories of thieves and swindlers, including "hookers," who snatched linen and clothes with a long pole from windows, "priggers of prancers" (horse thieves), and "Abraham men," who "feign themselves to be mad." The theft of goods worth more than twelve shillings could bring the death penalty, but more often offenders were publicly whipped, branded, mutilated by having an ear cut off, or sent to serve as oarsmen in the galley ships. Women were often treated more harshly than men, unless they were pregnant. Although only about 10 percent of those convicted of capital crimes were actually executed, such punishment was particularly brutal, including slow strangulation by hanging and being slowly crushed to death by weights.

The English upper classes, convinced that most crimes went unpunished, became obsessed with maintaining order, a fact reflected in several of Shakespeare's plays, in which ordinary people appear as potential threats to social order. Many Elizabethans believed that social order depended on the maintenance of social hierarchy and the securing of obedience to the moral authority of government. Thus, the Tudors formulated a doctrine of obedience to authority, basing their arguments on religious teaching.

Elizabethan literature and drama constantly returned to the theme of a moral law based upon the necessity of social order. In Shakespeare's *The History of Troilus and Cressida,* Ulysses proclaims:

> The heavens themselves, the planets, and this centre
> Observe degree, priority, and place,
> [. . .]But when the planets
> In evil mixture to disorder wander,
> What plagues and what portents, what mutiny!
> [. . .]And hark what discord follows. . . .

Many in the middle and upper classes believed that the slightest offense against the monarchy contained the seeds of rebellion; in 1576, a woman was burned at the stake for saying that Elizabeth was "baseborn and not born to the crown." Fear of disturbances and challenges to authority contributed to the development of a sense of national consciousness of England's elite, just as the defeat of Spain's Armada in 1588 led to pride in being both Protestant and English.

In 1598, Parliament passed the first "poor law," followed by another in 1601. These laws recognized for the first time the principle that the needy ought to receive some sort of assistance from the community in which they live. Justices of the peace, under the supervision of the clergy, were to oversee the distribution of assistance to the poor. The poor laws also specified the establishment of poor houses for the incarceration of the poor who would not or could not work (including the aged, sick, and insane).

The Elizabethan Theater

In 1576, two theaters opened in London, followed by others in a number of provincial towns. Putting aside the repertory of religious allegories and miracle and morality plays that had been staged in royal castles, country manor houses, or entire towns, they staked their survival on their ability to attract audiences that would pay to see actors perform. More than 2,000 different plays were staged in London between 1580 and 1640, mainly romances and dramas. During that period, more than 300 playwrights produced enough work to keep 100 acting companies working in London or touring provincial towns.

The plays of William Shakespeare (1564–1616) reflected uncertainty, ambivalence, and even disillusionment about contemporary English society. He was born in Stratford-on-Avon, where his father made gloves and was able to provide him with a primary school education. Shakespeare moved with his wife to London to become an actor, and in the late 1580s he began to write plays. He found first patronage and then unparalleled

(*Left*) William Shakespeare (*Right*) The Globe Theater, London, 1616.

success, angering rivals. Shakespeare became part owner and actor in the Lord Chamberlain's Men, an acting company of the Globe theater, which held an audience of 3,000 and hence was the largest of London's six private theaters. Seats at such theaters cost at least six times more than the cheapest tickets at the public theaters, which included places for the "penny stinkards" who stood in the uncovered pit below the stage.

Audiences shouted for what they liked and hooted at what they did not. Fights were not infrequent, both inside and outside of the theater. The playwright Christopher Marlowe (1564–1593) died in a brawl in an inn under mysterious circumstances; the actor and playwright Ben Jonson killed another actor in a duel. Because of their rowdy reputations, most London theaters stood outside the city walls. London officials sometimes tried to close down the public theaters because they thought that disease spread easily among assembled crowds and because of complaints about profanity and lewdness on stage.

An Emerging Empire of Trade

During the later years of Elizabeth's reign, bitter battles for influence and power within Elizabeth's inner circle belied the appearance of relative harmony. Elizabeth died in 1603, the forty-fifth year of her reign, leaving England a substantially more unified, effectively ruled, and powerful state that had begun to look across the oceans in the interest of expanding trade. Over the next few decades, England slowly began to develop a trading and then settlement empire in North America—as did France—while gradually extending its influence across other oceans, as well. This increasingly brought England into competition with France, which began to colonize Nouvelle France (now Quebec).

The development of English overseas trade allowed London to replace Antwerp as Europe's leading center of trade. London's Merchant Adventurers competed with Spanish and Portuguese rivals for spices and other products that fetched increasingly handsome prices at home. They traded textiles and other manufactured goods for slaves, gold, and ivory from the African and Brazilian coasts. Above all, West Indian sugar from Barbados entered the English domestic market in lucrative quantities. English merchants traded in India and Indonesia. In 1600, Queen Elizabeth chartered the East India Company with the goal of competing with Dutch traders.

To compete with the Spanish, who already had a colonial empire that stretched several thousand miles from what is now the southern United States to Tierra del Fuego at the southern tip of South America, Raleigh sought to establish a colony in Virginia between 1584 and 1587. Despite the failure of a first settlement on Roanoke Island, a permanent colony finally succeeded at Jamestown in Virginia, a full century after Spain took possession of its colonies in Mexico and Latin America. Tobacco began to reach England in the first decades of the seventeenth century. Tobacco was, to an extent, the equivalent of what silver was to the Spanish Empire, because of its great role in the economic development of the English colonies. Whereas the Spanish arrived in the Americas as conquerors, the English came intent on developing trade. Gradually, the English began to arrive in North America as permanent settlers. The Virginia Company, a joint-stock company, received in 1606 a royal charter to settle the region of Chesapeake Bay. The Virginia Company brought the first slaves to North America ten years later, although it was not until late in the century that a full slave system emerged. In 1625 the English throne proclaimed Virginia part of "Our Royal Empire." The Puritan settlement in Plymouth followed in 1620, and the Massachusetts Bay Company received its charter in 1629. Unlike the case of Spain, where colonization followed the impulse of a strongly centralized state and the Roman Catholic Church, English colonies reflected the Reformation, as Protestants, including Protestant dissidents like the Puritans, led the way as they sought religious freedom for themselves. In contrast to the Spanish Empire, English America remained extremely rural, despite the slow growth of Boston and New York (6,000 residents and 4,500, respectively, in 1692, at a time when Mexico City already boasted more than 100,000 people). The rising English population encouraged more emigrants to the New World, despite the high cost of the difficult trip across the Atlantic. In the developing colonies, settlers moved westward to take available land, pushing Native Americans farther back. Disease, along with guns, helped them. John Winthrop, the governor of Massachusetts, noted in 1634, "For the natives, they are all near dead of the smallpox, so as the Lord hath cleared our title to what we possess."

The English arrive in what would become Virginia.

Unlike that of the Spanish Empire's colonies in the Americas, the absorption of the emerging colonies of North America into what became an English and then a British Empire (following England's formal union with Scotland as Great Britain in 1707) proceeded at a much slower and unpredictable pace, following the vicissitudes of trans-Atlantic trade instead of conquest and tight incorporation into England. The number of ships that went back and forth between England and the American colonies doubled to more than 1,000 per year between the 1680s and the 1730s, a round-trip voyage of 100 days under the best of circumstances. There was no English equivalent of the Council of the Indies, which oversaw the Spanish Empire in the Americas. In England's North American colonies, administrative institutions, representative assemblies—eight of which had been established by 1640—and judicial systems developed at their own pace without a phalanx of royal officials. The local administration of the English colonies continued to be influenced by regional differences, without the centralized distribution of resources that characterized the Spanish Empire. A sense of political participation developed in the English colonies, at least among men of property. With this went the growing sense that the colonies were a place of liberty, as many colonists arrived seeking religious freedom. Tensions were almost inevitable between the colonies, with their emerging sense of liberty and separateness, and Britain, which tried to extract more revenues from the colonies (see Chapter 11).

Again in contrast to Spain, which developed an empire marked by the firm alliance of Church altar and an authoritarian throne, the English felt less of a mission to bring Christianity to indigenous peoples. Moreover, unlike Catholicism in the case of the Spanish Empire, the established English religion, Anglicanism, was just one religion among others in the English colonies. By 1675, only an estimated 2,500 Native Americans had been converted to Christianity. In the Spanish Empire, many colonists undertook inter-ethnic marriages and thus helped bring about a considerable mixed population, allowing social mobility for a select few. In contrast, English settlers from the beginning sought to exclude and push back the indigenous population. Fearful of cultural mixing and of those they continued to consider "savages," most of whom showed no interest in assimilation, the settlers drove them farther west.

THE DECLINE OF SPAIN

The "decline" of the overstretched Spanish Empire was first noted in 1600. Had the Spain of the Catholic kings fallen from God's favor? Castilians themselves still regarded Spain as a haven of peace and prosperity compared to the rest of Europe, which was wracked by religious wars.

The Dutch Revolt

The decline of Spanish power began with the Dutch revolt. In the Netherlands, Dutch nobles and officials resented higher taxes imposed by the Spanish crown. Above all, many Dutch were angered by the Spanish king's attempt to promote the Catholic Reformation by imposing the Inquisition in a land where most people were now Calvinists. In the early 1560s, resistance first began against the presence of Spanish garrisons.

In 1567, Philip II appointed the duke of Alba (1507–1582) to restore order in the north with 10,000 Spanish troops. The ruthless Castilian ordered the execution of prominent Calvinist nobles on the central square of Brussels, established military courts, imposed heavy new taxes, and virtually destroyed self-government in the Netherlands. But Alba's reign of terror as governor also helped transform the resistance of Dutch nobles and officials, led by William of Orange (1533–1584), into a national revolt.

In the Southern Netherlands (Belgium), Alba's Council of Troubles, known to the Dutch as the "Council of Blood," executed thousands of people from 1567 to 1573. In 1572, rebellion became full-fledged insurrection. Spanish troops dominated on land, but Dutch ships controlled the seas. When a Spanish army undertook a siege of Leiden, southwest of Amsterdam, the people of the town opened the dikes, and Dutch ships sailed over the rushing waters to drive the Spaniards away. But Spanish victories

Prince William of Orange leading the revolt in the Netherlands against higher taxes from the Spanish crown. The Dutch revolt signified the decline of Spanish power.

in the Southern Netherlands followed. There Catholic nobles began to have second thoughts about continuing a struggle launched by Dutch Protestants. They detached the southern provinces from the rebellious federation. In 1579, the Dutch provinces formed the Union of Utrecht, and two years later they declared their independence from Spain as the Dutch United Provinces.

For the moment, Spain, which was also at war against France, could supply its armies because Alba's armies had recaptured some of the Southern Netherlands, while Philip II maintained peace with England. As the Dutch revolt wore on, however, the problems of fighting a war a thousand miles away plagued the Spanish king. Military contractors or entrepreneurs recruited mercenaries; Italians, Burgundians, Germans, and Walloons made up much of the Spanish army.

Spanish routes for troops, supplies, and bullion to the Netherlands had to be maintained through a combination of diplomatic charm, cunning, and coercion. As allegiances and the fortunes of war eliminated first the Palatinate and then Alsace and Lorraine as routes through which armies could pass, the Spanish forged the "Spanish Road" as a military corridor (see Map 5.3). It began in Genoa, went overland across the Alps, and then passed through Lombardy and Piedmont, Geneva, Franche-Comté, Lorraine and,

MAP 5.3 THE SPANISH ROAD   The route taken by the Spanish armies, supplies, and money to the Netherlands was long and difficult, as it passed through mountainous terrain and many states.

finally, the duchy of Liège, with Spanish agents assuring supplies along the way.

Spain's acute problems of recruiting and supply were exacerbated by dubious efforts to save money—for instance, charging sharpshooters for powder and shot. The army's guarantee to carry out the written wills made by soldiers also seems to have been a curiously self-defeating approach to inspiring confidence. Desertions and mutinies—the largest involving non-Spanish troops—occurred with ever more frequency as troops demanded payment of back wages, better and more regular food, and decent medical care. By 1577, the Spanish army in the Netherlands, unpaid for months, had dwindled in size from 60,000 to no more than 8,000 men.

Throughout the long war, the superior Dutch fleet kept the Spanish ships in port. The ships of "sea beggars," as they were called, harassed Spanish ships. The English navy, allied with the Dutch in 1586, controlled the English

Channel. When the Spanish fleet sailed north in 1588, the result was the disastrous defeat of the Armada. At the beginning of the seventeenth century, the Dutch gradually fell back behind protective town fortifications and natural barriers formed by rivers. The war became a series of long Spanish sieges against frontier towns defended by brick fortifications, bastions, and moats—a defensive system that had its origins with the Italian city-states. With the defense having a marked advantage, towns could be conquered only by being starved out.

France withdrew from the war in 1598, and England withdrew six years later. A truce between the Spanish and the Dutch, signed in 1609, lapsed in 1621. In Holland the "war party" won the upper hand. Led by Maurice of Nassau (1567–1625), the son of William of Orange, who had been assassinated in 1584, the war party appealed to Calvinist religious orthodoxy by calling for a crusade against Catholicism that would also free the Southern Netherlands from Spanish rule. Army officers and merchant traders wanted to keep the struggle against Spain going as long as possible. It dragged on, draining the Spanish economy.

Economic Decline

Economic decline—above all, that of Castile in the middle decades of the seventeenth century—underlay Spain's fall from a position of European domination. But decline is, of course, relative. Spain remained an important state. Yet its population, which had risen to well over 6 million people during the last half of the sixteenth century, fell by almost a quarter to about 5.2 million by the middle of the seventeenth century, as harvest failures, plague, smallpox, war, and emigration took their tolls.

The "price revolution," the sharp rise in inflation during the sixteenth century in Europe, may well have affected Spain less than some parts of northern Europe, but it still had adverse effects on the Spanish monarchy. Gold and silver from the Americas accelerated inflation by increasing the supply of money, as did royal monetary policies of currency debasement. The monarchy, which had declared bankruptcy in 1557, suspended payments in 1575, and again in 1596, renegotiating loans at more favorable rates. From 1568 to 1598, Spain had five times the military expenditures of the Dutch, English, and French combined. The economy slipped into stagnation. To one noble it already seemed that "the ship is sinking."

Forced to borrow money from foreign bankers at disadvantageous interest rates, the Spanish state attempted to find new sources of revenue. To raise funds, the crown imposed a tithe, or assessment of a tenth of the most valuable piece of real estate in each parish, and in 1590 the Castilian Cortes agreed to an extraordinary tax assessed on towns. An excise (sales) tax was imposed on consumption. This undermined the economy by encouraging the middle class to abandon business in favor of the acquisition of perpetual privileges—and thus tax exemptions—as they obtained noble status.

The monarchy's massive expulsion of the Moriscos in 1609 proved counter-productive. The king succumbed to pressure from the Catholic Church and from wealthy families eager to seize Moorish land. The region of Valencia lost one-third of its population, including many skilled craftsmen and farmers.

Nobles added the lands of indebted peasants to their large estates (*latifundia*), but they showed little interest in increasing the productivity of their land, in contrast to their English counterparts. They turned fields into pastureland or simply left them untended. Farmers were hampered by a state-imposed fixed maximum for grain prices, which discouraged ambitious agricultural initiatives. Spain became dependent on imported grain. Royal policies also favored sheepherding over farming—because it was easier to collect taxes on sheep than on agricultural produce. But fine woolens manufacturing suffered from competition with foreign textile imports, especially lighter cloth brought from France and the Netherlands.

"Conquered by you, the New World has conquered you in turn, and has weakened and exhausted your ancient vigor," a Flemish scholar wrote a friend in Spain. The Spanish colonies themselves became a financial drain on the crown because of the cost of administering and defending them. The flow of Latin American silver, which had paid less than a quarter of the crown's colonial and military expenses, slowed to a trickle beginning in the 1620s. Spain had never really developed commerce with the empire to the same extent as the English, who had made trade the basis of their maritime empire, enormously developing the colonial market. In the Spanish Empire, the market for Spanish goods, already limited by the poverty of the colonies, shrank with the precipitous decline in the Indian population (caused, above all, by disease; see Chapter 1). Unlike in the English colonies, emigration to the New World from Spain had slowed to a trickle by the early eighteenth century, in part because economic opportunities in Spanish-held territories were relatively limited. This was compounded by the prohibition of non-Spanish migration to Spain's American colonies. The colonies had also developed their own basic agricultural and artisanal production and relied far less on Spanish goods. The Atlantic ports of northern Castile suffered competition not only from Seville and Cádiz, but from Spain's own colonies, and above all, from England and the Netherlands.

Although the burden of taxes in Castile increased by four times between 1570 and 1670, the Spanish crown proved less efficient in collecting taxes than the monarchs of France and England. Increased taxes on the poor generated more discontent than income. Spain's Italian subjects resisted contributing money for distant wars that did not concern them. No more tax income came to Spain from the Netherlands.

Contemporary Spaniards lapsed into a morose acceptance of decline. The novelist Miguel de Cervantes (1547–1616) had fought and been wounded

El Greco's *Burial of the Count Orgaz,* 1586.

with the king's armies at the Battle of Lepanto (1571). Several years later, he was captured by Turkish pirates and spent five years as a slave before managing to return to Spain. *Don Quixote* (1605–1615) is on one level a humorous tale of a zany noble intent on bringing true chivalry back to Spain, accompanied by his sensible, subservient squire, Sancho Panza. On a deeper level, however, it is the story of national disillusionment in the face of perceived national decline. The dramatist Pedro Calderón de la Barca (1600–1681) portrayed in his plays the floundering Spanish aristocracy struggling to preserve its honor. Nobles and churchmen, the two pillars of Spain, purchased the paintings of the increasingly gloomy Greek-born artist El Greco (1541–1614). His *Burial of the Count Orgaz* (1586) shows figures gazing up at a vision of celestial glory, the splendor of which is heightened by the dismal scenes below them on earth.

An Empire Spread Too Thin

Spain's mounting economic problems were exacerbated by the fact that the empire's interests were spread so widely, not only in Europe, but across the seas. Philip IV (1605–1665), who succeeded to the throne in 1621, was intelligent and had a keen interest in the arts, but he was stubborn. He chose as his chief adviser Gaspar de Guzmán, the duke of Olivares (1587–1645), an Andalusian noble whose family had, like Spain itself, suffered reverses. The short, fiery, and increasingly obese Olivares sketched ambitious plans to shape the rebirth of Spanish might. Confronted with the economic strength of the Dutch rebels, as well as that of the English, Olivares sensed that Spain could not remain a power without a marked economic resurgence. "We must devote all our efforts," he had written, "to turning Spaniards into merchants," like the English. The Count Duke, as he was called, mastered his master, convincing the indolent king that only hard work and reform could restore the glories of the not-so-distant past. He would tutor the king, whose chamber pot he once ceremoniously kissed, in the fine art of monarchy.

The Count Duke espoused the growth of monarchical power and state centralization. His motto "one king, one law, one money" generated resistance, in the latter case because of the by then notorious instability of the Castilian currency. Olivares sought to subject all of Spain to the laws and royal administration of Castile, promising the king that, if he did so, he would become the most powerful prince in the world.

Olivares wanted to force Dutch capitulation to restore the monarchy's reputation, afraid that the Dutch rebellion might begin a chain reaction that would destroy the empire. He persuaded the king to allow the truce with the Dutch to lapse in 1621, thus necessitating massive expenses for land and sea warfare. To preserve the "Spanish Road," Olivares sought to bolster, at great expense, Spanish interests in northern Italy and in Austria. But France cut the Spanish supply routes in Savoy in 1622 and then in Alsace nine years later. Intermittent hostilities with France lasted from 1628 to 1631.

Spain could now ill afford such conflicts. In 1628, Dutch pirates captured a Spanish fleet loaded with silver. This enormous loss made it imperative that the crown find new resources with which to wage war. But for the first time, Castile's monarchs could not establish credit with foreign investors. Increased taxation, the flotation of short-term loans through bonds, the sale of yet more privileges, and the imposition of new financial obligations on Aragon and the Italian territories all proved inadequate to the task of financing expensive wars.

Its interests gravely overextended, Spain's position weakened. English ships began to nip at its imperial interests in the Americas. Dutch warships took on the proud Spanish galleons in the West Indies. Three decades of intermittent warfare with France began in 1635, as the Thirty Years' War (see Chapter 4) became a struggle between competing dynasties. As more and more bullion from the Americas had to be diverted to pay military expenses in the Netherlands and Italy, the monarchy demanded new contributions from Catalonia and Portugal (which had been merged with Spain in 1580), as Spain had assumed the expensive and ultimately extremely damaging responsibility for protecting Portuguese shipping around the world. Tumultuous tax riots broke out in Portugal, where the upper classes resisted Spanish authority.

Olivares's decision to demand more taxes from Catalonia proved fateful. Faced with resistance, he ordered the arrest of several Catalan leaders. Catalan nobles put aside their differences, and a full-scale revolt against Castilian rule began in 1640. Catalan and French forces together defeated the Spanish army. A year later, Andalusian nobles were foiled in a plot to create an independent kingdom there. Nobles in Madrid hatched plots against Olivares. Portugal reasserted its independence in 1640. Three years later, Philip packed off the despondent Olivares into exile.

However, the illusion of Don Quixote was maintained—that the restoration of traditional aristocratic and ecclesiastical values would restore Spanish power and prestige. Olivares established two court academies intended to train young nobles in the art of government. Heeding the advice of churchmen, he censored the theater and books, prohibiting certain kinds of fancy clothing and long hair. Over the long run, Spanish rulers weakened parliamentary traditions. Soon the Cortes was convoked only on ceremonial occasions. The crown continued to extend its reach and solidify its authority against possible provincial rebellions. In Catalonia, Barcelona surrendered to royal troops in 1652. Catalan nobles accepted the supremacy of the crown in exchange for an affirmation of social hierarchy and royal protection against ordinary Catalans who resented their privileges. The Aragonese nobles, too, accepted this compromise.

Ironically, given the intense perception of Spanish decline, the last years of Philip IV and the reign of his pathetic successor, Charles II (ruled 1665–1700), sustained a period of great cultural accomplishment in the arts and literature. But this, too, may have been generated by the prevailing mood of introspection. Olivares put dramatists and a small host of other writers to work in the name of glorifying the monarchy and imparting a sense of purpose that he hoped would revive Spain. Philip IV added more than 2,000 canvases to what already was a rich royal art collection, including many by Italian masters. He covered the palace walls with grandiose paintings of battle scenes. Diego Velázquez (1599–1660), the court painter, undertook forty somber portraits of the vain king, a commentary on the monarchy's fading glory and disillusionment.

King Philip IV of Spain.

In the meantime, the Dutch rebels, aided by increased commercial prosperity, had fought the Spanish armies to a draw. The Treaty of Münster, which was part of the Westphalia settlement of 1648 that ended the Thirty Years' War, officially recognized Dutch independence after a struggle that had lasted three-quarters of a century. The provinces of the Southern Netherlands, which were overwhelmingly Catholic, remained a Habsburg possession.

The Spanish monarchy, overstretched by its vast empire in the Americas, had not learned that it could not fight effectively on a variety of fronts. In contrast, the French monarchy was concentrating its efforts in Italy, for the moment realizing the wisdom of fighting on one front at a time. Thus, subsequent Spanish victories in the north against French armies were not enough, for when the French turned their attention to Spain, they held their own. The Treaty of the Pyrenees, signed between France and Spain in 1659, established the border between these countries that has lasted, with only a few minor changes, until this day. Spain also gave up Milan to Austria, and Naples and Sicily to the Italian Bourbon dynasty. The Portuguese, aided by the English, turned back several halfhearted invasions by Spanish armies, and in 1668 Spain recognized Portugal's independence. Ten years later, France occupied the Franche-Comté, the last major Spanish holding in northern Europe. By 1680, when the depression that had lasted almost a century ended, Spain was no longer a great power. This was because of agricultural and manufacturing decline, to be sure, but, above all, because the Spanish crown had overreached its ability to maintain its vast and distant empire.

Conclusion

The development of trade across the Atlantic Ocean to the Americas was part of European economic expansion during the sixteenth century. Following the union of the crowns of Castile and Aragon, Spain grew into a great power. Philip II expanded the Spanish Empire, which, in the Americas stretched from what is now the southwestern United States to the southern tip of Latin America, and in Europe included the Netherlands and several Italian states. In England, the Tudor monarchy overcame the country's religious divisions in the wake of the English Reformation to strengthen its authority. In this, it resembled the ruling Valois dynasty of France, another "new monarchy" that had enhanced its reach, efficiency, and prestige. Burgeoning trade, manufacturing, and agriculture in the Elizabethan Age underlay England's growing prosperity, even as social polarization, reflected in the crises of the 1590s, became more apparent.

The surprising English naval defeat of the Spanish Armada in 1588 symbolized not only the rise of England but in some ways anticipated the decline of Spanish power. Spain's rulers had expanded their vast empire and imperial interests beyond the ability of the state to sustain them. When silver from the Americas slowed to a trickle, Spain's own limited natural resources and inability to collect taxes efficiently, combined with demographic stagnation that began early in the seventeenth century, as well as, arguably, resistance from Aragon and Catalonia, prevented a revival of Spanish preeminence. The long revolt of the Netherlands ended with recognition of Dutch independence in 1648. That the Dutch Republic and England, two trading nations, had emerged as European powers reflected the shift of economic primacy to northwestern Europe.

CHAPTER 6

ENGLAND AND THE DUTCH REPUBLIC IN THE SEVENTEENTH CENTURY

    England and the Dutch Republic were anomalies in the seventeenth century. At a time when aggressive European monarchs were forging absolute states (see Chapter 7), these two seafaring, trading nations maintained representative governments.

    The Stuart monarchs' flirtation with absolutism in England brought bitter discord, resistance, and civil war. In the Dutch Republic, which had earned its independence in 1648 after a long war against Spanish absolute rule, the prosperous merchants who dominated the economic and political life of the country brushed aside the absolutist challenge of the House of Orange, which wanted to establish a hereditary monarchy.

    In both England and the Netherlands, religious divisions accentuated the struggle between absolutism and constitutionalism. Both the protracted revolt of the largely Protestant Dutch against Catholic Spain and the English Civil War echoed the religious struggles between Catholics and Protestants during the Thirty Years' War (1618–1648) in Central Europe (see Chapter 4). The Dutch had risen up in open rebellion in 1566 in part because the Spanish Habsburgs attempted to impose the Catholic Inquisition on what had become a Protestant country. In England, Kings James I and Charles I attempted to return the English Church to the elaborate rituals that many people associated with Catholicism, thereby pitting the monarchy against Parliament. This constitutional crisis led to the defeat and execution of Charles I in 1649, the fall of the monarchy, and in 1688, to the "Glorious Revolution," which brought King William III and Queen Mary to the throne. Parliament, which historically represented landed interests, succeeded in balancing and constraining royal authority. By virtue of Parliament's victory in the English Civil War, England remained a constitutional monarchy. England's new monarchs agreed to a Bill of Rights, which affirmed the civil liberties of English people and the rights of Parliament.

The emergence of England and the Dutch Republic, both predominantly Protestant states, as great powers reflected the vitality of the middle classes in both nations, the relative unity of the two states, and the location of both rising powers on the Atlantic. England's international commerce developed rapidly. And as Amsterdam emerged as a banking center and first port of call for international trade, the Dutch Republic enjoyed the golden age of its culture.

CONFLICTS IN STUART ENGLAND

Conflicts between the Stuart kings and Parliament, in which religious conflict played an important part, led to the English Civil War, which helped define the constitutional and political institutions of modern Britain. The monarchy tried to enhance its authority at the expense of Parliament by attempting to impose extralegal taxes without the consent of Parliament. But the English gentry, whose status and influence came from ownership of land, emerged from the period with their parliamentary prerogatives intact.

Conflicts between James I and Parliament

King James I (1566–1625) succeeded his cousin Queen Elizabeth to the English throne in 1603. As King James VI of Scotland, he had overcome court factionalism and challenges from dissident Presbyterians. After he also became king of England, the two countries were joined in a personal union. The first Stuart king of England, James was lazy, frivolous, and slovenly, particularly enjoying hurling jelly at his courtiers. But there was more to him than that. He was an intelligent and well-read blunderer, once described as "the wisest fool in Christendom." Before coming to the throne, James had sketched out a theory of divine right monarchy. And in a speech to Parliament in 1609 the king had called "the state of monarchie . . . the supremest thing upon earth: for Kings are not only God's Lieutenants upon earth, and sit upon throne, but even by God himselfe they are called Gods." James described Parliament as nothing but "cries, shouts, and confusion." Relations between the monarch and Parliament degenerated rapidly.

The English monarchy found itself in a precarious financial position, with Queen Elizabeth's war debts at least partially to blame. James brought to court like-minded dandies, most of whom proved not only unpopular with Parliament but incompetent as well. In the last years of his reign, James became increasingly dependent on his young, handsome favorite, George Villiers, the duke of Buckingham (1592–1628). A relative newcomer to court circles, Buckingham convinced the king to sell peerages and titles, offices, monopolies, and other privileges to the highest bidder. Opposition to the monarch's attempts to raise money in such ways mounted within Parliament.

Although it met only sporadically and at the king's pleasure, Parliament transformed itself from a debating society into an institution that saw itself as defending the rights of the English people. The House of Commons, lashing out at the beneficiaries of royal monopolies, impeached on charges of bribery Lord Chancellor Francis Bacon (1561–1626), philosopher of science and once the king's friend. Here, too, there was a principle at stake: the accountability of ministers to Parliament.

English foreign policy contributed both to the monarchy's mounting debt and to the emerging political crisis. Queen Elizabeth had denied that Parliament had the right to discuss matters of foreign policy unless invited by the monarch to do so. Parliament still insisted on that right. Thus, James favored peace with Spain, but Parliament clamored for war because Catholic Bavaria, an ally of Habsburg Spain, had invaded the Protestant Upper Palatinate. And in 1621, asserting its right to influence foreign policy, Parliament refused to provide more funds for the conflict, setting the stage for the greatest constitutional crisis in English history.

Parliament denounced the monarch's attempt to arrange a marriage between his son, Charles, the heir to the throne, and the daughter of Philip IV of Spain. As dynastic marriages were an essential part of foreign policy, cementing or building alliances, members of Parliament objected to a royal foreign policy that seemed pro-Spanish and therefore pro-Catholic. Parliament declared its right to discuss the proposed marriage, and thus foreign affairs. But James defied Parliament by stating that it could not discuss matters of foreign policy, denying that the privileges of Parliament were "your ancient and undoubted birthright and inheritance." Rather he described them as "derived from the grace and permission of our ancestors and us."

James's wedding plans for his son fell through in 1623, however, when the Spanish king refused to allow Charles, who had gone to Madrid, even to set eyes on his daughter. But two years later, James then arranged Charles's marriage to another devout Catholic, Henrietta Maria of France, the daughter of Henry IV and Maria de' Medici. The secret price of this liaison included the king's promise that he would one day allow English Catholics, who numbered 2 or 3 percent of the population, to practice their religion freely. In a country in which anti-Catholicism had been endemic since the English Reformation of the mid-sixteenth century, James seemed to be taking steps to favor Catholicism.

James was succeeded upon his death by his son, Charles I (ruled 1625–1649). The young king was indecisive and painfully shy, traits compounded by a stammer. Even more than his father, Charles rejected the view that his appointments to ministries and other important offices should represent a wide spectrum of political and religious views. He stubbornly refused to oust the duke of Buckingham.

(Left) King James I. *(Right)* The young Charles, heir to the throne and later Charles I.

RELIGIOUS DIVISIONS

King Charles I once claimed, "People are governed by the pulpit more than the sword in time of peace." In the seventeenth century, no other realm of life so bitterly divided Europeans as religion. In England, religious divisions helped accentuate and define the political crisis. The Established or Anglican Church faced a challenge from the Puritans, a dissident religious group of Calvinists that had emerged during Elizabeth's reign.

Many Puritans were more sure of what they were against than what they were for. Puritans were strongly attracted by the Calvinist idea that each individual was predestined by God through His grace to be saved or not to be saved. They emphasized preaching and the individual's personal understanding of the Bible, spiritual devotion, discipline, and sacrifice as the basis of religion. Because they emphasized the personal worth of the individual minister, not the value of an ecclesiastical title, Puritans opposed the role of bishops in the Church of England. They wanted authority to be taken away from bishops and given to local synods (ecclesiastical councils made up of clerical and lay leaders). They de-emphasized the sacraments and wanted worship to be simpler than the contemporary Anglican Church services. Relentlessly hostile to Catholicism, Puritans held that elaborate church accoutrements in the Church of England—such as stained-glass windows and ornate altar rails—smacked of the Roman papacy.

Puritans did not choose the name by which they came to be known in the late sixteenth century, which was originally intended as a term of abuse. Considering themselves "the godly," they believed that they represented the true Church of England. They constituted not more than 10 percent of the population, and perhaps a third of all gentry, but their influence grew. University graduates who had embraced Puritanism formed "a godly preaching ministry" in many parishes, providing opportunities for Puritans to preach and win converts.

The Puritans were increasingly hostile to those who espoused a kind of Protestantism known as Arminianism. At first no more than a handful of ecclesiastics with the king's ear, Arminians soon came to wield considerable power. Charles I became an Arminian, and so did the duke of Buckingham. English Arminians, like their Dutch counterparts, rejected the Calvinist idea of predestination, which Puritans accepted, and, unlike the latter, believed that an individual could achieve salvation through free will. Arminians also accepted rituals that to the Puritans seemed to replicate those of the Catholic Church, and they emphasized the authority and ceremonial role of bishops, which Puritans opposed with particular vehemence. The Arminians emphasized royal authority over the Church of England. Increasingly they seemed to be proponents of royal absolutism.

The king's aggressive espousal of Arminianism enhanced the influence of William Laud (1573–1645), bishop of London. In 1633, Charles named Laud to be the head of the Church of England as Primate of England (archbishop of Canterbury). The pious, hard-working, and stubborn son of a draper, Laud warned Charles that the religious extremes of Catholicism and radical Puritanism both posed threats to the Established Church. An Arminian, Laud espoused High Church rituals, and because of this, the Puritans thought that he was secretly working to make Catholicism the established religion of England. Under Elizabeth I and James I, Catholics had remained a force in some sectors of English life. Fear of a "popish plot" to restore Catholicism as the religion of the English state existed at all levels of English society. Landowners whose families had purchased ecclesiastical lands during the Reformation now worried that Laud might return them to the Catholic Church. Catholicism and "popery" was popularly identified with the Spanish Inquisition, the Saint Bartholomew's Day Massacre in France, and the duke of Alba's "Council of Blood" in the Netherlands.

Charles I and Parliament Clash

Charles's fiscal policies deepened popular dissatisfaction with his reign. In 1625, the king decreed a forced loan on landowners, which he levied without Parliament's consent and which he insisted be paid within three months, an unprecedented short period of time. The next year, he ordered the imprisonment of seventy-six gentlemen who refused to meet the royal demand. Parliament refused to consent to the levies unless Charles met its demands for fiscal reform. The king convoked three Parliaments in four years, but dissolved each when it refused to provide him with funds. Parliament continued to demand that Charles appoint ministers it could trust and began impeachment proceedings against the duke of Buckingham. However, Buckingham disappeared as a source of irritation to Parliament when a disgruntled naval officer who had not been paid assassinated him in 1628.

Charles again asked Parliament to provide him with more funds. In response, Parliament promulgated the Petition of Right, which it forced Charles to accept in return for the granting of a tax. This constrained the king to agree that in the future he would not attempt to impose "loans" without Parliament's consent, and that no "gentlemen" who refused to pay up would be arrested—nor would anyone else be imprisoned without a show of just cause. The Petition of Right, which was initially put forward in 1628 by Sir Thomas Wentworth (1593–1641), then an opponent of the crown and one of the men imprisoned for refusing to pay the forced loan, was a significant document in the constitutional evolution of England. It defined the rights of Parliament as inalienable and condemned arbitrary arrest, martial law, and taxes imposed without its consent.

Angered by the Petition of Right and by Parliament's insistence that customs duties were a violation of the Petition, Charles ordered Parliament's dissolution in 1629. Because it was the role of the speaker of the house to communicate with the king on behalf of Parliament, members of the Commons physically held the speaker in his chair so he could not leave. They proceeded to declare that anyone who attempted to collect funds not levied with the approval of Parliament would be considered "a capital enemy to the kingdom and commonwealth," as would anyone who sponsored "innovation of religion," which is what Puritans considered Laud's espousal of elaborate High Church ceremonies. A defiant Parliament then disbanded.

For the next eleven years, Charles ruled without Parliament and tried to raise monies in new and controversial ways. Inflation had increased not only the royal debt but also the cost of ships and arms for waging war. The monarchy had exhausted its credit. Unlike James, Charles had some scruples about peddling privileges, but none at all about other means of raising funds. He fined gentlemen who did not attend his coronation. Most controversially, Charles ordered that "ship money" again be imposed without Parliament's consent on inland towns beginning in 1634.

Charles's high-handed royal policies led to a rebellion in Scotland. The king had seized lands from Scottish nobles, and, at Laud's instigation, in 1637 he ordered the imposition of the Anglican Book of Common Prayer on the Scottish Presbyterian Church (established as the Scottish national church in the 1560s). The Scots had never been pleased with the union with England that had been weakly forged in 1603 when James VI of Scotland ascended the English throne as James I. They demanded that Charles allow a general church assembly to consider the prayer book. In 1638, some Scottish leaders signed the *National Covenant,* attacking the pope and the prayer book and swearing to defend their religion and liberties. Faced with the resolution of Scots to maintain the Presbyterian Church, Charles convoked the

Riot in St. Giles' Cathedral, Edinburgh, when the bishop begins to read from the Anglican Book of Common Prayer.

church assembly in Scotland, but he also began to prepare for an invasion of Scotland. In the meantime, Scottish nobles and landowners began evicting Anglican bishops and taking over churches. The Scots rose up in arms.

This was a turning point in the dramatic reign of King Charles I. Desperately needing funds to defeat the Scots, in 1639 the king demanded that the city of London help pay for the war. After several small allocations, London finally consented to lend the crown a large sum, but only on the condition that Charles convene Parliament and allow it to sit for a reasonable period of time.

Nobles and gentry led resistance to royal policies from the beginning; some were already in touch with the rebellious Scots, who in 1640 occupied the northeastern English port of Newcastle without resistance. Running short of cash and facing mutinies in the royal army, in April 1640 the king summoned Parliament for the first time in eleven years. But when it refused to allocate money for the war against Scotland until Charles agreed to consider a list of grievances, the king dissolved this "Short Parliament" after less than two months. Charles I's defiance of Parliament initiated a full-fledged constitutional crisis.

The English Civil War

The political crisis of the Stuart monarchy became a constitutional conflict about how England was to be governed. To the king's opponents, Parliament existed to protect fundamental English liberties that had been established under the Magna Carta in 1215. By this reasoning the king did not have the right to dispense with its counsel and its traditional authority to allocate royal finances, nor did he have the right to impose taxes without historical precedent. While Parliament, led by Puritans, was not yet claiming sovereignty, it was clearly asserting its traditional role as a balance to royal authority.

Defenders of Parliament believed Laudian religious reforms and the collection of ship money to be the work of power-crazed men perhaps manipulated by the pope. Justices of the peace resented the usurpation of their authority by various decrees of martial law and by royal courts that impinged on regional courts. Local officials believed that the king's lieutenants were exceeding their traditional authority over military affairs by bypassing established routines of local approval of military levies. London merchants felt aggrieved that they were not able to export cloth because of royal control over cloth exports through the monopoly of the Merchant Adventurers (see Chapter 5). The monarchy alienated other Londoners by allowing some craftsmen to operate outside the structure of the London guilds and by attempting to force the city to provide more money for the war with Scotland. The sale of the right to collect royal customs generated controversy as well, particularly as the government sold more privileges to pay off those who "farmed" taxes.

In the meantime, Charles surrounded himself with confidants, advisers, artists, and musicians, whose sense of royal decorum and aesthetic tastes seemed to suggest the influence of continental Catholicism. The queen brought to the court Flemish artists who emphasized the religious themes of the Catholic Reformation, leading critics to believe that a plot was afloat "to seduce the King himself with Pictures, Antiquities, Images & other vanities brought from *Rome*."

Those who consistently supported Parliament became known as the supporters of "Country," while those who supported virtually unlimited monarchical prerogatives were identified with "Court." Titled nobles, of whom there were about 1,200, generally supported Charles. Gentry formed the core of the political opposition to the king. During the previous century, many gentry had extended their landholdings, and men enriched by commerce or service in the law or army had become part of the gentry through the purchase of land. The roots of confrontation may have come from the struggle of these economically dynamic gentry to obtain political power commensurate with their rising station in English life. Some gentry of lesser means who had fallen upon hard times may have blamed the monarchy for their plight and hence supported Parliament.

The English Civil War has been called the "Puritan Revolution," even though its causes extended beyond the question of religion and Puritans were not alone in resisting the monarchy. There were indeed many Puritans in Parliament, including the body's leader, John Pym (1584–1643). A brilliant speaker and debater, Pym was a zealot, an impetuous and perhaps even paranoid man whose strong convictions were in part defined by an obsession that a "popish plot" existed to restore Catholicism to England. Puritans were

PYM.

John Pym.

numerous among the lesser gentry in eastern England, areas that took the side of Parliament during the Civil War.

As the political crisis grew in the 1630s, the authority of Anglican bishops, their appointment as state officials, and their right to nominate ministers also smacked of "popery." Charles I echoed the famous statement of his father, James I, "No bishops, no king!"—an assertion that would come back to haunt him. Laud expanded the power of ecclesiastical courts, which tried people accused of offenses against the Church of England. This reminded some people of the Spanish Inquisition.

Moving toward Conflict

Having dissolved the "Short Parliament" in May 1640, Charles again convoked a newly elected Parliament the following October. The crown's strengthening of the army with Catholic Irish regiments, commanded by Wentworth, who was now a supporter and adviser of the king and had been named the earl of Strafford, confirmed to credulous ears that a "popish plot" was in the works. Ordinary people smashed altar rails and shattered stained-glass windows. The English army suffered defeat in Scotland; the war required yet more funds. Led by Pym, Parliament turned its wrath upon Charles's advisers. It indicted Strafford, who was tried and executed in London before a rejoicing throng. Parliament denounced as illegal the most unpopular royal acts during the previous eleven years and abolished some of the courts controlled by the monarchy. Parliament proclaimed that it could only dissolve itself, and that in the future the king would have to summon it every three years. In the meantime, Irish peasants rose up against the English in 1641 and killed many Protestant landlords. The Irish rebellion highlighted the rights of Parliament by making urgent the issue of who controlled the militia.

In November 1641, Parliament passed the Grand Remonstrance. Presenting what Parliament considered a history of royal misdeeds, the document denounced "a malignant and pernicious design of subverting the fundamental laws and principles" of English government. It called for religious and administrative reforms. Its passage by a narrow margin indicated that Parliament remained divided over how far to carry its opposition to royal policies.

Puritans, who narrowly controlled the House of Commons, wanted to reform both church and state. Wealthy nobles began to form a solid bloc around the cause of the king, fearing that reform might weaken their influence. Shortly after the passage of the Grand Remonstrance, the high sheriff of Lancashire called upon "gentlemen" to take arms with their tenants and servants on behalf of the king "for the securing of our own lives and estates, which are now ready to be surprised by a heady multitude." In some places, fighting began that month, as both sides fought for control of the militias.

The king attempted a bold coup against Parliament in January 1642. He personally led several hundred armed soldiers into Parliament and ordered the arrest of Pym. Forewarned by someone, Pym and other leaders had left the House of Commons before Charles arrived, but they remained in London where they were protected by artisans and craftsmen. The latter opposed the crown's support of monopolies and for religious reasons supported Laud. Charles, fearing for his safety in London, where people had become more forceful in their support of Parliament, headed north with his family to more friendly country, and his supporters left Parliament. In June, Parliament's "Nineteen Propositions" denounced the confrontational royal policy. In August 1642, Charles mobilized his forces at Nottingham.

Taking Sides

As civil war spread, Parliament's soldiers came to be known as "Roundheads" for the short, bowl-shaped haircuts many of them wore. The king's "Cavaliers" liked to think of themselves as fighting the good fight for God and king against those who would shatter social harmony by making "subjects princes and princes slaves." But so far as civil wars go, there was little actual fighting. Winter interrupted relatively short "campaign seasons." There were only four major battles (see Map 6.1). The two sides fought to a draw on October 23, 1642, at Edgehill, south of Birmingham. When a royal military advance on London was turned back, Charles set up headquarters in Oxford, fifty miles northwest of London. In February 1643, the king rejected Parliament's terms for a settlement. When a second royal march on London failed, both sides intensified massive propaganda campaigns to win support. The war became a war of words, among the first in history. More than 22,000 newspapers, newsletters, pamphlets, broadsides, sermons, and speeches were published between 1640 and 1661.

Yet life in thousands of villages was disrupted by requisitions, plundering, and general hardship. About 10 percent of the English population was forced to leave home during the war. Many counties—perhaps most—were neutral, as local leaders struggled to maintain control and keep their counties free of fighting and devastation.

Without London's credit institutions, Charles financed the war with gifts and loans from nobles, selling more titles, and forced levies. The Roundheads, in keeping with Parliament's resistance to monarchical centralization,

MAP 6.1 THE ENGLISH CIVIL WAR   Major battles during the English Civil War, as well as Cavalier and Roundhead strongholds.

kept civil, fiscal, and military authority relatively decentralized in regions under its control. Parliament raised funds through heavy excise and property taxes, and confiscated the property of some prominent families supporting the king's cause. A regional military structure developed, based on associations of counties pledging mutual assistance to the parliamentary cause.

Parliament drew considerable support from the most economically advanced regions where commercialized agriculture had developed through deforestation, the draining of marshland, and acts of enclosure, and where cloth manufacturing had brought prosperity, particularly in the south and east. Charles I retained the allegiance of most of northern and western England, regions of more traditional agriculture and social hierarchy. In some places, villages became sites for religious and political struggle. For example, in regions where traditional festive rituals had survived the assault of Puritans, who considered them frivolous, disruptive, and ungodly spectacles that brought drinking, dancing, and sexual freedom, support was strong for the king, whose supporters—wealthy country gentlemen—encouraged such merriment.

Oliver Cromwell and the New Model Army

In 1643, Parliament allied with the Scots, many of whom were Presbyterians. John Pym's sudden death at the end of the year did not lessen Parliament's resolve to force the king to capitulate. In July 1644, the Roundheads and Scots defeated the Cavaliers at Marston Moor, near York. About 45,000 men fought in this battle, the largest of the English Civil War. This gave Parliament control of northern England. Scottish participation only added to the determination of the "war party" to whom Charles listened.

Oliver Cromwell.

Oliver Cromwell (1599–1658), who led the Roundheads to victory at Marston Moor, emerged as the leader of Parliament. Cromwell, born into a modest gentry family, never lost what more well-heeled gentry considered his rough edges. Several years before being elected to Parliament in 1640, he had undergone—perhaps during serious illness—a deep spiritual conversion, becoming convinced that God had chosen him to be one of the Puritan elect. Cromwell displayed idealism as well as the stubbornness of someone who is convinced that he is always right.

Combining three armies, Parliament formed the New Model Army in 1645. Cromwell instilled strict discipline, and the Roundhead soldiers' morale improved with regular wages. Unlike its predecessors, the New Model Army won grudging good will in the counties by paying for supplies and not plundering, in contrast to the king's army.

Divisions within Parliament

Two political groups emerged in Parliament: Presbyterians and Independents. Presbyterians, a majority within Parliament, were moderates. Originally a pro-Scottish group that had rallied behind John Pym, most (despite the name "Presbyterians") were Puritans. Opposed to the bishops' authority, they rejected religious toleration and wanted an established national Calvinist Church. They were ready to accept a negotiated settlement with the king.

The Independents were militant Puritans who desired more drastic changes than the Presbyterians. They wanted the church to be a loose alliance of congregations that would choose their own ministers, a more radical position than that of the Presbyterians. The Independents were less willing to compromise with the king on the issue of parliamentary prerogatives.

Crowds watch Puritan soldiers leaving London, c. 1647. Note the "roundheads" and the armed preacher urging them on.

They opposed the creation of a new established church and favored toleration of some religious dissent. Some of them even desired more far-reaching political reforms that would protect individual rights. Cromwell's rise to leadership reflected the ascendancy of the Independents in Parliament.

Cromwell purged Presbyterian commanders within the New Model Army, replacing them with Independents loyal to him. Singing psalms as they rushed fearlessly into battle, Cromwell's "Ironsides," as his troops were called, maintained an air of invincibility. In June 1645, the New Model Army routed the royalists. Charles surrendered to the Scots a year later, hoping to obtain a less draconian peace than if he capitulated directly to Parliament. But the Scottish army soon withdrew from England and left the king in the custody of Parliament in February 1647.

Radicals

As the war dragged on, England fell into virtual anarchy amid growing resentment over the billeting of soldiers, food shortages, and rising prices. The English Civil War unleashed forces that seemed to challenge the foundation of social and political order. During the siege of royalist Oxford, a hungry sentry called down to the besieging forces, "Roundhead, fling me up half a mutton and I will fling thee down a lord!" At times the Roundheads appeared to hold back as if wary of the consequences of victory. Even some gentry who had taken the side of Parliament feared that a crushing victory might unleash "turbulent spirits, backed by rude and tumultuous mechanic persons [i.e., ordinary people]" and attacks against property by the mob, "that many headed monster."

In such an uncertain climate, new religious groups proliferated. Baptists did not believe that children should be baptized, reasoning that only adults were old enough to choose a congregation and hence be baptized. Some Baptists permitted couples to marry by simply making a declaration before the congregation.

"Levellers" were far more radical. They called for new laws that would protect the poor as well as the wealthy. Levellers, many of whom had been Baptists or Puritans, found adherents among small property owners, London artisans, and the ranks of the New Model Army "wherein there is not one lord." Yet, while the Levellers proposed a new English constitution and demanded sweeping political reforms that would greatly broaden the electoral franchise, they still based these rights on property ownership, which they defined as men having "a permanent fixed interest in this kingdom," excluding wage laborers and servants. Women were also prominent in Leveller petition campaigns, but calls for female enfranchisement were extremely rare.

Smaller groups of radicals soon went even farther. The "Diggers," who called themselves the "True Levellers," denied the claim of Parliament to speak for Englishmen and opposed the private ownership of land. They espoused agrarian reform and began a brief colony that began to share wasteland with the poor and the landless. The "Ranters" rejected the idea of heaven, hell, and sin, and postulated that true salvation could be found only in drink and sex.

To some people in mid-seventeenth-century England, the world indeed seemed "turned upside down." Some radicals opposed not only hierarchical authority, but also paternal authority within the family. The assumption that the king ruled his nation as a husband and father directed his wife and children had been prominent in early modern political theory. Now some pamphlets denounced the subjugation of women to their husbands.

Parliament's Victory

Pressured by the Presbyterians, who feared the radicals of the New Model Army, Parliament ordered the disbandment of part of it without paying the soldiers. The army, however, refused to disband, and instead it set up a general council, some of whose members were drawn from the lower officer corps and even the rank and file, perhaps reflecting Leveller influence.

The New Model Army considered Parliament's attempts to disband it to be part of a plot against the Independents. A few regiments mutinied and prepared a political platform, the *Agreement of the People,* written by

London Levellers. This text anticipated later theorists by claiming that all "freeborn Englishmen," not just property owners, were the source of political authority and that "the poorest man in England is not at all bound in a strict sense to that government that he hath not had a voice to put himself under." Cromwell ruthlessly restored order in the New Model Army, subduing mutinous Leveller regiments and ordering several leaders shot.

In November 1647, King Charles escaped the custody of Parliament and fled to the Isle of Wight. Against the opposition of Presbyterians who hoped that some compromise could still be reached with the king, the House of Commons passed a motion that no further addresses should be made to King Charles. The implication was that Parliament alone should proceed to establish a new government without Charles's participation or consent, probably indicating that Cromwell and many other members of Parliament had already decided that Charles I should be put to death and a republic declared.

In May 1648, Presbyterian moderates joined Cavalier uprisings in southern Wales and southern England. Charles had been secretly negotiating with the Presbyterian Scots, hoping that they now would join an alliance of Anglicans and members of Parliament who had become disillusioned with Cromwell's radicalism. But the New Model Army turned back a Scottish invasion in August, and besieged royalist forces in Wales surrendered. The king was placed under guard on the Isle of Wight, "more a Prisoner," as an observer put it, "than ever . . . and could not goe to pisse without a guarde nor to Goffe [play golf]."

A detachment of the New Model Army, under Colonel Thomas Pride, then surrounded the Parliament house and refused to let Presbyterians—and some Independents as well—join the other members. "Pride's Purge," which took place without Cromwell's consent or knowledge, left a "Rump Parliament" of about a fifth of the members sitting.

The Rump Parliament, dominated by Independents, appointed a High Court to try the king on charges of high treason. Charles refused to defend himself and was found guilty. Charles I was executed at Whitehall on January 30, 1649, the first monarch to be tried and executed by his own subjects. Charles's beheading had immediate international repercussions; one power after another severed diplomatic relations with England.

The Puritan Republic and Restoration

The Rump Parliament abolished the monarchy and the House of Lords. It established a Puritan republic, the Commonwealth of England, with Cromwell as its leader. In 1649, Cromwell brutally put down the Irish uprising that had gone on for eight years. The Act of Settlement in 1652 expropriated the land of two-thirds of the Catholic property owners in Ireland, assuring the ascendancy of English Protestants in that strife-torn land for

Eyewitness depiction of Charles I's execution, January 30, 1649.

the next 300 years. The Scottish Protestants did not fare any better for having supported Charles, however belatedly, as Cromwell then conquered Scotland in 1650–1651. Having defeated both the Irish and the Scots, Cromwell then fought wars against the Dutch Republic from 1652 to 1654 and Spain from 1655 to 1659, with an eye toward reducing the power of both of these economic rivals.

The Rump Parliament met until 1653. It would not dissolve itself and so Cromwell, torn between his determination to assure a "godly reformation" in England and a mistrust of political assemblies, dissolved it in a military coup. The Long Parliament (if the Rump session is counted) had lasted since 1640. Cromwell now picked 140 men to serve as a new Parliament. This body came to be called the Barebones Parliament, named after one of its members, a certain "Praise-God Barbon," a leather merchant.

England became a military dictatorship. The army council dissolved the Barebones Parliament six months later and proclaimed a Protectorate under a new constitution, the Instrument of Government. Cromwell took the title "Lord Protector" and held almost unlimited power. The contention of the philosopher Thomas Hobbes (1588–1679), who had supported Charles I against Parliament, that the natural state of mankind is one of war, "everyone against everyone," seemed now to apply to England.

The Puritan republic turned out to be as oppressive as the monarchy of the Stuart kings. Cromwell imposed taxes without parliamentary approval and purged Parliament when it disagreed with him. When Parliament produced its own constitution, Cromwell sent its members packing in 1655.

But, like Charles I before him, he was obliged to recall Parliament the following year to vote money for war, this time against Spain.

Although Cromwell granted *de facto* religious freedom to all Puritan sects (including the Presbyterians, Independents, and Baptists), he continued to deny such freedom to Anglicans and Catholics. He did, however, allow Jews, who had not been allowed in England since 1290, to return in 1655. But Cromwell lost support as a result of financial impositions necessary to fight wars and supply an army of 50,000 men in England. The Lord Protector proved to be a better military administrator than a civilian one. Cromwell also alienated people through his exhortations that people behave in "godly" Puritan ways, as set forth in a code enforced by the army. Cromwell began to wear armor under his clothes and took circuitous routes in order to foil assassins who might be stalking him.

In the meantime, Cromwell claimed to be a humble caretaker of government who would keep order until godly righteousness prevailed. In 1657, a newly elected Parliament produced another constitution and offered Cromwell the throne of England. He refused, perhaps because he believed God had spoken to him against this and because a monarchy would alienate elements in the army. But he accepted the terms of the "Humble Petition and Advice," introducing a second house of Parliament (a nominated House of Lords) and a quasi-monarchical position for the Lord Protector, including the right to name his successor. Cromwell then dissolved Parliament because republicans in it were hostile to an evident monarchical direction. A year later, Cromwell died, succeeded by his considerably less able son, Richard (1626–1712), the New Protector. After Richard, several military successors stumbled on, backed by remnants of the New Model Army.

Increasingly, however, it seemed to the upper classes that only the restoration of the Stuart monarchy could restore order in England. Charles (1630–1685), heir to the throne of his executed father, lived in exile in The Netherlands. Armed force would still play a deciding role in this tumultuous time. General George Monck (1608–1670), a former royalist officer who now commanded the army in Scotland, had shrewdly kept Scottish tax money to pay his soldiers. His army became the only reliable force in England. After Parliament tried to assert control over the army, Monck marched with his forces on London and dissolved Parliament. New elections returned an alliance of royalists and Presbyterians, giving Parliament a moderate majority inclined to accept a restoration. When Charles issued a conciliatory proclamation, Parliament invited him to assume the throne of England. Eleven years after his father's execution, he crossed the English Channel in May 1660 and was crowned King Charles II on April 23, 1661.

Charles II, who disbanded the New Model Army, manifested considerable charm, energy, courage, unfailing good humor, and loyalty to those who had remained loyal to him (with the notable exception of the queen, to whom he was anything but faithful). He could also lash out vindictively when he believed himself betrayed. He earned the affection of most of his subjects

The coronation of King Charles II in 1661.

because the return of monarchy seemed to end the extended period of division and chaos. He used grand royal ceremonies to help restore faith in the monarchy, even attempting to cure sufferers of scrofula with the "royal touch" of his hand, as had his predecessors centuries earlier.

Although the English Civil War was a victory for parliamentary rule, in some ways the Restoration turned the clock back to before the conflict. The Church of England again became the Established Church. The crown refused to extend official toleration to other religions, and the Church of England expelled Presbyterian ministers. Once again the king, chronically short of money, depended on Parliament for funds.

The way now seemed clear for England to continue to expand its commerce and influence in a climate of social and political peace. Between 1660 and 1688, the tonnage hauled by English ships more than doubled, as the merchant fleet established regular trade routes to Newfoundland, Virginia, and the Caribbean. In 1664, a small English force seized the Dutch colony of New Amsterdam, which became New York City. Tobacco, calico, furs, sugar, chocolate, and rum brought from the New World changed habits of consumption. London became a booming port, and the East India Company emerged as a powerful force in shaping royal policy. Lloyd's of London began to insure vessels sailing to the New World in 1688. By then almost half of

England's ships were trading with India or America. Exports and imports increased by a third by 1700.

England's foreign policy entered a new, aggressive period in support of English manufacture and commerce. To undermine Dutch commercial competition, Parliament passed a series of Navigation Acts between 1651 and 1673, requiring that all goods brought to England be transported either in English ships or in those belonging to the country of their origin. This led to three wars with the Netherlands, in 1652–1654 (undertaken by Cromwell), 1665–1667, and 1672–1674.

THE GLORIOUS REVOLUTION

The highly charged issues of royal authority and Catholicism, which had sparked the English Civil War, led to another constitutional crisis and planted the seeds for the Glorious Revolution of 1688, when Parliament summoned a new king to rule England. Then the following year Parliament passed the Bill of Rights, which enshrined the rights of Parliament and the English people, and above all, men who owned property.

Stuart Religious Designs

After the return of the Stuarts to power, religion once again surfaced as a divisive issue in England, threatening to shatter the political unity seemingly achieved with the Restoration. Charles II had returned if not with strong Catholic sympathies at least with the conviction that he owed toleration to Catholics, some of whom had supported his father. Again, a Stuart king's seemingly provocative policies generated determined opposition from Parliament, which asserted its prerogatives.

Charles favored Catholics among his ministers and seemed to be trying to appeal to Dissenters in order to build a coalition against the Church of England. In response, Parliament passed a series of laws against Dissenters (1661–1665), known as the Clarendon Code. The Act of Corporation (1661) required all holders of office in incorporated municipalities to receive communion in the Anglican Church. The Act of Uniformity (1662) stated that all ministers had to use the Anglican Book of Common Prayer. Nonconformists had to take an oath that they would not try to alter the established order of church and state in England. Hundreds of Quakers, members of a pacifist group formed in 1649, refused to pay tithes or take oaths and were incarcerated, left to die in prison.

In 1670, Charles II signed a secret treaty of alliance with Louis XIV of France. He promised the king of France that he would declare himself a Catholic when the political circumstances in England were favorable. In return, he received subsidies from the French monarch. Charles ended restrictions on religious worship and laws that had been directed at

Catholics and Dissident Protestant groups. The hostile reaction to his decision, however, forced the king to reinstate the restrictive measures. In 1673, Parliament passed the Test Act, which largely superseded the Clarendon Code and excluded non-Anglicans from military and civil office.

Many people in England suspected that there were plots afoot to restore Catholicism as the state religion. Although Charles II's agreement with Louis XIV remained secret, in 1678 a strange man named Titus Oates loudly claimed the existence of a plot by the Catholic Church against England. Oates claimed that the Jesuits were preparing to assassinate the king and slaughter all English Protestants. They then would proclaim James, Charles's devout Catholic brother, king. (James was heir to the throne since Charles had no legitimate children, although he had a good many who were not.) Oates had made it all up, as the king knew perfectly well. But the monarch could not speak up because of his own secret promise to Louis XIV of France to restore Catholicism to England.

In the 1670s, two factions had emerged in Parliament that in some ways echoed the split between "Court" and "Country" before the Civil War. Members of Parliament who supported the full prerogatives of the monarchy, some of them trumpeting the theories of divine-right monarchy, became known as Tories, corresponding to the old "Court" faction. Those members of Parliament who espoused parliamentary supremacy and religious toleration became known as Whigs (corresponding to "Country"). Whig leaders orchestrated a plan to exclude James from the royal succession because of his Catholicism. During the ensuing Exclusion Crisis (1678–1681), the Tories defended James as the legitimate heir to the throne of England. When in 1679 some members of Parliament tried to make Charles's illegitimate son heir to the throne, Charles dissolved Parliament. In three subsequent parliamentary elections, Whigs profited from the mood of anti-Catholicism to take a majority of seats.

Parliament's passage in 1679 of the Habeas Corpus Act reflected Whig ascendancy. This act forced the government to provide a quick trial for those arrested. By establishing the legal rights of individuals accused of crimes, it further limited monarchical authority. The Habeas Corpus Act was thus part of the century-long struggle of the House of Commons for the maintenance of its constitutional role in England's governance.

In 1681, Charles II attempted, like his father before him, to rule without Parliament. Two years later, a number of Whigs were charged with plotting to kill both the king and his brother, and the king had them executed. On his deathbed two years later, Charles proclaimed his Catholicism.

Thus, in 1685, Charles II's brother assumed the throne as James II (1633–1701). In Scotland and in western England, royal armies crushed the small insurrections that rose up in favor of Charles's illegitimate son (who was executed). Naive as he was devout, James forgot the lessons of recent history and began to dismiss advisers who were not Catholics.

The prince regent riding a horse along a street strewn with the heads of members of the opposition placed on large stones.

In 1687, James made Catholics eligible for office. The Dissenters also benefited from toleration, because the new king needed them as allies. The king did not denounce Louis XIV's revocation of the Edict of Nantes in 1685, which ended toleration for Huguenots (French Protestants, see Chapter 7). This made English Protestants even more anxious. When it became apparent that the queen was pregnant, James boldly predicted the birth of a son and Catholic heir to the throne. For the enemies of the king, the timing of the birth of a son and the fact that the only witnesses were Catholics inevitably sparked rumors that the newborn was not really the king's son but a surrogate baby.

Royal prerogative thus remained the central constitutional issue. James may have entertained visions of implanting monarchical absolutism, a tide that approached from the continent. Certainly he sought to restore Catholicism as the state religion. In April 1688, he issued a declaration of toleration and ordered the Anglican clergy to read it from the pulpit. When seven bishops protested, James put them in prison. However, when the bishops were tried in court, a jury declared them not guilty.

The "Protestant Wind"

One of James's Protestant daughters by a previous marriage, Mary (1662–1694), had married the Protestant Dutchman William of Orange (1650–1702), the stadholder (chief official) of the Netherlands. A group of Tories and Whigs, the "immortal seven"—six nobles and a bishop—invited William to restore Protestantism and, from their point of view, the English constitution. William, eager that England assist the Dutch in resisting Louis XIV's aggressive designs, prepared to invade England from the Netherlands. His followers flooded England with propaganda on behalf of his cause.

The context of European international politics seemed favorable to William. Louis XIV's revocation of the Edict of Nantes had outraged the Dutch, who worried that James's successful restoration of Catholicism in England might make the Dutch Republic more vulnerable to Catholic France. They believed that England was an indispensable partner in helping resist Louis XIV's grand ambitions. A friendly Protestant monarch on the throne of England might even reduce tensions stemming from the trade rivalry between the Dutch Republic and England.

The Catholic continental monarchs would not aid James II. Louis XIV's principal interest remained continental territorial expansion. Despite declaring war on the Dutch Republic, Louis limited his attacks to verbal bluster and the seizure of several Dutch ships in French ports. Emperor Leopold of Austria, another powerful Catholic monarch, was tied up fighting the Turks in the east.

James did little to prepare military defenses except to appoint Catholic officers in his new regiments and to bring more troops from Ireland. He relied on his navy to protect his throne. Hoping for a last-minute compromise, he promised to summon a "free" Parliament. But it was too late.

In a declaration promulgated early in October 1688, William accused James of arbitrary acts against the nation, Parliament, and the Church of England. Aided by a munificent wind—later dubbed the "Protestant wind"—that blew his ships to the southwestern coast of England but pinned James's loyal fleet farther away in the Channel or kept them in port, William landed at Torbay on the English Channel with a force of 15,000 men on November 5,

William III of England and Queen Mary, joint rulers of England.

1688. William marched cautiously to London, encouraged by defections from James's cause. Uprisings on William's behalf in several northern towns further isolated the king. James was in a state of virtual physical and psychological collapse. At the end of November, he promised to summon Parliament and allow William's supporters to sit. But riots broke out against his rule and against Catholics. In December, James left England for exile in France. Parliament, victorious again, declared the throne vacant by abdication and invited William and Mary to occupy a double throne.

The Bill of Rights

This "Glorious Revolution" of 1688, less dramatic than the English Civil War, was arguably of more lasting importance in the constitutional evolution of England. Parliament passed a Bill of Rights in 1689 that ratified the Revolution of 1688, ending decades of constitutional battles. Accepted by William and Mary, it became a milestone in English history. It was passed at a time when the rights and influence of representative bodies lay in shambles throughout much of the continent as absolute monarchs consolidated their power (see Chapter 7). The Bill of Rights reaffirmed the rights of Parliament and guaranteed the rights of property owners to self-government and of the accused to the rule of law. In particular, it reasserted Parliament's financial authority over government by enumerating what a monarch should not do and by reducing royal control over the army. The Toleration Act (1689) stipulated that Protestant Dissenters could hold public services in licensed meeting houses and could maintain preachers. Anglicanism, however, remained the Established Church of England, and only Anglicans could hold office. Catholics could not occupy the throne and, like Dissenters, they were excluded from government positions.

The Glorious Revolution pleased the English philosopher John Locke (1632–1704), friend of some of the wealthy landowners who sent James II into exile. Locke was specific about the ways in which the power of monarchs ought to be limited. "The end of government," he wrote, should be "the good of mankind." Locke argued that the rights of individuals and, above all, the ownership of property found protection when Parliament's rights limited monarchical prerogatives. Knowing of the bloody chaos of the Thirty Years' War (1618–1648) on the continent, Locke also advocated religious toleration and espoused the right of subjects to rise up against tyranny, as the English supporters of Parliament had against Charles I.

The Glorious Revolution reaffirmed the political domination of the gentry, whose interests Parliament represented above all. English monarchs named nobles to hereditary seats in the House of Lords, but wealthy landowners elected members to the House of Commons. The gentry's economic and social position was more secure than during the inflationary years of the first half of the century. Order and social hierarchy reigned, and the fear of popular disorder ebbed. Benefiting from the consensus of 1688, the elite of wealthy landowners, increasingly more open to newcomers than their continental counterparts, would continue to shape British political life in the eighteenth century. The English Civil War and the Glorious Revolution affirmed the principle of representation not only in England, but also in the North American colonies, an important legacy for the future.

THE GOLDEN AGE OF THE DUTCH REPUBLIC

The Dutch Republic of the United Provinces (usually known today as the Netherlands, or sometimes simply—and erroneously—as Holland, its most populated and prosperous province) was the other European power (besides

MAP 6.2 THE NETHERLANDS, 1648   At the conclusion of the Thirty Years' War, the Dutch war of independence also ended, with the northern United Provinces becoming the Dutch Republic and the southern provinces remaining under Spain as the Spanish Netherlands.

Poland) that defied the pattern of absolute and increasingly centralized rule that characterized seventeenth-century Europe. Spain ruled the Netherlands from 1516, when Holy Roman Emperor Charles V, who had inherited the territories of the dukes of Burgundy, became king of Spain. After a long, intermittent war that had begun in 1566 against Spanish rule (Chapter 5), the Dutch Republic officially became independent in 1648 (see Map 6.2 and pp. 98–202). The United Provinces, a confederation of republics, had been federalist in structure since the Union of Utrecht in 1579, when the provinces and cities of the Dutch Netherlands came together to form a defensive alliance against the advancing Spanish army. The Dutch Republic, from which William of Orange had launched his successful invasion of England in 1688, resisted the aspirations of the House of Orange for a centralized government dominated by a hereditary monarchy. Like their English counterparts, most people in the Netherlands did not want absolute rule, which they identified with the arbitrary acts of the Catholic Spanish monarchy.

The Structure of the Dutch State

The States General served as a federal legislative body of delegations from each of the seven provinces of the Dutch Republic. Each of the provinces held to traditions of autonomy, provincial sovereignty, and, since the Reformation, religious pluralism. Nobles received automatic representation in the States General. But their economic and political role in the Republic was relatively weak, except in the overwhelmingly agricultural eastern provinces.

The Dutch Republic was in some ways less a republic than an oligarchy of wealthy families who monopolized political power. No republican ideology existed until at least the second half of the seventeenth century. But Dutch citizens enjoyed some basic rights unavailable in most other states at the time. Provincial courts protected the Dutch against occasional arbitrary acts of both the central government and town governments. Solid fiscal institutions generated international confidence, permitting the Republic to raise sizable loans as needed.

The princes of the House of Orange served as *stadholder* of the Republic. A stadholder was at first appointed, and served as a political broker. He had influence, but not authority. He was not a ruler, and could not declare war, legislate, or even participate in the important decisions of the Republic. Many of the Orangist stadholders chafed under the restrictions on their authority, although they dominated some high federal appointments and named the sons of nobles to important positions in the army and navy. The Orangist stadholders dreamed of establishing a powerful hereditary monarchy. In 1650, William II (1626–1650), stadholder of five of the seven provinces, arrested six leaders of Holland and sent an army to besiege Amsterdam. A compromise reinforced the stadholders' power. But with William's sudden death several months later, the balance of power swung back to the regents (wealthy merchants and bankers) of the provinces. Any possibility of the Netherlands becoming an absolute state ended.

Expanding Economy

The Dutch economy developed more rapidly during the first two-thirds of the seventeenth century than did the economies of its competitors, England and France. The increased affluence brought by foreign trade helped the Dutch carry on the war against Spain. In 1609, following the signing of a truce with Spain, the Amsterdam Public Bank opened its offices in the town hall. The bank's principal function was to facilitate Amsterdam's burgeoning foreign trade by encouraging merchants to make payments in bills drawn on the bank. Foreign merchants were attracted to Amsterdam, particularly after mid-century, when bills of exchange became acceptable as currency.

Amsterdam's banking, credit, and warehousing facilities were soon unmatched in Europe. Although an ordinance in 1581 had included bankers among those occupations considered disreputable—along with actors, jugglers, and brothel keepers—and therefore excluded them from receiving communion in the Dutch Reformed Church, bankers came to be respected by the beginning of the seventeenth century. Good credit allowed the United Provinces to raise loans by selling negotiable bonds at low interest rates.

The Amsterdam Bourse in the seventeenth century. Merchants had fixed places at the Stock Exchange where they met to arrange various financial matters.

Canals and rivers expedited internal trade in the Dutch Republic. These boats along the Spaarne at Haarlem carried goods to the port, where they were loaded for distant trade.

The Dutch Republic, small in territory and population, expanded its agricultural resources during the first half of the seventeenth century. Workers and horses reclaimed much of the country's most fertile land from the sea. Increased productivity generated an agricultural surplus that was invested in commerce or manufacturing; an increased food supply sustained a larger population. Commercial livestock raising and capital-intensive farming became lucrative.

The Dutch Republic's population rose by a third between 1550 and 1650, to almost 2 million people, which made it Europe's most densely populated country after several of the Italian states. More than half of the population lived in towns. As Amsterdam became a major international port of trade and London's primary rival, its population rose from about 50,000 in 1600 to about 200,000 by 1670.

Early in the seventeenth century, construction of three large canals expanded Amsterdam's area by almost four times. These canals permitted boats to dock outside merchants' warehouses, where they were loaded with goods, which they then carried to the large ships of the port. Handsome townhouses reached skyward above new tree-lined streets along the canals. Built for bankers and merchants, the townhouses had narrow and increasingly ornamented facades, dauntingly steep staircases, and drains and sewers. The city spread out from the port along the semi-radial canals. The Dutch Republic benefited not only from relatively good roads, which expedited internal trade, but also from 500 miles of canals dug during the middle decades of the century.

Dutch traders steadily expanded their range and the variety of goods they bartered. They specialized in bulk goods carried by specially designed long, flat vessels that could be cheaply built and operated. The Dutch Republic's merchant fleet tripled during the first half of the century. Dutch shipbuilding boomed, aided by wind-powered sawmills. The Dutch Republic's 2,500 ships in the 1630s accounted for about half of Europe's shipping. Amsterdam became the principal supplier of grain and fish in Europe as the Dutch dominated the lucrative Baltic trade. Dutch ships hauled most of the iron produced in Sweden, and carried wheat and rye from Poland and East Prussia, dropping off what was needed for local consumption and then carrying what was left to France, Spain, and the Mediterranean. Capital investment and shrewd knowledge of markets made the herring trade a crucial part of Dutch prosperity. Dutch fishing boats were omnipresent in the rich North Sea fishing grounds. In 500 ships solid enough to stand up to the storms of the North Sea, Dutch fishermen worked in waters as far away as northern Scotland, the Shetland Islands, and Iceland. As many as 200 million herring a year were salted and packed in wooden casks, then exchanged for grain, salt, wine, and other commodities.

In 1602, a group of investors founded a private trading company, the Dutch East India Company, to which the government of the Dutch Republic granted a monopoly for trade in East Asia. When the Thirty Years' War and a Spanish embargo on Dutch commerce reduced continental trade, Dutch traders successfully developed trade overseas with India, Ceylon, Indonesia, and Japan. The Dutch East India Company proved to be stiff competition for the English company of the same name.

Tolerance and Prosperity

In contrast to England, where religious division led to civil war, the Dutch Republic remained a relative haven of toleration in an era of religious hatred. During the last decades of the sixteenth century, perhaps 60,000 Huguenots fled to the Dutch Republic to escape persecution in France and the Spanish Netherlands. Published works circulated throughout the Netherlands defending the rights of religious dissidents, including Mennonites, Lutherans, Quakers fleeing England, and Dutch Collegiants (a dissident Protestant group). Amsterdam's Jewish community numbered 7,500. Most were immigrants from the German states, and they spoke Yiddish among themselves, as well as German and Dutch; others had originally left persecution in Spain and Portugal. The municipal government rejected a request by Christian merchants that their Jewish competitors be restricted, as in many European cities, to a specific neighborhood, or ghetto. The

Amsterdam regents built 1,000 dwellings for refugees. Refugees from religious persecution in other countries contributed to the prosperity of the Dutch Republic.

Nonetheless, despite the religious toleration generally accorded in the Dutch Republic, the Dutch Reformed Church, a strict Calvinist religion, did persecute and discriminate against some religious groups. Dutch Arminians asked for protection from persecution in a Remonstrance (which gave them their most common name, the Remonstrants). Catholics, most of whom lived in the eastern provinces, also faced Calvinist hostility, although many had fought for Dutch independence. Jews were excluded from most guilds, and gypsies were routinely hounded and persecuted. Overall, however, toleration seemed less divisive to the Dutch than intolerance, and it seemed to make economic sense as well.

The Dutch Republic blossomed like the famous tulips that were so popular in Holland (the craze over this flower, originally imported from Turkey, reached such a fever pitch that a single tulip bulb could cost as much as the equivalent of three years' wages for a master artisan). To the eyes of a French visitor, Amsterdam was "swollen with people, chock-full of goods, and filled with gold and silver." The Dutch in the middle decades of the seventeenth century reached a level of prosperity unmatched in Europe at the time. Real wages rose during the last half of the seventeenth century while falling elsewhere. Dutch families enjoyed a relatively varied diet, consuming more meat and cheese—as well as, of course, fish—than households elsewhere in Europe. Amsterdam's market offered a plethora of colonial goods, such as coffee, tea, cocoa, ginger, and other spices; dried and pickled herring and other fish; a wide range of grains; finished cloth from Antwerp and Florence; Silesian linens; and English woolens. Dutch manufacturers, with windmills providing power, found lucrative outlets for draperies, worsteds, papers, books, and jewels. Even at the beginning of the century, Amsterdam had almost 200 breweries and more than 500 taverns.

Although prosperity reached far down the social ladder, the Dutch Republic also had its poor, who lived in the narrow streets around the Bourse (Stock Exchange), in poor farmhouses in the eastern flatlands, and in the huts of ethnic Frisian fishermen exposed to the onslaught of the waves and wind of the North Sea. The urban poor occasionally rioted and sometimes stole in order to survive. The proliferation of charitable institutions demonstrated Dutch compassion but also the desire to confine vagrants and beggars, as well as a capacity to lash out in brutal repression when patience with the poor grew thin. Beatings, floggings, branding, and even death remained common forms of punishment, and gallows stood at the main gates of large cities.

Yet despite prosperity, a sense of precariousness and vulnerability permeated the Republic. The armies of the ambitious king of France camped across the low-lying Southern Netherlands (now Belgium). The Republic had almost no natural resources and was subject to sudden calamities

Dike breach at Caevarden. Because so much land had been reclaimed from the sea, many of the Dutch lived in chronic fear of flooding.

brought by weather. A good part of the Dutch Netherlands would have been under water were it not for the famous dikes. These occasionally broke with catastrophic consequences long remembered (a flood in 1421 had claimed over 100,000 lives). A sense that disaster might be looming was reflected by the popularity in the Republic of novels and histories about disasters. This may explain the sense of solidarity and patriotic duty that brought people of various classes together against Spanish rule.

Seventeenth-Century Dutch Culture

Dutch painting in the golden age of the seventeenth century reflected not only the Republic's commercial wealth, but also its toleration and openness to secular styles and subject matter. The Dutch press enjoyed relative freedom; books were printed in the Republic that could not have been printed elsewhere. The first English and French newspapers were published in 1620, not in London and Paris, but in Amsterdam. Dutch publishers diffused knowledge of the Scientific Revolution (see Chapter 8). Dutch writers and poets discovered their own language, translated Latin authors, and popularized Dutch accounts of the revolt against Spain.

Dutch painting reflected the prosperity and taste of the middle class. Like the artists of the Renaissance, Dutch painters depended on the patronage of people of means, particularly wealthy Amsterdam merchants. Although Delft and several other towns each claimed their own style, the great port of Amsterdam dominated the art market. Some shopkeepers and craftsmen were prosperous enough to buy a painting or two, and some well-off peasants did as well.

Holland's regents, in particular, patronized Dutch painting. In contrast, the princes of Orange and some nobles patronized French and other foreign artists whose work reflected baroque themes associated with the Catholic Reformation found in the Southern Netherlands. Flanders became a northern outpost of the Catholic Reformation, encouraging religious themes with emotional appeal. In the Dutch Republic, by contrast, ecclesiastical artistic patronage was generally absent. Indeed, the Dutch Reformed Church ordered the removal of paintings from its churches.

Dutch painters looked to picturesque urban and rural scenes within their own country for inspiration. The Dutch school retained much of its cultural unity at least through the first half of the seventeenth century. Until 1650, the Republic remained relatively isolated from outside cultural influences, despite the arrival of refugees and immigrants. Very few Dutch artists and writers had the resources to travel as far as Italy or even France; even those who earned a comfortable living showed little inclination to go abroad. The group paintings of merchants or regents and municipal governments were usually commissioned by the subjects themselves, as in the case of Rembrandt van Rijn's *The Night Watch* (1642), a theatrically staged masterpiece presenting a group of city officials in uniform.

Rembrandt (1606–1669) was the son of a miller from Leiden. He was one of a handful of Dutch painters who amassed a fortune. Certainly, few artists have so successfully portrayed human emotions through the use of color, light, and shadow. Despite his posthumous fame, in his own time the brooding Rembrandt was a loner isolated from other painters. He bickered with his patrons and squandered most of what he made. Rembrandt increasingly became his own favorite subject, and he did at least eighty self-portraits, some of which reveal a thinly disguised sadness.

Dutch painters depicted everyday life. The prolific Jacob van Ruisdael (c. 1628–1682) mastered the visual effects of light on figures, trees, and household objects. The remarkable ability of Delft-born Jan Vermeer (1632–1675) to place simple scenes of ordinary people in astonishing light exemplifies the Golden Age of Dutch painting. Within the Dutch school of the seventeenth century, only Rembrandt frequently turned to the classical biblical themes that were so predominant in Flemish art. Although seascapes and naval scenes proliferated in Dutch painting, there were few canvases depicting battles, a favorite subject in absolute states, and those took their place on the large walls of noble châteaux in the distant countryside, not in the narrow houses of Amsterdam.

The Dutch considered the household a place of refuge and safety from the struggles of the outside world, as well as the basis of economic, social, and political order, and therefore worthy of artistic representation. Frans Hals (1580–1666) brought middle-class subjects and militia companies to life in remarkably composed individual and collective portraits. Paintings of fami-

A peasant family pausing to pray before mealtime.

lies at work, at play, or eating were particularly popular. Jan Steen (1626–1679) portrayed boisterous revelers of different means. Still lifes of platters of food became staples for Dutch artists, with titles such as *Still Life with Herring* and *Jug Still Life with Lobster*. The banquet became a favorite subject, with all of its accoutrements, such as oak table and chairs, iron cooking pans, elegant plates and drinking vessels, and its rituals, such as the prayer, the careful carving of the meat, and rounds of toasts.

The relationship between parents and children emerged as another familiar domestic theme. The Dutch painters also frequently portrayed servants, furniture and other household goods, and domestic pets. However, women on Dutch canvases appear more equal to men than they were in reality.

THE DECLINE OF THE DUTCH REPUBLIC

The relative decline of Dutch power is perhaps not surprising, given the greater economic resources and populations of France and England. England emerged in the second half of the century as the world's dominant commercial power, although the decline of Dutch trade was not complete until early in the eighteenth century.

The Dutch Republic tried to steer a course between England (its greatest commercial rival) and France, but this proved impossible. Wars against England in defense of Dutch commercial interests drained resources. Furthermore, Louis XIV of France had designs on the Netherlands. In 1667, France imposed damaging tariffs on Dutch goods and also forced the Dutch out of the cinnamon-producing island of Ceylon (now Sri Lanka) in the Indian Ocean. In Brazil, the Dutch West India Company failed to dislodge the Portuguese. Few Dutch demonstrated much enthusiasm for these distant places, and the Republic's colonial empire lagged behind those of England and Spain, to be sure, but also behind that of France.

With Spain weakened, Louis XIV coveted the Southern Netherlands, the conquest of which would place the Dutch in direct danger. Should France be able to open the Scheldt River (closed by the Spanish in 1585 with the goal of breaking the Dutch rebellion) to international trade, Antwerp's return to its former prosperity would be at Amsterdam's expense. In 1672, Louis XIV invaded the Dutch Republic, having signed a secret treaty with King Charles II of England (see Chapter 7). French armies quickly occupied all of the Republic except for two provinces, one of which was Holland. But the Dutch successfully defended the Republic, defeating the English fleet and pushing back the French army.

Taking advantage of the invasion, William of Orange (King William III of England in 1688) forced the States General to name him stadholder in 1672. He ordered the dikes opened, literally flooding the French into retreat. Royalist mobs murdered the leading official of the Republic and several influential regents of Holland who had dedicated themselves to keeping the stadholders in place. Supporters of the House of Orange eased into important political positions in that province. The Orangists controlled the Republic's foreign policy until the end of the century, but they still could not impose a monarchy on the provinces. With William's death in 1702, the main Orange dynastic line ended.

After the Glorious Revolution in England in 1688, the United Provinces allied with England and Sweden, fearing that Louis XIV of France might again invade. The alliance helped stave off the French threat in the last decades of the century, but at the same time it dragged the small country into a series of wars with France that lasted until the mid-eighteenth century, necessitating considerable spending on armies and southern fortifications.

The relative decline of Dutch influence in Europe could be first seen by about 1670 or 1680. Some luxury products, such as linen and Delft porcelain, continued to sell abroad, but Holland's textile industry and shipbuilding failed to keep pace with those of its rivals, above all England. Higher production costs (particularly wages) and a lack of technological innovation were at least partially to blame. Rivals imposed tariffs, which kept out many Dutch products. Dutch ships lost control of the Baltic trade. The Dutch faced competition in the herring market from England, France, and Sweden. The protectionist policies of Britain and Sweden protected their own fishermen while cutting off their domestic markets to Dutch herring. English warships destroyed Dutch ships in the wars fought between the two rivals. Furthermore, some Dutch entrepreneurs lent money abroad or invested in the colonies, land, government stocks, and even in English manufacturing, not in Dutch businesses. Investment in agriculture and land reclamation fell off.

Spain's golden age of art coincided with its decline as a great power. In contrast, Dutch painting languished with the nation's decline. Painters began looking abroad for inspiration and, in doing so, lost some originality. In the 1650s, the Amsterdam regents ignored the Dutch school when planning the construction and decoration of the new town hall, which combines Italian classicism and the Flemish baroque flamboyance. Some Dutch leaders now took pride in speaking French, believing it the language of good taste. French classicism overwhelmed Dutch literature and poetry. Although the French military invasion of 1672 failed, a cultural invasion succeeded. Dutch artists began to offer pale imitations of French works. There were fewer paintings of attentive and hardworking municipal and provincial officials.

The originality of Dutch political life also waned with relative economic decline. The great merchant families maintained increasingly tight control over the position of regent and other influential posts. A form of municipal corruption ("contracts of correspondence") allowed them to divide up or even purchase lucrative government positions. More regents were now major landowners and had little in common with merchants, who had vital interests in government policies.

Government became more rigid, more distant from the Dutch people, and less tolerant, persecuting religious dissenters and undertaking a witch hunt against homosexuals. The Dutch army became increasingly one of mercenaries, not citizens. The Dutch Republic's loss of vitality and economic primacy was accompanied by its decline in international affairs.

CONCLUSION

At the dawn of the eighteenth century, England and the Netherlands remained non-absolutist states. The victory of Parliament in the English Civil War, the Glorious Revolution of 1688, and the Bill of Rights of 1689, accepted by the monarchy, guaranteed the rights of Parliament and the rule of law. While the Netherlands entered a period of decline, as had Spain, Great Britain (as England became known in 1707 after the formal union with Scotland) would remain a great power in the eighteenth century, enriched by commerce and empire. In the meantime, the kings of Spain and the rulers of France, Prussia, Austria, Russia, and Sweden increased their authority over their subjects as continental Europe entered the age of absolutism.

CHAPTER 7

THE AGE OF ABSOLUTISM, 1650–1720

〜

In Louis XIV's France, architects and artists were paid to glorify the monarch. In 1662, the king chose the sun as his emblem; he declared himself *nec pluribus impar*—without equal. To Louis, the sun embodied virtues that he associated with the ideal monarch: firmness, benevolence, and equity. Henceforth, Louis XIV would frequently be depicted as Apollo, the Greek and Roman sun god.

The rulers of continental Europe, including Louis XIV (ruled 1643–1715), relentlessly extended their power between 1650 and 1750. The sovereigns of France, Prussia, Russia, Austria, and Sweden, in particular, became absolute rulers, in principle above all challenge from within the state itself. To the east, the power of the Turkish sultan of the Ottoman Empire was itself already in principle absolute. Rulers extended their dynastic domains and prestige, making their personal rule absolute, based on loyalty to them as individuals, not to the state as an abstraction. But at the same time, they helped lay the foundations for the modern centralized state. Absolute rulers asserted their supreme right to proclaim laws and levy taxes, appointing more officials to carry out the details of governance and multiplying fiscal demands on their subjects. They ended most of the long-standing privileges of towns, which had survived longer in Western Europe than in Eastern Europe, such as freedom from taxation, or the right to maintain independent courts.

The absolute state affected the lives of more people than ever before through taxation, military service, and the royal quest for religious orthodoxy. Absolute rule thus impinged directly on the lives of subjects, who felt the extended reach of state power through, for example, more efficient tax collection. A Prussian recalled that in school no child would question "that the king could cut off the noses and ears of all his subjects if he wished to do so, and that we owed it to his goodness and his gentle disposition that he had left us in possession of these necessary organs."

Absolutism was at least in part an attempt to reassert public order and coercive state authority after almost seventy years of wars that had brought economic, social, and political chaos. England and Spain had been at war in the last decades of the sixteenth century. Wars of religion had raged through much of Europe on and off for more than a century—above all, during the Thirty Years' War (1618–1648). The Dutch war of independence against Spain began in 1566 and did not officially end until 1648. The tumultuous decade of the 1640s was particularly marked by political crises. Wars had led to often dramatic increases in taxes, which quadrupled in Spain under Philip II, and jumped fivefold in France between 1609 and 1648. During the 1640s, the English Civil War led to the execution of King Charles I in 1649 (see Chapter 6). In France, the period of mid-century rebellion known as the Fronde included a noble uprising against the crown and determined, violent peasant resistance against increased taxation. The multiplicity and seemingly interrelated character of these crises engendered great anxiety among social elites: "These are days of shaking, and this shaking is universal," a preacher warned the English Parliament.

THEORIES OF ABSOLUTISM

The doctrine of absolutism originated with French jurists late in the sixteenth century. The emergence of theories of absolutism reflected contemporary attempts to conceptualize the significance of the rise of larger territorial states whose rulers enjoyed more power than their predecessors. France was a prime example of this trend. The legal theorist Jean Bodin (1530–1596) had lived through the wars of religion. "Seeing that nothing upon earth is greater or higher, next unto God, than the majesty of kings and sovereign princes," he wrote in the *Six Books of the Republic* (1576), the "principal point of sovereign majesty and absolute power [is] to consist principally in giving laws unto the subjects in general, without their consent." The ruler became the father, a stern but supposedly benevolent figure. Bodin, who like many other people in France longed for peace and order, helped establish the political theory legitimizing French absolute rule.

Almost a century later, the political philosopher Thomas Hobbes (1588–1679) emerged as the thundering theorist of absolutism. Hobbes had experienced the turmoil of the English Civil War (see Chapter 6). In *Leviathan* (1651), he argued that absolutism alone could prevent society from lapsing into the "state of nature," a constant "war of every man against every man" that made life "solitary, poor, nasty, brutish, and short." People would only obey, Hobbes insisted, when they were afraid of the consequences of not doing so. Seeking individual security, individuals would enter into a type of social contract with their ruler, surrendering their rights in exchange for

Non est potestas Super Terram quæ Comparetur ei Iob. 41. 24.

The illustration for the cover of the Englishman Thomas Hobbes's *Leviathan* (1651) depicts the absolute state. Note how the ruler's body is made up of the masses over whom he rules. England and then Great Britain, however, remained an exception to the absolutist wave that swept across continental Europe.

protection. A ruler's will thus became for Hobbes the almost sacred embodiment of the state. In France, Jacques Bossuet (1627–1704), bishop and tutor to Louis XIV, postulated that kings ruled by "divine right," that is, by virtue of the will of God. Unlike Hobbes's notion of authority based on a social contract, Bossuet held that the ruler's authority stemmed from God alone.

Yet theorists of absolutism recognized the difference between absolute and arbitrary or despotic rule. Inherent in their theories was the idea that the absolute ruler was responsible for looking after the needs of his people. Bossuet summed up: "It is one thing for a government to be absolute, and quite another for it to be arbitrary. It is absolute in that it is not liable to constraint, there being no other power capable of coercing the sovereign, who is in this sense independent of all human authority." But he went on, "it does not follow from this that the government is arbitrary, for besides the fact that all is subject to the judgment of God . . . there are also laws, in states, so that whatever is done contrary to them is null in a legal sense; moreover, there is always an opportunity for redress, either at other times or in other conditions." Thus, even according to one of the most determined proponents of absolutism, the monarch, whose legitimacy came from God, nonetheless was subject to limits imposed by reason through laws and traditions. Western monarchs recognized, at least in theory, the necessity of consulting with institutions considered to be representative of interests such as the Church and nobility: parlements (noble law courts), Estates, the Cortes in Spain, and Parliament, which had been victorious in the English Civil War in non-absolutist England, where the law remained separated from the will of the monarch.

CHARACTERIZING ABSOLUTE RULE

Absolute states were characterized by strong, ambitious dynasties, which through advantageous marriages, inheritance, warfare, and treaties added to their dynastic domains and prestige. Their states had nobilities that accepted monarchical authority in exchange for a guarantee of their status, ownership of land, and privileges within the state and over the peasantry, whether peasants were legally free, as in Western Europe, or serfs, as in Prussia, Austria, Poland, and Russia. The absolute states of Central and Eastern Europe—Prussia, Austria, and Russia—shared similar social structures: a strong nobility with ties to rulers who granted privileges in exchange for cooperation; a subservient peasantry in the process of losing remaining rights to rulers and landlords, including—by becoming serfs attached to the land they worked—that of personal freedom; and a relatively weak and politically powerless middle class. Unlike England and the Dutch United Provinces, these states had no representative institutions and few towns of sufficient importance to stand in the way of absolute rule.

The Commonwealth of Poland-Lithuania was an exception and thus did not fit the Russian or Prussian model. In 1386 the Kingdom of Poland and the Grand Duchy of Lithuania had been joined in a personal union (Warsaw became the capital in 1595). The Commonwealth of Poland-Lithuania was created in 1569 by virtue of the Union of Lublin. In the Commonwealth, the authority of the king was limited by the strength of the landed nobility—the *szlachta*, who dominated the Parliament (the Sejm). Particularly in northern Poland around the port city of Gdańsk, a concept of sovereignty emerged that paralleled similar important transformations in England and the Netherlands. The Commonwealth of Poland-Lithuania is thus sometimes referred to as a "gentry democracy." Here the parliamentary system, which had been founded in the fifteenth century, protected the personal freedom of the citizens of the monarchy.

Although some Western sovereigns were somewhat limited by representative bodies—diets, parlements, Estates—absolute monarchies nonetheless created an unprecedented concentration of governing power. Between 1614 and 1788, no king of France convoked the Estates-General, an assembly of representatives from the three estates—clergy, nobility, and commoners—that had been created early in the fourteenth century as an advisory council to the king. To take another example, the Portuguese assembly of nobles did not meet at all during the eighteenth century.

Monarchs and Nobles

In each absolute state, the relationship between ruler and nobles determined the specific character of absolutism. This delicate balance is reflected in the oath of loyalty sworn to the king of Spain by the Aragonese nobility: "We who are as good as you swear to you who are no better than we to accept you as our king and sovereign lord, provided you observe all our liberties and laws; but if not, not." Monarchs negotiated compromises with nobles, awarding titles and confirming privileges for obedience, or at least compliance. In some cases, nobles asserted independence vis-à-vis royal authority. But emphatic assertions of royal authority reduced nobles to the role of junior ruling partners in governance, dominating state and local government. Nobles frightened by the social and political turmoil that shook Europe during the first half of the century now more willingly served rulers as royal officials and military commanders.

"Tables of ranks" dividing nobles into distinct grades or ranks were established at the turn of the century by the kings of Sweden, Denmark, Prussia, and Russia, making it clear that noble privileges were bestowed by monarchs. Louis XIV of France asserted the right to monitor the legitimacy of all titles and even to confiscate noble estates. In 1668, he ordered the investigation of "false" nobles holding dubious titles. These measures helped the king maintain the loyalty of nobles, some of whom resented those who held titles they considered suspect. The great noble families thereafter enjoyed an even greater monopoly over the most lucrative and prestigious royal and ecclesiastical posts. Using the augmented power of the state, rulers also placated nobles by ending a turbulent period of peasant uprisings against taxes, obligations to lords, and the high price of grain. Insurrections occurred less frequently and were savagely repressed.

The gradual centralization of authority in Eastern Europe left nobles with even more autonomy than they had in the West, allowing Russian lords, Polish nobles, and Prussian nobles (*Junkers*) the possibility of further increasing their wealth and power through the extension of their estates, which were worked by serfs. Beginning in the late sixteenth century, such seigneurs made fortunes shipping grain to the West, where prices of cereal and food had risen dramatically in response to population growth. Royal decrees in Prussia and Russia and assembly legislation in Poland progressively limited the right of peasants to move from the land they worked, or even to inherit property. Ravaged by hard times, peasant proprietors had to sell their land to nobles. Impoverished and virtually powerless to resist, peasants lost their personal freedom, a process most marked in Russia. Thus, as feudalism disappeared in Western Europe, it became more prevalent in the East as lords dispossessed peasants from their land and the latter became serfs. The economic crises of the seventeenth century, including the Thirty Years' War and the decline in Western demand for grain imported from the East because of increased production in the West, only made conditions of life harder for serfs.

In the Ottoman Empire, absolutism was even more despotic. All lands were considered the sultan's private imperial possessions. He granted landed estates to those who served him, but because the sultan recognized no rights of property, no hereditary nobility could develop to challenge his authority. No representative institutions existed. Towns in the overwhelmingly rural empire had neither autonomy nor rights.

Expanding State Structures

Absolute monarchs extended their authority within their territories by expanding the structure of the state. The Renaissance city-states of Italy had created relatively efficient civil administrations and had set up the first permanent diplomatic corps. During the seventeenth century, the apparatus of administration, taxation, and military conscription gradually became part of the structure of the absolute states, which were increasingly centralized. The result was that in Europe as a whole, the number of government officials grew about fourfold. To fill the most prestigious offices, monarchs chose nobles for their influence more than for their competence. But some absolute rulers also began to employ commoners as officials to collect vital information—for example, to project revenues or to anticipate the number of soldiers available for war.

One result of these expanding ranks of officials was the tripling of tax revenues between 1520 and 1670 in France and Spain, and in England as well. To raise money, absolute rulers sold monopolies (which permitted only the holder of the monopoly to produce and sell particular goods) on the production and sale of salt, tobacco, and other commodities, and imposed taxes on trading towns. The rulers of France, Spain, and Austria also filled the state coffers by selling hereditary offices. James I of England doubled the number of knights during the first four months of his reign. Queen Christina of Sweden doubled the number of noble families in ten years. In addition, as royal power and prestige rose, the monarchs more easily found wealthy families to loan them money, usually in exchange for tax exemptions, titles, or other privileges.

Absolutism and Warfare

The regular collection of taxes and the expansion of sources of revenue increased the capacity of absolute rulers to maintain standing armies and fortifications, and to wage war. Absolute states were characterized by the

Table 7.1. The Size of European Armies, 1690–1814

	1690	1710	1756/60	1789	1812/14
Britain	70,000	75,000	200,000	40,000*	250,000
France	400,000	350,000	330,000	180,000	600,000
Habsburg Emp.	50,000	100,000	200,000	300,000	250,000
Prussia	30,000	39,000	195,000	190,000	270,000
Spain	na	30,000	na	50,000	na
Sweden	na	110,000	na	na	na
United Prov.	73,000	130,000	40,000*	na	na

*Drop reflects peacetime and non-absolutist character of the state.
na: Figures not available.
Source: Paul Kennedy, *The Rise and Fall of the Great Powers* (New York: Vintage, 1989), p. 99.

deployment of a large standing army capable of maintaining order at home and maintaining or expanding dynastic interests and territories. Absolutist statemaking and warfare had direct and indirect consequences for most of the European population. Kings no longer depended on troops provided by nobles or military contractors, thereby avoiding the risk that private armies might challenge royal power. Standing armies continued to grow in size during the eighteenth century (see Table 7.1). During the 1500s, the peacetime armies of the continental powers had included about 10,000 to 20,000 soldiers; by the 1690s, they reached about 150,000 soldiers. For the first time, uniforms became standard equipment for every soldier. The French army, which soon stood at about 180,000 men in peacetime, rose to 350,000 soldiers during the War of the Spanish Succession (1701–1714). The Russian army grew from 130,000 in 1731 to 458,000 in 1796. In contrast, England and the Dutch Republic, two non-absolutist powers, had relatively small armies, and, as sea powers, both depended on their navies.

As absolute monarchs consolidated their power, the reasons for waging international wars changed. The wars of the previous century had been fought, in principle, over the rivalry between the Catholic and Protestant religions, even if dynastic interests were never far from the surface. Now, although religious rivalries still constituted an important factor in international conflict (as in the case of the long struggle between the Muslim Ottoman Empire and the Catholic Habsburg Empire), "reasons of state" became a prevalent justification for the rulers of France, Prussia, and Russia to make war on their neighbors.

Warfare both encouraged and drew upon the development of credit institutions. But as the British and Dutch cases demonstrated, a state did not have to be absolutist to marshal sufficient resources to fight sustained wars. English colonial trade generated excise and customs taxes, permitting the expansion of the Royal Navy. The crown's reputation for repayment facilitated raising money through loans at home and abroad. Amsterdam's stature as a great banking center contributed to the ability of the Dutch government to fight extended wars. In contrast, the French monarchy lacked the confidence of wary investors, and despite the sale of privileges found itself in an increasingly perilous financial situation. Moreover, the French monarchy often had to pay higher rates of interest than private investors because it was a bad credit risk.

Even in peacetime, military expenditures now took up almost half of the budget of the European state. In times of war, the percentage rose to 80 percent, or even more. By the end of the sixteenth century, Philip II of Spain had allocated three-quarters of state expenditures to pay for past wars or to wage new ones. Appropriately enough, the bureau in Prussia that a century later would oversee tax collection itself evolved from the General War Office, making explicit the close connection between the extraction of state revenue and the waging of dynastic wars. Inevitably, there came a point even in absolute states when noble and other wealthy families upon which monarchies depended for financial support began to grumble.

Absolutism and Religion

An alliance with established churches helped monarchs achieve and maintain absolute rule. Absolute monarchs lent their authority and prestige to the established churches, the support of which, in turn, seemed to legitimize absolute monarchical power. In Catholic states in particular, the Church's quest for uniformity of belief and practice went hand in hand with the absolutist monarch's desire to eliminate challenges to his authority. The Church helped create an image of the king as a sacred figure who must be obeyed because he served God's interests on earth. In turn, absolute monarchs obliged the Church by persecuting religious minorities.

Absolute rulers also reduced ecclesiastical autonomy in their realms. The Catholic Church lost authority to their absolute monarchs. Yet the Church owned as much as two-thirds of the land in Portugal, at least one-tenth of the land in Spain, Austria, and France, half the land in Bavaria and Flanders, and considerable holdings in every Italian state. Moreover, the Church claimed the right to the tithe, the tax of 10 percent on annual resources. But absolute monarchs maintained authority over ecclesiastical appointments, in effect creating national churches, much to the consternation of the papacy in Rome. Signs of the victory of absolute rulers over the Catholic Church included eliminating the Inquisition in France and Spain, closing monasteries and expelling religious orders in France and Austria, assuming control over censorship, reducing ecclesiastical authority over marriage, and establishing the principle of state supervision over education.

The siege of Constantinople by the Turks in 1453 from a French manuscript illumination.

In France, the very existence of the French, or Gallican Church, defied papal claims to complete authority over the Church. By the Concordat of Bologna in 1516, the pope had given the kings of France virtual control (subject to papal confirmation) over the appointment of bishops in France and the right to overrule the judgments of ecclesiastical courts. This irritated French "ultramontane" clergy, who recognized only the authority of the pope "beyond the mountains," that is, over the Alps in distant Rome. The provincial parlements, or noble law courts, by contrast, remained defiantly Gallican. The Gallican Church itself was far more likely to remain loyal to the monarchy that defended its prerogatives, even if Gallicans themselves insisted that the pope and bishops retain spiritual authority, with the king having a monopoly only on temporal power.

Recognizing no distinction between church and state, the Turkish Ottoman Empire remained a theocracy. The sultan's subjects believed his despotic authority to be divine. The Muslim religious hierarchy, which included judges, theologians, and teachers, provided officials for the imperial administration. The supreme religious dignitary occasionally invoked religious law, of which he was the main interpreter, to counter orders of the sultan, but the latter's political authority remained absolute.

The expansion of the Ottoman Empire had been based upon the concept of the crusading "Holy War" against infidels, that is, non-Muslims. As the Turks destroyed the Byzantine Empire, capturing Constantinople in 1453, they confiscated many of the resources of the Orthodox Church and other Christian denominations. The Ottoman Turks enslaved prisoners of war, purchased slaves abroad, and imposed slave levies upon the Christians of the empire. Many Christian children had been trained as officials or soldiers and had converted to Islam. The empire also depended on the contributions of nonslave Christians, including skilled Greek sailors who made

Turkish galleys feared in the Mediterranean. Some joined the "janissary" infantry, a military corps that assumed police duties in periods of peace.

Yet the Ottoman Empire tolerated religious diversity. As long as non-Muslims did not resist Turkish authority, they were free to practice their religion and to become officials within the empire. In Albania (where alone conversions seemed to have been forced), Bosnia, and Herzegovina, many people, including some nobles, converted to the Muslim faith. Young Christians captured by Turkish fleets could convert to Islam to escape a life chained to benches as galley slaves. In contrast, Muslims captured by Christian powers remained galley slaves, even if they converted.

Monumentalism in Architecture and Art

Absolute monarchs utilized the extravagant emotional appeal of monumental architecture. They designed their capitals to reflect the imperatives of monarchical authority. Madrid, Berlin, Saint Petersburg, and Versailles were planned, shaped, and invested with symbols of absolute rule. These cities were laid out according to geometric principles. In contrast to the narrow, winding streets of cities that had evolved organically from medieval times, straight, wide boulevards were created in one fell swoop. These symmetrical boulevards symbolized the organized and far-reaching power of absolutism and the growth of the modern state. Royal armies paraded down boulevards to squares or royal palaces, around which were grouped government buildings and noble residences. Barracks housing standing armies also became a prominent feature of the new urban landscape.

Monarchs paid artists and architects to combine baroque elements with a more restrained, balanced classicism, influenced by the early sixteenth-century Roman style of the High Renaissance. This became known as the Louis XIV style. Thus, the facade completing the Louvre palace in Paris, the work of Gianlorenzo Bernini (1598–1680), drew on the architectural style of Roman temples, thereby linking Louis to the glories of Julius Caesar. Hyacinthe Rigaud's full-length

Hyacinthe Rigaud's *Louis XIV* (1701).

portrait of Louis XIV in 1701 shows a supremely confident and powerful king standing in a regal pose, wearing luxurious coronation robes, clutching his staff of authority, and looking with condescension at the viewer—his subject.

Absolutism in France

Absolutist France became the strongest state in early modern Europe. Francis I and Henry IV had extended the effective reach of monarchical authority (see Chapter 4). Louis XIII's invaluable minister Cardinal Richelieu had used provincial "intendants" to centralize and further extend monarchical authority. Richelieu's policies led to the doubling of taxes between 1630 and 1650, sparking four major waves of peasant resistance, including one uprising in the southwest in 1636 in which about 60,000 peasants took up arms, some shouting the impossible demand, "Long live the king without taxes!" Upon Louis XIII's death in 1643, the stage was set for Louis XIV to rule as a divine-right king of an absolute state. But before the young Louis could take control of the government, France would first experience the regency of his mother and the revolt known as the Fronde.

The Fronde: Taming "Overmighty Subjects"

Louis XIV was four years old at the time of his accession to the throne. His mother, Anne of Austria (1601–1666), served as regent. She depended on Cardinal Jules Mazarin (1602–1661) for advice. Mazarin, a worldly, charming, and witty Italian, always dressed in the finest red silk and was well known for his love of money. A master of intrigue, rumor had it that he and Anne had secretly married.

During the Regency period, Anne and Mazarin kept French armies in the field, prolonging the Thirty Years' War, which had become a struggle pitting the dynastic interests of France against the Austrian and Spanish Habsburgs (see Chapter 4). Most nobles, with much to lose from civil disturbances, remained loyal to the monarchy. But Mazarin's prolongation of the victorious struggle against Spain generated a political crisis.

Resistance to royal authority culminated in a revolt that shook the Bourbon monarchy at mid-century. Between 1648 and 1653, powerful "nobles of the sword" (those nobles who held ancient titles and whose forebears had gathered retainers to fight for the king) tried to regain the influence lost during the reign of Louis XIII. Ordinary people entered the fray, demanding lower taxes because of deteriorating economic conditions. The revolt became known as the Fronde—named for a slingshot boys in Paris used to hurl rocks.

Mazarin, whom many nobles considered a "foreign plotter" and an outsider like Anne of Austria, had borrowed money for the state from financiers. He did so against expected revenue from new taxes or the sale of offices.

Nobles were willing to suffer extraordinary levies in times of war. But now they complained bitterly that since the wars had ended supplementary impositions were needless. Furthermore, some of the oldest noble families had claimed for some time that they had been systematically excluded from the highest and most lucrative and prestigious offices. In fact, there was some truth in this claim, as the king feared the power of disloyal "overmighty subjects," preferring lesser nobles for military offices and skilled bureaucrats for some civil posts. Now nobles of the sword denounced Mazarin, his system of patronage, and his financier friends, some of whom had made fortunes supplying the royal armies.

In 1648, Mazarin attempted to secure the approval of the Parlement of Paris for increased taxes. The Parlement of Paris, the chief law court in France, was made up of nobles who had purchased their positions from the crown. Wanting to safeguard their privileges and power, the Parlement of Paris defied the Regency by calling for an assembly of the four sovereign courts of Paris to consider the financial crisis. Meeting without royal permission, the assembly proposed that the courts elect delegates to consider financial reforms in the realm. The provincial parlements joined the protest against what seemed to be unchecked royal authority. Financiers who had earlier purchased titles from the crown now refused to loan the state any more money.

When Mazarin ordered the arrest of some of the defiant members of the parlement in August 1648, barricades went up in Paris in support of the parlement. From inside the Louvre palace, Louis XIV, now nine years of age, heard the angry shouts of the crowds. Popular discontent forced the royal court to flee Paris in January 1649.

The role of the prince of Condé (Louis de Bourbon, 1621–1686), head of the junior branch of the Bourbon family, was crucial in the Fronde. Condé's great victory in 1643 over the Spanish at the battle of Rocroi in northern France, which ended any possibility of a successful Spanish invasion of the country, earned him the name of "the Great Condé." But as long as Mazarin had met Condé's demands for money and offices, the latter remained loyal to the young king and in 1648 marched to Paris with his army to defend him. Short-lived tax reforms bought time. But major uprisings against taxes, which had doubled in two decades as Richelieu and Mazarin had in turn raised money to wage war, broke out in several provinces. Relatively poor nobles, who resented that wealthy commoners were able to purchase titles, led other revolts. Condé himself changed sides in 1649 and supported the *frondeurs*.

Fearing Condé's influence, a Spanish invasion, and further insurrections, Anne and Mazarin found noble allies against Condé and early in 1650 ordered him imprisoned. Condé's arrest further mobilized opposition to Mazarin, whose enemies forced the minister to flee the country early the next year. A year later, Condé was released from prison at the demand of the Parlement of Paris. In September 1651, Louis XIV declared his majority and right to rule, although he was only thirteen. But he faced an immediate challenge from Condé, who marched to Paris in 1652 with the goals of reestablishing the great nobles' political influence and of getting rid of Mazarin (who continued to sway royal policy from his exile in Germany). However, finding insufficient support from the parlement, the municipal government, or ordinary Parisians, Condé fled to Spain. The boy-king recalled Mazarin to Paris.

Louis XIV restored monarchical authority by ending the nobles' rebellion and putting down peasant resistance against taxation. Louis made clear that henceforth the Parlement of Paris could not meddle in the king's business. And in 1673 the king deprived the twelve parlements of their right to issue remonstrances (formal objections to the registration of new royal ordinances, edicts, or declarations, which could be overridden by the king) before they registered an edict. The king also disbanded the private armies of headstrong nobles and tightened royal control over provincial governors.

Unlike the English Parliament's successful rebellion against the crown in defense of constitutional rule (see Chapter 6), royal victory in the Fronde broke French noble resistance to absolute rule. The king's predecessors had frequently consulted with prominent nobles about important matters. Louis XIV felt no obligation to do so. Yet the Fronde also demonstrated that the crown had to rule more subtly with respect to noble interests.

Mercantilism under Louis XIV

Following Mazarin's death in 1661, Louis XIV, now twenty-two years of age, assumed more personal responsibility. The state's firmer financial footing owed much to the cool calculations of Jean-Baptiste Colbert (1619–1683), controller-general of the realm, who directed administration, taxation, and public works. The grandson of a provincial merchant of modest standing, Colbert endured the hostility of the old noble families. His frosty personality led him to be dubbed "the North." He employed surveyors and mapmakers to assess the economic resources of the provinces. Whereas formerly only about a quarter of revenues reached royal coffers, now as much as four-fifths of what was collected poured into the royal treasury. Even though the direct royal tax on land (the *taille*) had been reduced, state revenues doubled, despite abuses and privileged exemptions (nobles and clergy did not pay the land tax).

Mercantilism underlay the economy of absolutist France, as it did royal economic policies in Europe. Mercantilists posited that all resources should be put into the service of the state and that a state's wealth was measured by its ability to import more gold and silver than it exported. Jealous of English and Dutch prosperity, Colbert became the chief proponent of French mercantilist policies, which emphasized economic self-sufficiency. He founded commercial trading companies to which the king granted monopolies on colonial trade, and levied high protective tariffs on Dutch and English imports. Louis XIV established the royal Gobelins tapestry manufacture on the edge of Paris and encouraged the textile industry and the manufacture of other goods that could be exported. He improved roads and oversaw the extension of France's network of canals, including the Languedoc Canal (Canal du Midi), which links the Mediterranean to the Garonne River and thus to the Atlantic Ocean.

Yet despite the growth of the French merchant fleet and navy, the French East India Company, established by Colbert in 1664, could not effectively compete with its more efficient and adventurous Dutch and English rivals in the quest for global trade. The monarchy had to bail out the company and later took away its trading monopoly. Moreover, trade within France remained hamstrung by a bewildering variety of restrictions and internal tariffs that in some places were not much different from those that characterized the hodgepodge of German states.

At the same time, while the king was a master of extracting revenue from his subjects, his greatest talent was for emptying the royal coffers with dizzying speed. Louis XIV and his successors plunged the monarchy into an ever-deepening and eventually disastrous financial crisis.

The Absolute Louis XIV

As Louis XIV grew into manhood, he looked the part of a great king and played it superbly. Handsome, proud, energetic, and decisive, the king's love of gambling, hunting, and women sometimes took precedence over matters of state. But he also supervised the work of the high council of his prominent officials, and, although a spendthrift, he closely monitored the accounts of his realm.

The king became a shrewd judge of character, surrounding himself with men of talent. He consciously avoided being dependent on any single person, the way Louis XIII had been on Richelieu, or his mother on Mazarin. During a visit to the château of Vaux-le-Vicomte, built by the unpopular minister of finance Nicolas Fouquet, Louis was served with solid gold tableware and viewed large pools filled with seawater and even saltwater fish. The king promptly ordered Fouquet arrested and took the magnificent château for himself.

Having affirmed his authority over Paris, Louis dissolved any remaining pretensions of autonomy held by the elites in the major provincial towns. One result of the Fronde was that the monarchy expanded the narrow social base on which state power had previously rested. Louis selected governors, intendants, and bishops who would be loyal to him. Mayors became officials of the state who had to purchase their titles in exchange for fidelity to the king. Wealthy merchants now preferred to seek ennoblement rather than try to maintain municipal privileges that seemed increasingly archaic. The presence of royal garrisons, which towns once resisted, not only affirmed the sovereign's authority but were welcomed by local elites as protection against plebeian insurrection. Troops were also good for local business. In 1667, Louis took another important step in affirming his authority by appointing a lieutenant-general of police for Paris, who was given extensive authority ranging from powers of arrest to responsibility for street cleaning and fire fighting. Paris soon had street lighting—thousands of glass-enclosed candles—during the early evening hours.

Louis XIV portrayed himself as God's representative, charged with maintaining earthly order. "*L'état, c'est moi*" ("I am the state"), he is said to have remarked. The royal propaganda machine provided ideological legitimacy by cranking out images of the king as a glorious monarch. At the same time, royal censors suppressed publications, prohibited imported books, and limited the number of printers. The goal of censorship was to protect the honor and reputation of the king and religion.

Louis XIV created the first French ministry of war and shaped it into an effective bureaucracy. The king and his ministers brought the noble-dominated officer corps under royal control, making seniority the determinant of rank and charging wealthy nobles handsome sums for the privilege of commanding their own regiments or companies. The ministry of war ordered the construction of military academies, barracks, and drilling grounds, and ordered the brilliant military engineer Sébastien le Prestre de Vauban (1633–1707) to fortify key border towns.

Louis XIV described himself as first seigneur of the realm. Nobles still insisted more than ever—though more quietly than at the time of the Fronde—that institutionalized noble privileges were necessary to counter the excesses of absolute authority. Nobles were almost completely immune from royal taxes (basically paying only indirect taxes) until Louis made them subject to two additional taxes (the *capitation*, a head tax, and the *vingtième*, a tax of 5 percent, usually only on land). They benefited from the economic development the monarchy encouraged, such as the construction of better roads and networks of canals that were largely underwritten by the state.

Since the time of Henry IV, offices had effectively become forms of hereditary property. Louis XIV's lavish sale of offices and titles—500 sold with a single edict in 1696—expanded the nobility. As one minister put it, "as soon as the crown creates an office God creates a fool willing to buy it." Few noble families now could trace their titles back more than several generations. This accentuated differences between nobles of the sword and nobles of the robe (many of whom had purchased their offices). The nobles of the sword dominated court life, but the king did not hesitate to dip into the ranks of commoners to find efficient, loyal officials, exempting them from taxation and providing lucrative posts for their offspring. A noble of the sword denounced the "reign of the vile bourgeoisie," that is, nobles of recent title and other relative upstarts he viewed as unworthy of prominent posts.

The château of Versailles, built by Louis XIV between 1669 and 1686.

Louis XIV at Versailles

Louis XIV never forgot hearing the howling Parisian mob from his room in the royal palace. Resolving to move his court to Versailles, twelve miles west of Paris, he visited Paris only four times during the seventy-two years of his reign. Realizing that an adequately fed population would be less likely to riot, Louis XIV and his successors worked to assure the sufficient provisioning of the capital.

The Sun King followed Colbert's admonition that "nothing marks the greatness of princes better than the buildings that compel the people to look on them with awe, and all posterity judges them by the superb palaces they have built during their lifetime." The staging ground for royal ceremonies was the monumental château of Versailles (constructed 1669–1686), surrounded by geometrically arranged formal gardens, interspersed by 1,400 fountains supplied by the largest hydraulic pumps in the Western world. Sculptures in the gardens made clear the identification of Louis XIV with the Greek and Roman sun god Apollo. In the vast château, the royal dining room was so far from the kitchen that the king's food often arrived at his table cold and, during one particularly cold winter, the wine froze before Louis could taste it. The château's corridors were so long that some nobles used them as urinals, instead of continuing the lengthy trek to a more appropriate place.

Louis summoned the greatest nobles of the realm to Versailles to share in his glory. There they could be honored, but none could become too powerful. More than 10,000 nobles, officials, and servants lived in or near the château. Each day began with the elaborate routine of dressing the king in the company of the richest and most powerful nobles. The ultimate reward for a loyal noble was to be named to a post within the royal household. Louis XIV allowed the nobles to form cabals and conspire, but only against each other.

For nobles at Versailles there was little else to do except eat, drink, hunt— in the company of the king, if they were favored—gamble, and chase around each other's wives and mistresses. Nobles also attended the expensive theatrical and operatic productions put on at royal expense. These included the works of Jean-Baptiste Molière (1622–1673) and Jean Racine (1639–1699), master of the tragic dramatic style, who drew themes from the classical Greek poets. Both Molière and Racine wrote effusive praise for the king into some of their plays, the latter dedicating his first great success, *Alexander the Great*, to Louis XIV.

Social struggles mark the plays of Molière. The son of an upholsterer, the playwright started a traveling theatrical company before settling in Paris. The lonely, unhappy Molière poked fun at the pretensions of aristocratic and ecclesiastical society, depicting the private, cruel dramas of upper-class family life. But his popular works also helped reaffirm the boundaries between social classes. He ridiculed burghers, whose wealth could purchase titles but not teach them how to behave as nobles. In *The Bourgeois Gentilhomme* (1670), the parvenu gives himself away with a social gaffe. Molière also detested hypocrisy, which he depicted in *Tartuffe* (1664), a tale of the unfortunate effects of unrestrained religious enthusiasm on a family. *Tartuffe* brought Molière the wrath of the Church, but he had an even more powerful protector in the king.

Louis XIV believed that his court stood as the center and apex of civilization. Indeed, French arts and literature had an enormous influence in Europe. Foreign monarchs, nobles, and writers still considered French the language of high culture. The château of Versailles encouraged imitation. Philip V of Spain, among others, ordered a similar palace built. The duke of Saxony rebuilt his capital of Dresden along neoclassical lines. The château of Versailles also served as a model for noble estates and townhouses built in the classical style.

Louis XIV's Persecution of Religious Minorities

One of the most salient results of the victory of absolute rule in Catholic states was the persecution of religious minorities. Such campaigns in part served to placate the papacy and the Church hierarchy in each Catholic state. Louis XIV had little interest in theology, although he was relatively pious. But as he grew older, the king brought into his inner circle a number

(Left) The symbol of the sun used to glorify the absolute ruler, Louis XIV. *(Right)* This caricature shows Louis XIV, the Sun King, as the exterminator of Protestantism.

of extremely devout advisers, and into his bedroom a fervently religious mistress.

Reversing the tolerant policies of Henry IV and Louis XIII, Louis XIV launched a vigorous campaign of persecution against Huguenots, closing most Protestant churches and initiating attempts to force conversions to Catholicism. In 1685, he revoked the Edict of Nantes, by which Henry IV in 1598 had extended religious tolerance to Protestants. This pleased the provincial estates in regions where Protestants were a forceful minority and memories of the wars of religion were still fresh. But the economic cost to France was considerable in the long run. Although the king forbade Huguenots from leaving France, many merchants and skilled craftsmen were among the 200,000 Huguenots who emigrated during the next forty years. Many went to England, Prussia, the Dutch United Provinces, and even South Africa.

With the motto "one king, one law, one faith," Louis XIV also persecuted Jansenists in his quest for religious orthodoxy. Jansenists were followers of Cornelis Jansen, bishop of Ypres in the Southern Netherlands (Belgium), who died in 1638. They could be found in France, the Netherlands, Austria, and several Italian states. Seeking reforms within the Church, Jansenists emphasized the role of faith and divine grace in the pursuit of salvation. Believing mankind to be fallen and hapless, incapable of understanding the will of God, Jansenists came close to accepting a Calvinist doctrine of predestination. Their enemies called them "Calvinists who go to Mass." However, Jansenists believed that one should completely withdraw from the world, given the certainty of sin and mankind's ignorance of God's will.

Notoriously ascetic, they criticized the Church for encouraging a lax morality by holding out the possibility of repeated penance and deathbed conversion.

The pope had condemned Jansenism in 1653, perhaps at the insistence of the Jesuits, the Jansenists' most determined enemy. Louis XIV began to persecute them in the name of "one faith" in 1709; he ordered the Jansenist community at Port-Royal outside of Paris evicted and its abbey burned to the ground. He convinced Pope Clement XI to issue a papal bull, *Unigenitus* (1713), which condemned Jansenism. The Parlement of Paris, however, refused to register the edict. Louis was still trying to force compliance two years later when he died. The king's attempt to impose religious orthodoxy in France fell short, indicating that absolute rule had its limits.

The Limits of French Absolutism

France, like other countries, was far from being a nation-state in which most people thought of themselves as French, as well as or instead of Norman, Breton, or Provençal, or from other regions with their own traditions. More than half the population did not speak French. Inadequate roads isolated mountain regions, in particular, limiting the effective reach of absolute rule.

The absolute monarchy stood at the top of a complex network of patronage based on personal ties that reached into every province and every town. But Louis XIV's intendants still had to take local networks of influence into consideration, using intimidation, cajoling, and negotiation to gain their ends in what was then Western Europe's most populous state.

The king played off against one another the jurisdictions and interests of the Estates, parlements, and other provincial institutions dominated by nobles. The provincial Estates were assemblies of nobles of the *pays d'état* (regions more recently integrated into France and retaining a degree of fiscal autonomy, including Brittany, Provence, Burgundy, and Languedoc), which represented each province. The Estates oversaw the collection of taxes and tended to the details of provincial administration and spending. They met annually amid great pageantry and carefully orchestrated ceremony that, like those at Versailles, reaffirmed social hierarchy. In principle, the Estates could refuse to provide the crown with the annual "free grant" (a subsidy provided by each region to the monarch), which was hardly "free," since the king informed the Estates of the amount of money he wanted. Louis XIV abolished the custom of allowing the Estates to express grievances before voting the amount of their "gift" to the monarchy.

The interests of the nobles also prevailed in the parlements, the sovereign law courts that registered, publicized, and carried out royal laws. The parlements, most of whose members were nobles, claimed to speak for their province in legal matters, asserting the right to issue binding commands in cases of emergencies. But, unlike the English Parliament, no national representative political institution existed in France. The Estates-General, which had met four times between 1560 and 1593, had not been convoked since 1614.

Even the king of France was not as omnipotent or omniscient as he would have liked to think. Jean Bodin had expressed his view that a ruler would be wise to avoid exercising full power—for example, to avoid interfering with his subjects' property. This seeming paradox is perhaps best symbolized by the king's phrase to the Estates of a province: "We entreat you but we also command you. . . ." Even the powerful Bourbons were bound by the so-called fundamental laws of the realm, as well as by those they believed God had established.

The Balance of Power

During the century beginning about 1650, the concept of a balance of power between states gradually took hold in many of the courts of Europe. Like the evolving European state system itself, the emergence of the concept arose in part out of the decline of religious antagonisms as a dominant cause of warfare. The quest of absolute rulers to add to their dynastic territories and the growing global commercial rivalry between the great powers increasingly shaped European warfare.

A diplomatic concept dating from the time of the Renaissance city-states of fifteenth-century Italy, the balance of power principle held that great powers should be in equilibrium, and that one power should not be allowed to become too powerful. The decline of one power could threaten the balance of power if, as a result, another power considerably enhanced its strength. Now the main threat to peace ceased to be religious division but rather the power of Louis XIV of France.

The Origins of International Law

Horrified by the Thirty Years' War, two northern European political theorists systematically analyzed questions of international relations, drawing on the recent history of Europe. They helped lay the foundations for the evolution of modern diplomacy. In 1625, the Dutch jurist Hugo Grotius (1583–1645) sought to establish the foundations of international law by arguing that laws to which nations were subject followed from nature and not from God. Samuel von Pufendorf (1632–1694), a German Protestant, found himself under arrest for eight months when he was caught up in the war between Sweden and Denmark. Pufendorf's *Of the Law of Nature and Nations* (1672) postulated legal principles for times of peace—which he argued should be the natural state—and for times of war. He claimed that only a defensive war was justified, pending international arbitration to resolve crises. The problem was, of course, that unless there existed some powerful, impartial body to adjudicate disputes between nations, each side in any conflict invariably claimed that its cause was just. European power politics swept away such theoretical considerations.

THE HABSBURG MONARCHY

The eighteenth-century French Enlightenment philosophe Voltaire only somewhat exaggerated when he dismissed the Holy Roman Empire, that cumbersome federal structure of Central European states that once served as a powerful protector of the papacy, as having ceased to be holy, Roman, or an empire. The Holy Roman Empire included almost 300 German states. Seven, and then in 1648, eight electors (princes and archbishops) selected the Holy Roman emperor, invariably the Habsburg ruler. But in a Europe increasingly dominated by absolute monarchs, the Holy Roman Empire seemed an anomaly.

In principle, the Holy Roman emperor still commanded the allegiance of the states of the empire. These included sizable states such as Austria, Bavaria, and Saxony, whose rulers oversaw elaborate courts, maintained standing armies, and paid for all this by levying taxes on their subjects and customs duties and tolls on merchandise being carried through their territories. The Holy Roman Empire also included many small principalities, duchies, and even archbishoprics barely extending beyond the walls of towns like Mainz and Trier. But in reality the empire had increasingly only a shadow existence, despite its mystique as the defender of Catholicism. The Treaty of Westphalia (1648), which concluded the Thirty Years' War (see Chapter 4), reflected the inability of the Holy Roman Empire to enforce its will, conduct foreign policy, or effectively maintain an army. During the long war, some German princes with powerful allies outside the empire had gone their own way. Indeed, the Treaty of Westphalia specifically empowered each member state to carry out its own foreign policy. The imperial Assembly of the Holy Roman Empire (the Reichstag) thus had virtually no authority to conduct foreign policy with other states. The imperial army was too small and difficult to mobilize to be effective, and the imperial court of law was powerless to enforce its decisions, depending entirely on the good will of the individual states.

The strongest state within the Holy Roman Empire, Habsburg Austria, extended beyond the boundaries of the empire itself. The Habsburgs had ruled Austria without interruption since the thirteenth century. The old Habsburg principle was "Let others wage war. You, happy Austria, marry [to prosper]." Advantageous marriages brought the dynasty the wealthy territories of Burgundy and the Netherlands in the fifteenth century. Charles V, who became Holy Roman emperor in 1519, added Hungary and Bohemia. Counting Spain and its far-flung possessions, he reigned over perhaps a quarter of the population of the European continent, as well as the Spanish Empire in the Americas.

When Charles V abdicated as emperor in 1558, he divided the Habsburg domains into two parts. His brother Ferdinand I inherited the Austrian Habsburg lands (including Austria, Hungary, and Bohemia) and succeeded him as the elected Holy Roman emperor. Charles's son Philip II became king of Spain. His empire included the Netherlands, dependencies in Italy, and colonies in the Americas. The Spanish and Austrian branches of the Habsburgs were henceforth two separate dynasties, although the interests of both as Catholic states and dynastic rivals of France sometimes converged.

The Austrian Habsburg monarchy exercised foreign policy and directed the army, but had less effective authority within its territories than the kings of France had within their realm. Nobles oversaw the court system and policing. When confronted with threats to their traditional prerogatives, nobles put aside differences, such as those between the great landowners and the lower nobility, and formed a common front to preserve their privileges against monarchical erosion.

Austria was the only power able to exercise its influence equally in both Western and Eastern Europe. The Austrian Habsburgs successfully implemented an effective state administration, expanded educational opportunities for the upper classes, and brought resistant or even rebellious nobles under dynastic control. But timely marriages were no longer enough. Throughout the sixteenth century and during the first half of the seventeenth century, the Habsburgs had been almost constantly preoccupied with politics within the German states. During the Thirty Years' War, however, the Habsburgs were unable to expand their domination throughout Central Europe. The Habsburgs remained vulnerable to French expansionism and to Turkish incursions, forcing the monarchy to address threats on two fronts.

That the Habsburg empire contained territories of different nationalities was a source of weakness. Leopold I, elected Holy Roman emperor in 1658 (ruled 1658–1705; Louis XIV was the opposing candidate), was simultaneously Holy Roman emperor, duke of Upper and Lower Silesia, count of Tyrol, archduke of Upper and Lower Austria, king of Bohemia, prince of Transylvania, king of Hungary, Slavonia, Dalmatia, and Croatia, and titular ruler of Lombardy, Styria, and Moravia (see Map 7.1). The monarch necessarily had to consider local political institutions. The Hungarian and Croatian provincial diets, or noble Estates, impeded Habsburg absolutism. Hungarians also resented German-speaking administrators and tax collectors, as well as the Habsburg armies stationed in Hungary to protect the empire from the Turks. In Bohemia, the scars of the religious conflicts between Catholics and Protestants during the Thirty Years' War healed very slowly. Bohemia and Moravia remained centers of Protestant intellectual ferment, despite Catholic domination. Bohemian nobles resented the fact that a decree in 1627 had abolished the elective monarchy, made the Bohemian crown a hereditary Habsburg possession, and brought the confiscation of their lands.

Hungary had been part of the Habsburg domains since the sixteenth century. The Hungarian crown included Hungary, Transylvania, and Croatia.

The Hungarian nobles, proud of their defense of the Habsburg empire against Turkish incursions, seized every opportunity to extract concessions from the Habsburgs. Unlike their Austrian counterparts, most of the Hungarian, or Magyar, nobles had become Protestant during the Reformation. Habsburg persecution of Hungarian Protestants helped spark an insurrection in 1679 that spread into Moravia, Slavonia, and Silesia. This led Leopold to promise the Hungarian Estates to restore some privileges of landowners that had been suppressed. But dissatisfied Protestants then called for Turkish assistance at a time when the Turks were preparing to attack Habsburg territories. The Ottoman army besieged Vienna, the Habsburg capital, in 1683. It was saved after two months by the arrival of a combined relief army of Austrians, Germans, and Poles under the command of the crusading King John Sobieski (ruled 1674–1696), Catholic ruler of Poland. Pope Innocent XI succeeded in convincing Emperor Leopold I, who saw himself as a prince of the Catholic Reformation, to lead a "Holy League" in 1684 against the Ottoman Turks. In the War of the Holy League (1686–1687), and in subsequent fighting, Habsburg armies recaptured most of Hungary and the eastern province of Transylvania from the Turks, as well as

Map 7.1 The Holy Roman Empire under Leopold I, 1658   The Holy Roman Empire was a polyglot state, made up of territories of different nationalities.

much of Croatia. The Peace of Karlowitz (1699) confirmed the Habsburg victory over the Turks. Although Ottoman garrisons remained in Belgrade and Turkish galleys still roamed the Mediterranean, the Ottoman threat to Central Europe had passed.

The Habsburg victory over the Turks consolidated the dynasty's authority over Hungary. In 1687, the Hungarian Estates were forced to declare that the Hungarian throne (the crown of Saint Stephen, named after Hungary's patron saint) would henceforth be a hereditary possession of the Habsburgs and no longer elective. Hungary thereby recognized the sovereignty of the Habsburg dynasty in exchange for several promises: the Hungarian Diet would be convened at regular intervals; Hungary would have its own administration; and Magyar nobles would continue to be exempt from royal taxation. Thus, although he consolidated Habsburg authority within the dynasty's domains, Leopold failed to impose centralized rule on Hungary. Hungary's special position within the monarchy revealed the limits of Habsburg absolutism and Austrian power.

The Habsburg monarchy, the least absolute of Europe's absolute states, was less successful than France in maintaining its power. In 1700, Austria's Habsburg dynasty lost its long-standing ties to Spain when that country passed from the Habsburg dynasty to the Bourbon dynasty with the death of the childless Charles II (ruled 1665–1700). France's defeat in the War of the Spanish Succession (1701–1714), which had been fought to determine who would inherit the Spanish Habsburg territories, enabled the Austrian Habsburgs to pick up some of the remaining pieces of the decimated Spanish Empire in Europe. However, during the eighteenth century Austria ceded its preeminence in Central Europe to Prussia.

THE RISE OF PRUSSIA

The presence of all the essential components of absolutism explain Prussia's rise as a major European power: a proud, ambitious dynasty, the Hohenzollern family of Brandenburg; privileged but loyal nobles, whose estates formed the base of the economy and who dominated a downtrodden peasantry devoid of rights; an increasingly centralized and efficient bureaucracy; and the emergence of a large standing army. Austrian defeats in the Thirty Years' War and vulnerability to French and Turkish challenges left the way open for a rival to emerge among the German states. Bavaria and Saxony were not strong claimants for primacy among the German states, with weak nobilities and lacking effective bureaucracies or large armies. The Catholic clergy undermined the authority of the Bavarian dukes. The attention of Saxony, subject to Swedish influence, was often turned away from German affairs eastward toward the volatile world of Polish politics.

MAP 7.2 THE RISE OF PRUSSIA, 1648–1720   Territories acquired by Brandenburg-Prussia.

The small north-central German state of Brandenburg-Prussia, stretching across the sandy marshes between the Elbe and Oder Rivers, seemed an unlikely candidate to rival Austria and to grow into a powerful absolute state. In 1618, Brandenburg's ruling Hohenzollern dynasty inherited East Prussia, which lay 100 miles to the east of Brandenburg along the Baltic Sea, bordered by Poland. It then absorbed several smaller territories in the Rhineland, more than 100 miles to the west (see Map 7.2). Consisting of three diverse, noncontiguous realms, Brandenburg-Prussia lacked not only defensible frontiers but also the network of prosperous trading towns of other states in Germany. During the Thirty Years' War, Swedish and Austrian armies took turns ravaging Prussia. But with the Treaty of Westphalia (1648), Prussia absorbed much of Pomerania on the coast of the Baltic Sea.

In one of the typical trade-offs that built absolute states in early modern Europe, Prussian nobles accepted Hohenzollern authority as a guarantee of their privileges. At the same time that Junkers were securing their privileges, Prussian peasants were losing their freedom, including their rights to free movement and often even to inheritance. During the late fifteenth and the sixteenth centuries, they became serfs, legally bound to a lord's estate, and could be sold with the land on which they worked. A burgher in a Prussian town in 1614 described serfdom as "this barbaric and Egyptian servitude . . . in our territory serfdom did not exist fifty or a hundred years ago, but lately, it has been brought in on a large scale, with the help of the authorities." The authority of the Hohenzollerns, however, stopped at the gate of the manor: Junkers retained rights of seigneurial justice over their peasants. Burghers, including merchants and skilled craftsmen, also stood powerless before nobles, in contrast to the middle class in England and the Dutch United Provinces, where they presented an imposing obstacle to the growth of absolutism.

Frederick William (ruled 1640–1688), the "Great Elector" of Brandenburg (so named because the ruler of Brandenburg had the right to cast a ballot in the election of the Holy Roman emperor), initially had neither a standing army nor the resources to raise one. Prussian nobles at first resisted the creation of a standing army, fearful that it might aid Frederick William in reducing their privileges. In 1653, Frederick William convinced the Junkers to grant him funds with which to build an army in exchange for royal confirmation of their privileges over the peasantry and their right to import goods without paying duties. Furthermore, the king agreed to consult the nobles on matters of foreign policy.

Then Frederick William turned to the business of augmenting state authority in his three fragmented territories. He extracted concessions from each of them, including more taxes and the right to recruit soldiers. The Hohenzollern family owned more than half of East Prussia, which provided considerable state revenue. The Great Elector established a centralized administrative bureaucracy, arguably the first modern efficient civil service in Europe. The Prussian bureaucracy was coordinated by an office with the suitably imposing name of "General Directory Over Finance, War, and Royal Domains." Prussian towns, which paid a disproportionate percentage of taxes, lost their representation in the provincial Estates. In 1701, the Great Elector's son Frederick III (his title as elector of Brandenburg) took the title of King Frederick I of Prussia (ruled 1688–1713).

Frederick William I (ruled 1713–1740), grandson of the Great Elector, succeeded Frederick III as elector of Brandenburg and king in Prussia. As a boy, Frederick William could not count to ten without his tutor's assistance, but upon his succession to the throne he continued the centralizing policies of his grandfather and father. The bad-tempered "Sergeant-King" wore his officer's uniform around the house and turned the royal gardens into a military training ground. Frederick William I was known for fits of screaming rage, calling everyone in sight "blockhead," sometimes beating officials with a stick, and knocking out the teeth of several judges whose sentences displeased him. Officials known as "fiscals" went around to ensure that the king's representatives served him well. But the king was astute enough to break with tradition by employing some commoners, many of whom served with uncommon loyalty and efficiency.

A Prussian official described, with some exaggeration, the feature that defined his country's absolutism and the emergence of Brandenburg-Prussia as a power: "What distinguishes the Prussians from other people is that theirs is not a country with an army. They have an army and a country that serves it." Military expenditures accounted for half of Prussia's state budget.

King Frederick William I increased the Prussian army from about 39,000 to 80,000 soldiers. He engaged only tall soldiers for his royal guard, those standing more than six feet in height, virtual giants at the time. One of his first royal acts was to abolish the luxury industries in Berlin, the capital, that catered to court and nobles, and to replace them with workshops that turned out military uniforms. The king ordered all young men in Prussia to register for military service and organized a procedure by which each regiment was assigned a specific region from which to recruit or conscript soldiers. Prussia established the first system of military reserves in Europe: soldiers drilled in the summer for two months. This meant that far more men in Prussia experienced military life than in any other country.

The Russian and Swedish Empires

Two other empires rose in eastern and northern Europe. Early in the sixteenth century, Muscovy was a relatively small state. It stood vulnerable to invasions by the Mongols, who had conquered what is now Russia in the thirteenth century, the Tatars of Crimea on the edge of the Black Sea, and by the kingdom of Poland-Lithuania. That kingdom and grand duchy had been joined in an enormous confederation in 1386, becoming the Commonwealth of Poland-Lithuania in 1569, with Warsaw becoming the capital in 1595. Twice the size of France, the confederation had only about 8 million inhabitants. Gradually, the duchy of Muscovy, where Orthodox Christianity had taken hold, emerged as the strongest of the states of Russia, absorbing Novgorod and other rivals and principalities late in the fifteenth century. By the early sixteenth century, the Russian Orthodox Church had become centered in Moscow, which now claimed the title of the third Rome (the second was Constantinople). Muscovy's ruler Ivan III (ruled 1462–1505) began using the title "lord of all Russia," a title that offended the more powerful state of Poland-Lithuania. In 1500 and again twelve years later, Ivan brazenly attacked Poland-Lithuania, capturing the fortress town of Smolensk, which guarded the upper Dnieper River.

The Expansion of Muscovy

The rise of Russia as an absolute state and empire began with the further expansion of Muscovy in the late sixteenth century. Tsar Ivan IV (ruled 1533–1584) became in 1547 the first to be crowned tsar of Russia. Muscovy conquered the Volga basin, driving back the nomadic Muslim Tatars, conquered the Don and Volga river basins to the south before they could be taken by either the Ottoman Empire or the Safavid rulers of Iran, absorbed parts of the Mongol states to the east, and unsuccessfully battled Poland-Lithuania for control of the Baltic territory of Livonia. Peasants, hunters, and fur traders expanded the domination of Muscovy into the cold and

Ivan the Terrible watching the beggars of Novgorod being tortured to death.

sparsely populated forest reaches of Siberia. Muscovy annexed the steppe khanates of Astrakhan and Kazan at mid-century, reaching the borderlands of China.

Ivan IV truly earned his sobriquet "the Terrible." He was raised in a world of violence marked by the bloody feuds of the Muscovite nobles, some of whom poisoned his mother when he was eight years old. Five years later, Ivan ordered a noble ripped apart by fierce dogs; as an adult, he had an archbishop sewn into a bearskin and thrown to hungry wolves. His goal was to assure himself a reliable military force and revenue. His means was to create a "service state" in which Muscovite nobles, the *boyars*, held their estates in exchange for agreeing to serve in an administrative or military capacity, thus receiving protection against peasant insurrections or other nobles. Allying with a group of military retainers, Ivan decimated noble families he viewed as too powerful or too slow to obey. Ivan alternated between moods of religious fervor, drunken passion, and stormy brutality. After being defeated in Lithuania in 1564, Ivan subjected his people to an eight-year reign of terror. He killed his own son with a massive blow to the skull and routinely ordered anyone who displeased him tortured to death.

Ivan's death in 1584 led, almost unimaginably, to an even worse period for Muscovy. The "Time of Troubles" (1598–1613) was a period of intermittent anarchy. Weak successors allowed nobles to regain control of the now sprawling country. Polish armies took Moscow in 1605 and again five years later. In 1613, the Assembly of Nobles elected the first tsar from the

Romanov family. The next two tsars restored order, regaining some of the lands lost to Poland-Lithuania and Sweden.

For most peasants, life itself was an endless "time of troubles" in the face of state taxation and brutalization at the hands of their lords. Revolts seemed endemic, some led by men who claimed to be the "true" tsar who would restore justice. One of the latter led a huge force of peasants, which captured several cities before being decimated in 1670.

Serfdom emerged as one of the fundamental characteristics of Russia. In times of dearth or crisis, many peasants traditionally had fled the region of Moscow to settle on the frontier lands of Siberia in the east or in Ukraine, standing between Russia, Poland-Lithuania, and a Tatar state on the Crimean peninsula—the word Ukraine itself means "border region." The resulting chronic shortage of rural labor, and the need to provide landed estates to loyal nobles, led the state in 1649 officially to establish serfdom, which had already become widespread in the late sixteenth century. The chronically indebted Russian peasants gave up their freedom in exchange for loans from the crown and from landlords. The Orthodox Church, a major landowner, also contributed to the expansion of serfdom. Nearly 90 percent of peasants in Russia were now bound to the land, assuring the state and nobles of a relatively immobile labor supply. In exchange for the tsar's support of this system, Russian nobles, like their counterparts in Prussia, pledged their service to the state.

In the meantime, the Commonwealth of Poland and Lithuania to the west, Swedish territories to the north, and the Ottoman Turks to the south blocked Russia's further expansion. The northern port of Archangel on the White Sea, its harbor frozen solid much of the year, offered Muscovy its only access to the sea. Polish territories included much of today's Belarus and Ukraine. Most landowners in Ukraine were Polish Catholics. Most Ukrainian peasants were, like Russians, Orthodox Christians and spoke a language similar to Russian. Peasant revolts rocked Ukraine in the late 1640s, and, after an uprising that drove back the Polish army, Ukraine accepted Russian sovereignty in 1654. Under the Treaty of Andrussovo (1667), which concluded a war with Poland, Russia absorbed Ukraine east of the Dnieper River. To the south, several peoples resisted incorporation into Russia as well as into Poland-Lithuania. These included Turks, Crimean Tatars (an ethnic Turkic group), and Cossacks, a warrior people living on the steppes of southern Russia and Ukraine.

The Rival Swedish Empire

In the 1640s and 1650s, Swedish kings added to their dynastic holdings the regions of Denmark and Norway, Estonia and Lithuania, and West Pomerania in northern Germany. Like the Habsburg empire, the kingdom of Sweden encompassed a farraginous set of languages, including Swedish, Finnish, Latvian, Estonian, and German, the language of administration. Sweden was a relatively poor state, but revenues from lucrative copper mines, the sale of Swedish iron and steel—the finest in Europe—and trade with Muscovy and then Russia and the West generated enough revenue to finance expansion. But expansion had its costs: Queen Christina (ruled 1632–1654) raised money by selling almost two-thirds of the royal lands, with Swedish nobles becoming the main beneficiaries. Swedish peasants, who had their own Estate in the Swedish Diet (assembly), demanded in vain the return of all alienated lands to the throne. The lower Estates did not dare challenge royal prerogatives: "We esteem Your Majesty's royal power as the buttress of our liberties, the one being bound up in the other, and both standing or falling together."

Emboldened by his fledgling empire, King Charles XI (ruled 1660–1697) in the 1680s established absolute rule in Sweden. He overcame the resistance of the wealthiest nobles by winning the support of their jealous colleagues of lesser means, as well as that of the burghers, clergy, and peasants, who increasingly sought royal protection against the most powerful nobles. His son Charles XII (ruled 1697–1718) became king at the age of fifteen. He snatched the crown during his coronation and placed it on his own head, and never convoked the Estates. Having been instructed only in warfare as a youth, he remained a headstrong military man who acted by impulse, not reflection, relying on military force to achieve Swedish ends. Instead of turning Sweden's full military attention toward Denmark, which sought to recapture lost provinces from Sweden, he spent five years campaigning against Russia (see p. 277), a quest that took him into the Ottoman Empire, where he sought assistance against Russia. But during Charles XII's reign, the crown added to its wealth by reclaiming land that had been sold to nobles in the previous decades. Gradually the Swedish monarchy established a bureaucracy and increased state revenue. But when Charles XII was killed in a war in Norway, leaving no heir, the Swedish nobility succeeded in imposing a parliamentary regime based on the prerogatives of the Estates and marked by complicated political struggles. In 1772, however, King Gustavus III (ruled 1771–1792) overthrew the parliamentary system, supported by some nobles, and reimposed absolute rule, albeit with a new constitution that reduced the power of the Senate and the Diet. Gustavus III portrayed himself as a "patriot king" protecting peasants from avaricious nobles. By then, however, Sweden's empire was a fading memory and Gustavus's aristocratic enemies organized his assassination in 1792.

Peter the Great Turns Westward

In Western Europe so little was known about "barbaric" Russia that Louis XIV sent a letter to a tsar who had been dead for twelve years. Peter the Great (ruled 1682–1725) first imposed order on a state torn by bloody uprisings; then he created an enormous inland Russian Empire. Whereas Ivan the Terrible and several of his successors had been turned back by

Poland and Turkey, Peter's wars brought territorial acquisitions at the expense of Sweden, Poland, and the Turks. No European state more dramatically increased its territory than Russia, which expanded its frontiers at a rapid pace between the 1620s and 1740s. During the seventeenth century, Russian territory increased from 2.1 to 5.9 million square miles, even if in the distant reaches of north Asia this included little more than a series of trade routes.

As a boy growing up in the violent world of Russian court politics, Peter was schooled in all manner of guns, ballistics, and fortifications, and he was fascinated by sailing. Wearing a military uniform, he became tsar at the age of ten after a bloody struggle, which he witnessed firsthand, between the clans of his father's two widows. Seven years later, Peter killed members of his own family whom he perceived to be a threat to his rule.

Tsar Peter, who wore shabby clothes, worn-out boots, socks he had darned himself, a battered hat, and very long hair, stood close to seven feet tall and suffered from chronic back problems compounded by frenetic energy. Facial tics became most apparent when he was anxious or angry, which seemed to be most of the time, as he lashed out with clubs or fists. On several occasions he carried out public executions himself with an axe.

When he was twenty-five, Peter visited Western Europe incognito, dressed as a humble, giant workman. He preferred the company of ordinary people (his second wife was a Latvian peasant), enjoyed wood turning and fire fighting, and was most comfortable in simple Russian wooden houses. In the West, he shocked statesmen and nobles with his dress and coarse manners, snatching meat from dining tables. In London, Peter and his entourage virtually destroyed a rented house with wild parties—the tsar loved to dance and drink—leading an English bishop to worry aloud that this "furious man had been raised up to so absolute an authority over so great a part of the world."

Peter was not an uncritical admirer of the West, but he borrowed Western technical knowledge as he sought to copy absolutism. In London he became fascinated by the use of mathematics in shipbuilding, and four months on the Dutch docks taught him ship carpentry. Impressed with the military strength and administrative efficiency of the Western powers, Peter emulated what he considered to be more "rational" organization. His turn toward the West represented a monumental cultural change that was secular in character. He ordered nobles to become educated, told his guards and officials to shave off their beards, encouraged the use of glasses, bowls, and napkins at meals, and ordered a Western book of etiquette translated into Russian. Furthermore, he ordered nobles to build Western-style palaces, and he demanded that women wear bonnets, petticoats, and skirts. German and, to a lesser extent, French became the language of court. Purchasing German and Italian paintings and statues, Peter began the royal collection that would later become the renowned Hermitage Museum in St. Petersburg, and he also created the Russian Academy of Science and the Moscow School of Mathematics and Navigation.

Peter the Great trimming the long sleeves of the boyars, symbolically reducing noble power in the Russian Empire.

Peter retained a marked ambivalence about the role of tsar, maintaining a "Drunken Assembly," a kind of mock parallel government of people he trusted with strange statutes and rituals. Presided over by a pretend "prince-pope," the "All Jesting Assembly" undertook boisterous, bawdy farces that mocked religious ceremonies. Yet Peter the Great's reforms reflected the influence of Western absolutism on the Russian state. He believed that it was his role to help his people achieve the best living conditions possible. He thus came to a conception of the common good that he closely identified with Russian patriotism. At the time Peter became tsar, only three books considering nonreligious themes had been translated into Russian—a grammar book, a law code, and a military manual. Translations of Western books followed at Peter's instigation, including works by John Locke. The tsar sent Russian students abroad to learn and, in doing so, helped move Russia away from a uniquely religious culture.

Fearing the military superiority of his rivals, Sweden and Poland-Lithuania, Peter now raised the first Russian standing army, gradually replacing Western mercenary soldiers with Russian troops by implementing military conscription in 1705 in order to have an infantry to complement Cossack cavalrymen. Thereafter, one recruit—who would serve for life—had to be provided for every twenty peasant households. Peter brought in Western commanders to train his army and provided soldiers with uniforms and Western flintlock muskets with socket bayonets.

The bustling docks of Amsterdam and London had inspired Peter's interest in building first a river navy and eventually an oceangoing fleet. Skilled workers from Prussia and the Dutch Republic were hired to build warships, and Russian craftsmen were sent abroad to learn new skills. Russians gradually replaced Western Europeans as designers, builders, and ship commanders. By the end of the century, Russia had a naval fleet.

Military might, then, also underlay Russian absolutism. Even in peacetime, at least two-thirds of state revenue went to the army and navy. Peter forced nobles to send their sons to new military and engineering schools by decreeing they could not marry unless they did so. To pay for his army, the tsar tripled state revenues, imposing a direct tax on each male serf, or "soul." Landlords became responsible for the collection of these taxes. He established state monopolies on the production and sale of salt, oil, tobacco, rhubarb, and even dice, awarding the profitable right to collect these revenues to his favorite nobles, to "official" merchants, or to foreigners. The acquisition of new territories helped increase state tax revenues by three times. Hoping to expand Russian industry and attract gold and silver payments from abroad, Peter oversaw the exploitation of mines and the establishment of a metal industry in the Ural Mountains. But even absolute authority could not overcome a primitive transportation system, the lack of capital, and the absence of a sizable merchant class.

Peter succeeded in managing the often volatile politics of the court and the boyars, the 200 to 300 noble families (some of whom had as many as 40,000 serfs on their lands). While remaining an autocrat, Peter was nonetheless the first tsar to distinguish between his person as ruler and the state itself. Indeed, he made officials take two oaths, one to him and one to the state whose power he enhanced.

Tsar Peter reorganized the civil administration, dividing his domains into fifty administrative districts, each with a governor, although the effective reach of the state over such vast lands remained quite weak. He created a Senate, an administrative body charged with ruling in his absence during wartime and with overseeing state administration in times of peace. He experimented with councils, or committees, whose members could—if they dared—give him advice, representing the equivalent of government ministries. The tsar also put towns under the direct control of provincial governors, although they retained some measure of self-government. The Table of Ranks (1722) required all male nobles to enter state service and serve in the army, navy, or bureaucracy, and allowed commoners who rose through the bureaucracy or military to assume noble titles. Thus, the nobility also became an instrument of the state, and in Moscow nobles sought places on the boyar council (Duma), which met in the throne room of the palace.

The tsar's turn toward the West angered the old noble families of Moscow and the traditional Orthodox Church leaders, despite the fact that Peter himself remained quite pious. In particular, Peter faced the hostility of the Old Believers, dissidents who claimed authority over the tsars and resented that Peter subordinated the church to his state. They also opposed Greek and Byzantine liturgical forms, as well as the growing influence of baroque art and religious architecture imported to Russia from Central Europe. They considered such reforms, which constituted a "Russian reformation," sacrilegious. For example, they believed that the beards the tsar had ordered shaved had distinguished Russians from people in the West. Peter placed the Orthodox Church fully under state control, first by not naming a new patriarch (the head of the Russian Orthodox Church) upon the death of the incumbent in 1700 and later by simply abolishing the patriarchate. Peter overcame four uprisings and several conspiracies directed against him. In 1716–1718, he suspected his son Alexei, who was influenced by churchmen and boyars who did not support the tsar's wars, of being involved in a plot with the Habsburg monarchy against him. Peter ordered him tortured to reveal his accomplices, who were executed, and Alexei died in a prison cell.

MAP 7.3 THE EXPANSION OF RUSSIA   The state of Muscovy was expanded through the acquisitions of Ivan III, Ivan IV (the Terrible), and Peter the Great.

In the meantime, Peter the Great pushed back the neighbors who had blocked Muscovy's expansion: Sweden, Poland, and the Ottoman Turks. He added territory beyond the Ural Mountains, and along the Caspian Sea at the expense of the Turks (see Map 7.3). Peter dreamed of conquering the Turkish capital of Constantinople, which would give him control over its straits, the crucial passage between Europe and Asia leading to the Black Sea. Peter's new fleet sailed down the Don River in 1696, taking the Turkish port of Azov on the Sea of Azov, which gives access to the Black Sea. However, he was forced to surrender Azov back to the Turks after an unsuccessful war against them (1710–1711), thus remaining without access to the Black Sea.

Russia's role in European affairs, however, had remained minimal, despite its participation, with Habsburg Austria, Poland, and Venice, in the long series of wars against the Turks in the last decades of the seventeenth century. Russia joined Denmark and Saxony in attacking Sweden in the Great Northern War (1700–1721). The Russian ambassador in Vienna reported that once the news of Peter's victory arrived, "people begin to fear the tsar as formerly they feared Sweden." Peter's goal was to win a "window on the Baltic Sea" at Sweden's expense. The Swedes turned back the assault of a much larger Russian army at Narva (1700) in Estonia. But after Charles XII of Sweden passed up the opportunity to pursue the Russian army in order to invade Poland and Saxony, the Russian army conquered the mouth of the Neva River in 1703.

There Peter ordered the construction of a new capital city, where he forced nobles and wealthy merchants to build elegant townhouses. Saint

St. Petersburg, Peter the Great's new capital of the Russian Empire.

Petersburg offered a striking contrast to the chaos of tangled streets and shabby wooden buildings of Moscow, then by far the largest city in Russia. Built on coastal marshlands, Saint Petersburg reflected architectural ideas borrowed from the West, particularly Amsterdam. State offices, including army and military headquarters, occupied the centrally located islands. Symmetrical facades rose along the Neva River's south bank, near the ship-yards, admiralty, and fortresses. Unlike Moscow, churches did not dominate the skyline of Saint Petersburg. Geometrically arranged boulevards, squares, gardens, and baroque palaces completed the tsar's capital, which itself became a reflection of absolute rule.

Russia supplanted Sweden as the Baltic region's dominant power. In 1709 at the Battle of Poltava, Peter's army turned back an invading Swedish army in Ukraine, a battle that marked the end of Sweden's status as a great power and its domination of northern Europe, allowing Peter to annex eastern Ukraine and bringing the Black Sea into sight. Five years later Russian troops raided Sweden for the first time. After losing its German and Polish territories, Sweden then entered a period of constitutional struggles, as the nobility tried to reassert economic and social prerogatives lost to the monarchy (see p. 271). This allowed Russia to solidify its expansion. The Treaty of Nystadt (1721) confirmed Russian primacy in the Baltic region, adding Estonia and Livonia (the southeastern part of modern Finland) to Peter's empire and bringing Russia ever closer to European affairs.

By the time of Peter's death in 1725, the territory controlled by abso-lutist Russia had increased sixfold since the time of Ivan the Terrible. The Russian Empire, thirty times bigger than France, had joined the European state system.

Louis XIV's Dynastic Wars

As rulers of Russia, Sweden, Prussia, Austria, Turkey, and France sought to expand their territories, dynastic interests determined the choice of allies. Yet strong states were also likely to switch sides to gain the most beneficial terms from new allies. For example, in order to expand its influence in Cen-tral Europe, France needed an alliance with either Austria or Prussia. But inevitably such a coalition pushed the other German power into opposition, forcing it to look for allies against France. Usually this partner was England (Great Britain after the union of England and Scotland in 1707), France's rival in North America. Following the conclusion of hostilities that reworked borders, alliances frequently shifted, as rulers anticipated their next oppor-tunity to conquer new lands.

Louis XIV was determined that territorial gain and prestige should be the measure of his greatness (see Map 7.4). France was the continent's richest, strongest, and most populous state. The king of France sought to expand his kingdom's borders to what he considered to be France's "natural" frontiers, that is, the Pyrenees Mountains to the south and the Rhine River to the east.

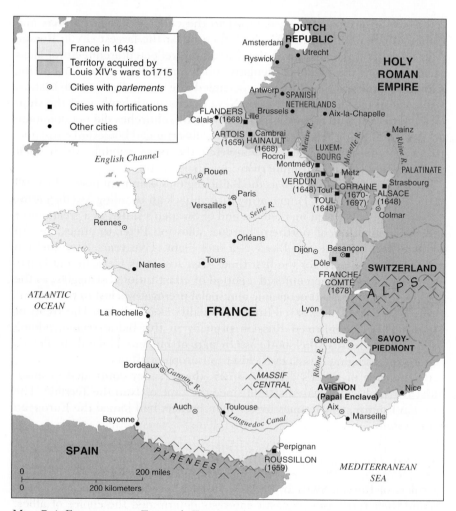

MAP 7.4 EXTENSION OF FRANCE'S FRONTIERS UNDER LOUIS XIV   Louis XIV sought to expand his dynastic territories through wars fought between 1643 and 1715.

International conditions seemed conducive to such grandiose plans. England had been divided by civil war in the 1640s, and its restored monarch, Charles II, faced mounting political opposition at home (see Chapter 6). To the north, Sweden confronted a Danish threat to its control of the Baltic Sea. In Central Europe, the Austrian Habsburgs confronted other German princes, as well as threats from Poland-Lithuania and the Turks.

Louis XIV's "grand strategy" was to contain the two Habsburg powers, Spain and Austria, by initiating a series of wars. Each conflict followed the king's violation of a previous agreement or formal treaty, and was accompanied by the claim that French aggression was "just." Each war was to pay for itself: French armies would force local populations to offer "contributions." The Treaty of the Pyrenees (1659), ending essentially a quarter of a century of hostilities with Spain, established the lasting frontier between the two states and confirmed France's status as the preeminent European power.

France again went to war against Spain in 1667. Louis wanted to annex Spain's French-speaking Franche-Comté to the east and the Spanish Netherlands (Belgium) to the north. When French armies invaded the Spanish Netherlands, England, fearful that Flanders and its Channel ports would fall to France, joined the Dutch Republic, Sweden, and Spain to turn back Louis XIV's armies. By the Treaty of Aix-la-Chapelle (Aachen) in 1668, France annexed Lille and part of Flanders. Four years later, Louis XIV invaded the Dutch Republic after assuring English neutrality by making secret payments to King Charles II. The Dutch fended off the French by opening up the dikes to create a barrier of water (see Chapter 6). After several more years of indecisive fighting and negotiations, France absorbed Franche-Comté and tiny parcels of the Southern Netherlands. Still the king of France was not satisfied. He conquered Alsace and Lorraine beyond his eastern frontier. Despite the opposition of a wary alliance of Habsburg Austria, Spain, Sweden, and Saxony, Louis XIV ordered the invasion of the Palatinate, intending to secure the Rhine River. This initiated the War of the League of Augsburg (1688–1697). England and the Dutch Republic (an alliance solidified by the fact that William III of Orange now was king of England) and a number of other German states joined the coalition against France.

After hesitating, in 1692 Louis made a foolish attempt to invade England. Dutch and English ships drove the French fleet onto rocks off the coast of Normandy; the two sea powers then enforced an economic blockade of France. Louis XIV retaliated by turning French privateers loose on his enemies' ships. French defeats as well as rising opposition in the Dutch Republic and England to the cost of the war forced both sides to negotiate. The Treaty of Ryswick of 1697 confirmed French gains in Alsace, but also made clear that the other European powers would ally again if necessary to keep France from further territorial acquisitions in the Southern Netherlands and the German states in order to preserve the balance of power.

The question of the succession to the throne of Spain soon presented Louis XIV with the greatest temptation of all. The Habsburg King Charles II of Spain had no direct heir. Louis opposed the candidacy of the Habsburg archduke Charles of Austria (son of Holy Roman Emperor Leopold I), hoping to end the virtual encirclement of France by Habsburg powers. Then Louis XIV, whose wife was the daughter of the late Philip IV of Spain, put forth his own claim to the throne.

When Charles II died in 1700, he left a will expressing his desire that his diminished empire remain intact, and that Louis XIV's grandson Philip of Anjou succeed him, but renounce any claim to the throne of France. However, on ascending the Spanish throne, Philip V (ruled 1700–1746) made clear that he favored the interests of his imposing grandfather. The Austrian Habsburg ruler Leopold I refused to accept Charles II's will as valid and invaded the Italian territories of the Spanish Habsburgs.

Louis XIV refused to rule Philip V out of the line of succession to the French throne, so that if Philip's elder brother, the duke of Bourgogne, died without male issue, Philip would then inherit the throne of France, and the kingdoms of France and Spain would be joined. The matter became pressing in 1712, when smallpox struck the French royal family, leaving only Bourgogne's youngest son as heir to the French throne. If the future Louis XV had died then, Philip would have become heir to both kingdoms.

The French king's obvious interest in the possibility of the two thrones being brought together drew Great Britain into the war. The Dutch Republic again had reason to fear French occupation of the Spanish Netherlands. If the French opened up the Scheldt River to trade, Antwerp would reemerge as a commercial rival to Amsterdam. This vital link to the English Channel had been closed since the Dutch formally received independence from Spain in 1648, thus preventing ships from reaching Antwerp. The alliance against France also included Austria, Prussia, and Portugal. The War of the Spanish Succession reflected the fact that European wars were taking on a global dimension (see Chapter 6), as the powers fought for markets as well as prestige. As in the War of the League of Augsburg, British and French forces also battled in North America.

The Rock of Gibraltar being captured by the English fleet during the War of Spanish Succession.

France fought with Bavaria and Spain as allies. The English commander, the duke of Marlborough (1650–1722), raised an army of English, Dutch, and mercenary troops. In 1704, at Blenheim in southern Germany, the allied armies, aided by Habsburg Austrian troops, crushed a combined French and Bavarian force. Louis XIV's armies retreated behind the Rhine River. Winning victories in the Spanish Netherlands in 1708 and 1709, the allied armies also drove the French from the Spanish Netherlands and out of the Italian peninsula. The English fleet captured Gibraltar (1704), which guards the entrance to the Mediterranean Sea. During the terrible winter of 1709–1710, France suffered military defeat and famine. The great kingdom of Louis XIV seemed on the verge of collapse.

But the French and Spanish armies revived their fortunes. Dynastic changes, too, helped Louis XIV's cause. In 1711, Archduke Charles of Austria became Holy Roman Emperor Charles VI (ruled 1711–1740). Should France and Philip V of Spain be defeated, the British and Dutch now confronted the possibility that Charles might one day become king of Spain, reviving the dynastic union that had made the Habsburg dynasty Europe's strongest power during the first half of the seventeenth century. It was now in the interests of Great Britain and the Dutch Republic to bring the war to an honorable conclusion. Louis XIV, weakened by age and illness and suffering the financial burdens of the war, agreed to negotiate.

Under the 1713 Treaty of Utrecht (confirmed by the Treaty of Rastatt in 1714, when Emperor Charles VI accepted peace), Habsburg Austria received the Southern Netherlands as security against future French ambitions and annexed Lombardy and Naples, replacing Spain as the paramount power on the Italian peninsula (see Map 7.5). The decline of Spain, which had now lost all of its European possessions beyond the Pyrenees Mountains, continued unabated. In North America, France ceded Newfoundland, Nova Scotia, and Hudson Bay to Great Britain.

Louis XIV had reigned so long that on his death in 1715 the throne passed to his great-grandson, young Louis XV (ruled 1715–1774), with affairs of state in the hands of a regent. Philip V kept the throne of Spain, but the monarchies of Spain and France would remain separate. Louis XIV was defeated by more than powerful alliances mounted against him. Britain had proved better able to sustain long wars; its more developed commerce and manufactures provided greater tax revenues. The non-absolutist British state collected taxes more efficiently than the absolute monarchy of France, where tax farmers kept part of the take. Britain's interests remained overseas, dominated by lucrative commercial concerns that were protected by the Royal Navy. France's foreign policy had led to costly wars on the continent.

France had been the preeminent power in Europe at the time of the accession of Louis XIV; this was no longer true at his death. The king's reputation had fallen victim to unrestrained ambition. Perhaps a lingering sense of failure explains why Louis XIV tried to burn his memoirs shortly before his

MAP 7.5 EUROPE IN 1721 Territorial realignments in Europe after the Treaty of Utrecht (1713), the Treaty of Rastatt (1714), and the Treaty of Nystadt (1721).

death (although they were rescued from the fire). On his deathbed, Louis confessed with uncharacteristic insight that perhaps he had "loved glory too much."

THE MODERN STATE

As they established absolute rule, the sovereigns of continental Europe constructed the modern state. While extending authority over their subjects and expanding their dynastic territories, they developed state bureaucracies and established large standing armies. They broke noble resistance to absolute rule, confirming their privileges in exchange for loyalty to the throne. This relationship between rulers and nobles thus remained essential to the functioning of most European states in the eighteenth century.

Following a period of relative stability, the structure of Western European society then began to change as the European economy entered a remarkable period of dynamic growth, particularly during the second half of the eighteenth century. This was the case above all in Britain, where the expansion of capital-intensive agricultural techniques, population growth, and a boom in manufacturing combined to begin the Industrial Revolution. The changing structure of society, in turn, would affect states by encouraging demands for political reform that began in the 1760s and 1770s and challenged the monopoly on political power by oligarchies and absolute rule itself. Traditional assumptions about science also came under attack. The methodology, discoveries, and culture of the Scientific Revolution helped create modern science.

PART THREE
NEW CULTURAL AND POLITICAL HORIZONS

During the late seventeenth century and the eighteenth century, Europe entered a period of remarkable intellectual and political ferment. Rejecting the weight of tradition, men and women of science developed the scientific method, a means of understanding based on systematic observation of natural phenomena and experimentation regarding causes and effects. Their successors, the philosophes—the thinkers and writers of the Enlightenment—believed their role was to bring progress to the world through the application of reason to their reflections on the nature of mankind. Influenced by growing religious skepticism and increased knowledge of the New World brought through overseas trade and the establishment of European empires, and drawing on expanding literacy, the philosophes espoused views of nature, mankind, society, and government that challenged some of the fundamental tenets most Europeans shared.

During this exciting period, Europe also entered a remarkable time of economic and social change. Increased agricultural productivity supported a larger population that, in turn, raised the demand for food and permitted the development of large-scale manufacturing in and around northern English towns.

Changes also came in the realm of political life. The public political sphere was transformed by the emergence of newspapers and learned associations, which facilitated political interest and discussion. Reform-minded people began to denounce unwarranted privilege and "despotism," and they celebrated the British model of constitutional monarchy and the successful rebellion of the American colonists against British rule. In a time of economic and social change, new cultural and political innovations began to transform Europe.

CHAPTER 8

THE NEW PHILOSOPHY OF SCIENCE

In 1633, ecclesiastical authorities summoned the astronomer and physicist Galileo Galilei (1564–1642) to Rome to face the Inquisition. The stakes were high. In the first year of the new century, the Italian Giordano Bruno (1548–1600), a Dominican friar accused of heresy who loudly proclaimed the virtues of scientific investigation, had been burned along with his books in Rome. Many Church fathers vehemently objected to Galileo's work on physics, for he, like Bruno, espoused an atomistic theory of matter that seemed to challenge the Catholic Church's view that during communion bread and wine become the body and blood of Christ. The Church also opposed Galileo's contention that the earth revolves around the sun. The papacy's political situation forced the Church's hand. Protestant armies had recaptured some of the lands in which the Catholic Reformation had appeared victorious. The papacy, its influence weakened by the Protestant Reformation and eclipsed by powerful dynastic rulers, could ill afford another defeat.

Pope Urban VIII, who before his elevation to the pontificate had been Galileo's friend, accused the astronomer only of supporting the views of the Polish scientist Copernicus, not of heresy. This would save Galileo from death but might also put the pope in a bad light for protecting the scientist. Although Galileo agreed to renounce these "errors" as heresies in order to avoid a death sentence, in 1633 he was still sentenced to a lifetime of house arrest. When guards returned him to his house, however, he cast a glance to the heavens and proclaimed of the earth, "See, it's still moving!"

The origins of modern science date to the seventeenth century, a period so marked by innovative thinking that it has been called the "century of genius." In several different corners of Europe, a few people struggled to understand the workings of the cosmos in a new way. Their own observations of the skies seemed to contradict explanations of the universe that had originated with Aristotle in the fourth century B.C. and, having acquired the authority of the Church, had been passed down for centuries. Breaking free of the bonds of tradition, these seventeenth-century thinkers developed the scientific method, a means of understanding based on systematic observation of natural phenomena and experimentation regarding causes and effects. But what we now know as the Scientific Revolution owed its impact less to new technology and inventions than to new ways of thinking about the universe.

CHANGING VIEWS OF THE UNIVERSE

The writings of the Greek philosopher Aristotle (384–322 B.C.) dominated European science for centuries. Then, in the sixteenth century, the Polish astronomer Copernicus observed the heavens and concluded that ancient and medieval science could not explain what he saw with his own eyes. Later in the century, his successors—above all, Galileo—made systematic mathematical calculations to explain celestial motion. In doing so, they created scientific methodology, which would also be applied to reach an understanding of the workings of the human body.

Ancient and Medieval Science

Aristotle believed that the earth was located at or near the center of the universe. He envisioned a hierarchical order of the cosmos comprised of a series of spheres that became progressively purer. Aristotle also believed that terrestrial bodies naturally moved toward the earth, the center of the universe, unless they were propelled in another direction. In this view, impetus imparted motion through contact with an object; when the contact ceased, the object simply stopped moving or fell back to earth. The natural tendency of all matter, then, was toward rest, regarded as a nobler state than motion. Because all motion had to be explained, a "mover" therefore had to be found for every motion.

In the second century A.D., the Greek astronomer Claudius Ptolemy (c. 85–165) published a massive work that became known as *Almagest* (from the Arabic for "greatest"), which summarized the conclusions of Greek astronomers and presented his own theories and observations. He described instruments such as the quadrant, invented by the Arabs, with which he tried to measure the orbits (which he believed to be spherical) of the sun, moon, and planets in the sky. Ptolemy accepted Aristotle's contentions, asserting that the earth was encased by a series of clear spheres—about eighty—revolving around it. The most distant sphere contained the farthest stars, which he believed were fixed points of light. Within those spheres, the moon was closest to the earth; next came the planets Mars, Venus, Jupiter, and Saturn. With minor variations, medieval thinkers still held Ptolemy's views.

Within the context of Christian theology, people of learning in the Middle Ages believed that scientific inquiry should serve theological ends through the study of nature to explain the mysterious ways of God. Church savants never raised the possibility that mankind could, with understanding, alter or master nature.

Aristotle's belief that the heavens and earth displayed two different kinds of motion—one toward the center of the earth, which seemed the natural state, but also an unnatural violent motion away from it—nicely fit the medieval Church's view that the universe consisted of good and evil. The earth, standing at the center, was heavy, corrupted not only by its weight but also by original sin and earthly misdeeds. Angels therefore were placed far off in a weightless existence in Heaven. The goal of human beings was to achieve the lightness of Heaven, God's domain, on the exterior edge of the universe.

The writings of the medieval poet Dante (1265–1321) reflected the prevailing influence of Aristotle's physics and Ptolemy's astronomy. Dante held that the universe comprised ten spheres surrounding the spherical, motionless earth. In his *Inferno*, Dante and the Roman poet Virgil travel to the core of the earth, then climb out to the other side, the Southern Hemisphere, where they find Purgatory. Hell lay at the earth's center, with Heaven in the distant tenth sphere. Dante and his contemporaries believed that the earth consisted of four elements: earth, water, air, and fire, the first two of which had a natural tendency to fall toward the center of the stationary earth.

Medieval European scholars seemed little interested in astronomy. Yet, to be sure, some medieval thinkers took significant steps toward modern science by embracing the study of natural phenomena and revering the

Virgil, Cicero, and the Three Giants in the Lost Circle, from Dante's *Devine Comedy (The Inferno)*, 1313.

scholars who studied such problems. Medieval scientists made lasting contributions in such fields as optics—inventing eyeglasses—and biology. They classified objects for study and espoused experimentation based on scientific procedures and the use of mathematics to verify theories. But even the contributions of the most brilliant medieval thinkers remained only in the realm of theory.

As the Renaissance drew on the discovery of classical prose, poetry, art, and architecture, Italian scholars of the period also turned to classical Greek scientific texts that had been recovered, edited, and printed. The Arabs had come into contact with classical learning centuries earlier, when they conquered the eastern reaches of the Byzantine Empire. Arab scholars, who also made significant original contributions in astronomy, mathematics, and medicine, preserved many ancient Greek and Roman texts, translating them into Arabic. Some of the manuscripts brought by Greek scholars to the West from Constantinople after its conquest by the Turks in 1453 suggested that mathematics could be applied in the quest for knowledge about the universe. Arab scholars had raised troubling questions challenging age-old views of the earth as they observed and even began to measure the heavenly phenomena they beheld. In this way, the texts of Ptolemy became subjects of renewed interest and study.

Ptolemy's view of the cosmos reflected the domination of Aristotle's theory of motion. Yet there had earlier been at least one dissenting voice. Archimedes of Syracuse (c. 287–212 B.C.) had challenged Aristotle's contention that rest was a natural state for all objects and that only the presence of an "active mover" could generate motion. This view was picked up again in the fourteenth century by thinkers at Paris and Oxford Universities. They observed that falling bodies move at an accelerating speed and that the accompanying presence of a "mover" simply could not be observed. A few scholars also rejected Aristotle's explanation that air itself served as a natural propellant. They observed that an arrow shot from a bow clearly was not continually propelled by air or anything else, but sooner or later simply fell to earth. The gradual development of a theory of motion, based on an understanding of the role of the mass of the moving object, along with the advances in the field of mathematics itself, provided the basis for new discoveries in astronomy and mechanics.

Copernicus Challenges the Aristotelian View of the Universe

The revolution in scientific thinking moved forward because of a cleric who kept his eyes toward the heavens, but not necessarily in pious contemplation. Nicolaus Copernicus (1473–1543) launched the strongest attack yet on the Aristotelian view of the universe. He was born near the Baltic coast in Poland. After the death of his father, Copernicus's uncle (a wealthy bishop) assumed responsibility for his education. From the University of Krakow, Copernicus went to Italy to study medicine and law. After learning Greek, he read medieval scientific and humanist texts. Also trained as a doctor and portrait painter, he devoted his life to observation and discovery.

Copernicus's *Concerning the Revolutions of the Celestial Spheres* was not published until he lay dying in 1543, the same year the work of Archimedes was first translated into Latin. Paradoxically, in view of the intense theological debate it would generate, Copernicus dedicated his study to the pope. Copernicus was troubled by the inability of the Ptolemaic system (itself a refraction of the Aristotelian view of the universe) to account for what his own observations, made with the naked eye, told him: that the planets, the moon, and the stars obviously did not move around the earth at the same speed. Nor did they seem to be in the spherical orbits Ptolemy had assigned them. That Mars seemed to vary in brightness particularly perplexed him. What Copernicus observed, in short, contradicted the fundamental assumptions of the Aristotelian and Ptolemaic universe.

Even before Copernicus, some thinkers questioned Aristotelian physics and the Ptolemaic cosmos, but they generally did not venture out of the realm of mere speculation. Nicholas of Cusa (1401–1464), a German bishop and theologian who wrote on astronomy, believed the earth might be in motion, but neither he nor anyone else in the period tried to make mathematical calculations that might prove or reject this bold theory. He suggested the possibility that the sun stands at the center of the universe and, by implication, that the universe is infinite and nonhierarchical in nature, unlimited by Aristotelian layers of spheres. The extraordinary Renaissance artist and humanist Leonardo da Vinci (see Chapter 2), who called wisdom "the daughter of experiment," had also suggested that the earth might move around the sun.

Copernicus concluded that the sun, not the earth, lies at the center of the universe and that the earth rotates on its axis once a day and revolves around the sun once every 365 days. "In the middle of all sits the Sun enthroned," he wrote. "How could we place this luminary in any better position in this most beautiful temple from which to illuminate the whole at once?" Copernicus's postulation was, like his critique of some of Ptolemy's conclusions, not totally original. But his assertions were bold, explicit, and, for many, convincing. Furthermore, they suggested that mathematics could verify astronomical theories.

The notion that the earth was just one of many planets rotating in circular orbit around the sun raised shocking questions about the earth's status. This perplexed and angered Catholic, Protestant, and Jewish theologians by seeming to reduce the standing of mankind. It seemed unbelievable that mere mortals peering into the heavens were themselves moving rapidly through the universe. Martin Luther, himself not given to accepting inherited wisdom without skepticism, said of Copernicus, "This fool wants to turn the whole of astronomy upside down!"

Copernicus did just that. Yet he seemed uninterested in carrying out his own systematic observations and made serious errors in some of his calculations. He could not explain why there was no constant wind from the east, which might be expected based on the assumption that the earth moved in that direction around the sun. Copernicus sometimes sought to answer his own doubts by turning to the teachings of the ancients and did not completely abandon the system of celestial spheres postulated by Ptolemy. Copernicus also continued to accept the notion that the spherical universe was finite, and that it perhaps was limited by the stars fixed in the heavens.

The Universal Laws of the Human Body

As scientists began to chart movements in the heavens, some scholars now began to question old assumptions about the human body. They contended that it is subject to the same universal laws that govern celestial and terrestrial motion. The Renaissance had generated interest in human anatomy. Most assumptions about how the body works had been passed down for centuries from the ancient world. Galen (129–c. 210), a Greek contemporary of Ptolemy, was the first person to develop theories about medicine based on scientific experiments. He carried out a number of experiments

Dissecting a cadaver at the University of Montpellier, 1363.

on apes, assuming that animal and human bodies were essentially the same in the arrangement of bodily organs. Like Aristotle, Galen believed that disease followed from an imbalance in the four bodily humors—blood, phlegm, yellow bile, and black bile. He held that two kinds of blood initiated muscle movement and digestion, respectively: bright red blood, which flowed up and down through the arteries, and dark red blood, which could be found in the veins. Doubting Galen's view of anatomy, Andreas Vesalius (1514–1564) published *On the Fabric of the Human Body* (1543). Arguably the founder of modern biological science, Vesalius rejected old explanations for the circulation of blood and began to dissect and study cadavers— in the Middle Ages, the Church had considered this to be sinful—and was the first to assemble human skeletons.

The English scientist William Harvey (1578–1657) largely solved the riddle of how blood circulates. Like the astronomers, he adopted a scientific methodology: "I profess," he wrote, "to learn and teach anatomy not from books but from dissections, not from the tenets of philosophers but from the fabric of nature." Harvey's accomplishment was in the realm of thought and owed virtually nothing to prior inventions. Indeed, he made his discoveries before the invention of the microscope, and he referred only twice in his experiments to a magnifying glass.

Harvey's theory of blood circulation pictured the heart and its valves functioning as a mechanical pump. Yet Harvey, like medieval thinkers, retained a belief that "vital spirits" were to be found in the blood. The long-term consequence of Harvey's work was, as in the case of Vesalius, to undermine further Aristotelian philosophy and medieval science and to help establish a basis for the development of modern biology and medicine in later centuries.

Brahe and Kepler Explore the Heavens

Tycho Brahe (1546–1601), a Danish astronomer, and Johannes Kepler (1571–1630), his German assistant, carried the search for an understanding of the way the universe works to a new stage of scientific knowledge. While studying philosophy at the University of Copenhagen, Brahe became fascinated with the heavens after observing a partial eclipse of the sun. Brahe, an odd-looking nobleman who had lost part of his nose in a duel and had replaced it with a construction of silver and gold alloy perched above his handlebar moustache, built an astronomical observatory on a Danish island.

Brahe rejected Copernicus's contention that the earth rotated around the sun. He claimed that if this were true, a cannonball fired from west to east (the direction Copernicus thought the earth moved) would travel farther in that direction, and a weight dropped from a tall tower would strike earth to the west of the tower because of the earth's movement. Brahe came up with a cumbersome compromise explanation that had the five known planets rotating around the sun, which in turn moved around the stationary earth.

In 1572, Brahe observed a bright exploding star. This and a comet sighted five years later irrevocably compromised the Aristotelian view of the universe as unchanging. Brahe compiled extensive data based upon his own observations, systematically charting what he could see of the planetary orbits and using mathematics to locate the position of the planets and stars. At the same time, his rejection of the Copernican view that the sun was the center of the universe and the fact that his calculations were often inaccurate remind us that the Scientific Revolution did not develop in a linear fashion. False turns and setbacks were part of the story.

Johannes Kepler, Brahe's assistant, was the son of a German mercenary soldier and an herb dealer with an interest in astrology (his mother would later be condemned to be burned at the stake for her dabblings in astrology; Kepler saved her life by undertaking a lengthy legal process). Kepler was a dazzling but strange individual: a rigorous astronomer and mathematician as well as a religious mystic and astrologer, who took credit for predicting not only a particularly harsh winter but also peasant uprisings in Germany.

Facing persecution from Lutheran theologians in 1596 because of his Copernican beliefs, Kepler briefly found protection from the Jesuits. But four years later, he was forced to leave a teaching position in Austria because he refused to convert from Lutheranism to Catholicism. Kepler moved to Prague and began to work with Brahe in 1600. On his deathbed, Brahe implored Kepler to complete his observation tables. Holy Roman Emperor Rudolph II, whose interest in science outweighed any concern

(Left) Tycho Brahe's system of planetary rotation, about 1560, (Right) Kepler's concept of an attractive force from the sun, early sixteenth century.

that Kepler was Protestant, appointed him to succeed Brahe as imperial mathematician.

Kepler shared Copernicus's belief that observers on earth were moving while the sun stood still. After carefully plotting the orbit of Mars, Kepler concluded that the orbits of the planets were "imperfect"—not circular, but rather elliptical. He also concluded that the planets were affected by some sort of force emanating from the sun. William Gilbert (1544–1603), an English scientist, had published a book on the magnet in 1600, the first study written by a university scholar and informed by laboratory experimentation. Gilbert's investigations of magnetic force provided a model for the development of a modern theory of gravitation. Kepler now decided that it was perhaps magnetic force that attracted the earth and sun to each other. He also determined that tides were the result of the magnetic attraction of the earth and the moon.

Based upon his mathematical calculations, Kepler postulated three laws of planetary motion, which he assumed were determined by the power, or specific magnetic attraction, of the sun. He used observation and mathematical calculations to demonstrate that the planets were a separate grouping with different properties from those of the fixed stars, and that Aristotle's crystalline spheres simply did not exist.

Kepler's discoveries, blows to Aristotelian and medieval science, also suggested that the hand of the prime mover—God—was not required to govern the movement of the planets. Even more than Copernicus's placing of the sun at the center of the universe, Kepler's conclusions challenged the theological assumptions of the Catholic Church. Nonetheless, the Scientific Revolution still occurred within the system of Christian belief. Kepler himself sought to glorify God by demonstrating the consistency, harmony, and order of divine creation as expressed in the working of the universe.

Francis Bacon and the Scientific Method

From England, Sir Francis Bacon (1561–1626), lawyer, statesman, and philosopher, launched a frontal assault on ancient and medieval metaphysics and science. Calling himself "a bellringer who is first up to call others to church," Bacon helped detach science from philosophy. Medieval scholasticism had focused, he argued, on abstract problems that were without practical consequences, such as the question of how many angels could stand on the head of a pin. So, too, had Renaissance humanism. Bacon rejected outright all arguments based on the weight of traditional authority, calling for "a total reconstruction of sciences, arts and all human knowledge."

Bacon carried out few experiments and made no discoveries that could have been considered significant by his own standards (he died after catching a bad cold while carrying out an experiment of marginal value: stuffing snow into a dead chicken). But Bacon announced the dawn of a new era in which humans would gradually begin to understand and then perhaps even overcome their physical environment. Through inductive reasoning—that is, proceeding from observation and experimentation to conclusions or generalizations—the truths of the universe would be revealed by discovery and scientific experiment, not by religion. "Arts and sciences," Bacon wrote in 1620, "should be like mines, where the noise of new works and further advances is heard on every side." Scientists should divide up the toil by specializing and working in cooperation to "overcome the necessities and miseries of humanity." Bacon's renown—he served for three years as King James I of England's Lord Chancellor (before being dismissed for accepting bribes)—helped create interest in science in England, although for the moment this was limited to a small number of people.

Galileo and Science on Trial

On the Italian peninsula, Galileo emerged as the dominant figure of the early stage of the Scientific Revolution. The scion of a wealthy family, he studied medicine and mathematics. Like Copernicus, he taught at the University of Padua, the leading center of scientific learning in Europe, at a time when virtually every other university showed little interest in scientific observation. That Padua was under the protection of Venice, which was hostile to the pope, facilitated its university's precocious role in the development of scientific methodology. Scholars in Padua hotly debated

(*Left*) Sir Francis Bacon. (*Right*) The feisty Galileo at age sixty.

Aristotelian explanations of motion as well as the question of the relationship between the natural sciences and metaphysics, or the nature of being. The latter debate was especially crucial, because on it hinged the question of whether scientific investigation could be independent of the Catholic Church, which considered revealed religion the only source of true knowledge.

New ways of thinking about the heavens, systematic observation, and scientific measurement had played a more significant role in the early stages of the Scientific Revolution than did the development of new technology. The invention of the telescope, however, led to further advances. Upon learning in 1609 that a man in the Netherlands had invented a "spy glass" that could magnify objects many times, Galileo constructed one of his own. This telescope enabled him to study Jupiter's moons, Saturn's spectacular rings, some of the innumerable stars of the Milky Way, and craters on the moon. His observation of spots that seemed to move on the surface of the sun led Galileo to conclude that the sun, too, rotated. That sunspots seemed to change also challenged the traditional view of the static nature of the universe.

Galileo undermined the Aristotelian theories of motion. He demonstrated that the earth was in perpetual rotation and that balls of varying weights will pick up speed at the same rate as they fall, so therefore their speed is not determined by their mass. From such experiments, he developed a theory of inertia: a body moving at a constant speed in a straight line will continue to move until encountering another force. He demonstrated that air and clouds move with the earth as it rotates around the sun, while appearing immobile to an observer also moving with the earth. The rooms in his house that he set aside for experimentation served as the first university laboratory.

Unlike other scholars, Galileo did not disdain seeking practical information from craftsmen and artisans. He consulted workers who built cannons, soldiers who fired them, and people who made compasses, astrolabes, quadrants, and other scientific instruments for navigation. He began to investigate water pumps and other means of regulating rivers, as well as planning the construction of stronger military fortresses. Nonetheless, Galileo did not care whether or not his discoveries reached ordinary people. Moreover, he claimed that "the mobility of the earth is a proposition far beyond the comprehension of the common people." And he believed that the "all-too-numerous vulgar" ought to be kept in darkness, lest they "become confused, obstinate, and contumacious."

At first, Galileo tried to reconcile his findings and those of Copernicus with early Church texts. But the feisty Galileo's insistence that the universe was mathematical in its very structure and subject to laws of mechanics that could be discovered left him open to attacks by ecclesiastical authorities. In 1610, he wrote Kepler, "Here at Padua is the principal professor of theology, whom I have repeatedly and urgently requested to look at the moon and planets through my glass, which he obstinately refused to do. Why are you not here? What shouts of laughter we should have at this glorious folly!" In 1616, the pope condemned Galileo's proposition that the sun is the center of the universe and warned him not to teach it. Undaunted, Galileo published his *Dialogue Concerning Two World Systems—Ptolemaic and Copernican*, in which he taunted Aristotelians by presenting a lengthy dialogue between those espousing the respective systems of Ptolemy and Copernicus. A certain Simplicio took the side of Ptolemy in the dialogues; the character's very name outraged the Church by intimating that a farcical character symbolized the pope. This led to Galileo's condemnation by the Inquisition in 1633. But from house arrest in his villa in the hills above Florence, Galileo continued to observe, experiment, and write, publishing his texts in the Netherlands. When he went blind in 1638, the pope refused to allow him to go to Florence to see a doctor. Despite his blindness, he continued his scientific investigations until his death four years later.

Descartes and Newton: Competing Theories of Scientific Knowledge

Two brilliant thinkers, one French and the other English, accepted Galileo's revision of classical and medieval systems of knowledge. But they offered contrasting theories of scientific knowledge. René Descartes sought to discover the truth through deductive reasoning. Across the English Channel, Isaac Newton followed his countryman Bacon's insistence that the way to knowledge was through scientific experiment. One amazing discovery after another added to the foundations of the "new philosophy" of science. Science played a major part in the quest for demonstrable truth and authority during and following the period of intense social and political turmoil that lasted from the 1590s until the mid-seventeenth century (see Chapter 4).

Descartes and Deductive Reasoning

The reclusive French philosopher René Descartes (1596–1650) shared Bacon's and Galileo's critiques of ancient and medieval learning. But he offered a different methodology for understanding the universe, espousing deductive reasoning, that is, deducing a conclusion from a set of premises, not from scientific observation.

In 1637, Descartes published *Discourse on Method*. In this deeply personal account, he discussed his rejection of the scientific teaching he had encountered as a young man. Too much of what he had learned had been handed down from tradition without critical commentary. He defiantly "resolved no longer to seek any other science than the knowledge of myself, or of the great book of the world."

Any person, Descartes claimed, has to begin as a blank slate in order to understand the world through deductive reasoning. "I think, therefore I am" (*Cogito, ergo sum*) was his starting point, the postulation of a self-evident truth and the assertion that the ability to think is the basis of human existence. Then each problem has to be separated, he argued, into "as many parts as may be necessary for its adequate solution," moving from the simplest idea to the most difficult, in the same way as a mathematical proof is formulated. Cartesianism (the philosophy of Descartes and his followers) held that the world could be reduced to two substances: mind and matter, "thinking substance" and "extended substance." Matter—defined as an infinite number of particles that fill all space, leaving neither void nor vacuum—could be discovered and described mathematically, as could the laws of motion. Beginning with the certainty of his own existence, Descartes argued that the existence of the material universe and God could be deduced. "Begin with the smallest object, the easiest to understand," he insisted, "and gradually move to a knowledge of those that are the most complex."

René Descartes.

This materialist approach to knowledge left little or no room for ancient or medieval learning. As a sign of this break, Descartes published his works in French, identifying Latin with scholasticism and ecclesiastical doctrine. Like Kepler, Descartes viewed God as a benevolent, infinitely powerful clockmaker, who created the universe according to rules that the human mind could discover with proper reasoning. God then stepped back, according to this view, forever absent from the actual workings of what He had created.

Mathematics, Descartes argued, demonstrates "the certainty and self-evidence of its reasonings." It therefore stood as the foundation of all science. Eventually a rule for every phenomenon could be discovered. Descartes thus subordinated experimentation to reason in the quest for truth. One of the stream of savants who went to meet Descartes recalled that "many of them would desire him to shew them his Instruments . . . he would drawe out a little Drawer under his Table, and shew them a paire of Compasses with one of the Legges broken; and then, for his Ruler, he used a sheet of paper folded double."

The Newtonian Synthesis

Sir Isaac Newton (1642–1727) built upon the thought of Kepler, Galileo, and Descartes to effect a bold synthesis of the Scientific Revolution, to which he added his own extraordinary discoveries. Newton's *Principia, The Mathematical Principles of Natural Philosophy* (1687) was the first synthesis of scientific principles. Newton synthesized the empiricism of Galileo and others with the theoretical rigor and logic of Descartes, thereby laying the foundations for modern science, which is based on both theory and experimentation.

Newton conducted some of his experiments while living on his prosperous family's farm. There, sitting under a tree, ruminating about celestial motion, Newton observed a falling apple, which led him to recognize that the force that caused objects to fall to earth was related to planetary motion. Newton demonstrated that earthly and celestial motion are subject to laws that could be described by mathematical formulas, the science of mechanics. Going beyond Kepler's three laws of planetary motion, Newton postulated a theory of universal gravitation, the existence of forces of attraction and repulsion operating between objects. Newton concluded that Kepler's laws of planetary motion would be correct if the planets were being pulled toward the sun by a force whose strength was in inverse proportion to their distance from it. The moon, too, seemed to be drawn to the earth in the same way, while the pull that it exerted determined the ocean tides. Every particle of matter, Newton concluded, attracts every other particle with a force proportional to the product of the two masses, and inversely proportional to the square of the distance that separates them.

Newton combined the insights of his predecessors with his own brilliant discoveries. He correctly calculated that the average density of the earth is about five and a half times that of water, suggested that electrical messages activate the nervous system, and anticipated some of the ideas that two centuries later would form the basis of thermodynamics and quantum theory. Newton was the first to understand that all colors are composed of a mixture of the primary colors of the spectrum. He explained the phenomenon of the rainbow, calculated sound waves, and invented calculus (with Gottfried Leibniz, concurrently but separately). In the late 1660s, he also constructed the first reflecting telescope (previous

Sir Isaac Newton.

telescopes had used a refracting lens). Newton's first paper on optics, published in 1671, proposed that light could be mathematically described and analyzed. Some scientists still consider this paper as the beginning of theoretical physics.

Unlike his predecessors in the development of science, Newton became wealthy and a hero in his own time. He was elected to Parliament in 1689 representing the University of Cambridge, (where he was a professor), became warden of the Royal Mint, and was knighted by the king. However, Newton remained a remote, chaste, humorless figure who published his discoveries with reluctance and initially only when it seemed that rivals might first take the credit for a discovery. He brazenly accused those working on similar problems of copying him, and was ungenerous in acknowledging what he had learned from others. Newton's fame marked the victory of the scientific method, however, over ancient and medieval thought. The eighteenth-century English poet Alexander Pope went so far as to compare Newton's accomplishments with those of God on the first day of creation: "Nature and Nature's laws lay hid in night; God said, Let Newton be! and all was light!" Newton was given a state funeral and buried in London's Westminster Abbey.

The Newtonian synthesis of scientific thinking and discovery spread rapidly from England to the continent. Newton's followers clashed with Cartesians, the followers of Descartes. Newton rejected Descartes's materialism, at least partially because it seemed to leave open the possibility that the world was made up totally of matter and that God did not exist, although the French philosopher never made such an assertion. For his part, Newton believed that God had to intervene from time to time to keep the great clock of creation running, lest it run down. That Newton continued to produce manuscripts on theological questions reflected his own belief that there seemed to be no necessary contradiction between science and religious faith.

Like Descartes, Newton insisted on the explanatory power of abstract reasoning. But despite his postulation of theories that could not be demonstrated by the scientific method, such as his description of gravity as a force that operates between two objects in space, where possible Newton sought to confirm them experimentally. Until at least 1720, some tension remained between the English scientific groups (who insisted on the necessity of experimentation) and their French and German Cartesian counterparts. Yet this was a creative tension, based on a common acceptance of the primacy of scientific inquiry.

The Cartesians found an ally in the Spanish-born Dutch philosopher and mathematician Baruch Spinoza (1632–1677), who also believed that thought and matter formed the two categories of reality. While making his living grinding lenses for glasses, he found both a philosopher's introspective isolation—arguing in a Cartesian manner that human understanding advances through inner reflection—and stimulation from the new physics.

Expelled from the Jewish community of Amsterdam in 1656 for refusing to participate in religious ceremonies, Spinoza, a proponent of human liberation, called for toleration of all beliefs.

The northern German philosopher and mathematician Gottfried Leibniz (1646–1716) agreed with Descartes and rejected Newton's suggestion that God had to intervene from time to time in the operations of the universe, believing this idea to be demeaning to the Creator's divinity. For Leibniz, the universe was, like God, infinite in space and time. The bodies of humans and animals ran like clocks, set in motion, like the universe itself, by God. Leibniz's popularity helped perpetuate the Cartesian challenge to Newton, notably in France. His deductive postulation of the infinite nature of the universe and his Cartesian insistence that God created the universe to run without further divine intervention according to the mathematical laws Newton had discovered became the hallmarks of the "new philosophy."

THE CULTURE OF SCIENCE

A "culture of science" developed in Western Europe and gradually spread eastward. By the 1660s, letters, newsletters, and periodicals linked Europeans interested in science. Gradually a "republic of science" took shape, spawning meetings, lectures, visits by traveling scholars, correspondence, book purchases, personal libraries, and public experiments. Above all, the formation of learned associations provided a focal point for the exchange of scientific information and vigorous debates over methodology and findings, expanding the ranks of people interested in science. Only a few decades after Galileo's condemnation, Louis XIV of France and Charles II of England granted patronage to institutions founded to propagate scientific learning. Attracted by scientific discoveries, rulers realized that science could be put to use in the interest of their states.

The Diffusion of the Scientific Method

Although most scientific exchange still occurred by correspondence, savants of science also traveled widely seeking to exchange ideas and learn from each other. For example, the Czech scholar Comenius (Jan Komensky, 1592–1670), a member of the Protestant Unity of Czech Brethren, left his native Moravia in the wake of religious persecution during the Thirty Years' War. After more than a decade in Poland, he began to visit scholars in many countries. For seven years, he traveled in the German states, the Netherlands, England, Sweden, and Hungary. Publishing hundreds of works, he proposed that one day scientific knowledge should be brought together in a collaborative form.

Learned associations and scientific societies had already begun to appear in a number of cities, including Rome and Paris, in the 1620s. In

London, a bequest made possible the establishment of Gresham College, which became a center for scientific discussion and research. In Paris, Marin Mersenne (1588–1637), a monk who had translated Galileo's writings into French, stood at the center of a network of vigorous scientific exchange that cut across national boundaries of states. He organized informal gatherings, attended by, among others, Blaise Pascal (1623–1662), a gloomy young physicist and mathematician who originated the science of probability.

In England, above all, the culture of science became part of public life during the period from 1640 to 1660, with the vocabulary of science joining the discourse of the English upper classes. Newton's prestige further spurred interest in scientific method. In several London coffeehouses, Newtonians offered "a course of Philosophical Lectures on Mechanics, Hydrostatis, Pneumatics [and] Opticks." Exchanges, debates, and even acrimonious disputes reached an ever wider scholarly audience. In England, pamphlets and books on scientific subjects were published in unprecedented numbers.

The Royal Society of London for Improving Natural Knowledge was formed in 1662 under the patronage of Charles II. Its diverse membership, which included merchants, naval officers, and craftsmen, reflected the growing interest in science in England. Members included Edmund Halley (1656–1742), an astronomer who catalogued and discovered the actual movement of the stars and who also discovered the comet that bears his name; the philosopher John Locke (1632–1704), founder of British empiricism, who held that laws of society, like those of science, could be discovered; and Christopher Wren (1632–1723), a versatile architect who rebuilt some of London's churches (including St. Paul's Cathedral) in the wake of the fire of 1666, but who was also a mathematician and professor of astronomy.

The Royal Society, to which Newton dedicated *Principia* and of which he served as president, took its motto from one of the letters of the Roman writer Horace: "The words are the words of a master, but we are not forced to swear by them. Instead we are to be borne wherever experiment drives us." The Royal Society's hundred original members doubled in number by 1670, its weekly meetings attracting visiting scholars. The *Philosophical Transactions of the Royal Society* published some of the most important work of members and foreign correspondents, especially in the field of mathematics.

The natural philosopher Margaret Cavendish, the duchess of Newcastle (1623–1673), participated in debates about matter and motion, the vacuum, magnetism, and the components of color and fire. The author of books on natural philosophy, as well as a number of plays and poems, Cavendish also hosted the "Newcastle circle," an informal gathering of distinguished scientists that received Descartes. But she worked in isolation, which she attributed not only to the fact that she was shy, but to her sex. Despite the

The Newcastle circle hosted by the duke and duchess of Newcastle. Margaret Cavendish, the duchess, is seated on the far right crowned with laurels.

evidence of her own achievements, she accepted, at least in her early years, the contemporary assumptions that women had smaller and softer brains than men, and thus were somehow unfit for science and philosophy. Few men of science would have agreed with the assertion in 1673 by one of Descartes's disciples in France that "the mind has no sex." This bold statement reflected Descartes's belief that thought transcended gender differences—and, therefore, having sense organs equal to men's, women should be recognized as their equals. But although Cavendish was permitted to attend one session, women were formally banned from the Royal Society—this would last until 1945—and they were excluded from English universities.

Yet as an interest in scientific theories and discoveries became influential among the educated upper classes, women also wanted to be informed about science. Several women assisted their husbands in scientific experiments. In Italy, it was more common for women to participate in the scientific life of their cities. Laura Bassi Veratti (1711–1778) studied philosophy at the University of Bologna and was elected to the Academy of Sciences, where she regularly presented her work—although she published very little. She received the title of university lecturer, but because of her gender she was not allowed to teach in public, only at home (which was very common in Italy). Later, however, after having studied mathematics, Bassi was named professor of experimental physics, experimented with fluid mechanics and electricity (perhaps even before Benjamin Franklin conducted his

Testelin's tapestry of the establishment of the French Royal Academy of Science, 1666, and the Foundation of the Observatory, 1667.

studies), was allowed in the last years of her life to teach in public, and thanks to surprising patronage from prelates in Rome was even able to gain access to the scientific studies that the pope had placed on the Index of Forbidden Ideas or Books. Laura Bassi remained an active participant in the scientific community.

In 1666, the French Royal Academy of Science held its first formal meeting in Paris. Like the English Royal Society, the French Academy enjoyed the patronage of the monarchy, which even provided the Academy with an astronomical observatory. Branches of the Academy began in several provincial cities. Unlike members of its English counterpart, those in the French Academy spent much time eating and drinking—one of them complained that too much time was wasted at the fancy dinners that preceded scholarly discussion.

Although some writers deliberately had used Latin because they believed that knowledge ought to remain the preserve of the educated few, with the gradual ebbing of Latin as the language of science, language barriers became a greater obstacle to the diffusion of ideas and research. Galileo had written in Italian to attract a wider audience among the elite, but also to remove science from Latin, the language of religious discourse. Newton wrote *Principia* in Latin, in part because only then could his work be read by most continental scholars. Newton's *Optics*, by contrast, appeared first in English, then in Latin and French translations. Gradually during the eighteenth century, each country's vernacular became the language of its scientists.

By the end of the seventeenth century, the ideas of Descartes had overcome Calvinist opposition to find their way into Dutch university curricula. But the further east one went in Europe, the weaker was the impact of
the Scientific Revolution. Scientific inquiry lagged in Poland, in part because
of the success of the Catholic Reformation, which restricted the free flow
of scholarly thought. Several printing houses in Gdańsk owned by Protestants began publishing scientific works in the second half of the seventeenth century. Leibniz enjoyed popularity in the Habsburg domains, at
least partially because he served several German rulers in a diplomatic
capacity, and perhaps also because his contagious optimism and belief that
God had preordained harmony found resonance in the diverse and scattered
kingdom. Nonetheless, theological and devotional literature still dominated
the shelves of university, monastic, and imperial libraries. The few publications on science remained strongly Aristotelian.

Some savants in the East did become aware of the debates in the West
on the scientific method. Protestant thinkers in Hungary and Silesia, for
example, were gradually exposed to the ideas of Bacon and Descartes by traveling scholars from Western Europe, and a few Hungarians and Silesians
learned of the new ideas by visiting Dutch universities. Some Bohemian and
Polish nobles began to include books on the new science in their private
libraries, one of which eventually comprised over 300,000 volumes and
10,000 manuscripts. Theoretical and practical astronomical work spread in
the Habsburg lands, carried on in some cases by Jesuits. Mathematics, optics,
and problems of atmospheric pressure, too, were the focus of debate. Holy
Roman Emperor Ferdinand III (ruled 1637–1657) studied military geometry, constructing arithmetic toys for his children.

Russia's distant isolation from Western culture was compounded by the
Orthodox Church's antipathy toward the West and, therefore, opposition
to scientific experimentation. There was, to be sure, acceptance of some
practical knowledge from the West, for example relating to the military,
mining, or metallurgy, which largely arrived with foreign merchants and
adventurous craftsmen. Seventeenth-century Russia had no gifted scientists and no scientific societies. Until the reign of Peter the Great, virtually
all books published in Russia were devotional in character, and Russian
culture was essentially that of a monastery. Foreign books began to appear
at court only after about 1650, many arriving from Poland and Ukraine. At
that point, however, the Orthodox Church, having suffered a schism,
launched another campaign against Western ideas, denouncing secular
knowledge as heresy and science as the work of the Antichrist. But gradually some nobles began to be exposed to ideas from the natural sciences.
These were the Russian nobles who were dissatisfied with Church learning
and eager to know more, for example, about the geography of their own
expanding state. The literate classes in Russia would thereafter in many
ways remain divided between those interested in ideas coming from the
West (most of what was known in the West was available in Russia by

1725) and those who rejected them in the name of preserving what they considered Russia's uniqueness as the most dominant Slavic state.

The Uses of Science

The seventeenth-century Scientific Revolution was above all a revolution in thought. Technological inventions that would change the way people lived lay for the most part in the future. But during the second half of the seventeenth century, scientific experimentation led to the practical application of some discoveries. Thanks to Newton, longitude could now be easily established and ocean tides accurately charted. Voyages of discovery, commerce, and conquest to the Americas increased the demand for new navigational instruments. Dutch scientists and craftsmen led the way in producing telescopes, microscopes, binoculars, and other scientific instruments.

But gradually, too, physicians, engineers, mariners, instrument makers, opticians, pharmacists, and surveyors, many of them self-educated, began to apply the new discoveries to daily life. Robert Hooke (1635–1703), another member of the Royal Society, improved the barometer, which measures atmospheric pressure, and augmented the power of the microscope by adding multiple lenses. This allowed him to study the cellular structure of plants. Biologists began to collect, categorize, dissect, and describe fossils, birds, and exotic fish, adding to contemporary understanding of the richness and complexity of the world around them.

As Francis Bacon had predicted, governments began to tap science in the service of the state. Absolute monarchs on the continent sought out scientists to produce inventions that would give them commercial and military advantages over their rivals. In France, Jean-Baptiste Colbert, Louis XIV's minister of finance, sought to steer the Royal Academy of Science toward the study of what he considered useful subjects that might benefit French commerce and industry, ordered the collection of statistics, and commissioned people to make reliable maps of the provinces and colonies. English government officials also began to apply statistics to administrative and social problems.

Tsar Peter the Great (see Chapter 7) was convinced by his trip to Western Europe that Russia would have to borrow from the West. He corresponded with Leibniz, who convinced him that empirical science, along with the creation of a system of education, would bring progress. The tsar wanted to refute the Western view that "[Russians] are barbarians who disregard science." Peter's campaign of westernization, which included opening his country to Western scientific ideas, made Russia a great power. The sciences that interested Peter were those that were useful in statemaking: mechanics, chemistry, and mathematics all aided in building ships and improving artillery. Peter established the Russian Academy of Sciences and the Moscow School of Mathematics and Navigation, which produced the first generation of Russian explorers, cartographers, and astronomers.

Science and Religion

As scientific discoveries led more people to doubt religious authority that was based on faith alone, points of tension not surprisingly continued to emerge between science and religion. This was particularly the case with the Catholic and Orthodox Churches. There seemed to be a close association between Protestant countries and advances in science, given the precocious role of England and, to a lesser extent, the Netherlands in the emergence of a culture of science. This contributed to the debate over whether Protestantism itself was more conducive to scientific inquiry.

Theological concerns still dominated the curricula at most universities, despite the role of science at the University of Padua, and the University of Cambridge, where by the 1690s both Newton's theories and those of Descartes were taught. Universities contributed relatively little to the diffusion of the scientific method. During the seventeenth century as a whole, their enrollments declined as the European population stagnated. In Catholic countries, canon law, and in Protestant states, civil law predominated in universities, which trained Church and state officials, respectively. The number of German universities more than doubled to about forty during the seventeenth century. The impetus for their creation came from Lutheranism and Calvinism, however, not from an interest in science.

The University of Padua in Italy, pictured at about the time Galileo taught there.

Catholic universities continued to be the most traditional. Following Descartes's death in 1650, the University of Paris, which had about 30,000 students and was the largest university on the continent, forbade a funeral oration for him. Almost three decades later, the archbishop of Paris declared that "in physics it is forbidden to deviate from the principles of the physics of Aristotle . . . and to attach oneself to the new doctrines of Descartes." The University of Paris continued to exclude the new philosophy until the 1730s. Experimental physics as well as botany and chemistry were absent from university study throughout Europe.

The salient role of Protestants in the diffusion of scientific method reflected differences between the theological stance of the Catholic Church and the more liberal ethos of the Protestant Reformation. Catholic theologians left little room for innovation or experimentation. The Protestant belief that an individual should seek truth and salvation in his or her own religious experience through a personal interpretation of the Bible encouraged skepticism about doctrinal theology. The emphasis on individual discovery seemed to lead naturally to empiricism. While Protestant theologians also could be rigid and unyielding, there was no Protestant equivalent to the papal Index of Forbidden Ideas or Books or the mechanism of the Inquisition.

Scientists in Catholic states, confronted by ecclesiastical denunciations or by reports of miracles that seemed to fly in the face of logic, found support in Protestant lands. The Protestant Dutch Republic, fighting a long civil war against Spanish rule, emerged as a center of toleration, where most books could be published. When Descartes learned of the condemnation of Galileo's work, he fled France for the Netherlands, where he published *Discourse on Method*. Francis Bacon had been among the first to associate the Scientific Revolution with the Protestant Reformation. Indeed, many Protestants believed that scientific discovery would lead to a better world and that the wonders of nature were there to be discovered and to give greater glory to God. Yet Jesuits in Bohemia protected Kepler (who had faced persecution from Protestant theologians), provided he limited himself to speculation about astronomy and mathematics and avoided what they considered to be theological questions.

The development of a scientific view of the world in England may be better understood in the context of decades of social, intellectual, and political crisis during the mid-seventeenth century. The campaigns of Parliament and of Puritanism against Charles I's seeming moves toward absolutism and Catholicism attracted political and religious reformers (see Chapter 6). Many who considered the Catholic Church an obstacle to scientific inquiry opposed Charles I as they sought a climate of freedom. The reformers' triumph in the English Civil War may have emboldened Newton and other proponents of the new philosophy. Moderate Anglicans, like the Puritans before them, insisted that science could bring progress. They encouraged the creation of the Royal Observatory, founded by Charles II

Astronomers using a telescope at the Royal Observatory of London.

at Greenwich in 1675. Newton and other members of the Royal Society almost unanimously supported the exile of the Catholic King James II to France and the Glorious Revolution of 1688. Censorship was relatively rare in England, where political and ecclesiastical authority was not so centralized.

By way of contrast, state censorship, encouraged by the Catholic Church, had formally begun in France in 1623, five years after the sovereign law court of Toulouse had ordered a defrocked monk burned at the stake for denouncing belief in miracles after studying at the University of Padua. Thereafter, each new manuscript had to be submitted to a royal office for authorization to be published. Six years later, separate offices were established for literature, science, and politics, with ecclesiastics having veto power over books treating religious subjects.

Yet, to be sure, not all churchmen in France adamantly waged a war on science. Some French Jesuits were open-minded about the scientific method. Jansenists, forming a dissident movement within the Church, also favored scientific discovery, discussion, and debate (see Chapter 7).

CONSEQUENCES OF THE SCIENTIFIC REVOLUTION

The Scientific Revolution seemed to push theology into the background. Even though the earliest exponents of scientific method never doubted

God's creation of the universe, the idea that mankind might one day master nature shocked many Church officials. Descartes's materialism seemed to suggest that humanity could live independently of God. Faith in the scientific method indeed had distinct philosophical consequences: "If natural Philosophy, in all its parts, by pursuing this method, shall at length be perfected," Newton reasoned, "the bounds of moral philosophy will also be enlarged." The English poet John Donne had already come to the same conclusion in 1612. "The new philosophy," he wrote prophetically, "calls all in doubt."

The men and women of science espoused the application of the scientific method to the study of nature and the universe. It was but a short step to subjecting society, government, and political thought to similar critical scrutiny. The English philosopher John Locke claimed that society was, as much as astronomy, a discipline subject to the rigors of the scientific method. Moreover, the Scientific Revolution would ultimately help call absolutism into doubt by influencing the philosophes, the thinkers and writers of the eighteenth-century Enlightenment. The philosophes' belief in the intrinsic value of freedom and their assertion that people should be ruled by law, not rulers, would challenge the very foundations of absolutism.

CHAPTER 9

ENLIGHTENED THOUGHT AND THE REPUBLIC OF LETTERS

"What is the Enlightenment?" wrote the German philosopher Immanuel Kant. His response was *Dare to know!* Have the courage to make use of your own understanding," as exciting a challenge today as in the eighteenth century. During that period of contagious intellectual energy and enthusiastic quest for knowledge, the philosophes, the thinkers and writers of the Enlightenment, espoused intellectual freedom and the use of reason in the search for progress. Unlike most scientists of the preceding period, they wanted their ideas to reach the general reading public. Education therefore loomed large in this view of their mission. Their approach to education was not limited to formal schooling, but instead took in the development of the individual and the continued application of critical inquiry throughout one's life.

The Enlightenment began in Paris but extended to much of Western Europe, including the German states, the Dutch Republic, Great Britain, and as far as North America. The works of the philosophes reached Poland and Russia. Orthodox Christian intellectuals carried the Enlightenment's celebration of science and humanism into the Balkans. The philosophes' writings helped confirm French as the language of high culture in eighteenth-century Europe. Indeed, it was reported from Potsdam that at the court of Frederick the Great of Prussia "the language least spoken is German." But French was hardly the only language of philosophic discourse. In Italy, those influenced by the new thinking used the ideas of the philosophes to attack clerical and particularly papal influence in political life. In Britain, the philosopher David Hume and economist Adam Smith, father of free-market liberalism, represented the thought of the "Scottish Enlightenment."

The Enlightenment can be roughly divided into three stages. The first covers the first half of the eighteenth century and most directly reflects the influence of the Scientific Revolution; the second, the "high Enlightenment," begins with the publication of *The Spirit of Laws* (1748) by Charles-Louis de Montesquieu and ends in 1778 with the deaths of François-Marie Voltaire and Jean-Jacques Rousseau; and the third, the late Enlightenment, influenced by Rousseau's work, marks a shift from an emphasis on human reason to a greater preoccupation with the emotions and passions of mankind. This final stage also features new ideas relating the concept of freedom to the working of economies, best represented by the thought of Adam Smith. At this time, too, several monarchs applied the philosophes' principle that rulers should work for the good of their subjects. But these experiments in "enlightened absolutism" were most noteworthy for rulers' organizing their states more effectively, further enhancing their authority. This third period also brought the popular diffusion of the lesser works of would-be philosophes seeking to capitalize on an expanding literary market. These works, too, were influential in undermining respect for the authority of the monarchy of France and thus indirectly contributed to the French Revolution.

Enlightened Ideas

The philosophes espoused views of nature, mankind, society, government, and the intrinsic value of freedom that challenged some of the most fundamental tenets Europeans had held for centuries. Slavery, for example, violated the principle of human freedom. The implications of Enlightenment thought were revolutionary, because the philosophes argued that progress had been constrained by social and political institutions that did not reflect humanity's natural goodness and capacity for material and moral improvement. Although many philosophes saw no or little incompatibility between science and religion, they were skeptical of received truths passed down from generation to generation. Thus, they challenged the doctrinal authority of the established churches and launched a crusade for the secularization of political institutions.

It is to the Enlightenment that we trace the origins of many of our modern political beliefs: the idea that people should be ruled by law, not rulers; the belief that a separation of powers ought to exist within government to prevent the accumulation of too much power in a few hands; the concept of popular sovereignty (legal authority should be wholly or at least partly based in the people, reflecting their interests, if not their consent); and the assumption that it is the responsibility of rulers to look after the welfare of the people. The consequences of such modern views of sovereignty, political rights, and the organization of states would be seen in the French Revolution and the era of liberalism in the nineteenth century.

Intellectual Influences on Enlightened Thought

Like all intellectual and cultural movements, the Enlightenment did not emerge spontaneously. Creating what David Hume (1711–1776) called "the science of man," the philosophes reflected the influence of the Scientific Revolution, whose proponents had espoused the scientific method in the study of nature and the universe. Sir Isaac Newton, the brilliant English scientist and theoretician (see Chapter 8), emphasized that science—reason and experimentation—holds the key to understanding nature, and that mankind discovers knowledge not through religious teaching but through "observation, analysis, and experiment."

Two thinkers linked the Scientific Revolution and Enlightenment thought: John Locke and Georges-Louis Buffon. Locke (1632–1704) claimed that philosophy was, as much as astronomy, a discipline subject to the rigors of the scientific method and critical inquiry. The son of a landowner and a member of the British Royal Society, Locke maintained a strong interest in medicine. After returning from Holland, where he had gone into self-imposed exile during the political crisis swirling around the throne of King James II, Locke remained close to the government of King William and Queen Mary (see Chapter 6).

Locke believed that the scientific method could be applied to the study of society. In *An Essay Concerning Human Understanding* (1690), Locke postulated that each individual is a *tabula rasa*, or blank slate, at birth. Believing that all knowledge is sensory, Locke denied the existence of

John Locke (*left*) and Georges-Louis Buffon (*right*), who both linked the Scientific Revolution and Enlightenment thought.

inherited abilities and rejected the idea that humanity is stained by original sin, a view held by the Catholic Church. He anticipated that the discovery of more laws of nature would be the basis of secular laws on which society should be based. He was confident that humanity might thereby be able to improve social conditions.

Locke had asserted the dignity of the individual in contending that every person has the right to life, liberty, and property (though he excluded slaves in the Americas from such innate rights). He argued that monarchies were based on a social contract between rulers and the ruled. People had to relinquish some of their liberty in exchange for security. But, unlike Thomas Hobbes, who famously believed that individuals should surrender their rights to the absolute state of unlimited sovereignty in exchange for protection from the "state of nature," Locke insisted that mankind's liberty and rights stemmed from the laws of nature. He became a leading proponent of educational reform, freedom of the press, religious toleration, and the separation of political powers.

Locke's interest in the relationship between nature and the social order led him to consider issues of gender. The assumption that the king ruled his nation as a husband and father ruled his wife and children had been prominent in early modern political theory, only briefly challenged by a handful of radicals during the English Civil War in the mid-seventeenth century. Locke argued against the contemporary vision of the state in which "all power on earth is either derived from or usurped from the fatherly power." He denied the appropriateness of the analogy between the family and the state as patriarchal institutions. Rejecting the contemporary view that Adam held supremacy over Eve, he viewed marriage, like government, to be organized by social contract. However, Locke went no further than that, and his espousal of equality within marriage remained only an ideal. In everyday life, he believed that women should defer to men. But Locke's analysis of the family as an institution nonetheless helped stimulate intellectual interest in the social role of women.

Georges-Louis Buffon (1707–1788) linked the Scientific Revolution to the Enlightenment. Buffon, whose initial presentation to the French Royal Academy of Science was a study of probability theory applied to gambling on hopscotch, became the curator of the Royal Gardens. Surrounded by monkeys and badgers in his laboratory, he carried out experiments, some of which worked, such as his study of the burning effect of the sun through glass, and some of which did not, including his study of the emotional life of birds. Buffon's experiments with cooling metals led him to build a large forge near his home in Burgundy.

The philosophes acknowledged their debt to the late-seventeenth-century proponents of the scientific method. Voltaire saluted Newton for having called on scientists and philosophers "to examine, weigh, calculate, and measure, but never conjecture." Hume insisted that all knowledge came from critical inquiry and scientific discovery and that the ability to reason distinguished mankind from other animals. Many philosophes, reflecting the influence of the Scientific Revolution, considered religion, the origins of which they found not in reason but in faith and custom, to be a social phenomenon, like any other to be studied scientifically. Hume blasted away at the idea of religious truths revealed through the Bible.

The very universality of their principles led some of the philosophes to suggest that a sense of morality—of what is right and wrong—might vary across cultures because it emerged from the nature of mankind, not from religious teaching. Denis Diderot, influenced by Locke, argued that sensory stimulation—or in the case of people who are blind, sensory deprivation— shapes individual moral responses, and that moral principles for a blind man might be somewhat different from those of someone who could see. He described the people of distant Tahiti as forming a rational social order without the benefit of any ecclesiastical doctrine. Hume called for a "science of morals" to serve the interests of Christians.

The Republic of Ideas

The philosophes' calls for reform were sometimes subtle, sometimes boldly forceful. Yet they did not lead insurrections. Their pens and pencils were their only weapons as they sought to change the way people thought. They communicated their ideas in letters, unpublished manuscripts, books, pamphlets, brochures, and through writing novels, poetry, drama, literary and art criticism, and political philosophy.

The philosophes glorified the collegiality and interdependence of writers within the "republic of letters," what the men and women of the Enlightenment sometimes called the informal international community of philosophes. By the mid-eighteenth century, Voltaire claimed with some exaggeration that the professional writer stood at the top of the social summit. He, Montesquieu, and Diderot accepted election to the prestigious French Royal Academy, revealing their ambivalence toward the monarchy that they attacked, however subtly, in their work. The most famous of the philosophes gained money as well as prestige, although Voltaire and Montesquieu were among the few who could support themselves by writing.

The philosophes may have shared the fundamental ideas of the Enlightenment, but significant differences existed among them. They came from different social classes, generations, and nations. And they often disagreed, like people in any republic, arguing in person, by letter, and in their published work. They could not agree, for example, whether the ideal state was an enlightened, benevolent monarchy, a monarchy balanced by a parliamentary body representing the nobility, or a kind of direct democracy. Their views on religion also varied. Montesquieu, Voltaire, and Rousseau were deists. Because scientific inquiry seemed to have demonstrated that the persistent intervention of God was unnecessary to keep the world in motion, they viewed God as a clockmaker who set the world in motion according to the

Voltaire presiding (with his arm raised) over a dinner gathering of philosophes, including Denis Diderot, who is sitting at the far left.

laws of nature and then left knowledge and human progress to the discovery and action of mankind. In contrast, Diderot became an atheist.

For all the variety and richness of the republic of letters, four philosophes dominated Enlightenment discourse with startling ideas about society, religion, and politics: Montesquieu, Voltaire, Diderot, and Rousseau. Each is well worth considering separately.

Montesquieu

Montesquieu (Charles-Louis de Secondat; 1689–1755) inherited a feudal château near Bordeaux and a small income upon the death of his father. He studied law and later inherited from a wealthy relative more property and the title of baron de Montesquieu, as well as the presidency of the noble parlement, or provincial sovereign law court, seated at Bordeaux.

In 1721, after moving to Paris, Montesquieu published *Persian Letters*. In the form of reports sent home by two Persian visitors to Paris, his work detailed the political and social injustices of life in the West. By casting this critique of eighteenth-century France in the form of a travelogue, Montesquieu was able to dodge royal censorship. The work irritated ecclesiastics who resented its insinuation that the pope was a "magician." As for the king of France, the Persians reported that he "is the most powerful of European potentates. He has no mines of gold like his neighbor, the king of Spain: but he is much wealthier than that prince, because his riches are drawn from a more inexhaustible source, the vanity of his subjects. He has undertaken and carried on great wars, without any other supplies than those derived from the sale of titles of honors." But beneath the satire of the *Persian Letters,* Montesquieu was arguing the point that nature reveals a universal standard of justice that applies for all people in all places at all times, in Islamic Persia as in Christian France.

Montesquieu's ideas reflected the increased contact between Europeans and much of the rest of the world. Merchants, soldiers, missionaries, and colonists had followed the first European explorers to, among other places, the Americas and Asia. Published accounts of travel stirred the imagination of upper-class Europeans who were interested in societies and cultures that lay on the fringes of or beyond their continent. America and China, in particular, fascinated Europeans who had read about them. Yet in *Persian Letters,* Montesquieu manifested doubts about the quest for colonies: "empires were like the branches of a tree that sapped all the strength from the trunk." He also offered the first critical examination of the institution of slavery by a philosophe. He rejected slavery as an extension of despotism, concluding that "slavery is against natural law, by which all men are born free and independent" because "the liberty of each citizen is part of public liberty." Thus slavery compromised "the general good of men [and] that of particular societies."

The Spirit of Laws (1748) inaugurated the high Enlightenment. Montesquieu applied the principles of observation, experimentation, and analysis, which lie at the heart of scientific inquiry, to the social and political foundations of states. He described the relationship between climate, religion, and tradition, and the historical evolution of a nation's political life. Laws, he argued, are subject to critical inquiry and historical study because they develop over time. Historians, freeing themselves from the influence of the Church, could now study "general causes, whether moral or physical."

The British political system fascinated Montesquieu, who spent two years in England. He was impressed by the historical role of Parliament, a representative body unlike French parlements (law courts), despite the similarity of their names. The English Parliament seemed an "intermediate power" that had during the English Civil War prevented Britain from becoming either a monarchical despotism or a republic, which Montesquieu identified with chaos. His point was that each political system and legal tradition evolved differently. He feared that the French monarchy was showing signs of becoming despotic because it lacked the separation of powers found in England. Only constitutionalism could combine the guarantees for order (offered by monarchy) with those of freedom. Montesquieu believed that noble rights and municipal privileges, which had been eroded by royal absolutism in France, could stave off monarchical despotism. Montesquieu held that the sovereignty of the king came not from God, but from the people.

Voltaire

Brilliant, witty, and sarcastic, Voltaire (François-Marie Arouet, 1694–1778) was the most widely read, cited, and lionized of the philosophes. He was the son of a notary who had enhanced his family's position through a favorable marriage. Voltaire's parents, who wanted him to be a lawyer, sent him to Paris to be educated by the Jesuits. Instead, the brash, ambitious young man made a name for himself as a dramatist and poet—though many of these early works are quite forgettable. Voltaire developed a pen as quick and cutting as a sword. Some of his early works were banned in France; everything he ever wrote was forbidden in Spain.

Like Montesquieu, Voltaire reflected the Anglophilia of the philosophes of the early and high Enlightenment. He extolled Britain, its commercial empire, relative religious toleration, and freedom of the press. Voltaire believed that the only representative body that might guarantee the natural rights of the king's subjects in France would be the equivalent of the British House of Commons. Whereas Montesquieu looked to the nobility to protect people from monarchical despotism, Voltaire counted on the enlightened monarchs of centralized states to protect their people against the self-interest of nobles.

Voltaire claimed that the political organization of each state was at least partially determined by its specific history and circumstances. As science should study the world of nature, so should the philosophe trace the separate development of nations. This line of reasoning convinced him that Montesquieu was wrong to think that the British political system could be successfully transplanted to France.

Voltaire reserved his most scathing attacks for the Church, an institution, like the parlements, which seemed to block the development of freedom in his own country. His motto was an impassioned cry against the teaching of the Church—*"Écrasez l'infâme!"* ("Crush the horrible thing!"). Of monks, he once said, "They sing, they eat, they digest." The pope and the Parlement of Paris both condemned his polemical *Philosophical Dictionary* (1764). His attacks were clever and devastating; for example, his pithy description of the Chinese as having "an admirable religion free from superstition and the rage to persecute" was read by virtually everyone as suggesting that in France the opposite was true. Voltaire believed that God created the universe and then let it operate according to scientific laws. He espoused a natural religion based upon reason.

Voltaire intended *Candide* (1759) to be an indictment of fanaticism and superstition. In the short tale, the cheerful optimist Candide bumbles from disaster to disaster. Here Voltaire confronts the seeming contradiction between the goodness of God and the evil in the world. He writes about the earthquake that ravaged Lisbon in 1755, killing thousands of people and destroying much of the Portuguese capital. If God is all good and omniscient, why, Voltaire reasoned, would He allow such an event to occur? But Voltaire nonetheless believed that religion was beneficial because it offered people hope, and therefore made their lives more bearable. It also kept them in line: "If God did not exist, one would have to invent him. I want my attorney, my tailor, my servants, even my wife to believe in God, and I think that I shall then be robbed and cuckholded less often."

Voltaire's fame spread when he took up the cause of a man who seemed wrongly accused of murder. In 1761, Jean Calas, a Protestant from Toulouse, stood accused of killing his son, who had been found hanging in the family basement. The young Calas had intended to convert to Catholicism. Convicted by the Parlement of Toulouse, the father was tortured to death, though it seemed likely that his son had committed suicide. Several years later, the parlement reversed its earlier decision—too late, alas, for Jean Calas. But the Calas Affair helped put the philosophes' critique of religious intolerance into the limelight of public opinion.

Voltaire's energetic interest in the Calas Affair reflected his insistence that progress is somehow inevitable without human action. He concludes *Candide* with the famous, though seemingly ambiguous, advice that "one must cultivate one's own garden," as he did at his rural retreat. But Voltaire was counseling anything but a withdrawal into the sanctuary of introspection. He called for each person to follow the path of light and do battle with those institutions that seemed to stand in the way of humanity's potential. In 1764 he predicted, "Everything I see scatters the seeds of a revolution which will definitely come. . . . Enlightenment has gradually spread so widely that it will burst into full light at the first right opportunity, and then there will be a fine uproar. Lucky are the young, for they will see great things."

Diderot

Denis Diderot's monumental *Encyclopedia* best reflected the collaborative nature of the Enlightenment, as well as its wide influence. Diderot (1713–1784), the son of an artisan, was something of a jack-of-all-trades, a man of letters who wrote plays, art criticism, history, theology, and philosophy. Educated by the Jesuits (like Voltaire), he flirted with the idea of becoming a priest, and for a time supported himself by writing sermons for bishops. Unlike Montesquieu and Voltaire, Diderot underwent a rugged apprenticeship in the "republic of letters." He penned a pornographic novel to earn enough to indulge the fancies of his mistress. But he also questioned how, through centuries of male domination, women, despite their capacity for reproduction, had come to be considered inferior to men. Diderot claimed that laws that limited the rights of women were counter to nature.

The *Encyclopedia,* on which Diderot worked for twenty-five years and to which he contributed 5,000 articles, stands as the greatest monument of the Enlightenment. At the heart of the project lay the philosophes' insistence that knowledge is rational and that it follows the laws of nature. Social and political institutions should be submitted to standards of rationality. All things, as Diderot put it, are equally subject to criticism. By elevating mankind to the center of human inquiry, the 140 authors of the *Encyclopedia*—including Rousseau, who penned 344 articles—sought to achieve Diderot's goal, "to change the general way of thinking," as well as to bring glory to France.

Voltaire had set a goal for the Enlightenment itself: to educate the literate and intellectually curious of the social elite, and perhaps people farther down the social scale as well. The *Encyclopedia* at least partially fulfilled that goal. Published over a period of more than twenty years beginning in 1751, it consisted of 60,000 articles and 2,885 illustrations in 28 volumes. Subtitled "A Classified Dictionary of the Sciences, Arts and

Depiction of an eighteenth-century canal with locks, from Denis Diderot's *Encyclopedia*.

Trades," this first such compilation in the West was a bold attempt to organize and classify all knowledge gathered from "over the face of the earth." Its authors insisted that by learning more about the universe, men and women could improve the world. This marked a departure from the assumption that mankind's ability to penetrate the secrets of the universe was limited. Montesquieu contributed sections on artistic taste, Rousseau on music, Voltaire on literature, and Buffon on nature. Diderot gave particular credit to the everyday contributions of artisans by describing how and why ingeniously simple tools and machines could make tasks easier.

The *Encyclopedia* generated sufficient excitement that advance sales alone financed its publication. It earned its publishers a handsome profit. After the first edition, subsequent editions with less expensive paper and fewer illustrations became available at about a sixth of the original price. Lawyers, officials, and *rentiers* (people living from property income) were more likely to own a copy than merchants or manufacturers, who could afford the volumes but seemed less interested. What began as a luxury product ended up on the shelves of the "middling sort."

The philosophes wanted the *Encyclopedia* to carry the Enlightenment far beyond the borders of France. Although only about one in ten volumes

MAP 9.1 DIFFUSION OF DIDEROT'S *ENCYCLOPEDIA* Subscriptions to Diderot's *Encyclopedia* throughout Europe.

traveled beyond the country, its pattern of distribution in the 1770s and 1780s reflected the success of the enterprise (see Map 9.1). The *Encyclopedia*'s prospectus and booksellers' advertisements assured potential buyers that ownership would proclaim one's standing as a person of knowledge, a philosophe. In northern Germany and Scandinavia, customers were described as "sovereign princes" and "Swedish seigneurs." A few copies reached African settlements, including the Cape of Good Hope. Thomas Jefferson helped promote the *Encyclopedia* in America, finding several subscribers, among them Benjamin Franklin. King Louis XVI of France owned a copy. There was an Italian edition, despite the opposition of the Church. However, in Spain, Inquisition censorship frightened booksellers and buyers alike, and in Portugal only a few copies got by the police.

The *Encyclopedia* implicitly challenged monarchical authority. Jean-Jacques Rousseau wrote enthusiastically about representative government and even popular sovereignty, and came close to espousing a republic. After initially tolerating the project, French royal censors banned Volume 7 in 1757, after an unsuccessful assassination attempt on Louis XV. Diderot, whose first serious philosophical work had been burned by the public executioner, was briefly imprisoned. In the 1770s, the French state again tolerated the *Encyclopedia,* which it now treated more as a commodity than as an ideological threat to monarchy or Church. The small subsequent skirmishes fought over the volumes had more to do with rivalries between publishers, between those privileged with official favor and those without. In this way, Diderot's grand project symbolized the ongoing political struggles within the French monarchy itself.

Rousseau

The place of Jean-Jacques Rousseau (1712–1778) in the Enlightenment is far more ambiguous than that of Diderot and his *Encyclopedia.* Rousseau embraced human freedom, but more than any other of the philosophes, Rousseau idealized emotion, instinct, and spontaneity, which he believed to be, along with reason, essential parts of human nature.

The son of a Geneva watchmaker, Rousseau, a Protestant, went to Paris as a young man in the hope of becoming a composer. The arrogant, self-righteous Rousseau received an introduction into several aristocratic Parisian salons, informal upper-class gatherings at which ideas were discussed, where he became friendly with Diderot. In 1749, the Academy of Dijon (an academy in France was a regular gathering of people to discuss ideas, and, as we shall see below, a way that enlightenment thought spread) sponsored an essay contest on the question of whether the progress of science had strengthened or weakened morality. Rousseau's first-prize essay concluded that primitive or natural humanity had embodied the essential goodness of mankind and that for humanity to be happy, new social and political institutions would be necessary.

Portrait of Jean-Jacques Rousseau.

Exiled by the Parlement of Paris because his writings offended monarchy and Church, Rousseau returned to Geneva. Following the condemnation of his writings there in the early 1770s, he abandoned his children in an orphanage—as his father had abandoned him—and set off to visit England. Rousseau remained a contentious loner, quarreling with other philosophes. He assumed that when his former friends disagreed with his ideas, they knew that he was right but simply refused to admit it. In his *Confessions* (the first volume of which appeared in 1782), he appealed to future generations to see how contemporary thinkers had misinterpreted or misrepresented him.

In *Discourse on the Arts and Sciences* (1750), Rousseau argued that civilization had corrupted the natural goodness of man, which he called the "fundamental principle" of political thought. The intemperate quest for property had disrupted the harmony that had once characterized mankind in its primitive state by creating a hierarchy of wealth. Rousseau's idealization of relatively primitive, uncomplicated, and, he thought, manageable social and political groupings led him to believe that a republic, such as his own Geneva, alone offered its citizens the possibility of freedom. As free people in primitive societies joined together for mutual protection, enlightened people could associate for their mutual development in a kind of direct democracy. However, Rousseau remained suspicious of representative government, believing that people might ultimately vote themselves into slavery by electing unworthy representatives. He remained vague on how people were to be organized and governed.

In *The Social Contract* (1762), Rousseau tried to resolve the question of how people could join together in society to find protection and justice and yet remain free individuals. Locke had described the relationship between a ruler and his people as a contractual one. Hobbes, in contrast, had argued that individuals could find refuge from the brutality of the state of nature only by surrendering their rights to an absolute ruler in exchange for safety. Rousseau imagined a social contract in which the individual surrenders his or her natural rights to the "general will" in order to find order and security. By "general will," Rousseau meant the consensus of a community of citizens with equal political rights. Citizens would live in peace because they would be ruled by other citizens, not by dynastic rulers eager to expand their territorial holdings.

Although *The Social Contract* remained largely unknown until after the French Revolution of 1789, it offered an unparalleled critique of contemporary society. Rousseau summed up his thinking with the stirring assertion that "men are born free yet everywhere they are in chains." Whereas Voltaire and other philosophes hoped that rulers would become enlightened, Rousseau insisted that sovereignty comes not from kings or oligarchies, or even from God, but through the collective search for freedom.

Rousseau thus helped shape the final period of the Enlightenment, which anticipated nineteenth-century romanticism by giving emotion more free play. "Everything is good as it comes from the hands of the Author of nature, but everything degenerates in the hands of man," Rousseau's novel *Émile* (1762) began. It described what he considered to be the ideal natural, secular education, as the young Émile is gradually exposed by his tutor to nature during walks to explore brooks and mills. Rousseau intended such wonders to stimulate Émile's emotions, which were to be developed before his sense of reason, "the one that develops last and with the greatest difficulty." Émile's primitive virtue needed to be preserved against the vices of culture, but also developed as an end in itself so that he would become an autonomous individual. Rousseau assigned Sophie, Émile's chosen "well-born" spouse, an education appropriate to what Rousseau considered a woman's lower status in life. Yet, even Rousseau's insistence on the capacity of women for intellectual development was ahead of its time. The novel became a literary sensation.

Voltaire ridiculed Rousseau's espousal of primitiveness as virtue: "I have received, Monsieur, your new book against the human race, and I thank you. No one has employed so much intelligence turning men into beasts. One starts wanting to walk on all fours after reading your book. However, in more than sixty years I have lost the habit."

THE DIFFUSION AND EXPANSION OF THE ENLIGHTENMENT

The groundwork for the Enlightenment lay not only in the realm of ideas, such as those of the Scientific Revolution and Locke, but also in gradual social changes that affected the climate of opinion. These changes, especially but not exclusively found in France, included challenges to and even the decline of organized religion in the eighteenth century, at least in some regions, and the emergence of a more broadly based culture.

Religious Enthusiasm and Skepticism

During the first half of the seventeenth century, the Catholic Reformation engendered a slow but steady religious revival in France, Spain, and the Habsburg domains. The founding of new religious orders and monasteries and the popularity of the cults and shrines of local saints reflected religious intensity. The established churches still retained formidable authority and prestige.

The development late in the seventeenth century of Pietism among Protestants in the northern German states, emphasizing preaching and the study of the Bible, reflected, however, growing dissatisfaction with established religions and the existence of considerable religious creativity. Disaffected by abstract theological debates and by the Lutheran Church's hierarchical structure, Pietists wanted to reaffirm Protestant belief in the primacy of the individual conscience. Like English Puritans and French Jansenists (a dissident group within the Catholic Church), they called for a more austere religion. Pietists wanted a revival of piety and good works, and asked that laymen take an active role in religious life. Bible reading and small discussion groups replaced the more elaborate, formal services of the Lutherans, helping expand interest in the German language and culture among the upper classes. But by the last quarter of the eighteenth century, Pietist influence had waned, reflecting not only the diffusion of Enlightenment thought but also the fact that Lutheranism remained the state religion in the northern German states, maintaining a hold on the universities.

In Britain, religious practice seems to have increased among all social classes during the seventeenth century. The Anglican Church of England was the Established Church, but Britain also had about half a million non-Anglican Protestants, or Dissenters, at the end of the eighteenth century. Some middle-class Presbyterians, Congregationalists, Unitarians, Baptists, and Quakers sent their sons to private academies. Oxford and Cambridge Universities admitted only Anglicans. Anti-Catholicism remained endemic in England, where there were about 70,000 Catholics in 1770, most in the lower classes.

Although many Baptists, Congregationalists, and Quakers, among other Dissenters, had traditionally been laborers, no one religion held the allegiance of many ordinary people in England in the eighteenth century until the ministry of John Wesley (1703–1791). An Anglican trained in theology at the Univer-

John Wesley, who preached Methodist evangelism to the ordinary people of England.

sity of Oxford, the brooding Wesley began to believe that his mission was to infuse ordinary people—who seemed ignored by the Established Church—with religious enthusiasm.

Wesley never formally broke with the Anglican Church nor claimed to be setting up a new denomination. Yet that was the effect of his lifetime of preaching directly to ordinary people on grassy hills and in open fields and of writing religious tracts directed at ordinary Britons. Wesley attracted about 100,000 followers to Methodism. Stressing personal conversion, Methodism suggested that all people were equal in God's eyes. This offended upper-class Englishmen and -women, not the least because Methodists shouted out their beliefs and sometimes publicly confessed sins that the upper classes thought best left unnamed. A duchess explained that she hated the Methodists because "it is monstrous to be told that you have a heart as sinful as the common wretches that crawl on the earth."

Methodist evangelism was both a dynamic and a stabilizing force in British society. There was little or nothing politically or socially radical about Wesley, as shown by his unwillingness to break formally with the Established Church. Far from preaching rebellion, Wesley encouraged work, self-discipline, and abstinence from dancing, drinking, and gambling.

The Anglican Church, in turn, began to seek more followers among the lower classes. It established the Society for the Promotion of Christian Knowledge and Anglican Sunday schools, which provided poor children with food and catechism. The evangelical Hannah More (1745–1833), the "bishop in petticoats," abandoned the material comforts of upper-class life for the challenges of bringing religion to the poor.

Despite all of the evangelistic efforts, by the middle of the eighteenth century religion seemed to play a significantly smaller role in the lives of people of all classes, particularly in regions with expanding economies and relatively high literacy rates. The numbers of men and women entering the clergy in France declined, and male and female monastic orders lost a third of their members between 1770 and 1790 alone. Fewer wills requested that Masses be said for the deceased or for souls in Purgatory. A Venetian theologian at mid-century claimed that the people of his state had become "de-christianized." In France, popular dislike of the exemption of the clergy from taxes increased, although the Church still provided the monarchy a sizable yearly contribution from its great wealth. Thus, the philosophes who challenged the role of the established churches in public life were addressing many readers who had lost interest in organized religion.

Expansion of the Cultural Base

The expanding influence of the middle classes in England and northwestern Europe also began slowly to transform cultural life, expanding interest in literature, music, and the arts. The increasing number of literary associations reflected this change. A rise in literacy expanded the size of the potential audience of the philosophes. By the end of the century, perhaps half of the men in England, France, the Netherlands, and the German states could read. A smaller proportion of women—between a third to a half of the female population of these countries—was literate. The rate was considerably lower in southern Europe, and relatively few people could read in Eastern Europe, Russia, and the Balkans. Opportunities for women, even those from noble families, to obtain more than a minimal education remained quite rare, although several German states began schools for girls. Even Marie Antoinette, queen of France and one of the wealthiest people in the world, made frequent grammatical and spelling errors.

Publishers fed the growing appetites of readers eager to know what events were taking place in their own country and abroad. Newspapers published one or two times a week summarized events transpiring in other countries. The number of English periodicals increased sixfold between 1700 and 1780. In the German states, the number of books and magazines published grew by three times during the last decades of the eighteenth century. Novels gained in popularity at the expense of books on theology and popular piety. Sentimental novels presented syrupy stories of domestic life and tender love. English female novelists gave women an unprecedented public voice in Britain, presenting their heroines as affectionate companions to their husbands and good mothers. Diderot and the German dramatist and critic Gotthold Lessing (1729–1781) called for the theater to portray the lives and passions of ordinary people, instead of only kings and queens, princes and princesses. However, traditional literature, such as religious tracts, popular almanacs, and folktales, remained the most widely read literature.

The Enlightenment had a direct influence on the growing popularity of history. Reflecting their interest in understanding human experience, the philosophes helped create history as a modern discipline. Since the classical Greeks, there had been relatively little interest in history in Europe. Church fathers espoused the primacy of theology and viewed the world as little more than a test to prepare Christians for the afterlife. But now all human experience, including non-Western cultures, emerged as suitable for historical inquiry. Edward Gibbon (1737–1794) was inspired to undertake his *History of the Decline and Fall of the Roman Empire* (published over a period of twelve years beginning in 1776) by visiting the coliseum in Rome. Natural science, too, developed a following.

The number of lending libraries, as well as reading circles or clubs, some organized by resourceful booksellers, increased. In Paris, London, Milan, Berlin, and other large cities, lending libraries rented books for as short a period as an hour. Small private libraries became more common. Reading, which heretofore had largely been a group activity in which a literate person read to others—in the same way that storytellers spun their yarns—became more of a private undertaking.

BIBLIOTHECÆ LUGDUNO-BATAVÆ CUM PULPITIS ET ARCIS VERA IXNOGRAPHIA.

The library of the University of Leyden in the Netherlands, 1610.

While some of the most significant works of the Enlightenment were virtually unknown outside the republic of letters, others became the best-sellers of the age. Montesquieu's *The Spirit of Laws* went through twenty-two printings—approximately 35,000 copies—in the first eighteen months after publication in 1748. Buffon's thirty-volume study, *The System of Nature* (1749–1804)—despite its bulk—also enjoyed prodigious success. Voltaire's *Candide* was reprinted eight times the year of its publication in 1759. Abbé Guillaume Raynal's *The Philosophical and Political History of European Colonies and Commerce in the Two Indies* (1770) was reprinted seventy times to supply an eager market. It described the colonization of the New World, Asia, and Africa, including the development of the slave trade, which Raynal denounced in no uncertain terms.

The Arts

The philosophes sought the same status and freedom for artists that they demanded for writers. They believed that the arts had to be not only unfettered by censorship but also subject to critical inquiry. Some philosophes worked toward a philosophy of art, but they did not espouse a single theory. The distinguished English portrait painter Joshua Reynolds (1723–1792) believed that classical rules preserved from antiquity had to be followed. But David Hume, among other Enlightenment figures, emphasized the aesthetic appreciation of art, rejecting formal rules or standards for art imposed by royal academies or ecclesiastical influence.

The secularization of culture could be seen in the development of rococo, a new and generally secular decorative style. It evolved from the highly ornamental baroque style that had characterized the art and architecture of the Catholic Reformation, particularly in Austria and Bavaria. Closely tied to noble taste, rococo's popularity in France reflected the fact that many nobles now spent more time in elegant townhouses. However spacious, such urban residences afforded them less room than they enjoyed in their countryside châteaux. They therefore lavished more attention on decoration.

The rococo style—sometimes called Louis XV style—began in France but also became quite popular in the German and Italian states. Like the baroque, it featured flowing curves, thus suggesting rocks and shells (*rocailles* and *coquilles*, thus its name). Rococo stressed smallness of scale, reducing baroque forms to elegant decorative style. It utilized different materials, including wood, metal, stucco, glass, and porcelain, brought for the first time from China during the eighteenth century and reflecting the growing interest in Asia. It combined texture and color with spirited and even erotic subject matter. Elements drawn from nature, such as birds and flowers, replaced religious objects as decorative elements.

Engraving depicting the grand rococo style that was popular in France in the eighteenth century.

Although Greek mythology and religious themes remained popular, eighteenth-century painters found new sources for artistic inspiration. The French painter Jean-Antoine Watteau (1684–1721) influenced the artistic move away from traditional religious subjects laden with didactic meaning toward lighter, more secular themes. Adopting a more realistic style than baroque painting, he depicted elegantly dressed noble subjects at leisure. Painters adopted the rococo style, emphasizing smallness of scale. As the market for painting widened, scenes of nature and everyday life also became popular, as they had a century earlier in the Netherlands.

William Hogarth's *Gin Lane* (1751) is a commentary on the deleterious impact of alcohol on the poor of eighteenth-century London.

In France, the Academy of Painting and Sculpture organized the first public art exhibition in Paris in 1737, bringing together viewers of different social classes. The expanding middle-class art market and the growing secularization of artistic taste was nowhere more apparent than in Britain. William Hogarth (1697–1764) portrayed everyday life in London with affection and satire. He was as adept at conveying the elegance of London's parks as the depravation of the city's notorious "Gin Lane." He poked fun at the hearty Englishman putting away pounds of roast beef (Hogarth himself died after eating a huge steak), the dishonest lawyer, the clergyman looking for a better post while ignoring his pastoral duties, and the laboring poor drowning their sorrows in cheap gin, a plague that led the government to raise the tax on alcohol.

Music

The taste for music moved beyond the constraints of court, ecclesiastical, and noble patronage. Opera's great popularity in the seventeenth century had been closely tied to ornate opera houses constructed at European courts. Composers and their music passed from court to court. Court composers were considered the equivalent of favored upper servants. The German composer George Frideric Handel (1685–1759) gratefully accepted the patronage of several English aristocrats as well as King George II. When someone asked Franz Joseph Haydn (1732–1809), who worked as *kapellmeister* (orchestra director) for the fabulously wealthy Esterházy family of Hungary, why he had never written any quintets, he replied, "Nobody has ordered any."

In the early 1750s, Rousseau penned stinging attacks on French opera. Readers understood his strident language as he intended—he was denouncing court and aristocratic taste itself. Rousseau compared the Royal Academy of Music's monopoly on French music to a ruthless Inquisition that stifled imagination. Rousseau's critique generated a storm of controversy because it seemed to be nothing less than a denunciation of the social and cultural foundations of contemporary French society. Like his philosophical works, Rousseau's operatic compositions extolled the simple, unpretentious life of rural people.

In England, concerts were held at court or in the homes of wealthy families; in Italy, they were sponsored by groups of educated people who gathered to discuss science and the arts; and in Switzerland, concerts were sponsored by societies of music lovers. The public concert also emerged in some German cities early in the eighteenth century. Gradually public concert halls were built in the capitals of Europe. Handel began to perform his operas and concerts in rented theaters, attracting large crowds. By the 1790s, Haydn was conducting his symphonies in public concerts in London.

The short, brilliant life of Wolfgang Amadeus Mozart (1756–1791) reflected the gradual evolution from dependence on court and aristocratic patronage to the emergence of the public concert. Mozart began playing the harpsichord at age three and composing at five. In 1763, his father took him and his sister on a tour of European courts that would last three years, hoping to make the family fortune, with mixed results. Mozart returned to Paris in 1778 at his father's insistence that he "get a job or at least make some money." The temperamental Mozart failed to make his way in the social world of Paris: "I would wish for his fortune," a contemporary wrote, "that he had half as much talent and twice as much tact."

Thereafter Mozart resided in his native Salzburg, where he served as unhappy court

The young Wolfgang Amadeus Mozart at a pianoforte.

musician of an unpleasant archbishop. Mozart wrote church music and light music, including a hunting symphony for strings, two horns, dogs, and a rifle, before resigning after quarreling with his patron. Mozart spent money as rapidly as he made it and was constantly in debt, unable to attract the lavish court, noble, or ecclesiastical patronage he desired. But his schedule increasingly included public concerts. Unlike Handel, Mozart died a poor man at age thirty-five and was buried in an unmarked pauper's grave in Vienna.

A prolific genius, Mozart moved away from the melodious regularity of his predecessors to more varied and freely articulated compositions. The operas *The Marriage of Figaro* (1786) and *Don Giovanni* (1787) demonstrated Mozart's capacity to present characters from many walks of life, revealing not only their shared humanity but their personal moods and expectations. *The Magic Flute* (1791), his last opera, expressed his belief in the ability of mankind to develop greater virtue and a capacity for love. Mozart thus shared the confident optimism of the philosophes.

The Spread of Enlightened Ideas

Salons, academies, and Masonic lodges helped spread Enlightenment thought. Salons, which brought together people of means, noble and bourgeois alike, in private homes for sociability and discussion, were concentrated in Paris, but they were also found in Berlin, London, and Vienna, as well as in some smaller provincial towns. The English historian Edward Gibbon claimed that in two weeks in Paris he had "heard more conversation worth remembering than I had done in two or three winters in London." The salons of Paris were organized and hosted mainly by women, who selected topics for discussion and presided over conversations. In Warsaw, Princess Sophia Czartoryska's salon played an important role in conveying Enlightenment ideas to Polish elites. In London, women hosted similar gatherings, some composed exclusively of women.

In Paris Madame Marie-Thérèse Geoffrin hosted artists on Monday and men of letters on Wednesday. "I well remember seeing all Europe standing three deep around her chair," recalled one of her visitors. Her husband sat silently at the other end of the table while his wife put the philosophes through their paces. One night, a regular guest noted that the place where the silent man usually sat was empty and asked where he was. "He was my husband," came the laconic reply, "and he's dead."

Salon guests could discuss the work of the philosophes without fear of police interference. By the middle of the century, political discussions increasingly captured intellectuals' attention. Not all ideas discussed, of course, were of equal merit. In the 1780s, a German scientist, Franz Mesmer (1734–1815), proclaimed the healing properties of electromagnetic treatments. "Mesmerism" attracted considerable interest in the salons of Paris, where the nature of the "universal fluid" that Mesmer and his disciples

An actor reading from a work of Voltaire at the salon of Madame Geoffrin. Note the bust of Voltaire, then in exile.

believed linked the human body to the universe, was debated. The French Academy of Science vigorously denounced Mesmerism as nothing more than resourceful charlatanism.

In France and in some Italian cities academies played a similar role to that of the salons. These were not "academies" in the sense of offering an organized curriculum, but rather formal gatherings taking place about every two weeks of people interested in science and philosophy. Meetings consisted of reading minutes and correspondence, followed by lectures and debates. The academies also helped spread Enlightenment ideas by bringing together people, including some clergymen, eager to discuss the works of the philosophes. Unlike the salons, women (with several exceptions) were not elected to the academies.

The French academies served two masters: the king and the public. They depended on royal intendants, governors, and other state officials for funding and meeting places. The monarchy believed that the academies served the public interest because members discussed questions of contemporary importance. Some academics sponsored essay competitions in the arts and sciences; during the decade of the 1780s, more than 600 such competitions were held. Topics increasingly reflected Enlightenment influence, such as "religious intolerance and the role of magistrates in the defense of liberty."

Many members of the provincial academies began by mid-century to think of themselves both as representing public opinion in their role as informal counselors to the monarchy, and interpreting the sciences and philosophy for a more general audience. Thus the academies contributed to the development of a sense that reforms in France were possible.

Masonic lodges, another medium for the ideas of the philosophes, had begun in Scotland, perhaps as early as the sixteenth century, as stonemasons' guilds. They now brought together freethinkers and others who opposed the influence of the established churches in public life. Masonic lodges proliferated in Europe during the middle years of the eighteenth century. Members took vows of secrecy, although their meetings, membership lists, and rituals were widely known. In some places women were admitted as affiliated or adopted members. Members held a variety of political opinions, but they shared a general faith in progress, toleration, and a critical view of institutionalized religion. In Scotland in particular, clubs, coffeehouses, and taverns also provided the setting for discussion of the new ideas.

Still, several obstacles limited the dissemination of Enlightenment ideas. Books and even pamphlets were expensive. Censorship, although erratic and varying greatly from place to place, also discouraged publication. In France and Spain, among other countries, censored books were burned, and those who published material officially considered blasphemous could be, at least in principle, sentenced to death. Far more frequently, officials closed printers' shops. Even the relatively tolerant Dutch Republic banned Diderot's

A gathering of a Masonic lodge in Vienna. Masonic rituals included the use of allegorical symbols, blindfolds, and swords.

Philosophic Thoughts as an attack on religion. In the face of a spate of publications critical of monarchy, aristocracy, and the Church, Louis XV (ruled 1715–1774) promulgated censorship laws in 1757 that were much harsher than those regulating the book trade in England. The French monarchy also controlled what was published through the licensing of printers, booksellers, and peddlers.

ENLIGHTENED ABSOLUTISM

The philosophes believed that the success of any state depended on the degree of freedom and happiness it was able to assure its people. As David Hume put it, a state is justified by the good that is done in its name. Voltaire and Diderdot, in particular, believed in "enlightened absolutism." They wanted enlightened monarchs to impose reforms that would benefit their subjects. Leopold II of Tuscany (1747–1792), the most significant reformer of his era, went so far as to declare that "the sovereign, even if hereditary, is only the delegate of his people." Rousseau, however, warned that absolutism and enlightened thinking were incompatible. However, some rulers applied Enlightenment "rationality" to statecraft, with the goal, above all, of making their regimes more efficient.

Reform of Jurisprudence

Cesare Bonesana, the marquis of Beccaria (1738–1794), had the greatest influence on his era as a reformer influenced by the Enlightenment. A noble from Milan, Beccaria became a professor of political philosophy in Habsburg Austria and ended his career advising the state chancellory on such diverse topics as agriculture, mining, and trade. He made his reputation, however, with his ideas on crime and punishment.

In *On Crimes and Punishment* (1764), Beccaria, who had read Montesquieu, Buffon, Diderot, and Rousseau, applied their analysis to the issues at hand. He argued that the state's task was to protect society while respecting the dignity of all people. This meant that the rights of those accused of crimes, too, had to be protected. Beccaria wanted standard procedures to govern criminal trials, so that rich and poor would stand equal before the law. The Italian philosopher's assumption that the accused is innocent until proven guilty has remained, along with the tradition of English constitutional law and trial by jury, a cornerstone of Western judicial systems.

Beccaria argued that the punishment for a given crime should not be linked to the religious concept of sin, but rather rationally determined by an assessment of the damage done to society. He argued that "it is better to prevent crimes than to punish them." His principles reflected the origins of utilitarianism, the influential social theory of the first decades of the nineteenth century that held that laws should be judged by their social utility.

Beccaria opposed torture to extract confessions or render punishment. Barbarous punishment, instead of protecting society, seemed only to encourage disrespect for the law and more awful crimes. This led him to object to capital punishment, lamenting the enthusiastic crowds that were attracted to public executions. Leopold II of Tuscany (who admired Beccaria), Gustavus III of Sweden, and Frederick the Great of Prussia banned torture—clear examples of the influence of enlightened thought on contemporary rulers.

Educational Reform

Education in the widest sense was central to the program of the philosophes. The Empress Catherine the Great of Russia (ruled 1762–1796) admired and read Montesquieu and Voltaire, hosted Diderot, and purchased the latter's library for a handsome price. Born a German princess, she was contemptuous of Russian culture and preferred French. She seemed to heed the advice she had received from Diderot: "To instruct a nation is to civilize it." Catherine established a school for the daughters of nobles. Without eliminating censorship, she authorized the first private printing presses and encouraged the publication of more books.

A few other monarchs implemented educational reforms, but they did so at least partially to assure a supply of able civil servants. In 1774, Joseph II (1741–1790) established a structured, centralized system of education from primary school to university, which doubled the number of elementary schools in Bohemia. In Poland, the Seym created the Commission for National Education in 1773 to serve as a ministry for education, overseeing Poland's universities in Krakow and Vilnius, as well as all secondary and parish schools. During this period in Central and Eastern Europe, textbooks appeared in the Magyar, German, Croatian, Slovak, Ukrainian, and Romanian languages.

Empress Catherine the Great.

Religious Toleration

Although the eighteenth century was a period of relative religious peace, intolerance could still be intense. In England, Catholics, in particular, suffered legal discrimination (see

Chapter 11), and could not vote or be elected to the House of Commons. French Protestants had no civil rights; their births, baptisms, and marriages were considered not to have occurred unless registered by a Catholic priest. Protestants suffered discrimination in Hungary and the Catholic Rhineland. In Austria, in 1728 the bishop of Salzburg gave 20,000 Protestants three days to leave their homes, and royal edicts forced Protestants out of Upper Austria and Styria during the next decade.

Europe's 3 million Jews suffered intolerance and often persecution all across Europe—especially in Eastern Europe. Jews could not hold titles of nobility, join guilds, or hold municipal office. In many places, they could own land, although in some German states they needed special permission to buy houses. They were excluded from agricultural occupations and certain trades in France, Eastern Europe, and Russia. The Habsburg monarchy required Jews to stay inside until noon on Sundays, and in 1745 it suddenly ordered the thousands of Jews living in Prague to leave. In Vienna and Zurich, Jews were confined to ghettos, and in several German towns they were not allowed inside the city walls. Although the Swedish government allowed Jews to build synagogues beginning in 1782, they could reside only in certain cities, and were forbidden to marry anyone who was not Jewish, to purchase land, or to produce handicrafts.

Because moneylending had been one of the few professions Jews were allowed to practice, Polish, Russian, and Ukrainian Jews faced resentment from peasants who often owed them money. In Poland the Catholic Church often led the way in persecution; rumors that Jews were ritually sacrificing Christian children during Passover found credulous ears. In 1762, Ukrainian peasants killed at least 20,000 Jews in the bloodiest pogrom of the century. Yet, by about 1750, Western Europe seemed to be entering a more tolerant age. For one thing, intolerance generated periodic rebellions, which took state funds to put down. But a more humanitarian spirit could also be felt.

Some of the rulers who undertook religious reforms were inspired by a desire to strengthen their authority. This was the case in the expulsion of the Jesuits from several countries, which highlighted the struggle between the popes and Catholic monarchs. The Jesuits had been closely identified with the papacy since the inception of the order during the Catholic Reformation. They had gained great influence as tutors to powerful noble families and in the Spanish, French, and Portuguese colonies in the Americas. Catholic kings perceived the Jesuits as a threat to their authority.

In Portugal, King John V's strong-willed minister, Sebastião, the marquis of Pombal (1699–1782), enhanced the monarchy's authority at the expense of the great noble families and the Church. When Jesuits criticized the regime for, among other things, orchestrating anti-Semitism, Pombal accused them of exploiting the indigenous population of Paraguay, where they virtually ran the colonial state. After Pombal falsely accused the order of planning the king's assassination, the monarch expelled the Jesuits from

Jesuits being expelled from Spain, 1764.

Portugal in 1759. Ten years later, Pombal ended the Inquisition's status as an independent tribunal, making it a royal court. Other rulers followed suit, including Louis XV of France in 1764. The expulsion of the Jesuits from some of the most powerful Catholic states reflected the diminishing power of the papacy in the face of absolute monarchs determined to retain control over what they considered to be national churches.

In Spain, Charles III (ruled 1759–1788) ordered universities to include instruction in science and philosophy. In 1781, Spain carried out its last execution of a person accused of heretical religious beliefs. Charles then reduced the feared Spanish Inquisition to a series of legal hurdles governing publishing. Like the kings of Portugal and France, Charles III in 1776 expelled the Jesuits in part because their near-monopoly on education seemed to pose a threat to the monarchy's control over the Church. In Italy, Leopold II also reduced the authority of the Church in Tuscany, ending the tithe and crippling the Inquisition. Catherine the Great's enlightened approach to religion could be seen in her termination of official (or "government") persecution of Old Believers, the dissident sect within the Russian Orthodox Church. And when Jews came under tsarist rule for the first time after the first Partition of Poland in 1772 (see Chapter 11), she initially placed Jewish merchants and other townspeople on an equal basis with their Christian neighbors. However, protests brought Catherine to adopt more restrictive measures. In 1794 she introduced double taxation for Jews. Louis XVI granted French Protestants most civil rights in 1787. And in Great Britain the following year Parliament reduced some restrictions on

Catholics—although they still could not hold public office. Nonetheless, London crowds shouting "No popery!" attacked the property of Catholics during the "Gordon riots," in which almost 300 people were killed. In 1792, however, the first legal Catholic church in England since the sixteenth century opened its doors in London.

Protestant states seemed most receptive to religious toleration. In the northern German states and Swiss cantons, the ideals of the philosophes provided support for religious toleration that had grown out of the sixteenth-century Reformation. The quest for religious tolerance played an important part in German enlightened thought. In his drama *Nathan the Wise* (1779), Gotthold Lessing argued that people of all religions are members of the human family. In Catholic Austria, Joseph II's relaxation of censorship permitted a spate of pamphlets and brochures calling for toleration of Protestants. The king's Edict of Toleration (1781) extended some toleration to non-Catholics. The edict included Jews, who were now "free" to bear the burden of a "toleration tax" and to pay an assessment on kosher meat. Joseph also ennobled several Jews, incurring the wrath of other nobles. Moreover, for the first time, Protestants could enter the Habsburg civil service.

Frederick the Great

The German states appeared to be the most fertile ground for enlightened absolutism. German philosophes remained closely tied to the existing order, looking to the individual states and to religion for reforms. They were less critical of the state than their French counterparts. For Immanuel Kant (1724–1804), the Enlightenment meant the liberation of the individual intellectually and morally, but not politically or socially. The individual should think critically, but also obey.

Frederick II of Prussia (ruled 1740–1786 and known as Frederick the Great), wanted to be remembered as an enlightened ruler. A man of considerable intelligence, he turned his court into a center of learning for the nobility. "Sans Souci," his rococo château in Potsdam outside Berlin, had French formal gardens and was considered the height of civility. Frederick, a flute-playing "philosopher-king," made Voltaire the centerpiece of his palace for two years. Voltaire praised Frederick for having transformed "a sad Sparta into a brilliant Athens." But the French philosophe soon grew disenchanted with the cynical, manipulative Prussian king, who coolly invaded the Habsburg territory of Silesia in 1740, in the first year of his reign. Voltaire angered Frederick by lampooning a royal favorite, and when the king ordered his hangman to burn the offending tract publicly, Voltaire took the hint and left Potsdam in 1752.

But Frederick again borrowed Enlightenment discourse when he claimed that one of his major tasks was "to make people as happy as is compatible with human nature and the means at my disposal." He once

Frederick the Great playing the flute at Sans Souci.

claimed somewhat disingenuously that he was nothing more than the "first servant" of his people as king: "I well know that the rich have many advocates, but the poor have only one, and that is I." Frederick freed the serfs of the royal domains (1763) and ordered the abolition of the lords' right to punish their own serfs physically. Judicial reforms ended some flagrant abuses by magistrates. The Prussian king relaxed censorship and abolished capital punishment, except in the army. Yet he refused to emancipate Prussian Jews, while continuing to depend on loans from them. Nonetheless, the Prussian Code, finally completed and promulgated in 1794, eight years after Frederick's death, granted "every inhabitant of the state . . . complete freedom of religion and conscience."

Frederick the Great's "enlightened" reforms were, above all, intended to make the Prussian state more powerful, not more just (see Chapter 11). He made Prussia a more efficient absolutist state. Frederick intended his law code to enhance the reach of the state rather than to make his people equal before the law. When he freed the serfs of the royal domains, it was because he needed them in the army. Nobles (Junkers) dominated most of the plum positions as military officers and high officials. Yet some commoners did in fact rise to important posts, including some army officers, who were subsequently ennobled. Frederick improved the state bureaucracy by introducing an examination system to govern entry. In the courts of justice, candidates had to pass the most difficult examinations, and in Berlin only a third of all judges were nobles.

Prussian law reinforced the distinction between noble and commoner. The Prussian Code divided Prussian society into noble, bourgeois, and common estates. Frederick bolstered the position of Prussian nobles because he was determined to prevent any erosion of their status as the landowning class. He refused to ban serfdom on private estates, and he created institutions that would provide credit to nobles in financial difficulty. Nobles were not permitted to sell their lands to non-nobles, and marriages between nobles and commoners were not recognized.

The Prussian monarch's *Essay on the Forms of Government* (1781) offered a recipe for enhancing the efficiency of the absolute state. Frederick's view of the world bound the state and the individual subject together. When their mutual interests could not be reconciled, however, the Prussian state always took precedence. As Voltaire had discovered for himself, Frederick the Great's reign reflected the limitations of enlightened absolutism.

Rural Reforms

Several other European rulers tried to improve conditions of rural life. Leopold II, who promulgated a new code of laws in 1786 and established a new and more independent judiciary, ended some restrictions on the grain trade, freeing the price of grain. These moves were popular among merchants and wealthy peasants, but not among poor people, who depended upon bread to survive. Following the disastrous decade of the 1770s, marked by hunger and disease, Austrian Queen Maria Theresa banned the mistreatment of peasants by their lords and tried to limit seigneurial obligations. As she put it, sheep must be well fed if they are to yield more wool and milk. Her son Joseph II abolished serfdom in 1781, converting peasant labor obligations into an annual payment to the lord, and ended obligations of personal service to the lord. Henceforth a peasant could marry and/or leave the land without the lord's permission. Peasants, at least in principle, could also turn to the state for support against an oppressive lord; they could even take the lord to court. However, Joseph II's Serfdom Patent encountered resistance among landowners and regional powers in the eastern regions of the empire. The nobility of Bohemia simply refused to enact any of the provisions, while nobles in Transylvania neglected to inform the peasants of any changes in their condition. In Hungary, the estate owners insisted that their peasants were not actually serfs but simple tenants and therefore not covered by the law. In the German-speaking parts of the empire, the Serfdom Patent granted the serfs legal rights but left most of the financial obligations of the old system intact. And in Tuscany, as in the Habsburg domains, aristocrats and state officials sabotaged Leopold's reforms.

Reasons of state lay behind even these seemingly enlightened reforms. By restricting labor obligations in some parts of the empire, peasants now owed the state even more taxes and were subject to a longer term of military service. Peasants, though legally free, remained indebted to their lords. Thus, "enlightened" reforms had little effect on the lives of most peasants.

Joseph II announced that he wanted the Habsburg state to follow "uniform principles," which included a reorganization of the imperial bureaucracy. He taxed Church property, abolished some monastic orders, and forced a reorganization of the Church within the Habsburg domains. None of the "enlightened" rulers gave up any of his or her monarchical prerogatives.

Catherine the Great, influenced by Montesquieu's *The Spirit of Laws,* wanted the nobility to serve as an "intermediary body" standing between the crown and its subjects. Catherine hoped that by clarifying their rights, nobles might contribute to the functioning and glory of her state. The Charter of the Nobility of 1785 formalized the relationship between the autocratic state and the nobles, recognizing the nobility of blood as equal to that of service. It confirmed their security of property, the right to hold serfs, and immunity from arrest and confiscation of property by the state. For the first time, nobles could travel abroad without the permission of the emperor. Local elective councils of nobles could henceforth send petitions to the tsar or empress, but the latter had no obligation to respond. Catherine herself turned against Enlightenment thought, however, fearing that it might become a tool of those opposed to absolute rule. Like Voltaire's experience at the court of Frederick the Great, Diderot's confidence in Catherine ended in disappointment when, to his chagrin, he learned that the empress had imprisoned those with whom she disagreed.

CURRENTS OF THE LATE ENLIGHTENMENT

The late Enlightenment contained several currents. British economists applied the concept of freedom for the first time to the workings of the economy. Meanwhile, on the continent, philosophes turned away from the preoccupation with rationality and the laws of nature. The mark of human freedom was no longer the exercise of reason but the expression of the emotions. Rousseau himself had begun this turn toward what he called "reasoned sentimentality" by stressing the importance of emotional development and fulfillment. In a related development, a number of writers began to "discover" and embrace their own national cultures, seeking their origins in medieval poems and songs. And in France, when there were no more Voltaires or Rousseaus, a generation of would-be philosophes, mediocre writers who attacked the institutional structure of the French monarchy, influenced public opinion. All of these developments served to undermine the established order (see Chapter 11). The late Enlightenment's emphasis on the historical roots of national culture provided a way of conceptualizing national identity, a transformation that would, for example, have enormous consequences in Europe in the nineteenth century and beyond.

Enlightened Thought and Economic Freedom

The philosophes' quest to discover the laws of nature and society led several of them to try to establish a set of laws that could explain the working of the economy. This search led away from mercantilism, which had formed the basis of seventeenth- and early eighteenth-century economic theory, to the emergence of classical economic liberalism. Mercantilist theory held that states should protect their economies with restrictions and tariffs that would maintain a favorable balance of trade, with more gold and silver flowing into a nation than going out.

The "physiocrats" believed that land, not gold and silver, was the source of all wealth. They wanted to end state interference in agriculture and the commerce of farm products. Writing in Diderot's *Encyclopedia*, François Quesnay (1694–1774), a French doctor and economist, called on the monarchy to free the grain trade and end arbitrary controls on prices, which states sometimes imposed to preserve public order. He and other physiocrats insisted that higher prices for goods would encourage production, thereby bringing about lower prices over the long run. The physiocrats also encouraged wealthy landowners to put science to work to increase farm yields, and wanted enlightened rulers to free the agricultural economy from tolls and internal tariffs. In England, where commercial agriculture was already well developed, the physiocrats attracted an interested following.

Adam Smith admiring his book, *The Wealth of Nations*.

However, when the oddly named Anne-Robert Turgot (1727–1781), Louis XVI's controller-general, freed France's grain trade from controls in the early 1770s, disastrous shortages accompanied a series of bad harvests (see Chapter 11). Hoarding contributed to much higher prices; grain riots followed, and the experiment soon ended with the old strictures and controls back in place.

Adam Smith (1723–1790), a Scottish professor of moral philosophy at the University of Glasgow, argued against some of the hallmarks of mercantilism in his *An Inquiry into the Nature and Causes of the Wealth of Nations* (1776). In the name of freeing the economy from restraints, he opposed guild restrictions and monopolies, as well as trade barriers and other forms of protectionism. Such bold proposals flew in the face of contemporary economic thought, which held closely to regulated monopolies and remained suspicious of free-market competition. Merchants looked to the state to provide financial, political, and military protection. The Scottish philosopher's optimistic doctrine came to be known universally by its French name, *"laissez-faire,"* or "leave alone." Each person, Smith insisted, should be "free to pursue his own interest his own way." If "left alone," Smith argued, the British economy would thrive naturally, generating domestic and foreign markets. The "invisible hand" of the unfettered economy would over time cause the forces of supply and demand to meet, determining the price of goods. By overcoming that "wretched spirit of monopoly," which made people less energetic, the "virtue of the marketplace" would also enhance social happiness and civic virtue. This was a common theme in the Scottish Enlightenment—Scottish philosophes were particularly concerned with how civic virtue and public morality could be inculcated in a society being slowly transformed by commerce and manufacture.

German Idealism

While in England the late Enlightenment brought an emphasis on economic freedom, on the continent it was marked by subjectivism and a greater emphasis on emotion, a shift already reflected by Rousseau's "reasoned sentimentality." The basic tenet of German idealism was that we perceive and understand the world through the medium of our ideas, and not through the direct application of our senses. Kant was the foremost proponent of this school. Born an artisan's son in the Prussian town of Königsberg, Kant's *Critique of Pure Reason* (1781) affirmed that rational inquiry into nature leads to knowledge. In his memorable analogy, reason is like a judge who "compels the witness to answer questions which he himself has formulated." But for Kant, reason alone was not the basis for our knowledge of the world. Instead, each person understands the world through concepts that cannot be separated from his or her unique experience. This philosophy undermined faith in the rational objectivity and universalism that had characterized the high Enlightenment. German idealism invited the subjectivity and relativism of early nineteenth-century romanticism.

In the eighteenth century, writers became interested in discovering the roots of national cultures; Sweden, Denmark, Russia, and Poland all discovered their "national" literatures, written in their own languages. The first Czech national theater opened in Prague in 1737. Gotthold Lessing proudly wrote in German and called for a national theater. Scottish readers eagerly saluted the "discovery" by the poet James Macpherson (1736–1796) of the work of an imaginary Gaelic bard of the third century, Ossian. Macpherson's publication in the early 1760s of what he claimed were translations of the poet he called the Gaelic Homer set off a bitter debate, one that contributed to the emergence of Scottish romanticism.

Composers began to borrow from popular culture, especially from folk music not necessarily religious in inspiration. The first Jewish periodicals were published in Königsberg in the century's last decades, and the first Jewish school established in Berlin in 1778. The emotional search for and enthusiastic identification with national cultures contributed, as in the case of Scotland, to the development of romanticism, and very gradually of nationalism. Nationalism would help undermine the established order in several continental states, notably France, where the established order was based on allegiance to a monarchical dynasty and often to established religion as well, and not yet necessarily on national identity.

The Enlightenment and Public Opinion

Public opinion, a concept we take for granted, did not always exist. But it began to take shape in French, English, and several other European languages in the eighteenth century (see Chapter 11). During the 1770s, more people in France discussed the pressing political issues of the day than ever before. Lawyers helped establish the concept of public opinion when they sought a wide spectrum of support for the parlements. Louis XV had decided to replace these provincial noble law courts in 1768 with malleable institutions more directly under royal control. Public opinion forced the king to restore the parlements six years later. Public opinion, to which opponents of the monarchy and increasingly the court itself now appealed, provided a forum in which political ideas were increasingly discussed. These ideas were shaped by Enlightenment discourse on political sovereignty and the limits of absolute rule.

A number of the treatises published during the late Enlightenment dealt with contemporary political issues, in the tradition of Voltaire's broadsides at the time of the Calas Affair, which had exposed the consequences of intolerance and persecution to public opinion. As the financial crisis of the French monarchy worsened during the 1780s, such publications would help make the question of reform an increasingly national issue.

Forbidden Publications and the Undermining of Authority

Some of the fringe members of the republic of letters, whom Voltaire had dismissed as mere "scribblers," also undermined respect for the monarchy and the royal family. Whereas the milieu of the philosophes earlier in the century had been elegant salons, the would-be philosophes of the last period of the Enlightenment hung around cheap cafés, lived in rooms high above the street, and dodged creditors by frequently changing addresses. At the same time, they insisted that royal censorship blocked their ascent to better things. Some made a modest living peddling forbidden publications. While claiming common cause with the major philosophes against the unenlightened institutions of France, some wrote pornography or penned pieces slandering prominent people, including the royal family, and a few kept afloat by spying on other writers for the police. There had been such publications before the 1770s and 1780s, but never so many of them, and never had they been so widely read.

Banned books reached France through the efforts of resourceful shipping agents, transporters, bargemen, dockers, and peddlers, who smuggled books published in Switzerland or the Austrian Netherlands to French booksellers willing to circumvent the controls of the booksellers' guild and the state. In 1783, the crown redoubled its efforts to stem the tide of smuggled books and to still the clandestine presses within France. These publishers undercut the legitimate Parisian book trade because they published banned books and produced cheaper editions of acceptable works. Moreover, royal officials were concerned about the effects of these smuggled satires on public opinion.

Was there any connection between the high-minded philosophes and their "successors," who included the authors of *Venus in the Cloister, or the Nun in a Nightgown; Christianity Unveiled;* and *Margot the Campfollower?* In fact, the envious and mediocre descendants of the philosophes in some ways continued their predecessors' work by undermining respect for the authority of the Church, the aristocracy, and, above all, the monarchy.

Moreover, certain themes of the Enlightenment did find their way into their work. They joined their far more illustrious predecessors in attacking the foundations of the French monarchy. Frustrated authors attacked the privileges, for example, of the printing and booksellers' guild, which they blamed for keeping them from reaching the stature they desired. Their identification of censorship with despotism, though self-serving, was nonetheless effective, as they argued that only its abolition could permit the free exchange of ideas. Political events and scandals kept the presses of the literary underground turning, fanning popular critiques of the monarchy, Church, and nobility.

LEGACY OF THE ENLIGHTENMENT

The Enlightenment philosophes celebrated reason, while acknowledging the passions, and were suspicious of pure faith. Steeped in respect for science and reason and confident that humanity would discover the truths of nature, they were optimistic about human potential. The philosophes' belief in progress, which Kant insisted was a sign of modernity, separated them sharply from the Catholic Church, in particular. Yet, they were not as naive, uncritical, or foolish as Voltaire's Candide, who thought progress inevitable. The philosophes believed that the combination of thought, study, education, and action would lead to a better future. States, they thought, were not ordained by God but by mankind and, like other phenomena, should be subject to critical scrutiny.

The philosophes' belief in human dignity led them to oppose all forms of despotism. Most spoke out against religious intolerance, torture, and slavery. (Yet an effective campaign against slavery, launched by the English abolitionists of the Society for the Abolition of the Slave Trade in 1787, stood independent of the Enlightenment). Furthermore, some Enlightenment thinkers and writers recognized that contemporary assertions about the inequality of women contradicted their understanding of nature.

Some philosophes had strong reservations about the ability of individuals to develop equally. "As for the rabble," Voltaire once said, "I don't concern myself with it; they will always remain rabble." Those with power and influence first must be enlightened, they reasoned, so that eventually everyone could develop through education. However, Diderot, Montesquieu, and Voltaire supported the right to divorce, but also opposed equal status for women.

In their commitment to individual freedom the philosophes influenced the subsequent history of the Western world. Whereas most people in the eighteenth century still considered the monarchy to be the repository of the public good, the philosophes proclaimed that the public had rights of its own and that freedom was a good in itself. Enlightenment thought helped create a discourse of principled opposition that would shake the foundations of absolutism. If the philosophes themselves were not revolutionaries, many of their ideas in the context of eighteenth-century Europe were indeed revolutionary.

CHAPTER 10

EIGHTEENTH-CENTURY ECONOMIC AND SOCIAL CHANGE

The great English landowners did as they pleased in the eighteenth century. More than one gentleman had an entire village demolished or flooded because it stood in the way of his landscaping plans. Another wrote, "It is a melancholy thing to stand alone in one's own country. I look around, not a single house to be seen but for my own. I am Giant, of Giant's Castle, and have ate up all my neighbors." Fences and servants kept venturesome interlopers far away. Some men of great means gambled fantastic sums on horse races. Sir Robert Walpole's estate guests drank up £1,500 of wine a year, the combined annual wages of more than 100 laborers. English nobles seemed particularly vulnerable to overeating. A certain Parson Woodforde carefully entered in his diary the day of his death, "Very weak this morning, scarce able to put on my clothes and with great difficulty get downstairs with help. Dinner today, roast beef, etc."

At about the same time, in Switzerland, a peasant lived a very different and arguably more productive life. Jakob Gujer, who was called Kleinjogg (Little Jake) by his friends, inherited an indebted small farm and transformed it into something of a model enterprise, where he grew vegetables and new crops and raised cattle. It is said that when the duke of Württemberg came to see the famous peasant, Kleinjogg told him how flattered he was that a prince should pay a visit to a humble peasant. The prince, teary eyed, replied, "I do not come down to you, I rise up to you, for you are better than I." To which Kleinjogg is alleged to have answered with tactful deference, "We are both good if each of us does what he should. You lords and princes must order us peasants what to do, for you have the time to decide what is best for the state, and it is for we peasants to obey you and work with diligence and loyalty." But there were few peasants with the means and initiative of Kleinjogg on the continent. In England, there were relatively few peasants left at all.

349

Although in some ways society remained the same as in earlier centuries, economic, social, and political developments transformed Europe during the last half of the eighteenth century. To be sure, these transformations were uneven and regionally specific, affecting England and northwestern Europe the most, while bypassing much of Central and Eastern Europe. In economically advanced regions, some of the traditional checks on population growth became less imposing. Increased agricultural productivity supported a larger population that, in turn, expanded the demand for food. Manufacturing developed in and around northern English towns, leading to the beginning of what we know as the Industrial Revolution.

In a related change, distinctions within the highest social estates or orders were becoming less marked in Western Europe. Moreover, increased wealth generated some fluidity between social groups, contributing, in particular, to the dynamism that made Britain the most powerful state in the world. In France, too, wealth increasingly blurred lines of social class without, however, eliminating them entirely. Distinctions in title no longer necessarily corresponded to patterns of wealth distribution. By contrast, social barriers remained much more rigidly defined in Central and Eastern Europe.

The Social Order

In much of early modern Europe, social structure was marked by birth into particular estates, or orders, which conferred collective identities and privileges. Each order was legally defined, with specific functions and rights conferred to it by virtue of being part of the order, not through individual rights. The nobility was a privileged order, with special rights accorded by rulers and law, such as exemption from taxation. Noble titles were hereditary, and stemmed in principle from birth, although in reality many families during the century were able to purchase titles. The clergy was also a privileged order and, like the nobility, generally exempt from taxation. In France, the "third estate" was simply everyone who was neither noble nor a member of the clergy, and included peasants and townspeople, all of whom were subject to taxation. Within and between these estates, or orders, some degree of social movement was possible, particularly in Western Europe. The extent of social mobility that existed within the "societies of orders" was debated by contemporaries, as it has been subsequently by historians.

Nobles

In most of the continental European states (with the exception of the Dutch Republic and Switzerland), nobles dominated political life during the eighteenth century, although in most of these states they numbered no more than 2 to 3 percent of the population. They accounted for a much larger percentage in Russia, Spain, Poland, and Hungary, which together probably accounted for almost two-thirds of the nobles in Europe. In Spain's northern provinces and in Poland, more than 10 percent of the male population held noble titles. In Hungary, what may have been the first accurate census in European history in 1784 counted more than 400,000 people claiming to be nobles, about 5 percent of the population. In France, by contrast, there were only somewhere between 25,000 and 55,000 noble families.

Hungarian noblemen in the eighteenth century.

The vast majority of nobles drew their wealth and status from land they owned but that other people worked ("I am idle, therefore I am," went a Hungarian saying about Magyar nobles, spoofing the words of the French philosopher Descartes). Noble landlords owned between 15 and 40 percent of the land, depending on the country, and an even higher percentage of productive land. In Prussia, only nobles could own land that was exempt from taxes; in Poland, commoners could not own any land at all. Russian commoners lost the right to own property to which serfs were legally bound. Austrian nobles held half of the arable land in the Habsburg domains, hiring agents to collect what peasants owed them. Nine thousand nobles owned a third of all Swedish land. In the Italian states, the nobility's share of the wealth was even more than that of the Catholic Church.

Many continental nobles retained specific rights, often called seigneurial rights, over the peasantry. Nobles drew income in rent (cash), kind (crops), and dues (often labor) owed them by virtue of their social status and ownership of land. Some dispensed justice in their own courts. Peasants were obligated to pay to have their grain ground in the lord's mill, to bake bread in his oven, and to squeeze grapes in his press. The burden of seigneurial dues and debts left peasants with little or sometimes nothing left to pay state taxes and church taxes (tithes), or to feed their families, which might well include parents and unmarried sisters, brothers, and children.

Nobles proved remarkably adept at maintaining their privileges while adapting to the challenges and possibilities resulting from the growth of the centralized state. Such privileges included being exempt from virtually all taxation, as were nobles in Prussia, Poland, Hungary, and Russia, or exempt from the direct tax on land. Other noble privileges included the nobles' right to bear a family coat of arms, to wear certain clothing and jewelry, to occupy special church pews near the altar (in some places Mass could not start until the local nobles had taken their accustomed places), to receive communion before anyone else, and to sit in specially reserved sections at concerts and on special benches at universities. Commoners were expected to bow, curtsy, or tip their hats when a noble walked by, gestures upon which nobles increasingly insisted. The right to duel over family "honor" in some states and the right to wear a sword were honorific privileges that served to distinguish nobles from their social inferiors.

There were significant differences in the wealth and status of European nobles, however. The wealthiest, most powerful nobles considered themselves "aristocrats," although this was not a legal category. They were proud possessors of the most ancient titles (in France, they were the nobles of the sword, whose titles originated in military service to the king), and many of them were members of the court nobility. Aristocrats viewed themselves as the epitome of integrity, honor, and personal courage, and the embodiment of elite culture. The *grands seigneurs* in France and the *grandees* in Spain were identified by their great wealth and ownership of very large estates. But the wealthiest nobles may have been the great landed magnates of East Central Europe. Prince Charles Radziwill of Poland was served by 10,000 retainers and a private army of 6,000 soldiers. Another Polish nobleman's property included 25,000 square kilometers of land, territory about four-fifths the size of today's Belgium. A single Russian prince owned 9,000 peasant households.

On the other hand, in every country there were also nobles of modest means who eagerly, even desperately, sought advantageous marriages for their daughters, and state, military, and church posts to provide a living for their sons. Demographic factors put pressure on poorer nobles, because now more noble children survived birth and childhood. Many Sicilian, Polish, and Spanish nobles owned little more than their titles. About 120,000 Polish nobles were landless, many so poor that they were referred to as the "barefoot nobility." The *hobereaux* were the threadbare nobles of France. Spanish *hidalgos* depended on modest state pensions, and some were so poor that it was said that they "ate black bread under the genealogical tree." In Spain, these impoverished nobles retained the right to display their coat of arms and to be called "Don" ("Sir"), and freedom from arrest for debt. But until 1773 they were not permitted to engage in manual work, and hence they had few ways to emerge from poverty.

Nobles who could afford to do so tried to maintain an aristocratic lifestyle, keeping up châteaux (manor houses) on their rural estates, some also owning elegant townhouses with gardens designed to recreate the illusion of a rural manor. Some nobles of lesser means attempted to keep an aristocratic lifestyle, going into debt as a result.

The British Landed Elite

In Britain, there were only about 200 families that claimed noble title. Yet the percentage of English land owned by nobles rose from about 15 to 25 percent, a far larger percentage than in either France or the German states. Unlike their continental counterparts, British nobles had to pay property taxes, and the only special privileges that peers retained (besides their vast wealth) were the rights to sit in the House of Lords and, if accused of a crime, to be tried there by a jury of their equals. Because in Britain only the eldest son inherited his father's title and land, younger sons had to find other sources of income. One such source was the Anglican Church and its twenty-six bishoprics, the plums of which were reserved for the younger sons of peers and which offered considerable revenue and prestige. Whereas in the previous century about a quarter of Anglican bishops had been commoners, by 1760 only a few were not the sons of nobles.

Although only nobles could sit in the House of Lords, the British ruling elite of great landowners was considerably broader. British landowners became even more prosperous during the eighteenth century, particularly after about 1750, when they raised rents on their estates and amassed fortunes selling agricultural products. Wealthy newcomers who owned large chunks of land also joined the elite. The ownership of landed estates conferred "gentry" status, which a broad range of families claimed. At the time of the Glorious Revolution of 1688, the landed elite numbered about 4,000 gentry families.

The wives of gentlemen oversaw governesses and domestic servants while instructing their children in the responsibilities of family, religion, and social status—to behave politely, but confidently. It was considered poor form to show too much emotion, to be too enthusiastic, and, above all, to be overly passionate, sensual or, worse, licentious. One did not seek openly to convert the lower classes to better manners and virtue, but rather to set a good example. The writer Horace Walpole (1717–1797) once claimed he attended church only to set a good example for the servants.

Young gentlemen were tutored at home, or they attended secondary schools, such as Westminster and Eton, boarding schools that characterized a gradual shift to out-of-home education throughout Europe for elites. Oxford and Cambridge Universities then beckoned some, although few actually graduated. Scottish universities, in contrast, offered more dynamic thought and research. Young gentlemen were expected to know something about the classics and contemporary poets. Yet, to many if not most wealthy families, academic knowledge seemed superfluous, even suspect. When Edward Gibbon (1737–1794), the historian of ancient Rome, presented one of his books to a duke, the latter exclaimed, "Another damned thick square book! Scribble, scribble, scribble, eh Mister Gibbon?" A wealthy dowager offered her grandnephew and heir a handsome annual stipend if he would "chuse to travel" and thus forsake "one of the Schools of Vice, the Universities." The goal of the "grand tour" of the continent, servants in tow, was to achieve some knowledge of culture and painting. Such trips further enhanced the popularity in Britain of the classical style of architecture, so called because it emulated classical Greek and Roman edifices.

The Clergy

Although in France, Prussia, and Sweden the clergy was technically the first order or estate, the clergy did not really form a separate corporate entity, but rather reflected the social divisions between rich and poor that characterized European life. Most village priests and ministers had prestige and local influence, but they shared the poverty of their parishioners. Yet in many places, the material advantages of being a priest (including exclusion from some taxes) attracted the sons of peasant families. On the continent, the members of the French clergy were likely to be the most literate, Russian Orthodox priests the least.

The lower clergy, drawn from the lower middle class, artisans, or the relatively prosperous peasantry, resented the undisguised ambition, greed, and arrogance of the bishops. Wealth and rank, not piety, usually determined such selections, as in the Italian states, where bishops were invariably drawn from the families of the great landowners. Even so, few monarchs were as brazen as King Philip V of Spain, who named his eight-year-old son to be archbishop of Toledo. Many bishops did not take their responsibilities seriously. In the 1760s at least forty bishops resided in Paris, only one of whom was, in principle, supposed to live there.

Although some parts of Europe, especially regions in France, had already become "de-christianized," meaning that religious practice and presumably belief had declined (see Chapter 9), in most places religion still played an important part in village life. The clergy baptized children,

A baptism performed in Italy, a religious ritual that maintained its importance in most Catholic places.

registered their births, married couples, and buried the dead. Priests and ministers supervised charitable activities and provided certificates of good behavior for those leaving to search for work elsewhere. Religion offered consolation to many impoverished people: everyone could go to church, even if the poor were restricted as to where they could sit or stand. In general, the quality of the parish clergy seems to have been quite high in the eighteenth century (when compared to the next century), due in part to efforts to improve clerical training. Nonetheless, many parish priests were still caught between liturgical demands and the persistence of popular superstitions shared by all social groups—for example, the duchess of Alba in Spain tried to cure her son's illness by having him ingest powder from the mummified finger of a saint.

The "Middling Sort"

Most of those people who engaged in commerce, trade, and manufacturing were known as the "middling sort" by the English and the "bourgeoisie" by the French. The term "bourgeois" evolved from the medieval sense of "privileged townsmen" (in earlier times they had been exempt from having to pay taxes to territorial rulers; see Chapter 1).

The middle classes ranged from wealthy entrepreneurs, who had developed the economies of trading and manufacturing cities, to struggling retail merchants, craftsmen, and innkeepers, who made barely enough to hang on to their businesses. Purchasing land and titles when they could, the wealthiest commoners owned about a quarter of the land in France and most of the land in Switzerland. Great Britain had already become the proverbial "nation of shopkeepers," with one shop for every thirty or forty people.

In Western Europe, the middle decades of the eighteenth century brought an expansion of the liberal professions, particularly in the number of lawyers. Men trained in law took positions in state bureaucracies and law courts. In England and France, some of the best students, or at least the best connected, became barristers; this gave them the right to plead in court, which attorneys (solicitors), their subordinates, could not do. Distinguished medical schools produced few physicians, not yet a profession viewed with great respect. Beneath them were surgeons, some of whom were former barbers. Military surgeons tended to be a cut above the others, their skills honed in the heat of battle. Despite the fact that some universities taught anatomy, surgical techniques were learned on the job.

To some nobles, "bourgeois" was an expression of contempt, seen in the sense of a seventeenth-century play in which a protagonist is jeered by a young nobleman: "Bourgeois is the insult given by these hooligans to anybody they deem slow-witted or out of touch with the court." In the eighteenth century, the term had not lost the sense provided by a seventeenth-century dictionary: "Lacking in court grace, not altogether polite, overfamiliar, insufficiently respectful."

Triumphant merchants at table. Note that one of the merchants is smoking tobacco, a new fad. Note also the aristocratic wig on the dog on the right.

Peasants

In 1787, the peripatetic Englishman Arthur Young was traveling in Champagne in northern France when he encountered a peasant woman who looked to be about sixty or seventy years of age. To his astonishment, she gave her age as twenty-eight, a mother of seven children who survived by virtue of "a morsel of land, one cow and a poor little horse." Each year her husband owed 42 pounds of wheat to one noble, and 168 pounds of oats, one chicken, and a cash payment to another noble. He also owed taxes to the state. The woman, old before her time, stated simply that the "taxes and seigneurial obligations" were a crushing burden, one that seemed to be getting worse.

Peasants still formed the vast majority of the population on the continent: from about 75 percent (Prussia and France) to more than 90 percent (Russia). Peasants were the source of the wealth that sustained the incomes of crown, nobility, and church. Peasants stood at the bottom of society, condemned as "a hybrid between animal and human" in the words of a Bavarian official. An upper-class Moldavian called peasants "strangers to any discipline, order, economy or cleanliness . . . thoroughly lazy, mendacious . . . people who are accustomed to do the little work that they do only under invectives or blows." Such cruel images were particularly prevalent in regions where lords dominated peasants of another ethnic group, as in Bohemia, where German landowners drew on the labor of Czech peasants.

The village was the center of the peasant's universe. Village solidarities helped them pull through as best they could in hard times, through harvest failures, epidemics, and wars. Villagers viewed outsiders with suspicion. Folk songs celebrated peasant wisdom and wiliness, as humble rural people outfoxed naive and bumbling outsiders, whose wealth could not impart common sense.

All peasants were vulnerable to powerful outsiders in the overlapping and interdependent systems of domination that characterized early modern Europe. The state, nobles, and churchmen extracted taxes, produce, labor, and cash. The proportion of peasant revenue in kind or cash that disappeared into the pockets of nobles, officials, and clergy ranged from about 30 percent (France) to 70 percent (Bohemia). Rulers extracted money, commodities, and labor payments, imposing additional taxes when they were at war.

The peasantry was not, however, a homogeneous mass. In Western Europe, where almost all peasants were free, a peasant's status depended upon the amount of land, if any, owned or controlled through leases. In northern France, Flanders, southwestern Germany, Switzerland, and Sweden, many peasants owned or rented plots of sufficient size and productivity to do well enough in most years. Swedish peasants owned about a third of the cultivable land in their country. Recognized formally as a fourth estate, the Swedish peasantry maintained a degree of independence perhaps unique in Europe. Charles XII of Sweden bragged that he would rather be the most miserable Swedish peasant than a Russian noble unprotected by law from the whims of the tsar. Rural industry—for example, linens—provided supplementary income for peasant families in parts of France, Switzerland, and in German states. In Zurich's hinterland in the 1780s, about a quarter of the population spun or wove at home for the cotton and silk industries.

Many landowning peasants were constantly in debt, borrowing against the often empty hope of the next harvest. Sharecroppers worked land owned by landlords in exchange for one-third to one-half of what was produced. Landless laborers scraped by, if they were lucky, working on rural estates. All over Europe, some peasants took to the road as peddlers. Seasonal migrants left their homes in the Alps, Pyrenees, and other mountain regions each year for construction work in Milan, Lyon, Barcelona, or other large cities, or to work in the grain fields in the summer or in the vineyards in the fall.

Serfdom had largely died out in Western Europe. Yet many free peasants continued to be subject to some kind of seigneurial justice. In France, thousands of manorial courts still existed in 1789, providing lords with additional income by virtue of legal fees and fines assessed on peasants. Most of these courts, presided over by nobles, occupied themselves with minor offenses such as poaching and trespassing, civil suits for debt, and family matters such as inheritances and guardianships.

In addition to taxes on land and salt, peasants also owed obligatory labor service, usually work on roads, in France, Denmark, Sweden, Switzerland, Poland, Russia, and some German states. Obligations varied from only a couple of days in parts of France to as much as 200 days per year in Denmark. In Eastern Europe, peasant children were sometimes required to work in the service of the lord. Other obligations included the duty to provide the lord's household with a certain amount of food—for example, a chicken or goose on a holiday, or even just a few eggs—to provide food for the lord's dogs, or to spin or weave cloth for the lord's household. To these were added mandatory payments to the seigneur upon transfer of land held by peasants with hereditary tenure. When a peasant with such tenure died, the lord claimed both money and the best animals the peasant owned.

The conditions of peasant life became worse the farther east one traveled. Peasants in Russia and Eastern Europe lived in hovels made of earth, clay mixed with straw, branches, twigs, and sometimes caked manure. Floors were of mud and beds of straw. Only well-off peasants could afford wood as building material.

The farther east one went, too, the more authority lords wielded over peasants. Most peasants east of the Elbe River were serfs, some of whom had to take an oath of loyalty to their seigneur, as during the Middle Ages. There were some free peasants in the Habsburg domains and in Poland, but very few in Russia. The number of people who lost their freedom by becoming serfs had increased so much in eastern Prussia and Brandenburg that the German term for serfdom had become the same word for slavery.

Gallows stood near some Prussian manor houses, symbolizing the judicial prerogatives nobles held over serfs, including the right to dispense corporal punishment. In Poland, nobles could have their serfs executed until late in the eighteenth century. Russian lords could torture serfs, as long as they did not die immediately from such treatment, or they could send them into exile in Siberia. In Poland, a noble convicted of murdering a peasant paid only a small fine.

In Russia, proprietary serfs remained personally bound to the land of the nobles and, after Catherine the Great's Charter of 1785, to the nobles themselves. Lords could sell serfs, give them away—for example, as part of a dowry—or lose title to them through gambling. Serfs could be sold individually or as a family to another noble, or be exchanged for animals. Lords could refuse permission for their serfs to marry or to choose a certain occupation. A good number of serfs took their chances in setting out to seek their freedom in the vast expanses of Siberia. In Russia, as well as in Central and Eastern Europe, a few serfs managed to put together enough money to purchase their freedom.

In Russia, a poll tax on males (called "souls"), from which only nobles were excluded, added to the dependence of the "bonded people" to the

A family of serfs paying homage to their lord. Note the wife kissing the noble's hand.

state. Villages were collectively responsible for the payment of taxes. Moreover, all male peasants could be conscripted into army service for terms of twenty-five years, a life sentence for most soldiers.

Possibilities for peasant resistance were limited; yet the "weapons of the weak" were not insignificant. These ranged from sullen resentment and foot-dragging to arson, or even insurrection. All nobles in an idle moment— and there were many—pondered the possibility of a massive uprising of "the dark masses." As the legal and material conditions of the serfs deteriorated, rebellions were endemic in eighteenth-century Russia. During the reign of Catherine the Great, the Cossack Emelian Pugachev appeared on the Siberian frontier claiming to be "Tsar Peter III" (the real Peter III had spoken of reforms but had been dethroned and then murdered). He led several million peasants against their lords in 1773 and 1774. Pugachev's followers included Cossacks, Old Believers (dissidents persecuted by the Orthodox Church and doubly taxed), miners from the Ural Mountains, and desperate serfs. About 3,000 landowners perished in the Pugachev rebellion before it was crushed.

In Bohemia and Moravia, 40,000 royal soldiers were required to put down peasant uprisings in 1775. And in the middle of the next decade, about

30,000 Transylvanian peasants rose up after a false rumor spread that those enlisting in the Habsburg army would gain freedom from serfdom. They demanded the abolition of the nobility and burned several hundred manor houses to make their point. The uprising ended with the torture of several of the leaders, parts of whose bodies were nailed to the gates of towns.

The Beginnings of the Industrial Revolution

The Industrial Revolution began in England during the eighteenth century. For the most part, its early stages brought an intensification of forms of production that already existed: small workshops and cottage-industry manufacturing, the production of goods at home. Technological innovation played a part, but in the beginning its role was not as large as has sometimes been assumed. Ultimately, however, a new source of power, the steam engine, would replace animal and human power, and in the nineteenth century manufacturing increasingly would be characterized by factory production.

The growth in manufacturing itself depended on two interrelated factors: agricultural productivity, then the principal source of wealth, and population growth. The two were so closely linked that it is sometimes difficult to know which followed which. An increase in agricultural productivity permitted the European population to increase during the century. At the same time, greater demand for food encouraged capital-intensive farming, including specialization of cash crops (such as olives, grapes, and raw silk) and the raising of cattle and poultry for the market. Greater profits from agriculture generated a surplus of funds that could be invested in manufacturing. In turn, a larger population, with some of the growth concentrated in and around cities and towns, increased the demand for manufactured goods and provided a labor supply for town-based and rural industry.

Stagnation and Growth in Agriculture

New agricultural methods, first applied in the middle of the seventeenth century, helped raise farm yields, in England above all, aided by the application of natural and artificial fertilizers. Gradually the practice of leaving part of the land fallow every other or every third year gave way to crop rotation, which helped regenerate the soil. Landowners planted fodder and root crops such as clover and turnips. This provided food for animals as well as for human beings, in addition to enriching the soil by helping it absorb and retain nitrogen.

By 1750, English agricultural yields had increased to the point that almost 15 percent of what was produced could be exported abroad (although about a third of the British population still did not have enough to eat). On average, at the end of the seventeenth century an acre of agricultural land yielded perhaps 2.5 times more food in England than in France. Agriculture's contribu-

Measuring land in preparation for enclosure.

tion to the British gross national product reached a peak of 45 percent in 1770, and then only slowly was overtaken by English manufacturing as its place in the economy rose remarkably. Increased farm profits provided capital not only for further investment in agriculture but also in manufacturing (although landowners were still more likely to invest in government bonds than in speculative ventures).

One of the impediments to the expansion of agricultural production in England had been the widespread existence of open fields or common lands, which made up about half of the arable land in 1700. Beginning in the sixteenth century, on request from landowners, acts of Parliament permitted the "enclosure" of common land, transforming open fields or land that was communally owned into privately owned, fenced-in fields that could be more intensively and profitably farmed by individual owners (see Chapter 5). Between 1760 and 1815, 3,600 separate parliamentary acts enclosed more than 7 million acres of land, more than one-fourth of the farmland of England. Over two centuries, enclosure acts forced perhaps half of English small landholders from the land, swelling the ranks of agricultural laborers. Small tenant farmers, too, suffered, as many could not afford to pay rents that rose rapidly after about 1760. The poorest members of the rural community lost their age-old access to lands on which they had gleaned firewood, gathered nuts and berries, and grazed animals. Before enclosure, it was said, a "cottager" was a laborer with land; after enclosure, he was a laborer without land. The Irish-born writer Oliver Goldsmith commented with playful, bitter irony:

> The law locks up both man and woman
> Who steals the goose from off the common,
> But lets the greater felon loose
> Who steals the common from the goose.

Agricultural change came far more slowly on the continent. Most producers remained at the subsistence level, farming small plots without an agricultural surplus that they might have used to expand their holdings or improve farming techniques. Primitive farming techniques (including wooden plows that barely scratched the surface of rocky terrain) characterized the mountainous and arid land of southern Italy and Sicily, the Dalmatian coast, southern France, much of Spain, and the Balkans. Peasants lacked farm and draft animals and therefore fertilizer, meat, and milk. Markets and transportation networks remained inadequate to the task of agricultural modernization.

On the continent, a bewildering variety of land tenures and agricultural practices under which they were held seemed to set rural poverty in stone. Most continental farmland remained divided into small strips, and each year more than one-third of arable land may have lain fallow, with crops rotated between fields. Traditional peasant agricultural methods also blocked a major expansion of production. "Slash and burn" tillage survived in some parts of Europe where peasants simply burned the stubble on their land once the harvest had been taken in, replenishing the soil with ash.

The studied attention many English country gentlemen gave to their lands may be contrasted with the approach of many French, Spanish, and Prussian nobles, content to sit back and live from revenue extracted from peasants. While the state had an interest in increasing farm output to generate additional tax revenue, most royal officials, seigneurs, and churchmen looked first to better ways of extracting peasant surpluses, not to improving yields. Nobles resisted occasional royal attempts to reduce the peasants' obligations, or to change them, such as by commuting labor service to payments in cash or in kind. Furthermore, much of what peasants managed to produce they owed to landlords, the state, and to a lesser extent, the Church. "Why should I build a better house," asked a Bavarian peasant, "so that my seigneur can line his pockets with the requisite fees to be paid?"

Serfs had even less interest than other peasants in innovation. In Central and Eastern Europe, an old adage went "there is no land without a lord" because in most places only a noble, the crown, or the Church could own land. The absence of independent peasant proprietors left a formidable obstacle to agricultural development.

Changes on the continent comparable to those taking place in England were mainly confined to northwestern Europe. In northern France, Flanders, the Dutch Republic, Schleswig-Holstein, parts of northern Italy, and Spanish Catalonia, the fertile land and sufficient capital facilitated investment in commercial agriculture. Moreover, these were regions generally farmed by people who owned the lands on which they worked, and who therefore had more incentive to augment production. But even in the less densely populated countryside of Eastern and southern Europe, more land was brought into cultivation, as in Russia where the population pushed into the steppes of the eastern frontier lands.

Other factors, too, contributed to improvements in Western European agriculture. During the eighteenth century, Europe as a whole experienced warmer, drier weather, particularly in the summers, in stark contrast to the unusually cold and damp seventeenth century. This had a salutary effect on population, agricultural yields, and commerce. Land reclamation projects helped expand the amount of land under cultivation. The Dutch continued to reclaim land from the sea, and land reclamation added significantly to the amount of land under cultivation in the Southern Netherlands (Belgium) and Brandenburg.

Though not to the same extent as in England, the enclosure of separate strips of land and the sale or consolidation of common lands in northwestern Europe permitted the development of "agricultural individualism," as more land passed to peasant-owners. Beginning in the 1760s, state policies created small farms owned by peasants, helping transform Danish agriculture from the stagnation of serfdom to relative prosperity. Royal decrees encouraged enclosure and forced the commutation of labor obligations to rent payments.

Gradually some techniques that characterized agricultural improvements in England reached the continent. Innovative landowners and tenant farmers began to implement crop rotation (growing foliage crops to improve the fertility of fields), replacing the old three-field system so that little or no land lay fallow. As in England, turnips, potatoes, and rice enhanced dietary nutrition. Yet many peasants remained prisoners of tradition, refusing to plant or eat potatoes (Russian peasants called them "apples of the devil"), despite the fact that they can grow almost anywhere under any conditions. The cultivation of sugar beets (from which sugar can be made), the tomato (despite the fact that some peasants believed it to be poisonous), and chestnuts (the "bread of the poor") also spread, sustaining population growth.

Animal husbandry also benefited from improved techniques. Oxen, mules, and especially horses could pull plows more easily than peasants. More cattle provided manure for fertilizer, and meat and milk for nutrition. Sheep-raising developed rapidly, providing both food and wool.

Some landowners formed societies to discuss agriculture, and a handful began model farms. Such groups included nobles, wealthy bourgeois, and clergy. French physiocrats, who believed that land was the source of all wealth, urged landowners to make their property more profitable and encouraged state policies to free the price of grain. Publications on agriculture dramatically increased in number.

A few continental rulers took steps to intervene in the interest of agricultural progress. The elector of Bavaria in 1762 offered farmers an exemption from taxes for ten years in the hope that they would plant foliage crops in their fallow fields. Several princes in the German Rhineland encouraged the selective breeding of cattle. In 1768, Queen Maria Theresa of Austria ordered the division of common pasturelands in some parts of the Habsburg territories and the establishment of agricultural societies.

Population Growth

The European population rose from about 120 million to about 190 million people during the eighteenth century (see Table 10.1). Historians have long debated the causes and consequences of this demographic revolution, studying parish registers of births, marriages, and deaths. Europe's birthrate increased, particularly after about 1740, and the number of deaths each year—the mortality rate—declined even more rapidly. These changes came first and foremost in densely settled regions of soaring agricultural productivity: England, the Netherlands, Flanders, northern Italy, and northern France (see Map 10.1). This suggests that an increase in agricultural production was the most important factor in explaining why the European population began to rise.

Plagues and epidemics, as well as chronic malnourishment, still intervened periodically to check population growth. Many monarchs ascended the throne because elder siblings had died young, as did Frederick II of Prussia, who came to the throne because his two elder brothers did not live past their first birthdays. Poor people were particularly vulnerable to infection, and rates of infant mortality remained high. Epidemics such as influenza, typhus, smallpox, and the plague occasionally ravaged populations. In 1719, 14,000 people in Paris died of smallpox. Malaria epidemics occurred frequently in Spain during the 1780s and 1790s. During the plagues of 1781–1783 in Salonika (Thessalonika) in the Ottoman Empire, more than 300 people died every day. Whooping cough alone killed at least 40,000 children in Sweden during a period of fifteen years in the middle of the century, and more than 100,000 people died of bacillary dysentery in Brittany in one year. In Moscow, half the population died of disease early in the 1770s. Some states tried to close their frontiers and ports to prevent the arrival of disease, or to put those arriving into quarantine, but

TABLE 10.1. EUROPEAN POPULATION, 1700–1800 (MILLIONS)

	1700	1750	1800
Great Britain	9.0	10.5	16.5
France	19.0	21.5	28.0
Habsburg Empire	8.0	18.0	28.0
Prussia	2.0	6.0	9.5
Russia	17.5	20.0	37.0
Spain	6.0	9.0	11.0
Sweden	1.5*	1.7	2.3
United Provinces	1.8	1.9	2.0

*Data for Sweden is from Franklin D. Scott, *Sweden: The Nation's History* (Carbondale, Ill.: University of Southern Illinois Press, 1988), p. 260.
Source: Paul Kennedy, *The Rise and Fall of the Great Powers.* (New York: Vintage, 1989), p. 99.

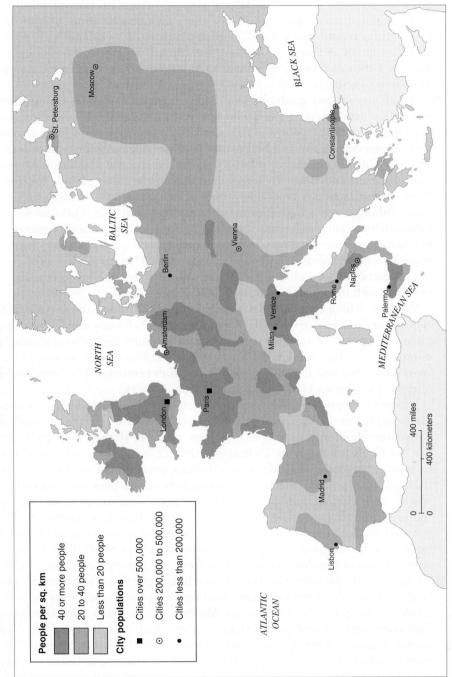

MAP 10.1 POPULATION IN 1780   Distribution of the European population in 1780.

People per sq. km

- 40 or more people
- 20 to 40 people
- Less than 20 people

City populations

- ■ Cities over 500,000
- ⊙ Cities 200,000 to 500,000
- • Cities less than 200,000

ATLANTIC
OCEAN

NORTH
SEA

BALTIC
SEA

BLACK SEA

MEDITERRANEAN SEA

Moscow ⊙

St. Petersburg ⊙

Constantinople ⊙

Vienna ⊙

Berlin •

Amsterdam ⊙

Milan • Venice •

Rome •

Naples ⊙

Palermo •

London ■

Paris ■

Madrid •

Lisbon •

0   400 miles

0   400 kilometers

often to no avail. Famine, following several successive harvest failures, accentuated disease, particularly for those at opposite ends of the life cycle—infants and the elderly. Hardship turned into calamity. In 1769 alone, as much as 5 percent of the population of France may have died of hunger. Cities and towns remained unhealthy places where more people died than were born.

Yet life expectancy gradually rose as diseases and epidemics ravaged the population less often and less murderously. In general, people of means lived longer than the poor. But the average life expectancy for French men and women during the last half of the century still was only twenty-nine, and in Sweden, a country of relative longevity, it stood at about thirty-three years for men and thirty-six for women during the same period. Vaccinations against smallpox gradually proved effective, at least in Western Europe, although mass inoculations were not yet available. Quinine water helped people survive fevers. Scientific and medical societies encouraged towns to supervise waste removal and to take greater care when burying the dead, forbidding inhumations within town walls. The expansion of the cotton industry provided clothing, especially underwear, which could be more easily washed than wool and other materials.

Warfare, which had checked population growth during the seventeenth century, became less devastating. Armies became professionalized, and more under the control of stronger dynastic states. Military discipline and supply improved, sparing civilians the long, bloody conflicts (such as the Thirty Years' War) that had taken a heavy toll in earlier centuries. The New World offered new sites for battles between the great powers.

Economic opportunity, such as the expansion of cottage industry, encouraged couples to marry earlier—in their early twenties in England—and to have more children. Contemporaries were aware of the rise in population. For the English clergyman Thomas Malthus (1766–1834), the rise of the European population was alarming. Malthus predicted in his *Essay on the Principle of Population* (1798) that natural checks on population growth—plague and disease, famine, war, and infant mortality, what he called "nature's auditing with a red pencil"—would become less significant. He believed that population would "increase beyond the nourishment prepared for it," that is, the food supply would grow only arithmetically (2-3-4-5, and so on), whereas population would henceforth multiply exponentially (2-4-8-16-32 . . .). To be sure, the rise in population put more pressure on the land, particularly where most land holdings were small and often too subdivided to be profitably farmed. Yet Malthus did not take into consideration rising agricultural productivity, nor the fact that some people had already begun to limit the size of their families. We have only hints of this, such as when the British writer James Boswell referred delicately to his sexual encounters "in armor." In France, coitus interruptus is credited with bringing about a small decline in the birthrate after 1770. But birth control was unreliable, to say the least.

Manufacturing: Guilds and Domestic Industry

The workshop remained the basis of manufacturing in eighteenth-century Europe. In most countries, merchants and artisans were organized into corporate guilds by the goods they sold or produced. Guilds conferred a type of privilege, because rulers awarded them monopolies over the production or sale of certain products, particularly luxury goods. Masters' guilds and associations of journeymen gave rights and status to craftsmen; they limited and oversaw the training of boys as apprentices, beginning at the age of twelve or thirteen. In France, journeymen perfected their skills while completing a "tour of France," the origin of the modern bicycle race. A journeyman stopped in a number of cities over a period of several years; he was housed in the craft association's "mother house" before returning home with skills acquired from serving many masters, and with hope of one day becoming a master himself.

It was, however, becoming increasingly difficult for a journeyman to become a master, particularly if he did not have a father or other male relative to smooth the way with money. By the 1770s, Spanish and French skilled trades, in particular, had become glutted. Parisian guilds faced competition from outsiders who escaped corporate controls, such as craftsmen who lived on the outskirts of the city and produced cabinets and other goods more cheaply than their Parisian rivals, whose goods were taxed.

Since at least the sixteenth century in England, partially to circumvent the guilds, some merchant-manufacturers had looked to the countryside for workers to produce goods. This shift to domestic industry (also known as proto-industrialization, the cottage industry, or the putting-out system) contributed to what would eventually become a worldwide revolution in manufacturing. The early stages of the Industrial Revolution showed an increase in domestic industry rather than a shift to new forms of production. New technology would only gradually lead to mechanization and the standardization of tasks previously done by hand.

Britain's manufacturing base expanded early in the eighteenth century. Indeed, if in 1500 about a quarter of the people of England worked in non-agricultural occupations, by 1750 the proportion had increased to about half. The quest for profit was considered perfectly respectable, the manufacturer worthy of emulation. Daniel Defoe (1680–1731) described the Yorkshire countryside in 1720 as "one continuous village" in which were "scattered an infinite number of cottages or small dwellings, in which dwell the workmen which are employed, the women and children of whom are always busy carding and spinning." Home workers carded, spun, or wove with equipment (spinning wheels and looms) that they either owned or, in most cases, rented. Hand spinning continued throughout the century to be the largest source of female employment. Master clothiers, or merchant-manufacturers, provided domestic workers with raw materials, such as wool or Indian cotton purchased at a cloth hall, later coming back

Carding and spinning at home.

to collect and pay for the goods that had been completed. They would then transport the goods to the next stage in the production process, for example, to a dyer. Low pay rates in the countryside encouraged the persistence of rural industry. At the end of the eighteenth century, hand-knitted stockings produced by rural Scottish families still cost less than those knitted on a power loom.

As the cottage industry was organized by household, women had a major, even determining, role in the organization of the household economy, including training young children. There were both male and female wool spinners. One man, later a successful inventor of textile machinery, recalled, "my mother taught me to earn my bread by carding and spinning cotton, winding linen or cotton weft for my father and elder brothers at the loom, until I became of sufficient age and strength for my father to put me into a loom." Many families of home spinners, weavers, glove-makers, and shirt-buttoners also worked the land—theirs or someone else's—part time. Rural industry paused at harvest time.

Inventions

Technological change contributed to the Industrial Revolution. Between 1660 and 1760, 210 new inventions were patented in England; during the next twenty-nine years, there were 976. But inventions at first had little to do with increased productivity. They were probably less important than the infusion of investment capital into manufacturing and the expansion of the number of workers in the textile industry, the leading edge of the Industrial Revolution. Some inventions were only gradually diffused, or their importance not recognized until later. No invention, however, was of greater long-term significance than the steam engine, invented by James Watt (1736–1819), a Scot who made musical instruments. Watt added a separate condenser to a primitive steam engine, resulting in a more powerful engine, which he patented in 1769. Yet, like its predecessor, Watt's costly invention was first used only to drain mines, making it possible to dig deeper shafts and to rapidly increase coal production, so essential to the Industrial Revolution. Slowly, the steam engine was put to use in manufacturing.

In 1709, Abraham Darby, a foundry man, came up with a process to smelt iron ore into cast iron by using coke (coal residue) instead of charcoal. This process spread only slowly; in 1775, there were still only thirty-one blast furnaces in Britain. Moreover, charcoal smelting continued to be important, further depleting Britain's forests. In 1784, Henry Cort (1740–1800), an ironmaster, invented the "puddling and rolling" process in iron casting. Molten metal in a furnace was raked to remove carbon and other impurities, producing wrought iron, which was far stronger than cast iron. Iron bridges replaced their flimsy predecessors. Iron made new buildings sturdier and basically fire-resistant. Cast-iron railings and gates began to appear on landed estates and in elegant townhouses. Low-cost iron made possible sturdier plows and other farm implements that, in turn, significantly increased the demand for iron.

Improvements in the spinning wheel and basic looms had already accelerated textile production in the late seventeenth and early eighteenth centuries. The stocking frame produced lighter and more fashionable cotton and silk stockings that replaced the heavier woolen hose of the upper classes. John Kay (1704–1764) invented the "flying shuttle" (patented in 1733 but

(*Left*) James Watt. (*Right*) The steam engine.

not diffused for more than twenty years), which ultimately made it possible to weave at a much greater speed, doubling productivity. But Kay's invention, too, has to be seen in the context of traditional manufacturing: its principal effect was to increase the productivity of hand-loom weavers.

Gradually machines powered by water and then by steam eliminated bottlenecks in textile production. In about 1764, James Hargreaves (c. 1720–1778), a carpenter and weaver, invented an apparatus known as the spinning jenny, which wrapped fibers around a spindle (a long, slender pin). Drawing on medieval technology, Hargreaves multiplied the number of thread spindles a worker could operate from one to eight, and then soon to eighty spindles. In 1769, Richard Arkwright (1732–1792), a former barber turned entrepreneur, borrowed some money from a publican and patented a mechanized "water frame," which, combining spindles and rollers, became the first spinning mill. The water frame turned out a strong, coarse yarn of quality that transformed the cotton industry and increased production of wool worsteds (combed wool). With the exception of its water-powered rollers, Arkwright built his power spinning machine out of the same components as the ordinary spinning wheel that had been found in Europe since medieval times. He had his portrait painted with his hand touching his famous spinning machine, as the same painter might have formerly depicted a country gentleman standing with his hand resting on a fence, his hunting dogs sitting at his feet.

Cottage industry, artisanal workshops, and factory production often coexisted within the same industry. With the gradual mechanization of spinning, weaving could only keep pace with the rapid expansion of the number of hand-loom weavers. Even a rudimentary power loom, invented in 1784, was too expensive to compete with domestic industry, which continued to be based on the availability of an inexpensive workforce. Hand-loom weavers survived well into the middle decades of the nineteenth century.

Richard Arkwright with his famous water frame at his fingertips.

The inventions that slowly revolutionized the textile industry did not inevitably lead to factory production. Like framework knitting, the first spinning jennys and mules were small enough to be adaptable to workshops and even some houses, where skilled workers and their apprentices used stronger, more reliable hand-operated machinery or tools.

The factory, however, slowly became the symbol of the new industrial age in England. One of Arkwright's textile mills in the early 1770s had 200 workers, and ten years later it had four times that number. An ironworks employed more than 1,000 workers by 1770, a concentration previously seen only in great shipyards. In 1774, Watt and Matthew Boulton (1728–1809), a toymaker, went into business in Birmingham producing engines and machine parts in the largest factory in the world. It was not a single structure but rather a number of adjacent workshops, which drew on the work of about 20,000 men, women, and children in the countryside around Birmingham.

The development of the factory at first had relatively little to do with technological imperatives. Manufacturers preferred bringing workers under one roof so that they could more easily supervise them, imposing the discipline of factory work on people used to having their schedule defined by the rising and setting of the sun and the passing of the seasons. When a defective piece of pottery emerged from the kilns, the pottery manufacturer Josiah Wedgwood (1730–1795) would storm over and stomp on it with his wooden leg, chiding his workers. "Thou shalt not be idle" was Wedgwood's eleventh commandment; "Everything gives way to experiment" his favorite maxim. His goal was to train his workers so thoroughly as "to make such machines of the men as cannot err." Putting workers in factories facilitated such a goal. By the middle of the eighteenth century, factory manufacturing had begun to alter the northern English landscape. "From the Establishment of Manufacturers, we see Hamlets swell into Villages, and Villages into Towns," exclaimed a gentleman in the 1770s.

Expanding British Economy

The production of manufactured goods doubled during the last half of the eighteenth century in Britain. Cotton made up 40 percent of British exports by the end of the century. India's domination of the world market for textiles ended. The production of iron followed in importance, along with wool and worsteds, linen, silk, copper, paper, cutlery, and the booming building trades.

Despite its relatively small size, Britain's significant economic advantages over the nations of the continent help explain why the manufacturing revolution first began there. Unlike the German or Italian states, Britain was unified politically. People living in England spoke basically the same language. France and the Italian and German states still had internal tariffs that made trade more costly, whereas in Britain there were no internal tariffs once the union between England and Scotland had been achieved in 1707. Weights and measures in Britain had largely been standardized.

Great Britain was by far the wealthiest nation in the world. Its colonies provided raw materials for manufacturing and markets for goods produced by the mother country. English merchants supplied slaves snatched from the west coast of Africa for the plantations of the West Indies in exchange for cotton. The amount of raw cotton imported from India increased by twenty times between 1750 and 1800. Beginning in the 1790s the United States provided Lancashire manufacturers with cotton picked by southern slaves.

England's stable banking and credit arrangements facilitated the reinvestment of agricultural and commercial profits in manufacturing. London's banks, particularly the giant Bank of England, were profitable and respected. Merchants and manufacturers accepted paper money and bills of exchange with confidence. Gentry invested in overseas trade expeditions and in manufacturing without the reticence of continental landowners. London's financial market could provide information twice a week on what investments were worth in Amsterdam and Paris. Joint-stock companies, which had begun in the late seventeenth century, offered limited personal liability, which meant that in the case of a company's financial disaster, individual investors would be liable only to the extent of their investments.

Expanded demand for manufactured goods led to a dramatic improvement in Britain's roads. A new process of road surfacing—macadamization—improved travel on the main routes. Turnpikes were extended and improved; investors formed "turnpike trusts," repairing the highways and turning a profit by charging a toll. In 1700, it took fifty hours to travel from Norwich to London by coach; by 1800, the journey could be achieved in nineteen hours. The daunting trek to the Scottish city of Edinburgh from London had been reduced to a mere sixty hours of travel.

England's water transportation was also unmatched in Europe, a gift of nature. Rich coal and iron ore deposits lay near water transportation. By 1800, Britain was extracting about 90 percent of the world's coal. No part of England stands more than seventy miles from the sea. Navigable rivers facilitated the transportation of raw materials and manufactured goods; so did canals built in the middle decades of the century, including a ninety-mile-long canal linking Manchester to the Mersey River and the Irish Sea.

The British government offered businessmen more assistance than any continental rivals could anticipate from their own governments. The Royal Navy protected the merchant fleet, which tripled in size during the first three-quarters of the century. Navigation Acts forced foreign merchants to ship export goods to Britain in British ships. Bowing to pressure from woolens producers, the British government in 1700 had imposed protective tariffs on imported silk and calico, undercutting imports from India. Agreements with the Dutch Republic and France in the late 1780s reduced trade tariffs with those states, which helped British exports. Political influence kept taxes low on business. Other British strategies were even more imaginative: a law dating from the late seventeenth century required that all corpses be dressed in woolens for burial, a clever way of helping woolens manufacturers.

Yet the British government rarely interfered in operations of the economy in ways that businessmen might have considered intrusive. Adam Smith (1723–1790) emerged as the first economic theorist of capitalism (see Chapter 9). Smith rejected the prevailing theory of mercantilism and extolled economic liberalism. He also observed that the greater division of labor was increasing productivity. Taking a famous example, he argued that a single worker could probably not make a single common pin in one day, but that ten workers, each repeating the same task, such as straightening the wire, or grinding its point, could make hundreds of pins in a workday. Smith's logic anticipated the age of factory manufacturing.

Expanding Continental Economies

On the continent, too, particularly in the West, manufacturing expanded rapidly in cities, towns, and the countryside. Continental European manufacturing was characterized by small-scale production and cottage industry (taking advantage of an almost endless supply of laborers). France did not lag far behind Britain in the production of manufactured goods, and it remained the principal supplier of Spain and its empire. Despite bewildering differences in, for example, weights and measures, currencies (even within large states), and calendars (Russia's was eleven days behind that of the West), European commerce developed rapidly during the eighteenth century.

Global trade also contributed to the economies of the Italian and German states, and to those of Spain, Portugal, and France (see Map 10.2). Increased trade with the wider world brought new products—Chinese silk and porcelain, Indian cotton, West Indian sugar and rum, East Indian tea, South Seas spices, and much more. In the chancy sweepstakes of the globalization of colonial trade, traders and their investors could make considerable fortunes, but they could also easily be ruined when a sudden storm or pirate attack destroyed a ship and its cargo.

Bankers, investors, shipbuilders, wholesale and retail merchants, insurance underwriters, transporters, and notaries profited from the marked increase in international trade. Some of the prosperity trickled down to more ordinary folk as well, providing work, for example in prosperous port towns, for carpenters, dockers, haulers, and artisans, who supplied luxuries for wealthy merchants.

Considerable obstacles remained, however, to further economic development on the continent. Traditional suspicion of paper money, the problems of obtaining credit and raising investment capital, and periodic government debasing of currencies created hurdles for those undertaking long-distance commerce. London and Amsterdam were alone in having respected banks, credit facilities, relatively low interest rates, and insurance companies.

MAP 10.2 TRADE FROM COLONIES TO EUROPE, c. 1775   Exports from the colonies to Europe, including the value of the trade.

Even in Western Europe, Britain's South Sea Bubble (see Chapter 11) and the collapse in 1720 of John Law's bank in France scared off investors. Capital remained for the most part in the hands of wealthy families and small groups of associates who loaned money to states, pushing up the cost of credit. The absence of investment capital led the Prussian and Austrian monarchies to supply capital for some manufacturing enterprises. Guilds held monopolies on the trade and production of certain products; international tariffs and tolls complicated trade between the many small states in Central Europe. Furthermore, as we have seen, relatively few nobles took an active interest in manufacturing, although exceptions were to be found in France, the Austrian Netherlands, and Russia, where some nobles developed coal mines and invested in the iron industry. Despite the development of the copper and iron industry of the Ural Mountains, in the Russian Empire the possibilities for increased manufacturing were limited by the monumental distances between population centers and natural resources, as well as an inadequate transportation network that had barely changed since the time of Ivan the Terrible in the sixteenth century.

SOCIAL CHANGES

Urban growth, particularly after 1750, was one of the most visible changes engendered by the rise in population and the expansion of trade and manufacturing, as well as the continuing centralization of state power. Other changes included the rise of the "middling sort" and the greater vulnerability of the laborer who was displaced by enclosure and forced to move from place to place in search of work.

The Growth of Towns and Cities

Although Europe remained overwhelmingly rural, cities and towns grew faster than the population as a whole, meaning that Europe, particularly the West, slowly urbanized. Cities grew as people moved to areas where there was work, or for the poorest of the poor, where they might find charity. New manufacturing centers served as magnets to which those who had no land or prospects were drawn. By the end of the century, Europe had twenty-two cities with more than 100,000 people (see Table 10.2).

The British urban population (any settlement of more than 2,500 people qualified as "urban") grew from slightly less than 20 percent of the population in 1700 to more than 30 percent in 1800, when London's population reached nearly a million people, nearly twice that of Paris. London was the world's largest port, the center of banking, finance, insurance, manufacturing, exports, and empire. In the eighteenth century, a fifth of the British population spent part of their lives in London. Two-thirds of the residents of London had been born outside of the city, migrants who had come to the

TABLE 10.2. EUROPE'S LARGEST CITIES AT THE END OF THE EIGHTEENTH CENTURY

City	Population	City	Population
London	950,000	St. Petersburg	270,000
Paris	550,000	Vienna	230,000
Naples	430,000	Amsterdam	220,000
Constantinople	300,000	Lisbon	180,000
Moscow	300,000	Berlin	170,000

capital in search of opportunity. Indians and blacks had also begun to appear in the imperial capital.

Some contemporaries believed that wickedness and crime increased almost inevitably with larger cities and towns. In the case of London, the book *Hell Upon Earth, or the Town in an Uproar* (1729) was subtitled "The Late Horrible Scenes of Forgery, Perjury, Street-Robbery, Murder, Sodomy, and Other Shocking Impieties." It denounced "this great, wicked, unwieldy, over-grown Town, one continued hurry of Vice and Pleasure, where nothing dwells but *Absurdities, Abuses, Accidents, Accusations.*"

London's emerging social geography reflected the paradox that Britain was both an aristocratic and commercial society. Bloomsbury Square and Bedford Square, elite districts in West London, near Westminster, the seat of Parliament, were largely aristocratic creations, as nobles developed some of their land. At the same time, commercial London also expanded rapidly along with the British Empire. Near the burgeoning docks of the East End on the River Thames, dilapidated buildings housed the poor.

As England's economic dynamism began to shift northward with increased manufacturing, Liverpool, a teeming port on the Irish Sea, "the emporium of the western world," and Manchester, a northern industrial town, developed rapidly. By 1800, Manchester had become the "metropolis of manufactures," with 75,000 inhabitants and growing industrial suburbs.

Continental cities, too, added population. In France, the growth of Paris, above all, but also Lyon, Lille, Bordeaux, and other cities was deceptive, as only about 10 percent of the population lived in towns of more than 5,000 people in 1789, compared to 25 percent in England. In the German states, there had been but twenty-four towns with more than 10,000 people in 1500; by 1800, there were sixty of them. In Berlin, royal officials, lawyers, and soldiers accounted for about 40 percent of the Prussian capital's 140,000 inhabitants in 1783. In southern Italy, Naples was barely able to support its impoverished population of more than 400,000 people. No other town in southern Italy had 10,000 inhabitants. In Rome, the clergy constituted about half the population of 160,000 people. East Central and Eastern Europe and the Balkans had relatively few cities. In the middle of the eighteenth century, only three cities within the vast Russian Empire had more than 30,000 inhabitants: Moscow, Saint Petersburg, and Kiev. Yet the Polish capital, Warsaw, which had only 7,000 inhabitants in the mid-sixteenth century, had grown to 150,000 a century later.

As cities developed, those with money and leisure time found more to do. The largest English towns sported theaters and concert halls, gentlemen's clubs, scientific societies, and racetracks. Towns took pride in their development, publishing guides for visitors and directories listing the names of shops. Elegant buildings of brick and stone replaced tottering woodbeamed medieval structures. Streets were widened, paved, and cleaned, at least in wealthy neighborhoods. Dublin, Boston, and Calcutta offered smaller versions of English urban society, sporting private clubs and municipal pride, at least for British residents.

Wealthy merchants and bankers lived in elegant townhouses near the docks in Hamburg, Nantes, and Genoa, bustling port cities of international trade. Expanded trade and urban growth engendered consumerism. Paris became the European capital of luxury goods, as French nobles continually raised the standards of conspicuous consumption. Polish lords traded grain for luxury goods from Western Europe. In Sweden, such luxury reached court, aristocrats, and wealthy bourgeois, but a diplomat in 1778 estimated the market for such goods in Sweden to be only 70,000 people of a population of 2.5 million. Thomas Jefferson, who espoused simplicity in life, nonetheless paid for a stream of luxury goods from London and Paris to be shipped to Virginia.

Noble and wealthy bourgeois alike insisted on personal prerogatives of taste, for example, in decoration and food. It became a compliment to say

Elegant shops on Capel Street in Dublin.

that someone or something reflected "urbanity." Three-cornered hats, along with wigs, which wealthy commoners as well as nobles increasingly favored, and stockings emerged as symbols of respectability. Cafés took their name from the coffee served there, a drink only people of means could afford. Upper-class men and women became concerned as never before with modesty; "water closets" became more common. A code of conduct served—with income and private space itself—as a barrier between wealthy and ordinary people.

The eighteenth-century consumer revolution extended to the poor, as well. By the mid-seventeenth century, resourceful households in northwestern Europe were finding ways to purchase consumer goods that would make their lives somewhat more comfortable. Families drew upon the labor of women and children, as well as longer working hours by husbands. Now the number of ordinary families able to acquire household utensils and even books and cheap prints increased dramatically. Different kinds of apparel were available even to the very poor. Many mill hands now had a change of clothes. Some servant girls wore silk kerchiefs, and an occasional laborer sported a watch, for which he paid the wages of several weeks. Even some infants deposited at foundling homes had been dressed in printed cottons. For very ordinary people with a little money or some credit, taverns and bars provided cheap liquor and sociability. For people with neither, there was the street.

Social Movement within the Elite

With the growth of manufacturing, trade, and cities came concomitant social changes, including mobility of the "middling sort." Bankers and wealthy merchants aspired to social distinction and an aristocratic lifestyle. In Paris, wealthy merchants purchased elegant townhouses and mingled with nobles. In Barcelona, members of the trading oligarchy earned the right to carry swords like nobles. The bourgeoisie of the Austrian Netherlands demanded the same privileges Habsburg rulers had granted to Belgian nobles. Noble titles could be purchased in most European states, providing a relatively easily obtained means of social ascension, without eliminating the distinctions between nobles and commoners. As the rising cost of warfare (larger armies to equip, train, and send into battle, and expensive fortifications to maintain) and reduced tax revenue during hard economic times weighed heavily on royal coffers, the sale of titles and offices swept more commoners into the nobility in France, Austria, and Castile. The number of French nobles doubled between 1715 and 1789, and relatively few noble families could trace their origins back more than a couple of generations.

In Britain, on the other hand, it was rare for commoners to move into the nobility. The sale of offices had never been as widespread in England as on the continent, at least not since the English Civil War in the mid-

Notice the marked contrast between the poor worker and the elegant member of the gentry in this English etching from the eighteenth century.

seventeenth century, and the purchase of noble titles was nonexistent. Yet the crown occasionally elevated spectacularly successful, wealthy commoners into the peerage with hereditary noble titles (baron, viscount, earl, marquis, and duke), which carried with them a seat in the House of Lords. The monarchy rewarded other landed gentlemen with various titles, including knight (a nonhereditary title) and baronet (a hereditary title, granted less frequently), both of which carried the title of "Sir." Very few people, however, ever rose from trade into a peerage, or even to the upper gentry.

Entry into the British elite, however, was generally more open than into its continental counterparts. Gradual shifts in social structure in English society, beginning in the seventeenth century, contributed to the nation's social stability. No legal or cultural barriers in Britain prevented bankers, manufacturers, merchants, and urban professionals from ascending through wealth to social and political predominance as "country gentlemen" through the purchase of landed estates that made them gentry.

Daniel Defoe, who wrote *Robinson Crusoe* and other novels for an expanding middle-class readership, claimed that "men are every day starting up from obscurity to wealth." Trade and manufacturing in England were honored occupations. Unlike on the continent, where second and third sons often were automatically relegated by their fathers into Church or military posts, many of these sons marched proudly into business. A Manchester cobbler wrote in 1756:

> See, as the Owners of old Family Estates in your Neighborhood are selling off their patrimonies, how your townsmen are constantly purchasing; and thereby laying the Foundation of a new Race of Gentry! Not adorn'd, its true, with Coats of Arms and a long Parchment

Pedigree of useless Members of Society, but deck'd with Virtue and
Frugality.

In France, Denmark, and Sweden, tensions remained between old noble
families and those more recently ennobled, whom the former viewed as
boorish newcomers. The number of ennobled commoners in the eighteenth
century may not have been significantly greater than that in the previous
century, but those who were ennobled were wealthier. However, the older
noble families still controlled the most important and lucrative offices in
the royal bureaucracy, the Church, and the army.

The French army began to phase out the purchase of commissions in the
late 1770s, and early in the next decade nobles demanded and received royal
assurance that the crown would respect their monopoly on the most prestigious military titles. Directed against newcomer nobles, the Ségur Law of
1782 asserted that no one could be appointed to a high post in the army who
could not demonstrate at least four generations of nobility on his father's
side. However, barriers between the bourgeois and nobles in many states
were starting to break down. In some places, a small number of nobles
entered commerce or manufacturing. The expansion of trade and manufacturing led more continental
nobles to seek new sources of
wealth. French and Russian
nobles were principal owners
of mines. Swedish nobles contributed to the modest expansion of manufacturing in their
country. In eighteenth-
century Spain, little stigma
was attached to noble commercial ventures, perhaps
because there were so many
nobles. In contrast, in Prussia, Poland, and Hungary
most nobles still considered
participation in commercial
activity (above all, retail commerce) or manufacturing to
bring derogation, implying a
loss of status and honor.

This painting depicts a socially mobile French
merchant and banker receiving envoys from
Joseph II, the Holy Roman Emperor, requesting a loan.

The Changing Condition
of the Poor

For millions of people, only a
thin line stood between hav-

ing enough to eat and hunger or starvation, between occasional employment and begging, and between relatively good health and sudden illness
and death. If both partners were young, healthy, and could occasionally
find work, marriage increased the odds of survival in "an economy of
makeshifts." But economic crisis often pulled a couple apart, as one partner might be forced to leave to look for work elsewhere.

At the end of the eighteenth century, almost 30 percent of the British
population depended on some sort of poor relief; more than a million people were classified as "paupers" in England and Wales. Laborers, some of
whom had been chased from village common lands by parliamentary acts of
enclosure, wandered in search of work. Yet residents of a given village or
neighborhood were far more likely to benefit from local charity than outsiders, often feared as thieves or worse. Beggars in Austrian law were
referred to as "push people," because authorities sought to push them away.

Meager harvests and bitter winters periodically took terrible tolls on the
poor, with indigents found frozen to death in church doorways, barns, or
fields. When food shortages occurred or the police expelled beggars from
large cities, country roads swarmed with young children who had been
abandoned, told by their parents to make their way as best they could. The
elderly, particularly widows, were often the poorest of the poor, unable to
move elsewhere, depending on neighbors little better off than themselves.

The poor were perpetually undernourished. Bread remained the basis of
the diet of the vast majority of Europeans—white bread for people of means;
black bread, porridge or gruel made from rye, potatoes, or buckwheat for
everybody else. Vegetables—peas and beans, and cabbage in Central and
Eastern Europe—were prized as occasional additions to soup or porridge.
Poor people rarely consumed meat, except for heavily salted meat that
could be preserved. The orphanage of Amsterdam, a prosperous city,
served meat and fish twice a week and vegetables once a week. But dried
peas, beans, porridge, or gruel comprised most meals there. Fish and shell-
fish were common only at the sea's edge for ordinary people (especially
because they were not allowed to fish in most rivers and ponds). Water,
often not very clean, was the drink of necessity; wine and beer were
beyond the budget of most people. Swiss peasants prosperous enough to
drink coffee and eat chocolate were the exception in Europe. Yet overall,
ordinary people experienced a modest improvement in diet and health during the eighteenth century.

Charity, however impressive, fell far short of relieving the crushing poverty,
particularly in France, where it provided only about 5 percent of what was
needed. During the Catholic Reformation, the Church had emphasized
the importance of charitable works in the quest for eternal salvation. Most
Protestants, too, believed in the importance of good works—after all,
Christ had washed a beggar's feet. Parishes and, in Catholic countries,
monasteries and convents regularly provided what relief they could afford
to the poor, particularly around Christmas and during Lent. Hospices and

other charitable institutions cared for the sick, invalids, and the elderly as best they could. But during hard times the number of abandoned infants increased dramatically, far beyond the capacity of institutions to care for them.

Social Control

By the middle of the eighteenth century, many upper-class Europeans believed that they had entered an age of clamoring crowds and even riots. In the 1770s and 1780s, particularly, the lower orders seemed increasingly less deferential. The poor protested the purchase and removal of grain from their markets at prices they could not afford. They stopped wagons, seized grain, and sold it at what they considered to be the "just price," a sum that would permit even the poor to buy enough to survive.

Work stoppages by craftsmen became more widespread. Following a London strike by journeymen tailors protesting cuts in their pay, the British Parliament passed the first Combination Act in 1721. The law established wages and working conditions for tailors and allowed the jailing of striking workers without benefit of a trial. Seeing that many craftsmen and skilled workers were leaving Britain, some for the colonies, Parliament then passed legislation forbidding their emigration.

Protecting Property in Britain

The British Parliament represented the interests of wealthy landowners, who consolidated their property during the eighteenth century and alone could elect members of the House of Commons. Thus, in 1723, Parliament passed without discussion a law that added fifty capital offenses against property.

Hunting was a badge of living nobly. It was a domesticated, usually non-lethal—at least for the hunters—version of warfare. The exclusive right to hunt was a vigilantly guarded prerogative of any and all who could claim noble status. But acts against poaching were invoked more often to protect property rights. Wealthy English landowners set brutal mantraps—including trap-guns—and snares that maimed poachers who snuck onto their property, including in the "deer parks" established on land that had once been common land. The felonies listed under the Black Act, among them the blackening of one's face as a form of disguise—hence the law's name—included poaching game or fish, chopping down trees, or gleaning branches blown down in storms. Henry Fielding (1707–1754) called attention to such a felony in his novel *The Adventures of Joseph Andrews*: "Jesu!" said the Squire, "would you commit two persons to Bridewell [prison] for a twig?" "Yes," said the Lawyer, "and with great leniency too; for if we had called it a young tree they would have been both hanged."

The concern for protecting property could be seen in the Marriage Act (1753), which forbade clandestine marriages. It specifically sought to protect property against ambitious men who might be tempted to try to elope with the daughters of wealthy property owners. Parliament also passed a law permitting divorce by parliamentary act—which none but the very wealthy and well-placed could seek—at least partially because gentlemen wanted to be free to divorce wives who shamed them with adultery or who could not produce heirs to inherit their estates.

A gamekeeper snags a poacher.

Subordination and Social Control

People of means debated strategies of social control with increasing urgency as economic crises widened the gap between rich and poor. During 1724–1733, the French state undertook a "great confinement" of paupers, beggars, and vagrants in workhouses, where they were to learn menial trades under conditions of strict discipline. The subsequent reorganization and expansion of royal efforts at policing the poor represented an increase in the reach of the state. Yet temporary programs of poor relief were common on the continent, as were periodic repressive campaigns against beggars and vagrants. Since the beginning of the seventeenth century, English parishes or townships provided charity to those wearing the requisite "P" for pauper. In order to keep indigents off the road, towns established workhouses, where the poor would be forced to work in exchange for subsistence. A 1782 English law replaced workhouses with somewhat more humane "poorhouses." In 1795, the Speenhamland system, so called after the parish in which it was conceived, provided for a sliding scale of assistance, determined by the current price of bread and wage rates. But such programs merely scratched the surface as the problem of poverty entered public discourse to an unprecedented degree.

Britain did not undertake the kind of largely successful campaign found in some places on the continent to limit the number of capital crimes to those that threatened life or the state. Parliament added almost two hundred capital offenses to the law between 1688 and 1810, sixty-three of

A public hanging at Tyburn in London.

them between 1760 and 1810. About mid-century, two young men were arrested for poaching. Their wives went to the landlord's estate to beg his merciful intercession. The lord, moved to tears, said that their husbands would be returned to them. True to his word, he sent the two corpses to the wives. But English juries, in particular, hesitated to convict those accused; only about two hundred criminals were executed each year. Executions drew huge throngs at London's Tyburn. Corporal punishment, such as branding or being exhibited in stocks to public contempt, was far more common. Children were worked and punished as adults, though not all as harshly as the seven-year-old girl who was hanged in Norwich for stealing a petticoat. England was relatively under-policed, particularly when compared to France (Paris had four times more policemen than London, which was twice its size).

Authorities everywhere tended to lump the poor into one of two broad categories—"deserving" and "undeserving," that is, whether they were considered worthy of pity and charity. Among the latter were "false beggars" who simulated horrifying wounds or injuries with the skill of a makeup artist and, clutching at the clothes of the wealthy passing by, received a few cents as his benefactors scurried away as rapidly as possible. These categories reflected the belief that many, if not most, of the poor were destitute because they were lazy and that stiff punishment would be enough to end begging.

In small bourgs, villages, and the countryside, people feared bands of thieves, whose threat of arson could intimidate, as a fire would destroy a harvest or a farm in a matter of minutes. Brigandage was rampant in southern Italy and in Sicily. In the grain-rich Beauce region south of Paris, some bandits were known as *chauffeurs* because they held their victims' feet to the fire to force them to reveal the hiding place of their valuables. Yet many poor people considered some bandits as heroic Robin Hoods, who stole from the rich to give to the poor.

A CENTURY OF CONTRASTS

The eighteenth century was a period of contrasts. Musical performances at court and in châteaux and elegant townhouses took place while peasants and rural day laborers struggled to survive, toiling in fields they rarely owned or working as dock or market porters, chimney sweeps, or common laborers in town. The well-heeled financier, wholesale merchant, manufacturer, or lawyer in Paris, Amsterdam, Barcelona, or Vienna lived in a vastly more cosmopolitan world, increasingly shaped by consumerism, than did their counterparts in the relatively few cities and towns in Prussia, Russia, and the Balkans. In many ways a century still dominated politically by nobles, the eighteenth century also was a dynamic period of economic and social transformation, beginning with the Industrial Revolution in England. Commerce and manufacturing increased on the continent, as well. Developing trade across oceans changed patterns of consumption in Europe. Trade remained the basis of the British Empire, which stretched across the world. Rivals Spain and France, too, were colonial powers.

Economic and social changes brought remarkable political consequences during the 1760s and 1770s. English country gentlemen who invariably supported court policies and those who sometimes opposed them began to look and act like political parties. And the domination of political life by an oligarchy of landowners came under challenge from ordinary people without the right to vote. In the North American colonies, the king's subjects protested the fact that they were taxed without representation, and they rebelled against British rule.

On the continent, denunciations of unwarranted privilege began to be heard, including calls for reform of the French absolute monarchy. Public opinion gradually began to see parlements as blocks against absolute rule and defenders of the rights of the "nation," a term that increasingly came into use. Elsewhere on the continent, too, opposition to entrenched privilege became more insistent.

CHAPTER 11

EIGHTEENTH-CENTURY DYNASTIC RIVALRIES AND POLITICS

King George III (ruled 1760–1820) proclaimed that he "gloried in the name of Britain." Indeed during his reign, despite his personal failings, a nationalist cult developed around the British monarchy, significantly after the empire suffered its biggest loss, that of the thirteen American colonies.

The king projected the image of an ordinary family man, surrounded by his homely wife and fifteen children. Less interested in goings-on in Hanover, his family's dynastic home, than his predecessors, he won popular affection in Britain. "This young man," assessed the writer Horace Walpole, "don't stand in one spot with his eyes fixed royally on the ground, and dropping bits of German news; he walks about and speaks to everybody." The king's domesticity also made him a target for the gentle spoofs of caricaturists. His nervousness led him to bombard almost everyone he encountered with questions, ending with "hey, hey?" By the last decade of the century, symptoms of a hereditary disease made George III appear to be quite mad.

Early in his reign, King George III held strongly to royal prerogatives, even within the context of the British constitutional monarchy. Yet not only did British nationalism develop rapidly with him on the throne, but the idea developed in and beyond Parliament that a party of opposition formed an essential part of the parliamentary system of representation.

The nature of the European state system itself also underwent fundamental change in the eighteenth century as the rivalries between Great Britain, France, Spain, and the Dutch Republic (the United Provinces) broadened to a global scale. Whereas Europe in the period of Louis XIV had been marked by frenetic war-making—much of it at his instigation—and the pursuit of alliances against France, Europe's dominant state, the wars fought between the great powers in the middle of the eighteenth century reflected a more even distribution of power. This balance of power was increasingly affected not only by events overseas but also by those in Eastern Europe. There, Russia expanded its empire at the expense of the Ottoman Empire, and Russia, Prussia, and Austria dismembered Poland in a series of Partitions, the last in 1795.

The increasingly global nature of conflicts between empires put strains on the structures of states in Europe. They were forced to reorganize themselves to become more efficient. In Britain, as the role of the House of Commons expanded and political parties emerged, newspapers and organizations in which politics was discussed created public opinion, transforming the public sphere as more people demanded political reform. A precocious sense of British national identity and patriotism developed.

Reform movements and even uprisings in Europe alarmed rulers and intrigued intellectuals, who in increasing numbers denounced unwarranted privilege and despotism. American colonists rose up against British rule. Public opinion on the continent demanded reform; in France, the parlements began to defend the "nation" against monarchical despotism. As contemporaries sought explanations for movements that sought to limit monarchical authority, the Bavarian envoy in Vienna went so far as to claim in 1775 that "the spirit of revolt has become universal."

THE EIGHTEENTH-CENTURY STATE SYSTEM

In eighteenth-century Europe, the powers danced together in temporary partnership until the music changed and old partners were deserted and new ones embraced. The eighteenth-century state system was a pattern of rivalry and alliance in which powerful states vied for dynastic and global power. Few borders or thrones were secure from challenge by other rulers coveting more territory. Rulers sought to expand their power through marriage, inheritance, alliances, or warfare. Other states sought to maintain the balance of power, so that one state did not grow more powerful at the expense of the others. Spain, France, the Dutch Republic, Sweden, Poland-Lithuania, the Holy Roman Empire, and the Ottoman Empire found themselves with less power than in the seventeenth century, while Britain, Russia, and Prussia continued to extend their reach.

The emergence of a global economy increasingly linked to colonial trade engendered rivalries as Britain, France, Spain, and the Dutch Republic battled for commercial and colonial advantage, preparing the way for European expansion in the nineteenth century. The wars between the great powers spilled into the Americas and India. The powers were motivated by the hope of economic gain and reflected the primacy of the economic theory of mercantilism, which assumed that there was a finite amount of wealth available in the world, and that the might of any state depended on its success in bringing in more gold than it paid out.

In the meantime, dynastic rivalries remained a major source of conflict. George I from the German state of Hanover succeeded to the throne of England in 1714, but his German origins and interests complicated British foreign policy and led to unsuccessful attempts by the Catholic Stuart pretenders to take back the British throne. On the continent, Frederick the Great of Prussia and Maria Theresa of Austria locked horns in a battle of expansion for the former and survival for the latter. The other great powers lined up in alliances on the side of each.

Global Rivalries

As voyages of discovery opened up new horizons to Europeans, the stakes of colonial rivalry between the great powers rose. During the seventeenth century, England, the Dutch Republic, France, Spain, and Portugal had gradually expanded their trading routes across the seas. Coffee, tea, molasses, ginger, indigo, Indian calicoes, tobacco, and other colonial products—for the most part luxury goods—fetched high prices at home. The discovery of gold in Brazil in 1694 and 1719 further whetted the appetites of commercial companies. By the end of the seventeenth century, Dutch and French traders began to sail to China in greater numbers. There the K'ang-hsi emperor and the Ch'ing dynasty had expanded toward the south even while affirming Chinese cultural unity, even within the context of a vast and varied land. The Chinese rulers manifested little interest in the traders from the West. (When a diplomat representing King George III of Britain arrived in China to try to convince the emperor to begin diplomatic relations with his country and brought presents from England, the emperor's message to him said "I set no value on objects strange and ingenious.") Ambitious European merchant-traders still brought back spices and fine silks from Asia, but sea routes had largely supplanted the old land trade routes that had stretched through the Middle East and Central Asia. Chinese prints, porcelain, silk, and rugs became popular in Western Europe.

In the eighteenth century, the British East India Company established new posts in South India and Bengal. Parliament licensed the company to operate as a military force. Ships of the British East India Company carried Chinese porcelain, silks, spices, and tea to England in exchange for silver and, increasingly, opium grown in India. British traders exchanged slaves taken from West Africa and textiles and other manufactured goods for colonial products. If at the middle of the eighteenth century there were about 3 to 4 million Europeans living in British, French, Spanish, and Portuguese colonies in America, several times that number of slaves had been carried there by European ships from Africa.

Spain still had the largest empire. It included the largest Caribbean islands, the Philippines in the Pacific, and most of South America except for

The trading post established by the British East India Company in Surat, India, late eighteenth century.

Brazil, which belonged to Portugal. The Dutch had bases on the northern coast of South America, West Africa, South Africa (their colony at the Cape of Good Hope was the only permanent European settlement at the time in South Africa), the island of Mauritius in the Indian Ocean, the Indian subcontinent, and Southeast Asia, where they conquered three Islamic states in the late seventeenth century. The Dutch were also in Japan, which in the late sixteenth and early seventeenth century had expanded trade in East Asia and Southeast Asia. The Dutch presence in Japan during the 1630s and 1640s had been limited to the port of Nagasaki, as Japan rejected more than superficial contacts with foreigners. As in the case of China, the Japanese exhibited little knowledge of or interest in other cultures.

French forts and settlements dotted the North American colony of Nouvelle (New) France. French trappers established posts on the Mississippi River, with the port of New Orleans at its mouth far to the south. The territories claimed by the French, on which they had only scattered military and trading posts, almost tripled in size by the middle of the eighteenth century, but by the 1760s the French population of Nouvelle France stood at only about 80,000 people.

Global rivalries led to conflicts between the great powers. French and British armies and navies battled in North America, the West Indies, and India, believing that the loss of Canadian furs, Caribbean spices, or Indian jewels might be a damaging blow to prosperity and prestige. Spanish colonial rivalry with Britain led to the only war ever fought over an ear. Both Spain and Britain insisted that their colonies ship goods only on vessels flying their flag. Since 1713 the Spanish had granted the right to Britain to supply its colonies with 4,800 slaves each year; in exchange for this sale, a single English ship each year could trade at one Spanish colonial port. Illegal trade, however, continued as before. The Spanish navy sank several British ships, and in 1731 one of its vessels accosted an English frigate suspected of smuggling. A Spanish sword cut off one of the ears of the captain, Jenkins. The incident led to the "War of Jenkins's Ear" in 1739 after a member of Parliament whipped up anti-Spanish sentiment by waving the severed ear in the air during a speech. The war, highlighted by the successful Spanish defense of the port of Cartagena in what now is Columbia, went on with neither side claiming victory, a settlement coming only with the conclusion of the War of the Austrian Succession (see pp. 394–396).

The Hanoverians and the Stuarts in Great Britain

In 1702, Queen Anne (1665–1714), the Protestant daughter of James II, succeeded her brother-in-law, William III, to the throne of England. Despite eighteen pregnancies and five live births, Anne had no surviving children. The House of Commons had passed the Act of Succession in 1701 to prevent any future restoration of the Catholic Stuart line to the throne. By this act, which broke strict rules of dynastic succession, the Protestant ruling dynasty of Hanover, related by blood to the English royal family, would become the English royal line upon Anne's death.

In 1707, the Act of Union created the Kingdom of Great Britain, which took the Union Jack as its flag, and linked Scotland to England and Wales. Scotland received seats in the House of Commons, but fewer than its population should have warranted. Parliament's goal in formalizing the dynastic union was fear that Scotland might seek to summon Queen Anne's exiled Catholic half-brother (James III; the Stuart son of James II) to be king of Scotland, instead of going along with England and Wales's awarding of the throne to the house of Hanover. Ireland, in which English Protestants owned seven-eighths of the land, continued to pay dearly for having supported the Catholic monarch James II after the Glorious Revolution of 1688 had evicted him from the throne. Legal restrictions prevented Irish Catholics from being merchants, lawyers, or members of the Irish Parliament, the powers of which were strictly limited. In England itself, Parliament had not extended the Toleration Act of 1689 to Catholics. British Catholics could not vote, be elected to Parliament, or hold state offices; they also were subject to special taxes, could not possess weapons,

George I, the Hanoverian king of Great Britain who never learned English.

be admitted to Oxford or Cambridge Universities, or worship freely, at a time when Protestant Dissenters—that is, Protestants not belonging to the Church of England—were able to rise to respectable positions within the British state.

The Hanoverian George I (1660–1727), a distant cousin of Queen Anne, became king in 1714. He never learned English, brought some of his own advisers from Hanover, was stubborn and obese (some of his subjects referred to their monarch as "King Log"), and may have ordered the murder of his wife's lover in Hanover. All of this was more easily forgiven by wealthy Englishmen than his apparent indifference toward the crown he wore, seemingly demonstrated by the fact that he spent long periods in his beloved Hanover.

The Hanoverian dynasty's accession to the throne complicated British foreign policy. The Treaty of Utrecht (1713), the first of two treaties that concluded the War of the Spanish Succession (1701–1714, see Chapter 7), confirmed Britain's colonial supremacy, adding Newfoundland, Nova Scotia, the Hudson Bay territory, and New Brunswick, as well as Gibraltar and the island of Minorca to the empire, and it also granted the right to trade in Spanish colonial ports. But George I looked with disfavor on the treaty because it had not advanced the interests of Hanover. Furthermore, some in Parliament considered the compromise treaty as too much of a compromise and thus humiliating for Britain. It was ratified by the House of Lords only because Queen Anne had created enough new peers to assure passage.

The new Hanoverian dynasty was threatened by remaining support for the Catholic Stuart dynasty. In 1715, the intransigent supporters (Jacobites) of James III rose up in Scotland. Although by the Treaty of Utrecht the king of France had officially renounced support for James, Catholic France still wanted him on the British throne. But troops loyal to George I quickly quelled the rebellion.

George II (1683–1760) became king in 1727. Like his father, he was courageous and had led troops into battle in the German states. But unlike his father, he took the time to learn English (although it remained decidedly his second language). He spoke it with a strong accent that his subjects mocked ("I hate bainting and boetry!" he once announced). He had a stiff, tedious personality, displaying impatience and a bad temper. On one occasion he bellowed, "I am sick to death of all this foolish stuff, and wish with all my heart that the devil may take all your bishops, ministers, Parliament, and the devil take the whole island—provided I can get out of it and go to Hanover!"

In 1745, the dreamy pretender Charles Edward Stuart (1720–1788) planned an invasion of England, similar to the one his father had undertaken thirty years earlier. "Bonnie Prince Charlie" landed in Scotland with a small army of enthusiasts. Adding Scottish clansmen from the Highlands to his force, he then marched into England with about 9,000 men. The threat to the throne was serious enough to give birth to the British anthem "God Save the King," which dates from this time.

But Charles Edward found in England almost no support for his cause. The young pretender hesitated a hundred miles from London and then retreated to Scotland. Many highlanders deserted his ranks as English troops ravaged their country, defeating Bonnie Prince Charlie at Culloden Moor near Inverness in April 1746. It was the last battle fought on British soil to this day. The pretender hightailed it back to France. The government ordered the execution of two Scottish peers who had thrown their support to the pretender, and forbade the wearing of kilts or tartans, symbols of the highlanders. Thereafter, a handful of Jacobites continued to celebrate Stuart birthdays. They toasted "the king over the water" living in French exile by holding their glasses of spirits over another glass filled with water.

The Prussian-Austrian Dynastic Rivalry in Central Europe

Prussia threatened Habsburg interests in Central Europe. Charles VI (ruled 1711–1740), the decent but mediocre Holy Roman emperor, had never recovered from the Habsburg loss of Spain in the War of the Spanish Succession. He remained obsessed with keeping the remaining Habsburg lands together. As Charles had no son, he spent years during his reign trying to bribe or otherwise convince the other European powers to recognize the integrity of the Habsburg inheritance upon his death. In 1713, he tried to get them to recognize the Pragmatic Sanction, which asserted the indivisibility of the Habsburg domains and recognized the right of female as well as male succession, should Charles have no sons.

When Charles VI died without a male heir, his twenty-three-year-old daughter Maria Theresa (ruled 1740–1780) assumed the Habsburg throne. While Maria Theresa could, as a woman, be archduchess of Austria and queen of Hungary and Bohemia, she was barred from becoming Holy Roman empress, thus opening up the question of imperial succession. The young queen had little money, no army, almost no bureaucracy, and bad advisers, and hence was in a poor position to defend her throne against aggressive hostile powers. France and Prussia, despite having pledged to uphold the Pragmatic Sanction, were each preparing to dismember the Habsburg Empire.

Frederick the Great, King of Prussia.

The immediate threat to Maria Theresa came from the Prussian King Frederick II (ruled 1740–1786). As a young man, Frederick had little in common with his raging father, Frederick William I. The royal son was intelligent, played the flute, enjoyed reading, preferred French to his native German, and as a boy expressed little interest in the army. At the age of eighteen, he tried to run off to England to catch a glimpse of his intended English bride. When young Frederick's scheme, planned by his best friend—and perhaps his lover—was foiled, the furious Frederick William decided to have his son executed. When dissuaded by his officials, Frederick William made the young prince watch from a prison cell the decapitation of his friend. Forced by his father to serve in the royal bureaucracy and as an army officer, Frederick became an aggressive absolute monarch.

Frederick, called "the Great" by his subjects, worked twelve hours a day lovingly overseeing minute details of army administration. His own physical courage was legendary—six times horses were killed beneath him in battle. At the same time, he eschewed an extravagant court life.

Frederick the Great's "enlightened" reforms (see Chapter 9) made Prussia a more efficient absolutist state. He improved the state bureaucracy by introducing an examination system. Talented commoners could be awarded positions in the courts of law. "Old Fritz" strengthened the Prussian economy by establishing state-operated iron- and steelworks, ordering the construction of more canals to haul goods, and encouraging the establishment of workshops in Berlin to produce textiles, glass, clocks, and porcelain. Because he ordered officials to accumulate stocks of grain in good times,

Prussia never suffered the desperate periods of dearth that occurred in France. With careful budgeting, Frederick the Great managed to pay for his wars, closely monitoring state tax revenues and expenses. He refused to undertake expensive loans, sell noble titles and privileges, or impose new levies on the peasantry, policies that were wreaking financial and social havoc in France.

Frederick continued the exemptions of the Junkers from many taxes and preserved their domination of the bureaucracy and army. He personally planned educational reforms with an eye to improving the performance of his officials. Nobles oversaw regional government, as well as the collection of taxes. But Frederick also wanted to keep the Junkers in a position of subordination to the crown. Noble army officers could not marry or travel abroad without the king's authority. He tolerated no appeal of royal decisions. In a society with a relatively rigid social structure, aristocratic and military virtues were henceforth inseparable in Prussia, a fact fraught with significance for modern German history.

Conflicts between the Great Powers

The rise of Prussia and Russia (see Chapter 7) carried European dynastic rivalries and warfare into Central Europe. The War of the Austrian Succession (1740–1748) revealed the fundamental principle in eighteenth-century power politics: the balance of power. The unchecked success of any one power seeking to expand its territory inevitably brought a combined response from the other powers to maintain a rough balance between the states. The expansion of Prussian power engendered the "Diplomatic Revolution" of 1756, when Austria and France put their long-standing rivalry aside to join forces against Prussia and Britain in the Seven Years' War (1756–1763). The long, costly war between France and Britain was truly global in extent, as both powers battled in North America (where the war became known as the French and Indian War), the Caribbean, and in India. The armies that fought in the war were larger and better drilled than ever before. At the same time, the French and British navies played a greater role in transporting troops and supplies, as well as guarding commercial vessels in the global struggle.

The War of the Austrian Succession

The War of the Austrian Succession reflected naked absolutist aggression. Frederick the Great coveted Silesia (now part of Poland), a Habsburg territory south of Prussia and then squeezed between Saxony, Poland, and Austria. With its textile, mining, and metallurgical industries, Silesia was a relatively wealthy province within the Habsburg domains. Frederick II had come to the throne in the same year as Maria Theresa and quickly sought to take advantage of the lone queen in a world of kings. Confident that the recent death of the Russian empress would preclude Russian assistance to Austria, Frederick sent his army into Silesia.

Frederick the Great was the latest in the line of aggressive Prussian kings who identified the interests of the state with a powerful army complemented by a centralized bureaucracy able to raise money through taxes. The Habsburg monarchy embodied, by contrast, the complexity of Central Europe. Austrian Germans dominated the administrative structure of the empire of many different peoples and languages. The multiplicity of privileges (particularly those of Magyar and Croatian nobles), traditions, and cultures undermined the authority, resources, and efficiency of the state. The Habsburg Empire also lacked the trading and manufacturing base of Great Britain and the Dutch Republic, foremost among the non-absolutist states, or of France or even Prussia. Mercantilists in Austria hoped that foreign trade would add to the coffers of the state, but the overwhelmingly rural Habsburg lands had little to export.

Maria Theresa's troubles were not limited to Silesia. The nobles of Bohemia, the richest Habsburg province, rebelled against Habsburg rule, offering the throne to the ruler of Bavaria, Austria's rival in southern Germany. Dependent on the good will of the provincial Diets, no Habsburg monarch could be sure of having either sufficient support from the Estates or money with which to raise an effective army.

Now, with Prussian troops occupying Silesia, Maria Theresa traveled to Hungary to ask for the support of the Hungarian Diet, which had agreed to the Pragmatic Sanction in exchange for recognition of Hungary's status as a separate kingdom within the Habsburg Empire. Dressed in mourning clothes following the recent death of an infant daughter and clutching one of her sixteen children to her, Maria Theresa convinced the Diet to provide an army of 40,000 men. The Magyar nobles held out their swords to her, shouting their promise to give "life and blood" for her. The gesture could not restore Silesia to the Habsburgs, but it may have saved the Habsburg monarchy. Aided by Hungarian troops, imperial forces put down the Bohemian revolt.

Fearing a disproportionate expansion of Prussian power in Central Europe, other states now joined an alliance against Frederick the Great. Yet, confronted by Austria, Russia, Sweden, Piedmont-Sardinia, and Denmark, states with a combined population twenty times that of Prussia, the Prussian army more than held its own, with the help of France as well as Spain and Bavaria, each hoping to help bring about the disintegration of the Habsburg Empire. France joined the anti-Austrian coalition because it coveted the Austrian Netherlands (Belgium); Spain participated because it wanted to recapture influence in Italy at Habsburg expense; and the king of Piedmont-Sardinia cooperated because he coveted Milan. Frederick, satisfied for the moment with the acquisition of Silesia, withdrew from the war in 1745 after the Peace of Dresden. But Britain was drawn into the

Aristocratic officers safely above the carnage at the Battle of Fontenoy, 1745.

conflict by its need to protect the dynastic territory of Hanover from Prussia and France. Indeed, at Dettingen in 1743, King George II became the last British monarch to fight in battle. His horse was spooked and rode off with its frightened royal rider still astride. In North America, a British force captured the French fort of Louisbourg, which guarded access to the Saint Lawrence River. France's army defeated the combined Dutch and British forces in the Battle of Fontenoy in what is now Belgium in 1745, the bloodiest battle of the century until the French Revolution. Fifteen thousand soldiers were dead or wounded among the 95,000 soldiers who fought at Fontenoy. In 1748, the inconclusive Treaty of Aix-la-Chapelle ended the War of the Austrian Succession (see Map 11.1). French forces withdrew from the Austrian Netherlands in return for the English abandoning the captured fort of Louisbourg. The northern Italian city of Parma passed to a branch of the Spanish Bourbons, and Piedmont-Sardinia absorbed parts of the duchy of Milan.

The Seven Years' War

The Seven Years' War (1756–1763) was remarkable for several reasons. First, it was arguably the first truly global conflict. The commercial interests of France and Britain clashed in North America (where the two powers claimed large reaches of the American interior as far as the Mississippi River

MAP 11.1 THE WAR OF THE AUSTRIAN SUCCESSION, 1740–1748   Major battles and territorial changes at the end of the war.

and had been at war since 1754), the Caribbean, and India (see Map 11.2). Second, for the first time we can speak of a war not just of kings but self-consciously of nations, at least in the cases of Britain and France. Both states underwent a surge of patriotic enthusiasm, marked, for example, in the case of France by calls for "patriotic gifts" to support the war. In Britain, the sense of being "Briton" developed among all classes, accentuated by an overwhelmingly popular war against Catholic France. In both countries there were calls for the more efficient management of the war, seen as part of pursuing national interests, arguably for the first time.

Prussia's gains in the War of the Austrian Succession engendered the Diplomatic Revolution of 1756. France had previously undertaken alliances with Prussia and the Ottoman Empire to counter the threat of Austrian

MAP 11.2 THE SEVEN YEARS' WAR, 1756–1763 Areas of conflict, including battle sites, during the Seven Years' War, as well as territorial changes at the end of the war.

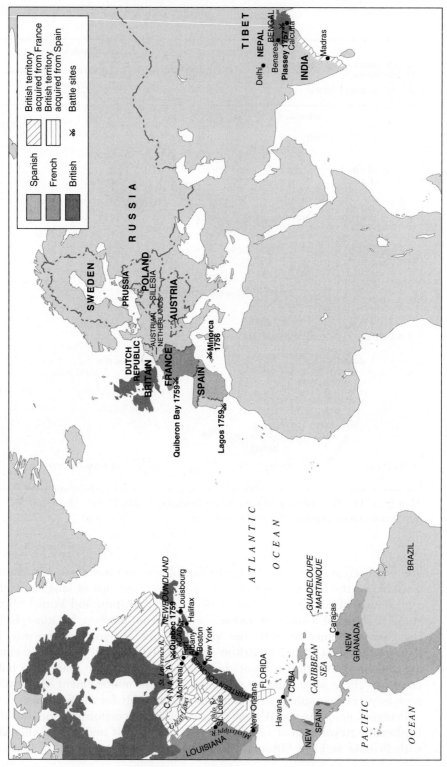

and Russian expansion and was thus determined that Poland survive as an independent state. The Diplomatic Revolution of 1756 now ended more than a century of intermittent warfare between France and the Austrian Habsburgs. Alarmed by the expansion of Prussian power, Austria now allied with France, and then Russia, with the goal of recapturing Silesia. The cost of France's support would be its future annexation of the Austrian Netherlands and Austrian neutrality in the war between Britain and France (which in 1756 had been going on in North America for two years). Frederick the Great, determined to keep Silesia, turned to Britain, France's enemy. To France and Russia, Britain's sudden and shocking alliance with Prussia seemed a betrayal, even as France reversed its century-old opposition to Habsburg interests. Having changed partners, the great powers went to war again.

In 1757, Frederick defeated a large French army and then a Habsburg force. But a Russian army attacked from the north, occupying Berlin, while more Austrian troops marched on Prussia from the south. Prussia's situation seemed desperate, leading the king to compare his state to "a man with many wounds who has lost so much blood that he is on the point of death." But as luck would have it, Peter III became tsar of Russia in 1762, succeeding Empress Elizabeth, Frederick's determined enemy. The new tsar admired the Prussian king and called the Russian troops home. At the cost of perhaps 300,000 soldiers, Prussia preserved its full independence.

The rivalry between the European powers in India took the shape of a struggle between the British and French East India Companies against the background of intrigues and warfare among Indian rulers. The Mughals had conquered most of the subcontinent in the seventeenth century, but along the southern coast, where Mughal control was limited, the European trading network had continued to expand. In the meantime, India became the largest producer of textiles in the world, threatening the production of English cloth. The Mughal Empire collapsed during the first half of the eighteenth century following invasions from Iran and Afghanistan. Bengal, the wealthiest part of the Indian subcontinent, became autonomous. The resulting political chaos in the 1740s aided the subjection of India by Britain, even if in 1750 there were only about 5,000 British residents (and 20,000 soldiers) in the subcontinent.

Robert Clive (1725–1774), the son of a provincial gentleman and lawyer, led troops of the East India Company and Indian mercenaries into Bengal. There the prince preferred French to British traders and in 1757 had incarcerated more than a hundred British subjects in a room so small and stuffy that most of them died—the "Black Hole of Calcutta." That same year, Clive's force defeated the prince's army at Plassey, north of Calcutta. After putting a pliant puppet on the Bengali throne, Clive continued to use British troops to further not only the interests of the British East India Company, but himself as well. He became very rich through imperial acquisitions and secured a British peerage. By 1761, the stage was set for

General Wolfe's forces scale the heights of the Plains of Abraham in Quebec.

British control of most of the Indian subcontinent, with the British navy preventing French traders and soldiers from receiving sufficient supplies. The East India Company's great successes opened up new trade between Britain, India, and South China, a vast new market.

In what became Canada, there was much more at stake because Britain and France were fighting for control of a vast territory. In this struggle, France had a decided disadvantage. Even after more than a hundred years as a colony, at mid-century "New France" had a French population of only about 80,000 people, for the most part clustered in three towns along the St. Lawrence River—Montreal, Quebec, and Trois-Rivières. By contrast, the thirteen British colonies already had more than 2 million residents. British incursions into their territory led Native Americans to ally informally with the French. During the French and Indian War (1754–1763), British troops forced over 10,000 French-speaking Acadians living in Nova Scotia and New Brunswick to emigrate. Many of them settled in the French colony of New Orleans, where the word "Cajun" emerged as a corruption of the French "*acadien.*"

The British navy accentuated its advantage on the seas by seizing 300 French merchant ships and capturing 8,000 sailors even before hostilities formally began. Despite the capture by French troops of several forts in the Great Lakes region, British ships reduced French reinforcements and supplies to a trickle, also besting a French fleet at Quiberon Bay off the coast of Brittany in 1759.

In 1759, General James Wolfe (1727–1759) led an audacious, successful British attack on the French near Quebec, his forces climbing up the cliffs from the St. Lawrence River to surprise their enemy. British forces captured Fort Duquesne in 1758, driving the French from the Ohio River Valley, and in 1760 took Montreal. In the Caribbean, the British picked off French islands and their small garrisons one by one.

War left all the combatants exhausted. The British national debt had doubled. The French monarchy entered a period of financial crisis. The Seven Years' War ended the domination of France on the continent and cleared the way for the expansion of the British Empire. By the Treaty of Paris of 1763, Austria recognized Prussia's absorption of Silesia in 1740 in exchange for Saxony's retention of independence. The Southern Netherlands, however, remained an Austrian Habsburg territory. The settlement in North America and the Caribbean was much more far-reaching. Canada became British. France retained fishing rights on the Grand Banks off Newfoundland, but accepted British claims to territory east of the Mississippi River, and those of Spain to all territory west of the Mississippi. This enormous western region, known as the Louisiana Territory, stretched from the almost tropical climate of New Orleans to the freezing plains of central Canada. France retained the Caribbean islands of Martinique and Guadeloupe, only because English colonists feared competition from sugar produced on those islands if they became British. Spain ceded Florida to Britain (though only, as it turned out, until 1783).

Britain then tried to mend fences in Europe, where the balance of power had been preserved. However, Austrian troops occupied Bavaria, leading to the brief War of Bavarian Succession (1778–1779). The resistance of Prussia and Saxony foiled the Habsburg plan. Like Franco-British enmity, Austro-Prussian rivalry for domination of German-speaking Central Europe continued unabated.

Armies and Their Tactics in the Eighteenth Century

Long after monarchs succeeded in putting an end to private noble armies, warfare remained part of noble culture. Military schools in France, Russia, and several German states trained the sons of nobles in the skills of war. In Prussia, Frederick William I believed that any attempt to allow commoners to become officers would be "the first step toward the decline and fall of the army." Noble officers had much more in common with the officers of the enemy than with their own troops, who were conscripted or impressed from the lower classes. Indeed, the Habsburgs often appointed foreign nobles as officers in its army. Officers captured during a war were treated to a nice glass of wine and a good meal, and then exchanged for their own officers who had fallen into enemy hands. War was fought over territory. In some ways, it seemed like a game of chess played between aristocrats in a manor house parlor. It is said that the French officers at the Battle of Fontenoy in 1745 gallantly shouted to their British counterparts, "Fire first, *messieurs les anglais!*" before the slaughter began.

Recruitment practices differed in the various European states. The Prussian army's military recruitment system was the most comprehensive. Each of its regiments was assigned a district from which to draw recruits. In France, military recruitment was placed directly under the control of the state bureaucracy, which relieved officers of the responsibility for filling a quota of recruits. In Russia, each commune (*mir*) had to provide at least one soldier. Throughout Europe, certain categories of the population were exempt from service, including prosperous farmers, the servants of French nobles, Russian merchants, and, in some countries, men with families. England was alone among the major powers in not having a standing army, at least in principle.

Yet mercenaries still sometimes provided the bulk of eighteenth-century European armies, the notable exception being France. Military service provided those who joined up with regular meals, shelter, and adventure. Swiss guards served the French royal family as well as the popes in Rome, and their countrymen fought with a variety of armies. The Dutch army included a brigade of Scottish highlanders. Military service could still provide respectability. Criminals and other men with something unpleasant in their past often turned up as soldiers. Non-military officials, servants, wives, children, and prostitutes accompanied armies: "We are a marching brothel," assessed one British commander.

Desertion remained widespread, affecting up to 35 percent of an army, despite threats of mutilation for those caught leaving. During the Seven Years' War, about 62,000 soldiers deserted the Habsburg army, 70,000 left the army of France behind, and 80,000 Russian soldiers disappeared into the night. Tightly packed formations served to discourage desertions, as they were intended to do, because soldiers were under more constant control. Harsh, even brutal, discipline in army camps complemented that in the field. Frederick the Great was not alone in believing that "[the soldier] must be more afraid of his officers than of the dangers to which he is exposed." Although strategies for supplying troops improved during the century, armies rarely moved far from their supply camps. The lack of commitment and unreliability of mercenary and levied troops often helped end fighting.

Military technology had evolved slowly since the invention of gunpowder. In the seventeenth century, the soldier wielding a bayonet, a musket topped with a razor-sharp knife, had pushed the pike man, a foot soldier armed with only a spear-like weapon, off the battlefield. Other significant changes in warfare in the seventeenth century included improved flintlock muskets, with cartridges and iron ramrods that permitted riflemen to fire three times per minute and increased their range. Handheld firearms became practical weapons for the first time. Artillery pieces were also lighter and more mobile, with somewhat greater range. The training of artillery officers improved.

Soldiers in the eighteenth century were now far better trained and disciplined than in the previous century; armies were far larger than ever before. The discipline and efficiency of troops in formation won or lost battles. Muskets, inaccurate beyond a short distance, were fired in deadly volleys by rows of soldiers taking turns reloading. Cavalry charges, which generally took place on the flanks of battle with the goal of neutralizing the enemy's cavalry, usually were over quickly.

New tactics had brought greater maneuverability in the sixteenth and seventeenth centuries, including linear formations involving coordinated movements that required well-trained and disciplined troops. In the eighteenth century, even greater troop mobility was achieved by combining line and column formations in a "mixed order." Moreover, the British and Prussian armies were the first to create a light infantry division that could engage the enemy more rapidly, often fighting with bayonets. Yet defense still dominated in battle, as symbolized by the impregnable fortresses along the northern frontier of France built in the late seventeenth century. Line formations were more conducive to defense than offense.

Following the unrestrained carnage of the Thirty Years' War (1618–1648), warfare became somewhat more civilized, or at least somewhat more predictable, with fewer civilian casualties. Prisoners of war, even commoners, were kept in relatively decent conditions and were sometimes exchanged for their counterparts. The development of logistical support and professionalized, well-drilled armies meant that soldiers no longer had to live off the land. The goals of warfare were now generally restrained by traditions of monarchical and aristocratic civility. Once victory was achieved, there seemed no reason to pursue one's enemy to finish him off. Civilians were now generally spared in times of war.

Navies

British statesmen knew that to maintain superiority over France on the seas, their enemy had to be kept busy on the continent, whether by direct military operations or by large subsidies paid to France's enemies among the German states. The Royal Navy had begun to grow in size during the second half of the seventeenth century. As its role in protecting commerce increased, it expanded further, from 105 ships in 1750 to 195 in 1790, while the smaller French navy increased only modestly in size to 81 warships, 9 more than those of the Spanish navy.

Building on earlier improvements in sails, rigging, charts, and navigational techniques, the size and quality of ships improved. Shipbuilding drew on scientific assistance from experts in mathematics and navigation. The British first added copper to hulls, which made their ships sturdier. Short-barreled cannon of greater caliber proved deadly in close combat.

Navies were also beset by problems of desertion, at least when ships were in port. Almost one-fourth of the men who joined the British navy between 1776 and 1780 deserted—many of whom had been dragged to the docks by press-gangs. Shipboard disease killed many sailors, despite the use of lemon juice to counter scurvy, an illness caused by a vitamin C deficiency.

As the British naval supremacy established the basis for the expansion of commerce and empire, there were few decisive naval confrontations in the eighteenth century. "Do you know what a naval battle is?" asked a French minister. "The fleets maneuver, come to grips, fire a few shots, and then each retreats . . . and the sea remains as salty as it was before." The cost of full-fledged battles seemed too high; ships were enormously expensive to build and maintain. Fifteen times more British sailors died of disease between 1774 and 1780 than succumbed to battle wounds.

POLITICAL CHANGE IN GREAT BRITAIN

In England, the Glorious Revolution of 1688 had put an end to fifty years of social and political turmoil. The Bill of Rights of 1689 guaranteed Parliament's right to approve taxation and prohibited the monarch from suspending or dispensing with laws. Parliament also maintained control of military funding and the size of the army. Only with the consent of Parliament could a standing army be raised in peacetime (even though this in itself was technically unconstitutional and the House of Commons had to annually approve funding). Thus, the political struggles of the seventeenth century had demonstrated that the king had to work with Parliament in governing the nation. In turn, the state served as a guarantor of rights of property and patronage. The rights of Parliament and the elective nature of the House of Commons, even if based on an extremely narrow electoral franchise, distinguished British political life from that of its continental rivals.

The period of "aristocratic consensus" that followed the Glorious Revolution was not as free from political contention as the term suggests. But it brought major changes in British political life. The interests of wealthy property owners were represented in the House of Commons, which gradually became a far more important political forum than the House of Lords, which only represented peers. It also became more difficult for the king to manage the House of Commons.

Political differences between Tories and Whigs (see Chapter 6) became more consistent. The former were now clearly identified with the prerogatives of the throne, the latter with the rights of Parliament. Whigs believed that the role of Parliament was to defend liberty, property, and the rule of law and thereby preserve the British constitution against possible abuses of power by the throne. In the words of the Irish-born political theorist Edmund Burke (1729–1797), the British "mixed constitution" (which balanced the institutions of monarchy, the House of Lords, and the House of Commons), stood as an "isthmus between arbitrary power and anarchy." During this period, there emerged a sense that opposition within Parliament to government policies was an intrinsic part of a political process in which competing interests were struggling for primacy. Moreover, during the eighteenth century, political life began to spill beyond the narrow confines of the British political elite as ordinary people demanded a voice in political life with increasing insistence. In Britain's North American colonies, a similar and in some ways parallel struggle for liberty began, leading to the American War of Independence (1775–1782).

Expanding Central Government in Britain

Britain was justly renowned for its political preoccupation with liberty. An essential part of eighteenth-century British identity included the victory of Parliament during the English Civil War in the mid-seventeenth century in defense of constitutional monarchy. Yet, as with the continental powers France, Spain, Austria, and Russia, in non-absolutist Great Britain, too, the powers of central government expanded, creating what has been called a "British version of the fiscal-military state, complete with large armies and navies, industrious administrators, high taxes and huge debts." By the end of the eighteenth century, the British state had perhaps ten times more revenues than a century earlier. At the same time, the increasingly global nature of trade and warfare made greater demands on the state's administrative abilities. The growth, greater centralization, professionalization, and efficiency of military and civilian administration permitted Britain to replace France as the strongest power on the globe. British landed, financial, commercial, and manufacturing interests followed British military engagements across the globe with rapt attention. Britain's financial community, centered in what would become called "The City"—London's financial district—became ever more tied to and financially dependent on Britain's wars in Europe and abroad. The British Empire became closely linked not only to British prosperity but also identity.

Between 1680 and 1780, Britain built and consolidated its empire. The British army and navy tripled in size. The power and reach of the treasury also increased, along with its capacity to raise money for foreign wars and imperial conquest. As the economy grew rapidly, the British state raised and efficiently collected taxes, including land taxes, excise taxes (on commodities), and customs taxes, which provided an increasing share of revenue. The government borrowed as never before, increasing the national debt. Britain's bureaucracy also grew in size and complexity. Government officials became more professional, technical expertise more important, and government offices more clearly defined. Civil service posts offered educated men chances for social advancement.

The British government, like its continental rivals, continued to confront the problem of paying off the massive national debt amassed by loans that financed dynastic and trade wars. The government spent more than three-quarters of its expenditures on the army, navy, or paying back debts from previous wars. In 1719, the government had awarded the South Sea

Company the right to take over the national debt. The South Sea Company had been founded in 1711. Two years later, the government had awarded it a monopoly over the slave trade with Latin America and favorable conditions for European trade. But because of the intermittent fighting with Spain during the War of the Spanish Succession, any profits from such trade seemed in the distant future. Needing a rapid infusion of capital, the directors of the company offered stock for sale on attractive terms. They bribed some potential purchasers and developed ties with high government officials.

With the help of unscrupulous investors, many of whom were holders of part of the national debt who wanted to get their money back, the company converted the debt owed them by the state into company shares. The directors parlayed the price of the stock higher. The scam worked as long as there were enough investors whose funds could be used to pay dividends to those who had bought shares earlier. But the profits were all based on the sale of the stock rather than on real commercial gains.

A fever of speculation seized England. Smaller companies started up overnight, most of them insolvent or strangely organized, such as one literally limited to women dressed in calico. One joint-stock company (made up of shareholders who would divide profits according to the amount of their investments) was created for "a purpose to be announced." The speculative craze ended with a jolt in 1720. With no gains of any kind forthcoming, the "South Sea Bubble" burst in September of that year. It was the

1720 cartoon showing how speculation caused shares in the South Sea Company to rise, which would eventually lead to the South Sea Bubble.

first great financial crash (and coincided with the bursting of smaller speculative "bubbles" in Amsterdam and Paris).

The financial scandal hung over political life when Robert Walpole (1676–1745) became chancellor of the exchequer in 1721, a post he would hold for more than twenty years. The son of a gentry landowner of relatively modest means, the short, ruddy-cheeked Walpole was energetic and ambitious, making himself quite rich at state expense. In office, he was determined to restore political confidence to Britain. Parliament passed a law that allowed only companies chartered by the government to sell stock shares to the public. Walpole created a sinking fund (intended to retire the debt by paying off, or "sinking," part of it each year). This helped restore confidence. George II trusted Walpole's judgment, and the latter survived the wrath of some members of Parliament (MPs) who disliked his unpopular financial reforms, including greater taxes on imports and on salt, and his goal of keeping Britain out of war.

Walpole perfected the system of political patronage, virtually managing the House of Commons and making the Anglican Church part of a state structure that would last more than a century. He placed MPs loyal to him—"placemen"—in well-paying governmental positions, some of which were veritable sinecures. In return, they voted with the government. On the local level, the bigger fish became county lord-lieutenants and the smaller fry justices of the peace. One tombstone epitaph flaunted the harvest of political patronage reaped by a well-connected lady lying therein: "By means of her alliance with the illustrious family of Stanhope, she had the merit to obtain for her husband and children twelve appointments in church and state," not a bad haul. Walpole also worked to isolate Jacobites, smoothing the Hanoverian succession to the British throne.

However, Walpole's support in Parliament eventually began to crumble. His attempt to extend the excise tax to wine and tobacco failed in 1733, after generating riots. William Pitt the Elder (1708–1778) led a coalition of "boy patriots" against Walpole. Specifically, they objected to his inaction against Spain, whose ships were harassing British ships in the Atlantic. After being forced by public outcry to declare war on Spain in 1739—the War of Jenkins's Ear—Walpole resigned two years later.

The duke of Newcastle (Thomas Pelham-Holles, 1693–1768), whose notorious incoherence led him to be known as "Hubble-Bubble," succeeded Walpole and ably manipulated the patronage of his position. Then Pitt became prime minister. The "Great Commoner" Pitt was a lonely, unstable man who alternated between feverish excitement and dark depression. He was demagogic, arrogant, and ruthless, commanding respect through fear.

The Role of the House of Commons

The British monarch could declare war or make peace, call or dissolve Parliament, and appoint whomever he or she wanted to serve as cabinet minister, officer, bishop, general, or admiral. The cabinet and government officials carried out the functions of state. But they did so against the backdrop of ongoing practical compromises between Parliament and the monarch.

During the early decades of the eighteenth century, the House of Commons gradually emerged as an epicenter of political life. Unlike the House of Lords, all of whose members were nobles, members of the House of Commons were elected by Britain's narrow electoral franchise based on landed wealth. Although still dominated by "gentle," or landed, interests, the number of merchants elected to the Commons increased, for families that had made fortunes in business, whether they were titled nobles, nontitled gentry, or commoners, invested their money in land. Wealthy MPs could easily control blocs of votes in their countries through patronage. In 1776, only 5,700 men in Britain elected half of the members of Commons, most of whose members were routinely reelected every seven years. In only three boroughs did more than 4,000 men have the right to vote, and in several others, fewer than 15 men could cast ballots. Thus, one lord confidently assured his son in 1754, "Your seat in the new Parliament is at last absolutely secured and that without opposition or the least necessity of your personal trouble or appearance." Some MPs were returned from "rotten" and "pocket" boroughs. Rotten boroughs ranged from the infamous "Old Sarum," which had no inhabitants but two representatives in Commons, and another that had been under water for centuries, to those with several hundred voters almost as easily managed. Pocket boroughs were in the pocket of the MP because his election was uncontested.

Some of England's growing industrial towns were not represented in Parliament. Many urban elites no longer bought the idea that their interests were "virtually represented" by MPs from districts represented in the House of Commons. Furthermore, emerging political discontent reflected alarm that the role of the House of Commons as the defender of the constitution against possible tyrannical abuse was being compromised by institutionalized patronage and outright corruption, symbolized by rotten and pocket boroughs.

The Development of Party Politics in the 1760s: Whigs and Tories

Whigs and Tories had governed in reasonable harmony during the Robert Walpole era. But after Walpole, many Whigs came to believe that ministers ought to be acceptable to Parliament as well as to the king. In contrast, Tories traditionally took the view that the prerogatives of king and Church had to be maintained at all costs.

After coming to the throne in 1760, George III gave the impression that he intended to rule without Parliament. When the king refused to declare war on Spain in 1761 during the Seven Years' War, Pitt resigned as prime minister. Subsequently, the king appointed his former tutor, the aristocratic, aloof Scotsman John Stuart, the earl of Bute (1713–1792), as secretary of state and then as prime minister. But Bute was an unpopular choice because he was not an MP, had little political experience and even less influence, and did not want Britain to undertake hostilities against Spain.

The king's appointment of his "dearest friend" seemed to Whigs to violate the unwritten agreement that the king act with Parliament's consent. Determined opposition merely served to strengthen the king's resolve. The press castigated Bute, and crowds in the street howled against him. Rumor insisted that he owed his controversial appointment to having been the lover of the king's mother. On the verge of a nervous breakdown, Bute resigned in 1763.

Bute's appointment, raising the question of ministerial responsibility, divided Commons along ideological lines. George III turned against the Whig country gentlemen who no longer could be counted upon to support him on all matters. The king insisted on the monarchy's independence and particularly on his right to choose whomever he wished as minister.

MPs representing the interests of the "country gentlemen" began to use the term "party," but without the trappings of formal organization that would come late in the next century. Although they traditionally upheld the rights of Parliament, Whigs, to be sure, remained loyal to the throne, even if King George accused them of being otherwise. While the issues dividing Tories and Whigs remained in some ways the same as those that had characterized the Walpole period, or even the English Civil War, the emerging notion of political parties was probably of more lasting significance than the political groupings themselves.

The term "party" had existed since the time of the Glorious Revolution of 1688; it had the sense of a group of people sharing a belief on a specific matter of political controversy. It had been somewhat synonymous with "faction," which since the 1670s had the negative connotation of a cabal of individuals working for their own interests. With the exception of the Jacobite Tories, however, the differences between Whigs and Tories were vague and uncertain during the reign of the first two Georges. George III's seeming determination to create a government above parties revived the solidarity of the old Whigs. The idea developed that a party of parliamentary opposition formed an essential part of the parliamentary system of representation.

George III insisted that it was his duty to defeat the forces of "faction." Burke, for one, rejected the king's efforts to discredit the concept of "party." In *Thoughts on the Cause of the Present Discontents* (1770), he defined a party as "a body of men united for promoting by their joint endeavors *the national interest* upon some particular principle in which they are all agreed." He believed that political parties stood as the basis of representative government and therefore of political order. A newspaper article in 1770 went even further: "Opposition, in parliament, to the measures of government, is so far from being in itself an evil, that it has been often productive of good to the state." Parties alone could ensure the preservation "of responsible government," specifically, the notion that ministers ought to be acceptable to Parliament. This concept of a loyal parliamentary opposition did not exist in France or anywhere else on the continent. Nor, for that matter, did it exist in all constituencies in Britain; in many places, politics, dominated by family ties and outright patronage, went on as before.

George III could count on about a third of the members of Commons for unconditional support, at least partially because they held court-appointed posts. Unfailing voters for "court" became increasingly known as Tories, particularly to the Whig opposition. Supporters of the government rejected the term, as they did all labels, but at the same time they lent credence to the concept by cohesively defending a patriarchal society based on the prerogatives of monarchy, aristocracy, and the Anglican Church.

In 1766, George III turned to Pitt, who was immensely popular, again to serve as prime minister; he hoped to split the Whigs, because the "Great Commoner" was alienated from aristocratic Whigs. Pitt lost support even among his political friends by accepting a peerage, becoming duke of Chatham. Vigorous debates among Whigs, principally between the imperious Pitt and the duke of Newcastle and his followers, however, did not diminish the emerging notion of "party" that most Whigs now accepted. For Whigs, the most significant issue remained the extent to which the king could act without the support of Parliament.

The Rise of British Nationalism

Although king and Parliament had been bitterly divided during the crises that led to the English Civil War and the Glorious Revolution, they were thereafter unified in the quest for British commercial and international predominance. During the eighteenth century, a strong sense of nationalism developed in Great Britain. This included pride in the nation's high degree of freedom and reverence for Parliament as the Protestant institution that had turned back the threat of Catholicism and prevented absolute rule.

The fear of Catholicism, endemic in England since the Reformation, fired British nationalism. Faced with the threat of French invasion during the Anglo-French wars, British patriots across the social spectrum embraced the British Isles as the chosen land of God. They boasted of Britain's prosperity and social stability while belittling France and Spain, Catholic powers.

William Pitt the Elder was an empire builder. Believing that the throne's Hanoverian interests were dominating foreign policy, and having made his reputation accusing Walpole of indifference to British interests abroad, Pitt turned his attention to expanding the colonies. "Who will laugh at sugar, now?" he thundered in 1759 to nobles who had scorned colonial trade. Horace Walpole (1717–1797), Robert Walpole's youngest son, a novelist and the beneficiary of lucrative posts that left him plenty of time to write, was among the few who had some doubts about all of this. "No man ever went to the East Indies with good intentions," the younger Walpole said, adding sarcastically that "it really looks as if we intended to finish the conquest of the world during the next campaign."

The lure of commercial profit and empire thus helped define British nationalism. As we have seen, the financial community of investors in London closely followed not only the vicissitudes of the economy but the ups and downs of British warfare. A good many financiers had, after all, loaned money to their state and therefore eagerly watched what was done with it. Foreign and colonial trade often depended on naval protection, further linking their interests to the Union Jack, the flag of Great Britain. The state itself depended on expanding commercial activity for tax revenue. Representatives of economic interest groups and lobbies made contacts in the London financial community and in government circles to put forward their views, for example, on excise and customs taxes. New patriotic societies, some of them drawing ordinary people into the wave of nationalist enthusiasm, sprang up.

The generally harmonious relationship between the landed elite and the commercial community was a source of social and political stability and of rising British nationalism. They joined together in the pursuit of empire. Nobles and gentry benefited from the expansion of state activity, diversifying their investments with loans to the crown. Unlike the continental powers, in Britain all subjects paid taxes. This afforded all social groups the sense of being Britons. At the same time (in contrast to the case in France), improved communications and the development of a national market aided the process of national integration in Britain.

Their commitment to the nation also enabled the British elite, proud of their freedoms and their country's more decentralized form of government, to accept a stronger state apparatus without complaining about infringements on their liberty. Thus, they did not feel the need for constitutional guarantees (based upon equality before the law) against arbitrary tyranny. The stronger state did not diminish the status of British landowners, and it in no way infringed on their personal freedoms within civil society.

Anglo-Irish, Scottish, and Welsh landowners became more integrated into a national British elite, as the increasing intermarriage among these groups indicated. Many Scots, though hardly all, began to see themselves as British, just as fewer English people considered Scots or Welsh to be outsiders who were potentially disloyal to the crown, views they continued to hold, however, of the Catholic Irish. The prerogatives of Parliament notwithstanding, the British monarchy and its army and navy became increasingly revered and celebrated as a rallying point for the nation.

CHALLENGES TO ESTABLISHED AUTHORITY

In the 1760s and 1770s, movements for reform emerged in several countries. In Britain, "liberty" became the watchword of political opposition to the government. In a parallel struggle on the other side of the Atlantic Ocean, the American colonists of Britain's thirteen colonies demanded "no taxation without representation," and then, when rebuffed, these "Patriots" rebelled against British rule in the War of American Independence. Elsewhere, similar reform movements on the European continent sought to reduce absolute rule (as in Denmark), prevent it from lapsing into despotism (as in France), or wanted to prevent the imposition of a stronger centralized authority (as in the Dutch Republic). Other movements for reform challenged what seemed to be unwarranted privileges, again most notably in France. In every Western country, more information about political events in other states was available through newspapers and gazettes, as well as from merchants, travelers, and diplomats. In Britain and parts of Western Europe, political clubs also reflected greater preoccupation with politics. These reform movements, then, influenced each other, however indirectly.

British Radicals

In the 1760s in Britain, ordinary people demanded electoral reform, and some even called for universal male suffrage. Reformers asked that constituencies be redrawn so that rapidly growing industrial regions in the north of England be appropriately represented in Parliament, and that London, which was grossly underrepresented, elect more MPs. Moreover, shouts for more liberties came from ordinary people without the right to vote.

John Wilkes (1727–1797), the son of a successful London malt distiller, was an MP of modest means and a Protestant Dissenter. Charming, witty, and reckless, Wilkes leapt into the public eye in 1763 with the publication of his newspaper, the *North Briton*. Issue number 45 attacked the government—and the king himself directly—for signing the compromise Treaty of Paris with France that year, ending the Seven Years' War. The king ordered "that Devil Wilkes, a trumpet of sedition," arrested for libel. Wilkes announced that he considered his arrest a blow against liberty and the constitution by the unjust, arbitrary power of government; it was "a question of such importance," as he declared at his trial, "as to determine at once, whether English Liberty be a reality or a shadow." The court freed Wilkes after a week in jail on the basis of parliamentary immunity. Wilkes triumphantly boasted that his fate was tied to "that of the middling and inferior set of people" in Britain.

Fearing prosecution for pornography—the government had dug up a bawdy old poem he had written—since the House of Commons had lifted parliamentary immunity, Wilkes left for France in 1764. Upon his return four years later, he was arrested, tried, and convicted, and then freed after thousands of people demonstrated on his behalf. Wilkes then stood for election in Middlesex, the county making up most of metropolitan London north of the Thames and outside of "The City." With the support of merchants and small manufacturers wealthy enough to be eligible to vote, Wilkes was reelected to Parliament. Four times he was elected, and four times Parliament refused to seat him because of his previous conviction. Cloaking himself in a patriot's garb, he became a rallying symbol for the campaign for the rights of the unrepresented in a time of economic hardship, grain riots, and work stoppages.

The phrase "Wilkes and Liberty" echoed in speeches, conversation, and song. In 1769, the Society of the Supporters of the Bill of Rights invoked the name of Wilkes as it called for the government to "restore the constitution." The number 45—the libelous issue of the *North Briton*—became a rallying cry. Wilkes's rather misshapen face appeared on posters, handbills, verses, cartoons, tea mugs, and dinner plates. He was elected sheriff of London in 1771 and even lord mayor three years later, though he was not allowed to occupy either position.

More "respectable" reformers now began to demand greater freedom of the press, specifically a redefinition of libel laws, so that the government could be criticized, and the right to publish parliamentary debates. They further demanded that Parliament meet each year and that MPs be required to live in the districts they represented. However, most Whigs now

(*Left*) John Wilkes, in an etching by William Hogarth. (*Right*) Wilkes's supporters take to the streets.

disassociated themselves clearly from Wilkes, in part because of his rather unsavory reputation and identification in upper-class eyes with "the mob." They were wary of demonstrations for universal male suffrage. Few Whigs were willing to go beyond insisting on the principle of ministerial responsibility.

Literary and "philosophical" societies, which had sprung up in most large towns, facilitated the emergence of an even wider political culture than that which had developed during the political crises of the seventeenth century. Inns and coffeehouses added special reading rooms to accommodate their clientele. By 1760, London printing presses, the number of which had increased from seventy-five in 1724 to about two hundred at the time of Wilkes's first arrest, churned out eighty-nine newspapers, four of which were dailies. Another thirty-five newspapers were published outside London. By 1790, there were fourteen daily London newspapers, and the number of provincial papers had multiplied by four times. Political pamphlets, handbills, and caricatures inundated the capital and the larger provincial towns. By the 1760s, artists stopped omitting the names of the targets of their satirical wit. Like its Whig opponents and the extra-parliamentary radicals, the government found itself obliged to utilize newspapers, pamphlets, brochures, and handbills to argue its case before public opinion.

American Revolutionaries

During the 1760s, another challenge to the British crown was smoldering far across the Atlantic Ocean in North America. The thirteen American colonies, many times the size of England, had become ever more difficult for the British government to administer. The population of the colonies, which took in 20 percent of British exports and supplied 30 percent of its imports, had grown by tenfold in just seventy years, from about 250,000 in 1700 to more than 2.5 million in 1775, compared to about 6.4 million people in England at the same time. Those arriving in the colonies found a land of opportunity. Many were able to purchase land that would have been beyond their means at home. Artisans and even common laborers commanded relatively high wages because of the shortage of labor in the colonies.

Over the decades in the eighteenth century, the residents of the colonies had developed a sense of living in a British-American society with its own distinct culture. The North American colonies had developed without the kind of centralized organization for economic exploitation and determination to conquer that had characterized the Spanish Empire. The English settlement colonies had been founded in the quest for trade and economic opportunity, as well as religious freedom, as in the case of Massachusetts Puritans, and religious toleration, as in the case of Maryland Catholics. Thus, the colonies' insistence on the liberty of "freeborn Englishmen" (and, after 1707, British subjects) was easily transferred into a demand for a more encompassing liberty that included rejection of the idea that British sovereignty could not be challenged. Merchants, lawyers, and wealthy landowners, like the Virginians George Washington (1732–1799) and Thomas Jefferson (1743–1826), who stood on top of the social hierarchy, led the colonists. They resented the continued presence of the British army and the attempt of British officers to try to impose on colonial forces the same standards of discipline that applied in Britain. The American colonists believed that they had the right to resist unjust laws in the name of liberty.

The quest of George Grenville (1712–1770), who had succeeded Pitt in 1763 as prime minister, for supplementary revenue aggravated the strained relations between the colonists and the mother country. In 1765, Parliament passed the Stamp Act, which forced Americans to purchase stamps for virtually anything printed. A year later, Benjamin Franklin (1706–1790) of Philadelphia made the colonists' case to the House of Commons. He argued that the act represented the unfair domination of England over another part of the empire. The House of Commons repealed the Stamp Act, but the government then initiated other taxes. Furthermore, Parliament proclaimed a Declaratory Act in 1766, which asserted its right to tax the colonies as it pleased. A year later, the Townshend Acts levied duties on colonial imports of paper, tea, and other products.

Some British Whigs began to identify themselves with the colonists, who took the name Whigs themselves, claiming that corruption was threatening Britain's constitutional balance between monarchy and Parliament. They saw the two movements as parallel struggles for freedom. For radicals in Britain, rotten boroughs symbolized the threat to liberty; for the American colonists, as expressed by John Adams, "liberty can no more exist without virtue and independence than the body can live and move without a soul." The colonists' claim that they were being taxed without having the right to representation played nicely into the hands of political radicals in Britain. American political pamphlets and brochures found an eager audience among British merchants, manufacturers, artisans, and others eager for representation in Parliament. Colonists lobbied in Britain, claiming that "the cause of America is the common cause of the realm . . . both countries have the same complaint, and therefore claim the same friends."

The British government was at first divided and uncertain in the face of an upsurge of demonstrations at home and agitation in the colonies. Popular protest quickly revealed the limits of the hold Britain had on its thirteen American colonies. In March 1770 in Boston, British soldiers fired on a crowd that was vociferously protesting the quartering of British troops in that city. The "Boston Massacre," which took five lives, outraged colonists. That year, George III appointed Frederick Lord North (1732–1792) as prime minister. North, an amiable, sensible man who got along well with the king, was skilled at putting together political coalitions and was a brilliant debater in the House of Commons. He sponsored the Tea Act of 1773. North hoped to aid the East India Company by allowing the company to

Paul Revere's depiction of the Boston Massacre.

ship a surplus of tea to the colonies, with the British government collecting its tariff when the tea arrived in American ports. The move would reduce the price colonists paid for tea but would maintain the British government's assertion that it could tax goods imported into the colonies. It would also threaten the interests of American smuggling, a widespread money-making operation.

On December 16, 1773, colonists dressed as Native Americans forced their way aboard British merchant ships docked in Boston and dumped the cargo of tea into the harbor. Parliament responded to the Boston Tea Party by passing the "Intolerable Acts," which announced that the port of Boston be blocked until the colonists had reimbursed the merchants and government for the tea dumped into the harbor. In September 1774, representatives from the colonies met in the First Continental Congress. Benjamin Franklin drew a distinction between "uncorrupted new states," by which he meant the colonies, and "corrupted old ones," one of which seemed to be waging war on liberty. More troops arrived from England. In April 1775, in the first open fighting between colonists and British regulars, the colonial militia held its own against British troops searching for weapons at Concord and Lexington, Massachusetts, and then in the pitched battle at Bunker Hill near Boston.

In his pamphlet *Common Sense* (1776), 100,000 copies of which circulated in the colonies, Thomas Paine (1737–1809) launched a devastating attack on the king. *Common Sense* reflected the influence of the Enlightenment, particularly Rousseau's notion of the "social contract." Paine reiterated Locke's argument that governments received "their just powers from the consent of the people." He helped convince delegates to the Second Continental Congress to adopt Thomas Jefferson's Declaration of Independence on July 4, 1776. It declared the equality of all people, based on "inalienable rights," and it asserted that the authority of government stems from the consent of the governed. It also stated that when governments violate the "unalienable rights" to "life, liberty, and the pursuit of happiness" of their people, they had the right to rebel.

American resistance became a war for independence. The Continental Congress appointed George Washington to command its troops. The British government hoped to recover the colonies at the lowest possible cost; military campaigns were therefore compromised by halfhearted and often inept leadership by the British commanders. The initial British policy of isolating and punishing the rebels quickly failed. There were too few British troops to fight a war on unfamiliar territory against an increasingly determined foe. Next, the British undertook conventional military operations. But the colonial troops simply scattered. In 1776, Washington's army managed to cross the Hudson River into New Jersey. By the time Admiral Richard Howe (1726–1799) tried to negotiate with the rebels at the end of 1776, the colonists refused to listen because they had no reason to negotiate. Washington captured Trenton that December.

In contrast to British soldiers, the colonial army was virtually self-sufficient and broadly supported by the colonists. It became far more than what a loyalist (someone who supported the British cause) dismissed as "a vagabond Army of Ragamuffins, with Paper Pay, bad Cloathes, and worse Spirits." The most significant battles of the war were fought in the classic European style of confrontations, not as engagements between hit-and-run patriots and British regulars. The brutality of the British soldiers in requisitioning goods and maintaining order in the territories they controlled was self-defeating. In the meantime, during the war more than 60,000 American loyalists left the United States, many resettling—some taking their slaves with them—in distant reaches of the British Empire, including Canada, the Caribbean, and Africa.

France signed an alliance with the American rebels in February 1778, agreeing to provide substantial loans in gold. The French monarchy realized that favorable commercial treaties with an independent United States might more than compensate for having lost all rights to territory east of the Mississippi River in 1763. Thereafter, the French navy harassed British supply routes. In 1779, Spain joined the war on the American side, hoping to recapture Gibraltar and the island of Minorca, off the east coast of Spain. Seeking to prevent the North American colonies from purchasing

Benjamin Franklin was a favorite of the French, a relationship that was representative of the alliance between America and France against the British.

Dutch supplies, the British also fought the Dutch Republic. Britain confronted the refusal of Russia, Sweden, Prussia, Portugal, and Denmark to curtail trade with the rebellious Americans.

Great Britain had overextended its capacity to wage war. Its naval advantage, the basis of its strength in modern times, had been eroded. Despite swelling the army to 190,000 men, campaigns on land went badly. On October 19, 1781, Lord Cornwallis surrendered his outnumbered army at Yorktown, Virginia, to a combined force of American and French troops. Britain officially recognized the independence of the American colonies by signing the Treaty of Versailles in 1783.

Having lost its richest colony, Great Britain did not want to lose any others. In 1774, as the resistance in the thirteen colonies became more determined, Parliament had passed the Quebec Act, in an effort to prevent tensions between the British Anglican conquerors and the Catholic population of Quebec from boiling over. The Test Act, which required all officials to take communion in the Anglican Church, was abolished in Quebec, and the Catholic Church was given the status of an established church. The British government also strengthened its control over its other colonies. The India Act (1784) created a board responsible to Parliament to which the East India Company had to report. Another parliamentary act in 1791 created more centralized administration in Canada, with a governor-general exercising far more authority than two colonial assemblies elected by restricted suffrage.

The British government looked to extend the empire further, ordering the systematic charting of the oceans and their winds and currents. James Cook (1728–1779) sailed around New Zealand and along the eastern coast of Australia in 1770, claiming half of the continent for Britain. He was killed by indigenous people upon arriving in Hawaii, showing the dangers of venturing into unfamiliar waters. In 1788 the African Institution was established in London to encourage the exploration of Australia, only some coastal regions of which were known. At the same time, British Evangelicals imagined the conversion of the peoples with whom commerce and empire brought the British into contact.

British sea power and growing commercial empire expanded global trade beyond the luxury goods that had dominated it, particularly with the beginning of the Industrial Revolution in England (see Chapter 10). English textile production began to outproduce India by many times. Mercantilism's hold on the economic thinking of states disappeared forever. Britain became the world's major supplier of capital.

In the meantime, the advent to power in 1784 of William Pitt the Younger (1759–1806) restored political stability in Britain. The next year, Pitt introduced a wide-ranging bill for political reform. It proposed to reduce the minimum tax required for the electoral franchise and to abolish thirty-six rotten boroughs, awarding their representation to manufacturing regions and cities. Opposition among the country gentlemen, as well as that of the king himself, however, led to the bill's defeat. But Pitt did manage to eliminate useless offices that had become sinecures, introduce more accurate accounting methods into government, and facilitated the collection of excise taxes. Despite the personal failings of George III, Britain emerged from the turbulent decades of the 1760s and 1770s with its constitutional monarchy strengthened.

The Parlements and the French Monarchy

In France, two interrelated struggles in the early 1770s challenged the nature of absolute rule. The first was against privileges held by nobles and other corporate groups. The second opposed royal policies and pretensions that seemed to verge on despotism. In a way, this debate somewhat paralleled political issues in Britain.

In France, reformers seeking to limit royal authority had a daunting task because of the absolute nature of monarchical rule. The kings of France nonetheless depended on the support of the parlements. These law courts were made up primarily of nobles, seated in Paris and in twelve provinces. Their principal function was to give royal edicts the force of law by registering them. By refusing to register them, the parlements could impede the functioning of the absolute state. Thus, when the king's edicts had to do with increased or new taxation, political opposition to royal policies sometimes emerged in the parlements.

The increased centralization of the French state had in itself helped create contact between more people and the officials of the king. The concept of a "public" emerged, to which the monarch was in some sense considered responsible and before which the layers of privilege in French society no longer seemed to some acceptable. The crises that embroiled the king and the parlements from the 1750s to the 1780s helped shift public opinion toward the view that the parlements represented the rights of the "nation," threatened by a monarchy that seemed to be ruling in a despotic way.

The issue of Jansenism set the parlements against royal absolutism by raising the constitutional issue of the right of the monarch to circumscribe the parlements' traditional prerogatives. The Jansenists (see Chapter 7) were a dissident group within the Catholic Church. The pope had condemned Jansenism in 1713 with the papal bull *Unigenitus*, which Louis XV supported. But Jansenists, with a considerable following in Paris, found support within some of the parlements, which identified with Jansenist resistance against what they considered the papacy's undue interference in French affairs.

The period of conflict between the parlements and the crown really began in 1749. The controller-general attempted to make the *vingtième* tax (a tax applying to both nobles and commoners) permanent, drawing heated opposition from the parlements. And the Church again sought, without success, to force the French clergy to accept the papal bull *Unigenitus*. Many bishops threatened that sacraments would be refused to laymen who did not have a certificate signed by a priest attesting that the person had made his or her confession to a priest who had accepted the papal bull. Seven years later, the pope tried to defuse the crisis by banning these certificates.

But this concession did not placate the Parlement of Paris. Many of the parlements were manipulated by a handful of Jansenist magistrates and lawyers who managed to convince their colleagues that French acceptance of the papal edict amounted to an abandonment of French sovereignty over the temporal affairs of the Church. The king, refusing to hear the parlements' grievances, made clear that he considered the parlements nothing more than rubber stamps, a means of promulgating his will. When the Jesuit order continued to crusade against Jansenism, the Parlement of Paris responded by ordering Jesuit schools closed in 1761, citing the fact that members of the order took a vow of obedience to the pope.

The successive crises over Jansenism may have weakened the authority of the French monarchy by allowing the Parlement of Paris, and several provincial parlements as well, to claim they were defending constitutional liberties and the independence of the Gallican (French) Church—since Jansenists saw themselves as part of it—against royal encroachment and against Rome. By weakening the authority of the Catholic Church in France, the crisis over Jansenism also eroded the prestige of the absolute monarchy. Jansenism ceased being a political issue after 1758, when the

Parlement of Paris won judicial authority over many ecclesiastical matters. But the self-proclaimed role of magistrates as representatives of public opinion and protectors of the sovereign political will of the nation against abuses of power was a legacy of the Jansenist crisis.

The layers of economic privilege in France had proliferated with the extension of state power, as each monarch sought revenues with increased desperation. Despite increasing calls for reform, even critics who vociferously challenged monopolies (for example, those maintained by guilds) did not intend to end privileges per se. Rather, many of them wanted a share of the privileges and wanted to eliminate "unjust" monopolies that seemed to benefit others unfairly. Wealthy commoners, enriched by the economic changes, sought the kind of privileges nobles enjoyed—above all, exemption from many kinds of taxation. Thus, the issue of taxation would mobilize some of the parlements against the monarchy because it raised questions about the layers of privilege within the French state and about the limits of absolute authority.

In 1771, Chancellor René-Nicolas de Maupeou (1714–1792) provoked the parlements by attempting to make the *vingtième* tax permanent. Many nobles feared that general tax increases might lead to peasant uprisings, in which nobles stood to lose the most. Facing mounting resistance, Louis XV abolished the parlements. He then created new, more docile law courts that would not resist royal authority, staffed by magistrates who did not own their offices.

Both sides in the conflict between the parlements and Chancellor Maupeou appealed to public opinion. A declaration of high-ranking nobles stated that the king had abused "the constitution of the government and the rights of the people" by trying to establish "a despotism without bounds, without limits, and consequently without rights." The nobility asserted its "right of assembly," recalling that "the nation, in its assemblies, had charged the parlements with defending its rights." Influenced by the ideas of the Enlightenment, lawyers called for judicial reform, religious toleration, and the end to the abuse of privilege. When the monarchy tried to silence the lawyers, the latter turned courtrooms into forums for political opposition. Lawyers explored notions of national sovereignty while putting forward the case of the parlements against the crown.

As the idea of the nation gradually entered political discourse, the possibility emerged that when the interests of the monarchy and the nation clashed, popular allegiance could ultimately pass exclusively to the nation. Some degree of popular identification with parlements as defenders of the nation against despotism would not be effaced. The Maupeou "coup" lasted only three and a half years, but it had far-reaching effects on the nature of the opposition to the monarchy. It demonstrated that the parlements were not powerful enough to protect "the nation" against royal despotism, suggesting to some that only a body such as the Estates-General, which had not been convoked since 1614, could do so.

Chancellor René-Nicolas de Maupeou (*left*) and his supporter, Anne-Robert Turgot (*right*).

Louis XV was no stranger to unpopularity. He was held to be lazy and indifferent, and rumor had him obediently following the orders of his favorite mistress. The Seven Years' War had exhausted the treasury. Furthermore, France had lost Canada and several Caribbean islands to Britain. This loss of prestige, as well as income, increased the number of the king's critics. The structures of absolute rule seemed inadequate to the task of managing and paying for the cumbersome French state.

Louis XV's death in 1774 did not resolve the crisis. Following demonstrations and a spate of publications in support of the parlements, the twenty-year-old Louis XVI (ruled 1774–1793) dismissed Maupeou and reinstated the parlements. Public opinion seemed to have helped turn back what was popularly conceived to be a despotic assault on restraints on absolute rule.

Convinced that the financial difficulties of the monarchy stemmed from the stifling effect of privileges on the economy, a new minister, Anne-Robert Turgot, undertook ambitious reforms (see Chapter 9). His goal was to cut away some of the web of privileges, thus making the monarchy more efficient. Turgot convinced the young king to issue royal edicts, despite the opposition of the Parlement of Paris. These ended noble and clerical tax exemptions, abolished the guilds, freed the internal commerce of grain (the price of which had been first set free in the 1760s), and exempted peasants from having to work a certain number of days each year repairing roads. Economic liberalization would, he hoped, increase agricultural production and manufacturing, thereby augmenting tax revenue.

But like Louis XV's attempts to override the traditional role of the parlements, Turgot's reforms aroused vociferous opposition. Nobles—with some significant exceptions—rallied against the proposed financial reforms. The parlements, still smoldering over their treatment by Maupeou and Louis XV several years earlier, refused to register—and thereby give the status of law to—the reforms of Turgot, who had supported Maupeou. Grain merchants and guilds voiced strident opposition. Ordinary people rose up in protest, blaming the freeing of the grain trade for the higher prices of flour and bread in a period of dearth. Accusations of hoarding abounded. Grain riots, in which women played the leading roles, swept across the country during the spring "flour war" of 1775. Lawyers once again insisted on the difference between absolute and despotic rule.

The king ended the most significant reform effort on the continent by dismissing Turgot in 1776. When the American colonists declared their independence from Britain, France allied with them, forcing Louis XVI to borrow ever more money at high interest rates and to sell more offices and titles (about 3,700 venal offices conferred noble title). This helped shift power within the nobility from the embittered "nobles of the sword" to "nobles of the robe," ennobled through the purchase of office or title. The latter had a different way of looking at the world, even as they embraced aristocratic privilege. The more recently ennobled families remained in some ways outsiders, their titles the result of worldly achievements, thus undercutting the very essence of noble status passed down by heredity. In the meantime, the French monarchy slid into an even deeper financial crisis.

Other Movements for Reform

In other cases, movements for reform came from below. In the Swiss Republic of Geneva, native-born artisans during 1765–1768 demanded equality with the citizens possessing political rights. They were rebuffed by wealthy Genevans, who tried to placate them with reductions in their taxes. An uprising in 1782 unseated the ruling oligarchy before the intervention of France, Sardinia, and the Swiss canton of Bern put an end to it.

In 1761, an uprising on the Mediterranean island of Corsica in the name of "fatherland and liberty" ended rule by the northern Italian port city of Genoa. France occupied Corsica seven years later. In 1770, the Greeks, with Russian assistance, rose up against Turkish domination. Russia was eager to enter the world of Mediterranean politics because it desired ultimately to conquer Constantinople. The accession of Catherine the Great in 1762 had ended a long succession crisis, palace plots, and assassinations, bringing stability to the Russian Empire. She sent an army and a small fleet in the hope that Greek success might encourage other peoples to rise up against Ottoman rule. Turkish troops crushed the revolt, but the Greek movement for independence, by virtue of the special place of classical Greece in the development of Western civilization, helped ignite Panhellenism.

In Denmark, where the king had imposed absolute rule in 1660 by suppressing the parliament and refusing to consult with the estates, a current of reform emerged early in the 1770s. In part, it was the inspiration of Johann Struensee (1737–1772), a German doctor, who convinced King Christian VII (ruled 1766–1808) to undertake reforms to strengthen the state economically so that, with Russian support, Sweden's residual Baltic ambitions could be thwarted. The king abolished censorship and the death penalty for thieves, extended religious toleration, and promised to undertake more agricultural reforms in the interests of creating a free peasantry. But the king's widowed mother and some nobles conspired against the reforms. Struensee was tried and convicted of, among other things, living "without religion or morality," and was executed in 1772. A decade later, however, the reforms Struensee had encouraged became part of a program for the future, a sign of the times.

Political struggles in the Dutch Republic—like the struggles between Whigs and the crown in Britain—were followed by the emergence of extra-parliamentary demands by ordinary people for political reform. The regents of the Dutch cities, defending the republic's federalism embodied in the Estates-General, opposed the policies of the bumbling William V of Orange (stadholder 1751–1795). The regents declared war on Britain in 1780 in the hope of weakening their commercial rival. As the war dragged on, they also sought to undercut the monarchical pretensions of William V.

In 1785, in the midst of political crisis, the Dutch Republic allied with France. The immediate goal was to counter the Austrian plan to reopen the Scheldt River and restore Antwerp to some of its former commercial glory, which would have undercut Amsterdam's prosperity. The possibility that France might annex the Southern Netherlands made the British government uneasy, further irritating the pro-British stadholder William V.

In the meantime, a radical "Patriot Party," primarily drawn from the middle class and artisans, put forward democratic reforms. Influenced by the success of the American revolutionaries, they demanded more democratic representation in the Estates. These Dutch reformers unseated the stadholder. Prussian King Frederick William II (ruled 1786–1797), whose sister was the stadholder's wife, sent an army in 1787, occupying Amsterdam and ending the challenge to William V's authority as stadholder. France seemed on the verge of offering the Patriots assistance, but distracted by a mounting political crisis, it backed down against the opposition of Prussia and Britain, powers that supported William V. The balance of power had once again been preserved. Dutch Patriot refugees poured into the Austrian Southern Netherlands and France.

The Austrian Netherlands, too, experienced political turmoil. Powerful nobles opposed to Austrian King Joseph II's enlightened reforms, which threatened their privileges, drove out Austrian troops in 1789. In the Austrian Netherlands, too, a movement for democratic reform emerged, calling for the transformation of the Estates into a representative assembly.

The Dutch (and, as we will see, French) mood seemed to be catching. Dutch Patriots invaded the Southern Netherlands in October 1789, driving away the Austrians. But a popular movement appealed to the nobles even less than did Austrian rule. Backed by the clergy and with the tacit support of most peasants, the nobles wrested control of the short-lived state from the urban-based reformers. The return of Austrian troops in 1790 occurred without resistance.

DECLINING POWER, DISAPPEARING STATE: THE OTTOMAN EMPIRE AND POLAND

The structure of international power in eighteenth-century Europe was not fundamentally changed by the quest for reform during the 1760s and 1770s. But in the new, more competitive European environment of the late eighteenth century, two other states that did not have access to the fruits of international trade and that were unwilling to restructure themselves lost their power in Europe: the Turkish Ottoman Empire and Poland. The Ottoman Empire, its power overextended and lacking a centralized structure of government, began to decline slowly but surely as its territories in the Balkans and Caucasus were eaten away by Austria and Russia. Poland, in which reforms had arguably come too late, fell prey to its aggressive absolutist neighbors: Russia, Prussia, and Austria, which divided up the state in three partitions in 1772, 1793, and 1795.

The Decline of Ottoman Turkish Power in Europe

In contrast to other absolute sovereigns, the Ottoman Turkish sultans ruled indirectly, governing through Islamic or village officials. Indeed, indirect rule itself may ultimately have hastened the decline of Ottoman absolutism. Like the Spanish Empire at its peak, the Ottoman domains were so extensive that they defied effective control. Insurrections, including some by the janissaries, the once-loyal court militia now increasingly subject to the influence of local elites, challenged the authority of the sultans—whose government in Constantinople became known as the Porte. Imperial officials, Muslim and Christian Orthodox alike, became notoriously corrupt, including the Greek-educated Phanariots, who served the sultans by collecting taxes, while making their families very wealthy. As the system of indirect rule declined in effectiveness, some local Christian and Muslim leaders commanded their own military forces, virtually independent of the sultan's authority in Constantinople. Sultans awarded large estates to those who served them well. This was precisely the same phenomenon that the absolute monarchs of France, Prussia, Russia, and Austria had overcome. However, the Ottoman Empire did not have a hereditary aristocracy. And unlike Russia and parts of Central and Eastern Europe, peasants within the

Sultan Selim III in his palace in Istanbul, with a line of followers stretching in front of him. The Turkish sultans ruled indirectly over a vast network of domains, a tactic that may have hastened the decline of Ottoman absolutism.

empire were free. But Turkish authority virtually collapsed in mountainous Montenegro and Bosnia, where the Turks battled Habsburg and Venetian forces. The government began to run out of money. Stop-gap measures, such as the debasement of the currency, failed to provide sufficient revenue.

Incapable sultans unwilling or unable to impose reforms further weakened the Ottoman Empire. As boys they lived in virtual isolation in a world of uncertainty among court eunuchs and palace intrigue. No regular pattern of succession had ever been established. Whereas Peter the Great of Russia undertook Western military reforms, the sultans did not. The Turkish economy, army, and navy could not keep pace with the Western powers. Turkish cavalrymen, with curved swords and magnificent horses, fell before Western artillery. The advice of officials who had been sent to Vienna and Paris to study methods of state went unheeded in Constantinople. Long wars fought against Persia in the east made it more difficult to repress disturbances in the Balkans. In some parts of the empire, a system of land inheritance replaced the old system, and new landowners began to force peasants into serfdom. European merchants took over Ottoman sea trade. The haphazard and inefficient collection of taxes, increasingly by dishonest tax farmers, engendered peasant resistance. As in the cases of China and Japan, Ottomans and the scholar class (*ulama*) showed little interest in Western ideas or technology. The single printing press in the empire, which dated only from the 1720s, was shut down sixty years later; no newspaper was published until 1828, and that in Cairo, not Istanbul. The classical literary tradition, as in China and Japan, continued to hold sway. The long decline of Ottoman power in Europe began when the Turks were turned back at the gates of Vienna in 1683. Austria's subsequent conquest of Hungary and Transylvania was confirmed by the Treaty of Carlowitz in 1699. However, the Turks continued to control the Black Sea by virtue of holding Constantinople and the straits. Major Ottoman defeats left the way open for continued Russian expansion. Although the Ottomans took advantage of inter-European wars to maintain their peripheral territories, in the 1760s this began to change. In 1774, following the destruction of the Turkish fleet in the Black Sea, the Ottoman Turks granted Russia the right to oversee Turkish authority in the Danubian principalities and to serve as the official protector of Christians living within its empire. In the meantime, in Morocco, Algiers, Tripoli, and Tunis, which remained nominally part of the Ottoman Empire, local dynasties set up shop. Yet we should not exaggerate the decline of the Ottoman Empire, which remained a power capable of effectively defending its interests well into the nineteenth century.

The Partitions of Poland

While the Ottoman Empire survived, Poland did not endure as an independent state (at least until the end of World War I). Poland was, for all intents and purposes, a republic. It had a king who was elected by citizens, a Senate (which included bishops and other important personages), and an elected Chamber of Deputies (the Sejm). The Sejm, which met every two years but which the king could convene in an emergency, elected the king for life and retained the right to pass laws, approve taxes, and ratify treaties. The king could not travel out of the country without the approval of the Sejm. Moreover, the "liberum veto" ("I freely forbid") accentuated the influence of the wealthiest nobles, who sometimes combined forces to block legislation. The rise of even more powerful aristocrats who owned vast estates exacerbated the impact of the "liberum veto" within the Sejm, preventing reforms that might have strengthened Poland.

During the first decades of the eighteenth century, the kingdom, its population reduced by wars and bubonic plague to only 6 million people, became increasingly dependent on Russia. Indeed, Poland's eclipse made possible Russia's gains in Ukraine. The War of Polish Succession (1733–1735) began when Russia attempted to impose its candidate on the Polish throne over the opposition of the Polish nobles. Because of France's interest in maintaining Sweden, the Ottoman Empire, and Poland as checks against

Austrian Habsburg domination of Central Europe, Louis XV proposed a candidate for the throne, his father-in-law, Stanislas Lesczinski, who had reigned as king of Poland from 1704 to 1709 and now had the support of most Polish nobles. But a Russian army forced the election of Augustus III of Saxony (ruled 1733–1763), the Austro-Russian candidate.

In 1763, the Polish throne again fell vacant with the death of Augustus III. A long period of legislative stagnation that accompanied the conflict between the Sejm and the Saxon kings ended the following year when the Sejm, reflecting Russian influence, elected as king the cultured, cosmopolitan Stanislas Poniatowski (ruled 1764–1795), one of the many lovers of the insatiable Russian Empress Catherine the Great ("many were called, and many were chosen," as one wag put it). Stanislas was somewhat influenced by Enlightenment thought. Sensing the necessity of reform, he hoped to advance manufacturing in Poland and looked to Britain as a model. He tried to end the liberum veto and to curtail the right of seigneurial courts to impose death sentences. He also established a number of schools. Only by such measures, he believed, could Poland escape poverty and backwardness. But some of the more powerful Polish nobles, who resented Russian influence, now opposed Stanislas and his reforms. They hoped that the French monarch or the Ottoman sultan might intervene on their behalf.

Catherine, like the Prussian king, feared that Stanislas's reforms might lead to a stronger, less subservient neighbor. Since 1764, Russia and Prussia had worked against an expansion of French influence in the Baltic, while preventing Poland from reviving its fortunes. Furthermore, Polish nobles had begun to persecute non-Catholics. Catherine, in the interest of the Orthodox Church, demanded that all non-Catholics be granted toleration in Poland. When Polish nobles formed an anti-Russian and anti-Orthodox confederation, Catherine sent troops into Poland. Ukrainian peasants took advantage of the chaos to rise up against their Polish lords. When they burned a Turkish town while chasing out Poles, Turkey entered the war against Russia (1768–74). Catherine annexed Wallachia and achieved Russia's dream since Peter the Great by reaching the Black Sea, annexing several territories at Turkish expense. In 1783, the Crimean peninsula, too, became part of the Russian Empire.

Alarmed by the expansion of the Russian Empire, Austria and Prussia demanded territorial compensation. Catherine suggested that the three powers might help themselves to parts of Poland. The First Partition in 1772 reduced Poland by about a third (see Map 11.3). Maria Theresa of Austria "wept and then took her share," the large province of Galicia, which lay between Russian Ukraine and Austria. Prussia absorbed West Prussia, which had formed a corridor separating East Prussia from the rest of the kingdom. Russia snatched large chunks of territory of eastern Poland.

The Polish Diet in 1791 voted what arguably was the first written constitution in Europe, a liberal document that established a hereditary monar-

MAP 11.3 THE PARTITIONS OF POLAND Poland at its greatest extent in 1660–1667, and the loss of territory to Austria, Prussia, and Russia during the Partitions of 1772, 1793, and 1795.

chy, abolished the system of noble veto, and proclaimed that all authority stemmed from the nation. Reflecting the influence of the French Revolution (see Chapter 12), Poland became a constitutional monarchy, with the king naming ministers but with the parliament and Poland's major towns retaining privileges.

But Poland's days were numbered as an independent state, particularly given the fact that its old protector, France, was in the throes of revolution and had lost influence in East Central Europe. When Poles rose up in 1792 against Russian authority in the part of Poland that had been absorbed by Russia twenty years earlier, Russian troops intervened. They were backed by Polish nobles who opposed the liberal constitution. Prussia refused to come to Poland's aid, receiving in exchange for looking the other way annexation of more Polish territory in the Second Partition in 1793. With the Third Partition in 1795, Prussia and Russia ended Poland's independence for more than a century. The Constitution of 1791, perhaps the most progressive constitution of the century, was torn to shreds. Russia's new gains drew its interests farther into Central Europe, and it now shared a border with the Habsburg monarchy. Poles were now subject to the authority of three different states. In the lands acquired by Prussia, serfs gained some protection against abuses by landlords, but, as in the case of lands absorbed into the Habsburg Empire, the Polish secondary-school system was ended, imposing the German language.

Conclusion

Some historians have argued that movements against absolutism and against privilege, such as the political unrest in Great Britain and the successful rebellion of its North American colonies, constituted a general Western "democratic revolution." But despite the quest for political change in several Western states, demands for universal male suffrage were rare, and calls for the extension of political rights to women even more so (an exception being Geneva in the early 1780s). Even in Britain, after a contentious decade marked by demonstrations for political reform, the most widespread riots of the 1780s were the anti-Catholic Gordon riots. In France, calls for reform were less an attack on the nobles, per se, than on privilege. The institutions of the Old Regime in continental Europe demonstrated not only resiliency, but also some capacity to undertake reform.

Nonetheless, denunciations in France against privilege, shaped in part by Enlightenment thought, would be revived in the late 1780s. The Seven Years' War and assistance to the Americans worsened the financial crisis of the French monarchy, as the increasingly global dynastic rivalries and wars placed further strains on European states. France entered a serious political crisis when critics of the monarchy accused the king of ruling despotically and attacked the layers of economic and social privilege that seemed to constrain effective government and constrict freedom. Demands for sweeping reform led to the French Revolution of 1789, which proclaimed the principle of the sovereignty of the nation. Once again, the eyes of Europe turned toward France.

PART FOUR

REVOLUTIONARY EUROPE, 1789–1850

The French Revolution of 1789 struck the first solid blow in continental Western Europe against monarchical absolutism on behalf of popular sovereignty. The roots of revolution extend back to the second half of the seventeenth century, an era of hitherto unparalleled absolute monarchical authority. The monarchs of France, Russia, Prussia, Austria, Spain, and Sweden had reinforced their authority to the extent that they stood clearly above any internal challenge to their power. Compliant nobles served as junior partners in absolutism, acknowledging the ruler's absolute power to proclaim laws, assess taxes, and raise armies, in exchange for royal recognition of their noble standing and protection against popular revolts. The governments of Great Britain and the Dutch United Provinces stood in sharp contrast to absolute states. In the English Civil War in the 1640s, Parliament had successfully turned aside the possibility of absolute monarchy in England, leading to the execution of King Charles II, followed after some years of turmoil by the Restoration of constitutional monarchy. In the Netherlands, the Dutch revolt against absolutist Spain led to the establishment of the Dutch Republic. The theory of popular sovereignty developed not only as an alternative to absolute rule but also as an extension of constitutional rule. In the dramatic events of the French Revolution that began in 1789, the theory of popular sovereignty became reality as ordinary people helped bring about the downfall of absolute rule and then, three years later, the monarchy itself.

True popular sovereignty was a short-lived experiment, however, as counter-revolution and foreign intervention led to the dramatic centralization of state authority. In 1799, Napoleon Bonaparte helped overthrow the Directory, the last regime of

the revolutionary era in France. An admirer of the Enlightenment, Napoleon claimed that he was the heir of the French
Revolution. But while Napoleon saw himself as a savior who
carried "liberty, equality, and fraternity" abroad, his conquest of
much of Europe before his final defeat left a mixed legacy for
the future. More than a fifth of all the significant battles that
took place in Europe from 1490 to 1815 occurred between the
coming of the French Revolution and Napoleon's final defeat in
1815.

Following Napoleon's defeat in 1815 at the Battle of Waterloo,
the Congress of Vienna created the Concert of Europe, the international basis of Restoration Europe, in the hope of preventing
further liberal and nationalist insurrections in Europe. But liberal and nationalist movements could not so easily be swept away.
During the subsequent three decades, "liberty" became the
watchword for more and more people, particularly among the
middle classes, who came to the forefront of economic, political,
and cultural life. Liberal movements were in many places closely
tied to the emergence of nationalism, the belief in the primacy of
nationality as a source of allegiance and sovereignty.

In the meantime, during the first half of the nineteenth century, the Industrial Revolution slowly but surely transformed the
way many Europeans lived. Dramatic improvements in transportation, notably the development of the railroad but also road
improvements, expanded the market for manufactured and other
goods. Rising agricultural production, increasingly commercialized in Western Europe, fed a larger population. Migrants poured
into Europe's cities, which grew as never before. Contemporaries,
particularly in Western Europe, sensed profound economic,
social, political, and cultural changes.

CHAPTER 12

THE FRENCH REVOLUTION

In 1791, King Louis XVI decided to flee Paris and the French Revolution. A virtual prisoner in the Tuileries Palace by the first months of the year, he had secretly negotiated for possible intervention on his behalf by the Austrian king and other European monarchs. The royal family furtively left the Tuileries Palace late at night on June 20, 1791, disguised as the family and entourage of a Russian baroness riding in a large black coach with yellow trim. But in an eastern town, the postmaster recognized the king, whose image he had seen on a coin. He rode rapidly to the town of Varennes, where the National Guard prevented the king's coach from going on. Three representatives of the National Assembly brought the royal family back to Paris. Near the capital, the crowds became threatening, and national guardsmen stood by the roadside with their rifles upside down, a sign of contempt or mourning.

The French Revolution mounted the first effective challenge to monarchical absolutism on behalf of popular sovereignty. The creation of a republican government in France and the diffusion of republican ideals in other European countries influenced the evolution of European political life long after the Revolution ended. Issues of the rights of the people, the role of the state in society, the values of democratic society, notions of "left" and "right" in political life, the concept of the "nation at arms," the place of religion in modern society and politics, and the question of economic freedom and the sanctity of property came to dominate the political agenda. They occupied the attention of much of France during the revolutionary decade of 1789–1799. The political violence of that decade would also be a legacy for the future.

The revolutionaries sought to make the French state more centralized and efficient, as well as more just. Napoleon Bonaparte, whom some historians consider the heir to the Revolution and others believe to be its betrayer, continued this process after his ascent to power in 1799.

Modern nationalism, too, has its roots in the French Revolution. The revolutionaries enthusiastically proclaimed principles they held to be universal. Among these were the sovereignty of the nation and the rights and duties of citizenship. The revolutionaries celebrated the fact that the Revolution had occurred in France. But wars intended to free European peoples from monarchical and noble domination turned into wars of French conquest. The revolutionary wars, pitting France against the other great powers, contributed to the emergence or extension of nationalism in other countries as well, ranging from Great Britain, where the sense of being British flourished in response to the French threat, to central and southern Europe, where some educated Germans and Italians began to espouse nationalism in response to the invading French armies.

THE OLD REGIME IN CRISIS

The French Revolution was not inevitable. Yet difficult economic conditions in the preceding two decades, combined with the growing popularity of a discourse that stressed freedom in the face of entrenched economic and social privileges, made some sort of change seem possible, perhaps even likely. When a financial crisis occurred in the 1780s and the king was forced to call the Estates-General, the stage was set for the confrontation that would culminate in the French Revolution.

Long-Term Causes of the French Revolution

The increasing prevalence of the language of the Enlightenment, stressing equality before the law and differentiating between absolute and despotic rule, placed the monarchy and its government under the closer scrutiny of public opinion. Adopting Enlightenment discourse, opponents accused Louis XV of acting despotically when he exiled the Parlement of Paris in 1771 and tried to establish new law courts that were likely to be more subservient than the *parlements*, the sovereign law courts, had been. Opponents believed that the king was trying to subvert long-accepted privileges. Following Louis XV's death in 1774, the young Louis XVI reinstated the parlements, which retained their right to register royal edicts.

As complaints mounted about noble privileges, guild monopolies, and corrupt royal officials, the implications of Enlightenment thought led to political action. In 1774, Controller-General of Finances Anne-Robert Turgot drew up a program to eliminate some monopolies and privileges that fettered the economy (see Chapter 11). However, the decree abolishing the guilds, among other decrees, generated immediate hostility from nobles, the Parlement of Paris, and from ordinary people, who rioted in Paris in 1775 because the freeing of the grain trade had brought higher prices in hard times. Two years later, Turgot's experiment ended. But some writers now began to contrast the freedoms Turgot had in mind with the corporate privileges that characterized the economy and society of eighteenth-century France.

France remained a state of overlapping layers of privileges, rights, traditions, and jurisdictions. Nobles and professional groups such as guilds and tax farmers (who generally had bought their offices and could pocket some of the taxes they collected) contested any plan to eliminate privileges. At the same time, the social lines of demarcation between nobles and wealthy commoners had become less fixed over the course of the eighteenth century. Despite increasing opposition from the oldest noble families who believed their ranks were being swamped by newcomers, in the fifteen years before 1789 almost 2,500 families bought their way into the nobility. Yet many people of means, too, resented noble privileges, above all the exemption of nobles from most kinds of taxes. Disgruntled commoners did not make the French Revolution, but their dissatisfaction helped create a litany of demands for reform. The monarchy's worsening financial crisis accentuated these calls.

The sharpest resistance to reform came from the poorer nobility. Among the "nobles of the sword," the oldest noble families whose ancestors had proudly taken arms to serve the king, some had fallen on hard times and clung frantically to any and all privileges as a way of maintaining their status. They resented the fact that the provincial parlements, in particular, had filled up with new nobles who had purchased offices—the "nobles of the robe"—and that power had shifted within the nobility from the oldest noble families to those recently ennobled.

The monarchy depended upon the sale of titles, offices, and economic monopolies for revenue and long-term credit. But by creating more offices—there were more than 50,000 offices in 1789—it risked destroying public confidence and driving down the value of offices already held.

Economic hardship compounded the monarchy's financial problems by decreasing revenue while exacerbating social tensions. Rising prices and rents darkened the 1770s and 1780s. A series of bad harvests—the worst of which occurred in 1775—made conditions of life even more difficult for poor people. The harvests of 1787 and 1788, which would be key years in the French political drama, were also very poor. Such crises were by no means unusual—indeed they were cyclical and would continue until the middle of the next century. Meager harvests generated popular resistance to taxation and protests against the high price of grain (and therefore bread). A growing population put more pressure on scarce resources.

Many peasants believed that their hardship was being increased by landowners. Something of a "seigneurial reaction" was under way as smaller agricultural yields diminished noble revenues, while inflation raised the costs of noble life. Noble landowners hired estate agents, lawyers, and surveyors to maximize income from their lands, and reasserted old rights over common lands, on which many poor peasants depended for pasturing animals and gathering wood for fuel. Many landlords raised rents and tried to force share-cropping arrangements on peasants who had previously rented land.

Although the feudal system of the Middle Ages had long since passed, remnants remained. Peasants were still vexed by seigneurial dues and cash owed to their lords. Many nobles still held some rights of justice over their peasants, which meant that they could determine guilt and assess penalties for alleged transgressions. Seigneurial courts were often used to enforce the landlord's rights over forests, lakes, and streams, and his exclusive rights to hunt and fish on his estate. The political crisis that led to the French Revolution would provide ordinary people with an opportunity to redress some of these mounting grievances.

The Financial Crisis

The serious financial crisis that confronted the monarchy in the 1780s was the short-term cause of the French Revolution. France had been at war with Britain, as well as with other European powers, off and on for more than a century. The financial support France had provided the rebel colonists in the American War of Independence against Britain had been underwritten by loans arranged by the king's Swiss minister of finance, Jacques Necker (1732–1804). Almost three-fourths of state expenses went to maintaining the army and navy, and to paying off debts accumulated from the War of the Austrian Succession (1740–1748) and the Seven Years' War (1756–1763), as well as from the American War of Independence. The monarchy was living beyond its means.

Where were more funds to be found? Nobles had traditionally enjoyed the privilege of being exempt from most, and the clergy from all, taxation. There was a limit to how many taxes could be imposed on peasants, by far the largest social group in France. In short, the financial crisis of the monarchy was closely tied to the very nature of its fiscal system.

The absolute monarchy in France collected taxes less efficiently than did the British government. In Britain, the Bank of England facilitated the government's borrowing of money at relatively low interest through the national debt. In France, there was no central bank, and the monarchy depended more than ever on private interests and suffered from a cumbersome assessment of fiscal obligations and inadequate accounting. French public debt already was much higher than that of Britain and continued to rise as the monarchy sought financial expedients.

The hesitant and naive Louis XVI was still in his twenties when he became king in 1774. Louis knew little of his kingdom, venturing beyond the region of Paris and Versailles only once during his reign. He preferred puttering around the palace, taking clocks and watches apart and putting them back together. He excelled at hunting. The unpopularity of Louis's elegant, haughty wife, Marie-Antoinette (1755–1793), accentuated the public's lack of confidence in the throne (whether or not she really snarled "Let them eat

(*Left*) Louis XVI. (*Right*) Marie-Antoinette.

cake!" when told that the people had no bread). The daughter of the Austrian queen Maria Theresa, Marie-Antoinette was married to Louis to strengthen dynastic ties between Austria and France. She never felt really at home in France. Unhappy in her marriage, Marie-Antoinette lived extravagantly and was embroiled in controversy. In 1785, she became entangled in a seamy scandal when a cardinal offered her a fabulous diamond necklace in the hope of winning favor. The necklace and some of the prelate's money were then deftly stolen by plotters, a strange scenario that included a prostitute posing as the queen. The "diamond necklace affair," as it was called, seemed to augment the public image of the king as a weak man, a cuckold. The queen's reputed indiscretions and infidelities seemed to undercut the authority of the monarchy itself. Her detractors indelicately dubbed her the "Austrian whore."

In the meantime, Necker continued to float more loans. But in 1781, some ministers and noble hangers-on convinced the king to dismiss Necker. Necker produced a fanciful account of the royal finances that purported to demonstrate that more revenue was coming to the state than was being spent. Necker hoped to reassure creditors that reform was unnecessary. Bankers, however, did not believe Necker's figures and some refused to loan the monarchy any more money until the state enacted financial reforms. The new finance minister, Charles-Alexandre de Calonne (1734–1802), demonstrated that Necker's calculations of royal finances were far-fetched. Yet Calonne spent even more money and put the royal treasury deeper in debt by borrowing from venal officeholders to pay off creditors now gathered at the royal door.

The parlements were certain to oppose fiscal reform, which they believed would lead to an increase in taxation through a general tax on land. They distrusted Calonne, whom they identified with fiscal irresponsibility and governmental arrogance that some believed bordered on despotism.

To sidestep the parlements, Calonne asked the king in February 1787 to convoke an Assembly of Notables consisting of handpicked representatives from each of the three estates: clergy, nobility, and the third estate (everybody else). The crown expected the Assembly to endorse its reform proposals, including new land taxes from which nobles would not be exempt. Calonne suggested that France's financial problems were systemic, resulting from a chaotic administrative organization, including the confusing regional differences in tax obligations. The monarchy's practice of selling the lucrative rights to collect, or "farm," taxes worsened the inefficiency. Calonne knew that the crown's contract with the tax farmers would soon have to be renegotiated, and that many short-term loans contracted by the monarchy would soon come due.

Denouncing "the dominance of custom" that had for so long prevented reform and encumbered commerce, Calonne proposed to overhaul the entire financial system. The Assembly of Notables, however, rejected Calonne's proposals for tax reform and refused to countenance the idea that nobles should be assessed land taxes. Moreover, the high clergy of the first estate, some of whom were nobles, also vociferously opposed Calonne's reforms. They, too, feared losing their exemption from taxation. The privilege-based nature of French society was at stake.

Nobles convinced the king to sack Calonne, which he did on April 8, 1788. Louis XVI replaced Calonne with the powerful archbishop of Toulouse, Étienne-Charles de Loménie de Brienne (1727–1794). Like his predecessor, Loménie de Brienne asked the provincial parlements to register—and thus approve—several edicts of financial reform, promising that the government would keep more accurate accounts. But the Parlement of Paris refused to register some of the edicts, including a new land tax and a stamp tax, which evoked the origins of the American Revolution.

The First Stages of the Revolution

Some members of the Assembly of Notables had been willing to accept fiscal reform and to pay more taxes, but only with accompanying institutional reforms that would guarantee their privileges. They wanted the king to convoke regular assemblies of the Estates-General—made up of representatives of the three estates—which had not been convoked since 1614. The king was in a difficult position. He needed to reduce the privileges of the nobles to solve the financial crisis, but to do so without their approval would lead to accusations of despotism, or even tyranny, the sometimes violent implementation of the structures of despotic authority. On the other hand, capitulating to the demands of the privileged classes in return for new taxes would compromise his absolute authority and suggest that his word was subject to the approval of the nation, or at least the nobility. The resolution of this dilemma would lead to the events that constituted the first stages of the French Revolution.

Convoking the Estates-General

The "noble revolt" began the French Revolution. In response to the refusal of the Parlement of Paris to register the land and stamp taxes, in August 1787 Louis XVI exiled its members to Troyes, a town east of Paris. Nobles and high clergymen protested vigorously. The provincial parlements backed up the Parlement of Paris. The Parlement of Grenoble refused to register the new stamp and land taxes and convoked its provincial estates (the assembly of nobles that represented the interests of the region) without royal authorization. The "revolt of the nobility" against the monarchy's attempt to force nobles to pay taxes spread. Provincial parlements demanded that the Estates-General be convoked. This revolt was not directed against the institution of the monarchy itself, but against what the nobles considered abuses of the rights and privileges of the nation committed by an increasingly despotic crown.

The monarchy sought compromise. Loménie de Brienne agreed to withdraw the new land and stamp taxes in exchange for maintaining the tax on income (the *vingtième* tax), which nobles and other privileged people had first been assessed in the late 1750s to pay for the Seven Years' War. He made clear, however, that the crown would be forced to settle its debts in paper money backed by royal decree. Louis XVI recalled the Parlement of Paris from exile in November 1787. But the king ordered new loan edicts registered without giving the parlement a chance to be heard. When the duke of Orléans, the king's cousin, interjected that such a procedure was illegal, Louis replied, "That is of no importance to me . . . it is legal because I will it." Louis XVI thus seemed to cross the line between absolutism and despotism.

In May 1788, the king ordered the arrest of two of the most radical members of the Parlement of Paris. He then suspended the parlements, establishing new provincial courts to take their place and creating a single plenary court that would register royal edicts. Resistance to the king's acts against the parlements came quickly. The Assembly of the Clergy, which had been summoned to decide on the amount of its annual gift to the crown, protested the abolition of the parlements. Riots in support of the parlements occurred in several towns, including Grenoble, where crowds expressed support for their parlement by pelting soldiers with stones and roof tiles.

On August 8, 1788, Louis XVI announced that he would convoke the Estates-General on May 1 of the following year. He hoped that he could avert royal bankruptcy if the Estates-General would agree to the imposition of the new taxes. Two weeks later, he reappointed Necker as minister of finance, a measure he believed would appease nobles, investors, and holders of government bonds, who had never objected to unrestrained borrowing.

But the convocation of the Estates-General helped unify public opinion against the king. That the nobles forced the crown to convoke the Estates-General became the first act of the French Revolution. Many people believed that the Estates-General, more than the parlements, would represent their interests and check royal despotism.

The question of how voting was to take place when the Estates-General met assumed increasing importance. Would each of the three estates—clergy, nobles, and the third estate—have a single vote (which would almost certainly quash any reform since the majority of nobles and clergymen were against reform), or would each member of the Estates-General be entitled to his own vote?

On September 25, 1788, the Parlement of Paris, which had been reinstated amid great celebration, ruled that voting within the Estates-General would take place by estate, as had been the case when the Estates-General had last met in 1614. Thus each of the three estates would have the same number of representatives and be seated separately. Henceforth, the parlements would be seen by many people as defending the prerogatives of their privileged members against the interests of the third estate, losing their claim to defend the nation against the king's despotism for having registered the royal decree that voting would be by estate.

Popular political writers now began to salute the third estate (which made up 95 percent of the population) as the true representative of liberty and of the nation against royal despotism. Others asked for some sort of representative assembly that would reflect "public opinion." The "patriot party," a coalition of bourgeois members and some liberal nobles, began to oppose royal policies, which they contrasted with the rights of the "nation." "Patriots" denounced the vested interests of the court and the nobles close to it. Political publications transformed these debates into national political issues. The Society of the Thirty, a group that included liberal nobles from very old families—for example, the Marquis de Lafayette (1757–1834), French hero of the American War of Independence—as well as a number of commoner lawyers, met to discuss, debate, and distribute liberal political pamphlets. They proposed that the third estate be entitled to twice as many representatives in the Estates-General as the nobility and clergy.

In January 1789, Emmanuel Joseph Sieyès (1748–1836), an obscure priest, offered the most radical expression of a crucial shift in political opinion. "We have three questions to ask and answer," he wrote. "First, What is the Third Estate? Everything. Second, What has it been heretofore in the political order? Nothing. Third, What does it demand? To become something therein." He contrasted the "nation" against royal absolutism and noble prerogative, demanding a predominant role for the third estate in political life.

The vast majority of the men elected to the Estates-General were residents of cities and towns, and two-thirds of these had some training in the law. Two-thirds of those elected to the first estate were parish priests, many of whom were of humble origin and resented the privileges of the bishops

(*Left*) The Marquis de Lafayette. (*Right*) The Abbé Sieyès.

and monastic orders. Some of the younger noble representatives elected to the second estate were relatively liberal. They wanted institutional reforms in the organization of the French monarchy that would permit them to check the power of the king, in much the same way as the Parliament in England served as a check on the English crown. In December 1788, the king agreed to double the number of representatives of the third estate but declined to give all members an individual vote.

The king asked the local assemblies, along with the first two estates, to draw up lists of grievances (*cahiers de doléances*), which the Estates-General would discuss. Thousands of grievances offered the monarchy a wide variety of opinions, ranging from concrete suggestions for reform to the considered opinion that the foul breath of sheep was ruining pastureland in Lorraine. More important, *cahiers* criticized monarchical absolutism and the intransigence of seigneurs, asked for a more consistent and equitable tax structure, and called for the creation of a new national representative body. A few of the *cahiers* denounced as an abuse of royal power the so-called *lettres de cachet*, documents issued in the name of the king that allowed a person to be arrested for any reason and imprisoned indefinitely. For example, one *cahier* demanded "that no citizen lose his liberty except according to law." However, some *cahiers* also reflected continued reverence for the king, while denouncing the rapacity and bad faith of his advisers and ministers. Most *cahiers* never reached the king.

On May 5, 1789, the nearly 1,200 members of the Estates-General (about 600 of whom represented the third estate) assembled at Versailles. The king greeted the first two estates, but kept the commoners waiting for two hours. When he finished his speech, members of the third estate violated protocol by boldly putting their hats back on, a right reserved for the two privileged orders. On June 17, the third estate overwhelmingly approved a motion by Sieyès that declared the third estate to be the "National Assembly" and the true representative of national sovereignty. The third estate now claimed legitimate sovereignty and an authority parallel, if not superior, to that of the king of France.

But, on June 20, as rumors circulated that the king might take action against them, representatives of the third estate found that their meeting hall had been locked for "repairs." Led by their president, Jean-Sylvain Bailly (1736–1793), an astronomer, the members of the third estate took the bold step of assembling in a nearby tennis court. There they took an oath "not to separate, and to reassemble wherever circumstances require, until the constitution of the kingdom is established and consolidated upon solid foundations." With principled defiance, the third estate demanded that defined limits be placed on the king's authority.

The king declared the third estate's deliberations invalid. Yet on June 23 he announced some substantial reforms, agreeing to convoke periodically the Estates-General, to abolish the *taille* (the tax on land) and the *corvée* (labor tax), to eliminate internal tariffs and tolls that interfered with trade, and to eliminate the *lettres de cachet*. He also agreed that the Estates-General would vote by head, but only on matters that did not concern "the ancient and constitutional rights of the three orders." To the radicalized members of the third estate, the king's concessions were not enough.

The Tennis Court Oath, June 20, 1789.

Louis XVI had dismissed Necker on June 22, but reversed himself after learning that thousands of people in Paris had invaded the courtyard of the Tuileries Palace in Paris to demand that Necker stay on. Necker's contention in 1781 that the kingdom's finances could be put on an even keel without raising taxes had increased his popularity, as had the fact that nobles were pushing for his recall. During these days, most of the clergy and a number of nobles had joined the third estate. Now, after threatening to dissolve the Estates-General by force, on June 27 the king ordered the remaining clergy and nobles of the first two estates to join the third. The new gathering began to constitute itself as the National Constituent Assembly.

Storming of the Bastille

Amid a shortage of food and high prices, many ordinary people now believed that a conspiracy by nobles and hoarders was to blame. Furthermore, the number of royal troops around Paris and Versailles seemed to be increasing. Rumors spread that the National Assembly would be quashed. On July 11, the king once again ordered Necker, who remained unpopular with the court, into exile. He and other ministers were dismissed because the king was convinced they were unable to control the demands for change coming from the Estates-General. Bands of rioters attacked the customs barriers at the gates of Paris, tearing down toll booths where taxes on goods entering the city were collected, thus making foodstuffs more expensive.

On the morning of July 14, 1789, thousands of people—mostly trades-men, artisans, and wage earners—seized weapons stored in the Invalides, a large veterans' hospital. Early that afternoon, the attention of the Paris crowd turned toward the Bastille, a fortress on the eastern edge of the city, where the crowd believed powder and ammunition were stored. For most of the eighteenth century, the Bastille had been a prison, renowned as a symbol of despotism because some prisoners had been sent there by virtue of one of the king's *lettres de cachet,* summarily and without a trial. On that hot sum-mer day, the Bastille's prisoners numbered but seven, a motley crew that included a nobleman imprisoned upon request of his family, a renegade priest, and a demented Irishman, who alternately thought he was Joan of Arc, Saint Louis, and God.

The crowd stormed and captured the Bastille, which was defended by a small garrison. More than 200 of the attackers were killed or wounded. A butcher decapitated the commander of the fortress, and the throng carried his head on a pike in triumph through the streets. The Bastille's fall would be much more significant than it first appeared. The king entered "nothing new" in his diary for that day, July 14. But the crowd's uprising probably saved the National Assembly from being dissolved by the troops the king had ordered to Versailles and Paris. Now unsure of the loyalty of his soldiers, Louis sent away some of the troops he had summoned to Paris, recognized both the newly elected municipal government, with Bailly serving as mayor,

The taking of the Bastille, July 14, 1789.

and a municipal defense force or National Guard (commanded by the Marquis de Lafayette), and capitulated to the popular demand that he recall Necker to office.

On July 17, 1789, the king came to Paris to be received by the municipal council at the town hall, accepting and wearing an emblem of three colors, red and blue for the city of Paris, and white for the Bourbons. By doing so, Louis XVI seemed to be recognizing what became the tricolor symbol of the French Revolution.

The Great Fear and the Night of August 4

News of the convocation of the Estates-General had brought hope to many rural people that the king would relieve their crushing fiscal burdens. They had expressed such hopes in the grievances they sent with their third estate delegates to Versailles. Now, upon news of the fall of the Bastille, between July 19 and August 3 peasants attacked châteaux. In some places they burned title deeds specifying obligations owed to lords. These peasant rebellions helped cause a subsequent panic known as the "Great Fear." Fueled by the rumor of an aristocratic "famine plot" to starve or burn out the population, peasants and townspeople mobilized in many regions of France. To repel the rumored approach of brigands sent to destroy crops, townspeople and peasants formed armed units to defend themselves and save the harvest. New local governments and National Guard units were established to institute reforms and to restore order as the effective authority of the state disintegrated. These events brought to local influence lawyers, merchants, and other "new men" who had formerly been excluded from political life.

News of peasant violence galvanized members of the National Assembly. On August 4, 1789, in an effort to appease the peasants and to forestall further rural disorders, the National Assembly formally abolished the "feudal regime," including seigneurial rights. This sweeping proclamation was modified in the following week: owners of seigneurial dues, or payments owed by peasants who worked land owned by nobles, would receive compensation from the peasants (although, in general, such compensation was not forthcoming and was subsequently eliminated). The Assembly abolished personal labor servitude owed to nobles, without compensation. The members of the National Assembly thus renounced privilege, the fundamental organizing principle of French society. Other reforms enacted the following week included the guarantee of freedom of worship and the abolition of the sale of offices, seigneurial justice, and even of the exclusive right of nobles to hunt. The provinces and cities, too, were required to give up most of their archaic privileges. In these ways, the National Assembly enacted a sweeping agenda that proclaimed the end of what soon became known as the Old Regime.

CONSOLIDATING THE REVOLUTION

The Assembly's decrees destroyed absolutism by redefining the relationship between subject and king. No longer would the king rule by divine right, or buy allegiance by dispensing privileges to favorites. Instead, he would be constrained by powers spelled out in a constitution. The Assembly promulgated the Declaration of the Rights of Man and Citizen, a remarkable document that proposed universal principles of humanity. It next established a new relationship between church and state, creating a national church, making Catholic Church property "national property," and compelling the clergy to swear allegiance to the nation. The National Assembly then turned to the long process of framing a constitution for the new regime, and is therefore sometimes also known as the Constituent Assembly.

In the meantime, Marie-Antoinette denounced the revolutionaries as "monsters," and some of the king's most influential advisers balked at accepting any weakening in royal authority. Fearing the influence of nobles at the court, crowds early in October marched to Versailles, returning to Paris with the king and the royal family. Henceforth, while many nobles, among others, fled France for exile and sought the assistance of the monarchs of

Europe against the Revolution, the king himself became vulnerable to the tide of Parisian popular radicalism. As nobles and clergy led resistance to the Revolution, the Parisian clubs made more radical demands.

The Declaration of the Rights of Man and Citizen

As it set out to create a constitutional monarchy, the Assembly promulgated the Declaration of the Rights of Man and Citizen on August 26, 1789. This set forth the general principles of the new order and intended to educate citizens about liberty. One of the most significant documents in Western political history, the Declaration reflected some of the ideas that Thomas Jefferson had enshrined in the American Declaration of Independence of 1776. Article One proclaims, "Men are born and remain free and equal in rights." The Enlightenment's influence is apparent in the document's concern for individual freedom, civic equality, and the sense of struggle against corporatism, unjust privilege, and absolute rule, a discourse based upon a belief in the primacy of reason. All people were to be equal before the law. All men were to be "equally eligible to all honors, places, and employments . . . without any other distinction than that created by their virtues and talents." No person could be persecuted for his or her opinions, including those concerning religion.

Proclaiming universal principles, the Declaration of the Rights of Man and Citizen clearly placed sovereignty in the French nation. The notion of rights stemming from membership in the "nation," as opposed to that in any corporate group or social estate, was a fundamental change. Laws were to reflect the notion of the "general will," an Enlightenment concept, which would be expressed by national representatives. The nation itself, not the monarch alone, was to be "the source of all sovereignty." The assertion of equality of opportunity, however, was not intended to eliminate all social distinctions. The preservation of property rights assured that differences due to wealth, education, and talent would remain and be considered natural and legitimate. The Declaration thus helped make wealth, not birth, blood, or legal privilege, the foundation of social and political order in modern France.

The Declaration invoked "universal man," meaning mankind. But at the same time, its authors excluded women from the Declaration and did not espouse or foresee equality of the sexes. Nonetheless, many men and women now began to greet each other as "citizen." Indeed, some calls for women's rights arose from the beginning of the Revolution.

The abolition of feudalism and the proclamation of the Declaration of the Rights of Man and Citizen were such monumental achievements that already in 1790 people were referring to the Old Regime as having been that which existed before the representatives of the Estates-General constituted the National Assembly. It remained, however, for Louis XVI to accept the Assembly's work.

"The Baker, the Baker's Wife, and the Baker's Little Boy"

The political crisis was by no means over. The king's closest advisers, the "court party," rejected any constitutional arrangement that would leave the monarch without the power of absolute veto. Royal authority was at stake. Speaking for the patriot party, Sieyès insisted, "If the king's will is capable of equalling that of twenty-five million people . . . it would be a *lettre de cachet* against the general will." The majority of the Assembly, having defeated a motion that an upper chamber like the British House of Lords be created, offered the king in September the power of a "suspending" veto over legislation. The king would be able to delay a measure passed by the Assembly from becoming law for up to four years.

When the king refused to accept these provisions and the decrees of August 4, a flood of pamphlets and newspapers attacked his intransigence. The radical journalist Jean-Paul Marat (1743–1793) quickly found a popular following for his new newspaper, *The Friend of the People*. A physician beset by financial woes, Marat was like one of the ambitious, frustrated "scribblers" whom Voltaire, forty years earlier, had scathingly denounced as hacks. Marat captured with stirring emotion and the colorful, coarse slang of ordinary Parisians the mood of those for whom he wrote. The rhetoric of popular sovereignty, some of it borrowed from the philosophe Jean-Jacques Rousseau, came alive in the outpouring of political pamphlets that undermined popular respect for Louis XVI and even for the institution of monarchy itself.

By October, some "patriots" were demanding that the king reside in Paris, echoing a number of *cahiers*. Like many of the most important events in the French Revolution, the "march to Versailles" began with a seemingly minor event. The officers of the Flanders Regiment insulted the newly adopted tricolor emblem at a reception in their honor attended by the king and queen. According to rumor, they shouted, "Down with the National Assembly!"

On October 5, women from the neighborhoods around the Bastille, having found little at the market, gathered in front of the town hall. From there, some 10,000 people, mostly women, left on foot for Versailles, hoping to convince the king to provide them with bread. Some of them occupied the hall of the National Assembly, where they claimed power in the name of popular sovereignty. Later in the day, a large force of national guardsmen led by Lafayette also arrived at Versailles, hoping to keep order and to convince the king that he should return with them to Paris. Louis cordially greeted the women in the late afternoon, promising them bread. That night Louis XVI announced his acceptance of the Assembly's momentous decrees of the night of August 4.

Nonetheless, violence followed at dawn. When people tried to force their way into the château, royal guards shot a man dead, and the crowds retaliated by killing two guards and sticking their heads on pikes. The crowd insisted that the royal family join it on the road to Paris. Some of the women

Women of Paris leaving for Versailles.

sang that they were returning to Paris with "The Baker, the Baker's Wife, and the Baker's Little Boy," reflecting the popular notion that the king was responsible for providing bread for his people. The National Assembly, too, left Versailles for Paris. By putting the king and the Assembly under the pressure of popular political will, the women's march to Versailles changed the course of the French Revolution.

Reforming the Church and Clergy

As the National Assembly set about creating a constitution that would limit the authority of the king, it proclaimed Louis "the king of the French," instead of the king of France, a significant change that suggested that he embodied the sovereignty of his people. Alarmed by such changes, the king's brother, the count of Artois, went into exile after the October Days, and was soon followed by more than 20,000 other émigrés, most of whom were nobles, other people of means, and clergymen.

The Assembly turned its attention to reforming the Church. The decrees of August had ended the unpopular tithe payments to the Church, and now the Assembly looked to the Church's wealth to help resolve the state's mounting financial crisis. On October 10, Charles-Maurice de Talleyrand (1754–1838), who had entered the priesthood at the insistence of his family and had been consecrated bishop early in 1789, proposed that Church property become "national properties" (*biens nationaux*). After the Assembly narrowly passed Talleyrand's measure on November 2, some 400 million francs in Church property—roughly 10 percent of the nation's land—began to be offered for sale at auction. The primary beneficiaries of the sale were urban bourgeois and prosperous peasants who could marshal enough cash to buy the land put up for sale.

To raise funds immediately, the Assembly issued paper money (*assignats*), which was backed by the value of the Church lands. Although the law required everyone to accept *assignats* in payment of debts, their value fell dramatically because of a lack of public confidence, and those who used the *assignats* to purchase Church lands or pay debts received a windfall. Even poor peasants were thus able to reduce their debts with inflated currency. Among the consequences of the sale of Church lands, and later of lands owned by noble émigrés, was that more land was brought under cultivation by peasants. The clearing of trees and brush to make room for crops and small-scale farming also put increased pressure on the environment.

The Assembly then altered dramatically the status of the Church itself. On February 13, 1790, it decreed the abolition of the religious orders, deemed politically suspect by many reformers. On July 12, the National Assembly passed the Civil Constitution of the French Clergy. The Assembly redefined the relationship between the clergy and the state, creating, in effect, a national church. Bishops, who could now only publish pronouncements with the authorization of the government, were to be elected by local assemblies at the local level. Ten days later, the king reluctantly accepted these measures affecting the Church.

The Church became essentially a department of the state, which henceforth would pay clerical salaries, the expenses of worship, and poor relief. In November 1790, the National Assembly proclaimed that all priests had to swear an oath of loyalty to the Revolution, and thus accept the Civil Constitution of the French Clergy. His authority directly challenged, Pope Pius VI denounced the Declaration of the Rights of Man and Citizen in March, and in April 1791 he condemned the Civil Constitution of the French Clergy.

The Civil Constitution of the French Clergy altered the course of the Revolution, largely because it was widely resisted and contributed directly to the growth of a counter-revolutionary movement. Between one-half and two-thirds of parish priests refused the oath, and the Assembly prohibited these disloyal, "non-juring" priests from administering the Church sacraments. Nonetheless, many continued to do so with popular support. The issue of the oath split dioceses, parishes, and some households. In some provinces, violence mounted against "non-juring" priests; in others, refractory priests received popular support and protection. Such issues were no small matter, as many Catholics, Louis XVI among them, believed themselves obliged by faith to refuse to take sacraments from the "juring" clergy, that is, those who had taken the oath.

The Reforms of 1791

The Constitution of 1791 formalized the break with the Old Regime by substituting a constitutional monarchy for absolute rule. Although the king retained only the power of a suspending veto, he would still direct foreign policy and command the army. Acts of war or peace, however, required the Assembly's approval.

But France was far from being a republic. In sweeping away the Old Regime, the Revolution had redefined the relationship between the individual and the state by stripping away hereditary legal privileges. Although all citizens were to be equal before the law, when the Assembly abolished titles of hereditary nobility in June 1790, it carefully distinguished between "active" and "passive" citizens. Only "active citizens," men paying the equivalent of three days' wages in direct taxes, had the right to vote in indirect elections—they would vote for electors, wealthier men, who in turn would select representatives to a new legislature (see Map 12.1). Critics such as Marat and the populist orator Georges-Jacques Danton (1759–1794) denounced the restrictive franchise, claiming that the Assembly had merely replaced the privileged caste of the Old Regime with another by substituting the ownership of property for noble title as the criterion for political rights. Rousseau himself would have been ineligible to vote.

In Europe, religious discrimination still characterized many states. In Britain, English Dissenters and Catholics could not hold public office and were excluded from certain professions; in Hungary and the Catholic Rhineland, Protestants faced discrimination. Jews faced intolerance and persecution in much of Europe, excluded, for example, from certain occupations or forced to live in specially designated places. In some parts of Eastern Europe and Ukraine, they suffered violence as well.

Now the National Assembly granted citizenship and civil rights to Protestants and Jews by laws in 1790 and 1791 (Protestants had already been granted civil rights in 1787). The Assembly abolished guilds, declaring each person "free to do such business and to exercise such profession, art or trade as he may choose." It subsequently passed the Le Chapelier Law on June 14, 1791, prohibiting workmen from joining together to refuse to work for a master. This law was a victory for proponents of free trade. The Assembly also passed laws affecting the family: establishing civil marriage, lowering the age of consent for marriage, permitting divorce, and specifying that inheritances be divided equally among children.

The National Assembly abolished slavery in France, but not in the colonies. This exception led to a rebellion by free blacks on the Caribbean island of Hispaniola in October 1790 against the French sugar plantation owners, many of whom were nobles. It was led by Toussaint L'Ouverture (1743–1803), a former slave who had fought in the French army. The National Convention (which would replace the Assembly in September 1792) abolished slavery in the colonies in 1794, hoping that the freed slaves

MAP 12.1 FRANCE BEFORE AND AFTER 1789 The map on the left indicates the provinces and provincial capitals in France before the Revolution. The map on the right indicates the administrative districts (*départements*) created in France in 1790.

The Three Estates hammering out the next constitution.

would fight against Britain. Half of Hispaniola—modern-day Haiti—became the first free black state.

In 1791, the call for equal rights for women was first made explicit in France when Olympe de Gouges (1755–1793), the daughter of a butcher, published *The Rights of Women*. "The law," she wrote, "must be the expression of the general will; all female and male citizens must contribute either personally or through their representatives to its formation." Encouraging women to demand their natural rights—and thereby evidencing the influence of the Enlightenment—she called on the Assembly to acknowledge women's rights as mothers of citizens of the nation. She insisted on women's right to education and to control property within marriage and to initiate divorce proceedings. Olympe de Gouges defined the nation as "the union of Woman and Man," and suggested that men would remain unfree unless women were granted similar rights, stopping short of demanding full political rights for women.

Resistance and Revolution

On July 14, 1790, the first anniversary of the fall of the Bastille, an imposing Festival of General Federation took place on the Champ-de-Mars, a royal parade ground in Paris. But there was no revolutionary consensus in France. In the south, nobles had already begun to organize resistance against the Revolution, and militant Catholics attacked Protestants, who tended to support the Revolution. By the summer of 1791, as the Assembly promulgated its constitution, open resistance to the Revolution had broken out in parts of the south and west, and in Alsace.

Such resistance prompted further calls for even more radical changes. Some of the revolutionaries, who did not accept the distinction between active and passive citizens, called for more democratic participation in political life. From where did this democratic thrust come? The monarchical state had rested on an intertwining network of groups—each with a set of privileges—at virtually every level of society. These included judicial, professional, administrative, and clerical groups, ranging from provincial Estates to artisanal guilds. Participatory and sometimes even democratic procedures within such bodies (or *corps*) may have instilled a tendency toward democracy that affected the course of the Revolution and pushed France toward a republic.

The first clubs were established by political factions among the deputies to the National Assembly. Some of the Assembly's most radical members split off to form the Jacobin Club, so-called because it met in the house of the religious order of the Jacobins. The Cordeliers Club brought together the radicals of Paris, while supporters of the cause of constitutional monarchy, whose members broke with the Jacobins in July 1791, gathered at the Club of the Feuillants. Monarchists formed royalist clubs. Moreover, some women began their own political clubs, such as the Club of Knitters, or joined the Fraternal Society of Patriots of Both Sexes. By 1793, there were at least 5,000 clubs in France. During the first years of the Revolution, however, there was little in France that was not political, and the political clubs were not the only place where political debate occurred. In Paris, there were also meetings of neighborhood "sections," which had first been defined as electoral districts for the convocation of the Estates-General.

Parisian revolutionaries became increasingly known as *sans-culottes*. They defined themselves by what they were without—the fancy knee britches, or *culottes*, which were associated with the aristocracy. The sans-culottes were shopkeepers, artisans, and laborers who were not opposed to private property, but who stood against unearned property, and especially against those people who seemed to have too much property, or who did not work for a living. They demanded that a maximum price be placed on bread, which alone absorbed more than half of the earnings of the average working family. Sans-culottes were for "the people," as they put it. They were defined by their political behavior. Even aristocrats could be sans-culottes if they supported the Revolution. Likewise, laborers or peasants could be called "aristocrats" if they seemed to

A female sans-culotte.

King Louis XVI wearing the Phrygian cap.

oppose the Revolution. In a world in which symbols played a crucial political role, sans-culottes could be identified by the Phrygian cap, a symbol of freedom drawn from the Roman Republic—close-fitting, red in color, with a tricolor emblem—in contrast to the three-cornered hat that had been worn by urban social elites. The language of the sans-culottes also quickly indicated who they were; they called everyone "citizen" and used the familiar (*tu* and never *vous*), egalitarian form of address. The political ideal of the sans-culottes was that popular sovereignty had to be practiced every day in direct democracy, in revolutionary clubs and in the sections.

The Flight to Varennes

Fearing the growing violence of the Revolution and counting on the support of the other monarchs of Europe, Louis XVI and his family tried to flee France in June 1791. The king's goal was to throw his support behind the foreign enemies of the Revolution and return to France to revoke the concessions that he had made. Apprehended by the National Guard in Varennes, the royal family was prevented from continuing their journey into exile and freedom.

The king's attempt to flee turned public sentiment further against him, and strengthened support for a republic. The day after his flight, the Cordeliers Club called for the establishment of a republic, but the majority of the Assembly feared civil war. On July 17, 1791, at the Champ-de-Mars in Paris, people came to sign (or put their "X" on) a petition resting on the "Altar of the Fatherland" that called on the National Assembly to replace the king "by all constitutional means." The National Guard opened fire, killing fifty people. Bailly, the moderate mayor of Paris, and Lafayette, the commander of the National Guard in Paris, declared martial law. However, even Louis XVI's formal acceptance of the constitution on September 14, 1791, could not stem the popular tide against the monarchy.

WAR AND THE SECOND REVOLUTION

The Revolution now entered a new, more radical phase. The king's flight seriously weakened the constitutional monarchists within the Assembly.

(*Left*) Georges–Jacques Danton. (*Right*) Maximilien Robespierre.

The leaders of the Parisian population—Danton, Marat, and Maximilien Robespierre—were Jacobins who had given up on the idea that a constitutional monarchy could adequately guarantee the liberties of the people. Elections brought to Paris a Legislative Assembly, which met on October 1, 1791. It replaced the Constituent Assembly, which had dissolved following the proclamation of the constitution the previous month. Republicans—now identified with the "left" as monarchists were with the "right," due to the location of the seats each group occupied in the Assembly—became a majority in March 1792.

In the meantime, French émigrés at the Austrian and Prussian courts were encouraging foreign intervention to restore Louis XVI to full monarchical authority. The republican followers of Jacques-Pierre Brissot (1754–1793), former radical pamphleteer and police spy as well as a flamboyant orator, called for a war to free Europe from the tyranny of monarchy and nobility. The members of this faction became known as the Girondins because many were from the district of Gironde, in which the major Atlantic port of Bordeaux is located. Under Girondin leadership, the Assembly's proclamations took on a more aggressive tone. The French declaration of war against Austria led to the Second Revolution, the formation of a republic, and, ultimately, a Jacobin-dominated dictatorship, which imposed the "Terror."

Reactions to the French Revolution in Europe

The French Revolution had a considerable impact on the rest of Europe. The early work of the National Assembly, particularly the abolition of feudal rights and the establishment of a constitutional monarchy found considerable favor among educated people in Britain, the Netherlands, and some German and Italian states. Some lawyers and merchants in other lands applauded, for example, measures taken to reduce the independence of the Catholic Church. The promulgation of the principles of national sovereignty and self-determination, however, threatened the monarchies of Europe. The threat posed by the French Revolution brought about a rapprochement between Austria and Prussia, rivals for domination in Central Europe, as well as a wary alliance between Great Britain and Russia.

The Prussian government's first reaction to the Revolution had been to try to subvert the alliance between France and Austria and to undermine Austrian authority in the Southern Netherlands (Belgium). In Vienna, the Habsburg emperor Leopold II was initially preoccupied with demands from the Hungarian nobility for more power. In 1789, a rebellion drove Austrian forces out of the Southern Netherlands and led to the establishment of a republic that survived only until Austrian troops returned in force in 1790.

In London, some radical Whigs greeted with enthusiasm the news of the fall of the Bastille and the first steps toward constitutional monarchy in France. But in 1790, the British writer Edmund Burke attacked the Revolution in *Reflections on the Revolution in France*. He contended that the abstract rationalism of the Enlightenment threatened the historic evolution of nations by undermining monarchy, established churches, and what he considered the "natural" ruling elite.

The Englishman Thomas Paine (1737–1809; see Chapter 11) wrote pamphlets denouncing monarchical rule and unwarranted privilege. *The Rights of Man* (1791–1792) defended the Revolution against Burke's relentless attack. Political societies supporting the Revolution, in which artisans played a major role, sprang up in Britain during the early 1790s. A small group of English women also enthusiastically supported the Revolution. Mary Wollstonecraft (1759–1797), a teacher and writer, greeted the Revolution with optimism, traveling to France to view events firsthand. Angered that the Assembly limited the right to education to men only, she published *Vindication of the Rights of Woman* (1792), the first book in Britain demanding the right for women to vote and hold elected office.

The rulers of the other European states felt threatened by the proclamation of universal principles embodied in the Declaration of the Rights of Man and Citizen. The Revolution also posed the threat of French expansion, now on behalf of carrying the revolutionary principles of "liberty, equality, and fraternity" to other lands. Besieged by exiles from France eager to tell tales of their suffering, the rulers of Prussia, Austria, Naples, and Piedmont

Olympe de Gouges (*left*), whose book *The Rights of Women* was published in France in 1791. It detailed the notion of equal rights that Mary Wollstonecraft (*right*) would take up the next year in Britain with the publication of her *Vindication of the Rights of Woman*.

undertook the suppression of Jacobin sympathizers in their states. In Britain, the seeming threat of foreign invasion helped affirm British national identity (see Chapter 11). Popular respect for the British monarchy and probably also for nobles soared as anti-French and anti-Catholic feelings came to the fore. Pitt the Younger's government lashed out at the development of popular politics in Britain, suspending the freedoms of association, assembly, and the press, as well as the writ of *habeas corpus*. "Coercion Acts" facilitated the arrest of those advocating parliamentary reform.

Thus, Louis XVI's virtual imprisonment in the Tuileries Palace in Paris and the thunderous speeches in the Assembly proclaiming the necessity of "a war of peoples against kings" worried the crowned heads of Europe. On August 27, 1791, Emperor Leopold II of the Holy Roman Empire (brother of Marie-Antoinette, who had not seen him in twenty-five years) and King Frederick William II of Prussia promulgated the Declaration of Pilnitz. It expressed their concern about the plight of the French monarchy and stated the common interest of both sovereigns in seeing order restored in France. Despite Robespierre's speeches warning the deputies that the Revolution must first deal with its enemies within France before waging war abroad, the Assembly, egged on by General Charles François Dumouriez (1739–1823), minister of foreign affairs, in April 1792 declared war on Austria. The stated reason was fear that an Austrian invasion from the Southern Netherlands was imminent. The declaration of war soon seemed a rash move, as the army had been devastated by the desertion of two-thirds of its officers (85 percent of its officers had been nobles before the Revolution). Moreover, Prussia soon joined with Austria in fighting the French. The early stages of the war produced French defeats at the hands of Austrian and Prussian armies.

A Second Revolution

The war sealed the fate of the monarchy and the royal family. As France faced the possibility of foreign invasion by Austria and Prussia, the popular fear that aristocrats and clergymen were betraying the Revolution brought down the monarchy. Early defeats on the northern frontier by Austrian troops and soaring bread prices (in part due to the requisitioning of food for the army) compounded popular anxiety and led to a new revolutionary groundswell, particularly in Paris.

In early April 1792, women marched through the capital demanding the right to bear arms. On June 20, a crowd stormed into the Tuileries Palace and threatened the royal family, shouting, "Tremble, tyrants! Here come the sans-culottes!" Strident calls for the end of the monarchy echoed in clubs and in the sections. On July 11, the Assembly officially proclaimed the *patrie,* or nation, to be "in danger," calling on all citizens to rally against the enemies of liberty within as well as outside of France. The Assembly encouraged the sections to admit the "passive" citizens who had previously been excluded because they had failed to meet tax requirements. Troops from Marseille, among volunteers called up to defend the front, sang a new revolutionary song, "The Marseillaise," penned by Rouget de Lisle. It became the anthem of the Revolution. In the meantime, the Jacobins pressed their attack against the monarchy.

In the Brunswick Manifesto (July 1792), Austria and Prussia warned the French that they would be severely punished if the royal family were harmed. All but one of the forty-eight sections of Paris responded by demanding that the king be immediately deposed. Popular discontent and Jacobin agitation came together in August. A radical committee overthrew the city council and established a revolutionary authority, the Commune of Paris. On August 10, sans-culottes from the Paris sections attacked the Tuileries Palace. The invaders killed 600 of the king's Swiss Guards and servants after they had surrendered. The royal family escaped and found protection in the quarters of the Legislative Assembly. The Assembly immediately proclaimed the monarchy suspended and ordered the royal family's imprisonment.

The popular revolution doomed France's first experiment in constitutional monarchy. On September 2, 1792, a Prussian army entered French territory and captured the eastern fortress town of Verdun. The proximity of the allied armies and the fear of betrayal at home led to the imprisonment in Paris of many people suspected of plotting against the Revolution. When a rumor circulated that the prisoners were planning to break out of prison and attack the army, mobs dragged the prisoners from their cells and killed them. During these September Massacres, more than 1,200 people, includ-

The September Massacre of 1792 in the abbey of Saint-Germain-des-Prés in Paris.

ing 225 priests, perished at the hands of crowds who acted as judges, juries, and executioners.

But just as Paris seemed vulnerable to foreign invasion, a ragtag army of regular soldiers and sans-culottes stopped the Prussian and Austrian advance with effective artillery barrages on September 20, 1792, near the windmill of Valmy, near Châlons-sur-Marne. The German poet Johann Wolfgang von Goethe, amazed by the victory of such ordinary people over a highly trained professional army, wrote, "From this time and place a new epoch is beginning." An officer trained under the Old Regime called the resultant warfare of the revolutionary armies a "hellish tactic," which saw "fifty thousand savage beasts foaming at the mouth like cannibals, hurling themselves at top speed upon soldiers whose courage has been excited by no passion."

The Revolution had been saved by the same people who had first made it. Delegates to a new assembly called the National Convention were selected by universal male suffrage in elections. The Jacobins dominated. The delegates arrived in Paris to draft a republican constitution. Their first act was unanimously to abolish the monarchy and proclaim the republic on September 21, 1792, even before news of Valmy had been learned.

The revolutionary armies of proud, loyal citizen-soldiers, however badly armed, pushed Prussian troops back across the Rhine and entered Mainz in October. On November 6, Dumouriez defeated the Austrians at Jémappes in the Austrian Netherlands, which was soon controlled by the French revolutionary army (see Map 12.2). To supply French troops, arms manufacturers turned out 45,000 guns in one year, and a Parisian factory produced 30,000 pounds of gunpowder every day.

MAP 12.2 EXPANSION OF REVOLUTIONARY FRANCE, 1792–1799 The map indicates French revolutionary army offensives and foreign anti-revolutionary army offensives. It also shows areas annexed by the French, areas occupied by the French, and dependent republics established by revolutionary France.

Emboldened by these unexpected military successes, the National Convention on November 19, 1792, promised "fraternity and assistance to all peoples who want to recover their liberty." French troops captured Frankfurt and occupied much of the Rhineland. The Convention also declared the outright annexation of the Alpine province of Savoy, belonging to the Kingdom of Sardinia, and the Mediterranean town of Nice, captured at the end of September. They declared them within the "natural frontiers" of France—a claim that contradicted the principles of popular sovereignty and self-determination contained in the annexation decrees themselves. On December 15, 1792, the Convention abolished all feudal dues and tithes in those territories occupied by French armies.

The governments of Britain and the Dutch Republic viewed the occupation of the Austrian Netherlands as a great threat. When it appeared that both states were considering joining Austria and Prussia in taking action against France, the Convention on February 1, 1793, declared war on Britain and the Dutch Republic. Spain and the Kingdoms of Sardinia and Naples joined this First Coalition against France.

When correspondence between Louis XVI and the Austrian government was discovered, his trial became inevitable. Accused of treason, the king defended himself with grace and dignity. He called on the Convention to look after his family as he had tried to watch over those of France. But with the words "one cannot reign innocently" ringing in the hall, the Convention condemned the king to death. On the morning of January 21, Louis XVI was guillotined. The huge throng roared its approval as the executioner held up the severed royal head, symbol of the Old Regime, for all to see.

As the Convention and the more radical Paris Commune vied for authority, the French Republic, still at war, began to split apart. The Girondins and the Jacobins quarreled bitterly. The Girondins were popularly identified with the economic liberalism that characterized the port cities and with the desire to carry the Revolution aggressively beyond the frontiers of France. Opposed to centralizing power in Paris, they wanted a significant

The execution of Louis XVI.

degree of local political control. The deputies of the far left, principally the Jacobins and their followers, sat on the raised side of the Tuileries Hall where the Convention met. The far left became known as "the Mountain" (their followers the *Montagnards*). The political center became known as "the Plain." Backed by the Parisian sans-culottes, the Jacobins insisted on the necessity of centralizing authority in the capital to save the Revolution from internal subversion and foreign armies. The Girondins, more moderate, believed that the Revolution had gone far enough. The Jacobins accused them of secretly supporting the monarchy and demanded swift punishment for traitors.

From the point of view of the Jacobins, those who were not for them were against the Revolution. The sense of vulnerability and insecurity was heightened by reverses in the field. The armies of the First Coalition defeated the French in the Austrian Netherlands in March 1793. Dumouriez then betrayed the Revolution, preparing to march his soldiers to Paris to put Louis XVI's son on the throne as Louis XVII. When his army refused to follow him, Dumouriez fled across the border to join the Austrians and other émigrés. In the meantime, the allies recaptured the left bank of the Rhine River.

Counter-Revolution

The Counter-Revolution began in regions where religious practice still seemed strong and where the Civil Constitution of the French Clergy had met with considerable resistance (see Map 12.3). A full-scale insurrection against the Revolution began in March 1793. This revolt in the western part of France became known as the Vendée, after the name of one of the most insurrectionary districts (the old provinces having been divided into *départements* in 1790). In August 1793, the revolutionary government decreed mass conscription, the *levée en masse,* which initiated the concept of the nation at arms: "Young people will go to battle; married men will forge arms and transport supplies; women will make tents, uniforms, and serve in the hospitals; children will pick rags; old men will have themselves carried to public squares, to inspire the courage of the warriors, and to preach hatred of kings and the unity of the Republic." The unpopularity of military conscription in defense of the republic also generated resistance.

South of the Loire River, the counter-revolutionary forces principally emerged from the relatively isolated bocage, or hedgerow country, where the old noble and clerical elites had been relatively unaffected by the economic changes of the past few decades, specifically the expansion of the market economy. In Brittany, which had enjoyed a relatively light tax burden during the Old Regime, the revolutionary government was hated for having ended that privilege, thereby increasing taxes. Both sides fought with a brutality, including mass executions and systematic pillage, that recalled the Thirty

MAP 12.3 THE COUNTER–REVOLUTION   The map indicates areas of federalism and counter-revolutionary activity, including major uprisings.

Years' War (1618–1648) in Central Europe. In insurrectionary areas during 1793–1794, perhaps a quarter of the population perished, as many as 250,000 people, in part because the revolutionary troops, facing guerilla warfare, saw local civilians as potential threats.

The Terror

Faced with foreign invasion and civil insurgency, the Jacobins further centralized government authority and implemented the "Terror" against those considered enemies of the Revolution. The Convention set aside a planned Constitution of 1793 (which was to have replaced the Constitution of 1791).

The rights of the accused were limited, and new special courts prosecuted anyone considered disloyal to the republic. On March 19, 1793, the Convention passed a law permitting the immediate trial of armed insurgents without a jury. The Jacobin-dominated Convention established a Committee of Public Safety of nine and then twelve members, which gradually assumed more and more power as it oversaw the Terror. The Convention also decreed a special war tax, including a forced levy on wealthy people, and in May 1793 imposed the "Maximum"—a maximum price on grain. These measures of centralization and government interference in the economy led to an irreversible break between the Jacobins, who believed in state controls, and the Girondins, who believed in economic freedom.

Military requisitions of foodstuffs accentuated hardship. Poor people rioted against the high price of grain. In Paris, the Society of Revolutionary Republican Women took to the streets, demanding laws against hoarding and calling for women to be granted citizenship. A group called the *enragés* (the "enraged") demanded that bakers be penalized if they charged more than the maximum price for bread.

In June, pushed on by crowds from the radical sections of Paris, the Convention expelled twenty-nine Girondin deputies, accusing them of supporting hoarders, and it ordered the arrest of some of them. Insurgents in Toulon turned over half of the French fleet to the British. In July, Charlotte Corday, a royalist noblewoman, stabbed Marat to death in his bathtub. Tax revenue and foreign trade fell by half. *Assignats,* more of which had rolled off the government presses as the financial crisis continued, plunged further in value.

Two young radical Jacobin leaders strode forward to take charge of the Terror. Louis Antoine Saint-Just (1767–1794), a precocious, icy young deputy whose mother had once had him incarcerated for running off with the family silver, waged war on royalists, hoarders, and Girondins. "Those who make revolutions by halves dig their own grave," he warned.

Maximilien Robespierre (1758–1794) emerged as the leading figure on the Committee of Public Safety. He knew that the Mountain drew its support from the sans-culottes, some of whom supported the Terror. But he also believed that the popular

Jacques-Louis David's *The Death of Marat.*

movement remained a threat to the orderly transformation of political life in France. Historians have offered interpretations of Robespierre that range from the view that he was a popular democrat who saved the essence of the Revolution from counter-revolutionaries to the suggestion that he was actually a precursor of twentieth-century totalitarianism.

Robespierre was the son and grandson of lawyers from the northern town of Arras. After his irresponsible father abandoned his family, Robespierre depended on scholarships for his schooling. At age eleven, he was chosen to read an address in Latin to the royal family at his school in Paris. It was raining and the royal family, it was said, without acknowledging the young student, ordered their driver onward. The royal coach splashed Robespierre with mud.

After completing his law degree, Robespierre defended a number of poor clients, including a man unjustly accused of stealing from an abbey. After he was elected to the third estate, Robespierre gradually established a reputation in Paris for his well-organized and thoughtful but colorless speeches. Contemporaries noted the prissiness of the impeccably dressed, slight man with very pale skin and chestnut hair always perfectly powdered. A favorite of the Parisian sans-culottes, the man they nicknamed "the Incorruptible" called in 1793 for "a single will" of the nation to save the Revolution.

Insurrections by supporters of the Girondins against the Jacobins and the authority of the Convention broke out in Lyon, Marseille, Bordeaux, and Caen, where merchants and lawyers played prominent roles in failed "federalist revolts" against centralized revolutionary authority emanating from Paris. Lyon fell to Jacobin troops on October 9, 1793, and bloody reprisals followed.

The "Law of Suspects" promulgated by the Convention in September deprived those accused of crimes against the nation of most of their remaining rights. The Convention banned clubs and popular societies of women. Olympe de Gouges was among the Girondins guillotined. Marie-Antoinette, though hardly a feminist, also went to the scaffold.

The Jacobins were so intent on destroying the Old Regime and building a new political world that they instituted a new calendar in October 1793. The old calendar gave way to a new republican calendar based upon "weeks," or cycles of ten days, and "months" taking their names from more secular notions of the changing of the seasons (such as *Germinal,* meaning "the budding," *Ventôse,* meaning "windy," and so on). September 22, 1792, the first year of the republic, became, retroactively, day one of the "year I."

The Jacobins adopted new revolutionary symbols to take the place of Old Regime symbols and to help maintain revolutionary enthusiasm. Following the execution of Louis XVI, the revolutionaries chose a female image for liberty and the republic, which was ironic in light of their denial of political rights to women. The female image of the republic appears gentle, non-threatening, and virtuous, representing the abstract virtues of liberty, popular sovereignty, community, and nation. Contemporaries contrasted republican virtue with the abuses of power that seemed to have characterized the Old Regime. They did so even as Jacobin representatives of the Revolution imposed their will wherever they were resisted in the provinces.

During the "year II" (which began in September 1793), radical revolutionaries undertook an ambitious campaign of "de-christianization," a war on religious institutions and symbols. They closed down churches and removed crosses standing in public places. The campaign failed, unable to overcome centuries of firmly implanted beliefs and traditions, even among many people who supported the Revolution. It also turned many clergy who had accepted the Civil Constitution away from the Revolution, generating further resistance.

Outside of Paris, "representatives on mission," armed with dictatorial authority in the name of the Convention, tried to maintain order. They worked with local "surveillance committees" and "revolutionary tribunals" of Jacobins. Some of these revolutionary officials sent counter-revolutionaries to the guillotine. "Revolutionary armies" of artisans and day laborers guarded requisitioned provisions for the military and oversaw the melting down of church bells for war use.

Yet the Terror was never uniformly implemented. Between 11,000 and 18,000 people perished at the hands of the Committee of Public Safety (a fraction, by comparison, of the deaths that had resulted from the Thirty

A Revolutionary Tribunal during the Terror.

Years' War or the American Civil War). About 300,000 royalists, Girondins, or other "enemies of the Revolution" were imprisoned for some period during the Terror. About 15 percent of those killed were nobles or clergy. Thus, nobles and clergy suffered disproportionately in terms of their number in the population as a whole (5 to 8 percent). However, artisans and peasants constituted by far the largest number of those dispatched by the revolutionary tribunals. The majority of these were arrested near the northern and eastern frontiers that had been invaded by foreign armies or in the counter-revolutionary west where civil war raged. During the winter of 1793–1794, perhaps as many as several thousand prisoners—including priests and nuns—captured from the counter-revolutionary armies of the Vendée were taken out into the swirling waters of the Loire River in boats that had holes bored in them and drowned at the orders of a cruel revolutionary official. In all, several thousand people perished.

In the meantime, the tide of the war had turned in favor of the aggressive French armies. Significant French victories on the battlefield undercut the argument that the Terror was necessary because of the immediate external threat to the republic. A French army defeated the Austrians in the Austrian Netherlands in June 1794, forcing them out of Belgium. Another French force reached the Rhine River and captured Mainz. A third French army recaptured Savoy from the Kingdom of Sardinia. The Spanish army retreated across the Pyrenees Mountains.

The Terror then struck the *enragés* leaders in March 1794 after they demanded even more economic controls and an intensification of the "de-christianization" campaign. They were brought before the Revolutionary Tribunal of Paris, condemned, and guillotined. The Committee of Public Safety then went after Danton and his followers, who believed that the Terror was no longer necessary, and thus had been labeled the "Indulgents." They too were condemned and guillotined. Real and imagined conspiracies provided the justification for the Terror, which now seemed without end. "Who will be next?" was whispered among even those loyal to the most radical members of the Committee of Public Safety. In May, Robespierre survived an assassination attempt.

Robespierre sought to establish a secularized "Cult of the Supreme Being" that would serve as a "constant reminder of justice" to bind the people to the new values of republicanism. With the elimination of the *enragés* and Danton and many of his followers, Robespierre devoted his energies to creating a "Republic of Virtue." Early in June 1794, the republic celebrated the "Festival of Reason." The cathedral of Notre Dame in Paris became a "temple of reason." A popular female opera singer, dressed as Liberty, wearing a Phrygian cap and holding a pike, bowed before the flame of reason. The painter Jacques-Louis David constructed huge statues of monsters like Anarchy and Atheism made of pasteboard. After Robespierre set fire to them, a statue of Wisdom rose out of the ashes.

The Terror took on a momentum of its own. Saint-Just warned, "We must punish not merely traitors, but also the indifferent." The Jacobins arrested the Marquis de Condorcet (1743–1794) for alleged counter-revolutionary activity. Condorcet, an influential philosophe of the late Enlightenment, had been elected to the Assembly in 1791. He believed that all people should have a voice in approving acts of government, albeit indirectly, and that all citizens should be equal before the law. He had campaigned against the death penalty and slavery, and he defended political equality and the rights of women. Condorcet died of apoplexy—or committed suicide—in his cell in the spring of 1794, shortly before he was to be executed. The Revolution seemed to have turned on and destroyed the enlightened reason that had arguably helped bring it about.

THE FINAL STAGES OF THE REVOLUTION

Moderate Jacobins and other members of the Convention, fearing that they might be next in line to be purged, overthrew the Jacobin dictatorship. They established a new government called the Directory, which ended the Terror. Caught between staunch Jacobins on the left and monarchists on the right, the period of the Directory was marked by great political instability, ongoing wars abroad, and economic hardship at home. Although the Directory consolidated some of the gains of the Revolution, it too would be overthrown by conspirators led by the Abbé Sieyès and one of the rising stars of the revolutionary army, Napoleon Bonaparte.

Thermidor

The Revolutionary Tribunal of Paris used new powers granted by the Committee of Public Safety in June 1794 to send 1,376 people to their deaths over a period of six weeks. Afraid that they would be next on Robespierre's list, moderates in the Convention began to plot against Robespierre and his allies. They were led by Paul Barras (1755–1829), a follower of Danton, and Joseph Fouché (1758–1820). On July 27, 1794 (the 9th of Thermidor), Robespierre haltingly addressed the Convention, calling for one more purge. But, anticipating his own downfall, Robespierre also murmured, "I ask for death." That night, Robespierre and Saint-Just were arrested at the virtually unguarded town hall of Paris. Robespierre attempted suicide, shattering his jaw with a shot.

Robespierre and the others were executed without trial, their fate as swift and pitiless as that of the Terror's victims. They were followed to the scaffold by more than a hundred of their allies. In the provinces, particularly in the south, the revenge against the Jacobins by their enemies was swift and brutal. Lazare Carnot (1753–1823), a talented military engineer, brilliant administrator ("the organizer of victory"), and one of the twelve members of the Committee of Public Safety, survived because he had opposed Robespierre. Moreover, the continuing war effort desperately required his administrative talent.

After dismantling the Paris Commune, the victors of Thermidor—the name taken from the period in the revolutionary calendar in which Robespierre fell—set about establishing a new national government. Order was only slowly and incompletely restored in the countryside. The Thermidorians greatly reduced the powers of the Committee of Public Safety on July 31, 1794, and then abolished it completely. In November 1794, Jacobin Clubs were banned.

The Directory: Politics and Society

In 1795 the Thermidorians produced a constitution that created a bicameral (two-house) legislative assembly and a collective executive of five directors. The latter provided the name "the Directory" for this period of the Revolution. The two assemblies included the Council of the Ancients (250 members), which discussed and voted on legislation proposed by the second assembly, the Council of Five Hundred. Two-thirds of the members of the new councils were elected from among the members of the existing Convention. The two councils elected the five directors who formed the collective executive authority, or Directorate. Beginning in 1797, one-third of the members of each council and one of the five directors were to be replaced each year.

People with property benefited from the Thermidorian reaction. By the Constitution of 1795, all male taxpayers could vote, but they selected electoral assemblies for which only about 30,000 men were eligible, a smaller group than in the indirect elections of 1789–1791. But although about 2 million men could vote (out of some 7 million men of voting age), the system of indirect election favored the selection of the wealthiest citizens to serve in the assemblies.

The period of the Directory was marked by a decided turn against the asceticism associated with Robespierre's Republic of Virtue. The *jeunesse dorée,* or gilded youth, drawn from the bourgeoisie and old nobility, set the social and cultural tone of the day. Wearing square collars and fancy clothes, wealthy young men smashed busts of Marat. The red-colored symbols of the sans-culottes—such as the Phrygian cap—quickly disappeared. Women who could afford to do so wore long flowing white robes of opulence and sensuality, with plunging necklines that would have horrified Robespierre. The familiar (*tu*) form of address, identified with section and club meetings, gave way to the formal *vous* more characteristic of the Old Regime. Crowds in which women played a prominent part demanded that churches be reopened. Boisterous social events amused the middle class; among them the macabre "Dance of the Victims," a ball to which only those with a relative who had perished in the Terror could be admitted. Some revelers turned up with their

The return of high society during the Directory.

hair cut away from the back of their neck, mimicking the final haircut of those about to be sent to the guillotine.

Under the Directory, the comforts of the wealthy, some of whom had made their fortunes during the Revolution (by buying Church lands or supplying the military), contrasted sharply with the deprivations of the poor. The economy lay in shambles. The winter of 1795 was cruelly harsh. The abolition of the Maximum spelled the end of cheap bread, which rose in price by thirteen times that spring in Paris. The price of basic commodities soared. Near Paris, people scrambled to eat the carcasses of dead army horses, and in mountainous areas people searched for berries and edible roots while trying to stay warm. Peasants suffered the military requisition of food supplies.

Instability

The Directory may have ended the Terror, but it brought neither stability nor peace to France, despite peace agreements concluded with Prussia in April 1795. Prussia accepted the French annexation of the left bank of the Rhine River, the Austrian Netherlands, and the Dutch United Provinces (which became the "Batavian Republic"). In the meantime, French armies continued to press forward against the Austrian armies in Central Europe and Italy. Mass desertion and heavy casualties drastically reduced the size of the French army, which, after reaching a million men in the summer of 1794, fell to less than 500,000 a year later.

War compounded social and political instability in 1795. That spring, the Directory repressed two small popular demonstrations by crowds demanding a return to controls on the price of bread. Encouraged by the Convention's move to the right, royalists also tried to seize power. The king's son had died in a Paris prison in June 1795, and so the count of Provence, Louis XVI's brother, was now heir to the throne. An army of nobles supported by the British landed at Quiberon Bay in Brittany on June 27, but French forces turned back the invaders with ease. On October 5, 1795, royalists attempted an insurrection in Paris, where they found support in the more prosperous districts. The government called in Napoleon Bonaparte (1769–1821), a young Corsican general, who turned away the insurgents with a "whiff of grapeshot."

Instability continued. François-Noël Babeuf (1760–1797), who was called Gracchus, plotted to overthrow the Directory. Influenced by Rousseau and espousing social egalitarianism and the common ownership of land, Babeuf concluded that a small group of committed revolutionaries could seize power if they were tightly organized and had the support of the poor. Babeuf organized the "Conspiracy of the Equals," finding support among a handful of Parisian artisans and shopkeepers. In May 1796, Babeuf and his friends were arrested; they were guillotined a year later after a trial. The Directory took advantage of the discovery of this plot to purge Jacobins once again.

Caught between the intransigent, dogmatic followers of Robespierre and the Jacobins on the left and the royalists on the right, and lacking effective and charismatic civilian leaders, the Directory's difficult tightrope act grew more precarious in an atmosphere of uncertainty, intrigue, and rumors of coups d'état.

In 1797, elections returned many royalists to the Council of Five Hundred. Fearful that they might press for peace with France's enemies in the hope of obtaining a restoration of the monarchy, the Directory government annulled the election results. The coup d'état of the 18th Fructidor (September 4, 1797) eliminated two of the directors, including Carnot. In May of the next year, the directors refused to allow recently elected deputies to take their seats on the Council of Five Hundred.

For all of its failures, the Directory did provide France with its second apprenticeship in representative government. The Constitution of 1795 was an important transition between the political system of the Old Regime, based primarily upon monarchical absolutism and noble privilege, and modern representative government grounded in the sanctity of property.

The Directory had rejected cautious British suggestions that a workable peace might be forged without France having to give up its conquests of the Rhineland and the Austrian Netherlands. Perhaps fearful that a more bellicose ministry in Britain might replace that of William Pitt the Younger if such a peace were signed, the French fought on.

Napoleon Bonaparte, who had swept aside the royalist insurrection, now commanded the Army of Italy, checking in with Paris only when it suited him. His armies overwhelmed the Austrian troops in northern Italy. The Treaty of Campo Formio (October 17, 1797) left France the dominant foreign power in Italy. This victory, and Napoleon's boldly independent diplomatic negotiations in the Italian campaigns, made him the toast of Paris. The Austrians joined the Prussians in recognizing French absorption of the left bank of the Rhine River and annexation of the Austrian Netherlands. Reorganized in July 1797 as the Cisalpine Republic, much of the north of Italy became a feeble pawn of France.

Despite these victories, years of war had exhausted the French nation and damaged the economy. France's financial situation deteriorated even further. Inflation was rampant, and the collection of taxes was sporadic at best. *Assignats* were now virtually worthless. Many bourgeois were dissatisfied, having lost money when the Directory cancelled more than half of the national debt in 1797.

In May 1798, Napoleon sailed with an army to Egypt, over which Turkey was sovereign; he hoped to strike at British interests in India. Fearing that France sought to break apart the Ottoman Empire and extend its interests in an area Russia had always wanted to dominate, Russia allied with Britain. Austria also joined the alliance, which became the Second Coalition (1799–1802). Austria hoped to undo the Treaty of Campo Formio and to prevent further French expansion in Italy, where French forces had sent the pope into exile and established a Roman Republic.

The combined strength of the Coalition powers for the moment proved too much for the overextended French armies in Italy. In Switzerland, a combined Russian and Austrian army defeated a French force. When Irish rebels rose up against British rule in 1798, France sent an invasion force to aid the insurgents, in the hope of launching an invasion of England. After the defeat of the Irish insurgents and French troops who landed ashore, a French fleet attempting to land more soldiers was defeated off the coast. British troops crushed a series of Irish rebellions in a bloody struggle in which 30,000 people were killed, and the British navy captured one of the French ships and turned back the rest.

In the meantime, coalition members quarreled over strategy and eventual goals. Russian Tsar Paul (ruled 1796–1801) withdrew from the Second Coalition in October 1799, as he was irritated with the British for insisting that the Royal Navy had the right to stop and search any vessel on the seas.

The Eighteenth Brumaire

The wily Abbé Sieyès (who once replied "I survived" when asked what he had done during the Revolution) became a director in the spring of 1799. He believed France needed a government with stronger executive authority.

Because the role of the army had grown enormously, he concluded that it would emerge as the arbiter of France's political future. In the face of endemic instability, Sieyès decided in 1799 to overthrow the Directory. The go-between was Talleyrand, the foreign minister. The career of Talleyrand provides another remarkable example of revolutionary survival; a detractor once claimed that Brie cheese was "the only king to whom he has been loyal." Sieyès contacted General Napoleon Bonaparte. On November 9, 1799 (the 18th Brumaire), General Bonaparte announced to the hastily convened councils that another Jacobin conspiracy had been uncovered and that a new constitution had to be framed to provide France with a stronger executive authority. The deputies were justly dubious. Some demanded his immediate arrest. Napoleon's response was incoherent and ineffective, but the quick thinking of his brother, Lucien, president of the lower assembly, saved Bonaparte from one of his few moments of indecision. Lucien rejected the call for a vote to outlaw Napoleon, and he ordered troops to evict members who opposed him. Those who remained delegated complete power to Sieyès and General Bonaparte. Would Napoleon, whose rise to power would have been almost unthinkable without the French Revolution, be the heir of the French Revolution, or its destroyer?

A contemporary British caricature of the 18th Brumaire: "The Corsican Crocodile dissolving the Council of Frogs!!!"

Perspectives on the French Revolution

The French Revolution, which began in Paris, swept across Europe. In France, it marked a significant break with the past, although, to be sure, important continuities from the Old Regime helped shape the modern world. In other countries, too, the Revolution effected major changes. These included in some places the abolition of feudalism, curtailment of clerical privileges, and establishment of a more centralized governmental structure. But while some people welcomed the export of the French Revolution, others did not, viewing "liberation" by the French as indistinguishable from conquest. The French presence engendered a patriotic response in Russia, Spain, and some of the German and Italian states, contributing to the emergence of nationalist feeling there.

   Like the contemporaries who witnessed the Revolution, modern historians also have had a variety of interpretations of it. Many of them still disagree as to the causes, effects, and significance of the Revolution, debating the dramatic events with some of the same passion as those who experienced it firsthand.

European Responses to the Revolution

In countries over which revolutionary armies swept, enthusiastic shouts for "liberty, fraternity, and equality!" echoed in German, Dutch, and Piedmontese, then disappeared in a sea of French muskets, military requisitions, and even executions. The revolutionary wave did bring about sweeping changes in some of the "liberated" territories, and these changes continued even as Napoleon consolidated his authority in France (see Chapter 13). Thus, in Piedmont, French control reduced the influence of the nobility and left a heritage of relative administrative efficiency. The abolition of feudalism in some of the conquered German states, northern Italy, and the Kingdom of Naples increased the number of property owners. The French conquerors proclaimed the rule of law and curtailed some of the influence of the clergy.

   But the French faced the realities of almost constant warfare and, increasingly, local resistance. As the wars dragged on and the economic situations of the "republics" grew worse, the benefits brought by the French seemed increasingly less important. Ruined merchants and former officials joined nobles and clerics in opposing rule by France or its puppets. As the Civil Constitution of the French Clergy led to a violent reaction against the Revolution in France, anticlerical measures in the occupied territories had the same effect. The peoples of the Rhineland, the Netherlands, and Flanders bitterly resented the revolutionaries' de-christianization campaign. Increasingly, the French presence bred contempt and hatred. Bavarian, Dutch, Piedmontese, Austrian, and Swiss patriots found willing listeners. The French occupation gave rise to general opposition and a new wave of national feeling among the conquered. In Great Britain, the French Revolution also contributed to the accentuation of British nationalism in the face of a perceived threat by its old Catholic enemy in a new guise.

The French conquests in Europe were themselves an exercise in statemaking, largely unanticipated and unwanted by the local populations. Between 1795 and 1799, the Directory established satellite "sister republics" directly administered by France. The Helvetic Republic (Switzerland), the Batavian Republic (the Netherlands), the Cisalpine Republic (Milan), and the Parthenopean Republic (the Kingdom of Naples) were founded with the goal of shoring up alliances against the other great powers. But in the Italian states, only the Cisalpine Republic generated any local enthusiasm for the French invaders, and then only briefly. People "liberated" from the rule of kings and princes found themselves governed by a revolutionary bureaucracy administered from Paris.

The French found support and hired officials principally from the middle class, which had already provided officials in the old state structure. But the French invasions gradually generated a hatred for the revolutionary invaders and in some places a concomitant nationalist response. This was especially true within the German states, where many writers and other people in the upper classes hoped one day that "Germany"—300 states, 50 free cities, and almost 1,000 territories of imperial knights of the Holy Roman Empire—would one day be politically unified.

Historians' Views of the Revolution

Marxist historians long dominated the historiography of the French Revolution. They have described the Revolution as the inevitable result of a bourgeois challenge to the Old Regime, dominated by nobles. Thus, Marxists have interpreted the Revolution in terms of the rise of the bourgeoisie and its struggle for social and political influence commensurate with its rising economic power during the eighteenth century. Marxists have insisted that the nobility compromised the authority of the absolute monarchy by refusing to be taxed; then, according to this interpretation, the emboldened bourgeoisie allied with urban artisans and workers to bring down the absolute monarchy. They have described the emergence of the bourgeoisie as the dominant social class in France, insisting on its growing role in the country's increasingly capitalist economy.

This traditional Marxist economic interpretation of the French Revolution has been largely discredited. Some historians have noted that differences between aristocrats and bourgeois, and within both social groups, had become considerably blurred during the eighteenth century; that most of the "bourgeois" members of the Estates-General were not drawn from commerce and manufacturing but rather from law; and that, in any case, the upper middle class and nobles by the time of the Revolution shared a common obsession with money, not privilege. Thus, one cannot accurately depict the Revolution as having been simply a victory for the bourgeoisie.

Moreover, the Revolution did not expedite capitalism but may even have retarded it, by launching France and Europe into a long series of costly wars.

Views critical of the "bourgeois revolution" thesis have also emphasized that within France the complex nature of local political power, divided among provincial Estates and parlements, and among various groups enjoying formal privileges or monopolies and municipalities, limited the actual prerogatives of absolute monarchy. Many historians now see the Revolution as affirming the victory of men of property—a rubric that included both nobles and bourgeois—over titled nobles born into status and power.

A related interpretation has seen the Revolution as part of an essentially democratic "Atlantic Revolution" stretching across the Atlantic Ocean. By this view, the American War of Independence was the first manifestation of an essentially political quest for popular sovereignty. It influenced, in turn, the French Revolution and subsequent attempts in other European countries to gain political rights, as well as movements for independence in Spain's Latin American colonies early in the nineteenth century.

More recently, another revisionist school has argued that a new political culture was already in place in the last decades of the Old Regime. An extreme version of this interpretation sees the French monarchy as a state well on the way to reforming itself through the collaboration of liberal nobles before the Revolution interrupted this process. One view sees in the 1750s and 1760s the origins of this new, revolutionary political culture, seen in the political and ideological opposition to Louis XV and particularly in the rhetorical violence of the Revolution's first year.

None of these varying interpretations, however, diminishes the significance of the French Revolution in transforming the Western world by providing its first modern European democratic experience. This is why its origins and nature continue to generate excitement and debate today, well more than 200 years after the fall of the Bastille.

CHAPTER 13

NAPOLEON AND EUROPE

~

The royalist, religious writer François-René de Chateaubriand once called his enemy Napoleon "the mightiest breath of life which has ever animated human clay." In a rare moment of introspection, Napoleon once remarked, "It is said that I am an ambitious man but that is not so; or at least my ambition is so closely bound to my being that they are both one and the same."

Yet, far more than his imposing will, Napoleon's career was shaped by and reflected the breathtaking changes brought by the French Revolution. Statemaking and the emergence of nationalism, accompanied by the increased secularization of political institutions, slowly but surely transformed the European continent.

An admirer of the Enlightenment, Napoleon claimed that he was the true son of the French Revolution. He personally supervised the writing of the new constitution, which made wealth, specifically propertied wealth, the determinant of status. Napoleon's reign was also a watershed in statemaking: he further centralized the French state and extended its reach, making it more efficient by codifying laws and creating new bureaucratic structures and a new social hierarchy based upon state service.

Napoleon saw himself as a savior who carried "liberty, equality, and fraternity" abroad, freeing the European peoples from sovereigns who oppressed them. From his final exile on the distant Atlantic island of Saint Helena, Napoleon claimed to have created European unity. But in the process of "liberating" other nations from the stranglehold of old regimes, he also conquered them.

NAPOLEON'S RISE TO POWER

Napoleon's rise to power should be seen in the context of the French Revolution. With the emigration of most of the officer corps during the early stages of the Revolution, a generation of talented generals had risen rapidly through the ranks by virtue of their remarkable battlefield accomplishments during the revolutionary wars that had raged across much of Western and Central Europe since 1792. During the Directory, generals became increasingly powerful arbiters in political life. Napoleon manipulated the consuls and ultimately overthrew the Directory.

The Young Bonaparte

Of the strategically important Mediterranean island of Corsica, Jean-Jacques Rousseau in *The Social Contract* (1762) wrote, "I have a presentiment that one day this small island will astonish Europe." The year before, the Corsican patriot Pascale di Paoli (1725–1807) had managed to evict the Genoese from Corsica. But in 1768 the French took Corsica. Carlo Buonaparte, one of Paoli's followers, remained on the island rather than join Paoli in exile in England.

On August 15, 1769, Buonaparte's wife, whose family could trace its noble origins back to fourteenth-century Lombardy, gave birth to a son, Napoleon, named after a cousin who had been killed by the French. It is one of the strange ironies of history that Napoleon would have been British had his father followed Paoli into exile. In 1770, the French government accepted the Buonaparte family as nobles. The island's governor arranged for the young Buonaparte to receive an appointment to the royal military school at Brienne, in Champagne, which Napoleon entered as a boy in 1779. There he was exposed not only to a rigorous program of study but also to the humiliating condescension of the other students. He was an outsider, and the other students mocked his strong Corsican accent—Napoleon's first language was the patois of his island, a mix of Genovese and Tuscan—and his relatively humble economic situation. During the summer of 1789, he penned a history of his island in which the French were portrayed as murderous exploiters and tormenters, and Corsicans their victims. Unusually bright but also brooding, melancholy, and at least once even suicidal, he earned appointment to the artillery section of the national military academy in Paris, passing the examinations in a single year.

Antoine-Jean Gros's painting of the young Napoleon in *Bonaparte at Arcole* (1796).

Napoleon and the Revolution

With the outbreak of the Revolution, Napoleon returned to Corsica in September 1789. There he helped organize the National Guard and drew up a petition to the National Assembly in Paris asking that Corsica formally become part of France, with its people enjoying the rights of citizenship. In this way, Napoleon distanced himself from those Corsicans who wanted independence, thus parting ways with his hero Paoli, who had returned from England and joined the island's royalists. Napoleon favored the Revolution for three reasons: he wanted to see a curtailment of the abuses of the Old Regime; he hoped that the Revolution might end his island's status within France as little more than a conquered territory; and he thought the Revolution might provide him with an opportunity for promotion.

Napoleon became a Jacobin. He commanded a volunteer force that on Easter Sunday, 1792, fired on rioters supporting the cause of the Catholic Church. When Paoli's victorious forces turned the island over to the English, the Buonapartes were forced to flee. Sent by the Committee of Public Safety to fight federalist and royalist rebels and their British allies in the south, in December 1793 Napoleon planned the successful artillery siege of the port of Toulon, which was held by British forces.

Useful political connections and the lack of direct involvement in the bitter factional struggles in Paris may have saved Napoleon from execution in the Terror or during Thermidor. The result was that Napoleon's star continued to rise (with the help of his own determined campaign to construct a heroic public image of his exploits), while some of his Jacobin friends went to the guillotine. In the Paris of Thermidor, Napoleon helped put down a royalist uprising on October 6, 1795. He attracted the attention of—and soon married—Josephine de Beauharnais, the lover of the corrupt Paul Barras, one of the directors, and the widow of a member of the National Assembly who had been guillotined during the Terror. In 1796, the directors made Napoleon commander of the Army of Italy. It now seemed appropriate to eliminate the Italian spelling of his name; Buonaparte became Napoleon Bonaparte. Spectacular successes against the Austrians and their allies in Italy, including at the Battle of Arcole (November 1796), made him the toast of Paris. He later recalled that, after victory over Austrian forces at the Battle of Lodi (May 1796), which opened the way to Milan, "I realized I was a superior being and conceived the ambition of performing great things, which hitherto had filled my thoughts only as a fantastic dream. I saw the world flee beneath me, as if I were transported in air."

Napoleon was now conducting military and foreign policy virtually on his own, pillaging and looting Italy of art treasures as he pleased in the name of "liberty." His forceful and virtually independent pursuit of the war, and the subsequent peace he arranged with Austria at Campo Formio on October 18, 1797, gave France control of the Austrian Netherlands, Venetia, and the satellite Cisalpine Republic in northern and central Italy. For the moment, only Great Britain remained as an enemy.

Dreaming of an eastern empire, Napoleon then turned his attention to the Middle East. In 1798, he set off on a spectacular voyage to Egypt, part of the Ottoman Empire, thus undertaking the first try by a Western power to occupy a country in the Middle East. He was accompanied by 35,000 soldiers and a shipload of scientists, including mathematicians, physicians, zoologists, and engineers, a few of the latter already dreaming of carving a canal through the Isthmus of Suez that would give the French an overwhelming advantage in trade with the Far East. In Cairo he founded the Institute of Egypt, which greatly influenced the origins of Egyptology. Thus, Napoleon cloaked his invasion as a "civilizing mission."

After pausing en route long enough to capture the island of Malta, Napoleon defeated Egyptian forces at the Battle of the Pyramids in July 1798. But the tiny British admiral Horatio Nelson (1758–1805), who could see out of only one eye, had lost an arm, and had few teeth left, trapped and destroyed the French fleet on August 1, 1798, in the Battle of the Nile. Russia and Austria, their respective interests threatened by French campaigns in the east, now formed a Second Coalition against France, which Turkey also joined. Temporarily stranded in Egypt because of the naval defeat, and with his officers having to use the Greek historian Herodotus's *Histories* as their guide to Egypt, the undaunted Napoleon set off to conquer Syria. In Palestine his army stopped at Jaffa, where it massacred the population. Forced to retreat to Egypt by dwindling supplies and disease, Napoleon achieved a final victory there over the Turks with the annihilation of several more villages and their inhabitants. Napoleon then returned to France.

In Paris, Abbé Emmanuel Sieyès was plotting to overthrow the Directory. Such a venture now required the participation of one of the powerful, popular young generals whom the incessant warfare had catapulted to prominence. Napoleon, who could be portrayed as the potential savior of France, now helped piece together a political constituency from among the quarreling factions of the Directory. With the coup d'état of the 18th Brumaire (November 9, 1799), Sieyès and Napoleon overthrew the Directory.

CONSOLIDATION OF POWER

After the overthrow of the Directory, the conspirators established a new government, the Consulate. It brought political stability to France. It did so by concentrating strong executive authority in the eager hands of Napoleon, who oversaw the drafting of a constitution and made peace with the Catholic Church. Designated "consul for life" in 1802, Napoleon crowned himself emperor two years later. In the meantime, he continued to wage wars against Britain, Austria, Russia, and Prussia, four rivals driven into coalitions by French expansion. By 1809, although he had failed in his goal of bringing Britain to its knees, a series of remarkable victories enabled Napoleon to forge a great empire, the largest in Europe since that of Rome.

Establishment of the Consulate

With the fall of the Directory in 1799, Napoleon Bonaparte, at the age of thirty, became first consul, the most powerful man in France in a new, stronger executive authority of three consuls, replacing the five directors. The Constitution of 1799, promulgated in December, gave lip service to universal suffrage, but reflected the authoritarian character Sieyès intended. Indirect election for each political institution reduced the political body of the nation to a small number of notables. A Senate, appointed by the consuls, chose men from a list of 6,000 "notabilities" to serve in a Tribunate. A Council of State, whose members were appointed by the first consul, would propose legislation. The Tribunate would discuss the proposed legislation, and a Legislative Body would vote on the laws but could not debate them. There was more than a little truth to the oft-repeated story that one man who asked what was in the new constitution received the reply, "Napoleon Bonaparte." The constitution was submitted to voters in a plebiscite (voters could vote either yes or no). More than 99 percent of the all-male electorate approved the document. The plebiscite became a fundamental Napoleonic political institution, embodying his principle of "authority from above, confidence from below."

The Consulate provided political stability by institutionalizing strong executive authority. France's districts (*départements*) each received an appointed prefect, whose powers, delegated by the central government in Paris, surpassed those of the intendants of the Bourbon monarchs. Napoleon's brother Lucien, as minister of interior, extended effective executive authority to the most distant corners of the nation, curtailing royalist and Jacobin opposition. Napoleon ruthlessly suppressed the press, reducing the number of newspapers in Paris from seventy-three to thirteen, cowing survivors with threats, or winning their allegiance with bribes.

The Concordat

Napoleon made peace with the Catholic Church, bringing it under state supervision. Deep hostility remained between priests who had sworn allegiance to the nation during the Revolution—the "juring" clergy—and those who had refused. Influenced by the Enlightenment, Napoleon believed the Church should not have an institutional role in the affairs of state. But he was also a cynical pragmatist. "There is only one way to encourage morality," he once said, "and that is to reestablish religion. Society cannot exist without some being richer than others, and this inequality cannot exist without religion. When one man is dying of hunger next door to another who is stuffing himself with food, the poor man simply cannot accept the disparity unless some authority tells him, 'God wishes it so . . . in heaven things will be different.'" An agreement with the Church also was intended to undercut popular support for the monarchist cause by restoring some of the Church's prerogatives, but not any that would threaten the government's authority. Napoleon thus shrewdly sought to detach the Church from the quest for a restoration of the monarchy.

With the death in 1799 of Pope Pius VI (pope 1775–1799), who had refused any accommodation with the Revolution, his successor, Pius VII (pope 1800–1823), was eager to end a decade of religious turmoil. In 1801, Napoleon signed a Concordat with the papacy that helped solidify some of the changes brought by the Revolution, declaring Catholicism "the religion of the majority of citizens" in France. A majority of bishops refused to accept the Concordat. The pope would henceforth appoint new bishops, but on the recommendation of the first consul, that is, Napoleon. The Church also abandoned all claims to those ecclesiastical lands that had been sold as "national property" during the first years of the Revolution. The Concordat helped restore ecclesiastical influence in France, reflected by an increase in religious observance and in the number of people entering the clergy. Napoleon also pleased the Church by abandoning the confusing official calendar put in place in 1793, reestablishing Sundays and religious holidays.

The Organic Articles, which Napoleon promulgated without consulting the pope, regulated the Gallican (French) Church's status in France and reduced the pope's authority. The Church would now be subject to virtually the same administrative organization and policing as any other organization;

Napoleon and Pope Pius VII signing the Concordat in 1801, reconciling the Catholic Church with France after the Revolution.

a "minister of religion" would sit with the other ministers in Paris. The state would pay clerical salaries. No papal bull could be read in France's churches without permission of the government, and the clergy would have to read official government decrees from the pulpit. Under Napoleon, the Church gained the freedom of religious practice, but at the expense of some of its independence. Primary-school students were required to memorize a new catechism:

> *Question:* What are the duties of Christians with respect to the princes who govern them, and what are, in particular, our duties toward Napoleon . . . ?
> *Answer:* . . . Love, respect, obedience, fidelity, military service. . . . We also owe him fervent prayers for his safety and for the spiritual and temporal prosperity of the State.

Napoleon granted Protestants and Jews state protection to practice their religion. An article of the Concordat guaranteed freedom of worship for people in both religions (who together made up less than 5 percent of the population, the vast majority of whom were Protestants). One set of Organic Articles supervised Calvinists, another Lutherans. An imperial decree in 1808 organized Judaism into territorial consistories, although rabbis, unlike priests and Protestant ministers, were not to be paid by the state.

Napoleon's settlement with the Church alienated some of his cautious supporters on the left, notably the group known as the Ideologues. After a solemn ceremony at Notre Dame Cathedral in Paris celebrating the Concordat, one general put it bluntly to Napoleon—"A fine monkish show. It lacked only the presence of the hundred thousand men who gave their lives to end all that."

Napoleon's Leadership

One of his staff would later describe Napoleon as an "ever-restless spirit." He ate rapidly and could work days on end with very little sleep. He dictated more than 80,000 letters in his extraordinary career. Napoleon seemed to absorb every bit of information that arrived in his office or field headquarters and rapidly mastered subjects related to military or administrative concerns. But he often ignored matters that did not particularly interest him, such as economics and naval warfare, in which France lagged behind Britain.

Napoleon was more than just an optimist. He believed that his wildest dreams of conquest and empire would inevitably become reality. Everyone feared his rages, although he could be surprisingly understanding and generous toward subordinates when he believed they erred. He delegated very little meaningful authority, mistrusting even his closest advisers, but he tolerated opposing viewpoints. Napoleon's style of leadership became ever more tyrannical. He made up his own mind, and that mind invariably chose war.

Wars of Conquest and Empire

Napoleon had brought stability to France, but France was still at war with the Second Coalition: Great Britain, Austria, and Russia. In February 1800, when Austria turned down his overtures for peace on the basis of the Treaty of Campo Formio (1797), Napoleon returned to the battlefield, retaking Milan and defeating an Austrian army in June 1800. With the Treaty of Lunéville (February 1801), Austria reaffirmed the conditions of the Treaty of Campo Formio, accepting French gains in Italy, as well as French control over the Southern Netherlands (Belgium).

With Austria defeated and Russia tied up by a war against the Ottoman Empire, the British government signed the Peace of Amiens in March 1802. France kept all of its significant gains on the continent, and Britain returned all of the French colonies it had captured. Great Britain gained only the end of hostilities.

In Central Europe, Napoleon was now free to dismember the Holy Roman Empire and to dictate the territorial reorganization of the small German states. France had absorbed the left bank of the Rhine River, fulfilling the nationalistic dreams of a France extending to its "natural frontiers." Since this expansion came at the expense of Prussia and Austria, these two powers had to be compensated. By the oddly named Imperial Recess of 1803, the two most powerful German states absorbed a number of small, independent German states, ecclesiastical territories, and most of the free cities. The rulers of Baden, Bavaria, Hesse-Kassel, and Württemberg, the other largest German states, also added to their domains. France's position in Italy also was solidified. Piedmont remained a French possession, with Napoleon naming himself president of the Italian Cisalpine Republic. After imposing a Federal Constitution on the cantons of Switzerland that transformed them into the Helvetic Republic, Napoleon forced a defensive alliance on that strategically important country. By 1802, France was at peace for the first time in a decade. Napoleon had brought his nation to a position of dominance in Europe not seen since the time of Charlemagne a thousand years earlier.

No longer satisfied with the title "first consul," in 1802 Napoleon became "consul for life," a change approved by another plebiscite. Napoleon then prepared the establishment of a hereditary empire in France. Although thousands of émigrés took advantage of a declared amnesty to return to France, an alleged conspiracy against Napoleon's life by a group of royalists in 1804 led him to act against the Bourbons and to expedite his plan to become emperor. Napoleon accused Louis de Bourbon-Condé, the duke of Enghien (1772–1804)—a member of the Bourbon family who had emigrated to Baden—of involvement in the conspiracy. French troops moved into Baden to arrest him. The duke was hurriedly tried and executed near Paris, despite the lack of any evidence of his involvement in plans to assassinate Napoleon. Public opinion throughout much of Europe was outraged. The German composer Ludwig van Beethoven crossed out the dedication to Napoleon of his Third Symphony ("Eroica," meaning "heroic") shouting, "So he is also nothing more than an ordinary man? Now he will trample on the rights of mankind and indulge only his own ambition; from now on he will make himself superior to all others and become a tyrant!" One of the royalist conspirators, before his own execution, lamented, "We have done more than we hoped to do; we meant to give France a king, and we have given her an Emperor."

The Tribunate, Senate, and another plebiscite quickly approved the change from the Consulate to an empire. On December 2, 1804, Napoleon was anointed emperor by Pius VII. Instead of waiting for the pope to crown him, Napoleon snatched the crown from the pontiff and placed it on his own head. A new constitution presented a telling contradiction: "The government of the republic is entrusted to an emperor." Once an unknown officer who had scraped by with little money amid the spendthrift glitter of Thermidor, Bonaparte began to wear a coat of red velvet that would have been fit for Louis XIV.

Napoleon was no more temperamentally suited to live with peace than with defeat. Jealous of Britain's naval and commercial supremacy in the

Jean-Louis David's *Emperor Napoleon Crowning the Empress Joséphine in the Cathedral of Notre Dame* (1805–1808).

Mediterranean and the Western Hemisphere, he began to goad Britain into a new war. Haiti, the western side of the island of Hispaniola, had proclaimed its independence from France in 1801 under the leadership of Toussaint L'Ouverture (see Chapter 12). In 1802, in response to pressure from sugar planters, Napoleon restored French control of Haiti and reinstituted slavery in the French colonies. French troops captured L'Ouverture and took him to France, where he soon died. However, tropical disease killed most of the French troops occupying Haiti, and the British prevented the arrival of reinforcements. The French army surrendered, and in 1804 Haiti, which had been France's richest colony, again became independent. With his plans to extend France's empire to the Caribbean having come to naught, Napoleon shouted "Damn sugar, damn coffee, damn colonies!"

Seeking to recoup the financial losses France had incurred from war, Napoleon sold the huge Louisiana Territory to the United States in 1803 for 60 million francs (then about 11 million dollars). In retrospect, this was a paltry sum for a territory that virtually doubled the size of what was then the United States. Napoleon's hope that its former colony would emerge as a rival to Britain also lay behind the sale.

In July 1805, Russia and Austria joined Britain to form the Third Coalition against Napoleon. Undaunted, Napoleon readied an army and ships at the port of Boulogne on the English Channel for an invasion of Britain. A French decoy fleet lured Horatio Nelson's fleet into pursuit, hoping to inflict a crushing defeat on the Royal Navy. But the hunter soon became the hunted. When the French fleet sailed from the Spanish Mediterranean port of Cádiz on October 21, 1805, it sighted the Royal Navy. Turning to sail back to port, the French vessels were left vulnerable to attack by two columns of ships that succeeded in breaking the French line. As Nelson lay dying of a wound (which might have been avoided, had he covered up his shiny medals and epaulets that attracted a French marksman's eye), his fleet earned one of naval history's most decisive victories at Cape Trafalgar, not far from Gibraltar. Any chance for a French invasion of England evaporated. Great Britain controlled the seas.

The French armies were more successful on the continent. They defeated the Austrians at Ulm in October 1805, capturing 50,000 troops. Napoleon finally coaxed the Russians and Austrians into open battle. At Austerlitz on December 2, 1805, Napoleon tricked his opponents into an attack on his intentionally weakened right flank. He then divided the two armies with a crushing attack at their vulnerable center. When the dust cleared after the battle, the Russians and their Austrian allies had suffered 30,000 casualties, the French fewer than 9,000. Austria asked for peace, giving up the remnants of imperial territories in Italy and Dalmatia. Napoleon's allies, Bavaria, Baden, and Württemberg, once again gained Habsburg territories.

In the wake of Austerlitz, the hesitant King Frederick William III (ruled 1797–1840) of Prussia abandoned his tentative agreement to join the Third Coalition, instead signing an alliance with France. In July 1806,

The Battle of Trafalgar.

Napoleon organized the Confederation of the Rhine, composed of sixteen German states, excluding Prussia and Austria (see Map 13.1). Napoleon named himself "Protector" of the Confederation, whose members agreed to accept French garrisons in southern Germany and to support Napoleon if war broke out again. This made the Holy Roman Empire even more irrelevant than it had been for a very long time. In 1806, Francis II (Francis I of Austria) simply dissolved the clumsy entity by abdicating as Holy Roman emperor.

As French power in Central Europe grew, the British government convinced Frederick William to join the alliance against Napoleon. But Napoleon's forces humiliated the Prussian army at Jena near Nuremberg on October 14, 1806, and then occupied Berlin. In February 1807, the French and Russian armies fought to a bloody draw in a Polish snowstorm. Had Austrian and British troops been sent to support the Russians, Napoleon might well have been soundly defeated. But Austria was still reeling from the defeat at Austerlitz, and the British were preoccupied with defending their commercial interests in the Western Hemisphere. Napoleon sent for fresh troops from France and added 30,000 Polish soldiers, some attracted by speculation that the emperor might create an independent Polish state.

After defeating the Russian army at the Battle of Friedland (June 1807), Napoleon met with Tsar Alexander I (ruled 1801–1825) on a raft in the middle of a river. Frederick William, the king of Prussia, paced anxiously on

MAP 13.1 THE EMPIRE OF NAPOLEON   This map shows the areas conquered by Napoleon, including dependent states and states incorporated directly into France or ruled by Napoleon's relatives.

the shore as he awaited the outcome. The news was indeed bad. By the Treaty of Tilsit (July 1807), Prussia lost territory in western Germany and in Poland, which became, respectively, the Kingdom of Westphalia and the Grand Duchy of Warsaw, the latter annexed by Napoleon's ally, Saxony. The king of Saxony became the grand duke of Warsaw by virtue of a personal union. Russia was forced to accept the territorial settlements in Western Europe as definitive. In return, the tsar received a promise of French support in Russia's current quarrel with the Ottoman Empire. France thus tacitly agreed to back Russia's long-standing ambitions in southeastern Europe. Finally, the tsar agreed to close Russian ports to British ships.

When Austria challenged Napoleon by invading Bavaria in 1809, Napoleon moved rapidly against Vienna, capturing the Habsburg capital. He then crossed to the left bank of the Danube River and defeated the Habsburg army in July at Wagram, a battle in which 300,000 men participated and 80,000 were killed or wounded. Defeat forced Austria to surrender Illyria to France and other territory to Bavaria and Russia, which was still technically but uneasily allied to France. With Austria defeated and weakened, Prussia discouraged and dismembered, Russia neutralized, and Britain once again left alone to challenge France, Napoleon's position in Europe seemed invincible. Through conquest, the establishment of satellite states, and alliances with smaller powers, Napoleon had constructed a vast empire.

The Corsican Warrior

Napoleon has been considered one of the most brilliant military leaders in modern history. Yet his talents lay not in originality but in his stunningly innovative adaptations of military strategies and tactics developed in the eighteenth century and during the Revolution. Before mass military conscription, warfare had usually involved relatively limited numbers of soldiers. Armies had not moved rapidly. Since the beginning of the Thirty Years' War (1618–1648), wars had been fought over dynastic honor, commercial rivalry, and disputed territories (see Chapters 7 and 11). Old Regime armies had consisted largely of mercenaries commanded by nobles. Most battles had been fought in precise, drilled ranks, by two relatively small armies in line formation directly facing each other.

In the eighteenth century, technological and tactical improvements in artillery augmented its importance in warfare. Artillery pieces became lighter and therefore could be moved more easily. Improvements in roads also helped expedite the movement of cannon, as well as troops. Properly positioned artillery, launching powerful shells, could now play a decisive role against infantry. The artillery became a more respected part of the army; talented officers, Napoleon not the least of them, found a chance for promotion that they would not have had elsewhere.

Warfare changed when armies were no longer made up of mercenaries but rather of "citizen-soldiers" with greater commitment to their cause. Thus, during the French Revolution, committed sans-culottes were first mobilized as citizen-soldiers in the *levée en masse* proclaimed in August 1792. They fought to defend the nation, winning the stunning victory over the Austrian army at Valmy (September 1792; see Chapter 12). The Revolution inaugurated a period of warfare in Europe in which more soldiers entered battle than ever before. Between 1800 and 1815, perhaps as many as 2 million men served in or allied with Napoleon's armies. Napoleon harnessed French nationalism to win the commitment of his armies.

The Prussian general and military writer Karl von Clausewitz (1780–1831) described how warfare, which he defined as "an extension of state policy by other means," had changed. Whereas the wars of most of the eighteenth century had been those of kings and of states, not entire peoples, now "war had again suddenly become an affair of the people, and that of a people numbering thirty million, every one of whom regarded himself a citizen of the state."

Napoleon's genius was his ability to organize, oversee, and assure the supplying of and communication between larger armies than had ever before been effectively assembled, and to move them more rapidly than anyone before him. "Everything is in the execution," as he put it. He built on the French innovation in 1792–1793 of using combat divisions that combined

French citizens drawing lots to determine who would be conscripted to fight in Napoleon's wars.

infantry, cavalry, and artillery, and he subdivided his armies into corps, each with its own sense of pride.

Napoleon founded a military school in 1803 that produced 4,000 officers by 1815—there were lots of vacancies as the wars took their toll. As in the administration of the empire, however, Napoleon refused to delegate responsibility for crucial strategic and tactical decisions to his subordinates. In the long run, this would cost him dearly.

The infantry remained the heart of Napoleon's armies and his military planning (there were never more than 4 artillerymen for every 1,000 foot soldiers). Napoleon perfected the "mixed order" formation developed in the eighteenth century, which combined stretching troops across the field in a thin line about three men deep and bunching them in columns not only for marching but also for attack. Napoleon kept some battalions in columns, others in lines, which allowed battlefield flexibility. When he saw the opportunity, he launched an attack by outflanking his opponent and striking against the enemy's lines of communication. When he confronted an army stretched out before him, skilled marksmen threw the opponent's advance forces into disarray. Napoleon then brilliantly assessed the opposing army's weakest point. The concentration of deadly artillery fire—Napoleon once referred to the twelve-pound cannons as his "beautiful daughters"—prepared the way for the assault of the infantry columns. The speed of his army's movements was such that Napoleon could rapidly attack and defeat part of an enemy army before reinforcements could arrive. Instead of stopping to celebrate victory, Napoleon sent his troops, particularly the cavalry, to pursue the enemy. Victory became a rout.

Napoleon's armies, unlike the professional armies of the Old Regime, lived off the land, simply requisitioning what they needed. This did not make the French troops very popular, even in those lands officially incorporated into the empire. But it did allow the imperial army to travel far afield, in great numbers, marching up to twenty miles a day. Such speed seemed incredible for the period, since each infantryman carried with him about sixty pounds of equipment.

Finally, Napoleon enjoyed intense loyalty from his officers and troops, even up to the bitter end. He took to the field with his troops and rewarded good work with promotions and decorations, sometimes given on the field of battle. The emperor's own courage was also a source of inspiration to his troops. During one battle, the Imperial Guard refused to fight until Napoleon had moved to a safer place. He treated his soldiers with demonstrable respect and even affection because they seemed willing to die for him. At least 400,000 did just that.

The Napoleonic adventure offered even the most humble soldier a chance for glory. Yet the risks of injury and death were considerable. Disease sometimes killed more soldiers than battlefield wounds. (Napoleon had the good fortune to be wounded only twice in his long military career.) Soldiering was a tough life. In good times, soldiers ate reasonably well—bread, vegetables,

Napoleon used titles and awards as pillars of the empire. Jacques-Louis David's *Oath of the Army after the Distribution of Standards* shows the eagerness of the army to defend Napoleon and the empire.

even some meat, and drank wine or rum. But after defeat, or when they were far inside inhospitable territory, soldiers were fortunate just to find enough to eat. Medical care remained inadequate, despite improvements that included caring for wounded soldiers while the battle was still raging, rather than afterward when it often was too late. Major surgery—including the countless amputations occurring after each major battle—was often fatal. Napoleon, however, remained far more concerned with able-bodied soldiers than with the wounded or sick.

THE FOUNDATIONS OF THE FRENCH EMPIRE

The Napoleonic empire was a significant episode in the long story of statemaking in Europe. Continuing the tradition of eighteenth-century monarchs, Napoleon sought to make state administration more efficient and uniform. His aggressive conquests brought centrally controlled, bureaucratic government and a centralized legal system to much of the continent. For this reason, it is possible to see him as the embodiment of "enlightened absolutism" awaited by the philosophe Voltaire.

Napoleon created a new social hierarchy based not on blood but on service to the state, particularly in the army and bureaucracy, and on ownership of property. Beyond French borders, the empire was based on an imperial system in which Napoleon made his relatives and marshals heads of state. Thus, he gave the throne of Westphalia to his brother Jérôme, as earlier he had transformed the Cisalpine Republic in northern Italy into a monarchy ruled by his stepson, Eugène de Beauharnais. He named his brother Louis king of Holland. His brother Joseph became king of Naples and later king of Spain. Everywhere that French armies conquered, Napoleon's daunting will imposed change.

Institutional Foundations: Imperial Centralization

Napoleon's Council of State, the most prestigious and important administrative body of the empire, oversaw finance, interior affairs, and war. Members advised the emperor and drew up laws and regulations for approval by the Legislative Body. Napoleon attached to the council a corps of young, bright, apprentice bureaucrats who would assume important administrative posts in the future. The Senate, Legislative Body, and Tribunate lost all but their ceremonial roles, and Napoleon completely eliminated the Tribunate in 1807. Even the members of the Council of State found their influence on the emperor increasingly reduced.

Napoleon established the Bank of France in 1800, which facilitated the state's ability to borrow money. He followed the Directory's policy of abandoning the grossly inflated paper money of the Revolution. This stabilized France's currency. He facilitated the assessment and collection of taxes, ordering a land survey of the entire country upon which direct taxes were to be based. And he expanded the number of indirect taxes collected on salt (which had also been a principal source of revenue for the Old Regime monarchy), tobacco, and liquor, as well as on goods brought into any town of over 5,000 inhabitants.

The empire followed the Revolution, and particularly the Directory, in making higher education the responsibility of the state. With about half the population illiterate, Napoleon believed that schools could create patriotic and obedient citizens through teaching secular values that would ultimately link education to nationalism. In 1802, Napoleon established state secondary schools (*lycées*), thirty-seven of which were operating six years later, for the relatively few boys who went to secondary school. Students read only textbooks approved by the emperor. In 1808, Napoleon created France's first public university system, charging it with "direct[ing] political and moral opinions."

Legal Foundations: The Napoleonic Code

Napoleon wanted to be known to history as the new Justinian, the Roman lawgiver. The Civil Code of 1804, which became known as the Napoleonic Code, may have been the emperor's most lasting legacy. Many of the *cahiers*, or lists of grievances submitted to Louis XVI on the eve of the Revolution, had asked that French laws be uniform. During the constitutional monarchy, the Convention had begun the process of codifying French laws, but it had been interrupted by the vicissitudes of the Revolution. While the fundamental division in French law had been between the written Roman law in the south and customary law based upon regional and local traditions in the north, there were many different legal codes in France. Napoleon ordered the Council of State to seek advice from a battery of lawyers to codify the laws of the land. Napoleon personally participated in many critical discussions and debates. The Napoleonic Code made the rights of property owners sacrosanct: the majority of the articles concerned private property.

The code, over 2,000 articles long, enshrined the equality of all people before the law and granted the freedom of religion. The subsequent Penal Code of 1810 proclaimed the "freedom of work," reaffirming the Le Chapelier Law of 1791 that forbade the formation of workers' or employers' associations (the latter were extremely rare). The "freedom" guaranteed in relations between employers and workers left workers legally subordinate to their employers and unable to strike. Furthermore, workers were required to carry small passports that had to be handed over to municipal officials, police, or employers when requested.

The Napoleonic Code reflected Napoleon's traditional attitudes toward the family. He considered the family the most important intermediary between the state and the individual, a means of guaranteeing social order. Rejecting scattered demands during the Revolution for the equality of women, the code reaffirmed the patriarchal nature of the traditional family. It made women and children legally dependent on their husbands or fathers. The code granted men control of family property. A woman could not buy or sell property or begin a business without her husband's permission, and any income she earned would pass to his descendants, not hers. A woman worker's wages, too, went to her husband, and women had no control over their children's savings. As during the First Republic, the state recognized divorce, but it was now more difficult to obtain. More articles in the Napoleonic Code established conditions for the sale of cattle than addressed the legal status of women. In cases of adultery, women risked penalties that were far more severe than those for men. Only adult males could officially witness a legal document. Napoleon complained: "In France women are considered too highly. They should not be regarded as equal to men. In reality they are nothing more than machines for producing children."

As in the Old Regime, parents could put their offspring in jail and retained authority over their children's marriages. The code required equal inheritance of all children (the parents could dispose of a certain percentage, based on a sliding scale, as he or she wished), ending primogeniture (inheritance by the eldest son) in northern France, where it still existed. Yet siblings often found ways to keep the family property together; one brother could buy out his brothers' shares in an inherited property. The end of primogeniture also may have provided an impetus for French couples to have fewer children in an effort to avoid further division of property.

The Napoleonic Code—despite its obvious inequities, imperfections, and the fact that it was sometimes promulgated by a conquering army—served as the basis for the codification of laws and the reorganization of judicial systems in Switzerland, Piedmont-Sardinia, and the Netherlands. At the end of his life, Napoleon claimed, "My glory is not to have won forty battles . . . but what nothing will destroy, what will live eternally, is my Civil Code."

Social Foundations: The Imperial Hierarchy

Napoleon once wrote, "My motto has always been: a career open to all talents." He considered the end of social distinctions by birth to be one of the most lasting accomplishments of the French Revolution. The empire favored the aspirations of the middle classes. The elimination of legal barriers to social ascension left wealth, largely defined by the ownership of property and service to the state (rewarded by grants of property, titles, and pensions), as the main determinant of status. Yet imposing obstacles to social mobility remained. It took wealth to acquire the background, education, and reputation to take one's place in the imperial hierarchy.

The army and the bureaucracy were the two pillars of the empire. Napoleon created an elite of "notables," as they were called, rewarding those who served him well with prestigious titles and lucrative positions. At the pinnacle of the new hierarchy were eighteen marshals, appointed in 1804 from the ranks of the Senate and including generals who had earned fortunes waging war. Napoleon began to restore titles abolished by the Revolution: prince in 1804, duke two years later, followed by count, baron, and chevalier. But unlike the titles of the Old Regime, these titles, which could be hereditary, did not stem from the ownership of a certain estate or château, but rather were awarded for service to the state.

Between 1808 and 1814, Napoleon created 3,600 titles. Yet Napoleonic notables totaled only one-seventh of the number of the nobles in France on the eve of the Revolution. Some of the new notables had already become rich through purchase of ecclesiastical and émigré lands sold during the Revolution. More than half of all men granted titles by the emperor had rendered service in the military. The emperor often repeated that "in the backpack of each soldier, there is a marshal's baton." The civil service was the second most important avenue to a Napoleonic title. Some Italians, Dutch, Germans, and others from conquered lands found that the French Empire offered them dignified and sometimes even lucrative careers.

In May 1802, Napoleon established the Legion of Honor to reward those who served the nation with distinction. It was, predictably enough, organized along military lines, with commanders, officers, and knights. Indeed 97 percent of those so decorated by Napoleon served in his military forces. Yet a former Jacobin member of the Council of State complained that the award, a decorated cross that could be displayed prominently on one's coat, was nothing more than a "bauble." Napoleon replied, "You may call them baubles, but it is by baubles that mankind is governed." The subjects of territories incorporated into the empire were eligible to receive the Legion of Honor. When Rome became part of Napoleon's immense empire, the following parody on the Legion of Honor appeared on the walls of the Eternal City:

> In fierce old times, they balanced loss
> By hanging thieves upon a cross.
> But our more humane age believes
> In hanging crosses on the thieves.

THE TIDE TURNS AGAINST NAPOLEON

French rule generated resistance in countries absorbed into Napoleon's empire through conquest. Napoleon manipulated factional splits in some countries, co-opted local elites where he could, brushed aside rulers as he pleased, and tried to establish compliant new regimes, some handed over to his brothers. But ultimately French rule over such an extended empire collapsed. Napoleon's failure to force British submission by strangling its economy with his "Continental System," which aimed to cut off Britain from its continental markets, kept his major enemy in the field, or more appropriately, on the high seas. In Spain, resistance against French rule became a full-fledged rebellion (the Peninsular War) that, with British assistance, sapped imperial resources. Moreover, French occupation of some of the German states gave rise to German nationalism, solidifying resistance. Prussian and Austrian military reforms led to stronger opponents in the field. And in a final ill-considered expansion of imperial aggression, Napoleon in 1812 decided to invade Russia. The destruction of his "Grand Army" in the snow-drifts and howling winds of Russia was the beginning of the end.

The Continental System

Knowing that the war was costing the British government huge sums (between 60 and 90 percent of the state's annual revenue), in November 1806 Napoleon announced his Continental System. It prohibited trade with Britain, which he hoped would strangle the British economy by closing all continental ports to British ships. French merchants and manufacturers, as well as the state, would earn fortunes supplying the captive markets of the continent. Increased hardship might even cause damaging unrest in Britain.

But the blockade of the continental ports was far easier said than done. The continental coastline is enormous, the British navy was strong (despite the loss of 317 ships between 1803 and 1815), and the merchants and smugglers resourceful. British merchants continued to find American markets for their goods. The banning of British imports did lead to the development of some important innovations in France (for example, the Jacquard loom for silk weaving and the planting of the sugar beet to compensate for the loss of sugar from the West Indies). But France's relative lack of available coal and iron ore, its lack of capital accumulation and investment, and the overwhelming allocation of the nation's material and human resources to war prevented French merchants from taking up the slack left by the absence of British goods in continental markets.

In response to Napoleon's Continental System, the British government's "Orders in Council" of November and December 1807 demanded that trading ships under all flags purchase a license in a British port. This decision placed Britain at loggerheads with the United States, one of France's principal trading partners. Napoleon retaliated with the Milan Decrees, threatening to seize any ship that had traded with Britain or that had even accepted a search by British authorities. Yet, in 1809, British imports could still be readily found on the continent. The French, suffering a sharp decline in customs revenue, began tolerating violations of the Continental System, even selling special licenses and placing hefty taxes on the importation of British goods to bring in more revenue. The blockade came completely apart in the midst of an economic depression that began in 1811.

Napoleon counted on Britain's deepening crisis with the U.S. government, which opposed the boarding and searching of its vessels by British

British Prime Minister William Pitt the Younger and Napoleon carve up the world.

inspectors, to bring Anglo-American relations to a breaking point. But even the War of 1812 between the British and the United States, which ended with the exhausted British capitulating, could not destroy the British economy. Moreover, the fact that French agents had encouraged an Irish insurrection against British rule in 1798 lingered in the memory of the British upper class, adding to their resentment of France. Tory governments, which governed Britain throughout the entire revolutionary and Napoleonic periods, remained committed to defeating Bonaparte (and repressing dissent at home), despite the staggering economic cost of the war.

The Peninsular War

Napoleon's obsession with bringing Britain to its knees led him into the disastrous Peninsular War (1808–1813) in Spain. In 1807, Napoleon had reached an agreement with Charles IV (ruled 1788–1808), the incompetent king of Spain, that permitted French troops to pass through his kingdom to conquer Portugal, Britain's ally (an arrangement that had functioned to guarantee Portugal's independence from Spain and had also provided Portuguese wine with a ready market for thirsty British people of means). A French army marched on Lisbon, and the Portuguese royal family fled to Brazil. An insurrection in March 1808 led to the abdication of Charles IV and the succession of his son Ferdinand VII (ruled 1808, 1814–1833) to the throne. Believing that the kingdom of Spain was on the verge of falling like an apple into his hands, Napoleon forced Ferdinand to abdicate that same year, and summoned his older brother, Joseph Bonaparte (1768–1844), from his wobbly throne in Naples to become king of Spain.

But Napoleon did not count on the resistance of the Spanish people. Ecclesiastical reforms imposed by Joseph and Napoleon, including the reduction in the number of monastic convents by two-thirds and the abolition of the Inquisition, angered the Church, which remained a powerful force in Spanish life. Napoleon found some allies among the urban middle class, but the Spanish nobility joined their old allies, the clergy, in opposition to the invaders. French forces were easy targets for the small, mobile groups of Spanish guerrillas, who attacked and then quickly disappeared into the Spanish landscape. British troops led by Arthur Wellesley, later duke of Wellington (1769–1852), arrived to help the Spanish and Portuguese fight the French. By 1810, about 350,000 French troops were tied up in the Iberian Peninsula. Fighting for "Church and king," Spaniards sustained what arguably was the first successful guerrilla war in modern Europe. Napoleon's "Spanish ulcer" bled France.

Stirrings of Nationalism in Napoleonic Europe

One of the lasting effects of the Napoleonic period was the quickening of German and, to a lesser extent, Italian national identity. The French revolutionaries had called for a war against the tyrants of Europe. But Napoleon

Francisco Goya's *The Third of May, 1808* depicts the execution of citizens of Madrid by French soldiers after the fall of the city during the Peninsular War.

seemed blind to the fact that the exportation of the principles of the French Revolution might encourage resentment and even nationalist feeling against the French in those countries conquered by his armies. Gradually the French discovered that nationalism was a double-edged sword. Some people in states conquered by French armies not only resented the occupation of their lands but they also began to long for the existence of a territorial state organized around their own nationality.

In any case, Napoleon sought to curry favor in each conquered state in exchange for support against his enemies. Napoleon may indeed have intended that Westphalia, created by the Treaty of Tilsit (1807) out of former Prussian territories and other smaller states that had fought against him, would become a model state. He ended serfdom and gave peasants the right to own land, to move through the kingdom as they pleased, and to send their children to school. But his principal goal was to bolster the Confederation of the Rhine's north flank against possible attacks against his interests.

Napoleon considered conquered territories sources for military conscripts and raw materials, or as potential markets for French goods. In Italy, French authorities forbade the importation of textile machinery and imposed disadvantageous tariffs, fearful of competition with their own industries. With the exception of Jacobin anti-clericals, intellectuals, and merchants who stood to profit from the French occupation, most people expressed little enthusiasm for the Napoleonic regime. In the Netherlands, the French occupation virtually brought the prosperous Dutch trading economy to a standstill. Poles soon began to doubt Napoleon's promise to reestablish Polish independence; some Polish nobles began to look to the Russian tsar for help, others to the king of Prussia. Among those territories conquered by Napoleon, open insurrections were relatively rare, although in the Austrian Tyrol, peasants sang nationalist songs as they fought against the French in 1813. The French armies waged war brutally against those who dared oppose them, burning villages and executing civilians, particularly in Spain, Tyrol, and southern Italy.

The impact of the French invasions on nationalism was perhaps clearest in the numerous German states. At first, some German intellectuals had praised Napoleon, but that soon changed. Attacks by German writers against French occupation mounted in 1807. That year, the French executed a Nuremburg bookseller accused of selling anti-French literature. Two years later, Napoleon escaped an assassination attempt by a young German student, the son of a Lutheran minister, who shouted "Long live Germany!" as he was executed. Gradually German writers espoused the view that people of the German states shared a common culture based upon language, tradition, and history. Only in the middle of the eighteenth century had German writers begun to write in their own language; before then, they considered French the language of culture. Like some composers, they began to discover elements of a common culture, drawing on language, literary texts, folk traditions, and other German cultural traditions to express themselves. This emotional quest for cultural and political institutions that would define "Germany" reflected some rejection of the rational tradition of Enlightenment thought identified with France.

Some German nationalists believed that the multiplicity of states in Central Europe stood in the way of eventual German unification. The Holy Roman Empire had been swept away in 1806. Napoleon destroyed the religious settlement imposed by the Treaty of Westphalia, which in 1648 had ended the Thirty Years' War. Napoleon may have helped the cause of German nationalism by eliminating some tiny states, increasing the territory of the middle-sized states at the expense of the former. About 60 percent of the population of the German states passed from one ruler to another during the revolutionary and Napoleonic eras. Yet in states such as Hanover and Württemburg, German particularism—local identity—was considered part of being German. Forty separate German states survived. Baden, Bavaria, and Württemberg, although much smaller and less powerful than Austria and Germany, emerged from the period with their independence and separate traditions for the most part intact.

Even though any possible political unification of Germany seemed distant, if not impossible, German nationalism nonetheless contributed to the determination with which the people of the German states resisted Napoleon. Johann Gottlieb Fichte (1762–1814) called on "the German nation," which he defined as including anyone who spoke German, to discover its spiritual unity.

In Spain, as we have seen, people of all classes came to view the French as invaders, not liberators. A constitution proposed by the Spanish Cortes in 1812 at Cádiz, which was not under French control, nonetheless reflected the influence of the French Revolution. It proclaimed freedom of the press, established an assembly to be elected by a relatively wide electorate, and abolished the Inquisition. But the constitution, although never implemented because of the eclipse of Spanish liberals in the wake of conservative reaction, was also a self-consciously nationalist document. Some Spaniards, too, were becoming more aware of their own shared linguistic, cultural, and historical traditions.

Military Reforms in Prussia and Austria

The successes of Napoleon's armies led Prussia (particularly in view of the devastating Prussian defeat at Jena in 1806), and, to a lesser extent, Austria, to enact military reforms. In 1807, a royal decree abolished serfdom in Prussia, with military efficiency in mind. Peasants were now free to leave the land to which they had been attached and to marry without the lord's permission. A decree three years later allowed peasants to convert some of the land they worked into their own property. Other reforms removed class barriers that had restricted the sale of land between nobles and non-nobles and that had served to keep middle-class men from assuming the military rank of officer (and had also prevented nobles from taking positions considered beneath their status). The Prussian military commander Baron Heinrich Karl vom und zum Stein (1757–1831) appointed some commoners to be officers and cashiered some of the more inept noble commanders. Stein established a ministry of war, taking away some important decisions from the whims of the king and his inner circle. In 1807, the Stein ministry abolished serfs' ties to the land, but the labor obligations and seigneurial dues of serfs remained in effect. This reform improved the loyalty of peasant-soldiers to the state. Stein called for greater patriotic participation in the national affairs of Prussia. Thus he and many other statesmen who resisted Napoleon continued to think in Prussian, not "German" terms. The elimination of most forms of corporal punishment enhanced troop morale, as did the rewarding of individual soldiers who served well. Stein also organized a civilian militia, which provided a proud, patriotic reserve of 120,000 part-time soldiers.

The Empire's Decline and the Russian Invasion

Napoleon now confronted the fact that he still had no legitimate children to inherit his throne. Although he loved his wife Josephine, he was as unfaithful to her during his lengthy absences as she was to him. Napoleon arranged for a bishop in Paris to annul his marriage—the pope having refused to do so—allowing him to remarry with the Church's blessing. Napoleon then considered diplomatically useful spouses. When the Russian tsar would not provide his younger sister, Napoleon arranged a marriage in 1810 with Marie-Louise (1791–1847), the daughter of Austrian Emperor Francis I. She had never even met Napoleon, but that in itself was not as unusual as the fact that the French emperor had an old enemy, the Archduke Charles (brother of Francis I and Napoleon's opponent during the 1809 war with Austria), stand in for him at the wedding ceremony, while he remained in Paris. Napoleon thus entered into a *de facto* alliance with the Habsburgs, Europe's oldest dynasty. Within a year, Marie-Louise presented Napoleon with a son and heir.

For the first time since Napoleon's remarkable rise to power, dissent also began to be heard openly inside France. Deserters and recalcitrant conscripts dodged authorities in increasing numbers beginning in about 1810. Royalist and Jacobin pamphlets and brochures circulated, despite censorship. Royalists objected to Napoleon's disdainful treatment of the pope, who excommunicated the emperor after France annexed the Papal States in 1809. Napoleon responded by simply placing Pius VII under house arrest, first near Genoa, and then near Paris in Fontainebleau.

Napoleon had become increasingly unable to separate options that were feasible or possible from those that were unlikely or indeed impossible to achieve. One of the emperor's ministers remarked: "It is strange that Napoleon, whose good sense amounted to genius, never discovered the point at which the impossible begins. . . . 'The impossible,' he told me with a smile, 'is the specter of the timid and the refuge of the coward . . . the word is only a confession of impotence' . . . he thought only of satisfying his own desires and adding incessantly to his own glory and greatness . . . death alone could set a limit to his plans and curb his ambition."

Napoleon's advisers now expressed their doubts about the emperor's endless plans for new conquests. Talleyrand had resigned as foreign minister in 1807, after the execution of the duke of Enghien. Talleyrand now symbolized the "party of peace," which opposed extending the empire past limits that could be effectively administered. In 1809, he began to negotiate secretly with Austria about the possibility of a monarchical restoration in France should Napoleon fall.

Napoleon's interest in expanding French influence in the eastern Mediterranean and his marriage to a Habsburg princess virtually assured war with Russia, which had reopened its ports to British and neutral vessels carrying English goods. Believing that he could enforce the continental blockade by defeating Russia, Napoleon prepared for war, forcing vanquished Austria and Prussia to agree to assist him. In the meantime, the tsar signed a peace treaty with the Ottoman Empire, freeing Russia to oppose Napoleon. Alexander I lined up the support of Sweden. There Jean-Baptiste Bernadotte

(1763–1844), once one of Napoleon's marshals, had been elected crown prince in 1810 and thus heir to the Swedish throne by the Swedish Estates (he would succeed the childless Charles XIII in 1818 as King Charles XIV). In return, the tsar offered Sweden a free hand in annexing Norway.

In June 1812, Napoleon's "Grand Army," over 600,000 strong, crossed the Niemen River from the Grand Duchy of Warsaw into Russia. Napoleon hoped to lure the Russian armies into battle. The Russians, however, simply retreated, drawing Napoleon ever farther into western Russia in late summer.

The Grand Army may have been the largest army ever raised up to that time, but the quality of Napoleon's army had declined since 1806 through casualties and desertions. Some of his finest troops were tied up in Spain. Half of the Grand Army consisted of Prussian, Italian, Austrian, Swiss, or Dutch conscripts. Officers now were by necessity more hurriedly trained. As the Grand Army was almost constantly at war, there was no chance to rebuild it to Napoleon's satisfaction.

In Russia, disease, heat, and hunger took a far greater toll on Napoleon's army than did the rearguard action of enemy troops. The Grand Army finally reached the city of Smolensk, 200 miles west of Moscow, in the middle of August; there the emperor planned to force the tsar to sign another humiliating peace. However, the Russian troops continued to retreat deeper into Russia. Napoleon's marshals begged him to stop in Smolensk and wait there. Tempted by the possibility of capturing Moscow, Napoleon pushed on until his army reached Borodino, sixty miles from Moscow. There the two armies fought to a costly draw in the bloodiest battle of the Napoleonic era, with 68,000 killed or wounded before the Russian army continued its retreat. Napoleon entered Moscow on September 14, 1812. He found it virtually deserted. Fires, probably set by Russian troops, spread quickly through the wooden buildings. Almost three-quarters of the city burned to the ground. The tsar and his armies had fled eastward.

Over 1,500 miles from Paris, without sufficient provisions, and with the early signs of the approaching Russian winter already apparent, Napoleon decided to march the Grand Army back to France. The retreat, which began on October 19, was a disaster. Russian troops picked off many among the retreating forces, forcing them to take an even longer route to Smolensk, 200 miles away. The Russians were waiting for Napoleon's beleaguered armies at the Berezina River, where they killed thousands of French soldiers. The emperor himself barely escaped capture by the Cossacks. The freezing winter then finished off most of what was left of Napoleon's Grand Army.

The retreat from Moscow was one of the greatest military debacles of any age. A contemporary described some of the French troops as "a mob of tattered ghosts draped in women's cloaks, odd pieces of carpet, or greatcoats burned full of holes, their feet wrapped in all sorts of rags . . . skeletons of soldiers went by, . . . with lowered heads, eyes on the ground, in absolute silence. . . ." Of the more than 600,000 men who had set out in June from

The retreat of the Grand Army in Russia, November 1812.

the Grand Duchy of Warsaw (Napoleon's defeat ended the hopes of Polish nationalists for independence), only about 40,000 returned to France in December. (Indeed, a mass grave of frozen soldiers of the Grand Army was discovered in Lithuania in 2003.) After racing ahead of the groans of the dying and the frozen corpses, Napoleon issued a famous bulletin that was sent back to Paris: "The health of the emperor has never been better."

Napoleon arrived at the Tuileries Palace in December 1812. In the wake of a military disaster of such dimensions that press censorship and duplicitous official bulletins (the expression "to lie like a military bulletin" became current) could not gloss over it, the mood of the French people soured.

Undaunted, Napoleon demanded a new levy of 350,000 more troops. This call, coming at a time of great economic hardship, was greeted with massive resentment and resistance. Instead of negotiating a peace that could have left France with the left bank of the Rhine River, Napoleon planned new campaigns and further expansion.

The Defeat of Napoleon

Napoleon now faced allies encouraged by his devastating defeat. In February 1813, Russia and Prussia signed an alliance, agreeing to fight Napoleon until the independence of the states of Europe was restored. Napoleon earned two costly victories over Russian and Prussian troops in the spring of 1813, but his casualties were high. Great Britain, still fighting the French in Spain, formally joined the coalition in June. Napoleon rejected Austrian conditions for peace, which included the dissolution of the Confederation of the Rhine, and Austria joined the coalition in August 1813. Napoleon's strategy of winning the temporary allegiance, or at least neutrality, of one of the other four European powers had failed.

In August 1813, Napoleon defeated the allies at Dresden, but then learned that Bavaria had seceded from the Confederation of the Rhine and joined the coalition against France. In October, his troops outnumbered two to one, Napoleon suffered a major defeat at Leipzig (in the Battle of the Nations) and retreated across the Rhine River into France. His armies, ever more filled with reluctant, raw recruits, lacked adequate supplies. An insurrection in the Netherlands followed by an allied invasion restored the prince of Orange to authority there. Austrian troops defeated a French army in northern Italy. The duke of Wellington's English forces drove the French armies from Spain and back across the Pyrenees. Forced to fight on French soil for the first time, Napoleon's discouraged armies were greeted with hostility when they tried to live off the land as they had abroad. Opponents of Napoleon, including some for whom a Bourbon restoration seemed a possibility, now spoke more openly in France.

Early in 1814, the allies proposed peace (perhaps insincerely, assuming the French emperor would refuse) if Napoleon would accept France's natural frontiers of the Rhine River, the Alps, and the Pyrenees. Napoleon stalled. An allied army of 200,000 moved into eastern France. In Paris, the Legislative Body approved a document that amounted to a denunciation of the emperor, though it never reached the public. Even Napoleon's normally dutiful older brother Joseph encouraged the members of the Council of State to sign a petition calling for peace.

The allies were determined not to stop until they had captured Paris. After overcoming stiff French resistance, the main allied force swept into the

(*Left*) Arthur Wellesley, the duke of Wellington. (*Right*) Charles Maurice de Talleyrand.

French capital in March 1814. Tsar Alexander I of Russia and King Frederick William III of Prussia rode triumphantly into the city. At Fontainebleau, Napoleon's marshals refused to join in his frantic plans for an attack on the allies in Paris and pressured him to abdicate. Talleyrand called the Senate into session. It voted to depose Napoleon. The allies refused to consider Napoleon's abdication in favor of his three-year-old son. Without an army and, perhaps for the first time, without hope, Napoleon abdicated on April 6, 1814, and then took poison, which failed to kill him. The long adventure finally seemed at an end.

MONARCHICAL RESTORATION AND NAPOLEON'S RETURN

The allies sought the restoration of the Bourbon monarchy. The French Senate, too, expressed its wish that Louis XVI's brother, the count of Provence, return to France as Louis XVIII. By the Treaty of Fontainebleau (April 11, 1814), the allies exiled Napoleon to a Mediterranean island off the coast of Italy. Bonaparte would be emperor of Elba. Marie-Louise refused to accompany him, preferring to be duchess of Parma, receiving the title by virtue of being a member of the Austrian royal family.

The Bourbon Restoration

The count of Provence entered Paris on May 3, 1814, as King Louis XVIII (ruled 1814–1815; 1815–1824). With more than a little wishful thinking, he announced that this was the nineteenth year of his reign (counting from the death of the son of Louis XVI, who had died in 1795 in a Paris prison without ever reigning). The allies worked out a surprisingly gracious peace treaty with France, largely thanks to Talleyrand's skilled diplomacy. The Treaty of Paris, signed on May 30, 1814, left France with Savoy and small chunks of land in Germany and the Austrian Netherlands—in other words, the France of November 1, 1792. France could now rejoin the monarchies of Europe.

Louis XVIII signed a constitutional "Charter" that granted his people "public liberties," promising that a legislature would be elected,

Louis XVIII, king of the French. Note the perhaps unconscious Napoleonic pose.

based on a very restricted franchise. Although the document affirmed monarchical rule by divine right, it confirmed some of the important victories of the Revolution, including equality before the law and freedom of expression and religion, although Catholicism would be the religion of the state (see Chapter 15). A coterie of fanatical nobles and their followers (the Ultra-royalists) convinced the king to enact some measures, however, that were highly unpopular. Many in France disapproved of the substitution of the white flag of the Bourbon family for the tricolor, the description of the Charter as a "gift" from the king to the French people, the retiring of 14,000 officers at half pay, the restoration of returned émigrés to high positions in the army, and the return to their original owners of national lands that had not been sold. But most of the French were simply exhausted from years of wars and sacrifice.

The 100 Days

In March 1815, just months after his exile, Napoleon boldly escaped from Elba and landed near Antibes on the French Mediterranean coast. He knew that he retained considerable popularity in France. Furthermore, so much time had passed and so many dramatic events had occurred since the execution of Louis XVI that one of the monarchy's staunchest supporters claimed, with some exaggeration, "The Bourbons were as unknown in France as the Ptolemies."

The word that Napoleon had landed in France stunned everyone. Marshal Ney, who had offered his services to the Bourbons, promised to bring Napoleon back to Paris in a cage. But upon seeing Napoleon, Ney fell into his arms. Regiment after regiment went over to Napoleon as he marched north. With Bonaparte nearing Paris, Louis XVIII and his family and advisers fled to Belgium, which had become part of the Kingdom of Holland. Soon Napoleon again paced frenetically through the Tuileries Palace, making plans to raise new armies.

It was not to be. The allies quickly raised an enormous army of more than 700,000 troops. Napoleon led an army of 200,000 men into the Austrian Netherlands, engaging Prussian and British forces south of Brussels on June 16, 1815. He forced the Prussians to retreat and ordered one of his generals to pursue them with his army. Napoleon then moved against the British forces commanded by Wellington, his old nemesis. The armies met near the village of Waterloo on June 18, 1815. Wellington had skillfully hidden the extent of his superior infantry behind a ridge. Napoleon watched in horror as a Prussian army arrived to reinforce Wellington. The general sent in pursuit of the Prussians, like all Napoleon's commanders, had been taught to follow Napoleon's directives to the letter and not to improvise. He held back until it was too late. When the imperial guard broke ranks and retreated, much of the rest of the French army did the same. The defeat was devastating and total.

The Battle of Waterloo, June 18, 1815.

Napoleon abdicated a second time. He surrendered to British forces near the western coast of France, while hoping to find a way to sail to America. This time the exile would be final. The allies packed Napoleon off to the small island of Saint Helena, in the South Atlantic, 1,000 miles away from any mainland. The closest island of any size was Ascension, a British naval base, some 600 miles distant. Louis XVIII returned to take up the throne of France a second time, 100 days after fleeing Paris.

On Saint Helena, Napoleon's health gradually declined. He died on May 5, 1821, his last words being "France, army, head of the army, Josephine." He died of an ulcer, probably a cancerous one, despite stories to this day that he was poisoned by arsenic.

Napoleon's Legacy

Napoleon's testament, a masterpiece of political propaganda, tried to create a myth that he saved the Revolution in France. "Every Frenchman could say during my reign,—'I shall be minister, grand officer, duke, count, baron, if I earn it—even king!'" And in some ways, Napoleon was indeed the heir to the French Revolution. He guaranteed the survival of some of its most significant triumphs. Napoleon considered his greatest achievement "that of establishing and consecrating the rule of reason." His Napoleonic Code proclaimed the equality of all people before the law (favoring, however, men over women), personal freedom, and the inviolability of property. Napoleon furthered the myth, and to some extent the reality, of the "career open to talent," which aided, above all, the middle class, but even peasants in some cases. He consolidated the role of wealth, principally property ownership, as the foundation of the political life of the nation. This increased the number of citizens eligible to participate in political life, however limited by imperial strictures. Furthermore, Napoleon helped turn nationalism into an aggressive secular religion, manipulating this patriotic energy and transforming it into an ideology inculcated by French schools.

Napoleon's reforms, built upon those of the French Revolution, extended into states conquered by his imperial armies. The French imposed constitutions and state control over the appointment of clergy, standardized judicial systems, and abolished ecclesiastical courts. Napoleon created new tax structures, standardized weights and measures, ended internal customs barriers, abolished guilds, and established state bureaucracies that were extensions of French rule in the "sister republics" founded by the Directory. In addition to abolishing serfdom and proclaiming equality before the law in Poland, the French occupation also ended residual peasant seigneurial obligations (such as the requirement to provide labor services to the lord) virtually everywhere, and abolished noble and ecclesiastical courts in northern Italy and the Netherlands. The Napoleonic Code proclaimed freedom of worship, and the French conquest of other European states, including Baden, Bavaria, and the Netherlands, helped remove onerous restrictions on Jews. But under pressure from French planters, Napoleon also reestablished slavery in Haiti in 1802.

Yet Napoleon's success in implementing reforms varied from place to place, depending on existing political structures, the degree of compliance by local elites, and the international situation. In southern Italy, for example, which Napoleon's armies conquered relatively late and where the structures of state authority had always been particularly weak, the French presence had little lasting effect. As the Napoleonic wave subsided, nobles and clergy regained domination over the overwhelmingly rural, impoverished local population.

Napoleon claimed from Saint Helena that he was trying to liberate Europe, but he had actually replaced the old sovereigns with new ones—himself or his brothers. "If I conquered other kingdoms," he admitted, "I did so in order that France would be the beneficiary." Wagons returned from Italy full of art and other treasures, which became the property of Napoleon and his family, his marshals, or the state. French conquests helped awaken nationalism in the German states and Spain.

To the writer Germaine de Staël (1766–1817), the daughter of the Swiss banker Jacques Necker, Louis XVI's minister, Napoleon "regarded a human being as an action or a thing . . . nothing existed but himself. He was an able chess player, and the human race was the opponent to whom he proposed to give checkmate." In the end, his monumental ambition got the best of him.

About 2 million men served in Napoleon's armies between 1805 and 1814; about 90,000 died in battle and more than three times that number subsequently perished from wounds or disease; over 600,000 were later recorded as prisoners or "disappeared." Reflecting in 1813, Napoleon put it this way: "I grew up on the battlefield. A man like me does not give a damn about the lives of a million men." Indeed, Napoleon's armies may have suffered as many as 1.5 million casualties. The Napoleonic Wars killed about one in five of all Frenchmen born between 1790 and 1795.

Napoleon's final legacy was his myth. From Saint Helena, he claimed, "If I had succeeded, I would have been the greatest man known to history." The rise of romanticism helped make the story of Napoleon, the romantic hero, part of the collective memory of Western Europe after his death. Long after Waterloo, peddlers of songs, pamphlets, lithographs, and other images glorified Napoleon's life as earlier they had the lives of saints. "I live only for posterity," Napoleon once said. "Death is nothing, but to live defeated and without glory is to die every day." Rumors of his miraculous return to France were persistent long after his death. So powerful was his legend that even the most improbable seemed possible.

Of the changes in the post-Napoleonic period that profoundly transformed the way Europeans lived, none arguably had more important social, political, and cultural consequences than the Industrial Revolution. Having begun in England in the middle decades of the eighteenth century, it accelerated in that country during the first decades of the nineteenth century. It spread to Western Europe in particular, but affected regions in other places as well. The Industrial Revolution and its critics would help shape the modern world.

CHAPTER 14

THE INDUSTRIAL
REVOLUTION

Manufacturing on a small scale had been part of the European experience for centuries. The economy of every region had depended to some extent on the production of clothes, tools, pots, and pans. Most production was carried out by men and women working in small workshops, hammering and shaping household goods, or by country women weaving or knitting clothes.

During the first half of the nineteenth century, the Industrial Revolution slowly but surely transformed the way many Europeans lived. In Western Europe, it became easier for entrepreneurs to raise money for investment as banking and credit institutions became more sophisticated. Dramatic improvements in transportation, notably the development of the railroad and steamship but also the construction of more and better roads, expanded markets. Rising agricultural productivity, increasingly commercialized in Western Europe, fed a larger population. Western Europe underwent a period of rapid urbanization: the number of people living in cities and towns grew more rapidly than did the percentage of people residing in the countryside, although the latter still predominated.

As the population expanded, demand increased for manufactured goods. The number of people working in industry rose. Mechanized production slowly revolutionized the textile and metallurgical industries, increasingly bringing together workers, including women and children, in large workshops and factories. Rural industry declined and, in some regions, disappeared. Rural producers in much of France, the uplands of Zurich in Switzerland, and Ireland, among others, lost out to more efficient urban, factory-based competitors. Slowly but surely factory production transformed the way Europeans worked and lived.

While many contemporaries were amazed and impressed by factory production of goods and watched and rode trains in wonderment and appreciation, others were shocked at what seemed to be the human costs of such a transformation. Poor migrants flooded into towns and cities,

A factory town in Germany in the 1830s.

which burgeoned as never before. Conditions of life in gritty industrial towns were appalling. At the same time, large-scale industrialization undercut many artisans, who lost protection when guilds were abolished under the influence of the French Revolution. Mechanization undercut their livelihood. At the same time, lurid but not inaccurate accounts of the awful conditions of workers (men, women, and children) in factories and mines began to reach the public. Calls for state-sponsored reform from state officials and middle-class moralists echoed far and wide. Moreover, many skilled workers in Western Europe not only protested harsh conditions of work and life but began to see themselves as a class with interests defined by shared work experience. During the 1830s and 1840s, workers began to demand social and political reform. Proclaiming the equality of all people, the dignity of labor, and the perniciousness of unrestrained capitalism, the first socialists challenged the existing economic, social, and political order.

PRECONDITIONS FOR TRANSFORMATION

We have come to call the transformation of the European economy the "Industrial Revolution." It began in England and parts of northwestern Europe during the eighteenth century (see Chapter 10). Early histories of the Industrial Revolution tended to emphasize the suddenness of the changes it brought; historians sought to identify the exact period of industrial "take-off" in each country, underlining the role of inventions, mechanization, and factories in the process. This led to an emphasis on "victors" and "laggards," "winners" and "losers" in the quest for large-scale industrialization, a preoccupation that blinded historians to the complexity of the manufacturing revolution.

Recent work, however, has de-emphasized the suddenness of these changes. Despite the importance of inventions such as those that gradually transformed textile manufacturing, the first Industrial Revolution was largely the intensification of forms of production that already existed. Most industrial work still was organized traditionally, using non-mechanized production. Rural industry and female labor remained essential components of manufacturing. Not until the mid-nineteenth century, when steam power came to be used in many different industries in Western Europe, did industrial manufacturing leave behind traditional forms of production. Handicraft production remained fundamental to manufacturing, as did domestic industry (tasks such as spinning, weaving, and product finishing done for the most part, but not exclusively, by women in the countryside). For example, the growth of the linen industry in Porto, Portugal, stemmed not from factories, but from the work of villagers in the countryside who were paid for spinning and weaving per piece. Even in England, the cradle of large-scale industrialization, craft production and rural "outwork"—work farmed out to cheap labor—remained important until the second half of the nineteenth century. Even in Britain at mid-century, the majority of British industrial workers were not employed in factories. In Germany there were twice as many "home workers" as workers employed in factories. In the Paris region in 1870, the average manufacturer still employed only seven people.

The Industrial Revolution could not have occurred without increased agricultural productivity, which sustained a dramatically larger population. In turn, an increase in population generated greater consumer demand for manufactured goods, now transported in many places by trains and steamships.

Demographic Explosion

The rise in population in Europe that began in the eighteenth century accelerated during the first half of the nineteenth century. Europe's population grew from an estimated 187 million in 1800 to about 266 million in 1850, an increase of 43 percent. Europe was then the most densely populated of the world's continents, with about 18.7 people per square kilometer in 1800 (compared to approximately 14 people in Asia and fewer than 5 in Africa and the United States), rising to about 26.6 fifty years later.

Industrializing northwestern Europe—Britain, Belgium, and northern France—had the greatest population increases (see Table 14.1). Britain's

Table 14.1. Estimated Populations of Various European Countries
from 1800 to 1850 (in millions)

Country	1800	1850
Denmark	0.9	1.6
Norway	0.9	1.5 (1855)
Finland	1.0	1.6
Switzerland	1.8	2.4
Holland	2.2	3.1
Sweden	2.3	3.5
Belgium	3.0	4.3 (1845)
Portugal	3.1	4.2 (1867)
Ireland	5.0	6.6
Great Britain	10.9	20.9
Spain	11.5	15.5 (1857)
Italy	18.1	23.9
Austria-Hungary	23.3	31.3
The German states	24.5	31.7
France	26.9	36.5

Source: Carlo M. Cipolla, *The Fontana Economic History of Europe: Vol. 3, The Industrial
Revolution* (London, 1973), p. 29.

population tripled during the nineteenth century. The population of predominantly agricultural societies rose as well. Sweden's population more
than doubled over the course of the nineteenth century. Russia's population
also grew substantially, from about 36 million in 1796 to about 45 million in
1815 to at least 67 million in 1851. The population of the Balkans rose from
about 10 million in 1830 to four times that ninety years later.

Nonetheless, disease and hunger continued to interrupt cycles of
growth well into the twentieth century. Cholera tore a deadly path through
much of Europe in the early 1830s and reappeared several times until the
1890s. During the Irish potato famine in the late 1840s, between 1 and 2
million people died of hunger in Ireland. Tuberculosis (known to contemporaries as "consumption") still killed off many people, especially workers
and particularly miners.

Overall, however, the mortality rate fell rapidly in the first half of the
century. Vaccination made smallpox, among other diseases, somewhat
rarer. Municipal authorities in some places paid more attention to cleanliness, sewage disposal, and the purity of the water supply, although the
most significant improvements did not come until later in the century.
Sand filters and iron pipes helped make water more pure. Improvements in
reservoirs, the first of which was built in 1806, increased the availability of
clean water.

Life expectancy increased in all classes. Individuals surviving their first years could anticipate living longer than their predecessors. Fewer women died young, thus prolonging the period during which they could bear children. Furthermore, wives were less likely to suffer the loss of their partner during this same period, and therefore were more likely to become pregnant. Yet poor people—above all, in cities—remained far more vulnerable than people of means to fatal illness. In Liverpool, half of all children born to the poorest families died before the age of five. In eastern and southern Europe, mortality and birthrates continued to be quite high until late in the century.

Despite the fact that infant mortality rates remained high until the 1880s, the chances of a baby surviving his or her first year of life rose because of rudimentary improvements in sanitation, such as a safer water supply and better waste disposal. "Wet-nursing," a common practice in which urban families sent babies to women in the countryside to be nursed, traditionally had taken a heavy toll on infants because of illness and accidents. Mothers, particularly poor ones, would not have sent their babies to wet nurses if keeping them at home did not also pose a risk. Many mothers needed to work to help keep the family economy afloat, and not all were, in any case, healthy enough to breast-feed or able to supply enough milk. Substituting cow's or goat's milk could be lethal, and also had been a cause of high mortality rates during the warm summer months. Now the practice of wet-nursing slowly declined. Fresh milk became more readily available, and by the end of the century people were aware that it must be sterilized.

The decline in mortality, particularly among infants, preceded and encouraged a fall in the birthrate in Western Europe. With more adults surviving childhood, the subsequent decline in birthrates had much to do with choice. The French birthrate, in particular, gradually fell, and then plunged dramatically beginning with the agricultural crisis of 1846–1847. Many farming families in France had fewer children so that inheritance would not be spread too thin.

Europe also enjoyed nearly a century of relative peace, broken only by brief and limited wars. A Swedish bishop, then, was not wrong to describe the causes of his overwhelmingly rural country's rise in population during the first half of the century as "peace, vaccine, and potatoes."

The Expanding Agricultural Base

Agricultural production sustained the rise in population (although more easily in western than in eastern or southern Europe). It also permitted the accumulation of capital, which could be reinvested in commercialized farming or in manufacturing. Capital-intensive production (larger-scale and market-oriented farming) underlay the agricultural revolution. More land gradually came under cultivation as marshes, brambles, bogs, and heaths gave way to the plow. Between 1750 and 1850 in Britain, 6 million acres— or one-fourth of the country's cultivatable land—were incorporated into larger farms.

Farm yields increased in most of Europe. England produced almost three times more grain in the 1830s than in the previous century. The elimination of more fallow land (land left untilled for a growing season so that the soil could replenish itself) helped. Some farmers raised cattle or specialized in vegetables and fruits for the burgeoning urban market. Farmers increased yield by using more intensive agricultural techniques and fertilizers, which, in turn, accentuated demand for sturdier manufactured agricultural tools.

During the first half of the century, continental visitors to England were surprised to find that, in contrast to the world they knew, relatively few small family farms remained. With the ongoing consolidation of plots, the number of rural people dependent on wage labor for survival rose. Farm work in 1831 remained the largest single source of adult male employment in Britain, employing almost a million men. Thus, the English countryside was peopled by a relatively small number of "gentlemen"—including British nobles—of great wealth who owned most of the country, landed gentry of considerable means, many yeomen (independent landowners and tenant farmers of some means), and landless laborers, who moved from place to place in the search for any kind of farm work. The tough lives of the latter reflected a too-often forgotten human dimension of the agricultural revolution, which increased the vulnerability of the rural poor.

On the continent, there was not as much consolidation of land as in England, but there, too, productivity rose as more land was brought into cultivation and fertilizers became more widely used. French agricultural production rose rapidly after 1815, as northern farmers with fairly large plots began to rotate their crops three times a year. In the south, where the soil was of a generally poorer quality, the land more subdivided, and much of it rocky, peasants planted vineyards, although the wine they produced hardly caused the owners of the great vineyards of Burgundy or the Bordeaux region to lie awake at night worrying. Farmers terracing hillsides, goats climbing up steep slopes, and the sounds of silkworms munching mulberry leaves as peasants anticipated the harvest of raw silk characterized some Mediterranean regions.

In Central Europe and parts of Eastern Europe, too, a modest increase in agricultural production occurred. In the German states, agricultural productivity rose more than twice as fast as the population between 1816 and 1865. Prussian agricultural productivity jumped by 60 percent during the first half of the century, partly because of improved metal plows and other farm implements, as well as because of information disseminated by new agricultural societies. As in Britain and France, root crops, such as turnips and the potato, added nutrition to the diet of the poor. Even in the impoverished Balkans, some peasants began to grow corn, potatoes, and tomatoes.

Yet in much of Europe, including Portugal, where two-thirds of the land was not cultivated, and the Balkans and Greece, subsistence agriculture continued as it had for centuries. In Russia, the rich Black Earth region, covering the middle Volga River area and much of Ukraine, still was undeveloped. During the first half of the nineteenth century, some of the larger estates, benefiting from fertilizer and even some farm machinery, began to produce and export more wheat and rye. The yield of potatoes and sugar beets increased dramatically during the 1830s and 1840s. Yet Russian farms could barely feed the empire's huge population in good times, and their output was grossly inadequate in bad times. Serfdom still shackled Russian farm productivity.

Trains and Steamboats

Besides the growth in population and the expansion of the agricultural base, remarkable improvements in transportation also contributed to the transformations of the Industrial Revolution. The first railroad train began hauling coal in northern England in 1820, and passenger train service began between Liverpool and Manchester in 1830. (It was macabre testimony to the novelty of the train that the British minister of commerce was run down and killed by a train after stepping out of a carriage.) Britain had about 100 miles of rail in 1830 and 6,600 in 1852. Railway construction employed 200,000 men by mid-century. Some observers compared the building of rail lines to the construction of the pyramids of ancient Egypt, as embankments, tunnels, and bridges transformed the countryside. The wonders of modern science were now clearly applied to daily life. In England railroad terminology was swiftly incorporated into the teaching of the alphabet, and board games and puzzles quickly embraced the train. Paintings, lithographs, drawings, and engravings took the magic of the railroad and the wonders of travel as themes. Giant railway stations became centers of urban activity, attracting hotels and commerce (see Map 14.1).

The railroad's development served as a significant catalyst for investment, catching the imagination of the middle classes, which identified the railway with progress that could be seen, heard, and experienced. Private investment completely financed British railways during this period. Whereas earlier investments in businesses had been largely the preserve of patricians, smaller companies undertaking railroad construction attracted middle-class investors. Railway booms accustomed more middle-class people to the benefits (up to 10 percent annually in 1846), as well as the risks, of investment. The value of the stock-in-trade of the London and North Western Railway had outstripped that of the East India Company by the mid-nineteenth century.

MAP 14.1 PRINCIPAL BRITISH RAILWAY LINES, 1851

The construction and operation of railroads also brought other benefits to the expanding British economy. Railroad construction spurred the metallurgical industry. Rail transport reduced shipping costs by about two-thirds, dramatically increasing consumption and, in turn, production. Trains carried "railway milk" from the countryside and frozen meat from the port of

The opening of the Stockton and Darlington Railway in 1825.

Southampton to London. Yet, at the same time, railways also entailed the destruction of large swaths of major city centers, displacing about 50,000 people in Manchester during a seventy-five year period, and many times that in London. Railway construction also brought continental states into the realm of economic decision making; in France, the government and private companies cooperated in building a railway system. In Belgium and Austria, the railway system was state owned from the beginning (see Map 14.2).

Railways became part of the social and cultural landscape. The relatively rapid pace of travel arguably helped spread the sense of being "on time," and in the 1850s Greenwich time, or "railway time," had become standard in Britain. Trains brought places much closer together, carrying newspapers and mail more rapidly than could ever have been imagined. The first trains could speed along at twenty-five miles an hour, three times faster than the finest carriages. An English clergyman described his first train ride in 1830: "No words can convey an adequate notion of the magnificence (cannot use a smaller word) of our progress . . . soon we felt that we were GOING. . . . The most intense curiosity and excitement prevailed." Railroad companies were quick to divide their cars into first-, second-, and third-class service, although at first the luxuries were limited to foot-warmers in winter. For people of more modest means, second- or even third-class carriages (called "penny a mile" travel in Britain, with train wagons not even sheltered from the elements until the mid-1840s) had to suffice. English seaside resorts lured middle-class visitors and some craftsmen and their families. Trains ran

MAP 14.2 PRINCIPAL CONTINENTAL RAILWAY LINES, 1851 More railway lines existed in the north than in the south of Europe, as industrialization proceeded more quickly in northern France, Belgium, the German states, and the northern Italian states than in southern France or southern Italy.

to German health spas and casinos, whose clientele a century earlier had been limited to princes and noblemen.

Yet some contemporaries already feared the environmental costs of the iron tracks and black soot pouring from locomotives. Fearing for nature, the British poet William Wordsworth (1770–1850) denounced the plan to build a line into the Lakes District: "Is then no nook of English ground secure / From rash assault?" In the 1870s the English writer John Ruskin (1819–1900) lamented railways that "slashed like a knife through the delicate tissues of a settled rural civilization. . . . Your railroad mounds, vaster than the walls of Babylon, they brutally amputated every hill on their way." Yet after mid-century the use of steel rails, more powerful locomotives, and innovations in engineering eliminated enormous excavations and earthworks, meaning less damage to the landscape.

Speed—at least relatively speaking—was also brought to rivers and oceans. In 1816, a steamship, combining steam and sail power, sailed from Liverpool to Boston in seventeen days, halving the previous best time for the journey. Steamboats, which began to operate on Europe's rivers in the 1820s and 1830s, revolutionized travel and transport. By 1840, the transport of Irish cattle and dairy products to England alone fully engaged eighty steamships. A constant procession of steamships traveled the Rhine River from Basel, Switzerland, to the Dutch seaport of Rotterdam.

At the same time, the contribution of improved, paved roads to the Industrial Revolution should not be forgotten. Here, too, the story of European economic development involved continuity as much as innovation, reminding us that in some significant ways the Industrial Revolution was based upon an innovative expansion of technologies and ways of doing things that were already in place.

The Great Western leaving Bristol in 1838 for its maiden voyage to New York. Steam power reduced the trip to nineteen days.

A Variety of National Industrial Experiences

During the first half of the nineteenth century, the Industrial Revolution affected Western Europe more than the countries in southern or eastern Europe. Furthermore, within states some regions underwent significant shifts toward a manufacturing economy: Catalonia, but not Castile in Spain; the Ruhr and Rhineland in the German states, but not East Prussia; Piedmont and Lombardy in northern Italy, but not southern Italy and Sicily (see Map 14.3).

Some regions that developed modern industries had the advantage of building on long-standing economic bases (see Table 14.2). This was true in Belgium, newly independent since 1831, which emerged with continental Europe's greatest concentration of mechanized production and factories. While Belgium's northern neighbor, the once-great trading power of the Netherlands, continued its relative economic decline, Belgium seemed to offer a blueprint for rapid industrial development. Like the Netherlands, it was densely populated and urbanized, which provided demand for manufactured goods and labor. Flanders had for centuries been a center of trade and the production of fine textiles. Belgian manufacturing boomed. Blessed with rich coal deposits, Belgium's railroad construction advanced rapidly, facilitating the transport of goods from Belgian ports to Central Europe.

Table 14.2. Manufacturing Capacity throughout Europe (thousands of horsepower of steam power)

Country	1800	1850
Great Britain	620	1,290
The German states	40	260
France	90	270
Austria	20	100
Belgium	40	70
Russia	20	70
Italy	10	20
Spain	10	20
The Netherlands	—	10
Europe	860	2,240

Source: Carlo M. Cipolla, ed. *The Fontana Economic History of Europe: Vol. 4(1), The Emergence of Industrial Societies* (London, 1973), p. 165.

In the Vanguard: Britain's Era of Mechanization

Why did the Industrial Revolution begin in England? Britain was well on the way to becoming the "workshop of the world" in the second half of the eighteenth century. Capital-intensive commercialized farming began to trans-

MAP 14.3 THE INDUSTRIAL REVOLUTION IN EUROPE, 1815–1860   Areas of industrial concentration and growth in Britain and on the continent.

form English agriculture earlier than anywhere else, feeding Britain's growing population. Britain was blessed with coal and iron ore deposits located
near water transportation, which made it possible for raw materials to be
transported to factories with relative ease. British commercial domination,
built in part on its rich colonial trade, provided capital for investment in
manufacturing. British entrepreneurs relied heavily on self-finance, and at
first banks played a relatively small role in long-term investment. However,
the government did encourage a precocious banking system that would
assume a greater role later in the century. It was far easier to begin a company in Britain than on the continent; after 1840, any number of people
could form a company in Britain simply by registering with the government.

The structure of British society also proved conducive to economic
development. There were fewer social barriers between wealthy landowning nobles, prosperous gentry, and eager entrepreneurs. Dissenters (non-
Anglican Protestants) were afforded basic toleration, and some became
manufacturers.

The British government adopted a general policy of non-interference in
business. But Parliament, which had protected British manufacturers by
enacting tariffs in the eighteenth century, now was able to reduce tariffs in
the 1820s, shrugging off foreign economic challenges. Parliament allocated
funds for England's burgeoning transportation network, aiding merchants
and manufacturers. Parliamentary acts of enclosure (facilitating the consolidation of arable strips of land and the division of common lands) helped
wealthy landowners add to their holdings, augmenting the productivity of
their land and permitting the accumulation of investment capital.

English cotton manufacturing, gradually transformed by mechanization,
led the Industrial Revolution and carried along other industries in its wake.
The popularity of cotton clothing spread rapidly, allowing poor people to be
more adequately clothed. Cotton fabric could be more easily cleaned and
was less expensive than wool, worsted, and other materials. Cotton clothing
joined silks and linens in the wardrobes of the wealthy.

The cotton manufacturer became the uncrowned king of industrial society in Britain, revered as the epitome of the successful entrepreneur, enriching himself while embellishing Britain's reputation. Between 1789 and
1850, the amount of raw cotton imported into Britain (much of it picked by
plantation slaves in the southern United States) increased by more than fifty
times, rising from about 11 million pounds per year to 588 million pounds.
During the same period, British production of cotton textiles increased from
40 million yards per year to 2,025 million yards. Cotton goods accounted
for about half of all British exports through the first half of the nineteenth
century.

In the British textile industry, spinning (the operation by which fibrous
materials such as cotton, wool, linen, and silk are turned into thread or yarn)
gradually had become mechanized during the last decades of the eighteenth
century (see Chapter 10). The advent of power looms and power weaving

Power looms in a British cotton factory, 1830.

(the process by which threads are interlaced to make cloth or fabric) removed the last bottleneck to fully mechanized production. The number of power looms in England multiplied rapidly, from 2,400 in 1813 to 85,000 in 1833 to 224,000 in 1850.

Industrialization in France

France was the world's second leading economy, although the wars during the revolutionary and Napoleonic periods had interrupted economic development. The revolutionary government had eliminated some hurdles for French businessmen by ending the tangle of regional customs barriers and tax differences. But France's coal deposits were less rich and more dispersed and were far from iron ore deposits and canals. Thus, transportation costs kept up the prices of raw materials. Demand was also less in France than in Britain because the French population rose by only 30 percent during the first half of the nineteenth century; in Britain the population had doubled during the same period. French agricultural production developed more slowly than that of Britain; small family farms remained characteristic. High agricultural tariffs did not encourage agricultural efficiency.

French banking facilities remained relatively rudimentary compared to those in Britain and the Netherlands. The primary function of the Bank of France, created by Napoleon in 1800, was to loan money to the state. The handful of private banks, which were run out of the deep pockets of wealthy families, preferred to make what appeared to be safer loans to governments.

Furthermore, banks—like investors—faced unlimited liability in the event of bankruptcy. Deposit banks were specifically denied the right to invest in private industry, except for investment in companies enjoying state concessions, such as those building the railways. Even normal business transactions were complicated by the fact that more than 90 percent of payments had to be made in specie (gold or silver). Until the late 1850s, the smallest banknote was worth 500 francs (the equivalent of almost a year's earnings for an unskilled worker). Banks thus had considerable difficulty attracting ordinary depositors.

The French state shared investors' suspicions of companies of any size, limiting the number of investment "joint-stock companies" that could be created. Furthermore, many companies were cautious family firms that invested profits in land rather than in the expansion of their businesses. With many peasant families still hiding their money in their houses or gardens, it was difficult to raise investment capital.

In France, too, textile production provided the catalyst for industrial development. At the same time, between the end of the Napoleonic Wars in 1815 and the beginning of the economic crisis of 1846–1847, the production of coal tripled, and that of pig iron doubled. But the reputation of French industry proudly rested on the production of luxury products, "articles of Paris" such as gloves, umbrellas, and boots, as well as fine furniture. Workshop production—for example of barrels, pipes, and watches—expanded into

A rural joiner's workshop in France.

many rural areas in response to increased demand, spurred by a modest level of urban growth. Rural industry, characterized by low capital investment, remained essential to French economic growth.

French manufacturers benefited from increased state assistance. The July Monarchy (1830–1848), the constitutional Monarchy brought by the July Revolution of 1830 (see Chapter 15), encouraged business interests, sometimes maintaining high tariffs that protected special interests—for example, those of textile manufacturers, who feared outside competition from British imports. Taxes on commerce and industry remained extraordinarily low. The government provided a decisive push in the launching of railways in France, purchasing the land and bridges along which the tracks were to pass and guaranteeing a minimum return on investments in railway development. Bankruptcy laws became less onerous, eliminating the humiliation of incarceration as a penalty. New legislation made it easy for investors to join together to form new companies with people to whom they were not related or, in some cases, did not even know—hence their name, "anonymous societies" (*sociétés anonymes*). The government also pleased businessmen by crushing insurrections by republicans and by silkworkers in Lyon in the early 1830s. Furthermore, strikes, legalized in Britain with the repeal of the Combination Acts (1799–1800) in 1824, remained illegal in France until 1864.

Industrialization in the German States

In the German states, industrialization lagged behind that of Britain and France. Three main factors undercut manufacturing in the German states: the multiplicity of independent states; the labyrinth of tolls and customs barriers, a veritable financial gauntlet through which any wagon or boat carrying merchandise had to pass; and virtual monopolies held by guilds over the production and distribution of certain products. The German states remained as a whole overwhelmingly rural, their percentage of rural population barely declining at all between 1816 and 1872. Furthermore, the harvest failure and subsequent agricultural depression of 1846, compounded by the Revolutions of 1848 (see Chapter 16), temporarily halted German economic development, like that of France, in its tracks.

Yet beginning in the mid-1830s, textile manufacturing developed in the three most demographically dynamic regions—the Rhineland, Saxony, and Silesia (see Map 14.3). Berlin emerged as a center of machine production. Coal mining and iron production developed in the Ruhr Basin, which had half of the coal riches of the entire continent. The Prussian state appointed directors to serve on the boards of private companies, brought technical experts from Britain to help develop industries, encouraged technical education, and founded associations for the encouragement of industrialization. In the 1840s, the Bank of Prussia began operating as a joint-stock credit bank to provide investment capital, the lack of which limited industrial development in the other German states.

MAP 14.4 THE ZOLLVEREIN (GERMAN CUSTOMS UNION), 1834   States and cities within the German Customs Union. Led by Prussia, it was the first attempt by the German states to reduce customs duties and to coordinate economic activity.

The German states took a major step toward an expansion of commerce and manufacturing when they formed the Zollverein, a customs union, in 1834 (see Map 14.4). The Zollverein was the brainchild of economist Friedrich List (1789–1846), a tanner's son who became an outspoken proponent of railway building. Calling a customs union within the German states and railway construction the "Siamese twins" of economic expansion, List proposed in 1819 the abolition of all tariffs within the German states, although, unlike many other liberal economists, he insisted that protective tariffs be raised to shield German industries from British imports. List, a fiery advocate for the political unification of the German states, believed that only through tariff reform could Germans save themselves from being "debased to be carriers of water and hewers of wood for the Britons . . . treated even worse than the downtrodden Hindu." The Zollverein included four-fifths of the territory of the German states. It contributed modestly to German economic and industrial growth, expanding markets for manufactured goods.

In the Ruhr Basin, young Alfred Krupp (1812–1887) began to manage his late father's small steel manufacturing firm in Essen at the age of fourteen. He served, in his words, as "clerk, letter-writer, cashier, smith, smelter, coke-pounder, [and] night watchman at the converting furnace." In 1832, his firm nearly closed for lack of business. In 1848 he melted down the family silver in order to pay his workers. Finally, an order from Russia arrived for machinery to produce knives and forks, followed by another for steel springs and axles for a German railway. In 1851 at the Crystal Palace in London, he exhibited axles for train coaches and cannon with a gleaming cast-steel barrel (his newest and ultimately most successful product). Thereafter, Krupp's steelworks became enormously successful, turning out guns of increasing size and quality. Krupp employed 72 workers in 1848, 12,000 in 1873.

Sparse Industrialization in Southern and Eastern Europe

Eastern and southern Europe remained sparsely industrialized, hampered by inadequately developed natural resources and insufficient government attention. Entrepreneurs faced the difficulty of raising investment capital in poor agricultural societies. There were regional exceptions, to be sure, such as the increasingly mechanized textile production of Piedmont and Lombardy in northern Italy and Catalonia in Spain, and pockets of industrialization in Bohemia and near Vienna.

Industrialization in Spain was slowed by inadequate transportation and laws that discouraged investment. Lacking navigable rivers, Spain also suffered the absence of a railway system until after the middle of the nineteenth century. A commercial code in 1829 established the right of the state to veto any proposed association of investors. Following the continent-wide economic crisis in 1846–1847, the state placed banking under the control of the Cortes (assembly) and forbade the creation of new companies unless investors could demonstrate that they would serve "public utility."

Russia had a relatively tiny middle class—with only about 160,000 merchants out of a population of about 57 million people at mid-century. However, the majority of the population were serfs (see Chapter 18) bound for life to land owned by lords. Their bondage made it difficult for entrepreneurs to recruit a stable labor force; industrial workers were among the hundreds of thousands of serfs who fled toward the distant eastern reaches of the empire.

Transportation in the Russian Empire remained rudimentary. The minister of finance from 1823 to 1844 opposed the building of railway lines, believing that they would encourage needless travel. Moscow and Saint Petersburg were joined by rail only in 1851. Serviceable roads—only about 3,000 miles of them—had been built with military, not commercial or industrial, considerations in mind. Rivers provided arteries of transportation, but the boats were not steam-driven and travel was slow. Three hundred thousand boatmen pulled barges up the Volga River, a trip of seventy-five days.

Early in the nineteenth century several major canals were constructed, including one joining Saint Petersburg to the Volga River. Internal and foreign trade expanded markedly in the first half of the nineteenth century, including grain and timber, much of it through Black Sea ports. However, coal and iron ore deposits lay thousands of miles from Saint Petersburg, Moscow, and Kiev and could be transported to manufacturing centers only with great difficulty and at daunting cost.

Some hostility toward industrialization—and toward the West in general—remained entrenched in Russia, in part orchestrated by the Orthodox Church. In the 1860s, there still was no generally accepted word in Russian for "factory" or even "worker." Industrial workers remained closely tied to village life. The state undertook only feeble efforts to encourage industrial development. The Council of Manufacturers was created in 1828, trade councils organized in the largest towns, and several technical schools were established.

Overall, despite these factors, the growth of Russian industry was significant during the first half of the nineteenth century, if only in and around Saint Petersburg, Moscow, and the Ural Mountains. The cotton industry developed rapidly, as did a number of traditional manufacturing sectors in response to population growth. The number of Russian industrial workers—a fifth were serfs who had to pay some of what they earned to their lords—increased from 201,000 in 1824 to 565,000 in 1860 out of a population of about 60 million. At the same time, Russia began to import and construct more machinery. However, spinning and weaving remained overwhelmingly cottage industries.

THE MIDDLE CLASSES

One should not exaggerate the cohesiveness of the European middle class. The size and influence of the middle class was far greater in Britain, France, Belgium, the German states, and the northern Italian states, whose economies and politics were slowly being transformed by the Industrial Revolution, than in Spain, the Habsburg monarchy, or Russia, which still were dominated by nobles.

In liberalism, the middle class found an economic and political theory that echoed the way they viewed the world, with the family as the basis of social order. Within the family, men and women occupied, at least in theory, separate spheres. Religion and education played privileged roles in middle-class families. At the same time, for all the frugality sometimes ascribed to the nineteenth-century middle class, bourgeois prosperity found expression in the development of a culture of comfort.

The family concert.

Diversity of the Middle Classes

The middle class expanded in size and diversity amid the ongoing economic transformation of Europe. It included all people who neither held noble title nor were workers or peasants depending on manual labor for economic survival. The terms "bourgeois" and "burghers" had first emerged in the Middle Ages to refer to residents of towns like Lübeck, Bremen, and Hamburg that enjoyed specific rights (such as immunity from some kinds of taxation) or even independence granted by territorial rulers. By the nineteenth century, the middle class made up roughly 15 to 25 percent of the total population in Western Europe but a far smaller percentage in Sweden, Eastern Europe, and the Balkans. The Russian middle class at the beginning of the century accounted for no more than about 2 percent of the population, including some intellectuals and Orthodox priests.

The nineteenth-century middle class encompassed a great range of economic situations, occupations, education levels, and expectations. It can be imagined as a social pyramid, topped by a small group of well-connected banking families, industrial magnates, and the wealthiest wholesale merchants, as well as a few top government ministers and ambassadors. Below this extremely wealthy group came lawyers and notaries (both part of what became known as "the liberal professions") and families drawing more modest incomes from businesses, rental properties, and lucrative government posts. In general it required some resources, connections, and access to credit to make money. Four out of five Berlin entrepreneurs were the sons

A middle-class couple out on a walk in Vienna.

of bankers, manufacturers, or merchants; their fathers brought them into the business or loaned them enough money to get started on their own. At the bottom of the pyramid stood the "petty bourgeoisie," at whose expense nobles and wealthy bourgeois made cruel jokes. This stratum included shopkeepers of modest means and expectations, wine merchants, minor officials, schoolteachers, café owners, and some craftsmen—especially those in luxury trades, such as goldsmiths and silversmiths—who proudly considered themselves middle class.

Many wealthy merchants and industrialists hungered for social prestige, which was still closely tied to owning land. The proportion of land owned by the middle class increased rapidly during the first half of the nineteenth century in Britain, France, and the German and Italian states. Since ownership of land (specifically the taxes paid on it) remained the basis of electoral enfranchisement in much of Western Europe, this further increased the political influence of the middle classes.

The landed elite—noble and non-noble—remained at the pinnacle of social status in Britain, although its share of the nation's wealth fell from about 20 percent to about 10 percent between 1800 and 1850. Some English "country gentlemen" still looked down their noses at those they scorned as mere "calico printers" and "shopkeepers," even if some peers now owed their titles to family fortunes made in commerce or industry a century earlier. Likewise, because in Britain the eldest son still inherited the entire family fortune, some second and third sons left country life to become businessmen, without feeling the sense of humiliation that their counterparts might have felt in Prussia. Many noble families were delighted to have their offspring marry the sons and daughters of wealthy businessmen.

The Entrepreneurial Ideal and Social Mobility

The entrepreneur emerged as a man to be revered and emulated. The Scottish philosopher and economist James Mill (1773–1836) became the political champion of the middle class, which he called "both the most wise and the most virtuous part of the community." Mill's 1820 *Essay on Government* denounced nobles for selfish attention to their landed interests: "They grow richer as it were in their sleep, without working, risking, or economizing. What claim have they, on the general principle of social justice, to this accession of riches?" In Spain, the middle class—bankers, manufacturers, and merchants in the prosperous port of Barcelona, and lawyers and civil servants in Madrid—considered themselves "the useful classes," in contrast to noble "idleness." Many middle-class families in England, the Netherlands, and some of the German states were influenced by evangelical Protestantism, which stressed the redeeming nature of hard work. In 1847, a Parisian newspaper defined what it meant to be bourgeois: "The bourgeoisie is not a class, it is a position; one acquires that position and one loses it. Work, thrift, and ability confer it; vice, dissipation, and idleness mean it is lost."

The notion of "respectability" gradually changed in Europe. Even in Prussia, schoolbooks that had early in the nineteenth century emphasized immutable social hierarchy and the necessity of obedience gradually shifted to discussions of the virtues of hard work, self-discipline, and thrift. Middle-class families viewed the expansion of their fortunes as the best assurance of respectability. Bankruptcy seemed a fate worse than death.

The ideal of the self-made man was born. Yet rapid social ascension remained difficult and fairly rare. There were, to be sure, spectacular success stories. The son of an ironmonger and saddler, the Welshman Robert Owen (1771–1858) began his career as a clerk and then sold cloth. Borrowing money to start up his own textile business, he became part owner of the large and prosperous New Lanark Mills in Scotland. Robert Peel (1788–1850), a British prime minister, is another case in point. His family had owned some land, his grandfather sold goods door to door, and his father became one of the most successful entrepreneurs in Lancashire. By 1790, Peel sat in Parliament as Sir Robert Peel, one of England's wealthiest men. To be sure, some degree of social mobility was also possible from the ranks of relatively prosperous master artisans. Yet hard times could cause petty bourgeois to tumble into the working class. The possibility of being afflicted by economic crises or personal disasters haunted such families.

Rising Professions

Urban growth swelled the ranks of lawyers, doctors, and notaries. For the most part, however, the aspirations of those in these professions remained higher than their incomes and prestige. In the novels of Honoré de Balzac (1799–1850), young middle-class men "kill each other, like spiders in a jar." Lawyers had less than sterling reputations even as their numbers increased. In the 1830s and 1840s, the French caricaturist Honoré Daumier (1808–1879) depicted lawyers as arrogant, self-satisfied, insensitive men far more interested in extracting fees than serving justice. However, in Britain—and

Daumier depicts a lawyer pleading his case.

elsewhere—the "pettifogging attorney" of the eighteenth century gradually was replaced by the "respectable lawyer" of the nineteenth. Notaries, too, gained in wealth and status with the growth of cities. They earned—though some of their clients would not choose that particular verb—fees that sometimes amounted to more than 10 percent of the value of property by registering and storing deeds of title. They prepared marriage documents, dowries, and wills. Notaries thus remained in most countries the financial equivalent of father-confessors, knowing—or at least guessing—most of the deepest secrets concerning their clients' fortunes.

The number of doctors rose rapidly in nineteenth-century Western Europe, although they still struggled to be recognized as professionals rather than members of a trade. While some brilliant researchers labored in obscurity, some notorious hacks received public plaudits. Among the latter was the decorated French doctor who claimed that he had proved that syphilis was not communicable—thus reassuring clients who paid for his soothing words. Doctors were limited in the treatments at their disposal, which also contributed to their profession's minimal prestige. Popular belief in age-old cures rooted in superstition persisted. The vast majority of the hospitals that existed in London at mid-century had been founded since 1800.

In Western Europe, doctors began to form professional associations. The British Medical Society began in 1832 with the goal of encouraging standardized training and professional identity. For the first time, in some countries surgeons now needed to have studied medicine in order to take up a scalpel, at least legally. The British Medical Act of 1858 standardized credentials for doctors, but did not require them.

Other professions also gradually commanded respect. In 1820, the Scottish writer Sir Walter Scott, assessing the future of a nephew, said that if the young man seemed fit for the army, he might well make his way there, but, if not, "he cannot follow a better line than that of an accountant. It is highly respectable." Newer professions in such fields as veterinary science and pharmacology were open to sons of artisans and peasants. Clergymen and schoolteachers were increasingly drawn from the middle classes. The growing reach of the state also required more officials and bureaucrats, providing attractive careers for middle-class sons.

MIDDLE-CLASS CULTURE

The middle classes believed that the family offered the best guarantee of social order. Most bourgeois held fast to the idea of separate spheres for men and women. Education and religious practice (however varied) provided a common culture for the middle classes. A wave of evangelical fervor swept over Britain in the late eighteenth and early nineteenth centuries, and a revival of religious enthusiasm was apparent in some places on the continent as well.

Marriage and Family

An astute choice of a marriage partner could preserve and even enhance a family's wealth and position through the acquisition of handsome dowries and wealthy daughters- and sons-in-law. There were fewer noblemen to go around. The disasters of what were considered ill-advised or inappropriate marriages ("misalliances")—that is, a union between two people far apart on the social ladder—continued to be a popular theme in novels and the theater.

Love could—and increasingly did—happily play a role in the choice of a mate. Prospective partners were more likely to insist that their views be taken into consideration in the arrangement of marriages. A Parisian woman told her father that she could not marry "someone that I do not love . . . in order to give myself a lot in life. . . . How could I hold onto him, if I do not love him and desire him?"

With an eye toward assuring the future of their progeny, some middle-class families began to practice contraception after about 1820, limiting their children to two. The economist Jean-Baptiste Say (1767–1832) encouraged family planning, warning that "one must increase savings accounts more than increase the number of children." Coitus interruptus certainly became more common, as well as other rudimentary forms of birth control.

The concepts of childhood and adolescence developed within middle-class families. The "children's room" and the "children's hour," when the young came forward to see their parents or meet guests, were middle-class concepts. In working-class and peasant households, there was no space for a separate room or quarters for children. Most working-class and peasant children had to begin work as soon as it was physically possible for them to do so. Many children who were apprentices did not live with their families, but with the masters of their chosen trade.

Because children, too, were an investment—and much more, of course— parents had to prepare them to take over family responsibilities, passing on self-discipline and self-reliance to their offspring. Germans called it *Bildung*, the training of cultivation and character, the subject of many nineteenth-century novels.

Separate Spheres and the Cult of Domesticity

To the nineteenth-century middle class, the family was the basis of order, what the English called the "nursery of virtue." Many men considered women "virtuous" when they remained in their domestic sphere, "angels" whose obligation was to provide comfort, happiness, and material order to their families. However, although many bourgeois insisted that women should work only when dire necessity left them with no alternative, many middle-class women worked in commerce, as unpaid clerks in their husbands' shops or as receptionists and secretaries in their spouses' law, medical, or notarial offices.

At the same time, the cult of domesticity also became increasingly fundamental to concepts of masculinity: men were to provide for and assure the future of the family. Yet during the middle decades of the nineteenth century the concept of British "manliness" came to emphasize physical strength. Men increasingly joined sports clubs. Oxford and Cambridge Universities evolved into defiantly masculine spaces that privileged athletic prowess. This trend perhaps reflected a response to the perceived threat of gradually increasing possibilities for women in British society, as well as a homosexual subculture at universities and in Britain's burgeoning urban world.

A woman's status remained closely tied to that of her father and her husband. In France, the Napoleonic Code made all men legally equal but left each woman subordinate to her husband's (or father's) will. On his accession to the throne in 1820, King George IV of Britain (ruled 1820–1830) tried to prevent his wife, Caroline, from becoming queen by blocking her return from Italy under threat of prosecuting her for adultery. But the king was forced to abandon his plan and accept his queen when women— particularly middle-class women—petitioned on her behalf, denouncing the king for promoting a double standard, since his own liaisons were notorious. A ballad urged women to rally behind Caroline:

Attend ye virtuous British wives
Support your injured Queen,
Assert her rights; they are your own,
As plainly may be seen.

A woman's separate sphere was inside the household and included supervising children and servants.

Middle-class women cared for their children, planned and oversaw the preparation of meals, supervised the servants, and attended to family social responsibilities. They exercised great influence over the education of their children, supplementing formal school instruction and taking responsibility for providing some religious instruction.

Middle-class British feminists began to challenge female legal and political subordination, debating the issue of "separate spheres" for women and men. Some women now demanded the right to vote. In *The Enfranchisement of Women* (published anonymously in 1851), Harriet Taylor Mill (1807–1858) stressed the injustice of considering anyone inferior, and therefore not deserving of the right to vote, by virtue of gender. Eighteen years later, her long-time companion and future husband John Stuart Mill (1806–1873) published *The Subjection of Women* (1869). Mill argued that women, like men, should be able to compete as equals in a society defined by market relations. Feminists demanded that married women be allowed to continue to have control over property they had brought with them into marriage. However, opponents of women's rights identified feminist movements with the violence of the French Revolution, or with surges of working-class militancy. Many upper-class Britons continued to view feminism as "unrespectable."

A Culture of Comfort

The European middle classes gradually shaped a culture based on comfort and privacy. Most bourgeois families were able to employ one or more servants and had apartments of several rooms. The wealthiest usually occupied the first floors of apartment buildings—but rarely the ground floor, where the concièrge lived—while less well-off neighbors had to hike further up the stairs.

A cross section of a Parisian apartment building, about 1850. Note that with the exception of the concierge's apartment on the ground floor, the farther you had to walk up the stairs, the less well off you were.

Kitchens and even dining rooms became separate rooms, as did attached offices for notaries, lawyers, and doctors. A distinct middle-class style of interior design slowly emerged, with national and regional variations. The accoutrements of the salon were likely to include an armoire or two, a chest of drawers, an elegant table and chairs, Limoges porcelain in France, Wedgwood china in England, crystal glasses, a clock, candelabras, a painting or print or two on the walls, all passed down from one generation to the next. The German decorative style offered wallpaper and sparse, austere furnishings and ornamentation. Pianos and other musical instruments became more common in the home and accompanied family singing. Flush toilets with running water began to replace outdoor privies and the chamber pots that had caused many unfortunate mishaps when emptied unceremoniously out windows.

Victorian Britons in particular embraced household possessions with a passion that verged on obsession. Leaving the simplicity of decoration behind, they began to fill up their residences with china, carpets, mantelpieces, statues, and garishly decorated fire-screens and teapots. They ascribed to furniture and items of interior decoration a kind of moral quality they believed suggested that their owners were living good lives. The Victorians' identification with their homes also arguably reflected the threat to class distinctions that was indeed very real in a century of enormous social change. Some of these novelties—such as antiques of fairly dubious origin or copies of colonial items purchased in curiosity shops—may seem to us in hindsight to be remarkable for their bad taste. But they enabled their owners to defy the trend of mass manufactured items, and try to reflect their status in Victorian society.

The old Roman saying that "clothes make the man" rang true of the nineteenth-century bourgeoisie. Middle-class men wore black suits, perhaps enlivened by a cashmere scarf. Their wives dressed only somewhat less simply; it was left to jewelry to suggest family wealth.

Expanding readership during the first half of the century encouraged a proliferation of novels, histories, poetry, literary reviews, newspapers, and political pamphlets, reflecting the diversity of middle-class interests. Reading clubs and bookshops flourished. Balzac's novels were first published in France as installments of lengthy serials—authors were often paid by the word—that appeared at the bottom of the front page of newspapers. Charles Dickens (1812–1870), too, first reached his public in monthly installments. *The Pickwick Papers* (1836–1837) attracted 40,000 regular readers in Great Britain.

Travel for pleasure became more common among the middle class. It also became a business. In 1835 in the German Rhineland, a young publisher named Karl Baedeker (1801–1859) published a guide to sites along the Rhine River. He soon published similar guides to Paris, German states, Austria, Belgium, and the Netherlands. In Britain, Thomas Cook (1808–1892) organized his first collective excursion in 1841 when he chartered a special train to transport a group of workers to a temperance meeting. Four years later, he began the first travel agency, building on demand for his services at the time of the Great Exposition of 1851 in London. Soon Cook was transporting groups as far as classical ruins in Italy and Greece. Middle-class families began to view travel as a means of self-improvement. They took in museums and other sights. In London, the National Gallery first opened its doors in 1824, about the same time as Berlin's Old Museum.

Education

Secondary education increasingly provided a common cultural background for the middle classes. Prussia's secondary schools (*Gymnasien*, or high schools) were arguably Europe's finest, offering a varied curriculum that included considerable religious instruction. In Britain, the victory of the entrepreneurial ideal was reflected in a gradually changing secondary-school curriculum. The English elite had long been exposed to a classical curriculum, as well as to Spartan discipline featuring corporal punishment. Reforms undertaken by Thomas Arnold (1795–1842), headmaster at Rugby School, were intended to spur students on to better performances by stimulating academic competition through examinations and prizes. Arnold's reforms reinvigorated the existing English "public"—in the United States they would be considered private—secondary schools, and new ones were established.

Many businessmen, however, still believed that experience was the best preparation to carry the family torch. Prosperous French shopkeepers sometimes pulled their children out of school at age eleven or twelve, viewing what they learned there as irrelevant to the tasks that lay ahead. Some entrepreneurs of family firms preferred to send sons to other companies, sometimes even in other countries, to obtain practical experience.

Secularized education, sponsored by states, only slowly undermined the role of religion in public life. In France, the Chamber of Deputies approved a law in 1833 (the Guizot Law, named after the French politician who sponsored it) specifying that each village was to have a primary

The Reading Lesson, by Jean-François Millet.

school. Private schools operated by the clergy continued to exist, and in many places provided the only schooling. In Catholic countries, middle-class families sent girls to convent schools to learn about drawing, music, and dance. However, state educational systems, staffed by lay teachers, gradually eroded ecclesiastical control of education. In France, liberals and republicans opposed a pronounced role for the Church in public life, demanding public schools that would teach secular, nationalistic values. In the German states, ecclesiastical and secular authorities battled it out, but the established churches retained greater influence over public education. The clergy still controlled schools in Spain and the Italian states. Yet in 1847 Piedmont became the first European state to establish a ministry of public education.

The educational systems of early nineteenth-century Europe did provide many more people than ever before with basic reading and writing skills. The literacy rate in Western Europe moved well above 50 percent. But social barriers remained daunting. Relatively few families could afford to send their children to secondary schools, which could provide them with more advanced skills needed for better-paying employment. In France in the early 1840s, only two of every thousand people attended a secondary school. Some working-class families still resisted even sending their children to primary school, not only because they could ill afford the modest costs involved, but because they needed their children's wage contributions, however small, to the family income. For women, very few formal opportunities existed for secondary schooling.

More young men went to university in order to prepare for careers in law, medicine, the church, or the civil service. Even in Russia, the number of university students tripled, from 1,700 in 1825 to 4,600 in 1848—still precious few in a population of more than 50 million.

Religion

Religious ideals still played an important part in the middle-class view of the world. Although disenchantment with organized religion permeated novels in Britain, France, and the German states, contemporary writing rarely challenged common assumptions that closely linked Christianity and morality. Biblical references abounded even in the treatment of secular subjects, because they were understood by all literate people. In the German states, as in the Scandinavian countries, the middle classes were more likely to go to church than other social groups. Throughout Europe, women manifested a much higher rate of religious observance than did men.

Many middle-class men and women deplored the materialism that seemed to have lured some of their own away from church. The novels of Jane Austen (1775–1817), the daughter of a clergyman, were highly successful at least partially because she affirmed that character, moral rectitude, and proper conduct, including control of the passions (in short, "respectability"), were not the preserve of wealthy landowners and titled nobles, many of

Evening prayer in a Viennese middle-class household.

whom were concerned only with wealth and status. Virtue could also be found among the men and women of the middle class.

The English middle class also viewed religion as a way of "moralizing" workers by teaching them self-respect. By the mid-nineteenth century, more than 2.6 million children attended Sunday schools, many created by the working-class communities they served. They provided the children of workers with educational, social, and recreational opportunities not otherwise available. Indeed the middle class did not have a monopoly on "respectability" and the virtues of hard work and discipline.

The Ambiguities of Liberalism: Voluntarism versus State Intervention

Clubs, societies, and other voluntary associations became part of middle-class life. Some, organized exclusively for leisure activities, manifested an upper-class sense of social distinction, such as the exclusive clubs of west London and the Anglophile Jockey Club of Paris. French bourgeois increasingly joined sociable "circles," and German university students formed dueling fraternities (*Burschenschaften*). Middle-class women formed their own clubs, among the few public opportunities open to them.

Charitable activities emerged as an important facet of middle-class life in nineteenth-century Europe, in many places remaining closely tied to organized religion. Growing public awareness of the appalling conditions in which many workers and their families lived engendered impressive charitable efforts among the more privileged. Such associations joined manufacturers, merchants, and members of the professions in northern English industrial towns in seeking to "moralize" the lower classes by shaping their conduct (for example, by encouraging them to attend church and to drink less). In 1860, there were at least 640 charitable organizations in London alone, more than two-thirds of which had been established since the beginning of the century.

Despite the growing tradition of voluntarism and liberal rejection of state interference, fear of popular insurgency could temper liberalism. Anxious bourgeois were reassured by the greater professionalization of police forces both in France and in Britain, where Home Secretary Robert Peel (a future prime minister) organized an unarmed municipal police force in London. They became known as "bobbies" in his honor. At mid-century Berlin had only 200 policemen to watch over a population of 400,000, which they did with military precision and occasional brutality. In British, German, French, and Italian cities, and in the United States, as well, civilian national guards were established, with membership limited to property owners. Such forces on occasion supplemented the police, national police, and regular

A charity providing halfpenny dinners to children in London.

HALFPENNY DINNERS FOR POOR CHILDREN IN EAST LONDON.

army units, and could be called upon to quell local disturbances and protect property.

By about 1830, some Western European liberals became aware of some of the social consequences of laissez-faire economic policies. They did not object to the wealthy becoming even wealthier, but worried that the poor were becoming too poor. Some of Jeremy Bentham's followers, among others, began to espouse government-sponsored social reform. Liberals crusaded against slavery, portraying the institution as incompatible with morality and British freedom. Such campaigns also reflected evangelical Christianity.

Differing views circulated on education for the poor. The British writer Hannah More (1745–1833) believed that poor children should learn how to read so that they could study the Bible, but not to write, because such a skill might make them reject their social subordination. Thomas Malthus (1766–1834), the English clergyman who predicted that the rise of population would rapidly outdistance the ability of farmers to provide enough food, believed that education would make ordinary people "bear with patience the evils that they suffer," while realizing the "folly and inefficacy of turbulence." Middle-class liberal reformers, however, shared far more optimistic views of education. The National Society campaigned for universal education in Britain. Henry Lord Brougham (1778–1868) believed that progress would be served if working men were educated. In 1826, he founded the Society for the Diffusion of Useful Knowledge, which made available to ordinary people cheap pamphlets and other publications of "improvement literature." Brougham and his followers founded a number of schools called Mechanics Institutes, most of them short-lived, which hammered home the entrepreneurial ideal to artisans and skilled workers. But educational reform in Britain proceeded slowly, at least partially because the state provided little direction.

Many poor children in Britain attended Sunday schools, charity schools, or "dame" schools (essentially day-care centers that charged a fee). The state did no more than provide inspectors for schools built by towns or parishes that could afford to do so or that had received random government grants. On the continent, compulsory primary education existed only in Switzerland, beginning in the 1830s.

The English philosopher John Stuart Mill became a forceful proponent of greater government intervention on behalf of social reform. He was appalled that relatively few people of means seemed concerned about the awful conditions of working-class life. In his *Principles of Political Economy* (1848), Mill rejected Adam Smith's cheery optimism about the "invisible hand," and called on the state to assist workers by encouraging their cooperative associations. Mill's *On Liberty* (1859) argued that the individual is the best judge of his or her own interests, but he encouraged a retreat from pure economic liberalism even in his spirited defense of individual freedom. Moreover, John Stuart Mill's espousal of causes such as women's rights and his participation in union campaigns for economic justice reflected this evolution of liberalism away from laissez-faire principles to a political theory concerned with economic, social, and political justice.

IMPACT OF THE INDUSTRIAL REVOLUTION

The Industrial Revolution, to be sure, changed the way people lived. Yet one should not overestimate either the speed or the extent to which these fundamental changes occurred in the nineteenth century. Even in Britain, France, and Prussia, the three most industrialized European powers, factory workers comprised between only 2 and 5 percent of the population in 1850. In many places, industrial workers—particularly miners—returned home to work in the fields part of the year, or even part of the day.

Continuities on the Land

Most rural people in Europe were not landowners. Landless laborers outnumbered any other category of the rural population, and their numbers increased dramatically in nineteenth-century Europe. Agricultural wages fell, and rural under- and unemployment became chronic. Landlords hired workers on a disadvantageous short-term basis. The abolition of serfdom in 1807 on the Prussian great estates east of the Elbe River increased the number of rural laborers scrambling to find farm work there. The increase in population put more pressure on the rural poor. Yet, even when peasants owned land, they were by no means guaranteed a decent life, because many plots were too small to be profitable, or the land was of poor quality. In Prussia and southern Spain, the number of landless laborers soared as owners of small farms were unable to survive and sold off their land.

Rural protest increased in the first two decades of the nineteenth century. In 1830, a hard year, travelers found people who had died of hunger on the roads, nothing in their stomachs but dandelions. In southern and eastern England, wealthy landowners had begun to use threshing machines, which left many hired hands without work. Grain passed through the rollers of these portable machines and then into a revolving drum. Threshing machines could be set up in any barn or field and operated by one or two horses. Farm workers, whose labor as threshers or "flailers" was no longer needed, began to smash threshing machines. The protesters were sometimes supported by local artisans, whose own livelihoods were threatened by mechanization, or by small landowners who could not afford the machines and were being driven out of business by their wealthier colleagues who could.

Some of the scrawled threats landowners received were signed "Captain Swing" (for example, "Revenge for thee is on the wing, from thy determined Captain Swing!"). Swing emerged as a mythical figure symbolizing popular

Bread riots in England, 1830.

justice, created to give the impression that the laborers were numerous and organized enough to force the landowners to renounce—as a few did—use of the machines. Authorities weighed in to make arrests, exiling some people to Australia, and executed nineteen men. Other similar attacks occurred between 1839 and 1842 in Wales when poor people attacked tollgates and tollhouses in the "Rebecca riots," which were also named after an imaginary redresser of social wrongs. In Portugal, women played a major role in an uprising in 1846 that followed a government attempt to enclose land and force peasants to register land they owned.

Rural poverty weighed heavily, especially on the continent. The Prussian political theorist Karl von Clausewitz, traveling in the Rhineland during the brutal winter of 1817, came upon "ruined figures, scarcely resembling men, [prowling] around the fields searching for food among the unharvested and already half rotten potatoes that never grew to maturity." Conditions of rural life in Eastern Europe may even have worsened since the eighteenth century. Russian serfs and Balkan peasants still lived in wooden huts. In Sweden, the small red cottages of farming families were notoriously cramped; many people depended on their parishes to provide assistance in hard times. Rural people drew warmth from fireplaces during the day and from animals with which many shared quarters at night. There were few windows because they let in wind and rain (in Sweden, some windows were still covered with animal membrane), or because farmhouses had been built that way to reduce the tax on doors and windows, as in parts of France. A traveler described the hovels in which Romanian peasants lived: "holes dug in the earth, over which a propped roof is thrown—covered rarely with straw, generally with turf."

The farther east one went in Europe, the more peasants remained fettered by obligations to lord and state. Russian serfs needed permission to leave their villages. In Silesia, peasant families still owed lords more than a hundred days of labor a year, for which they were to provide a team of animals; they were obligated to repair roads and to make various payments in kind. Peasants also paid the equivalent of a third of their produce to the lord or to the state in taxes. Such obligations, particularly to lords, were often deeply resented. More than a hundred Russian landlords or their stewards were murdered by their peasants and serfs between 1835 and 1855. In 1846, peasants in Austrian Galicia rose up and slaughtered their lords. Even when entrepreneurial landlords began commuting such payments in labor and in kind into cash, this did not end subsistence agriculture in parts of Central Europe and most of Eastern Europe and the Balkans.

The rural poor ate rye bread, porridge, and vegetables such as potatoes in northern Europe, cabbage in Central and Eastern Europe and in Russia, and onions and garlic in France. For many people, meat was little more than a distant memory of a wedding feast. When they could afford to eat meat, poor people were most likely to eat tripe, pigs' ears, or blood sausage. Most peasants who owned animals could not afford to slaughter them. Fish was relatively rare on peasant plates, except near the sea or a lake or pond in which they were allowed to fish or could get away with it (although even the English and Scandinavian poor could afford herring, fished in enormous quantities in the Baltic Sea). Water, however contaminated, remained the drink of necessity for the poor; in southern Europe they drank poor-quality wine, and in northern Europe they drank beer when they could, or cider, although both were relatively expensive.

Urbanization

The first half of the nineteenth century brought about a marked urbanization of the European population, as the percentage of people living in towns and cities rose rapidly (see Table 14.3). In 1750, two British cities had more than 50,000 inhabitants (London and Edinburgh); in 1801 there were eight, and by mid-century, twenty-nine. London's population rose from about 900,000 in 1800 to 2,363,000 in 1850. At mid-century, half of the population of Britain resided in towns. French and German urbanization proceeded at a significantly slower pace than that of Britain and Belgium. In 1851, only a quarter of the French population lived in urban areas, which were then defined as settlements of at least 2,000 people.

Yet Paris grew from about 550,000 in 1801 to a million inhabitants in 1846. Stockholm's population multiplied by four, from 75,000 in 1800 to 350,000 at the end of the century. Smaller towns grew rapidly, as well, such as Porto in Portugal, which doubled in size in sixty years. Industrial towns grew most rapidly, but commercial and administrative centers, too, gained population.

Table 14.3. Population of Major European Cities

City	1800	1850
London	900,000–1,000,000	2,363,000
Paris	547,000 (1801)	1,053,000 (1851)
Vienna	247,000	444,000
Naples	350,000	415,000 (1871)
Saint Petersburg	200,000	485,000
Moscow	200,000	365,000
Berlin	172,000	419,000
Liverpool	77,000	400,000
Birmingham	73,000	250,000
Leeds	53,162	172,023
Manchester	25,000 (1772)	367,000

In general, the farther north and particularly east one went in Europe, the fewer and smaller the towns. In Austria, more than four of every five people lived in the countryside, and in Sweden, nine of ten. In Russia, serfdom tied peasants to the land. Furthermore, there was in general less manufacturing in Eastern Europe, and therefore fewer manufacturing towns and trading ports. The Russian Empire had only three cities of any size—Saint Petersburg, Moscow, and Kiev; parts of Moscow were still indistinguishable from the rural world, dotted with wood or mud huts inhabited by peasant workers. Yet even in the Russian Empire, the percentage of people living in towns and cities almost doubled during the first half of the century.

As cities grew, streets may have been better illuminated than ever before, thanks to gas lighting, but poorer districts became much more crowded. Only a fifth of the buildings in Paris were connected to the city's water supply, and in these only the first floor or two (carriers hauled tubs of water up and down staircases). Crimes against property increased rapidly with urban growth, especially during periods of hardship. Between 1805 and 1848, indictable offenses in England and Wales multiplied by six, although part of this dramatic jump may reflect the result of better policing, and thus reporting. To the upper classes, rapid urban growth itself seemed threatening.

As urban centers became ever more densely packed, industrial suburbs developed. The urban periphery offered more available land; proximity to railways, canals, and rivers; and a ready labor supply perched on the edge of the city, where the cost of living was cheaper. After the Revolution of 1830, one of French King Louis-Philippe's ministers warned that the factories and industrial workers of the periphery "will be the cord that wrings our neck one day." Within cities, the European middle classes withdrew into privileged elite quarters, leaving workers and other poor people in separate, disadvantaged neighborhoods.

Social segregation intensified within cities. Industrial pollution, including smoke and other smells, altered residential patterns, driving some middle-class families to new quarters. At the same time, some people of means in industrial cities moved to newly developing middle-class suburbs. Country-side secondary residences, retreats from the bustle of urban life, became more common. Although most European suburbs were plebeian, in England some middle-class people of means moved to exclusive suburbs, such as the villa neighborhoods on the edge of London and Manchester. A poem in 1851 described a suburb of Birmingham, England: "See Edgbaston, the bed of prosperous trade, Where they recline who have their fortunes made; Strong in their wealth, no matter how possessed, There fashion calls, and there at ease they rest." The wealthy in London enjoyed vast public gardens, com-fortable theaters, and elegant shopping arcades, a jolting contrast to the mis-ery of the East End. Public gardens like Copenhagen's Tivoli and Berlin's Tiergarten, as well as Paris's Champs-Elysées, developed so middle-class denizens could observe and be seen. Cafés catered to people of means—coffee was expensive—while cabarets, selling cheap drink, attracted more ordinary people.

On the Move

As more people died than were born in most large cities, immigration of peasants and unskilled workers accounted in almost every case for urban growth. Thus, only about half of the residents of London and Paris and only about a quarter of those in the even more rapidly growing northern English industrial towns had been born there. The majority of immigrants were poor.

Most migrants moved to town because they knew someone there, usually relatives or friends from home who might be able to help them find a job, and perhaps put them up until they found a job and their own place to live. People tended to live in the same neighborhood as others from their regions, such as the sooty "Little Ireland" in the midst of the largest factories of Manchester in which many of the 35,000 Irish of the city lived in cellars, or the infamous Irish "rookery" of St. Giles in central London. The discrimina-tion faced by the Irish in London was reflected in Elizabeth Gaskell's *North and South* (1855), in which the villains are Irish. Among the English of all social classes, "Paddy" became a racist stereotype of the Irish character, depicted as ignorant, superstitious, lazy, drunken, and potentially violent. Anti-Irish feeling in Victorian England was linked to anti-Catholicism, which, after generating violence and riots in the 1850s and 1860s, only slowly declined in the last part of the century.

Between 1816 and 1850, at least 5 million Europeans booked passage across the seas, particularly during the "hungry forties," which struck Cen-tral and Eastern Europe and Ireland particularly hard. One and a half mil-lion people of Ireland's population of approximately 8 million left their homeland between 1835 and 1850 (and somewhere between 1 and 2 million people died of hunger on the Emerald Isle), particularly during the potato famine in the 1840s. An Irish migrant to London remembered:

> I had a bit o' land, yer honor, in County Limerick. . . . It was about an acre, and the taties was well known to be good. But the sore times came, and the taties was afflicted, and the wife and me—I have no children—hadn't a bit nor a sup, but wather to live on, and an igg or two. I filt the famine a-comin'. I saw people a-feedin' on the wild green things. . . . The wife and me walked to Dublin . . . and we got to Liverpool. Then sorrow's the taste of worruk could I git, beyant oncete 3 [shillings] for two days of harrud porthering, that broke my back half in two. I was tould, I'd do betther in London, and so Glory be to God! I have—perhaps I have.

Following the Irish, Germans were the next largest group of emigrants. After 1820, Norway sent more emigrants to the United States than the number of people living in the country in that year. At the same time, hundreds of thousands of Russian migrants pushed toward the eastern reaches of the empire in the quest for land.

Improvements in transportation expanded the distance people could travel to find work. Seasonal migration took men greater distances to work in towns

This British cartoon from 1850 depicts the expectations of migrants.

HERE   AND   THERE;
Or, Emigration a Remedy.

and cities during the warmer months of the year, while their wives cared for the children and whatever land they might have at home. Before the middle of the nineteenth century, seasonal workers still may have accounted for as much as a third of the workforce.

INDUSTRIAL WORK AND WORKERS

The English novelist Charles Dickens dubbed the grim, sooty industrial cities of England "Coketown." After completing his novel *Hard Times* (1854), an account of working-class life, Dickens wrote that "one of Fiction's highest uses" is to "interest and affect the general mind in behalf of anything that is clearly wrong—to stimulate and rouse the public soul to a compassionate or indignant feeling that *it must not be.*"

Middle-class socialists and workers themselves also began to criticize passionately some of the consequences of large-scale industrialization. The growing awareness among some workers that they formed a class apart followed directly from their growing sense that they were vulnerable to the vicissitudes of capitalism.

Gender and Family in the Industrial Age

In Western European nations, domestic service remained the largest category of female employment at the middle of the century, employing in Britain 1.3 million women, nearly 40 percent of women workers. Working up to eighteen hours a day, servants slept under staircases and in attics, but ate relatively well. They had a higher rate of literacy than did working-class women in general and better prospects of marrying above their social class.

Country women spun and wove wool, linen, and cotton; sewed, embroidered, and knitted stockings by hand; and worked in fields or gardens, while looking after children. Such cottage work on the continent allowed country people to maintain the traditional rural family economy well into the nineteenth century. Urban women worked as laundresses, seamstresses, or street merchants and peddlers, and some kept boardinghouses.

Female labor remained central to large-scale industrialization. Women were employed in many of the industries, both rural (where their labor had long been predominant in cottage industry) and urban, that expanded during the industrial age. Although only a relatively small percentage of women worked in factories, a gradual shift to larger textile and clothing workshops and factories occurred in England, above all, as well as in parts of France, Belgium, and the Prussian Rhineland. In France, women accounted for 35 percent of the industrial workforce. With the expansion in power-loom weaving, women with experience as cottage laborers found employment in textile mills. While there were a number of important predominantly male industries, such as iron production, the leather trades, building, and mining, women did work in these industries as well. The textile industry was the second largest employer of women (hiring 22 percent of all female workers). In general, women everywhere worked for about half of what their male counterparts earned. As in the pre-industrial period, many, if not most, female factory workers were young and single.

Many male workers bitterly resented the arrival of women in the workplace. This challenged traditional gender roles, including that of patriarchy, in that women's work had long been assumed to be at home. What came to be called the "struggle for the breeches" began in Britain. One of the significant developments brought about by the Industrial Revolution may have been the slow change from the conception of gender as hierarchical to one as representing different but complementary spheres.

Thus, despite significant continuities, wage labor altered family life and the structure of communities. Wage labor made young women and men less dependent on their parents, enabling many to marry earlier. But marriage still remained to some extent an economic relationship; moreover, some couples delayed wedlock until both partners could accumulate the skills or assets to maintain an independent household. A sharp rise in illegitimate births (in Paris, about 33 percent of all births, 45 percent in Stockholm) seems to have been another effect of the rise in employment opportunities and wages for unmarried couples in "free unions," or common-law marriages, although many women who gave birth were unattached.

Working-class families were presented with a dilemma: with the growth of factories and the consequent separation of home and work, women had to balance the need for the additional income factory work could provide with caring for young children. Many mothers left the workforce to care for children for at least a time. But since the family economy also depended on their wages, they generally returned to work as quickly as possible.

Hundreds of thousands of European women worked full- or part-time as prostitutes. Prostitution presented a hierarchy of conditions of life and wages, ranging from confident high-class courtesans to poor girls beckoning clients from dark doorways. Some women, including many who were married, were able to earn much more money selling sexual favors than they could earn in textile mills or in domestic service.

To middle-class moralists, prostitutes symbolized moral failure and the dangers of modern life. Yet it was the increase in middle-class male demand for prostitution that increased the number of prostitutes in Europe's burgeoning cities. Governments therefore accepted prostitution as a "necessary evil." They sought to police brothels and the comportment of prostitutes in order to keep the profession hidden as much as possible from public view, while trying to limit the ravages of venereal disease by ordering prostitutes to have regular medical checkups. The number of prostitutes in London was so difficult to determine that estimates for the 1840s vary from 7,000 to 80,000. In Saint Petersburg, there were over 4,000 registered prostitutes in 1870.

Child Labor

Children had always worked in agriculture, given such tasks as caring for farm animals, scaring birds away from crops, and gleaning at harvest time. At a very young age, many had also learned to assist in domestic textile production, preparing wool for spinning and raising silkworms. Now in factories, their smaller size made children useful for certain tasks, such as mending broken threads or climbing on machinery to extract something impeding its operation. Teenage girls were particularly adept at calico printing. In Britain during the early 1830s, youths less than twenty-one years of age made up almost a third of the workforce.

As in cottage industry, factory work often employed entire families, with adult males supervising other family members. Children's low wages—about a quarter of what their fathers earned—nonetheless represented a significant contribution to the family economy. One man recalled "being placed, when seven years of age, upon a stool to spread cotton upon a breaker preparatory to spinning," an elder brother turning the wheel to put the machine in motion.

Factory work was often dangerous. An English factory inspector reported that the children working at a punching machine risked losing their fingers: "'They seldom lose the hand,' said one of the proprietors to me, in explanation, 'it only takes off a finger at the first or second joint. Sheer carelessness . . . sheer carelessness!'" An eight-year-old girl who worked as a "trapper" in the mine pits, opening ventilation doors to let coal wagons pass, related, "I have to trap without a light, and I'm scared. I go at four and sometimes half-past three. . . . Sometimes I sing when I've light but not in the dark. I dare not sing then."

Young children working in a factory.

Some contemporaries believed that long days of labor instilled discipline, whereas idleness would turn children into sinners and criminals. But Methodists, among other British evangelical Protestants, wanted to save children from exhausting and sometimes dangerous work. A British law passed by Parliament in 1833 forced employers to start part-time schools in factories employing children, although in some cases the owners simply designated a worker to be "teacher," whether or not he could read or write very well. The 1833 Factory Act in Britain banned work by children less than nine years of age and limited labor by older children to eight hours (subsequent legislation in 1847 limited older children and women to a ten-hour day). In 1841, France's first child labor law banned factory work for children under eight years of age and limited the workday to eight hours for those eight to thirteen years old and to twelve hours for those thirteen to sixteen years old, banning child labor at night and on Sundays and holidays. The law, however, was extremely difficult to enforce, and was routinely circumvented by employers and ignored by parents who needed the additional family income, however small.

The Laboring Poor

In 1838, a British member of Parliament described a cotton mill:

> [It was] a sight that froze my blood. The place was full of women, young, all of them, some large with child, and obliged to stand twelve hours a day. Their hours are from five in the morning to seven in the evening, two hours of that being for rest, so that they stand twelve hours a day. The heat was excessive in some of the rooms, the stink pestiferous, and in all an atmosphere of cotton flue. I nearly fainted. The young women were all pale, sallow, thin, yet generally fairly grown, all with bare feet— a strange sight to English eyes.

The northern industrial cities of England in particular attracted the attention of horrified observers. There were, to be sure, people of means in Manchester, but Friedrich Engels (1820–1895), a German Rhinelander, sought and found the grim face of unrestrained capitalism there:

> At the bottom flows, or rather stagnates, the Irwell, a narrow, coal-black, foul-smelling stream, full of debris and refuse. . . . Above the bridge are tanneries, bonemills, and gasworks, from which all drains and refuse find their way to the Irk, which receives further the contents of all the neighboring sewers and privies . . . here each house is packed close behind its neighbor and a bit of each is visible, all black, smoky, crumbling, ancient, with broken panes and window-frames. The background is furnished by old barrack-like factory buildings. . . . [Beyond] the background embraces the pauper burial ground, the station of the Liverpool and Leeds railway, and, in the rear of this, the Workhouse . . .

of Manchester, which, like a citadel, looks threateningly down from behind its high walls and parapets on the hilltop, upon the working people's quarter below.

The satanic mills of Manchester.

The "cheerful" school of historiography has argued that the Industrial Revolution, at least during the first half of the century, by increasing employment and lowering the price of some goods, almost immediately improved the way ordinary people lived. By contrast, other historians have embraced the view that industrial capitalism was making conditions of life even worse for workers and their families as the number of people depending on wage labor increased faster than did job possibilities and pay.

During the first half of the century, the incomes of many artisans, as well as women workers, fell as trades were flooded with the end of guild restrictions and increasing mechanized production. Women workers such as spinners were often the first to experience unemployment because of the new technology. Wages in many industries were extremely volatile; boom periods could come and go with numbing suddenness. Even good years were broken in many industries by "dead seasons" when there was no work. The gap between the rich and the poor increased. In England, many middle-class heads of household earned three or four times as much as even a skilled worker. In the late 1820s in Paris, more than three-quarters of people who died left virtually nothing to heirs, because they had next to nothing and, in any case, they could not afford to have a will drawn up by a lawyer.

On the continent, the poorer a family was, the greater the percentage of its income that was spent on food, primarily bread. Clothing accounted for the second largest category of expense, followed by lodging. All other expenses, including heat, light, tools, supplies, and recreation, had to come out of less than 10 percent of the family income. Most migrants to cities no longer benefited from the kind of community support they had received during hard times in their villages. Recourse to the neighborhood pawn shop was part of the experience of the majority of urban working-class families.

English workers tended to be better off than most of their continental counterparts. Paternalism, the tradition by which employers took some responsibility for helping their workers by providing some supplementary assistance in addition to their salaries, seemed rare in the new factory towns. But some manufacturers did pay slightly higher wages, provided decent housing, and insisted that their workers' children attend school. However, such laudable efforts affected the lives of relatively few workers.

The nineteenth-century urban poor probably lived in more miserable housing than their counterparts in the previous century. Buildings in industrial cities, built hurriedly and as cheaply as possible, quickly became dilapidated tenements. Many workers lived amid terrible smells from raw sewage, garbage, industrial pollution such as sulfurous smoke, and putrid rivers and streams. Warm summers brought outbreaks of serious diseases like typhus and dysentery. Between 1848 and 1872 in Britain, a third of all people died of contagious diseases. Despite attempts to improve water supplies and construct sewer systems in several large English cities, the decline in mortality was barely felt in the heart of industrial cities, where tuberculosis remained a great killer.

Many children either died or were abandoned at an early age. At mid-century, about 26,000 infants were abandoned each year in both Moscow and Saint Petersburg, and about a fifth of all babies in Warsaw. The most fortunate of the abandoned were left at the doors of charitable organizations created by states, municipalities, and churches. Some babies were left with notes such as this one found in Rouen in 1831: "It is with the greatest pain that I separate myself from my son, after the great suffering I have gone through to keep him in his present state. . . . I hope to see him again as soon as I can take him back for good." Sadly, this would usually not be the case.

A poor family blocks their landlord from invading their cellar apartment, which they share with a donkey and some rats.

Foundling homes were overcrowded and notoriously unhealthy. In four towns in one Russian province, more than 90 percent of all of the children taken in by orphanages died within a few years.

Great Britain was the first state to have a national policy of poor relief. Against the background of the French Revolution, the Speenhamland system established in 1795 supplemented the wages of laborers with funds generated from property taxes ("poor rates"). Doles were based on the price of bread and the number of dependents for whom each head of a poor family had to provide. But this arrangement had the drawback of encouraging landowners to pay lower wages, while assuring them of an inexhaustible supply of cheap field hands. It also may have encouraged poor families to have more children, as payments were adjusted to family size.

The Poor Law Amendment Act of 1834 ended the Speenhamland system. It established workhouses in which poor people without jobs would be incarcerated. Workhouses were organized like prisons, their occupants exposed to harsh discipline in the hope that they would find any kind of possible work in order to avoid being sent back. Towns enforced laws against begging in order to force the unemployed poor into workhouses. When families were taken in, husbands were separated from their wives, children from their parents, and all were herded into dormitories. Inmates were forced to work at simple tasks and were given used clothes and dreadful food. The stigma of being poor was such that one influential official even tried to stop the ringing of church bells at pauper funerals. In 1841, despite organized opposition and although application of the law varied greatly, more than 200,000 people were workhouse inmates in Britain.

Class Consciousness

During the first half of the nineteenth century, many workers began to consider themselves members of the working class, with interests that were different from those of their employers and the middle class. They began to have a sense of community based on a belief in the dignity of labor. This class consciousness did not spring up overnight, and it is difficult to fix a certain point in time when it did develop. Moreover, certainly not all workers became conscious of themselves as a class apart. Great differences in skills and work experience remained among workers in different countries and even among workers in the same region, or city, and between male and female workers. Other identities continued to be important to workers, such as those of family and motherhood, cultural identity (Flemish, Venetian, Welsh, etc.), religious adherence, and village and neighborhood solidarity.

Urban artisans were the first workers to begin to express class consciousness, sharing the frustrations and goals of other workers. This process began early in the nineteenth century in England, although it was not until the early 1830s that one can speak of a cohesive class identity; it began in the

1840s in France and in some areas of the German states, and later in other countries.

Large-scale industrialization had deleterious consequences for many trades, threatening the control craftsmen had maintained for centuries over their work. Changes in artisanal production were a Europe-wide phenomenon. Artisans had traditionally organized themselves by trades into guilds, which enabled them to control entry into their trades, the training of apprentices, and production, even if guild controls had not been able to protect all workers from market forces (for example, from rural cottage production). Shoemakers, masons, and tailors, among those in other trades, retained their own craft organizations. Rival associations within the same trade sometimes engaged in bitter, violent battles. Furthermore, even within trades, hierarchies of skill and remuneration remained.

As a number of states followed France's lead in 1791 by banning guilds in the name of economic liberalism, the number of artisans expanded rapidly because there were no legal restrictions to entering a given craft. Journeymen, having completed their apprenticeships, were more uncertain than ever before about whether they would become masters and would employ their own journeymen and take on apprentices. In Prussia, the number of masters increased by only about half between 1816 and 1849; the number of journeymen and apprentices aspiring to a mastership more than doubled during the same period. Artisans' confraternities and trade associations (some of which governments tolerated, even if they were technically illegal) facilitated the emergence of working-class consciousness (although in places where they helped to maintain trade exclusiveness, they may have delayed its emergence).

"De-skilling" reduced the income and status of workers like tailors and skilled seamstresses by taking away opportunities for them to work for piece rates and wages they had once earned. For example, competition buffeted tailors as never before. Merchant-manufacturers, some of them former tailors who had been able to save some money, put work out to master and journeymen tailors, but asked them to perform a single task, such as making sleeves, in return for less money than if they had tailored an entire suit. Tailors' incomes plunged during the 1830s and 1840s. Many master tailors were driven out of business or forced by necessity to become subcontractors in their own trade. Mechanization also gradually began to undercut tailors by producing ready-made clothes.

The gradual mechanization of some trades brought protest. Already in 1811 and 1812, glove makers in Nottingham, England, smashed a thousand stocking-frames that deprived them of work. One of their leaders—perhaps fictitious—was a man called Ned Ludd. Machine-breaking "Luddites" yearned for a return to the old economic and social order, before mechanization, as had the "Captain Swing" rebels in 1829–1830.

In 1836, a mob burned down a textile factory in Barcelona, Spain, denouncing machinery as "the devil's invention." Mechanical looms reduced Silesian hand-loom weavers to desperate poverty. Movements of social protest and gradual political involvement infused communities of workers with a sense of moral struggle against economic and political forces they could not control.

Workers' views of themselves drew upon a corporate language of the Old Regime that gave primacy to the idea of work as a value in itself and of the community of workers as a moral entity. Many workers concluded that they, not entrepreneurs with capital, were the source of wealth and were being exploited. Other workers also began to feel a sense of class consciousness because they collectively suffered unemployment or reduced wages. Residential patterns and leisure haunts (pubs, cabarets, music halls) contributed to solidarities among such workers.

Workers' Associations and Social Protest

Workers' associations helped shape working-class consciousness and militancy. In Britain, craft-based "friendly societies" had more than a million members in 1815. More than 32,000 such organizations existed in 1872. Their counterparts were journeymen's associations and "mutual aid societies" in France and in the German states.

Fledgling trade unions developed in Britain, particularly after 1824 when Parliament repealed the Combination Acts (1799–1800), which had banned unions. Members sought to protect wage rates and conditions within their trades. Yet, even in prosperous periods when workers could afford dues, less than a fifth of workers belonged to such associations during the first half of the century, and the vast majority of these were more skilled craftsmen. Many of these men believed they had little in common with unskilled workers, who, in any case, could not afford union dues and who lacked job stability.

Some trade associations, including a minority organized by and for women, provided assistance when a member fell sick (paid out of membership dues) and assured members that they would be spared the indignity of a pauper's grave. They also provided funds to assist workers who refused to agree to conditions imposed by employers or masters. These payments had to be made covertly because strikes remained illegal in most places.

Artisans led movements of social protest. They had a much higher level of literacy than did unskilled workers—printers were an obvious example, but tailors and shoemakers were often literate, as well as many seamstresses, who were often self-educated. Literate workers read newspapers and brochures and related the news to those who could not read. The emergence of political movements seeking universal male suffrage (or even universal suffrage) and significant social reforms aided the development of a sense of class by emphasizing the language of "liberty, fraternity, and equality," a heritage of the French Revolution.

Francis Place (1771–1854), a tailor who had been a member of one of the workers' associations sympathetic to the French Revolution, became a

Socialism as a symbol of hope for the working poor, about 1848.

leader of the English workers' movement. Some workers began cooperative stores, hoping to put aside funds to finance cooperative villages. Trade unionism made considerable headway between 1829 and 1836. In the latter year, the first national union, made up of spinners, was founded. Some trade union members undertook producers' cooperatives within their trades, but most of these were short-lived.

The period from 1815 to 1850 was arguably the most socially turbulent period in modern British history. Skilled workers joined with middle-class radicals to demand political reform. William Cobbett (1763–1835) helped galvanize radical opinion with his journal, the *Political Register*. Artisans and skilled workers led massive demonstrations in 1831 and 1832, which pressured Commons and the House of Lords to pass the Reform Bill of 1832 (see Chapter 15). By expanding the number of those eligible to vote, the Reform Bill temporarily diffused middle-class dissatisfaction. The continued exclusion of working men from voting contributed to working-class consciousness in Britain, because in this way Parliament had legally defined workers as a separate, inferior class. At about the same time, middle-class and working-class support for factory reform, marked by public meetings, petitions, and demonstrations, led to the acts of Parliament in the 1830s limiting work hours for children and then women. Amid hardship, more workers took to the streets in protest to demand political reform.

Yet, even in Britain, the most industrial nation, major impediments limited working-class militancy. Methodism (see Chapter 9), which won thousands of converts among workers, preached discipline and the acceptance of one's fate on earth. More important, solidarities within specific trades remained stronger than those that cut across trades. Furthermore, unskilled workers lacked the organization and resources of craftsmen, some of whom continued to do very well, the English "aristocracy of labor." Gradually, too, the utopian vision of rebuilding British political life while bringing social justice faded. Many if not most workers came to accept capitalism as inevitable, while demanding a fairer share of its benefits.

French and German artisans were more militant than their British counterparts, who accepted the tradition of the politics of reform. German craftsmen desperately struggled to try to protect their trades from being flooded by newcomers. Many French workers, now seeing themselves as members of a "confraternity of proletarians," struck against employers in the 1830s and 1840s. They also supported bourgeois republicans in their push for electoral reform, in the hope that a republic would enact reforms on their behalf.

THE ORIGINS OF EUROPEAN SOCIALISM

As large-scale industrialization gradually transformed economy and society in Western Europe, the 1830s and 1840s brought lively discussion, heated debate, and startling transformations in thought. The rapid increase in wage labor influenced the emergence of new political forces that, proclaiming the equality of all people, sought dramatic social and political change. One of the most salient results of the growing preoccupation with the condition of workers was the birth of the movement known as socialism.

Utopian Socialists

Utopian socialists, most of whom were French, provided an original critique of the changes brought by the Industrial Revolution. Their ideas were in part shaped by their reaction against the social consequences of economic liberalism. The name "utopian" reflects their dreams of creating a perfectly harmonious way of life. But their importance comes not from their sometimes quirky theories, however intriguing they may be, but from the fact that many workers found an explanatory power in the critical reaction of the utopians to liberalism and capitalism. This accentuated their determination to put forward demands for social and political reform.

Utopian socialists agonized over the living conditions of the laboring poor. The "social question" was the miserable living conditions of many if not most workers. Rejecting the "egotistic" individualism of the spirit of acquisition, utopian socialists envisioned a gentle world of cooperation. In some ways children of the Enlightenment, utopian socialists were also optimistic champions of the power of science and technology to construct new social and political institutions.

Count Claude-Henri de Saint-Simon (1760–1825) posited a "religion of humanity," arguing that religion should "direct society toward the great end of the most rapid amelioration possible of the lot of the poorest class." In 1820, Saint-Simon published a provocative parable. Speaking hypothetically, he asked what the consequences for France would be if all of its dukes and duchesses, princes and princesses, bishops and priests, and other luminaries of altar, throne, and château sank in a terrible shipwreck. As tragic as that event would be, he had to admit that the loss to society would be inconsiderable. However, if France, in a similar tragedy, were to lose all of its most learned men, talented bankers, artisans, and productive farmers, the result would be disastrous. The timing of his parable was most unfortunate, because soon after its publication in 1820 the heir to the throne of France, the duke of Berry, fell to an assassin's knife (see Chapter 15). Saint-Simon was charged with offending the royal family, but he was acquitted by a jury.

Saint-Simon postulated a hierarchy, or order of status, based not on blood, but on productivity. Believing that history moves through discernible stages, he asserted that mankind could anticipate a future in which science would solve the material problems of humanity in harmony with an era of moral improvement. For this to happen, people of talent must be freed from the fetters of restraint imposed by uncaring, unproductive monarchs, nobles, and priests.

Contemporary and historical appraisals of Charles Fourier (1772–1837), Saint-Simon's mystical rival, have ranged from sanctifying him as a genius of great insight to ridiculing him as a paranoid crackpot. Fourier claimed that at a very early age he discovered that the art of selling was the practice of lying and deception. At his father's insistence, he went off to Lyon as a young man to start a business that quickly failed. Fourier spent the rest of his life preparing a grand scheme for improving the condition of humanity. His cosmology rested upon his conclusion that history moved in great cycles toward a more perfect future. This planet's next stage would be based upon mankind's discovery that the principles of cooperation and harmony would free everyone from the repression of bourgeois individualism. Having determined that there were 810 distinct personality types, Fourier proposed that they be organized into "phalanx" communities made up of 1,620 people, one man and one woman of each personality type. The phalanx would channel the "passions" of each person in socially productive ways, while individuals would benefit from the opportunity to express their deepest proclivities. In the "phalanstery," the place where the utopians would live, crime would become a distant memory, because criminals' supposed penchant for blood would be safely fulfilled in certain occupations, such as by becoming butchers. With everyone so satisfied, it would not matter that differences in wealth would remain. Fourier sat in his apartment everyday at noon, await-

A drawing of a phalanstery contemplated by Charles Fourier.

ing the wealthy man who would come, he hoped, to finance the first phalanstery. No one ever showed up.

While Fourier dreamed and waited, the wealthy British industrialist and
philanthropist Robert Owen acted. Believing that education and environment could shape a spirit of cooperation, Owen built a mill in New Lanark,
Scotland. He provided decent housing for his workers and established
schools for their children. Like Fourier, for whom human progress demanded
the emancipation of women, Owen espoused the equality of women,
although he emphasized not political rights but rather the special qualities of
motherhood. Likewise, an Englishman named William Thompson penned in
1825 the *Appeal of One Half of the Human Race, Women, Against the Pre-
tentions of the Other, Men.*

No utopian socialist had a greater popular following than Étienne Cabet
(1788–1856) in France. Cabet, too, sought to apply the principles of Christianity to the extreme social problems of the day. His novel *Voyage to Icaria*
(1840) described an imaginary city of wide streets, clean urinals, and social
harmony, a vision of organized economic and social life so attractive that
even the bourgeoisie would be converted peacefully to the principles of
cooperation and association. Cabet's "communist" newspaper had 4,500
subscribers in the early 1840s, and almost certainly reached twenty times
that number. Artisans, their livelihoods threatened by the abolition of the
guilds and mechanization, were particularly intrigued by Cabet's ideas. A
few of them set sail with Cabet for the New World, founding several utopian
colonies in Texas and Iowa.

Another group of utopian socialists represented the scientific, or technocratic and even authoritarian tendencies inherent in Saint-Simon's overwhelming respect for science and insistence that the state lead the way
toward material progress. Prosper Enfantin (1796–1864)—called "Father"
by his followers—left Paris for Egypt with a small group in search of the
Female Messiah; one of the traveling party, Michel Chevalier, came back

with the idea of building a canal through the Isthmus of Suez, thus joining the Red Sea and the Mediterranean, a project later achieved in 1869 by Ferdinand de Lesseps, another Saint-Simonian.

Practical Socialists

Some utopian socialists carried Saint-Simon's analysis a crucial step further. They relegated the bourgeoisie into the category of non-producers, because they possessed capital, while workers seemed to them to be the real producers by virtue of their labor. In France, a group of Saint-Simonian women in 1832 founded a newspaper, *La Tribune des Femmes,* that vowed only to publish articles by women, proclaiming that the emancipation of women would come with the emancipation of the worker.

Gender discrimination led Flora Tristan (1801–1844) to socialism. When the French government confiscated her Peruvian father's fortune upon his death and declared Flora to be illegitimate because it refused to recognize her parents' marriage in Spain, she had to take a series of makeshift jobs. When she separated from her abusive husband, French law decreed that he receive custody of their children, although she later won custody when he started to abuse them, too. Tristan campaigned against women's inequality within marriage and before the law. Linking feminism and socialism, she campaigned for female emancipation with impassioned speeches and forceful prose.

Louis Blanc (1811–1882) looked to governments to give scientists a free hand in applying their talents to the betterment of the human condition. The state should also guarantee workers the "right to work," that is, employment in times of distress and a decent wage in the face of unchecked competition. The state should provide credit to workers so that they could form producers' associations within their trades, thereby eliminating the middleman who skimmed off profits that he had not earned. Blanc believed that these workshops would serve as the basis for the reorganization of society along cooperative lines. Blanc's socialism was predicated on increasing workers' influence on government through the establishment of universal suffrage.

In sharp contrast to Blanc, Pierre-Joseph Proudhon (1809–1865) looked not to the strengthening of the state but to its abolition to create a better world. Proudhon, a typesetter, had grown up among landowning peasants in eastern France. He believed that the very existence of the state itself was a principal reason why capitalism exploited workers. In 1840, he published a fiery pamphlet that answered the question "What Is Property?" with the resounding reply "Theft." Not surprisingly, this frightened property owners in France, even though Proudhon defined property as unearned profit that came to employers from the labor of their workers, and not property per se. Proudhon wanted workers to organize themselves into small, autonomous groups of producers that would govern themselves. By preaching the abolition of the state, Proudhon was arguably the first anarchist.

Karl Marx and the Origins of "Scientific Socialism"

The economic and political theorist Karl Marx (1818–1883) also read the utopian socialists, but although admiring their critique of capitalist society he found them naive and "unscientific." Born in 1818 in the Rhineland, Marx studied philosophy at the University of Berlin. When in 1843 his career as a journalist came to an abrupt halt after his radical newspaper ran afoul of the Prussian government, he went to Paris. There he read the histories of the French Revolution and the utopian socialists.

Proudhon destroying property as seen by a hostile caricaturist.

After Marx lambasted the French monarchy in a series of articles, the French police expelled him. He befriended Friedrich Engels, the Rhineland German whose prosperous, conservative family owned a cotton mill in Manchester, England. Marx visited industrial Lancashire, then the greatest concentration of industry in the world. His observation of evolving capitalist society led him to conclude that capitalism was but a stage in world history.

Marx applied the concept of dialectical stages of the development of ideas and institutions, developed by the German philosopher Georg Wilhelm Friedrich Hegel (1770–1831), to the progression of world history. The French Revolution had marked the definitive overthrow of feudal society, represented by the power of the aristocracy and the Church; for Marx, this was a bourgeois revolution. Just as the nobility and the bourgeoisie had battled in the eighteenth century, so the victorious bourgeoisie, who controlled the means of production (capital, raw materials, and equipment needed to produce goods), and the proletariat were in the process of fighting it out in the middle decades of the nineteenth century. English commercial capitalism had brought the bourgeoisie to power, which in turn had facilitated the growth of industrial capitalism. By creating a proletariat, however, capitalists had sown the seeds of their demise. Inevitably, socialism would replace capitalism when the proletariat seized power. The end of private property and pure communism would follow.

But that moment, Marx thought, lay in the future, awaiting the further concentration of capitalism and the development of a larger, class-conscious proletariat aware of its historical role. Marx called his socialism "scientific socialism" (in contrast to utopian socialism), because he thought that it was inevitable, based on what he considered the scientific certainty of class struggle.

Marx believed that a revolution by workers would be prepared by the organizational efforts of a group of committed revolutionaries, so he formed the Communist League. In 1848, he published the *Communist Manifesto,* which resounds with the provocative exclamation, "The proletarians have nothing to lose but their chains. They have a world to win. Working men of all countries, unite!"

CONCLUSION

Europeans could not help but be impressed with the rapid pace of economic change during the first half of the nineteenth century. Trains truly revolutionized commerce and travel, bringing distant places closer together. Cities grew rapidly, their railway stations bringing in more agricultural goods produced with capital-intensive farming. More people worked in industry than ever before. Factories now dotted the landscape, although traditional workshop and cottage production remained essential.

Yet many upper-class contemporaries were worried by what seemed to be teeming, increasingly disorderly cities. The Industrial Revolution, to be sure, had generated material progress—indeed, opulence for some people—but it also seemed to have increased wrenching poverty and dissatisfaction among workers.

In the meantime, having defeated Napoleon at Waterloo, the European powers—Britain, Prussia, Austria, and Russia—set about trying to restore the prerogatives of ruling dynasties, nobles, and the established churches. Liberal and national movements struggled against conservative ideology in Restoration Europe. Liberalism, above all, seemed to reflect the desires of the middle classes, whose numbers and influence expanded so rapidly in the decades following the end of the Napoleonic era.

CHAPTER **15**

LIBERAL CHALLENGES TO RESTORATION EUROPE

$\sim\!\!\!\!\sim\!\!\!\!\sim$

At the Congress of Vienna of 1815, representatives of the allies who had defeated Napoleon—Austria, Russia, Prussia, and Great Britain—came together to reestablish peace in Europe. They hoped that by imposing a treaty on France and creating an international mechanism, the Concert of Europe, they could prevent Europe from again being shaken by revolution in France or elsewhere. The Congress represented conservative impulses, standing against the liberalism and nationalism that espoused organizing states along ethnic or national lines and demanded reforms in the name of the popular sovereignty that conservatives blamed for the French Revolution and Napoleonic era.

Early nineteenth-century Vienna was a perfect setting for a gathering of the representatives of Europe's sovereign powers. The Schönbrunn Palace on the outskirts of the Habsburg capital and Vienna's own elegant baroque buildings still reflected the grandeur of absolutism and traditional court life, despite the years of warfare that had virtually bankrupted the Austrian monarchy.

At the Congress, which met between September 1814 and June 1815, the Austrian hosts staged elaborate dinners, elegant balls, and festive fireworks displays, and organized hunts helped relieve boredom. Artists stood ready to paint the portraits of the members of the diplomatic delegations. Aristocratic guests amused themselves by trying to guess which of the hundreds of maids and porters were spying for the Austrians. The antics of some representatives provided as much comic relief as irritation. A Spanish diplomat insisted that his country should have the right to several small Italian states. The other representatives were so annoyed by this demand that they invited him to go on a ballooning excursion, and sent him off in the general direction of the Alps.

What the English poet George Gordon, Lord Byron (1788–1824), called "that base pageant," the Congress of Vienna provided an opportunity for the informal discussions that had always been an important part of traditional

The Congress of Vienna.

European diplomacy. In fact, the Congress met officially but once, to sign the final treaty, which had been negotiated in smaller formal and informal gatherings of the various delegations. In the wake of the many territorial changes that had occurred during the previous twenty-five years, the representatives redrew the map of Europe, particularly of Central Europe, putting old rulers back on their thrones.

After Napoleon's final defeat in 1815—the Congress of Vienna continued to meet during the 100 Days—a protracted struggle among the conservative forces, monarchies, nobles, established churches, and liberals took place in Europe. "Liberalism" as an economic and political philosophy implied the absence of government constraints that could interfere with the development of the individual. It was a philosophy perfectly suited to the middle classes in "the bourgeois century." The middle classes were an extremely diverse social group that ranged from merchants and manufacturers of great wealth to struggling shopkeepers (see Chapter 14). Rapid population growth swelled the number of lawyers, notaries, and other middle-class professionals. The entrepreneur came to be revered. Moreover, the middle classes' liberal emphasis on individual freedom found expression not only in economics and politics but also in the literature, art, and music of romanticism, which celebrated individual fulfillment through subjectivity and emotion. Boasted one German liberal, "We are the times."

Liberal movements were in many places closely tied to the emergence of nationalism as a source of allegiance and sovereignty. Nationalism was usually defined by language and cultural traditions, and the quest to establish national states whose borders would correspond to patterns of ethnic residence. Nationalism threatened the territorial settlements effected by the Congress of Vienna. The Habsburg Austrian monarchy itself ruled eleven major nationalities without a state of their own, including Hungarians and Poles, who had once had fully independent states. In the meantime, German and Italian nationalists began to call for national political unification.

THE POST-NAPOLEONIC SETTLEMENT

The allied representatives to the Congress were determined to ensure that France could not again rise to a position of domination in Europe. Thus, even before Napoleon's first defeat and abdication in 1814, representatives of Prussia, Austria, Russia, and Great Britain formed a coalition, the "Quadruple Alliance," intended to prevent France or any other state or political movement from threatening the legitimate sovereigns of Europe.

The Treaty of Paris

The Treaty of Paris was signed in March 1814, thus before the Congress of Vienna. Charles-Maurice de Talleyrand (1754–1838), who had served Napoleon with flexibility rooted in an uncanny sense of survival, became the intermediary. He exploited tensions among the allies, especially between Prussia and Austria. The victorious powers agreed to restore the Bourbons to the throne of France in the person of the count of Provence, brother of the executed Louis XVI, who took the throne as Louis XVIII. The allies might well have forced the French to sign a draconian treaty. But they were dealing not with the defeated Napoleon but with the restored Bourbon monarch, whose throne they wanted to solidify against liberal challenges within France.

France retained lands incorporated before November 1, 1792, including parts of Savoy, Germany, and the Austrian Netherlands, as well as the former papal city of Avignon. France gave up claims to the remainder of the Austrian Netherlands, the Dutch Republic, the German states, the Italian states, and Switzerland. It lost to Britain the Caribbean islands of Trinidad, Tobago, Santa Lucia, and part of Santo Domingo. The allies demanded no reparations from France. Yet difficult territorial issues remained to be resolved in central and southern Europe.

Diplomatic Maneuvering at the Congress of Vienna

The Congress of Vienna was almost entirely the work of diplomats representing Austria, Prussia, Great Britain, and Russia. The goals were threefold: to redistribute territory in the wake of the French revolutionary and Napoleonic Wars, to achieve a balance of power that would prevent any one

British Foreign Secretary Viscount Robert Castlereagh.

state from becoming too powerful and potentially aggressive, and to make future revolutionary movements impossible. At the beginning, defeated France played only the role of a very interested observer (although French was the official language of the conference). But Talleyrand's wily off-stage negotiations gradually brought France to the position of a full-fledged participant in the deliberations.

The dominant figure in Vienna was the Austrian chancellor Prince Klemens von Metternich (1773–1859). Born in the German Rhineland, Metternich was the son of a noble who had served at the court of the Habsburg monarch. Forced to flee his homeland by the French invasion in 1792, he subsequently entered the diplomatic service in Vienna, rising to become the minister of foreign affairs in 1809. Metternich was a handsome dandy with immaculately powdered hair as at home in the social whirl of formal receptions and magnificent balls as in the petty intrigues of high society. He could bore people in five languages. But he was a determined, calculating practitioner of tough-minded diplomacy. Metternich dominated international affairs of the continent until 1848.

Foreign Secretary Viscount Robert Castlereagh (1769–1822) represented Britain. Aloof and painfully shy, Castlereagh, whose passion was sheepherding, went to Vienna in the hope of establishing Britain as the arbiter of European affairs. Now Europe's greatest power, the British Empire included one of every five people in the world. The British government sought the elimination of the French threat to its commercial interests as well as security. Moreover, Castlereagh and Metternich both viewed the prospect of Russian expansion in Central Europe with anxiety. Only Russia now seemed in a position to disrupt Europe through unilateral acts.

Tsar Alexander I of Russia (ruled 1801–1825) wanted the allies to affirm formally what he considered the religious basis of the European alliance. Alexander I was, above all, a deeply religious man who occasionally lapsed into an intense mysticism and overwhelming unhappiness as he became increasingly reactionary. Alexander I drafted a document that became the basis for the Holy Alliance. It asserted that the relations of the European sovereigns, "the delegates of Providence," would thereafter be based "upon the sublime truths which the Holy Religion of Our Savior teaches." Emperor Francis I of Austria and Frederick William III of Prussia signed the document, but the British prince regent—the future George IV (ruled 1820–1830)—begged off. Castlereagh called it "a piece of sublime mysticism and nonsense." Prussia, Russia, and Austria promised mutual assistance wherever established religions and peace were threatened. In the moral claims of the Holy Alliance lay justification for the repression by the allies of any liberal and national movements in Europe.

The Congress System

The Congress of Vienna drew a map of Europe that lasted for several generations (see Map 15.1). Under Metternich's stern leadership, what became known as the Congress system restored the principle of dynastic legitimacy and the balance of international power in Europe. The future of Poland, which had lost its independence when it was last partitioned by Russia, Prussia, and Austria in 1795, stood at the top of the list of contentious issues. Russian troops occupied much of Poland, which Tsar Alexander wanted to annex to the Russian Empire. Great Britain, France, and Austria, fearing increased Russian and Prussian power in Central Europe, formed an alliance to head off any attack in Central Europe by Russia or Prussia. In May, the Kingdom of Poland was proclaimed by the Congress. It was to include lands Austria and Prussia had seized during the earlier partitions. But "Congress Poland," as it came to be known (made up of about 20 percent of Poland's territory before the first partition of 1772; see Chapter 11), was despite a constitution nothing more than a Russian protectorate, with the tsar himself occupying the Polish throne. Moreover, large parts of what had been independent Poland remained in Prussia and in the Austrian Empire. Russia also held on to Finland, which it had conquered during the Napoleonic Wars. To balance Russian gains in the east, Prussia received the northern half of Saxony, which had cast its fate with Napoleon, as well as Polish-speaking Posen and the port city of Gdańsk.

In comparison with the debates over Poland and Saxony, the resolution of remaining territorial issues seemed easy. Prussia received territories on the left bank of the Rhine River to discourage French aggression to the east. The Prussian Rhineland was now separated from the eastern Prussian provinces by the states of Hanover and Hesse-Kassel. Prussia also received Swedish Pomerania and parts of Westphalia, but lost its outlet to the North Sea with the return of East Friesland to Hanover. Other buffers against France along its eastern border included Switzerland, reestablished as a neutral confederation of cantons, and the Kingdom of Piedmont-Sardinia, enlarged to include Genoa, Nice, and part of Savoy.

Most territorial settlements were made without the slightest consideration of local public opinion. Although the allies emphasized the principle of legitimacy in the territorial settlement, they never hesitated to dispense

MAP 15.1 EUROPE AFTER THE CONGRESS OF VIENNA, 1815   Changes in boundaries of states after the Congress of Vienna.

with a number of smaller legitimate princes whose claims would have inter-fered with the creation of buffers against France. The republics of Genoa and Venice disappeared from the map.

The Congress placated Britain by awarding the former Austrian Nether-lands (Belgium) to the Dutch, leaving a state friendly to Britain on France's northern border. The former stadholder of the Dutch Republic became King William I. But Castlereagh's plan to link the Dutch throne to the British monarchy by engineering the marriage of a British princess to the Dutch royal family failed, at least in part because the intended groom became roy-ally drunk in the presence of the intended but most unwilling bride.

Austria was well compensated for the loss of the Austrian Netherlands with Lombardy and Venetia in Italy, much of Galicia, and Illyria on the coast of Dalmatia. The grand duchies of Parma, Modena, and Tuscany, too, had close family links to Vienna. The Congress restored the Bourbon dynasty to the throne of the Kingdom of the Two Sicilies (Naples and Sicily). There, Ferdinand I introduced a constitution, but signed an alliance with Austria and promised not to introduce any further reforms without the latter's per-mission. Austrian garrisons and secret police in each Italian state helped assure Austrian domination of northern Italy.

Napoleon's remarkable escape from Elba in March 1815 and the dra-matic episode of the 100 Days (see Chapter 13) did not change the most important aspects of the Congress's shuffling of European territories. The second Treaty of Paris, signed in November 1815 following Napoleon's defeat at Waterloo in June, however, pushed France back from its 1792 borders to those of 1790. Furthermore, the allies now exacted reparations totaling 700 million francs from France. Their armies would occupy France until the debt was settled.

Napoleon's victories in Central Europe had led to the end of the Holy Roman Empire in 1806. On June 9, 1815, the Congress created a German Confederation of thirty-five states loosely joined by a Federal Diet (Bun-destag), or governing body, that would meet in Frankfurt. In addition to Prus-sia and Austria, the Confederation also included the states of Bavaria, Hanover, Württemberg, the two Hesses, and Baden, and the independent, or "free," cities of Hamburg, Frankfurt, Bremen, and Lübeck. The Confed-eration did not, however, include the non-German lands of the Austrian Empire. Members of the Confederation pledged to assist each other if any of them were attacked or in any way threatened. But it was unlikely that unanimity could ever be achieved among the member states, or that states could be compelled to obey a decision made by the Confederation. The Diet merely afforded Metternich a means of bullying the smaller states. The Ger-man Confederation was anything but an affirmation of a move toward Ger-man national unification. German states, large and small, were proud of their traditions of autonomy, or what was known as "German particularism." By virtue of its Rhineland acquisitions, Prussia emerged as a rival for Austria's leadership of the Confederation and for dominance in Central Europe.

The Concert of Europe

To preserve the settlements enacted at Vienna, the five major European powers (Great Britain, Prussia, Austria, Russia, and France) formed a "Concert of Europe." In this extension of the Congress of Vienna, representatives of the powers would meet annually. If necessary, they would join together to put down movements that could threaten the *status quo*. Metternich's Austria had the most to fear from national claims for independent states. Austria was both a state in the German Confederation and the most important province within its empire of many nationalities. The Austrian Empire stretched from the stately elegance of Vienna through the plains of Hungary, to isolated Romanian and Croatian villages. German was the language of the imperial bureaucracy, and of many of the towns, but one could find eleven major languages within the borders of the empire. The Habsburg monarchy depended on the support of the nobles of the favored nationalities—principally Austrian, Hungarian, and Croat— and the German-speaking middle classes. Metternich exploited the fear that the upper classes of the favored nationalities felt toward any awakening from the lower classes, particularly of other ethnic groups. This kept most Magyar (Hungarian) nobles loyal to the Habsburg dynasty, although some desired ultimate independence.

Tensions remained between the allies. Prussia and particularly Austria feared that Russia was seeking to expand its influence in the Balkans, especially among peoples of the Orthodox faith. Metternich therefore was willing to use Austrian armies to maintain the *status quo,* but he sought to avoid any joint Congress military action that might bring Russian armies into Central Europe or the Balkans. He thus wanted to keep alive the Austrian alliance with Britain against any future French, Prussian, or Russian aggression.

Castlereagh, on the other hand, was less concerned by Russia's expanded interests in Central Europe than about containing France. But he had reservations about the appropriateness of the Quadruple Alliance's intervention in the internal affairs of European states. The British participated in the annual gatherings of representatives of the Concert powers, but gradually withdrew from the Congress system. At Aachen in 1818, the allies agreed to withdraw their remaining troops from France, which, having paid off the war debts, now joined the Holy Alliance.

Restoration Europe

The monarchs, diplomats, and nobles at the Congress of Vienna were guided by conservative principles of monarchical legitimacy, with the right to the thrones of Europe to be determined by hereditary succession, and by close ties to the prerogatives of the established churches.

The Restoration of Monarchs, Nobles, and Clergy

Monarchs, nobles, and clergy returned to power, prestige, and influence. In the Kingdom of Piedmont-Sardinia, the members of the ruling House of Savoy came back wearing powdered wigs in the style of the eighteenth century, and the religious orders returned in force. In Lombardy-Venetia, consultative assemblies were established in Milan and Venice, but they did little more than assess taxes. With the exception of Baden, in the German states such bodies routinely approved legislation without limiting the power of the sovereign. The governments of the German states that had been occupied by France completely purged the remnants of Napoleonic administration, annulled French-inspired legislation, and imposed strict censorship.

When the French left the Papal States, Pope Pius VII immediately tried to exorcise all traces of French influence. Administrative reforms undertaken during the occupation ended; so did street lighting and even vaccinations, which were identified with the godless French. The clergy reclaimed most public offices. In Tuscany the duke ordered the colors of Giotto's portrait of Dante altered, fearing that observers would see in them the French tricolor flag.

The French Revolution had by no means eliminated noble influence in the states of Europe. Even in Britain, where the lines between landed and business wealth were more blurred than anywhere else, nobles still dominated the House of Commons. In France, the Bourbon monarchy restored nobles to political primacy. An electoral system based on landed wealth gave them a disproportionate advantage. In Spain, nobles were particularly numerous, although many of them were relatively poor. Sweden still counted about 12,000 nobles in the middle of the nineteenth century. In the Italian states, nobles still held sway in declining or stagnant walled towns like Palermo, Naples, and Rome, as they did in the countryside. Even in industrializing Milan and in Turin, nobles dominated the civic administration.

The farther east one went, the more nobles still dominated economic, social, and political life. Nobles (Junkers) owned 40 percent of the land of Prussia and retained their stranglehold over the officer corps. The army defiantly brushed aside possible competition from the Landwehr, the civilian reserve force commanded by mere commoners—merchants, teachers, and bureaucrats. In Russia, the officer corps remained a noble stronghold, reinforced by the aristocracy's near monopoly on appointments to military academies and to important posts in the civil service. In Austria, where the greatest 300 to 400 hereditary aristocratic families remained close to the Habsburg throne, 70 percent of those in top official posts had noble titles in 1829, and twenty years later the percentage had grown even more. Austrian Chancellor Metternich warned Tsar Alexander I about the dangers of the "intermediate class," which prospered by adopting "all sorts of disguises."

Postcard depicting the Houses of Parliament in Budapest.

Indeed, noble style and distinction retained great influence. In the architecture of public buildings and palaces, noble taste still predominated, as in the enormous neo-Gothic Parliament in Budapest, where nobles held sway as for centuries. In much of Europe, public buildings and statues affirmed aristocratic values and moral claims that had characterized the old regimes. European nobles retained close ties to the established churches, which still deferred to aristocratic status.

During the revolutionary era, the established churches, particularly the Catholic Church, had suffered. Europe now witnessed a marked religious revival, as in the Lutheran northern German states. In France, the old religious confraternities were revived; pious families contributed money to rebuild churches, monasteries, and convents destroyed or damaged during the Revolution. In Britain, the Established (Anglican) Church rejected the notion of divine-right or absolutist monarchy, yet most British conservatives believed the existing social order represented by the Anglican Church to be God-given and immutable. They strongly opposed (Protestant) Dissenters and, above all, Catholics.

Conservative Ideology

The conservative ideology of Restoration Europe drew on several sources. A theory of organic change held Christian monarchies to be, as a French writer put it, "the final creation in the development of political society and of religious society." Conservatives insisted that states emerged through gradual growth and that monarchical legitimacy stemmed from royal birthright, confirmed by the sanction of religion. Catholic and Protestant conservatives insisted that the established churches provided a moral authority that complemented that of traditional monarchical institutions of government, which alone could maintain order. In Russia, the mystical Tsar Alexander I believed fervently that the Orthodox Church had an important role in keeping his people subservient. In the German states, Pietism broke with Protestant orthodoxy to teach that mankind was essentially sinful and required a repressive state to keep in line. Europe's conservative monarchies, depending on noble support, therefore sought to reestablish the privileges that the French Revolution and Napoleon had swept away.

A French writer, Joseph de Maistre (c. 1754–1821), emerged as a theorist of the alliance of throne and altar. Rejecting the concept of "natural rights" associated with Enlightenment thought, de Maistre argued that a king's power could never be limited by his subjects, because that power came only from God. De Maistre blamed the Revolution on the philosophes who had shaken the faith that underlay the absolutism of hereditary monarchy. To de Maistre, "the first servant of the crown should be the executioner." Most conservatives saw no difference between reform and revolution, believing that reform would inevitably lead to revolution and radical change. They stood adamantly opposed to political claims stemming from any notion of individual freedom, popular sovereignty, or membership in any particular national group.

Yet conservatives confronted the problem that their support was limited to a very narrow social and political base in a Europe that was slowly being transformed by the Industrial Revolution. It was testimony to the influence of the revolutionary era that the restored monarchy in France under Louis XVIII granted a Charter to the French people promising essential liberties. Moreover, the French monarchy, as well as that of Piedmont-Sardinia and even Metternich's Austria, utilized the bureaucratized state apparatus inherited from Napoleon to repress liberals, instead of restoring the less-centralized ruling structure that had typified Old Regime Europe.

LIBERALISM

Nineteenth-century liberalism was more than an economic and political theory: it was a way of viewing the world. Liberals—the term became current in the late 1830s—shared a confidence that human progress was inevitable, though gradual. From the Enlightenment, the bourgeoisie inherited a faith in science, which they held to be a motor of progress. Liberalism reflected middle-class confidence and economic aspirations.

Liberals and Politics

"Liberty" became the watchword for the increasingly liberal middle classes, who protested their exclusion from political life in most European states. Liberals believed that all individuals should be equal before the law because—reflecting Enlightenment influence—they held that individuals are born good, free, and capable of improvement. Economic liberals for the most part believed in "laissez-faire," that the economy should be allowed to operate freely without state interference. (In contrast, liberals in more recent times want states to protect and assist ordinary people, particularly the poor.) Nineteenth-century liberals wanted government by constitution and by elected legislative bodies (such as the British Parliament and the French Chamber of Deputies) that would reflect some degree of sovereignty, with authority resting to some extent in the popular will rather than from monarchical legitimacy. Moreover, liberals demanded such civil liberties as freedom of the press and of assembly, and education for the lower classes, so that individuals could develop to their full capacities.

Liberals gradually replaced the discourse emphasizing the rights of man—which had emerged from the Enlightenment of the eighteenth century and the French Revolution—with that of the legally defined rights of the citizen or subject. They put their faith in political and social rights embodied in constitutions, defined by law, and guaranteed by the state. Middle-class voters trusted elected legislative bodies to ensure that their rights as property owners could not be trampled by monarchs and aristocrats. They opposed electoral systems that were so narrowly constructed that only the wealthiest men were allowed to vote, as in Britain, France, and Prussia. Their goal was the expansion of the electoral franchise. But most liberals during the first two-thirds of the nineteenth century did not believe that all people should vote, but rather that eligibility to vote should stem from the amount of property owned, and that only such men—and not women—of property should hold the electoral franchise.

Laissez-Faire

Adopting the maxim that "that government is best which governs least," liberals sought to place limits on state authority. In particular, they rejected government interference in the operations of the economy. Many liberals therefore opposed protectionism—state-imposed duties on imports. They followed the theories of Adam Smith (1723–1790), author of *The Wealth of Nations* (1776). Their motto was "laissez-faire" ("let do as one pleases"), which meant that government should allow the "invisible hand" of supply and demand to bring change. Smith had argued that the unrestricted functioning of the free economy would ensure the pursuit of private interests. This would, in turn, serve the public interest by creating more wealth. Smith contended that a new social hierarchy would emerge if the economy were allowed to follow its natural course. With their investments augmenting the general good, businessmen would supplant nobles and churchmen as the men to whom ordinary people deferred. Indeed, this was increasingly what was occurring in Western Europe.

Utilitarianism formed another cornerstone of the entrepreneurial ideal, indeed of liberalism in general. Jeremy Bentham (1748–1832) was its most influential exponent. In 1776, he posited that laws should be judged by their social utility, or whether or not they provided "the greatest good for the greatest number" of people. His famous standard question about any law or government institution was "Does it work?" Bentham's utilitarianism reflected the relatively decentralized government of Britain and a pervasive belief among the king's subjects that a government that made few demands and that served efficiently counted among the "liberties" of freeborn Britons.

Adam Smith's successors gradually made a science out of speculations about the operations of the economy, insisting that the laws they postulated about the development of capitalism were based on scientific certainty. They optimistically pointed to the ongoing economic and social transformation of Britain in the manufacturing age. The theories of Smith and Bentham had a great impact on British businessmen. The social status of an individual increasingly came to be measured in terms of utility.

In 1817, the British economist David Ricardo (1772–1823) published *Principles of Political Economy and Taxation*. Ricardo assumed the existence of an "iron law of wages," which held that, if wages were left to the laws of supply and demand, they would fall to near subsistence level. This was certainly more cheering news for manufacturers than for workers. Elected to Parliament in 1819, Ricardo became a hero to the middle class. He reassured liberals by telling them that the "invisible hand" of the economy would bring continued economic growth, with the bulk of entrepreneurial profits going into employers' pockets. Through the Political Economy Club, the *Westminster Review* (first published in 1824), and newspapers, the ideas of Bentham and other liberals reached a wide audience. Liberal economists earned academic appointments at the University of Edinburgh and the University of London (founded in 1828 by religious Dissenters). Economic liberalism found proponents in France and the German states.

Middle-class entrepreneurs did not always agree on what specific economic policies they favored. In the 1820s, Tory governments in Britain bored the first holes in the wall of protectionism by reducing the duty collected on Baltic timber, which had been kept high to favor Canadian exporters, and by establishing sliding scales for tariffs tied to the price of wheat in England. Many French industrialists demanded that the government maintain high tariffs to keep out British manufactured goods and machinery. Businessmen everywhere demanded improved transportation networks. Most liberals like Ricardo demanded the "freedom of work," that is, that nothing constrain free agreements between employers and their workers. Many industrialists opposed state-imposed limits to their authority within the workplace, including regulations concerning safety and child labor. They considered their factories to be their castles, in which they could do what they pleased.

British liberals believed that a strong state compromised political freedom. The French Revolution had, after all, culminated in Jacobin state centralization and Napoleonic despotism. Continental liberals remained more "statist," accepting a more active role by government, particularly in the German states, and in Spain, where they relied on a powerful state to counteract the influence of nobles and clerics.

ROMANTICISM

Romanticism, emphasizing imagination and emotion in personal development, began to emerge as a literary, artistic, and musical movement in the late eighteenth century. In 1798, the English poets Samuel Taylor Coleridge (1772–1834) and William Wordsworth (1770–1850) penned a manifesto calling on poets to abandon the classical style based on Greek and Roman models that characterized eighteenth-century court and aristocratic life and instead express their emotional response to nature. During the romantic era, swooning and fainting came into vogue because they seemed to be honest expressions of emotion.

Conservative Origins

Romanticism first contributed to the conservative revival. After initially being intrigued by the French Revolution's apparent victory over the strictures of the Old Regime, the early romantic writers had become disillusioned by its violent turn. Coleridge had been among the first to sing the praises of the Revolution, but turned against it when French armies began pouring across the frontiers more as conquerors than as liberators.

Many of the early romantic writers were individuals of religious faith who rejected Enlightenment rationalism. "I wept and I believed," wrote the French writer François-René de Chateaubriand (1768–1848), relating his re-conversion to Catholicism after the turmoil of the revolutionary and Napoleonic eras. Disillusionment with the French Revolution helped German romantic writers discover in nationalism a means of individual fulfillment. Nationalism, too, marked a reaction against Enlightenment rational tradition. Johann Gottfried von Herder (1744–1803), the son of a Prussian schoolteacher, was one of the impassioned leaders of the *Sturm und Drang* (Storm and Stress) movement, a rebellion by young German writers against Enlightenment thought. Calling for the study and celebration of German literature and history, Herder argued that it was through the passionate identification with the nation that the individual reached his or her highest stage of development. All Germans would be bound together by an awareness of and identity in a common history, culture, and above all, language as p⸝ a *Volk*, or living and evolving "national community." Herder thus h⸌⸜ invent the idea of a national culture. At the same time, his insistence on the existence of different racial types, shaped by climate, history, and cultural traditions, would influence the evolution of racism later in the century. In Central and Eastern Europe, which was constituted in many areas by a patchwork of nationalities, romanticism celebrated the historical authenticity of the cultural traditions and languages of ethnic peoples. From there it would be a short step to argue that nationalities should have their own independent state.

Romantic Literature and Painting

Romantics defined freedom as the unleashing of the senses and passion of the soul. They searched for the "heroic genius" who fulfills himself in spite of constraints placed on him by the state, religion, or societal convention. Johann Wolfgang von Goethe (1749–1832) evoked the impassioned battle raging in the mind of the heroic individual. Goethe's hero in *Faust* (1790) struggles to make his way against a society that fails to understand him.

Like Faust, romantic writers and artists were, at least at the beginning, literary and academic outsiders. Many were loners, without established professional positions, overwhelmed by what they considered the tragedy of their unrequited search for individual fulfillment because less-gifted people did not comprehend their brilliance. Romantics bared the suffering of their souls. The English poet Percy Bysshe Shelley (1792–1822) penned his loftiest tribute to the poet (and, thus, himself) in "Hymn of Apollo":

> I am the eye with which the Universe
> Beholds itself and knows itself divine;
> All harmony of instrument or verse,
> All prophecy, all medicine is mine,
> All light of art or nature;—to my song
> Victory and praise in its own right belong.

Romantic painters sought to convey feeling through the depiction of the helplessness of the individual confronted by the power of nature—gathering storms, surging seas, and immense, dark forests, portrayed with deep, rich colors. In France, Théodore Géricault (1791–1824) reached the public eye with his *Officer of the Chasseurs Commanding a Charge* (1812), p. 584, an almost worshipful painting of a Napoleonic officer in the heat of battle. Géricault became obsessed with shipwrecks, a subject that reflected his volatile personality. He sought out real-life survivors of such tragedies in order to paint his powerful *The Raft of the Medusa* (1818–1819), depicting a shipwreck off the West African coast.

Théodore Géricault's *Portrait of an Officer of the Chasseurs Commanding a Charge* (1812).

Romantic Music

The romantics also believed that music, like painting, was poetry capable of releasing torrents of emotion in listeners. Whereas romantic literature sought and achieved a sharp break with the rules of classical literature, romantic musical compositions built on the traditions of the eighteenth-century masters, helping the public rediscover them. The compositions of Ludwig van Beethoven (1770–1827) bridged the classical and romantic periods, with a foot firmly in each. The son of an alcoholic court musician in the Rhineland town of Bonn, Beethoven was a homely, isolated, brooding man.

Beethoven's music followed classical rules of structure and harmony. The German romantic composer Richard Wagner would later say that, as Beethoven became increasingly deaf, he was "undisturbed by the bustle of life [hearing only] the harmonies of his soul." Beethoven's audiences struggled to understand his music, which increasingly seemed to defy traditional structures and harmonies. A critic reacted to one of Beethoven's symphonies, "The composer . . . takes the majestic flight of the eagle, then he creeps along rock-strewn paths. After penetrating the soul with a gentle melancholy he immediately lacerates it with a mass of barbarous chords. I seem to see doves put in together with crocodiles!" Beethoven's symphonies and string quartets were widely played in Europe, and his sonatas helped popularize the piano. The instrument, which continued to be improved, became more resonant and was established as a single solo instrument. Part of the growing popularity of the piano may have stemmed from contemporary fascination with fast-moving machines. Whereas only two decades earlier Mozart had struggled to make ends meet, Beethoven enjoyed wealth and fame, freeing himself from the old patronage system of court and church.

Although opera remained the most popular form of musical expression, drawing crowds with its extravagant staging and elaborate, expensive costumes, romantic music grew in popularity during the first half of the nineteenth century. The public flocked to public concerts, and more musicians could now make a living from their performances. Musicians wrote music for public concerts. The musical "virtuoso" became a phenomenon, going on

The celebrated Niccolò Paganini in concert, early nineteenth century.

concert tours and traveling by train. No one was more popular than the Italian composer and violinist Niccolò Paganini (1782–1840). Paganini's performances, the musical effects he produced, and his frenzied appearance suggested to one observer that he was engaging in witchcraft. Music also assumed a greater role in private life. Not only did more people play the piano, but concerts in middle-class homes became common.

STIRRINGS OF REVOLT

The Congress of Vienna resembled the Dutch boy gamely trying to dam the deluge by plugging up the holes in the dike with his fingers. During the first half of the century, virtually every country in Europe experienced a confrontation between the old political order, represented by the Congress of Vienna, and nascent liberalism.

In France and the German states, liberal bourgeois demanded political rights for a wider number of people. Newspapers and political pamphlets deftly sidestepped the heavy hand of censorship to challenge the restored prerogatives of conservative regimes. In Britain, middle-class spokesmen confronted conservatives and what conservatism's enemies referred to as "Old Corruption," a political system based upon the patronage and influence of wealthy landowners. On the continent, the middle classes clamored for constitutions.

In the German and Italian states and Belgium, liberalism was closely associated with emerging groups of nationalists. Intellectuals, lawyers, and students called for the creation of independent states based upon ethnicity. This was anathema to the powers represented at the Congress of Vienna, particularly the leaders of the polyglot Russian and Austrian Empires. Demands for new states organized around the principle of nationality—as opposed to monarchical or princely sovereignty—would threaten the very existence of these empires.

Liberal Revolts in Spain, Portugal, and Italy

The first test for the Congress system came in Spain. Upon his return to Madrid in 1814, King Ferdinand VII (ruled 1808–1833) declared that he did not recognize the liberal constitution that had been drawn up by the Cortes (assembly) in 1812. It provided ministers responsible to the Cortes and defined sovereignty as residing "essentially in the [Spanish] Nation," the union of all Spaniards in both hemispheres. It guaranteed the right of property, freedom of the press, and freedom from arbitrary arrest.

Ferdinand VII imposed strict censorship, welcomed back the Jesuit religious order, and repressed Masonic lodges. Furthermore, he refused to convoke the Cortes, which he had promised to do upon his return. Ecclesiastics and nobles reclaimed land they had lost during the Napoleonic period. The Inquisition, the Catholic Church's institutionalized apparatus to maintain religious orthodoxy, returned to Spain, and the police again began to arrest alleged heretics.

Thus the Spanish monarchy remained inextricably allied with noble and ecclesiastical privilege. The clergy accounted for about 30 percent of adult Spanish males, many living in monasteries that dotted the countryside. The aristocracy and the Church owned two-thirds of the land, much of it as unproductive as its owners, who collected revenue from those tilling the soil. Yet the vast majority of peasants supported the established order, believing the word of the village priest to be that of God. The small number of nobles and bourgeois who read the country's few newspapers—the majority of the population remained illiterate—found little except, as one traveler put it, "accounts of miracles wrought by different Virgins, lives of holy friars and sainted nuns, romances of marvelous conversions, libels against Jews, heretics and Freemasons, and histories of apparitions."

The allies were delighted to have a "legitimate" sovereign back on France's southern flank, although Spain had long since ceased to be a European power. Moreover, the Spanish Empire had begun to disintegrate. French occupation and the Peninsular War, with the king in exile (see Chapter 13), had weakened Spain's hold over its Latin American colonies. Rebellions against Spanish rule broke out in the colonies, beginning in Argentina in 1816. Simón Bolívar (1783–1830), a fiery Creole aristocrat educated in European Enlightenment ideals, led an army that liberated his native

Venezuela in 1821 and defeated Spanish troops in Peru in 1824. The example of the War of American Independence in North America provided inspiration. Spanish forces, lacking resources and badly led, were obliged to fight over enormous stretches of wildly varying territory. Spain recognized the independence of Mexico in 1821. Of the overseas empire that had stretched from North America to the southern tip of South America in the sixteenth century, Spain retained only the Caribbean islands of Cuba and Puerto Rico, as well as the Philippines in Asia.

Against this background, a revolt broke out in Spain in 1820. Army officers who led the insurrection against Ferdinand were soon joined by merchants and lawyers. The king now agreed to convoke the Cortes and abide by the liberal constitution of 1812. Metternich and Tsar Alexander I of Russia, supported by Prussia, demanded allied armed intervention; so did Louis XVIII of France, eager to prove himself a reliable ally. Great Britain, however, remained adamantly opposed to any intervention in Spanish internal affairs, first as a matter of principle, and secondly because of fear that the presence of foreign troops in Spain might jeopardize British commerce or increase French influence on the Iberian Peninsula.

Meanwhile, the fires of liberalism also spread to Portugal. Liberal army officers took advantage of the continued absence of King John VI, who had fled to Brazil during the Napoleonic Wars, to rise up against the British-backed regent in 1820. They drafted a liberal constitution, based on that penned in Spain in 1812. That same year, a military coup d'état led to the return of King John from Brazil as a constitutional monarch. The constitution proclaimed that year guaranteed religious toleration, civic rights, and the sanctity of property. The influence of this revolution, which undercut the influence of the Church, led to civil war from 1832 to 1834 between royalists and an alliance of liberals and radicals, and then in 1851, after some forty different governments and another coup d'état, to the establishment of a

A secret meeting of the members of the Carbonari, Italy c. 1815–1830.

parliamentary system of government based on a restricted electoral franchise.

In 1820 an insurrection also broke out in Italy. Army officers and merchants in Naples and Sicily revolted against the rule of King Ferdinand I, another monarch who had been restored to his shaky throne by the allies. Some of the revolutionaries were members of a secret society, organized along military lines, known as the "Carbonari." These "charcoal-burners" took their name from their practice of swearing each new member to secrecy by tracing a charcoal mark on his forehead. The Carbonari, originally formed to fight Napoleon's armies, now directed its fervor against the monarch placed on the throne by the Austrians. However, Austrian troops put down the revolt, and another in the Kingdom of Piedmont-Sardinia.

In response to what they perceived as the liberal threat, in 1820 the Russian, Prussian, and Austrian governments signed an agreement at the Congress of Troppau in Austrian Silesia. Based on the "principles of the [Holy] Alliance," it proclaimed the right of the signatories to intervene militarily in any country in which political changes were brought about by revolution. Following the suicide of Castlereagh (who suffered unpopularity and perhaps also blackmail over a sexual matter) in 1822, Britain further distanced itself from the Congress system. That year, the remaining Congress powers reconvened in the northern Italian town of Verona. Britain's withdrawal cleared the way for military action in Spain to restore King Ferdinand VII to his throne. With the support of Russia, Prussia, and Austria, a French army took to the field for the first time since Waterloo, but in very different circumstances. It crossed the Pyrenees Mountains in 1823 and captured Madrid. The grateful king of Spain renounced the Constitution of 1812 and ordered the torture and execution of his opponents.

In December 1823, U.S. President James Monroe, fearing that the Concert powers might try to help Spain restore its authority over its former Latin American colonies, issued a proclamation that became one of the bases of subsequent American foreign policy. Stressing that the political systems of the European powers were different from its own, the Monroe Doctrine warned that the United States would "consider any attempt on their part to extend their system to any portion of this hemisphere as dangerous to our peace and safety."

Stirrings in Germany

In the German and Italian states, liberals and nationalists were often the same people. Members of student fraternities demanded a united Germany. In 1817, a large convocation of student associations celebrated the three-hundredth anniversary of Martin Luther's revolt against the papacy by burning books deemed anti-patriotic. In 1819, a German student murdered an arch-conservative historian and dramatist commonly believed to be in the pay of the Russian tsar. Metternich persuaded Emperor Francis I

Nationalist German students in 1817 burning books and other objects deemed anti-patriotic.

of Austria and Frederick William III of Prussia to impose the Carlsbad Decrees, which the Diet of the German Confederation unanimously accepted. These muzzled the press and dissolved the student fraternities. Teachers fired in one state were to be blacklisted in other member states. Metternich convinced Frederick William to renounce any form of "universal representation" in his kingdom. The episode seemed to clinch Metternich's victory over constitutionalism in the German states.

Cracks in the Congress of Europe: The Greek Revolt

The Greek revolt in 1821 against the Ottoman Turks shattered the Congress system. Austria and, above all, Russia hoped to extend their influence in the Balkans at the expense of the Ottoman Empire. In the late eighteenth century, Catherine the Great had seen Russia's role in the Balkans as protecting Christians there against the Islamic Turks. Moreover, Russian nationalists coveted Constantinople, the gateway to Asia and the Black Sea. Britain feared a potential threat to British control of India and was wary of Russian influence in Afghanistan. Austria, threatened by Russian interest in the Balkans, also feared Russian designs on Constantinople. The Greek revolt put the Congress powers in a bind. Christian Europe traditionally considered the Turks savage infidels. But, at the same time, the Congress powers had to recognize the Ottoman Empire as the historically "legitimate" sovereign of the Greeks. Support for the Greek rebels would represent a renunciation of the *status quo*, a principle upon which the Congress system had been based.

The Greek revolt grew out of a small Greek nationalist movement that had developed at the end of the eighteenth century. Prince Alexander Ypsilantis (1792–1828), a former general in the Russian army, founded a secret nationalist organization in 1814, the "Society of Friends." He counted on the tsar's support for a Greek uprising. (Russia had encouraged a Greek insurrection in 1770, one that had been crushed by Turkish forces.) In 1821 Ypsilantis organized a revolt in Turkish Moldavia, hoping that Romanians would also rise up against Ottoman domination and that Russia would aid the cause of the insurgents. But when Romanians did not rebel and the tsar disavowed the rebels, the Turks crushed the initial Greek uprising. Several weeks later, further revolts against the Turks broke out in mainland Greece and on several Aegean islands. The Congress powers, including Russia, immediately condemned the insurrection.

However, the Greek revolt caught the imagination of writers in Western Europe. Romantic writers espoused national self-consciousness. Members of the philhellenic movement (scholars and intellectuals who had become passionately interested in classical Greece) embraced the Greek revolt as a modern crusade for Christianity and independence against what they con-

Eugène Delacroix's *Massacre at Chios*, 1824.

sidered Turkish oppression of the birthplace of Western civilization. The English poets Byron and Shelley took up the cause of Greek independence. Shelley, who called the poet the "unacknowledged legislator of the world," also supported Irish independence from Britain.

The Greek insurgents massacred thousands of Turks in 1821, but it was the brutal Turkish repression of the Greeks that caught the attention of Western conservatives and liberals alike. In 1822, the Turks massacred the entire Greek population of the island of Chios, after having executed a year earlier the patriarch of Constantinople in his ecclesiastical robes on Easter Sunday. The French romantic painter Eugène Delacroix (1798–1863) celebrated the Greeks' struggle for national sovereignty in his painting *The Massacre at Chios* (1824), p. 590. The British government also had come to the view that peace could best be maintained by the creation of an autonomous Greek state. In 1827, Britain, France, and Russia signed the Treaty of London, threatening the Turks with military intervention if they did not accept an armistice. When the Turks refused, a combined naval force destroyed the Turkish fleet at Navarino.

Russia declared war on the Ottoman Empire in 1828 and occupied the Balkan territories of Moldavia and Eastern Wallachia. However, military obstacles and the self-interested disapproval by Britain and France of Russian plans for dismembering the Ottoman Empire forced Russia to agree to the Treaty of Adrianople (1829). Moldavia and Wallachia became protectorates of Russia, further pushing back the Ottoman Empire's European territories and expanding Russian influence in the Balkans. In 1832, the Greeks finally gained independence. The treaty between Britain, France, Bavaria, and Russia placed Greece under the "guarantee" of "protecting powers" and selected a young Bavarian prince to be king of Greece (Otto I, ruled 1833–1862).

The Decembrist Revolt in Russia

At his succession to the throne after the assassination of his autocratic father in 1801, Tsar Alexander I seemed liberal and idealistic. Scarred by the hatred between his father, Tsar Paul, and his grandmother, Catherine the Great, and by the assassination of Paul, Alexander had at least been aware of the plot. Because he was somewhat familiar with Enlightenment thought, some Russian liberals welcomed Alexander's accession to the throne, seeing him as a potentially charming reformer. He surrounded himself with a committee of advisers who advocated reform and began his reign by granting amnesty to thousands of people condemned by his father, relaxing censorship, abolishing torture in judicial investigations, and allowing more Russians to travel abroad. During the Napoleonic Wars, Tsar Alexander had taken steps to make his regime more efficient, including the creation of a council of state, the formation of centralized ministries directly responsible to the tsar, and the organization of local governments. Yet, an enormous social, economic, and legal gulf separated the Russian aristocracy from the millions of destitute serfs bound to the lands of their lords. Most Russian nobles feared that any reform would threaten their prerogatives. Early in his reign in 1803, the tsar gave permission to the nobles to free their serfs but few chose to do so.

However, Tsar Alexander I became increasingly reactionary. In 1809, he rejected a proposed constitution. Conservative elements regained power and introduced coercive measures. Universities and schools were closely monitored to root out liberals; study abroad was banned; and censorship was applied with ruthless efficiency. At the same time, he continued the aggressive policies of Peter the Great and Catherine the Great in the late seventeenth and eighteenth centuries, expanding the empire by adding Georgia at the expense of the Turks.

But liberal reform had advocates in Russia, including some young nobles who had been educated in Western Europe (before foreign study was prohibited) and a handful of army officers who had lived in France during the allied military occupation after Napoleon's fall. They were bitterly disappointed by Alexander I's reactionary turn. By 1820, two loosely linked conspiratorial "unions," as they were called, had been formed. The educated nobles of the Northern Union hoped that Russia might evolve toward British constitutionalism. The military officers of the Southern Union had a more radical goal: to kill the tsar and establish a republic.

Tsar Alexander's sudden death in December 1825 seemed to offer the conspirators their chance. The tsar had two brothers. Constantine, the eldest, had quietly yielded his succession to the throne in favor of his younger, more

Decembrists gathering in December 1825 at Senate Square in Saint Petersburg.

reactionary brother Nicholas. The Northern Union nonetheless convinced the Saint Petersburg garrison to support the succession of Constantine. Troops occupied a central square in the capital, shouting the name of their favorite, until Nicholas ordered troops loyal to him to fire. A hastily planned insurrection by the Southern Union was also put down. The leaders of the Decembrists, as they came to be known, were executed.

Hard-working and willful, Nicholas I (ruled 1825–1855) believed that his power to govern came directly from God. Nicholas tightened the grip of the police on education in an attempt to exclude Western ideas from Russia. In 1833, the minister of education proclaimed the doctrine of "Official Nationality": autocracy, orthodoxy, and official [Russian] nationality were the intertwined principles of the state. The new tsar did not approve of serfdom because it was inefficient, but he feared that its abolition could lead to peasant insurrection. Nicholas did, however, order the codification of Russian laws in the first decade of his reign and encouraged reforms improving the conditions of state serfs. The arrival of liberal ideas from the West encouraged debate and calls for reform within the Russian intelligentsia, encouraging a group of reform-minded men within the imperial bureaucracy.

France: The Bourbon Restoration and the Revolution of 1830

In a contemporary French lampoon of the return of the Bourbons to the throne, a majestic eagle—the symbol of Napoleon—sweeps out of the Tuileries Palace in Paris as a somewhat plump, unsightly duck waddles in, followed by its ungainly brood. The contrast between the image of Napoleon's bold achievements and the stodgy and pious Restoration was sharp indeed. The Bourbons returned "in the baggage of the allies," as it was said.

Upon the return of the Bourbons to power in May 1814, Louis XVIII promulgated a Charter that, in effect, made France a constitutional monarchy. The Charter recognized equality before the law and accepted the Napoleonic Civil Code. It established an assembly consisting of a Chamber of Deputies and a Chamber of Peers. The king would name members (whose appointment would be for life and hereditary) of the Chamber of Peers, as well as ministers, who would be responsible only to him. The Chamber of Deputies would be elected in a complicated two-stage process, based on an extremely narrow electoral franchise.

The restored Bourbon monarchy maintained the centralized state bureaucracy; recognized all Napoleonic titles, decorations, and even pensions; and promised that property purchased during the Revolution as "national" would remain in the hands of the new owners. Moreover, the Charter offered freedom of the press. The government could levy no taxes without the consent of the Assembly.

The Catholic Church would still be subject to Napoleon's Concordat (see Chapter 13), but was returned to its privileged position, and Catholicism again became the official state religion, although the Napoleonic

Code's guarantee of the free practice of religion to Protestants and Jews was reaffirmed. The religious orders returned to France in force, and the observance of Sunday and Church holidays became obligatory.

Ultra-royalists, or "Ultras," the most fanatical royalist enemies of the Revolution, had after Waterloo launched the "White Terror," so called because of the color of the Bourbon flag, against those who had supported Napoleon. In the election for the Chamber of Deputies in August 1815, the Ultras easily defeated more moderate royalists sponsored by the government. Some of the Ultras referred contemptuously to Louis XVIII as "King Voltaire" because of his Charter, which they viewed as a compromise with the Revolution. They demanded that the "national property" be returned to its original owners.

Louis XVIII dissolved the Ultra-dominated Chamber of Deputies in 1816, and new elections produced a somewhat more moderate Chamber. In 1820, a madman assassinated Charles, the duke of Berry, the king's nephew and the only member of the Bourbon family capable of producing an heir to the throne. France was plunged into mourning. The Ultras cried for revenge, accusing the liberals of being ultimately responsible for the assassination. The king dismissed the moderate government, restored more stringent censorship, and altered the electoral system to reduce the influence of bourgeois voters living in towns.

Soon, however, the church bells stopped their mournful cadence and rang out in joy. It turned out that the duke's wife had been pregnant at the time of his death. Royalist France celebrated the birth of a male heir, "the miracle baby," as he came to be called, the duke of Bordeaux (later known as the count of Chambord). Confident that God was with them, the Ultras, at least for the moment, retained the upper hand.

Upon Louis XVIII's death in 1824, his reactionary brother, the count of Artois, took the throne as Charles X (ruled 1824–1830). Rumors spread that the pious king was going to allow the Catholic Church to collect the tithe, that is, require French subjects to pay 10 percent of their income to the Church. The Chamber of Deputies passed a law making sacrilege—any crime committed in a church—a capital offense. That no one was ever executed for such an offense did not diminish public outrage. The government financed the indemnification of those who had lost land during the Revolution by reducing the interest paid to holders of the national debt, most of whom were middle class.

Many in France retained an allegiance to Napoleon's memory. Former Napoleonic soldiers, particularly those officers pensioned off on half pay, looked back on the imperial era as their halcyon days. In 1820–1821, some joined the Carbonari, a secret society named after its Italian equivalent, and plotted to overthrow the Restoration. Some merchants and manufacturers believed that the Restoration monarchy paid insufficient attention to commerce and industry, listening only to rural nobles.

Honoré Daumier's caricature of the less-than-inspiring members of the French Chamber of Deputies.

Amid an economic crisis that had begun with the failure of the harvest the previous year, elections in 1827 increased liberal strength in the Chamber of Deputies. Two years later, Charles X threw caution to the wind, appointing as his premier the reactionary Prince Jules de Polignac (1780–1847), one of only two members of the Chamber of Deputies who had refused an oath of allegiance to the Charter granted by Louis XVIII.

The opposition to the government of Charles X received a boost from a new generation of romantic writers. In the preface to his controversial play *Hernani* (1830), the production of which caused a near riot outside the theater, Victor Hugo (1802–1885) clearly set liberalism and romanticism against the established order of the restored monarchy:

> Young people, have courage! However difficult they make our present, the future will be beautiful. Romanticism, so often badly defined, is . . . nothing less than *liberalism* in literature. . . . Literary liberty is the daughter of political liberty. That is the principle of this century, and it will prevail.

In 1828, liberals formed an association to refuse to pay taxes in protest of the government's policies and worked to ensure that all eligible to vote registered to do so. Benjamin Constant (1767–1830), a Swiss novelist, political essayist, and member of the French Chamber of Deputies, demanded that the electoral franchise be extended. He espoused a philosophy of liberalism based on a separation of powers and "a government of laws and not men" that would protect property and other freedoms from tyranny (he had both Napoleon and arbitrary monarchical rule in mind).

In response to Charles's bellicose speech opening the 1830 session of the Chamber, 221 deputies signed an address to the throne that attacked the government in no uncertain terms. When the king dissolved the Chamber, the liberal opposition won a majority in the new Chamber. In the meantime, Charles had sent an army to conquer Algeria, whose ruler was a vassal of the sultan of Turkey. But not even news of the capture of Algiers on July 9, 1830, could end vociferous opposition. The king and Polignac then settled on a move that they hoped would bring an end to the crisis. Instead, it brought revolution.

On July 26, 1830, Charles X promulgated the July Ordinances, shattering the principles of the Charter of 1814. He dissolved the newly elected Chamber of Deputies; disfranchised almost three-quarters of those currently eligible to vote; ordered new elections under the newly restricted franchise; and muzzled the press. Demonstrations on July 27 led to skirmishes with troops. Parisians blocked the capital's narrow streets with barricades. Fired upon in the street and pelted by rocks and tiles thrown from rooftops, the king's soldiers became increasingly demoralized.

Early on July 30, liberals put posters around Paris calling for Louis-Philippe to be the new king. From the family of Orléans, the junior branch of the royal Bourbon family, Louis-Philippe, the duke of Orléans, had the reputation for being relatively liberal, having fought in the revolutionary armies. His father (known as Philippe Égalité) had in the National Assembly voted for the execution of Louis XVI. Louis-Philippe had expanded his horizons by drinking bourbon in Kentucky. Liberals offered the throne to Louis-Philippe (ruled 1830–1848), who became "king of the French"—the title, rather than "king of France," was intended to convey that the king's authority came from the people. Charles X abdicated on August 2. Louis-Philippe agreed to a revised version of the Charter, and the tricolor flag of the Revolution replaced the white flag of the Bourbons.

Despite its revolutionary origins, the new liberal monarchy won relatively quick acceptance from the other European powers. Catholicism ceased to be the official religion of the state, although it remained the nominal religion of the vast majority of the population. The new Orleanist regime almost doubled the number of voters, but France was still far from being a republic. Many of those enfranchised by the revised Charter were drawn from the middle class. Lawyers and men of other professions significantly increased middle-class representation in the legislature. The government helped stimulate economic growth and industrial development by improving roads and implementing other policies that benefited manufacturers and merchants. The rallying cry of François Guizot, historian and prime minister (1787–1874, prime minister 1840–1848), to the middle class was "Enrich yourselves!" Known as the "July Monarchy," after the month of its

Eugène Delacroix's *Liberty Leading the People* (1830). Note the female image of liberty and the presence of the top-hatted bourgeois and the heavily armed street urchin, neither of whom actually fought in the Revolution.

founding, the Orleanist reign also came to be known and lampooned as "the bourgeois monarchy." The portly Louis-Philippe himself contributed to this image, surrounding himself with dark-suited businessmen and carrying an umbrella, that symbol of bourgeois preparedness.

The Orleanist monarchy could claim neither the principle of monarchical legitimacy asserted by the Legitimists (supporters of Charles X's Bourbon grandson) or that of popular sovereignty espoused by republicans. Legitimists launched several small, failed insurrections in western France. In Paris, crowds of workers, disappointed by the government's lack of attention to their demands, sacked the archbishop's palace in 1831. Silk workers in Lyon rose up against their employers and the state in 1831 and 1834. Following an uprising by republicans in Paris, the Chamber of Deputies passed a law in 1835 severely restricting the right to form associations, and the next year it passed another law again fettering the press.

Louis-Philippe survived an assassination attempt in 1835; a plot by a secret organization of revolutionaries, the "Society of the Seasons," to overthrow him in 1839; and another attempt to kill him in 1840. Less serious—for the moment—seemed attempts in 1836 and 1840 by Louis Napoleon Bonaparte, Napoleon's nephew, to invade France with a few loyalists and

Louis-Philippe receiving black-suited members of the Chamber of Deputies, who present him with the act by which they confered the crown on him.

rally support. The cult of Napoleon, accentuated by the vogue for the literature of romanticism, served only to highlight what seemed to be the mediocrity of the July Monarchy.

Other Liberal Assaults on the Old Order

The French Revolution of 1830 directly encouraged liberal and national movements in other countries. Liberal successes followed in Belgium and Switzerland, but not in Spain.

Independence for Belgium

The Dutch Netherlands had achieved independence from Spain in the seventeenth century. The Southern Netherlands was Belgium, largely Catholic, and divided between Flemish speakers in the north and French-speaking Walloons in the south (see Map 15.2). Brussels, the largest city in Belgium, lies within Flemish Belgium, but had many French speakers.

What Belgians called "Dutch arithmetic" left Belgium with fewer seats in the Dutch Estates-General than its population should have warranted. Catholics had to contribute to Protestant state schools and paid higher taxes. In the late 1820s, Belgian liberals allied with Catholics against the Protestant Dutch government demanding that ministers be responsible to the Estates-General and taxes be reduced. Dutch King William I (1772–1843) granted only more press freedom.

MAP 15.2 THE BIRTH OF BELGIUM, 1831–1839 The boundaries of the Dutch
Republic and Belgium, including within Belgium the areas that were Protestant and
Catholic, as well as Flemish and Walloon areas. The Grand Duchy of Luxembourg
was created in 1831 and united with the Netherlands in the person of the grand duke,
King William I of the Netherlands.

Following the arrival of news from France of the July Revolution, the
Brussels opera presented a production about an insurrection in Naples in
1648 against Spanish rule. So inspired, the audience left the theater to
demonstrate against a government newspaper and other symbols of Dutch
authority. Workers, suffering unemployment and high prices, put up barricades, and were soon joined by units of bourgeois militia from outside Brussels. A halfhearted military attack floundered when inexperienced Dutch
troops panicked as the ranks of the defenders swelled. After three more
days of fighting, the Dutch troops withdrew to the north. The Dutch bombardment of Antwerp convinced more Flemish to support the rebels.

In early October 1830, a provisional government declared Belgium independence. A Belgian Congress offered the throne to one of Louis-Philippe's sons, but he was forced to decline because Britain would not tolerate such French influence in Belgium. The Congress then offered the throne to a German prince, Leopold of Saxe-Coburg (who was a British subject, the widower of Princess Charlotte of England). Leopold was crowned King Leopold I (ruled 1831–1865) in July 1831. The European powers guaranteed Belgium's independence, and when the Dutch took Antwerp in August 1831, French military intervention returned that city to the new nation. Belgium became a constitutional monarchy with a parliament of two houses, both elected by about one of every thirty males.

Liberal Successes in Switzerland

Another liberal success came in Switzerland, which the Congress of Vienna had reestablished as a federation of semi-autonomous cantons. Because of Switzerland's long tradition of decentralized government, the allies had been willing to tolerate a constitution that allowed relatively extensive political freedoms. However, fearing that some cantons might become havens of liberalism, the Congress powers forced the Swiss cantons in 1823 to restrict freedom of the press and curtail the activities of foreign political exiles.

The 1830 revolution in France inspired the quest for constitutional guarantees of freedom, more efficient government, and limits on the political influence of Protestant and Catholic clergy in Switzerland. In December 1830 the federal Diet initiated a period of "regeneration." The constitutions of ten cantons were liberalized, guaranteeing freedom of expression and giving all adult men the right to vote, a victory unique at that time.

But Metternich was not far away. Austria pressured the German-speaking Swiss cantons to oppose secularization. During the winter of 1844–1845, when the canton of Lucerne announced that the Jesuit order would again be welcome within its borders, liberals rebelled. Seven Catholic cantons withdrew from the Swiss Confederation, forming a separate league (*Sonderbund*). In 1847, the other cantons declared war on the Sonderbund and, in what amounted to little more than a skirmish, defeated the Catholic cantons within a month. In 1848, Switzerland adopted a new liberal constitution, becoming a federal state with universal male suffrage.

NATIONALIST DREAMS

Nationalism also gradually emerged as a force for change in Central and Eastern Europe within the context of multinational empires. Nationalism was closely tied to liberalism in that exponents of both ideologies demanded far-reaching political change that threatened the state systems (see Map 15.3).

MAP 15.3 LIBERAL REVOLTS Liberal or nationalist uprisings in Congress Europe. Arrows indicate intervention by conservative Congress powers to suppress revolts.

Intellectuals demanded that national boundaries correspond to linguistic frontiers.

The Revolt in Poland

The Congress of Vienna had left about 20 percent of pre-Partition Poland as "Congress Poland" with its own army, but within the Russian Empire. The tsar was king of Poland. Tsar Alexander I granted the Poles the Constitutional Charter of 1815, which provided for a parliament of two houses—a Senate of appointed members drawn from noble families and Catholic bishops, and a lower house (the Sejm) elected by people of means. Neither assembly, however, possessed real authority. In 1820, Alexander forbade the Sejm from meeting for five years as punishment for opposing Russian policies, which included imposing disadvantageous customs barriers on Polish grain.

Some Poles hoped that France, in the wake of the July Revolution, would send forces to help them expel the Russians. However, the issue of Polish independence interested only French republicans, not the liberal monarchists who had brought Louis-Philippe to power. However, Polish military cadets rose up in Warsaw in November 1830. Russian troops withdrew in the hope

Polish insurgents rising up against Russia in 1830–1831.

that the municipal government could restore order. In January 1831, a large crowd surrounded the Sejm, which declared that the Russian tsar (Nicholas I) was no longer king of Poland. A provisional national government formed. The Sejm, however, refused to attempt to mobilize peasants in support of the insurrection, fearing that they might demand land reform and attack their lords instead of the Russians. In August 1832 the tsar's troops surrounded Warsaw. Tensions between moderates and radicals erupted into violence, making its defense even more difficult. Warsaw fell to Russian troops in the autumn, and about 10,000 Poles fled Russian oppression. Émigré Polish artists and musicians enriched cultural life in Western Europe capitals. The composer Frédéric Chopin (1810–1849) moved to Paris in 1831, hoping to make his fortune. Although he was not really a political refugee, ardent nationalism infused his music, as he drew upon Polish folk themes and dances.

The privileges that had been accorded "Congress Poland" disappeared. Nicholas I abolished the constitution that Poland had enjoyed within the Russian Empire, as well as the Sejm and the Polish army. Encouraged by Russian measures against the Poles, Prussia and Austria withdrew concessions they had earlier given to the Poles in the territories they had absorbed in the 1790s.

Uprisings in Italy and Spain

Popular stirrings in the Italian states, beginning with movements in Bologna and the Duchy of Modena, started as protests against inefficient and corrupt rule. Rebels in Parma literally locked Duchess Marie-Louise out of the city by shutting the gates until an Austrian army arrived in March 1831 to let her back in. Several cities in central Italy that declared their independence from the Papal States proclaimed the "United Provinces of Italy."

Like the Poles, insurgents against Austrian rule in several towns within the Papal States unrealistically counted on help from French armies, who again would march with a tricolor flag since the fall of the Bourbons. With Austrian troops approaching from the north, an army of volunteers marched toward Rome, defeating the pope's army. But by then Austrian forces had taken Modena, Parma, and Ferrara. A papal army mopped up resistance, sacking several towns, and Austrian troops had to return to save the local populations. The Italian insurrections collapsed without winning popular support.

Giuseppe Mazzini (1805–1872), a lawyer by training and an energetic revolutionary by temperament, emerged as a guiding spirit in the quest for Italian unification under a republic. Mazzini wanted to bring peace to Europe by liberating all peoples. He was one of the first to suggest that the states of Europe might evolve into a loose federation of democratic states based on the principle of nationality. Mazzini believed that a defeat of Austria in northern Italy would serve as a first step toward creating a federation of European democratic republics. Rejecting the Carbonari's conspiratorial tradition, he was convinced that he could expand his nationalist organization, Young Italy, whose membership was limited to individuals under forty years of age. Jailed and then expelled from one country after another, he launched futile insurrections in 1834–1836 and in 1844. However, Mazzini kept the cause of Italian nationalism alive.

Some Italian nationalists began to look to the liberal Kingdom of Piedmont-Sardinia, Italy's strongest state, to effect national unification. But Austria still dominated the Italian peninsula, which included small states that were proud of their independence. The dream of Italian unification remained for the most part limited to a small number of middle-class intellectuals.

In Spain, King Ferdinand VII married Maria Christina, a liberal Neapolitan princess, in 1830. Their daughter Isabella became the heir to the Spanish throne. But nobles and churchmen insisted that a woman could not rule Spain. After the king's death in 1833, civil war broke out between liberals and conservatives (the Carlists), who supported the cause of the late king's brother, Don Carlos. Maria Christina, ruling as regent, promulgated a constitution in 1834 modeled on the French Charter of 1814. In 1843, General Ramón Narváez (1800–1868) seized power, promulgating a conservative constitution and stifling the press. On his deathbed he boasted, "I have no enemies, I have shot them all."

German Nationalism in Central Europe

In the German states, liberals faced an uphill battle. Constitutions implemented during the Napoleonic period had been gradually weakened or withdrawn. Electoral assemblies were selected by limited franchise and had almost no power. However, the wave of liberal and nationalist movements encouraged by the revolutions of 1830 reached Central Europe. Popular disturbances forced the rulers of Hanover and Hesse-Kassel to make political concessions. In Saxony, a liberal constitution was enacted following uprisings in Leipzig and Dresden, and liberals won a constitution in the northern German state of Brunswick.

The Polish revolt against Russia in 1831 fueled the imagination of German university students. The movement culminated in a huge meeting in 1832 of 30,000 people at the ruins of a château near the University of Heidelberg, where speakers saluted popular sovereignty. Police foiled an attempt by students to seize Frankfurt, the meeting place of the Federal Diet of the German Confederation. The Confederation's Diet responded by passing "Ten Articles," which brought the universities under surveillance, coordinated police repression of liberals in the German states, prohibited public meetings, and stipulated that any state threatened by revolution would be assisted by the others.

Yet liberalism in the German states slowly gained momentum among professors, students, and lawyers during what later became known as the

Vormärz ("Before March") period, that is, the period of ferment that preceded the Revolution of March 1848 (see Chapter 16). The French Revolution of 1830 influenced these "Young Germans." The poet Heinrich Heine (1797–1856) had rushed to Paris after the fall of the Bourbon dynasty. His *French Conditions* sharply contrasted the mood of apparent intellectual freedom and optimism of Paris with that of the repression and gloomy resignation liberals faced in the German states, which had no revolutionary tradition. German liberals remained political outsiders, confronting a pervasive respect for ideological conformity.

Yet German liberalism became increasingly linked to the pursuit of German unification, despite the challenge posed by German particularism, the tradition of many small, independent states. The philosopher Georg Wilhelm Friedrich Hegel (1770–1831) made explicit the close connection between the development of German nationalism and the reverence for a strong state as the embodiment of national sovereignty, which characterized German liberal thought. For Hegel, nationalism was the equivalent of a secular religion that had the potential of shaping a new morality. Hegel's state is overwhelming, even frightening, subsuming individual rights to its power.

Liberal economic theory attracted German merchants and manufacturers, who objected to the discouraging complexity of customs tariffs that created a series of costly hurdles along roads and rivers. As German manufacturing developed, particularly in the Rhineland, businessmen supported a proposed German Customs Union (Zollverein), which, following its creation in 1834, removed some tariff barriers in seventeen states. To liberal nationalists, the Zollverein seemed to offer a basis for the eventual political unification of Germany. It breathed life into the movement for political reform. But those who hoped that Prussia and the other German states would move toward constitutionalism were disappointed. Prussian King Frederick William IV (ruled 1840–1861) refused to establish a Diet representing all of Prussia. When he finally did convoke a United Diet in 1847, it was not popularly elected and was to serve the king only in an advisory capacity.

CRISIS AND COMPROMISE IN GREAT BRITAIN

In Britain, demands for political reform, specifically the expansion of the electoral franchise to include more middle-class voters, would be the true test of the ability of the British elite to compromise in the interest of social and political harmony. Three hundred thousand soldiers demobilized after Waterloo found little work, and many of them depended on poor relief. Amid popular protest, working people joined clubs organized by radicals demanding universal suffrage. Poor harvests in 1818 and 1819 brought high prices and grain riots and machine breaking. The popular radicalism of the 1790s had led to the government's dissolution of radical "corresponding societies" and the suspension of *habeas corpus*, which made it possible to arrest people

The Peterloo Massacre in Manchester, 1819.

without charging them with anything. The Combination Acts (1799–1800) made strikes illegal while reinforcing existing laws against trade unions. Ordinary people now demanded political reform. On August 16, 1819, a crowd of some 60,000 men and women gathered near Manchester to demonstrate for the right to form political organizations and to assemble freely. Deputized local constables moved in to arrest the main speaker. Then soldiers gunned down protestors, many dressed in their Sunday best, killing eleven and wounding hundreds of others. The ugly incident entered history as "Peterloo," a shameful victory not over Napoleon at Waterloo but over Britain's defenseless laboring poor. Parliament passed Six Acts that, reviving the repressive legislation of the era of the French Revolution, included suspending *habeas corpus* and imposing further restrictions on the press. That year the government broke up the "Cato Street Conspiracy," a plot by radicals to assassinate members of the Cabinet as they attended a dinner in London.

The late 1820s were also bleak years for the English poor. Crimes increased in Britain, particularly against property, reflecting hard times. Artisans and skilled workers demanded higher wages and organized more unions within crafts—for example, those representing skilled engineering workers. Parliament abolished the Combination Acts in 1824, making strikes legal. Workers formed more "friendly societies," which, in exchange for modest fees, offered minimal assistance when a member became ill, or paid for burial upon death to avoid the indignity of a pauper's grave. The friendly societies and other clubs of workingmen generated interest in reform, against a backdrop of hardship, industrial disputes, demonstrations, and the wave of food riots and machine breaking that spread in 1829–1830 through southern England.

Religious and Electoral Reform

However, there would be no revolution in nineteenth-century Britain. The landed elite, which dominated Parliament, supported by manufacturing interests, enacted reforms that defused social and political tensions by bowing to middle-class demands. Even if many Tories believed that electoral reform would be a dangerous precedent, the fear of popular protest and perhaps even revolution led them to compromise. Reforms passed by Parliament contributed to the emergence of a liberal consensus in Victorian Britain that lasted throughout the century. Religion, too, may have played a part. The government allocated funds for the construction of more Anglican churches in working-class areas. At the same time, Methodism, along with other churches within the "New Dissent," won many converts, arguably reducing social tension. Bible societies and other evangelical associations interested in the plight of the poor increased dramatically in number.

In 1828, despite vociferous opposition from the Established Church, Parliament repealed the Test and Corporation Acts, which had forced anyone holding public office to take communion in the Anglican Church. Catholic emancipation had emerged as a major political issue at least partly because it was linked to the problem of Catholic Ireland. There a reform movement had begun and organized protests against English Protestant domination. Insurgency seemed endemic. Catholics of means had not been able to vote until 1793 in Ireland (and the franchise was subsequently made even more restrictive). The Irish Parliament had been eliminated in 1800, although Ireland was represented in British Parliament. Finally, in 1829, Parliament passed the Catholic Emancipation Act, which removed the legal restrictions that had kept Catholics from holding office or serving in Parliament.

In Britain, political liberalism continued to be closely linked to the movement led by Whigs, the party most attached to constitutional monarchy and the rights of Parliament, for electoral reform. Only one of fifteen men in Britain had the right to vote. Businessmen resented being underrepresented in the House of Commons. The electoral system remained a patchwork that reflected the interests of local elites and particular communities that had gradually developed in England since the fourteenth century. The industrial north sent few men to Parliament because electoral districts had not changed since before the Industrial Revolution. No one represented the industrial centers of Manchester and Birmingham in Parliament. Wealthy merchants in those cities were no longer content with indirect, "virtual representation" through members of Parliament who claimed to have their interests in mind. In contrast, some sparsely populated rural districts still were represented in Parliament. Dunwich, the most notorious of these "rotten boroughs," had been covered over by the sea since the twelfth century. "Pocket boroughs" were electoral districts "in the pocket" of a wealthy landowner routinely returned to Parliament (see Chapter 11).

With news of France's Revolution of 1830, the British upper classes rallied together, fearful, as they used to say, that when France sneezed, the rest of Europe might catch a cold. Amid shows of armed force by the government, organized protest was limited to an enthusiastic rally in the Scottish city of Glasgow to celebrate the news of the French and Belgian revolutions. In England, crowds gathered to hear the popular radical William Cobbett (1763–1835), whose weekly newspaper, the *Political Register*, aimed at "journeymen and labourers" spoke on behalf of the extension of the electoral franchise to all men.

The Reform Bill of 1832

The general election following George IV's death in 1830 reduced the conservative majority in Parliament. A broadly based campaign for electoral reform swept the country; some of the 5,000 petitions that were brought to Parliament attacked in patriotic language the selfishness of the landed elite. The new prime minister, Earl Charles Grey (1764–1845), a Whig, knew that any reform bill that passed the House of Commons would never get through the House of Lords as then constituted. In 1831, Lords rejected a bill sponsored by the government that would have eliminated many "rotten" and "pocket" boroughs. Public meetings protested this defeat, particularly in the cities of the industrial north and Scotland, which had no representation in Commons. When the House of Lords rejected a second reform bill in October 1831, demonstrators massed in London and a riot in Bristol ended in twelve deaths.

By this time, more Tories had come around to Grey's view that only the passage of some sort of electoral reform bill could save Britain from a revolution. They feared an alliance between frustrated businessmen and radicals, supported by workers, as had occurred in France in 1830. The Whigs proposed a third bill, which Commons passed in March 1832, and sent it on to Lords. The duke of Wellington tried and failed to form a ministry. Grey, who again became prime minister, convinced the new king, William IV (ruled 1830–1837), to threaten to create enough new peers to get the reform bill through the House of Lords, whose peers did not want to see their ranks contaminated by "instant lords." Wellington agreed not to oppose its passage, and the bill passed.

The Reform Act of 1832 was a turning point in the history of modern Britain. The landed magnates agreed to lower the minimum franchise requirement, almost doubling the size of the electorate. Britain was far from a democracy—only about one of every five adult male citizens was now eligible to vote—but the British Parliament now more accurately reflected

Britain's emerging industrial society. In the early 1840s, 15 percent of the members of the House of Commons were businessmen, and 35 percent had some other connection to commerce and industry, such as serving on the board of directors of enterprises. A larger percentage of men could now vote in Britain than in France, Belgium, the Netherlands, or Spain.

The new electorate, as the Tories had feared, increased Whig strength. Commons passed two reforms in 1833 influenced by the Reform Act. In part a response to growing opposition to slavery by religious Dissenters, Evangelical Protestants, and political radicals, anti-slavery societies launched a nationwide campaign against slavery in the British Dominions. Britain had withdrawn from the slave trade in 1808, and six years later 750,000 people had signed petitions in Britain calling for the abolition of slavery. However, in 1830 there were still 650,000 slaves in the British West Indies, and slaves in British colonies in Africa and Asia (as well as in the United States). Ladies' associations distributed campaign literature and organized a boycott of sugar produced by slaves in the West Indies. The campaign was successful. In 1833, Parliament abolished slavery in the British Empire.

The second reform measure, also passed in 1833 (see Chapter 14), prohibited work by children under nine years of age, limited the workday of children from nine through twelve years to eight hours a day (and a maximum of forty-eight hours per week), and that for "young persons" ages thirteen to eighteen to twelve hours a day (to a maximum of sixty-nine hours per week).

The Poor Law followed in 1834. Able-bodied individuals would no longer receive assistance from parishes, but would be incarcerated in "well-regulated" workhouses. And the Municipal Corporations Act of 1835 eliminated the old, often corrupt borough governments, creating elected municipal corporations responsible for administration. This again reflected the growing political influence of the English middle classes, particularly in industrial areas. These reforms allowed many more Whigs, including Dissenters, to assume positions of responsibility in local government, another blow to the domination of public life by the old aristocratic oligarchy and the Established Church.

Chartism and the Repeal of the Corn Laws

The Chartist movement reflected the strength of reformism in Britain. Whereas some French and German workers dreamed of revolution, their English counterparts took out their quill pens. In 1836, William Lovett (1800–1877), a cabinetmaker, founded the London Workingmen's Association for Benefiting Politically, Socially, and Morally the Useful Classes. Two years later, Lovett and Francis Place, a London tailor, prepared the "Great Charter." It called for the democratization of political life, including universal male suffrage, annual elections, equal electoral districts, the secret ballot, and salaries for members of Parliament, so that ordinary people could serve if elected. Chartists objected to the monopoly of wealth and political influence in Britain by a small percentage of the population, wealthy landowners and the captains of industry. The Chartist movement remained overwhelmingly peaceful, its members committed to acting as a "moral force" in British life. Chartism was in some ways a movement that looked back into a past its members imagined as being more moral than the period in which they lived. Chartist leaders attempted to attract women to the movement by recognizing the contributions of women workers to the family economy—despite the resentment of many male craftsmen in working-class families that the gender roles of many women seemed to be changing and that some men now found themselves working alongside them. Some Chartists sought to convince hard-drinking and often wife-beating male workers to be more respectable. (However, Chartist leaders rejected feminist pleas that their movement include demands for the rights of women.) A small "Physical Force" group emerged within the Chartist movement in northern England, threatening strikes and even insurrection if Parliament did not yield, but this group remained small and relatively unimportant.

In 1839, Parliament summarily rejected a Chartist petition with almost 1.3 million signatures. Undaunted, the Chartists tried again in 1842 when the National Chartist Association carried a giant scroll with 3.3 million signatures to Westminster. Once again, Parliament turned the Great Charter away. Thereafter, Chartism declined as a movement, despite a brief revival in 1848.

Yet Parliament enacted another significant reform. Passed by a conservative-dominated Parliament in 1815 and 1828, the Corn Laws had

Photograph of the final Chartist demonstration at Kensington Common, April 10, 1848.

imposed a sliding tariff on imported wheat (then known as "corn"). When the price of wheat produced in Britain fell below a certain level, import duties would keep out cheaper foreign grain. Foreign grain could be imported virtually free of import taxes only when the price of wheat stood at or above a certain level. The laws protected landowners, but were detrimental to the interests of businessmen who imported or sold imported grain and, above all, to ordinary people, who were forced to pay higher prices for bread. Failed harvests in 1839–1841 brought great deprivation, as parishes cut back on allocations to the poor. The "Great Hunger" in Ireland, caused by the potato famine that began in 1845, brought mass starvation (see Chapter 14).

The issue of the repeal of the Corn Laws pitted proponents of laissez-faire economic policies against wealthy property owners, Whigs against Tories. British manufacturers and spokesmen for the poor denounced the entrenched "bread-taxing" and "blood-sucking" oligarchy. In 1839, the Anti–Corn Law League started up, joining businessmen, Whig politicians, and political radicals, who believed that the repeal of the Corn Laws would be a major step toward universal male suffrage. John Bright (1811–1889) argued that the repeal of the Corn Laws would be a major step toward political democracy. The son of a Quaker cotton mill owner, Bright, although not an MP, incarnated British liberalism, as he thundered against aristocratic privilege and its close ties to the Established Church. He warned, "Until now, this country has been ruled by the class of great proprietors of the soil. Everyone must have foreseen that, as trade and manufactures extended, the balance of power would, at some time or other, be thrown into another scale. Well, that time has come."

SEARCHING FOR POTATOES IN A STUBBLE FIELD.

A destitute, hungry Irish family searching for potatoes in a stubble field during the potato famine.

As with the 1832 Reform Act, it took a change of heart by a Conservative government to get a repeal bill passed. Prime Minister Robert Peel, whose smile it was said resembled the gleam of silver plate on a coffin, was himself the conservative son of a cotton manufacturer. Believing in free trade, he had pushed through reductions in and even the elimination of some tariffs, including those on imported raw cotton. The Irish potato famine helped push him to undertake the dismantling of the Corn Laws. Repeal would be an act of political courage, as he was bound to fall from power. Peel now believed only such a move could forestall a popular insurrection. In 1846, Parliament repealed the Corn Laws, reducing duties on wheat and other imported agricultural products. Having bitterly divided the Conservative Party, Peel was forced to resign the same day, a victim, his supporters insisted, of doing the right thing.

CONCLUSION

Between 1820 and 1850, liberals and nationalists challenged the conservative post-Napoleonic settlement. Revolutions brought a liberal monarchy to France and independence to Belgium. In Great Britain, political and economic liberalism triumphed within the context of the nation's reformist tradition. The Reform Act of 1832 incorporated many more middle-class men into the political arena. British workers remained committed to peaceful protest. Liberals also gained ground in the German and northern Italian states, where middle-class proponents of German and Italian national unification became more vocal.

At the same time, cultural and nationalist movements began to develop among Czechs, Serbs, and other peoples within the Habsburg domains. However, the Prussian and Austrian monarchies, to say nothing of the Russian tsar, whose troops had crushed the Polish insurrection in 1831, stood as formidable obstacles both to reform and national movements. Nonetheless, the Concert of Europe no longer existed. Political momentum was with those seeking to break down the bastions of traditional Europe, as the dramatic Revolutions of 1848 would clearly demonstrate.

CHAPTER 16

THE REVOLUTIONS
OF 1848

~~~

The year 1848 was the year of barricades in Europe, the "springtime of the peoples." Few took note when an uprising occurred in January 1848 in Palermo, Sicily, against King Ferdinand II of Naples. But when a revolution drove Louis-Philippe from the throne of France in February, nationalists exiled in London, Brussels, Paris, and Zurich excitedly returned to their native lands, convinced that their time had come. Everything seemed possible.

The establishment of a republic in France became the catalyst for revolutionary movements in Central Europe. In the face of clumsy attempts by governments to repress opposition by force, street insurgency and barricades forced the rulers of Prussia, Austria, and several other German and Italian states to accept more liberal constitutions when confronted by determined crowds. The existence of the Habsburg monarchy was threatened by insurrections against its rule. People in Lombardy and Venetia in northern Italy, and Czechs, Poles, and South Slavs put forth demands for autonomy. In Austria, liberals demanded political reforms, while some German speakers sought inclusion in a unified Germany. Magyar nobles forcefully asserted demands for Hungarian autonomy. Turkish and Russian troops put down an uprising by Romanian nationalists in Bucharest. Of the European powers, only Britain (the most economically and politically advanced) and Russia (the most economically backward) did not experience revolutions. Yet in Britain, the Chartist petition campaign for the extension of political rights revived in 1848 with news from the continent. Daniel O'Connell (1775–1847), a barrister, had stimulated national awareness among Irish peasants. The radical Irish Confederation grouped militants determined to work for independence. The government feared an Irish uprising and searched ships arriving from the United States for weapons. In several countries, monarchs capitulated to liberal demands. In Sweden, the king appointed a new, more popular government. Danish nationalists pressured their king to grant a liberal constitution. The Netherlands received a new constitution in October

1848, and popular pressure forced the expansion of the Belgian electoral franchise.

A common process was present in the revolutions in France, the German states, and in the Habsburg lands: initial mobilizations of liberals, republicans, and nationalists coalesced into movements against existing regimes (see Map 16.1). In each revolution, the hard times of the 1840s, marked by harvest and business failures, had increased popular dissatisfaction with conservative or moderate regimes. Essentially middle-class movements, they drew on the support of artisans and craftsmen, members of trade organizations who believed that political change would lead to social reforms that would benefit their trades. Following initial victory, ranging from the overthrow of the Orleanist monarchy in France to political concessions in Austria and Prussia, however, the ensuing struggle to implement change led to a split between moderates and radicals. Then followed the gradual but convincing victory of counter-revolution, in which the armies of the reactionary Tsar Nicholas I of Russia would play an important role.

REVOLUTIONARY MOBILIZATION

The late 1840s brought food shortages in Europe, including the tragic Irish potato famine. Unemployment plagued manufacturing towns. Yet, however widespread, economic discontent was not enough in itself to bring about the wave of revolutions that occurred in 1848 (if this was the case, the Irish would have risen up). Rather, hard times provided an impetus to political opponents of existing regimes, which were preoccupied with food riots and other popular protest.

Critics and political opponents included liberal reformers asking for moderate political changes, such as a lessening of restrictions on the press, or, in states with elected assemblies, an expansion in the electoral franchise so that more men could vote. German nationalists stood ready to push for the unification of the German states. Republicans and socialists demanded more radical reforms, including universal male suffrage and social reforms to ameliorate the condition of the laboring poor. Radical reformers also included nationalists within the Austrian Habsburg lands, principally Hungarians, who wanted their own independent state. When a spark ignited the fires of protest, moderates and radicals joined forces in revolution. The sudden overthrow of the July Monarchy in France provided that spark.

The February Revolution in France

In France, the liberal Orleanist monarchy, which had been established by the Revolution of 1830, seemed to have more enemies than friends. It was caught between nobles insisting that the monarchy lacked dynastic legiti-

MAP 16.1 MAJOR REVOLUTIONS, 1848–1849   The map shows areas of rebellion and centers of revolution during the turbulent period of 1848–1849.

macy and republicans demanding a regime based on popular sovereignty. Republicans had begun to campaign for electoral reform in 1840–1841, as the country reeled from a disastrous harvest. France had also suffered international humiliation in 1840 after King Louis-Philippe seemed to back the Ottoman governor of Egypt, Mehmet Ali, who rebelled, with the support of Russia, against the Turkish sultan with the hope of establishing an Egyptian empire. When the other European powers, particularly Britain, opposed Mehmet Ali, fearing that his autonomy and recent conquests threatened the stability of the Ottoman Empire, France had to back down to avoid war.

Republicans mounted another campaign for electoral reform in the midst of another cyclical economic crisis that began with the disastrous harvest of 1846. Workers demanded the right to vote and state assistance for their trades. The electoral reform campaign was to culminate in a giant reform banquet on February 22, 1848, in Paris. François Guizot, the premier, banned the event. In protest, demonstrators marched through the streets of central Paris. The next day, large crowds assembled in the pouring rain. The Paris National Guard, drawn from the middle class, refused to disperse the demonstrators by force. Louis-Philippe dismissed Guizot. But that evening, amid continuing boisterous protests, troops panicked and fired on a crowd, killing forty people. The crowds carried the bodies through the streets, and workers (primarily craftsmen) began to construct barricades. King Louis-Philippe abdicated, hoping that the Chamber of Deputies would crown his

The February Revolution of 1848 in Paris.

young grandson, the count of Paris. It was too late. The victorious crowd proclaimed the Second French Republic at the town hall.

The Chamber of Deputies selected a provisional government, headed by nine republicans. A crowd at the town hall pressed for the addition of two well-known socialists supported by the radicals: the socialist Louis Blanc and a worker. The provisional government immediately proclaimed universal male suffrage and abolished slavery in the French colonies.

The revolution spread to the provinces. Enthusiastic crowds planted "liberty trees," intended to commemorate a new era, a ritual borrowed from the French Revolution. Legitimists wanted a Bourbon Restoration. Nor could the Orleanists be counted out, for Louis-Philippe had several able sons in exile. Both shades of monarchists could count on the support of local notables (nobles or wealthy bourgeois). Furthermore, Napoleon Bonaparte's nephew, Louis Napoleon Bonaparte (1808–1873), had a coterie of supporters who honored his uncle's memory. At a time when the prominent poet Alphonse de Lamartine (1790–1869) complained that "France is bored," the legend of Napoleon remained strong among many former soldiers, peasants, and students.

Republicans were themselves divided between staunch republicans, who had opposed the Orleanist regime all along, and moderates, who accepted the republic only after its proclamation. Socialists hoped that the republic would be but the first step toward a "democratic and social republic." Louis Blanc and other socialists were committed to the "right to work," as they put it, believing that the government should assume responsibility for providing employment in times of economic crisis, as well as encouraging or even subsidizing workers' associations.

Because of France's revolutionary tradition, the fledgling republic had to reassure the other powers of Europe that the French would not try to export their revolution, as had occurred in the 1790s. The other powers feared that the new regime might publicly support Polish independence or Italian or German nationalism, spurred on by the presence in Paris of political exiles advocating these causes. Some French nationalists called for the annexation of Savoy and Nice (parts of the Kingdom of Piedmont-Sardinia), which France had claimed off and on for centuries. Volunteers formed a ragtag army with this acquisition of territory in mind. But Lamartine, the new republic's minister of foreign affairs, assured the European powers that the French had only peaceful intentions.

With elections for a constituent assembly approaching, political interest was widespread among people previously excluded from political life. In Paris, more than 200 political clubs, mostly republican and republican-socialist, began to meet, and almost that many newspapers began publication, joined by others in the provinces. When George Sand (the pen name of Amandine Dudevant; 1804–1876), a writer and activist for women's rights, was locked out of her apartment, she discovered that all three of the neighborhood locksmiths were at club meetings. Representatives from the clubs went into the provinces with the goal of wooing the overwhelmingly rural electorate away from the influence of local notables who favored a monarchy.

The economic crisis immediately widened the gap between moderate republicans and socialists. Unable to secure credit, many businesses closed. Government bonds plunged in value, and the Paris Stock Exchange temporarily shut down. Artisans were left without clients, laborers without work. More than half of the workforce in the capital was unemployed. Younger and more marginal workers were enrolled in an auxiliary paramilitary police force, the Mobile Guard, organized by the provisional government to help maintain order. Short of funds, the provisional government raised direct taxes on an emergency basis by 45 percent, the 45 centimes tax.

With more provincial workers arriving in Paris every day looking for assistance, the provisional government opened "National Workshops," paying unemployed workers to repair roads and level hills. Many well-off Parisians began to grumble about the new government having to support unemployed workers. The government finally agreed to restrict the workday to a maximum of ten hours in Paris and twelve hours in the provinces. At the request of the socialists, the government also established the "Luxembourg Commission" to study working conditions.

By undermining existing political structures, the 1848 revolution called into question all social institutions, including the existing gender hierarchy. In Paris, women formed a number of clubs. *The Women's Voice* and several other newspapers begun by women called for reforms, including equality of women before the law, the right to divorce, and better working conditions. Petitioners demanded that the republic extend the electoral franchise to

A Paris women's club in 1848.

women. This groundswell of demands for change frightened the upper classes.

April elections brought a conservative majority, including many monarchists, to the Constituent Assembly, which would draw up a new constitution. Radical republicans and socialists won only about 100 of 900 seats. The republicans were hurt in the countryside by the provisional government's tax hike. Many rural people resented the demands of urban workers, including low bread prices and the maintenance of National Workshops. The euphoria of February gave way to anxiety.

Revolution in the German States

Unlike the Revolution of 1789, that of 1848 spread rapidly from France into Central Europe. While liberals bided their time, young German radicals, few in number, became more restive. During the "hungry forties," in which perhaps 50,000 people died of disease in Prussian Silesia alone, riots against grain merchants and tax collectors occurred in many German states. Craftsmen formed trade associations and mutual aid societies. Although these organizations offered only minimal assistance during times of unemployment and strikes, they provided an apprenticeship in political ideology.

The differences in tactics between German liberals and radicals were clear and significant. Both groups, sometimes sharing newspaper offices, political clubs, and even associations of gymnasts and rifle enthusiasts, demanded an end to all remaining feudal obligations owed by peasants to nobles, the end of political repression, the granting of a constitution, freedom of assembly and the press, and expansion of the electoral franchise. Liberals, however, rejected universal male suffrage. Radicals, some of whom were socialists, believed that only revolution could move the German states along the path to a new, more liberal political order, and perhaps to unification.

The news in late February 1848 of revolution in France convinced rulers of the German states to make concessions to liberals. In Bavaria, word of the February Revolution arrived at a time when students had begun protesting the rule of Ludwig I (ruled 1825–1848). As Bavarian demonstrators built barricades and demanded a republic, Ludwig granted freedom of the press and other liberties. When this failed to placate his opponents, the king abdicated in favor of his son. The sovereigns of several smaller states, including Hanover, Württemberg, Saxony, and Baden, also named prominent liberals to ministerial positions. These were the "March governments" of 1848, formed not out of conviction but rather from fear of revolutionary contagion.

Everyone waited to see what would happen in Prussia and Austria, the two largest and most powerful German states. In the Prussian capital of Berlin, demonstrators agitated for liberal political reforms and in favor of German nationalism. Prussian King Frederick William IV responded by convoking the United Diet (Parliament). On March 18, 1848, he replaced his conservative

Germans putting up barricades in the streets of Altenburg during the Revolution of 1848.

cabinet with a more liberal one. The king promised to end press censorship and grant a constitution. He further stated that the Prussian monarchy would take the lead in pushing for a joint constitution for the German states.

But as troops moved in to disperse the throngs, someone on one side or the other fired shots. Students and workers put up barricades. The next day the army attacked the insurgents, killing 250 people. As in Paris, the shooting of civilians by troops drove the situation out of control. Women were among the casualties. The king sent the troops out of the capital and appealed for calm. Intimidated by the disturbances, he met with representatives of the crowd, authorized the formation of a civic guard, and ordered the release of imprisoned liberals. He paid homage to those killed in the "March Days" and announced that "Prussia is henceforth merged with Germany."

Most of the Berlin insurgents had been artisans, as in the February Revolution in Paris. Although some of them were vaguely nationalist and wanted Prussia to lead the way toward the unification of Germany, most had economic goals. During the "hungry forties," mechanized production had undercut tailors, whose handmade clothes could not compete with mass-produced garments. Cabinetmakers and shoemakers had lost the security afforded by guilds. Now these artisans demanded state protection. Workers in other German states, too, mounted protests, principally in the more industrialized

Rhineland. Transport workers who had been put out of work attacked railroads and steamships on the Rhine River, forcing temporary government concessions.

As in Paris, clubs and workers' associations began meeting in several German cities in March. A Club of Democratic Women and a congress of workers both demanded equal rights for women. The German political theorist and revolutionary Karl Marx hurried back to the Rhineland from Belgium, convinced that the revolution he awaited was at hand.

Disturbances broke out in the German countryside. In the Black Forest, peasants attacked noble manors. In early March, the rural poor defied laws forbidding them to use royal and noble forests, and now hunted game and pastured their flocks as they pleased. Some peasants seized and destroyed old documents that had recorded feudal obligations and forced lords to sign formal renunciations of old privileges. Outbreaks of violence occurred even in Brandenburg, where the iron will of the Prussian nobles, the Junkers, had rarely been tested. Several wary German princes formally relinquished long-held rights. Armies, militias, and police hesitated to enforce the laws or obligations that affected the peasantry for fear of sparking a bloody uprising like the one that took place in Polish Galicia in 1846.

Revolution in Central Europe

There were relatively few liberals to trouble the sleep of the feeble-minded Habsburg ruler, Ferdinand I (ruled 1835–1848), who could barely sign his name to the reactionary decrees put before him. Liberals, most of whom were Austrians seeking political change or Czechs desiring more rights for their people, opposed Habsburg autocracy, not Habsburg rule itself. They wanted constitutional reform, the complete emancipation of the peasantry, greater efficiency in the administration of Habsburg lands, and, like Western liberals, freedom of the press and expansion of the electoral franchise.

Although Hungary, over which Ferdinand ruled as king, had an even smaller middle class than Austria, it did have several prominent Hungarian nobles who espoused liberalism and supported constitutional reform. Their chief goal, however, was the creation of an independent Hungary. Lajos Kossuth (1802–1894), a lawyer from a lesser noble family, emerged as the leader of Hungarian liberals who had been influenced by British and American constitutional liberalism. Whereas some Magyar leaders believed that Hungary could survive as a nation only within the Austrian monarchy, Kossuth saw Hungary's junior partnership with Austria as an obstacle to liberal reform and to Magyar nationalism. Most nobles were unwilling, however, to support reforms that would inevitably undercut their special privileges. Elsewhere in the Austrian monarchy, small nationalist groups, such as the Polish Democratic Society, Young Italy, and the Italian Carbonari, also demanded national independence from Habsburg rule.

News from Paris encouraged liberals and radicals in the imperial Habsburg capital of Vienna. On March 13, 1848, crowds composed largely of students and artisans demanded reform. Troops opened fire, killing several demonstrators, by now a familiar scenario. Klemens von Metternich, the seventy-five-year-old Austrian premier, was not optimistic: "I am not a prophet and I do not know what will happen, but I am an old physician and can distinguish between temporary and fatal diseases. We now face one of the latter." The Imperial Council advised Ferdinand to sacrifice Metternich. The guiding light and symbol of the post-revolutionary restoration left Vienna in a rented carriage, beginning his journey to the safety of London amid the spectacle of joyous crowds parading through the streets in triumph. The crown capitulated to protesters' demands and authorized the formation of a National Guard, with a separate battalion (the Academic Legion) for Vienna's students. Workshops, similar to those in Paris, provided many workers with temporary employment.

The emperor then announced several important political concessions, including freedom of the press and the expansion in the narrow electorate for the Diet. Ferdinand hurriedly granted constitutions to Austria, Moravia, and Galicia, adding lower houses to the Diets that were to be elected indirectly by men wealthy enough to pay taxes. When demonstrators protested these requirements, the crown reversed itself, creating a single house of parliament to be elected by universal male suffrage in each province. In the elected Austrian parliament, the monarchy's ethnic minorities combined would outnumber German speakers.

Vienna explodes in the Revolution of 1848.

Ferdinand then attempted to renege on his promises and ordered the universities closed and abolished the Academic Legion within the National Guard. But again barricades went up in Vienna, and again Ferdinand was forced to relent.

The Habsburg realm had remained under the grip of feudalism, particularly in Galicia and Transylvania. Now fearing rural rebellions on which liberals and nationalists might capitalize, the emperor in September decreed the abolition—effective the following year—of all remaining feudal and seigneurial obligations, including the onerous *robot,* the yearly obligation of labor service—sometimes a hundred days working in the fields or on roads—that peasants owed lords. The crown would compensate the lords for their losses. Many landowners had already converted the labor obligation into peasant cash payments. The Austrian parliament also took credit for these dramatic changes.

Meanwhile, the Hungarian nobles proceeded as if the Habsburg monarchy no longer existed. Kossuth demanded virtually complete Hungarian autonomy. He and his allies proclaimed the "March Laws," under which the delegates to the Hungarian Diet were to be elected by male property holders. The cabinet would be responsible to Hungary's Diet. The emperor of Austria would remain the king of Hungary, but Hungary would maintain a separate army and conduct its own foreign policy. The Habsburg court, reeling from reverses on all sides, had little choice but to approve the changes. The new Hungarian government immediately proclaimed freedom of the press, established a civilian guard, and affirmed the abolition of the *robot* for peasant landowners, while maintaining it for landless peasants.

Although asserting its own autonomy from the Habsburg Empire and abolishing serfdom, the Hungarian Diet virtually ignored the autonomy of the other nationalities within the Hungarian domains, including Croats, Slovaks, Serbs, and Romanians, some of whose intellectuals viewed the revolutions of 1848 as the victory of the idea of the nation. Croats, the largest of the non-Magyar nationalities in Hungary, were particularly resentful at not having been consulted. The narrow electoral franchise, based on property owned and taxes paid, excluded most people of the poorer nationalities from election to the Diet. So did the requirement that each representative speak Hungarian, one of Europe's most difficult languages (although Latin had remained the official language of Hungary until 1844).

The Magyars' problem of national minorities became the Habsburg dynasty's hope for holding its empire together. The imperial government began to mobilize the Croats against the Hungarians, whom the Serbs and Romanians also resented. In March, the emperor appointed Joseph Jelačić (1801–1859) as the new governor-general for Croatia. Jelačić refused to cooperate with the Hungarians. In retaliation, the Hungarians refused to send troops to help the imperial army battle Italian insurgents. Ferdinand then withdrew the concessions he had made in March to Hungarian autonomy.

Another challenge to the monarchy, again revealing the complexity of Central Europe, came in Bohemia, populated by both Czechs and Germans. In March, Czech nationalists revolted in Prague, demanding that Bohemia, like Hungary, become an autonomous state only loosely tied to the old monarchy. They wanted the Czech language to be made equal to German, which remained the language of the army, the bureaucracy, and commerce. They also wanted to expand the borders of Bohemia eastward into Moravia, where many Czechs lived. At the same time, many Bohemian Germans looked eagerly toward possible unification with the German states to the north. In the meantime, Emperor Ferdinand left Vienna for Innsbruck in May 1848, fearing that revolutionary students and workers might make him a prisoner in his own palace.

Revolution in the Italian States

In the Italian states, March brought insurrections against Austrian rule in Lombardy and Venetia, and against conservative regimes in the other states, notably the Papal States. In Tuscany, the grand duke bowed to reformers by promulgating a constitution. King Charles Albert (ruled 1831–1849) of Piedmont-Sardinia met some liberal demands by creating a bicameral parliament to be selected by a small minority of adult males, easing press censorship, and establishing a civilian guard in Italy's strongest state. The revolutions in the Italian states, too, were animated by different goals: bourgeois liberals called for political reform and Italian unification, radicals wanted a republic, and workers demanded some tangible benefits for themselves.

On March 18, 1848, 10,000 people marched to the palace of the Austrian governor-general in Milan carrying a petition calling for liberal reforms, echoing those in Paris, Berlin, and Vienna. Barricades went up, and five days (known as the "Five Glorious Days") of bitter street fighting followed. The poorly armed people of the city, whose arsenal included medieval pikes taken from the opera house, drove away the Austrian army of Count Joseph Radetzky (1766–1858). Radetzky became a major figure in the counter-revolution at age eighty-one (and was energetic enough to have fathered a child only two years before). Now in Milan, as insurgents established a provisional republican government, he found his army weakened by the desertion of many Italian soldiers.

Suddenly, much of Italy, particularly the Austrian-controlled north, seemed on the verge of a liberal and national revolution. Other towns in Lombardy rose up against Austrian rule. Venetians forced Habsburg troops to leave their city and declared a republic. In Naples, liberals forced a constitution on King Ferdinand II (ruled 1830–1859).

Many Italian nationalists now looked to King Charles Albert of Piedmont-Sardinia for leadership in the political unification of Italy. Yet, despite pleas for armed assistance from Lombardy and Venetia, Charles

Albert hesitated to send his army against the Habsburg forces. He felt that if the Italian peninsula were to be unified, it should be on his terms, not as a result of rioting commoners. The Piedmontese king feared the specter of popular insurgency in northern Italy. He also worried that if Piedmont launched a war against Austria, the new French republic might take advantage of the situation to invade Savoy and Nice.

The outpouring of anti-Austrian sentiment in Piedmont and the opinions of his advisers convinced Charles Albert to change his mind. The Piedmontese army, swollen by volunteers from Tuscany, Naples, and Parma, and even the Papal States, marched unopposed through Lom-

Giuseppe Mazzini dreaming of a unified Italy.

bardy, defeating the Austrian army. But instead of crossing the Po River and cutting off Radetzky from supplies in Venetia, Charles Albert decided to consolidate his gains in Lombardy, with an eye toward annexing that territory to Piedmont.

In Lombardy itself, no one seemed able to agree on what should happen next. Wealthy landowners wanted little more than a loose union of Lombardy with Piedmont. Middle-class nationalists hoped to drive the Austrian army from Italy and establish a unified state, perhaps even a moderate republic. Radicals were disappointed when the charismatic nationalist leader Giuseppe Mazzini supported Charles Albert, instead of forcefully arguing in favor of a republic. In a hurried plebiscite, the people of Lombardy approved union with Piedmont.

The other Italian states hesitated. Some rulers mistrusted Charles Albert, fearing (with reason) that he wanted to expand Piedmont at their expense. Traditional tensions between northern and southern Italy surfaced. Furthermore, the pope helped stymie the movement for Italian unification. Before the revolutions, the new pope, Pius IX (pope 1846–1878), had initiated a few modest reforms in his territories, releasing some liberals jailed by his predecessor. Some nationalists had even begun to think that Italy could be unified around papal authority. But the pope was hardly about to oppose the Catholic Habsburg dynasty on which the papacy had depended for centuries. Pius IX then announced that he would not support the war against Austria.

Meanwhile, the newly elected French Constituent Assembly unanimously approved a motion calling for the liberation of the Italian states. A French volunteer legion stood ready on the frontier, hoping that its help against Habsburg armies would bring French annexation of Savoy and Nice, as

Charles Albert had feared. But facing British opposition and with enough to worry about at home, the new French republic for the moment stayed out of the Italian fray. Nonetheless, the beleaguered Austrian court seemed resigned to losing Lombardy, and willing even to abandon its claim on Venetia, provided that Piedmont would not directly annex either territory.

Benefiting from better troop morale and reinforced by soldiers arriving from Austria, Radetzky believed he could defeat the nationalist armies of the Italian states, which fought with more enthusiasm than experience and lacked effective organization and supplies. One Piedmontese commander complained that the nationalists did "nothing, except to drown themselves with flowers, dancing, singing, shouting, and calling each other 'sublime,' 'valorous,' and 'invincible.'" Radetzky's army defeated the Piedmontese-led army of Italian nationalists at Custoza near Milan in early August 1848. The people of Milan then scornfully turned against Charles Albert, who slipped out of the city late at night and returned to his capital of Turin. From safer ground, the hesitant king negotiated an armistice with Austria, hoping in vain that he could retain Lombardy for his Kingdom of Piedmont-Sardinia.

The Elusive Search for Revolutionary Consensus

The Revolutions of 1848 generated resistance almost immediately from the political and social forces that had the most to lose from their success. In Prussia, the king and nobles feared being toppled from their privileged positions. In the Habsburg lands, where nationalism was the most significant factor in the revolution, the emperor and his army resisted. In France, the upper classes generally opposed radical changes. The ultimate success of the counter-revolution throughout Europe was aided by the revolutionaries' mixed aims. The split between liberals and radicals worked to the advantage of those who wanted a return to the way things had been before the spring of 1848.

Crisis in France

In France, the political crisis intensified as the provisional government faced competing demands. On May 15, 1848, an attempt by the political clubs of the far left to dissolve the Constituent Assembly and declare a "social" republic of the people failed. The provisional government now began to arrest radical republicans. With the provisional government rapidly running out of money and credibility, on June 23, 1848, the Assembly announced that the National Workshops would be closed in three days. Enrolled unmarried men were to be drafted into the army and married workers sent to work in the provinces. Parisian workers rose up in rebellion.

For three days the "June Days" raged in the workers' quarters of central and eastern Paris. General Louis Cavaignac (1802–1857) put down the

ATTAQUE DE LA BARRICADE PLACE MAUBERT

Troops attacking a barricade in Paris during the June Days, 1848.

uprising with brutality, using regular army soldiers, the Mobile Guard, and National Guard units, some of whom arrived from conservative provinces by train and steamboat, symbols of a new age. More than 1,500 insurgents were killed, some summarily executed. The provisional government deported more than 4,000 workers to Algeria or other colonies, and sent thousands of people to prison.

Karl Marx believed that the June Days were a dress rehearsal for a future proletarian revolution that would pit workers against the bourgeoisie. The short, bloody civil war, however, was more complicated than that. Some younger workers, including artisans, fought alongside unskilled proletarians in the Mobile Guard, which helped put down the uprising. Some radical bourgeois supported the workers.

The Assembly immediately passed legislation to curtail popular political movements. New laws limited freedom of the press and assembly and closed political clubs, specifically banning women from membership. The Luxembourg Commission was quickly disbanded. Cavaignac became provisional chief executive of the republic.

Attention now focused on the presidential elections instituted by the new republican constitution that was finally promulgated in November 1848.

Louis Napoleon Bonaparte quickly emerged as a leading candidate, largely because of the reputation of his uncle, Napoleon. Although one wag cruelly dubbed him "the hat without the head," it was testimony to the magic of the Napoleonic legend that Louis Napoleon had been elected to the Constituent Assembly in April 1848, after returning from exile. Many people believed that he could restore political stability. Cavaignac, the other major candidate, was the favorite of those who wanted to combine social order with a very moderate republic. The minister of the interior of the provisional government, Alexandre-Auguste Ledru-Rollin (1807–1874), was the principal candidate of the socialists, while Lamartine, a moderate, also ran, but both were identified with the provisional government and the unpopular 45 centimes tax. Outside of Paris many people had never heard of either one of them, but just about everyone had heard of Napoleon. Louis Napoleon also won the support of many people who were for the republic. Like his uncle, he was assumed to have good will toward all people in France. On December 10, 1848, Louis Napoleon was overwhelmingly elected president of the Second Republic. Some skeptics were already wondering whether he, like his uncle, would serve as the heir to a revolution, or its executioner.

The Frankfurt Parliament

In the German states, liberals and radicals gradually split as conservative forces gathered momentum. Shortly after the February Revolution in Paris, a group of German liberals, meeting in Heidelberg, invited about 500 like-minded figures to form a preliminary parliament to prepare elections for an assembly that would draft a constitution for a unified Germany. Most liberals wanted the German states to be united under a constitutional monarchy. Radicals, however, wanted nothing less than a republic based on universal male suffrage, and some of them joined a brief insurrection in the Rhineland state of Baden. To conservatives, and to some of the liberals as well, this insurrection raised the specter of "communism," amid rumors that radicals would divide the great estates among landless peasants.

The remainder of the members of the preliminary parliament announced elections for a German Constituent National Assembly, the Frankfurt Parliament. But, distinguishing their liberalism from that of the departed radicals, only male "independent" citizens in the German states would be eligible to vote; some states used this vague qualification to exclude men who owned no property. The Diet of the German Confederation accepted the plans for the election of the Frankfurt Parliament.

In May 1848, more than 800 elected delegates of the German Constituent National Assembly filed into Frankfurt's St. Paul's Church, which was decked out in red, black, and gold, the colors of early German nationalist university student organizations. State, municipal, and judicial officials, lawyers, university professors, and schoolteachers comprised about two-thirds of the Frankfurt Parliament. Since about a third of the delegates had some legal training, many people began to refer to the gathering as a "parliament of lawyers," whose members debated far into the night, confident that their deliberations would shape the future of the German states. Many were oblivious to the fact that poor acoustics rendered their speeches inaudible to people sitting in the back.

In electing Heinrich von Gagern (1799–1880) president, the delegates chose a man who symbolized the liberal and nationalist idealism of 1848. He had been one of the founders of the nationalist fraternities and a leader of the liberal opposition in his native Hesse. Although not of great intellect, Gagern offered an imposing physical presence and carried out his difficult tasks with dignity. He confidently gave the false impression that the unity of the delegates was assured and that German unification lay just ahead.

The Frankfurt Parliament in 1848.

The Frankfurt Parliament operated outside any state structure. It lacked the support of the rulers of Prussia and Austria, and, for that matter, of Bavaria and Württemberg. Without an army, it could not impose its will on any of the German states. Furthermore, considerable division existed over what shape the proposed unified Germany would take. Would it be a centralized state, or only an expansion of the German Confederation? How would sovereignty be defined? Who would have the right to vote?

Amid flowery speeches celebrating German national destiny, the problem of nationality immediately surfaced. Some delegates wanted Austria excluded from a united Germany, leery of the problem posed by non-German speakers within their state. Among these exponents of this "smaller German" (*Kleindeutsch*) solution, some wanted German unification around Protestant Prussia, fearing the inclusion of Catholic Austria. The more liberal "greater German" (*Grossdeutsch*) group wanted a unified Germany to include all states and territories within the German Confederation. Some wanted Austria's inclusion to counter possible Prussian domination, as well as that of northern Protestants.

After months of debate, a compromise solution appeared to be a victory for the "smaller German" plan. On October 27, 1848, the Frankfurt Parliament voted that any German state could join the new Germany, but only if it did not bring with it territories having non-German populations. Unless Austria was willing to separate itself from Hungary, it would have to remain outside a united Germany. For the moment, the Austrian government, struggling against resistance to its authority from Hungary and the northern Italian states of Lombardy and Venetia, regarded the Frankfurt Parliament's German nationalism as another threat to its survival.

The Frankfurt Parliament put aside its liberalism when it came to the question of Poland. When a Polish uprising against Prussian rule broke out, a parliamentary delegate rose to denounce Polish nationalism, insisting on "the preponderance of the German race over most Slav races" and calling for "[German] national egotism" and "the right of the stronger." The Frankfurt Parliament voted overwhelmingly in favor of armed Prussian repression of the Polish uprising, also expressing support for the Habsburg monarchy's crushing of the rebellious Czechs.

The Prussian parliament (which had been elected by universal male suffrage after the March insurrection in Berlin) had also gathered in May 1848 to begin to draft a constitution for Prussia. Amid urban and rural unrest, the parliament voted to make the civic guard a permanent institution, which challenged noble control of the army officer corps. It also abolished the Junkers' special hunting privileges and banned the use of all noble titles in anticipation of the abolition of formal class distinctions.

The Junkers, however, were not about to stand by and watch Prussia drift toward a constitutional monarchy or republic. They vowed to defend "God, the King, and the Fatherland," which they identified with their immunity from taxation and other prerogatives. Encouraged by the reaction to the June Days in France, Frederick William dismissed his liberal cabinet, sent troops to Berlin, and then in December dissolved the parliament. He declared martial law and disbanded the civic guard. Prussian troops crushed opposition in the Rhineland and Silesia.

While counter-revolution gathered momentum in Prussia, the middle-class liberals of the Frankfurt Parliament, powerless to effect German unification on their own, failed to build a base of popular support among workers and peasants. They feared the lower classes perhaps even more than did the Prussian nobles: one member of the Parliament described universal male suffrage as "the most dangerous experiment in the world." Thus, the Frankfurt Parliament rejected craftsmen's demands for protection against mechanization and an influx of new practitioners into their trades as being incompatible with economic liberalism. Since the eighteenth century, German guilds had gradually lost their autonomy to the regulatory authority of the states. The influx of apprentices and journeymen into trades had reduced the opportunity for journeymen to become masters. By turning a deaf ear to workers' demands, the Frankfurt Parliament lost a significant source of popular support. Furthermore, any hope of winning the allegiance of German peasants probably ended when the Parliament proclaimed that peasants must compensate their former lords in exchange for their release from remaining obligations.

Frustrated by the Parliament's moderation and general dawdling, in September 1848 several hundred workers charged into St. Paul's Church and tried to persuade the Parliament to declare itself a national convention of republicans. Austrian, Prussian, and Hessian troops had to rescue the delegates.

After six months of debate, the Frankfurt Parliament proclaimed in December 1848 the Basic Rights of the German People. Influenced by the American Declaration of Independence and the French Declaration of the Rights of Man and Citizen, it proclaimed the equality of "every German" before the law; freedom of speech, assembly, and religion; the end of seigneurial obligations; and the right to private property. Jews gained legal equality. The support of Prussia and/or Austria would be necessary to implement the Basic Rights of the German People and to form a united Germany. "To unite Germany without [Prussia and Austria]" would be, as a contemporary put it, "like two people trying to kiss with their backs turned to one another." But Austria's opposition to the Frankfurt Parliament became even stronger. Nationalism was antithetical to the monarchy's existence. The Frankfurt Parliament could do nothing as the Austrian government executed one of its delegates for having led an uprising in Vienna in October 1848. The Habsburgs encouraged other German states to disregard the Parliament and to proceed with their own counter-revolutions. The emperor made it clear that Austria would only consider joining a united Germany if the entire Habsburg monarchy, with its many non-German nationalities, was included. The Parliament had already rejected such a possibility.

In April 1849, the Frankfurt Parliament promulgated a possible constitution for a united Germany. It proposed the creation of a hereditary "emperor of the Germans" and two houses of Parliament, one representing the individual German states, the other elected by universal male suffrage. Austria, Bavaria, and Hanover rejected the proposed constitution.

The only chance for the constitution to succeed was to convince the king of Prussia to become king of a unified Germany. Frederick William had occasionally voiced vague support for German nationalism. The Parliament sent a delegation to Berlin to offer Frederick William the German crown. A Prussian noble shouted: "What, you bring an imperial crown? You are beggars! You have no money, no land, no law, no power, no people, no soldiers! You are bankrupt speculators in cast-off popular sovereignty!" When the head of the delegation asked for a glass of water in the royal palace, he was denied even that. Frederick William refused to accept a "crown from the gutter," a "dog collar" offered "by bakers, and butchers, and reeking with the stench of revolution."

Before the Prussian parliament could approve the constitution proposed by the Frankfurt liberals, the king dissolved it on April 28, 1849, declaring a state of emergency. He then implemented new voting restrictions that greatly favored the conservatives in subsequent parliamentary elections. Henceforth, the wealthiest 3 percent of the Prussian population elected one-third of the representatives; the next wealthiest 10 percent elected another third; and the remaining 87 percent of men elected the final third of the Prussian parliament. Liberal abstentions and popular indifference further assured conservative domination of the new parliament, which created an upper house of nobles, officials, churchmen, and other members to be selected by the king. Divided by indecision, lacking popular support, and facing Prussian and Austrian opposition, most of the Frankfurt parliamentarians went home. The Frankfurt Parliament, which embodied the hopes of German liberals and nationalists, ended in abject failure. Germany would not be unified by liberals.

Counter-Revolution

With the lack of consensus among the revolutionaries, counter-revolution now gained the upper hand in the Habsburg Empire and in the German and Italian states. In the Habsburg lands, the initial period of optimism gave way to a grim realization of the complexity of Central Europe. Ethnic conflicts broke out among Hungarians, Croats, and Serbs, as well as between landowners and peasants.

Counter-Revolution in Habsburg Central Europe

The confusion of competing national claims and rivalries within the Habsburg lands eased the task of counter-revolution within the Austrian Empire. If freedom was a central concern of the revolutionaries, it meant different things to different people. Magyar nobles wanted more autonomy for Hungary; Viennese journalists wanted freedom from press censorship; artisans wanted freedom from the competition of mechanized production; peasants wanted freedom from labor obligations owed to nobles. Czechs demanded freedom from German domination as well as their own national autonomy within the Habsburg domains.

Czechs hosted a Pan-Slav Congress in Prague in June 1848 to promote the rights of and bolster a union of Slavs within the Habsburg Empire and Central Europe. The assembled national groups could agree only on their common dislike for Habsburg policies. Each group had a different plan for the reorganization of the empire, one that would favor its own interests. Frantisek Palacký (1798–1876), a Czech historian, declared that if Austria did not exist, it would have to be invented, because otherwise small ethnic peoples such as the Czechs would be submerged by Germans or Russians. Often considered the father of Czech nationalism, Palacký therefore supported increased autonomy for the Czechs within a strong Habsburg state. Finally, the Pan-Slav Congress issued a vague statement in June 1848 that

Croatian regiments loyal to the Habsburg emperor attack Viennese revolutionaries, October 1848.

condemned the Germans for having oppressed the Slavic peoples and called for the reorganization of the Austro-Hungarian monarchy into a federation that would take into consideration the rights of each nationality.

While the Pan-Slav Congress, like the Frankfurt Parliament, was discussing lofty national questions, ordinary people were hungry. On June 12, 1848, barricades went up in Prague, manned by artisans and the laboring poor. Prince Alfred Windischgrätz (1787–1862), the Habsburg imperial governor, ended the insurrection four days later, bombarding Prague with cannon fire. Meanwhile, in northern Italy, the Habsburg imperial army defeated the Piedmontese forces, which had moved to assist the revolutions against Austria-Hungary, and Jelačić's Croatian army defeated Hungarian revolutionary forces.

In August, Emperor Ferdinand returned to Vienna and was welcomed by the middle classes. When he began to shut down the workshops, which had been established to provide work for the unemployed, the workers rose up, as they had in Paris, before being crushed by the National Guard. Two months later, workers rebelled again. Ferdinand fled Vienna for a second time, taking his court to Moravia. The imperial armies under Windischgrätz bombarded Vienna, killing more than 3,000 people. Once again, enthusiastic revolutionaries proved no match for the professional armies of the established powers. The emperor imposed martial law, closed the political clubs, dissolved the National Guard, and reestablished censorship. Arrests, trials, and executions followed. The emperor appointed a council of advisers (the *Reichsrat*), but was under no obligation to consult it.

Emperor Ferdinand appointed Prince Felix zu Schwarzenberg (1800–1852) as head of government on November 21, 1848. This ended the period of political uncertainty within Austria that had followed the March insurrection. Schwarzenberg convinced the hapless emperor to abdicate his throne in December 1848 in favor of his eighteen-year-old nephew, Francis Joseph (ruled 1848–1916). Placing his faith in the army, the new emperor was determined to assure the dynasty and its empire's survival.

Prince Schwarzenberg enhanced the effectiveness of the imperial bureaucracy by appointing able commoners to important posts. He hoped to win the support of Hungarian moderates, albeit without recognizing the rights of nationalities. Alexander Bach (1813–1893), a lawyer of noble origins, was first appointed to be minister of justice and then of the interior, and reformed the Habsburg legal system. At the same time, he implemented a system of carefully coordinated bureaucratic surveillance, spying, and repression—known as the "Bach system"—that helped root out political opposition.

But the Schwarzenberg government still had to deal with the Austrian parliament. That body, from its exile in the town of Kremsier, had produced a draft for a liberal constitution. The constitution approved the emancipation of the peasantry and sought to establish a decentralized, multinational state under a constitutional monarchy that would recognize all languages. It would have made ministers responsible to parliament. But the liberal Kremsier constitution was never implemented. Schwarzenberg suddenly dissolved the parliament in March 1849, ordered the arrest of some of the deputies, and imposed his own constitution. It made virtually no concessions to the non-German nationalities within the Habsburg domains and restored Hungary to its pre-1848 position. Furthermore, Schwarzenberg, with the young emperor's consent, intended to delay putting his constitution into effect until the revolutionary crisis had passed.

In April 1849, the Hungarian Diet refused to recognize Francis Joseph's ascension to the Habsburg throne and thus his sovereignty over Hungary. In turn, the young emperor refused to recognize Ferdinand's concessions to Hungary. The liberal Hungarian leader Kossuth tried to rally support in Hungary against Austria. The Hungarians defeated the imperial forces twice in the spring, taking Budapest and driving the Habsburg army out of Transylvania.

On April 14, 1849, the Hungarian Diet proclaimed Magyar independence and made Kossuth president of the newly formed Hungarian republic. As the Habsburg Empire's survival was now defiantly threatened, Francis Joseph called on the Russian tsar for help. The recent European revolutions had made Nicholas I even more reactionary. Having previously granted small reforms (see Chapter 15), he now forbade Russian students from traveling abroad, drastically reduced the number of government scholarships, ordered that philosophy and constitutional law be dropped as university subjects, and reinforced censorship of all publications. Thus without hesitation the Russian tsar sent 140,000 troops into Hungary and Transylvania. Kossuth frantically implored the Frankfurt Parliament for assistance, but that body had no army. The British government disliked the Russian intervention in Central Europe, but it wanted to preserve the Habsburg monarchy as a buffer against French and, above all, Russian interests. Hungarian resistance ended in August as Russian and Austrian forces advanced. Kossuth escaped to Turkey, never to return to Hungary. Austria executed thirteen Hungarian generals for treason, imprisoned thousands of people, and imposed martial law. The "Patent" of December 31, 1851, officially restored imperial absolutism.

An early photograph of the Hungarian noble, lawyer, and patriot Lajos Kossuth.

One by one in the other German states, the "March ministries" of 1848 fell from power as rulers abrogated constitutions granted that spring. Even where constitutions remained on the books, the counter-revolutions orchestrated by rulers with the help of nobles left parliaments and assemblies with little or no effective power. Scattered radical insurrections failed. After being chased from his duchy in June 1849, the grand duke of Baden returned to oversee the trials of more than 1,000 people. The German Revolution of 1848 was over. On August 23, 1851, the German Confederation annulled the Basic Rights of the German People, the major work of the Frankfurt Parliament.

Prussian-Austrian Rivalry

Now that the German revolutionaries had been swept away by the juggernaut of counter-revolution, Prussian King Frederick William IV proposed the creation of a "Prussian Union." It would consist of two "unions": the larger would include the states of the defunct German Confederation, as well as non-German Austrian territories; the smaller would be a confederation of all German-speaking lands, including those of Austria. In proposing these clumsy structures, a loose confederation based both on conservative political premises and an expansion of Prussian influence, Frederick William took advantage of the insurrections against Austrian authority in Hungary and northern Italy. Austria, Bavaria, and Württemberg all expressed immediate opposition to the plan. The Habsburg dynasty no more wanted to see an expansion of Prussian influence in Central Europe than it had desired German unification under the liberal auspices of the Frankfurt Parliament. On September 1, 1849, Austria unilaterally proclaimed the revival of the old German Confederation, pressuring member states to withdraw all the concessions to constitutionalism and liberalism they had made in 1848.

As Prussia and Austria both sought to assure the victory of counter-revolution as well as to secure a dominant position in Central Europe, relations between the two powers deteriorated further. In September 1849, the prince of Hesse asked the reconstituted German Confederation for assistance when his own people rebelled against the withdrawal of a liberal constitution he had earlier granted. The government of Prussia, however, objected to the involvement of the Confederation in Hesse because Hesse stood between two parts of Prussia. Prussia, which had the right to move troops through Hesse, threatened to send an army there if the Confederation tried to intervene. But the Russian tsar, now wary of a possible expansion of Prussian power in Central Europe, forced Prussia to back down. In October, the German Confederation, with secret Russian backing, sent Bavarian and Hanoverian troops to Hesse, but Prussian forces blocked their way. However, the Prussian government backed away from war, agreeing to drop plans for a Prussian Union. The Prussian government signed the "humiliation of Olmütz" (November 29, 1850), in which Prussia agreed to demobilize its army.

The Counter-Revolution in the Italian States

The counter-revolution in Central Europe and particularly in Austria spelled doom for Italian revolutionaries. And as in the German states and in the Habsburg Empire, those espousing liberal reforms and the cause of nationalism were too few, scattered, and divided by divergent and even conflicting goals. When Habsburg forces were fighting in Hungary, a nationalist "war party" in Piedmont-Sardinia pushed King Charles Albert toward a resumption of hostilities with Austria. The Piedmontese army crossed into Lombardy, but Austrian forces under General Joseph Radetzky defeated it at Novara in March 1849. Fearing that Radetzky's strengthened army would invade Piedmont, Charles Albert asked for peace and abdicated in favor of his son, Victor Emmanuel II. The new king signed an armistice with Austria in Milan in August, renouncing Piedmontese claims to Lombardy.

In 1848, revolutionaries had challenged the authority of the pope in the Papal States. In August, workers in Bologna rose up against Pope Pius IX. But the pope's forces prevailed. The next outbreak of opposition to papal authority came in Rome itself. Fearing an insurrection, Pius named a new, more liberal government, which announced the imposition of a tax on Church property. After one of the government's leaders was assassinated in November 1848, crowds stormed into the streets, calling for a declaration of war against Austria. Pius appointed more liberals to his government and called for parliamentary elections, before fleeing in disguise. From Naples, he called for the overthrow of the government he had appointed under duress.

In Rome, the new cabinet met many of the workers' demands, setting up charity workshops and ending the grain tax. The new government confiscated Church property, turning some buildings into apartments for poor workers. In elections for a Constitutional Assembly, the radicals won an overwhelming victory. On February 9, 1849, the Assembly proclaimed

Pope Pius IX puts aside the liberal mask of Christ, revealing his true conservative face.

the Roman Republic. The pope immediately excommunicated from the Catholic Church some of the republic's officials. The republic, in turn, abolished the Inquisition and proclaimed freedom of the press and the secularization of university education.

Some Italian nationalists now were beginning to think of the Roman Republic as a center around which the peninsula could be unified. Mazzini's arrival in Rome in early March 1849 to join the revolutionary government confirmed the pope's fears in this regard. With the armies of the Habsburgs tied up with struggles in Central Europe, the pontiff had to look elsewhere for a strong army to come to his rescue. Although Piedmont, the strongest Italian state, did not want a Roman Republic, the pope did not solicit Piedmontese assistance, fearing that if its forces came to the rescue, they might never leave.

Beset by severe economic shortages and inflation and discouraged by the news of the Piedmontese defeat at Novara in March, leaders of the Roman Republic now learned that the French were coming to try to restore the pope's temporal power. Louis Napoleon Bonaparte was eager to consolidate the support of French Catholics. He also did not want Austrian influence in Italy to go unchallenged. With the approval of the French Constituent Assembly, an army of 10,000 French troops disembarked near Rome, and then, embarrassingly enough, had to retreat when they met fierce resistance.

Giuseppe Garibaldi (1807–1882), a more strident—and organized—republican nationalist than Mazzini, arrived with a corps of volunteers from Lombardy to help the besieged republic. As pro-papal forces sent by the king of Naples and the Spanish government approached Rome, the French army began to shell the Eternal City in early June 1849. The Constitutional Assembly capitulated a month later. French troops then occupied Rome, dissolving the Assembly and the clubs and reviving press censorship. The pope returned to Rome in April 1850.

Of all of the governments formed by revolutions and uprisings in the Italian states in 1848, only the Venetian Republic now survived. But having defeated the Piedmontese in March 1849, the Austrians blockaded and bombarded Venice. The Venetian Republic capitulated on August 22, 1849.

The Italian revolutions were over. The only liberal regime that remained was in Piedmont. Austria retained Lombardy and Venetia. The king of Naples, the grand duke of Tuscany, and the pope were back in power. Italian unification remained a dream of northern middle-class nationalists. The multiplicity of states and lack of strong popular support for unification—reflected by the gap between liberals' and workers' goals—had for the moment proven too powerful.

The Agony of the French Second Republic

In France, the election of Louis Napoleon as president in December 1848 seemed to guarantee a return to political stability. Yet even as better economic times gradually returned, the "democratic-socialists," whose supporters had been primarily drawn from France's largest cities and some smaller market towns, expanded their appeal in the countryside. They particularly gained followers in the south, winning support among many peasants, for whom the low prices of agricultural depression had brought hard times. Taking the name of the far left during the French Revolution, the Montagnards called for the establishment of progressive taxation, higher wages, the abolition of the tax on wine, the creation of credit banks for peasants, and free and obligatory primary schools. The democratic-socialists effectively used written political propaganda to reach ordinary people; stories, songs, lithographs, and engravings spread the popularity of radical candidates. In the legislative elections of May 1849, the left won almost a third of the seats in the Constituent Assembly, harnessing the heritage of the French Revolution in regions in which it had found enthusiastic support.

Encouraged by the strength of the left in the Chamber of Deputies and in Paris, Ledru-Rollin, who had been a candidate in the presidential election, attempted to provoke an insurrection on June 13, 1849. His pretext was the Assembly's readiness to send a French army to support the pope, which the left claimed violated the new constitution, because French troops would be violating the freedom of the Romans. However, intervention in Rome earned Louis Napoleon the gratitude of conservative Catholics; Ledru-Rollin's

Uprooting a liberty tree in Paris.

uprising discredited the left among the upper classes. But by-elections in the spring of 1850 reflected the growing popularity of the democratic-socialist program in some places.

Backed by the "party of order," Louis Napoleon's government claimed that a massive plot threatened social order. Symbols of the French Revolution itself, including singing "The Marseillaise," became illegal. The government also outlawed red caps and belts, because red was identified as the color of the left. The police felled liberty trees one by one. The government curtailed the freedoms of assembly and association and banned many workers' associations, including some that had been granted state funds in 1848 to establish producer and consumer cooperatives. National Guard units in many towns were disbanded. Mayors and schoolteachers were replaced if they supported the left, and cafés identified with the democratic-socialist cause were closed. Many radical republican and socialist leaders were jailed. These included Jeanne Deroin (1810–1894), a socialist seamstress and feminist, who in 1849 had tried to run for election despite the fact that women were ineligible for election and could not vote. In March 1850, the Assembly passed the Falloux Law, which allowed the Catholic clergy to open secondary schools and permitted them to serve on education committees. One of the practical consequences was that villages now could turn operation of their schools over to the clergy.

In May 1850, the Constituent Assembly ended universal male suffrage by adding a residency requirement that disqualified many workers who traveled from place to place to find work. This reduced the electorate by one-third, eliminating 3 million voters. Many of the disenfranchised lived in the larger cities, where Napoleon and his candidates had not fared well. The repression succeeded in smashing the left in much of France.

In some southern and central regions, the repression drove the left into secret societies, whose members, mostly artisans and peasants, swore an oath of allegiance to defend the "democratic and social Republic." These societies, which started in towns, gradually spread into the surrounding countryside. This occurred particularly where economic growth during the preceding two decades, including cash-crop agriculture and rural handicrafts, had brought more rural artisans and peasants regularly into market towns.

The constitution limited the presidency to one term of four years. Although Louis Napoleon's term as president was, in principle, nearing an end, he had no intention of stepping aside. On December 2, 1851, the anniversary of his uncle's victory at Austerlitz and the coronation of Napoleon Bonaparte as emperor, Parisians awoke to read an official poster that announced the dissolution of the Constituent Assembly. The secret societies then undertook the largest national insurrection in nineteenth-century France. More than 100,000 people took up arms in defense of the republic. But the ragged forces of artisans and peasants armed with rusty rifles and pitchforks were easily dispersed by troops before they got very far. Military courts tried over 26,000 democratic-socialists, and almost half that many went into exile.

Yet support for the coup by Louis Napoleon was overwhelming in France as a whole. The plebiscite that followed the coup approved the takeover by more than 10 to 1. The Paris stock market soared. Louis Napoleon proclaimed a new constitution. On December 2, 1852, he took the title Napoleon III, emperor of the French.

THE LEGACY OF 1848

The glacial winds of reaction brutally chilled the "springtime of the peoples." The wave of repression dashed the hopes of liberals, republicans, and nationalists throughout Europe. It has often been said, with the advantage of hindsight, that in 1848, at least with reference to Prussia and the other German states, European history reached its turning point and failed to turn.

European states became even stronger after the Revolutions of 1848. The revolutions had succeeded at first because the French, Prussian, and Austrian authorities lacked sufficient military preparedness. All three quickly learned their lessons. With the defeat of the revolutionaries came the end of

The generals who crushed the insurgency within the Habsburg Empire: Jelačić, Radetzky, and Windischgrätz.

the era of civic or national guards, which had been demanded by the people of Berlin, Vienna, and Paris. Professional armies enforced the counterrevolution, restoring Habsburg authority in Bohemia, Hungary, and northern Italy; the Prussian army crushed the last gasps of revolution in the German states; and the French army put down subsequent resistance to Louis Napoleon's coup d'état. Louis Napoleon's plebiscite reinforced the centralized character of the French state.

Nonetheless, the Revolutions of 1848 marked the first time workers put forward organized demands for political rights. Moreover, radical peasants in southern France helped dispel the myth of the inevitably conservative peasant. Although the Revolutions of 1848 ultimately failed, they left crucial political legacies. The period was one of political apprenticeship for republicanism in France and nationalism in the German and Italian states. Portugal completed a liberal revolution begun in 1820 with the establishment of a parliamentary government. The revolutions were not only separate national phenomena but also part of a common process that anticipated the emergence of mass politics in the last decades of the nineteenth century. While many of the goals of the revolutionaries centered on middle-class demands for liberal reforms, such as freedom of the press, the Revolutions of 1848 also had a popular quality characterized by demands for universal male suffrage, as well as by a few calls for political rights for women. Hundreds of thousands of ordinary people participated, if only somewhat briefly, in political life. The mid-century revolutions influenced the subsequent political evolution of each country that had had a revolution in the spring of 1848.

Great Britain provides the counterexample. However, in Britain, too, the experience of 1848 was revealing in that there was no revolution in 1848. In Britain, political reform followed compromise, not revolution. In contrast to their French counterparts before the Revolutions of 1830 and 1848, English middle-class liberals avoided at all costs prodding workers into street confrontations with authority, fearful of unwittingly unleashing an uncontrollable insurrection. Chartism, the mass petition movement in the 1840s for universal male suffrage, had its last gasp in 1848. The British government arrested suspected radicals, sent 8,000 troops into London in anticipation of a movement on April 10 that never occurred, and appointed 150,000 civilian "special constables." Businessmen, anticipating trouble from a Chartist demonstration, hauled out hunting rifles and barricaded their offices. In any case, with the exception of a very small radical component in favor of the use of "physical force," the Chartists were gradualists. The Irish nationalist movement, dormant since a failed insurrection in 1798, reawakened in 1848, in part because of the revolutionary enthusiasm of Irish immigrants then living in the United States. British authorities searched ships arriving from the United States for weapons and funds intended for potential insurgents. But the presence of the British army, as well as the emigration of great numbers of Irish to the United States, limited Irish nationalists' efforts in that revolutionary year to one minor uprising. A possible alliance between the radical Irish Confederation and "physical force" Chartists never took place. At the same time, elite fears of Irish insurgency contributed to the persistence of anti-Catholicism in British national identity, as the press denigrated the Irish "Paddy" as drunken, untrustworthy, and potentially revolutionary.

The counter-revolution in Europe scattered a generation of committed republicans, nationalists, and socialists throughout much of the world. Thousands of Frenchmen were exiled to Algeria, while German and Italian political exiles left for the United States. They spread the ideas of republicanism, nationalism, and socialism.

The Habsburg monarchy, too, survived the liberal and nationalist challenges of 1848. The young Habsburg Emperor Francis Joseph bragged to his mother, "We have thrown the constitution overboard and Austria has now only one master." The Austrian government had adroitly manipulated ethnic tensions, using a Croatian army against a Hungarian uprising. The situation was so complicated that a Hungarian noted "the King of Hungary declared war on the King of Croatia, and the Emperor of Austria remained neutral, and all three monarchs were the same person." Hungary, in which perhaps as many as 100,000 people were killed during the fighting in 1848–1849, remained within the monarchy as Austria's junior partner. But peasants were now free from labor obligations previously owed to landowners. Although the liberal Kremsier constitution had been tossed aside, the Austrian constitution of March 1849 did establish a parliament. Yet the goals of many Hungarians, Czechs, Poles, and other ethnic groups remained unachieved. On the Italian peninsula, Habsburg control of Lombardy and Venetia, the existence of many other separate states, and the indifference of most people to Italian nationalism remained daunting obstacles to Italian unification. Even in failure, however, the revolutions in the Italian states had only made Italian nationalists more determined to work for national unification. Likewise, the defeat of the Hungarian and Bohemian revolutions, as well as the failure of the radical revolution in Vienna, by no means ended challenges to the Habsburg monarchy.

The Revolutions of 1848 accentuated support for German nationalism. A Prussian minister recognized that "the old times are gone and cannot return. To return to the decaying conditions of the past is like scooping water with a sieve." The revolution did produce a Prussian constitution and an elected assembly, however, which the king only slightly modified in 1849–1850, when he again took control. The failure of the Revolutions of 1848 in Central Europe suggested to many Germans that unification could only be achieved under the auspices of either Prussia or Austria. German unification under any auspices would potentially entail a drastic change in the European state system, altering the balance of power, especially in Central Europe.

PART FIVE

THE AGE OF MASS POLITICS

In 1850, Great Britain, France, and Russia were the three major European powers. However, the unification of Italy and Germany during the 1860s and early 1870s shifted the balance of power in Central Europe and dramatically changed international dynamics. Moreover, amid rising national consciousness, ethnic minorities within the Habsburg Empire, in particular, demanded more rights, setting the stage for further conflict in Europe.

During the nineteenth century's last three decades, much of Europe entered a period of remarkable economic, social, political, and cultural change. During the Second Industrial Revolution, scientific and technological advances ushered in a period of rapid economic growth. Steel and electricity transformed manufacturing. Cities grew rapidly, their wide boulevards lined with department stores, cafés, and newspaper kiosks. The emergence of spectator sports and flashy cabarets symbolized the fin-de-siècle period. However, some of the rebellious writers and artists of the avant-garde worried that Western civilization was moving too rapidly and seemed out of control.

On the continent, political parties developed, which helped bring about the age of mass politics. Despite a general improvement in the quality of life, the difficult conditions of the laboring poor encouraged the creation of Socialist parties. Socialists were elected to many European parliaments. Trade unions put forth demands and engaged in strikes. In Britain, the Labour Party started up early in the twentieth century, supported by workers demanding social reform. In Russia, liberal critics of the tsarist autocracy became bolder. The humiliating defeat of Russia by

Japan led to the Russian Revolution of 1905. This forced short-lived political reforms and encouraged reformers and revolutionaries alike.

For more than half a century, liberals had championed the interests of the middle class, basing the right to vote on the ownership of property. They did so in the context of constitutional government, pushing for the rights of legislative assemblies. In the three decades following the largely unsuccessful 1848 revolutions, liberalism prevailed in Great Britain, France, Austria, Italy, Greece, and Sweden. The British Parliament, which in 1867 had greatly extended the right of men to vote, approved the secret ballot in 1872, and in 1884 enfranchised almost all remaining adult males. France became a republic early in the 1870s, and universal male suffrage subsequently was adopted in Germany, Belgium, Spain, Austria, and Italy. Without the liberals' determination to expand the franchise, universal male suffrage in much of Western Europe, followed by political democracy in many states, would not have occurred. Liberal democracy emerged as the dominant form of European politics from the second half of the nineteenth century to the present day.

However, in the last decades of the century, liberalism was on the defensive, attacked from left and right. Nationalism increasingly became part of the expanding contours of political life within states and between them. During the French Revolution and Napoleonic era, nationalism had been an ideology identified with the political left. Liberals had believed that laissez-faire economic policy and parliamentary government combined with an expansion of the right to vote (but not necessarily universal male suffrage) would provide a firm base for the establishment of nation-states. During at least the first half of the nineteenth century, liberalism and nationalism were closely entwined; liberals and nationalists were often the same people, as in Britain, France, and Italy.

By the end of the century, many nationalists, convinced that their people were superior to any other, trumpeted the primacy of the nation over claims of popular sovereignty or belief in human equality. Nationalism became an ideology championed, above all, by right-wing parties. Cheap newspapers glorified the nation for eager readers. "Jingoism" came to define the swaggering self-assurance of nationalists committed to expanding the power of their nation. At the same time, waves of strikes and demonstrations frightened conservatives from Norway and Sweden to Austria and Spain. The fear of socialism, espousing internationalism, pushed social elites and some in the middle class to the nationalist right. Anti-Semitism fed on aggressive nationalism.

Nationalism merged easily with imperialism, which was predicated on the assumption that the people of one nation were superior to others, and therefore entitled to dominate "inferior" peoples through the expansion of empire. The "new imperialism" of the powers began in the 1880s. By 1914, they had divided up three-quarters of the world's surface. Imperialism helped sharpen international rivalries. Entangling alliances led the European powers into two heavily armed camps, linking Germany and Austria-Hungary against Britain, France, and Russia. The growth of nationalism in the Balkans fueled the rivalry between Russia and Austria-Hungary, each backed by strongly committed allies.

CHAPTER 17

THE ERA OF NATIONAL UNIFICATION

During the first half of the nineteenth century, small groups of German and Italian nationalists agitated for the political unification of their respective peoples. Liberals and nationalists were often the same people sharing the same goals. Many revolutionaries in 1848 had demanded national unification, notably the lawyers and professors of the Frankfurt Parliament in the German states and the Italian liberals and nationalists opposing Austrian domination of northern Italy. But the outcome of the 1848 revolutions notwithstanding, Germany and Italy were not unified by the popular movements that typified the revolutions that in 1848 brought a republic to France, forced constitutional changes in Prussia and Austria, and sparked insurrections against Austrian control of northern Italy.

Italian unification came, not because of the utopian nationalism of Giuseppe Mazzini nor because of the frenzied dashes of Giuseppe Garibaldi and his followers into the south, but rather largely as a result of the expansion of Piedmont-Sardinia, the peninsula's strongest and most liberal state. Italy was unified politically under the liberal auspices of the Piedmont-Sardinian monarchy, the House of Savoy.

The case of Germany was very different. German unification was effected by autocratic Prussian King William I and Chancellor Otto von Bismarck through shrewd manipulation of both diplomacy and warfare. "Most countries have an army," it was said, but "Prussia is an army with a country." The German Empire, like the Prussia that forged it in "blood and iron," was defiantly reactionary, flying in the face of currents of European liberalism.

Without question, the emergence of Italy in the 1860s and of Germany in 1871 changed the history of modern Europe. Germany emerged as a great power, Italy as a would-be great power. And the Austro-Hungarian monarchy increasingly was confronted by demands from its ethnic minorities for their own independence, which remained a factor for instability in its domestic and international politics. In some ways, the Habsburg monarchy seemed an anachronism, out of place in the age of nationalism.

The Political Unification of Italy

The Austrian statesman Klemens von Metternich once whimsically remarked that Italy was "a mere geographical expression." Since the end of the Roman Empire, Italy had been politically disunited, a cacophony of competing voices from different regions and peoples.

Marked differences in economic development compounded political fragmentation. Northern Italy has always been considerably more prosperous than the south. The Habsburg monarchy also presented a formidable obstacle to Italian unification, as it retained Venetia and Lombardy, and dominated Parma, Tuscany, and Modena in north-central Italy (the rulers of the latter two states were members of the Austrian royal family). The pope's influence and temporal control over the Papal States around Rome posed another barrier to Italian unification. Furthermore, Italy lacked a tradition of centralized administration. Powerful local elites dispensed patronage, constituting unofficial parallel governments in much of the south and Sicily. Finally, these structural barriers to unification were accompanied by disagreement among elites and nationalists about whether a unified Italy would be governed by a monarchy (constitutional or not), a republic, or even by the pope.

Although many forces were working against Italian unification, some factors promoted the ultimate Risorgimento ("Resurgence") of Italy. Nationalist sentiment developed among the liberal aristocracy and the upper middle classes, particularly among northern lawyers and professors. It was fanned by nationalist brochures and newspapers, the memory of the failures of the Revolutions of 1848, and a common hatred of Austria, the latest of the outside powers that had held parts of Italy since the end of the fifteenth century. Most Italian nationalists envisioned a Risorgimento independent of the pope and the Catholic Church.

Leadership for Italian Unification

There seemed to be two possible sources of leadership for Italian unification. First, Victor Emmanuel II (ruled 1849–1878) of the House of Savoy, king of Piedmont-Sardinia (the Kingdom of Sardinia), wanted to unify Italy by gradually extending his control over the peninsula. Piedmont-Sardinia was far and away Italy's most prosperous region, boasting a significant concentration of industrial production, fine sources of water power, and accessible markets. It had inherited from the French revolutionary and Napoleonic eras a relatively efficient bureaucracy.

King Victor Emmanuel II, poorly educated and uncouth, loved horses and hunting more than anything else, with the possible exception of his sixteen-year-old mistress, the daughter of a palace guard. In 1852, Victor Emmanuel at least had the good sense to appoint Count Camillo di Cavour (1810–1861) to be his prime minister.

(*Left*) King Victor Emmanuel II of Piedmont-Sardinia. (*Right*) Count Camillo di Cavour.

Born into a family of Piedmontese nobles during the Napoleonic occupation, Cavour was a pampered child who grew up to be headstrong, somewhat lazy, and bad tempered. His older brother inherited the family title of marquis, and Cavour entered a military academy, where he did well in mathematics and engineering. In the army, he became enamored of political radicalism. Upon hearing of the July Revolution of 1830 in France, Cavour ran through his barracks in Genoa waving a paper knife, shouting "Long live the Republic! Down with all tyrants!" Cavour's political radicalism was unlikely to win him promotion in the army. He resigned his commission as a military engineer, pleading poor eyesight and bad health, the latter at least partially due to a lifelong pattern of eating and drinking too much.

Cavour read widely in economics and politics and traveled to France and England, both of which impressed him with their prosperity and efficient administration. Cavour's first language remained French, although his command of Italian improved. On his property, he made a good deal of money by utilizing crop rotation, land drainage, and mechanized farm machinery. Triumphs in banking and business followed, but none brought the morose Cavour happiness. In his early twenties, he wrote in his diary that he thought of suicide because he believed his life was "without purpose, without hope, without desire." Yet he found a compelling goal: the unification of the Italian peninsula.

Cavour came to espouse aristocratic liberalism. He became determined to effect political unification by gradually expanding the constitutional monarchy of Piedmont-Sardinia. An idealist of vision and courage, Cavour was also capable of ruthlessness and unscrupulous trickery, all of which would be necessary to achieve Italian unification. He bragged that he liked to reduce political problems to graphs on which he had plotted all possible factors and outcomes.

Elected to the Piedmontese Parliament in 1849 in the new constitutional government, named minister of commerce and agriculture the following year and prime minister in 1852, he initiated the first of a series of loose coalition liberal governments based on the political center, standing between the noble and clerical right and the republican left.

Cavour's policies helped stimulate the Piedmontese economy. He facilitated the availability of credit for businessmen, helped attract foreign capital by lowering tariffs, built railways, and strengthened the army. Reflecting Piedmontese liberal secular values, Cavour made the clergy subject to the same civil codes as everyone else and taxed Church property. Like the liberalism of the French Orleanist monarchy and the early Victorians in Britain, however, Cavour's liberalism stopped well short of republicanism.

A second, more popular nationalist tradition survived the broken dreams of "the springtime of the peoples," the Revolutions of 1848. Giuseppe Mazzini remained its spokesman. The Genoese-born Mazzini had as a boy watched Piedmontese patriots leave for exile after an ill-fated revolutionary uprising in 1820–1821. Mazzini frequently dressed in black (often in the company of his pet canaries, who wore yellow), vowing to remain in mourning until Italian unification could be achieved. The failure of conspiratorial uprisings led him to espouse a nationalist movement that had a wider range of support, with the goal of establishing a republic that would implement social reforms. While he was a determined enemy of monarchism and aristocratic privilege, Mazzini believed that classical liberalism was devoid of moral values, and he rejected socialism as overly materialistic. He embraced unification as a moral force that would educate and uplift the people of Italy, providing a common faith and purpose that would unlock their potential and make them worthy of democracy.

Mazzini believed that the unification of Italy had to be the work of the people themselves, and should not be achieved merely through the expansion of the Kingdom of Piedmont-Sardinia. Drawing on the conspiratorial tradition of the Carbonari, Mazzini's secret society, "Young Italy," hoped to mobilize the European masses, beginning in the Italian states, to rise up for nationalism and democracy. He thus supported the goals of other nationalist groups in Europe, including Hungarians, Poles, and Slavs in the hope that "Young Europe," a brotherhood of nations, would eventually come into existence.

Mazzini was undaunted by the failures and repression that followed the Revolution of 1848, including the ill-fated attempt to proclaim the Roman Republic in 1849. However, these debacles discredited his movement among the middle classes. Four years later, Cavour tipped off the Austrians that Mazzini was planning an insurrection in Lombardy. King Victor Emmanuel II congratulated Austrian Emperor Francis Joseph on the success of the subsequent repression. Yet Mazzini's effective propaganda kept the Italian question alive in European diplomatic circles while attracting the interest of lawyers and liberal landowners in some of the northern Italian states.

Alliances and Warfare to Further Italian Unification

Italian unification would be impossible as long as Austria dominated much of northern and central Italy. Having first concentrated on reforms within Piedmont-Sardinia, Cavour next began a series of diplomatic moves that he hoped would bring the support of Great Britain and France. Specifically, he wanted to form an alliance with France against Austria that would further the cause of Italian unification. Austria was not about to withdraw from Lombardy on its own, and Piedmont-Sardinia was too weak to defeat the Habsburg army alone. Cavour initiated commercial agreements with France, as well as with Great Britain, trying to impress both powers with Piedmont-Sardinia's political and economic liberalism.

In March 1854, France and Great Britain joined the Ottoman Empire in opposing Russia in the Crimean War (1853–1856). The cagey Cavour worked to make the war serve the interests of Piedmont-Sardinia and Italian unification. Cavour informed the French and British governments that Piedmont-Sardinia would be willing to join the coalition against Russia in exchange for a role in determining new frontiers in Eastern Europe at the war's end. Knowing that Britain needed more troops for the fight, Cavour sent 15,000 soldiers to Crimea in January 1855. Mazzini, on the other hand, bitterly opposed intervention as irrelevant to his vision of a united republican Italy. Piedmont-Sardinia signed the Peace of Paris in 1856, which ended the Crimean War, an occasion Cavour used to focus diplomatic attention on the Italian situation.

Cavour was now eager to ally with imperial France in the interest of working toward Italian unification. Despite a failed assassination attempt against him by an Italian nationalist republican in 1858, French Emperor Napoleon III was eager to extend his country's influence in Italy and hoped to annex Savoy and Nice from Piedmont-Sardinia. He proposed marriage between Victor Emmanuel's fifteen-year-old daughter and his own young cousin, Prince Napoleon Bonaparte. Such an alliance would help cement relations between France and Piedmont-Sardinia, not a happy situation for the Austrians (nor necessarily for the young bride).

Cavour devised an agreement with France against Austria, which was signed in July 1858 at Plombières, a spa in eastern France. Napoleon III now agreed to support Piedmont-Sardinia in a war against Austria. In January 1859, Piedmont-Sardinia and France formalized the Plombières agreement in a treaty. Then the ruling dynasties were united in youthful marriage (the princess had agreed to marry the young Frenchman if "he is not actually repulsive to me"). Russia, Austria's rival in the Balkans, was happy to sit this one out in exchange for French acceptance of a possible revision of the

Pope Pius XI on the special train given to him by Napoleon III, who protected papal temporal independence.

Peace of Paris, which had in 1856 deprived Russia of the right to have a fleet in the Black Sea. In turn, Russia would look the other way if events in Italy altered the settlements enacted by the Congress of Vienna in 1815.

Austria provided an excuse for war, announcing that it would draft men from Venetia and Lombardy into the imperial army. Piedmont-Sardinia, in turn, made it known that it would accept deserters from Austrian conscription, and it mobilized troops in March. But the British government lobbied so effectively for a peaceful solution that Cavour denounced a "conspiracy of peace" and threatened to resign. Napoleon III hesitated, asking Piedmont-Sardinia to demobilize its troops. Austria saved the situation for Cavour by issuing an ultimatum to Piedmont-Sardinia on April 23, 1859, hoping that other German states would support it. With Austria now appearing as the aggressor, Prussia and the other German states felt no obligation to come to its aid. After Piedmont-Sardinia rejected the ultimatum, Austrian troops invaded Piedmont, which brought France into the war. Napoleon III himself led 100,000 troops into northern Italy; many of the troops went by train, the first time that a railway played a major part in warfare.

The French and Piedmontese defeated the Habsburg army at Magenta and then at Solferino in June 1859, driving the Austrians out of Lombardy (see Map 17.1). But the French feared that a crushing defeat of Austria might yet bring Prussia and other German states into the war against France, with the bulk of the French armies still in northern Italy. Furthermore, Cavour

MAP 17.1 THE UNIFICATION OF ITALY, 1859–1870   The unification of Italy by Piedmont-Sardinia included territory acquired in 1859, 1860, 1862, and 1866.

had sparked several nationalist insurrections against the Austrians in Tuscany, Bologna, Modena, and Parma, whose rulers fled, leaving the duchies under Piedmontese control. Further revolts in the Papal States failed; the pope's Swiss mercenaries recaptured Perugia, looting the city and shooting unarmed civilians. It became apparent to the French emperor that if Piedmont-Sardinia were *too* successful, Victor Emmanuel's expanded kingdom might become a rival instead of a grateful, compliant neighbor. Without consulting Cavour, Napoleon III arranged an armistice at Villafranca with Emperor Francis Joseph of Austria in July.

Cavour and Victor Emmanuel now believed that France had betrayed them. Austria lost Lombardy to Piedmont-Sardinia but would retain Venetia. By the Treaty of Turin on March 24, 1860, Napoleon III agreed to Piedmont-Sardinia's annexation of Tuscany, Modena, Parma, and Bologna, in addition to Lombardy. In exchange, Piedmont-Sardinia ceded Savoy and Nice, which passed to France after a plebiscite. With the exception of Venetia, almost all of northern and central Italy had now been united under the constitutional monarchy of Piedmont-Sardinia.

Garibaldi and the Liberation of Southern Italy

The colorful republican revolutionary Giuseppe Garibaldi (1807–1882) now leapt onto the stage. Born in Nice (and, like Cavour, a French speaker), the charismatic and courageous Garibaldi had joined Mazzini's Young Italy movement in 1833. After twelve years in exile in South America, he fought against the Austrians in Lombardy in 1848 and against the French in Rome in 1849. The war of 1859 provided him with another opportunity to fight Austria. Angered that the Villafranca armistice had cut short what he considered a war for Italian unification, Garibaldi formed an army of volunteers, hoping to drive the Austrians from Venetia and the French from Rome. But an ill-prepared attack on Rome failed completely.

In April 1860, a revolt began against Francis II, the Bourbon monarch of the Kingdom of the Two Sicilies (Naples and Sicily), as a protest against the milling tax and the high price of bread. Secretly encouraged by Cavour (who

Giuseppe Garibaldi.

planned to send Piedmont-Sardinia's army to Rome later to rescue the pope) and openly urged on by Mazzini, Garibaldi landed in Sicily with an army of 1,000 "Red Shirts." Sicilians welcomed him as a liberator. Garibaldi's followers outfought the larger Neapolitan army, taking Palermo on May 27, 1860. This success swelled Garibaldi's ragtag army of nationalists and adventurers.

Garibaldi then announced that he was assuming dictatorial power in Sicily on behalf of King Victor Emmanuel II of Piedmont-Sardinia. In August, Garibaldi's army returned to the Italian peninsula. Aided by a popular insurrection, the Red Shirts took Naples, Italy's largest city, in September. Garibaldi's victories now put Piedmont-Sardinia in a difficult situation. If Garibaldi marched against Rome, France might declare war because of the threat to the pope. If Garibaldi moved against Venetia, which seemed inevitable, Austria would almost certainly fight again, perhaps this time with Prussia's support. Cavour sent Piedmontese troops into the Papal States the same day that Garibaldi's troops took Naples. The ostensible goal was to join Garibaldi, but the real intention of the expedition was to stop the adventurer's dramatic independent operations. The combined forces of Piedmontese troops and Garibaldi's army put an end to papal resistance and that of the royal Bourbon family of Naples.

Italy Unified

Plebiscites in October in Naples, Sicily, and the Papal States demonstrated overwhelming support for joining the expanding Italian state of Piedmont-Sardinia. The annexation of these states angered Napoleon III, as Cavour had promised that an international conference would provide arbitration. Now only Venetia—still Austrian—and Rome and its region—the shrinking kingdom of the pope—remained unincorporated into the new Italy.

Victor Emmanuel II of Piedmont-Sardinia triumphantly entered Naples with Garibaldi in November 1860. He took the title King Victor Emmanuel II of Italy in March 1861. Garibaldi, whose daring exploits had made these events possible, retired in semi-exile. On June 6, 1861, Cavour died at age fifty-one, depriving Italy of his effective decision making and political acumen. Depending on one's point of view, Italy had lost either the great hero of the Risorgimento or a scheming Machiavellian—probably something of both.

Two more conflicts completed the political unification of Italy. In 1866, Austria went to war with Prussia, its rival for the leadership of the German states. Italian troops, allied with Prussia, moved into Austrian Venetia. When Prussian forces defeated the Austrians in July (see pp. 666–67), Venetia became part of Italy.

The final piece in the Italian jigsaw puzzle fell into place when French troops left Rome in 1870 at the beginning of the Franco-Prussian War. Italian troops occupied Rome, making it the capital of the new Italian state. On May 13, 1871, the Italian Parliament passed the Law of Papal Guarantees, which reduced the holdings of the pope to the Vatican, barely larger than Saint Peter's Basilica and its adjoining ecclesiastical buildings.

Limits to Unification

During the next decades, the limits to Italian unification became increasingly apparent. The Italian state, despite its phalanx of civil servants and police, seemed irrelevant to many, perhaps even most, of the people now called Italians. Most remained loyal to their families, towns, regions, and to the Catholic Church (particularly in central and southern Italy), as well as to powerful local leaders, families, or factions. Almost 70 percent of the population was illiterate in 1871 and 50 percent in 1900, even though the peninsula now shared a common written Italian language. In 1860, almost 98 percent of the population of Italy spoke dialects in daily life and not Italian. Schoolteachers sent to Sicily from the north were taken for Englishmen. A French writer related that in Naples in 1860 he heard people shout "Long Live Italy!" and then ask what "Italy" meant.

Resistance to the Italian state came naturally. In southern Italy, the crime organizations of the Camorra of Naples and the Mafia of Sicily, with similar codes of honor, served as the real basis of authority. Family feuds and vendettas, often accompanied by grisly violence, went on as before. "Italy" was seen as a northern ploy to bilk money through taxes, or to draft the sons of southern Italians into the army, or to undercut what seemed to be legitimate local influence and ways of doing things. To the poor farmers and impoverished laborers trying to scratch out a living, local notables at least could provide what they considered "justice" for the poor. Moreover, brigands had traditionally received assistance from the local population, who viewed them as fellow resisters to the state, if not Robin Hoods. The state managed to drive bands of brigands out of business in the 1870s, but only through a savage repression that killed more Italians than all the wars of the Risorgimento combined, intensifying suspicion and mistrust of the state.

The liberal free-trade policies of Cavour, who had never been farther south in Italy than Florence, further served to concentrate industry in the triangle formed by Milan, Turin, and Genoa by driving out smaller and less efficient manufacturers, accentuating the gap between north and south. The south became even more dependent on poor agriculture. Northerners dominated Italian politics, as they had Italian unification, treating the people of the south as colonial underlings. Far fewer southerners were eligible to vote than northerners. Mass emigration, principally to the United States and Argentina, could only partly resolve the problems of overpopulation and poverty.

In the meantime, the popes portrayed themselves as Roman prisoners of a godless state. The Church had refused to accept the Law of Papal Guarantees of 1871, which gave it title to the Vatican and the authority to make ecclesiastical appointments within Italy. The popes not only refused to recognize Italy's existence, but they banned the faithful from running for electoral office or even voting. While some Italian Catholics simply ignored such stern papal warnings, others systematically abstained from casting a ballot. The state paid the salaries of the clergy, but it also confiscated Church property. Secular reforms removed the teaching of theology from the universities, closed convents and monasteries, made priests eligible for military conscription, banned public religious processions, and made civil marriage obligatory. The attitude of the Church hierarchy and prominent laymen to the Italian state was reflected by the headline of a Catholic newspaper after the death of King Victor Emmanuel II in 1878: "The king is dead, the pope is well."

Italian Politics

The king of Italy ruled through a premier and parliament. The electoral franchise was small: only about 600,000 men (2.5 percent of the population) were eligible to elect members of the Chamber of Deputies before the expansion of the franchise in 1882, after which 2 million men, about 10 percent of the population, could vote, and in 1912, when the number eligible to vote was doubled. Italian governments lurched from one political crisis to another in the 1880s, buffeted by rampant corruption as well as rapidly changing coalitions—a process that became known to critics as *trasformismo*—"transforming" political opponents into allies. King Umberto I (ruled 1878–1900) stood aside until his intervention became absolutely imperative. Italy's king was lazy, so uneducated that he did not even like to sign his own name if someone was watching, and considered himself above politics.

The arrogant Premier Francesco Crispi (1819–1901) built political alliances between northern industrialists, who were anticlerical and wanted high tariffs, and southern landowners, who also favored protectionism. Crispi used the army against strikers and demonstrators and used the police to cow opponents daring to organize electoral opposition against him. In 1894, he ordered the disfranchisement of nearly a million voters and banned the Italian Socialist Party. His authoritarian methods angered even the king, who wryly admitted, "Crispi is a pig, but a necessary pig."

In 1901, King Victor Emmanuel III (ruled 1900–1946) signed a decree granting the premier authority over cabinet posts. Upon becoming premier in 1903, Giovanni Giolitti (1842–1928) brought relative stability to Italian political life. Giolitti was a master of *trasformismo,* making party labels essentially meaningless by building a series of makeshift but effective coalitions. Giolitti won the loyalty of enough deputies to remain in office through negotiations, cajoling, promises of jobs and favors, threats, and outright bribery. With the motto "neither revolution nor reaction," the premier's balancing act depended on votes from the anticlerical Radicals, a party based in the north, who supported increased administrative efficiency and liked the premier's opposition to socialism. But Giolitti also depended on southern Catholic moderates, and therefore opposed any land reform on behalf of the rural poor that would break up large estates. His government also had to appease the Church by refusing to meet the anticlerical demands of the Radicals. (In 1904, the Church relaxed its anti-republican stand enough to allow practicing Catholics to vote in elections if their participation would help defeat a Socialist candidate.) Giolitti also sponsored legislation that turned over education in southern Italy to the clergy. The premier left the Mafia and Camorra alone because they could bring him votes in any region or town they controlled, ordering on one occasion the release of more than a thousand *mafiosi* from prison in exchange for their votes.

The Rise of Italian Nationalism

In a country wrought by political division, aggressive nationalism appeared as one means of bringing Italians together. Crispi had favored a policy of forceful colonialization, fearful that Italy would be left out while the other powers snatched up territory (see Chapter 21). He prepared an invasion of the East African state of Abyssinia (now Ethiopia) from the Italian colony of Eritrea in 1896, circumventing parliamentary opposition and refusing to heed the warning of generals that such a move might fail. When the Abyssinian tribesmen Crispi had referred to as "barbarians" crushed the Italian army at Adowa, he resigned. Italian nationalists then began to claim the territory of Trentino in the Austrian Tyrol and the Adriatic port of Trieste as "Unredeemed Italy" (*Italia Irredenta*). In 1911, while Giolitti was premier, Italy launched a war of conquest in Libya, establishing a colony there (see Chapter 22). Giolitti's social reforms had frightened employers and many other conservatives, and the ranks of the anti-parliamentary right swelled. Nationalist candidates demanded further aggressive moves in the Mediterranean. Although the war in Libya went reasonably well for Italian troops, the right objected to the fact that it seemed mismanaged, and the left did not want the invasion at all. Both left and right moved farther away from Giolitti's Liberal center. The Libyan war thus directly undid Giolitti's political system. With the Socialists divided by the Libyan war and unwilling to be "transformed" into temporary political partners, Giolitti now had to turn to Catholic leaders. Giolitti convinced Catholics to support his Liberal candidates if the Liberals agreed to end the campaign against Church schools and for legalized divorce. Angered by Giolitti's promises to the Church, the left tripled its vote, forcing him from office in March 1914. A nationalist proclaimed that the role of his new party was to teach Italians to respect "international struggle," even if the result was war. The Italian liberal state had survived many challenges, but even greater ones lay ahead.

The Unification of Germany

The unification of Germany would not come through liberal auspices. In the German states, too, growing nationalist sentiment existed within the middle class. Yet, as in the case of Italy, there were also formidable obstacles to German unification. First, in the wake of the Revolution of 1848, the upper classes were wary of any change that might threaten the *status quo*. They particularly feared the strong nationalist feeling unleashed by revolution, the extension of which might lead to, they reasoned, the proclamation of the equality of all citizens. Second, it was still not clear around which power, Austria or Prussia, Germany could achieve national unification. Some believed in the "small German" solution in which Prussia might effect German unification and exclude Austria. Other German nationalists supported the "big German" ideal, whereby Austria would dominate an expanded German Confederation. Third, in both Prussia and Austria, the 1850s brought repression that made it clear to most nationalists that German unification would not come under liberal auspices. The repression following the Revolutions of 1848 had scattered thousands of German democrats and socialists across Europe and as far as the United States.

As in the case of Italy, where unification had been achieved primarily through the efforts of one relatively strong and prosperous state, in the German states Prussia held several trump cards toward achieving German unification, including territorial additions in the industrializing Rhineland after the Napoleonic Wars and a relatively strong economic position, which had been bolstered by the Zollverein customs union. Furthermore, Prussia's population was quite homogeneous, as it was almost entirely German-speaking and Protestant. The Prussian royal family, the Hohenzollerns, benefited from the internal stability brought by an effective administrative bureaucracy and were supported by an ambitious, powerful landed nobility, the Junkers, who dominated the officer corps of the Prussian army. Prussia already represented an example of successful statemaking. The expansion of Prussian power therefore seemed to many Prussians to be perfectly natural. Catholic Austria, on the other hand, dominated a multinational population. The Habsburg monarchy had much to lose by the encouragement of national movements that might catch fire among the varied peoples within the imperial boundaries.

All German nationalists, however, did not agree on what political form a unified Germany should take. Most Prussian Junkers had been unrelenting in their opposition to the liberal movements that had championed popular sovereignty during the 1848 revolutions. They rejected the liberalism of Rhineland industrialists, eager to enhance their own political power. Many liberals, particularly republicans from the more liberal southern German states, wanted a unified Germany to have a parliamentary government free from domination by either autocratic, aristocratic Prussia or imperial Austria. Yet, despite Prussia's autocratic and militaristic traditions, some nationalistic republicans still hoped Prussia, not Austria, would lead Germans to unification. Prussian Junkers also feared that if the "big German" plan for unification came to be, their influence would be greatly diluted by Austrian influence. Nonetheless, Austria continued to attract the interest of German nationalists who mistrusted Prussia. Many southern Germans wanted the Habsburg monarchy to champion the cause of the smaller German states, leading to a decentralized federation, not domination by Prussia.

William I, Bismarck, and the Resolution of the Constitutional Crisis

The first step in the unification of Germany was the ascension to power of a monarch equal to the task. In 1858, the pious William I (1797–1888) became regent for his brother, Frederick William IV, who was declared insane. Crowned following Frederick William's death in 1861, William I made clear from the outset of his reign that, unlike his predecessor, he would look beyond the small group of reactionary Prussian Junkers and bring some more moderate conservatives into his cabinet. William I promised to rule constitutionally. Voters—men of at least moderate wealth—responded by turning out in unprecedented numbers to vote. Liberals won a clear victory in the 1858 elections to the Prussian Parliament, which brought to that assembly a good number of men enriched by the economic boom in the early 1850s. Liberals who favored German unification now had a public forum in which to be heard. Many businessmen believed that German unification would be good for them, as the Zollverein customs union had benefited them in the 1840s.

In the meantime, the Austrian war against Piedmont-Sardinia and France in 1859 divided Prussians. Some were torn between dislike for Austria and irritation with French Emperor Napoleon III for helping engineer the outbreak of war. Austria was a member of the German Confederation and had the right to expect assistance from fellow members. But Austria was also Prussia's major rival for power within the German states. Prussia remained neutral in the war, but Italy's move toward unification greatly impressed German nationalists. Those who looked to Prussia to forge German unity welcomed Austria's defeat.

In 1858, several "Pan-German" associations had been formed as pressure groups supporting German unification. The largest and most influential, the National Union (*Nationalverein*), wanted a constitutional and parliamentary German state. The Prussian government remained suspicious of the National Union because many of its members favored the extension of political freedom within the German states. As in the old Frankfurt Parliament, its members were overwhelmingly middle class, including intellectuals, lawyers, officials, and small businessmen, but also included several industrialists. The National Union rebuffed an attempt by workers' organizations to join in 1863, but contributed to the resurgence of political liberalism within Prussia by demanding an effective constitution that would limit the domination of the monarchy and the Junkers.

The question of army reform raised the issue of parliamentary control over the budget. The Prussian constitutional crisis that followed became a critical step in the unification of Germany along lines that turned out to be anything but liberal. The Prussian military mobilization in 1859 during the Austrian war against Piedmont and

William I.

France had revealed serious inadequacies in the Prussian army. The minister of war proposed expensive reforms of the army: expansion of the officer corps, increasing the number of recruits, and an extension of the time of service to three years. Prussian liberals wanted all citizens to serve in the army, but also hoped that the National Guard (*Landwehr*) would replace the professional, Junker-dominated army as the foundation of the Prussian military, thus forging a link between the army and the people.

The Prussian Parliament did not enjoy many prerogatives in autocratic Prussia, but it did have the right to approve new taxes. In response to government pressure, in 1861 the parliament, despite its liberal majority, passed a provisional bill that gave the army the money it needed until the reform could be considered. Liberal approval of the provisional bill was a fateful event in German history because it provided parliamentary sanction to the virtually unchallenged power of the Prussian army.

Some leaders among the liberal opposition then formed the German Progressive Party. Liberals declined to vote for the new military budget when the minister of war refused compromise. After William dismissed parliament, new elections returned another liberal majority, which rejected a second army budget. Seeking to overcome parliamentary opposition, the king turned to a strong-willed and intransigently conservative Junker, Count Otto von Bismarck (1815–1898), appointing him prime minister in 1862.

Bismarck was the son of a dull Junker father and a lively, intelligent mother from a family of middle-class bureaucrats. In his Berlin school, Bismarck was more noted for dueling scars earned in student fraternities than for academic success. After receiving his law degree, he passed the entrance examination for the Prussian bureaucracy. Bismarck was appointed Prussian representative to the German Confederation in Frankfurt in 1851. He was sent to Saint Petersburg as ambassador in 1859, perhaps to mute his noisy denunciations of Austria.

As prime minister of Prussia, Bismarck was convinced that he could create a new German state that would not be too large for Prussia to dominate, nor too democratic for the tradition of the Hohenzollern monarchy. He wanted to create a modern, bureaucratic state that would be strong and secular. He cleverly used political parties when it suited his purposes. For the next three decades, he doggedly held on to personal power. Bismarck's shrewd manipulation of domestic and international politics dominated relations among the European powers. The "iron chancellor" patiently made uncanny assessments of every possible option and then moved with determination to strengthen Prussia's position. Bismarck's type of politics came to be known as *Realpolitik,* the pursuit of a nation's self-interest based on a realistic assessment of the costs and consequences of action. Inherent in *Realpolitik* was an absence of moral or ethical considerations, overrun by Bismarck's unshakable determination to enhance the power of the Prussian monarchy and nobility, and therefore of Germany.

Bismarck was a very complex man, both a man of iron and one easily moved to tears. He once said of himself: "Faust complains of having two souls in his breast. I have a whole squabbling crowd. It goes on as in a republic." A large man, he looked like a senior military officer stuffed into a uniform that was too small. At times outgoing and charming, Bismarck could also lapse into moods of intense, gloomy isolation. He was unforgiving toward those who crossed him: "If I have an enemy in my power, I must destroy him." He once said that he sometimes spent whole nights hating. Bismarck could never contain his disdain for parliamentary liberalism: "The position of Prussia in Germany will be determined not by its liberalism but by its power. . . . Not through speeches and majority decisions are the great questions of the day decided—that was the great mistake of 1848 and 1849—but through blood and iron."

Bismarck now announced that the government would operate without constitutional authorization. It did so for four years, using tax money previously voted to finance army reforms. In June 1863, Bismarck struck against the liberal Progressives by restricting freedom of the press, refusing to confirm the election of Progressive mayors, and banning discussion of political issues in municipal council meetings. The fact that both public opinion and even Crown Prince Frederick William opposed these measures did not dissuade him in the least. Nor did the election of even more liberals to the parliament in October 1863. In the meantime, Bismarck's stridently anti-Austrian policy helped split the liberal parliamentary opposition.

Alliances and Warfare to Establish Prussian Leadership

Russia and France were the two powers that would be most threatened by a unified Germany. The 1863 Polish revolt against Russian domination presented Bismarck with a perfect opportunity to ingratiate himself to the tsar. Whereas the other major powers sympathized with the Poles, Bismarck immediately voiced support for Russia. "Hit the Poles so hard that they despair for their lives," Bismarck advised. The Prussian government then signed an agreement with Russia, in which they agreed to assist each other in pursuing insurgents across their respective frontiers. Austria, which also had a sizable Polish population within its borders, found its relations with Russia soured.

Bismarck's first war was fought against the Danes in 1864 over Schleswig-Holstein, two duchies that included the Baltic port of Kiel (see Map 17.2). British Prime Minister Lord Palmerston (Henry John Temple, 1784–1865) once said that only three men truly understood the problem of Schleswig-Holstein: one was dead, one had gone mad, and the third, Palmerston himself, had forgotten it all. The duchies were ruled by the king of Denmark although not incorporated as part of the kingdom of Denmark. Holstein, which lies between Prussia and Schleswig, was almost entirely German-speaking and belonged to the

MAP 17.2 THE UNIFICATION OF GERMANY, 1866–1871 The unification of Germany by Prussia included territory acquired after the Austro-Prussian War (1866) and the Franco-Prussian War (1870–1871).

German Confederation, whereas both German and Danish speakers lived in Schleswig, which was not part of the Confederation. In 1848, the king of Denmark had declared the union of Schleswig with Denmark, and revolution broke out in both duchies. The Danish army occupied Schleswig. During the summer, a Prussian army on behalf of the German Confederation intervened in defense of the revolutionary provisional government in Holstein, which demanded autonomy. International opinion (particularly in Britain and Russia) rallied to the cause of the Danes. After some fighting, the Prussian forces withdrew. Following Swedish mediation, the provisional government of Holstein was dissolved by the Armistice of Malmö (August 1848). Although they were administered by a Danish-German commission, the two duchies essentially retained their former status. Prussia's defeat seemed a defeat for the cause of German nationalism. A small war followed in 1849–1850 between Prussian and Danish troops, ended by another armistice that left the status of Schleswig and Holstein up in the air.

Prussian coastal battery during the war against Denmark, 1864.

The London Protocol of 1852 placed Schleswig-Holstein under the authority of the Danish king, but forbade their incorporation into Denmark. In March 1863, however, the Danish king enacted a new constitution that seemed to incorporate Schleswig into his kingdom. Bismarck, capitalizing on the wave of nationalistic support, then found an ally in Austria. Prussia issued Denmark an ultimatum in January 1864, demanding that the new constitution for Schleswig be redrawn. The Danish government, incorrectly assuming that because of Schleswig's strategic importance, France and Britain would rush to its defense, rejected the ultimatum and found itself at war with Prussia and Austria. To no one's surprise, the Danes were easily beaten. The Treaty of Vienna (October 1864) established the joint administration of Schleswig-Holstein by Prussia and Austria—Austria would administer Holstein, and Prussia would administer Schleswig. This awkward arrangement left Prussia with a military corridor and communications line through Austrian-controlled Holstein and use of the port of Kiel.

Bismarck now viewed a military showdown with Austria as inevitable, even desirable. Yet, while preparing for that eventuality by currying the favor of the smaller German states and working to isolate Austria further from the other European powers, he blithely tried—and failed—to tempt Austria into making an agreement that would formally divide their influence in the German states into north-south spheres. Bismarck persuaded Napoleon III that France would receive territorial compensation in the Rhineland if it would stay out of an Austro-Prussian war. The French emperor tried to play both sides. Convinced that Austria could defeat Prussia, he signed a secret treaty with the Habsburg monarchy that would give the French Venetia and establish a French protectorate in the Rhineland after an Austrian victory.

Bismarck then drew Italy into a secret alliance, signed in April 1866, by promising it Venetia in the event of a Habsburg defeat. Italy promised Prussia assistance if there was war with Austria, knowing that a Prussian victory would add the last large chunk of the Italian peninsula to Italy (see p. 657).

Exaggerating reports of Austria's military preparations, Bismarck denounced Austria's "seditious agitation" against Prussia in Schleswig-Holstein. After Bismarck had secured the temporary alliance with Italy and assured France's neutrality, Prussian troops entered Holstein. Austria allied with some of the smaller states (including Hanover, Saxony, and Hesse-Kassel) of the German Confederation. Prussia left the German Confederation, which then voted under Austria's leadership to send troops against the Prussian army.

Within three weeks, Prussian troops had defeated the South German and Hanoverian armies in the Austro-Prussian War (1866). The Prussian army bested the Austrian forces in the Battle of Sadowa (or Königgrätz) in eastern Bohemia on July 3, 1866. Almost 1 million soldiers fought in the battle. Superior military planning as well as the rapid mobilization, deployment, and concentration of troops, talented officers, and more modern weapons— particularly the breech-loading "needle gun"—brought the Prussian army success.

The North German Confederation

In the aftermath of a victory most people did not expect, Bismarck restrained the Prussian officer corps, many of whom wanted to push on to Vienna. Bismarck realized that he would ultimately need the support of the South German states, some of whom had been allied with Austria, if Germany was to be unified under Prussian auspices. Moreover, the chancellor did not want to provide France or Russia with an opportunity to enter the conflict. The Treaty of Prague (August 1866) eliminated Austria as a rival for the domination of the German states. The German Confederation was dissolved. The Habsburg monarchy recognized the North German Confederation (see Map 17.2), a new union of twenty-two states and principalities north of the Main River, with a constitution and a parliament (Reichstag), which Prussia would dominate with William I as president and Bismarck as federal chancellor. Bavaria signed an alliance promising to join Prussia if it were attacked by France, which had been alarmed by the relatively easy Prussian victory. Schleswig-Holstein became part of Prussia. By virtue of the annexation of Hanover, Frankfurt, Nassau, and Hesse-Kassel, Prussia was no longer divided into two separate provinces. The Berlin government intimidated, bribed, or cajoled these smaller states into compliance.

Bismarck left no doubt that he considered the North German Confederation a provisional solution until Germany could be united under Prussian leadership. In the meantime, the old Zollverein customs union, which included the South German states, was expanded to include an assembly of elected delegates. Bismarck received support from Prussian businessmen who would profit from the removal of customs barriers and the centralization of railway networks. As long as unification brought material progress, it did not seem to matter to them that the traditional class system and restricted political life that characterized Prussia would form the basis of a united Germany. Bismarck was the man of the hour, the Prussian state a dynamic force with which to be reckoned.

Bismarck's bitter quarrel with the liberals over the military budget disappeared in the enthusiasm. Some members of the Progressive Party and other liberals still espoused "a vigilant and loyal opposition" at home. But liberal newspapers willingly accepted the triumphs of Prussian foreign policy and military might. Some liberals were so elated by the prospect of German unification that they left the more hesitant Progressive Party and formed the nationalistic National Liberal Party, which supported Bismarck. At the same time, some of the South German states were moving closer to Prussia through economic and military alliances.

The Franco-Prussian War and German Unification

Prussian victory in the Franco-Prussian War of 1870–1871 completed the unification of the German states, with the exception of Austria. Napoleon III foolishly seized upon the issue of the Hohenzollern candidacy for the vacant Spanish throne as an occasion to go to war against Prussia. Bismarck fanned the embers of the crisis he had hoped would lead to a war he considered inevitable and necessary. His carefully planned diplomacy was never more evident. The Russian tsar warmly remembered Prussian support during the Polish rebellion of 1863. The Austrian government had not forgiven France for joining Piedmont-Sardinia in the war of 1859. Italy still resented the loss of Savoy and Nice in 1860 to France. Bismarck played his real trump card with the British, coolly revealing documents proving that the French emperor had in 1866 demanded Belgium and Luxembourg as compensation for Prussia's increased power. This ended any chance of support for Napoleon III by the British government, which would never tolerate a potentially hostile power in Belgium. France went alone to war against Prussia. Following the surrender of French armies at the end of August and the beginning of September, Prussian forces besieged Paris. French resistance continued until January 28, 1871 (see Chapter 18).

Bismarck signed a convention with the provisional French government, awaiting the election of a National Assembly in France that could conclude a peace treaty. Bolstered by a surge of nationalist sentiment in the South German states as well as in Prussia, Bismarck demanded the annexation of Alsace, where German speakers predominated (although they did not necessarily want to be incorporated into a united Germany), and much of Lorraine.

The German Empire was officially proclaimed at Versailles on January 18, 1871. King William I of Prussia became Emperor William I of Germany. The North German Confederation and its constitution provided the framework for German unification. The German Empire took on the auto-

Prussian troops move to cut a French railway line in the Franco-Prussian War.

cratic political structure of Prussia, dominated by Prussian nobles and military officers. For their part, industrialists and merchants trusted that unification would provide a boost to large-scale industrialization in the new Germany. Hamburg merchants thus traded the traditional independence of their city for the economic advantages of operating within a centralized state. Bismarck had harnessed economic liberalism to the goals of conservative political nationalism. Although many Germans remained indifferent to unification and others preferred the particularism of their region, over the long run, most Germans came to accept with growing enthusiasm the politically unified state that had been forged by Bismarck's spectacularly successful statemaking. The result was a critical shift in the balance of power in Europe.

The empire had a parliament, but the Reichstag had little real authority. Its members, elected by a franchise system that in Prussia grossly over-represented landed interests, could not hold cabinet posts. The chancellor was responsible not to the Reichstag, but rather to the emperor. The Reichstag could not propose legislation. Foreign policy and military affairs remained in the hands of the emperor and the chancellor. The Reichstag's control over the budget could not limit the prerogatives of the throne. Each of Germany's twenty-five states sent a delegate to a federal council (*Bundesrat*), over which the chancellor presided. Although each German

William I and Bismarck celebrate the proclamation of the German Empire in the Hall of Mirrors at Versailles.

state—for example, Bavaria, which had a relatively liberal constitution—retained considerable administrative autonomy, as well as in some cases its own prince, the nature of the German imperial government remained authoritarian. Germany's growing economic power was therefore unaccompanied by the evolution toward effective parliamentary government that characterized Britain and then France, as well as to some extent Italy.

Junkers dominated the army and civil service. In exchange for loyalty, they were exempt from most taxation, receiving what amounted to state subsidies for their immense estates. Inevitably, as in England, noble economic clout declined with the agricultural depression and with the remarkably rapid industrialization of Germany, but Prussian Junkers retained their full measure of political power.

Unlike their counterparts in Victorian England and France, the German middle class largely remained outside political life in the German Empire, as they had been in Prussia before unification. Most middle-class Germans willingly acquiesced to imperial authority and noble influence. The subsequent rise of the German Social Democratic Party, founded in 1875 (see Chapter 20), was, in most cases, enough to keep the German middle class loyal to the empire.

Nationalist versus Internationalist Movements

Chancellor Bismarck hated the Catholic Center and Social Democratic parties, doubting their loyalty. The Catholic Center Party was founded in 1870 to lobby for the rights of Catholics, who made up 35 percent of the German population, most living in Bavaria and the Rhineland. In 1870, the pope asserted the doctrine of papal infallibility. To Bismarck, this meant that one day the pontiff might simply order German Catholics to not obey the government. In 1873, Bismarck launched a state campaign against Catholics, the *Kulturkampf* ("cultural struggle"). Priests in Germany henceforth had to complete a secular curriculum in order to be ordained, and the state would now recognize only civil marriage. Subsequent laws permitted the expulsion from Germany of members of the Catholic clergy who refused to abide by discriminatory laws against Catholics. An assassination attempt against Bismarck by a young Catholic in 1874 and papal condemnation of the *Kulturkampf* the following year only hardened the chancellor's resolve.

Gradually, however, Bismarck realized that he might in the future need the support of the Catholic Center Party against the Social Democrats. The chancellor quietly abandoned the *Kulturkampf,* although Catholics were still systematically excluded from high civil service positions, as were Jews. The state helped German Protestants purchase bankrupt estates in Prussian Poland so that they would not fall into the hands of Catholics, who made up most of the population there. Alsace and the parts of Lorraine annexed from France, where Catholics formed a solid majority, were administered directly from Berlin instead of being considered a separate state of the Reich.

Bismarck became obsessed with destroying the socialists, who improved their gains in the elections, although they still held only a couple of seats in the Reichstag. Two attempts to kill Emperor William I in 1878 provided Bismarck with an excuse for his war on the socialists, although neither would-be assassin had even the slightest contact with socialist leaders. The Reichstag obliged Bismarck by passing antisocialist legislation that denied socialists the freedoms of assembly, association, and the press. The police arrested socialists, shut down their newspapers and periodicals, and intimidated workers into quitting trade unions.

A contemporary image of Bismarck pitted against the pope in the German chancelor's campaign against German Catholics.

William II and German Nationalism

Following William I's death, Frederick III, a man of foresight and tolerance, reigned for only 100 days, tragically dying of throat cancer. In 1888, William II (ruled 1888–1918) became emperor. William held that "a society is only strong if it recognizes the fact of natural superiorities, in particular that of birth." He boasted, "We Hohenzollerns derive our crowns from Heaven alone and are answerable only to Heaven."

The German emperor compensated for a withered left arm with a love of military uniforms and swords. His education had proceeded in a hit-or-miss fashion that mostly missed. William's favorite reading included the pseudo-scientific racist ramblings of the English writer Houston Stewart Chamberlain. William II considered himself an expert on military affairs, but was not. He was lazy, yet talked at great length superficially about any conceivable subject, rushing to conclusions without reflection. His lack of tact—he invariably referred to the diminutive King Victor Emmanuel III of Italy as "that dwarf"—was a common topic of conversation in imperial circles.

Bismarck lasted two years as William's chancellor. When Bismarck in 1890 sought a pretext to launch another campaign of repression against the Social Democrats, the emperor, wanting to cultivate as much popularity as possible, preferred to win mass support by sponsoring more legislation that would improve working conditions. After an unpleasant confrontation, Bismarck resigned.

William II (*left*) and Emperor Francis Joseph of Austria-Hungary (*right*).

The iron chancellor's less able successors were unable to keep William from impulsively antagonizing Germany's rivals. The emperor's personal foibles became increasingly important as international relations entered a new and dangerous stage. He personally contributed to the rise of aggressive German nationalism and the Anglo-German naval rivalry. William zipped around Germany and the North Sea eagerly reviewing troops and christening ships. He enthusiastically supported the expansionist goals of the Pan-German and Naval Leagues. He asserted, "I believe, as it is written in the

Bible, that it is my duty to increase [the German heritage] for which one day I shall be called upon to give an account to God. Whoever tries to interfere with my task I shall crush."

The alliance between Conservatives, National Liberals, and the Catholic Center Party provided the German emperor with a conservative base within the Reichstag. The National Liberals wanted a strong, secular state, and mistrusted parliamentary democracy. The resulting alliance between industrialists and agriculturists ("iron and rye") led to protectionist economic policies that began in 1879 and culminated in 1902 with a tariff that imposed a 25 percent duty on manufacturing and food imports. Liberalism continued to be closely tied to the defense of small-town interests.

In the meantime, the German conservatives became increasingly nationalistic and anti-Semitic. Following the economic crash of 1873, two years after Jews had received full legal emancipation with the proclamation of the empire, newspapers selected Jewish bankers, industrialists, and rival publishers as scapegoats. The operatic composer Richard Wagner and his circle of friends were outspokenly anti-Semitic. Wagner believed that the theater (and composers) stood as a center of German emotional national culture, which he did not believe included Jews. Some Germans identified Jews with liberalism and socialism. In 1892, the German Conservative Party made anti-Semitism part of its party platform, despite the fact that most Jews were fully assimilated into German society. A Jewish industrialist remembered in 1911 that "in the youth of every German Jew there comes a painful moment that he never forgets, the moment when he realizes for the first time that he has entered the world as a second-class citizen and that neither his efforts nor his accomplishments will free him from this status."

Yet, the Social Democrats won more seats in the Reichstag in 1912 than any other party. But many Social Democrats also were engulfed by the mood of aggressive nationalism that swept much of Germany, heightened by rivalry with Great Britain and by the Second Moroccan Crisis of 1911, which brought Germany and France close to war (see Chapter 22). Socialist deputies voted for the prodigious augmentation of funds for naval expansion, but did so in part because the issue of direct versus indirect taxation was at stake, and they wanted to establish the principle of direct taxation so as to end the tax privileges of wealthy families. Unlike French or Italian socialists, German socialists manifested little anti-militarism, giving every sign that they would support the government in time of war, particularly against Russia. The German Empire embodied the decline of liberalism and the rise of aggressive nationalism in late nineteenth-century Europe.

NATIONAL AWAKENINGS IN THE HABSBURG LANDS

Whereas Germany and Italy were politically unified when astute leaders mobilized nationalist feeling within the upper classes and successfully carried out an aggressive foreign policy, nationalism threatened the very existence of the Habsburg monarchy. Ethnic tensions within the Austro-Hungarian Empire, the second largest European state, were in many ways those of Europe itself. In the meantime, the unification of Germany, as well as that of Italy, altered the balance of power in Central Europe. Unified Germany, not Austria, was now unquestionably the strongest state in Central Europe. Moreover, the absorption of Lombardy and Venetia into the new Italian state had come at the expense of the Austrian Habsburgs.

Diversity and Cohesion in the Habsburg Empire

The provinces that formed the Habsburg domains represented extraordinary linguistic, cultural, and historical diversity (see Map 17.3). Eleven

MAP 17.3 NATIONALITIES IN THE HABSBURG EMPIRE   The diverse nationalities and lands encompassed by the Habsburg Empire during the 1860s and 1870s.

TABLE 17.1. ETHNIC COMPOSITION OF THE AUSTRO-HUNGARIAN EMPIRE IN 1910 (IN MILLIONS)

Ethnic Group	Population	Ethnic Group	Population
Germans	12.0	Serbs	2.0
Magyars	10.1	Slovaks	2.0
Czechs	6.6	Slovenes	1.4
Poles	5.0	Italians	0.8
Ukrainians	4.0	Bosnian Muslims	0.6
Romanians	3.2	Others	0.4
Croats	2.9		

major nationalities lived within the territorial boundaries of the empire; these included Czechs in Bohemia and Slovaks to their east; Poles in Galicia; Slovenes, Croats, Muslim Bosnians, and Serbs in the Balkans; Romanians and Ukrainians in the southeast; and Italians in the Alpine Tyrol, as well as Jews and Gypsies. But by far the two largest national groups were the Germans (35 percent of the population), living principally in Austria but numerous also in Bohemia, and the Hungarians, or Magyars (23 percent). The traditional Hungarian crown lands formed the largest territory in the empire, divided into Hungary, Croatia, Transylvania, the Vojvodina, and the Military Frontier. Yet the Germans and Hungarians were outnumbered by the various Slavic groups, who together accounted for about 45 percent of the empire's population. Czechs comprised 23 percent of Austria's population. In Hungary, Romanians (with 19 percent of the population) formed the next largest group after the Magyars (see Table 17.1). Inadequate transportation networks accentuated the insular and overwhelmingly rural nature of many ethnic regions—for example, there was no railroad between Vienna and the Croatian capital of Zagreb.

How did this polyglot empire hold together as long as it did among all of the competing ethnic rivalries and demands? The answers tell us something of the process of statemaking from the point of view of the nonnational state. First, the tradition of the Habsburg monarchy itself was an important force for cohesion, rooted in centuries of Central European history. Emperor Francis Joseph, who was eighteen when he came to power in 1848, had taken the second part of his name from his enlightened ancestor Joseph II to invoke the tradition of the House of Habsburg in those revolutionary times. As a Hungarian statesman put it during the Revolutions of 1848, "It was not the idea of unity that had saved the monarchy, but the idea of the monarchy that saved unity."

Second, the Habsburgs depended on the support of the German middle class and of the enormous German-speaking bureaucracy. The most salient cultural traditions (for example, music) of the imperial capital, Vienna, were overwhelmingly German. Viennese liberals celebrated their domination of

Austrian political and cultural life during the 1850s and 1860s by building a broad modern boulevard, the Ringstrasse. The grand artery was built on the traces of the city's fortifications, which Francis Joseph had ordered dismantled in 1857, since they had long since lost all military function except to separate the wealthy center of the city from the proletarian suburbs. The new boulevard also took shape with military motives in mind—troops could be moved rapidly in the event of a working-class rebellion. The architecture of central Vienna reflected the taste of the aristocracy and the Catholic Church. In contrast, public buildings (including the university, the opera, and the parliament building) and residences of manufacturers and bankers that bordered the Ringstrasse reflected the secular cultural tastes of the Viennese upper classes.

The empire's largest Czech and Austrian towns were largely German-speaking; in Prague, Germans outnumbered Czechs by more than three to one, although the percentage of Germans there declined during the second half of the century with the migration of more Czechs to the city. German was also the official language of the army (and of the secret police). To get anywhere, one had to speak German, a fact learned by non-German migrants to the cities. The German middle class also benefited from free-trade policies, and profited from the beginnings of industrial concentration in Bohemia.

Third, the monarchy enjoyed the support of Austrian and Hungarian nobles, as well as their Croatian, Polish, and Italian counterparts, landed nobles of ethnic groups with long histories of political sovereignty. The latter three nobilities depended on the Habsburg monarchy to maintain their

A view of Vienna and its Ringstrasse, 1873.

prerogatives vis-à-vis ethnic minorities within their territories and against the peasants of their own nationality. Thus, the small Croatian nobility, which needed the cooperation of the Habsburgs for the retention of their own privileges in Croatia, had a long tradition of military service to the dynasty. (In 1868, Croatia received semi-autonomous status within the empire.) The monarchy therefore depended on the preservation of the status of the favored nationalities, above all, the Germans and Magyars, from the challenges of other national minorities within the lands of their domination, such as Slovenes, Slovaks, Ukrainians, Serbs, and Czechs.

Fourth, Catholicism, the religion of the majority of the peoples of the Habsburg domains, was another factor for unity in Austria. The centuries-old support of the Catholic Church for the Habsburg dynasty also undercut nationalist movements among predominantly Catholic nationalities like the Slovaks, Croats, and above all, the Poles. In the newly unified Germany, by contrast, the religious division between the Protestant north and the Catholic south represented at least a potential force for disunity.

Fifth, the imperial army retained considerable prestige (although, lacking adequate funds, it had proved more dashing on the parade ground than on the battlefield, as defeats by the French in 1859 and the Prussians in 1866 had demonstrated). The army helped hold the monarchy together. German speakers dominated the officer corps, as they did the bureaucracy, holding 70 percent of military positions. Habsburg officers prided themselves on an esprit de corps (addressing each other by the familiar *Du* form, and not the more formal *Sie* that persisted in the German army). Soldiers drawn from the different nationalities continued to serve loyally in the army, which rarely intervened in local strikes, in contrast to the situation in France, where the army was unpopular with workers. Francis Joseph, whose long rule was shaped by the fact that he had come to power as his monarchy seemed to be breaking apart, was as devoted to the army as it was to him.

Repression of Nationalism in the Habsburg Empire

In the 1850s and 1860s, nationalism among the ethnic minorities remained limited to a relatively small number of intellectuals and people from the liberal professions, particularly Poles and Hungarians. As a Czech nationalist put it at a meeting of writers in Prague, "If the ceiling were to fall on us now, that would be the end of the national movement." Most nationalists at first aimed at a cultural and linguistic revival.

The Habsburg monarchy feared that demands for autonomy, or even outright independence, would pull the empire apart. Nationalism, which had frequently been tied to political liberalism, could also challenge the empire's authoritarian structure. The success of German and Italian nationalism also threatened the empire's territorial integrity by raising the possibility that the very small Italian and, above all, the German-speaking parts of the empire might prefer inclusion in Italy or Germany, respectively.

Alexander von Bach

Furthermore, Hungarians, the second-largest ethnic group within the empire, demanded political influence commensurate with the size of the Magyar territorial domains.

After the mid-century revolutions, the Habsburg monarchy, like the German states and France, continued an unrelenting repression of liberal and national movements. Beginning with Francis Joseph's accession to the Habsburg throne, the monarchy entered a period of "neo-absolutism," codified in the "Patent" of December 1851. Alexander von Bach (1813–1893), the minister of the interior (and essentially prime minister without the title), put some of the most potent tools of the state to work, including a hierarchy of officials and police sent out from Vienna into the imperial provinces. The nobles, some of whom resented the abrogation of peasant obligations after 1848, in general welcomed the restoration of Habsburg authoritarianism. But they also had lost some of their regional privileges and prerogatives to the state.

In 1855, Bach signed a Concordat with the Catholic Church, restoring many of its privileges and extending ecclesiastical authority, including the right of prelates to judge the clergy. As in France, the Church made a comeback. The monarchy eliminated civil marriage and restored the Church's *de facto* control over education. Protestants were not allowed to teach in Catholic schools, and new restrictions limited the right of Jews to acquire property. A contemporary cynically described the Bach system: "The administration was run by a standing army of soldiers, a kneeling one of those praying in church to be acceptable to the government, and a crawling one of informers."

Political Crisis and Foreign Policy Disasters

In the wake of the defeat of Austrian forces in Italy and amid mounting hostility between Germans and non-Germans and the growing unpopularity of neo-absolutism, in August 1859 Francis Joseph dismissed Bach as the head of government. He then promulgated a new constitution, the October Diploma of 1860, which reestablished a form of conservative federalism. The provincial assemblies received new authority, placating the nobles. Nonetheless, the October Diploma did not satisfy the Hungarian aristocrats, who lacked the influence and political role enjoyed by German speakers who had benefited from the Bach system.

Anton von Schmerling (1805–1893), minister of the interior, drafted the February Patent of 1861, a constitution that established a bicameral parliament in which all the empire's nationalities were to be represented. Yet the number of non-German representatives, as elected by the diets of the respective crown lands, would not equal those of the Germans, as electoral restrictions favored urban elites. Magyars, Croats, and Italians refused to participate in the first election, and Schmerling dissolved the regional parliaments. The February Patent perpetuated the most salient elements of Bach's neo-absolutism, placing virtually no constitutional limitations on the emperor's power. Francis Joseph even suspended the constitution in 1865.

While Bach's neo-absolutism made internal enemies, foreign policy failures seriously undermined the monarchy's international position. The Habsburg monarchy's status as a power in European affairs declined as relations with Russia and Prussia deteriorated. In 1863, Schmerling expressed sympathy for the Poles in their struggle against Russia (in contrast to Bismarck's response, as we have seen). This pleased the Poles within the Habsburg Empire but angered Tsar Alexander II. When Francis Joseph went to war with Prussia in 1866, he could not look for support from the tsar, or from the British or French, who resented the fact that Austria had joined Prussia against Denmark two years earlier.

Prussia's victory over Austria cast doubt on the efficiency of Bach's neo-absolutism and encouraged the other preeminent nationalities—particularly the Magyars, but also the Croats and Poles—to demand a greater share of political power, since the monarchy seemed to be floundering under the domination of German speakers. Humiliated twice in seven years on the field of battle, some of Francis Joseph's subjects blamed the authoritarian structure of neo-absolutism for the defeat. Liberals called for the implementation of constitutional government.

Creation of the Dual Monarchy

The empire's military defeats heightened Magyar demands for more power. Fearing the possible alliance of German liberals with the Magyars, Francis Joseph in 1865, a year before the defeat at the hands of Prussia, met the Magyar demand for the reincorporation of Transylvania into Hungary. He had already asked Ferenc Deák (1803–1876) to propose a solution that would reconcile Magyar demands with imperial power. Deák, a wealthy Magyar noble and lawyer, believed that Hungary's identity as a nation depended on the continued existence of the Habsburg monarchy. The emperor realized that as long as the Magyars remained dissatisfied and uncooperative, he could not contemplate a war of revenge against Prussia.

The Compromise (*Ausgleich*) of 1867 created the Dual Monarchy of Austria-Hungary. The Hungarian Parliament proclaimed Francis Joseph constitutional king of Hungary, as well as emperor of Austria. The bureaucracy in Vienna would continue to carry out matters of finance, foreign policy, and defense. Hungarian now became the language of administration in Hungary, and the Magyar domains henceforth had their own constitution, parliament, and bureaucracy. The halves of the Dual Monarchy would negotiate economic tariffs every ten years. The parliaments of Austria and Hungary elected representatives to the Imperial Assembly, or Delegation.

The *Ausgleich* left intact the dominance of German speakers in Austria and of Magyars in Hungary. While in principle recognizing the equality of all nationalities, the new constitution nonetheless maintained the disproportionate advantage enjoyed by Austria's Germans in the Austrian Imperial Council (Reichsrat) in Vienna. The emperor routinely appointed Germans to important ministries, and he could easily circumvent parliamentary opposition by ruling by decree when parliament was not in session, or by refusing to sign any piece of legislation he did not like.

The Hungarian Constitution of 1867 allowed the Magyar nobles to hold sway in the Hungarian Parliament, since the emperor's powers as king of Hungary were now more limited. Hungarian ministers were not responsible to Francis Joseph, but rather to the Hungarian Parliament's lower house, which was elected by leading Magyar property owners. Thus the *Ausgleich* was a victory for Hungarian liberalism. The Nationality Law of 1868 gave the peoples of each nationality the right to their own language in schools, church, and in government offices, but it did not recognize any separate political ethnic identity. The Croats and the South Slavs particularly resented the settlement. Growing tensions were reflected by the claim of one of the Austrian architects of the *Ausgleich* that "the Slavs are not fit to govern; they must be ruled." Many Serbs increasingly identified with Russia, which saw itself as the protector of all Slavs.

Ethnic Tensions and Nationalist Movements in the Dual Monarchy

In Austria-Hungary, ethnic tensions generated continued political division, stemming principally from Hungarian resentment of Austrian preeminence within the Dual Monarchy and the demands of subordinate nationalities. Beginning in the 1870s, Croatia, which was technically part of Hungary, sent five representatives to the sixty-member imperial Delegation, while the Slovaks, Serbs, and other minorities were left out. The Hungarian government relentlessly carried on with a program of Magyarization, ranging from dissolving non-Magyar cultural societies to banning non-Magyar names for villages and streets. Hungarian remained the official language and the government refused to allow administrative or cultural autonomy of the other nationalities. To an extent, the Magyarization campaign in Hungary was a reaction by Hungarians to this growing Pan-Slavist movement, combined with Hungary's resentment of its junior status in the Dual Monarchy.

Count Eduard von Taaffe (1833–1895), Austrian prime minister from 1879 to 1893, balanced off the competing interests of the varied nationalities. Czech nobles and intellectuals earlier in the century had worked toward a literary and linguistic revival,

An image in a Pan-Slav journal published in Vienna, *Slavic Papers*.

compiling and publishing Czech dictionaries and books of Czech grammar. Czech nationalists demanded recognition of the historic Kingdom of Bohemia. But opposition from German speakers in Bohemia, and from Magyars, who feared similar demands from minorities within Hungary, led Francis Joseph to refuse such recognition. While ignoring demands by Slovenes and other smaller national groups for concessions to their languages, Taaffe placated the Czechs, the third largest ethnic group, by declaring their language on an equal footing with German in the state administration in Bohemia and Moravia in 1880. He also encouraged Czech schools and established a university in Prague (1882). But intellectuals within the "Young Czech" movement wanted national independence. In 1893 Taaffe resigned over the issue of increasing the number of eligible voters in Austria. One of his successors would later resign after the government had to declare martial law when Czechs demonstrated against the withdrawal of an edict, following protests by German speakers, that ordered officials to know both German and Czech.

As movements of cultural nationalism grew, they almost inevitably added the goal of national independence. Since the Third Partition in 1795, Poles had been a subject people in the empires of Germany, Austria-Hungary, and Russia, where troops had crushed the Polish insurrection of 1863 (see Chapter 18). Polish nationalism revived during the 1880s, but the relatively favored position of Poles in Austrian Galicia (where they held sway over Ukrainians in eastern Galicia) and the dispersion of the Polish people in three empires reduced any immediate Polish threat to the Habsburgs.

The absorption in 1878 of Bosnia and Herzegovina into the Habsburg Empire added a large Serb, as well as Muslim, population at a time when the Pan-Slav movement was growing in Russia and the Balkans. This increased demands from South Slavs—principally Serbs, Croats, and some Slovenes—that they be allowed to form an integral third part of the monarchy. Serbia had been virtually independent within the Ottoman Empire since 1828, when a Serb official who had put down a Serb insurrection was named hereditary prince of Serbia. Now, with Serbia's independence formalized in 1878, many Serbs in Austria-Hungary wanted to be attached to Serbia.

Hungarians demanded that their language be put on an equal footing with German in the army. At the turn of the century, Emperor Francis Joseph threatened to dissolve Hungary's parliament and to declare universal suffrage, believing that giving in to Hungarian demands would have meant the end of the Dual Monarchy. Relations between the aging Habsburg emperor and the Hungarian Parliament deteriorated, just as the Balkan Wars (1912–1913; see Chapter 22) and rampant South Slav nationalism soured relations between the Austro-Hungarian Empire and Russia. A visitor to the lower house of the Austrian Parliament in March 1914 recalled in amazement: "About a score of men, all decently clad, were seated or standing, each at his little desk. Some made an infernal noise violently opening and shutting the lids of these desks. Others emitted a blaring sound from little toy trumpets; others strummed Jew's harps; still others beat snare drums. . . . The sum of uproar thus produced was so infernal that it completely drowned the voice of a man who was evidently talking from his seat in another part of the house, for one could see his lips moving, and the veins in his temple swelling. Bedlam let loose! That was the impression on the whole."

CONCLUSION

The unification of Italy and that of Germany had both largely been effected by the expansion of the most powerful of the states that would become part of the unified state that resulted. Yet the two cases were different, despite appearances. Camillo di Cavour first had transformed Piedmont-Sardinia into a liberal monarchy through reforms, before achieving the unification of Italy. Liberal Italy then struggled from one political crisis to the next, despite reforms, its expanding electoral franchise—which more than doubled in 1912—arguably adding even more divisions to those provided by the gap between north and south. The advent of Giovanni Giolitti as premier in 1903 stabilized Italian politics. At the same time, socialists, growing in strength, opposed the liberal regime from the left, while nationalists attacked from the right.

Whereas Cavour had achieved Italian unification through liberal political means, Otto von Bismarck had harnessed economic liberalism to the goals of conservative political nationalism in achieving the unification of Germany. Liberals had relatively little influence in unified Germany. Although having universal male suffrage, Germany remained dominated by reactionary monarchs supported by reactionary Junkers, its Reichstag almost powerless against autocracy, despite the growth of a mass socialist party.

In the wake of the Revolutions of 1848, nationalism had proven itself a major force for unification in both Germany and Italy. In the Habsburg lands, in sharp contrast, nationalism was a force that came to challenge the very existence of the empire. In the age of militant nationalism, ethnic tensions within the Austro-Hungarian Empire would become those of Europe. In contrast, each of Europe's three other powers had been politically unified for centuries. Of the three, Britain and Russia had had no revolution in 1848. In contrast, France, the third, emerged from the tumultuous period with an authoritarian empire. In the next chapter, we will consider Britain, Russia, and France during the great period of change, 1850–1914.

THE DOMINANT POWERS IN THE AGE OF LIBERALISM: PARLIAMENTARY BRITAIN, TSARIST RUSSIA, AND REPUBLICAN FRANCE

The Crystal Palace, a vast structure built of glass and iron in London's Hyde Park, housed the Exposition of 1851, the first world's fair. It stood 1,848 feet long, 408 feet across, and 66 feet high, and included a million square feet of glass, 3,300 columns, and 2,300 girders, all of identical size so they could be prefabricated. Gaslight provided illumination, and, for the first time, public toilets were installed for the convenience of visitors. The machinery on exhibit, above all, captured the attention and imagination of observers, including Queen Victoria herself. To the British subjects of Queen Victoria, the Great Exposition of 1851 represented the ascendancy of the British constitution, free trade and manufacturing, and Christianity.

Great Britain was the quintessential liberal state. Britain's long tradition of constitutional monarchy, with the remaining authority of the monarch more than balanced by Parliament, reflected its liberalism and economic prosperity. There had been no revolution in 1848 in Europe's most liberal

The Crystal Palace, symbol of the new industrial age.

nation. In the parliamentary constitutional monarchy, reform in 1867 expanded the number of those males eligible to vote.

Besides Britain, the other dominant powers during the age of liberalism were France, which was more slowly entering the industrial age, and Russia, which despite some significant reforms remained an autocracy antithetical to liberalism. France during the period 1852–1870 was a highly centralized empire, with Emperor Napoleon III determined to bring economic progress through the strong involvement of the state. Napoleon III implemented universal male suffrage in the first year of his reign. Following a disastrous war against Prussia (1870–1871), the empire fell, replaced by the Third Republic, another liberal regime in which executive authority was left weak, in this case out of fear that yet another Napoleon might emerge.

In contrast, Russia remained an autocracy, a state in which the absolute authority of the tsar was limited only by bureaucratic inefficiency and the impossibility of reaching into every corner of the vast empire. Russian nobles dominated the peasant masses, and unlike Britain and France, Russia had no representative political system and only a tiny middle class, despite economic growth. Tsar Alexander II shocked many of his own nobles by emancipating the serfs in 1861. But unlike the political reforms enacted in Britain and France, the tsar's reforms did not significantly alter the autocratic nature of the Russian Empire. Yet Russia, too, was transformed by new ideas and increasingly courageous opponents of autocratic authority. And, like France, imperial Russia also had to worry about the consequences of a unified Germany.

Victorian Britain

In 1840, young Queen Victoria (1819–1901) married the German Prince Albert (1819–1861) of Saxe-Coburg-Gotha. They were happily married, although she described sex as "giving way to the baser passions." She warned one of her daughters who was about to be married that a bride was "like a lamb led to the slaughter," and that there would be times when she would simply have to submit to her husband's urges and "think of England." Victoria bore children only because she thought it part of her duties as queen. She raised her children with little visible affection, as if managing a business from afar. Yet the queen projected a maternal image both in Britain and in the colonies over which she also ruled.

Albert's tendency to be narrow-minded, socially awkward, and tactless irritated cabinet ministers and other highly placed people. He hovered about the government, dashing off letters and memoranda when the mood struck him, meddling when he could. Although Victoria made clear from the beginning that she would serve as a queen without a king, her devotion to Albert sparked some anti-German feeling in Britain.

Prince Albert organized the Great Exposition of 1851 in London. In his opening prayers, the Anglican archbishop made the connection between Britain's prosperity and the era of relative peace that had prevailed since the end of the Napoleonic Wars in 1815. More than this, Great Britain seemed special. The historian Thomas Macaulay wrote in the wake of the Revolutions of 1848 on the continent: "All around us the world is convulsed by the agonies of the great nations. . . . Meanwhile, in our island, the course of government has never been for a day interrupted. We have order in the midst of anarchy."

At the Great Exposition of 1851, more than 6 million visitors—most from Britain but a good many from the continent and beyond—could choose among more than 100,000 exhibits (half from Britain and its colonies) put forward by 14,000 exhibitors. The exhibits were categorized into raw materials, machinery, manufactured goods, and fine arts, and ranged from useful household items to huge guns exhibited by the Prussian industrialist Krupp. These seemed somewhat out of place in a venue where many assured themselves that science and industry offered hope for continued peace in Europe.

The Great Exposition celebrated the industrial age, Britain's primacy in manufacturing, and the "working bees of the world's hive." Its catalogue intoned, "The progress of the human race . . . we are carrying out the will of the great and blessed God." Most of the visitors to the Great Exposition, ranging from the wealthy and famous to the poor folk paying just one shilling to enter, arrived by railroad.

When Albert died of typhoid in 1861 at age forty-two, Victoria was devastated. She retreated into lonely bereavement and isolation, ignoring most public duties. Only gradually did Victoria reemerge to provide a focal point for a nation in the midst of a great transformation during the second half of the century.

Victoria knew virtually nothing about the lives of her subjects and instinctively disapproved of factory reforms and increased opportunity of education for the lower classes (fearing that it would lead them to want to raise their station in life). But the queen remained the personification of the "respectability" that gave her name to the Victorian age. "Respectability"—inculcated by education and contemporary literature—centered on the family and strict rules about public comportment. But it meant different things to families of different strata: three servants for a comfortable middle-class family, a parlor off the kitchen for breakfast for a lower-middle-class family, and avoiding a pauper's funeral for a lower-class family.

The Victorian Consensus

"Victorian," a term first used in 1851, the year of the Great Exposition, evokes a sense of the contentment and confidence that middle-class Britons enjoyed. The Victorian consensus was formed around the capitalist entrepreneurial ethic, emphasizing self-reliance and faith in progress. In the Victorian entrepreneurial ideal, the individual demonstrated his moral worth through hard work, in contrast to the evils of the old system of patronage. Competition would determine those who were fit to rule, not aristocratic monopoly or unearned privilege, and not working-class demands for a greater share in the prosperity of the nation that middle-class Britons believed their hard work had created.

In 1859, the belief in the virtues of rugged individualism received a boost from the publication of *On the Origin of Species* by Charles Darwin (1809–1882). Darwin, the son of a domineering father, overcame chronic anxiety, self-doubt, and severe depression to undertake determined, systematic research and analysis on the evolution of living organisms. His bold book argued that some animal species survived and evolved by virtue of being better adapted to existing conditions, while others disappeared because they were less "fit." By implication, Darwin's work seemed to suggest that the state should stand back and let individuals alone to compete on the playing field of life. This was more good news for many confident Victorians, but not for churchmen, for Darwin's book taught that mankind evolved from other animal forms over millions of years, thus challenging the Bible's description of God having created the world in seven days. Darwin's research and analysis were a major event in the battle between science and religion in nineteenth-century Europe.

Religious images and references permeated Victorian social and political discourse. Entrepreneurs believed that they were doing God's work by becoming successful and rich. Many Victorians insisted that the pervasive influence of religion more than prosperity explained the apparent social harmony of their age. Thus, many Britons were surprised and even shocked by the

A contemporary impression of Darwin looking at human ancestry.

results of a government survey of every church in England and Wales on a Sunday morning in 1851. Out of a population of almost 18 million people, only slightly more than 7.2 million had attended church. Moreover, if everybody in England and Wales had decided to attend church, only 58 percent of the population and only 30 percent of Londoners could be accommodated. Between 1841 and 1876, the Anglicans built 1,727 new churches and restored more than 7,000 old ones; among their rivals, Congregationalists and Catholics doubled the number of their churches, and Baptists multiplied their churches by five.

The Church of England, closely identified with the British elite, remained a target for liberal reformers. Parliament had repealed the Corporation and Test Acts in 1828, eliminating two significant discriminatory laws that had kept Dissenters (non-Anglican Protestants) who refused to take communion in the Anglican Church from holding office. Parliamentary decrees in 1854 and 1856 allowed non-Anglicans to attend Cambridge and Oxford Universities. Catholics, most of whom were Irish immigrants—in addition to a small number of nobles whose families had converted to Catholicism—still faced popular suspicion, however, reflecting the deep roots of anti-Catholicism in British national identity.

Many middle-class Victorians wanted to make the lower classes more "moral." Congregationalist and Baptist evangelicals (as well as Methodists) won converts among the lower classes, perhaps because leaders of these churches demonstrated far more interest in the conditions of the poor than did the Church of England. Temperance movements proliferated in a wave of concern about lower-class drunkenness—one-third of all arrests were for drunk and disorderly conduct. The Charity Organization Society, founded in 1869, promoted charitable giving to those who steered clear of drink. And in 1875, the Salvation Army began its work, offering assistance to those who would participate in religious revival services.

The Crimean War

In 1854, Britain found itself involved in a major war that ended the long peace that had lasted almost without interruption since Napoleon's defeat in 1815. (Indeed the period is sometimes known as the Pax Britannia, in part because Britain's naval domination helped discourage conflict.) Britain entered the Crimean War (1853–1856) to support the Turks against Russia, which had intervened in 1841 against Mehmet Ali, the governor of Egypt (see Chapter 16). In 1853, Russian forces occupied the Ottoman Danubian principalities of Moldavia and Wallachia (see Map 18.1) to solidify Russia's position in the Balkans.

The Russian Empire had since the late eighteenth century sought control over the Straits of Constantinople, which divide Europe from Asia and could provide the Russian navy with access to the Aegean and Mediterranean Seas. Such ambitions inevitably brought conflict with the Ottoman Empire, which had controlled virtually the entire Balkan region until the early nineteenth century.

Following defeat after the Greek revolt in the 1820s, Ottoman rulers had undertaken a series of major reforms of the army (after having replaced the janissary corps—the Turkish sultan's militia that had originally been formed of Christians who converted to Islam, slaves, and members of other nationalities—with a more European army in 1826) and

MAP 18.1 THE CRIMEAN WAR, 1853–1856   Russian, British-French-Piedmontese, and Austrian troop movements involved in this war between the great powers.

imperial administration. Sultan Mahmud II (ruled 1808–1839) had reorganized the treasury and ordered a census of the empire in 1831. Mahmud II's successors decreed further reforms during the period known as Tanzimat—the "Reorganization"—that lasted from 1839 to 1878. By the Rose Chamber (Gulhane) Decree of 1839, the sultan guaranteed the life and property of all Ottoman subjects and their equality before law, while initiating military conscription and a more organized system of taxation. Other changes followed: the establishment of penal and commercial codes, the reform of justice, and the implementation of more central government control over regions, reducing the autonomous power of the governors through the creation of a more modern bureaucracy. Such reforms pleased the governments of Britain and France, in part because Ottoman markets were now more open to foreign trade, but also because these governments viewed the stability of the Ottoman Empire as necessary to tempering Russian dreams of further expansion toward Constantinople and the Bosporus and Dardanelles straits.

A century earlier, perhaps as much as 80 percent of the population of the Ottoman Empire in Europe had been Christian. Each religion had the right to worship freely, and non-Muslims had access to Islamic courts. Christians and Muslims got along for the most part very well. The structure of the empire had for centuries encouraged the conversion of Christians to Islam, because Christians were considered second-class subjects and faced a heavier tax burden then did Muslims. Intermarriage was fairly frequent. In the late eighteenth century, the sultans had begun to tighten their control over the various religions in the empire. Each religious community—Greek Orthodox, Jewish, and Armenian—was organized into what became known as the "millet" system. In the middle of the nineteenth century, the sultan brought the hierarchy of Muslim religious and cultural leaders (the *ulema*) under administrative control. In addition, stories of persecution of Muslim minorities in Russia and suspicion of the Western powers toward Islam contributed to the gradual emergence of Islamism in the Ottoman Empire. Religious leaders began calling for a return to the fundamental values of Islam.

At the same time, however, Turkish economic development brought the emergence of a group of prosperous merchants who turned away from and even rejected the organization of communities along religious lines. Officials (*memurs*) replaced the old Ottoman ruling class, which had originally been drawn from the servants of the sultan's household, who had held positions in the imperial administration and army. The Ottoman ministries of the interior, finance, and foreign affairs, among others, reflected Western influence.

Yet the continued decline of the Ottoman Empire seemed probable. Egypt appeared on the verge of achieving independence. Russia stood poised like a vulture to profit from its once-powerful rival's weakness, a situation that came to be called the "Eastern Question." Russia presented itself as the protector of Slavic and Orthodox Christian interests in the Balkans, encouraging agitation against the Turks. Christian minorities within the Ottoman

Empire in the Balkans began to exert nationalist claims, dreaming of their own independent states. This challenged the Islamic character that had existed for centuries as an essential part of the empire.

With interests in Afghanistan, Britain was ill disposed to the expansion of Russian influence. Increased British trade with the Ottoman Empire had become another factor in British support for the Turks. Napoleon III of France, eager for a military victory to solidify support for his regime, also stood ready to stop Russian expansion by supporting the Ottoman Empire. The French emperor saw himself as the protector of the Catholic Holy Places of Judea, which were under Ottoman authority. To placate Catholic supporters, Napoleon III demanded at least Catholic equality with the Orthodox religion in Jerusalem's Church of the Holy Sepulcher. This Russia refused, demanding the right to veto any changes in the status not only of the Holy Places but also in the situation of the entire Ottoman Christian population.

The Ottoman Empire declared war on Russia in October 1853. Russian Tsar Nicholas I's fleet defeated the Ottoman fleet in the Black Sea, setting fire to the sultan's wooden ships with incendiary shells. But the tsar's confidence that Britain and France would soon quarrel because of conflicting interests proved ill founded. With British public opinion eager for the flag to be shown even after the withdrawal of Russian troops from Moldavia and Wallachia, the British Royal Navy sailed into the Black Sea. Not to be outdone, Napoleon III, too, sent warships.

Britain and France declared war on Russia in March 1854. British and French forces first moved against the Russian port of Sebastopol on the peninsula of Crimea on the edge of the Black Sea. Invulnerable to sea attack, Sebastopol could only be stormed from land. The rusty invading armies lay siege to Sebastopol. The French army seemed better trained, as well as better fed and supplied than that of the British. The senior British commander, a veteran of Waterloo forty years earlier, persisted in referring to the Russians as "the French." Most British officers owed their commissions to the fact that they were aristocrats, not because of particular competence. One commander spent each night on his private yacht anchored offshore, dining on meals prepared by a French chef while his men shivered in the wind and mud of the Crimean winter and ate ghastly rations.

Far more men died (about 600,000) of disease than in battle, although Alfred Tennyson (1809–1892), Britain's poet laureate, helped make famous the "Charge of the Light Brigade," in which British cavalry rode into "jaws of death" at Balaklava. The first war correspondents sent dispatches by telegraph to eager readers in Britain and France, where interest in the distant siege dramatically increased newspaper circulation.

Into this maelstrom ventured Florence Nightingale (1820–1910). The daughter of a prosperous family, she had shocked her parents by becoming a nurse, an occupation that had a reputation as providing a refuge for "disorderly" women. Nightingale volunteered for service in a Constantinople hospital after hearing of the appalling conditions endured by the

(*Left*) The charge of the Light Brigade at Balaklava. (*Right*) Florence Nightingale.

wounded and those sick with cholera and dysentery. She bombarded the government with highly detailed information on what was wrong and what was needed. Raising funds through private contributions, she succeeded in improving conditions in the hospital. Nightingale had to overcome the conviction of officers that she would "spoil the brutes," that is, the sick and wounded enlisted men, as well as overcoming prejudices against a woman making forceful demands on the government. The government several years later enacted a series of reforms to improve food and health care for the men in its army. In part a result of Florence Nightingale's highly publicized work throughout the remainder of her career, nursing emerged as a more respected profession.

The Crimean War ground to a halt after Sebastopol finally capitulated in September 1855. The Peace of Paris (March 1856) guaranteed the autonomy of the Danubian principalities of Moldavia and Wallachia (which became independent Romania in 1878), the independence of Turkey, and the neutrality of the Black Sea. The Crimean War left little doubt that Victorian Britain remained Europe's strongest power.

The Liberal Era of Victorian Politics

Britain entered a period of relative social harmony. The repeal of the Corn Laws in 1846 convinced many workers that they could place their trust in political reform, which is one reason there was no revolution in Britain in 1848 (see Chapter 16). Middle-class reformers had broadened their appeal to include the most prosperous segments of the working class. Most British workers seemed to accept the belief that hard work and savings would inevitably be rewarded. Most Victorians of all social classes increasingly felt themselves part of a nation with which they could identify.

British workers, including many union members, joined "friendly societies," or as they were increasingly called, "self-help associations." Membership in such groups rose from less than a million in 1815 to 3 million in 1849 and 4 million in 1872, four times that of unions. They provided members with minimal assistance in times of unemployment or illness and a decent burial. Preaching individual self-help and respectability, such organizations did not offer the socialist vision common among workers in France, Belgium, or the Rhineland. They helped inculcate a sense of what the British called "respectability," which discouraged militancy.

Like the friendly societies, Britain's "new model unions" also embodied the concept of self-help. Members of these unions first and foremost saw their organizations as representing craftsmen and skilled workers of specific crafts, such as carpenters and printers from the "aristocracy of labor" who could afford dues. They constituted about 15 percent of the working class, standing apart from the mass of unskilled laborers. Some of them taught in Sunday schools, working men's colleges, reading rooms, and improvement societies. Even when local unions within a single trade joined to form national organizations, there was no talk of revolution or even of eventually restructuring British economic, social, and political life. Strikers in the 1860s were increasingly willing to accept arbitration boards and to compromise to achieve limited goals.

Benefiting from the 1832 enfranchisement of more middle-class men, the Whigs governed Britain for most of the 1850s and 1860s. Henry John Temple (1784–1865), the Viscount Palmerston, who began his political career as a Conservative, led the Whigs. The notorious philandering of the shrewd and feisty "Lord Cupid," as he was known to his detractors, stood out in an age of public prudishness. Palmerston outraged Queen Victoria by trying to seduce one of her ladies-in-waiting in Windsor Castle.

Palmerston held together a coalition of Whigs who were determined to uphold laissez-faire economic policies. Dissenters, Catholics, and liberal Anglicans wanted the Anglican Church to lose its status as the Established Church of England. Gradually these Whigs began to be referred to as the Liberal Party.

Palmerston's bellicose saber-rattling won him personal popularity. Crowds cheered when he ordered the blockade of the Greek port of Piraeus in 1850 to enforce claims against the Greek government by Don Pacifico, a British-born Portuguese Jew whose house an Athens mob had destroyed. Palmerston boastfully compared the might of classical Rome and Victorian Britain, which had remained one of the "protecting powers" of Greece since its independence in 1832. Following the overthrow of King Otto in 1854, Britain, France, Bavaria, and Russia selected a Danish prince to rule Greece as King George I, while placating Greek nationalists by awarding one of the Ionian islands to Greece.

After glorying in Britain's victory in the Crimean War, Palmerston then lurched into a short war against China in 1857, after the Chinese government seized a pirate ship that had formerly been registered under the British flag. Rebuffed by a majority in Commons and opposed by pacifist political radicals outside of Parliament, Palmerston refused to resign and called for a general election. Basing his campaign on an appeal to patriotism, he won the day.

William Gladstone (1809–1898) then became the leader of the Liberal Party. Gladstone was the son of a wealthy and unscrupulous merchant who had made a fortune in trade with India and the West Indies. The young Gladstone was deeply religious and wore his moral vision of the world on his sleeve, going out into the night to try to convince prostitutes to abandon their trade. Gladstone sought to impose his own self-discipline and sense of Victorian Christianity on the nation. During his early years in government, he worked to assure laissez-faire economic policies, campaigning for the abolition of even the very modest income tax.

As chancellor of the exchequer, Gladstone had waged war against extravagance and waste in government. In contrast to his Conservative rivals, he opposed colonization as being too expensive. Queen Victoria loathed Gladstone, blaming him for almost every domestic and international problem. She resented his *de facto* campaign to reduce the already limited role of the monarchy in the constitutional government of Britain. Having supported the repeal of the Corn Laws in 1846, he wanted to make the Liberals the party of reform.

Robert Peel had split the Conservatives by supporting the repeal of the Corn Laws in 1846. After Peel's death in 1850, Benjamin Disraeli

(*Left*) William Gladstone, Liberal prime minister. (*Right*) Benjamin Disraeli.

(1804–1881) became the leader of the Conservatives and Gladstone's great rival. A Jew who had been baptized into the Anglican Church, Disraeli seemed an unlikely leader of a party dominated by landed wealth. But he was an energetic, skilled politician and an impressive orator who had the good sense to realize that further Conservative attempts to revive economic protectionism were doomed. Unlike Gladstone, Disraeli got along famously with the queen, whom he flattered on every possible occasion. Victoria depended upon Disraeli for advice much as she had on Albert. (As Disraeli lay dying, the queen wrote to ask if she might visit the Conservative leader. "It is better not," Disraeli replied. "She'd only ask me to take a message to Albert.")

The Reform Bill of 1867

Since 1832, the majority of British subjects had regarded further political reform as a certainty. A growing number of middle-class voters, hoping to end disproportionate aristocratic influence in British political life, supported some expansion of suffrage. Workers wanted universal male suffrage. As for Queen Victoria, she insisted that she "cannot and will not be the queen of a democratic monarchy." John Bright (1811–1889), who represented Manchester and then Birmingham in the House of Commons, campaigned for electoral reform. In 1866, the National Reform Union, whose membership was overwhelmingly middle class, and the Reform League, which many craftsmen joined, allied with Bright's parliamentary radicals. Their goal was household suffrage, that is, the right of the adult male head of family to vote.

Gladstone, typically, was convinced that political reform was not only expedient but also moral. "You cannot fight against the future," the Liberal leader taunted Conservatives in Parliament. "Time is on our side. The great social forces . . . are against you." But he wanted to let down the electoral drawbridge only long enough to let in artisans and skilled workers, the "aristocracy of labor," but not all males.

Conservatives feared that the enfranchisement of more people would add to the ranks of the Liberals and eventually lead to subsequent legislation that might weaken the political influence of wealthy landowners. The Liberal government proposed a bill to reduce the minimum amount of tax one had to pay to be eligible to vote both in the countryside and in towns, where the rate would be set lower. The proposed reform would still exclude ordinary workers and other poor people. However, the House of Lords rejected the bill because a majority of members opposed any change.

Disraeli, who had predicted that "pillage, incendiarism, and massacre" would follow universal male suffrage in Britain, now believed that electoral reform that maintained some exclusions was not only inevitable but that his Conservative Party could benefit from it. Disraeli took a "leap in the dark," proposing that the vote be given to each head of a household and that the minimum countryside tax requirement be further lowered. Under Conservative auspices, the Reform Bill of 1867 passed, like that of 1832. This doubled the ranks of voters but still left Britain short of universal male suffrage.

In France at the same time, every adult male could vote during the Second Empire, to be sure. But there Emperor Napoleon III cynically manipulated universal male suffrage by presenting government-sponsored candidates and utilizing that old Bonapartist tool, the plebiscite. The German Empire, too, had universal male suffrage, but the Reichstag (assembly) had little real authority. In Russia, there were no national elected bodies at all, and local assemblies (*zemstvos*) initiated in 1864 were elected by local electoral colleges but were dependent upon officials named by the tsar. In Italy, only a small percentage of adult males were eligible to vote, by virtue of their ownership of property. The reformed electoral system in Britain not only enfranchised many more voters, but gave them more influence, because the House of Commons exercised great authority in Britain's constitutional monarchy. Here, too, Britain seemed to lead the way in the gradual emergence of democratic politics.

Disraeli's Conservatives, however, failed to woo many of the new voters. The Liberals won a large majority in Parliament, boosted by support from workers who now could vote. The major goal of the Chartist campaign more than two decades earlier had been reached.

Another act of reform in 1884 added 2 million more voters to the rolls by enfranchising agricultural laborers. With women still excluded from the vote, the only adult males who could not vote were those without a fixed residence, sons living at home with their parents and not paying rent, and domestic servants. The Redistribution Act of 1885 disenfranchised some underpopulated districts while increasing representation of many urban areas. However, the establishment of single-member constituencies compensated Conservatives, balancing potential Liberal gains in urban areas.

Other Victorian Reforms

The Victorian consensus rested upon a strong belief that the "invisible hand" of the economy would generate economic growth. Many Victorians had believed the Poor Law of 1834 was self-defeating because it provided minimal resources to the poor for which they had not worked. But increasingly aware of the devastating poverty of millions of workers, most middle-class Victorians by mid-century had changed their minds about the role of government in society. Edwin Chadwick (1800–1890), a journalist and associate of Jeremy Bentham, had drafted the Poor Law. His *Report on the Sanitary Condition of the Laboring Population of Great Britain* (1842) served as an impassioned plea for government action after cholera had ravaged poor urban neighborhoods. Largely thanks to Chadwick's efforts, Parliament passed laws facilitating the inspection of rooming houses, where many poor workers resided. Thereafter, parliamentary commissions began to call upon experts to gather information and assess conditions of British life. The age of statistics had arrived.

Regulatory agencies began to spring up. In 1848, Parliament created the national General Board of Health. Chadwick's revelations about public health—or rather, the lack of it—encountered ferocious opposition from those who were against any government intervention as a matter of principle. "We prefer to take our chance on cholera and the rest than be bullied into health," groused *The Times*. Yet, by the time Chadwick was driven to resign from the General Board of Health in 1854, the right of the state to intervene in matters of health had been established. Parliamentary acts in the 1860s extended regulations of working conditions in mines and in factories with more than fifty employees and where women and children worked. The Public Health Act of 1866 gave local government more authority to assure a cleaner water supply. Five years later, state inspectors for the first time obtained legal access to workplaces. Parliament soon established health boards in towns and country districts, even if local business and political interests often combined to foil the efforts of reformers. Yet, reform leagues, such as the National Education League became part of British political life.

Victorious in elections following the passage of the Reform Act of 1867, the Liberals ended the purchase of army commissions, enacted land reform in Ireland, and the government recognized the legal existence of trade unions. When the Conservatives returned to power in 1874, they, too, sought to woo the allegiance of workers from the Liberals by getting Parliament to approve a number of reforms, including a law that forbade labor by

Street disinfectors in London, 1875.

uneducated children. Yet considerably more than altruism lay behind a shift in middle-class attitudes. Manufacturers also knew that demand for their products depended on workers having money to spend. In Great Britain, the "age of optimism" became the "age of improvement."

Queen Victoria once asked someone to define "bureaucracy," a term she did not know. "That, Madam," came the reply, "is something that they have in France." Yet the Victorian state expanded. In 1841, the British government—the least centralized of the major European powers—had employed 40,000 men and 3,000 women; by 1911, 271,000 men and 50,000 women worked for the state. The administration of the Poor Law itself served to strengthen the role of government in local affairs. Municipal councils took over the task of administering local government from the justices of the peace, who had served in such capacity since the sixteenth century. Municipalities were now responsible for education, as well as for health, housing, roads, and policing. Service in local government, once little more than another honor awarded a landed gentleman, now required the participation of paid officials.

With increased responsibilities, the British civil service became professionalized. The government administered competitive examinations on which appointment and promotion depended. However, these exams did not democratize entry into the civil service. Applicants who had attended one of the expensive, elite public schools (so called because they accepted students from all over Britain, provided their families could afford the steep tuition) had a far greater advantage on the examinations than those who had not.

As the role of the British state thus expanded considerably during the middle decades of the century, the era of laissez-faire liberalism came to a close. Speaking of her father, Gladstone's daughter remembered, "I was accustomed to hear him utter the word 'Government' in a tone that charted it with awe and made it part of my effective religion."

Mass Politics Come to Britain

Out of office following passage of the 1867 Reform Act, Benjamin Disraeli sought to accommodate Conservatives to the era of mass political life. Realizing that his party, long closely tied to the British landed elite and the Anglican Church, would have to outbid their Liberal rivals for votes, he created a modern national party organization. Disraeli made British nationalism and imperialism part of the Conservative Party platform, suggesting that the Liberals would weaken Britain. When the Turks and Russians began to quarrel over the Balkans, Disraeli supported the Turks, despite the massacre of about 10,000 to 15,000 Bulgarians in 1876 by Turkish troops. Gladstone, however, was horrified by the bloodbath and made a political issue of the Balkans. It was easy enough for him to do so: Britain had less to fear from the Ottoman Empire in decline than from an aggressively expansionist Russia.

The Conservative Party now reflected an important change in modern British political life. The traditional split between "city" and "country," which had characterized politics since the seventeenth century, had largely ended. The Conservatives now found new support among some of the wealthiest businessmen, who abandoned the Liberals. Furthermore, many aristocrats were themselves now actively involved in the management of banks and modern industries. The English business elite that had been formed during the first decades of Victoria's reign became as conservative as the aristocrats they emulated. A contemporary assessed this evolution when he wrote: "Our territorial nobles, our squires, our rural landlords great and small, have become commercial potentates; our merchant princes have become country gentlemen." Some wealthy businessmen deserted the Dissenters to join the Established Anglican Church. This new Conservative political culture, supported by a faithful minority of nationalist "Tory workers," survived the economic and social changes that were transforming Britain.

Gladstone himself embarked on whistle-stop "Midlothian" campaigns—so named for one of his first stops in 1879. His audiences were made up of anyone who wanted to come to the railroad station to hear him. This forced Conservatives even more to put aside their feelings that such appeals to ordinary people were vulgar, or too "American."

Yet the Conservative Party remained the party of great landed wealth. The law of primogeniture helped keep huge estates intact. Because of parliamentary districting, the countryside remained overrepresented in Parliament, again to the advantage of landed gentlemen. In 1871, about 1,200 people owned a quarter of the land of England, and the holdings of 7,000 families amounted to half of the country. Landed gentlemen dominated the House of Commons until 1885, the cabinet until 1893, and the aristocratic House of Lords well into the twentieth century.

Irish Home Rule

The Liberals continued to be faced with the problem of Ireland, which reflected the dilemmas of national identity in late nineteenth-century Europe. In 1868, William Gladstone had announced that the most pressing mission of his new government was to "pacify Ireland." A year later, the Liberal prime minister pushed through both houses of Parliament a bill that disestablished the Church of Ireland (which had become part of the United Church of England in 1800), since Ireland was 80 percent Catholic. This meant that the Episcopal Church in Ireland no longer received state support.

To many Irish, it seemed that only by owning land could Irish peasants reach any degree of prosperity. The Irish Land Act of 1870 provided tenants with compensation for improvements they had undertaken and protected them from being evicted from property without just cause. But English

Protestant landlords were not about to turn over land in Ireland to the peasants who rented from or worked for them. The fall in the price of agricultural commodities made it more difficult for tenant-farmers to meet their rent payments. In 1879, the Irish Land League, drawing on the remnants of the secret Irish Republican Brotherhood (known in Gaelic as the Fenians) and sworn to win independence, began to pressure Parliament for land reform.

Gladstone's determination to make Ireland his ongoing moral crusade met with opposition within his own Liberal Party, which depended on support from Whig landowners in Ireland to maintain a parliamentary majority. Charles Stewart Parnell (1846–1891), a Liberal Irish Protestant, began to build a small parliamentary coalition in favor of Home Rule, which meant the establishment of a separate Irish Parliament, but not outright independence. The Irish Catholic Church supported Home Rule. Parnell's program, however, fell short of the demands of the Land League, which wanted immediate and sweeping land reform, and the revived Irish Republican Brotherhood, which insisted on complete Irish independence.

During 1879–1882, Irish farmers undertook a "land war" of protest. Irish tenants and laborers began to shun farmers who took over the leases of peasants evicted for nonpayment of rent. A certain Captain Boycott, the agent of a large landowner, was one of the first targets; his name became synonymous with such a strategy. The British government replied with repression, suspending the writ of *habeas corpus* in Ireland in 1881. However, that same year, Gladstone also pushed through a bill (by threatening to dissolve Parliament) protecting any Irish tenant from eviction who could pay one year's back rent. Parnell was sent to prison for his violently anti-British speeches. Moreover, opposition to Home Rule mounted in Parliament among MPs who argued that concessions had encouraged violence. A year later, the British government ordered Parnell's release from prison, in the hope that he would help end disorder in Ireland in exchange for the future passage of another bill to help Irish tenants.

In 1882, Irish republicans hacked to death two British officials who had been walking in Phoenix Park in Dublin. The assassinations shocked the English public. In response to the murders, and to more than thirty other deaths in Ireland at the hands of Irish republicans, a Coercion Act facilitated the British government's repression of the republicans by eliminating some rights of those arrested. Five of those responsible for the Phoenix Park assassinations were arrested and hung.

Gladstone (who served as prime minister four different times) proposed Home Rule in 1886, but the issue divided the Liberal Party and the bill failed. Joseph Chamberlain (1836–1914) led the defection of the "Liberal Unionists" over Home Rule. Parnell fell into disgrace three years later when news broke of his affair with Kitty O'Shea, the wife of a Liberal Irish MP active in the campaign for Home Rule. Another bill failed in 1893, defeated in the House of Lords.

New Contours in British Political Life

Queen Victoria's longevity—she ruled the vast British Empire with dignity from 1837 until 1901—symbolized British social and political stability. She endeared herself to her people on the occasion of her silver jubilee in 1887 by wearing a simple bonnet (albeit one with diamonds) instead of her crown. The Prince of Wales inherited the throne as King Edward VII (ruled 1901–1910). Edward could not have been more different from his mother, with whom he constantly battled and whom he often embarrassed. Edward "the Caresser" indulged his extravagant tastes in beautiful women, prize horses, good food, fine wines, and gambling.

The Conservatives returned to power in 1895. Like their counterparts in France and Germany, the British Conservative Party became even more aggressively nationalist, imperialist, and resolutely antisocialist. The Liberal Unionists had allied with the Conservatives over Home Rule. In 1895, their leader Joseph Chamberlain joined the Conservative government as colonial secretary.

Frustrated by the Conservative government's refusal to initiate parliamentary bills of social reform and by employers' attempts to weaken the unions by hiring non-union labor, British trade unionism entered a more aggressive phase during the last two decades of the nineteenth century. The Trades Union Congress (created in 1868) had provided a forum for organized labor, although the financial resources of unions became even more depleted.

Now, a more militant "new unionism" was characterized by the organization of semiskilled workers, including many iron and steel factory workers. In 1887, for the first time since the last Chartist marches in London in 1848, English workers went into the streets in great numbers to protest, demonstrating against unemployment and the high cost of living. On November 13—"Black Monday"—store owners slammed their doors shut amid a "red fear" in central London, again the first since 1848. The police attacked crowds of workers, killing 2 and wounding about 100 protesters.

In 1889, following a victory by gas workers in a London strike that achieved the eight-hour workday, dockworkers struck for a minimum wage. They were led by Ben Tillett (1860–1943). Born in Bristol, Tillett had at the age of seven begun cutting slabs of clay in a brickyard, then ran away with Old Joe Barker's Circus as an acrobat, before joining the merchant marine and then the navy. Finding work as a dockyard laborer, he helped organize thousands of unskilled laborers in a massive strike. Australian workers sent funds that helped tide the strikers over. After five weeks, the dockworkers won a minimum wage and overtime pay. Tillett's dockworkers' union soon had 30,000 members.

But hundreds of thousands of casual laborers, including those living in London's teeming East End, still were not unionized, nor in friendly societies. For them the independence of the skilled worker remained only a

(*Left*) Ben Tillett, organizer of the Docker's Union. (*Right*) James Keir Hardie, founder of the Independent Labour Party.

dream. Strikes in 1897–1898 (including Britain's first national walkout, which ended in the workers' defeat) revealed the growing reach of the new unions.

The state went on the offensive against the unions. In 1901, in resolving a railway case in Wales, the Taff Vale decision of the House of Lords made unions and their officers legally responsible for losses sustained by companies during strikes. This encouraged the creation of the Labour Party. First organized in 1900 (taking its name in 1906), the Labour Party had its origins in the small Independent Labour Party, which had been founded in 1893 by MP James Keir Hardie (1856–1915). This rough-hewn Scottish miner had provoked the House of Commons by chiding members for sending a congratulatory message to the queen on the birth of a great-grandson instead of a message of condolence to the families of several hundred miners killed in an accident in a mine shaft in Wales. The Labour Party now vowed to represent workers in Parliament and specifically to bring about the repeal of the Taff Vale decision.

A split within the Liberal-Unionist-Conservative bloc brought ten years of Conservative government to an end. Some political leaders, including Joseph Chamberlain, campaigned for protective tariffs, believing that they would increase British prosperity by creating a large imperial market. Many Conservatives, including Prime Minister Arthur Balfour (1848–1930), believed that voters preferred traditional free trade policies, identified with lower food prices. Unable to resolve the split within his party, Balfour resigned in December 1905, and the Liberals swept to victory the following year. Promising to repeal the Taff Vale decision, they garnered many working-class votes. The Labour Party, which had managed to win only one seat in 1900, now sent twenty-nine MPs to the House of Commons. Under the Liberal government, Parliament reversed the Taff Vale decision with the Trade Disputes Act of 1906, which legalized picketing and relieved unions of the legal responsibility for financial losses caused by strikes.

In 1908, Herbert Asquith (1852–1928) became Liberal prime minister. Like the Conservatives, he supported British imperial causes. But the dynamic, ambitious, and charismatic Welshman David Lloyd George (1863–1945) was the rising star of the Liberals. A man of modest origins who preferred to speak his native Welsh than English, Lloyd George had come into the public eye for his opposition to the Boer War (see Chapter 21), although in general he supported the empire. While crusading against the Conservative Party, Lloyd George worked to continue the Gladstonian reformist tradition. He wanted to counter the drift of union members toward the Labour Party by bringing workers, middle-class men, and businessmen into an alliance that would support Liberal social and political reforms. The Liberal government established local boards to set minimum industrial wages, involving the British government in bargaining between employers and workers to an extent hitherto unseen.

In 1909, Lloyd George (who was chancellor of the exchequer) proposed a budget that called for increased public benefits to be partially funded by taxes on inheritance and on unearned income and uncultivated land. These "supertaxes" (which were in fact quite small) would fall on the richest families of the nation. He compared the costs of maintaining "a fully-equipped duke" to that of a new battleship, depicting the aristocratic families as parasitical leeches maintained at public expense.

In the Osborne judgment of 1909, the House of Lords had ruled in favor of a railway worker who had sued his union with the goal of keeping union funds from being used to support Labour candidates for the House of Commons or to pay them while they served. (MPs began to receive salaries several years later.) Like the Taff Vale case, the Osborne judgment struck a damaging blow against the unions. In a climate of social confrontation, the House of Lords then provocatively vetoed the 1909 budget, which it viewed as an attack on the wealthy, thus exercising a right that it had not used for decades. Asquith called the House of Lord's veto a "break with the constitution and a usurpation of the rights of the Commons." He dissolved Parliament, confident of winning the new elections.

The Liberals did indeed return to power early the next year with the help of Irish nationalists and the Labour Party. Asquith's Parliament Act of 1911 proposed to eliminate the right of the House of Lords to veto any financial bill. Many Britons viewed the passage of such a bill as a final blow to noble privilege. The act also specified that any bill that the House of Lords did not pass after it had been approved on three occasions by the House of Commons would become law if two years had passed since it had first been introduced in Parliament.

When Asquith threatened to ask King George V (who had succeeded to the throne in 1910) to create enough new peerages to pass the bill, the House of Lords, despite the opposition of intransigents, the so-called Die-hards, approved the Parliament Act in 1911. The House of Lords thus eliminated its own constitutional veto, completing the long revolution in British political life that had begun with the passage of the Reform Act of 1832, which had first reduced the disproportionate power of British nobles. The House of Lords then reversed the Osborne judgment.

In 1911, a walkout by seamen, stevedores, bargemen, and ship repairers spread rapidly in London, Manchester, and Liverpool. The prospect of a food shortage forced the government's hand. Through binding arbitration, the strikers won raises. A national rail strike ended in compromise settlements. When the Miners' Federation called the first general coal strike, more than 800,000 men went out, which left another 1.3 million without work. The miners gained a minimum wage, but when dockers failed to achieve their strike goals in 1912, Britain's largest wave of strikes to date ended in failure. That many strikes ended in defeat may have helped turn British workers further toward parliamentary reformism. In any case, collective bargaining had become commonplace in the 1890s, with conciliation and arbitration boards established in many localities.

Irish Home Rule, still a major political issue, now seemed almost inevitable. Irish politicians, peasants, and poets shared the burst of nationalist sentiment characteristic of the first decade of the twentieth century. The Gaelic League popularized Irish music and encouraged people to speak Gaelic, not English. The poet William Butler Yeats (1865–1939), who helped create a native Irish theater in Dublin, contributed to a literary nationalism that sometimes glossed over class differences among the Irish: "Parnell came down the road and said to a cheering man: / 'Ireland will get her freedom, and you shall still break stone.'" Such literature also tended to romanticize the Irish as peasants made virtuous by poverty and hard work. In the collection of short stories *Dubliners* (1912) by James Joyce (1882–1941), the countryside appears as an idyllic escape from the confusion of Ireland's rapidly growing, impoverished metropolis, which had once been his home.

If some Irish nationalists would accept nothing less than complete independence from Britain, others advocated Home Rule. Irish Protestants living in Ulster, who outnumbered Catholics there by two to one, opposed any measure of Home Rule, which they identified with Catholic "Rome Rule." In 1913, Ulster Protestants formed a paramilitary army of volunteers. At the same time, an Irish Republican Army added men and arms. Century-old wounds split open again, and Ireland seemed on the verge of civil war. In September 1914, Parliament passed a Home Rule Bill, despite the intransigent opposition of the House of Lords. But with Britain—and all the powers of Europe—going to war, the details were left for the uncertain future. Liberal Britain, too, was being swept into international events it could not control.

Tsarist Russia

Autocratic Russia—an absolutist state based upon an alliance of the tsar and the nobles—in the nineteenth century presented a particularly sharp contrast with Great Britain, with its long tradition of parliamentary rule and commercial and manufacturing prosperity. Since the sixteenth century, the Russian tsars had slowly expanded their empire through the conquest of vast stretches of territories and peoples to the south and into Asia. Like the Austro-Hungarian Empire, the much larger Russian Empire was multinational. Ethnic Russians formed less than half of the population. Ethnic resistance to the empire and to the Orthodox Church—for example, from Polish Catholics—increasingly challenged Russian domination.

Since the brief and ill-fated Decembrist uprising of 1825 (see Chapter 15), Russia had seen no major reforms, except the emancipation of state-owned serfs in the 1840s. The structure of the state remained the same, with no institutional constraints on the tsar's authority. Yet liberal ideas from the West had begun to filter into Russia via intellectuals. Alienated from a society built upon serfdom, which legally bound most peasants to the land of their lords, some of them believed revolution inevitable. Moreover, serfdom not only was inhumane, it was also economically inefficient. This helped convince the tsar that only through reform and the emancipation of the serfs could Russia compete with the West.

Stirrings of Reform in Russia

Serfs lived in villages in which patriarchs served as intermediaries between the lords and the community and, like the gentry, administered harsh physical punishments to serfs who failed to obey. Only about 5 percent of the empire's population resided in towns. Russia had a very small middle class and a tiny group of intellectuals and educated commoners. The intelligentsia believed that only revolution could bring change.

Nicholas I (ruled 1825–1855), who had become tsar just after the Decembrist revolt of 1825, was obsessed with keeping Russia sealed off from Western ideas, which he blamed for the rebellion of military officers. The Revolutions of 1848 in Western and Central Europe increased the determination of the Russian autocracy to stifle internal dissent. The ministry of education oversaw a policy of tight censorship and repression by the fearsome Third Section, the political police. But the police found it impossible to seal off the colossal empire entirely. More than 2 million foreign books entered Russia just in the 1847–1849 period, most ending up in Saint Petersburg and Moscow.

In Eastern and eastern Central Europe, the Russian and Polish intelligentsia stood as separate social groups who felt responsible for leading the fight for social and political change and for national independence. Many were gentry who could survive well enough without a university position or government post. Part of an educated elite, they could afford to write, even if the public audience they reached was small indeed. Unlike their counterparts in Western countries, they were not absorbed into the liberal professions and maintained their identity as a group.

During the 1830s and 1840s, some gentry were overwhelmed with guilt that they were well off while the masses suffered. Alexander Pushkin (1799–1837), whose mother exiled two serfs to Siberia with a nod of her head after they failed to bow as she passed by, attacked serfdom in his short stories. Steeped in a variety of intellectual currents, the intelligentsia brooded in small groups, or "circles," in Saint Petersburg and in Moscow over how Russia might emerge from autocracy and relative backwardness.

Several important writers emerged from this underground hotbed of intellectual and creative ferment. Fyodor Dostoyevsky (1821–1881), who adhered to populism and the Pan-Slavist cause, presented brilliant psychological depictions of his characters. These included disturbing portraits of troubled individuals like himself whose actions reflected not rationality but aberration, even madness, in such novels as *Crime and Punishment* (1866) and *The Brothers Karamazov* (1879–1880). Sentenced to death by the authorities in 1849 for participation in a reading circle that discussed socialism, he was hauled out of jail early one morning, blindfolded, placed before a firing squad, and then, after a cruelly staged mock execution that understandably shattered his nerves, sent to prison in Siberia. He described his own suffering, but also that of Russian society, in the crucial years following defeat in the Crimean War. Count Leo Tolstoy (1828–1910), another great Russian realist writer, was a wealthy landowner who served in the Crimean War. He emerged as a moral voice against violence. His monumental *War and Peace* (1869) depicts the struggle between his country and the West.

Pyotr Chaadayev's *Philosophical Letters* slipped by the censors in 1836. Chaadayev (1794–1856) presented a thinly veiled condemnation of Russia's cultural history. Officials declared him to be mad, and the police hounded him for the rest of his life. He pessimistically provoked heated discussion by suggesting that cultural backwardness would keep Russia from joining the ranks of civilized nations. *Philosophical Letters* opened the debate between "Westernizers"—those Russian intellectuals who, like Tsar Peter the Great in the seventeenth century, looked to the West for a model for progress—and "Slavophiles," who believed that Russia could never be reconciled with Western values. Like Westernizers, most Slavophiles were social critics of autocratic Russia. Westernizers like Chaadayev regarded the development of parliamentary institutions and industrialization in Britain,

France, and the German states as a model for Russia to emulate. In contrast, Slavophiles cherished the specificity of Russia's defining institutions: the Orthodox Church, the village commune (the *mir*), and even tsardom itself. They argued that Russia could avoid the traumas of Western industrial development because in the village it already possessed the basis for a future socialist society. The peasant commune, with a variety of communal buildings (a wind or water mill, a grain supply store, tavern, and a workshop), enabled peasants to adapt their lives to unbelievably difficult conditions imposed by nature, the state, and the lords. The *mir* seemed to provide both a moral vision and revolutionary potential.

Vissarion Belinsky (1811–1848) and Alexander Herzen (1812–1870) forcefully made the case that Russia had to follow the example of the West to emerge from backwardness. Belinsky, the son of a doctor, had been expelled from university for writing an article denouncing serfdom. When the writer Nikolay Gogol (1809–1852) refused to criticize the autocracy, Belinsky circulated his *Letter to Gogol* (1847), which helped define the Westernizer position by blasting Gogol's respect for "orthodoxy, autocracy, and nationality," the dominant triad of the Russian Empire: "Advocate of the knout [whip], apostle of ignorance, champion of obscurantism and reactionary mysticism, eulogist of Tartar customs—what are you doing? Look at what is beneath your feet; you are standing at the brink of an abyss."

Herzen, a landowner's son, had vowed to carry on the work of the Decembrist martyrs. Arrested and exiled for participation in a student discussion group, Herzen traveled to France. Returning to Moscow in 1840, he espoused the French Jacobin and socialist tradition and the belief in the inevitability of progress. In *From the Other Shore* (1855), written in voluntary exile in Paris after the Revolution of 1848, Herzen expressed confidence that Russia, even while following the lead of the West, would take its own path to socialism. Socialism could be easily established in Russia because the village commune already existed as a community of social equals in the face of autocratic and noble exploitation. Herzen implored Russian officials to struggle for peaceful liberal reform. Interestingly enough, both radical reformers and the men of the tsarist state shared a suspicion of Western "bourgeois" political and social life. The Slavophile current of reformism thus had much more in common

Alexander Herzen.

with the tsarist autocracy than it cared to admit. Unlike the Westernizers, the Slavophiles celebrated the religious faith of the Russian masses, believing that an era of social harmony and equality had existed in Russia before Peter the Great transformed the Russian state in the late seventeenth century by importing Western ideals and bureaucracy. "We are a backward people," wrote one young Slavophile, "and therein lies our salvation. We must . . . not repeat the stale old lessons of Europe."

The Emancipation of the Serfs

The emancipation of the serfs in 1861 by Tsar Alexander II (ruled 1855–1881) was the most ambitious attempt at reform in Russia during the nineteenth century. Serfdom dictated the organization of taxation, the army, the courts, and virtually every other institution of government. Indeed, the state had little active presence in the village—as the peasants put it, "God is in heaven and the tsar far away." Because landowners had a virtually unlimited source of labor, many showed little inclination to try to increase agricultural yields.

Alexander II, who succeeded his father Nicholas I as tsar in 1855, was shocked by Russia's defeat in the Crimean War. The tsar and some of his officials began to believe that his country could not compete with the West if the serfs were not emancipated. Despite an increase in agricultural laborers hired for wages, Russian industrial development and effective agricultural production required free wage labor that could be taxed. Even if some lords had attempted to increase the productivity of their land, serfs only worked halfheartedly—and who could blame them. Most Russian peasants still used the wasteful three-field system (with one field left fallow each year).

Serf rebellions—more than 1,500 during the first half of the century—periodically shook the empire. Many serfs had joined the army during the Crimean War, believing that they would be freed upon returning home. The flight of thousands of serfs toward the open spaces of the east, or to Crimea, undermined the agricultural economy upon which Russia depended. As rumors spread that the tsar, whom many peasants considered the father of his people, would end Russia's "peculiar institution," peasant rebellions became even more widespread. Intellectuals continued to denounce serfdom, as did bureaucrats, at least in private. Tsar Alexander II told assembled landowners, "It is better to abolish serfdom from above than to wait until serfs begin to liberate themselves from below." Some nobles now believed emancipation inevitable. In 1858, a Slavophile noble wrote the tsar that the "abolition of the right to dispose of people like objects or cattle is as much our liberation as theirs."

On April 5, 1861, Russia became the last European state to abolish serfdom. Alexander II emancipated the 22 million serfs by a proclamation made through the Orthodox Church. For two years, however, the old sys-

Peasants hailing Tsar Alexander II after the emancipation of the serfs in 1861.

tem remained essentially in place. But serfs then received land through the commune—the *mir*—which was administered by male heads of household. The state compensated nobles for their land, and peasants had to repay the state through annual redemption payments. Yet nobles lost in the emancipation, as in many cases they received bonds of little value, as well as losing the value of the serfs. Peasants were no longer dependent upon the whims of landlord justice. Yet many peasants, who had wanted complete and immediate freedom without compensation ("We are yours," went an old serf proverb, "but the land is ours.") were disappointed by the terms of their freedom. Furthermore, as the villages were collectively responsible for land redemption payments and taxes (although the lords' household serfs were freed without land and owed no payments), former serfs were rather like hostages to their own villages. Instead of owing labor to the lords, they now owed taxes to the state, which would be collected by the communes. They were dependent upon the village patriarchs for permission to go find work elsewhere. Peasants flocked to the cities, which grew by leaps and bounds.

In tsarist Russia, the serfs were freed practically without bloodshed, while in the United States the slaves found freedom only after one of the most violent struggles—the Civil War (1861–1865)—of the nineteenth century. Unlike the southern landed elite in the United States, who went to war in defense of slavery, the Russian nobility capitulated without resistance to emancipation. Despite the vast expanse of the Russian Empire, the tsarist state exercised more centralized authority than did the relatively weak central government in the United States. Moreover, Americans considered private property more of an absolute right than did even Russian nobles, who wanted, above all, to extract services from peasants. After emancipation, the vast wealth of the Russian nobles could still pay for such services.

More reforms followed. Alexander II rooted out some incompetent ministers and officials and asked the ministry of finance to keep regular budgets. In 1864, the tsar decreed the establishment of district or village assemblies called *zemstvos*. These would elect delegates to regional assemblies. Six years later, he created similar urban institutions called *dumas* (councils), with the authority to assess taxes and to organize public services and education. But the ministry of the interior controlled the *zemstvos*, and provincial governors ignored them, some treating their members as seditious agitators. Moreover, wealthy landowners elected the members of the *zemstvos*; their votes were given more weight than those of townsmen and peasants, yet the *zemstvos* provided some political apprenticeships to ordinary people.

Russian law had been codified in the 1830s, but the emancipation of the serfs necessitated an expanded administrative apparatus, since millions of people were now subject to the justice of the state. The tsar introduced regional and lower courts modeled on those of Britain, as well as public trial by jury. In 1864, for the first time, a separate judicial branch of government came into existence in Russia, although the tsar could override any court decision. A jury system was established, along with the possibility of appeals. Yet peasants were not judged in the same courts as social elites.

Thus, the essential structure of the Russian Empire remained the same. The army was no longer made up of loyal, poorly supplied, illiterate, beaten serfs but rather of loyal, poorly supplied, illiterate, beaten peasants. In the past, few soldiers had been expected to survive the twenty-five-year term of service. Indeed, wives of soldiers had the right to remarry three years after their husbands left for military service. Alexander II established a Prussian-style general staff, took steps to modernize weapons, and reduced the term of military service to six years, followed by nine years in the reserves and five years in the militia. Alexander also ordered the elimination of some forms of corporal punishment, including the brutal—and often fatal—floggings.

However, the arbitrary power of the tsarist state and its Third Section police to repress dissent remained largely intact. Most political cases were handed over to trial by secret court-martial. Alexander restored the censorship apparatus, which was temporarily weakened in the years before the emancipation, to full strength. Moreover, the tsar had no intention of creating any kind of national representative institution that would undercut his authority. Russian reform had its limits.

The Expansion of the Russian Empire

Following defeat in the Crimean War and as stipulated by the Peace of Paris (1856), Russia relinquished Moldavia, Wallachia, and Bessarabia and had to accept the neutrality of the Black Sea, further frustrating imperial designs in southeastern Europe (see Map 18.2). Russia now confronted nationalist movements among peoples within the empire. After two years of public demonstrations, an uprising in Poland occurred in 1863. Rebels proclaimed a "national government" before being crushed by Russian troops. Tsar Alexander II cracked down, ordering the confiscation of some Polish lands as punishment for participating in the revolt, closing most monasteries, and not permitting the creation of *zemstvos* (elected councils) or juries in law courts, reforms he had applied to Russia. Poland was transformed into a province with all illusions of autonomy ended. Poles felt the effect of the repression even in Prussia, where the government forbade the sale of lands to Poles or Catholics (priests had been among the insurgents). In the Ukraine, Polish national consciousness helped inspire emerging Ukrainian identity. In response, in 1863 the state forbade the publication of nonfiction works in the Ukrainian language.

In the Ottoman Balkans, Russian troops intervened on behalf of Bulgarians, who were fellow Slavs. The rising of pan-Slavism as an ideology was increasingly apparent. Pan-Slavism enthuastically proclaimed that all Slavs were in the same family. In Herzegovina, peasants had rebelled against Ottoman tax collectors and soldiers. In the subsequent Russo-Turkish War (1877–1878), a Russian army drove toward Constantinople. Austro-Hungarian forces and the British navy readied to prevent the Russians from reaching the Dardanelles strait. Defeat forced the Ottoman Empire to sign the Treaty of San Stefano (1878) with Russia. Then the other powers called for an international conference to discuss the matter. German Chancellor Otto von Bismarck presided at the Congress of Berlin (1878). Bulgaria became a principality, but remained a vassal state of the sultan of Turkey. At Disraeli's insistence, the Congress of Berlin reduced the size of Bulgaria. Greece received Thessaly, which it had claimed, thus moving the Greek border to the edge of Macedonia, claimed by Bulgaria, Serbia, and Greece. There were then few Bulgarian nationalists, despite the fact that Bulgaria received its own Orthodox Church in 1870; not many decades earlier most educated people there had considered themselves Greek. The fact that Russia would clearly dominate Bulgaria—Russians held key government posts—and the rising mood of Pan-Slavism (a movement aimed at promoting the interests and unity of all Slavs) in the Balkans alarmed Austria-Hungary and Britain. The Congress of Berlin also recognized Serbia, Montenegro, and Romania as independent states, further reducing Ottoman territory in Europe. Russia received a small part of Bessarabia, which allowed it to control the mouth of the Danube River. But Russian Pan-Slavs, in particular, believed themselves aggrieved by Britain and betrayed by Bismarck's

MAP 18.2 THE EXPANSION OF RUSSIA   After territorial losses under the Peace of Paris (1856), Russia turned eastward, expanding through Central Asia toward the Far East and its port at Vladivostok.

Germany. Likewise, Bulgarian nationalists would increasingly feel that they had been cheated out of land in Macedonia that they believed Bulgaria had been promised by Russia.

Alexander II then turned his attention toward Central Asia and the Middle East. Russian armies conquered Turkistan in 1859–1860, annexed Tashkent in 1866, and then reached Afghanistan. The wars that subdued the Muslim mountain people of the Caucasus ended in 1860. The expansion added about 5 million Muslims to the empire. Russian expansion now seemed to impinge upon British interests near India, the gem of its empire. The British army invaded Afghanistan, and in 1881 put a puppet ruler on the throne. In the Far East, Russian forces moved across Siberia, where the discovery of gold in the 1830s had attracted tens of thousands of settlers, to go with the ever-expanding convict population, giving the Russian navy access to the Pacific Ocean at Vladivostok.

The Russian Empire now included about one-seventh of the world's land mass. This eastward expansion eventually brought conflict with China. The Chinese emperors would be powerless in the face of Russian demands, as they were when confronted by those of Britain. Surprisingly, Japan, which emerged from centuries of isolation following the Meiji Restoration in 1868, would prove to be a far tougher adversary for Russia.

Nihilists and Populists

Revolutionaries replaced the conscience-stricken gentry of the 1830s and 1840s as the principal critics of the Russian autocracy. They were drawn from a variety of social backgrounds, including the sons and daughters of nobles, merchants, peasants, and Orthodox priests. Convinced that one spark might ignite a wave of rebellion, they struck out on their own or in very small groups.

Some Russian revolutionaries found the old debates between the Westernizers and Slavophiles irrelevant. Nihilists accepted no dogmas, but above all rejected the materialist doctrines of the West. They also disavowed many Russian traditions, and thus repudiated the Slavophiles. Some of them viewed the Orthodox Church as an institution of oppression, whereas others remained fervent believers.

Nihilists saw in the Russian masses an untapped revolutionary force, believing that the emancipation of the serfs had aided their cause by creating an independent peasantry, which might be more likely to rise up against its oppressors. Like the conscience-stricken gentry before them, the nihilists believed in the power of literature to effect change. In 1863, Nikolay Chernyshevsky (1828–1889), a former seminarian, published *What Is to Be Done?*, a novel that had an enormous impact on several generations of intellectuals. Chernyshevsky described committed people of action as "rational egoists" who would form a disciplined vanguard of change. Because nihilists did not feel bound by moral codes, they believed they could take whatever

(*Left*) Michael Bakunin, professional anarchist. (*Right*) Karl Marx, founder of Communism.

action seemed necessary to achieve their goals. In the 1860s, groups of nihilists turned to violent revolution, plotting the assassination of state officials and the tsar. The police infiltrated and drove groups like "Land and Freedom" and "The Organization"—with its central committee called "Hell"—underground, particularly after a student attempted to kill Tsar Alexander II in 1866.

In the meantime, Michael Bakunin (1814–1876) became the most famous anarchist of his or any other time. Anarchists rejected the very existence of the state, thereby quarreling bitterly with socialists, who wanted not to destroy the state but to take it over. A professional revolutionary who complained, "Karl Marx is ruining the workers by making theorists out of them," Bakunin left behind comfortable noble origins. He was a man of enormous energy who slept only a couple of hours a day, eating, drinking, and smoking cigars almost constantly, organizing and plotting between bites, gulps, and puffs. Once calling himself "the devil in the flesh," Bakunin defined the "social question" as "primarily the overthrow of society." That he set out to do. He led the police on a chase from Paris in 1847 to Dresden and other stops in Central Europe in 1848, that year of revolution. Arrested and imprisoned in Russia, he was exiled to Siberia, managed to escape in 1861, reached Japan, and then arrived in London via the United States.

Bakunin believed that "destruction is a creative passion" and, like the nihilists, that the peasant masses had untapped revolutionary potential. Marx insisted that peasants, unlike the industrial proletariat, could never be truly revolutionary because they could not be class-conscious. Anarchists, in turn, rejected Marx's belief that a militant working class organized in a centralized party could make a revolution, fearing that Marxists wanted to replace a bourgeois state with a proletarian state, a state all the same.

Unlike revolutionary nihilists and anarchists who dreamed of a spontaneous peasant uprising, Sergei Nechayev (1847–1882) held that a small, tightly organized revolutionary group could begin the peasant revolution that would sweep away autocratic oppression. "The revolutionary is," Nechayev wrote, "a doomed man. He has no personal interests, no affairs, sentiments, attachments, property, not even a name of his own. Everything in him is absorbed by one exclusive interest, one thought, one passion—the revolution." After murdering one of his colleagues, Nechayev was arrested and sent to prison, where he died.

During his anguished life, Nechayev had battled the populists (*narodniki*). The populists developed their doctrine in response to nihilism and retained the Slavophiles' faith in the Russian peasantry. They were romantic collectivists who idealized the Russian peasant community. In contrast to Chernyshevsky, who wanted to teach the peasants, the populists wanted to learn from them. In the early 1870s, several thousand young Russians, who had been members of circles of intellectuals, went from Saint Petersburg and Moscow into the countryside. Many had been influenced by Peter Lavrov (1823–1900), who lamented in his *Historical Letters* (1869) that the gap between the intellectuals like himself and peasants had become even greater over the previous decades. These upper-class Russians resembled the conscience-stricken gentry of the 1830s and 1840s. "Going to the people" and dressing like peasants, they also wanted to prepare revolution by helping to educate the peasants. Some of those attracted to direct revolutionary action worried that the emancipation of the serfs might create a class of conservative peasant proprietors. Time seemed to be running out for Russia to take its own path to socialism before capitalism became entrenched in Russia, as it had in Western Europe.

In 1878, a revolutionary populist shot and wounded the governor-general of Saint Petersburg. Another attack that year, carried out by the "disorganization section" of Land and Freedom, struck down the head of the Third Section police. A wave of strikes by industrial workers convinced the terrorists that revolution was not far away.

Twice more, Tsar Alexander II escaped assassination attempts. In the hope of placating his enemies without destroying the foundations of the autocracy, Alexander disbanded the Third Section. He dismissed the minister of education, whose restrictive policies on university admission were unpopular, and announced the formation of a new consultative assembly. But in 1881, members of "People's Will" struck, hurling a bomb near Alexander's sleigh. When the tsar foolishly stepped from the sleigh to inspect the damage, another man threw a bomb that killed him. However, the assassination did not prove to be the revolutionary spark anticipated by those who carried it out. Millions of the tsar's subjects mourned the ruler who had freed them.

Alexander III's Empire

Following his father's assassination, Alexander III (ruled 1881–1894) was in no mood to contemplate any liberalization of imperial institutions. Public opinion existed in the Russian Empire, but mass political life did not. The assassination led to a curtailment of the powers of the *zemstvos*. Judicial authority shifted to the police, putting political trials in the hands of military courts. For the moment, exile was the only safe place from which to criticize the autocracy. Small colonies of political refugees, most of whom were socialists, lived in Geneva, Paris, and London.

Professors and teachers were brought under stricter state control, and tuition was increased to discourage commoners from going to school. The police could arrest and imprison anyone without reason. The resulting political trials may have actually helped the cause of reformers and revolutionaries by serving as tribunals where the autocratic regime was discussed and political issues were brought into the open. What went on in courtrooms helped shape Russian opinion, even when political trials were moved into military courts.

The Russian Empire late in the nineteenth century was enormous. More than a hundred times the size of Great Britain and three times larger than the United States (to which Russia had sold Alaska in 1867), its population doubled from about 74 million inhabitants in 1861 to about 150 million by 1905. It was now comprised of almost 200 nationalities who spoke 146 languages. Russians made up 40 percent of the population of the empire. Ukrainians, Poles, and Belorussians made up the next largest national groups, followed by Lithuanians, Latvians, Estonians, Finns, Romanians (in Bessarabia), Crimean Tatars, Armenians, Georgians, Azeri (in the Caucasus), and the Muslim peoples of Central Asia.

Alexander ordered a vigorous campaign of "Russification" in the western empire. The tsar banned the use of languages other than Russian in school, and forbade publication in, for example, the Ukrainian language, despite the fact that it was spoken by 25 million people. At the same time, the Russian Orthodox Church launched campaigns against non-Orthodox religions, which held the allegiance of almost a third of the people of the empire. New laws enforced restrictions against Jews, who in principle where supposed to be confined to the "Pale of Settlement" in Poland. In 1899, the Finnish Assembly was reduced to a "consultative" voice, and Russians replaced Finns in most key administrative positions.

"Russification" firmed the resolve of nationalist groups to persevere in their demands for recognition. In Russian Poland, opposition grew more daring. Poles were linked by long-standing cultural bonds, based on language and Catholicism. Polish identity had survived the end of an independent Poland with the Third Partition of 1795 by Russia, Austria, and Prussia. Moreover, the cause of Polish independence had been kept alive by Poles forced to flee abroad after the ill-fated insurrections of 1831 and

1863. Two strong movements then developed. National Democrats sought to build up the strength of the Polish nation within the context of the Russian Empire, viewing Prussia and then Germany as the principal enemy. Polish Socialists, in contrast, wanted to organize another uprising, one that they hoped one day would lead to an independent and socialist Poland in which the rights of non-Poles would also be recognized.

Unrest, Reform, and Revolution

The majority of the population of the Russian Empire was poor: the average per capita income was more than four times higher in Britain, three times higher in Germany, and twice as high in the Balkan states. If by 1910, 70 percent of children aged 7 to 11 were likely to attend school for at least one year, about 60 percent of the population remained illiterate. In 1897, only 1 percent of the population had attended secondary school for any amount of time.

Yet literacy in European Russia and the Baltic region, in particular, was rising, and with it the number of people who wanted reform. The reading public grew dramatically in size around the turn of the century, especially in Saint Petersburg and Moscow. Even seasonal workers and peasants migrating to Siberia began to carry books with them. The taste for literature expanded from religious books and the emerging classics of the Russian literary tradition (above all, Gogol and Tolstoy) to relatively liberal magazines and newspapers.

Liberals had played a role in the expanding domain of Russian public opinion since the heady days of the 1860s and the emancipation of the serfs. The Russian army's poor performance in the war against Turkey (1877–1878) proved that military reforms instituted following the Crimean War had been inadequate. Expanding opportunities for education, increased government bureaucratization, and industrial development increased the professional middle class. This, combined with the expansion of heavy and light industry, and urban growth, seemed to make autocracy an anachronism.

Liberals included a smattering of gentry, leaders of local assemblies (the *zemstvos* and the municipal *dumas*), and, above all, members of the professional classes, including economists, *zemstvo* agronomists, physicians, lawyers, teachers, and students. Some state bureaucrats, too, sought a middle way between state and noble intransigence and revolutionary insurgency, hoping that the tsar would grant political reforms to complement the gradual modernization of the Russian economy. Some were encouraged by laws slightly reducing the long work day (1897) and providing the first factory insurance law (1903). Liberals in the Union of Liberation demanded an extension of the powers of the *zemstvos*, whose limited authority had been curtailed in 1890, but imagined little more than active consultation between those bodies and the tsar.

New revolutionary groups, however, still believed the autocracy incapable of reforming itself and that only revolution could bring reform. The populist Socialist Revolutionaries became the largest radical group, with growing support among peasants, whom Socialist Revolutionaries, like some of their optimistic predecessors, believed would one day overthrow the tsar. In the meantime, national movements developed in Poland, Finland, Ukraine, and the Baltic region. In the distant Muslim reaches of the empire, religion provided a new cohesiveness.

Marxists founded the Russian Social Democratic Workers' Party in 1898. They were confident that one day, though probably not in their lifetimes, the Russian proletariat would be sufficiently numerous and class-conscious to seize power. But this seizure of power could only occur, they believed, after a democratic revolution had successfully overthrown the Russian autocracy. Marxists claimed vindication for their view that peasants had no true revolutionary potential when, despite the terrible suffering and deaths of millions of peasants during the famine that followed the severe drought and epidemics of 1891–1892, the countryside remained quiescent.

By 1900, the tsar's police had succeeded in disbanding most of the revolutionary groups within the empire, deporting their leaders to join the groups in exile, sending them to Siberia, or putting them in prison. Most revolutionaries shared a belief that their country was far from revolution.

Lenin and the Bolsheviks

Vladimir Ilyich Ulyanov, known as Lenin, was born in the Volga River town of Simbirsk on April 22, 1870, more than 400 miles east of Moscow. His father served as the director of primary schools for the province and, as a result of loyal service, he obtained non-hereditary membership in the nobility; Lenin's mother, whose family had originally been German, was the daughter of a doctor. Older brother Alexander, who joined the revolutionary group "People's Will," was executed in 1887 for participation in a plot to kill Tsar Alexander III. Lenin briefly attended university, but was expelled for participating in a student demonstration. During the next six years, Lenin read widely in history and philosophy, including the works of Marx and Friedrich Engels, and received a degree in law from the University of Saint Petersburg.

In 1895, Lenin went to Austria, France, and Switzerland, meeting Russian political exiles and socialists from many countries. Back in Saint Petersburg two years later, he was charged with organizing and writing articles in a clandestine newspaper (*Iskra*, or *Spark*) and exiled to Siberia. When his term of banishment ended in 1900, he moved to Switzerland. As a virtually penniless exile, he bore his situation with good humor. Lenin's few interests outside of politics and revolution included chess, hunting, bicycling, and mountain hiking. But he viewed most recreational activities—even, at times, simple conversation—as interfering with revolutionary struggle. There was nothing about Lenin's appearance that would have attracted the attention of tsarist spies or Swiss and French police. An Englishman said that "he looked more like a provincial grocer than a leader."

Lenin combined a powerful ability to theorize with a facility for adapting to changing circumstances. His steely resolve would carry him to cold fury when colleagues or rivals failed to agree with him. "He who does not understand this does not understand anything!" was a typical Lenin rejoinder. A vigorous polemicist, he could be impatient and churlish in speech, cutting and sarcastic with his potent pen.

In 1902, Lenin, who had taken his name as a pseudonym the previous year, published *What Is to Be Done?* In this pamphlet (with the same title as the work by Chernyshevsky), Lenin established what would become the basic tenets of a new revolutionary party. Lenin believed that Marxist analysis could be applied to a backward, authoritarian nation with a relatively undeveloped working class and a small bourgeoisie. "The one serious organizational principle for workers in our movement must be strictest secrecy," he wrote, and "the strictest choice of members and the training of professional revolutionaries." He rejected all compromise with liberals and reform socialists, viewing as self-defeating the struggle of workers for small economic gains, crumbs tossed from the posh table of the ruling class. Rejecting the common Marxist view that the social experiences of workers would lead them to revolutionary consciousness, Lenin believed that only a minority of workers would achieve consciousness and that these should join with intellectuals in a party that would direct the masses.

Lenin and his followers became known as the "Bolsheviks," or "majority" (although much of the time in the years that followed they were not), and their rivals were known as the "Mensheviks," the "minority." The Mensheviks believed that a proletarian revolution lay in the future, but not until a bourgeois uprising had first succeeded in overthrowing the tsarist state. Mensheviks believed that their role was to mobilize support for their party through propaganda, while undertaking timely alliances with liberal groups. They objected to the high degree of party centralization upon which Lenin insisted.

The Russo-Japanese War (1904–1905)

In the meantime, the Russian Empire lurched toward war with Japan. It had begun to covet Chinese Manchuria and the peninsula of Korea. The acquisition of Manchuria would permit Russia to construct a more direct rail link to the ice-free Russian port of Vladivostok; that of Korea would protect the new port from possible attack and provide still more ports. In 1894, Japan goaded China into a war. By the Treaty of Shimonoseki (1895), the victorious Japanese took the island of Formosa (Taiwan) and gained Chinese recognition of Korea's independence. This placed the peninsula under direct Japanese influence. Japan also acquired the Liaodong (Liaotung)

Three Manchurian men crouch before the hulks of Russian ships sunk during the Russo-Japanese War.

peninsula in southern Manchuria but was forced by Russia, Germany, and France to return it.

Russia viewed the expansion of Japanese interests in the Far East with concern. In 1898, Tsar Nicholas II (ruled 1894–1917) signed a treaty with China and obtained a concession to build the Manchurian railway and to construct a port at Port Arthur on the tip of the Liaodong peninsula, providing a source of conflict between Japan and Russia. Japan, in turn, signed a treaty in 1902 with Great Britain, Russia's rival for influence in Afghanistan. Britain would remain neutral if Japan and Russia went to war against each other. But Britain would join Japan in any conflict that allied Russia with any other power in a war against Japan.

In February 1904, Japanese torpedo boats launched a surprise attack on the Russian fleet at Port Arthur, destroying a number of ships while the Japanese army drove Russian forces away on land. In March 1905, Japanese troops defeated the Russians in the bloody Battle of Mukden where, for the first time, two armies faced each other across trenches dug for protection. Two months later, the Japanese navy pounced on the Russian fleet, which had spent nine months at sea. The Battle of Tsushima ended with nineteen Russian ships sunk, five captured, and six forced to neutral ports. Only three ships of the Russian fleet reached Vladivostok.

How could the Russian Empire be defeated by a small island nation in Asia? Only a single-track railway line stretching across thousands of miles supplied the Russian forces. The Russian army was poorly commanded and fought with outdated artillery and rifles. By the Treaty of Portsmouth (New Hampshire), signed in September 1905 at a conference hastily arranged by U.S. President Theodore Roosevelt, Japan took over Russia's lease of the Liaodong peninsula and Chinese concessions in Manchuria. Russia accepted Japanese influence over Korea. A new world imperial power was born.

The Revolution of 1905

Many of the tsar's subjects had blamed government inaction for the murderous famine of 1891–1892, which had captured world attention. In 1902, peasants attacked noble property in some districts, and a wave of industrial strikes followed the next year. Liberals organized support for political reform by sponsoring banquets similar to those employed by French republicans just before the Revolution of 1848. Dissent mounted against forced Russification among subject nationalities, most notably the Poles and the Finns. Marxist groups were particularly active in Poland—where the issue of Polish nationalism versus internationalism was hotly debated—and in the Jewish Pale—those provinces where Jews were allowed to settle and where they faced endemic anti-Semitism and occasional bloody pogroms.

Shocking defeats in the distant Russo-Japanese War increased calls for liberal reform. A wide-ranging social and political alliance for change extended across classes. For the first time, liberals and socialists (except for Bolsheviks and Mensheviks), gentry, intellectuals, professionals, and workers, and both Russians and non-Russians came together in common opposition to autocracy, embracing a loose ideology of reform. After the assassination of his minister of the interior in July 1904 by a Socialist Revolutionary, Nicholas II appointed a more moderate successor in the hope of calming dissent. Moreover, the tsar allowed a national congress of *zemstvos* and *dumas* to take place. It called for the establishment of a national parliament.

In the meantime, the Russian labor movement remained small and faced constant police harassment. Skilled factory workers supplied the majority of labor militants. At the turn of the century, the police had authorized government-controlled labor associations in the hope of undercutting revolutionaries by encouraging workers to concentrate on economic grievances and achieve some small victories through negotiation or conciliation, as strikes remained illegal. But such halfway measures gave workers useful organizational experience.

In January 1905, a strike by 100,000 factory workers brought Saint Petersburg to a standstill. In Warsaw, a general strike brought violence and reprisals by troops. On January 22, an Orthodox priest, Father Gapon, led a march of workers to the tsar's Winter Palace, carrying a petition asking for "justice" and political reform. Troops blocked their way. When the marchers locked arms and refused an order to disperse, a commander barked out the order to fire.

More than 300 marchers, including women and children, fell dead, and perhaps 1,000 or more were wounded. "Bloody Sunday" helped shatter the myth that the tsar was the Holy Father manipulated by selfish nobles and wicked advisers. Bolsheviks and Socialist Revolutionaries, the latter particularly influential in the countryside, encouraged more strikes. A violent faction of the Socialist Revolutionaries carried out a particularly bloody series of terrorist attacks and assassinations. Nicholas dismissed his liberal minister of the interior. The tsar's uncle fell to an assassin's bullets. Strikes spread to Poland, where they were bolstered by the nationalist movement, and to Ukraine, Latvia, and Estonia. In some parts of Russia and in the Baltic provinces, peasants attacked the homes of wealthy landowners. In the southeastern borderlands, Muslim leaders announced the formation of an All-Russian Muslim League. Workers began to organize trade unions in huge numbers and newspapers appeared in open defiance of censorship. In June, sailors on the battleship *Potemkin* mutinied on the Black Sea, killing the captain and several officers.

With the bulk of the army fighting the Japanese in Manchuria, Nicholas appeared to choose the path of reform, appointing Sergei Witte (1849–1915) as prime minister. Witte was eager to make Russia a modern industrial power, and he believed that he could do so if the tsar granted minimal reforms. He persuaded Nicholas to rescind redemption payments to the state for land acquired when the serfs were emancipated in 1861, to allow Poles and Lithuanians to use their own languages, to allow religious toleration in Poland, to return political trials to regular courts, and to abolish some restrictions on Jews.

Russian troops fire on the workers, Bloody Sunday, January 1905.

Even more important, Nicholas's October Manifesto of 1905 created a national representative assembly, the Duma, to be chosen by universal male suffrage, and promised freedom of the press. Some state officials and most nobles, however, viewed these particular reforms as unacceptable, associating them with the parliamentary regimes of the West. But progressive nobles and businessmen were encouraged by the sudden, unexpected turn of events. Some staunch liberals, some of whom had participated in the *zemstvos,* took the name of the Constitutional Democratic Party (known as the Kadets). They demanded constitutional rule, insisting that even the promised reforms left the essential structures of autocracy unchanged. In the meantime, the Mensheviks had championed the establishment of Saint Petersburg workers' councils, known as *soviets.* These were neighborhood councils made up of delegates from factories, shops, trade unions, and political parties who helped organize strikes, which became legal in December. The Mensheviks now were willing to collaborate with the liberals to bring further reforms to workers and peasants.

But a violent uprising in Moscow in December 1905 brought on vigorous counter-revolution. Witte ordered the arrest of many of the workers' leaders. The *soviets* no longer were free to meet. Army units returning from Manchuria crushed nationalist demonstrations in Poland and Georgia and brutally restored order in the Russian and Ukrainian countryside. In the Baltic provinces of Latvia and Estonia, punitive expeditions ordered by the tsar killed over 1,000 people while crushing strikes and rural unrest. Fanatical Russian nationalists known as the Black Hundreds, perhaps instigated by Orthodox priests, unleashed a wave of violence against Jews (and against Russian, German, and Polish property owners, as well) which lasted more than a year. The Black Hundreds were led by small traders and agricultural laborers who feared that economic change would cost them what limited security they had and by police who opposed political reform. In the Black Sea town of Odessa, drunken mobs aided by the local police murdered 800 Jews, injured more than 5,000 others, and left twice that number homeless. The tsar himself intervened to prevent Witte from prosecuting the police there, praising the "mass of loyal people"; they had struck out against "troublemakers." Jews could be conveniently blamed for agitating against autocratic rule.

Against this turbulent backdrop, the Duma had met for the first time in April 1906. The U.S. ambassador described the gathering in the Winter Palace of the members of the Duma, who were dressed "in every conceivable costume, the peasants in rough clothes and long boots, merchants and tradespeople in frock coats, lawyers in dress suits, priests in long garb and almost equally long hair, and even a Catholic bishop in violet robes." The majority of the Duma members were Kadets (Constitutional Democrats), largely because the Marxist Mensheviks and Bolsheviks and the Socialist Revolutionaries refused to participate in the election.

As the Duma debated land reform, an issue on which the tsar refused any compromise, Nicholas decreed the establishment of an upper assembly, the State Council. With members to be drawn from the high clergy, the army, or other loyal institutions, it would counteract the influence of the Duma. The tsar then dismissed Witte and announced that he would promulgate any decree he pleased while the Duma was not in session. When the Kadets petitioned Nicholas to abolish the State Council, make ministers responsible to the Duma, and turn over some noble estates to the peasants, he dissolved the first Duma.

The Revolution of 1905 ended in failure, but its memory could not be effaced. The tsar had been forced to grant a parliament and the promise of limited civil rights. Many people within the Russian professional class, particularly bureaucrats and lawyers, remained sympathetic to the reforms after they had been undone by the tsar.

The Revolution of 1905 heightened the divisions among exiled Russian socialists. Mensheviks contended that compromise with bourgeois reformers would increase socialist support within Russia. Lenin and the Bolsheviks, on the other hand, believed that the failed revolution had clearly demonstrated that the Russian proletariat in the large cities was already a revolutionary force, and that the first stage of Marx's promised revolution could be achieved if workers and peasants joined together.

Nicholas II named Peter Stolypin (1862–1911) prime minister, and in June 1907 ordered the dissolution of a second elected Duma even though it was more conservative than the first. The tsar established military field courts

Tsar Nicholas II presides over the opening of the Duma.

that could summarily convict and sentence civilians accused of violent political crimes. This law resulted in nearly 1,000 hangings before it expired six months later. Liberals dubbed the ropes of the gallows "Stolypin's neckties."

After Nicholas changed the rules of election to increase the power of noble votes at the expense of peasants, workers, and non-Russians, a third Duma was elected in 1907 that was more to the tsar's liking. It was dominated by the "Octobrists," who believed that the tsar's promises in the October Manifesto of 1905 represented sufficient reform and wanted to stop at that. The repression and Russification campaign went on.

Stolypin nonetheless undertook rural reforms beginning in 1906, hoping that they might defuse the political intensity of the agrarian question and reduce unrest without the confiscation of land owned by the gentry. His goal was to create a class of prosperous peasants (*kulaks*) while increasing agricultural production by allowing peasants to leave their villages and set up independent farms. He hoped that the enclosure of common lands and a consolidation of holdings would expand the number of peasant plots. Indeed, a considerable amount of land passed from communal to private ownership. The number of prosperous peasants increased. Yet prices for farm products fell, and even peasants with fairly large plots of land still had to struggle to survive. By 1914 more than 5 million Russians had crossed the Ural Mountains, most of them peasants attracted by the possibility of land—Siberia thus became something of the equivalent of the American West.

In 1911, Stolypin was assassinated. Although the government of course claimed the assassin was a Jew, the minister may have been killed with the approval of the tsar at the instigation of noble advisers who considered him too liberal and rejected any agrarian reforms.

A surge of industrial strikes and peasant violence over the next three years demonstrated continued popular dissatisfaction. With political parties now legal, although facing police constraints, and the press in principle free, Liberals, Socialist Revolutionaries, and Menshevik and Bolshevik Social Democrats mobilized support against the regime. Indeed, the growing popularity of Bolsheviks among organized urban workers—revealed in their victories in trade union elections—reflected deepening impatience with the path of moderate reform.

FRANCE: SECOND EMPIRE AND THIRD REPUBLIC

In the meantime, Europe's traditionally most revolutionary country remained France. Following the Revolution of 1848, Louis Napoleon Bonaparte completed his destruction of the Second Republic with his coup d'état on December 2, 1851. The following year he proclaimed himself emperor as Napoleon III, with the overwhelming support of the upper classes and many peasants.

Emperor Napoleon III was a small man with a prominent nose who appeared lethargic. He reminded some people of a sphinx, and a contemporary of "a melancholy parrot." An unimpressed visitor from the United States described the French ruler as "a long-bodied, short-legged man, fiercely mustached, old, wrinkled, with eyes half closed, and such a deep, crafty, scheming expression about them!" Indeed, like his legendary uncle Napoleon Bonaparte, Napoleon III consistently demonstrated considerable energy when it came to behind-the-scenes intrigue and the pursuit of women.

During the Second Empire (1852–1870), wealthy businessmen became the equivalent of an imperial aristocracy in France, money standing as the measure of value that blue blood had been in the early modern period. Enjoying access to the emperor, some of them lived in Parisian residences and owned country houses that would have made eighteenth-century aristocrats drool with envy. The empress set the tone for Parisian fashion, while critics condemned the "triumphant vulgarity and appalling materialism" of the "imperial festival."

Yet Napoleon III set out to pull the nation together. France was the only European power with universal male suffrage, however distorted by government pressure. The emperor promoted economic growth, encouraged urban rebuilding projects (see Chapter 19), created institutions that provided credit, and constructed more railways. Moreover, in 1859 Napoleon III initiated the "liberal empire," encouraging a series of reforms, including authorizing a liberal trade treaty with Britain in 1860 and permitting the legalization of strikes in 1864.

The Authoritarian Empire

Napoleon III ruled with the help of a handful of worldly, trusted cronies who held ministries or who served on the Council of State. Ministers were responsible to the emperor, who alone could propose legislation. The state clamped down on the remnants of political opposition, maintained press censorship, and sponsored "official" candidates in the elections held every six years for the Legislative Body, the lower house of the National Assembly. Hand-picked notables made up its upper chamber, the Senate. Napoleon III's men built a Bonapartist party from the remnants of Orleanism, that is, from those conservative bourgeois who had supported the July Monarchy (1830–1848). They rallied to Napoleon III, who promoted economic growth and promised to maintain social and political order. The French state, more than its decentralized British counterpart, could buy political support by dispensing patronage, through prefects, the most powerful local officials. The Second Empire thus further centralized economic and political power in France.

A good many Legitimists—that is, the supporters of the Bourbon royal family and its exiled pretender, the count of Chambord—supported the emperor. Like his uncle, Napoleon III had made peace with the Church.

A cartoon critical of Napoleon III, shown limping behind a vulture after his defeat in the Franco-German war (*left*), stands in stark contrast to the Bonapartist propaganda early in his dictatorship declaring "The Glory of Napoleon III" (*right*).

The clergy remained grateful that during the Second Republic over which Napoleon had presided as president and then destroyed, the Falloux Law of 1850 had returned much control over education to them.

Economic Growth

The rate of French economic growth was such during the 1850s that economic historians sometimes use it as an example of an industrial "take-off." French exports doubled between 1853 and 1864. Never before had any state taken such a direct role in stimulating the economy through encouragement and investment. Government officials coordinated the efforts of the ministries of agriculture, commerce, and public works, while keeping in close touch with wealthy bankers and industrialists who backed the regime.

French entrepreneurs had often found it difficult to raise investment capital. Most companies remained family concerns, hesitant to open investment possibilities to outsiders. Napoleon III encouraged the creation of state mortgage banks. In 1852, the Péreire brothers, who were Protestants like many French bankers, created the Crédit Mobilier, an investment bank. Selling shares to raise capital until its collapse in 1867, it provided loans to businessmen. Other smaller deposit banks, too, attracted large and medium-sized investors. A mortgage bank (the Crédit Foncier), another one of Napoleon III's pet projects, aided the development of the agricultural sector.

At the same time, some major French industries reached a scale of production and concentration comparable to that of their British rivals. The

The opening of the Suez Canal, 1869.

metallurgical industry, in particular, underwent unprecedented growth. But most French industries remained relatively small in scale, producing luxury goods such as gloves, umbrellas, silk, jewelry, and fine furniture.

France became a major exporter of capital. French investors financed the construction of Russian, Spanish, and Italian railroads, as well as providing other timely loans to Portugal, Austria-Hungary, and Mexico. Ferdinand de Lesseps (1805–1894), an engineer, raised enough money through loans (half through public subscription) to finance the construction of his brainchild, the Suez Canal, which opened with suitable fanfare in 1869. Yet the chief beneficiary of the canal was not France but Britain, the world's leading trader, which had by far the most to gain by considerably reducing the journey to and from India and the rest of Asia (see Chapter 20).

State encouragement of economic development may be most clearly seen in the French railways. The Bank of France, which had seventy-four branches by 1870, provided financial aid to the companies that for the most part completed the main railway lines that helped stimulate the country's commercial and manufacturing boom. The state guaranteed investors a minimum profit. Between 1851 and 1869, the railway network expanded by five times, reaching almost 10,000 miles of track. French railroads became one of the largest employers in Europe.

The "Liberal Empire"

In 1859, Napoleon III announced his intention to "crown the [imperial] edifice with liberty." He would diffuse opposition by implementing some of the very reforms his opponents on the left desired. Five republicans had been elected to the Legislative Corps two years earlier. In 1860, the

National Assembly received the right to discuss the emperor's annual address—an exercise in sheer boredom, as he was a notoriously poor speaker. That same year, France and Britain signed a liberal trade agreement lowering tariff barriers between the two nations. In France the Cobden-Chevalier Treaty of 1860 was the idea of the emperor himself and an adviser, Michel Chevalier (1806–1879), who had been a utopian socialist as a young man. The treaty provided a sliding scale on import duties, aiding, for example, Bordeaux wine producers selling to England. The National Assembly received the right to approve the imperial budget. The liberalization of political institutions helped republicans increase their support. Press controls were relaxed, and the right to strike was established in 1864. Also in 1864, several French artisans were among the founders in London of the first international workers' organization, the First International, in the hopes of strengthening socialist movements within individual countries.

Foreign policy ultimately undid Napoleon III. In 1859, he joined with Count Camillo di Cavour of Piedmont-Sardinia to draw Emperor Francis Joseph of Austria into a war (see Chapter 17). The French army defeated the Austrians in northern Italy at Magenta and at Solferino, where the emperor himself commanded the French troops on horseback, if at a safe distance from the actual fighting. By the Treaty of Turin (1860), France gained Savoy and Nice (the latter after a plebiscite), both long coveted. Napoleon III then ordered the expansion of French control in Senegal and sent troops to protect missionaries in Lebanon and distant Indochina, annexing Cochin-China as a colony.

An imperial adventure in Mexico, which was in the midst of a civil war, ended in fiasco. The emperor believed that Mexico could become a profitable market for French exports of textiles and wine, and in 1861 he sent troops to protect French financial interests there. When order was restored, the French troops stayed. In 1864, Napoleon III proclaimed his protégé, Austrian Archduke Maximilian (1832–1867), the brother of Habsburg emperor Francis Joseph, to be emperor of Mexico. The United States protested that French intervention represented a violation of the Monroe Doctrine (1823), which had declared the Western Hemisphere off limits to the European powers. The Mexicans, understandably enough, did not want an Austrian emperor. Three years later, Mexican patriots defeated the French forces, who disembarked, leaving Napoleon III's hapless protégé to his own devices. Maximilian was executed in June 1867, a blow to the French emperor's international prestige.

A year earlier, the French emperor had made an error in foreign policy that would come back to haunt him. As Prussia and Austria drew closer to war in 1866, Napoleon III believed that Habsburg Austria would prevail. Bismarck quickly rejected Napoleon III's demand that Prussia compensate France with Rhineland territory. The French emperor then boldly insisted that Prussia go along with a possible French annexation of Belgium and Luxembourg (see Chapter 17). After an international conference a year

Edouard Manet's *Execution of Maximilian* (1867).

later guaranteed Luxembourg's independence, Napoleon III's dreams of territorial compensation from Prussia disappeared. But the cagey Bismarck had the French emperor's written demand tucked away in a drawer.

In June 1868, the emperor's authorization of a law permitting freedom of assembly helped mobilize opposition among monarchists, republicans, and socialists alike. Napoleon III's advisers wondered aloud if he had not sown the seeds of imperial demise by granting liberal reforms. Early in 1870, strikes spread. The emperor invited opponents to join the government and to begin drafting a more liberal constitution, one that would make ministers in some way "responsible" to the Legislative Corps. Napoleon III then reverted to a plebiscite, with a craftily worded statement in May 1870 by which those who wanted more extensive changes were forced to abstain, or to vote "yes" as if they approved of the emperor's policies. The plebiscite, in which "yes" overwhelmed "no," thus partially concealed the depth of opposition to imperial policies.

To the end, Napoleon III manifested a bizarre combination of perceptive foresight and bad judgment. When the Spanish throne fell vacant after a military coup deposed Queen Isabella II of Spain in 1868, one of the candidates was Prince Leopold, a Catholic prince of the ruling Prussian dynasty, the Hohenzollerns (see Chapter 17). Napoleon III threatened war with Prussia if it did not withdraw the Hohenzollern candidacy, which risked, if successful, leaving France with Hohenzollerns on two sides. He then ordered his ambassador to extract a letter from the king of Prussia apologizing to France and promising that Prussia would never revive the candidacy of

Prince Leopold. In July 1870, the French ambassador harangued Prussian King William I in a garden in the spa town of Ems. The king sent Bismarck a telegram stating what had occurred. After learning that the Prussian army was ready to fight, Bismarck embellished the king's telegram—the Ems Dispatch—to make the graceless diplomacy of the French seem positively insulting. Prussian public opinion reacted with anger. Bismarck's expectation that it would "have the effect of a red cloth on the Gallic bull" was justified; the incident increased popular support for war against France, which declared war on July 19, 1870. Württemberg, Hesse, Baden, and, more hesitantly, Bavaria joined the Prussian side. Napoleon III went to war against Prussia without allies.

The Franco-Prussian War and the Siege of Paris

The Franco-Prussian War was a French debacle. As French troops slowly mobilized, Prussian armies moved quickly into northeastern France. The speed of the Prussian attack and the competence of its generals more than made up for superior French rifles and recently developed machine guns. In August, Prussian troops cut off the fortress of Metz from the rest of France. When Marshal Marie-Edme de MacMahon (1808–1893) moved north in an attempt to relieve Metz, the Prussians cut him off. At the end of August, the main French force foolishly retreated to the fortress town of Sedan not far from the Belgian border. Sedan was soon surrounded by Prussians, who captured the emperor, so sick that he could barely sit on his horse. In Paris on September 4, 1870, crowds proclaimed a republic, and a provisional government was formed. Prussia allowed Napoleon III to leave for exile in Britain.

The Prussian army besieged Paris, its population swollen with soldiers and national guardsmen. As hunger invaded the capital, dogs and cats disappeared from the streets, finding their way to some of the finest tables. Zoo animals, too, were eaten, including two elephants admired by generations of Parisian children. An attempt to break through the Prussian lines north of the city at the end of October failed miserably. Still, Paris hung on.

In the meantime, Louis-Adolphe Thiers (1797–1877), who had served as Orleanist prime minister during the 1830s, wanted Bismarck's help in facilitating the establishment of a very conservative republic at the war's conclusion, or even a monarchy. The provisional government negotiated with Bismarck in the hope of obtaining an armistice on favorable terms. On January 28, 1871, ten days after the proclamation of the German Empire at Versailles (see Chapter 17), Bismarck and Thiers signed an armistice.

Some French leaders protested, demanding that the French army keep fighting. In February 1871, French voters elected a monarchist-dominated National Assembly, charged with making peace with Prussia and with establishing a new government. The newly elected National Assembly officially elected Thiers to be chief executive of the provisional government.

Jules Favre, peace negotiator, and Adolphe Thiers, provisional head of the government, accede to the loss of Alsace-Lorraine, France's right arm. They drag the weeping female image of France away from the "social republic."

By signing the Treaty of Frankfurt (May 10, 1871), France lost Alsace and some of Lorraine to the new German Empire. Prussian troops would occupy Paris and retain garrisons in eastern France until a large indemnity had been paid off. The National Assembly's choice of Versailles, the home of the Bourbon monarchs, as the temporary capital stirred popular anger and suspicion. Parisians, who had held out against the Prussians for four months, resented the ease with which the provinces had seemed to capitulate. Wealthy Parisians who had left Paris at the beginning of the siege returned from the safety of the countryside. Landlords insisted that back rents be paid immediately, angering renters, many of whom were unemployed workers who had managed to hang on during the siege.

The Paris Commune

Early in the morning on March 18, 1871, Thiers sent a small detachment of troops to the butte of Montmartre in Paris to seize cannon that had belonged to the National Guard, many of whose members were socialists, during the siege. Women at the market alerted the neighborhood; a crowd surrounded the detachment and put two generals up against the wall and shot them. Thiers ordered his troops to surround the capital. A second siege of Paris began, this one a civil war.

During the Prussian siege, socialists had placed bright red posters on the walls of the capital calling for the establishment of the "Paris Commune" to defend Paris. The leaders of the Commune were drawn from a variety of political persuasions: Jacobins, socialists, and republicans who wanted Paris to become again the capital of an anticlerical republic. Some Communards had been democratic-socialist activists during the Second Republic; others were followers of the revolutionary Auguste Blanqui (1805–1881), who believed that revolution could be achieved only by a small cell of determined men seizing power. There were also a good many anarchists, who hoped that independent Paris would serve as a model for a society of producers existing without the tyranny of the state.

Revolutionary clubs sprang up. The Communards organized Paris's defense and enacted a number of significant social reforms. These included the creation of a Labor Exchange, a place for workers to gather and find out about jobs; the abolition of night baking (a grievance of bakers) because of long hours and little sleep; the establishment of nurseries for working mothers; and the rights of workers' organizations to receive preference when the

A cartoon dedicated to the National Guard during the Paris Commune. Note the woman standing tall.

municipality contracted work. The Commune recognized women's unions—indeed the role of women in the Commune exceeded that of any previous revolutionary movement in France. Given the severity of the circumstances, with cannon shelling the city, it is remarkable how much the Communards accomplished in such a short time.

Much smaller uprisings occurred in Lyon, Marseille, and several other towns. These movements reflected a combination of middle-class dissatisfaction with Bonapartist centralization, republican enthusiasm, and socialist mobilization. But the provinces provided no help to the Paris Commune; rather, conservative regions sent volunteers to fight for the Versailles forces.

On May 21, 1871, the troops of Thiers's Versailles government poured into Paris through the western gates, left open for them by monarchist sympathizers. During the "bloody week" that followed, Thiers's army, aided by the recently constructed boulevards (see Chapter 19), overwhelmed neighborhood after neighborhood, blasting through barricades. Summary executions occurred throughout Paris, particularly after a rumor began that female incendiaries were burning banks and the homes of the wealthy. The Communards retaliated by executing some hostages, including the archbishop of Paris. About 15,000 to 25,000 Parisians were summarily executed or dispatched after hurried military trials.

For the left, the Commune seemed to be a glimpse of the future proletarian revolution (although Paris largely remained a city of artisans and skilled workers). To conservatives, the Commune offered a frightening glimpse of plebeian insurrection, affirming their resolve to oppose movements for social and political change with force.

REPUBLICAN FRANCE

The National Assembly elected in February 1871 had a monarchist majority. Yet most people in France wanted a republic. Gradually the Third Republic took hold, at first extremely conservative, then moderate, and beginning in 1899, radical, under the guidance of the socially moderate but stridently anticlerical Radical Party. Yet the republic had to overcome dramatic challenges from the far right, which rejected parliamentary rule and dreamed of recapturing Alsace-Lorraine from Germany.

Monarchists and Republicans

The Bourbon pretender to the throne of France was the count of Chambord, a lazy man of mediocre intelligence who lived in an Austrian castle and amused himself by playing cards and telling dirty jokes and anti-Semitic stories to his cronies. The Orleanist pretender to the throne was the relatively dashing count of Paris. Yet Chambord seemed to hold the upper hand, for his was the old Bourbon royal line. But, unlike the count of Paris, he was childless. A compromise, by which Chambord would become king with the count of Paris as his heir, fell through when the former refused to be king under the tricolor flag, which he identified with the French Revolution.

The close association of monarchism with the Catholic Church led many people to agree with the assessment of the radical republican Léon Gambetta (1838–1882) that "clericalism, there is the enemy." Republicans opposed the political domination of the "notables," the wealthiest men in France. The republic found a groundswell of support from those Gambetta called "the new social strata," the shopkeepers, café owners, prosperous peasants, craftsmen, and schoolteachers. The charismatic Gambetta's whistle-stop tours of the provinces reflected the rise of mass politics in France.

Thiers resigned under monarchist pressure as provisional head of state in 1873. Prussian troops marched out of France that year after the French government finished paying off the war indemnity, raised by loans and a public subscription. The monarchists, seeing their majority in the National Assembly eroding with each by-election, elected as president Marshal MacMahon, a hero of the Crimean War and the Italian War of 1859, who favored a monarchist restoration. The new government of "Moral Order," closely tied to the Church, undertook a massive purge of republican mayors, censored newspapers, closed hundreds of cafés, and banned public celebration of the French Revolution on July 14.

For the moment, the government of France was a republic with monarchist political institutions. In January 1874, the National Assembly passed the Wallon Amendment by one vote, stating that henceforth "the president of the Republic" would be elected by the Senate and the Chamber of Deputies. The lower house drafted a republican constitution in 1875, but one that seemed so vague that the state could easily enough have been converted into a monarchy.

Universal male suffrage determined the composition of the Chamber of Deputies. Each district elected a single representative. This gave monarchists an advantage, as local notables would be the most likely beneficiaries from last-minute political negotiations before the second ballot in each election. The Senate would be elected indirectly through a system that was radically tilted to over-represent conservative rural interests. Yet, despite heavy-handed governmental and ecclesiastical pressure on voters, more than twice as many republicans were elected as monarchists to the Chamber of Deputies in 1876. MacMahon was therefore forced to select a moderate republican, Jules Simon (1814–1896), as premier.

The republican majority in the National Assembly sought to limit the power of the president who was, after all, a monarchist. In 1877, MacMahon initiated a political crisis (the Crisis of May 16) by forcing Simon's resignation and naming a monarchist in his place. When the Chamber of

Deputies withheld its approval, MacMahon dissolved it and called for new elections. He embarked, with the help of the Church, on a bitter campaign to defeat Gambetta and the republicans.

However, France's voters returned republicans again, although with a smaller majority. MacMahon named a republican premier, and then resigned in 1879. Henceforth, the role of the executive authority would be weak because republicans feared that some Napoleonic character might try to impose his rule—indeed that threat lay ahead. With the constitutional privilege of dismissing government cabinets that had lost the confidence of the majority of its members, the Chamber of Deputies would dominate the political life of the French Third Republic. In 1881, the Chamber of Deputies passed a bill granting full amnesty to exiled Communards.

The Third Republic

The governments of the new republic reflected the center of the political spectrum, that of the "Opportunists," so called because many of them accepted a very conservative republic while preferring something more to the center. Resolved to hold the center against the monarchists and the Church on the right, and the anticlerical Radicals and the socialists to their left, the Opportunists retained the support of peasants by implementing high agricultural tariffs. The Méline Tariff, supported by industrialists and farmers, went into effect in 1892.

The Opportunist republic guaranteed freedom of the press, legalized public gatherings without prior authorization, and gave municipal councils the right to elect their own mayors (with the exception of Paris, not allowed to have a mayor—until 1977—for fear he might become too powerful). The president served as something of a chairman of the board to the Chamber of Deputies. He shook hands with everybody, intrigued pleasantly, and helped form coalitions. Governments came and went, giving an exaggerated image of parliamentary instability and impotence.

Because the republic had only gradually taken root in the 1870s and had been strongly contested by conservatives, the educational reforms of the 1880s had the goal not only of making France more literate but also more republican. Jules Ferry (1832–1893) sponsored laws that made primary education free and obligatory. The state allocated money to build village schools. Although some priests and nuns stayed on to teach in what were technically lay schools, the debates over the laicization of public schools ensured the animosity of many prelates and practicing Catholics against the "godless" republic.

General Boulanger and Captain Dreyfus

Amid growing social and political division, during the 1880s the parliamentary center began to melt under pressure from right and left. Nationalism became a potent political ideology. Bonapartists emerged from obscurity to tout Napoleon III's cousin, Prince Napoleon Bonaparte (1822–1891), as a potential savior. Some nationalists began to think that the republic was too weak to ever recapture Alsace and much of Lorraine from Germany. This concern with "revenge" against Germany reflected the passing of nationalism from the liberal left to the right wing in France.

The Boulanger Affair was in some ways the birth certificate of the new right in France, the Dreyfus Affair its baptism. In 1887, French rightists began to place their hopes of overthrowing the republic on the dashing figure of General Georges Boulanger (1837–1891), who had risen rapidly through the ranks to become minister of war. His bellicose noises about recapturing Alsace-Lorraine pleased nationalists while irritating Bismarck. Conservatives now were convinced that they had found the man who could overthrow the republic, restore the monarchy, or establish a dictatorship. Flattered by all of the attention, Boulanger allowed his name to be put forward as a candidate for the Chamber of Deputies.

The political movement on behalf of Boulanger was arguably the first mass political campaign in France. Funds provided by a wealthy royalist widow helped inundate the country with electoral posters and busts and statues of the dashing general. His supporters battled their political enemies in the streets, bringing unprecedented violence into an electoral campaign and drawing on rising nationalist anti-Semitism, although there were only about 80,000 Jews in a population of 40 million in France. For example, Parisian shopkeepers, frustrated by the economic depression, fearful of workers' consumer cooperatives, and losing clients to department stores, swung their support to right-wing nationalist parties, convinced by right-wing polemicists that "Jewish capitalists" were responsible for their plight.

Boulanger was elected in by-elections in several districts, but because he was in the army, he was ineligible to serve in the Chamber of Deputies. At this point, no one was sure what exactly Boulanger represented, no one probably less than the general himself. If his campaign money came from the right, many of his votes at first came from the left. The Opportunist government sent Boulanger to central France to remove him from the political limelight of the capital.

A political scandal cast a further shadow on the government, giving another twist to the term "opportunist." A prostitute revealed that the Legion of Honor medal was being peddled to the highest bidder. It turned out that one of the most successful salesmen was Daniel Wilson, the ruthless son-in-law of President Jules Grévy, who resigned.

All of this added to a feeling among some observers that the Third Republic was already at the end of its rope. The government declared General Boulanger retired. But this now left him free to run for the Chamber of Deputies, and he was elected deputy from Paris. To his right-wing followers, it seemed that a perfect occasion for a coup d'état had arrived. In January 1889, triumphant crowds gathered in the street, calling out Boulanger's name while he sat in a restaurant quietly eating dinner. But his moment passed. Two years later, government officials convinced the naive general that they held evidence that could lead to his conviction on charges of state treason. Boulanger caught a train to Belgium and, on the grave of his late mistress, took out his army pistol and blew out his brains.

Having survived Boulanger, the republic then received an unexpected boost from its old enemy, the Catholic Church, whose "rallying" (the *Ralliement*) to the republic began with an archbishop's toast in 1891 in Tunisia. Henceforth, the moderate republicans could draw on political support from the Catholic right against the socialist parties.

Another scandal gave the anti-parliamentary right a new focus for opposition. In 1881, a French company had begun to dig the Panama Canal under the direction of Ferdinand de Lesseps, who had overseen the construction of the Suez Canal. This canal proved to be even more challenging to build because of difficult terrain and malarial conditions. Company officials bribed government officials in the hope of gathering sufficient support to get the Chamber of Deputies to approve a loan that would be financed by a national lottery. The Chamber of Deputies obligingly approved the plan, but the financial campaign fell short. When the company went broke in 1889, more than half a million investors lost their money.

In 1892, Édouard Drumont's right-wing newspaper *La Libre Parole* published a series of revelations about the scandal. Drumont had earlier published a book in which he claimed that Jewish financiers were conspiring to dominate France. Now, the fact that some of the directors of the defunct company had been Jewish helped generate support for the League of Patriots, founded in 1892, a nationalist and anti-Semitic organization of the extreme right. The next year an indulgent court acquitted all but one of those implicated in the scandal.

The suicide of General Boulanger.

The next scandal was such a series of dramatic events that it became known for years simply as "the Affair." It pitted right against left; the army, Church, and monarchists against republicans and, in time, socialists; and family against family.

Alfred Dreyfus (1859–1935) was the son of an old Jewish family from Alsace. His family had been peddlers and then textile manufacturers. They were assimilated Jews, proudly considering themselves French. Following the annexation of Alsace by Germany in 1871, the Dreyfus family moved to Paris. In 1894, evidence surfaced—from a wastepaper basket in the office of a German military attaché—that someone in the French army had been passing secret information to the Germans about French military operations. Circumstantial evidence pointed to Captain Dreyfus—the writing on a list of documents that had been prepared to be handed over to a German contact resembled Dreyfus's handwriting. Maintaining his innocence, Dreyfus refused the arresting officer's offer of a loaded pistol with which he could kill himself. A hurriedly convened and secret court-martial found him guilty of treason. Dreyfus was stripped of his rank and sent to Devil's Island off the coast of South America.

However, confidential documents continued to disappear from French army offices. Two years later, a new chief of army intelligence, Lieutenant Colonel Georges Picquart, determined to his own satisfaction that the original list of documents had not been penned by Dreyfus, but by Major Walsin Esterhazy. Picquart, who was an unlikely hero in this case because he made no secret of his anti-Semitism, presented his evidence. But high-ranking officers believed that it was better to have an innocent Jew languishing in increasing depression on Devil's Island than to compromise the army's public image. The army packed Picquart off to a post in Tunisia, and a military court acquitted Esterhazy, despite overwhelming evidence of guilt.

(*Left*) Édouard Drumont's anti-Semitic newspaper *La Libre Parole* (*The Free Word*), 1893. (*Right*) Captain Alfred Dreyfus.

The novelist Émile Zola now took up Dreyfus's case. In January 1898, he wrote an article in a daily newspaper with the bold headline *"J'accuse!"* ("I accuse!"), denouncing the army and the government for covering up the reality of the case. The political right and the Church hierarchy jumped in on the side of the "anti-Dreyfusards," seeing the Dreyfus Affair as a conspiracy of Jews and Freemasons to destroy France by undermining the prestige of its army. A Catholic newspaper demanded that all Jews be deprived of their citizenship. Action Française, a right-wing nationalist and monarchist organization led by Charles Maurras (1868–1952), an anti-Semitic novelist, jumped into the fray against Dreyfus. Socialists demanded a new trial.

Another officer soon discovered that some new documents had been added to the Dreyfus file. They had been quite badly forged by Lieutenant Colonel Hubert Henry, who hoped they would lead to a new conviction of Dreyfus. Confronted with the evidence, Henry committed suicide in a military prison. In 1899, the army retried Dreyfus, once again finding him guilty, but with "extenuating circumstances." Dreyfus returned, a broken man, to Devil's Island. However, the president of France gave Dreyfus a presidential pardon that year, which allowed him to return to his family, although Dreyfus was not fully exonerated until 1906, when his military rank was restored.

The Radical Republic

Dreyfus's return to France provided the republic with a badly needed period of stability and boosted the Radical Party. The Dreyfus Affair had helped forge a working alliance between the Radicals, who were anticlerical moderate republicans, and socialists, which moved the republic to the left. In the Radical government formed in 1899, Alexandre Millerand (1859–1943), a reform socialist, became minister of commerce, despite the bitter opposition of many socialists who objected to a socialist serving in a "bourgeois" government.

In contrast to Britain, where the Anglican Church had always stood behind the government, in France the dominant religion had—at least until 1891— stood against the regime. The Radicals moved to separate church and state against conservative opposition. In 1902, the Chamber of Deputies, with socialist support, passed legislation exiling religious orders from France. In 1905, church and state were formally separated in France. During the next two years, the state took possession of all ecclesiastical property and assumed responsibility for paying the salaries of priests. Despite papal condemnation and the resistance of some clergy and parishioners, a *modus vivendi* evolved, with parish councils leasing churches from the state.

The Radical Premier Georges Clemenceau (1841–1929) embodied aggressive French nationalism. The man who later became known as "the Tiger" had been born into a family of modest noble title. His father was a prominent republican who had been exiled by Napoleon III. Clemenceau was a wealthy bully and a formidable dueler who hated socialists, unions, and the Catholic Church as much as he did his American ex-wife, whom he had followed by a detective, jailed, and deported. In 1907, he sent troops to crush a determined strike by small property owners and vineyard laborers in the south.

In 1911, Radical Premier Joseph Caillaux (1863–1944), unlike Clemenceau, sought accommodation with Germany. The French Socialist Party launched a campaign against militarism and particularly against the extension of the term of military service from two to three years. Antimilitarism remained popular among workers because of the role of troops in the repression of strikes. But the Second Moroccan Crisis between Germany and France that same year (see Chapter 22) gave rise to another wave of nationalism. Besieged by the press for his pacific stand, Caillaux's government fell the following year. Raymond Poincaré (1860–1934), an outspoken nationalist, became premier in 1912 and then president a year later. He eagerly anticipated the chance to win back Alsace and Lorraine, and he firmed up French support of a Russian role in the Balkans. Poincaré's nationalism seemed in tune with the times.

CONCLUSION

The second half of the nineteenth century brought about significant political change to the three European powers that had been the strongest at mid-century. In Britain, the second Reform Bill of 1867 expanded the electoral franchise, and another law in 1884 followed suit. After the collapse of the Second Empire in 1870 and the Paris Commune the following year, France emerged as a republic. In Russia, Tsar Alexander II's emancipation of the serfs in 1861 did not change the fundamental institutions of autocracy. Yet some reforms did follow, even as critics of the tsarist state grew more vocal, and the Revolution of 1905 challenged the foundations of autocracy. In the meantime, Britain's economic strength and great navy left it in a position to dominate international affairs. Having defeated Austria and then France, Prussia emerged as the leader of a unified and powerful Germany, dominant in Central Europe. At the same time, the Second Industrial Revolution brought remarkable technological advances, increased mass production, and ever larger cities now bathed in electric light.

CHAPTER 19

RAPID INDUSTRIALIZATION AND ITS CHALLENGES, 1870–1914

~~~

Jeanne Bouvier was a peasant girl born in 1865 in southeastern France. Her father earned his living by tilling the fields and as a barrel maker, an occupation closely tied to wine production. But in 1876, disease began to destroy the vineyards of the Rhône River Valley. Jeanne's family was forced to sell its land and possessions and travel to find work, pushed along by poverty and unemployment. From age eleven to fourteen, Jeanne worked thirteen hours a day in a silk mill. Four other jobs in various towns and villages in her region followed until Jeanne's mother took her to Paris, where the first job she found lasted only a week. Like so many other single, female migrants to city life, she then worked as a domestic servant. A cousin showed her how to do hat-trimming work. When that trade collapsed because of changes in style and the economic depression, she became a skilled dressmaker in a Parisian workshop and then developed her own clientele. Jeanne Bouvier became a Parisian. When she returned home to her native village, Jeanne spoke French, and not the patois in which her old friends conversed. She had become an urban woman.

In 1900, the French Catholic writer Charles Péguy expressed the opinion that Europe had changed more in the previous thirty years than it had since the time of Jesus Christ. The period 1870–1914 was indeed one of rapid economic and social change in much of Europe. Rail networks extended their reach into the countryside, carrying manufactured goods and returning with meat, vegetables, fresh milk, and fruit for burgeoning cities. The speed and capacity of steamships brought American cereal grains, cattle, and meat to Western European ports, reducing their prices.

Technological advances helped propel the Second Industrial Revolution, which beginning in the 1850s and 1860s swept across much of northern, western, and central Europe, as well as the United States, and some of southern and eastern Europe. New manufacturing processes spurred the emergence of the chemical, electrical, and the steel industries. "Big business" took shape as larger companies controlled a greater share of markets.

Technological advances and mechanized factory production transformed the way millions of people worked and lived. Electric lights turned night into day in cities and towns. A permanent working class that had broken its ties with the countryside developed. However, rural areas were also changing as agricultural productivity increased. Large, productive farms whose lands were enriched by chemical fertilizers and cultivated with mechanized equipment encouraged more efficient regional agricultural specialization. Improvements in agriculture were less apparent in the Russian Empire, Eastern Europe, and the Balkans, although in Hungary, where the great magnates and other nobles still owned much of the land, the use of agricultural machinery, the rotation of crops, and product specialization also brought greater yields.

Declining mortality rates led to an increase in Europe's population. Longer life expectancy followed better nutrition—a more varied diet with greater caloric consumption—as well as improved sanitation and purer water supplies. Living conditions gradually improved for most people. Wages continued to rise. Mass education elevated rates of literacy. The middle class expanded in size and complexity. An expansion in white-collar jobs—including positions as clerks, tram ticket collectors, and schoolteachers, among many others—offered peasants and workers chances for social mobility, particularly in Western Europe.

An elegant London department store, late nineteenth century.

Many workers now had a little money and time left over for leisure activities. Bicycles, sports, and, early in the new century, movies became part of the lives of millions. Nonetheless, in many regions—including much of southern Italy, Spain, Portugal, Russia, and the Balkans—wrenching poverty remained common, and mobility into the middle class remained exceptional at the turn of the century.

Emigration to other countries emerged as one of the most significant social phenomena of the age, particularly during the depression that lasted from 1873 into the mid-1890s. Peasants and laborers, in particular, left Europe in hope of economic opportunity in the United States, Canada, and Latin America. Great Britain, Germany, and Ireland had provided most of the earlier waves of emigrants—for example, during the "hungry forties" marked by the Irish potato famine. Now Italians, in particular, headed overseas in great numbers, along with Scandinavians.

The last years of the nineteenth century—the fin de siècle—would be remembered after World War I as the "Belle Époque"—the "good old days"— a period of material progress and cultural innovation. New inventions like the telephone and automobile promised an even better life ahead.

The Second Industrial Revolution

Steel led the Second Industrial Revolution. Then electricity accelerated European economic growth, providing, in the century's last two decades, power for industry. The Second Industrial Revolution brought a stunning variety of technological innovations that ultimately improved the everyday lives of most Europeans. In large cities, subways and, increasingly, automobiles made people more mobile. At the same time, new discoveries in the physical sciences—particularly chemistry—and the development of germ theory and bacteriology led to advances that improved agriculture, as well as public health, making possible longer lives.

The Second Industrial Revolution seemed impervious to an economic depression that began in 1873 and lasted until the mid-1890s. It was marked by falling prices and punctuated by financial panics, although not by prolonged unemployment or economic stagnation. Following a fever of speculation, particularly in Germany, banks failed in Vienna. The speed with which the crisis spread to other financial capitals reflected the extent to which improvements in transportation and communication had extended the links of an increasingly global economy. British foreign investment doubled between 1900 and 1914, and within Europe the volume of trade increased by twenty-five times between 1820 and 1913. Increasingly, the price of grain and other essential commodities became more constant with the development of a global market for foodstuffs. Agricultural prices fell virtually everywhere in Europe, in part because imported grain from the

United States and Canada flooded markets. In industrialized countries, tariffs became the focus of impassioned political debate, even in Britain, where economic liberalism remained the prevailing credo. Governments responded to the depression by imposing protective tariffs, in the interest of native industries and agriculture, in Austria (1874), Russia (1875), France (1892), Italy (1887), and Germany (1902).

New Technology and Scientific Discoveries

In 1856, the English inventor Henry Bessemer (1813–1898) developed a new method for forging steel from pig iron by forcing air through the molten metal to reduce its carbon content. The result was steel that was less expensive to produce than it had been by the old method and that could be turned out in greater quantities (see Table 19.1). Other related discoveries over the next twenty years permitted the production of steel of a more consistent quality, lowering its price by two-thirds.

Steel's strength, durability, and flexibility gave it a marked advantage over iron. Steel improved the size, quality, standardization, and precision of machinery. Just three years after Bessemer's discovery, the first British ship constructed of steel slid into the sea. Larger, sturdier, and faster than their predecessors, steel ships transformed naval warfare.

Medical advances enhanced the already soaring prestige of science and the professional stature of its practitioners. In much of Europe, a trip to the doctor was no longer seen as the first stop on the way to the undertaker. Anesthesia, which had already been discovered in the United States in the 1840s, made surgery less painful. The French scientist Louis Pasteur (1822–1895) discovered that just as various types of fermentation were caused by different kinds of germs, so were many diseases. His development of germ theory in the 1860s brought a virtual revolution in health

TABLE 19.1. ANNUAL OUTPUT OF STEEL (IN MILLIONS OF METRIC TONS)

Year	Britain	Germany	France	Russia
1875–1879	0.90	—	0.26	0.08
1880–1884	1.82	0.99	0.46	0.25
1885–1889	2.86	1.65	0.54	0.23
1890–1894	3.19	2.89	0.77	0.54
1895–1899	4.33	5.08	1.26	1.32
1900–1904	5.04	7.71	1.70	2.35
1905–1909	6.09	11.30	2.65	2.63
1910–1913	6.93	16.24	4.09	4.20

Source: Carlo Cipolla, ed., *The Fontana Economic History of Europe*, vol. 3(2) (London: Collins/Fontana Books, 1976), p. 775.

Louis Pasteur in his laboratory.

care. Pasteur's experiments demonstrated that the spoilage of food could be avoided by destroying microbes that were already present and preventing the arrival of others (thus, the "pasteurization" of milk). Pasteur's studies of specific bacteria and viruses led to the immunization of animals and helped end a silkworm blight. Wilhelm Röntgen (1845–1923), a German scientist, discovered the X-ray in 1895. Then another German, Robert Koch (1843–1910), discovered and isolated the tuberculosis bacillus.

The development of bacteriology, which infused the hygienic movement with the certitude of science and helped create preventative medicine, reduced mortality by encouraging, for example, sewage works. Sewer systems ensured a cleaner water supply, reducing some contagious diseases. People became less tolerant of foul smells. Rat poison killed off disease-carrying rodents.

The Electric and Chemical Revolutions

Electricity made possible the invention of the electromagnetic telegraph, the undersea cable, and the telephone. Yet electricity remained little more than a scientific curiosity until relatively late in the century. The bottleneck remained the generation of electricity. Werner von Siemens (1816–1892), a German, invented the first self-excited electromagnetic generator in 1867, which made possible the production of electrical energy, and three years later the first generator of direct current (a ring dynamo) followed. Germany took the lead in the production of power generators. Thomas Edison (1847–1931), an American scientist, invented the incandescent lamp in 1879. Two years later, the first electric power stations began operation in England, and during the following decades electricity gradually entered European homes. Electric alternators and transformers and improvements in cable and insulation provided means by which electric power could be generated and diffused. Yet, well into the twentieth century, in many parts of Europe electricity still remained a luxury.

For all their efficiency, water power, coal, and gas had placed limits on the location of factories. Electric power, however, could be transported with relative ease, which ultimately enabled countries not well endowed with natural resources to industrialize partially. The steel, textile, shoe-making, and construction industries, among others, came to depend upon electric power. In Europe, as in the United States, the first results of the electric age were particularly striking in heavy industry—for example in electrochemistry (aluminum) and metallurgy (electric furnaces). The burgeoning German electrical manufacturing industry helped Germany to challenge Britain for European manufacturing primacy.

The sewing machine, developed by the American Isaac Singer (1811–1875), began to be found in industry and homes in the 1850s, well before the use of electricity became common. The mechanization of the production of ready-made garments rapidly extended consumer markets, setting styles and reducing the price of clothing. But the impact of the sewing machine also demonstrated continuities in industrial work. For the garment industry—attracting Jewish immigrants to Paris and, above all, New York—remained largely tied to home work, as well as to sweatshops. Women, and some men, too, turned out ready-made cloaks and dresses. Machines that could do band stitching, make buttonholes, or embroider led to a further specialization of labor. Singer marketed his machine as a device that would liberate women from tedious work. But the sewing machine also bound many women to the hectic pace of piecework, and to payments for the machine itself, usually purchased on time-payment plans.

By 1900, other electrically powered household appliances—refrigerators, fans, and vacuum cleaners—were generally available to those families that could afford to have their houses wired for electricity and could pay for the appliances.

The development of chemistry also brought lasting advances. In Germany, university chemical research and teaching developed precociously. German companies benefited from synthetic organic chemistry, manufacturing dyes, soaps, and pharmaceuticals, further improving sanitation and public health. Fritz Haber (1868–1934) discovered the nitrogen-fixing process, by which atmospheric nitrogen could be converted into compounds. By 1913, he and his colleagues were able to transform ammonia into nitric acid by oxidation, which made possible the industrial production of fertilizers and explosives. Advances in chemistry helped transform agriculture, the textile industry, and engineering.

In Western Europe, powerful industrial giants began to emerge. The development of economic cartels dealt a blow to the liberal era of free trade. Cartels are formal agreements by which competitors within the same industry protect profits by sharing markets, regulating output, fixing prices, and taking other measures to limit competition. Cartels permitted a few large companies to dominate production and distribution, enabling heavy industries to protect themselves during periods of falling prices and high unemployment by controlling production and setting prices. In Germany, mining cartels set production goals and kept prices artificially high. In France and Great Britain, informal agreements among industrialists achieved virtually the same results as formalized cartels. The return to protective tariffs aided

Women working on a sewing machine and sewing by hand.

cartels, protecting them from competition from abroad. Even where there were no cartels, the concentration of business in larger companies continued, in part because in industries such as metallurgy and chemicals, expensive machinery made "start-up" costs prohibitive for smaller firms.

Regional Variations

The industrial boom of the Second Industrial Revolution was perhaps most dramatic in Germany. By 1890, both Germany and the United States had surged ahead of Britain in metallurgical production. By the turn of the century, German factories turned out more steel than Britain and France combined, and Germany's chemical industry was the most modern in the world. In 1900, Britain produced twice as much sulphuric acid as Germany; in 1913, the proportion had been reversed. Germany's national product more than tripled between unification in 1871 and 1914.

Germany enjoyed the advantage of starting to industrialize after its rivals, thereby being able to employ the most modern equipment in factories specially built to accommodate technological advances. By contrast, some British factories, most of which had been built early in the century (and some even before), seemed to be crumbling.

German banks played a more direct role in German industrialization than did their counterparts in other countries. While providing investment capital, large investment banks acquired large blocks of industrial shares, particularly in heavy industries like coal mining, electricity, and railways. Having entered industry to assure proper business management of companies to which they loaned money, the banks earned big profits and paid high dividends to those who had invested in them. German banks themselves became industrial entrepreneurs. This also favored the trend of German industry toward cartels, which controlled production and prices.

German universities were more numerous and of better quality than any others in Europe at the same time, despite their authoritarian structure and their acquiescence in discrimination against Jews, Catholics, and socialists. They emerged as centers of scientific research, particularly in chemistry. By contrast, English employers tended to look down their noses at academic training as a poor substitute for work experience, just as universities in Britain were relatively slow to adopt a more practical curriculum.

Great Britain remained the world's greatest economic power, but British manufactured goods stacked up at the docks as demand declined abroad and prices fell. By the mid-1880s, some of the countries that had purchased British goods were able to meet consumer demand at home with their own production. In the century's last decades, shiploads of foreign-made goods began to undercut British production, which was unprotected by tariff walls. Instead of depending upon British shipping, German, Italian, and French merchants now took advantage of the Suez Canal, opened in 1869, to send their own ships to Asia to make purchases and sell goods directly.

In the Russian Empire, the economy remained overwhelmingly agricultural. Despite the development of Ukraine as a major producer of wheat, the famine of 1890–1891, to which the novelist Leo Tolstoy helped focus international concern, killed millions of peasants. Absentee ownership of large estates, peasant plots that continued to be farmed at subsistence level as they had been for centuries, and village communal lands hindered agricultural development. Farmers in some places lacked even enough horses to pull plows. Yet Russian agriculture gradually increased its productivity, doing so without the capital-intensive farming that characterized much of Western Europe. Russian increases in harvest yields were comparable to those of France and Germany by 1900, making possible the increased export of grain and other foodstuffs. The Peasant Land Bank, created in the 1880s, helped thousands of peasants purchase land, and a thriving cooperative movement beginning at the turn of the century brought some prosperity.

Russian industries still confronted the serious physical impediment of sheer distance between resources, manufacturers, and markets. Coal deposits lay far from centers of manufacturing. Weak banking structures limited the accumulation of investment capital, and the Orthodox Church viewed investment as usurious and therefore dishonest.

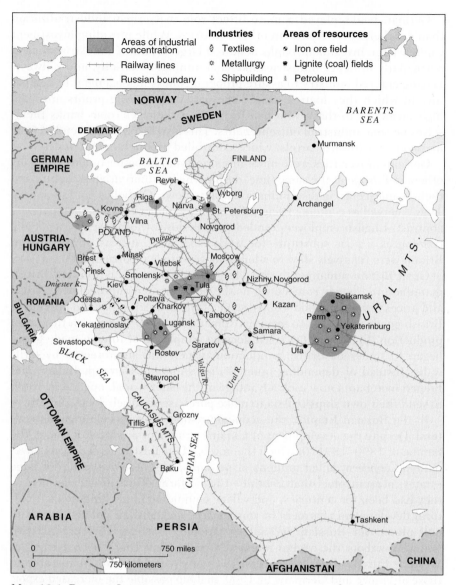

Map 19.1 Russian Industrialization, 1870–1914   Areas of industrial concentration, including kinds of industry and resources.

Yet Russian industry also developed rapidly beginning in the mid-1890s, benefiting from advanced technology imported from Western Europe (see Map 19.1). Foreign investment in Russia, above all from France, more than doubled during the 1890s. Although textiles still represented the largest branch of Russian industry, heavy industries, particularly metallurgy, boomed. The state helped develop heavy metals and fuel production,

TABLE 19.2. PRODUCTION OF COAL AND STEEL IN RUSSIA (IN THOUSANDS OF TONS)

Year	Coal	Steel
1860	695	257
1880	3,276	289
1890	6,015	857
1900	16,155	2,711
1910	25,000	3,017
1913	36,038	4,918

Source: Arcadius Kahan, *Russian Economic History: The Nineteenth Century* (Chicago: University of Chicago Press, 1989), p. 21.

including oil. The output of steel increased fourfold during the last decades of the century (see Table 19.2). By 1914, Saint Petersburg had become one of the largest concentrations of industry in Europe, with more than 900 factories. The growth of light industry and the expansion of the market contributed considerably to the country's economic growth, permitting exports to Asian neighbors. Russian foreign trade tripled between 1885 and 1913. The length of Russia's rail lines increased by three times between 1881 and 1905, and its banks developed in size and scale. By the turn of the century, railroads at last linked Russia's major cities and facilitated the shipping of grain to the empire's northern ports.

The Russian working class grew from about 2 million industrial workers in 1900 to about 3 million by 1914 (compared to over a 100 million peasants). Yet many Russian industrial workers still labored part-time in agriculture. In 1900, peasants made up two-thirds of the population of Saint Petersburg, a city of more than 1.4 million people. They retained strong ties to their villages, which remained their legal residences. The rural commune still carried out functions of local authority, including many fiscal obligations (assuring the payment of taxes and redemption payments on land gained at the time of the emancipation of the serfs in 1861), policing (including overseeing the division of communal lands), and rudimentary welfare functions.

In most of Europe's industrializing countries, the growing manufacturing sector coexisted with small-scale production (see Map 19.2). In France, the production of high-quality handicrafts, centered in Paris, continued to dominate industry. Traditional small-scale manufacturing also persisted alongside regionally specific heavy industries in Spain (Catalonia and the Basque region), Austria-Hungary, and Italy, where little large-scale industry could be found south of the triangle formed by Milan, Turin, and the port of Genoa. As in Russia, most of the investment in Spanish industry came from abroad because agriculture generated inadequate surpluses for significant industrial investment. In the Austro-Hungarian monarchy, the dynamism of

MAP 19.2 AREAS OF INDUSTRIAL CONCENTRATION, 1870–1914 Various regions industrialized more quickly than others, with indus-trial concentration likely to be found where there were coal fields and rivers.

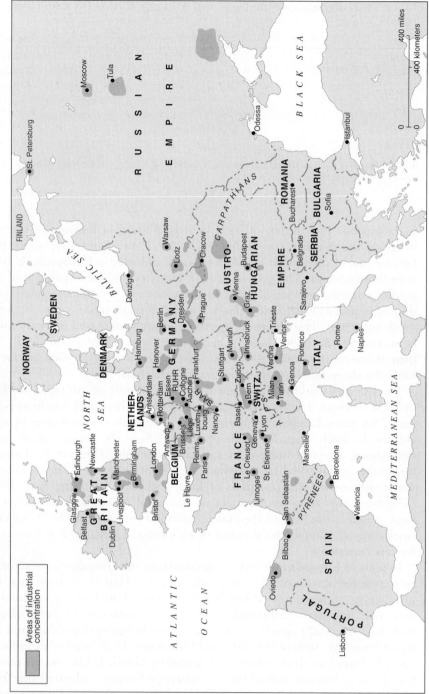

Areas of industrial concentration

Bohemia and Moravia contrasted sharply with the small-market ways of Austria and the Hungarian plain. In the Balkans, where major rail lines were not in place until the late 1880s, poor roads and the daunting mountains limited the emergence of vibrant regional market economies. In many places, mules remained the best way to transport goods. Yet even in overwhelmingly rural Bulgaria, the value of industrial production multiplied by three times just between 1904 and 1911, and the railway network increased rapidly after 1880.

Travel and Communications

Electric power led to the construction of modern public transportation systems, first trams and then subways. Mass transportation transformed residential patterns in large cities. The London underground railway had already opened without electricity in 1863, making it possible for employees and workers to live much farther from their jobs. In 1900, the first Paris subway—the *métro*—began operation on the right bank of the Seine River, and other lines soon followed. Four years later, the first sections of New York City's subway began operation.

In 1885, Carl Benz (1844–1929), a German engineer, built upon the invention of the internal combustion engine. He added a primitive carburetor and constructed a small automobile. The first automobiles were very expensive, the tires alone costing more than an average worker's annual wages. In 1897, Rudolf Diesel (1858–1913), a German, produced the first successful engine fueled by kerosene, which could power larger vehicles. By the turn of the century, four-cylinder engines powered automobiles.

Automobile manufacturing quickly became a major catalyst for industrial growth and the implementation of new production methods, stimulating the production of steel, aluminum, rubber, and tools. The petroleum industry slowly developed, although at the time only the oil reserves in Romania were known and exploited (the first oil refinery in Europe had been built there in 1857). Little by little some industrialists and statesmen began to grasp the economic and strategic significance of oil, particularly after the discovery in 1908 of rich oil fields in Persia (Iran).

Automobile manufacturers shifted from the limited production of elite cars, above all, the British Rolls Royce, to less expensive models. Henry Ford (1863–1947), who began his company in Detroit in 1903, produced more than 15 million "Model T" Fords, which even some of his own workers could afford to purchase. Worried by American competition, the French car manufacturer Louis Renault (1877–1944) looked for ways to cut production costs. Assembly-line production made it possible to construct cars in segments. Workers mounted components on stationary chassis frames lined up along the factory floor. They used hand files to shape engine parts for expensive cars since interchangeable parts were not yet available. The assembly

An early automobile assembly line.

line reduced the time it took to produce each car from twelve hours to one and a half hours.

The automobile transformed travel. Elegant horses and fancy carriages owned by people of means no longer monopolized travel. However, until it was repealed in 1896, the British "Red Flag Act" restricted the speed of motor vehicles to two miles per hour and required three people carrying red warning flags to accompany each vehicle, a decided inconvenience. In 1896, the speed limit was raised to fourteen miles per hour.

Car travel necessitated better roads. Early drivers required not only thick goggles to protect themselves against dust but also whips to keep away startled dogs. Gradually, government authorities ordered the paving of roads, and gas stations began to dot the landscape. In 1900, the Michelin Company in France, one of the first to shift from producing bicycle to automobile tires, published its first guide for travelers, listing garages, hotels, and restaurants. Michelin successfully lobbied for signs along roads indicating distances. The number of cars in Paris tripled between 1906 and 1912. Traffic jams became a way of urban life. Motorized taxis and then motorized fire engines raced by their horse-drawn predecessors.

The cult of speed next took to the air, after centuries of dreams had brought only balloon ascents and short glider flights. In 1900, a retired German general, Count Ferdinand von Zeppelin (1838–1917), built the lumbering dirigible airship that still bears his name. After years of experimentation with propellers and small engines, Orville and Wilbur Wright, two American bicycle manufacturers, launched the first successful flight in 1903. They then took their air show to England, France, and Germany, where the crown prince of Prussia began to consider the military uses of the airplane.

More Europeans could now travel for leisure than ever before. Middle-class vacations became more common. The travel business boomed. Health spas and resorts, which had developed since the mid-1800s, became even more popular in Western Europe. Spas claimed that their thermal waters offered healing and sustaining properties that facilitated the circulation of blood, attacked gout—the encumbering malady of people who were too well fed—or in some other way restored to equilibrium the human body victimized by modern life.

Mediterranean, North Sea, and English Channel resorts offered casinos and beachfront promenades. English coastal towns like Brighton and Blackpool attracted visitors oblivious to the rain. The tourist pier and arcade took shape. English nobles, who could afford to flee the British winter, "discovered" Nice. Upper-class Italians began to frequent their own Riviera, Belgians the port of Ostend, and Germans the Baltic resorts. Vacationers from many countries discovered the Alps and sent the first postcards back to envious friends. Partially spurred on by tourism, photography emerged as a major visual art. The relatively light Kodak camera appeared in 1888. Bretons began to refer to French-speaking tourists as "Kodakers."

A revolution in communications also slowly transformed life. The telegraph had already increased the availability of news from around the world, with the help of press agencies like Havas, the Associated Press, and Reuters. The telephone, invented by Alexander Graham Bell (1847–1922) in 1876, reached private homes. Germans made 8 million telephone calls in 1883, 700 million in 1900. Fifteen years after Thomas Edison invented the gramophone in 1876, a number of virtuosos had made their first scratchy recordings. The Italian Guglielmo Marconi (1874–1937)

pioneered the first wireless voice communication in the 1890s; by 1913, weekly concerts could be heard on the radio in Brussels. Silent motion pictures, first shown in 1895, became an immediate hit, sometimes accompanied by a piano. Early viewers watched brief scenes of modern life, such as a train beginning to move. Longer films with plots and action followed. The Austro-Hungarian army began to experiment with motion pictures, using cameras to study the flight of artillery shells.

Women at work at a telephone switchboard.

Further Scientific Discoveries: "A Boundless Future"
and Its Uncertainties

The astonishing advances of late nineteenth-century science led one researcher to exude that "science strides on victoriously towards a boundless future." The creation in 1883 of a worldwide system for patenting reflected a veritable torrent of new inventions. Scientists had already concluded that cells form the basis for life. This knowledge led scientists to understand more about the principles of heredity. At the same time, new discoveries revealing nature's complexity began to temper the infectious optimism of the age. Fin-de-siècle scientists realized that the more they understood about the world, the more there was left to know about such basic principles as matter, light, and energy. Mathematicians and especially physicists began to rethink fundamental assumptions about the universe.

Radioactivity was discovered in Paris in 1896. Marie Curie (1867–1934), a Polish-born chemist carrying out research with her husband, Pierre Curie (1859–1906), isolated radium, a radioactive element, in 1910. Marie Curie, who was refused entry to the French Academy of Science because of her gender, won two Nobel Prizes. Her rival, Ernest Rutherford (1871–1937), a New Zealander, discovered two kinds of radiation, which he called the alpha and beta rays. He posited the disintegration of radioactive atoms, which is the phenomenon of radioactivity. Rutherford used this discovery to

(*Left*) Pierre and Marie Curie. (*Right*) Ernest Rutherford, who is holding the apparatus that he used to break up the nucleus of the nitrogen atom.

postulate the structure of the atom, with a positively charged nucleus and negatively charged electrons circling around it.

"Particle theories" in physics cast doubt on contemporary assumptions about the universe. They demonstrated the complexity of motion, light, and matter, which appeared to consist of electrically charged particles. Since the time of Sir Isaac Newton in the seventeenth century, scientists had believed that any two objects, whether the sun and the earth, or a coffee cup and a bowl of sugar, acted on each other through gravitational force. There seemed no mechanism for transmitting action but rather only empty space between the two. James Maxwell (1831–1879), a British scientist, solved the "action at a distance" problem for the case of electromagnetic forces. His theory of electromagnetic fields postulated that one object creates an electrical field around particles, which in turn exerts forces on electrically charged objects, and that light itself consists of electromagnetic waves. The German scientist Max Planck (1858–1947) discovered that radiant energy is emitted discontinuously in discrete units, or quanta. Planck's quantum theory, not finalized until 1925, challenged the fundamental scientific understanding of energy that had survived almost intact since Newton's day. More than this, it seemed to add an element of chance to the story of the universe, suggesting that its operations were not absolutely predictable. Here, too, scientists now realized that they knew considerably less about the nature of matter and about the universe than they had long assumed.

These discoveries were only a beginning. The much more difficult problem of gravity remained. In Switzerland, German-born Albert Einstein

Albert Einstein explaining his theories to a stunned audience.

(1879–1955), whose modest position as a patent examiner of other people's discoveries belied his genius, sought to carry physics beyond Newton's theory that space and time were absolute quantities. In 1905, Einstein postulated a special theory of relativity, arguing that the velocity of light was both constant and independent of the velocities of the source and observer of light.

Einstein also postulated the relationship between mass and energy in his equation: $E = mc^2$ (energy equals mass multiplied by the square of the speed of light). In the mid-twentieth century, this formula would provide the key for the controlled release of energy from the atom. Einstein's search for an exact description of the laws of gravitation led him in 1915 from his relatively simple special theory of relativity to his general principle of relativity, which postulated that the laws of nature operated in exactly the same way for all observers. His theory supplanted traditional theories of gravitation, which saw gravity as a property of objects interacting with each other. Rather, Einstein believed that they interacted with space. Yet Einstein and other scientists remained ill at ease with the element of chance suggested by Planck's quantum theory. Trying to explain his conclusion that the universe could not operate in a random way, Einstein later insisted: "God does not play dice." Both Planck's theory, by suggesting a role for chance, and Einstein's staggering achievements themselves left open as many questions for the future as they resolved, not the least of which would later be terrifying new applications of the German scientist's famous formula to the hydrogen and atom bombs.

Social Change

Between 1870 and 1914, the population of Europe increased by half, rising from 290 to 435 million (see Table 19.3). By the end of the nineteenth century, one of every four people in the world was a European. The urban population of most countries grew rapidly. More "white-collar" positions,

Table 19.3. Population Growth in Major States between 1871 and 1911 (population in millions)

	c. 1871	c. 1911	% increase
German Empire	41.1	64.9	57.8
France	36.1	39.6	9.7
Austria-Hungary*	35.8	49.5	38.3
Great Britain	31.8	45.4	42.8
Italy	26.8	34.7	29.5
Spain	16.0	19.2	20.0

*Not including Bosnia-Herzegovina.
Source: Colin Dyer, *Population and Society in Twentieth Century France* (New York: Holmes and Meier, 1978), p. 5.

such as clerks and salespeople, became available, and service employment drew migrants to cities. Increased factory production altered the physical structure of industrial cities, which were characterized by greater social segregation within their limits. Working-class suburbs grew rapidly on the outskirts of towns. Overseas emigration, particularly to the Americas, rose rapidly and did not slow down even with the end of the economic depression in the mid-1890s.

Demographic Boom

Europe's population grew rapidly because the continent passed from the traditional pattern of high birthrates and high death rates to low rates of both births and deaths. Mortality rates fell during the second half of the nineteenth century, particularly among children. Births outnumbered deaths, despite the fact that fertility rates fell beginning in the 1860s, or even before. Infant mortality declined, particularly in Western and Central Europe, because of greater medical understanding of chest and stomach infections, as well as a general improvement in the standard of living. Many poor people now lived in warmer, drier accommodations, although improvements still lagged behind in large, dirty, industrial cities.

With infant mortality greatly reduced, more couples sought to control the number of children they had (see Table 19.4). Although Britain's Queen Victoria had nine children, poor families often had more children than upper-class couples, who limited themselves to two or three offspring because they wanted to devote more resources to the education and inheritance of each child. In France, officials and nationalists worried about their country's unique plunging birthrate. The French population grew by only about 15 percent from mid-century until 1914. The division of farmland into small plots may be a partial explanation—another child ultimately meant a further subdivision of land because France no longer had primogeniture (inheritance by the eldest son).

Contraception became more widespread, although the methods were very traditional ones. Coitus interruptus was the most common method, although

TABLE 19.4. THE DECLINE IN FAMILY SIZE (NUMBER OF CHILDREN) IN ENGLAND AND WALES

Year	Family Size
1861–1869	6.16
1871	5.94
1876	5.62
1890–1899	4.13
1900–1909	3.30
1910–1914	2.82

Source: E. A. Wrigley, *Population and History* (New York: McGraw-Hill, 1969), p. 197.

it was hardly flawless. Rudimentary condoms made of animal intestines were superseded in the 1880s by rubber condoms, although these still were relatively expensive, and were used primarily for protection against disease rather than for birth control. As families sought to limit the number of children and single women encountered unplanned pregnancies, abortion became more common, in part because contraception methods remained very hit or miss. A quarter of pregnancies probably ended in abortion, even though abortions were both illegal and extremely dangerous. Women seeking to terminate a pregnancy took all sorts of concoctions rumored to be effective, or put themselves at the mercy of quacks.

In some places, however, births to unmarried couples or to single mothers increased rapidly. Young female migrants to the city were vulnerable to the advances of men promising marriage or promising nothing at all. Unplanned pregnancies followed. A sizable percentage of the population of most countries—about 10 to 15 percent—never married or entered into permanent or long-term relationships. Unmarried women were especially common in Scotland, Ireland, and in Brittany in France, from which more males than females migrated to urban, industrial regions.

Improving Standards of Living

Living standards improved for ordinary people in every industrialized country. Standards of living were far higher in northern Europe than in southern and eastern Europe, greater in Britain than in France, with Germany closing the gap with both of its rivals. In Britain, real wages (taking inflation into account), which had increased by a third between 1850 and 1875, again rose by almost half during the last three decades of the century. Workers enjoyed higher levels of consumption because the price of food fell as agricultural production increased and transportation improved. Working-class families still spent half of their budget on food, but this was less than during previous centuries. This left more money to spend on clothes, with something occasionally left over. Small-town shops were better supplied than ever before, and ready-made clothes sold on market day alongside manufactured household utensils.

More grain and meat, arriving in refrigerated ships, reached Europe from Australia, Canada, the United States, and Argentina. Meat ceased to be a luxury. The average German had consumed almost 60 pounds of meat in 1873, 105 pounds in 1912. Germans consumed on average three times more sugar at the end of the century than thirty years earlier. People who lived a good distance inland—and who were of some means—found that fish reached them before the ice keeping the fish fresh had melted. The poor, too, now enjoyed a more varied diet, consisting of more vegetables, fruit, and cheese. As the diet of ordinary people improved, and thus their nutrition, people gradually became taller. Still, workers almost everywhere remained chronically undernourished and vulnerable to childhood diseases.

The average European laborer was still shorter than the average middle-class person.

Migration and Emigration

European migration was part of a worldwide movement of men and women in what was becoming a global labor force. Migration—both permanent and seasonal—within Europe continued to be significant. In France, in particular, many rural regions of marginal agriculture lost population to cities and towns. Seasonal work took hundreds of thousands of laborers across borders for part of the year as construction and harvest workers. Some Italian laborers known as "swallows" spent four weeks a year traveling to and from Argentina to work the harvests.

Permanent migration to the city did not end the contact between the migrants and their rural origins. Many industrial workers still went back to their villages to help with the harvest, and many miners were also part-time farmers. Thus, migration was a two-way street, at least when patterns of movement involved relatively short distances. When migrants returned home for visits, they brought with them not only stories about what they had experienced in the cities and towns where they now lived, but different ways of speaking, knowledge of birth control, the habit of reading, a taste for sports, and greater political awareness and interest.

Immigrants from Europe await a ferry for New York City, having passed through the entry point at Ellis Island.

Overseas emigration increased dramatically during the nineteenth century's last decades, the result of economic stagnation, marginal and overcrowded agricultural regions, religious persecution, and the hope of finding a better life. Between 1850 and 1880, about 8 million Europeans emigrated, most to the United States. Russia and Eastern Europe sent an increasing number of impoverished people abroad. Between 1890 and 1914, about 350,000 Greeks—one-seventh of the population of Greece—left their country, most for good. Emigration from Europe was itself facilitated by the transportation revolution, as steamships carried millions of people to a new life across the oceans.

With improving economic times in the late 1890s, emigration slowed down from Germany, while remaining high from Ireland and increasing dramatically from Italy. During the first decade of the twentieth century, emigration from Europe rose to between 1 and 1.4 million people each year. Most of those packing themselves onto overcrowded steamers went to the United States: Italians and Irish to New York, Boston, and Philadelphia; Portuguese to Providence and New Bedford; Germans and Bohemians to Chicago, Milwaukee, and Philadelphia (see Table 19.5); Poles to Chicago and Detroit. In 1907, due to their sheer number, Italian emigrants sent back enough money to cover half the commercial deficit of their native country. Pushed by crop failures and pulled by the U.S. Homestead Act of 1862 (which virtually guaranteed land in the American West), waves of Swedes, along with Norwegians and Finns, began to emigrate to the northern United States. By the 1930s, 3 million Swedes had changed countries, leaving a population of about 6 million at home. Hundreds of thousands of Portuguese left for Brazil in search of jobs as laborers, following the abolition of slavery in that country in 1888.

Between 1871 and 1914, more than 1.5 million Jews left Russia and Polish Russia for the United States, fleeing poverty and periodic anti-Semitic violence. Many left their homes with little more than a few cherished items and great hopes. One Jewish emigrant from a village in Belarus remembered that his family carried empty suitcases as they left home—they did not want the

TABLE 19.5. EMIGRATION TO THE UNITED STATES, 1871–1910

	1871–1880	1881–1890	1891–1900	1901–1910
Germany	718,000	1,500,000	505,000	341,000
Ireland	437,000	656,000	388,000	339,000
England/Scotland/Wales	548,000	807,000	272,000	526,000
Scandinavia	243,000	655,000	372,000	505,000
Italy	56,000	307,000	652,000	2,000,000
Austria-Hungary	73,000	363,000	574,000	2,145,000
Russia/Baltic states	39,000	213,000	505,000	1,597,000

Source: Leonard Dinnerstein and David M. Reimers, *Ethnic Americans: A History of Immigration and Assimilation* (New York: Harper and Row, 1977), p. 11.

other people they met along the way to know that they owned virtually nothing to carry. Tens of thousands of Jews moved westward to European capitals, such as London, where they lived in the East End. Most Jews retained their cultural traditions and religion and spoke Yiddish as their first language. They were considered outsiders by many people in Vienna, Berlin, Budapest, Paris, and other cities (even in some cases by assimilated Jews). The Zionist movement for the establishment of the Jewish homeland in Palestine emerged partially in response to the rising tide of anti-Semitism in Europe. The movement's founder was Theodor Herzl (1860–1904), a gifted journalist and German-speaking Jew from Budapest who had moved to Vienna.

Although many families left together for overseas destinations, many married men went alone, hoping either to send for their families when they could afford to do so, or to return after saving some money. In new homes, migrants forged new collective identities, a process shaped not only by their own ethnic backgrounds and solidarities but also by conditions in their new homelands. Many never saw their families again. Migrants to the United States from southern Italy were the most likely to return permanently, with almost two-thirds eventually going back.

The Changing World of Work

By 1900, more than half of all industrial workers in Britain, Germany, and Belgium were employed in firms with more than twenty workers. Artisans, skilled workers, and unskilled workers often found themselves in the same factory. Most industrial workers came from proletarian families and grew up with few or no illusions about finding a more secure way of earning a living. But "proletarian" was also a state of mind. Many workers took pride in their work and in their social class. "I was born in the slums of London of working-class parents," a contemporary recalled, "and although I have attained a higher standard of living, I still maintain I am working class." Yet enormous differences in skill, remuneration, and quality of life continued to exist among workers.

Mechanization eliminated or reduced demand for some trades. Skilled glassworkers were no longer needed when the Siemens furnace, which permitted continuous production, was adapted to the production of bottles in the 1880s. Porcelain painters lost their jobs to unskilled female laborers when factory owners started using decals that could be applied to plates and then baked on. Steam laundries left many washerwomen without clients.

New professions brought some workers higher status. Engineers, capable of designing, overseeing, and repairing machinery, became fixtures in factories. In the 1880s, some engineers still had received training as apprentices, but by the first decades of the twentieth century, many had received university training in their chosen profession.

Women's work remained closely tied to their stage of life. Many young, unmarried women became servants upon arrival in the urban world, trying to

Derbyshire pit boys outside the mines in Britain.

save enough money for a modest dowry, in the hope of marrying someone of a slightly higher social class. By the end of the century, servants accounted for more than half of female workers in Britain.

Most female industrial workers were still employed in small workshops or at home, but more women became factory workers. Even in the Habsburg Empire, which was much less industrialized than Germany or Britain, about 900,000 women worked in factories, largely in unskilled jobs. Most earned only about half the wages of their male counterparts for, in some cases, the same jobs. Women workers were usually the last hired and the first fired. Despite harsh working conditions and relatively low wages, some women saw factory work as bringing an improvement in wages and conditions over agricultural labor, cottage industry, or domestic service. A Belfast woman in 1898 remembered her time in a linen mill: "Wonderful times then in the mill. You got a wee drink, got a join [pooled money with others to buy food], done your work and you had your company."

Industrialization and the Working-Class Family

Moralists bemoaned the effects of industrial work, arguing that the uprooting of families from villages put them at risk in cities and factories characterized by vice and immorality. Despite laws controlling child labor (see Chapter 14), at the turn of the century many thousands of children, including those between the ages of eight and fourteen, were still working in factories (the young above age fourteen worked as adults). Moralists believed that only education, marriage, the habit of saving money, and a return to the old ways could save family life. Women, they claimed, were being taken away from their reproductive function, and from family life itself. Working-class families in cities were indeed much less likely to live with their extended families—that is, with parents and sometimes grandparents and in-laws—than were country people. More families tended to be broken up early when children sixteen years or younger left villages in search of work in the cities, leaving aging parents to fend for themselves as best they could. Furthermore, long hours in the factory for parents and children alike seemed to erode parental authority. Moralists blamed increasingly homogeneous working-class neighborhoods, where drinking and domestic violence seemed rampant.

Many women of child-bearing age who could afford to do so, or who had no other choice, tended children full time. But once their offspring were old enough to care for themselves, many working-class mothers returned to factory work. Others worked at home, doing piecework and caring for their children at the same time. Many women thus alternated between industrial wage labor and child rearing.

As ever in the European experience, many women still were forced by economic circumstances into prostitution, in large cities, towns of modest size, and even villages. Some of the tens of thousands of prostitutes in Paris, London, Berlin, and Vienna worked in elegant brothels, under the direction of a "madam," who allowed them only a couple days off per year. Others worked on their own, waiting for customers in bars, doorways, windows, and parks. Most prostitutes were working-class women—some of whom were married—unable to find industrial work. Many were young, having had to leave school early to support younger siblings.

Henri de Toulouse-Lautrec's *In the Salon at the Rue des Moulins* (1894) depicts French prostitutes.

Prostitutes began to be perceived more than ever before as a chronic danger to public health. Complaints from the middle class increased (which was ironic, since middle-class men constituted a significant portion of the clientele for prostitutes). Socialist parties, however, expressed little interest in prostitution as an issue of reform, although they blamed capitalism for the low wages or unemployment that forced many women into prostitution.

In 1864, the British Parliament had passed the Contagious Diseases Act, which required medical examination of prostitutes. The goal was to stop the spread of venereal disease, particularly syphilis, by hospitalizing prostitutes found to be infected. If a woman refused medical examination, she could be prosecuted. The Contagious Diseases Act had the ironic effect of transforming prostitution from a temporary profession for many struggling working-class women to a dead-end, permanent job because the law publicly branded them as prostitutes.

Josephine Butler (1828–1906), the devoutly religious wife of a clergyman and president of an association encouraging higher education for women, led a well-organized, determined campaign in Britain and then on the continent against the Contagious Diseases Act. Some opponents of the act objected that the law called only for the inspection of prostitutes, not their clients; others opposed extensive police regulatory authority. Butler espoused the right of women to regulate their own sexuality. Parliament repealed the Contagious Diseases Act in 1886, and passed a law that banned brothels, forcing prostitutes to operate in tolerated "red-light" districts, where they were often subject to violence. Almost all of the victims of the still unidentified London killer "Jack the Ripper" were prostitutes.

In France, too, laws placed prostitutes under greater regulatory control. Gradually, the belief that morality could be legislated ebbed in Europe. Charitable institutions more willingly provided assistance to unwed mothers and their offspring, increasingly considering their sad situations as a social, not a moral, problem.

Teeming Cities

In 1899, an American statistician—the profession itself was another sign of the times—noted that "the concentration of population in cities [is] the most remarkable social phenomenon of the present century." Britain and Germany led the way, but France, Austria, Switzerland, Italy, Sweden, and even Spain and Serbia also had high rates of urban growth. Classic "factory towns" such as Manchester, Saint-Étienne, and Essen grew rapidly in size, but so did the population of other towns, swollen by service workers and state and commercial employees.

Rural industry, which had provided spinning, weaving, and finishing work for hundreds of thousands of people—above all, women—on a full- or part-time basis, gradually disappeared during the last half of the century. Manufacturing, including home production in the garment industry, now became overwhelmingly concentrated in urban centers. Mechanized agriculture and falling agricultural prices reduced demand for farm laborers, encouraging migration to towns in search of work in the booming service sector or in industry. The population of Istanbul doubled in forty years, reaching 850,000 by 1886, swollen by the influx of Muslim refugees from Russia and the Balkans. Warsaw's population grew by more than four times from about 160,000 in 1850 to almost 800,000 people in 1911; two-thirds of the Polish city's buildings had been built in the nineteenth century. In Central and Eastern European cities like Prague and Tallinn, Czechs and Estonians, respectively, arrived in greater numbers from the countryside, changing the ethnic composition of these places.

Although some working-class families now lived in marginally more spacious lodgings, many densely packed urban neighborhoods became ghastly slums. London had its infamous "back to back" row houses, with little or no space between the houses and room for little more between the rows than outdoor toilets, if that, and garbage heaps. For most British workers, a parlor (a family room), a sign of "respectability," remained only a dream. In Glasgow, Scotland, a third of the city's families lived in one room, as more and more highlanders crowded into tall tenement dwellings.

As Paris became ever more crowded, Emperor Napoleon III had undertaken a massive rebuilding project in Paris during the 1850s and 1860s. He entrusted the planning to Baron Georges Haussmann (1809–1891). Together they planned the most extensive project of urban renewal since the rebuilding of London following the great fire in the seventeenth century and that of Edo (Tokyo) in Japan at about the same time following the great conflagration of 1657.

Napoleon III and Haussmann wanted to facilitate the expansion of commerce and industry through the creation of long, wide boulevards, which would be lined by symmetrical apartment buildings. It was not a coincidence

(*Left*) Tenement housing in Glasgow. (*Right*) Company housing near mines in northern France.

that some of the new arteries cut through some of the most traditionally revolutionary neighborhoods, providing troops quick access into the narrow streets in eastern Paris where ordinary people had risen up during the June Days in 1848, as well as during the French Revolution. This made it more difficult to erect barricades. The impressionist painter Auguste Renoir (1841–1919) would lament the transformation of these old Parisian neighborhoods and the new symmetrical buildings that lined the boulevards, "cold and lined up like soldiers at review." It seemed an appropriate image to accompany the further consolidation of state power. Glittering department stores and fancy cafés stood along the elegant boulevards, showcases to imperial monumentalism but also to modern life. Large iron structures provided space for Les Halles, the refurbished market of central Paris.

Napoleon III also wanted to make Paris a healthier place. Some of the broad boulevards replaced narrow, winding streets, cutting through unhealthy neighborhoods. Aqueducts were built to provide cleaner water for residents. Four hundred miles of underground sewers (which emptied into the Seine River northwest of Paris) improved health conditions in a city that had been recently ravaged by cholera.

Although the massive rebuilding provided jobs for many workers, it also forced many thousands of workers and their families to leave the central city for the cheaper rents of the inner suburbs, particularly those to the north and northeast—which were annexed to Paris in 1860—or to increasingly industrialized suburbs farther out, themselves emerging symbols of the Sec-

Emperor Napoleon III (*left*) and Baron Georges Haussmann, viewed as either the rebuilder of Paris or the "Alsatian Attila" (*right*).

ond Industrial Revolution.
The cost of all these projects was enormous and far
exceeded original esti-
mates. Speculators made a
fortune, tipped off as to
where the next demolitions
would take place.

Paris had already reached
well over a million inhabitants. By 1900, nine European cities had populations
that large. London dwarfed
them all, growing from 1.9
million in 1841 to 4.2 million in 1891. Between one-
fifth and one-sixth of the
population of Britain lived
in London, which was
larger than the next seven
largest English cities and
Edinburgh combined. The

Paris before Haussmann: Charles Marville's photograph of the Rue Traversine. Notice the drainage
ditch in the center of the cobblestone street.

sprawling imperial city seemed almost ungovernable, an imposing labyrinth
of different jurisdictions with 10,000 people exercising varying degrees of
authority. Unlike Paris, which was for the most part administered by the
centralized French state, London only had an effective local government
after the establishment of the London City Council in 1889.

The largest port in the world, London also remained a center of international banking, finance, and commerce, and the administrative nerve center of the British Empire. The influence of "the City"—London's banking
and finance district—extended around the world, channeling investment
capital to innumerable countries within and beyond the empire. Half the
capital that left Europe passed through London. The largest merchant
marine fleet in the world carried woolens and other textiles to China,
machine parts and hardware to Russia, toys to New York, settlers to
Canada, and soldiers and sailors to India, and it imported Australian wool,
Chicago beef, Bordeaux wines, Portuguese port, and Cuban cigars.

London was also a center of small-scale production and finishing in
shops usually employing only a few skilled and semiskilled workers each,
such as in the clothing industry, furniture making, engineering, and printing. The bustling East End docks employed a vast force of "casual labor"—
that is, semiskilled and unskilled laborers who worked when work could be
found. Two million people lived in the East End. There, and elsewhere, the
homeless slept where they could, in empty or half-collapsed buildings,
under bridges and railroad viaducts. To upper-class Londoners, the East

End, about which they knew nothing except "from hearsay and report," was a morass of tangled slums "as unexplored as Timbuktu." Residents of these districts spoke a cockney dialect that was difficult for outsiders to understand, or with a thick Irish brogue, or in Yiddish.

The Hungarian capital of Budapest revealed not only the social and ethnic complexity of the Austro-Hungarian Empire but also the increased social segregation characteristic of the modern city. This city on the Danube River grew from a population of about 120,000 in 1848 to 280,000 inhabitants in 1867 and almost 900,000 people in 1914. By then, Hungarian, which had been spoken by a minority of the population of the capital at mid-century, had become the language spoken by the vast majority of people. Many Germans and Jews had emigrated or been assimilated. The complexity of social differences was such that five forms of salutation were current, depending upon whom one was addressing. These ranged from the ultimate deference of "Gracious Sir," through the only slightly less groveling "Dignified Sir" or "Great Sir," all the way down to the considerably more common "Hey, you!"

Many social theorists were convinced that the rapid growth of cities bred crime (see Chapter 20). But, in fact, urban growth in some places seems to have significantly increased only crimes against property. Crime rates in Glasgow fell during the last half of the century, despite the petty extortion carried out by youth gangs like the Penny Mob, the Redskins, and the Kelly Boys. Many contemporary observers inveighed against cities as promoting an anonymous, alienated mass of people. Yet relatives and friends who had the same dialect or accent or religion encouraged others to move to the city and served as conduits for information about jobs and lodgings. The resulting "chain" migration created "urban villages" that mitigated against uprooting and lawlessness. Neighborhoods of Irish in Liverpool and London, and Italians and Irish in Boston and New York, provided solidarities that made the city seem less anonymous to newcomers.

Social segregation within European cities became more pronounced. Elevators carried wealthy occupants of apartment buildings to refurbished dwellings in the upper stories, where poorer people had once lived. Families of means lived along Vienna's Ringstrasse and near the parks of west London. As more suburbs developed around the edge of Europe's larger cities, some, particularly outside London, catered to middle-class people who could commute into the city, happy to live in small houses that offered more room and fresh air. These suburbs, unlike most center cities, reflected some degree of planning and improved water and gas supply, among other municipal services.

But European suburbs became even more mostly a plebeian phenomenon. Factories were constructed on the edge of cities so that manufacturers could take advantage of more space, proximity to railways and canals, somewhat lower cost of land and raw materials (avoiding the taxes that were still levied on goods brought into some cities), and the availability of cheap labor (see Chapter 14). Railway lines and factories on the edge of town were surrounded by poor-quality, low-rent housing, usually owned by absentee landlords. More and more workers commuted daily into town to work—some still on foot, others by tram, subway, train, and later bus. Modest suburbs even developed around the small Estonian capital of Tallinn in the Russian Baltic provinces, where peasant workers settled on the edge of town.

With urban growth in cities came civic pride. Municipal governments built celebratory historical monuments, constructed new hospitals and town halls, sponsored bands, and created beautiful parks complete with ornate bandstands. They prided themselves on an increasingly diverse municipal cultural life, including occasional music festivals and perhaps even a museum. The proliferation of voluntary associations, such as clubs and choral societies, also came to be taken as symbols of urbanity as cities and towns continued to grow, transforming the lives of millions of Europeans.

At the same time, homosexual subcultures developed in most large cities, and in some smaller places (a German writer first used the term "homosexuality" in 1868). Same-sex acts had first been decriminalized in France in 1791, but gays and lesbians largely remained in the shadows, although readily identifiable hotels, restaurants, bars, parks, and gardens provided places for them to meet. If the prostitution of women was very much out in the open, that of men was always less obvious. Public attitudes toward homosexuality remained generally intolerant. This was reflected by the fact that the English philosopher Jeremy Bentham (1748–1832) penned many pages defending same-sex relations, but never dared publish them, and by occasional high-profile trials. The Scientific-Humanitarian Committee, established in Berlin in 1897, was the first organization founded to support homosexual rights.

Social Mobility

The middle classes swelled during the Second Industrial Revolution, taking their places in Europe's burgeoning cities. Lower-middle-class occupations, in particular, expanded rapidly. (That the lower middle class had some degree of self-awareness was revealed by the fact that in 1899 the first— and last—World Congress of the Petty Bourgeoisie took place in Brussels.) Architects required draftsmen; companies needed accountants and bookkeepers; and the London underground and Paris subway had to have agents. Furthermore, the expansion of governmental functions generated thousands of jobs: tax collectors, postal workers, food and drug inspectors, and recorders of official documents. The number of schoolteachers increased dramatically between the 1870s and 1914—five times more in Italy, thirteen times more in England. (Table 19.6 represents the rapid growth in the number of state employees.) In Britain, the proportion of the population classified as lower middle class grew from about 7 percent in 1850 to 20 percent in 1900. Clerks working for banks, railroads, utility companies, and

Table 19.6. Number of Public Servants (Non-Military)

	1881	1901	1911
Great Britain	81,000	153,000	644,000
France	379,000	451,000	699,000
Germany	452,000	907,000	1,159,000

Source: Norman Stone, *Europe Transformed 1878–1919* (Cambridge, Mass: Harvard University Press, 1984), p. 130.

insurance companies considered themselves above the working class and therefore "respectable." With the optimism of the age, they viewed such employment as a first step to one day owning their own store. They did not wear work clothes and did not do manual labor and they made a little more money than workers.

In European cities, women found jobs as department store clerks, stenographers, and secretaries. There were twelve times as many secretaries in 1901 as there had been two decades earlier; women, who held only 8 percent of post office and government clerical positions in 1861, accounted for more than half in 1911. They now used metal pens that replaced the age-old quill, and then the typewriter, invented in the 1880s. Nursing became a respected profession. Cafés and restaurants employed hundreds of thousands of women.

Gains made by workers seemed paltry when compared to the fortunes being made by industrialists, and even the salaries earned by management personnel. These gnawing disparities aided unions and socialist parties in their quest for the allegiance of workers, many of whom walked to and from work while horse-drawn cabs raced by, carrying well-heeled occupants. Indeed, during the mid-1890s, real wages, which had risen for several decades, entered a period of decline.

Dizzying "rags to riches" tales (especially popular in the United States and Russia) suggested that hard work could lead to better conditions of life. Emigrants to the United States arrived with fantastically high expectations of what life would be like. Inflated expectations often brought disappointment, as social mobility was extremely limited, particularly for first-generation immigrants. During the last decades of the century, 95 percent of American industrialists came from upper- or middle-class families, and not more than 3 percent were the sons of poor immigrants or farmers. Among immigrants and native-born workers in the United States, the most common form of social advancement was within the working class, not into a higher social group.

Despite movement in Western European countries into clerical and other lower-middle-class jobs, however, there were fewer possibilities of movement by workers into the middle class during the hard years of the 1880s than there had been during the middle decades of the century. Low wages and periodic unemployment for industrial workers made saving and the ownership of apartments or houses, both essential components of

Clerical work toward the end of the nineteenth century.

mobility, extremely difficult to achieve. Craftsmen and skilled workers had a far better chance for social ascension than did unskilled workers. As in the United States, those who did move up to middle-class employment were the exceptions. The vast majority of marriages in Europe took place between partners considered social equals. Working-class women were more likely than their brothers to achieve some social mobility—for example, by marrying a clerk or railroad station employee.

CULTURAL CHANGES: EDUCATION AND RELIGION

In every country, states took enormous strides to bring education to more people. More children went on to secondary school, now including some girls. The state's increased role in education in Western Europe contributed to a growing secularization of public life. At the same time, the established churches lost the allegiance of many ordinary Europeans.

Education

Literacy rose rapidly during the last decades of the century in Europe as more governments enacted educational reforms. Literacy rates were higher in western—above all, northwestern Europe—than in southern and eastern Europe, although progress was notable in Russia around the turn of the century.

In Britain, Parliament passed, over Anglican opposition, the Education Act of 1870, which placed education in the hands of the state by permitting local education boards to create schools in districts where neither the Established Church nor its Dissenting Protestant rivals had established a school. (With the help of state grants, the Anglicans had far outdistanced their competitors in building new schools; only ten years earlier they had controlled 90 percent of the elementary schools in England and Wales.) In 1880, Parliament passed a law requiring that all children between five and ten years of age attend primary school, up to age twelve beginning in 1899, and in 1891 primary education became free. Truancy officers in working-class neighborhoods encountered resistance from parents who preferred the supplementary income from their children's work to their schooling. State inspectors maintained educational standards, requiring villages to provide better facilities for their schools and accommodations for teachers. Besides familiarizing young people with "the letters," primary schools in late Victorian Britain sought to teach them how to be "good Englishmen" and "good English wives," idealizing social harmony in Britain while espousing British "superiority" over the indigenous peoples of the empire (see Chapter 21).

In France, the Ferry Laws (passed 1879–1881, named after Minister of Education and then Premier Jules Ferry) made primary schools free, obligatory, and secular for all children from age three to thirteen. Each region was required to operate a teacher-training school. Bretons, Provençaux, Gascons, Basques, Catalans, and people speaking regional patois learned French, which became spoken by most people, although bilingualism remained common. In Italy, Italian ceased to be a language spoken only by the upper class.

The percentage of people able to read and write still varied considerably from country to country. More men could read and write than women, more urban residents than rural people. In France, where 40 percent of military conscripts had not been able to read or write at mid-century, the percentage had fallen at the turn of the century to only 6 percent. In contrast, in Dalmatia, on the Adriatic coast, only 1 of every 100 conscripts could read and write in 1870, and in Spain 70 percent of electors were illiterate in 1890. In 1860, 75 percent of Italian men and almost 90 percent of women could neither read nor write and depended on public letter writers to pen what correspondence they required. By 1914, 75 percent of all Italians were literate. Yet in southern Italy and Sicily, more than half of the children in many places still did not attend school regularly or at all. In Germany, by the turn of the century less than 1 percent of the population remained illiterate. In Russia, illiteracy fell from about 90 percent of the population in the 1860s to about 75 percent by 1910. Whereas the older, illiterate generation of Russians mistrusted education ("You can't eat books"), fearing that literacy would erode village religious culture (and perhaps also deference to elders), younger peasants ridiculed their superstitious parents and welcomed self-improvement through education.

During the 1870s and 1880s, the issue of female education surged to the forefront in Western Europe. Only women whose families were able and willing to pay the required fees received secondary education. In France, women were allowed to teach boys, but men were not permitted to teach girls. Both lay teachers and nuns instructed girls in the domestic mission of women, stressing gender differences and promoting deference to their future husbands, as in other countries. A female German Social Democrat later recalled that the education she had received had been so "that I might one day be able to provide my husband with a proper domestic atmosphere." Schooling for boys and girls alike emphasized patriotic, secular, and politically conservative themes. Female teachers of girls were to be considered morally irreproachable and thoroughly secular mother figures within their communities.

In Western Europe, more young people attended secondary schools, the number tripling in Germany and quadrupling in France between 1875 and 1912. Many families viewed education as a way of improving the employment and marriage possibilities for their daughters.

Yet secondary education in general remained possible only for families of some means. Moreover, existing educational systems reinforced social distinctions of class, counseling "patient resignation" to one's economic and social condition. Secondary schools taught skills that led to good jobs, but they drew very few children from the lower classes. In England, boarding schools founded in the 1860s and 1870s catered to middle-class students, while the sons of "gentlemen" attended the nine old elite "public"—that is, private—schools.

Although the number of university students tripled in Europe during this period, university education remained limited to a tiny proportion of the population drawn from the upper classes. At the University of Cambridge at mid-century, 60 percent of the students were sons of landowners or clergy. In all of Britain, there were only 13,000 university students in 1913 in a total population of 36 million people, although the percentage of university students drawn from the middle classes had greatly increased and technical colleges began to attract more students. In Prussia, for example, only 1 in 1,000 university students had parents who were workers. The Russian tsars reversed the European trend during the course of the century, making it more difficult for non-nobles to attend secondary school and university. Yet, overall, the number of universities increased—for example, in Hungary, where three new ones opened their doors.

Despite this, only very slowly were women admitted to universities. In the 1860s, a few women were medical students in Paris, and the first female students appeared at the University of Zurich in 1867. In the 1870s, there were already women's colleges in England and women began university study in Denmark and Sweden. In Germany, where professors constituted the "intellectual bodyguard" of the Hohenzollern dynasty, women did not attend university until the late 1890s. Upon seeing a woman in his lecture course, the historian Heinrich von Treitschke stopped speaking. He escorted her out the door. Only in 1909 did women obtain the right to study in any German university. At the University of Cambridge, the Senate in 1897 voted overwhelmingly to deny women the right to take a Cambridge

A protest opposing the admission of women to the University of Cambridge in 1881 demonstrates the unwillingness of many to erase gender distinctions in education.

degree. Women could not receive degrees or have full privileges as students at Oxford until 1920 and at Cambridge until 1948.

The Decline of Religious Practice

In a century of vigorous state secularization, particularly in Western Europe, many clergy viewed the period of rapid social change at the turn of the century with anxiety. The institutional influence of churches on states had declined dramatically in most of Europe. More than this, in some places, the influence of organized religion on society continued to wane. Secular education, espousing the cult of the nation, accelerated this trend, even though many people in Catholic countries still attended Church schools. However, fewer people went to church than earlier in the century. In London a survey at the turn of the century revealed that less than 20 percent of the population regularly attended services, a marked decline. In Spain, Galicia, the Basque provinces, and much of Castile remained devout, while much of southern Spain did not.

The first Catholic sociologists of religion found a sharp rise in "de-christianized" regions, as demonstrated by rates of couples not having church marriages or being slow to have their children baptized, or the decline in religious vocations. By the 1890s, the Church considered some

Catholic faithful at the Grotto of Lourdes.

regions in France, and most working-class districts of large European cities, to be "missionary" areas, in this way defined like China or the Congo. The loss of the Church's hold on ordinary people was reflected in the decline in the birthrate, explicable in part by increased use of birth control. Furthermore, an increasing number of French people called upon the clergy only at the time of baptism, marriage, and death (and thus were sometimes referred to as "four-wheeled Catholics," in reference to the wagons that carried an individual to each important occasion).

Yet the decline of religious practice in Europe was neither linear, nor did it occur everywhere. A revival of popular religious enthusiasm occurred in some places between 1830 and 1880, particularly among the upper classes. In Sweden the "Great Awakening" brought the revival of popular religion. In Catholic countries, lithography and printing presses helped rekindle devotion, spreading the news of religious shrines. Women were more apt to attend church than men (although in part this resulted from the fact that women live longer than men). The cult of the Virgin Mary also contributed to the feminization of religion in Catholic countries, perhaps encouraging more young women to enter convents.

The growing cult of miracles was part of a revival of popular religion, particularly in France, Italy, and Spain. Near the French town of Lourdes in the central Pyrenees, Bernadette, a peasant girl later canonized by the Church, announced in 1858 that the Virgin Mary had appeared to her.

Churchmen and their followers believed that the apparition explained the miraculous cures that seemed to occur at Lourdes, despite the skepticism of scientists. Religious pilgrimages by train to sites of miracles became big business. In the first decade of the new century, more than a million people came to Lourdes each year, many hoping to be cured of illness and disease. The popularity of pilgrimages reflected the resiliency of the Catholic Church, even in a time of growing doubt.

The Consumer Explosion

During the last decades of the nineteenth century, consumerism developed in the countries of Europe, again with considerable country-to-country variation. The new leisure activities of the Belle Époque themselves reflected the Second Industrial Revolution. Sports—principally soccer and rugby, bicycle and automobile races, and track and field—attracted participants and spectators and encouraged the formation of clubs.

Department stores reflected and helped shape the burgeoning consumer culture. First in London, Paris, and Berlin, department stores transformed the way many families shopped. They attracted prosperous clients in search of quality ready-made clothes that were less expensive than those stitched by tailors. The stores were monuments to the dynamism of bourgeois culture, displaying in their windows products that reflected material progress. Seeking to increase the volume of sales, department stores also stocked more inexpensive clothing, while adding umbrellas, toothbrushes, stationery, and much more. All of this required the organization into departments overseen by trained managers, which typified the Second Industrial Revolution. The expanding clientele of department stores included the families of shopkeepers, civil servants, and clerks of more modest means, and gradually workers as well. On an average day in the 1890s, 15,000 to 18,000 people entered the "Bon Marché"—still a Parisian landmark. Glossy catalogues in color, advancing advertising techniques, permitted shoppers to make purchases in the comfort of their homes. Advertisers began to direct their appeals at the "new woman," the housewife of taste, who had the time to create the model home and had some money to spend.

The owners of department stores wanted shopping to become an experience in itself, like a visit to a world's fair—except that one could now buy some of the displayed wonders of human innovation. Architects aimed at monumental and theatrical effects. The great department stores were enormous, stately structures topped with cupolas, with iron columns and an expanse of glass giving shoppers a sense of space and light. Shoppers could walk up grand staircases to observe the crowds below. Department stores became tourist sights, with dazzled visitors themselves becoming part of the spectacle. To Émile Zola, department stores had become the "cathedrals of modernity." For women of means, the commercialization represented by the department stores of the West End of London became a liberating experience, a veritable zone of pleasurable consumerism.

The actress Sarah Bernhardt dramatically laid out in the Art Nouveau style in a coffin.

Leisure in the Belle Époque

During the Belle Époque, there was more to do than ever before for those with time for leisure and money to spend. The French capital set the tone for style in Europe, if not the world. Dance halls, cafés, and café-concerts, the latter offering the performances of musicians, singers, poets, comedians, jugglers, acrobats, female wrestlers, and snake charmers, lined the *grands boulevards*, attracting throngs of Parisians and tourists alike. Hundreds of thousands of Londoners and Parisians attended the theater at least once a week. The tango and the turkey trot, imported from the Americas, were banned in some establishments. German Emperor William II forbade officers from dancing these steps while in uniform.

The talented and beautiful actress Sarah Bernhardt (1844–1923) embodied images of fin-de-siècle Europe. The daughter of a Dutch immigrant, she became famous for her dramatic expressiveness and ability to communicate tears to an audience through her supremely evocative voice. Bernhardt learned her trade from the traditions of the popular boulevard theater. Renowned for her dramatic gestures (as a young woman she asked a photographer to take a picture of her in a coffin) and for a variety of sexual liaisons, Sarah Bernhardt's worldwide fame was such that the American circus entrepreneur P. T. Barnum, upon hearing that she risked the amputation of a leg, offered her a fortune if she would allow him to take it on the road and exhibit it with his famous circus.

Sports in Mass Society

Sports emerged as a prominent feature of mass society during the last decades of the century, a phenomenon linked to modern transportation and to a general increase in leisure time. The first automobile race was held in 1894 in France. Some of the cars were powered by electricity, others by gasoline or even steam. Cycling competitions also generated enormous public interest. Sporting newspapers catered to fans. Competition between two cycling clubs led to the first Tour de France race in 1903, in which riders covered almost 1,500 miles in nineteen days.

Not only did people watch bicycle races, many rode bicycles themselves, both for leisure and as a source of transportation. A simple mechanism, the bicycle nonetheless reflected the technological innovation and mass production of the Second Industrial Revolution. By the late 1880s, bicycles were lighter, more affordable, and more easily repaired or replaced. Their manufacture became a major industry, with 375,000 produced in France by 1898 and 3.5 million in 1914.

Both men and women rode bicycles. But some men complained that the clothes women wore while riding bicycles were unfeminine. Some worried that female cyclists might compromise the middle-class domestic ideal of the "angel of the house." Moralists were concerned that the jolts of rough paths and roads might interfere with childbearing, or even lead to debauchery by generating physical pleasure. The president of a feminist congress in 1896, however, toasted the "egalitarian and leveling bicycle." It helped free women from the corset, "a new Bastille to be demolished." The bicycle may have also changed what some people considered the feminine ideal from plumpness to a more svelte line.

Team sports also quickly developed as a leisure activity during the second half of the nineteenth century. The two most popular team sports in Europe, football (soccer in the United States) and rugby, both began in England. Rugby, which developed at Cambridge and Oxford Universities in the 1860s, was an upper-class sport. Football had much earlier origins, perhaps going back to when Vikings and Russians used to "kick the Dane's head around"—literally. But football, which also had university origins, evolved into a plebeian sport, like boxing, which was to English workers what rowing, cricket, and golf became to the upper classes. Professional football began in England in 1863; eight years later, there were fifteen clubs playing for the championship. The new century brought the first major brawl between supporters of rival teams: a match between the Catholic Celtics and the Protestant Rangers of Glasgow ended with the stadium burned to the ground. In 1901, 111,000 spectators watched the English Cup Final.

Baron Pierre de Coubertin (1863–1937), a French noble who feared that the young men of his country were becoming soft, organized the first modern Olympic Games, held in Athens in 1896 in homage to the Greek creators of the Olympiad. An Anglophile, he revered the contemporary image of hard-riding, athletic upper-class Englishmen playing sports at Eton and Cambridge and then going on to expand the British Empire.

There was more to the rise of sports and the cult of physical vigor than simply games and fun. The development of sports culture also reflected the mood of aggressive nationalism. The popularity of Darwin's theory of the evolution of species led to a growing preoccupation with the comparative characteristics of specific races, or peoples. "Social Darwinists" misapplied the theory of "survival of the fittest" to society, including international sports competition. Games became hotly competitive. Moreover, the development of feminism in Western Europe may have contributed to what has been called a "crisis of masculinity," by which many men saw the strengthening of the "weaker sex" as the weakening of men. By this view, growing interest in sports competition was an affirmation of masculinity. Furthermore, the emerging interest in the times it took to run distances may have reflected fascination with scientific management.

Robert Baden-Powell, founder of the Boy Scouts.

The burgeoning interest in sports touched, above all, the young. In Germany, "wandering youth" clubs (*Wandervogel*) became popular, sending young boys out to camp under the stars. In Great Britain, Robert Baden-Powell (1857–1941) founded the Boy Scouts. After being rejected for admission to the University of Oxford and finding his vocation among young men in the army, Baden-Powell in 1908 organized the Boy Scouts in the hope of developing "among boys . . . a spirit of self-sacrifice and patriotism, and generally to prepare them to become good citizens." The uniform Baden-Powell had worn in South Africa—a Stetson hat, neckerchief, and khaki shorts—became that of the Boy Scouts, and their motto, "Be prepared."

Interest in sports touched all classes and reflected class differences. The poet Rudyard Kipling (1865–1936), who disliked sports in general, called cricket players (who tended to be from a loftier social class than his own) "fools." Football players, most of whom were from the working class, he dismissed as "oafs." People of great means were no longer the only people able to enjoy sports. While the upper classes had their own sporting associations, which retained a preference for horse racing—"the sport of kings"—working-class cycling and gymnastic clubs also began to spring up in the 1880s in Western Europe, particularly as workers won a shorter workweek and workday.

CONCLUSION

The Second Industrial Revolution transformed the way many Europeans lived. Electricity brought light to growing cities and towns, along whose boulevards, tramways and automobiles now carried passengers. Most Europeans could now read and write, but they were—at least in Western Europe—less likely to go to church regularly than earlier generations. Most people lived longer and better than ever before. At the same time, economic and social inequalities generated union organization, the growth of mass political parties—notably a variety of socialist movements—and waves of social protest. Nationalism became a political force in many countries during the last three decades of the nineteenth century and the beginning of the twentieth century, engulfing not only the industrialized constitutional monarchies and republics of western and southern Europe but also the empires of central and eastern Europe.

The rapid pace of material progress and scientific and technological advances generated innovative, complex cultural responses during the remarkable years that brought the nineteenth century to a close and saw the dawning of the modern world in the first years of the twentieth century.

CHAPTER 20

POLITICAL AND CULTURAL RESPONSES TO A RAPIDLY CHANGING WORLD

$\sim\!\!\!\!\sim$

As European economies were being transformed by the Second Industrial Revolution, states faced organized challenges from political movements that rejected the economic, social, and political bases of those states and demanded sweeping changes. Government officials, social reformers, and politicians had to confront the difficult conditions of many workers and their families—"the problem of problems," as it was called in Britain. Some states began to enact social reforms to improve the quality of life for workers and other poor people.

At the same time, the growth of large socialist parties that wanted to capture control of the state was one of the salient signs of the advent of mass political life. Marxist socialists believed that inevitably a working-class revolution would bring down capitalism. Reform socialists, in contrast, believed that electoral victories could lead to a socialist state, and that along the way to ultimate victory socialists could exert pressure on states to improve conditions of life for ordinary people. Anarchists did not want to seize the state, but rather to abolish it. Believing that violent acts would provide a spark that would unleash a social revolution, a number of anarchists launched a campaign of terrorism at the turn of the century, carrying out political assassinations. In parts of Europe, trade unionists known as syndicalists (from the French word *syndicats*, trade unions) believed that trade unions would provide not only the means by which workers could take control of the state but also a blueprint of how society would be organized after a successful revolution.

The late nineteenth and early twentieth centuries also brought remarkable cultural achievement in Europe from Britain to Russia, as writers and artists reacted to and against changes in the world they saw around them. Beneath the tangible progress and increased prosperity of late-nineteenth- and early-twentieth-century Europe lurked cultural pessimism and artistic rebellion, a modernist critique of the idea of progress itself. In 1904, the German sociologist Max Weber wrote that "at some time or another the color changes, the importance of uncritically accepted viewpoints is put in doubt, the path is lost in the twilight." To some, the fin de siècle seemed to be such a time.

State Social Reform

In general, Karl Marx's gloomy prediction that workers' wages and overall conditions of life would continue to decline had not been borne out in late-nineteenth-century Europe. Yet economic uncertainty and grinding poverty seemed to have engendered a social crisis of unmatched proportions. Descriptions of the dreary slums of blackened manufacturing towns reached many readers through novels and surveys of working-class life. Beginning in about 1870, as a result of the far-reaching, visible impact of large-scale industrialization, states gradually began to intervene to assist the poor. States and charitable organizations increasingly came to consider poverty a social and not a moral problem. The political left in Western European states demanded measures of social reform. In France and Italy, programs of subsidies for unwed mothers overcame the opposition of the Catholic Church. Germany, Austria-Hungary, and Sweden then implemented short paid maternity leaves for women who had insurance. Unpaid maternity leaves were made possible in some other places. Organized assistance for the elderly lagged behind, in part because of the traditional assumption that families were responsible for their care.

Confronted with the increased militancy of workers, some Western European employers sought to maintain worker loyalty through paternalistic policies. They encouraged workers to form savings associations by matching whatever small sums the working-class families could put aside for the future. A minority of manufacturers started funds for insurance and pension plans, or provided basic company housing (especially in mining communities). Yet such paternalistic policies, largely confined to Western Europe, were far from being generalized. Some social reformers, many politicians, and most workers demanded state intervention to protect workers from some of the uncertainties and hardships of their labor.

Imperial Germany, not republican France or parliamentary Britain, first provided workers some protection against personal and family disaster stemming from work-related accidents. Germany's domineering Chancellor Otto von Bismarck sought to outbid the Catholic Center Party and the

Social Democrats for working-class support. Determined to preserve his own power and the autocratic structure of the empire, Bismarck carried out domestic policies based upon compromise and conciliation between middle-class political interests and working-class demands. The German chancellor thus placed socialists in the delicate position of either opposing bills that would benefit workers or appearing to compromise their ideologically based refusal to collaborate with the autocratic imperial government. The Sickness Insurance Law of 1883 covered all workers for up to thirteen weeks if their income fell below a certain level. Deductions withheld from workers' wages provided most of the funds. A year later Bismarck announced a state-run insurance program that would incorporate existing voluntary plans. It would compensate workers for injury and illness, as well as provide some retirement funds. Other laws required that all workers be insured against accidents and disability, with half of the funds paid by employers, and provided pensions for workers who lived until seventy years of age. By the turn of the century, many German workers received medical care, small payments when they were ill or injured, and, if worse came to worse, a decent burial. By 1913, 14.5 million German workers had insurance.

In comparison to Germany, Britain's social policies were out of an earlier era. Workhouses, which had been created by the Poor Law of 1834, still carried a social stigma, even if conditions had somewhat improved by the end of the century. Families were separated, and inmates were forced to wear uniforms, attend chapel, participate in group exercises, and sustain periods of silence, all with the goal of learning "discipline." A contemporary surveyor of working-class life noted that "aversion to the 'House' is absolutely universal, and almost any amount of suffering and privation will be endured by the people rather than go into it." The vast majority of the inmates of the workhouses were not the able-bodied unemployed, but were children, the infirm, single mothers, the aged, or the insane. But although public opinion had already turned against workhouses, the Poor Law, slightly reformed, remained on the books until 1929.

The first Victorian social reforms had been largely limited to establishing minimum health standards. The Factory Act (1875) then reduced the workweek in large factories to fifty-six hours. The Artisans' Dwelling Act, passed the same year, defined unsanitary housing and gave the state the right to order the demolition of slum buildings that fell below a minimum standard. However, these laws were only very randomly enforced.

By the turn of the century, many Conservatives, most Liberals, and virtually all members of the new Labour Party (founded in 1900, but taking its name only six years later) accepted the right and the obligation of government to undertake reforms, thus ending classic liberal government non-interference in the working of the economy. The Workmen's Compensation Law (1897) made employers responsible for bearing the cost of industrial accidents; another act extended the same protection to agricultural workers. Liberal governments provided lunches to poor children and passed the Old

Dinnertime in an English workhouse, which provided relief for unemployed workers experiencing the dislocation and social transformation accompanying the Second Industrial Revolution.

Age Pension Act (1908), which provided some income for workers over seventy years of age whose incomes fell below a paltry sum per week. In 1908 the "deserving" poor in Britain could receive small old-age pensions. As a result of the National Insurance Bill (1911), workers' friendly societies administered insurance payments based on voluntary (and thus unlike the German case) employee wage deductions. The law's most salutary effect was to provide more workers and their families with direct medical treatment. Yet a third of the British poor still received no assistance of any kind. Moreover, government assistance to unemployed workers in Britain was less well organized and less generous than that in France.

In France, pushed by Radicals and Socialists, the Chamber of Deputies between 1890 and 1904 passed laws that eliminated obligatory special identity papers, or internal passports, for workers, created a system of arbitration for strikes, banned female night work, established employers' legal liability for industrial accidents, reduced the workday to ten hours for women and children, established a minimum age for industrial workers, and mandated an obligatory weekly day of rest. It also affirmed the right of the state to monitor conditions of work and hygiene in factories (although inspection was in many areas nonexistent), passed a workmen's compensation law with modest pension benefits, and provided limited medical care for working-class families. With the exception of Belgium, Sweden, and a smattering of other countries, in most of Europe workers could only dream of such reforms.

The Trade Union Movement

The trade union movement grew rapidly in Western Europe, above all among male skilled workers. The goals of unions were to raise wages and improve conditions, while increasing the number of members. By 1914, 3 million workers had joined unions in Britain, 1.5 million in Germany, and 1 million in Italy. The number of white-collar unions also increased, such as those organizing schoolteachers and postal clerks. In 1913, there were more than 400,000 union members in Austria, a country of only 6 million inhabitants. French unions proliferated after they were legalized in 1884. In 1895, French unions formed the General Confederation of Labor (C.G.T.), with the goal of unifying the trade union movement. The C.G.T., to which about a third of French unions belonged, renounced participation in politics and espoused revolutionary principles. Union membership in France reached 2.6 million in 1914. May Day demonstrations and festivals, with red flags flying, vigorous political debates, consumer cooperatives, and informal networks provided by factory work and cafés, also helped maintain solidarity among workers.

However, most European workers did not belong to unions, although many supported strikes and believed in union goals. The 1875 Trade Union Act ended many limitations on unions in Britain, but by the turn of the century only about 25 percent of British workers were organized, 10 percent were in France, and even less in Italy. Several factors limited the expansion of union membership. Considerable gaps remained between the work experience, salary, organizations, and expectations of skilled and unskilled workers. Many workers moved from place to place, following employment opportunities. Those with urban roots were far more easily organized than recently arrived migrants from smaller towns or villages. Differences and tensions between workers of different national groups also served to divide workers, such as between Irish and English workers in London, German and Czech workers in Prague, or Belgian and French workers in northern France.

The union organization of female workers lagged far behind that of men. Women made up 30 percent of the British labor force, but only about 7 percent of union members. Almost all female workers were relegated to relatively unskilled and low-paying jobs and confronted chronic vulnerability to being dismissed. Most women worked in unskilled jobs, such as making boxes, knotting fish nets, making buttonholes, and doing food-processing work. Furthermore, many male workers refused to accept women as equals and claimed that they were taking jobs away from men (a French union that admitted women as members included the following regulation: "Women may address observations on propositions to the union only in writing and by the intermediation of two male members"). Women also had to take responsibility for their children, something male union members often failed to recognize. Yet women workers also struck in the face of tougher working conditions, low wages, and, occasionally, sexual harassment.

Between 1890 and 1914, strikes increased dramatically, particularly in Western Europe, becoming a social fact of modern life. Workers hoped that they could force government officials to pressure employers to bargain with them. They struck when employers seemed most vulnerable; for example, when they had recently received relatively large orders for products. The vast majority of strikes were undertaken by skilled, organized workers in large-scale sectors such as textiles, mining, and metallurgy, whose unions had resources upon which to fall back. Strike movements reflected a more generalized sense of class consciousness among many—but hardly all—workers.

Strikes reflected not only growth in union membership but also changes in the organization of industrial work. In addition to low wages and the length of their workday, workers also resented factory foremen. Representing the company's interests, the foremen sought to impose industrial discipline on workers, some of whom had worked on farms or in domestic industry and had more or less controlled their own time. Now they were forbidden to enter and leave the factory as they wished when they had nothing to do, or in some cases even to talk on the job.

Techniques of scientific management of assembly-line production—"Taylorism," after Frederick W. Taylor (1856–1915), the American engineer who developed them—included careful counting of the number of units assembled by each worker in an hour. Many workers objected. Such industrial discipline placed factory workers more directly under the control of factory managers by measuring worker performance, tying pay scales to the number of units produced, which put more pressure on workers. Taylorism wore out workers. Noting that virtually all the factory workers employed by a Philadelphia manufacturer who had become enamored of scientific management were young, a British visitor asked repeatedly where the older workers were. Finally, the owner replied, "Have a cigar, and while we smoke we can visit the cemetery."

Socialists

The Socialist First International Workingmen's Association was founded in 1864 in London. Members represented a bewildering variety of experiences and ideologies. Karl Marx emerged as the dominant figure in the International. He was convinced that the unprecedented concentration of capital and wealth meant that the final struggle between the bourgeoisie and the working class was relatively close at hand. Marx's inflexible beliefs ran counter to the views of the majority of French members, some of whom were anarchists, and to the moderate, reformist inclinations of the more prosperous British workers, as well as their German colleagues.

The First International was dissolved in 1876 amid internal division, having been weakened by repression in many countries. Nonetheless, socialism emerged as a major political force in every major European nation. In 1889, at the centennial of the French Revolution in Paris, delegates to a socialist congress founded the Second International. At its congresses, socialists discussed strategies for pushing governments toward reform and for coordinating international action (for example, to achieve a shorter workday), while debating differences over doctrine and strategy.

During the last two decades of the nineteenth century, mass socialist parties developed in France, Germany, Italy, and Belgium. By the end of the first decade of the twentieth century, every Western European state had working-class representatives in their national assemblies.

Socialists proclaimed themselves internationalists. Contending that workers in different nations shared common interests, they believed a revolution would put the working class in power. But socialists remained divided. For Marxist adherents of his "scientific socialism," emancipation of the workers from capitalism could only be achieved by the conquest of the state through revolution and the subsequent establishment of a socialist society. Reform socialists believed that political participation could win concrete reforms that would improve conditions of life for workers until socialists could take power. Reformists participated in the political process, even at the cost of being accused by revolutionary socialists of propping up "bourgeois" regimes by doing so. Legislation in many countries had brought improvement in conditions of work, however unevenly felt. The extension of the franchise also offered hope that progress might come without a revolution that, given the strength of states, seemed to even some revolutionaries to be increasingly unlikely.

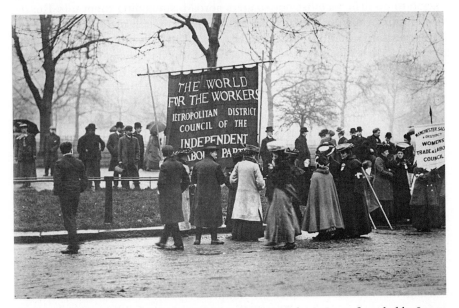

A gathering of members of the British Independent Labour Party, founded by James Keir Hardie in 1893.

The emergence of socialists as contenders for political power reflected economic, social, and political changes in individual countries and had relatively little to do with the influence of the Second International. Yet the debates and divisions that obsessed European socialists revolved around common questions. What should be the relationship between socialism and nationalist movements? Could socialists, proclaiming international solidarity among workers, support demands for Polish independence from the Russian, German, and Austro-Hungarian Empires, or those by Czechs and other nationalities for independence from the latter? Czech socialists with national aspirations for their people challenged the domination of the Austrian Social Democrats by German speakers who seemed oblivious to Czech demands. Should socialists oppose imperialism in all its forms (see Chapter 21), or should they hope that the colonial powers might gradually improve the conditions of life of Africans and Asians, who might become adherents to socialism? Finally, amid rising aggressive nationalism, socialists were divided on what response they should take in the event of the outbreak of a European war.

In the Russian Empire, Marxists were "Westernizers," in that they looked to "scientific socialism" as a model for political change in their country (see Chapter 18). They counted on Russia's industrial workers to launch a revolution, but only after Russia had undergone a bourgeois revolution anticipated to bring the middle class to power. In the 1880s, socialists formed reading groups of intellectuals and students—and at least one that was made up of workers—in the imperial capital of Saint Petersburg. Exiles began to publish socialist newspapers abroad, smuggling them into Russia.

Reformism dominated socialist movements in much of northern Europe. Great Britain's handful of socialists were virtually all intellectuals and reformists. In 1884, a group of intellectuals formed the Fabian Society, which took its name from the Roman dictator Fabius, known for his delaying tactics. Committed to gradualism, the Fabians took the tortoise as their emblem. The Fabians were influenced by an American writer, Henry George. The author of the best-selling *Progress and Poverty*, George argued that the great gulf in Britain between rich and poor could be lessened by the imposition of a "single tax" on land, which would force wealthy landowners to pay more taxes. The "single taxers" believed that socialism could be gradually implemented through reform.

Most German socialists did not accept Marx's contention that the working class could only take power through revolution. In 1863, Ferdinand Lassalle (1825–1864), the son of a Prussian merchant, had formed the first (very small) independent workers' party in any of the German states. Lassalle only lived a year more—killed in a duel at age thirty-nine by the fiancé of the woman he loved. In 1875, the German Social Democratic Party (SPD), was founded. Despite official proscription in 1878, it slowly grew into a mass political party. The SPD's program included reformist demands such as proportional representation, political rights for women, and the eight-hour workday for workers. Eduard Bernstein (1850–1932), the son of a Berlin plumber who became a railway engineer, helped the reformists carry the day by forcefully rejecting in his *Evolutionary Socialism* (1898) the Marxists' insistence that capitalist society was on the verge of final collapse. He thus became a leading socialist "revisionist" who believed that the party should continue to push for reforms, not revolution. The SPD became a major reform socialist party.

The SPD's popular vote in the elections for the Reichstag rose from less than 10 percent in 1884 to almost 35 percent in 1912, and the SPD was the largest German political party in 1914. Women, who could join the party following the passage of a national law on associations in 1908 but who still were not permitted to vote, added to the ranks of the SPD, which had more than a million members in 1914. The SPD worked to build cradle-to-grave social institutions that would give members a sense that they belonged to a special culture, establishing consumer cooperatives, choral societies, and cycling clubs. Unlike French socialists, the SPD not only developed a close alliance with the trade union movement but also helped found some unions.

The SPD became the largest and best-organized socialist party in Europe; it published more than a hundred newspapers and magazines, and it held regular political meetings and social events. The party's organization and reformism influenced the evolution of similar parties in Belgium, Austria, and Switzerland. The SPD remained, however, caught in the paradox of struggling for social and political reform in a society—that of imperial Germany—that remained in many ways undemocratic.

In France, that country's revolutionary tradition and, above all, the memory of the Paris Commune of 1871, encouraged some French socialists to believe that revolution would bring them to power. The Parisian socialist Jules Guesde (1845–1922), rigid, humorless, and doctrinaire—he was known as "the Red Pope"—espoused Marxist socialism. In 1883, Guesde formed a defiantly Marxist political organization, the French Workers' Party, the first modern political party in France. Guesde viewed electoral campaigns as an opportunity to propagate Marxian socialism, although his followers joined the battle for an eight-hour workday and other reforms. The rival reform socialists espoused political pressure to win all possible social reforms through the ballot box. During elections, revolutionary and reform socialists often put their differences behind them, winning control over the municipal governments of several industrial cities. But the results in France of "municipal socialism," while subsidizing some services for ordinary people, were limited by the strongly centralized state.

When the reform socialist Alexandre Millerand (1859–1943) accepted a cabinet post in 1899, the split between revolutionary and reform socialists again lay bare. In 1905, Jean Jaurès (1859–1914), a former philosophy professor whose energy, organizational skills, and stirring oratory swept him to national prominence, achieved the unification of French socialists with the formation of the French Section of the Working-Class International (SFIO), although the differences between Guesdists and reformists could not be swept under the rug. The socialists became the second largest party in France, holding in 1914 a fifth of the seats in the Chamber of Deputies.

In Italy, socialists had to overcome the entrenched power of local elites, repression (including the jailing in 1887 of the first Italian socialist deputies), and the strong attraction of anarchism, particularly in southern Italy. The Italian Socialist Party, founded in 1892, made few inroads in Italy's impoverished south. By 1912, the revolutionary faction had gained control of the party.

In Spain, real power still lay in the hands of powerful local government officials and landowners, men of great local influence (the *caciques*) who rigged elections to the Cortes, backed by the Catholic Church and the army. The Spanish Socialist Party, founded in 1879, gained a sizable following only in industrial Asturias and the Basque region. In contrast to Germany, France, and Italy, the first Spanish socialists were not elected to Parliament until 1909.

Christian Socialism

In Catholic countries, the Church still provided an alternative allegiance to the nation-state. However, the secularization of state and social institutions, along with nationalism itself, reduced the Church's influence in some Catholic countries. Papal pronouncements seemed to stand steadfastly against social and political change, and particularly against the emergence of the nation-state and parliamentary forms of government. In a papal encyclical, the *Syllabus of Errors* of 1864, Pope Pius IX had condemned the very idea that "the Roman Pontiff can and ought to reconcile himself and come to terms with progress, liberalism and modern civilization." In 1870, the Church proclaimed the doctrine of papal infallibility, which stated that in matters of faith and morals the pope's pronouncements would have to be taken as absolute truth. The Church backed monarchical regimes in Spain and Portugal, opposed the newly unified state in Italy, and, at the beginning of the French Third Republic, lent tacit support to monarchist movements in France.

Breaking with his predecessors, Pope Leo XIII (pope 1878–1903) accepted the modern age. His encyclical *Rerum Novarum* (1891) called attention to social injustice, recognizing that many workers were victimized by "the inhumanity of employers and the unbridled greed of competitors." One of the unintended effects of *Rerum Novarum* was the development of "Christian Socialist" movements in France, Germany, Belgium, and Italy in the 1890s, although the Church itself generally repudiated them. Christian Socialists hoped to bring employers and workers back to the Church. Some clergy and laymen and -women organized clubs, vacation colonies, sporting clubs, and charities, and helped workers rent gardens so that they could grow vegetables and fruit. And many Catholics took the pope's encyclical as authorization to participate in national political life. Catholic unions tried to counter socialist influence by bringing together workers, employers, and honorary members drawn from local elites. These "mixed" or "yellow" unions drew the unrestrained opposition of most trade unions.

The Anarchists

While socialists wanted to take over the state, anarchists wanted to destroy it. Anarchism was never more than a minority movement. Yet the dramatic increase in the reach of European states in the nineteenth century encouraged the development of anarchism, a philosophy with few roots in earlier periods. Anarchism was the very antithesis of a philosophy of political organization because anarchists associated politics itself with a tacit recognition of the state's existence.

While many anarchists like Michael Bakunin (see Chapter 18) believed in the violent overthrow of the state, others believed that voluntary mutualism would eventually make the state superfluous. Peter Kropotkin (1842–1921), a geographer and the son of a Russian prince, held a vision of a gentle society of equals living in harmony without the strictures of the state. Kropotkin's desire for anarchist communism was rooted in his firsthand views of the misery of the Russian masses and his own experience living in the Jura Mountains of Switzerland and France in the 1860s, where watchmakers and peasants seemed to coexist in relative prosperity and the state seemed distant. Kropotkin, like Jean-Jacques Rousseau, espoused the primitive as a natural end in itself. He believed that each person was born a *tabula rasa* (blank slate)—an idea theorized by John Locke—and then corrupted by society and, above all, by the state.

Anarchism gained some adherents in France, the most centralized state in Europe, but above all in Italy and Spain, two countries in which the nation-state appeared to many people as a foreign intruder, and in Argentina, influenced by Spanish and Italian immigrants. Improvements in transportation and increased immigration brought anarchists, including some exiles, to new countries, with London serving as a particular place of refuge for continental anarchists. Anarchists were among recent immigrants in the United States during the last decades of the century, four of whom were hung after the Haymarket riots in Chicago in 1886. In contrast, anarchism found very few followers in Germany, where socialists as well as supporters of the imperial monarchy respected the state, and in Great Britain, the least centralized but also one of the most nationalist states in Western Europe.

A loose organization of anarchists, the International Working-Class Alliance, known as the "Black International" because of the color of the anarchist flag, maintained contacts among anarchists in France, Spain, Italy, and the United States. But, for the most part, anarchists formed small groups or struck out on their own. Among poor peasants in the rugged

(*Left*) The assassination of French President Sadi Carnot by an Italian anarchist, 1894. (*Right*) Peter Kropotkins's publication *The Spirit of Revolt*.

southern Spanish province of Andalusia, anarchism took on a millenarian character stripped of most of the trappings of religion. Andalusian anarchists told the story of one of their own who, as he lay dying, whispered to one of his religious relatives to summon a priest and a lawyer. Relieved that the anarchist seemed at the last moment to be accepting the conventions of religion by accepting the last rites of the Church and drawing up a will, relatives sent for both. When they arrived, the anarchist beckoned them to stand on either side of his deathbed. As they leaned forward, one to hear his confession, the other to write down his will, the anarchist proclaimed, "Now, like Christ, I can die between two thieves."

In the 1880s and 1890s, a wave of anarchist assassinations and bombings shook Europe. To violent anarchists, the goal of "propaganda by the deed" was to spark a revolution. Bakunin's Italian disciple Enrico Maletesta (1853–1932), who had a following in Italy, Spain, and Argentina, expressed the bitter frustration of anarchists who had virtually nothing: "Do you not know that every bit of bread they [the wealthy] eat is taken from your children, every fine present they give to their wives means the poverty, hunger, cold and even perhaps the prostitution of yours?" Bakunin had believed that a single violent act might shock people into a chain-reaction revolution. "A single deed," Kropotkin once said, "is better propaganda than a thousand pamphlets." Barcelona became the "capital of bombs" in the 1890s. Anarchists killed six heads of states beginning in 1881, when members of

People's Will assassinated Tsar Alexander II. Other victims included King Umberto I of Italy, who was killed in 1900 (not long after saying that assassination was "a professional risk"), and President William McKinley of the United States, gunned down the following year.

From 1892 to 1894, a wave of bombings terrified Paris. "One does not kill an innocent person in striking the first bourgeois one sees," an anarchist told a shocked judge. François Claudius Ravachol, an impoverished worker, threw one of the bombs. "See this hand," Ravachol told the horrified judge and jurors, "it has killed as many bourgeois as it has fingers!" More attacks followed. In March 1893, an unemployed worker unable to feed his family threw a small bomb into the Chamber of Deputies, slightly injuring several members. He wanted to call attention to the plight of the poor. French President Sadi Carnot (1837–1894) turned down an appeal for mercy for the perpetrator. Next, Émile Henry, a young intellectual, tossed a bomb into a café near the Saint-Lazare railroad station, killing one man and injuring about twenty other people. In June 1894, an Italian anarchist assassinated Carnot. The wave of anarchist attacks subsided in France, but continued in Spain, where the government tortured and executed militant anarchists. In France, Italy, and Spain, harsh government repression itself brought a reaction against such policies, and soon the state gave anarchists fewer martyrs to avenge. With the rise of mass socialist parties and unions, anarchism faded further into the fringes of popular protest, except in Italy and, above all, Spain.

Syndicalists

At the turn of the century, syndicalism emerged as an ideology that held that union organization could provide a means for workers to seize control of their industries. Reflecting some anarchist influence, free associations of producers would eventually replace the state. Like revolutionary socialists and anarchists, syndicalists rejected participation in political life. Syndicalism, which was centered in France, Spain, and Italy, was sometimes called anarcho-syndicalism, because of its opposition to the existence of the state.

A retired engineer who proudly wore the prestigious legion of honor awarded by the French state, Georges Sorel (1847–1922) seemed an unlikely candidate to plan any revolution. But Sorel's *Reflections on Violence* (1908) encouraged direct syndicalist action against capitalism and the state, until a "general strike" by workers would bring both to their knees. By the general strike, Sorel meant a series of simultaneous walkouts that would shut down factories and lead to revolution.

The period 1895–1907 is sometimes referred to as "the heroic age of syndicalism" in France because so many strikes spread through so many industries there, as elsewhere in Europe. More than 1,000 strikes in France occurred in 1904 alone. During the "revolt of the south" in 1907, vineyard owners and vine-tenders aggressively protested the state tax on drink. In

Italy, Italian anarchists participated in the waves of strikes and insurrections in Sicily in 1893–1894. In Milan in 1898, fighting pitted the industrial suburbs against soldiers, and nearly 200 workers were killed and hundreds were wounded. Violent disturbances during "Red Week" shook the Italian Adriatic town of Ancona in June 1914 after police shot two people to death while preventing a crowd leaving an anti-militarist demonstration from marching into the downtown area. Even the normally peaceful Swedish capital of Stockholm was stirred by a general strike in 1909. It failed.

Anarcho-syndicalists dominated the labor movement in Barcelona, particularly among dockworkers, who confronted brutal police repression orchestrated from Madrid. Waves of strikes took place in Catalonia in 1902, 1906, and 1909, the latter followed by a bloody insurrection ("Tragic Week"). But gradually, revolutionary rhetoric gave way to the pursuit of concrete economic gains, particularly in Italy and France. In the end, at least in Western Europe, reformism won out.

The Quest for Women's Rights

Everywhere in Europe, women remained subordinate to men in legal rights. They were excluded from most universities, could not vote (in contrast, several U.S. states gave women the vote before 1914), and had limited or no control over family financial resources. Women made very little progress entering the professions because some men feared the advent of the "new woman," who demanded the same access to education and opportunity as men. The term "new woman" came from the title of a lecture given by the Italian feminist Maria Montessori (1870–1952), a doctor and originator of innovative schools (which still exist) that stress the encouragement of creativity in children. Still, the beginnings were difficult. When a female Greek scientist gave her inaugural lecture at the University of Athens, male students disrupted her lecture with shouts of "Back to the kitchen!" Women demanding equal rights faced daunting opposition. Queen Victoria of England called demands by women for equal rights "on which her poor feeble sex is bent . . . a mad, wicked folly . . . forgetting every sense of womanly feeling and propriety." The biologist T. H. Huxley (1825–1895) insisted that women were less intelligent than men. The claims of such bad science bolstered opposition to the women's movement.

Right-wing political parties opposed women's suffrage on principle. Moderate republicans claimed that women could not understand political issues. Socialists in Catholic countries feared that if women had the right to vote, they would support clerical candidates, although socialist parties and unions threw their support to women workers laboring for better wages and conditions. However, some women contended that social reforms would be inadequate as long as women were without the right to enter universities or vote.

The feminist movement (a name that only gradually took hold in Europe and the United States) developed very slowly in Europe. It was most active in Britain. There the first women's political organizations were created in the 1860s, and women gained the right to vote in municipal elections in 1864 and for county and parish councils six years later. Women also gained the right to enter university and made headway in achieving property rights for married women, child custody, and the right to initiate divorce. The movement for women's rights in Britain coincided with the "new imperialism" that began in the 1880s (see Chapter 21). Concern among feminists with the condition of indigenous women in the empire, particularly in India, where British women had more occasion to meet their counterparts and viewed them as backward victims of barbaric religious and cultural practices, helped shape British feminism. British feminists came to see themselves as the saviors of women in the colonies, while identifying themselves with the good of their empire, a special place in the "civilizing mission." As one put it, "We are struggling not just for English women alone, but for all the women, degraded, miserable, unheard of, for whose life and happiness England has daily to answer to God."

In 1889, the first International Congresses on Women's Rights and Feminine Institutions took place in Paris. By 1900, more than 850 German associations were working for women's rights, including improved educational and employment opportunities and equal wages. Near the end of the nineteenth century, British women's groups presented to Parliament a peti-

In 1913, the suffragette Emily Davison throws herself before the king's horse at the Derby at Epsom Downs and is killed.

tion with more than a quarter of a million signatures calling for reform. As more occupations opened up to women, the campaign for women's suffrage widened. The International Women's Suffrage Alliance encouraged organizations in a number of countries. A more militant group of feminists undertook a campaign of direct action. Emmeline Pankhurst (1858–1928) founded the Women's Social and Political Union in 1903. Members protested the lack of female suffrage by breaking shop windows on London's fashionable Oxford Street, tossing acid on golf putting greens (a sport then identified with aristocratic British males), and bombing the house of Liberal Party leader David Lloyd George (1863–1945). Other "suffragettes," as they were called, went on hunger strikes upon being arrested. In 1907, British women gained the right to serve in local government. In the most dramatic incident, a suffragette carrying a banner proclaiming "Votes for Women" hurled herself in front of a horse owned by King George V at the 1913 Derby at Epsom Downs and was killed.

CULTURAL FERMENT

Europeans had many reasons to be optimistic at the turn of the century. Since the fall of Napoleon in 1815, Europe had enjoyed a relatively long period of peace broken only by short wars with limited goals, including the bloody Franco-Prussian War (1870–1871). Literacy had risen rapidly, particularly in western and northern Europe. Nation-states, increasingly secular in character, commanded the loyalty of their populations. Advances in science and technology were transforming the way people lived. The standard of living had generally risen, and, at least in most of Europe, white-collar jobs provided hope of better things for more people. Furthermore, somewhat shorter working hours for employees, including many workers, left more time for leisure activities.

During the 1850s and 1860s, scientific progress and social change was reflected in the emergence of realism as the dominant cultural style for artists and writers. Then, beginning in the last decade of the nineteenth century, more technological advances and the emergence of a more urban world brought both a cultural crisis of previously unparalleled dimensions and remarkable achievements in the arts. More scientific discoveries and new theories about the functioning of the universe continued to tear away some of the old certainties. Social scientists tried to find explanations for the working of society and the inner world of the individual. At the same time, some writers and artists began to turn away from rationalism, materialism, and positivism. In France, Henri Bergson (1859–1941) emerged as the philosopher of irrationality. Challenging materialism and positivism, Bergson popularized the idea that each individual and each nation had a creative "dynamic energy," or vital force (*élan vital*), waiting for release. The "modernist" culture of the avant-garde turned against the century-old acceptance of rationality as one of the dominant values of Western culture. The notion of an avant-garde, a term taken from military tactics, implies a small group of people who see themselves in the forefront of artistic expression and achievement. Intellectuals and artists began to insist on the irrational basis of human nature, their work reflecting both uncertainty and cultural rebellion.

Realism

Influenced by the widening interest in science and the quickening pace of social change, some writers had in the middle decades of the century broken with literary traditions. Realism had emerged as the dominant European cultural style during the 1850s and 1860s. Charles Baudelaire (1821–1867) once described himself as the poet of modern life. Best known for his volume of poems *Les Fleurs du Mal* (1857; *The Flowers of Evil*), Baudelaire believed that art had to be the product of an exchange between the individual artist and contemporary society. The artist's own experience and self-discovery became critical in the emergence of modern literature. Baudelaire was fined in 1857 for "obscene and immoral passages or expressions." *Les Fleurs du Mal* became even more popular as his decadence and overt eroticism—he died of syphilis in 1867—angered officials and critics alike. Baudelaire was the consummate dandy and *"flâneur,"* the observer of modern urban life. Dressed in what modest elegance his small inheritance permitted, the flâneur strolled through Paris, finding beauty in its modern boulevards but also gazing at its hideous, even frightening aspects with objective detachment, both

reacting to and reflecting modern urban life. Baudelaire rebelled against bourgeois culture and conventional assumptions about artistic subjects and style. Rejecting the notion that absolute aesthetic values exist, Baudelaire was a crucial figure in the emergence of modern culture in the middle of the century.

In the 1850s, the Barbizon painters—so called because they gathered in a village of that name southeast of Paris—emphasized the painting of peasants, harvests, animals, and other symbols of village life. In doing so, they broke sharply with many of the long-accepted styles of painting, including romanticism. The development of photography during the 1840s may have contributed to the inter-

Charles Baudelaire, "the poet of modern life," in a photograph by Félix Nadar.

Jean-François Millet's *The Gleaners* (1857).

est in portraying artistic subjects with a vivid sense of actuality. Jean-François Millet (1814–1875), a Barbizon painter, painted peasants at work in such pieces as *The Gleaners* (1857) and *The Angelus* (1859), giving peasants a dignity that repelled many middle-class viewers who thought them unworthy of being painted.

Artistic style evolved far more rapidly than did official views of what constituted good art. Gustave Courbet (1819–1877) abandoned the idealization that still characterized painting. "Show me an angel," he scoffed at his critics, "and I will paint one." Taking as a compliment the assessment that he was "a democratic painter," he startled viewers by choosing ordinary workers as his subjects. Like Millet, Courbet shocked with his realism. *Burial at Ornans* (1849) portrays a family of some means looking rather unattractive, bored, or even indifferent as the body of a relative is being lowered into a grave in Courbet's hometown. *The Bather* (1853) shows a stout naked woman rising from a forest pool. Nudity did not bother many viewers—it was, after all, a staple of classical painting. Rather, viewers were upset by the fact that Courbet portrayed an ordinary-looking woman holding herself up very awkwardly. The artist seemed to be mocking the kind of classical scene painters had been expected to treat with reverence. When Napoleon III saw the exhibited painting, he struck the canvas with a riding-crop. Courbet, a political radical, believed that art should have a social purpose. He exacted some revenge in a later painting by depicting the emperor as a shabby poacher.

Realists continued to ruffle official feathers. The French police hauled the novelist Gustave Flaubert (1821–1880) into court, charging him with obscenity. His novel *Madame Bovary* (1857) evokes with flawless attention to detail the affair of a bored bourgeois housewife living in a small, dreary Norman town. Flaubert revealed the bohemian underside of bourgeois life. But like most writers and artists at the time, he also depended upon middle-class patronage for his work.

Gustave Courbet's *The Bather* (1853) in which the subject strikes an awkward pose.

The escapist science fiction fantasies of the French author Jules Verne (1828–1905) reflected contemporary fascination with developing sciences like geography, science, astronomy, and physics, as well as improvements in transportation and communication. Verne's *Around the World in Eighty Days,* first published in 1873, became a best seller. In Britain, Sir Arthur Conan Doyle's character of Sherlock Holmes emerged in the late 1880s as fiction's first truly scientific detective. The Norwegian playwright Henrik Ibsen (1828–1906) drew admiration and protest alike with works of unrelenting realism and concern with women's lives. His forceful dramas, such as *A Doll's House* and *Hedda Gabler,* offer realistic descriptions of the psychology and interaction of complex characters. Considered in some ways the father of modern drama, Ibsen privileged the themes of guilt and hypocrisy as he presented families in small-town life.

The French novelist Émile Zola (1840–1902) shocked critics with his evocation of working-class life, not only because the subject itself challenged traditional assumptions about literary worthiness but also because of his unabashed realism in depicting ordinary people as he saw them. Zola believed that naturalistic writing was a form of science. He went down into mine shafts in northern France so that he could offer a realistic depiction of the work there in his novel *Germinal* (1885).

Artists and writers who espoused the new realism confronted censorship in France. Napoleon III prohibited the historian Joseph Ernest Renan (1823–1892) from lecturing. Renan considered himself a proponent of "progressive ideas"—above all, a faith in science. His *Life of Jesus* (1863) offended the Catholic Church by presenting Christ as a historical figure, seemingly casting doubt upon his divinity. More than this, Renan argued that the Scriptures had to be studied like any other historical document.

Impressionism

During the French Second Empire, a group of artists developed impressionism, a remarkable artistic movement that lasted until the end of the century. Like the realists of the Barbizon school, impressionist painters rejected traditional religious and historical subjects and formal presentation. Instead, they depicted rural and urban landscapes, offering scenes from everyday existence, but generally integrated individual figures into landscapes. Embracing subjectivity, the impressionists preferred direct observation and the study of nature's effects to studio composition and imitation of classic styles. Édouard Manet (1832–1883), another dandy and flâneur, aspired to create what a contemporary called an art "born of today." The impressionists painted what they saw, and how they saw it at first glance, such as the way sunlight falls on inanimate objects (thus reflecting their interest in science). They put lighter and brighter colors on large canvases (which previously had usually been reserved for historical themes), applying many small dabs of paint to convey an impression of spontaneity, energy, and movement.

Although the impressionists did not begin to exhibit their paintings with the self-consciousness of an artistic group until 1874, their movement was shaped by official rejection. The Salon was a state-sponsored exhibition upon which artists depended in order to attract purchasers. In 1863, the jury for the official Salon turned down several canvases by Manet. After certain complaints reached the emperor, he allowed some of the paintings to be shown in other rooms. The "Salon of the Refused" included works by Manet, Auguste Renoir, and Paul Cézanne. Some critics raged against what they saw, but at least the public could now make up its own mind. Manet's *Olympia* (1863) generated a chorus of complaint. This study of a nude shocked public opinion—the outraged Empress Eugénie, not to be outdone by her husband, Napoleon III, who had attacked a Courbet canvas with a riding-crop, struck Manet's painting with her fan. Manet's *Déjeuner sur l'herbe* (1863) drew scathing commentary because it showed a nude female sharing a picnic with two fully dressed, upper-class males. Here, Manet, even more than the realists, challenged the hierarchy of subjects imposed by classicism.

Manet chose provocatively contemporary subjects, including very ordinary people, clients, and café waitresses enjoying themselves. He and his younger friend Claude Monet (1840–1926) painted the Gare Saint-Lazare, the point of entry each day for thousands of commuters, vacationers, and other visitors. Berthe Morisot (1841–1895), Manet's sister-in-law, placed her subjects, most of whom were women, in private gardens, in the Bois de Boulogne, boating on the Seine, and at the resorts of the Norman coast, which had been "discovered" by wealthy Parisians.

Édouard Manet's *Déjeuner sur l'herbe* (1863).

The rebuilding of Paris opened up new possibilities for the understanding of modernity. Impressionists found the great boulevards fitting subjects for their portrayal of modern life. The early impressionists were also influenced by the growing commercialization of leisure in Paris. Edgar Degas (1834–1917) followed wealthy Parisians to theaters, racetracks, cafés, and café-concerts, which offered entertainment that included vaudeville acts, poetry readings, comedians, and singers renowned for bawdy lyrics. Degas frequently chose female entertainers, most of whom were drawn from the popular classes, as his subjects. In the shadows of his ballet paintings lurk wealthy gentlemen awaiting their prey, like Napoleon III himself, who occupy the loges closest to the stage at the opera or stand in the shadows of the dressing rooms of the dancers, ready to claim their prizes. Degas, whose banking family had lost its money early in an economic depression, presented unflattering, dark stereotypes of Parisian speculators in *At the Stock Exchange* (1879). The increasing anonymity of the burgeoning city was also a frequent impressionist theme. Degas's *L'Absinthe* (1876–1877) shows two disconnected figures in a café. Such encounters with strangers seemed an intrinsic part of modern life.

Monet also manifested an uneasy ambivalence toward large-scale industry. In the 1870s, he lived in the industrializing Paris suburb of Argenteuil.

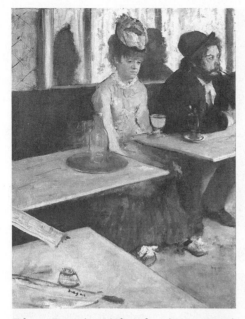

Edgar Degas's *L'Absinthe* (1876–1877) shows a woman and her companion with a glass of absinthe. Note how the lack of a table support helps draw the viewer's attention to the glass of absinthe.

His paintings of the town reflect a balance between leisure and industry (seen, for example, in a painting of sailboats on the Seine River with factory smokestacks in the background). Monet eventually tired of the hustle and bustle of urban life and moved down the Seine to the village of Giverny. There his garden and its pond and lily pads provided an ideal rural setting for his work. He never painted the railway tracks that ran through his property.

Social Theorists' Analyses of Industrial Society

Scientific advances contributed to the diffusion of the belief that human progress was inevitable and that it moved in a linear manner. This optimistic view became known as positivism. Auguste Comte (1798–1857) had already spread faith in the promise of science. Believing that scientific discovery had passed through three stages of development—the theological, the metaphysical, and the "positive" (or scientific)—Comte concluded that what he called "the science of society" could do the same. Society itself, he reasoned, like nature could be studied in a scientific manner and its development charted. Comte's positivism called for the accumulation of useful knowledge that would help students of society to understand the laws of social development.

Positivists challenged some of the central tenets of the established churches, particularly those of the Catholic Church, whose theologians held fast to a view of humanity as essentially unchanging. Darwinism (see Chapter 18) denied the literal biblical description of God creating the world in seven days. Clergy of many denominations, and many other people as well, were aghast to think that humanity could have descended from apes.

Now, in the face of rapid social change, intellectuals attempted to understand the structure of the society they saw changing around them. They did so by adopting the model of natural science and undertaking objective systematic analysis of observable social data. They gradually developed sociology, the science of society, which asked: How do societies hold together when confronted by economic and social forces that tend to pull them apart? The question itself expressed the cultural crisis of the fin de siècle. In 1887, the German Ferdinand Tönnies (1855–1936) published a groundbreaking work, *Community and Society (Gemeinschaft und Gesellschaft)*, which sought to synthesize and apply historical experience to understand the development of modern Western civilization.

Influenced by Tönnies and fascinated by the emergence of industrial society and the growth of the state, Max Weber (1864–1920), one of the fathers of modern social thought and sociology, sought to create an objective and thus "value-free" science of society that he thought held the key to guiding the future. Trained as a professor of law in Heidelberg, Weber became interested in the relationship between religion and society. *The Protestant Ethic and the Spirit of Capitalism* (1904–1905) defined the "spirit of capitalism" to be the assumption that whoever works hard in the pursuit of gain fulfills a moral obligation. He identified the origins of capitalism with Calvinist entrepreneurship in the sixteenth and seventeenth centuries. Weber observed the contemporary trend toward larger structures of government and the bureaucratization of state, business, and political structures, which he believed marked the victory of Enlightenment rationalism, as well as increased social stratification. But he worried that in the advancing impersonal age of bureaucracy, state officials would ignore political and social ideals. Weber's modern man seemed to be trapped in what he called "the iron cage of modern life." Theorist of a nervous age, Weber had a nervous breakdown before the turn of the century.

Doctors diagnosed more cases of hypochondria, "melancholy," and hysteria, paralyzing nervous disorders that many blamed on the complexities of modern life, which seemed to be overwhelming the nervous system. In particular, neurasthenia seemed to be a sign of the times, with its symptoms of extreme sensitivity to light and noise—two characteristics of urban life—fatigue, worry, and digestive disorders.

Alcoholism was ravaging many countries. In England, the "habitual soaking" of workers in beer worried reformers. A contemporary investigator claimed that it was not uncommon for some workers to spend a quarter of their earnings on drink. The dramatic increase in the production of wine in France (with the exception of the 1880s and 1890s, when the phylloxera disease ravaged vineyards), Italy, Spain, and Portugal flooded markets, greatly reducing its price. In parts of France, the average person (and thus the figure for adults would be even higher) consumed well more than sixty gallons of wine a year, in addition to beer, brandies, and absinthe, a licorice-tasting drink made from wormwood that is highly addictive. There were almost half a million establishments licensed to serve drink in France at the turn of the century—one for every 54 people, compared to one British "public house" for every 843 inhabitants.

French temperance movements were swept aside like tiny dikes by the torrent of drink. Nationalists, worried about the plunging birthrate, joined some doctors and reformers in claiming that France faced "racial degeneration" since its population might cease to reproduce itself because of the ravages of alcoholism. Some doctors blamed women for not doing their part to increase the French population, their attacks complementing surging resistance to the rise of feminism. For their part, some women began to put forward their role as republican mothers to bolster demands for more rights. Nationalists insisted that only by rallying around patriotic values could France avoid total collapse. In Britain, the temperance movement began earlier and was far stronger than in France. It was also much more closely tied to churches, as was the movement in Sweden, where in 1909 temperance societies had almost half a million members who signed pledges promising not to drink alcohol at all.

The use of opium and its derivatives—morphine (the popularity of which increased with its use as an anesthetic), laudanum (a mixture of wine and opium), and heroin—as well as cocaine and hashish, unfortunately became common among the artistic avant-garde, well before most people were aware of their devastating effects. These drugs arrived from Turkey, Persia, and India, with coca (from which cocaine is derived) brought from Peru and Bolivia. The painter Pablo Picasso (1881–1973) was for a period a hashish user, which may have influenced his dreamy rose-colored paintings of 1905–1908. Only in the latter years did the French government ban such drugs, in the wake of a number of drug-related suicides. Less dangerous, exoticism, mysticism, spiritism (including attempts to contact the souls of deceased people during séances), and a fascination with the occult became more popular than ever before, another sign of the rejection of science and the associated preoccupation with the irrational.

Modern life seemed to provide evidence that industrialization and urban growth had uprooted traditional values. Crimes seemed to be increasing. Seeking an explanation, the French social theorist Émile Durkheim (1858–1917) believed that the rapid, seemingly uncontrollable growth of large cities had destroyed the moral ties that had sustained the individual in traditional society. Durkheim believed that the waning of religious practice had undermined authority and therefore social cohesiveness. Durkheim's quantitative study of suicide led him to conclude that the stresses and strains of increasingly urban, industrial life were becoming more debilitating. He concluded that individuals lost in the faceless urban and

Two elegant morphine addicts, 1891.

industrial world suffered "alienation" (*anomie* in French). Yet he optimistically believed that social problems could be solved by studying them in a systematic, scientific manner.

Durkheim was hardly alone in thinking that urban growth, spurred on by the arrival of rural migrants, generated social pathology of which criminality was but one manifestation. In 1895, Gustave Le Bon (1841–1931) published *The Crowd,* in which he worried that modern life submerged the individual in the "crowd." Riots and strikes, he warned, were becoming part of the political process. He described crowds as lurching erratically, and sometimes dangerously, like drunks, at a time of a growing awareness of the ravages of alcoholism. Some nationalists now worried that their peoples were being undermined by "racial degeneration," which might compromise the natural process of evolution by hereditary debasement. Certain scientists claimed that significant racial differences could be identified within specific peoples, and that they accounted for soaring rates of crime, alcoholism, insanity, syphilis, and even popular political action. An Italian anthropologist believed that criminals showed inferior physical and mental development and contended that they could be identified by measuring their skulls.

Nietzsche's Embrace of the Irrational

Friedrich Nietzsche (1844–1900) emerged in this period as the most strident philosophical critic of Enlightenment rationalism. The son of a strict Protestant German minister who died when Nietzsche was young, he was raised by his domineering mother. He became a professor of classics in Basel, Switzerland. The tormented Nietzsche, forced by illness to leave the university, moved to the Swiss Alps and thereafter lived by his pen, but with little success. He suffered a mental collapse at the age of forty-five, after sending off telegrams to some of his friends signed "The Crucified." Nietzsche was briefly confined in an asylum toward the end of his life, leading one wag to comment, "At last, the right man in the right place."

Nietzsche hated all religions equally, believing that they had

Friedrich Nietzsche, philosopher of the irrational.

destroyed the individual's capacity for natural development and fulfillment by imposing uniformity. He became an atheist, proclaiming, "God is dead . . . and we have killed him." He claimed strenuously that religion was incapable of providing ethical guidance and that no single morality could be appropriate to all people.

Espousing "philosophy with the hammer," Nietzsche awaited the heroic superman who, as part of a natural nobility of "higher humanity," would rule through the "will to power." Although indirectly influenced by the contentions of Hegel and Darwin that mankind could continue to develop to a higher stage, Nietzsche's thought marked a total rejection of all previous philosophy. His "vital" force, which he believed could be found only in new philosophers like himself, would be morally ambivalent, idealizing power and struggle. The free man, wrote Nietzsche, "is a warrior." Yet for all of his talk about "master races" and "slave races" in a period marked by a growth of racism, he castigated the herd-like instincts of frenetic German nationalists and anti-Semites.

Freud and the Study of the Irrational

The Viennese doctor Sigmund Freud (1856–1939) stressed the power of the irrational, which he placed in the human unconscious. Freud was born in the small Moravian town of Freiberg (now in the Czech Republic) in the Habsburg monarchy, the son of a struggling Jewish wool merchant and his much younger wife. When Sigmund was three, his father's business affairs went from bad to worse, forcing the family to leave its tranquil, small-town existence for Vienna. The younger Freud never felt comfortable in the imposing imperial capital. But he benefited from the period of liberal ascendancy in Austria, where Jews had received full civil rights only in 1867. The Viennese middle class had helped make their city a cultural capital of Europe. That reassuring atmosphere changed with the stock-market crash in 1873, which began a period of economic depression and culminated in the election of an anti-Semite, Karl Lueger ("I decide who is a Jew," Lueger insisted), as mayor of Vienna in 1895.

After beginning his career as a research scientist in anatomy, Freud fell under the influence of the French neurologist Jean Charcot (1825–1893). From his scientific laboratory, Freud moved to the study of the irrational, or the "unconscious," convinced that it could be studied with the same systematic rigor as human anatomy. In the spring of 1886, he opened a small office in Vienna, treating patients with nervous disorders.

Freud developed the method of psychoanalysis, a term coined in 1896. It was based on the premises that the mind is orderly and that dreams offer codes that can unlock the unconscious. To Freud, a dream represented "the fulfillment of a [suppressed] wish"; it was the expression of an unconscious conflict. Freud encouraged patients to dream and to "free associate" in order to break down their defense mechanisms (the means by which

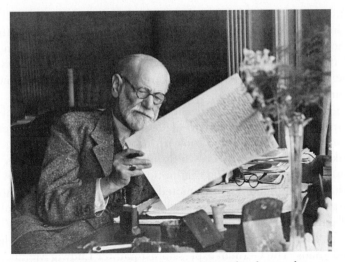

The Austrian psychoanalyst Sigmund Freud in his study.

individuals repress painful memories from childhood or even infancy). Sexuality, specifically the repression of sexual urges, formed the basis of Freud's theory of the unconscious. One of Freud's followers described the role of his mentor's "dream-work": "The mind is like a city which during the day busies itself with the peaceful tasks of legitimate commerce, but at night when all the good burghers sleep soundly in their beds, out come these disreputable creatures of the psychic underworld to disport themselves in a very unseemly fashion; decking themselves out in fantastic costumes, in order that they may not be recognized and apprehended." Psychoanalysis became both an investigative tool and a form of therapy, in which, very gradually—from several months to many years and at considerable financial cost—the patient could obtain self-awareness and control over his or her symptoms, such as hysteria.

Freud's theories of human development established the irrational as an intrinsic and sometimes even determining part of the human psyche. Psychoanalytic theory, which Freud claimed as a new science, emerged, along with Darwin's evolutionary theory and Marx's writings on capitalist development and revolution, as one of the foundations of twentieth-century thought.

Avant-Garde Artists and Writers and the Rapid Pace of Modern Life

Progress seemed to have a price. At the Paris Exhibition of 1900, which celebrated the dawn of a new century, an uneasy visitor noted, "Life seethes in this immense reservoir of energy . . . a too violent magnificence." In *The Wind in the Willows*, published in 1908 by Kenneth Grahame (1859–1932), the motor car threatens stability. Behind the wheel, Toad, the amphibian protagonist, turns into "the terror . . . before whom all must give way or be smitten into nothingness and everlasting night . . . fulfilling his instincts, living his hour, reckless of what might come to him." The airplane, rapidly rising and then swooping dangerously, seemed not only a soaring symbol of scientific advances but also of the uncertainty that unsettled some fin-de-siècle Europeans.

During the last ten years of the career of the French impressionist painter and anarchist Camille Pissarro (1830–1903), perhaps the preeminent painter of the countryside, he took up urban subjects, painting bridges, riverbanks, and boulevards, crowding myriad forms and figures into his panoramic views. Emphasizing the motion of transportation, walking, riding, loading, and unloading, he depicted the light, color, nervous movement, and energy of the city and its seemingly uncontrollable throngs, calling one series of paintings "Social Turpitudes."

Other painters also presented urban scenes in a harsh, jarring light that suggested chaos. The German expressionist painter Ludwig Meidner (1884–1966) insisted that painters ought to abandon the gentle, almost rural style that characterized impressionist urban scenes: "A street," he wrote, "is rather a bombardment of hissing rows of windows, of blustering cones of lights between vehicles of all kinds and thousands of leaping globes, human rags, advertising signboards and masses of threatening, formless colors."

Avant-garde writers and artists loathed the culture of the public, or what the English aesthete Oscar Wilde called the "profane masses." Popular culture seemed to be eroding the ability of high culture to survive the assault of mass manufacturing and teeming cities. Sharp reactions against the seeming uniformity of the machine age permeated the arts. The English craftsman and designer William Morris (1834–1896) believed that mass production was in the process of eliminating the aesthetic control craftsmen had maintained over production. Describing capitalism as a "defilement" and Victorian England as the "age of shoddy," Morris argued that the machine had become the master of both workers and design, instead of the other way around. Only a revolution in aesthetics could save art and architecture. Morris spearheaded the "arts and crafts movement" in Britain, espousing craft production that would create useful but artistic objects for the general public, thereby elevating taste to a new level.

The Avant-Garde's Break with Rationalism

Symbolism, which began as a literary movement in the early 1870s but had origins a decade earlier—the symbolists revered Baudelaire as a founding father—also reflected the discontent of writers with the materialism of the industrial age. Symbolists sought to discover and depict aesthetically the reality of human consciousness and identity. They believed that analogies existed between the human mind and the external world, and thus between the spiritual and natural worlds. They held that the links could be discovered through the exploitation of symbols, particularly through poetry. Thus some continuity existed between symbolism and the romanticism of the early nineteenth century, as symbolists sought to bring emotions to the surface through dreamlike states of consciousness.

In May 1913, the Russian aristocrat Sergey Diaghilev's ballet *The Rite of Spring* opened in Paris. For Diaghilev (1872–1929), who organized major art expositions and outraged conventional society by flaunting male lovers, art and life went hand in hand—they imitated each other. Diaghilev sought liberation in erotic ballets. Hitherto, ballet had retained absolute loyalty to classical subjects and presentation, immune to avant-garde challenge. Aesthetes in the audience hissed at the men and women of Parisian high society filing into the theater wearing tails and evening gowns. When the curtain went up, the dancers were jumping up and down, toeing inward in defiance of conventional ballet. The majority of the audience reacted with catcalls, hisses, and then screams of anger. An elderly countess scoffed that it was the first time that anyone—in this case, the dancers with their provocative performance—had ever made fun of her. The audience was shocked by the jarring, primitive music of the Russian composer Igor Stravinsky (1882–1971), who dispensed with the sentimental music that had invariably accompanied ballet. The avant-garde, however, cheered. Art and life had merged.

Thus, rejecting the idea that rationalism should underlie the arts and that objective standards could exist by which to assess literature, painting, and music, the writers, painters, and composers of the avant-garde rebelled against accepted cultural forms. They believed that these threatened to render the individual insignificant and powerless. Mass-circulation newspapers,

Scene from Sergey Diaghilev's *The Rite of Spring*, 1913.

the popular theater inevitably playing Gilbert and Sullivan in London or soapy popular operas in Paris, music halls, military band concerts in Hyde Park, and the cinema were the stuff of popular culture. The avant-garde wanted none of it.

Avant-garde artists accepted nothing as absolute, certainly not the traditional forms of cultural expression or morality. Showing Nietzsche's influence, some sought to transcend the limits of reason and moral purpose. Far more than even impressionist painters, the turn of the century avant-garde artists broke with the past. This was, to an extent, a revolt of the young—because of the rise in population, a larger percentage of the population was indeed young—and self-consciously so. In Austria, the avant-garde called themselves "The Young Ones." They were defiantly "modern," a term they embraced with passion. They paid less attention to their subjects than the response their work would elicit in their audiences. The French playwright Alfred Jarry (1873–1907) staged the play *King Ubu,* a mockery of an authority figure. The story of an avaricious oaf in desperate search of a crown, the farce ran one tumultuous night in December 1896; it began with one of the characters pretending to hurl human waste at the outraged audience.

The avant-garde did not write or paint for everybody. In Paris, a group of artists and writers called themselves "Bohemians"—gypsy wanderers. These avant-garde young men gloried in the condition of being outsiders, rebels against the dominant culture in the way that romanticism had been a revolt against the classical tastes of court and château, even rebels against the strictures of their own middle-class social origins. They sought to surprise with their spontaneity and creativity, and even to offend by creating a scandal. However, although the proponents of cultural modernism may have mocked bourgeois "respectability" and popular culture by sporting long hair, wearing strange clothes, and behaving erratically, they nonetheless sought public acceptance and patronage of their work.

Many, including a number who were homosexual, celebrated their individuality and tried to keep themselves in the public eye. The flamboyant Irish-born poet and dramatist Oscar Wilde (1854–1900), whose witty dialogues greatly improved British comedy, became a symbol of contemporary "decadence." When asked by a customs official if he had anything to declare on arriving in France, Wilde replied, "Only my genius." He faced prosecution in 1895 for his sexual orientation and was sentenced to two years' hard labor for "immoral conduct." He died a lonely, premature death in a small Parisian hotel in 1900.

New musical composition also reflected the contemporary discovery of the unconscious, as avant-garde composers moved defiantly away from traditional forms. Many abandoned the ordered hierarchical scale, in which certain tones held precedence. The composer Gustav Mahler (1860–1911) sought to release in his audience dreams and fantasies, which he believed could not be distinguished from real life, just as Freud sought to elicit them from the patients on his office couch. The French pianist and composer

Erik Satie (1866–1925) composed music by the dim light of lampposts as he returned in an alcoholic haze from his favorite cafés, where he would eat only foods white in color. Both Satie and his countryman Claude Debussy (1862–1918) set out to free music from all constraints. Satie's compositions, with fanciful titles like *Three Pieces in the Form of a Pear,* explored new relationships between chords that surprised listeners, outraging some while delighting others with their humor. The Austrian composer Arnold Schoenberg (1874–1951) began to break the patterns of traditional harmonies to write free atonal music, beginning with his String Quartet No. 2 (1908). He believed atonality realistically and subliminally followed the dictates, instincts, and sometimes suffering of his psyche: "What counts is the capacity to hear oneself, to look deep inside oneself. . . . Inside, where the man of instinct begins, there, fortunately, all theory breaks down." For Schoenberg, the self became a refuge from the outside world.

The artists, writers, and composers of the avant-garde believed that art could reveal what is hidden in the unconscious, and thus open up new vistas of experience that could be communicated to viewers and audiences. The poet Guillaume Apollinaire (1880–1918), whose work defied stylistic convention, wrote reviews of books that only existed in his mind. Master of ambiguity, he abandoned direct statement and even punctuation and conventional word order to encourage readers to find new meanings in his work. One contemporary, affirming the particularly close link between symbolism and music, urged writers to "drop a syllable into a state of pure consciousness and listen for the reverberations."

Postimpressionists painted subjects in ways that even more consciously than impressionism distanced the artist from the subject. Georges Seurat (1859–1891) claimed that painters could evoke emotions through the visual suggestions of discontinuous lines, colors, and tones. Symbolist writers, who believed that symbols would stimulate memory through free association, were intrigued by Seurat's paintings because they consisted of thousands of dots of color forming figures and landscapes. This bold style, called "pointillism," influenced by the development of photography, left Seurat's figures appearing strangely mechanical and separate from each other. This may suggest the alienation, social division, and isolation of modern urban life. Yet in *A Sunday on La Grande Jatte* (1884), Seurat may have sought to portray social cohesion through the social mix of bourgeois and workers enjoying a Sunday afternoon along the Seine River in Paris.

Expressionist painters used daring distortions, curious juxtaposition, and bold, unfamiliar color schemes to express what lay deep inside them and to obtain an emotional response in viewers. They were greatly influenced by the art of "primitive" societies. The French painter Paul Gauguin (1848–1903) abandoned a comfortable living as a stockbroker for the uncertainty of a career as a painter. His lengthy stay on the Pacific Ocean island of Tahiti shaped the appearance of his painting. Edvard Munch (1863–1944), a Norwegian artist who came to Paris in 1893, demon-

Georges Seurat's *A Sunday on La Grande Jatte* (1884).

strated Gauguin's influence. Munch's *The Scream* (1893) evokes the viewer's alarm and fear, because the subject's scream seems to fill the entire canvas. In Munich, which along with Dresden was the center of the German expressionist movement, the Russian painter Wassily Kandinsky (1866–1944) had by 1910 moved expressionism even farther away from surface reality, portraying the inner being in a simplified form with lines, dots, and intense colors.

Art Nouveau, a sinuous decorative style offering a synthesis between traditional and modern art, also reflected the anxiety and moodiness of the fin de siècle. Art Nouveau evinced contemporary fascination with psychiatry. Charcot, the French neurologist, had opened up the unconscious to investigation through hypnosis. The dreamlike flowing forms and shapes of Art Nouveau, then, complemented the growing awareness of the contours and fluidity of the mind and its dreams and fantasies.

Although drawing upon past decorative traditions in furniture, jewelry, glasswork, and ceramics, Art Nouveau also influenced architecture, seen in the houses and sweeping entrances to subway stations that Hector Guimard (1867–1942) designed in Paris, and in apartment buildings and the beginnings of a cathedral undertaken (and still unfinished) in Barcelona by Antonio Gaudí (1852–1926).

Leading cultural figures in France identified Art Nouveau's style with the republic, seeing in its highly crafted luxury products something that was very French. At the same time, it could be associated with the conservative republic because the style's rococo origins were rooted in an aristocratic

(*Left*) Antonio Gaudí's Casa Batlló in Barcelona. (*Right*) Gustav Klimt's *Judith II* (*Salome*) (1909).

tradition and, perhaps as well, seemed to affirm women's traditional role in household decoration at a time when more feminists were stepping forward to demand equal rights for women.

Vienna became a vital center of avant-garde cultural experimentation at the turn of the century. But after first enjoying state sponsorship of their art, the painters and writers of the avant-garde faced rejection in a climate of intolerance. Some intellectuals and painters then embraced aestheticism, which emphasized form and beauty as a way of surviving in an increasingly irrational, hostile world. The painter Gustav Klimt (1862–1918), among other Viennese artists, retreated into subjectivism, attaching primary value to individual experience. Yet in Vienna the aestheticism of the avant-garde was not a reaction against the resilient cultural values of the middle class. It was a reaction against political intolerance. Klimt and the "secessionists," like their counterparts in Munich, rebelled against what Klimt considered the unsatisfactory values and dangers of mass society. He sought to stimulate and shock viewers by using, for example, classical images in strange, unprecedented juxtapositions, presenting erotic fantasies and other representations of utopian escape.

In Paris, a disparate but supremely talented group of younger modern painters exhibited their work in 1905. A critic dismissed the show as "touches of crude colorings juxtaposed haphazardly; barbaric and naive games of a child who is playing with the 'box of colors.'" Another dubbed them the "fauvists," or wild beasts. The name stuck. The fauvists remained committed to experimentation with colors and lines on canvas in their quest for the liberation of both subject and painter. They also painted landscapes, including coastal resorts, with bright colors and open spaces. One hostile critic in 1905 described a fauvist's brush as having been "dipped in dynamite," affirming the perceived association between artistic and social, and even anarchist, rebellion in some minds.

Pablo Picasso (1881–1973) is widely considered to be the first painter of the modern movement. Influenced by his Spanish homeland, Picasso's work (especially the paintings of his "blue period") revealed the gloomy obsession with death that had characterized earlier Spanish painters. Picasso drew on his own intense subjectivity. His work was rarely shown in Paris, where he spent most of his career, in part because he mistrusted art dealers. His great influence came later.

(*Left*) The young Pablo Picasso in his studio. (*Right*) Picasso's *Les Demoiselles d'Avignon*.

Picasso's daring *Les Demoiselles d'Avignon* (1907), depicting five nudes, may mark the beginning of modernist art. Abstract painting is a subjective form of expression. "I paint objects as I think them, not as I see them," Picasso asserted. Above all, abstract art abandoned the artist's system of perspective that had endured since the Renaissance. In Picasso's work, one finds a fragmentation of perception and dismantling of realistic depiction in favor of products of the imagination—flat, distorted, and highly simplified geometric patterns of solid forms, and space divided by sharp angles.

Critics called the Spanish painter's style "cubism" because of his preoccupation with basic shapes, particularly the three-dimensional prism. Picasso considered the prism the fundamental component of reality. The influence of Georges Braque (1882–1963) on the cubist style contributed to the development of a second, "analytical" phase of cubism with an even greater emphasis on geometric shapes, now constructed from inanimate, pasted materials. The cubists became a more cohesive "school" than the fauvists, and relied more on light and shade than color to represent forms.

Futurist artists, most of them Italian, were inspired by technological change. In 1910, a futurist wrote, "All subjects previously used must be swept away in order to express our whirling life of steel, of pride, of fever and of speed." *Dynamism of a Cyclist* (1913) by Umberto Boccioni (1882–1916) depicts the frenetic energy of pedaling without actually showing the cyclist. The poet Filippo Tommaso Marinetti's "Manifesto of Futurism," which was published in 1909 in the aftermath of Wilbur Wright's triumphant airplane flights in France (following his first controlled airplane flight in Kitty Hawk, North Carolina, in 1903), proclaimed, "We want to sing the love of danger, the habit of energy and rashness. . . . Beauty exists only in struggle. There is no masterpiece that has not an aggressive character. . . . We want to glorify war—the only cure for the modern world."

CONCLUSION

Artists in the early twentieth century suffered the shrill denunciations of chauvinists. In France, the nationalist press denounced the cubists, several of whom, like Picasso, were not French, for artistic decadence, specifically for importing "foreign perversions" with the goal of weakening French morale. Insisting on eclecticism and experimentation, some Munich artists affronted German nationalists by insisting that art ought to be international in character and by bringing French and Russian artists—including Kandinsky—into their circle. The turn of the avant-garde toward irrationality came at a time when the rational structures that governed domestic political life and international relations seemed to be breaking down amid aggressive nationalism and militarism in Paris, Vienna, Berlin, and other European capitals.

Aggressive nationalism was closely linked to the "new European imperialism." Between the mid-1880s and 1914, the European powers raced each other to increase their domination of the globe. The European imperial powers included Great Britain and France, old rivals for colonies, as well as Germany and Italy, which also sought to extend what each considered its national interests. Imperial rivalries helped solidify international alliances, dividing Europe into two armed camps. The avant-garde had good reason, as it turned out, to be anxious.

CHAPTER 21

THE AGE OF EUROPEAN IMPERIALISM

In one of the odd twists in the long, bloody history of European imperialism, the vast Congo region in Central Africa was colonized by a monarch acting as a private citizen. When he was heir to the Belgian throne, Leopold II (ruled 1865–1909) had given one of his father's ministers a piece of granite with the inscription "Belgium needs colonies." And so when he was king of Belgium, Leopold organized the Congo Company to explore and develop Central Africa.

In 1879, Leopold sent the British-American journalist Henry Stanley (1841–1904) to the Congo. Stanley emerged with treaties signed with local rulers establishing Leopold's personal claim over the Congo. The Belgian king would now have his "piece of that great African cake."

An international conference of representatives of European states held in Berlin in 1884–1885 to discuss claims to African territory declared the Congo to be the "Congo Free State," with Leopold as its head. This "free state," recognized as the private possession of the Belgian king and as part of his business organization, received the status of a "mandate." The Berlin conference established this designation to signify that a European power accepted the "mandate" to govern a territory and to provide, in principle, for the welfare of its "backward people." The European powers agreed on ground rules governing the race for colonies. Henceforth no power could simply declare a region its colony unless it exercised effective control over the territory.

Despite Leopold's pledge that each colonial power would "undertake to watch over the preservation of the native races, and the amelioration of the moral and material conditions of their existence," the horrors perpetrated on the people of the Congo at Leopold's orders in his quest for ivory and rubber may have been unmatched in the annals of European imperialism. For the indigenous population, the colonial experience was hell on earth.

An American missionary reported a macabre way the Belgian soldiers had of trying to reduce the waste of bullets: "Each time the corporal goes

Bismarck and Disraeli meeting during the Congress of Berlin, 1878.

out to get rubber, cartridges are given to him. He must bring back all not used; and for every one used, he must bring back a right hand. . . . In six months, they had used 6,000 cartridges, which means that 6,000 people are killed or mutilated. It means more than 6,000, for the people have told me repeatedly that soldiers killed children with the butt of their guns."

The Belgian Parliament, stung by revelations of brutality uncovered by international investigations, demanded more humane standards. In 1908, it took the Congo away from Leopold and made it a colony of Belgium, a country one-eightieth the size of its colony.

FROM COLONIALISM TO IMPERIALISM

Imperialism is the process by which one state, with superior military strength and more advanced technology, imposes its control over the land, resources, and population of a less developed region. The repeated extension of Chinese control over the Vietnamese people of Indochina would fit most definitions of the term. At the same time, Japan emerged as an imperial power itself during the first decades of the twentieth century, as did the United States. Imperialism has above all characterized the relations of the European powers with Africa and Asia.

From the 1880s to 1914, the European powers expanded their direct control over much of the globe. Imperialism reflected and contributed to the development of a truly global economy: the manufacturing boom of the Second Industrial Revolution whetted the appetite of merchants seeking new markets and manufacturers seeking new sources of raw materials. The expansion of European empires during the period of the "new imperialism" generally included the exploitation of African and Asian lands with economic and strategic interests in mind.

Europeans had long visited, influenced, learned from, and conquered distant lands. Spain and Portugal began the first sustained European quest for colonies in the fifteenth century with excursions along the West African coast. During the sixteenth century, Spaniards built a vast colonial empire that stretched from what is now the southwestern United States to the southern tip of South America. In the seventeenth century, French traders, missionaries, and soldiers began small settlements in "New France" (present-day Quebec). The drive for colonies heightened the rivalry between Britain and France in the era of the American Revolution. After losing New France to Britain in the 1760s, France's modest empire included Algeria (conquered in 1830) and a few Caribbean islands, until the conquest of Indochina began during the Second Empire (1852–1870). During the early eighteenth and the nineteenth centuries, British merchants sought both raw materials and sizable markets for manufactured goods in Africa, India, and as far as Southeast Asia, China, and Japan.

In contrast to imperialism, colonialism from the last decade of the sixteenth century through the middle decades of the nineteenth century entailed economic exploitation and control, informal or formal, over territories. An essential element of colonialism was trade. Again, the British Empire provides the classic case. The British insisted on free trade, an open market that would allow English merchants to sell goods without tariff restrictions and return with luxury products—calicoes and spices from India, coffee, sugar, and rum from the Caribbean, and tobacco from Virginia—for the home market. European traders had established port facilities and made agreements with local rulers allowing them to trade freely (although Japan and China had only a few treaty ports providing trade access). North America, Australia, New Zealand, and parts of India, as well as some of the lands added to Russia's great inland empire in Siberia, Muslim Central Asia, and Northeast Asia, had become settlement colonies. However, relatively few Europeans had settled permanently in Africa or Southeast Asia, both of which had difficult tropical climates, or in China, which remained an independent state despite bullying by European powers. In these places the European presence remained generally peripheral, and staking out large chunks of territory as colonies seemed a daunting, expensive, and dangerous challenge. Despite their relative wealth and power, European imperial states lacked the resources for complete conquest and control.

Moreover, public opinion at home did not yet support massive colonial undertakings. In India, the British since the eighteenth century had drawn on a developed economic structure, credit networks, and, particularly in

Bengal, a full-fledged tax apparatus and local client armies to make possible conquest and absorption. With India as a base, Britain greatly increased its influence in the Persian Gulf, Arabia, and East Africa, after having forced China to open its ports following a quick military victory of 1842.

During the early nineteenth century, many of the original colonies of Spain and Portugal became independent. The Spanish Empire based on conquest, religious conversion, and the extraction of silver in the New World had largely disappeared by 1850. But Spain still held Cuba, Puerto Rico, and the Philippines. After Brazil, many times the size of Portugal, proclaimed its independence in 1822, Portugal was left with only toeholds in Africa, India, and East Asia.

The Dutch had established bases on the coast of West Africa (abandoned in 1872) and small island colonies scattered in the Caribbean, the Indian Ocean, and the Pacific. Dutch traders ended Portuguese control of Java, one of Indonesia's islands, and extended their own influence over the island in 1755. The Dutch gradually extended control over the rest of Indonesia. Britain and France had established bases on the west coast of Africa, despite its lack of natural harbors and estuaries. Both powers began to penetrate the giant continent during the nineteenth century—the British from the tip of South Africa, the French from Algeria and the coast of West Africa.

Yet only Britain, despite being only about the size of the island of Madagascar, still had a large empire by the middle of the nineteenth century. Despite the loss of thirteen of its American colonies, the British Empire still extended into so many corners of the world that it was tediously repeated that "the sun never sets on the British Empire." British imperialism rested in part on free trade, with the empire contributing to economic

A British colonial administrator settling a dispute between two indigenous chiefs on the Gambia River in West Africa.

domination. Britain's strength also rested on the pillars of its settlement colonies. In search of a more secure future or simply adventure, more than a million people emigrated from the British Isles in the 1850s alone, most of them to Australia, New Zealand, and Canada, as well as to the United States. Australia had become the world's largest exporter of wool by 1851, when the discovery of gold in New South Wales and Victoria brought another wave of immigrants dreaming of making their fortune, like those pouring into California at the same time. The Australian colonies and New Zealand received the right to maintain their own governments in the 1850s, under the watchful eye of the British Foreign Office, although Western Australia remained a convict colony until "transportation" to Australia ceased to be a punishment in England in 1865. Canada achieved Dominion status (that is, nominally autonomous within the empire) in 1867 with passage of the British North America Act by the British Parliament. The crown would grant Dominion status to Australia and New Zealand in 1907.

The "New Imperialism" and the Scramble for Africa

In the early 1880s, the hold of the European powers on the rest of the world was still relatively slight, as Map 21.1 demonstrates. Many leaders still could conclude that the cost of maintaining colonies outweighed the benefits. In 1852, British Prime Minister Benjamin Disraeli, later an outspoken advocate of imperialism, had referred to the colonies as "wretched" and "a millstone round our necks." William Gladstone, Disraeli's rival, reflected the prevailing liberal view when he pontificated, "The lust and love of territory have been among the greatest curses of mankind."

Distant, underdeveloped lands still seemed remote from urgent European interests. But this changed rapidly. Before the age of imperialism, Shaka, a renowned leader of the Zulus, who had established one of the two dominant African kingdoms in what is now South Africa, prophesied before his death in 1828 that his people would be conquered by the "swallows," white men who build mud houses. The prophecy came true.

The Second Industrial Revolution whetted the appetite of the powers for new sources of raw materials and markets for manufactured goods. The enormous resources generated by large-scale industrialization and the rapid spread of a contentious nationalism fueled the new imperialism. Despite rivalries between the powers, during this period they were not involved in wars with each other, allowing them to concentrate their energies and resources on imperial expansion, which new technological advances facilitated. Imperial powers Britain, France, Germany, and Italy no longer necessarily looked to preserve the balance of power on the continent, but rather to extend what each considered its national interests.

MAP 21.1 COLONIAL EMPIRES UNTIL 1880   Colonies of Britain, France, Russia, the Netherlands, Spain, Portugal, and the Ottoman Empire.

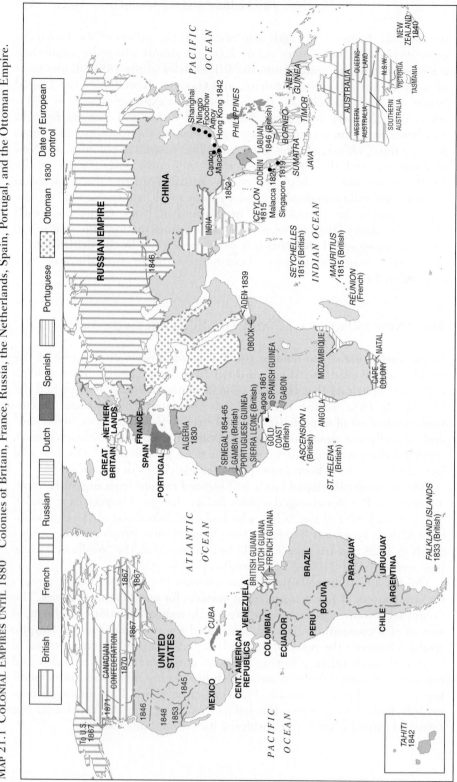

A British foreign minister recalled in 1891, "When I left the Foreign Office in 1880, nobody thought about Africa. When I returned to it in 1885, the nations of Europe were almost quarreling with each other as to the various portions of Africa which they should obtain." Another British foreign official would ask incredulously if his country sought to "take possession of every navigable river all over the world, and every avenue of commerce, for fear somebody else should take possession of it?" The colonial race extended even to the North Pole, first reached by the American Robert E. Peary (1856–1920) in 1909.

British and French Imperial Rivalry

A French colonial enthusiast assessed the "scramble for Africa"—the term was first used by a London newspaper as early as 1884—that began in the 1880s: "We are witnessing something that has never been seen in history: the veritable partition of an unknown continent by certain European countries. In this partition France is entitled to the largest share." Africa included about a fourth of the world's land area and a fifth of its population. Explorers plunged almost blindly into the uncharted and unmapped African interior. The source of the Nile River, the lifeline of Egypt, had been located in modern-day Uganda in 1862; most Western maps still showed blank spots for much of the continent's interior. Europeans discovered the bewildering complexity of a continent that included about 700 different autonomous societies with distinctive political structures.

France's imperial aspirations reveal some of the motives that fueled the new imperialism. After its humiliating defeat by Prussia during the Franco-Prussian War of 1870–1871, the gnawing loss of Alsace-Lorraine hung over France. German Chancellor Otto von Bismarck subtly encouraged the French government to pursue an interest in distant colonies, hoping it would forget about trying to retake Alsace-Lorraine. Indeed, French colonialism during the "new imperialism" was closely tied to a nationalist spirit that was linked with the idea of revenge against Germany.

At the Congress of Berlin in 1878, France agreed to abandon its claims to the island of Cyprus, while the British gave up claims to Tunisia. The French ambassador to Germany warned his own government in 1881 that if it failed to order bold action in Tunisia, France risked decline as a power, perhaps even "finding itself on a par with Spain." In March 1881, the French government claimed that raiders from Tunisia were harassing their troops in Algeria. French troops invaded Tunisia, which became a French protectorate two months later. Between 1895 and 1896, France also seized the island of Madagascar off the coast of East Africa and made it a colony (see Map 21.2).

French merchants and nationalists dreamed of an empire that would stretch across Africa. Railroads had begun to reach across continental Europe in the 1840s and 1850s. They became a symbol of modernity, but also

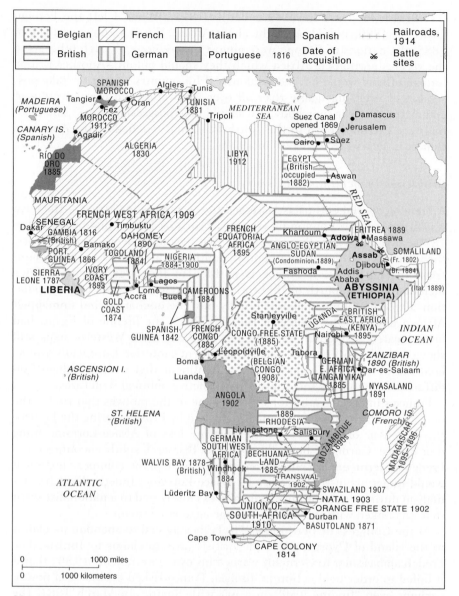

MAP 21.2 IMPERIALISM IN AFRICA BEFORE 1914   Belgian, British, French, German, Italian, Portuguese, and Spanish colonies in Africa and dates of European control.

of conquest, as in the case of the U.S. transcontinental railway. Not surprisingly, the railroad captured the imagination of imperialists. Cecil Rhodes (1853–1902), British entrepreneur and colonialist, reasoned that rails went farther and cost less than bullets. A French railway network was mapped out to connect Algeria and Senegal by crossing the Sahara Desert.

Most of the lines were never built, and, in any case, they could never have generated sufficient revenues to justify their enormous cost. France had little more than a series of forts to show for enormous expense. Yet British merchants on the coast of West Africa feared that French gains would lead to the loss of products such as palm oil and potential markets for their own goods in the African interior. The Franco-British rivalry in Africa heated up. Further French advances in western Sudan followed.

British and French rivalries in Egypt, a gateway to the markets and products of the Middle East, dated to the revolutionary years of the late 1790s. In 1869, a French engineer and entrepreneur, Ferdinand de Lesseps (1805–1894), completed a canal through the Isthmus of Suez, which connects the Red and Mediterranean Seas. The Suez Canal cut the distance of the steamship voyage from London to Bombay (now Mumbai) in half by avoiding the treacherous Cape of Good Hope at the southern tip of Africa. The severe financial difficulties of Ismail Pasha, the ruler (*khedive*) of Egypt, which was a part of the Ottoman Empire, brought Britain a stroke of incredibly good fortune. In 1875, Britain bailed out the bankrupt Ismail Pasha by purchasing a considerable portion of shares in the canal. Under British management, the number of ships passing through the canal rose from 486 in 1870 to 3,000 in 1882.

No power had a greater stake in the canal than Britain. The British government traditionally had sought to protect the land and sea routes to India by supporting the Islamic Middle Eastern states—above all, the Ottoman

British forces at rest around the Great Sphinx of Giza after defeating an Egyptian army at the Battle of Tel el-Kebir in 1882.

Empire—against Russian designs. With continuing social and political chaos in Egypt threatening the interests of British bondholders, in 1882 a British fleet shelled the Mediterranean port city of Alexandria. The British then established a protectorate over Egypt, still nominally part of the Ottoman Empire. The Egyptian *khedive* henceforth accepted British "advice." Over the next forty years, the British government repeatedly assured the other powers that its protectorate over Egypt would only be temporary. The French, who had loaned the *khedive* as much money as had Britain, were particularly aggrieved at the continued British occupation.

Central Africa became the next major focus of European expansion. In 1869, the *New York Herald* hired Henry Stanley to find the missionary and explorer David Livingstone (1813–1873), from whom there had been no word in almost four years. After a trip of fifteen months, he found the missionary in January 1871 on the shores of Lake Tanganyika and greeted him with that most understated Victorian salutation, "Dr. Livingstone, I presume?" Henry Stanley's subsequent long journey up the Congo River in 1879 to gain treaties for Belgian King Leopold II opened up interior Africa to great-power rivalry. In 1880, Savorgnan de Brazza (1852–1905), a French naval officer, reached Stanley Pool, a large lake Stanley had "discovered" in 1877. ("Stanley didn't discover us," one "native" put it reasonably, "we were here all the time.") Brazza returned with a piece of paper signed with an "X" by a king, which Brazza claimed granted France a protectorate over the territory beyond the right bank of the Congo River.

Although the French government first showed little interest, French nationalists made ratification of Brazza's "treaty" a major issue. Portugal then declared that it controlled the mouth of the Congo River. The British government demanded trade rights in the region. Leopold of Belgium voiced opposition to any French moves near his personal Congo territory. Amid continued resentment over British control of Egypt, the French Chamber of Deputies eagerly ratified Brazza's treaty. French colonial activity in West Africa continued unabated. Between 1880 and 1914, France's empire increased in size by twelve times, from 350,000 square miles to 4.6 million.

Germany and Italy Join the Race

Germany was the next power to enter the race for colonies. It did so despite the fact that Chancellor Otto von Bismarck at first viewed colonization as an expensive sideshow that distracted attention from the essential questions of power politics in European diplomacy. He once curtly rejected a German colonial explorer's plea for a more aggressive colonial policy: "Your map of Africa is very nice, but my map of Africa is in Europe. Here is Russia, and here is France, and we are in the middle. That is my map of Africa!"

The chancellor had routinely rejected pleas that Germany intervene in Africa on behalf of merchants, missionaries, and nationalistic adventurers.

The Germans in Africa. Cartoons originally appearing in the German journal *Jugend* in 1916 show an officer arriving to find chaos (*left*) and imposing military order (*right*).

The Colonial League, established in 1882, and the Society for German Colonization, a lobby of businessmen and other nationalists formed in 1884, pressured the government to pursue colonies. The German adventurer Karl Peters (1856–1918) sought an outlet for his financial interests and nationalist fervor through his East Africa Company. Peters's chartered company signed commercial agreements, built settlements, and assumed sovereignty over East African territories. These aggressive moves aroused the ire of British nationalists, exactly what Bismarck had hoped to avoid but, given the sudden intensity of nationalist and colonial fever at home, could not.

Bismarck gradually came to share the imperialist view that colonies might provide new markets for German products. But more than this, he realized that the establishment of colonies would solidify his political support within Germany. New markets could create jobs at home or abroad for unemployed German workers. Bismarck concluded that colonies could be administered indirectly at a relatively low cost.

The time also seemed right for the German government to appease its drooling colonial lobby, including merchants. The British Foreign Office was preoccupied with Islamic fundamentalist rebellions in the Sudan. France, with a new protectorate over Tunisia, was embroiled in debate over continued colonization in Indochina. In April 1884, Bismarck wired his consul in Cape Town, South Africa, ordering him to proclaim that the holdings of a German merchant north of the Orange River—the territorial limit of British colonial authority—would henceforth be the protectorate of German Southwest Africa. Britain acquiesced in exchange for Bismarck's acceptance of the British occupation of Egypt. That summer the German chancellor also decided to establish a protectorate over the Cameroons and Togoland in West Africa.

Bismarck, expertly playing off British and French interests against each other, called the Berlin Conference of 1884–1885 in response to a recent agreement signed between Britain and Portugal recognizing mutual interests. The Berlin Conference divided up the territory of the Congo basin between the Congo Free State (Leopold's private territory) and France (the French Congo), while declaring the Congo River open to all. French merchants penetrated Dahomey and the Ivory Coast, with French troops reaching the ancient trading town of Timbuktu (now in Mali) in 1894.

In 1885, Bismarck agreed to protect Peters's commercial enterprises in Tanganyika, which became German East Africa. Germany also established several coastal trading stations and the colony of Angra Pequena in German Southwest Africa, which merchants had portrayed with unerring inaccuracy as a territory of untapped wealth just waiting to be extracted.

To placate Britain, Germany recognized British interests in Kenya and Uganda and the protectorate status of Zanzibar in 1890. In exchange, Germany received a small but strategically important island naval station in the North Sea. The German colonial lobby was not happy: "We have exchanged three kingdoms for a bathtub!" moaned Peters. Nonetheless, by 1913, German colonies in Africa, including German East and Southwest Africa, Togoland, and the Cameroons, occupied over 1 million square miles, five times the size of Germany.

Italy was the last of the major European nations to enter the colonial fray. Its ravenous hunger for empire led Bismarck to note sarcastically that it proceeded "with a big appetite and bad teeth." In 1882, Italy established Assab, a small settlement on the Red Sea, and three years later it occupied Massawa, which in 1889 became the capital of the new Italian colony of Eritrea. Italian merchants hoped to force the adjacent African state of Abyssinia (now Ethiopia) to trade through Eritrea. In 1889, the Abyssinian emperor signed a treaty with Italy which the Italian government took to mean that Abyssinia was now an Italian protectorate. When the French began building a railroad that would link Abyssinia to French Somaliland and the Abyssinians attempted to cancel the treaty, Italian troops launched a war in 1894. The result was a disaster. In 1896, a general without adequate maps marched four badly organized columns of Italian troops into battle. The Abyssinians, some 70,000 strong, with Russian artillery advisers and French rifles, routed the Italian army in the hills near the coast at Adowa. Six thousand Italian soldiers were killed—many more than in the various wars that had led to Italy's unification—and several thousand were captured. The Italians became the first European army to be defeated in the field by Africans. Under the Treaty of Addis Ababa that same year, Italy was forced to renounce Abyssinia as a protectorate, although it kept the territory of Eritrea on the Red Sea.

Standoff in the Sudan: The Fashoda Affair

In 1898, the Anglo-French rivalry in Africa culminated in the standoff between French and British forces at Fashoda on the Nile River in the southern Sudan, nearly bringing the two powers to war. The French government resented the fact that Egypt served as a base for British initiatives in the hot, dry Sudan.

A fundamentalist Islamic and nationalist revolt led by a former Sudanese slave trader who declared himself to be the Mahdi (the Guided One) in the early 1880s challenged the nominal authority of the *khedive* of Egypt over Sudan. After the Mahdi and his followers (the Mahdists) began a holy war against Egypt and defeated Egyptian armies led by British officers, the British sent an expedition to the Sudanese capital of Khartoum to evacuate the Egyptian population. It was led by the dashing, eccentric British adventurer General Charles "Chinese" Gordon (1833–1885), so called because he had commanded troops that assisted the Chinese government in putting down the Taiping Rebellion in the 1860s. Besieged for ten months in Khartoum by the Mahdi's forces in 1884, Gordon was killed when the Mahdists stormed the garrison two days before a relief expedition from Britain arrived in January 1885.

Britain lost interest in Sudan until the French colonial lobby, still smarting from Britain's occupation of Egypt, sought a strategic foothold on the Nile River. In January 1895, Britain claimed the Sudan. The French government, in turn, announced that it considered Sudan open to all colonial powers. The British government responded that it would consider any French activity in Sudan "an unfriendly act."

In 1898, a British force commanded by Lord Horatio Kitchener (1850–1916) set out from Egypt for Sudan with the Upper Nile outpost of Fashoda

The charge of the dervishes (followers of the Mahdi) at the Battle of Omdurman in the Sudan, 1898.

as its goal. Kitchener and his army took revenge for Gordon's death, using machine guns to mow down 11,000 Mahdists at the Battle of Omdurman (September 1898) and retaking Khartoum. British troops desecrated the Mahdi's grave, playing soccer with his skull. At Fashoda, they encountered a French expeditionary force, which intended to establish a French colony on the Upper Nile. Kitchener handed his counterpart a mildly worded note of protest against the French presence, and the two commanders clinked drinking glasses, leaving their governments to fight it out diplomatically.

In both Britain and France, some nationalists demanded war. But the Dreyfus Affair (see Chapter 18) preoccupied French society; furthermore, as the French foreign minister lamented, "We have nothing but arguments and they have the troops." The Fashoda Affair ended peacefully when France recognized British and Egyptian claims to the Nile Basin and Britain recognized French holdings in West Africa. There seemed to be enough of Africa to go around. Only Abyssinia and Liberia, which had been settled in the 1820s by freed U.S. slaves, were independent African states.

The British in South Africa and the Boer War

In South Africa, Britain had to overcome resistance to its presence, first from indigenous peoples and then from Dutch settlers. The British had taken the Cape of Good Hope at the tip of South Africa from the Dutch in 1795. British settlers moved in, fighting nine separate wars against the Bantu people in the 1850s and 1860s. In 1872, the Cape Colony emerged from under the wing of the British Foreign Office, forming its own government, but remaining within the British Empire.

Known as the Boers, the Dutch settlers (Afrikaners) in South Africa were a farming people of strict Calvinist belief. The Boers resented the British abolition of slavery and the fact that the British allowed blacks to move about freely and to own property. In the "Great Trek" from the Cape Colony, which began in 1836 and lasted almost a decade, many Boers began to move inland to carve out states that would be independent of British rule (see Map 21.3). Overcoming Zulu resistance, Boers established the Natal Republic, a strip along South Africa's east coast. When the British intervened in support of the Zulus, the Boers left Natal, which became a British colony in 1843. The Boers crossed the Vaal River in search of new land. Slaughtering Zulus as they went, the Boers founded the Republic of Transvaal (later the South African Republic) and the Orange Free State, which the British recognized as independent in 1854.

The discovery of diamonds in the late 1860s, first in the Cape Colony and then west of the Orange Free State, attracted a flow of treasure seekers—at least 10,000 people—raising the stakes for control of South Africa. After annexing the Republic of Transvaal against the wishes of the Boers in 1877, the British gradually extended their colonial frontier northward, convinced that more diamonds and gold would be found beyond the Vaal River.

Map 21.3 South Africa, 1800–1910 The settlement of South Africa by the Boers and English, including the Boers' Great Trek and the 1910 boundaries of the Union of South Africa.

Cecil Rhodes orchestrated British expansion in South Africa, leading to conflict with the Boers, who still bitterly resented annexation into the British Empire. In 1880, the Boers rose up in revolt, their sharpshooters picking off British troops at Majuba Hill a year later. Unwilling to risk further trouble, William Gladstone's Liberal government recognized the political independence of the South African Republic. But, at the same time, the British tried to force the Boers to trade through the port of Cape Town by denying them access to the sea, reflecting the primacy of commerce in the British grand scheme.

The Boers in Transvaal were given a boost by the discovery in the mid-1880s of more gold deposits, which enabled them to buy weapons. Constructing their railway to Port Mozambique on the eastern coast, the Boers offered advantageous shipping rates to Natal and the Orange Free State, taking business away from British South Africa, and further souring relations between the Boers and Britain. Rhodes then subsidized an uprising in the Transvaal against the Boers. The British government followed Rhodes's advice to send a military excursion against the Boers in 1895, but the Boers fought off the "Jameson Raid" (lead by Leander Jameson) by 500 British cavalry with ease. The raid discredited Rhodes, but brought the British government even more directly into the crisis, particularly after Emperor William II of Germany sent Transvaal President Paul Kruger a congratulatory telegram after the failed Jameson Raid.

In 1899, the British goaded the Boers into a war that lasted three years. In order to depopulate the farms that supplied the rebels, the British imprisoned farmers' wives and children in camps in which thousands died. Some in Britain criticized these camps, although there had been few such outcries when the British had killed people of color during the wars against the peoples of India, Burma (Myanmar), and elsewhere in Africa. The outnumbered Boers evoked great sympathy in France and Germany, leaving the British government isolated diplomatically. The war shocked many people in Britain not only by the extensive, costly military campaigns it required (almost 400,000 British troops were sent), but also because of the hostile reaction the British conduct of the war engendered in other countries. In 1902, the Boers asked for an armistice. Thereafter, they were forced to take an oath of loyalty to the king of England. In 1906 and 1907, Britain granted the Republic of Transvaal and the Orange Free State self-government. In 1910, the Boers joined the British Union of South Africa

(*Left*) British troops in Pretoria, South Africa. (*Right*) Boer Commandos.

(which now included the Cape Colony, the Orange Free State, Transvaal, and Natal, and which was given Dominion status by the British at that time).

The new Boer government immediately proclaimed that it would "permit no equality between colored people and the white inhabitants either in church or state." Apartheid—the unequal separation of whites and blacks by law—was the result of the Boer policy of racial domination. It proved to be the most extreme consequence of the "scramble for Africa."

THE EUROPEAN POWERS IN ASIA

The European powers and the United States divided up much of the entire Pacific region in their quest for raw materials, markets, strategic advantage, and prestige. From the populous Indian subcontinent, Britain expanded its interests into and beyond Burma, accentuating a rivalry with Russia for influence in the region. In the meantime, the Dutch extended their authority in Indonesia, while the French turned much of Indochina into their protectorate. The Russian Empire had expanded well into Central Asia and to the Pacific Ocean. By 1900, only Japan, the emerging power in Asia, maintained real independence against European incursion, having accepted western modernization following the Meiji Restoration in 1868. Siam (Thailand) stood as a buffer state between British and French colonial interests, and the Western powers dominated China, forcing trade and territorial concessions on that weakening empire.

India, Southeast Asia, and China

Europe's quest for colonies and domination in Asia had begun even earlier than in Africa. During the Seven Years' War (1756–1763), British troops defeated the French in India. The British East India Company, responsible to the British Parliament, administered India. The Company ruled with the assistance of various Indian princes. The British recognized their local prerogatives in exchange for their obedience and assistance. Britain later expanded east from India into Burma, overcoming Burmese resistance in a war from 1824 to 1826, and then expanded south into Malaya (see Map 21.4).

Using India as a base, British merchants, backed by British naval power, worked to overcome barriers to trade with East Asia. In the 1830s, British traders had begun to pay for silks, teas, and other Chinese luxury goods with opium grown in India. In 1833, the East India Company lost its monopoly on trade with the east, and other English traders appeared in China selling opium. With opium addiction rampant in southern China, in 1839 the emperor tried to limit trade with foreigners, insisting that all such trade pass through Canton (now Guangzhou). The Royal Navy sent gunboats— hence the origin of the term "gunboat diplomacy"—to Canton to force Chinese capitulation in the short, one-sided Opium War (1840–1842). British

MAP 21.4 INDIA AND THE FAR EAST BEFORE 1914   Areas controlled by the British, French, Dutch, Portuguese, Germans, and Americans in Asia.

forces occupied Shanghai. By the Treaty of Nanking that followed in 1842, the first of the "unequal treaties," China was forced to establish a number of "treaty ports" open to British trade, including Canton and Shanghai, and it was required to grant Britain formal authority "in perpetuity" over Hong Kong (authority that lasted until 1997). British residents and European visitors received the rights of extraterritoriality, which meant that they were not subject to Chinese law. Britain and France together occupied Canton. Following hostilities in 1857 (see

Chinese men smoking opium.

Chapter 18), a combined British and French army forced China to open six more ports to British and French trade, including on the Yangtze River. The British trade route now ran from British ports to Bombay, Columbo in Ceylon (now Sri Lanka), Rangoon, and Singapore, dramatically assisted by the Suez Canal beginning in 1869.

In 1857, a revolt shook British rule in India, revealing some of the tensions between the colonialists and the colonized. Long-term causes of the mutiny of the Sepoys—Indian troops in the British army—included anger at the British policy of taking direct control over Indian states whose princes died without heirs. The immediate cause was the continued use of animal fat to grease rifle cartridges, a religious affront to both Hindu and Muslim soldiers. Other causes included low pay and resentment of British officers. Confronted with British intransigence, the Sepoys rebelled over a wide area, beginning near Delhi. In one place insurgents killed 200 British women and children. The rebels promised a return to Mughal power, as the emperor had been a mere figurehead since 1803. They found some support among local elites, particularly those who saw increased British authority to be a threat to Islam in areas of that religion. An extensive military campaign followed, involving almost 200,000 British and Indian soldiers. British authorities hanged rebels and burned a number of villages.

Following the mutiny, administration of India passed in 1858 from the East India Company to the British crown. Queen Victoria became "Empress of India" and British rule became more direct. Indian princes were guaranteed their lands if they signed agreements accepting British rule. The governor-general of India added the honorific title of "viceroy," as the

(*Left*) Ruins after the Sepoy Mutiny, 1857. (*Right*) Lord and Lady Curzon in Delhi, 1903.

monarch's personal representative, serving under the secretary of state for India. Lord George Curzon (1859–1925), who could trace his aristocratic family line back to the Norman Conquest of 1066, was one of the most forceful proponents of British imperialism. Viceroy of India before the age of forty, Curzon was determined to solidify British rule in India. He strengthened the northwestern frontier defenses against Russia, reduced the cost of government, and took credit for a modest increase in the Indian standard of living. The British government enacted educational reforms, initiated irrigation projects, reformed the police and judicial systems, and encouraged the cotton industry. Frightened by the Sepoy Mutiny, the British government also expedited railway construction in India in order to be able to move troops rapidly. From less than 300 miles of track in 1857, a network of 25,000 miles was established by 1900. By connecting much of the Indian interior with ports, railway development also encouraged production of Indian cotton, rice, oil, jute, indigo, and tea, which could now reach ports by train and then be exported to Britain. Railroads reduced the ravages of famine in India. So did the planting of new crops, such as potatoes and corn. The greater availability of food contributed to rapid population growth. The Indian subcontinent in the twentieth century would become one of the most populous places on earth.

But while some Indian merchants and manufacturers made money from expanded trading opportunities, others lost out. To assure a lucrative market in India, a country of almost 300 million people in 1900, the British at first banned some Indian manufactures that would compete with British goods produced at home, thereby destroying Indian village handicrafts such as textile weaving. Raw Indian cotton was shipped to England to be made into cloth there, and then re-exported to India. British tax collectors increased the indebtedness of Indian peasants in a vast nation beset by rising population, small holdings, and the increasing subdivision of land.

France made its first move to colonize Southeast Asia in the late 1850s. French and Spanish forces had bombarded the towns of Da Nang and Saigon (in present-day Vietnam) in joint retaliation for the execution of a Spanish missionary. When the Vietnamese counterattacked, a French admiral annexed three provinces. France attempted unsuccessfully to form a protectorate over northern Annam (the central part of Vietnam). In the early 1880s, the Emperor of Annam sought Chinese assistance against the French, invoking China's ancient claims to the region. An anti-foreign movement known as the "Black Flags," which included Vietnamese and Chinese brigands, harassed foreigners, aided by Chinese soldiers. In 1883, a French expedition captured the city of Hanoi in Tonkin in northern Vietnam. French troops sent from Cochin (the southern part of Vietnam) forced the Vietnamese to accept a protectorate that included all of Annam. In 1887, France created the Union of Indochina, which included Tonkin, Annam, Cochin, and Cambodia, and, in 1893, it unilaterally added Laos to French Indochina.

The colonial race extended to the islands of the South Seas. France claimed Tahiti and New Caledonia. Britain held the Fiji Islands, some of which served as refueling ports, but little else. Germany hoisted its flag over the Marshall Islands and Samoa. Smaller islands were sometimes bartered and traded as trinkets by the European powers in the various agreements signed to settle major disputes over the larger colonies.

Japan and China: Contrasting Experiences

In contrast to other Asian countries, Japan maintained real independence and gradually emerged as a power in Asia. Japan built up its army and navy after being opened to Western contact in the 1850s. The 1868 Meiji Restoration, ending a period of chaos, facilitated a remarkable Westernization of economic life in Japan. The new centralized state structure encouraged the development of international commerce and industry. Military conscription and the implementation of Western technology, assisted by Western technical experts, made it possible for Japan, with a modern army and navy, to emerge as a world power at the dawn of the twentieth century. Japan, too, then began to seek colonies in Asia.

In China, the Ch'ing (Qing) dynasty continued to be beset by internal division, as well as by the demands of the imperialist powers, and the government only slowly began to adopt Western technology. In the late 1860s, a few Chinese reformers had begun to favor building railways as a way of

modernizing the Chinese state. Yet conservative opposition to modernization continued within the imperial court. Some Chinese scholars believed
that railways damaged "the dragon's vein" across the landscape, threatening the earth's harmony. Imperial officials feared that in case of war
China's enemies would quickly seize the rail lines.

With colonial rivalries reaching a fever pitch in the late 1890s, the European powers sought to impose further trade and territorial concessions
on China. The Chinese government attempted to shore up the ability of
China to resist demands and incursions by Western powers by making use
of European and American science in a program of "self-strengthening."
Internal uprisings, notably the Taiping Rebellion in South China in the
1850s and 1860s, further encouraged such reforms. However, military
weakness made China an easy target for expansion of European influence.
The Sino-Japanese War of 1894–1895 led to an independent Korea (which
Japan made a protectorate and then annexed in 1910) and China's loss of
the island of Formosa (Taiwan) and part of Manchuria to Japan. Needing
loans to pay off a war indemnity to Japan, China was forced to make further trading concessions and disadvantageous railroad leases to Germany
and Russia.

Following the murder of two German missionaries in 1897, the German
government forced China in 1898 to grant a ninety-nine-year lease on the
north Chinese port of Tsingtao (Qingdao) on Kwangchow (Jiaozhou) Bay
and to grant two concessions to build railways in Shandong Province. Russia was eager to complete its own line to Vladivostok through Chinese territories, permitting it to open up the Chinese province of Manchuria, rich
in soybeans and cotton. Russia seized and fortified Port Arthur (Lüshun)
on the pretext of protecting China from Germany and compelled the Chinese government to lease Port Arthur and Dalian (Lüda) for twenty-five
years. The Chinese gave France a lease on Canton Bay and recognized
France's trading "sphere of influence" over several southern provinces.

The U.S. government now claimed to seek what it referred to as "an open
door" in China, in accordance with the principle of free trade. The powers
agreed not to interfere with any treaty port or with the interests of any
other power. China agreed to lease Britain some of the Shandong peninsula and several ports, and to guarantee a British trade monopoly on the
Yangtze River, the entry to much of central China. These forced concessions further weakened the ruling Ch'ing dynasty.

In northern China, many Chinese resented the foreigners, whom some
blamed for floods and a drought, events that also were taken to mean that
the "mandate of Heaven" of the ruling dynasty was at an end. The "Righteous and Harmonious Fists" was a secret anti-foreign society better known
as the Boxers, after the training practices of its members. Many of the Boxers believed they were immune to foreign bullets. The targets of their
wrath were missionaries who sought to convert the Chinese, railroads that
took work away from Chinese transporters, foreign merchants who flooded

the Chinese market with cheap textiles, bringing unemployment to the local population, and foreign soldiers, who often mistreated the Chinese.

In 1900, the Boxers attacked Europeans, Americans, and Chinese Christians in Shandong Province, cutting the railway line between Peking (Beijing) and Tientsin (Tianjin). These attacks spread quickly to the imperial capital and other parts of northern China. After the Boxers killed several hundred "foreign devils," British, Russian, German, French, Japanese, and American troops put down the rebellion. Their governments assessed the Chinese government a crushing indemnity of 67.5 million pounds.

The "scramble for concessions" went on. Russia's competition with Japan for Manchuria in northeastern China led to its shocking

A member of the "Righteous and Harmonious Fists" secret society that rose up against foreign influence in the Boxer rebellion in China in 1900.

defeat in the Russo-Japanese War of 1904–1905 (see Chapter 18). Following its victory, Japan took over and expanded the Manchurian railways. This humiliation, and the subsequent disadvantageous railway concessions granted to the European powers and Japan, intensified Chinese nationalist sentiment and contributed to the overthrow of the Ch'ing dynasty in 1911. In the meantime, Japan's aggressive imperialism in East Asia was well under way.

The United States in Asia

The United States, too, took colonies, believing that this was its right as an emerging world power. However, the American imperial venture in the Philippine Islands, an archipelago in the Pacific Ocean, was not all smooth sailing. During the Spanish-American War of 1898, fought largely over the Caribbean island of Cuba, the American admiral George Dewey (1837–1917) sailed into Manila Bay and defeated the Spanish fleet, capturing Manila. The United States had been helped by a Filipino nationalist,

Emilio Aguinaldo (1869–1964). But once the peace treaty ending the Spanish-American War was signed, President William McKinley announced that it would be "cowardly and discreditable" to leave the Philippines. In 1899, the Filipinos began a war of independence. U.S. troops defeated Aguinaldo's guerrilla forces after three years of fighting. American soldiers herded Filipinos into prison camps, torturing and executing some of those they captured. Aguinaldo himself was taken prisoner in 1901, and the insurrection, in which perhaps as many as 200,000 Filipinos died, ended the following year. The Philippines became a territory of the United States.

At the same time, the U.S. government did not want to be left out of the scramble for Chinese concessions. In 1899, Secretary of State John Hay announced his country's "Open Door Policy" with regard to China, and tried to convince the other powers to leave China open to all trade. Only the British government publicly expressed its agreement with this principle, but the scramble for advantage in China went on.

Map 21.4 demonstrates the remarkable impact of the scramble for colonies in Asia. Only Japan and Siam (Thailand) succeeded in really keeping their independence. The government of China was virtually helpless in the face of the imperial powers.

Domination of Indigenous Peoples

The eagerness with which many Europeans embarked on or applauded imperial ventures can be partially explained by their assumptions that non-Western peoples were culturally inferior. These were not new views, nor were they the only ones held. However, in early modern Europe, non-Western peoples—particularly Islamic peoples—had been viewed as enemies by virtue of their religions: Islam, Hinduism, and Buddhism, among others. The colonial powers assumed the right to exploit conquered "inferior" peoples and decide what was "best" for the colonized. British imperialists spoke of "the white man's burden," a phrase unfortunately immortalized by Rudyard Kipling's 1899 poem of the same name: "Take up the White Man's burden— / And reap his old reward: / The blame of those ye better, / The hate of those ye guard."

Nineteenth- and twentieth-century Western attempts to understand dominated or conquered peoples also reflected the intellectual and cultural processes of imperialism. What has become known as "Orientalism" began with the assumption that not only were Asian, African, and other colonized peoples different, but they were inferior as well. This was reflected by the Egyptian exhibit at an international exposition in Paris in 1900. There visitors could view what were presented as African and Asian villages, complete with "natives" on exhibit. An Egyptian visitor was outraged by the image that the hosts wanted to present of Cairo, his native city, as horribly old and run-down, such that "even the paint on the building was made dirty."

The competition for colonies also coincided with the emergence of pseudo-scientific studies that purported to prove the superiority of Western peoples (through, for example, measures of cranium size). Material progress represented by steamboats, railroads, and machine guns was assumed to follow logically from what was considered moral superiority. Thus a French prime minister insisted that "the superior races have rights over the inferior races." Imperial territories became a testing ground or laboratory for European science and technology.

Social Darwinism

In the eighteenth century, some of the philosophes of the Enlightenment had come to view cultural differences of

The British image of themselves in Africa, from *The Kipling Reader*, 1908: "A Young man . . . walking slowly at the head of his flocks, while at his knee ran small naked cupids."

non-Western peoples with interest, believing that they could learn from people who seemed in some ways different from themselves. In writing about the "propensity to war, slaughter, and destruction, which has always depopulated the face of the earth," Voltaire had noted that "this rage has taken much less possession of the minds of the people of India and China than of ours." Not all of the philosophes, to be sure, had been so enlightened in this respect: David Hume wrote in 1742, "I am apt to suspect the negroes and in general all the other species of men . . . to be naturally inferior to the whites." Likewise, social Darwinists in the nineteenth century did not believe that they could learn anything from non-Western peoples. Social Darwinists argued that what they regarded as the natural superiority of whites justified the conquest of the "backward" peoples of Africa and Asia. They misapplied theories of biological evolution to the history of states, utilizing the principle of "natural selection" developed by Charles Darwin, in which the stronger prevail over the weak. Another British scientist, Herbert Spencer (1820–1903), popularized these theories, uttering the chilling phrase "survival of the fittest." Nations, according to this view, must struggle, like species, to survive. Success in the international battle for colonies would develop and measure national mettle.

Cultural stereotypes of the peoples of the "mysterious" East or the "dark continent" of Africa held sway. These ranged from "childlike" (and therefore in need of being led) to "barbaric," "depraved," "sneaky," and "dangerous" (and therefore in need of constant surveillance). Lord Curzon called the Indian princes "a set of unruly and ignorant and rather undisciplined school-boys." British doctors contributed to a prevailing juxtaposition of the "African jungle," seen as a "hotbed of disease" (including stigmatized diseases like leprosy) by virtue of a lack of civilization, with the healthier "civilized" colonizers.

Even well-meaning critics of colonial brutality and other reformers assumed the inferiority of those they were trying to help. Josephine Butler, a feminist reformer, believed that Indian women stood lower on a scale of human development than did her British "sisters." Yet, at the beginning of the twentieth century, some feminist activists did begin to learn about and respect Indian culture and work closely with Indian women.

Imperial officials adopted racist ideology to justify colonialism and the brutalization of indigenous peoples. Colonial businessmen, as well as administrators, paid little attention to the damaging effects of colonialism on indigenous peoples, while simultaneously justifying their presence by claiming to "civilize" the people they dominated.

The experience of the Herero people in what had become German Southwest Africa provides perhaps the most egregious example of frightening Western attitudes toward indigenous peoples who stood in their way. A German official stated the goal of the colonial administration: "Our task is to strip the Herero of his heritage and national characteristics and gradually to submerge him, along with the other natives, into a single colored working class." In 1903, the Herero people, after losing their land to German cattle raisers and angered by the unwillingness of colonial courts to punish cases of murder and manslaughter against them, rose up in rebellion. The Germans killed about 55,000 men, women, and children, two-thirds of the Herero people, chasing survivors into the desert and sealing waterholes. The German official report stated: "Like a wounded beast the enemy was tracked down from one water-hole to the next until finally he became the victim of his own environment. . . . [This] was to complete what the German army had begun: extermination of the Herero nation."

Social Darwinism had other implications for the home countries. At the turn of the century, the U.S. historian Frederick Jackson Turner held that the westward expansion of the American frontier helped reduce discontent by providing land and opportunity to the surplus population of the East Coast. A French military administrator, Marshal Hubert Lyautey (1854–1934), once referred to Algeria and Morocco as the "French Far West." Some prominent Europeans began to believe that the powers could "export" their more economically marginal or politically troublesome population to the colonies. By "social imperialism," colonies would help countries easily dispose of their "least fit," such as unemployed or underemployed workers. Social tensions and conflict would be reduced, the ambitions of the working class for political power thus defused. Cecil Rhodes, as usual, put it most baldly: "If you want to avoid civil war, you must become imperialists." The British colonial armies alone absorbed thousands of "surplus" Scots and Irish, the latter making up about 40 percent of the non-Indian troops in India. By this view, then, colonies could serve as a social safety valve.

Technological Domination and Indigenous Subversion

Europeans employed technological advances in travel and weaponry in their subjugation of indigenous peoples. Railways aided imperial armies in their conquest and defense of colonial frontiers, although horses, mules, and camels still hauled men and supplies across African deserts and bush country. The steamship, like the train, lessened the time of travel to distant places. By the end of the century, thanks to the completion of the Suez Canal in 1869, linking the Mediterranean and Red Seas, British bureaucrats, soldiers, merchants, and tourists could reach India in about twenty days. The heliograph, which sent messages by means of a movable mirror that reflected sunlight, and then the telegraph speeded up communications and led to better coordination of troop movements. Observation balloons and, later, power searchlights aided European armies.

Advanced military technology invariably overcame open colonial rebellions. Along the South African frontier, Zulu warriors resisted the British advance in the late 1870s, earning several victories with surprise attacks. But by the 1890s, they were no match for cannon. The gunboat was the prototypical instrument of European power and enforcement, as it had proven to be in China during the Opium War in the early 1840s. The Gatling, or machine, gun and the single-barreled Maxim gun, which could fire rapidly without being reloaded, proved devastating. A contemporary quip described relations between colonists and the colonized: "Whatever happens we have got the Maxim gun, and they have not." A single gunner or two could fend off a large-scale attack, and British casualties were reduced to almost none. To soldiers, colonial battles now seemed "more like hunting than fighting."

The colonial powers tested new, lighter artillery that could be moved quickly and new, more powerful shells. The British developed the "dum-dum" bullet, which exploded upon impact, with the shooting of attacking "natives" in mind. (It took its name from the arsenal in Calcutta where it was developed.) For the most part, there was little to stop the European onslaught other than malaria and yellow fever carried by mosquitoes, and sleeping sickness carried by the tsetse fly.

Yet indigenous peoples could express resistance to powerful outsiders in other ways besides risking annihilation in open rebellion. The "weapons of the weak" ranged from riots and individual subversion to foot-dragging and gentle but determined defiance. The latter included pretending not to understand, or sometimes what Chinese called "that secret smile" that suggested not compliance but rather defiance in the guise of deference. Such play-acting in daily life offered only glimpses of the ridicule of Europeans that could be hinted at in theatrical productions, songs, dances, or other public expressions. Symbols, gestures, double meanings, and images were easily understood by the subordinate population, but sufficiently disguised from Europeans. These were small victories of political dissent, but victories nonetheless.

Imperial Economies

Once they had a foothold, the European powers established command, or "plunder," economies in three ways: they expropriated the land of the indigenous people; they used the soil and subsoil for their own profit; and they exploited the population for labor. The European powers imposed commercial controls over natural resources. Imperial powers routinely blocked long-standing trade routes that led to other colonies, preventing commercial exchanges from which their own merchants did not profit. European merchants, protected at home by high tariffs against foreign imports, maintained a monopoly on the sale of their manufactured goods in the colonies. Colonialists forced or, in the best circumstances, encouraged local populations to produce for the European market, discouraging or even forbidding the extraction of raw materials or production that would compete with that of the mother country. In Indonesia, for example, the Dutch employed the "culture" or "cultivation" system until 1870. They imposed production quotas on the indigenous population, organized forced labor, and ordered people in West Java to grow coffee when its price rose and to cut down spice-bearing

Trading ships in Calcutta at the end of the nineteenth century.

trees and plants when the price of spices fell. Local populations were forced over time to abandon traditional agricultural practices, ending up in a wage economy as poorly paid laborers. They also lost traditional rights to hunt, graze animals, and gather firewood on land they did not own, a process that had also characterized the early stages of capitalist agriculture in Western Europe.

In British Ceylon (Sri Lanka, captured from the Dutch during the Napoleonic Wars), Dutch Java, and German East Africa, indigenous people who could not produce formal, Western-style deeds or titles to their land lost it to the colonial power. In North Africa, the French government promoted the economic interests of French settlers, giving them the finest Algerian land. The government also ordered land owned collectively by Arabs to be sold as individual plots that only the French could afford to purchase. In Morocco and Tunisia, the French claimed "unexploited" land, such as that belonging to nomad peoples. In Algeria, the French government favored the Kabyles because their monogamous, sedentary, and mostly secular society with private property seemed to be more like republican France than did that of the nomadic Arabs. Above all, French colonial administrators sought to maintain order and collect taxes. One visitor found that "the head tax is above all a very effective agent of civilization," so that in one district "when a village could not or would not pay its taxes in full, the custom was to seize a child and place him in a village named 'Liberty' until the tax was paid." In some regions, taxes were collected through forced labor.

Portuguese colonists imposed conditions of virtual slavery in their African colonies in the nineteenth century. They kidnapped people from their colony of Angola, shipped them to the coastal island of São Tomé, and forced them to work on the cacao plantations for a "contract" period of five years, which few workers survived. In Angola, villagers who could not pay their taxes were required to work for the government for 100 days a year. Forced labor on mine and construction sites by colonial merchants and administrators alike was common; in the German Cameroons, about 80,000 Africans hauled goods for Germans on a single road in one year. Forced labor, which might be considered slavery in disguise, was widely practiced throughout most of the French colonies until 1946.

Colonial Administrations

European notions of the organization of states clashed with the way indigenous people lived. Almost all Africans lacked the European obsession with fixing exact boundaries, one that intensified in the age of nation-states and aggressive nationalism. For most Africans living in tribal societies, European notions of "boundaries" and "borders" established by colonial powers left many societies arbitrarily separated and sometimes interfered with the movements of migratory peoples. Colonial powers exploited tensions between peoples and tribes, purchasing the allegiance of temporary allies.

The British mastered the policy of "divide and rule," favoring and choosing officials from dominant ethnic groups to ensure cooperation. In India, the British effectively manipulated age-old tensions between Hindus, Muslims, and Sikhs to keep the Indian component of its army under control, ruthlessly repressing dissent.

How the European powers maintained control over colonies varied. Historians have distinguished between "formal" and "informal" imperialism, although the distinction is mainly one of degree, not kind. Britain, above all, took the path of informal imperialism by maintaining control through economic and military domination, without necessarily taking over political functions, as with indirect rule in India. But a "resident," or representative of Britain, retained ultimate authority. In formal imperialism, the European power assumed "protectorate" status over a territory, administering the colony directly.

The nature of a colonial "protectorate" changed during the scramble for Africa. Originally, the establishment of a protectorate meant that a colonial power defended its interests by controlling the foreign relations of a territory, leaving it to each ruler or chieftain to control his people. British colonial administration, headed by the Colonial Office in London with a relatively small staff, remained decentralized, like the home government itself. Colonial governors implemented policies. But gradually the colonial powers extended their authority over the local population through indigenous officials. In 1886, Britain assumed full sovereignty over most of its colonies. Local rulers found earlier agreements broken, and were increasingly treated as little more than intermediaries between the imperialists and their own people. Local systems of justice were left intact wherever possible—this, too, cost less money—but whites were subject only to the courts of the colonial power—a privilege called "extraterritoriality."

The British government wanted colonies to pay for themselves, with chartered commercial companies—which had launched British rule in Nigeria, Uganda, and what became Rhodesia—bearing the bulk of expenses in exchange for the right to extract profit. The British colonial administration directed railways and private capital toward regions where raw materials could be extracted or markets found. Imperial policy forced indigenous populations as well as colonists to produce revenues to pay for railroads, roads, and administrative officials.

The fate of the Ashanti kingdom in West Africa, which dated to the early eighteenth century, illustrates how informal control was transformed into more direct authority. In the early 1860s, British forces skirmished with the Ashanti people on the northern frontier of the Gold Coast, over which Britain had established a protectorate. After defeating the Ashanti in 1873–1874, Britain made the Gold Coast a crown colony, imposing more direct control. In 1891, the British proposed that the Ashanti kingdom itself become a protectorate. The king replied "my kingdom of Ashanti will never commit itself to any such policy; Ashanti must remain independent as of

British forces receiving supplies in 1874 during the Ashanti War, which led to the establishment of Ghana as a colony that same year.

old, at the same time to be friendly with all white men." Five years later, British troops occupied the Ashanti capital and deported the king when he could not come up with a huge sum in gold to buy continued independence. In a bloody sequel in 1900–1901, British troops crushed an uprising when the Ashanti refused to surrender the golden stool they treasured as the symbol of their people. In 1901, the Ashanti kingdom became a British colony.

African imperial ventures often began with the directors and principal shareholders of trading companies forging out territories from the underbrush and jungle. Following frenetic lobbying, the Royal Niger Company, with a charter from Parliament conveying administrative powers in 1886, began to develop what became Nigeria. To counter French moves in East Africa, the British government had authorized the Royal Niger Company to launch an expedition through the rain forests to reach Sudan. When German merchants, newcomers to Africa, began to establish trading posts to the east in the future Cameroons, the British government declared a protectorate over the Niger Delta.

The French government and the Royal Niger Company settled their respective claims through conventions. But when the Royal Niger Company went bankrupt in 1899, the British government took over administration of the territories. This scenario was common to the colonial experiences of France, the Netherlands, and Germany: merchant companies that had been granted state monopolies established trading interests in a new colony and then ran into financial difficulties, if not bankruptcy, necessitating the intervention of the imperial government itself.

Given the size of the British Empire, the number of colonial officials seems surprisingly small. Near the end of the nineteenth century, about 6,000 British civil servants governed India's 300 million inhabitants. The British colonial administration provided a career outlet for the sons of aristocrats, who became high-ranking administrators or officers in the navy and army. Eleven of the fourteen viceroys who served in India from 1858 to 1918 were peers by birth.

British officials recruited subordinates selectively from the colonial population, training, for example, upper-caste Indians to work in the administration of the subcontinent. In Nigeria, favored tribal chiefs assumed administrative functions. In the first decade of the twentieth century, at least partially in response to the first stirrings of Egyptian nationalism, the British government expanded the participation of Egyptians in running their country. In Malaya, the British "resident" was responsible for putting down disturbances that might threaten British control, while the local rulers were placed in paid administrative positions but had authority only in dealing with religious matters.

Many indigenous men who rose to positions of relative responsibility under the British managed to look and sound as much as possible like British gentlemen. But many Victorians disdained the Westernized Indian; they ridiculed the "babu," not because he seemed to be rejecting his own culture, but because they thought he could never be good enough to be British. At the same time, the British government often left intact the hierarchy of indigenous ruling elites, because this seemed more natural and made administrating the colonies easier.

French colonial rule differed from that of the British in ways that revealed contrasts between the British and French states. French colonial administration reflected the state centralization that had characterized France's development over the past century and more. Military control, more than commercial relations, formed the basis of its empire. The French colonial administration employed relatively more French officials and relied less on indigenous peoples than did its British rival.

The French colonial ministry then took a much greater role in economic decision making than its counterpart in the British Empire. The ministries of the navy and of commerce administered French colonies until the establishment of the colonial ministry in 1894. The French colonial civilian administration was staffed by bureaucrats, some trained at the Colonial School created in the 1880s. Africans and Vietnamese worked for the French governors-general as virtual civil servants. Like their British rivals, French colonial administrators also exploited pre-existing ethnic and cultural rivalries, using dominant groups to control their enemies. Thus, the French government used Vietnamese officials in key posts in Cambodia and Laos, and in Madagascar highland officials dominated the administration of their coastal rivals.

The French government directly ruled Algeria. Algerians could become French citizens, but with only limited rights. The sultan of Morocco and the bey of Tunisia still ruled their subjects, at least in name, although government and the exercise of justice remained in the hands of the French colonial administration. In Southeast Asia, the French government created the Union of Indochina between 1887 and 1893, which included Cochin, Tonkin, Annam, Cambodia, and Laos under a single governor-general, although France left pre-existing monarchies intact. The French government also centralized the administration of West Africa in 1895 by forming the federation of French West Africa, and in 1910 it established the federation of French Equatorial Africa, made up of its Central African colonies. Governors-general, based in Dakar and Brazzaville, served as the highest local administrative authority.

In the colonies, the British lived in isolation from the indigenous population. The upper class tried to replicate the world of the common rooms of Cambridge and Oxford Universities (more than a quarter of all graduates of Oxford's Balliol College at the turn of the century served in the empire) and of London gentlemen's clubs, served by Indian, African, or Asian waiters. British colonial women served only English recipes to their guests. In India, British "hill stations," which had begun as isolated sanitaria where the British could recuperate from tropical heat and illness, also provided commanding heights useful for surveillance. They became part of the imperial system, both as centers of power and closed British communities, "islands of white" that replicated the architecture and lifestyle of an English village. Indeed, in Kenya and Rhodesia, settler communities were organized around the sense of being "white" in unsettling and even dangerous surroundings; newcomers were discouraged from crossing racial lines because of the fear that such contact could undermine settler cohesion. In German African colonies, German women imagined themselves as cultural ambassadors, while colonial officials viewed them as representatives and even guarantors of German culture who would give birth and raise their children in the colonies as Germans.

Colonial urban architecture reflected the attempt to represent Western domination. In what became Vietnam in Indochina, the opera house built in Hanoi copied that in Paris. The French architects who planned the high Gothic vaulting of the cathedral in Saigon did not consider obvious differences in climate between France and Southeast Asia, providing insufficient ventilation. Outsized public buildings and long boulevards extended French authority in the form of architectural modernism into the daily life of French settlers and the local colonial population. In Madagascar, the medical school reflected design more appropriate to Lyon than a tropical island.

Yet one must also nuance the view that imperialists and indigenous peoples lived entirely in two different, necessarily antagonistic worlds. Some imperialists negotiated new cultural identities across East and West, for example by collecting (or accepting or extorting as gifts from princes or merchants) Hindu sculptures in India or various artifacts in Egypt, which to them represented the East. In doing so, they at least in some ways became part of two worlds. At the same time, Bengali patricians collected items that represented to them the European "other." Cross-cultural inter-action revealed more fluid boundaries between imperialists and the colo-nized, a process of negotiation, learning, and exchange. In acquiring objects that represented the colonized, imperialists helped transform their own identities. Some of what they collected, of course, now fills museums in London and Paris. Objects from the colonies became part of the material culture of imperialism, increasingly common in middle-class homes.

Assessing the Goals of European Imperialism

Someone once summed up the reasons for which the European powers expanded their horizons as "God, gold, and glory," or as the geographer, missionary, and explorer David Livingstone put it, "Christianity, Com-merce, and Civilization." Which, if any, can be singled out as the dominant impulse behind the "new imperialism"?

The "Civilizing Mission"

Most colonists insisted that God was on their side. Lord Curzon once gushed that the British Empire was "under Providence, the greatest instru-ment for good that the world has seen." A South African offered a more real-istic perspective when he commented, "When you came here we owned the land and you had the Bible; now we have the Bible and you own the land." The "civilizing" impulse still animated some European missionaries during the age of the "new imperialism." Thousands of Catholic and Protestant mis-sionaries went to Africa, India, and Asia in the name of God to win converts. In 1900, about 18,000 Protestant missionaries lived in colonial settlements around the world. French missionaries, both Catholic and Protestant, increasingly saw themselves as bringing the benefits of the French "civilizing mission" to indigenous people. Despite several decades of hostile relations with officials representing the secularized French Republic, French mission-aries gradually accommodated themselves to the imperial project their work helped sustain. Some British officials considered Anglican and Methodist missionaries to be nuisances. Most Dutch, Belgian, and Italian clergy made little pretense of bringing indigenous peoples "civilization," tending primar-ily to the spiritual needs of their troops and settlers.

One aspect of the "civilizing mission" continued to be the attempt of some reformers to limit or end abuses of indigenous peoples. In some places, the clergy helped force Europeans to end or at least temper abuses

Queen Victoria giving a Bible to a man wearing Central African garb.

carried out against local populations. Missionary societies may have been the "conscience" of European colonization, and a small conscience was better than none at all. For British reformers, the primary goal of the "civilizing mission" in the early part of the century had been to abolish slavery in the British Empire, which was achieved in 1833. In the 1880s, pressure from the British Liberal Party helped end the transport of Chinese laborers to work as indentured workers in South African mines. The British government was embarrassed by the treatment of Indian workers in Natal, a province of South Africa, which was brought to light by, among others, the young and future Indian leader Mohandas (Mahatma) Gandhi (1869–1948). French religious leaders launched a campaign against the remaining Arab slave trade in Africa. British officials protested the brutal labor practices of Portuguese and Belgian entrepreneurs. Yet the British government declined to press a campaign to reduce or eliminate the sale of arms and liquor to Africans, because both commodities were extremely lucrative to British merchants. Similarly, it had refused to stop the sale of Indian opium by British traders in China.

Lord Frederick Lugard (1858–1945), a British colonial official, came up with the term "Dual Mandate" to describe what he considered the "moral" and "material" imperatives of colonial powers. The European powers, he believed, had an obligation to "civilize" native populations and also to "open the door" to the material improvements brought by Western technology. They were establishing "trusteeships." In exchange, the Europeans would extract raw materials and other products. While imperialism became associated with conservative nationalism in Western Europe, a few socialists believed that empires could improve conditions of life for colonial peoples. In general, however, European socialists did not view the question of imperialism as one of their central concerns.

Earlier in the century, the French had seen their "civilizing" mission as the assimilation of colonial peoples into French culture: they would, it was commonly thought, become French. By the end of the century, however, the goal of assimilation had given way to a theory of "association," similar to Lugard's British Dual Mandate. This theory of association held that although colonial peoples were not capable of absorbing French culture, French colonialists would help them develop their economic resources, to the benefit of both. Only in urban settlements in Senegal in West Africa did newborn children automatically become French citizens; in 1914, Senegalese voters elected the first black representative to the French Chamber of Deputies.

The Economic Rationale

When missionaries arrived on the shores of Africa or Asia, they usually found that merchants and adventurers were already there looking for gold, ivory, and rubber. Indeed, Cecil Rhodes once stated that in the business of running colonies "philanthropy is good, but philanthropy at five percent is better." The discovery of new markets seemed absolutely necessary in the 1880s, particularly to British manufacturers, as one continental country after another adopted high protectionist tariffs. "If you were not such persistent protectionists, you would not find us so keen to annex territories," the British prime minister told France's ambassador to London in 1897. In the rather far-fetched opinion of Cecil Rhodes' brother, "The Waganda [of Uganda] are clamoring for shoes, stockings and opera glasses and are daily developing fresh wants," which would enrich British manufacturers and merchants peddling the products of the Second Industrial Revolution.

Writing in 1902 and influenced by the Boer War in South Africa, the radical British economist J. A. Hobson (1858–1940) called imperialism "the most powerful factor in the current politics of the Western world." He agreed that the great powers sought colonies because their economies required outlets for domestically produced manufactured goods and for capital investment. In Hobson's view, businessmen, particularly the finance sector based in London, virtually determined British imperial policy. Missionaries and soldiers helped them accomplish their goals. Hobson believed that the quest for colonies simply deferred the resolution of the central economic problem in Britain, because money that went into empire resulted in the underconsumption of industrial goods at home. If governments took action to raise wages and impose progressive taxation on wealth, a more equitable redistribution of wealth would allow ordinary people to purchase more goods. Imperialism would be unnecessary and China and other countries in Asia and Africa would be free to develop on their own. Hobson's views on imperialism anticipated critiques in our day of the economic and social consequences of globalization.

Hobson was not a Marxist, but his views in some ways echoed those of Karl Marx. In *Capital,* Marx, who never used the word imperialism, postulated that the bourgeoisie required "a constantly expanding market for its products." Subsequent Marxists therefore agreed with Hobson's linking of industrial capitalism and imperialism. Lenin, the Russian revolutionary leader, took Hobson's analysis a step further. He argued that the incessant expansion of capital inevitably brought with it colonial rivalries and war; in this final stage of capitalist development, "international trusts" would divide up the globe.

If Hobson, Rhodes, and Lenin had ever sat at the same dinner table, they would have disagreed about a good many things. But they would have agreed that there was a close connection between the great age of European imperialism and the quest for economic gain. The drive for colonies took on urgency in a period of mounting economic tariffs: there might not be, many thought, enough raw materials and markets to go around.

Merchant traders, like their seventeenth- and eighteenth-century predecessors, counted on finding rich mineral deposits and untapped markets in Africa and Asia. Gold and diamond discoveries in South Africa in the 1860s and again in the 1880s unleashed a stampede of prospectors and inspired colonists' dreams. Coastal traders generated further colonial expansion in West Africa. Trade in palm oil, used in large quantities for making soap and glycerin, replaced the slave trade.

Was the hope of economic gain the most significant factor in the frenetic European rush for colonies during the last decades of the nineteenth century? Did the colonial powers actually realize great wealth through their exploration and conquest?

To be sure, colonies provided some valued products for European markets. Ivory and rubber from Congo, palm oil from Nigeria, Dahomey, and the Ivory Coast, peanuts from French Senegal, diamonds and gold from South Africa, coffee from British Ceylon, and sugar from Malaya proved to be lucrative commodities. The rubber trade of French Indochina, Dutch Indonesia, the Congo, and British Malaya expanded rapidly with the popularity of the bicycle and particularly when automobiles took to the road. The British colonies of Nigeria and the Gold Coast produced 4 percent of the world's cocao in 1905 and 24 percent ten years later. The consumption of tea, most of it from China and Ceylon, increased by almost four times between 1840 and 1900.

Colonies provided an inviting market for manufactured goods from the mother country. Henry Stanley described the Congo not in terms of square kilometers but as "square yards of cotton to be exported." In the 1890s, about a third of all British exports and about a quarter of all investment went

Ivory from Africa became a valuable item on the European markets.

to its colonies, above all India, which imported cotton cloth and other textiles, iron, hardware, and shoes from Britain. Yet British capital investment abroad was still principally directed toward its lost colony, the United States, as well as toward other independent states such as Ottoman Turkey. British subjects also invested in the settlement colonies— Australia, New Zealand, and Canada, as well as India. The African colonies attracted very little British investment. There was more British trade with Belgium in the 1890s than with all of Africa.

Because colonial investments were risky, only a very small percentage of French and German investment was directed into their respective colonies. French investment abroad was overwhelmingly directed toward other parts of Europe, particularly Russia. Only about 5 percent of French investment reached its colonies in 1900; in 1914, France bought more goods from its colonies than it sold them in return. Less than 1 percent of German trade was with its colonies. By 1907, German investment in all German colonies fell slightly below the value of investments in a single large bank at home.

Imperial governments, which had to foot the bill for troops, supplies, guns, and administrative and other expenses, therefore became increasingly suspicious of the confident assurances of adventurers that incredible riches lay just a little farther up a barely explored African river or beyond the next oasis. In 1899, a French politician whose ardor for imperialism had waned defined the two stages of colonization as "the joy of conquest," followed inevitably, as after a fine restaurant meal, by "the arrival of the bill." The French colonial lobby, including provincial chambers of commerce in manufacturing cities and ports and geographic societies, pictured western Sudan as teeming with lucrative commercial opportunities. It turned out that this vast region of desert offered merchants little more than rubber, a little gold, some peanuts, and an occasional elephant tusk. The French government spent vast sums to administer and police an increasingly unwieldy empire. In the meantime, the exploitation of natural resources by the imperialists contributed to the economic and political underdevelopment of these regions once they became independent nations in the twentieth century.

Overall, however, the economic interpretation of the imperial race for colonies cannot be discounted. Key economic sectors did benefit substantially from raw materials and markets provided by the new colonies, as did individual businessmen. Nonetheless, an economic explanation for colonialism was only one factor—often a minor one—and is difficult to detach from a more dominant motivation.

Imperialism and Nationalism

The new imperialism was, above all, an extension of the search for security and power on the European continent in a period characterized by aggressive nationalism and bitter international rivalries. Even in the case of Great Britain, the imperialist power with the greatest economic investment in colonies, the international rivalry of the European powers was the strongest impulse for imperialism. Britain expanded its domination into new regions, not only in search of new markets, but to keep the French, Germans, or Russians from establishing bases and colonies that might threaten British interests. Britain's definition of its interests in Egypt, the pursuit of which helped launch the landgrab in Africa, had far more to do with fear of competition from its rivals than with economic motives.

Burma, absorbed by Britain after wars in 1824 and 1852 to protect India's eastern frontier against possible colonial rivals, is a case in point. When France declared its economic interest in Burma in the late 1870s, the British expanded their control over Upper Burma, fighting a third war with Burma in 1885. They packed off the reigning king to India, shipped his throne to a museum in Calcutta, turned his palace into a British club, and annexed Burma to the administration of India. Likewise, the establishment of a British protectorate over Afghanistan in 1880 can best be explained by a desire to place a buffer state between India and expanding Russian interests in the region. Britain's immediate goal in what contemporary diplomats called "the great game" between Britain and Russia in the Near East and Asia was to prevent Russian troops from occupying the high range of mountains in and adjacent to Afghanistan. Lord Curzon put the issues at stake for Britain succinctly: "Turkistan, Afghanistan, Transcaspia, Persia—to many these names breathe only a sense of utter remoteness. . . . To me, I confess, they are the pieces on a chessboard upon which is being played out a game for the domination of the world."

The nationalism that surged through all the European powers in the 1880s and 1890s fueled the "new imperialism." In 1876, when Britain opposed Russian moves toward the Turkish capital of Constantinople, a popular British song went: "We don't want to fight, / But, by Jingo, if we do, / We've got the men, / We've got the ships, / We've got the money too." The term "jingoism" came into use in English to mean fervent nationalism. Generations of British schoolchildren gawked at maps of the world that displayed colony after colony, however varied the structure and effectiveness of British control, colored red, the map color of Great Britain.

In Britain, the colonial experience became an important part of British national consciousness, pervasive in literature and in material culture. The same was true within each of the imperial powers. Newspapers, magazines, popular literature, and the publication of soldiers' diaries and letters carried home news from the colonies and made imperialism seem a romantic adventure. In 1880, the annual Naval and Military Tournament in London began to present reenactments of colonial skirmishes and battles. One play, *Siege of Delhi*, ended with an Irish officer falling in love and dancing a jig as the curtain falls on Indians about to be shot out of a cannon. In 1911, an Italian writer's enthusiasm for the feats of the Italian army in Libya included descriptions of the "lustrous" eyes of the Sicilian horses, which seemed, by their neighing, to be attempting to pronounce the word "Italy." A general's daughter exclaims in a novel about Egypt, "Let the peace-people croak as they please, it is war that brings out the truly heroic virtues."

From the drawing rooms of country estates to the wretched pubs of Liverpool and Birmingham, the British howled for revenge for the death of General Charles "Chinese" Gordon, killed in Sudan by the forces of the Mahdi in 1885. Few Europeans wept at the destruction of entire cultures and the deaths of hundreds of thousands of people at the hands of European armies. "Special artists" and then photographers began to travel with British colonial forces; movie cameras recorded Horatio Kitchener's 1899 campaign against the Boers in South Africa. At a time of rising political opposition in Great Britain to costly colonial commitments, the romanticization of British expeditionary forces helped win support for spending even more, and kept the Conservatives in power in 1900.

Voluntary associations pressured the colonial powers to devote more resources to the building of empire. In Great Britain, Germany, and France, geographic societies, associations that met periodically to listen to talks about exploration in Africa and Asia, sponsored voyages that charted unexplored—at least by Europeans—territories. In Germany and Britain, naval leagues whipped up enthusiasm for imperialism. The Pan-German League (founded in 1891) demanded more expenditures for warships. The champion of colonial lobbying groups, the Primrose League in Britain (founded in 1884), had 1.7 million members by 1906, drawn primarily from business, finance, the military, and government, the groups with the greatest stake in imperialism. The lengthy economic depression that gripped Europe between the mid-1870s and the mid-1890s, bringing low prices for commodities, accentuated such lobbying for aggressive imperialism.

To be sure, strident critics of imperialism could be found. In Britain, anti-imperialists were to be found among Liberal or Labour Party intellectuals, such as members of the "Ethical Union," formed in 1896. Like Hobson, who frequently addressed their meetings, they disparaged jingoism with passion. But with British victory in the Boer War, anti-imperialist voices grew fainter in Britain.

In France, anti-imperialists focused on the financial burden of expansion. A member of the Chamber of Deputies complained, "We are being drawn along in an irresistible process, like that of Time, by the mere force of a colonial expansionism which has got out of control." In the United States, the American Anti-Imperialist League joined together groups opposing the annexation of the Philippines as a territory. But everywhere the strident imperialist roar drowned out dissident voices. It contributed to the aggressive nationalism that fueled the increasingly bitter rivalries between the European great powers and further destabilized the continent.

CONCLUSION

In 1500, the European powers controlled about 7 percent of the globe's land; by 1800, they controlled 35 percent; in 1914, they controlled 84 percent. Between 1871 and 1900, the British Empire, which came to include one-quarter of the world's land mass and population, expanded to include 66 million people and 4.5 million square miles, the French Empire to 3.5 million square miles, and Germany, Belgium, and Italy to about 1 million square miles each. In Spain, with little left from its once mighty empire, the shock of losing the Philippines and Cuba to the United States in 1898 led to an intense period of introspection by intellectuals known as the "generation of 1898" who wanted to "regenerate" Spain. The Spanish government took new colonies in Morocco and the Western Sahara.

Aggressive nationalism shaped the contours of the new European imperialism from the early 1880s to 1914. Imperialism sharpened the rivalries of the great powers, while solidifying international alliances. Competing colonial interests brought France and Britain to the verge of war after the Fashoda Affair of 1898. Subsequent crises assumed even more dramatic dimensions. Infused with the same sense of struggle that seemed to engulf Europe, these crises would defy peaceful resolution.

PART SIX

CATACLYSM

The Great War began in August 1914. Germany and Austria-Hungary fought Great Britain, France, and Russia. Although most statesmen, military leaders, and ordinary soldiers and civilians believed that the war would be over quickly, it raged on for more than four years. A military stalemate, bogged down in grisly trench warfare on the western front, took the lives of millions of soldiers. In the war's wake, four empires fell. In 1917, a revolution overthrew the tsar of Russia, and then the Bolsheviks overthrew the provisional government, withdrew from the world conflict, and imposed Communist rule. The German Empire collapsed in November 1918 upon the victory of Britain, France, and their allies (including the United States since 1917). The multinational Austro-Hungarian and Turkish Ottoman Empires (which had joined Germany on the losing side) also collapsed.

The Versailles Peace Treaty, signed by the new German Republic in 1919, carved up the fallen empires, creating successor states in Central Europe—Poland, Czechoslovakia, and Yugoslavia. The treaties signed between the victors and the vanquished left a legacy of nationalist hatred in Europe that poisoned international relations during the subsequent two decades. Out of the economic, social, and political turmoil of the 1920s and 1930s emerged authoritarian movements that were swept to power in many European countries, beginning with Mussolini's Italian fascists in 1922. In Germany, Hitler's National Socialist Party—the Nazis—grew in strength with the advent of the Great Depression in 1929. The Nazis drew on extreme right-wing nationalism that viewed the Treaty of Versailles as an unfair humiliation to Germany. In the Soviet Union, Joseph Stalin became head of the Communist Party following Lenin's death in 1924; he purged rivals within the party, launched a campaign of rapid industrialization, forced millions of peasants into collective farms, and ordered the slaughter or imprisonment of those who resisted. Britain and France retained their parliamentary forms of government, despite economic, social, and political tensions.

In this Europe of extremes, the search for political stability after World War I proved elusive. After coming to power in 1933, Hitler rearmed Germany and disdainfully violated the Treaty of Versailles by reoccupying the Rhineland in 1936 and forging a union with Austria. The same year, Hitler and Mussolini supported a right-wing nationalist insurrection in Spain against the Spanish Republic. They sent planes, advisers, and war materiel to aid General Francisco Franco's military forces, which were victorious three years later. After Hitler's initial aggressive moves against Czechoslovakia were unopposed by Britain and France, the German dictator brazenly sent German troops to occupy all of Czechoslovakia in 1938.

Just weeks after shocking the world by signing a nonaggression pact with Stalin's Soviet Union, Hitler began his long-planned invasion of Poland, which quickly fell. And after a brief "phony war" of inaction in the West, in the spring of 1940 Hitler invaded France, the Netherlands, and Belgium. Japan's sudden attack on the U.S. military bases at Pearl Harbor, Hawaii, on December 7, 1941, brought the United States into World War II. Over 17 million people were killed in the fighting, and another 20 million civilians perished, including more than 6 million Jews systematically exterminated by the Nazis during the Holocaust. The war finally ended in 1945, after the defeat of Germany, Italy, and Japan. Europe and the entire world entered a new and potentially even more dangerous period, one in which nuclear arms made the threat of another world war even more horrible.

CHAPTER 22

THE GREAT WAR

"The lamps are going out all over Europe. They will not be lit again in our lifetime." So spoke Sir Edward Grey, the British foreign secretary, in early August 1914, as the Great War began. His last-ditch diplomatic efforts to prevent war having failed, Grey was one of the few to share an apocalyptic vision of a conflict that most people thought would be over by Christmas. Few observers anticipated that this war would be more destructive than any ever fought. International peace conferences held in The Hague in 1899 and 1907 had considered ways of reducing atrocities in war, but they failed to take into account that future wars might be different from those of the past. Not even Grey could have foreseen the 38.2 million casualties, the downfall of four empires, and the shifts in Europe's economic, social, cultural, and political life after the war that made the period before the war seem like "the good old days."

The Great War was the first large-scale international conflict since the Napoleonic era. It involved all the great powers, with Italy entering the war in 1915, albeit without much popular enthusiasm, and the United States entering in 1917. Before the war ended, it would also draw a host of minor states into the monstrous struggle. The catastrophic conflagration was set off by a spark—the assassination of Austro-Hungarian Archduke Francis Ferdinand in Sarajevo, the capital of Bosnia, on June 28, 1914, by a Serb nationalist. In little more than a month, war engulfed the powers of Europe through the decades-old system of entangling alliances that interwove their fates. And while these alliances did not make a general war in Europe inevitable—in fact, the situation in Europe seemed much more precarious in 1905 and 1911 than it did in 1914 before the assassination—most heads of state, diplomats, and military planners expected a major war in their lifetimes. Some were relieved, and others delighted, when it began. Few were surprised.

ENTANGLING ALLIANCES

Among the national rivalries in Europe, none seemed more irreparable than that between Germany and France. However, none was potentially as

LE NEZ DE LA TRIPLICE
imité du « Laocoon » antique

Cartoon satirizing the alliance between Germany, Austria-Hungary, and the Turkish Ottoman Empire (1896).

dangerous as that between Russia and Austria-Hungary, which was focused on the Balkans. It was accentuated by the presence within the Habsburg Empire of South Slav peoples who looked to Russia as the protector of all Slavs. In the meantime, Russia, with its long-standing goal of increasing its influence in the Balkans, fanned the flames of Pan-Slavism. Germany and Austria-Hungary became firm allies, with their alliance directed, above all, against Russia. In 1882, Italy joined the two Central European powers to form the Triple Alliance, which was revived in 1891 and 1902. By 1905, growing German and British economic and military rivalry helped drive together France and Britain, the oldest rivals in Europe. Russia, France, and Britain formed the Triple Entente. Entangling alliances left the great powers of Europe divided into two armed camps. Because of this alliance system, the outbreak of war between any two rivals threatened to bring all of the powers into the conflict.

Irreconcilable Hatreds

The German Empire, proclaimed at Versailles in the wake of the French defeat in the Franco-Prussian War of 1870–1871, had absorbed Alsace and most of Lorraine. The French never reconciled themselves to the loss of two of their wealthiest provinces. Although most Alsatians spoke a German dialect, Alsace had been an integral and strategically important part of France since the seventeenth century. Most people living in the parts of Lorraine annexed by Germany spoke and considered themselves French. The growing rivalry between France and Germany over colonial interests added to mutual mistrust.

Francis Joseph (1830–1916), the elderly emperor of Austria-Hungary, was a plodding man of integrity who had assumed the throne in 1848 and who had once told Theodore Roosevelt, the president of the United States, "You see in me the last monarch of the old school." Respected by his people, he remained a largely ceremonial figure identified with the survival of the polyglot Habsburg state in an age of nationalism. Francis Joseph bore a series of family tragedies with dignity: the execution in 1867 of his brother Maximilian in Mexico, where he was briefly emperor, his son's suicide in 1889, and his wife's madness, separation, and assassination. Throughout his reign, fifteen years longer than even that of Queen Victoria of England, the Habsburg emperor had been determined that the imperial army be strong and that his dynasty maintain international prestige.

(*Left*) An Alsatian woman learning to goose-step in a caricature from the German satirical review *Simplicimus*. (*Right*) The aging Emperor Francis Joseph of the Habsburg monarchy.

Irreconcilable hatreds existed in the Austro-Hungarian Empire, which was made up of a great many different nationalities. The Austrians and the Hungarians, who dominated the other nationalities of their territories (see Chapter 17), were satisfied, but other peoples were not. Thus Czechs, Slovaks, Poles, and others resented Austrian and Hungarian domination. And Romanians were unhappy with Hungary's vigorous campaign to "Magyarize" public life at the expense of non-Hungarian minorities.

The South Slavs were the most dissatisfied peoples within the Austro-Hungarian monarchy. The southern territories of Austria-Hungary included South Slav peoples—majorities in some regions—who resented subservience to the monarchy. These included Slovenes, Croats, and Serbs (see Map 17.3).

During the mid-nineteenth-century revolutions, the Russian army had bailed out the then-youthful Emperor Francis Joseph, invading Hungary in 1849 and defeating its rebellious army (see Chapter 16). But by the turn of the century, the Russian government was eagerly fanning Pan-Slav fervor in the Balkans, stirring ethnic tension in the southern regions of the Habsburg domains. In the mountainous Habsburg Balkan territories of Bosnia and Herzegovina, which included Orthodox Serbs, Muslims, and Catholic Croats, many Serbs were committed to joining Bosnia to Serbia. The implication of Pan-Slav nationalism, that Slavs sharing a common culture ought also to share a common government, threatened the very existence of the Habsburg monarchy. The threat of Russian-oriented Pan-Slavism made Austria-Hungary even more dependent on Germany, as it contemplated the possibility of one day being drawn into a war against Russia.

For centuries Russia had coveted the strategically crucial Dardanelles strait, as well as the narrow Bosporus strait of Constantinople, controlled by the Turkish Ottoman Empire. Russian mastery over the straits that separate Europe and Asia would allow it to control entry to the Black Sea and afford it easy access to the Mediterranean. Russia's defeat in the Crimean War (1853–1856) by Britain, France, and the Ottoman Empire had only temporarily diminished Russian interest in the region. British policy in the Balkans had long been predicated on keeping the straits from Russian control.

The Alliance System

The alliance system of late-nineteenth-century Europe, then, hinged on German and French enmity, the competing interests of Austria-Hungary and Russia in the Balkans, and Germany's fear of being attacked from both east and west by Russia and France (see Map 22.1). Great Britain stood independent of any alliance until undertaking an Entente with France in 1904. Colonial rival of both Germany and France and the opponent of Russian expansion, Britain ultimately came to fear the expanding German navy more than French colonial competition or Russia.

MAP 22.1 EUROPE IN 1914   Highlighting Alsace and the part of Lorraine occupied by Germany before the outbreak of the Great War.

The foundation of nineteenth-century diplomacy lay in the assumption by each continental power that alliances with other great powers would protect it by forcing any nation considering war to face at least two hostile powers. Bismarck captured the urgency the European great powers felt about the necessity of alliances, and the delicate nature of the balance of power itself: "All [international] politics reduces itself to this formula: Try to be *à trois* (three) as long as the world is governed by the unstable equilibrium of five great powers"—Germany, Austria-Hungary, Russia, Britain, and France.

The diplomats of the great powers were the heirs of Klemens von Metternich, the Austrian leader who dominated international relations in the three decades following Napoleon's defeat in 1815. Many of them were conservative nobles determined, at least in Germany, Austria-Hungary, and Russia, to hold the line against forces of democratization in their own states. War to some extent became an instrument of domestic politics. Diplomats believed that the great powers ought to make decisions in the interest of the smaller ones. They embraced nationalism as a principle, but only when considering the rights of the great powers. If they allowed smaller powers some rights, they ascribed the non-European peoples (with the exception of the United States and Japan, the only non-European powers) none at all.

Germany and Austria-Hungary against Russia

Germany at first enjoyed good relations with Russia, another autocratic power. In 1873, Bismarck forged the Three Emperors' League, an alliance between Germany, Austria-Hungary, and Russia; by the alliance, the three rulers pledged to consult each other in order to maintain the peace "against all disturbances from whatever side they might come." But it was difficult to gloss over tensions between Austro-Hungarian and Russian interests in the Balkans. When Russia sought and found occasions to extend its influence in that region, Austria-Hungary reacted with concern. In 1875, a revolt against Turkish rule had broken out in the Balkan provinces of Bosnia and Herzegovina. Following Russian intervention against and victory over Turkey in the bloody Russo-Turkish War (1877–1878), the Congress of Berlin in 1878 left Bulgaria nominally under the authority of the Ottoman Empire but also subject to Russian influence. The Austro-Hungarian government would henceforth administer Bosnia and Herzegovina, although they would remain within the Ottoman Empire. But this had the effect of potentially antagonizing Russia, because both territories had populations of Serbs, who looked to Russia for leadership. Moreover, in part because Britain and Austria-Hungary feared that Bulgaria might serve Russian interests, the Congress of Berlin recognized the creation of the independent states of Serbia and Romania (consisting of Walachia and Moldavia) as buffers against further Russian ambitions in the Balkans. Montenegro also gained independence, and the Ottoman Empire ceded the Mediterranean island of Cyprus to British occupation. The Ottoman Empire not only lost considerable territory in the Balkans (including much of the empire's Christian population) but now faced two new small but hostile states. Moreover, hundreds of thousands of Muslim refugees fled Serbia, Bulgaria, and Bosnia and Herzegovina, pouring into the diminished Ottoman territories. By 1879, about half of the 1.5 million Muslims who had lived in Bulgaria were no longer there; 200,000 had died, and the others had taken refuge in Turkey.

In 1879, fearing Russian expansionism, Bismarck forged the Dual Alliance, the cornerstone alliance between Germany and Austria-Hungary, predicated on German support for Habsburg opposition to an expansion of Russian interests in the Balkans. Although the details of the alliance remained secret, its general outlines were well known. The alliance became one of the central factors of European diplomacy for the next thirty-five years. When Italy allied with Germany and Austria-Hungary in 1882, the Triple Alliance was formed. Italy was not a great power, but it wanted to be one. The Italian government also wanted support for its aggressive imperial ambitions, which were directed toward the Mediterranean region, particularly North Africa. There France stood in the way, having occupied Tunisia in 1881 before the Italians could get there (see Chapter 21), and Italy now sought support against France.

Germany's alliance with Austria-Hungary made the Three Emperors' League virtually meaningless. Germany and Austria-Hungary each agreed to come to the aid of the other in the event of a Russian attack. Bismarck had intended Germany's alliance with Austria-Hungary to force Russia to seek better relations with Germany. But it had the effect of driving Russia further away. Moreover, Austria-Hungary's alliance with Germany had the potential to make instability in the Balkans a threat to European peace by putting Russia at odds not only with Austria-Hungary, but with Germany as well.

In a caricature of the alliance system, Otto von Bismarck is depicted as a puppet-master controlling the emperors of Russia, Austria-Hungary, and Germany.

Germany Encircled: Russia and France Ally

The last thing Bismarck wanted was for his alliance with Austria-Hungary to drive Russia and France together. Such an eventuality might one day leave

Germany confronting the necessity of fighting a war on two fronts, Bismarck's nightmare. In 1881, he resurrected the Three Emperors' League, which again allied the tsar of Russia with the emperors of Germany and Austria-Hungary. Despite considerable points of tension with the Habsburg monarchy, the Russian government entered this alliance as a hedge against Austro-Hungarian expansion in the Balkans toward the straits of Constantinople. The result was that Bismarck's resourceful diplomacy left Germany allied, in one way or another, with all of its potential enemies except France. As on the eve of the Franco-Prussian War of 1870–1871, France stood without allies.

Yet several factors seemed to draw Russia and France together, despite great differences in their political systems. Both France and Russia stood outside the Triple Alliance, which joined the powers of Central Europe with Italy. Russia, too, faced diplomatic isolation, despite the Three Emperors' League, because its Balkan interests clashed with those of Austria-Hungary. Russia hoped that an alliance with France would limit German support for the ambitions of the Habsburgs in southeastern Europe. Cultural ties between the Russian aristocracy and France remained strong; many Russian nobles still preferred to speak French.

French investment in Russia increased dramatically in the late 1880s and early 1890s. French bankers seized the opportunity to provide capital at attractive interest rates for Russian railway and mining development, and French investors enthusiastically purchased Russian bonds. By 1914, about one-fourth of all French foreign investment was in Russia. In contrast, Bismarck and his successors made it a policy to discourage and even to forbid German loans to Russia, although they invested in the Austro-Hungarian and Ottoman Empires. German private investors usually lacked the capital to undertake such loans. At the same time, German and French financial cooperation was extremely limited. French and German capitalists saw each other as rivals.

Franco-Russian ties were further solidified by Tsar Alexander III's visit to Paris during the Exposition of 1889. Yet the French left was outraged by government overtures to the autocratic and often brutal tsarist regime. For their part, Russian Tsar Alexander III and his successor Nicholas II were uncomfortable with close ties to a republic.

As the Russian government blamed Austria-Hungary for opposing what they considered its natural influence in the Balkans, the Three Emperors' League lapsed. In 1887, Germany and Russia signed a Reinsurance Treaty, by which each pledged to remain neutral if the other went to war, but it did not cover the most likely contingency of all—war between Russia and Austria-Hungary—because Germany was already committed to aid Austria-Hungary if Russian forces attacked. The young, headstrong Kaiser William II dismissed Bismarck as chancellor in 1890. Bismarck's successors were increasingly anti-Russian and failed to prevent Russia's alliance with France.

In 1892, Russia and France signed a military treaty by which each pledged a military response if the other were attacked by Germany or by one or more of its allies. A secret formal alliance followed in 1894. The alliance was essentially defensive in nature: the French no more encouraged Russian moves in the direction of the Balkans than the Russians wanted to see France embark on a war of revenge to recapture Alsace-Lorraine from Germany. But the Dual Alliance, as it was called, countered the Triple Alliance. It defeated the most essential thrust of Bismarck's foreign policy by ending France's diplomatic isolation.

Anglo-German Rivalry

During the 1890s, the possibility of Britain joining the Dual Alliance of France and Russia seemed remote. Whereas Germany and Britain had some competing colonial interests—for example, in Africa—the interests of France and Britain clashed in West Africa and Indochina, and France was jealous of British influence in Egypt. When a French force encountered a British army unit in 1898 on the upper Nile at Fashoda, war between the two seemed a distinct possibility (see Chapter 21) before the French government backed down. Furthermore, Afghanistan, lying strategically between British India and Russia, was a particular point of tension between those two powers.

The British government had long made it clear that it sought no alliance with anyone and that it would stand alone, its empire protected by the great British navy. But the British government signed the Entente Cordiale ("Friendly Agreement") with France in 1904. Britain did so for several reasons. The hostile reaction from every power in Europe to the Boer War (1899–1902; see Chapter 21) fought by British troops in South Africa demonstrated that it was one thing to stand in proud isolation from the continent, but another to have no friends at all. Furthermore, Britain's relations with Germany soured markedly. Germany's pointed criticism of Britain's war with the Boers strained relations between the two powers. In 1895, Kaiser William II, in his inimitably clumsy way, had sent a telegram congratulating the president of the Boer Republic of Transvaal in southern Africa on the Boers' successful stand against a British attacking force. This unleashed a storm of nationalistic fury in Britain and Germany.

Neither Anglo-German cooperation in the suppression of the Boxer Rebellion in China in 1900, nor a joint operation to force Venezuela to pay some of its foreign debts in 1902, significantly improved Anglo-German relations. Gradually, the British began to realize the growing extent of German influence in the Turkish Ottoman Empire. British military planners feared that Germany might be able to move troops more quickly overland into the Middle East than the Royal Navy could by ship.

German economic growth and the doubling of its foreign trade during the last three decades of the nineteenth century had begun to make some in Britain anxious, although Britain still accounted for about 45 percent of world investment. It also inspired a campaign to establish an empire-wide tariff barrier that would encourage trade within the British Commonwealth, while keeping foreign goods out.

Above all, it was the Anglo-German naval rivalry that pushed Britain toward a rapprochement with France. German military spending had already quadrupled between 1874 and 1890 (in a period of little inflation). In 1897 the Reichstag allocated funds for the accelerated expansion of the German navy over six years. William II's uncontrolled enthusiasm provided no small degree of impetus—the vain kaiser loved breaking bottles over the bows of brand new ships of war. Admiral Alfred von Tirpitz (1849–1930) belligerently cited the strength of the British navy as the *raison d'être* for the passage of the bill to build up the German navy. The nationalistic Pan-German League and the Naval League whipped up popular enthusiasm for the navy. The new German fleet began to include some of the biggest, fastest, and widest-ranging warships ever built.

Britain reacted quickly when confronted with the sudden and almost unexpected naval competition. In 1906, the fastest and most powerful battleship in the world, the *Dreadnought,* took to the sea. Germany began to build comparable ships of war, and wild British estimates had the Germans turning out even more, leading to a brief panic in 1909 that a German invasion of Britain was near.

British-French Rapprochement

The British government took a hesitant step toward ending its diplomatic isolation by signing a treaty in 1901 with the United States, which permitted the latter to construct the Panama Canal. By undertaking an alliance with Japan in 1902, Britain sought to counter Russian ambitions in East Asia. The Russo-Japanese War of 1904–1905 helped push Britain toward France (see Chapter 18). The Russian Baltic fleet, embarking on a disastrous voyage around the world to confront the Japanese navy in the Yellow Sea, sank several British fishing trawlers in the North Sea, somehow mistaking them for Japanese ships. Germany expected that France would immediately support Russia, with whom it was allied. Yet, to almost everyone's surprise, French Foreign Minister Théophile Delcassé (1852–1923) helped mediate between Russia and Britain. Russia's defeat in East Asia confirmed that Britain had far more to fear from Germany than from Russia.

The Entente Cordiale reached between Britain and France in 1904 had the immediate goal of eliminating points of tension between the two powers: Britain recognized French interests in Morocco in exchange for the French recognition of British control over Egypt; both sides accepted the existence of neutral Siam in Indochina standing between French Indochina and British-controlled Burma; and they settled a centuries-old dispute over fishing rights off the coast of Newfoundland.

The First Moroccan Crisis (1905)

The First Moroccan Crisis solidified the rapprochement between Britain and France, while highlighting the role of imperial rivalries in international politics. Germany had only modest commercial interests in Morocco, but German Chancellor Bernhard von Bülow (1849–1929) convinced William II to test the recently concluded Anglo-French agreement and perhaps force the British government to leave France to its own devices while casting Germany as defender of Moroccan sovereignty. In March 1905, the German kaiser arrived in Tangier aboard a yacht. William II demanded that Germany receive from Morocco the same commercial benefits as any other trading partner.

The French government reacted with fury, but backed down when British support for war seemed highly unlikely. Germany also pulled away from possible conflict, seeing that only Austria-Hungary took its side. The crisis ended with an international conference in the Spanish town of Algeciras in January 1906. Germany recognized the primacy of French interests in Morocco. This left the German government determined that another humiliation must not be suffered. The incident also seemed to confirm the bellicose and bullying nature of German foreign policy to both France and Britain. Anti-German feeling intensified in France among political moderates as well as those on the nationalist right. French and British generals and admirals began to draw up joint contingency plans for combined warfare against Germany.

The Algeciras Conference, and particularly the policies of Russian Foreign Minister Alexander Izvolsky (1856–1919), also brought Russia and Britain closer together. For Izvolsky, Russian interests were in the Balkans, where they competed with those of Austria-Hungary, not in Asia, where British interests lay. Set on the road to recovery from the disastrous Russo-Japanese War by British loans, the Russian government was now eager for better relations with Britain. The British government had long viewed Russian economic influence in Persia (Iran) and Afghanistan as threatening to its interests because a strong Russian presence in Persia might one day compromise the sea route to East Asia, and because Afghanistan served as a buffer between Russia and British India. In 1907, taking

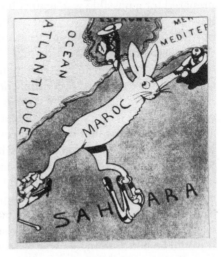

France and Germany quarrel over Morocco (1905).

advantage of the collapse of the shah's authority, the two powers divided Persia (Iran) into three zones—a Russian zone, a British zone, and a neutral zone—and agreed to respect each other's zone of influence. The Russians accepted British influence in Afghanistan, and both powers agreed to stay out of Tibet. Russia hoped that Britain might support, or at least tolerate, its interests in the Balkans, and its ultimate desire of controlling Constantinople. The elimination of some of the tensions between Britain and Russia strengthened the Franco-British Entente Cordiale.

THE EUROPE OF TWO ARMED CAMPS, 1905–1914

The inclusion of Russia in what was increasingly known as the Triple Entente moved Europe toward a clear division into two camps. Cordial relations, however, continued between Tsar Nicholas II and his cousin, German Kaiser William II. The German emperor was also the grandson of Queen Victoria of England—a standing joke in Berlin went that William feared no one except God and his English grandmother. But in the Europe of entangling alliances, blood relations were subordinate to the logic of great-power interests and alliances.

The German government could find little reassurance in Italy's nominal alliance with Germany and Austria-Hungary. Improved relations between Italy and France confronted Germany with the prospect that Austria-Hungary would be its only dependable ally.

Should Austria-Hungary cease to be a power or, in the worst-case scenario, completely collapse because of national movements from within, Germany might be left alone, encircled by enemies. The German high command prepared for a possible war against both France and Russia, a war that would have to be fought on two fronts. This left the German government in the position of having to support its troubled Habsburg ally unconditionally in the Balkans.

Moreover, the German government, like the other great powers, began to see military strength in a different way in 1904–1905. German military planners, concerned that Russia was rapidly reconstituting its army in the years following its humiliating defeat in the Russo-Japanese War of 1904–1905, continued to build their forces, as did Austria-Hungary. The powers increased ranks of soldiers and sailors, and almost frantically improved weapons, aided by technological advances in warfare, including artillery that could be fired more rapidly, machine guns, telephones, and even airplanes, at first intended essentially for reconnaissance. Moreover, the German government demonstrated that it was increasingly willing to use the threat of war as a tool of diplomacy. This new approach reflected a growing sense that it would be better to fight a war sooner rather than later, while Germany still had what appeared to be a favorable military balance of power. In the meantime, the public in every major power followed international politics with increasing care and were attentive to the capacity of their armed forces. Thus, perceptions of the balance of military power came into play in the international crises that led to war in 1914.

The Balkan Tinderbox

The Balkans increasingly became the key to maintaining peace in Europe (see Map 22.2). In 1897, Russia and Austria-Hungary had agreed informally to respect the *status quo* in the region. However, cultural and political nationalism continued to grow among the South Slavs living within the Austro-Hungarian Empire, in Serbia, or under Ottoman rule. In the Balkans, the vast majority of peoples had remained indifferent or ignorant of nationalist identities until at least the beginning of the twentieth century. Religious identities—Greek, Russian, or Bulgarian Orthodox, Muslim, Catholic, or Jewish—had always defined a sense of community, along with regional and village identities. Then, encouraged by the new states carved out of what had been Ottoman territory, national identities began to take hold. This made southeastern Europe ever more the focus of the rivalry between Austria-Hungary and Russia.

When a bloody revolution led to the assassination of the king and queen of Serbia in 1903, Russia quickly recognized the new king, Peter, hoping that Pan-Slav elements would dominate. Fearing any delay would push Serbia closer to Russia, Austria-Hungary recognized the *fait accompli*. The Serb parliament voiced its unqualified support for Russian ambitions in East Asia and its disastrous 1904–1905 war against Japan. Serb nationalists began to call for union with Serbs in Macedonia, which was still part of the Ottoman Empire and was peopled by Macedonians, Serbs, Bulgarians, Sephardic Jews, and Greeks, who had largely gotten along in the past. As Greek and Bulgarian Orthodox churches battled for the allegiance of peasants, the strident, aggressive calls of various nationalist groups helped create a nationalism that had previously existed on only a superficial level among elites. Now Greek, Bulgarian, and Macedonian armed groups operated inside Macedonia, as did Bulgarian and Macedonian nationalists. Provocative addresses to minorities worsened ethnic tensions in the region. Religion became much more identified with emerging national identities.

Relations between Serbia and Austria-Hungary further deteriorated. When Serbia tried to lessen its economic dependence on Austria-Hungary (the destination of almost all Serb exports) by signing a commercial treaty with Bulgaria, Vienna responded by forbidding the importation of Serb livestock. Thus began an economic battle in 1906 that became known in much of Europe as the "Pig War," as the humble pig formed a basis of Serbia's fragile agricultural economy. The Serbs resourcefully found new markets for their pigs. The Habsburg government, despite the lack of Hungarian support for economic retaliation, responded in 1908 by announcing the construction of a new railroad that would further isolate Serbia economically. Serb

Map 22.2 The Balkans, 1914   The Austro-Hungarian Empire and the Balkan states, including territory acquired in the Balkan Wars of 1912–1913.

nationalists viewed Bosnia and Herzegovina as South Slav states that should, with Russian encouragement, become part of Serbia.

Instability in Turkey

Political instability in Turkey in the early 1870s had further whetted the appetites of both Russia and Austria-Hungary for the Balkans, amid financial crisis, poor harvests, and the opposition of religious conservatives to secularization. Following the Crimean War (see Chapter 18), Britain and France had condescendingly invited the sultan "to participate in the advantages of public law and the system of Europe," while insisting on further Western reforms. The Ottoman default on foreign loans in 1875 led six years later to the administration of the Ottoman public debt being placed under the control of European administrators. The Ottoman governor of Egypt was constrained to sell his shares of the Suez Canal to the British government for a quarter of their real value, leading Egypt to bankruptcy.

Turkish Sultan Abdülhamid II (ruled 1876–1909) agreed to a constitution upon his ascension to the throne in 1876, consolidating some of the reforms of the past several decades. The constitution established parliamentary rule and guaranteed personal freedom and equality before the law. The sultan hoped to discourage the powers from intervening in Ottoman affairs on the pretext of forcing political reform. But in 1878 he suspended the constitution and dissolved the parliament it had established. The secret police rooted out potential opposition. During Abdülhamid's rule, foreign trade increased, agriculture developed, railway lines and paved roads more than doubled, and public schools increased in number. But his reign was also marked by the brutal repression of non-Muslim peoples of the Ottoman Empire. About 200,000 Armenians (who made up about 6 percent of the empire's population) were slaughtered in 1894–1895 in eastern Anatolia in response to Turkish fears of Armenian nationalism, encouraged by Russia. Moreover, the empire continued to be beset by financial problems, above all, high-interest debt owed to foreign bondholders. Influenced by Western political ideas and reflecting the emergence of a generation of Turkish intellectuals, a group of nationalists in 1889 founded the Committee of Union and Progress, finding support in the bureaucracy and army. In July 1908, these "Young Turks," as they were called, revolted in the name of "order and progress" and forced the sultan to restore the constitution of 1876. One of their leaders was Mustafa Kemal (later known as Atatürk, 1881–1938). The Young Turks wanted to unify and modernize the Ottoman lands, while preventing Western intervention on behalf of the Armenians. Abdülhamid II was deposed in 1909 when he tried to plot a counter-revolution, and gradually a Western-like bureaucracy was put in place.

The Young Turks, 1908.

The chaos within the Ottoman Empire seemed to promise the realization of the Russian dream of opening the straits of Constantinople to Russian ships, and perhaps only Russian ships. The Austro-Hungarian government faced the possibility that lands still held by the Ottoman Empire might be added to Serbia and Romania, further destabilizing the Balkans. This pushed Russian and Austro-Hungarian relations toward a breaking point.

The Bosnian Crisis of 1908

Turkish instability led to the Bosnian Crisis of 1908. In 1878, the Congress of Berlin had authorized Austria-Hungary to occupy Bosnia and Herzegovina, although both territories technically were still part of the Ottoman Empire. Austria-Hungary had done so, at the risk of bringing more Slavs into the empire, not only to solidify its position in the Balkans but to prevent Serbia from absorbing them. The Russian government had been secretly negotiating with Austria-Hungary to trade Russian acceptance of the absorption of Bosnia and Herzegovina for Austria-Hungary's support for the opening of the Bosporus and the Dardanelles straits to the Russian fleet. In October 1908, a day after Bulgaria, nominally under Ottoman sovereignty, declared its independence, the Austro-Hungarian government suddenly announced that it would directly annex Bosnia and Herzegovina, fearing the influence of the Young Turks there. The annexation was a clear violation of the agreements reached at the Congress of Berlin in 1878. The Russians reacted with rage. Serbia, furious that two territories in which many South Slavs lived were to be incorporated into the Habsburg Empire, mobilized its army with Russian support. Austria-Hungary responded in kind. The annexation also considerably strained relations between Austria-Hungary and Italy, nominal allies, because of Italian strategic and economic interests on the Adriatic coast. Pressured by Germany, Turkey received financial compensation in exchange for accepting the *fait accompli*.

The resolute opposition to war by Hungarian leaders within Austria-Hungary, as well as the opposition of the heir to the Habsburg throne, Archduke Francis Ferdinand (1863–1914), helped defuse the crisis. Not only would war be expensive, victory might well add a considerable South Slav population (from Serbia) to Hungarian territories. Furthermore, despite diplomatic bluster, Russia was not ready to fight, and its ally France was unwilling to go to war over the Balkans, where it had no interests. Lacking French or British support, the Russian government backed down, forcing Serbia to recognize the Austro-Hungarian annexation of Bosnia and Herzegovina.

War had been avoided, but the European powers had drawn significant conclusions from the Bosnian Crisis. Italy remained allied with both Central European powers, but both Berlin and Vienna viewed Italy's commitment to the alliance as uncertain. Italy's problematic status as an ally thus further firmed up Germany's alliance with Austria-Hungary. German and Austro-Hungarian military commanders met to plan for hostilities with Russia,

France, Serbia, and possibly—given its announced interests in Tyrolean Austria and Dalmatia—Italy. The German government demanded that Russia recognize Austria-Hungary's annexation of Bosnia and Herzegovina. The Russian government, viewing itself as a victim of German bullying, now sought a closer relationship with Britain. With German shipyards rapidly producing the most modern and heavily armed fighting ships at a frightening pace, British officials quickly gave up their reservations about the Entente Cordiale with France.

The Bosnian Crisis left deep scars on Russian relations with Austria-Hungary. Serb relations with Vienna worsened. The Habsburg government presented poorly forged documents to support claims that Serb authorities were trying to stir up the Slav populations within the empire. However, in fact, several groups of devoted Serb nationalists, including "The People's Defense" and "The Black Hand," received tacit support from the Serb state, as well as Russian encouragement.

The Second Moroccan Crisis (1911)

Germany also provoked the Second Moroccan Crisis. France had established a virtual protectorate in Morocco, which violated the Algeciras agreements of 1906. Using a local rebellion against the new Moroccan sultan as an excuse, a French army marched on the town of Fez, allegedly to protect French settlers. When the French government did not offer to compensate Germany because France had added another protectorate to its empire, the German emperor sent a small gunboat, the *Panther,* to the port of Agadir. It arrived on July 1, 1911, with demands that Germany receive the French Congo as compensation for France's claiming Morocco as a protectorate. France refused, bolstered by its closer relations with Britain, Russia's increased stability, and a wave of nationalist sentiment at home. Even German moderates seemed angered at what appeared to be a British commitment to preventing Germany from finding its "place in the sun."

The Second Moroccan Crisis, like the first, passed without war. In November 1911, Germany agreed to recognize Morocco as a French protectorate in exchange for 100,000 square miles of the French Congo. But the crisis further solidified Europe's competing alliances. Britain and France now formalized the agreement by which each pledged to aid the other in case of an attack by Germany. In April 1912, the British and French admiralties established zones of responsibility for their fleets—the French in the Mediterranean and the British in the English Channel and the North Sea. The arms race intensified.

The Balkan Wars

The Bosnian Crisis of 1908 had demonstrated that events in the Balkans could carry Europe to war. In 1911, the Turkish Ottoman Empire provided the kindling for another international flare-up. Late in the year, Italy invaded Libya, part of the Ottoman Empire, in what became known as the Tripoli War, overcoming resistance in October 1912. France acquiesced to the Italian seizure of Libya in exchange for Italian recognition of Morocco's status as a French protectorate. Another piece of the Ottoman Empire had been swallowed up.

Serbia, Bulgaria, Montenegro, and Greece had formed the Balkan League with the intention of freeing the Balkans from Ottoman rule. Encouraged by the difficulty the Turkish army had in putting down an insurrection in Albania in 1910 and by the Turkish defeat in Libya, they declared war on Turkey in 1912. The First Balkan War lasted less than a month, with the Balkan League emerging victorious. However, the success of the Balkan states worried the Austro-Hungarian government. Russia and the Austro-Hungarian monarchy seemed on a collision course in the Balkans. Serbia, Bulgaria, and Greece each annexed Ottoman territory (for Greece, which increased its territory by 70 percent, this new territory included the prize port of Salonika). Only one small chunk of the once enormous Ottoman Empire now remained on the European side of the straits (see Map 22.2).

Yet Russia and Austria-Hungary had avoided war. New foreign ministers, Sergei Sazonov (1861–1927) of Russia and Leopold Berchtold (1863–1942) of Austria-Hungary, helped defuse the crisis. Austria-Hungary's goals were to see that no Balkan state became so strong that it could generate nationalist agitation within its territories, and to prevent Serbia, Russia's friend, from gaining a port on the Adriatic. In the interest of peace, Britain and France supported Austria-Hungary's call for the creation of the independent state of Albania on the Adriatic, which would prevent Serbia from having its port. The German government viewed these issues as sufficiently grave to warrant its unconditional support for Austria-Hungary. The Treaty of London of May 1913 divided up most of the remaining Ottoman holdings in southeastern Europe among the Balkan states.

However, Bulgaria felt aggrieved by the fact that Serbia and Greece had ended up with large parts of Macedonia and attacked both states. Serbia and Greece, with the assistance of Romania and the Turks, quickly defeated Bulgaria in 1913 in the Second Balkan War. With the Peace of Bucharest, Serbia received the parts of what had been Ottoman Macedonia, which Bulgaria was to have received; Greece gained more territory on the Aegean coast as well as Crete, where Greeks had risen up against Turkish rule on two previous occasions and which Greece tried to occupy in 1897 before being easily defeated by Ottoman forces. The small Muslim state of Albania came into existence. Serbia emerged from the Balkan Wars larger, stronger, more ambitious, and angry that Austria-Hungary had frustrated its quest for an Adriatic port. It also may have emerged with the impression that there were limits to Germany's support for Austria-Hungary, since the German government had at least appeared to restrain the Habsburg government's aggressive response to Serbia's demand for a port.

"The Vortex—Will the powers be drawn in?" This image of the Balkan Wars, 1912–1913, had a ring of prophetic accuracy.

South Slav nationalism gained more adherents in the Balkans. After backing down against Austria-Hungary for the second time (the first having been the Bosnian Crisis in 1908), Sazonov irresponsibly placated the Serbs by telling them that their promised land lay inside the frontiers of Hungary. Some Serb political leaders sympathized with the young fanatics of "The People's Will" and "The Black Hand" nationalist organizations. In 1910, a boy who had been taught to shoot a gun by a Serb officer attempted to use it on the Austrian governor of Bosnia; the youth committed suicide after failing, becoming a martyr in Serbia. A few Habsburg personages, possibly including the Archduke Francis Ferdinand, may have been willing to consider the South Slavs as partners in a tripartite empire—the mere suggestion of which infuriated almost all Magyars and most Austrians. But the Austro-Hungarian government considered the South Slav nationalists to be threats who would ultimately have to be crushed. Because of the Balkan situation, the German military command once again turned its attention to readying its army, reacting to Russian measures of military preparedness. But in 1914 Europe seemed far less close to war than it had been in 1905 and 1911, the years of the two Moroccan Crises.

THE FINAL CRISIS

The powers of Europe were poised for conflict, divided into two armed camps by two rival alliances. While the outbreak of war was probably not inevitable—although many nationalists and military planners believed it to be—it was likely. Furthermore, once two powers seemed on the verge of war, the entangling alliances that pitted the Triple Alliance against the Triple Entente seemed likely to bring all of the European powers into the conflict. The crisis that precipitated World War I occurred in the Balkans, when Serb nationalists assassinated the Archduke Francis Ferdinand of Austria. Europe's diplomatic house of cards collapsed and the Great War began.

Assassination in Sarajevo

Archduke Francis Ferdinand was heir to the Habsburg throne. His first love was his commoner wife, Sophie; his second, hunting—he bragged of having killed 6,000 stags in his lifetime and of having bagged 2,763 seagulls on a single day. The archduke was not considered particularly pro-German, and probably had more sympathy for the problems of the South Slavs than any member of the royal family. Hungarians disliked him, fearing that when he came to the throne, he might eventually grant the South Slavs the same status as the Austrians and Hungarians. But many Serb nationalists would accept nothing less than an expanded independent Slavic state, or what they called Greater Serbia.

On June 28, 1914, Francis Ferdinand and his wife were on an inspection tour of the army in Sarajevo, the capital of Bosnia. As the archduke's motorcade approached the center of the city, a small bomb exploded under the archduke's car. The motorcade continued to the town hall, where the archduke expressed his indignation at the attempt on his life. When the motorcade departed, the drivers had not been informed of a change in route chosen to avoid the tangle of streets in central Sarajevo. When the first several vehicles began to turn into a narrow street, the military governor ran ahead, ordering their drivers to back up. Gavrilo Princip (1895–1918), a young member of the Black Hand Serb nationalist group, saw his chance, as

On an inspection tour of the army in Sarajevo, capital of Bosnia, Archduke Francis Ferdinand and his wife bathe in a warm welcome. They were assassinated a few hours later.

he happened to be only a few feet from the archduke's car. He opened fire, killing Francis Ferdinand and his wife.

Although the Serb government had been aware of the Black Hand nationalist organization and some individual officials had supported it, the Austrian description of the youthful killers as puppets whose strings were pulled in Belgrade was incorrect. Nonetheless, Serb newspapers virtually celebrated the death of the Habsburg heir. In Vienna, even those who had disliked the archduke for having married a commoner now mourned the couple fervently.

The Ultimatum

Within the Habsburg imperial administration, many officials immediately took the view that the chance to crush Serbia had arrived, and that, unlike 1908 and 1912, this time the opportunity would not be missed. The usually indecisive Austrian foreign minister, Leopold Berchtold, who had opposed war during the Balkan Crisis of 1912, now took a hard line.

From Berlin, William II urged retaliation, blaming Serbia for the assassination. German Chancellor Theobald von Bethmann-Hollweg (1856–1921) stubbornly held the view that Germany's strength must be paramount. ("Necessity knows no law," he once said.) Bethmann-Hollweg was now determined to stay the course with a numbing fatalism undoubtedly accentuated by the recent death of his wife. He advised his son not to plant his estate with trees that would take a long time to grow, because they would please only the Russians, whom by then he expected to have occupied northeastern Germany. He expected a war and wanted Russia to appear the aggressor. In Berlin, the German government gave an Austrian official a "blank check" to act with knowledge of full German support, that Germany would, if necessary, fight both France and Russia if those two powers intervened once Austria had declared war on Serbia. In this case, Bethmann-Hollweg expected Britain to remain neutral.

But for the moment, Austria-Hungary waited. Berchtold convinced the Hungarian leaders to support war against Serbia, promising that no Slavs from territories taken from defeated Serbia would be incorporated into Austria-Hungary. The Hungarian Social Democrats ended their opposition to the war. On July 21, 1914, Russian Foreign Minister Sazonov, encouraged by Maurice Paléologue, the French ambassador, warned Austria-Hungary against taking any military measures against Serbia.

On July 23, 1914, almost a month after the assassination, the Austrian ambassador in Belgrade presented a lengthy ultimatum to Serb officials. It denounced what it claimed was Serb activity aiming to "detach part of the territories of Austria-Hungary from the Monarchy." Austro-Hungarian demands included the end of all anti-Habsburg publications, the dissolution of all Serb nationalist organizations, and a purge of officials and army officers to be named by Austria-Hungary. The Serb reply was expected within forty-eight hours. Grey, the British foreign secretary, called the ultimatum "the most formidable document ever presented by one independent state to another."

The Serb government was in a no-win situation. Serbia's small army was no match for that of Austria-Hungary. Its options were either to capitulate completely to the ultimatum and suffer a humiliating diplomatic defeat, or, as one official put it, to die fighting. This made Serbia almost totally dependent upon Russian intervention.

The ultimatum sent shock waves through the capitals of Europe. Upon learning its contents, Sazonov exclaimed, "It's the European War!" He blamed Germany, claiming that the ultimatum was part of a German plan to keep Russia from reaching Constantinople. Some of Tsar Nicholas II's advisers saw war as a means of rallying the support of the Russian Empire behind the tsar. Yet others remembered Russia's disastrous defeat in the Russo-Japanese War, which had contributed to the outbreak of the Revolution of 1905 (see Chapter 18). Sazonov's first concern was to mobilize French support against Austria-Hungary, believing that a united show of strength would force the Central European allies to back down. From the Russian point of view, if Austro-Hungarian influence expanded in the Balkans, German influence would soon be manifest in the straits, because a coup in Turkey in 1913 had brought the Ottoman Empire even closer to Germany. French President Raymond Poincaré's state visit to Saint Petersburg from July 20 to July 23 seemed to indicate that France would stand by Russia, and Sazonov received quick assurance from the French ambassador of full French support.

On July 25, 1914, two days after the Austro-Hungarian ultimatum, the tsar placed the Russian army on alert, a stage that would normally precede mobilization. Such a step was fraught with consequences for the military planners of each power. Mobilization meant preparing an army for war, calling up reserves, declaring martial law in frontier areas, readying the railways for hauling troops and supplies, and accelerating the production of munitions. In these circumstances, a Russian decision to mobilize would be tantamount to an act of war in the eyes of German military planners.

The Schlieffen Plan

Germany's plan for war against France had been drawn up in 1905 by Count Alfred von Schlieffen (1833–1913), a former chief of the German general staff. Based on the assumption that it would take Russia, France's ally, several weeks to prepare its armies to fight, the Schlieffen Plan called for the German armies to use a lightning attack to knock the French out of the war. Then the German forces would be able to confront the Russian army attacking in the east. The German attack on France would require its forces to violate Belgian neutrality in order to bypass the sturdy fortifications the French had constructed on their eastern frontier after the

Franco-Prussian War of 1870–1871. German troops would march through the flat terrain of Belgium and the Netherlands, and turn south once the last soldier on the northern flank had brushed his sleeve against the English Channel. A pincer movement southward would encircle Paris from the northwest, and then turn to trap the French armies that had moved into Alsace-Lorraine. France would surrender. Schlieffen and his successors recognized that the plan would probably bring Great Britain into the war because that nation would never accept the violation of Belgian neutrality and the possible presence of an enemy power just across the Channel. But German commanders believed that the war on the continent would be over before the superior British navy could make a difference and that the small, volunteer British army posed little immediate threat. Then there would still be time to ship enough of the victorious army to the east to defeat the Russians as they rolled slowly toward Germany. This was the solution to Bismarck's nightmare, a simultaneous war on two fronts.

The French high command had its own plan for war. "Plan XVII" called for a rapid attack by two French armies into Alsace-Lorraine, as the Germans expected. With the bulk of the German army tied up by French and British troops in Belgium, and, at worst, northern France, the way to Berlin would be open. The French army was itching to redeem itself. Unlike Germany, which had to contemplate fighting a war on two fronts, the French army enjoyed the advantage of being able to focus its full attention on Germany. Marshal Joseph Joffre (1852–1931) had overseen French plans for the war. (When asked in 1911 if he thought about war, he replied, "Yes, I think about it all the time. We shall have a war, I will make it, and I will win it.") To the French high command, *élan,* or patriotic energy, was expected to bring victory: "The French army . . . no longer knows any other law than the offense," announced one of Joffre's disciples; "[we need only] to charge the enemy to destroy him." The French plan counted on the Russian army attacking Germany from the east by the sixteenth day of mobilization.

The British government suggested that, following Russian mobilization, the other powers help arrange a peaceful solution. Britain was unwilling to back Russia, a move that at this point might have made both Austria-Hungary and Germany consider backing down. The German government still assumed that the British would remain neutral in a war between France and Russia against Germany and Austria-Hungary.

The Russian government continued to believe that its resolute support for Serbia might well be enough to force Austria-Hungary to reconsider. Austria-Hungary and Germany were laboring under the same kind of illusion about Russia. Both believed that a show of unconditional support—Germany's "blank check" to Austria-Hungary—would force Russia to pull back. Yet Germany's aggressive support for its ally, combined with the bellicose prodding of the Russian government by the French ambassador, had just the opposite effect.

The Serb government therefore ordered military mobilization on July 25, 1914, confident of full Russian support. It then presented a formal reply to the Austro-Hungarian ultimatum just before the forty-eight hours had elapsed. It was surprisingly conciliatory. The Serbs accepted five of the demands without reservation; four others they would accept pending discussion and some further explanation. They rejected only one outright—that Austro-Hungarian representatives collaborate in the investigation of the Serb "plot" against the Habsburg Empire.

The Austro-Hungarian government viewed anything less than total compliance as unsatisfactory. It ordered military mobilization against Serbia, but stopped short of declaring war. The British again proposed a meeting of the powers in the hope of avoiding conflict in the Balkans, or at least keeping it limited to the Balkans. This the German government rejected, believing that Britain would not go to war unless it appeared that Germany was intending to conquer and absorb France.

"A Jolly Little War"

Austria-Hungary declared war on Serbia on July 28, 1914, exactly one month after the archduke's assassination. The declaration claimed an unsatisfactory Serb response to the Austro-Hungarian ultimatum, as well as an attack on Austro-Hungarian troops along the Bosnian frontier, an event that never took place. In a final attempt to avert war, British Foreign Secretary Edward Grey asked if Germany would participate in a last-ditch attempt to negotiate a settlement to the crisis. Germany accepted, but at the same time did nothing to try to forestall an Austro-Hungarian invasion of Serbia. If anything, Bethmann-Hollweg egged his ally on. In Saint Petersburg, the Austro-Hungarian declaration of war generated popular support for Serbia. An American diplomat reported tersely, "Whole country, all classes, unanimous for war."

On July 28, the same day as the Austro-Hungarian declaration of war, Bethmann-Hollweg sent a telegram to Vienna suggesting that its ally find a way to make it appear that, if a European war followed, it would be Russia's fault. And finally he warned that if Russia continued to support Serbia, Austria must stay the course, even if it led to war, or else forever renounce its status as a great power.

By the time the British cabinet discussed the Serb crisis on July 24, it was clear that Germany would not restrain Austria-Hungary. The Liberals, who had come to power in 1905, had long opposed entangling international alliances and large military expenditures, and they were divided over British intervention. Many Liberals and most Labourites disliked the idea of fighting alongside tsarist Russia. The government was beset by a number of pressing political issues, including the Home Rule Bill for Ireland—on July 16, British troops had fired on rioters in Dublin. The Royal Navy was placed on alert.

Bethmann-Hollweg now sent a sealed envelope to the German ambassador in Brussels, which was to be presented to the Belgian government when the order came. It contained a demand that German troops be allowed to march through Belgium. But, for the moment, there still seemed to be hope. William II sent a telegram to the tsar expressing his desire for peace. He signed it, "your very sincere and devoted friend and cousin, Willy."

Russian ministers and generals had debated since July 28 whether the crisis called for a limited mobilization of a million soldiers on the Polish and Galician frontiers, or a full mobilization. On July 29, word reached Saint Petersburg that the Austrians had bombarded Belgrade from the Danube. After twice changing his mind, Nicholas II ordered a full mobilization on July 30 for the following day. The tsar's diary entry for that day read: "After lunch, I received Sazonov. . . . I went for a walk by myself. The weather was hot. . . . I had a delightful bath in the sea." The Russian mobilization put an end to any hope for a negotiated settlement to the crisis. In Vienna, Francis Joseph declared general mobilization against Russia and Serbia.

A mood of anxious excitement prevailed in Paris. The army had already readied France's frontier defenses, but French troops were pulled back several kilometers from the frontier to avoid any incident with German units. In France, only the Socialist Party spoke out against the imminent outbreak of the international war. Many socialists still hoped that French and German workers would lay down their weapons and refuse to fire on fellow proletarians. Anti-militarism ran deep in some of France, not only because the army took sons away from farms, industrial work, and families, but also because the French government used the army to break strikes. The government maintained a list of socialists and other leaders of the left to be arrested in the event that war was declared.

In the meantime, the Russian and French ambassadors demanded assurance of British military support. The French ambassador even asked if the word "honor" would be stricken from British dictionaries if Britain refused to join France and Russia. Britain asked both Germany and France for a guarantee that Belgian neutrality (which had been accepted by Britain, France, Austria, Prussia, and Russia in 1839) would not be violated. Germany did not reply, Bethmann-Hollweg having earlier referred to the old guarantee as "a scrap of paper."

In Berlin, even the Social Democratic newspapers now accepted war as inevitable. Helmuth von Moltke (1848–1916), chief of the German general staff, pushed for an immediate attack on France, fearing that should Russian mobilization proceed any further, the Schlieffen Plan might fail. On July 31, 1914, Germany warned Russia to suspend mobilization at once. Germany demanded that France guarantee its neutrality in the event of a Russo-German war, and that German troops be allowed to occupy a number of French frontier forts as a show of French good faith. This no French government could accept. When no response was heard from either Russia or France, on August 1 the German army mobilized.

The relentless logic of the entangling alliances and military plans propelled Europe to war, as if the great powers were being pitched forward on an enormous wave. In Britain, Grey's frantic attempts to arrange a direct negotiation between Russia and Austria failed. The struggle of socialists in many countries to rally opposition against the war fell far short. On July 31, a rightist assassinated the popular French socialist leader Jean Jaurès. But Jaurès, too, had apparently just come to the conclusion that he should support the war against autocratic Germany. The Austrian socialist leader Victor Adler predicted: "Jaurès's murder is just the beginning. War unchains instincts, all forms of madness."

Of the powers, only Italy was not committed by alliance to fight, unless its allies in the Triple Alliance were attacked, and Italy could now reasonably claim that Austria-Hungary and Germany were launching hostilities. France ordered mobilization after receiving the impossible German demands. Germany declared war on Russia that same day, August 1. This obliged France, by virtue of its alliance with Russia, to fight Germany. German troops invaded Luxembourg, claiming falsely that a French attack on them was imminent and that they needed to seize the small duchy's railroads to defend themselves. On August 2, the German ambassador in Brussels handed the Belgian government the letter requesting permission to march armies through its territory. The negative reply came the next morning. Britain assured France that the Royal Navy would defend its Channel ports. On August 3, Germany declared war on France, falsely claiming that French planes had attacked Nuremberg. When Moltke's army marched into eastern Belgium and the German government ignored the British government's formal demand that they withdraw, Britain declared war on Germany on August 4, 1914. Enthusiastic crowds toasted departing soldiers in Paris and Berlin. The German crown prince anticipated "a jolly little war."

The Outbreak of War

When war was declared, eager commanders put long-standing military plans into effect. The German general staff counted on a rapid victory against France in the west before the giant Russian army could effectively be brought into action in the east. German troops outflanked French defenses by invading Belgium. However, this violation of Belgian neutrality brought Britain into the war on the side of France and Russia. Thus, the Great War pitted the Triple Alliance (Germany and Austria-Hungary, minus Italy, which for the moment remained neutral) against the Triple Entente (France, Great Britain, and Russia). These alignments had been shaped by the international tensions of the past decades.

(*Left*) French soldiers depart for war. (*Right*) British men surge toward a recruiting office.

Opening Hostilities

The Schlieffen Plan dictated the course of the opening hostilities. It was as if Schlieffen's "dead hand automatically pulled the trigger." However, Moltke had eliminated the Netherlands from the invasion plan and reduced the strength of the attacking force in order to bolster German defenses in Alsace-Lorraine. The French high command, which had known the basics of the Schlieffen Plan for years, did not believe the German army could move rapidly through Belgium, in part because the attacking forces would have to overcome the imposing fortress at Liège. The French also doubted that reserves incorporated into the German army could quickly become an able fighting force. In any case, the French command expected a frontal attack between the Meuse River and the hills of the Ardennes in northeastern France. The French generals also underestimated the speed with which their enemy could attack.

Although the Belgian army fought bravely against vastly superior strength, Liège fell on August 16 after a massive bombardment, followed by the fall of Namur. The Belgian army retreated north to Antwerp. Moltke then deployed seven divisions to prevent the Belgian army from escaping, further weakening the attacking forces that Schlieffen had anticipated would move as rapidly as possible toward the English Channel.

General Alexander von Kluck, commander of the First German Army, turned his troops toward the Belgian town of Mons. He hoped to force the French to surrender before they could bring up more troops from the Paris region. French advances in Alsace now convinced Moltke to divert troops to that border region from the primary attacking force, which intended to

Old and new combat in World War I.

encircle the French capital. Both the French and German high commands still considered success in Alsace critical to their strategies and to morale at home.

The British Expeditionary Force of 100,000 troops arrived to take its place on the French flank on August 20. One British soldier who went off to war in the summer of 1914 reassured his family, "At least the thing will be over in three weeks." But by August 24, the Allied (Entente) armies were rapidly retreating. At Mons and then Le Cateau, the British army fought its biggest battles since Waterloo in 1815. Yet retreat did not yet spell defeat. The Germans, fatigued by the pace of their march, also suffered from Moltke's indecision and inadequate communications. Kluck's army was already spread too thinly across a wide front. Now Moltke, surprised by the relatively rapid Russian mobilization and told of an early Russian victory on the eastern front, ordered four divisions to confront the surprisingly rapid Russian advance.

Nonetheless, the German armies managed to fight to within thirty-five miles of Paris (see Map 22.3). The French government provisionally withdrew to the safety of Bordeaux, just as they had been forced to do during the Franco-Prussian War. But despite heavy losses, Joffre was able to reinforce his defensive positions around Paris. This was in part possible because the French had concluded a secret treaty by which Italy, whose commitment to Germany and Austria-Hungary was defensive in nature, agreed to remain neutral if Germany attacked France. The German government, unaware of the treaty, still hoped Italy would join Germany and Austria-Hungary. Joffre

MAP 22.3 THE GERMAN ADVANCE, 1914 The Germans moved quickly into Belgium and France, largely following the Schlieffen Plan of 1905.

could thus count on troops that otherwise would have been needed in southeastern France to halt a possible Italian invasion.

At the dawn of air warfare, a French reconnaissance pilot noticed Kluck's army changing direction as it swept toward a point southeast of Paris, leaving its flank open. The French army rushed every available soldier into action, some arriving at the front in requisitioned Parisian taxis. When the Germans crossed the Marne River on September 5, the French counterattacked. Two German armies retreated, fearing that the French might take advantage of a sizable gap between their forces. It was the end of the Schlieffen Plan, and of the offensive war that the German generals had planned. The British poured through another gap between German armies, forcing the Germans to retreat forty miles to the Aisne River. There, on September 14, the Germans fortified their position by digging deep defensive trenches. Like the Battle of Valmy in 1792 during the French Revolution, the Battle of the Marne saved France in 1914.

The Germans then tried to outflank the British and French forces in what amounted to a race for the sea, as the Allied armies kept pace, holding much of Picardy and Flanders, before both sides ran out of space. The British and French, too, dug in.

A series of attacks and counterattacks in the fall took frightful tolls, with neither side able to break through. In November 1914, the last open battle of the western front was fought in the mud around Ypres in Belgium; British forces prevented the Germans from reaching the French Channel ports. By the end of the year, the German and French armies had combined casualties of 300,000 killed and 600,000 wounded. The British Seventh Division arrived in France in October with 400 officers and 12,000 soldiers; after eighteen days of fighting around Ypres, it had 44 officers and 2,336 men left. In a special British battalion of football players, originally brought together to play exhibition matches near the front and then sent to fight like everybody else, only 30 of 200 men survived.

THE CHANGING NATURE OF WAR

The German and Allied armies stared at each other across a broad front that reached from the English Channel to Switzerland. Two long, thin lines of trenches ended dreams of rapid victory based upon a mastery of offensive tactics. Few analysts had considered the possibility of a frozen front that would rarely move more than a few hundred yards in either direction and along which several million soldiers would die.

Besides trench warfare, new weapons dramatically changed the nature of battle. During the war, poison gas, hand grenades, flamethrowers, tanks, military airplanes, and submarines entered the arsenals of both sides. A new scale of warfare required an unparalleled, total mobilization of the home front to sustain the war effort.

Trench Warfare

Spades for digging trenches and rows of tangled barbed wire became more important than the rifle and bayonet, weapons of attack. Soldiers on both sides dug about 6,250 miles of trench in France. The front-line trenches were six to eight feet deep and about fifty yards to a mile apart. They were supplemented by support trenches several hundred yards to the rear and linked by communications trenches. Small fortress-like "strong points" held the line together even if part of the system was overrun. Sandbags and rows of barbed wire protected the trenches from attack. As the months passed in sectors where the front lines were immobile, the trenches became more elaborate, offering electricity and a certain minimal level of comfort. When there was no fighting, the soldiers confronted boredom. The French theater star Sarah Bernhardt, who had herself lost one leg to amputation (because of several bad falls) was carried on a stretcher near the front so she could entertain soldiers by reciting poetry. Some soldiers read voraciously to pass the time; the British poet Siegfried Sassoon was only half kidding when he remembered, "I didn't want to die, not before I'd finished reading *The Return of the Native* anyway." Since they were below ground, trenches offered soldiers some protection from rifle or pistol fire, but not from direct artillery hits. The periscope, sticking up from the trench below, provided the only safe way of looking across at the enemy lines without being shot by enemy snipers.

The front-line soldier lived amidst the thunder of barrages and the scream of falling shells. Persistent lice, mice, and enormous rats were his constant companions in the stagnant water of the trenches. So, for many, was venereal disease, contracted in the brothels near the front. A British soldier described a night in the trenches in January 1916:

> Lights out. Now the rats and the lice are the masters of the house. You can hear the rats nibbling, running, jumping, rushing from plank to plank, emitting their little squeals behind the dugout's corrugated metal. It's a noisy swarming activity that just won't stop. At any moment I expect one to land on my nose. And then it's the lice and fleas that begin to devour me. Absolutely impossible to get any shut-eye. Toward midnight I begin to doze off. A terrible racket makes me jump. Artillery fire, the cracking of rifle and machine-gun fire. The Boches [Germans] must be attacking. . . . Everything shakes. Our artillery thunders away without pause. . . . I doze off so as to get up at six. The rats and the lice get up too; waking to life is also waking to misery.

The cold and wind tore into the troops, especially in winter. "Before you can have a drink," one soldier wrote home, "you have to chip away the ice. The meat is frozen solid, the potatoes are bonded by ice, and even the hand grenades are welded together in their cases." The German army had been so sure of an easy victory that it had not equipped its men with high lace-up boots or adequate coats. German troops prized the British soldiers' sheepskin coats and removed them from enemy corpses when they had the chance. After battle, the screams of the wounded and dying filled the air; groans in German, French, and English from no-man's-land grew increasingly faint, but sometimes lasted for days.

Death was everywhere. It numbed. An Austrian soldier, a violinist, wrote: "A certain fierceness arises in you, an absolute indifference to anything the world holds except your duty of fighting. You are eating a crust of bread,

Paul Nash's *We Are Making a New World*, a tormented painting
evoking the pockmarked landscape around Ypres in Flanders.

and a man is shot dead in the trench next to you. You look calmly at him for
a moment, and then go on eating your bread. Why not? There is nothing to
be done. In the end you talk of your own death with as little excitement as
you would of a luncheon engagement." Hundreds of thousands of soldiers
suffered shell shock, psychologically devastated by the battle raging around
them.

On the western front, as both sides believed that a breakthrough was possible, massive attacks were preceded by an intensive bombardment of enemy
positions. Such bombardments, lasting hours and even days, clearly indicated
where the next attack could be expected, allowing the enemy to bring up sufficient reserves to prevent a breakthrough. Both sides adopted the use of
"creeping barrages," which moved just ahead of the attacking army to soften
resistance. The shelling mangled the terrain, leaving huge craters, thereby
creating unanticipated obstacles to the attacking troops. The attackers then
faced the most effective weapon of trench warfare, the machine gun—a
defensive weapon that mowed down line after line of advancing soldiers carrying rifles, bayonets, and pistols that they often never had a chance to use.

Piles of the dead filled shell craters left by the first barrages. If attacking
Allied troops managed to reach, take, and hold the first line of trenches,
they confronted fresh reinforcements as well as an even more solid second
line of defense. The defensive lines could bend, but then snap back against
attacking forces that soon outran their cover. Joffre's second offensive in
Champagne in 1915 illustrated this situation well. The French offensive
ran right into the second line of defense, took enormous casualties, and

(*Left*) French soldiers wearing gas masks prepare to attack. (*Right*) Victims of a German gas attack lining up at a field hospital.

then faced a vigorous counterattack. The Germans lost 75,000 killed and wounded, the French 145,000, for not more than a few miles of ravaged land. Still, Joffre ordered another attack. The result was the same.

Soldiers also faced new, frightening perils. German attacks against British positions around Ypres featured a horrifying new weapon, mustard gas, which, carried by the wind, burned out the lungs of the British soldiers. A member of the British medical corps wrote, "I shall never forget the sights I saw by Ypres after the first gas attacks. Men lying all along the side of the road . . . exhausted, gasping, frothing yellow mucus from their mouths, their faces blue and distressed. It was dreadful, and so little could be done for them." The gas mask soon offered imperfect protection—"this pig snout which represented the war's true face," as one combatant put it.

War in the Air and on the Seas

Airplanes became weapons of combat. In the first months of the war, airplanes were only used for reconnaissance in good weather; in 1915, techniques evolved and pilots began to photograph enemy trenches. Some pilots kept carrier pigeons in a cage, so that, if they had to ditch their planes, they could scribble their approximate location on a paper and send the information back to headquarters with the bird. Pilots fired pistols and hurled hand grenades and even bricks at enemy planes and troops before both sides discovered that machine guns could be mounted and timed to fire between the blades of the plane's propellers.

By the end of 1916, dashing and brave "aces," such as the German Red Baron, Manfred von Richthofen, and beginning in 1917 the American Eddie Rickenbacker, chased each other around the skies in fighter planes, cheered on by the trench soldiers below. When Richthofen was shot down behind British lines in April 1918, he was buried by his enemies with full military honors. Although the "dogfights" of combat in the skies had a romantic dimension, the airplane soon began to terrorize civilians. Paris and London were bombed several times during the war, as the speed and capacity of the first warplanes increased; the Rhineland German cities suffered heavy bombardments later in the conflict. By the war's end, Germany had produced more than 47,000 aircraft, France more than 51,000, and Britain more than 55,000 planes.

With the European powers fighting a land war unlike any ever seen, and conflict having taken to the skies, the seas remained relatively quiet. The British navy retained control, and the famed and feared German dreadnoughts stayed in port. The British navy won a series of initial encounters as far afield as the coast of Chile, the Falkland Islands near Argentina, and the Indian Ocean. German battleships trapped in the Mediterranean at the beginning of the war took refuge in Constantinople and were turned over to the Turks. The German navy took them back when Turkey entered the war in November 1914 on the side of the Central Powers (Germany and Austria-Hungary). Turkey was again pitted against its old enemy, Russia. The Austro-Hungarian navy, based in Trieste, was small and its influence was limited to the Mediterranean. The British admiralty, which possessed the German code book—plucked from the Baltic Sea by Russian sailors—

German and British planes in a dogfight high above the trenches.

awaited a major confrontation. Certain that the German fleet was going to sail from Wilhelmshaven, the British Grand Fleet lay in wait. At Dogger Bank on January 24, 1915, the Royal Navy sunk a German battleship. The British blockaded the principal German ports, neutralizing the kaiser's proud fleet.

Late in the 1880s, several countries had experimented with underwater warfare. At the turn of the century, the U.S. Navy was the first to commission a submarine. Although all of the powers had submarines by the time of the Great War, those of Germany made the greatest impact. The German navy believed that its fleet of submarines, which brought another fearful dimension to warfare, could force Britain to pull out of the war by sinking its warships and by preventing supplies from reaching the British Isles from the United States. In September 1914, a German submarine, or "U-boat," sank three large British armored cruisers off the coast of Belgium. U-boats, 188 feet long and with a range of 2,400 miles, could slip in and out of ports undetected. Yet ships carrying supplies to Britain continued to get through.

The Home Front

The waging of war on such an unprecedented scale required the full support of the "home front," the very concept of which emerged during the war. Sustaining the massive war effort depended first on mobilizing enough soldiers and food to supply the front, and then on producing enough guns and shells. It also depended on maintaining morale at home. Popular enthusiasm increasingly fed on a deep hatred of the enemy. German propagandists portrayed the war as a fight for German culture, besieged by Russian barbarians and the dishonorable French. A German soldier wrote, "We know full well that we are fighting for the German idea in the world, that we are defending German feeling against Asiatic barbarism and Latin indifference." British propagandists depicted the Allies as defending law, liberty, and progress against German violations of national sovereignty and international law. French propagandists had the easiest case to make: Germany had, after all, invaded France.

Such propaganda mixed elements of myth and truth. By the end of 1914, false tales of Germans impaling children and raping nuns were horrifying British and French readers. The German high command had instructed officers to ignore provisions of the Hague Conventions that sought the humane treatment of soldiers and civilians during war, which Germany had signed. Rumors had spread that civilians had killed German soldiers. The German army executed 5,500 Belgian civilians in two months, including in Louvain, where troops panicked when they heard shots fired in the distance by French troops and mistook them for action by Belgian citizens. The Germans then burned the library of the University of Louvain, which included rare manuscripts, for good measure. Austrian soldiers massacred, mutilated, and raped villagers in Serbia, as did Russian troops in East Prussia and Galicia. These actions, reflecting the brutalization of war and the banalization of death, foreshadowed a new kind of war—a total war in which civilians were not spared.

At the outbreak of hostilities in Britain and France, shops owned by people with German-sounding names were pillaged (in the latter case, some victims were French Alsatians for whom the war, at least in part, was supposedly being fought). A publication for French schoolchildren told this story: "Your little brother in your presence has lied to your mother. You take him aside and tell him, 'Do you want to behave like the Krauts?'" The younger boy confesses, now understanding that "the French don't lie." A publication for girls informed them that "pillage is a German word." German propaganda similarly smeared their enemies, particularly the British, who supposedly used dum-dum bullets that exploded upon impact and gouged out the eyes of German prisoners.

The outbreak of the war pushed aside bitter political divisions at home. In France, competing parties proclaimed a "sacred union," and the socialist Jules Guesde became minister of commerce. There was little public criticism of the way the war was being run until later in the conflict when casualties mounted. In Germany, too, socialist opposition to militarism based on class solidarity quickly turned to patriotic support. In Russia, at least in the first few years, only the tsar's will seemed to matter. In Austria-Hungary, the ability of the imperial bureaucracy to supply its multinational army, the prestige of which had helped keep the Habsburg Empire together, seemed almost miraculous. Tensions between the empire's nationalities remained beneath the surface, at least in the war's early years.

A poster showing support from the home front.

In Britain, the angry quarrels over strategy among the generals, as well as between them and the cabinet, were well hidden from the public. A volunteer army was raised with remarkable enthusiasm and speed, aided by an effective recruitment poster sporting the face of Lord Horatio Kitchener, the secretary of war. On a single day in September 1914, 33,000 men joined up. By the end of the year, the British had 2 million men in uniform. The volunteer force that German Kaiser William II had called "a contemptible little army" fought very well. In 1916, Britain began military conscription.

David Lloyd George (1863–1945), the Liberal politician who headed the wartime Ministry of Munitions, skillfully oversaw the transition from peacetime to wartime industrial production, using the powers specified by the Munitions of War Act of May 1915. The act forbade strikes and provided for the requisition of skilled workers for labor in factories, which were converted to the production of war materiel. Supplying the front with shells alone was a monumental task. In the opening months of the war, 500 German trains crossed the Rhine every day to supply troops. The nineteen-day artillery barrage at the third Battle of Ypres in 1917 expended all shells carried to the front by 321 trains, the output of a year's work for 55,000 armament workers.

The war spurred other changes in daily life at home. As heavy drinking became more widespread, legislation restricted the operating hours of British pubs. Some complained that the war had brought Britain a loosening of morals, frivolous dress and dancing, and an increase in juvenile delinquency. Daylight savings time was introduced for the first time to conserve fuel. A successful campaign for voluntary rationing of essential commodities such as sugar allowed the British to avoid mandatory rationing until early 1917, when hoarding contributed to shortages. The government instituted a coupon system, but price controls on essential commodities served to ration food.

Suffragette leaders, who had put aside their campaign for women's right to vote, threw their support behind the war. Millicent Garrett Fawcett (1847–1929), a leading British feminist, appealed to the readers of a suffrage magazine: "Women, your country needs you. . . . Let us show ourselves worthy of Citizenship," proclaiming that she considered pacifism almost the equivalent of treason.

THE WAR RAGES ON

Early in 1915, the French general staff predicted that its army would break through the German lines. However French attacks in the spring in Champagne and then in Artois further north brought enormous casualties but little progress (see Map 22.4). A British assault at Neuve Chapelle on March 10 gained 1,000 yards at a cost of 13,000 casualties. The British lost almost 300,000 men in 1915 alone; the Germans, who had a much larger army, suffered at least 610,000 casualties. Both nations' casualties, however daunting, paled alongside those of the French, who suffered 1,292,000 killed and wounded in 1915. French infantrymen were not helped by the fact that their uniform pants were, at least in the early stages of the war, bright red, which could be more easily seen through the morning mists than the German gray.

Italy had remained neutral at the outbreak of the war but gave in to street demonstrations and entered the war on the Allied side through the secret Treaty of London, signed in April 1915. Britain and France held out as bait territories many Italian nationalists claimed as part of "Italian Irredenta" ("unredeemed lands"), including the Tyrol in the Alps and Istria along the

MAP 22.4 THE WESTERN FRONT, 1914–1917 Major battles from 1914–1917, and location of trenches at the end of 1915 and at the end of 1917.

northern Adriatic coast. Italian nationalism, as well as the desire of powerful Italian businessmen to find new markets in the Balkans, had proved stronger than Italy's pre-war commitment to its former allies. Austria-Hungary now found itself, like Germany, fighting a war on two fronts. The Italians attacked with the port of Trieste as their goal. The struggle between Britain and Turkey—which was also allied with the Central Powers—carried the war into the Middle East. Japan, coveting several German islands in the Pacific and the German naval base at Kiao-chao, and seeking sanction for its interest in northeastern China, entered the war on the Allied side in 1914. What began as a European war became a world war.

The Eastern Front

In the wide-open spaces of the eastern front, the Russian armies had advanced into eastern Prussia despite the incompetence of the Russian general staff, intense animosity among commanders, hopelessly archaic equipment, and communications so inadequate that the Germans could easily listen to Russian officers discussing tactics on the telephone. In late August 1914, German forces trapped a Russian army almost 200,000 strong at Tannenberg in East Prussia, killing, wounding, or capturing 125,000 soldiers. Two subsequent military victories ensured that Russian forces would remain outside of German territory for the duration of the war. On the more confident German side, sixty-seven-year-old General Paul von Hindenburg (1847–1934), a stolid Prussian who had been called out of retirement, and the determined General Erich Ludendorff (1865–1937) embellished their reputations in these battles.

The Austro-Hungarian army, which had no joint plan of military coordination with its German ally, found the huge Russian army an imposing foe. Too many divisions had been diverted to the punitive invasion of strategically unimportant Serbia. In September 1914, the Russians captured the fortress of Lemberg in Galicia from the Austro-Hungarian armies and took 100,000 prisoners (see Map 22.5). Many of these were conscripted Slavs who felt more allegiance to Russians, their fellow Slavs, than to their German-speaking officers.

In January 1915, the Habsburg forces launched an offensive against the Russian army in the Carpathian Mountains. Although the offensive looked good on a map, the reality was otherwise. Snow-covered mountains posed a daunting obstacle: supplies had to be moved over ice or freezing marsh; low clouds obscured artillery targets; and soldiers had to warm their rifles over fires before they could use them. When the Russians counterattacked, the Germans had to send troops to support their ally in the Carpathians, and as a result they lost over 350,000 men. With the stalemate in the west, the Germans wanted to defeat the Russians before the latter could vanquish the Habsburg army. In May 1915, a massive German attack drove the Russian army back almost 100 miles. The Russian retreat, which had been orderly in the beginning, turned into chaos. A million civilians moved eastward with the Russian armies. An observer remembered that "while thousands of people trudge along the railway lines they are passed by speeding trains loaded with couches from officers' clubs, and carrying quartermasters' bird cages." The Russian retreat from the Carpathian Mountains gave the Austro-Hungarian forces some badly needed breathing room. German forces reached Brest-Litovsk in August 1915, ending 100 years of Russian control of Poland.

MAP 22.5 THE EASTERN, ITALIAN, AND BALKAN FRONTS Russian and Austro-German advances and battles along the eastern front; Austro-Hungarian and Italian armies face off along the Italian front; and Turkish and Allied armies clash on the Balkan front.

The War in the Middle East, Africa, and the Far East

British military and political leaders were divided between those who believed that victory would have to be won in the west, and others who pushed for a series of dramatic strikes against Germany or its allies on Europe's periphery. The latter included Winston Churchill (1874–1965), the First Lord of the Admiralty, and Lloyd George. Such victories might also even expand the British Empire, thus such a campaign would please the colonial lobby at home. This strategy angered the French government, which bitterly opposed any reduction of British support on the western front.

Churchill and Lord Kitchener planned an attack on Germany's ally, Turkey. When the Turks entered the war on the side of Germany and Austria-Hungary in November 1914, they closed off the Dardanelles strait, which separates the Aegean Sea from the Sea of Marmara. This cut off an important route for supplies to Russia through the Black Sea. Turkish forces also tied up Russian troops in the Caucasus Mountains. Turkey posed a potential threat to the Suez Canal. The British high command planned an assault on the Dardanelles strait. If everything went well, a British success might bring an end to the power of the pro-German faction in the Turkish government. Moreover, a successful campaign could open up a route to Russia through the Black Sea. With Turkey out of the war, Churchill reasoned, the German effort in the Balkans could be undermined, and Bulgaria would stay out of the conflict.

In April 1915, British ships sailed through the Dardanelles, destroyed several Turkish ships, and disembarked five divisions of troops on the beach of Gallipoli (see Map 22.5). British soldiers hurled themselves against the well-defended heights held by the Turks. British troops managed to dig in,

British troops massing during the ill-fated Gallipoli campaign.

and in August launched an assault that failed miserably. In the meantime, British, French, and German submarines were active during the campaign, forcing both sides to adapt supply tactics to the new threat. After committing more than 400,000 men, half of whom were killed or wounded, the British were fortunate to evacuate their remaining forces in January 1916. Amid harsh criticism of the campaign's humiliating failure, Churchill and Kitchener lost influence. To this day, the Gallipoli Campaign remains controversial. Some historians consider it an imaginative, even brilliant stroke that might have won the war. Others agree with most contemporaries who believed that it was a needless diversion dictated by British colonial interests in the Middle East and for which Australian and New Zealander troops paid a disproportionate price.

Still hoping to knock Turkey out of the war, the Allies tried to coax Bulgaria into the war on their side. But in October 1915 Bulgaria joined the Central Powers, who promised Bulgaria all of Macedonia, which the Allies could not because of Serb claims there, as well as much of Thrace. Austro-Hungarian and Bulgarian forces thus controlled an important part of the Balkans. A month later, a Franco-British force landed in Salonika, Greece, to try to aid Serb troops. But within two months, the German, Austro-Hungarian, and Bulgarian armies had crushed the Serb army, which by 1916 had suffered 100,000 deaths of the 450,000 men serving in 1914. The Germans called Salonika their "largest internment camp," since that campaign tied up half a million Allied troops fighting the Bulgarians. In the meantime, British troops fought a desert war against the Turks in Palestine and Mesopotamia.

Smaller British forces were occupied fighting for the German colonies in Africa (see Map 22.6). German Togoland fell in August 1914, German Southwest Africa in 1915, and the German Cameroons in 1916. In German East Africa (Tanganyika), combat continued for the duration of the war, pitting German troops against British and South African soldiers, and both sides against mosquitoes and disease. In Asia, Japanese forces captured the fortress and port of Tsingtao (Qingdao) from a German garrison, and seized the undefended German islands of the Marianas, Carolines, and Marshalls in the North Pacific.

The Western Front

Following Gallipoli, the British again focused on the western front. Southern England was so close to this front that officers who had lunch in private railroad cars before leaving Victoria Station could be at the front—and perhaps dead—by dinner. When British miners managed to blow up a previously unconquerable ridge near Messines in western Belgium, it was said that the explosion could be heard in Kent.

General Douglas Haig (1861–1928) was named commander in chief of the British army in France in December 1915. He agreed with Joffre's plan

MAP 22.6 THE WORLD WAR   The expansion of the war beyond Europe to the German colonies in Africa and the Far East.

for a mighty offensive in the vicinity of the Somme River. The assault would have to await the arrival of more British soldiers and good weather. The German army, too, had big plans. The new German commander in chief, General Erich von Falkenhayn (1861–1922), planned an assault on the fortresses surrounding Verdun in eastern France. Falkenhayn had no illusions about breaking through the French lines, but he believed that with a massive attack on Verdun, the Germans could "out-attrition" the French, who, by virtue of a lower birthrate, could not afford to lose as many soldiers as their more populous enemy. Falkenhayn assumed that France would lose five men for every two German soldiers killed. Realizing that even more German victories on the eastern front would not necessarily knock Russia out of the war, and doubting the ability of Austria-Hungary to hold off both the Russians on Germany's eastern front and Italy in the south, the German command needed to force the French to sue for peace.

After nine days of delay because of bad weather, the German artillery began to bombard the French forts stretched around Verdun across a front of eight miles on February 21, 1916 (see Map 22.4). Some of the guns weighed twenty tons; it took nine tractors to move each piece and a crane to load the shells. The French prepared to hold Verdun at all costs. Its loss would be a potentially mortal blow to French morale. In the damp, chilling mists of the hills northeast of Verdun, hundreds of thousands of men died, killed by shells that rained from the sky, machine guns that seemed never to be stilled, or bayoneted in hand-to-hand fighting within and outside the massive cement forts. French troops were supplied by a single "sacred road" on which trucks and wagons arrived from the town of Bar-le-Duc. Verdun was truly a national battle, in part because a new system of furloughs meant that nearly everyone in the French army spent some time in the hell that was Verdun.

The French army held. General Philippe Pétain (1856–1951), the new commander, became a hero in France. But the cost of this victory came close to fulfilling Falkenhayn's expectations. The French lost 315,000 men killed or wounded; 90,000 died at the appropriately named "Dead Man's Hill" alone. The Germans suffered 281,000 casualties. A French counterattack in the fall recaptured several of the forts the Germans had taken, and again the casualties mounted. In all, the French suffered 540,000 casualties and the Germans 430,000 at Verdun. At one of the forts, Douaumont, one can still see plaques put up by proud, grieving relatives after the war, one of which reads, "For my son. Since his eyes closed mine have not ceased to cry."

The Battle of Verdun, while extremely important as a symbol of French resistance, merely postponed plans for a huge British offensive on the Somme River, supported by a similar French thrust. After a week's bombardment, the assault began on July 1 in the hills and forests along a front of eighteen miles.

Allied troops climbed out of the trenches at dawn to the whistles of their officers and moved into no-man's-land. Artillery barrages had chopped up the terrain over which the attackers had to struggle but left intact most of the German barbed wire, too strong for British wire cutters. German machine gun emplacements had also survived the barrage. Many British soldiers managed only a few yards before being hit, falling with the sixty-six pounds of equipment they were carrying. A captain sought to inspire his men by jumping out of the trench and leading the attack by dribbling a soccer ball across no-man's-land. He was shot dead far from the goal. The Germans moved up reserves to wherever their lines were bending. The British commanders sent wave after wave of infantrymen "over the top" to their death; corpses piled up on top of those who had died seconds, minutes, or hours before. Of 752 men in the First Newfoundland Regiment, all 26 officers and 658 men were killed or wounded within forty minutes. Sixty percent of the Tenth Battalion of the West Yorkshires died in the initial assault. At the end of the first day of the Battle of the Somme, about 60,000 soldiers of the 110,000 British soldiers had become casualties, including 19,000 killed. (There were more British soldiers killed and wounded in the first three days of the Battle of the Somme than Americans killed in World War I, the Korean War, and the Vietnam War combined, and three times more killed than in fifteen years of war against Napoleon.)

When the disastrous offensive finally ended in mid-November 1916, Britain had lost 420,000 men killed and wounded. The French lost 200,000 men in what was primarily a British offensive. It cost the Germans 650,000 soldiers to hold on. This was almost 200,000 casualties more than at Verdun. Such losses helped convince the German high command that only a campaign of unrestricted submarine warfare against ships supplying Britain might bring victory. Yet the maximum German retreat was a few kilometers; in most places, Allied gains were measured in yards. A sign left over one mass grave said, "The Devonshires held this trench, the Devonshires hold it still." The British poet Edmund Blunden, who survived the Battle of the Somme, tried to answer the question of who had won: "By the end of the [first] day both sides had seen, in a sad scrawl of broken earth and murdered men, the answer to the question. No road. No thoroughfare. Neither race had won, nor could win, the War. The War had won, and would go on winning."

Futility and Stalemate

Futility and stalemate also prevailed on the mountainous Austro-Italian front, where in 1916 there were *twelve* different Battles of the Isonzo River, where the Habsburg armies had well-developed defensive positions. The Italian army considered one of these, the sixth, a great victory because it moved three miles forward. After half a million casualties, the Italians were still only halfway to Trieste. In the twelfth Battle of Isonzo in 1917—more widely known as that of Caporetto 1917—Austro-Hungarian and German forces broke through the Italian lines, capturing more than 250,000 troops.

British soldiers wearing gas masks firing a machine gun during
the Battle of the Somme, 1916.

On the eastern front, General Paul von Hindenburg claimed that there
was no way of gauging the number of Russians killed with any accuracy:
"All we do know is that, at times, fighting the Russians, we had to remove
the piles of enemy bodies from before our trenches, so as to get a clear field
of fire against new waves of assault." In June 1916, the Russian offensive
pushed back the Austrians by combining smaller surprise attacks by specially
trained troops, without the preliminary barrages, against carefully chosen
targets. But the arrival of more German troops minimized Russian gains.
Each side lost more than 1 million men in these encounters.

In 1916, the British poet Isaac Rosenberg, who would later be killed in the
war, wrote "Break of Day in the Trenches," one of the most haunting poems
to come out of the war.

The darkness crumbles away.
It is the same old druid Time as ever,
Only a live thing leaps my hand,
A queer sardonic rat,
As I pull the parapet's poppy
To stick behind my ear.
Droll rat, they would shoot you if they knew
Your cosmopolitan sympathies.
Now you have touched this English hand
You will do the same to a German
Soon, no doubt, if it be your pleasure

To cross the sleeping green between.
It seems you inwardly grin as you pass
Strong eyes, fine limbs, haughty athletes,
Less chance than you for life,
Bonds to the whims of murder,
Sprawled in the bowels of the earth,
The torn fields of France.
What do you see in our eyes
At the shrieking iron and flame
Hurled through still heavens?
What quaver—what heart aghast?
Poppies whose roots are in man's veins
Drop, and are ever dropping;
But mine in my ear is safe—
Just a little white with the dust.

The winter of 1916–1917 was bleak. There seemed few families on either side who had not lost a relative or friend at the front. On the Allied side, there was some cheer when Romania joined the war in exchange for the promise of some Hungarian territory with a significant Romanian population once the Central Powers had been defeated. But Falkenhayn, removed from the western front in disgrace after Verdun, quickly defeated the Romanian army. The war eroded the resources and morale of Bulgaria and Turkey. In December 1916, both states issued declarations expressing willingness to discuss terms for peace. The following March, Emperor Charles I (ruled 1916–1918) of the Austro-Hungarian Empire, who assumed the throne after Francis Joseph's death in November 1916, sent the Allies a peace proposal, without having consulted Germany. It included a willingness to recognize French claims to Alsace-Lorraine. But talk of a compromise peace was hushed and, at least in Vienna, deemed unpatriotic.

Unlike the French and British, the Germans realized that victory by breakthrough was extremely unlikely, if not impossible. To the Allies, a compromise peace seemed out of the question given that enemy troops were occupying much of the north of France. The complete withdrawal of German troops required a total victory that would guarantee France's future security. Increasingly criticized for the staggering casualty rate, Joffre was replaced by General Robert Nivelle (1856–1924) as commander in chief of the French forces in 1916. Nivelle insisted that a breakthrough on the western front could be achieved.

In Britain, Lloyd George became prime minister in December 1916. Even after staggering losses on the Somme, he agreed with British commanders that military victory was possible if the Allies cooperated more closely. The British government thus rejected a peace note sent by Germany on December 12, the aim of which was to force an end to the war by splitting apart Britain and France.

Soldiers and Civilians

In some ways, life in Britain and in the other combatant powers seemed to go on as before, which increasingly outraged soldiers returning from the front. Elegantly dressed people of means dining in the finest restaurants or watching the races at Derby and Ascot contrasted dramatically with the returning trainloads of badly wounded soldiers, and with the rationing of coal and food. A newspaper headline in 1917 gave equal emphasis to its two lead stories: "Battle Raging At Ypres. Gatwick Racing—Late Wire." Some big businessmen found the war very profitable, amassing fortunes on war supplies: Anglo-Persian Oil, which had lost money in 1914, enjoyed profits of 85 million pounds in 1916, 344 million in 1917, and over 1 billion in 1918. Profits of rubber companies increased fourfold.

In every belligerent country, women made contributions to the war. Nurses served courageously at the front and were acclaimed as heroines. Women took over many of the jobs of men who left to fight, or who had been wounded or killed. These included the enormous, back-breaking tasks of working the land. Over 1 million British women stepped into jobs from which they had previously been excluded, ranging from skilled and semi-skilled jobs in munitions factories ("Shells made by a wife may save a husband's life" went one poster in Britain) to positions as tram conductors and

Russian sharpshooters in a trench on the eastern front.

gas-meter readers. A visitor to Berlin in March 1916 reported "no men any-where, women are doing everything."

But women workers, as in the past, received lower wages than their male counterparts, allowing many employers to reduce expenses and increase their profits. In France and Austria, women workers struck in 1917 and 1918 to protest working conditions. Everywhere, shortages and economic hardship made women's tasks of managing the household economy that much more difficult, including standing in line for hours at stores. Crowds of women demonstrated against high prices in Italy in 1917.

Censorship, particularly in the first year, prevented the population from knowing about the staggering death tolls, or about the strategic blunders of the generals. "The war, for all its devastating appearances, only seems to be destructive," one Parisian newspaper assured its readers in November 1914, and in July 1915 it asserted that "at least [those killed by German bayonets] will have died a beautiful death, in noble battle . . . with cold steel, we shall rediscover poetry . . . epic and chivalrous jousting." Other papers emphati-cally related that "half the German shells are made of cardboard, they don't even burst," and that "Boche corpses smell worse than [those of the] French."

The British poet Robert Graves wrote that "England looked strange to us soldiers. We could not understand the war-madness that ran wild every-where. . . . The civilians talked a foreign language; and it was newspaper lan-guage." Lord Northcliffe, the press baron named by the British government to provide the public with reports of the war, described the trenches, "where health is so good and indigestion hardly ever heard of. The open-air life, the regular and plenteous feeding, the exercise, and the freedom from care and responsibility, keep the soldiers extraordinarily fit and contented." A French newspaper headline in December 1916 read, preposterously enough, "Among the many victims of gas, there is hardly a single death." A French captain wrote to protest newspaper accounts of heroic fighting and glorious death on the battlefield: "How does [the civilian] picture us combatants? Does he really believe we spend our time brandishing great swords with heroic ges-tures and yelling 'Long live France!' at the top of our lungs? When will these ladies and gentlemen in civilian life spare us their fantasies?"

The men in the trenches forged close bonds with those with whom they served. They bitterly resented senior officers who barked out deadly orders from the safety of requisitioned châteaux behind the front lines, and they detested government propagandists and censors. On leave, soldiers headed together to music halls, cabarets, and bars, hoping to forget a war they felt uncomfortable trying to describe to civilians who knew so little about it.

More than this, embittered soldiers occasionally felt more sympathy for those in the opposite trenches than for the politicians and generals at home. On Christmas Day, 1914, on the western front in France, German and British soldiers spontaneously declared their own one-day truce, some meeting in no-man's-land to exchange greetings, souvenirs, and even home addresses. In one or two places, soldiers from both sides played soccer.

A year later, a British soldier was executed for ignoring orders that such an event was not to recur. There were even occasional informal arrangements between units that had been facing each other across no-man's-land for several months, agreeing not to fire during mealtimes, or entertaining each other in verse or song. A British writer later recalled calmly discussing Nietzsche with a German he had captured just minutes after almost killing him. One prevalent rumor in both trenches had an entire regiment of German, French, and British deserters living under no-man's-land in tunnels, coming out only at night to rob corpses and steal food and drink from both sides. They, many soldiers said, were the lucky ones.

It was impossible to hide the effects of the war. In all combatant countries, women in mourning clothes were an increasingly frequent sight, clutching telegrams that began, "Be proud of X, who has just died like a brave man. . . ." Illegitimate births rose rapidly. In Germany, state governments, except for that of Prussia, for the first time allowed "illegitimate" birth certificates and gave unmarried or widowed women the right to call themselves *Frau* (Mrs.) instead of *Fraulein* (Miss).

As casualties mounted and the fighting ground on, opposition to the war emerged, particularly in Britain. Elsewhere in Britain, a relatively small number of pacifists and conscientious objectors protested against the war. Some of them were prosecuted and imprisoned. In 1916, when Britain adopted military conscription, pacifists became more vocal. In *No Conscription Leaflet No. 3*, the writer Lytton Strachey (1880–1932) warned, "The Cat kept saying to the Mouse that she was a high-minded person, and if the Mouse would only come a little nearer they could both get the cheese. The Mouse said, Thank you, Pussy, it's not the cheese you want, it's my skin."

Irish Republicans opposed Britain in order to gain Ireland's independence. The Germans encouraged Irish Republican preparations for an insurrection in Dublin set for Easter Sunday, 1916. Sir Roger Casement (1864–1916), an Irish nationalist who had denounced the brutal conditions under which indigenous laborers worked in imperial colonies, tried to form an Irish Legion and urged the Germans to send military assistance to those working for independence in Ireland. But seeing that the Germans had no plans to offer substantial help, he landed on the Irish coast with the help of a German submarine with the goal of convincing Irish Republicans to call off the insurrection, but was arrested immediately. The Easter Rising went ahead, but ended in dismal failure after five days of bloody fighting with 450 insurgents killed. Casement was among those executed, traitor to the British, hero to many Irish.

In Germany, Clara Zetkin (1857–1933), a militant socialist, went to jail because she refused to stop denouncing the war and tried to mobilize working-class women against a struggle between capitalist states that pitted worker against worker. Rosa Luxemburg, a Polish socialist living in Germany, also went to prison for her efforts to turn more members of her party against the war.

When Dutch socialists initiated a peace conference in Stockholm in December 1917, Britain prohibited British citizens from attending. The poet Siegfried Sassoon, wounded at the front, returned to England and publicly declared, "I believe the War is being deliberately prolonged by those who have the power to end it. I am a soldier, convinced that I am acting on behalf of soldiers." After being incarcerated in a mental asylum, he returned to the front because of his allegiance to his comrades. There he was wounded again.

In the meantime, the French government faced different problems on the home front than those confronting Britain. The German armies occupied some of France's richest agricultural land and industrial centers of the north and northeast. Refugees from the war zone arrived in Paris and, increasingly, the south carrying their remaining possessions. But the French home front held together, despite ebbs and flows in morale as the war went on and on. Although there was grumbling about peasants who profited from price rises for commodities, or about specialist workers exempt from conscription because munitions factories required their skills, and about other "shirkers" who escaped service, there were relatively few signs of opposition to the war in France, particularly early on. The government's decision in the war's first month to provide some financial assistance to families with husbands, brothers, and sons in uniform was popular. The French gradually adapted to the war. With the German army deep inside France, close to Paris, capitulation was unthinkable, as was even a negotiated settlement.

The German home front also held together. Posters showed an ogre-like British "John Bull" with the caption "This man is responsible for your hunger." However, in 1917 signs of war weariness increased as casualties reached astronomic levels and rumors spread that the campaign of unrestricted submarine warfare against the Allies was failing. Open criticism of

Berliners hunt for food.

officials became more common. In July, the Reichstag passed a resolution by a large majority asking the government to repudiate a policy of annexation and commit itself to seeking a peace of reconciliation. But the Reichstag had little influence in what amounted to a military government. In Germany, when William III dismissed Chancellor Bethmann-Hollweg in 1917, he gave Generals Hindenburg and Ludendorff even more power.

THE FINAL STAGES OF THE WAR

In 1917, two events of great consequence changed the course of the war. Reacting in part to the German campaign of unrestricted submarine warfare against Allied shipping, the United States entered the war in April on the Allied side. And Russia, where the February Revolution toppled the tsar (see Chapter 23), withdrew from the war after the Bolsheviks seized power in October. Meanwhile, the French armies seemed on the verge of collapse. Widespread mutinies occurred. And a massive German offensive that began in March 1918 pushed Allied forces back farther than they had been since 1914, before grinding to a halt in the face of stiff resistance. The stage was set for the final phase of the war.

The United States Enters the War

In 1916, Woodrow Wilson had been re-elected president of the United States on the platform "He kept us out of war." The U.S. government had adopted a declaration of neutrality, but American popular sympathy generally lay with the Allies, even though the German government tried to capitalize on American resentment of the British blockade, which entailed searches of American ships. U.S. bankers made profitable loans to both sides, but far more funds went to the Allies than to the Central Powers.

On May 7, 1915, a German submarine sank the British cruise liner *Lusitania* off the coast of Ireland. The ship was, despite U.S. denials, carrying American-made ammunition to Britain; 128 U.S. citizens were among the almost 1,200 killed. The United States, already outraged by the recent German introduction of mustard gas into combat, protested vigorously, and on September 1 the German government accepted the American demand that it abandon the unrestricted submarine warfare. Germany, wanting to keep the United States neutral, adopted a policy of warning liners before sinking them, providing for the safety of the passengers.

The fact remained that only with submarines could Germany prevent Britain from maintaining total control of the high seas. In 1916, the German fleet left port to challenge the British Royal Navy. The German admiralty hoped to entice part of the main British fleet into a trap by offering a smaller fleet as a target off the Norwegian coast. German submarines lay in wait, along with a sizeable surface fleet. The British, who had broken the German code, hoped to have the last laugh when the entire Grand Fleet suddenly appeared. The German and British fleets stumbled into each other off the coast of Denmark, in the Battle of Jutland, May 31–June 1, 1916. In a heavy exchange of gunfire, the British lost fourteen ships and about 6,000 men; eleven German ships were sunk and about 1,500 men were killed. Both sides claimed victory, but British losses were heavier, surprising and embarrassing British naval leaders (such that one admiral turned to a junior officer and stammered, "Chatfield, there seems to be something wrong with our bloody ships today!"). Yet in the end, it was the German fleet that fled, leaving the Royal Navy in control of the seas for the duration of the war.

The continuing success of the British blockade led Germany to announce on February 1, 1917, that its submarines would attack any ship in "war zones." In March 1916, the U.S. government had forcefully protested the sinking of the British ship *Sussex* in the English Channel, with the loss of American lives. Germany agreed to the "*Sussex* pledge," reaffirming the agreement to give up unrestricted submarine warfare. But pressure came from the German high command to turn loose the submarine fleet, now 120 strong, as the only hope for knocking Britain out of the war. This was a calculated risk, like the invasion of Belgium in 1914, because it would surely entail American intervention. Two weeks earlier, the United States had intercepted a coded telegram from the German foreign secretary, Arthur

(*Left*) Allied tanks stuck in the mud. (*Right*) A German U-boat surfaces.

Zimmermann, to his ambassador to Mexico. The "Zimmermann telegram" brazenly offered Mexico German help in taking back the states of Texas, Arizona, and New Mexico if it would go to war against its powerful northern neighbor. With more Americans killed in submarine attacks, Wilson used the telegram to bolster support for a declaration of war on April 6, 1917. Wilson promised a war that would "make the world safe for democracy." The United States turned its industrial might toward wartime production and drafted and trained an army that reached 4 million, of which half was in France by November 1918. The entry of the United States into the war tipped the balance fatally against Germany.

During 1917, German submarines sank one-fourth of all ships sailing to Britain. Half a million tons of shipping were sunk in February, three-quarters of a million in March, and nearly 1 million tons in April, when 350 British ships were sunk. But in the midst of despair, the British admiralty discovered that heavily escorted convoys could get through. Submerged mines at the entrances to the Channel also helped reduce the German U-boat threat. Within a few months, the first American troops reached the continent, along with a steady stream of military supplies.

Russia Withdraws from the War

The second remarkable event of 1917 was the Russian Revolution. The eastern front had stabilized following the Russian offensive at the end of 1916, as the Russian and Austro-Hungarian armies were depleted and exhausted. The Russian home front seemed on the verge of collapse. In February 1917, amid a chorus of demands for political reform, strikes and bread riots in Petrograd spread rapidly. Tsar Nicholas II abdicated on March 15. The head of the provisional government, Alexander Kerensky (1881–1970), had no intention of abandoning the war effort, and he ordered the commander in chief to launch another offensive on July 1. But "peace, land, and bread" became the motto of the soldiers. Many deserted or refused to obey their officers. Within a matter of weeks, a German counterattack pushed the Russians back nearly 100 miles.

As the Russian provisional government faced opposition from many sides, the Bolsheviks aimed to seize power and then take Russia out of the war as quickly as possible. They expected revolutions to break out in other countries as well, beginning with Germany. The German government desperately wanted to force the Russian provisional government to make peace as soon as possible, so that the German high command could turn its full attention to the western front before the American entry into the war could turn the tide. With this in mind, they allowed exiled Bolshevik leader Vladimir Lenin (1870–1924) to return to Russia from neutral Switzerland through Germany and Finland.

On November 6 (October 24 by the Old Russian calendar), the Bolsheviks overthrew the provisional government. The German army, facing little opposition, had captured Riga, the fortified capital of Latvia, and was advancing along the Baltic coast. The Germans were happy to comply with Lenin's request for an immediate armistice. In return, the German government wanted the revolutionary government to agree to the independence of Finland, Poland, Galicia, Moldavia, and the Baltic states of Estonia, Latvia, and Lithuania. Their goal was to create a series of small buffer states between Germany and Russia that they could dominate. The Allies understandably worried that such a peace between Germany and Russia would make it difficult to obtain peace in the west, as the German army could devote all its attention to that front.

The French and British governments feared the effect Russia's withdrawal from the war, in the wake of a revolution, might have on workers and socialists at home, as well as on the war's outcome. French Prime Minister Georges Clemenceau and British Prime Minister Lloyd George denounced the Bolsheviks, but relatively few people in Russia wanted the war to continue. In December, the Bolsheviks unilaterally declared the war over and signed a temporary armistice with Germany. When the revolutionary Russian government did not agree to the German terms for a formal armistice, the German armies marched into the Russian heartland. They reached the Gulf of Finland—only 150 miles from Petrograd—as well as the Crimean peninsula in the south, and advanced far into Ukraine. The Germans then offered a cessation of hostilities in return for virtually all Russian war materiel they could carry with them. They also again demanded the independence of the border states of the Russian Empire. The Bolsheviks abandoned Russian claims on Poland, Ukraine, and what would become Estonia, Latvia, and Lithuania. In March 1918, the Treaty of Brest-Litovsk officially ended Russian participation in the war.

Offensives and Mutinies

The year 1917 brought another major Allied offensive in the west. General Nivelle of France convinced his British counterpart in February that the long-awaited knockout punch was at last possible if a British attack would divert German forces along the Aisne River. But the British attack ran headlong into the impenetrable German second line of defense, the "Hindenburg Line." On April 16, Nivelle sent 1.2 million soldiers into battle along the Aisne River in miserable weather. Allied tanks, which had been introduced into battle for the first time in 1916, became stuck in the mud or in shell craters. Ten days later, French losses totaled 34,000 dead, 90,000 wounded, and 20,000 missing. Soldiers sang, "If you want to find the old battalion, I know where they are, I know where they are—They're hanging on the old barbed wire. I've seen 'em, I've seen 'em, Hanging on the old barbed wire." Nivelle again promised the increasingly anxious government in Paris that the breakthrough was just around the corner. More troops were sent into the meat grinder.

For the first time, soldiers resisted. Some French regiments were heard "baaing" like sheep led to the slaughterhouse as they marched past their commanding officers. On May 3, mutinies broke out. By the end of the month, they had spread to other regiments, even though soldiers who refused to go over the top knew they could be summarily shot. They reasoned that they were going to die anyway. Some regiments elected spokesmen, who declared that they would defend the trenches against German attacks, but would not participate in any more foolish assaults. The mutinies affected half of the French divisions along the western front, and at the beginning of June, only two of twelve divisions holding the line in Champagne had been unaffected. More than 21,000 French soldiers deserted in 1917.

Some soldiers were summarily shot where the officers retained the upper hand; 23,000 others were court-martialed, 432 sentenced to death, and 55 executed. Some generals blamed socialist "agitators" and peace propaganda. General Pétain, the hero of Verdun, knew otherwise, and at least tried to improve the conditions of daily life for the soldiers. The Nivelle offensive ground to a halt.

In the meantime, Haig planned another British offensive around Ypres, the "fields of Flanders." The goal was to push the Germans back from the coast to Ghent. Haig had not bothered to inspect the front himself, nor did he pay attention to the pessimistic reports of his intelligence staff. He had not reported estimates of German troop strength to the war cabinet in London. The battle began in heavy rain; the preliminary barrage turned the chalky soil into something like the consistency of quicksand. In the Battle of Passchendaele ("They died in hell, they called it Passchendaele"), named after a devastated village, the British gained four miles in exchange for 300,000 dead or wounded. One soldier determined that, in view of such gains, it would take 180 years to get to the Rhine River. The offensive ended. Haig kept his command.

Morale plunged during the winter in Germany and France. A writer was surprised to see a soldier who had lost an arm drunkenly begging on a Parisian boulevard, muttering, "Peace, Peace." Shortages became worse, rationing more vexing. Occasionally, in the south of France were heard sarcastic references to "Paris's war," or to the blond refugees from the embattled northern departments known as "the Krauts (boches) of the North." The French armaments minister faced shouts of "Down with the War!" when he visited a factory. There were waves of strikes in 1917. But Georges Clemenceau rallied the war effort after again becoming prime minister. He used troops against strikers, as he had before the war. He ordered the arrest of those calling for peace without victory, including his minister of the interior. A cartoon in Britain—unthinkable until 1917—pictured the encounter of two enlisted soldiers at the front. One said, " 'Ow long you up for, Bill?" "Seven years," was the reply, to which the first soldier said, "You're lucky—I'm duration."

Compounding this bleak picture for the Allies was a combined Austrian and German offensive in Italy, strengthened by the arrival of German troops from the Russian front. They pushed the Italian army back seventy-five miles in the Battle of Caporetto on the Isonzo River in October 1917, taking three-quarters of a million prisoners. Despite 200,000 casualties and twice that many desertions, the Italians held along the Piave River, just twenty miles from Venice. The Allies coordinated their war efforts. In October 1917, they established a Supreme War Council, which held regular meetings of the prime ministers of France, Britain, and Italy, as well as a representative sent by President Wilson.

Better news for the Allies came from the Middle East. The discovery of oil there prior to the war had dramatically increased the stakes for influence in the region. During the war, the British took advantage of Arab resentment—particularly by Muslim fundamentalists—of the Turks, who had ruled much of the Middle East for centuries. They stirred up revolts beginning in June 1916. The writer T. E. Lawrence (1888–1935), a British colonel, coordinated attacks against the strategically important Turkish railway that led from the sacred city of Medina to Damascus.

In the last decades of the nineteenth century, more Jews in Europe had begun to long for a homeland in Palestine, which was part of the Turkish Ottoman Empire. By 1914, 85,000 Jews had moved there. The British government in principle supported the Zionist movement for a Jewish state. On November 2, 1917, the Balfour Declaration expressed British willingness to support the future creation of a "national home" for the Jews in Palestine, once the Turks had been defeated, provided that such a state would recognize the rights of the Arab populations who already lived there. This declaration partially contradicted the Sykes-Picot Agreement of 1916, which had secretly divided Syria and other parts of the Middle East into British and French zones of influence. The British government hoped that the eventual creation of a Jewish state in Palestine could serve as a buffer between the Suez Canal and Syria, the latter controlled by France. In December 1917, a British force captured Jerusalem. The Central Powers' ally Turkey seemed on the verge of collapse.

The German Spring Offensive

In the spring of 1918, the Germans launched their "victory drive," their first major offensive since 1914. But Austria-Hungary showed signs of virtually dissolving, with major national groups openly calling for independence. The United States now had 325,000 troops in Europe. They were commanded by General John Pershing (1860–1948), who had won early fame for leading a "punitive expedition" (which turned out to be a wild-goose chase) against the Mexican bandit Pancho Villa. He had also served in campaigns against the Sioux in the American West, and had fought in the Philippines and Cuba. Pershing, a tall, tough, stubborn commander, insisted that

his troops remain independent, fearing that French and British generals
would lead them to slaughter.

Emboldened by the withdrawal of revolutionary Russia from the war,
Ludendorff decided on a massive German assault along the Somme River,
thereby avoiding the mud of Flanders and the hills and forts of eastern
France around Verdun. On March 21, 1918, after a brief bombardment of
five hours to maintain some element of surprise, 1.6 million men attacked
the Allied defenses in five separate offensives over a front of forty miles
(see Map 22.7). When the weather cleared at noon, British pilots observed
that the Germans had succeeded in breaking through the Allied lines. Five
days later, some German units had pushed forward thirty-six miles. The
Germans now advanced in Flanders, moving forward with relative ease
against troops from Portugal, which had recently entered the war on the

Map 22.7 The German Offensive, 1918   The spring offensive of 1918 in which
the Germans attacked the Allies in five separate offensives along the western front.

Allied side. Ludendorff hurled all available reserves into the battle. It looked as though the Germans would take the Channel ports. The Germans bombarded the French capital with their giant gun, "Big Bertha," which could lob shells, each weighing up to a ton, twenty-four miles through the air before they fell to earth with deadly impact. Late in May 1918, the offensive pushed French troops back to Reims, and then as close to Paris as the Marne River in early June. The French stopped the German advance short of Paris. In the gloom of the Allied headquarters, French Marshal Ferdinand Foch (1851–1929) assumed command of the combined French, British, and American armies.

However, the Germans had outrun their cover and supplies, and faced fresh Allied reserves. On July 15, 1918, another major German attack was repulsed. Ludendorff's offensive, which he viewed as the last chance to win the war, had failed. France was not about to negotiate for an armistice. Morale plunged in Germany, amid extreme shortages of food, gas, and electricity. Rationing became more stringent and black markets spread. Inflation was rampant, pushed by the circulation of more paper money, as gold and silver were withdrawn to prevent hoarding. In January 1918, 400,000 workers in Berlin went on strike, demanding a democratization of the government and peace. Carefully couched criticism of the war and of Kaiser William II began to appear in the press. Socialists became bolder. Demonstrations took place in several cities, including Berlin.

The Allies counterattacked in July 1918. The British used their tanks with increasing effectiveness to go over craters and barbed wire and to protect the advancing infantry. Coordinated attacks on the German lines began on August 8, 1918, when the British moved forward eight miles north of the Somme River. A month later, the Germans had been pushed back to the positions they had held at the start of the Ludendorff spring offensive.

The Allies were now confident that they would win the war, probably in 1919 if all went well. Ludendorff advised the kaiser to press for an armistice before it was too late. With the Allies gaining ground, on October 4, 1918, Germany's new chancellor, Prince Max von Baden (1867–1929), a liberal monarchist, asked President Wilson for an armistice based on the American president's call for "peace without victory." The Reichstag passed laws making ministers responsible to it and not to the kaiser. It was a revolution of sorts. Given the circumstances, Kaiser William II could do virtually nothing.

The situation for the Central Powers worsened on the Italian front. His armies in retreat, Austro-Hungarian Emperor Charles I seemed little inclined nor able to continue the war as desertions mounted. There was now little doubt that the defeat of Germany and Austria-Hungary was near.

The Fourteen Points and Peace

On January 8, 1918, in an address to a joint session of the U.S. Senate and House of Representatives, President Wilson set out a blueprint for permanent peace. His "Fourteen Points" were based upon his understanding of how the Great War had begun and how future wars could be avoided. The first point called for "open covenants, openly arrived at," in place of the secret treaties whose obligations had pulled Europe into war. Wilson also called for freedom of the seas and of trade and the impartial settlement of colonial rivalries. Other points included the principle of nonintervention in Russia; the return of full sovereignty to Belgium and of Alsace-Lorraine to France; autonomy—without mentioning independence—for the national groups within the Austro-Hungarian Empire; and the independence of Romania, Serbia, Montenegro, and Poland. The last of the Fourteen Points called for the establishment of an organization or association of nations to settle other national conflicts as they arose. If the desire of the European peoples to live in states defined by national boundaries had been one—if not the principal—cause of the war, then a peace that recognized these claims would be a lasting one. Or so thought Wilson, and many other people as well.

Germany now appeared willing to accept Wilson's Fourteen Points as grounds for an armistice, hoping to circumvent the British and French governments, which clearly would demand unconditional surrender and were not terribly interested in Wilson's idealism. The British, for example, opposed the point calling for freedom of the seas. As Wilson considered what to do with the German proposal for an armistice, a number of U.S. citizens were killed when a U-boat again sank a British ship off the Irish coast. An angry Wilson then replied to Prince Max that the German military authorities would have to arrange an armistice with the British and French high command, and not with him. Germany called off unrestricted submarine warfare and tried to convince Wilson that recent changes in the civilian leadership in Berlin amounted to a democratization of the empire. Foch and Clemenceau demanded unconditional surrender of the German fleet and occupation of the Rhineland by France.

The collapse of the Central Powers accelerated. When French and British troops moved into Bulgaria in September 1918, Bulgaria left the war, as did Turkey the next month. British forces occupied Damascus and Constantinople. When the Austro-Hungarian Empire also tried to get Wilson to negotiate an armistice based on the Fourteen Points, which trumpeted the sanctity of the nation-state, Czechs in Prague proclaimed an independent Czechoslovakia. Croats and Slovenes announced that they would join the Serbs in the establishment of a South Slav state of Yugoslavia. Hungary, too, proclaimed its independence, as if the Great War had been something forced on it by the Austrians. Facing no opposition, the Italian army finally managed to advance into Habsburg territory. Austria-Hungary signed an armistice on November 3, 1918. German sailors mutinied in the Baltic port of Kiel and riots rocked Berlin. An insurrection in Munich led to the declaration of a Bavarian Republic.

On November 7, 1918, an ad hoc German Armistice Commission asked the Allies for an end to hostilities. Two days later, a crowd proclaimed the

German Republic in Berlin. William II blamed socialists and Jews for the overthrow of the empire and then fled across the Dutch border. On November 11, 1918, a representative of the provisional German government and General Foch signed an armistice in a railroad car in the middle of the forest near Compiègne, north of Paris. Celebrations in London, Paris, and New York lasted for days. The mother of the poet Wilfred Owen received news that he had been killed as the church bells of her village were ringing for victory. A French veteran, tiring of the street festivities in his town, went at dusk to a cemetery. There he came upon a woman crying next to the tomb of her husband. Their small boy was with her, playing with a tricolor flag. Suddenly the boy cried out, "Papa, we've won!"

THE IMPACT OF THE WAR

There had been nothing like the Great War in history. About 6,000 people had been killed each day for more than 1,500 days. On average, more than 900 French and 1,300 German soldiers were killed each day during the more than four years of war. Nearly 74 million soldiers were mobilized. Of the 48 million men who served in the Allied armies, at least 18 million were casualties, not including the hundreds of thousands listed as missing. The Central Powers mobilized 25.5 million men and had 12.4 million casualties, again not counting the missing. In all, approximately 9.4 million men were killed or "disappeared," 21.2 million wounded (of whom an estimated 7 million may have been left permanently disabled), and 7.6 million prisoners of war. Many—perhaps millions—of civilians died from war-related causes, principally related to not having enough to eat. As Table 22.1 shows, the Austro-Hungarian, Russian, and French armies suffered proportionally more than the other major combatants. Of all French troops mobilized during the war, 16.8 percent were killed (compared to 15.4 percent of German soldiers). Furthermore, about 50 million people died in a worldwide influenza epidemic in 1918–1919 that killed more people in Europe than did the war.

But sheer numbers, however daunting, do not tell the whole story. Of the wounded who survived, many were condemned to spend the rest of their lives—shortened lives, in many cases—in veterans' hospitals. Soldiers who had lost limbs or who were mutilated in other ways became a common sight in European cities, towns, and villages after the war. Europe seemed a continent of widows and spinsters; so many men were killed in the prime of life that the birthrate fell markedly after the war. Support for families of the dead soldiers and invalids unable to work strained national budgets. War cemeteries stretched across northern France and Belgium. Warfare had changed. The Battle of Verdun had lasted ten months, that of Gallipoli more than eight months, and the Battle of Somme in 1916 more than five

TABLE 22.1. CASUALTIES IN THE GREAT WAR

ALLIED POWERS

Country	Mobilized	Dead	Wounded	POW/ Missing	Total	% Casualties
Russia	18,100,000	1,800,000	4,950,000	2,500,000	9,250,000	51.10
France	7,891,000	1,375,800	4,266,000	537,000	6,178,800	78.30
G.B., Emp. and Dom.	8,904,467	908,371	2,090,212	191,652	3,190,235	35.83
Italy	5,615,000	578,000	947,000	600,000	2,125,000	37.85
U.S.	4,273,000	114,000	234,000	4,526	352,526	8.25
Japan	800,000	300	907	3	1,210	0.15
Romania	1,000,000	250,706	120,000	80,000	450,706	45.07
Serbia	750,000	278,000	133,148	15,958	427,106	56.95
Belgium	365,000	38,716	44,686	34,659	118,061	32.35
Greece	353,000	26,000	21,000	1,000	48,000	13.60
Portugal	100,000	7,222	13,751	12,318	33,291	33.29
Montenegro	50,000	3,000	10,000	7,000	20,000	40.00
Total	48,201,467	5,380,115	12,830,704	3,984,116	22,194,935	46.05

CENTRAL POWERS

Country	Mobilized	Dead	Wounded	POW/ Missing	Total	% Casualties
Germany	13,200,000	2,033,700	4,216,058	1,152,800	7,402,558	56.08
Austria-Hungary	9,000,000	1,100,000	3,620,000	2,200,000	6,920,000	76.89
Turkey	2,998,000	804,000	400,000	250,000	1,454,000	48.50
Bulgaria	400,000	87,500	152,390	27,029	266,919	66.73
Total	25,598,000	4,025,200	8,388,448	3,629,829	16,043,477	62.67
Grand Total	73,799,467	9,405,315	21,219,152	7,613,945	38,238,412	51.81

Source: J. M. Winter, *The Great War and the British People* (London, Macmillan, 1985), p. 75.

months (in which 4 million soldiers fought, of whom more than a quarter were killed, captured, or "disappeared"). The carnage was not limited to the European continent. In response to Armenian demands for an independent state, in 1915 the Turks forced 1.75 million Armenians to leave their homes in Turkey; more than a third of them perished without water in the desert sun on the way to Syria.

The flower of European youth—or much of it—had perished in the war. There were other costs as well. The economic structure of northern France and part of Belgium had been chewed up in the fighting. The German economy, which was devastated by the war, would be further crippled by the terms of the peace treaty (see Chapter 24). The Carnegie Endowment for International Peace made a brave attempt to calculate the war's actual

A widow in mourning before her husband's grave at the
end of World War I.

cost, coming up with a figure of $338 billion dollars after establishing a
rough value for property and even lives lost.

No one could begin to measure other dimensions of the war's impact.
The psychological damage to the generation of survivors can hardly be
measured. "Never such innocence again," observed the British writer Philip
Larkin, referring to the period before the war. The post-war period, rampant
with hard times and disappointments, caused many people to look back even
more on the pre-war period as the "Belle Époque," the good old days.

Woodrow Wilson was not alone in thinking that the Great War was the
war to end all wars. Many people reasoned that no one could ever again
wish such a catastrophe on humanity. The American writer F. Scott
Fitzgerald took a friend to a battlefield in the north of France: "See that little stream—we could walk to it in two minutes. It took the British a month
to walk to it—a whole empire walking very slowly, dying in front and pushing forward behind. And another empire walked very slowly backward a
few inches a day, leaving the dead like a million bloody rags. No European
will ever do that again in this generation." He was wrong.

CONCLUSION

The Great War had several causes, with none alone standing as a sufficient cause. To be sure, the entangling alliances of the European great powers were undeniably a principal factor in the outbreak of hostilities. Aggressive nationalism spilled out of the opposing alliances during this period. Schoolchildren throughout much of Europe were taught that their country was the greatest nation in history, and that their rivals and enemies were craven reptiles. The imperial rivalries of the great powers—above all, in Africa—helped make the alliance system more rigid, sharpening rivalries between Germany and Britain and France. Nationalists strongly believed that having colonies helped define status as a great power: by such reasoning, states had to expand their military forces and be prepared to defend their empires as they would their own borders.

Military planners (who were, after all, nationalists themselves) in Germany, Austria-Hungary, France, and, to a lesser extent, Russia, all considered war not only inevitable but desirable. To one British writer, "War . . . is the sovereign disinfectant, and its red stream of blood . . . cleans out the stagnant pools and clotted channels of the intellect." In Germany, an official in the chancellery wrote that "the hostility that we observe everywhere [is] the essence of the world and the source of life itself." War would be the ultimate test by which the fit—individuals and nations—would be measured. "Give me combat!" rang out from the dueling fraternities in Heidelberg to the gymnastic and shooting clubs of Paris.

For those who had been lucky enough to survive, how much greater the disappointment, disillusionment, and bitterness that would follow. One contemporary observer did not mince words: "The World War of 1914–1918 was the greatest moral, spiritual and physical catastrophe in the entire history of the English people—a catastrophe whose consequences, all wholly evil, are still with us." Soldiers returned home to find skyrocketing prices and unemployment awaiting them. In Britain, parents whose sons had died as foot soldiers in France or Belgium learned that families of aristocratic officers had complained that their sons had been buried alongside ordinary people. Politicians who had put aside their differences during the war in a common effort for victory—such as the "Sacred Union" in France—reverted to bitter disagreements that were compounded by the dilemmas posed in the peace settlement. The problems of making peace and putting Europe back together again, as well as paying for the war, would not be easily resolved. U.S. participation in the war and, particularly, the Russian Revolution, which we will examine in the next chapter, would each have a profound impact on Europe's future. War became the continuing experience of the twentieth century.

CHAPTER 23

REVOLUTIONARY RUSSIA AND THE SOVIET UNION

W hen Nicholas II (1868–1918) was crowned tsar of Russia upon the death of Alexander III in 1894, he decided to hold a great public festival on a huge field outside of Moscow, considered the sacred center of the empire. Convinced that it was his duty to uphold the principles of autocracy, Nicholas was sensitive to the tsar's traditional role as the Holy Father of all his people. He wanted to reaffirm the ties that bound his subjects to him, and he to them. The festival attracted enthusiastic crowds numbering in the hundreds of thousands. It featured rides, fortune telling, and other staples of Russian popular festivals. But in the stampede to get free beer and coronation souvenirs, more than 1,200 people were crushed to death and between 9,000 and 20,000 injured. Celebration had turned to tragedy. And during the coronation itself, the heavy chain of the Order of Saint Andrew dropped from Nicholas's shoulders to the ground. Many people—perhaps even the superstitious tsar himself—saw these events as bad omens for the tsar's reign.

Not bad omens, however, but rather the failure to implement meaningful political reform brought down Nicholas II and the Russian autocracy in 1917. First, the Revolution of 1905 led to reforms but did not alter the autocratic nature of the regime. This revolution forced Tsar Nicholas II to grant increased freedom of the press and to create an elected Duma (assembly). These reforms had disappeared, for all intents and purposes, when the tsar regained the upper hand in the counter-revolution that began in 1906, yet the Revolution of 1905 demonstrated the vulnerability of even a police state to popular mobilization. In August 1914, the Russian Empire went to war, and the conflict itself encouraged those who demanded political reform. In February 1917, the tsar abdicated. Then, after six months of uncertainty and political division, the Bolshevik (October) Revolution overthrew the provisional government. Russia withdrew from the Great War. The "dictatorship of the proletariat" became that of Vladimir Lenin's Communist Party. Upon Lenin's death in 1924, Joseph Stalin consolidated his personal authority in the Soviet Union, ruthlessly establishing state socialism (see Chapter 25).

The Russian Revolution of 1917, like that of 1905, was not the kind of revolution that the Russian populists or anarchists had predicted—massive uprisings of the peasant masses against lords and imperial officials— although peasant rebellion was an essential ingredient in both revolutions. Nor did it correspond to Karl Marx's prediction that a successful bourgeois revolution would be followed by a revolution undertaken by an industrial proletariat. War played a catalytic role in the Russian Revolution of 1917: Russia's shocking defeat in the Russo-Japanese War (1904–1905) and, above all, the horror of the Great War created hardships that increasingly undermined the legitimacy of the tsarist regime.

WAR AND REVOLUTION

Reformers were still biding their time when Russia went to war in 1914. However, Lenin (see Chapter 18) was dumbfounded when most socialists in other countries supported their nation's mobilization for war. Among Russian socialists, "defensists" (Mensheviks and most Socialist Revolutionaries) argued that Russian workers should defend their country against German attack. "Internationalists" (including Bolsheviks) opposed the war, viewing it as a struggle between capitalist powers in which workers were but pawns.

Lenin took the war as a sign that capitalism might be ripe for what he thought was its inevitable fall. "Imperialism is the last stage," he wrote, "in the development of capitalism when it has reached the point of dividing up the whole world, and two gigantic groups have fallen into mortal struggle." He believed that if revolution were to break out in several countries, the fall of Russian autocracy and capitalism could be near, even without the true "bourgeois revolution" Marx had predicted. Even if the Russian working class was less developed than those of Western nations, the corresponding weakness of the Russian bourgeoisie could facilitate a successful revolution. This revolution would be followed by the establishment of a dictatorship of the proletariat, that is, by a mobilized working class led by its most dedicated elements, his party, the Bolsheviks. The revolution would then spread to other countries, where the working classes would follow the example of the first successful socialist revolution.

Russia at War

The Great War became a catalyst for demands for reform within Russia, first in the management of the war itself, and then in Russian political life.

The war had begun with an upsurge of patriotism and political unity, with the tsar blessing icons and the faithful kneeling before him. A Bolshevik noted bitterly that amid shouts of "'God Save the Tsar!' our class struggle went down the drain." Within a year, however, the war had shattered the "sacred union" that represented a patriotic consensus in 1914. Liberals renewed demands for political reform. Workers agitated for higher wages and better working conditions. By 1917, 15 million men had been drafted into the army, the vast majority of whom were poor peasants. It proved difficult to transform peasants who were more used to holding rakes than rifles into soldiers. Sent by high command into battle ill equipped, Russian losses were staggering.

In the interest of the war effort, the government allowed national organizations to exist that earlier had been forbidden. These groups became the organizational base for the liberal opposition. Liberal *zemstvo* representatives established a committee, the Union of *Zemstvos*, to organize relief for the sick and wounded; an organization of municipal governments, the Union of Towns, was also created.

In the spring of 1915, liberal Duma members began to express open dissatisfaction with the way the war was being run. Russia's factories experienced difficulties in meeting military needs; the army lacked sufficient rifles and artillery shells. The tsar permitted industrialists to form a War Industries Committee, to which delegations of workers were added, in order to expedite wartime production.

The war gradually transformed Petrograd (the new name given to Saint Petersburg, because it sounded more Russian), accentuating social polarization. By 1916, most of Petrograd's workers, who made up 35 percent of

Tsar Nicholas II, holding an icon, blesses his troops.

the population, were producing war materiel, swelling the ranks of metal, textile, and chemical workers. More peasants flocked to the capital, as did waves of refugees from the war zones of Russian Poland and the Baltic states.

As Russian society strained under the pressures of war, liberals demanded that the Duma be allowed to meet and that Tsar Nicholas dismiss a number of reactionary ministers. With military defeats—none more disastrous than that at Tannenberg (August 1914), where 100,000 Russian troops were captured—followed by humiliating retreats weighing on him, the tsar established a Council for National Defense. He summoned the Duma to meet in July 1915 and replaced four ministers. In August, some liberal members of the Duma formed a "Progressive Bloc" committed to working with the tsar in the hope of encouraging reform.

The melancholy, ineffectual tsar remained extremely superstitious. Seventeen was his unlucky number: on January 17, 1895, the day of his first speech as tsar, an elderly noble had dropped a traditional gift of bread and salt, a bad omen, and on October 17, 1905, he had been constrained to sign a constitution. But he retained the respect and distant affection of most of the Russian people. Tsarina Alexandra, in contrast, was loathed by many of her subjects. Born in Germany, she was the granddaughter of Queen Victoria and had been raised in England before marrying Tsar Nicholas in 1894. She had converted from Anglicanism to the Russian Orthodox Church. The illness of their only son, Alexei (1904–1918), a hemophiliac and the heir to the throne, increasingly weighed on the royal couple.

As she became ever more conservative, Alexandra extended her influence over her weak-willed husband. Nicholas dismissed ministers on the whims

Tsarina Alexandra with Grigory Rasputin (center).

of the tsarina. ("Lovey, don't dawdle!" she wrote her husband, urging him to fire one of them.) When he met in an emergency session with his Council of Ministers, the tsar followed Alexandra's instructions to clutch a religious icon. Nicholas then dismissed his liberal ministers. Many Russians wrongly believed that Alexandra was actively working for the interests of Germany, although no German agent could have served Germany as well. In the meantime, Nicholas had assumed command of the army. Liberals feared this could lead to more military disasters, and would also take the tsar away from Petrograd, leaving imperial decision making even more subject to the influence of Tsarina Alexandra.

Alexandra's great favorite was Grigory Rasputin (1872–1916), a debauched "holy man." Claiming occult power and the ability to heal Alexei's hemophilia, Rasputin had moved gradually into the inner circle of court life. On one occasion, he predicted that one of Alexei's spells would shortly subside, and it did. To the consternation of the tsar's ministers, the influence enjoyed by the man the tsarina called "our friend" became a matter of state. In December 1916, noble conspirators, who feared Rasputin's influence on military operations, put what they thought was enough poison into his many drinks to kill a cow. When Rasputin seemed almost unfazed, they shot him repeatedly and smashed his skull in a protracted struggle.

Food shortages eroded the revival of the workers' patriotism that had accompanied the beginning stages of the war. The growth of public organizations, which opened up a larger public sphere for discussion and debate, helped mobilize opposition to autocracy. Cooperative associations formed by workers to resist high prices had 50,000 members by the end of 1916. Some workers on the War Industries Committee pushed for greater militancy. The Bolsheviks found support among industrial workers. Attacks on the management of the war rang out in the Duma, as well as in the Union of Towns and the Union of the *Zemstvos*. In December 1916 the latter passed a resolution calling on the Duma to stop cooperating with the tsar and demanded ministerial responsibility. Liberals remained paralyzed, however, cowed by tsarist repression amid increased worker militancy.

For the moment, the tsar and the liberals needed each other. Outright revolution or violent repression seemed equally dangerous to both. The state needed the continued participation of voluntary committees and agencies of local self-government in order to keep the state from collapsing into shortage-induced anarchy. Liberal-dominated committees and agencies required the centralized apparatus of the state to carry out their work.

Food shortages reached a peak during the harsh winter of 1916–1917. Peasants hoarded their grain. Police repression of strikes helped close the ranks of workers against the government. In Lithuania, nationalists demanded autonomy within the empire, and some nationalist agitation occurred in other Russian borderlands as well. In 1916 Muslims in Turkistan in Central Asia rose up in arms against Russian rule after the government attempted to move a quarter of a million people to factories near the front. Increasing anger at the continued arrival of Russian settlers in Turkistan also played a role in the unrest. These occurrences revealed the complexity of the problem of nationalism in the Russian Empire.

Alexander Kerensky, (1881–1970), a lawyer, and leader of the Socialist Revolutionaries (see Chapter 18), denounced the war in a speech whose daring rhetoric had never been heard in the Duma. Some loyal nobles now urged reforms. But Nicholas replaced members of the Progressive Bloc with uncompromising reactionaries. He and his family withdrew into retreat, leaving the government floundering like a rudderless boat in high seas.

The February Revolution

The Russian Revolution that took place in Petrograd in February 1917 grew out of the massive discontent with hunger and deprivation, and amid mounting frustration at tsarist intransigence against reform. Like most large European cities, Petrograd's neighborhoods reflected social segregation. The upper- and middle-class residential districts and the palatial buildings of imperial government lay on and near a long street called the Nevsky Prospect. This central artery was lined with banks, hotels, restaurants, cafés, a giant department store, and offices. The streetcars did not run as far as the muddy streets of the workers' districts, nor in many cases did the city's water mains or electric power lines. Epidemics were still frequent in Petrograd, as in Moscow and other Russian cities, which were characterized by acute overcrowding and inadequate sanitation.

Revolutionary organizations prepared a massive general strike in early 1917, the anniversary of Bloody Sunday in 1905. During January and February, almost half of the capital's 400,000 workers went out on strike, including munitions workers at the Putilov factory—the largest factory in Europe with 30,000 workers. Yet the Petrograd garrison of about 160,000 soldiers still seemed adequate to the task of maintaining order, even though most were raw recruits. Demonstrators demanded that a provisional government be appointed with the power to enact major reforms. Food lines stretched longer in Petrograd, Moscow, and other cities in temperatures that reached forty below zero. Bread riots, in which many women and young people participated, became a daily occurrence.

On February 23 (all subsequent dates in this chapter refer to the Old Russian calendar, which was thirteen days behind the Western calendar), more determined demonstrators took to the streets. Workers in the Putilov munitions factory tore up factory rule books and created committees to represent their interests to the company. Female textile workers led the way out of the factories.

On February 25, a general strike closed down Petrograd. While Petrograd's Duma debated ways of dealing with severe food shortages, crowds of ordinary people poured into Petrograd's center. Military attention was focused on the front. Tsar Nicholas then ordered the commander of the garrison to suppress demonstrations. Street fighting began and spread in the city. The attitude of soldiers, most of whom were peasants or workers, now became crucial. Many were shocked when ordered to fire on insurgents. When a commanding officer tried to restore order by reading a telegram from the tsar, he was shot while trying to flee the barracks. Thousands of soldiers and some officers went over to the insurgent side, and a number of officers and soldiers who continued to resist were summarily executed after being captured.

Miserable conditions of war, the unpopularity of the officers (who addressed the rank and file as masters had spoken to serfs), awful food,

Bolshevik soldiers marching at the Kremlin in Moscow, 1917.

and empathy with the demands of the workers for "bread and peace" explain the massive defection of soldiers. Sailors mutinied on ships of the Baltic fleet. The capture of the Petrograd arsenal put thousands of rifles as well as ammunition into the hands of workers. The insurgents controlled Petrograd, the capital of Russia.

Nicholas, who was away at his seaside resort with his family, now ordered the Duma to dissolve. Some of its members drawn from privileged society obeyed, but the majority simply moved to a new meeting place. They voted to remain in Petrograd—a move not unlike the Tennis Court Oath of the third estate during the first period of the French Revolution, a precedent of which they were keenly aware. The Duma then elected a provisional committee, whose mandate was to restore order. In the meantime, the liberals, who tried to walk a tightrope between a desire for reform and a fear of the masses, now were in the position of trying to contain the revolution they had helped set in motion.

The Russian Revolution of February 1917 was unplanned and its outcome uncertain. But the soil was fertile. Experienced in strikes, Socialist Revolutionary, Menshevik, and Bolshevik activists helped impart a sense of direction to the movement. Their goal, unlike that of the liberals, who wanted only reform, was the overthrow of the tsarist regime. Amid the turmoil of sudden change effected by groups who did not necessarily agree on what should happen next, the provisional committee began to function as a provisional government, organizing a food supply commission and a military commission to try to bring the soldiers roaming through the city under some control.

On February 27, in response to calls in the streets, the Petrograd Soviet of Workers' and Soldiers' Deputies was created—*soviets* were councils that had been established during the Revolution of 1905. Members of the organization included several hundred workers, some of whom the demonstrators had freed from jail (where they had been placed for their political or trade union activities), as well as soldiers. They elected officers, discussed ways to defend Petrograd against a possible German attack, and sent representatives to encourage the formation of soviets in other cities. Menshevik leaders took the lead in the Petrograd Soviet's creation as Bolshevik leaders held back, fearing that a large and effective soviet might make it more difficult for their party to direct worker militancy.

Hoping to overwhelm the rebellion with his presence, the tsar now decided to return to Petrograd. He spent almost two full days aboard his private train, critical moments in the February Revolution. On the train, the tsar received an erroneous report that insurgent troops held the next stations and that they would refuse to let his train through. Nicholas then went to the northern military front, hoping to find a loyal army ready to march on Petrograd. In disbelief, he learned that Moscow, too, had fallen almost overnight to insurgents. His generals made no effort to save the

Workers at the giant Putilov factory in Petrograd vote during a meeting of the Petrograd Soviet.

regime. They believed the tsar's cause lost and that only his abdication could prevent civil war, and perhaps military defeat at the hands of Germany as well.

Nicholas II abdicated on March 2, 1917, leaving the throne to his brother, Prince Michael. He did so with characteristic calm and fatalism—scribbling in his diary that day, "All around me—treason and cowardice and deceit." A few hours in revolutionary Petrograd convinced Prince Michael to refuse to succeed his brother. The Soviet placed the tsar and his family under house arrest until the summer, when they were taken by train to a small Siberian town. The Russian autocracy had fallen in a matter of days, with only about a thousand people killed. No legions of faithful peasants had risen up from the land of the black earth to save the "Holy Father."

The Provisional Government and the Soviet

The provisional government and the Petrograd Soviet were left in the awkward position of serving as dual or parallel governments. The provisional government included Constitutional Democrats, liberals who had demanded only that the tsar initiate political reforms. The Petrograd Soviet, in contrast, consisted largely of workers and soldiers who had helped overthrow the tsar. The relationship between the moderate provisional government and the radical Soviet would ultimately affect the course of the Russian Revolution itself. For the moment, the Petrograd Soviet promised to accept the provisional committee's authority. Both the provisional government and the Soviet met in the same palace, with Kerensky, named minister of justice but also a member of the Soviet, running back and forth between the two bodies, trying to smooth relations between them.

On March 8, the provisional government granted civil liberties, including the right to strike, democratized local government, announced that it would convene a constituent assembly to establish a constitution, and amnestied political prisoners. The Petrograd Soviet, now with 3,000 members and an executive committee meeting virtually around the clock, demanded immediate economic and social reforms. The provisional government and the Soviet quickly became the focus of attention of competing political groups—Liberals, Socialist Revolutionaries, Mensheviks, and Bolsheviks—all of whom wanted to shape Russia's future.

The Army

In the meantime, the army was the last functioning imperial institution. On March 1, the Petrograd Soviet issued Order Number One, which claimed for the Soviet the authority to countermand orders of the provisional government on military matters and called for the election of soldiers' committees in every unit. In fact, such elections had already widely occurred, a remarkable attempt to democratize army life. In some places on the front, soldiers had refused to obey officers and, in a few cases, beat them up or even shot them. The soldiers wanted peace. Yet the danger that the military front might collapse against German pressure seemed quite real. Desertions increased in the first month of the Revolution. For the moment, however, the Bolshevik promise of "land and peace" seemed a distant prospect. As soldiers put it, "What good is land to me if I'm dead?"

The United States, first, and then Great Britain, France, and Italy quickly gave diplomatic recognition to the provisional government, hoping that the Revolution would not drastically affect the Russian military commitment to hold the eastern front. But in a few places on the front, Russian troops fraternized with astonished German and Austro-Hungarian soldiers.

The Revolution Spreads

As news of the Revolution and the abdication of Tsar Nicholas II spread, ordinary people in the vast reaches of what had been the Russian Empire attacked and disarmed police stations, freed political prisoners, and created provisional governing bodies. Yet it sometimes took weeks for "commissars of the revolution" to arrive. In some industrial regions, workers had already occupied factories, demanding higher wages, an eight-hour day, and control over production. But in most places, the situation remained unclear. One Russian reflected: "We feel that we have escaped from a dark cave into bright sunlight. And here we stand, not knowing where to go or what to do."

With Petrograd and much of European Russia caught between war and revolution, some of the minority peoples of the empire began to demand more favorable status. Their demands were as myriad and complicated as the old Russian Empire itself. Among the nationalities, some nationalists sought only cultural autonomy; others wanted some degree of political freedom within the context of a federal structure; still others demanded outright independence. Such demands soured relations in regions where ethnic and religious tensions had persisted, sometimes for centuries. In the steppes of Central Asia and in the northern Caucasus, fighting broke out between Russian settlers and the Cossacks (who had begun to settle the regions in large numbers following the emancipation of the serfs in 1861), the Kazakh-Kirghiz, the Bashkirs, and other Turkish peoples. Thousands of people perished in these struggles. In the Baltic states of Lithuania, Latvia, and Estonia, nationalist movements grew rapidly.

The provisional government's goal was to hold the empire together until a constituent assembly could be elected to establish the political basis of the new state. Its declaration of civil rights for all peoples had made each nationality in principle equal. In some places, representatives of the new regime immediately turned over administrative responsibility to local committees or individuals. But elsewhere, local peoples set up their own institutions of self-rule in the hope of maintaining order. In some places,

Alexander Kerensky (front center) head of the provisional government, with troops in Petrograd, 1917.

nationalist movements competed with Socialist Revolutionaries, Mensheviks, and Bolsheviks for allegiance.

Kerensky's provisional government announced that Poland, which had been an independent state until the Third Partition by Russia, Prussia, and Austria in 1795, would again become independent, in the hope of undermining German and Austro-Hungarian troops who occupied most of Poland. In neighboring Belarus—like Poland, a battleground—a national committee led by Socialist Revolutionaries demanded autonomy and established a Rada (council).

The situation in Ukraine was particularly complicated. The provisional government feared that if it granted Ukrainian autonomy, other nationalities would demand similar treatment. Shortly after the tsar's abdication, Ukrainian socialists had formed a soviet. On March 4, 1917, nationalists and socialists established the Ukrainian Central Council. Centuries-old resentment of Russia, based on cultural and linguistic differences, rose to the surface. As more radical nationalists gathered in Kiev, the Rada convoked a Ukrainian National Congress, which began to draft a statute for autonomy. Ukrainian soldiers formed their own military units. Serving as a *de facto* provisional government in Ukraine, the Rada broadened its social and national base by including non-Ukrainian residents. In the meantime, nationalism began to grip Ukrainian peasants, and many of them occupied lands owned by Russian or Polish landlords.

In regions with sizable Muslim populations, national movements were divided between religious conservatives, Western-looking liberals, and leftist Socialist Revolutionaries. The first All-Russian Muslim Congress, which began on May 1, 1917, reflected these divisions. Islamic conservatives attempted to shout down speakers advocating rights for women, but

Westernizers predominated, passing the measure. The congress announced the future formation of a religious administration that would be separate from the state.

Besides the enormous challenge of assuring the food supply—by ordering the army to curtail the unpopular requisitioning of grain—the provisional government had to make sure that the military front held. At the same time, the provisional government faced increasing pressure from the Soviet for economic and social reforms, above all, land reform. The provisional government authorized the formation of local food supply committees and "land committees," which were charged with gathering information in order to draft a land reform measure for the Constituent Assembly. Liberals also wanted land reform, but insisted that it be carried out in a deliberate, legal manner. Peasants, however, wanted action, not committees.

An All-Russian Congress of Soviets began at the end of March 1917 in Petrograd. Bringing together representatives of other soviets that had sprung up after the Revolution, this congress transformed the Petrograd Soviet into a national body, establishing a central executive committee dominated by members of the Petrograd Soviet.

A groundswell of opposition to Russia's continued participation in the war gradually drove a wedge between workers and soldiers and the provisional government. Nonetheless, at the All-Russian Congress of Soviets, the Bolsheviks' call for an immediate end to the war was easily defeated. Mensheviks and the Socialist Revolutionaries were willing to continue the war, but on the condition that the provisional government work for peace without annexations of land from Russia's enemies.

The issue of the war led to the provisional government's "April Crisis." The minister of foreign affairs, a leader of the Kadets (Constitutional Democratic Party), added a personal note to an official communication to the Allies that called for "war to decisive victory," evoking Russia's "historic right" to take Constantinople. Protests by the Petrograd Soviet and demonstrations against the war led to his resignation from the government at the beginning of May. The April Crisis led to the formation of the first coalition government, which reflected the push to the left. The provisional government now accepted the Petrograd Soviet's demand that "peace without annexations" be henceforth the basis of Russian foreign policy.

Worsening material conditions radicalized many workers, particularly in trade unions that had sprung up since February 1917. Workers organized factory committees and strikes. In the countryside, the poorer peasants operated on the simplest principle of all: those who work the land ought to own it. Many children or grandchildren of former serfs began to occupy the land of the lords for whom they had worked, sometimes killing landlords or former imperial officials in the process. Indeed, the percentage of landless peasants may have fallen by half during the 1917–1920 period. Soviets sprung up in the countryside as civil authority disappeared. In some villages, the Orthodox Church could no longer compel obedience. A priest reported, "My parishioners will nowadays only go to meetings of the soviet, and when I remind them about the church, they tell me they have no time."

Lenin's Return

The German government expedited Lenin's return to Russia from Switzerland, where he had been in exile since 1900. The Bolshevik leader's return might exert further pressure on the provisional government to sue for peace, allowing the German army to concentrate its efforts on the western front. After passing through German territory in a sealed railway car to assure that he had no contact with the German population, Lenin arrived in Petrograd in early April 1917.

Lenin gradually rallied the Bolshevik Party around his leadership, based on the following propositions: (1) Russian withdrawal from the war, the continuation of which he viewed as a serious obstacle to a Bolshevik victory; (2) no support for the provisional government; (3) a call for revolution in the other countries of Europe; and (4) the seizure of large estates by the peasantry.

In his "April Theses," Lenin argued that wartime chaos had allowed the bourgeois and proletarian revolutions to merge in a dramatically short period of time. The overthrow of the autocracy had suddenly and unexpectedly handed power to a weak bourgeoisie. The bourgeoisie, holding power through the provisional government, could be in turn overthrown by the proletariat, supported by the poorest peasants. Local power would be held by workers, soldiers, and peasants through the soviets, but under Bolshevik Party guidance. The soviets would provide the basis on which a new state could be constructed through the "dictatorship of the proletariat and peasantry." It sounded so simple.

Aided by the provisional government's division and growing unpopularity, Bolshevik support grew among the factory committees, Red Guards (newly created factory workers' militias), sailors at the naval base of Kronstadt, and soldiers within the Petrograd garrison. The failure of the existing provisional government to provide either peace or land undermined its support among peasants. It was powerless to resolve industrial disputes or to put an end to land seizures. In the meantime, Menshevik leaders warned that continued Bolshevik radicalism might push conservatives toward launching a coup d'état.

The July Days

Although neither troop morale nor the military situation boded well, in mid-June Kerensky announced a Russian offensive in Galicia. This was to reassure conservatives and moderates that military discipline had been restored, and to convince the Allies that Russia remained committed to winning the war.

On July 3, 1917, the Bolsheviks rose in insurrection. They had been encouraged by their increasing popularity among workers, the ongoing agrarian revolution, and widespread dissatisfaction with the war. Nearly 100,000 soldiers who feared being sent to the front joined the chaotic uprising. However, sensing defeat, the Bolshevik Central Committee tried to call off the insurrection the next day. Most troops remained loyal to the provisional government, and the insurrection failed.

These "July Days" hardened political lines in Russia. The provisional government ordered the arrest of Bolshevik leaders, and troops closed down party headquarters and the offices of the Bolshevik Party's newspaper, *Pravda* (Truth). Kerensky became prime minister of the second coalition government, depending even more on support from the liberal Kadets. Lenin fled to Finland.

The provisional government now believed that the Bolsheviks were finished. Kerensky tried to portray Lenin as a German agent, noting that the Bolsheviks in exile had received some German money. Kerensky's government disarmed army regiments it considered disloyal, reinstated the death penalty for military disobedience, and staged a state funeral, replete with national and religious symbolism, in honor of soldiers killed at the front.

But the repressive measures undertaken against the Bolsheviks were relatively ineffective because of the disorganization of the judicial apparatus, the rapid turnover of government officials, and the support the Bolsheviks enjoyed in the working-class districts of Petrograd. Many Bolshevik leaders escaped arrest and others were soon released from jail. The repressive measures further discredited the provisional government, which seemed to be using the July Days as an excuse to undertake a counter-revolution.

Doubting the revolutionary potential of the soviets, many of whose members and leaders remained Mensheviks and Socialist Revolutionaries, the Bolsheviks turned to the factory committees to consolidate their support. Bolshevik newspapers and brochures in factories denounced the provisional government and accused moderate socialists of counter-revolution.

The Kornilov Affair

Disillusioned by Kerensky's indecision, frustrated by the ineffectiveness of the repression against the Bolsheviks, and frightened by peasant land seizures, Russian conservatives, including some military officers and Kadets, began to think in terms of a coup d'état.

General Lavr Kornilov (1870–1918), newly appointed commander in chief of the army and a tough Cossack, seemed the obvious candidate to overthrow the provisional government. Prelates of the Orthodox Church sent him icons in the hope that the military could restore religious principles to Russia. In early August 1917, a "Conference of Public Figures," including influential leaders drawn from industry, commerce, banking, and the military, pledged Kornilov their support.

Kerensky organized a Moscow State Conference, which he hoped would mobilize support for his second coalition government. Most of the delegates (some of whom were leaders of trade unions, as well as bankers, representatives from the state dumas, military leaders, and professional people) now believed only a military dictatorship could save Russia from the soviets and from having to pull out of the war. German troops had captured Riga, a major Baltic seaport, posing a direct threat to Petrograd.

Kerensky wanted Kornilov to form a military government that could restore order, but he believed that the general would remain loyal to him and to the idea of establishing a democratic republic. Kornilov probably wanted to seize power and impose a right-wing military regime. A confusing exchange led each leader to misconstrue what the other meant. Kerensky demanded Kornilov's resignation as commander in chief and, when the latter refused, called on the army to remain loyal to the provisional government. On August 27, Kornilov issued an ultimatum to the provisional government declaring that "the heavy sense of the inevitable ruin of the country commands me in this ominous moment to call upon all Russian people to come to the aid of the dying motherland."

Bolsheviks, Mensheviks, and Socialist Revolutionaries formed a committee against counter-revolution. Workers reinforced security around their factories. Bolsheviks were among those receiving arms at the arsenals in anticipation of a stand against a military coup. But no coup d'état took place, and probably nothing specific had actually been planned. However, by raising the specter of counter-revolution, the Kornilov Affair aided the Bolsheviks, who portrayed themselves as the only possible saviors of the Revolution.

THE OCTOBER REVOLUTION

The provisional government seemed both incapable of solving the worsening economic crisis and unwilling to take Russia out of the war. The workers of Petrograd were organized and armed, their demands increasing. Only the Bolsheviks promised in their program to turn over to the soviets some degree of political power. The radicalized All-Russian Executive Committee of the Soviets now approved the Bolshevik demand that a "democratic" republic be declared by a government "of representatives of the revolutionary proletariat and peasantry" from which Kadets, moderate constitutional democrats, would be excluded.

The Bolsheviks Seize Power

After returning to Petrograd in disguise, on October 10 Lenin convinced the Bolshevik Central Committee that a second insurrection could succeed. Kerensky believed a Bolshevik insurrection imminent, but he vastly underestimated the party's influence with the Petrograd workers, the soviets, and some army units. Bolshevik propaganda hammered away at the theme that their party was untainted by support for the provisional government. Even if a majority of soldiers or of the population of Petrograd or of Russia did not necessarily favor the Bolsheviks, Lenin's assessment that they would not oppose their seizure of power proved correct.

Late on October 24, 1917, Kerensky shut down Bolshevik newspapers and sent troops to hold the bridges over the Neva River. About 12,000 Red Guards launched the insurrection, supported by factory committees in Petrograd's industrial districts. Leon Trotsky (Lev Davidovich Bronstein, 1879–1940) coordinated the uprising. Trotsky, the revolutionary son of a wealthy Jewish farmer, had borrowed his alias from one of his prison guards. Bolsheviks repelled an attack by army cadets loyal to the provisional government, the only serious fighting of the October Revolution. The regiments upon which Kerensky had counted remained in their barracks, their neutrality striking a blow for the insurrection.

The provisional government collapsed. Kerensky left Petrograd the same day in a car borrowed from the U.S. embassy, hoping in vain to rally military support at the front. That night, the battleship *Aurora*, under the control of revolutionaries, lobbed a couple of shells toward the Winter Palace, where the last ministers of the provisional government were holding out. The provisional government surrendered after eight months of existence. The Bolsheviks held power in Petrograd.

The October Revolution had occurred as if in slow motion. There were fewer people killed than in the February Revolution or even the July Days.

The Bolsheviks seize the Winter Palace, October 1917.

Life went on in many districts of the city as if nothing unusual was occurring. Restaurants, casinos, theaters, and the ballet remained open, although banks closed and streetcars were hard to find. Shares on the stock market, which had risen in anticipation of a military coup d'état during the Kornilov crisis, declined. John Reed, an American sympathetic to the Bolshevik takeover, recalled that in Petrograd's fancy quarters "the ladies of the minor bureaucratic set took tea with each other in the afternoon, [each] carrying her little gold or silver or jeweled sugar-box, and half a loaf of bread in her muff, and wishing that the tsar were back, or that the Germans would come, or anything that would solve the servant problem . . . the daughter of a friend of mine came home one afternoon in hysterics because the woman streetcar conductor had called her 'Comrade.' "

Most Mensheviks and many Socialist Revolutionaries walked out of the All-Russian Congress of Soviets to protest the Bolshevik insurrection. On October 26, the remaining members approved the Bolshevik proposal that "all local authority be transferred to the soviets." The Central Committee of the Congress of Soviets, all Bolshevik except for some leftist Socialist Revolutionaries, now ran the government.

In Moscow, Russia's second city, the insurrection began after the first reports from Petrograd arrived. There, too, the Bolsheviks found support in workers' neighborhoods. After a week of fighting, the forces of the provisional government surrendered. In the vast reaches of the former Russian Empire, a "revolution by telegraph" took place. Commissars representing the Bolsheviks went into the provinces (see Map 23.1). In industrial regions, where the Bolsheviks already dominated some soviets, it was easy enough to establish a military revolutionary committee to assume local power. In the countryside, the Bolsheviks cultivated support among the poorest peasants. Socialist Revolutionaries, with considerable influence among peasants, believed that they could coexist with the new Bolshevik-dominated government. But the Bolsheviks manipulated ethnic, social, and political tensions, purging the soviets of non-Bolsheviks and pushing aside not only the local institutions of self-rule that had spontaneously sprung up after the February Revolution but also their nominal allies, the Socialist Revolutionaries.

In Ukraine, the situation remained calm at least partially because the Bolsheviks had early in the Revolution made an agreement with Ukrainian nationalists. In the distant borderlands where ethnic Russians were a minority, however, strong anti-Russian national feeling often made it extremely difficult for the Bolsheviks to take control.

The Bolsheviks were a small minority in Russia at the time of the October Revolution. "We shall not enter into the kingdom of socialism in white gloves on a polished floor," Trotsky had warned shortly before the October Revolution. The revolutionary government, under Lenin's leadership, seized banks, closed down newspapers, and banned the liberal Constitutional Democratic Party. In December, a new centralized police authority, the

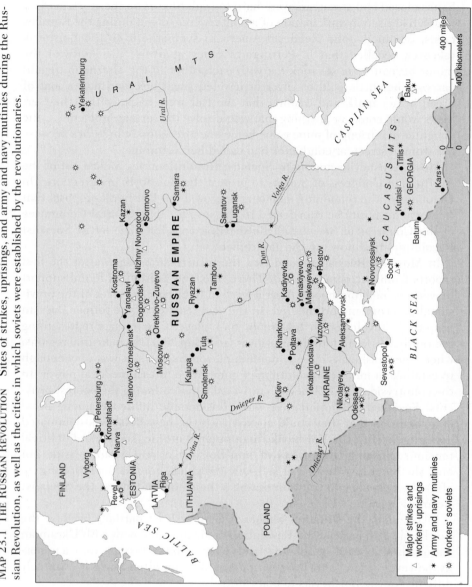

MAP 23.1 THE RUSSIAN REVOLUTION Sites of strikes, uprisings, and army and navy mutinies during the Russian Revolution, as well as the cities in which soviets were established by the revolutionaries.

Cheka, began to arrest those who disagreed with the Bolsheviks. It rapidly proliferated into a large organization with virtually unlimited power. Arbitrary arrests led the eminent writer Maxim Gorky to ask, "Does not Lenin's government, as did the Romanov government, seize and drag off to prison all those who think differently?"

In elections for the Constituent Assembly, the Bolsheviks were supported only by the left wing of the Socialist Revolutionaries. The Bolsheviks won just 29 percent of the vote, compared with 58 percent for the Socialist Revolutionaries. When the elected deputies arrived early in January 1918, the Bolsheviks forced the assembly to adjourn the next day. It never met again. Red Guards fired on protesters.

That month, Lenin proclaimed the "Declaration of the Rights of the Toiling and Exploited People," which stated that the goal of the revolutionary government was "the socialist organization of society and the victory of socialism in all countries." The third All-Russian Congress of Soviets established the Russian Socialist Soviet Republic, a federation of "soviet republics." But, as in the Russian Empire, Russia's interests, even under Bolshevik communism, remained paramount.

The Peace of Brest-Litovsk

After the Bolsheviks took power, Trotsky, now "People's Commissar for Foreign Affairs," offered Germany an armistice, signed early in December 1917. However, Trotsky broke off negotiations for a permanent peace agreement because of draconian German demands. In mid-February, German troops captured Kiev and much of Ukraine and Crimea, as well as some of the Caucasus region. On March 3, 1918, the Bolshevik government signed the Treaty of Brest-Litovsk with Germany, giving up one-fourth of the area of what had been imperial European Russia, containing some of its most fertile land and most of its iron and steel production. The Bolsheviks also agreed to German occupation of Estonia, Lithuania, and Latvia and agreed to pull Russian troops out of Ukraine and Finland. Angered by the treaty and demanding rapid attention to the agrarian question, the leftist Socialist Revolutionaries ended their cooperation with the Bolsheviks. The Germans then occupied all of Finland and Ukraine, setting up puppet regimes in both states.

CIVIL WAR

The Russian Civil War began in 1918 when Kornilov and other generals raised armies to fight the Bolsheviks (see Map 23.2). The anti-Bolshevik forces became known as the "Whites" because they shared a common hatred of the Bolsheviks, the "Reds." The White armies held Central Asia and Siberia, territory east of Moscow, and the Caucasus Mountains. A legion of 50,000 Czechoslovak troops, which had surrendered earlier in the war, operated as an anti-Bolshevik force along an extensive stretch of territory into Siberia, holding the crucial trans-Siberian railway. The White army played upon anti-Semitism by denouncing Trotsky and other Bolshevik leaders because they were Jews. A wave of pogroms spread through Ukraine and parts of Russia. More than 2 million people fled abroad to escape the Russian Revolution and the ensuing Civil War.

MAP 23.2 THE RUSSIAN CIVIL WAR   Boundaries of areas controlled by the Whites and the Reds during the Russian Civil War, including advances by the White and foreign armies.

Ukraine passed back and forth between Bolshevik and nationalist control in bloody fighting, falling again briefly into the hands of the Germans. A huge peasant army led by the anarchist Nestor Makhno (1889–1934) allied with the Bolsheviks and controlled parts of Ukraine after the Germans had fallen back. In Siberia, General Alexander Kolchak (1874–1920), backed by Britain and France, established a dictatorship that claimed to be the new government of Russia.

In February 1918, the Soviet government proclaimed the nationalization of all land. Food shortages and famine spread that summer. The Bolsheviks reacted to the crisis by implementing "War Communism." The state appropriated heavy industries and gradually put an end to private trade. The Bolsheviks forcibly requisitioned food and raw materials, turning poor peasants against more prosperous ones, known as "kulaks." Peasants from whom grain was being taken sometimes reacted with shock—after all, before the October Revolution the Bolsheviks had loudly proclaimed their support for immediate land reform. Now soldiers were confiscating their grain. Many peasants resisted. War Communism may have saved the Revolution, but it took a terrible toll, leading to a dramatic decline in industrial production.

Bolshevik guards moved Nicholas II and his family to Ekaterinburg, a town in the Ural Mountains, as rumors spread that the Czech legion or monarchist generals were planning to rescue them. On July 17, 1918, they

Lenin addressing the troops leaving for the front during the Civil War, 1920. Trotsky is in uniform standing to the right of the podium, and was later removed from this famous photo on Stalin's order after he was purged.

were brutally executed on the orders of the local soviet, an act evidently approved by Bolshevik leaders.

The Allies, particularly Britain, provided supplies to the White armies. In August, British, American, and Canadian soldiers landed in the northern port of Murmansk, claiming that such measures were necessary to prevent Russia's northern ports from falling to the Germans. Allied suspicion of the new Bolshevik government strengthened their decision to intervene. British troops attacked Soviet forces, and American troops landed at the icy northern port of Archangel. Japanese troops moved into Siberia, where the Bolsheviks had little effective control, remaining there until 1922.

Allied intervention helped rally popular opinion against the Whites, whose wanton brutality, including routine rape and murder (some victims were forced to kneel and kiss portraits of the tsar before being killed), exceeded that of the Bolsheviks. Whites filled three freight cars with bodies of Red Guards, sending them along to the Bolsheviks, who were starving, with the wagons labeled "fresh meat, destination Petrograd." However, the Whites had no monopoly on savagery, as in some places Red forces massacred peasants and Cossacks. In Finland, after a bitter civil war between local Reds and Whites, the "White Terror" took 80,000 victims among those who had supported the Revolution. Moreover, the Russian nationalist calls of White leaders for an "indivisible" Russia alienated other national groups, aiding the Bolsheviks, who falsely promised to respect the rights of non-Russian nationalities.

Following attempts on the lives of several Bolshevik leaders, including Lenin, the "Red Terror" began in September 1918. Government decrees gave the Cheka almost unlimited authority and set up forced labor camps to incarcerate those considered enemies. While many victims were indeed working for the overthrow of the regime, many others were simply Mensheviks, Socialist Revolutionaries, or others who held political beliefs that displeased the Bolsheviks.

Fighting the Whites required the mobilization of 5 million men. The Red Army defeated the largest White army in Ukraine during the summer of 1919 and turned back a final march on Moscow in October. General Alexander Kolchak's White army held out until late that year. The Civil War continued in 1920, and in the Pacific region fighting lasted into 1922.

In 1920, Józef Piłsudski, commander of the Polish army, sought to take advantage of apparent Soviet weakness in the wake of the Civil War by creating a federation of independent states, including Lithuania, Ukraine, and Belarus, under Polish leadership. Having defeated the White armies, Lenin planned a Soviet attack on Poland. But the Polish army invaded Ukraine, until the Red Army repelled the attack and pushed Polish forces back into Poland. However, Polish peasants and workers refused to join the Red Army. Piłsudski's forces surrounded the Soviet army on the edge of Warsaw in August 1920—the "miracle of the Vistula" River. This put an end to the possibility of the Soviet army pushing toward Berlin and linking up with a revo-

The White army executes suspected Bolsheviks during the Civil War.

lution in Germany. The Treaty of Riga in March 1921 ended the hostilities between Poland and the new Soviet government, which had been largely at the expense of Ukraine. While much of Ukraine was left within the Soviet Union, 5 million Ukrainians now found themselves living in Poland.

THE SOVIET UNION

The Revolution seemed to offer peasants in Russia hope. After destroying the authority of the imperial regime in the countryside, they then broke the power of the landlords. Many peasants feared the Whites, and they therefore went along with the demands of the Soviet regime, hoping that "peace and land" would follow. The Bolsheviks were able to install a centralized state authority to mobilize the countryside against the counter-revolution. Like the old imperial elites, the Bolsheviks mistrusted the peasants, their notions of family and village ownership of land, their sense of collective responsibility, and their eagerness to market what they produced. The Civil War established a precedent for the use of mass terror to enforce the party's will in rural areas. Gradually, Bolshevik commissars reestablished Bolshevik authority over Ukraine and border lands such as Georgia and Turkistan.

A constitution promulgated in July 1918 promised freedom of speech and assembly, as well as the separation of church and state. The "dictatorship of the proletariat" became that of the Bolsheviks. Marxist theory promised the "withering of the state" once socialism had been constructed, and Lenin himself warned against the growing power of the bureaucracy, which he had helped create. But the Soviet state did anything but wither.

MAP 23.3 THE SOVIET REPUBLICS, 1922–1939 Soviet Socialist Republics (SSRs) and their capitals in the Union of Soviet Socialist Republics.

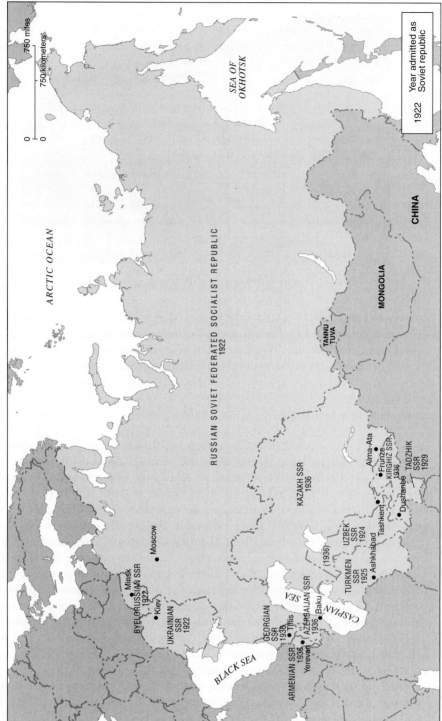

The Union of Soviet Socialist Republics was created in 1922. It included Russia, Belarus, Ukraine, and Transcaucasia (Georgia, Armenia, and Azerbaijan, which all became separate republics in 1936), to which Uzbek (Uzbekistan) was added in 1924, Turkmen (Turkistan) in 1925, Tadzhik in 1929, and Kazakh (Kazakhstan) and Kirghiz in 1936 (see Map 23.3).

Democratic Centralism

For Lenin, "democratic centralism," which had referred to decisions taken by the Bolshevik Party, was also a goal in itself in the organization of the socialist state. In the summer of 1918, the Bolsheviks took the name of the Communist Party, a name Lenin had favored during the war as a way of more clearly differentiating the more radical Bolsheviks from the Mensheviks, their socialist rivals. Lenin's concept originally called for open and free discussion and debate on policy issues, but once party leaders made a decision all dissent had to end and all party members were to unite around the party line. Major decisions and discipline would thus come from the top. The structure suffocated the democratic apparatus on the local level, which henceforth received orders that flowed downward and outward from the central party apparatus in the name of the state.

The Communist government did not tolerate workers' self-management, a goal of many people who had helped overthrow the tsarist autocracy. A group called the Left Communists had opposed signing the Treaty of Brest-Litovsk with Germany, arguing that Russia should lead a revolutionary war against the capitalist powers. Furthermore, they denounced the growing centralization of power. In response, Lenin acidly denounced "Left Infantilism and the Petty Bourgeois Spirit" in the summer of 1918, referring to those who criticized the abandonment of the principles of workers' self-management. Now "workers' control" meant state control.

In June 1919, the Bolsheviks nationalized most of the large-scale industries. In early 1921, at the end of the Civil War, worker discontent erupted in strikes and demonstrations in some industrial centers. In March 1921, the Red Army crushed a revolt at the Kronstadt naval base, where sailors demanded freely elected soviets. Massive strikes rocked Petrograd after Bolshevik authorities rebuffed workers' demands for better working conditions and more control over their shops and factories. Party officials pushed the soviets out of the way as the state turned against the idea of workers' self-management. In 1922, someone asked Trotsky, "Do you remember the days when you promised us that the Bolsheviks would respect democratic liberties?" Trotsky replied, "Yes, that was in the old days." That same year, when protests occurred in one region against the confiscation of Orthodox Church treasures, Lenin himself suggested that demonstrators be shot: "The more [of them] we manage to shoot, the better. Right now we have to teach this public a lesson, so that for several decades they won't even dare to think of resisting."

The New Economic Policy

Lenin and the other Bolshevik leaders debated how socialism could be implemented in a vast, poor country of many nationalities. The new Soviet government had to repair the massive disruption done to the economy by the Great War and subsequent Civil War. More than 7 million people died of starvation and sickness during a famine in 1921–1922. Moreover, the war against Poland and the loss of territory also accentuated the gravity of the economic situation. With the economy in near total collapse, Lenin recognized that communist ideology, which called for the abolition of private ownership, for the moment would have to be sacrificed. Market incentives would have to be tolerated, perhaps for some time.

Furthermore, War Communism had collapsed because of the resistance, active and passive, of peasants and workers. The cities and army had only been fed because the state had been able to requisition or commandeer supplies in the vast countryside. At a time of severe famine, the government needed to feed the population and build up a surplus of raw materials and food supplies. After the threat from the White armies had ended, peasants had violently resisted grain requisitioning. Against this background, in March 1921, Lenin announced a "New Economic Policy" (NEP). Although the state maintained its centralized control over the economy, the NEP permitted peasants to use the land as if it were their own and allowed trade of produce at market prices, although the state retained control of heavy industries. The goal was, above all, to encourage peasants to bring their crops to market. Lenin called this a temporary "retreat" on the road to socialism. Some merchants whose stores had been nationalized during the Civil War were now allowed to manage them again, and the government permitted small-scale, privately owned manufacturing. Lenin even invited foreign investment in mining and other development projects.

The NEP revived the economy. The amount of land under cultivation and industrial production gradually began to reach pre-war levels. In towns, small businesses run by "nepmen" prospered, and kulaks gained. But if the NEP brought economic concessions, there were virtually none in the political realm. The Bolsheviks further consolidated their hold over most government functions, claiming to be serving the interests of the working class by protecting them against the Western Allies. They declared all other political parties illegal, although Lenin claimed that this ban would be only a temporary measure, like the NEP itself. The Bolsheviks continued the campaign against Socialist Revolutionaries, as well as Mensheviks. In 1924, the state limited the entrepreneurship of "nepmen" and, three years later, of kulaks.

In the meantime, Joseph Stalin (1879–1953) emerged as an important figure in the Soviet hierarchy. Stalin—an alias taken from the Russian word for "steel"—was born Joseph (Soso) Dzhugashvili in Georgia, beyond the Caucasus Mountains in the southern reaches of the Russian Empire. His father was a tough cobbler who may have been killed in a tavern brawl, his mother a religious woman who worked as hard as her husband drank. The young Stalin entered an Orthodox seminary in 1894 in the Georgian capital of Tbilisi. Stalin rebelled against the conservatism of the Orthodox Church. In the seminary, Stalin learned Russian, secretly read Marxist tracts, and joined a radical study circle, for which he was expelled. Arrested in 1902 and exiled to Siberia the next year, Stalin escaped and returned to Georgia. There he sided with the Bolsheviks against the Mensheviks (see Chapter 18). The Bolsheviks' hardened secrecy appealed to the young Georgian's acerbic personality. More arrests, jail terms, exile to Siberia, and escapes followed in rapid succession over the next seven years. In 1912, Vladimir Lenin appointed Stalin to the Bolshevik Central Committee, and, after yet another escape from prison, he became editor of *Pravda*.

At the time of the February Revolution, Stalin was a prisoner in Siberia, 600 miles from even the trans-Siberian railway. He managed to return to Petrograd and, after the October Revolution, helped Lenin draft the "Declaration of the Rights of the Peoples of Russia," which promised the peoples of the former Russian Empire self-determination. During the Civil War, he served on the military revolutionary council and quarreled with Trotsky over military strategy.

Trotsky had surprisingly little talent for the ruthless political infighting that was as natural to Stalin as breathing. An intense intellectual and powerful orator, Trotsky considered Stalin a "mediocrity." Stalin remained suspicious of "cosmopolitan"—often an anti-Semitic code word for Jewish—intellectuals such as Trotsky. Espousing "permanent revolution," Trotsky believed that socialism in the Soviet Union could only be victorious following world revolution and that the capitalist nations of the West were ripe to be overthrown by proletarian revolutions. The Communist International had been founded in 1919 to help organize and assist revolutionary Communist parties in other countries. Lenin had believed that workers would overthrow one Western state after another. But this had not happened. The German Revolution of 1919 and the revolutionary government of Béla Kun in Hungary had been crushed (see Chapter 24). The International also promised to help colonial people win independence from imperialist domination.

The problem of the status of the 180 nationalities in the Soviet Union became ever more pressing. Lenin's support for national self-determination had been principally intended to undermine the provisional government and win the support of non-Russian nationalities. Furthermore, concerned with the Soviet Union's image in the colonial world, he wanted to give the impression that the various peoples enjoyed a degree of sovereignty. He still believed that national differences posed a threat to the revolution and that they would become irrelevant in the communist state. Stalin, who served as commissar for nationalities (1917–1923), wanted the peoples of the old imperial state incorporated into the existing Russian state. During the Civil War, he had crushed what he called "the hydra of nationalism" in his native Georgia. Russian interests prevailed within the party, and thus within the government. The

Vladimir Lenin (*left*) with Joseph Stalin (*right*) in a photo doctored by Stalin, who was eager to exaggerate his close association with Lenin.

republics created within the Soviet Union in 1922 and thereafter enjoyed virtually no autonomy. The official line was that communism had brought stability by eliminating ethnic tensions and that nationalism would disappear in the new socialist world. If Soviet policies encouraged the survival of some local languages, one reason was to ensure that state bureaucratic directives could be read by Soviet citizens. The Constitution of 1924 would declare the states of the Soviet Union equal, but the reality was completely otherwise.

In May 1922, Lenin suffered a stroke. His illness set off a struggle of succession infused with personal as well as ideological rivalries. Stalin had demonstrated forceful independence while remaining loyal to the party, and a capacity for organization. The previous month, the Central Committee had named Stalin to the recently created post of general secretary, which allowed him to appoint allies to various important posts and to repress dissent within the party. Stalin kept Lenin isolated as much as possible from visitors. In December, a day after suffering a second stroke, Lenin dictated his doubts about Stalin: "Comrade Stalin, on becoming general secretary, concentrated boundless power in his hands, and I am not sure whether he will always know how to use this power with sufficient caution." Lenin also warned against the expansion of the bureaucracies of both the Communist Party and the state.

Lenin's death in January 1924 consolidated Stalin's position. He placed his own men on the Central Committee and made party appointments throughout the Soviet state. He took every occasion to leave the impression that Lenin had handpicked him to be the next Communist Party leader, later doctoring photos so that he appeared to have been constantly at Lenin's side. Under Stalin, the Soviet Union became even more of a totalitarian regime. The promised "dictatorship of the proletariat" became that of the Communist Party and that of Joseph Stalin.

CHAPTER 24

THE ELUSIVE SEARCH FOR STABILITY IN THE 1920s

In the preface to his novel *The Magic Mountain* (1924), Thomas Mann (1875–1955) wrote that it took place "in the long ago, in the old days, the days of the world before the Great War." Mann sets up a parallel between a Swiss sanatorium and European civilization. In the sanatorium, rationality (Enlightenment thought and democracy) confronts irrationality (the aggressive nationalism of the right-wing dictatorships). In *The Magic Mountain,* which was an allegory for the post-war era, Mann expressed the mood of despair prevalent among European intellectuals in the 1920s: "For us in old Europe, everything has died that was good and unique to us. Our admirable rationality has become madness, our gold is paper, our machines can only shoot and explode, our art is suicide; we are going under, friends."

The Great War swept away the empires of Germany, Austria-Hungary, Turkey, and even before the end of the war, Russia. The Treaty of Versailles, signed in 1919 by a frail new German Republic, and the accompanying treaties signed by the victorious Allies and Germany's wartime partners, did not resolve national rivalries in Europe. Dark clouds of economic turmoil, political instability, and international tension descended on Europe in the two decades that followed the war. The specter of revolution frightened Europe's business and political leaders. Communist parties sprung up in one country after another, even though outside of the Soviet Union Bolshevism only triumphed briefly in Hungary and Bavaria. Although Europe experienced a brief return to relative prosperity and political calm after 1924, the Wall Street Crash of 1929 ended that short period of hope. The search for what U.S. senator and future president Warren G. Harding called "normalcy" proved elusive, if not impossible, in the 1920s.

The Great War helped unleash the demons of the twentieth century, as parties of the political extremes sprang up to threaten parliamentary

The Big Four deciding the future of Europe, 1919. Left to right: Vittorio Orlando of Italy, David Lloyd George of Great Britain, Georges Clemenceau of France, and Woodrow Wilson of the United States.

governments. Fascist and other extreme nationalist groups (see Chapter 25), intolerant of those considered outsiders and committed to aggressive territorial expansion, carried their violence into the streets. Many members of these organizations were former soldiers who vowed to replace democracies and republics with dictatorships. In Eastern Europe and the Balkans, parliamentary rule survived only in Czechoslovakia. Moreover, ethnic rivalries within nations, many inflamed by the Treaty of Versailles, intensified social and political conflict. The post-war treaties could not create new states that satisfied all nationalities.

The End of the War

Even before the representatives of the victorious Allies (along with those representing a host of smaller states) met in Versailles in 1919 for a peace conference, the German and Austro-Hungarian Empires had collapsed, rocked by revolutions. Amid social and political turmoil, the leaders of the great powers set out to reestablish peace in Europe. But the Treaty of Versailles reflected the determination of Great Britain and France to punish Germany for its role in unleashing the conflict. Representatives of the new German Republic were forced to sign a clause essentially accepting full blame for the outbreak of the war, and to agree to pay an enormous sum in war reparations to the Allies, but the amount and schedule of German payments was established only in 1921.

Despite the idealistic belief of U.S. President Woodrow Wilson that the Great War had been the "war to end all wars" and that an era of collective security had begun that would prevent future wars of a similar magnitude, the Paris Peace Conference left a legacy of bitterness and hatred that made it even more difficult for the German Republic to find stability because of massive dissatisfaction with the terms of the treaty. Furthermore, the individual treaties between the Allies and Germany's former wartime partners left several nationalities, notably Hungarians, dissatisfied with the establishment of new states constituted out of the old empires; the newly drawn borders often left them on what they considered the wrong side of frontiers. Nationalists in Germany, above all, but also those in some other countries, were determined to revise or abrogate the post-war peace settlements.

Revolution in Germany and Hungary

The end of the war brought political crises in Germany and Hungary. In the face of defeat, the German Empire came apart at the seams. In late October 1918, German sailors mutinied at two Baltic naval bases, demanding peace and the kaiser's abdication. In southern Germany, socialists led by Kurt Eisner (1867–1919) proclaimed a Bavarian socialist republic in early November. The new chancellor, Prince Max von Baden, called on William II to abdicate, as the socialists threatened to leave the emergency coalition cabinet if he did not do so. William abdicated on November 9. Von Baden then named Friedrich Ebert (1871–1925), a member of the left-wing Social Democratic Party, to succeed him as chancellor.

That same day, a German commission met with Allied representatives to begin drawing up terms for an armistice. On November 9, 1918, another Social Democrat, Philip Scheidemann (1865–1939), fearing that radical revolutionaries would declare a socialist state, proclaimed the German Republic. That night, William II fled into the Netherlands. On November 11, 1918, Germany signed the armistice with the Allies, ending the war. Chancellor Ebert named a provisional government, which was dominated by Social Democrats but with members of the more radical Independent Social Democratic Party also represented.

From its very beginning, the new German Republic was under siege from left and right. Inspired by the success of the Bolshevik Revolution in Russia, workers began to set up "workers' and soldiers' councils" and demanded higher wages and better working conditions. Workers also angered the army by calling for the dismissal of the right-wing General Paul von Hindenburg from the military high command on which he had served since 1916, and by demanding the abolition of the special military schools for officers that for generations had sustained Prussian militarism.

The right posed a more serious threat to the fledgling republic, a threat the Treaty of Versailles would strengthen. Germany had very weak democratic traditions. Monarchism and militarism ran deep, particularly in Prussia.

Furthermore, demobilized soldiers, many of whom were anti-republican, still held their weapons. Ominously, a veteran wrote that he believed the Great War of 1914–1918 was "not the end, but the chord that heralds new power. It is the anvil on which the world will be hammered into new boundaries and new communities. New forms will be filled with blood."

The head of Germany's Supreme Army Command offered the chancellor the army's support, but on condition that the new government not only order the army to maintain order but also to fight "Bolshevism." Ebert accepted and, in doing so, made the new republic virtually a prisoner of the army. Some generals had already begun to enlist demobilized soldiers into right-wing paramilitary units known as the "Free Corps."

Within the new government itself, a rift developed between the Social Democrats and the Independent Social Democrats, who demanded immediate assistance for workers and wanted the government to organize a militia loyal to the republic. When Ebert refused, the Independent Socialist Democrats left the governing coalition, weakening the shaky government. The new minister of defense turned over security operations to the army, and continued to encourage the Free Corps. To the left, this seemed like leaving the fox to guard the hen house.

Workers in Berlin mounted huge demonstrations against the security police. In January 1919, police and soldiers put down an uprising by the Spartacists, a group of far-left revolutionaries who took their name from the leader of a revolt by Roman slaves in the first century B.C. Military units hunted down the Spartacists, murdering Karl Liebknecht and the Polish Marxist Rosa Luxemburg, two of their leaders, who had just founded the German Communist Party.

The German Republic's first elections in January 1919 provided a workable center-left coalition of Social Democrats (who held the most seats in the Reichstag), the Catholic Center Party, and the German Democratic Party. The Reichstag elected Ebert president, and he in turn appointed Scheidemann to be the first premier of the Weimar Republic. The Reichstag met in Weimar, a small, centrally located town, chosen to counter the Prussian aristocratic and militaristic traditions identified with the old imperial capital of Berlin.

Hungary also soon became a battleground between the competing ideologies of the post-war period. Demobilized soldiers and former imperial officials were among those stirring up trouble. Hungarian nationalists feared, with good reason, that the victorious Allies would award disputed territories from pre-war Hungary to Czechoslovakia, Romania, and Yugoslavia. With the collapse of the Austro-Hungarian Empire in the autumn of 1918, Count Mihály Károlyi (1875–1955) led an unopposed revolution of liberals and socialists that proclaimed Hungarian independence. Károlyi favored a republic and initiated a program of land reform by turning over his own estate to peasants. Other wealthy landowners, however, prepared to defend their vast estates against land-hungry peasants. In March 1919, Béla Kun (1886–c. 1937), a Communist journalist, took advantage of the post-war chaos, seized

Karl Liebknecht addresses his supporters in January 1919, shortly before his assassination. (*Right*) Leaders of the Hungarian Communist movement, including Béla Kun, on the right, after they were overthrown.

power, and tried to impose a Soviet regime by means of a "Red terror." He announced a more extensive land-reform policy, established collective farms and labor camps, and nationalized banks, insurance companies, and large industries. Inflation and food rationing soared and the Hungarian currency lost 90 percent of its value. In July 1919, Kun attacked Romania, with the goal of retaking territory with a large Hungarian population. His forces also invaded Slovakia and proclaimed a brief Soviet republic there.

The Romanian army drove Kun's forces back, invading Hungary and marching to Budapest to help overthrow him. Admiral Miklós Horthy (1868–1957), a former Habsburg naval officer (with not much to do, as Hungary would lose its access to the sea), seized power in 1920, with the title of regent and head of state. He encouraged attacks against Jews—Kun was Jewish as was the head of his secret police—claiming that they were Bolsheviks, and he ordered the execution of thousands of workers and Communists. Backed by the Hungarian upper classes, he declared his determination to see Hungary maintain its previous borders.

The Treaty of Versailles

In this volatile atmosphere, delegates from twenty-seven nations and the four British Dominions (Canada, South Africa, Australia, and New Zealand) gathered for the Paris Peace Conference in the château of Versailles. As they convened in January 1919, the representatives of the "Big Four"—Prime Minister David Lloyd George of Britain, Prime Minister Georges Clemenceau of France, President Woodrow Wilson of the United States, and Prime Minister Vittorio Orlando of Italy—agreed that Germany, the nation they believed responsible for the war, should assume the financial burden of putting Europe back together again.

Beyond this area of agreement, the "Big Four" powers went to Versailles with different demands and expectations. France, which had suffered far greater losses than Britain, Italy, or the United States, demanded a harsh settlement that would eliminate Germany as a potential military threat. The diminutive, elderly, and thoroughly vindictive Clemenceau, a combative loner nicknamed "the Tiger," realized the dangers of a punitive peace settlement. But he was also mindful that the quest for security against Germany dominated French foreign relations and weighed heavily upon domestic politics. Defeated Germany was still potentially a stronger state because of its economic capacity and larger population.

France's victory had been Pyrrhic. More than 1.3 million Frenchmen were killed in the Great War. France seemed a country of crippled or traumatized veterans, widows dressed in mourning black, and hundreds of thousands of children left without fathers, for whom pensions would have to be paid. Much of the north and northeast of the country lay in ruins; factories and railways had been destroyed in a region that contained 70 percent of the country's coal. The state had to borrow money from its wartime allies and from its citizens at high interest rates to pay off those who had purchased war bonds.

Clemenceau demanded that Germany's military arsenal be drastically reduced and that French troops occupy the Rhineland until Germany had paid its reparations to the Allies. These payments would be based on a rough estimate of damages caused to the victorious powers by the war. Many in France wanted to go further, demanding annexation of the left bank of the Rhine River, or the creation of an independent Rhineland state that would serve as a buffer against further German aggression.

The British, represented by the Liberal Lloyd George, came to Versailles with more flexible views than the French. Britain had been spared almost all the physical devastation suffered by its cross-Channel allies. Still, the British had suffered horrific loss of life, and they had borne more than their share of the war's financial costs. The British government thus supported France's position that Germany had to be contained in the future. The slogan "Squeeze the German lemon 'til the pip squeaks" was current. However, Lloyd George now concluded that it was in Europe's interest to restore the fledgling German Republic to reasonable economic strength. Moreover, Britian also was wary of a possible increase in French power that could upset the future balance of power in Europe. In view of the perceived threat posed by the Russian Revolution, Lloyd George reasoned that Germany could emerge as a force for European stability.

Italian Prime Minister Vittorio Orlando (1860–1952) came to Versailles assuming that his country would receive territories of the former Austro-Hungarian Empire promised by the Allies in 1915, when Italy had entered the war on their side—namely, the port of Trieste; the strategically important Alpine region around Trent (the South Tyrol), which would give Italy a natural boundary; and Istria and northern Dalmatia on the Adriatic coast (see Map 24.1). Italy had entered the war in part with the goal of generating Italian nationalism, and its allies arguably considered Italy's war effort to have been lamentable. President Wilson found acceptable Italian annexation of the first two, which had sizable—although, except in the case of Trieste, not majority—Italian populations. As a result, Italy extended its frontiers to the Brenner Pass and to Trieste. But Wilson staunchly opposed Italian demands for Istria, northern Dalmatia, and the strategically important Adriatic port of Rijeka (known to its Italian minority as Fiume), which Italy had omitted from its demands in 1915, but now claimed. Italian nationalists denounced the "mutilated peace" of Saint-Germain that had not allowed annexation of all of the territories the Italian government had anticipated receiving.

Wilson's position on Italy's territorial demands reflected one of the broad principles this high-minded son of a Presbyterian minister brought with him to Versailles as representative of the United States. Wilson stood for national self-determination, the principle that ethnicity should determine national boundaries, and went to Versailles hoping to "make the world safe for democracy." This was manifest in his Fourteen Points (see Chapter 22). The U.S. president hoped that diplomacy would henceforth be carried out through "open covenants of peace," not the secret treaties that he held responsible for the Great War. Wilson believed that if the victorious powers applied "the principle of justice to all peoples and nationalities . . . whether they be strong or weak," Europe would enter an era of enduring stability.

The U.S. president's main concern at Versailles was with the creation of a League of Nations, which began in 1920, to arbitrate subsequent international disputes. He was less concerned with forcing a punitive settlement on Germany. In Wilson's opinion, the Great War had been fought largely over the competing claims of national groups, thus it was not right to separate Rhineland Germans from Germany.

Wilson believed that the outbreak of the Great War had demonstrated that the diplomatic concept of a "balance of power," by which the predominant strength of one power was balanced by alliances between several other powers, was unequal to the task of maintaining peace. Henceforth, Wilson wanted the United States to assume an international role, joining Great Britain, France, Italy, and Japan as permanent members of the League of Nation's Council. The League would stand for collective security against any power that would threaten the peace.

Yet idealism and reality were at odds at Versailles. Among the leaders of the three main victorious powers, Wilson's idealism contrasted with the determined realism of Lloyd George and Clemenceau. During four

Territory lost by:
- Germany
- Bulgaria
- Austria-Hungary
- Russia
- Plebiscite areas remaining in country
- Demilitarized zone

Map 24.1 Territorial Settlements After World War I Territories lost by Germany, Bulgaria, Austria-Hungary, and Russia as a result of the treaties ending the Great War.

months, the British and French leaders wrestled with public pressure at home for a harsh peace, which they had to balance against the possibility that a draconian settlement might push defeated Germany, Austria, and Hungary in the direction of the Soviet Union. The French and British views prevailed in what was called the "victor's peace." Moreover, both Lloyd George and Clemenceau, unlike Wilson, enjoyed the full support of their constituents.

By the "war guilt clause," Article 231 of the treaty, Germany accepted full responsibility for "the loss and damage" caused the Allies "as a consequence of the war imposed upon them by the aggression of Germany and her allies." Many Germans were outraged in April 1919 when they learned of the treaty that Germany had been forced to accept. The Allies seemed to be punishing the new German Republic for the acts of the old imperial regime, which arguably had, with Austria-Hungary, done more to start the war than the other powers. Premier Scheidemann resigned rather than sign the treaty. The next Social Democratic government signed it a week later, on June 28, 1919, but only after the Allies had threatened to invade Germany. The Treaty of Versailles returned to France Alsace and the parts of Lorraine that had been annexed by Germany after the Franco-Prussian War of 1870–1871 (see Map 24.2). French troops would occupy the parts of Germany that stood on the left, or western, bank of the Rhine River, as well as occupy for fifteen years a strategically critical strip of land along its right bank. These territories were to remain permanently demilitarized. France would retain economic control over the rich coal and iron mines of the Saar border region (which would be administered by the League of Nations) for fifteen years, at which time the region's population would express by plebiscite whether it wished to become part of France or remain German (the latter was the result in 1935). Germany also had to cede small pieces of long-contested frontier territory to Belgium (Eupen and Malmédy). Moreover, Germany lost its colonies.

In the east, Germany lost territory to Poland, which became independent for the first time since 1795. Poles had been forced to fight in the armies of the German, Austro-Hungarian, and Russian Empires during the war, and thus had been pitted against each other. During the war, both Russia and Germany had promised Poland independence. Indeed, in November 1916 the Central Powers had reestablished the Polish kingdom viewing it as a potential buffer against Russia. In September 1917 they appointed a "Regency Council" with no real power but with the goal of representing Polish Society, with an eye toward Polish autonomy, in the quest for Polish support. In the meantime, Polish nationalists campaigned for support for Polish independence in Britain, France, and the United States. During the war, Józef Pilsudski (1867–1935), one of the leaders of the Polish independence movement during the last decade of the Russian Empire and a leading member of the Polish Socialist Party, commanded a "Polish Legion." Allied with the Central Powers for tactical reasons, it fought against Russian forces in

MAP 24.2 AREAS OF FRENCH AND GERMAN DISPUTES, 1920s   Border areas, including the Rhineland and the Saar Basin, that were occupied by Allied troops or were part of a demilitarized zone after the Great War.

the hope of winning independence. In January 1918, one of Wilson's Fourteen Points was an independent Poland. On Armistice Day, November 11, 1918, Poland became independent. The Treaty of Versailles awarded Poland much of Pomerania, constituting what the Germans would call the "Polish Corridor" (Eastern Pomerania, which had been annexed by Prussia during the late-eighteenth-century partitions of Poland) that led to the Baltic Sea and divided East Prussia, which remained German, from the rest of Germany. The port city of Danzig (Gdańsk) became a free city under the protection of the League of Nations. Poland's new frontiers were settled in 1921 and accepted by the League of Nations two years later.

The German army was to be reduced to 100,000 volunteer soldiers. The German navy, now blockaded by the British fleet, would be limited to twelve warships, with no submarines. Germany would be allowed no air force.

Furthermore, Germany was to pay a huge sum—132 billion gold marks, the estimated cost of the war to the victorious Allies—in war reparations. (There was a precedent: France had been required to pay an indemnity to the German Empire following defeat in the Franco-Prussian war of 1870–1871). The Weimar Republic would be required to turn over to the Allies much of its merchant fleet and part of its fishing fleet and railroad stocks, among other payments. The German Baltic shipyards were to build ships at no cost to the Allies. Each year, Germany was to give the Allies more than one-fourth of its extracted coal as further compensation.

But how was the new Weimar Republic to raise the remainder of the reparations? Tax revenues were low because the economy was so weak, and powerful German industrialists opposed any new taxes on capital or business. The outflow of reparations payments in gold fueled inflation. Government

A German woman using worthless paper money to light her stove during the runaway inflation of 1923.

expenses far outweighed income, exports rapidly declined, and prices began to rise far faster than in other countries, destabilizing the new Weimar government.

The English economist John Maynard Keynes (1883–1946) left the British delegation to Versailles in protest of what seemed to be the draconian treatment afforded Germany. He warned, "If we aim deliberately at the impoverishment of Central Europe, vengeance, I dare predict, will not limp." In particular he denounced the reparations payments in his book *The Economic Consequences of the Peace* (1919), prophesying accurately the failure of the Versailles settlement. The reparations issue poisoned international relations in the 1920s.

The Allies counted on German payments to help them remedy their own daunting economic problems. The promise of German reparations enabled the British and French governments to accede to conservative demands that taxes not be raised or levies imposed on capital. But, in fact, Germany paid only a small portion of the reparations and received more in loans from the other powers than it ever returned in reparations. Germany received three times as much in loans from the Allies than it paid out. Reparations did not ruin the German economy, but their psychological impact in Germany damaged the very republic the Allies wanted to stabilize. The bitter resentment harbored by German right-wing parties toward the reparations compromised the ability of the Weimar Republic to survive.

France wanted the League of Nations to enforce the Treaty of Versailles and to ensure German payment of reparations. (Germany was not permitted to join the League of Nations.) But without an army, the League had no way of enforcing its decisions against member—or, for that matter, non-member—states that chose to ignore its principles or decisions.

After his six-month stay at Versailles, President Wilson returned to the United States to fight for Senate ratification of the treaty. But the elections of November 1918 had given Wilson's Republican opponents control of the Senate. A mood of isolationism swept the country. A majority of senators opposed U.S. membership in the League of Nations, fearing that the treaty would commit the nation to entanglements in Europe. Influenced by the large numbers of German, Italian, and Irish American constituents, some senators believed the treaty to be too harsh on Germany, insufficiently generous to Italy, and irrelevant to Irish demands for independence from Britain. The U.S. government refused to participate in the various international organizations set up to enforce the treaty and to air economic and security concerns. In November 1919, the U.S. Senate refused to ratify the Treaty of Versailles.

The absence of both the United States and the Soviet Union from the League doomed it to failure. The new Soviet government had not even been invited to Versailles. There were two reasons for this: (1) the Bolsheviks had simply declared an end to the war in 1917 and withdrawn troops from the front; and (2) Great Britain, France, and the United States had sent troops and military supplies to support the anti-Bolshevik forces in the Civil War in Russia.

Even among the victorious powers, the treaty generated some apprehension. It seemed a precarious peace. Keynes recalled, "Paris was a nightmare, and every one there was morbid. A sense of impending catastrophe overhung the frivolous scene; the futility and smallness of man before the great events confronting him; the mingled significance and unreality of the decisions." When Marshal Ferdinand Foch of France read the treaty, he exclaimed, "This isn't a peace, it's a twenty year truce!" He was right.

Settlements in Eastern Europe

A series of individual treaties, each named after a suburb of Paris, sought to recognize the claims of ethnic minorities of each country, in some cases redrawing national boundaries (see Map 24.1). But each also left the defeated country feeling aggrieved. "Revisionist" or "irredentist" states wanted the revision of the agreements in order to regain territory they believed should be theirs.

Bulgaria, allied in the war with Germany and Austria-Hungary, lost territory on the Aegean coast, ceded to Greece by virtue of the Treaty of Neuilly (November 1919), as well as small pieces of land to Romania and parts of Thrace that had been won in the Balkan Wars. By the Treaty of Saint-Germain (which specifically forbade Austrian union with Germany), Vienna was reduced to being the oversized capital of a small country, Austria. By the Treaty of Trianon (June 1920), Hungary lost two-thirds of its territory, 60 percent of its total population, and 25 percent of its ethnic Hungarians. Romania received more Hungarian territory than was left to Hungary, and one-third of its population now consisted of Hungarians, Germans, Ukrainians, and Jews. The treaty left 3.4 million Hungarians living beyond the borders of Hungary, hardly Wilsonianism in action. The Hungarian response to the treaty that ended the war is best summed up by the contemporary slogan "No, no, never." Moreover, 1 million Bulgarians—16 percent of the population—now lived outside of Bulgaria.

The Treaty of Sèvres (August 1920), the most harsh of the treaties with Germany's wartime allies, dismembered the Turkish Ottoman Empire. Britain, France, Italy, and Greece all coveted—as had the Russian and Habsburg empires in previous centuries—parts of the old Ottoman Empire that had stretched through much of the Middle East. Now the treaty awarded Smyrna, the region around present-day Izmir on the Anatolian peninsula, and much of Thrace to Greece; the island of Rhodes to Italy; Syria (then including Lebanon) to France, under a mandate from the League of Nations; Iraq and Palestine to Britain, also under mandate from the League of Nations; and Saudi Arabia to Britain as a protectorate (see Map 24.3). Italian troops occupied Turkish territory even as the peace conference was proceeding; Greek forces moved into Smyrna and into Thrace.

In Turkey, the Italian and Greek occupations generated a wave of nationalist sentiment. Mustafa Kemal Pasha (1881–1938)—known as Atatürk—organized armed resistance against the foreign incursions. Turkish forces pushed Greek units out of Smyrna in 1922 and threatened a neutral zone occupied by British troops. When the British government prepared to intervene, an exchange of populations was arranged. The Treaty of Lausanne of 1923 recognized Turkey's independence, ending the European role in administering the country's international debts. Turkey was left with a little territory on the European side of the Bosporus, as well as the Sea of Marmara and the Dardanelles strait, which themselves were declared open to all nations. The treaty called for the exchange of Turkish and Greek populations. Greece had to withdraw from the Anatolian peninsula, and at least 1 million Greek refugees moved from Turkey to Greece. Almost 400,000 Muslims were forced out of Greece, ending up in Turkey. Turks now comprised about 1 percent of the population of Greece; only about 3,000 Greeks remained in Turkey in a population of 70 million people. The Kurds, an ethnic minority within Turkey and Iraq, were still without an independent state. Atatürk became president of the Republic of Turkey, establishing his capital at Ankara in the interior of the Anatolian peninsula. The last Ottoman ruler left Turkey for the French Riviera. Seeking to Westernize and secularize his country, Atatürk promulgated legal codes separating church and state, implemented compulsory education and the Latin alphabet, required Turkish families to take Western-style names, and prohibited Turks from wearing the fez (a traditional brimless hat).

NATIONAL AND ETHNIC CHALLENGES

President Wilson's espousal of ethnicity as the chief determinant of national boundaries had unleashed hope among almost all the Eastern European peoples for independent states based on ethnic identities. The Treaty of Versailles accentuated the role of nationalism as a factor for political instability in Europe after the Great War. At the same time, the failure of the peacemakers at Versailles to address the demands of peoples colonized by the European powers left a legacy of mistrust.

The National Question and the Successor States

The Treaty of Versailles acknowledged the existence of "successor" states out of the ruins of the Austro-Hungarian Empire, as well as out of the territories that had belonged to defeated Germany and the defunct Russian Empire. The creation of these new states by the Treaty of Versailles in theory followed the principle of nationalism—that ethnicity should be the chief determinant of national boundaries—which had helped cause the Great War. However, the principle of nationalism was not applied to the former Russian

Empire, as the Treaty of Versailles did not concern itself with the nationalities of Russia, ostensibly a victorious power, although now transformed into a Communist state. In the north, Finland finally gained its independence after having been for centuries subject to Swedish and, since the beginning of the nineteenth century, to Russian rule. The three Baltic states of Latvia, Estonia, and Lithuania also became independent of Russia (see Map 24.1). The largest of these successor states were Yugoslavia in the Balkans and Czechoslovakia and Poland in Central Europe. Referring to the new states and redrawn boundaries, Winston Churchill complained, "The maps are out of date! The charts don't work any more!" The creation of smaller national states (which Lloyd George referred to as "five-foot-five nations"), whose boundaries were largely determined by ethnicity, added to the number of independent states in Europe. This number had decreased since 1500 as absolute monarchies had expanded their territories, and with German and Italian unification in the nineteenth century. But after the war, that trend was suddenly reversed. In 1914, there had been fourteen currencies in Europe; in 1919, there were twenty-seven.

The signatories at Versailles also had the strategic containment of communism in mind when they recognized the existence of the new nation-states as buffers—or what Clemenceau called a "cordon sanitaire" that would help contain the spread of Bolshevism from the Soviet Union. After the armistice, the Allies allowed German armies to remain inside Russia, Ukraine, and Poland to prevent the Red Army from carrying the Russian Revolution into Central Europe. German troops held railway lines in the Baltic states in order to thwart any attempted Bolshevik takeover there.

Seeking collective security against Hungary, which demanded revision of the Treaty of Versailles in order to win back territory lost to its unwanted new neighbors, as well as against Germany, the three nations of Czechoslovakia, Romania, and Yugoslavia formed the Little Entente by signing alliances in 1920 and 1921. (Poland sometimes worked with these states to achieve mutually beneficial goals but did not formally join the alliance.) Moreover, all three states depended on a series of defensive alliances that each had signed with France—Czechoslovakia in 1924, Romania in 1926, and Yugoslavia the following year. (Poland had signed a treaty with France in 1921.) The French government viewed such alliances with the Eastern European states as a means of countering a revival of German power, as well as a check on the Soviet Union. In 1934, Romania, Yugoslavia, Greece, and Turkey signed a Balkan Entente, intended to counter any revisionist territorial claims by Bulgaria.

The Allies applied Wilson's idealized formula of "one people, one nation" unequally when it came to those states that had fought against them in the war. The "Polish Corridor" dividing East Prussia from the rest of Germany contained a sizable—but not majority—German population. Mineral-rich Upper Silesia, claimed by Poland and with a large Polish population, was divided between Germany and Poland after a plebiscite. But in parts of Austria, where German-speaking majorities might have wanted to join Germany, the Allies specifically disallowed plebiscites. The Allies also refused Hungarian demands for plebiscites, which they accorded to Germany in East Prussia (which voted overwhelmingly to remain in Germany) and Schleswig (which was divided between Denmark and Germany).

Including part of the old Habsburg Balkan domains as well as the kingdoms of Serbia and Montenegro, Yugoslavia (called the Kingdom of Serbs, Croats and Slovenes until 1929) was the most ambitious attempt to resolve the national question through the creation of a multinational state in which the rights of several nationalities would be recognized. After complicated negotiations in 1917, the Serb government and a Yugoslav Committee made up of Croat and Slovene leaders in exile had agreed to form a new South Slav state when the war was concluded. They set up a provisional government even before an armistice had been signed. The new parliamentary monarchy would include Serbia, Montenegro, Croatia, and Slovenia (which lies between northern Italy and Austria), as well as Bosnia-Herzegovina and the smaller territory of Kosovo, two regions in which a majority of the population had converted to Islam during centuries of Turkish rule. Yugoslavia also absorbed part of Macedonia, which was populated by Bulgarians, Greeks, and Macedonians.

From its beginning, Yugoslavia was caught in a conflict between the "Greater Serb" vision of Yugoslavia, in which Serbia would dominate, and a federalist structure in which all nationalities and religions would play equal, or at least proportional, roles. Serbs, who are Orthodox Christians, were the largest ethnic group in Yugoslavia, but they still only made up 43 percent of the total Yugoslav population, with the Catholic Croats accounting for about 23 percent. Belgrade became the capital of Yugoslavia, as it had been of Serbia. Middle-class Serbs held almost all of the key administrative, judicial, and military positions. Concentrations of Serbs lived in Croatia, and Croats in Serbia, further complicating the rivalry between the two major peoples of the new state, who spoke essentially the same language, although the Serbs use the Cyrillic alphabet. Other major ethnic groups within Yugoslavia included Hungarians, Romanians, Bulgarians, Greeks, Germans, and gypsies.

Beginning in 1919, the League of Nations signed so-called national minority treaties with Poland, Czechoslovakia, and Yugoslavia (and later Greece and Romania), which agreed in principle to assure the protection of ethnic minorities. However, these treaties could not really be enforced. Moreover, ethnic rivalries were compounded by religious differences. For example, Poland included about 1.5 million Belorussians and 4 million Ukrainians, who, unlike the Catholic Poles, were largely Orthodox Christians. Poland also had the largest population of Jews in Europe—3 million. Moreover, about 1 million Germans, overwhelmingly Protestant, now lived in Poland.

The case of Czechoslovakia illustrates the complexity of the national question. In 1916, a National Council, made up of both Czechs and Slovaks, became a provisional government. The Slovak philosopher Tomáš Masaryk (1850–1937), who had spent the war years making contacts in London in the hope of advancing the cause of an independent Czechoslovakia, became the president of the new state in 1918. He was extremely popular among both Czechs and Slovaks. But Czechs and Slovaks together made up only 65 percent of the population of the new country. Three million Germans living in the Sudetenland found themselves included within the borders of Czechoslovakia, as did 750,000 Hungarians. Furthermore, Slovaks complained that promises of administrative and cultural autonomy within the Czechoslovak state were never implemented.

Facing similar economic, social, and political tensions, Poland became a dictatorship. Pilsudski became head of state in 1918. He commanded the Polish army that defeated in August 1920 the Soviet force that had reached the suburbs of Warsaw. "The miracle of the Vistula" River saved the independence of Poland, as well as that of the Baltic countries. Pilsudski pursued the policy of building a Federation of Poland and Ukraine, as well as Belarus and the Baltic states, regions that had been conquered by the Russian Empire and would form a bloc. But the Polish economy lay in ruins. No rail links between Warsaw and other major cities survived the war; tracks from Germany and Austria simply stopped at the Polish border. Inflation was rampant: a dollar was worth 9 Polish marks at the end of the war, and 10 million at the peak of the hyperinflation of 1923! (The zloty was introduced as the currency of Poland in 1924.)

The new Polish government faced the challenge of unifying the three parts of the country that had been part of three different empires. Deep divisions endured between nobles, who although many were greatly in debt owned most of the land and had subverted central authority in virtually every period of Polish history, and the peasants, who demanded land reform and were well represented in parliament. There were two main political blocs (and many smaller parties): National Democracy, the largest party of the right, which cooperated with a centrist Polish Peasant Party, and the Socialists and other parties on the left. In the 1922 parliament, there were eighteen different political parties. As no party ever enjoyed a solid parliamentary majority, governments fell on an average of almost two a year. Yet many peasants did receive land after World War I, although the process went increasingly slowly. Legislation limited the holdings of land that could be held by a single landowner to about 100 acres (three times that in the eastern regions), and about a third of Polish land changed hands. Pilsudski refused to stand for election for president in 1922 on the grounds that the constitution would not grant him sufficient executive authority. Although not by instinct a man of the right, he saw himself above political parties. However, he allied with leading conservatives and criticized the parliamentary regime, calling for a "moral regeneration" of Polish life.

Many Poles held the parliament responsible for the economic disaster of the post-war years and considered Marshal Pilsudski a hero. In 1926, Pilsudski, backed by the army and supported by Socialists fed up with the weak government and its policies, overthrew Poland's parliamentary government. After saying that he would have to wait to see whether Poland could be governed "without a whip," he imposed authoritarian rule, although political parties in principle continued to function and the press was relatively free. In 1930 Pilsudski arrested leaders of a center-left opposition group who demanded his resignation and the restoration of parliamentary government, and a new constitution followed in 1935, providing for stronger executive authority. After Pilsudski's death a month after the promulgation of the constitution, authority passed to a group of army officers who had been with him from the beginning.

The post-war period brought considerable instability to Greece and the Balkans. In Greece, which had only come into the war in 1917 on the side of Britain, France, and Russia, King Alexander died in 1920, after being bitten by his pet monkey. When parliament deposed his successor, Greek political life lurched into uncertainty accentuated by the arrival of 1.5 million Greeks expelled from Turkey and Bulgaria. In Greek Macedonia, refugees now made up half of the population. In the small, isolated Muslim state of Albania on the coast of the Adriatic Sea, moderate reformers battled proponents of the old ways against a backdrop of Italian territorial claims and bullying. The Prime Minister, Harvard-educated Ahmed Zogu, fearing for his life, fled to Yugoslavia in 1924. The next year, backed by Yugoslavia, he invaded his own country with an army, assumed the presidency of the Albanian Republic, and set up a dictatorial monarchy in 1928 (ruled 1928–1939).

In Bulgaria, King Boris III (ruled 1918–1943) was head of the country in name only. Alexander Stamboliski (1879–1923), leader of the Agrarian Union Party, elbowed opponents aside to become premier in 1919. He signed the Treaty of Neuilly, agreeing to try to prevent Macedonian nationalists from using Bulgarian territory to organize attacks inside Greece. Stamboliski assumed dictatorial powers in 1920. Army officers helped engineer a coup d'état in 1923, with the support of the king. Stamboliski fell into the hands of Macedonian nationalists, who cut off his right arm, which had signed the Treaty of Neuilly, then stabbed him sixty times, decapitating him for good measure. The army killed about 20,000 peasants and workers who wanted reform. It was a sign of the times in the Balkans.

Colonial and National Questions

The peace treaties failed to address the rights—or lack of them—of people living in the colonies of the European powers. Some of these peoples demanded national independence. Representatives of ethnic, religious, and national groups—including the Irish, Persians, Jews, Arabs, Indians from the subcontinent, Vietnamese, Armenians, and American blacks—went to Versailles in the hope of attaining recognition of their national rights. Lloyd George belittled these outsiders as "wild men screaming through the keyholes." The Allies refused to allow Ho Chi Minh (1890–1969), a young Vietnamese, to read a petition that asked that the Rights of Man and Citizen be applied to the French colonies. Only the representatives of Zionist groups—Jews who wanted the creation of a Jewish national state in Palestine—and their anti-Zionist Jewish rivals ever made it into the conference halls, and then only briefly. Women's groups, too, in vain sent representatives who hoped to be heard at Versailles.

Britain, still the world's largest colonial power, refused to accept President Wilson's plan that the League of Nations or some other international board arbitrate the future of colonies. The British government refused to recognize the right of self-determination. Still, the war had altered the relationship between Britain and its colonies, as well as that between France and its empire. The dramatic contraction of world trade during the postwar era, and above all during the Great Depression that began in 1929 (see Chapter 25), provided impetus to emerging independence movements. Imperial governments had long and loudly proclaimed that empire brought economic benefits to colonial peoples. Now such benefits were hard to find, as Britain, in particular, abandoned a cornerstone of the construction of its empire: free trade. The Dominions (Britain's original "settlement colonies" of Canada, South Africa, Australia, and New Zealand) had borne a great financial and material burden in the Great War, and a considerable loss of life as well. While they were not fully independent, a delegation from each had signed the Treaty of Versailles, and each had a government responsible to its own citizens and had become a member of the League of Nations. The "British Commonwealth" was created in 1926 and formalized in 1931. In this union of Britain and the Dominions, each state would be independent and not subordinate to Britain but united by common allegiance to the crown.

The powers created the "mandate system" to deal with Germany's colonies. The colonies were placed under the nominal authority of the League of Nations but were actually administered by Allied powers. Through this system, Britain increased the size of its empire by a million square miles, for example, by adding the former German colony of Tanganyika and parts of Togoland and the Cameroons as "mandate" colonies (see Map 24.3).

In Palestine, both Arabs and Jews had reason to be disappointed by the settlement. In 1915, in order to encourage Arab resistance against Turkey, the British government had promised some Arab leaders that after the war Britain would support an independent Arab state. But a year later, the British and French governments had secretly drawn up plans to divide the Middle East into two spheres of influence. Moreover, in the 1917 Balfour Declaration (see Chapter 22), Britain had promised to help Jews create a "national home" in Palestine, without necessarily promising to establish a

Map 24.3 Mandates Under The League Of Nations   German colonies became mandates of the League of Nations and administered by Allied powers after the Great War.

Jewish state. Once the war ended, the promises disappeared at Versailles. Britain established mandates over Trans-Jordan (which would later become Jordan), as well as over Iraq (which became nominally independent in 1932) and Palestine, each of which was ruled by a viceroy responsible to the colonial office in London. Britain maintained informal control over Egypt through the sultan and Egyptian ministers and the Suez Canal even after nominal Egyptian independence in 1922. Following an agreement made in 1916 between Britain and France, the French also established a mandate over Lebanon and Syria, where troops put down a revolt in 1925–1927.

But the British government could no longer put aside the challenge of the Irish movement for independence. The imposition of military conscription in Ireland in 1918 had angered Irish who felt no allegiance to the empire. The Irish Republican Army, which was organized from remnants of the rebel units disbanded after an ill-fated Easter Sunday insurrection in 1916, gained adherents amid high unemployment, strikes, and sectarian violence between Catholics and Protestants in largely Protestant Ulster (the six counties of northeastern Ireland). In a mood of mounting crisis, British Liberals wanted to begin negotiations as soon as possible with Irish political leaders. Conservatives, in contrast, wanted to crush the Irish Republicans. In the 1918 elections to the House of Commons, Irish voters elected a majority of members of Sinn Féin ("We Ourselves" in Irish Gaelic), the Irish Republican political organization. Sinn Féin members refused to take their seats in Parliament and then unilaterally declared a republic. Parliament finally passed the Government of Ireland Act in 1920, dividing Ireland into two districts. The Catholic district in the south—most of the island—was to become a crown colony. Largely Protestant Ulster remained part of Britain.

Most Catholic Irish, however, wanted nothing less than complete independence. The British government kept about 50,000 troops and 10,000 police in Ireland, including the "Black and Tans," a special police force that terrorized the Irish population supporting the Irish Republicans. More than a thousand people were killed in fighting during 1921, half of whom were British policemen or soldiers ambushed by the Irish Republican Army. In January 1922, the British Parliament went a step further, creating the Irish Free State, a Dominion within the British Commonwealth, although many Irish Republicans demanded the severance of all formal ties to Britain and the creation of the Irish Republic (which would come in 1948). Ulster, or Northern Ireland, remained within the United Kingdom. Continuing sporadic sectarian violence in Ulster proved that tensions between the Protestant majority and Catholic minority, which did not accept British rule, would not subside.

The Great War accentuated other nationalist movements for independence. Total war had brought the mobilization of men and resources from the colonies. This led to considerable resentment among indigenous peoples. In Egypt, following the arrest of an Egyptian nationalist, more than a thousand people were killed in the repression that followed an uprising. In India, which the British viewed as the key to sustaining the Empire (providing a vast reservoir of soldiers for the army), a growing Indian national movement developed. It was led by Mahatma Gandhi, who merged Hindu religion and culture with peaceful political resistance. Gandhi adapted Western-style propaganda techniques to the Indian struggle. Unlike the Indian National Congress, which had since the 1880s sought greater autonomy for India within the British Empire, Gandhi and his followers, who included many Indian Muslims, sought outright independence. Following riots in 1919, Indians held a protest in Amritsar in Punjab against the Rowlatt Acts, which allowed the government to forgo juries in political trials. The British army

Houses set ablaze in Ireland by the Black and Tans of the Royal Irish Constabulary, about 1920, during the fight for Ireland's independence from Great Britain.

retaliated by massacring 400 Indian civilians. Like the Sepoy Mutiny of 1857 (see Chapter 21), the incident exacerbated the mutual suspicion and mistrust that had existed between the Indians and British for decades. Bengali groups undertook terrorist attacks against British residents.

France also confronted and repressed revolutionary nationalist movements in its colonies of Indochina, Tunisia, Morocco, and the African island of Madagascar, as it did moderate groups asking only for the extension of political rights. During and following World War I (until the 1930s), most of the nationalist movements in the French colonies sought reform from within the colonial framework, not outright independence through revolution.

Japan strengthened its position as the only Asian great power and growing empire. Japanese armies were already taking advantage of the turmoil that followed the Russian Revolution to grab land from the old Russian Empire in Asia. Furthermore, Great Britain, France, and Italy had secretly agreed in 1917, in exchange for active Japanese support against the German navy, to back Japanese demands for concessions China had been forced to grant Germany in 1898 and 1899 (see Chapter 21). The members of the Chinese delegation to Versailles in 1919 had not been aware of the 1917 agreement; nor did the Chinese delegates know that their warlord premier had secretly agreed, in return for loans, to grant Japan a full concession to build railways in the northeast province of Shandong (Shantung). When the Allies publicly agreed to Japanese claims, demonstrations and riots erupted in China. The May 4 (1919) movement in China, named for the day of the first major demonstrations in Beijing against the Treaty of Versailles, accentuated the development of Chinese nationalism and resentment against foreign domination.

The United States, eager to protect its interests in Asia and wary of the alliance between Japan and Britain, which was determined to maintain its empire, agreed to join the Washington treaties of 1921–1922. These called for "consultations" between the three powers, as well as France, when events in Asia required them. A subsequent Nine-Power Treaty that included Belgium, the Netherlands, Portugal, and Italy, as well as China, guaranteed China's independence and territorial integrity.

ECONOMIC AND SOCIAL INSTABILITY

Because of the relief and—for the victors—exhilaration with which many Europeans greeted the end of the Great War, the 1920s has often been described as "the roaring twenties." Europeans thrilled to quests for record speeds or landmark travel by air and automobile. They gathered around radios, lined up to attend movies, dressed in more casual clothing styles than ever before, crowded into cabarets and clubs, and danced late into the night.

However, the two decades following the Great War were above all marked by tremendous economic and social instability. The continent was wracked by inflation and unemployment, factors that exacerbated international tensions and rivalries and poisoned domestic political life—particularly in Germany, but also in a number of other states reeling from the impact of the war. In Western Europe, after the long, bloody war finally ended and with the Russian Revolution fresh in mind, workers (and some women's groups as well) put forward demands for better living conditions. At the same time, economic and social elites were determined to overcome the challenge to their power launched by organized labor and the political parties of the left. But one of the results of the long ordeal of a war that had necessitated the mobilization of virtually all of the economic resources of the combatant powers was a growing determination among the parties of the political left that states ought to increase the services they provided their citizens. The origins of the welfare state may in part be traced to the immediate post-war period.

Social Turmoil

The staggering economic disruption caused by the war contributed to the international disorder that ensued at its end. Soaring inflation and unemployment destabilized European political life. The conflict cost more than six times the national debts of all countries in the entire world from the end of the eighteenth century until 1914.

Manufacturing and agricultural productivity fell dramatically during the conflict. Only countries far from the battlefields, such as the United States, Canada, India, and Australia, experienced economic growth. But they, too, could not escape high inflation and unemployment when the war ended. European states had borrowed vast sums of money to pay for the war; governments now began to print money to pay it back. This accelerated inflation (See Table 24.1). Prices were three times higher in 1920 in Britain than before the war, five times higher in Germany, and, in an ominous sign of things to come, 14,000 times higher in Austria and 23,000 times higher in Hungary. Workers resented the widening gap between themselves and the wealthy.

The British press carried stories about well-placed entrepreneurs who had amassed fortunes selling war materials to the government, living it up while others died for their country and everyone else tightened their belts. The Conservative politician Stanley Baldwin referred to businessmen elected to Parliament in the first post-war election as "hard-faced men who looked as if they had done well out of the war."

French steel magnates and German arms producers, among others, had emerged from the war with huge profits. These were enhanced by cartel arrangements within their industries that allowed them to monopolize production and set prices. War production had benefited large companies more than small ones, as in Germany, where the War Raw Materials Corporations provided essential materials to large enterprises. The chemical giant I. G. Farben had been formed in Germany by joining together a number of smaller firms. Industrialists enjoyed greater prestige and political influence than ever before. With governments playing the leading role in establishing economic priorities, allocating resources, and recruiting labor during the war, fewer people now embraced the old classic liberal principle of laissez-faire. Some businessmen and state officials, particularly in Germany, Italy,

Table 24.1. Index of Wholesale Prices (1913 = 10)

	1914	1915	1916	1917	1918	1919
Germany	106	142	153	179	217	415
France	102	140	189	262	340	357
Great Britain	100	127	160	206	227	242
Italy	96	133	201	299	409	364
Canada	100	109	134	175	205	216
United States	98	101	127	177	194	206

Source: Gerd Hardoch, *The First World War 1914–1918* (Berkeley: University of California Press, 1977), p. 172.

and France, had been impressed by the degree of wartime cooperation between state, business, and labor. They now believed these arrangements should be permanent. They hoped that corporate entities could be established in each major industry to coordinate production, ending competition between companies. They called themselves "corporatists" and their ideas "corporatism." Corporatists in Germany, France, and Italy believed that by creating cartel-like corporations that joined all people dependent on one industry, ruinous competition between companies and conflict between bosses and workers could be eliminated in the interest and prosperity of the "national economic community." Such cartel arrangements might well reduce or even eliminate the social and political tensions inherent in capitalist economies by forging an organized alliance of interests, including those of the state, big business, and labor.

However, Europe's business elite greeted the post-war era with some anxiety. For more than a half century, European economic elites had worked to preserve their power against the mounting challenge of organized labor and the political parties of the left. They did so, for example, by trying to maintain the elite character of higher education, pressuring governments to maintain high tariff barriers at the expense of consumers, seeking to limit government intervention in factory conditions, or trying to maintain legislation that restricted the right to strike. Above all, many people of means had wanted to keep their countries from adopting universal male suffrage or becoming democracies. Despite their efforts, however, the role of parliamentary bodies had expanded in every Western country during the last decades before the war, as universal male suffrage had come to France, Italy, Belgium, Norway, Sweden, and even imperial Germany.

Women's movements were one of the forces for democratization that gained considerably during the war. Having suspended their suffrage campaigns for the duration of the conflict, women's groups now demanded recognition for their wartime contributions—when they had taken the place of conscripts in factories and fields. After the war, women won the right to vote in Germany, Sweden, and several other countries in Western Europe, as well as in the newly created Eastern European states of Czechoslovakia, Poland, and Hungary. The legal position of women was probably strongest in Britain. Women voted for the first time in the British elections of December 1918, and the first woman was elected to the House of Commons soon after. The Sex Disqualification Act of 1919 opened the way for women to enter professions from which they had previously been excluded. However, women who had taken men's jobs during the war gradually lost or abandoned their employment, many returning to domestic service. During the 1920s, the percentage of British working women declined for the first time in many decades. Nonetheless, a greater variety of jobs became available to women. During the next two decades, many women found work in textile factories, commerce, transport, and in new jobs within the service sector (as hairdressers, department store clerks, or telephone operators). For many women, such jobs represented an advance in opportunity and working conditions.

The labor movement gained strength in the immediate post-war period. In France, the General Confederation of Labor, which had recruited hundreds of thousands of new members after the war, reached 2 million members in 1920, although the proportion of unionized workers remained small when compared to the proportion in Britain. In Italy, more than 3 million workers joined unions in the first two years of peace. Unions mounted massive campaigns to make the economy more democratic, a goal that was more revolutionary than bread-and-butter issues like hours, wages, and working conditions. Strikes spread in all Western countries. Some Britons began to think that their nation, which, unlike its continental rivals, had avoided insurgency and revolution in the nineteenth century, might now be vulnerable to an uprising by dissatisfied workers influenced by the Bolsheviks. In Glasgow, workers demanding a forty-hour workweek raised the Communist red flag on the town hall.

If anything, the mobilization of workers in defense of their interests contributed to conservative victories in the post-war elections. Britain's Conservative Party had swept to victory in the "khaki" elections (so called because of the color of British army uniforms) in December 1918. The influence of business interests also helped bring conservatives to power in Germany, Italy, and France in post-war elections. The French Employers Association printed thousands of posters showing a Bolshevik with a blood-stained knife between his teeth. The "National Block," drawing upon a wave of patriotism following the victory of the blue-clad French soldiers, in 1919 brought a strongly nationalist majority to the "horizon blue" Chamber of Deputies. Many French conservatives, who before the war dreamed of a monarchical restoration or the overthrow of the republic by a military man, now supported the republic, as long as it was a conservative republic. A general strike failed completely in May 1920. Union efforts failed to obtain the nationalization of key industries, such as French railroads, or German and British coal mines. Factory councils, which workers hoped would meet with employers to set production targets, wages, and conditions, had within a few years been eliminated in Germany, never got off the ground in France, and were quickly banned in Italy. In Britain, an attempt to call a general strike, organized by the "triple alliance" of railway workers, miners, and dockworkers—the three largest unions—fizzled completely on April 15, 1921, "Black Friday" for British workers. Rates of unionization fell. "Corporatist" rhetoric about how bosses and workers within the same industries shared the same goals gradually disappeared in Germany and France. Employers still called the shots with the notable exception of those in the Soviet Union, where the state exercised increasing control.

The Left and the Origins of the Welfare State

The Great War was a devastating experience for the international socialist movement, which had in 1914 split into pro- and anti-war factions. The German Social Democrats and the socialist parties of France, Italy, and Belgium had rallied to the war effort of their respective countries despite opposition to what they saw as a war between capitalists. The Russian Revolution of 1917, too, divided socialists. The unexpected victory of the Bolsheviks in Russia suggested to some that socialists could come to power through a tightly organized, hierarchical party structure. In France, at the Congress of the French Socialist Party in Tours in December 1920, three-fourths of the delegates supported joining the Third Communist International, which had been founded in Moscow

The French reaction to the Russian Revolution is illustrated by this anti-Bolshevik poster: "How to vote against Bolshevism."

in 1919 to encourage the organization of Communist parties in all countries. They founded the French Communist Party. Those remaining loyal to the French Socialist Party continued to accept reformism and thus loyalty to the republic, as well as to the democratic organization of their party.

Léon Blum (1872–1950) led the French Socialist Party. A Jew born into comfortable circumstances in Paris, Blum was a literary critic and intellectual who took a law degree and became a civil servant. Like his hero Jean Jaurès, the French socialist leader assassinated in 1914 on the eve of the war, Blum was an idealist for whom socialism followed philosophically from what he considered the humanism of the French Revolution. Blum remained convinced that socialism would be achieved through the electoral process.

For Communists, the economic malaise of the 1920s seemed proof that capitalism's defeat was near. Within two years, the French Communist Party grew as large as the Socialist Party. In 1922, on orders from Moscow, the party purged intellectuals from its membership. The Communist Party attracted many followers in the grim industrial suburbs of Paris, the "red belt" around the capital. Communist-dominated municipalities provided social services, such as unemployment relief, as well as light and drinking water for residents living in hastily constructed, insalubrious dwellings. In contrast, the British Communist Party, founded in 1920 and repudiated by the Labour Party, never attracted more than a few thousand followers.

Reformism dominated the parties of the left in post-war Europe. The German Social Democratic Party and the French Socialist Party participated in parliamentary alliances that underlay, respectively, the Weimar Republic and French moderate center-left governments. The British Labour Party, closely allied with the trade unions, emerged as the second largest party in Britain after the war. All three parties depended, to a large extent, on the support of the reformist labor movements in their respective countries. In some ways, unions had become interest groups like any other, bargaining with governments and employers. To this extent, the Communist critics of union reformism may have been correct when they warned that reformism served to integrate workers into the structure of the capitalist state.

The emerging outlines of the welfare state in the 1920s reflected the pressure of the parties of the left and of trade unions. At the same time, the origins of the welfare state must be seen in the context of earlier programs of social reform adopted in most countries in the decades before the Great War (see Chapter 20). While the Communist parties of Europe espoused, at least in principle, working-class revolution, socialists and most union members demanded that states provide certain minimum protection for workers. Scandinavia, Denmark, Sweden, and Norway evolved into social democracies, implementing pathbreaking social services. The socialist municipal government of Vienna constructed an attractive working-class apartment complex that provided communal facilities such as laundries, bathhouses, and kindergartens.

In Britain, Prime Minister Lloyd George had promised demobilized soldiers "a country fit for heroes to live in." The reality was considerably less grand. However, pressured by the Labour Party, which now held the second largest number of seats in the House of Commons, the Housing and Town Planning Act of 1919 provided town councils with subsidies to encourage the construction of cheap row houses. This eliminated some slum overcrowding and provided many working-class families with centralized heating and bathrooms. Within old city limits, "council" flats paid for by town councils provided more modest lodgings for some of the poorest workers. In 1920, the British government expanded unemployment insurance coverage to include most industrial workers, and in 1925, Parliament granted pensions to war widows and orphans, major steps in the emergence of the British welfare state. In France, the Chamber of Deputies in 1930 provided insurance for 10 million workers.

Political Instability

In October 1919, Italian Prime Minister Orlando reflected the uncertainty prevalent in the immediate post-war period when he stated that the growing disillusionment threatened Europe "like a blind whirlwind of destruction and disordered violence." The economic crisis that followed the war and the political instability it helped engender were nowhere clearer and ultimately more damaging than in Germany, where the new Weimar Republic sought to steer an even course between threats from the left and the right. Moreover, in Britain and France, states with established parliamentary governments, the subsequent division between left and right was also bitter.

Germany's Fragile Weimar Republic

The newly elected German Reichstag adopted the red, gold, and black flag of the ill-fated 1848 Frankfurt Parliament (see Chapter 16). The civil strife in which the Weimar Republic made its start influenced its constitution, approved by the Reichstag in July 1919. The constitution left the German president, who was to be popularly elected, considerable powers. Serving a term of seven years, he could dissolve the Reichstag and call for new elections. Although ministers would be responsible to the Reichstag, the president retained the power to suspend the constitution to restore order and to rule by decree, leaving the republic vulnerable to the president's authority.

Challenges to the republic came from the left and the right. In Bavaria, Kurt Eisner's rebel socialist republic collapsed. Following Eisner's murder by a rightist gunman in February 1919, Bavarian leftists rose up again in Munich in April to proclaim a Soviet-style republic. When a general strike paralyzed Berlin in early March, members of the Free Corps and regular German soldiers from Prussia gunned down several thousand workers and socialists.

The new German Republic desperately needed political stability. But many members of several key social groups, including bureaucrats and university professors who had received their posts under the empire, were against the republic from the beginning. Magistrates handed down absurdly light sentences to members of the Free Corps arrested for murder.

Groups of army officers began to plot against the republic during the summer of 1919. Conservative politicians and businessmen attempted a coup d'état, or "putsch," led by Wolfgang Kapp, a former Prussian imperial bureaucrat, with the goal of overthrowing the republic. On March 20, 1920, the rebels took over Berlin. The conservative parties proclaimed their support for the new government. In Bavaria, right-wingers seized power after forcing the resignation of the socialist government that had come to power the previous April. Chancellor Ebert appealed to the workers to defend the republic. They responded by launching a general strike that shut down much of the country. When some Berlin army units wavered, the Kapp Putsch collapsed.

But the threat to the republic was not over. The center and center-left parties of the Weimar coalition all suffered substantial losses in subsequent elections, while the conservative parties and radicals gained. When the Social Democrats withdrew from the government, the republic depended on a shaky coalition of Center Party politicians and moderate right-wing parties less committed than the Social Democrats to the republic they now governed. As Germany's economy floundered in ruinous inflation, political instability and violence mounted. Right-wing groups and parties sprang up, among them the National Socialists (Nazis), led by Adolph Hitler (see Chapter 25).

Walther Rathenau (1867–1922), the new foreign minister, was determined to negotiate the reparations issue with the British and French governments. Rathenau then shocked Britain and France by signing a statement of mutual friendship with the Soviet Union, the Rapallo Treaty (April 1922), in the hope of countering Western pressure. The Soviet Union received German technical assistance, which it paid for by helping Germany evade some of the military stipulations of the Treaty of Versailles. Subsequently, German officers provided technical assistance to the Soviet army. The Soviets, winning diplomatic recognition and German acquiescence to its repudiation of debts contracted under tsarist rule, renounced any future war reparations from Germany. Two months later, right-wing nationalists murdered Rathenau.

The German mark plunged dramatically in value. The Weimar government informed the Allies that it could not meet the schedule of reparations payments in gold or cash, but that it would continue payments of coal and other natural resources. With the United States pressuring Britain and France to repay their war debts, the Allies grew all the more determined that Germany pay up. France's new prime minister, Raymond Poincaré (1860–1934), threatened a military occupation of the Ruhr Valley industrial district if Germany failed to meet the reparations schedule. He accused Germany of deliberately withholding payments and trying to force the Allies to make concessions by ruining its own currency.

Britain and France, however, could not agree on a common policy. The French refused a German request for a moratorium on reparations payments so that the German currency (the mark) could be stabilized. The resentful German government, backed by virtually all political parties except the Communist Party, called on the miners of the Ruhr region to stop working for the Allies. This seemed to confirm Poincaré's contention that Germany was sabotaging repayment of its war debts.

On January 11, 1923, against the advice of the British government, French and Belgian troops occupied the Ruhr. When the German government began to finance the passive resistance in the Ruhr by simply printing more money with which to pay its miners not to work, inflation in Germany spiraled completely out of control, as Table 24.2 luridly demonstrates.

In 1923, Germans wheeled shopping carts filled with literally trillions of marks down the street to pay for a single loaf of bread. A half pound of

TABLE 24.2. THE MARK AND THE DOLLAR, 1914–1923

Date	Rate: 1 dollar =
July 1914	4.2 marks
January 1919	8.9
July 1919	14.0
January 1920	64.8
July 1920	39.5
January 1921	64.9
July 1921	76.7
January 1922	191.8
July 1922	493.2
January 1923	17,972.0
July 1923	353,412.0
August 1923	4,620,455.0
September 1923	98,860,000.0
October 1923	25,260,208,000.0
November 15, 1923	4,200,000,000,000.0

Source: Gordon Craig, *Germany 1866–1945* (New York: Oxford University Press, 1978), p. 450.

apples went for 300 billion marks. Employees asked to be paid their wages each morning so that they could shop at noon before merchants posted the afternoon price rises. Spiraling inflation wiped out people with fixed incomes and small savings they had put aside for retirement. Many of those who believed that they had done their patriotic duty by buying war bonds during the war now blamed the Weimar Republic when those bonds became worthless. The poor found staples and other goods not only ridiculously expensive but often unavailable at the market as farmers hoarded produce. Nonetheless, those people who were able to pay off bank loans with wildly inflated currency or to invest in property did well. The rich got richer. In such an atmosphere, the German Communist Party attracted bitter, discouraged workers in great numbers, undercutting the Social Democrats.

In August 1923, Ebert turned to Gustav Stresemann (1878–1929) to form a government. Stresemann, a former monarchist converted by right-wing violence to the republic, governed by decree with the support of the Social Democrats. He convinced miners to go back to work and to cease their passive resistance in the Ruhr Valley. France and Belgium ended the occupation after a nine-month period that had been as financially damaging to those nations as it was ruinous to Germany. Government printing presses stopped cranking out billion-mark notes and issued a new mark. The hyperinflation in Germany ended.

Stresemann hoped to meet the Allied demands as much as possible, and in doing so, open the way for Germany's return to respectability as a European

power. He hoped that this might clear the way for future Allied concessions, namely on Germany's disputed eastern frontier with Poland. Stresemann convinced both Britain and France to provide loans to help Germany
emerge from the economic crisis.

In 1924, a League of Nations commission, chaired by an American
banker, Charles G. Dawes (1865–1951), extended the schedule for payment of German reparations. The Dawes Plan left the Reichsbank partially
under the direction of an American commissioner who was to oversee German payments, but it did not lower the amount Germany was expected to
pay. Meanwhile, the United States had reduced the debt the Allies owed it
by percentages ranging from 30 percent (Britain) to 80 percent (Italy).
Still, the Dawes Plan improved relations between the Allies and Germany
and, with the revival of the European economy beginning in 1924, the
reparations issue receded in importance. The Weimar Republic seemed to
find stability as the economy finally began to improve. German industries
became more competitive, and unemployment began to decline.

Stresemann's discreet and effective diplomacy, now as foreign minister,
paid off. By the The Treaty of Locarno (really five separate treaties), signed
in 1925 between Great Britain, France, Belgium, Italy, and Germany, the
signatories pledged to settle all future controversies peacefully and guaranteed Germany's western borders as settled at the end of the war. At Locarno,
France also signed security treaties with Czechoslovakia and Poland to offset
to some extent the fact that Germany's eastern borders were not guaranteed,
which the German government refused to include in the agreement. European leaders and newspapers now began to use the phrase "the spirit of
Locarno" to refer to a mood of increasing international cooperation. The following year, Germany became a council member of the League of Nations in
return for agreeing that it would not seek to alter its western boundaries
with France and Belgium.

Nonetheless, German right-wing parties could never forgive Stresemann
for collaborating with the socialists. The opponents of the republic seemed
almost more vehement in their denunciations of Weimar when it succeeded
than when it failed, for success might generate stability and survival. Even
after what appeared to be a diplomatic victory for Weimar, German elections reflected the renewed strength of the right; the old Prussian warrior
General Hindenburg was elected president upon Ebert's death in 1925.

The Established Democracies: Britain and France

Britain and France were, to be sure, not immune from the political tensions
of the post-war period. Britain, in particular, remained a class-segregated
society. Nowhere in Europe was the concentration of wealth so marked as
in Britain. The top 1 percent of the population possessed two-thirds of the
national wealth, and one-tenth of 1 percent owned a third of the land in
England. Education, occupation, dress, accent, the newspapers one read,

and leisure activities all defined and revealed the social class to which one belonged. The distance between the elegant country gentleman and the Yorkshire factory worker, or the top-hatted London banker and the cloth-capped East End docker, remained as great as in the eighteenth century.

The Labour Party benefited from the decline of the Liberal Party, whose major nineteenth-century issue, free trade, now appealed to relatively few voters. Labour gained the support of most new voters. In 1924, James Ramsay MacDonald (1866–1937), a skilled orator who moved in the most elegant social circles, formed the first Labour government. However, the fall of MacDonald's government after several months demonstrated the resilience of British Conservatives, assisted by a widespread fear in Britain of communism. Conservatives had denounced MacDonald after his government became the first to accord official recognition to the Soviet Union. The press fanned the flames of a "red scare," similar to one then sweeping the United States. A newspaper published a letter it claimed had been written by Grigory Zinoviev, the head of the Communist International, detailing for British Communists ways of destabilizing the government. In fact, the letter was a forgery, the work of a Polish anti-Bolshevik. Returned to power, the Conservatives were determined to restore financial stability and to reject working-class demands. The government put Britain back on the gold standard in 1925, which meant that pounds sterling could be exchanged for gold according to a fixed rate of exchange. But this depleted the amount of gold reserves available to back the British currency and led to the pound's overvaluation. British products became more expensive on the international market, particularly when the other European powers stabilized their own currencies at lower rates. British manufacturing, the key to prosperity for more than a century, remained sluggish, its markets increasingly challenged by goods from the United States and Japan. The United States had become the world's leading creditor nation. New York City was now the new center of international finance.

In Britain, tensions between industrialists and workers came to the fore in 1926. The mines still employed over 1 million workers. After the war, the mining companies had reduced wages and lengthened the workday. A government commission in March 1926 recommended that firms implement safer working conditions, but that the miners accept lower wages. The miners rejected these conclusions with the slogan, "Not a minute on the day, not a penny off the pay." The Trade Union Council launched a general strike of miners in defense of the unions in May 1926. The vast majority of unionized workers in Britain went out in solidarity. The strike enraged the upper and middle classes, inconvenienced by the shutdown of all public transportation. Conservative Winston Churchill castigated the strikers as "the enemy," demanding their "unconditional surrender" as if he were talking about a German bunker in the war. The Labour Party was sympathetic to the plight of the workers, who truly suffered during the strike for defending their principles, but it maintained a safe political distance. Businessmen and students from Oxford and Cambridge Universities drove buses and trucks carrying people in and out of London while troops hauled food. After two weeks, most workers returned to their jobs, although the miners remained on strike for seven months. The strike was broken. A year later, Parliament passed the Trade Disputes Act, which forbade "sympathy strikes," walkouts in support of striking workers by those in other industries. This amounted to a crushing defeat for British workers.

When the French franc, long considered invulnerable to economic shocks, collapsed in value in a financial panic in 1924, the rightist government in France collapsed with it. A coalition of Radicals and Socialists, sharing little more than anticlericalism, formed a left-center government. But this alliance broke apart when the Socialists suggested a sizable tax on capital as a solution to the economic crisis. Ministries came and went with bewildering regularity.

In 1926, the conservative Poincaré returned as premier. He raised taxes on consumption, which the wealthy preferred to levies on capital, because the burden did not fall on them. The franc stabilized, as wealthy Frenchmen brought assets back from abroad and began to buy francs, which then rose rapidly in value. Poincaré became known as the savior of the French currency. But his idea that political consensus existed in France was, like the belief that France was the most powerful country in Europe, only an illusion. Many ordinary French men and women believed that a "wall of money" still held the country hostage and, along with an entrenched bureaucracy, prevented social reform. With an institutionally weak presidency, the Chamber of Deputies increasingly came to be seen as a debating

A barricade during the London General Strike, 1926.

society incapable of responding effectively to domestic and international crises. Political and social tensions encouraged the disillusionment with democracy felt by parties of the political extremes such as the French Communist Party on the one hand, and the fledgling right-wing fascist movements intrigued by Benito Mussolini's seizure of power in Italy on the other (see Chapter 25).

ARTISTS AND INTELLECTUALS IN THE WASTE LAND

The effects of the Great War could also be clearly seen in European intellectual and artistic life, as writers and painters wrestled with the consequences of a devastating struggle that stood as a great divide between the present and a world that was no more. A veteran of the trenches described the war's cataclysmic destruction as "a cyclopean dividing wall in time: a thousand miles high and a thousand miles thick, a great barrier laid across our life." The resulting cultural uncertainty reflected the economic, social, and political chaos of the period.

The defiant modernism of artists and intellectuals in the wake of the war was part of a revolt against traditional cultural conventions within the arts but also against the strictures of bourgeois society. In Britain, for example, people still read Victorian novels and romantic poetry, but such texts seemed to offer no explanation for what had gone wrong in Europe. Horrified by the war, many artists and writers now rejected the social conventions that had inculcated the values of nationalism and blind obedience. In the wake of the war, the "outsiders" of the Belle Époque had become, at least in the realm of the arts, "insiders." To be sure, most of the dramatic changes in artistic expression that followed the war had their origins in the pre-war years—for example, the adoption of psychological, subjective themes and approaches to painting and writing (see Chapter 20). The war had destroyed not only millions of lives but many of the signposts by which artists and writers defined reality. The American writer Gertrude Stein (1874–1946), who bounced back and forth between her artist and writer friends in London and Paris, called the war's survivors "a lost generation." In a 1922 lecture, the French poet Paul Valéry (1871–1945) said, "The storm has died away and still we are restless, uneasy, as if the storm were about to break . . . among all these injured things is the mind. The mind has indeed been cruelly wounded. . . . It doubts itself profoundly."

The bleak 1922 poem *The Waste Land,* by American-born poet and critic T. S. Eliot (1888–1965), reflected the disintegrating impact that the war had on Europe.

A heap of broken images, where the sun beats,
And the dead tree gives no shelter, the cricket no relief,
And the dry stone no sound of water. . . .

Hooded hordes swarming . . .
Falling towers
Jerusalem Athens Alexandria
Vienna London
Unreal

The Dadaists, a group of artists and writers who had gathered in Zurich in 1916, were the first to rebel against the absurdity of the slaughter of 1914–1918 by rejecting all artistic convention. They penned and painted nonsense; some wrote poems that consisted of words gathered from newspapers. It was all nonsense, but no more, they argued, than the war itself.

The artists and writers of the post-war generation stressed the primacy of subjectivism. Like soldiers emerging from the ghastly trenches, they looked into themselves in their quest to comprehend what seemed incomprehensible. Their subjectivism unleashed an imaginativeness that defined much of the new art.

The painters Piet Mondrian (1872–1944), Paul Klee (1870–1940), and Max Beckmann (1884–1950), among others, thumbed their noses at classical rules about painting, and even about what constituted art. Mondrian, a

French Dadaist painter Francis Picabia sitting on his "Dada"—or horse—among friends.

Dutch modernist painter, offered two-dimensional abstractions and straight lines forming grids. Klee's fantasies assumed unexpected shapes and distortions on the canvas; "the artist must distort," he contended, "for therein is nature reborn."

The expressionist movement, too, had its origins before the war. Beckmann rejected the label, but he defined the movement when discussing his own work: "What I want to show in my work is the idea which hides itself behind so-called reality. I am seeking the bridge which leads from the visible to the invisible." Expressionist poets rejected linguistic conventions in an attempt to communicate the emotion buried beneath the human exterior. Expressionist playwrights ignored long-established conventions of plot, character, and dialogue to represent what they considered to be unseen reality. In his modernist epic *Ulysses* (1922), the Irish writer James Joyce (1882–1941) abandoned long-accepted stylistic and narrative conventions to present the chaotic and seemingly unconnected—at least at first glance—"stream of consciousness" dialogue of three main characters, through which he revealed all their sensations and feelings. The novel's eroticism led it to be banned in Britain (but not in traditionally prudish Ireland) and in the United States until 1934.

In 1924, a group of nineteen painters and writers, led by the French artist and poet André Breton (1896–1966), published a "Surrealist Manifesto." In it they rejected "traditional humanism" and the respect for reason that seemed to have so manifestly betrayed mankind. They were not interested in rationality, which seemed defunct, but in what lay beneath it. The surrealists were obsessed with the crater-pocked landscape of churned-up earth, tree stumps, and twisted rubble in northern France and Belgium. They sought to shock audiences and viewers by expressing themselves in a way that was spontaneous and deeply personal, but still realistic. Breton's work sometimes defies interpretation because none was intended.

After four years in the trenches, the German surrealist Max Ernst (1891–1976) wrote that he had "died on the first of August 1914 and returned to life on the 11th of November 1918." Ernst joined a circle of Dadaists in Cologne. His 1933 painting *Europe after the Rain (I)* depicts with oil and plaster what appears to be a distorted, disfigured, and unsettling aerial relief map of Europe. It suggests the mutilation of the continent, which appears to be slowly swallowing itself. The surrealists were militant leftists, and they were also among the minority of Europeans who opposed colonial domination.

For his part, the Viennese doctor Sigmund Freud, founding father of psychoanalysis, believed that the war demonstrated the irrational nature of mankind. Freud's scientific analysis of the unconscious, translated into many languages during the 1920s, had begun to influence sociologists, political scientists, and cultural anthropologists. They applied ideas drawn from psychoanalysis to try to understand group behavior and social conflict. The war lent a sense of urgency to this enterprise. Freud also greatly influenced surrealists such as Breton, who drew images and words from his dreams.

Max Ernst's *Europe after the Rain (I)* (1933).

Some of Freud's early ruminations about the role of the unconscious in art were based on the haunting experience of seeing shell-shocked soldiers.

In 1928, Erich Maria Remarque (1898–1970), who had fought in the war, published *All Quiet on the Western Front,* the powerful pacifist novel about the trenches that quickly became a classic. In 1929, the British writer Robert Graves published his memoirs, focused on his experiences in the Great War. He called his book *Goodbye to All That.* The problem was that Europe could not say "goodbye to all that" and put the war behind it. Amid economic chaos and social and political turmoil in the two decades following the end of the war, one European dictator after another ended parliamentary democracy, imposed authoritarian rule, and suppressed political opposition. Fascist states, particularly Nazi Germany, poisoned international relations with nationalist bullying, making grandiose claims on the territories of other states. At the same time, in the Communist Soviet Union, Joseph Stalin consolidated his power. In what has been called the "Europe of Extremes," Europe entered an even more dangerous period in which it became increasingly clear that Woodrow Wilson's description of the Great War as the "war to end all wars" was meaningless in the Europe of economic Depression and dictatorship.

CHAPTER 25

THE EUROPE OF ECONOMIC DEPRESSION AND DICTATORSHIP

In 1922, Benito Mussolini became the first dictator to take power in Europe. By the end of 1925, fascist parties demanding the imposition of dictatorships had sprung up in many other nations. Other more traditional right-wing authoritarian movements, too, were on the rise. In Portugal, where junior army officers had overthrown the monarchy in 1910 and declared a republic, right-wing military officers staged a coup d'état in 1926. General Józef Pilsudski overthrew the Polish Republic the same year. All of the Eastern European and Balkan states became dictatorships in the 1920s and 1930s, with the exception of Czechoslovakia. In the meantime, Joseph Stalin transformed the Soviet Union into a totalitarian state. Amid the ravages of the Great Depression that began in 1929, Europe entered an even more dangerous period of instability. In 1933, a right-wing government came to power in Austria, and Adolf Hitler, leader of the National Socialist (Nazi) Party, became chancellor of Germany. The right-wing nationalist revolt against the republic of Spain began in 1936, starting a civil war that ended in 1939 with the victory of General Francisco Franco's right-wing nationalist forces. Britain and France were the only major powers in which parliamentary government was strong enough to resist the authoritarian tide. Democracy also survived in the smaller states of Belgium, the Netherlands, Switzerland, Denmark, Sweden, and Norway, despite the existence of small fascist movements in each.

Economies in Crisis

The global economic Depression that began in October 1929 had dramatic political consequences in Europe. Economic insecurity and accompanying social unrest undermined parliamentary rule. More and more people sought scapegoats who could be blamed for hard times: Jews, Socialists, Communists, ethnic minorities and other nationalities, big business. Under such circumstances, many people could be convinced that parliamentary government itself was to blame and that nationalistic dictatorships were the solution. Amid plunging confidence and general bewilderment, international cooperation became more difficult, particularly as the powers began to blame each other for adopting policies that adversely affected them. Germans castigated their wartime enemies for assessing massive, seemingly unjust reparations; people in Britain and France blamed Germany for not paying all the reparations; many Americans blamed their own former allies for not paying back loans. The vicious cycle of mistrust grew.

The Great Depression

By 1924, prosperity seemed to have returned to much of post-war Europe, at least in the Western states. But beneath the surface, the increasingly interdependent world economy had not recovered from the war. The wartime inflation greatly increased during the years that followed the armistice. At the same time, steel and iron prices fell sharply after the war when demand plunged for tanks, artillery pieces, and munitions. Overproduction and the increasing use of hydroelectricity and oil caused the price of coal to fall rapidly. Slowly some industrial jobs began to disappear.

European agriculture, particularly in Eastern Europe, was in a depressed state well before the Crash of 1929. More grain, meats, and other food sup-

(*Left*) The Wall Street Crash, October 1929. (*Right*) An unemployed Briton seeks work, 1930.

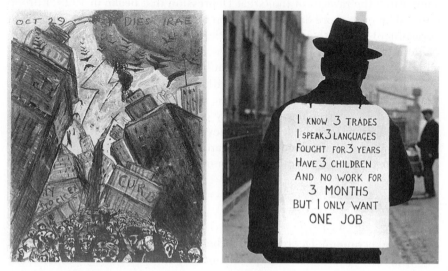

plies arrived on the continent from Australia, Argentina, Canada, and the United States. The price of locally produced agricultural goods fell. Lower farm incomes, aggravated by the burden of taxation, in turn reduced demand for manufactured goods.

European states reacted by erecting tariff barriers to try to protect their internal markets for domestic agricultural products. Countries like Bulgaria that depended on agricultural exports saw their foreign markets dry up, or they received less for what they sold. With less income and less Western investment, Eastern European and Balkan nations could not repay their wartime debts. Germany's defeat, the dismemberment of the Austro-Hungarian Empire, and the Russian Revolution significantly weakened the region's three largest pre-war trading partners.

The contraction of demand and price deflation probably would not have been enough to generate full-fledged economic disaster. But unrestrained financial speculation also undercut the world economy. In Germany, high interest rates attracted considerable foreign investment following the 1924 economic recovery. Credit was easily available, and companies issued huge amounts of stock shares based upon insufficient real assets. In the United States, a sizable reduction in demand for goods was already apparent by 1927. Wealthy people began to invest in highly speculative stocks.

Wartime loans and post-war debts made the finances of the larger powers more interdependent and helped destabilize the international economy. German reparations also adversely affected the world economy because, ironically, they accentuated the flow of capital into Germany. Following the Dawes Plan, which in 1924 extended the schedule of reparations, Germany borrowed $110 million from U.S. banks to meet its reduced reparations payments to the Allies, rather than paying them out of current income through higher taxes. German railroads served as collateral for the loans, which were immediately oversubscribed in New York. Like bonds and speculative investments, reparation loans diverted investment away from industry and ignited further foreign lending. Besides loans to pay reparations, other loans also poured into Germany. Most of this debt was short term rather than long term, which made Germany even more vulnerable to a sudden calling in of those loans. In 1928, U.S. banks refused to issue more loans to Germany, investing available funds instead in the Wall Street stock market, further undercutting German banks.

By early 1929, the U.S. economy was in recession. In late October, the New York stock market crashed. Thousands of large and small investors were ruined as stocks lost most of their value. American and British investors with assets still tied up in Germany now began to pull their money out as quickly as possible. German gold reserves were depleted, as banks owed far more money to creditors than they had assets. Table 25.1 shows the importance of the U.S.-German financial connection, which contributed to the fact that the Depression began earlier and production fell more in those two countries than in the other major powers.

Table 25.1. Indices of Industrial Production

Year	Germany	United States	France	Britain
1925	79.3	93.7	85.0	94.8*
1927	97.2	95.5	86.6	101.2
1929	101.4	107.2	109.4	106.0
1930	83.6	86.5	110.2	97.9
1931				
August	71.9	74.8	99.2	84.6
December	59.4	66.7	87.4	84.7
1932				
January	55.2	64.9	82.7	90.1
August	54.7	53.2	73.2	89.2

*For Great Britain, 1924.
Source: David E. Sumler, *A History of Europe in the Twentieth Century* (Homewood, IL: Dorsey Press, 1973), p. 145.

As unemployment mounted to unprecedented levels, the "roaring twenties" became the "threadbare thirties." Jobs disappeared and families were compelled to spend the savings they had so painstakingly amassed over the previous five years, even as manufacturing and agricultural prices continued to fall because of the dramatic contraction of demand. Manufactured goods piled up on the docks.

Confronted by a catastrophic fall in production and prices, as well as unemployment approaching 20 percent of the workforce, British government officials and economists debated strategies that might revive their floundering economies. There were no easy answers. The economic orthodoxy of the day held that the way out of the crisis was to reduce public expenditures. The inflation of the immediate post-war period, particularly the hyperinflation that had ravaged Germany in 1922 and 1923, frightened statesmen and economists away from even limited financial or fiscal expansion.

National policy options, too, were further constrained by the interdependence of the international economy, especially under the gold standard. For example, James Ramsay MacDonald's British Labour government first reacted to the Wall Street crash by increasing unemployment benefits and funding more public works, while raising taxes. These expenditures further increased the government deficit, already soaring because of reduced tax revenue. But the British government was then forced to reduce unemployment benefits in order to be deemed creditworthy by New York and Parisian bankers, in the hope of stabilizing the pound and maintaining the gold standard.

The international monetary system collapsed as the world economy plunged into dark Depression. Banks and private interests that had loaned money to Germany began to call in debts. Already reeling from agricultural Depression in Eastern Europe, the failure of the largest Austrian bank in May 1931 immediately brought the collapse of several German banks to which it owed money. A general financial panic ensued. U.S. President Herbert Hoover (1874–1964) suggested a moratorium on the repayment of all reparations and war debts, hoping that confidence and the end of the cycle of defaults would follow. The other powers accepted the moratorium in August 1931.

As the British economy floundered because of the decline in world trade, European bankers intensified the run on the pound. They exchanged their holdings of British pounds sterling for gold, 2.5 million pounds' worth per day during the summer of 1930, dangerously reducing Britain's gold reserves. As investors panicked, sterling quickly lost a third of its value.

With Labour not having a majority in the House of Commons, McDonald was forced to negotiate with the other parties, but the latter insisted on reducing the budget, including cutting unemployment benefits. This McDonald's Labour colleagues could not accept. But instead of resigning as everyone expected, McDonald formed a "National Government" of members from the three parties, although most Labour leaders declined to join him. He thus stayed on as prime minister. Worsening conditions forced the National Government to take Britain off the gold standard in September 1931. This meant that the Bank of England would no longer remit gold in exchange for pounds. This seemed like a step into the economic unknown. Wild fluctuations in the values of other currencies followed. This further discouraged business, and international trade declined even more steeply, but it did permit some domestic recovery. In April 1933, the United States, too, went off the gold standard.

In Britain, the Conservatives' deflationary measures, which sought to reduce expenditures, seemed to British voters to be the only way out of the crisis. In the elections of October 1931, the Tories won an overwhelming majority of seats in the House of Commons. Neville Chamberlain (1869–1940) now became chancellor of the Exchequer. His aloof manner, inveterate dullness, rasping voice, and whiny disposition did little to inspire confidence—one critic suggested that he had been "weaned on a pickle." Chamberlain promised a "doctor's mandate" to extract Britain from the economic crisis. The government imposed higher tariffs, further reducing consumer spending. Many members of the Labour Party called MacDonald a traitor for going along with deflationary measures because they included reducing unemployment benefits, and they proposed the nationalization of mining, the railways, and other essential industries as first steps toward the implementation of a more planned economy. But Labour's campaign ran headlong into traditional Conservative opposition and middle-class fear of socialism, as well as the orthodoxy of deflationary economic policies.

Across the English Channel, smaller-scale industries, artisans, and family farmers in France at first were sheltered from the Depression because they depended, above all, on local markets. France also had considerable gold reserves, which helped maintain business and consumer confidence and keep consumer spending at a relatively high level. The run on the British pound and the German mark, too, at first aided France, as gold exchanged by investors ended up in Paris. The franc initially remained stable, and undervalued, encouraging the purchase of French goods. But gradually French prices also fell and unemployment rose, again revealing the interdependence of the global economy. The Depression hit France only in 1932. French exports declined with the contraction of the world market, particularly because the franc, which had not plunged like the pound, was now overvalued, making French goods expensive abroad. But most French leaders considered devaluation to be anathema. "Who touches the franc," cautioned one newspaper, "touches France!" The French government, like that of Britain, stuck to classical economic remedies, ignoring demands for active state intervention to stimulate the economy both from right-wing corporatists who sought support for cartels and from left-wing socialists who called for the nationalization of crucial industries and more unemployment benefits.

Gradual European Economic Revival

In the rest of Europe, government leaders debated strategies that they hoped would pull their countries out of the Depression. The major powers acted in their own interests—establishing high tariffs and devaluing their currencies—without prior consultation with other governments. The U.S. government, like that of Britain, followed contemporary economic orthodoxy. Both sharply reduced government spending, cutting unemployment benefits and restricting credit. However, John Maynard Keynes (1883–1946), the English economist, insisted that recovery would depend upon just the opposite strategy: an increase in government expenditures, including deficit spending—for example, on public works—to stimulate consumer spending by reducing unemployment. Keynes argued that deflationary measures, such as cutting government spending, reducing unemployment benefits, or encouraging companies to limit production and thus keep prices artificially high, were counterproductive. They could prolong the Depression by reducing the demand for goods. With one-quarter of the labor force out of work early in 1933 and wages falling, there was insufficient demand to generate a manufacturing upswing in Great Britain, the United States, or anywhere else. But Keynes stood virtually alone, and most of what he had written was then still largely unknown.

Only very gradually did the Depression begin to recede in the industrialized countries. A modest recovery began in Britain in 1932. But it was not due to the dramatic improvement of British international trade upon which the Conservatives had counted. Rather, it followed a slow increase in consumer spending. Keynes had been right. Increases in 1934 and 1935

Reflecting the enormity of class divisions in Britain during the Depression, these working-class boys look in amazement at two Eton students outside a cricket ground.

of unemployment benefits and the restoration of government salaries to their pre-Depression levels helped. The subsidized construction of more houses pumped money into the economy, helping to increase consumer confidence. While some inefficient steel and textile manufacturers went under, others consolidated and became more efficient, perhaps benefiting from the imposition of higher tariffs on industrial imports. Real wages slowly rose. The imposition of quotas on agricultural imports aided farmers. As industry and agriculture gradually returned to prosperity, unemployment began to fall.

The German economy also slowly improved, at least in part because, after Hitler came to power in 1933, rearmament created many jobs. Business confidence slowly returned. In 1930, the Young Plan, named after its American originator, had extended the date by which Germany was to have paid all reparations to 1988. Then the Lausanne Conference of 1932 simply declared the end of reparations payments. In France, the Depression lingered longer than in any other European industrialized power. The government, constrained by weak executive authority, failed to act decisively until 1935, when it lowered taxes to encourage consumption, after trying to protect France with a wall of protectionism and productions quotas. When other countries devalued their currencies, France's comparative advantage disappeared, and demand for exports trailed off. Moreover, France's low birthrate, combined with the horrific loss of life during the war, reduced demand.

In the United States, where the Depression hit hardest, recovery came even more slowly. Franklin D. Roosevelt (1882–1945), elected president in 1932, implemented his "New Deal." It facilitated loans that saved banks, provided relief for the unemployed through public works programs, and provided assistance to farmers and to businesses. When Keynes learned of Roosevelt's plans, his assessment was that "Roosevelt was magnificently right" (though as someone noted Keynes might have said that he was "magnificently left"). Gradually, a return of consumer confidence, boosted by the president's low-key "fireside chats" by radio to the American people, improved the economy. But only with the entry of the United States into the Second World War in 1941, with its massive mobilization of economic resources in the production of war materials, did the Depression finally end its grip on the United States.

The Dynamics of Fascism

It is against the background of hard times that followed the Great War that the rise of fascism and other authoritarian movements must be seen both in the industrialized countries of Western Europe and in the largely agrarian states of Eastern Europe and the Balkans (see Map 25.1). Fascist parties developed in the 1920s as political movements seeking mass mobilization— but not political participation. There was nothing democratic about fascist organizations: they were hierarchically structured and, rejecting parliamentary rule, sought to bring dictators to power.

Several factors contributed to the rise of the extreme right, with none serving as a single explanation. If in the nineteenth century the middle class had stood as a bulwark of liberal values in Europe, this was no longer the case in the post-war climate. In Germany, Italy, and Austria, fascists found disproportionate support among the middle class, which had been ravaged by years of economic crisis. Middle-class families watched in horror as their pensions and modest savings disappeared. They feared union leaders, Socialists, and Communists, who all demanded an extension of public programs to aid unemployed workers. Many in the middle class feared such reforms would come at their expense. Big business in Italy and Germany, in particular, turned against parliamentary rule. But middle-class frustrations do not provide a sufficient explanation for the rise of authoritarian movements in Eastern Europe and the Balkans, where the middle classes were extremely small. Moreover, the middle classes in Britain and France endured many of the same economic frustrations, but only in France did a minority turn to authoritarian political movements.

Fascists, Nazis, and other authoritarian right-wing groups blamed parliamentary government itself for the weaknesses and failures of their states in the post-war years. They believed parliamentary regimes to be unstable and weak by their very nature, undercut by factionalism and class divi-

MAP 25.1 DICTATORSHIPS IN EUROPE, 1932–1937   States ruled by dictators before 1932; states that became dictatorships after 1932; remaining democracies in 1937.

sions. The states in which authoritarian dictators came to power lacked strong traditions of parliamentary democracy. Moreover, the seeming instability of parliamentary regimes in times of crisis during the 1920s contributed to the attractiveness of the idea of a strong leader—a dictator who would restore order and embody nationalist aspirations, fulfilling what some considered their nation's "historic destiny." Frenzied crowds, with arms raised in fascist salutes, greeted their authoritarian leaders as heroes. The irony was, of course, that fascist gangs themselves were largely responsible for creating the political turmoil that ultimately led to the destruction of parliamentary governments.

Fascism was less of an ideology per se than a violent plan of action with the aim of seizing power. Fascists most often defined themselves by denouncing who and what they were against, such as parliamentary democracy, rather than what they were for. Fascists did not put forward "programs" for authoritarian rule. They saw themselves as building a new social and political order based upon service to the nation. This idea of creating a new elite also distinguished fascist from authoritarian movements in Spain and Portugal, where nationalists tried to affirm the domination of traditional elites, such as nobles and churchmen, and remained suspicious of mass movements in general.

Fascist movements opposed trade unions, Socialists, and Communists with particular vehemence because all three emphasized class differences they believed were endemic in capitalist society, espoused working-class internationalism, and based their appeal primarily on the perceived needs of workers. Fascists, by contrast, viewed economic and social tensions as irrelevant, arguing that it was enough that all people shared a common national identity, and that this national community meant more than did economic disparities between social classes. Fascism would make such divisions obsolete. Mussolini and Hitler covered up the brutal realities of their rule by promising with vague rhetoric that the needs of the "national economic community" would be fulfilled. In the early 1920s, Mussolini had added "international finance capital" to his list of enemies, a holdover from the rhetoric of his days as a socialist before the war, trying to convince workers that he spoke for their interests, too. Like Mussolini, dictators Engelbert Dollfuss in Austria (1892–1934) and Antonio Salazar (1889–1970) in Portugal also added "corporatism" to their list of promises, announcing that associations of employers and workers would be formed within each industry. But fascist states remained capitalistic in nature, with big business accruing great profits and workers lagging far behind.

There was no single fascist ideology, and not all of the right-wing authoritarian movements in Europe in the 1920s and 1930s can be qualified as fascist. In Spain, Francisco Franco imposed a military dictatorship like that of Salazar in neighboring Portugal; both were predicated upon the influence of traditional elites, the Catholic Church, and the army. Yet, while sharing the anti-Bolshevism of fascist Italy and Nazi Germany, neither the Spanish nor the Portuguese dictatorship shared the expansionist ideology of those regimes, and both distrusted the kind of mass movement that helped sweep the Italian fascists and German Nazis to power. The agrarian populist authoritarian regimes of Eastern Europe may also be described as fascist states, or at least "para-fascist" dictatorships. Some of these also were aggressive, nationalist mass movements built upon anti-communism, anti-Semitism, and fierce opposition to parliamentary rule. Yet although inspired in some ways by Italian fascism and German National Socialism, they had no illusions about expanding their states beyond what each claimed as the "historic" limits of their nationality. Moreover, Stalin's Soviet Union, too,

An enthusiastic crowd, which includes many youths, greets Hitler at a rally at the Nuremberg stadium in 1937.

had become a state dictatorship, like the fascist regimes, but one organized at least on Communist rhetoric about creating a workers' paradise. Stalin, casting aside the claims of the many non-Russian nationalities, and for that matter, of the workers themselves, tolerated no opposition to or within the Communist Party. The Soviet Union was also a totalitarian state, with centralized control of all political functions by a dictator ruling through terror in the name of a single party.

Hatred of parliamentary and democratic rule, Socialists, Communists, and Jews helped give fascism an international character. In 1935, there was even a short-lived attempt to create a fascist international, similar to the Communist International (Comintern) on the other end of the political spectrum. Mussolini contributed funds to the Belgian, Austrian, and British fascist movements. But the stridently nationalist aspect of fascism worked against fascist internationalism. Yet fascist and right-wing authoritarian states found ready allies among similar regimes, as joint German and Italian assistance to the nationalist rebellion during the Spanish Civil War (1936–1939) solidified the alliance between Hitler and Mussolini.

Middle-class economic frustration, anti-parliamentarianism, upper-class fears of socialism, anti-Semitism, aggressive nationalism, and the belief that a dictator could bring order and national fulfillment were all present in European society before the Great War. But the cataclysmic experience of the war channeled them all in new and frightening directions, contributing to the proliferation of aggressive nationalism. For many veterans of the trenches, the experience of the war had made them increasingly indifferent to brutality and human suffering. To an extent, nationalism represented a continuation of the Great War—and the camaraderie of the trenches—now transformed into a race war against those considered internal or external enemies. In Germany, in particular, right-wing movements attracted demobilized soldiers, who had returned home with weapons, habits of military order, and experience with violence. Fortunate enough to have returned home from the war at all, demobilized troops found not a significantly better life to repay them for their sacrifices, but hard times driven by inflation. They kept right on marching. Paramilitary squads of war veterans destabilized political life in France and Italy, in victorious states, but above all in revisionist states that did not accept The Versailles Settlement (see Chapter 24). The Free Corps in Germany, the Home Guard in Austria, and the Cross of Fire in France denounced the "decadence" and "softness" of parliamentary regimes. They wanted continuation of war, the dominant experience in their lives, not peace.

Aggressive nationalism easily became racism. From the beginning, Hitler's National Socialism espoused German racial supremacy. Nazism manifested an unparalleled capacity for violence and destruction based upon the assumption that Nazis could assume the authority to determine who could live and who could die. Their principal target was Jews. This carried Nazi ideology and practice beyond other violent nationalist right-wing regimes. Germans were not alone in believing spurious literature proclaiming the superiority of their race and the degeneration of other races. Eastern European dictators denounced other ethnic groups and nations, which could be blamed for practically anything. Anti-Semitism also characterized authoritarian movements in Austria, Poland, Romania, and Yugoslavia, as well as in France and Belgium. Inspired by Hitler, Mussolini also added anti-Semitism to his nationalist ravings in 1938.

Fascism borrowed some symbols and rites that represented spiritual revolution (for example, "blood" and "martyrdom") from Christianity, replacing the latter with nationalism. Fascism became something of an all-embracing civic religion that sought to build a "national community." In a totalitarian way, fascism sought to eliminate the distinction between private and public life. Fascists sought to create the "new man" who would serve the nation (women were to remain at home) and a new elite defined by service to the state. Fascists emphasized youth and youthful energy, contrasting the "new men" with what they considered the old, failed political systems. Lining up behind authoritarian dictators whom they believed to be natural, aggressive leaders who incarnated their national destiny, fascists trumpeted the historical rights of, and duties to, the nation, which they believed outweighed any other rights. In their view this gave them the right to exclude from the national community—and, for some fascists, to kill—those they considered outsiders in the interest of racial "purity." They believed that this also gave them the right to expand their national frontiers toward what they considered their proper "historical" limits. They placed such struggles in the context of what they conceived of as a Darwinian struggle of the fittest that they would win, and celebrated what they considered to be the beauty of violence. When the film version of Erich Maria Remarque's *All Quiet on The Western Front* appeared in 1930, Nazis marched in protest and shut down some theaters.

Fascists did more than rule through terror—their dictatorships were also built upon popular consensus. Fascism created what has been called a "magnetic field" in Europe in the 1920s. Extreme right-wing movements won widespread support among millions of ordinary people in many corners of Europe, beginning in Italy.

Mussolini and Fascism in Italy

The economic and social tensions of the immediate post-war period destabilized Italy's liberal government. The dissatisfaction of Italian nationalists with the Treaty of Versailles accentuated a political crisis. This made Italy vulnerable to a growing threat from the far right.

Gabriele D'Annunzio (1863–1938), a bombastic, decadent poet, had in 1914 described war as perfect hygiene for the modern world. Having proclaimed, "I am not, and do not wish to be, a mere poet," he took matters into his own hands. In September 1919, the decorated war veteran who had lost an eye in combat swept into the Adriatic city of Fiume (Rijeka). He led a force of 2,000 men, many of whom were demobilized soldiers. D'Annunzio planted the Italian flag, forcing the Italian government to begin negotiations with the new Yugoslav state, which also claimed the Adriatic port. Both countries agreed that Fiume would be independent, but that most of Istria and northern Dalmatia would remain in Yugoslavia, as the Treaty of Versailles had specified. D'Annunzio's little republic lasted sixteen months, until Italian ships lobbed a few shells in the general direction of the city and sent the poet and his small force packing.

D'Annunzio had briefly stolen the thunder of another fervent Italian nationalist, Benito Mussolini (1883–1945). Mussolini was born to a family of modest means in northern Italy. His father, a blacksmith, was something of a revolutionary; he had taught himself to read from socialist tracts and named his son after the Mexican revolutionary Benito Juarez. The young Mussolini was a schoolyard bully quick to raise his fists and pull a knife, once stabbing a girlfriend. He had no close friends and was proud of it—"Keep your heart a desert," he once advised.

Mussolini read Karl Marx, and Friedrich Nietzsche, whose espousal of daring revolt and the "will to power" intrigued him. After a stint in the army, Mussolini proclaimed himself a socialist and anti-militarist and became a political journalist. He took to the streets to denounce Italy's

Italian dictator Benito Mussolini and his fascists, 1935.

colonial war against Libya (see Chapter 21). Late in 1912, Mussolini became editor of the Italian Socialist Party's newspaper, *Avanti!* At the outbreak of war in 1914, Mussolini led a chorus of socialists demanding that Italy remain neutral.

In October 1914, a small number of members broke away from the Socialist Party, demanding that Italy join the war. They took the name "fascists" from the Latin word *fascio*, meaning "a bundle of sticks," or, by extension, an association. When Italy entered the war in 1915, Mussolini joined the army. His views toward war were already changing. "Only blood," he wrote, "makes the wheels of history turn." The influence of Nietzsche was overwhelming that of Marx in his mind. Lightly wounded in 1917, he returned to journalism. At the war's end, Mussolini led the chorus of nationalist demands for a peace settlement favorable to Italian interests. In March 1919, he founded the National Fascist Party.

The post-war crisis of Italy's liberal state aided the fascists. The major parties of Italy—the Liberals, the Socialists, and the new Catholic Popular Party—struggled in vain to find consensus. While governments formed and fell in quick succession, severe economic difficulties followed the armistice. Hundreds of thousands of demobilized troops joined the ranks of the unemployed. Inflation soared, eroding middle-class savings and undercutting the already low standard of living of workers and landless peasants. Agricultural Depression compounded high unemployment.

As in Britain, France, and Germany, workers flocked to organized labor in Italy, and waves of strikes spread in 1919 and 1920. Peasant laborers demanded land and formed unions called "red leagues." In the south, thousands of poor families had begun to occupy some of the vast, often uncultivated holdings belonging to wealthy landowners. Banditry exploded in the south and Sicily.

During these "red years" of 1920–1922, many landowners and businessmen turned against parliamentary rule. The Liberal government had alienated the wealthy by proposing a progressive tax on income and a high imposition on war profits and outraged them by legalizing peasant land seizures. Wealthy industrialists helped bring the Italian fascists to power. In the north, ship owners and iron and mining magnates, as well as wealthy landowners, provided funds for Mussolini's fascists. Uniformed squads of fascists wearing black shirts intervened on behalf of big landowners and businessmen, attacking Socialists, Communists, and union members. Laborers and sharecroppers fought back against the fascists, but had little chance because the landowners supplied the *squadri* with weapons. The left was divided and hesitant.

Mussolini, now boasting a private army and a sizable claque, or "applause squad," of paid supporters, praised the "bath of blood" that swept parts of Italy. He reveled in rumors of a coup d'état associated with his name, cranking out violent articles denouncing parliamentary government.

In 1921, the Liberals, hoping to find a parliamentary mandate to impose order, offered the fascists qualified support and accepted them as electoral allies. Mussolini and several dozen other fascists were elected to the Italian Parliament. The fascist leader now had an ideal soapbox for his flamboyant oratory, as well as immunity from prosecution. The Liberal government of Giovanni Giolitti (see Chapter 17) resigned, succeeded by another coalition government.

The fascists were now a powerful political movement with prominent allies, money, newspapers, and hundreds of thousands of party members. Fascist thugs had carved out territories in which their word was law. They disrupted local political life, shattering the organization and support for the traditional parties. Mussolini, who took the title of the Duce, or "the leader," presented himself as a defender of law and order, blaming Socialists and the newly formed Communist Party for the turmoil for which the fascists were largely responsible. Fascists enjoyed the tacit support of many state and police officials, and fascist violence went unpunished.

For Mussolini, fascism was an ideology of violent confrontation, a means of winning and maintaining political power, more than a coherent doctrine of political philosophy. Italian fascists, as with their counterparts who would soon emerge elsewhere, advocated a strong, virulently nationalist, militarized state. Italy would fulfill its "historic destiny" by transforming the Mediterranean into "a Roman lake."

In October 1922, Mussolini made his move. He pressured indecisive King Victor Emmanuel III (ruled 1900–1946), a shy man who loved to hunt, wear military uniforms, and collect coins, to name him and several other fascists to cabinet posts. The king remained out of Rome for weeks at a time as the crisis built, hoping that it would simply go away. Even as he planned a coup d'état, Mussolini charmed members of the royal family. He told 40,000 fascists in Naples, "Either we are allowed to govern, or we will seize power by marching on Rome." The prime minister asked the king to declare martial law and to use the army to restore order by suppressing the fascists, who had seized control of several towns.

The king declared a state of emergency and then changed his mind even as thousands of black-shirted fascists surged toward Rome on the night of

October 27, 1922. Mussolini took a comfortable night train to the capital. When one politician refused the king's request to form a government, Victor Emmanuel turned to Mussolini. On October 29, the Duce became prime minister. Fascists celebrated in the streets by beating up political enemies and shutting down left-wing newspapers.

Despite the fact that his party held a small proportion of the seats in the chamber and could not claim the party allegiance of a single senator, Mussolini convinced both bodies to grant him full powers to rule by decree for a year. Many mainstream politicians endorsed him because the fascists promised to restore social order. They also assumed that Mussolini could not long survive once brought into respectable political life.

Mussolini's shrewd management of fascist newspapers and his ability to plant favorable articles in other papers through cajoling and bribery helped win further support. Aided by the intimidating tactics of the fascist militia, the National Fascist Party won enough votes in the 1923 elections to emerge as the majority party, at least with the support of the Catholic Popular Party.

Despite a major political crisis in 1924 that followed his implication in the murder of a Socialist deputy, Mussolini developed an almost cult-like following. The Duce encouraged the phrase "Mussolini is always right" and managed to convince millions of people that this was indeed the case. He was the first politician of the twentieth century to make use of modern communication techniques. Mussolini subsidized several films about his accomplishments; his rambling speeches, voluminous tomes, an autobiography, and several authorized biographies were sold in glossy editions. By the early 1930s, Italian journalists were required to capitalize He, Him, and His when referring to the Duce, as they did when mentioning God or Jesus Christ. All Italians at age eighteen had to take an oath to obey Mussolini. Italian press agents worked to enhance his image abroad. In Vienna, Sigmund Freud at first praised him; the American poet Ezra Pound remained an admirer. The U.S. ambassador saluted "a fine young revolution," and *Time* magazine put him on its cover eight times. To some foreign visitors, Mussolini's fascism seemed to offer a third way—namely, corporatism—that lay between unchecked capitalism and the contentious challenge of socialism and communism. The Duce became known abroad as the genius who managed to make Italian trains run on time, although, in fact, such a description applied only to those carrying tourists to the ski resorts in the Italian Alps.

Not long after Mussolini took power, however, French newspapers began to describe him as a Carnival Caesar. The tag stuck. The Duce strutted about, boasting egregiously, his eyes rolling and his chin jutting out as he piled falsehood upon exaggeration. He insisted that officials and assistants sprint to his desk, and ordered photographers to take pictures of him fencing, playing tennis, or jogging by troops he was reviewing. Mussolini obnoxiously boasted of his sexual energy and prowess. But despite his insistence that he be portrayed as dynamic, he was rather lazy. To some extent, the

Italian dictator was an actor, and the balconies from which he thundered speeches were his stage.

Mussolini planned an army of "eight million bayonets" and an air force that would "blot out the sun." But despite the dictator's attempt to project an image of fascism that emphasized youthful physical vigor, relatively little military training actually took place in Italy. The Italian army remained beset by inadequate command structures and poor training.

The Duce took over the most important operations of the state and was like an orchestra conductor trying to play all of the instruments at once. He warned ministers not to disagree with him because they might divert him "from what I know to be the right path—my own animal instincts are always right." Officials reported only what they thought Mussolini wanted to hear. The gap between Mussolini's assessment of Italy's military strength and reality widened.

Mussolini treated domestic policy as an afterthought, once claiming that "to govern [Italy], you need only two things, policemen, and bands playing in the streets." Yet while it is easy to emphasize the farcical aspects of Mussolini's rule, in Italy, as in other fascist states, there was nothing comical about the brutality of the police or about his provocative foreign policy, which made Europe an increasingly dangerous place.

In order to placate a potentially powerful source of opposition, Mussolini made peace with the Catholic Church, which had previously denounced the regime after fascist squads smashed Catholic workers' cooperatives along with similar Socialist organizations. In 1929, the Duce signed the Lateran Pacts with the Church, a concordat that left the Vatican an independent papal enclave within Rome. In exchange, the papacy for the first time officially recognized Italy's existence. The Italian dictator returned religious instruction to all schools, and banned freemasonry, literature that the Church considered obscene, the sale of contraceptives, and swearing in public. Mussolini won further Church support with his pro-natal campaign (which included a tax on "unjustified celibacy"), vague statements about the importance of the family, measures limiting Protestant publications, and fulminations against women participating in sports. The Duce now had his grown children baptized and his marriage recognized by the Church, ten years after his civil marriage to a wife with whom he no longer lived. Pope Pius XI called Mussolini "the man sent by Providence."

Like Hitler and Stalin, Mussolini sought to eliminate the boundary between private and public life. He wanted the "new Italian woman" to espouse the values of, and serve, the nationalist state. With the fascist motto, "Everything within the State, nothing outside the State," he viewed the family as an essential component of fascism. "The Nation is served even by keeping the house swept. Civic discipline begins with family discipline," advised an Italian children's book. But fascism could never overcome the inevitable tensions between family obligations and what fascists considered national duties. Mussolini and the fascists believed they were restoring old values. But the idea of women serving the nation-state was very new—for example, the attempt to create mass fascist organizations of women ranging from after-work recreational clubs to female paramilitary squads. The Duce disliked the fact that women had obtained the right to vote in Great Britain, Germany, and several other countries, and that more Italian women were going to work. In Italy's fascist state—as in Hitler's Germany—the place of women was, in principle, in the home, obeying their husbands and having babies.

Mussolini viewed corporatism (see Chapter 24) as a possible remedy to the economic problems that beset Italy. The Duce created twenty-two corporations, or assemblies, overseen, at least in theory, by a National Council of Corporations. Each corporation was based on a council of employers and employees. But Italian fascist corporatism had very little impact in Italy. Its chief practical consequence, at least until the early 1930s, was to swell the number of state bureaucrats hired to supervise creaky, inefficient, and largely superfluous organizations.

The Duce wanted to make Italy economically independent. State agencies invested in industries Mussolini considered crucial to the colonial and European wars he was planning. By 1935, no other European state, except Stalin's Soviet Union, controlled such a large portion of industry, with major shares in industries like steelworks and shipbuilding. Hydroelectricity and automobile manufacturing developed, but Italian industry still depended on raw materials imported from abroad, including copper, rubber, and coal.

Mussolini dubbed his most ambitious agricultural program the "battle for grain." But wheat production was uneconomical in many regions; by converting from labor-intensive crops to wheat, the Duce's pet program generated unemployment and reduced pasture and fruit-growing lands and the number of farm animals. High tariffs on grain imports raised food prices. Land reclamation and irrigation projects also failed. While Mussolini's speeches celebrated "blood and soil" (a constant refrain on the fascist and authoritarian right in inter-war Europe), the number of Italian peasant proprietors declined.

The failures of Mussolini's economic policies were compounded by the demands of military spending, which absorbed a full third of Italian income by the mid-1930s. While the state spent heavily on planes and submarines, Italy's per capita income remained about that of Britain and the United States in the early nineteenth century. Illiteracy remained high, particularly in the south. Under fascism, the gap between the more industrialized north and the poor south continued to grow.

The paradox of Italian corporatism was revealed in Mussolini's rhetoric that there were no social classes in Italy, only Italians. The Duce cheerily proclaimed the end of class struggle and bragged that he had done more for workers than any other leader. But employers and workers were certainly not on an equal footing. Their trade unions destroyed (replaced by fascist trade unions), their conditions of life basically unimproved, and strikes now

Italian women with gas masks line up for the Duce as part of a parade of 70,000 fascist women and girls in celebration of the twentieth anniversary of fascism in 1939.

illegal, most workers remained skeptical about Mussolini. The fascist government did limit the workday in 1923, and in 1935 it introduced a five-day workweek. But employers broke contracts with impunity. The conditions of life for sharecroppers and other landless laborers worsened.

In other respects, some things went on as before. In the south, where peasants particularly resented and resisted the state, the Mafia provided an alternative allegiance, a parallel underworld government. Mussolini failed to destroy the power of the Neapolitan and Sicilian Mafias, even though the number of Mafia-related killings fell dramatically. The Church also remained at least an alternative source of influence to fascism. A Catholic revival, which included a rapid rise in the number of priests and nuns, was independent of fascism. Pope Pius XI lost some of his enthusiasm for Mussolini's fascism, denouncing in the early 1930s "the pagan worship of the state." Few Italians paid attention to the Duce's attempts to convince Italians to stop singing in the streets, or his insistence that they dress babies in fascist black shirts. That not all Italians listened to Mussolini's bombastic rhetoric (nor to the Catholic Church) was demonstrated by the continuing fall of the birthrate (from 147.5 births per 1,000 in 1911 to 102.2 in 1936), despite the call of the Duce for more baby soldiers and the ban on the sale of birth-control devices. Massive emigration out of Italy continued throughout the 1920s and 1930s. However, overall, most Italians still supported Mussolini, if only passively.

Hitler and the Rise of the Nazis in Germany

Like Italian fascism, the rise of the Nazis became closely identified with the rise to power of a charismatic leader, Adolf Hitler (1889–1945). Hitler was born in the small Austrian town of Braunau, on the border with Bavaria. His father was a customs official of modest means. As a boy, the young Hitler lacked discipline and was, as a teacher remembered, "notoriously cantankerous, willful, arrogant, and bad-tempered. He had obvious difficulty in fitting in at school."

Hitler quit school in 1905. Turned down for admission to the School of Painting at the Academy of Fine Arts in Vienna, he nonetheless moved to the imperial capital where he lived in a hostel with little money and few friends. In the 1914 city directory, Hitler had himself listed as "painter and architect," although his painting amounted to earning a little money painting postcards for tourists.

Hitler was of average height with a large head, dark hair, broad cheekbones, and an unusually high forehead. Wearing baggy clothes and sporting his characteristic trimmed mustache, he was not an impressive-looking man. He had bad teeth and poor eyesight. Hitler was compulsive about daily routines, did not drink coffee or smoke, was a vegetarian, and took only an occasional drink. He enjoyed the company of women but may, in fact, have been impotent.

During this time in Vienna, Hitler expressed great hatred for the Social Democrats, not Jews, despite Vienna's rampant anti-Semitism. He moved to Munich and, as a German nationalist, cheered the proclamation of war. He joined the German army and was wounded in the leg in 1916, gassed in a British attack just before the end of the war, and decorated on three occasions for bravery. But his superiors found Hitler unfit for promotion to the officer corps, believing that he lacked leadership qualities.

Hitler would later recall "the stupendous impression produced on me by the war—the greatest of all experiences . . . the heroic struggle of our people." He claimed to have warned fellow soldiers that "in spite of our big guns victory would be denied" to Germany because of "the invisible foes of the German people," Marxists and Jews. The war accentuated Hitler's fanatical German nationalism and transformed him into a raging anti-Semite.

In 1918, Oswald Spengler (1880–1936) published the first volume of *The Decline of the West*. He blamed Germany's defeat on the decay of Western civilization. "We no longer believe," he wrote, "in the power of reason over life. We feel that life rules over reason." He anticipated that new, powerful leaders would emerge out of the maelstrom to destroy "impotent democracies." Spengler believed that the German race would emerge victorious in a biological struggle against its competitors. German culture would be embodied in a new state in which the individual would be subsumed in the racial nation.

By 1919, Hitler had constructed a view of the world that was strikingly similar to that of Spengler. Moreover, it was increasingly shared by many Germans. It was composed of racism, anti-Semitism, anti-communism, and aggressive nationalism. He believed that Germans were "Aryans," descended from a superior Caucasian people. That year, Hitler joined the German Workers' Party, a newly formed right-wing nationalist organization. The following year, when Hitler became the head of the organization, he renamed it the National Socialist German Workers' Party, or Nazi Party. Some Nazis now referred to Hitler as the "Führer," or "leader," as Mussolini was the Duce in Italy.

Nazis organized a paramilitary organization, the "storm troopers," known after 1921 as the S.A. (*Stürmabteilung*), led by the hard-drinking Bavarian Ernst Röhm (1887–1934). Like the Free Corps, the S.A. offered comradeship and an outlet for violence to frustrated right-wing war veterans. To its members, Hitler appeared to be a man of action, a survivor of the trenches—one of them.

Emboldened by their success at attracting adherents, the Nazis marched out of a Munich beer hall on November 9, 1923, planning to seize power and then march on Berlin. Troops loyal to the government put an end to the "Beer Hall Putsch." An anti-republican judge sentenced Hitler to five years in prison. He served only one year and emerged from prison a national figure. Hitler then built up the Nazi Party.

Some of the first Nazi storm troopers in 1922, with swastikas on their arms and flag.

In 1925, Hitler published *Mein Kampf* (*My Struggle*), which he had written in his comfortable jail quarters. Here he reiterated the claim, originally that of General Paul von Hindenburg and believed by many Germans, that Germany had been stabbed in the back by Jews and Communists during the war. It was easy to forget that the military front had collapsed before the home front, a convenient collective amnesia. "If, at the beginning and during the war," Hitler wrote, "someone had only subjected about twelve or fifteen thousand of these Hebrew destroyers of the people to poison gas— as was suffered on the battlefield by hundreds of thousands of our best workers from all social classes and all walks of life—then the sacrifice of millions at the front would not have been in vain." His identification of communism with Jews intensified his obsessive anti-Semitism. Hitler never strayed from the most salient themes of his appeal, believing that people could only absorb a few ideas, which must be hammered in over and over again. Germany would rearm and then conquer "living space" at the expense of the "inferior" Slavic peoples. Many Germans now believed that the problem was not that Germany had fought the war, but only that victory had been stolen from them.

In these early days, the Nazis, like Mussolini's fascists, drew much of their support from the middle class, which had been devastated by the hyperinflation of the early 1920s and turned against the Weimar Republic itself. Pensioners struggled to make ends meet; many small businessmen, shopkeepers, craftsmen, and clerks had to sell or pawn silver or other items of value that had been passed down in their families for generations. Many big businessmen were at first suspicious of Nazism's mass appeal. They preferred more traditional kinds of authoritarian ideas that appealed to their sense of social exclusiveness, such as a monarchy backed by the armed forces in the Prussian tradition. Middle-class businessmen of more modest means early on were more likely to back the Nazis. They looked to Hitler to protect them from "Bolsheviks" and did not care how he did so.

Slowly the Nazis built their party. They won less than 3 percent of the vote in the 1928 elections. But German political life was moving to the right, led by the powerful National People's Party, most of whose members were increasingly anti-republican but not yet necessarily attracted to the Nazis. They preferred a monarchy or military dictatorship. The death in October 1929 of Gustav Stresemann, Germany's able and respected foreign minister, removed a powerful voice of support for the republic, gravely weakening the Weimar coalition in the Reichstag. Socialists, too, were divided, despite considerable popularity—indeed the largest veterans' organization was that of the Socialist (SPD) Party. The political center disappeared as support for Weimar crumbled. The American Wall Street Crash in October 1929 compounded social and political instability. The economic hardship of the Great Depression swelled the ranks of parties committed to overthrowing parliamentary rule in Germany and other states.

Right-Wing Authoritarian Movements in Eastern Europe

In Eastern and Central Europe, parliamentary governments did not survive the instability wrought by the economic dislocation of the 1920s and 1930s, nor the bitter ethnic rivalries within these nations, which included states that already existed at the outbreak of the war (Romania, Bulgaria, and Greece, as well as Poland, once again independent) and the new state of Yugoslavia. Except for the kingdom of Yugoslavia, each of these multinational states had some sort of liberal constitution in the 1920s. But by the end of the 1930s, only Czechoslovakia had not become a dictatorship.

With the exception of Czechoslovakia, which included industrialized Bohemia, all of these countries were heavily agricultural, poor, and had high percentages of illiteracy. When compared with the countries of Western Europe, the countries of Eastern Europe had very small middle classes, except Czech Bohemia, parts of Serbia, and major cities like Budapest.

A daunting variety of conflicting economic interests could be found among the people of Eastern Europe, ranging from those of wealthy Hungarian landowners to Bosnian mountain dwellers scratching out a meager living from thankless land. In Eastern Europe, most peasants were not interested in politics and associated states with taxes. But they wanted land reform, and this demand brought them into the political process. After the war, the governments of the Eastern European states did implement ambitious land reform programs that reduced the number and size of the large estates, adding to the ranks of small landholding farmers. But populist agrarian parties, such as the Smallholders in Hungary and the Romanian National Peasant Party, were essentially single-interest parties that fell under the sway of fascist demagogues. Such agrarian parties vilified Jews as ethnic outsiders, mobilizing resentment against their economic roles as bankers, small businessmen, and shopkeepers. In Hungary, Romania, and Bulgaria, wealthy landowners, desperate to protect their estates against further land reform and frightened by the rise of small Communist parties, turned toward authoritarian rule. As political parties and ultimately parliamentary rule failed amid agricultural Depression, nationalism filled the gap, becoming ever more strident and aggressive.

Poland was the first Eastern European state to become a dictatorship. General Józef Pilsudski seized power in 1926, imposing a military dictatorship that survived his death in 1935 (see Chapter 24). The Yugoslav experiment in parliamentary rule ended abruptly in 1929, when King Alexander I (ruled 1921–1934) dissolved the assembly and banned political parties. That year, Croats established the Ustaša (Insurrection) Party, a right-wing nationalist party that demanded an independent Croatia. In 1934, King Alexander was assassinated, with the help of Ustaša members. Five years later, Croatia won status as an "autonomous" region with its own assembly, but this did not reduce Serb domination of the multinational state. In Yugoslavia, then, the principal battle was not between partisans of dictatorship

King Alexander I of Yugoslavia and French Foreign Minister Jean-Louis Barthou were assassinated while driving through Marseilles in 1934; the assassin was later lynched by onlookers.

and those of parliamentarian government, as in Germany, but between the authoritarian Serb government and a right-wing Croat organization.

In Hungary, Admiral Miklós Horthy (1868–1957), the head of state since 1920, appointed a fascist prime minister in 1932 but repressed the extreme right-wing parties when they threatened to seize power for themselves. Bulgarian political life was marked by assassinations and coups d'état followed by dictatorship in 1935. In Greece, republicans, monarchists, and military officers battled it out. In 1936, Greek King George II (1890–1947) gave his blessing to the dictatorship of General Ioannis Metaxas (1871–1941), who, in the fascist style, took the title of "leader." In 1938, Romanian King Carol II (1893–1953) established a dictatorship by suspending the constitution. He did so to protect his rule against a challenge from the fascist "Legion of the Archangel Michael" and particularly its murderous shock troops, the "Iron Guard," a fanatically Orthodox religious group with strong anti-Semitic prejudices. Romanian fascists drew upon peasant discontent created by agricultural deflation. The king's bloody suppression of the Legion and the Iron Guard only postponed the victory of fascism in Romania.

In Eastern Europe, only Czechoslovakia managed to achieve political stability as a parliamentary democracy, despite differences between Czechs and Slovaks. The two largest political parties, the Agrarian Party and the

Social Democratic Party, drew members from both peoples. By the late 1930s, it was apparent that the greatest threat to parliamentary rule in Czechoslovakia would come from Nazi Germany, as Hitler seized upon ethnic tensions in the Czech Sudetenland between the German-speaking population and the Czechs. Consequently, even Central and Eastern Europe's most stable country was not immune from destabilizing ethnic rivalries.

Fascism in Austria

In Austria, the undersized, German-speaking remnant of the Habsburg Empire, fascism was closely tied to German nationalism and anti-Semitism. Moreover, lying between Germany and Italy, Austria almost inevitably came under the influence of those states. During the 1930s, Mussolini wanted to absorb the Austrian Tyrol, although only the southern part was Italian speaking, and Hitler wanted Germany to annex all of Austria. The Nazi Party of Austria was eager to assist Hitler by destabilizing political life.

The split between right and left in Austria led to "Bloody Friday," July 15, 1927, when police killed a hundred striking workers during demonstrations in Vienna by Socialists protesting right-wing violence. Yet in Vienna social democracy was rooted in areas of public housing on the edge of the city. The contrast between the stately inner city, where some of the old Habsburg nobles still lived, and its political "red belt" of working-class housing could not be missed. Much of the tax burden fell on the Viennese middle classes, which were for the most part socially conservative, fervently Catholic, and overwhelmingly supportive of the conservative ruling Christian Social Party. Anti-Semitism had deep roots in Vienna as well as in provincial Austria. As everywhere, the Depression accentuated existing social and political tensions and violence.

The violent anti-parliamentary groups in neighboring Bavaria, where Hitler had got his start, served as a point of attraction for the Austrian Nazis. Members of the Austrian right-wing Home Guard wore traditional green woolen coats, lederhosen, and Alpine hats, but carried quite modern machine guns. The Social Democrats formed their own guard, determined to protect their members.

In 1933, Chancellor Dollfuss, a diminutive, awkward man who wore traditional Austrian peasant garb because he was proud of his provincial origins, dissolved the Austrian Parliament because it stood in the way of an authoritarian state. In February 1934, after Home Guard raids on workers' organizations and newspapers, the workers of Vienna, led by the Social Democrats, undertook a general strike. Fighting erupted when Dollfuss unleashed the Home Guard and army against the left. Army units attacked the industrial suburbs with artillery fire, killing several hundred workers during four days of fighting. Police closed down all Social Democratic organizations, and tried and executed some of their leaders. Dollfuss then banned all political parties except the fascist Fatherland Front.

The Popular Front in France against the Far Right

Fascist parties in France had their origins in the anti-republican national-ism of the late nineteenth century. The Great War and the economic and social frustrations of the post-armistice period, as elsewhere, contributed to the rise of the far right. War veterans were prominent in the Faisceau movement, which was founded in 1919 and emulated the newly created Italian fascist organization, and in the Cross of Fire, established in 1929. French fascist leaders included two renowned producers of luxury prod-ucts, the perfume magnate François Coty and the champagne baron Pierre Taittinger. The latter's Patriotic Youth movement, founded in 1924, counted more than 100,000 members by the end of the decade.

The rise in immigration to France increased xenophobia and racism. Beginning in 1935, more people died in France each year than were born there, and its population grew only because of the arrival of immigrants—Italians, Poles, Spaniards, and Belgians, as well as Jews from Eastern Europe. About 7.5 percent of the French population in the late 1930s con-sisted of immigrants—the highest percentage in Europe.

French fascists decried the existence of the Third Republic, which seemed to them an anomaly in a continent of dictators. Political power in France lay not with a strong executive authority but with the Chamber of Deputies. Governments came and went in turn, increasing rightist dissatisfaction. In 1934, a seamy political scandal offered the extreme right an opening for action. The appearance of government complicity in a fraudulent bond-selling scheme engineered by Serge Stavisky (1886–1934), a Ukrainian-born Jew, led to violent rightist demonstrations against the republic. On February 6, 1934, right-wing groups rioted, charging across the Seine River in Paris toward the Chamber of Deputies before being dispersed by troops, with casualties on both sides. But, unlike the right in Germany, Italy, or Spain, the French right did not have a dominating figure capable of uniting opposition to parliamentary rule. On February 12, millions of French men and women marched in support of the republic.

The formation of the Popular Front in France, an alliance between the Radical, Socialist, and Communist parties, must be seen in the context of the threat posed by the right not only in France but throughout Europe. Socialists and Communists had been at odds since the Congress of Tours in 1920. The split became policy when the Communist International (Com-intern) of 1927 adopted the tactic of "class against class," which tolerated no concessions to "bourgeois" parties, including the Socialist Party. But in the 1930s, the reality of the threat of the right to France overcame ideology. Stalin's fear of German rearmament led the Comintern to repudiate the "class versus class" strategy in June 1934. The French Communist Party was now free to join forces with the Socialist and Radical parties in a Popular Front to defend the republic against fascism. The three parties prepared a compromise program incorporating tax reform, a shorter workweek, increased unemployment benefits, support for the League of Nations and international disarmament, and the dissolution of the fascist leagues.

The Popular Front won a clear victory in the subsequent elections of May 1936. But the Communists refused to participate in the ensuing government, on orders from Moscow. Léon Blum (1872–1950) became prime minister of the Popular Front government. That the Socialist leader was Jewish intensified the rage of the extreme right. Shouts of "Better Hitler than Blum!" echoed in Paris.

As unions, encouraged by the Popular Front's pre-election promises, put forward demands for better work conditions, the largest strike wave in French history broke out across the country. For the first time, workers occupied plants, singing, putting on theatrical productions, and staging mock trials of bosses. The strikes, many by non-unionized workers, took both French labor organizations and the Communist Party by surprise. The Communists tried to bring the strikes to a speedy conclusion, fearful that defeat might hurt their influence with workers or help the Socialists. The Communist Party newspaper *L'Humanité* answered the workers' optimistic slogan "Everything is possible" with the headline "Everything is not possible!"

Blum convinced employers and union representatives to sign the "Matignon Agreements," establishing a forty-hour workweek, pay raises, and paid vacations. The strikes gradually ended. But the economy continued to falter in the face of intransigent opposition from employers and wealthy families shipping assets out of France. Moreover, the reduced workweek undercut production. Blum declared a "pause" in his reform program, and cut back social benefits and other state expenditures.

The Popular Front began to unravel. In March 1937, police fired on workers demonstrating against the rightist Cross of Fire group. The Communists denounced the government, which they had helped bring to power but never joined. The government had to devalue the franc several times because of the flow of gold abroad. Blum asked the Senate to grant him power to rule by decree. When the conservative-dominated Senate refused, he resigned in June 1937. For all intents and purposes, the Popular Front was over. A centrist government lurched on in France as the international situation worsened.

Fascism in the Low Countries and Britain

Fascism threatened even Belgium and the Netherlands, as well. In Belgium, the fascist party "Rex" (from the Latin for "Christ the King"), led by Léon Degrelle (1906–1994), drew on the frustrations of white-collar workers and shopkeepers, victims of the Depression who blamed competition from department stores and socialist consumer cooperatives for their plight. Economic malaise compounded tensions generated by the linguistic division between French-speaking Walloons and the Flemish speakers of Flanders, some of whom demanded Flemish autonomy. A wave of strikes tore through

Belgium in 1936, similar to the one in France at the same time. However, Belgian fascists never won more than 12 percent of the vote. The majority of the middle class remained loyal to parliamentary government. Banks and the Socialist and Catholic parties successfully pressured the government for action to assist the lower middle class by increasing credit available to small retailers and extending union rights to white-collar employees. The Catholic Church's condemnation of Rex in 1937 led many of the group's members to return to moderate Catholic parties.

Similarly, in the Netherlands, the Dutch National Socialist League, which emulated the Nazis, was condemned by both the Calvinist Reform Church and the Catholic Church. It won the support of only 8 percent of Dutch voters in 1937.

In the depths of the Depression, a fascist movement developed even in Britain, the home of parliamentary government. That there were considerably fewer immigrants in Britain than, for example, France, probably limited the appeal of the nationalistic far-right parties. However, Oswald Mosley (1896–1980) started a small fascist party in Britain. Born into a wealthy aristocratic family, Mosley left the Conservative Party in 1924 over his concerns about unemployment in Britain. The philandering Mosley proclaimed his new motto "Vote Labour, Sleep Tory." In 1931, he founded a small party with disastrous electoral results. Then, infatuated with Mussolini and the idea of corporatism, he attacked "international finance capital," as well as the Labour Party, and formed the British Union of Fascists in 1932, delivering violent speeches attacking Jews. Mussolini provided funds, as did Hitler, who served as best man at his second wedding. Mosley surrounded himself with black-shirted toughs, but he attracted more attention than followers (they never numbered more than 20,000). The British people once again avoided political extremes.

The Third Reich

In Germany, the Depression helped swell the ranks of not only the Nazi Party but also other parties and groups (including powerful army officers and big businessmen) committed to the end of parliamentary government. Political parties, labor unions, and voluntary associations crumbled before the Nazi onslaught. Nazi organizations enrolled millions of Germans.

The Collapse of the Weimar Republic

The Depression increased opposition to the Weimar Republic, particularly among the middle classes. The Nazis in 1929 were but one of a number of extreme right-wing groups determined to overthrow the republic. The Depression also further eroded the centrist coalition within the Reichstag upon which the republic had depended from the beginning. In March

1930, the last remnants of the Weimar coalition came apart under the pressure of the economic turmoil; the government, led by the Social Democrats, resigned. Social and political compromise seemed impossible. President Hindenburg began to rule by decree.

The new elections held in September 1930 confirmed the erosion of the parliamentary center. The Nazis received five times more votes than in the last elections, obtaining 18 percent of the popular vote and 107 seats in the Reichstag. The Communist Party, too, gained seats, while the Social Democratic Party remained the largest party with 143 deputies, although it lost seats, as did the moderate conservative parties. Bolstered by rising numbers of supporters, in 1932 Hitler ran for president against Hindenburg, winning 13.5 million votes to the general's 19 million and the Communist candidate's 4 million. The Nazi Party now had more than 800,000 members.

Traditional conservatives, including military men, not the least of whom was Hindenburg, turned against the republic. Franz von Papen (1879–1969), power broker of the traditional anti-parliamentarian right, became chancellor in June 1932. After elections for the Reichstag in November 1932, the Nazis became the largest party in the Reichstag (with 196 seats against 121 held by Social Democrats, 100 by Communists, and 90 by the Catholic Center Party). Although support for the Nazis had fallen by 2 million votes, the Nazis and Communists, both of whom rejected the Weimar Republic, had won more than half the votes cast.

Papen resigned as chancellor in December 1932. His successor, General Kurt von Schleicher (1882–1934), an enemy of Papen's who had arranged his fall, wanted to form a parliamentary majority by wooing some Nazis—but excluding Hitler—and even trade unionists, an improbable idea. When Schleicher's government resigned the next month, Papen, intriguing with Hitler, proposed a coalition government that would include the Nazis, with Hitler as chancellor. Hoping to transform Germany from a republic into a military authoritarian regime (perhaps through a monarchical restoration), Papen believed that Hitler could serve his purposes if the Nazis received only three of twelve cabinet posts. Once Hitler and the Nazis had helped assure the end of the Weimar Republic, they could be tossed aside. In Italy, Giolitti's Liberals had made the same fatal miscalculation in 1922 in their dealings with Mussolini.

Now joined by members of Hindenburg's family and staff, Papen convinced the president to appoint Hitler as chancellor, believing that he could control Hitler in his capacity as vice-chancellor. On January 30, 1933, Adolf Hitler formed the seventeenth—and last—Weimar government. "We've boxed Hitler in," was the way Papen memorably put it, "We have hired him."

Many Prussian nobles and generals still mistrusted Hitler. To the former, he seemed a vulgar commoner; to the latter, a mere foot soldier who made boastful claims of military expertise. But the generals had been taught, above all, to obey orders. Furthermore, Hitler's denunciations of Bolshevism appealed to their dislike of Russia, their enemy on the eastern front during the Great War.

Most wealthy businessmen still preferred more traditional nationalists like Hindenburg and Papen and worried about Hitler's unpredictability and his early denunciations of capitalists and promises to create a new elite. The Nazi Party found only one major donor among big businessmen; a group of industrialists even tried to convince Hindenburg to leave Hitler out of the cabinet. Although some big businessmen shared the Nazis' virulent anti-Semitism, they were uneasy with the foreign condemnation it brought, and concerned that it might one day undercut their markets abroad.

But big business nonetheless contributed to the fall of Weimar. Most Rhineland industrialists were no more in favor of parliamentary government than were Prussian Junkers. Hitler flattered business leaders and promised public order, which was good for business, even if achieved at gunpoint.

The Nazi State

Hitler's appointment as chancellor sparked a wave of systematic and brutal Nazi attacks on union members, Socialists, Communists, Jews, and some Catholics who opposed Nazism. Mussolini had consolidated his power over the Italian state in about three years. It took Hitler less than three months. During the night of February 27, 1933, a fire caused considerable damage to the Reichstag building in Berlin. The police arrested a deranged, homeless Dutch Communist, charging him with arson.

Citing an imaginary Communist plot, Hindenburg issued an emergency decree suspending virtually all individual rights. Penalties of imprisonment and even death could be imposed without due legal process as police arrested thousands of Communists. Hermann Göring (1893–1946), one of Hitler's long-time disciples and now minister of the interior in Prussia, authorized a new auxiliary police force made up of members of the S.A. and other paramilitary groups.

But the parliamentary elections of March 5, 1933, which Hitler promised would be the last held in Nazi Germany and which took place amid enormous Nazi intimidation, did not give Hitler the overwhelming majority he had anticipated—the Nazis emerged with 44 percent of the vote. Nonetheless, Hitler proceeded as if the vote had been unanimous. On March 23, the cowed Reichstag approved an Enabling Act, which extended the unlimited "emergency" powers of the Nazis. The liberal political parties of the Weimar Republic simply disbanded. In July 1933, Hitler banned all political parties except the Nazi Party. It tripled in size, with 2.5 million members by the end of 1933, adding so many people that the "old fighters" who had joined early in the 1920s began to grumble that the party was losing its so-called elite character.

The Nazis implemented a dictatorial state. In May 1933, they organized the state-controlled German Labor Front to replace the unions they had

Communists under arrest after the Reichstag fire of 1933.

decimated. Strikes were illegal. Hitler dissolved the state parliaments and took away the remaining autonomy of the individual German states, appointing Nazis to take over state governments. A new law empowered officials to dismiss subordinates whom they considered potentially disloyal to the Nazis, or who could not prove that they were of pure "Aryan" racial stock. In October, the first concentration camp began operation at Dachau near Munich for the incarceration of political prisoners.

Despite Nazi rhetoric about a racially pure community of Germans, Hitler was far from envisioning social equality, which he associated with socialism and communism. Still, for some Germans, the Nazi Party, and particularly the S.S. (*Schutzstaffel*, security units that guarded Hitler), provided a means of social mobility; military trappings conveyed the respectability many Germans associated with a uniform. Although the Nazis drew support from all social classes (although proportionately less support from workers), the Depression in particular drove desperate middle-class Germans into the Nazi fold.

Hitler needed the loyalty of Germany's army. But many German officers were becoming increasingly wary of the S.A., which was now almost 3 million strong and which seemed out of control. Its members openly competed with Nazi officials for appointments and influence. Röhm announced that henceforth members of his force could not be tried by courts and that they were not subject to police authority. Believing that Hitler would betray the party's radicalism, he foolishly bragged that he would free Hitler from his "stupid and dangerous" advisers.

The S.S. and the Gestapo (the Nazi secret police) crushed the S.A. on June 30, 1934. They killed at least eighty people, including Röhm. The "night of the long knives" also swept up some conservatives and military officers, as Hitler had feared trouble from the old right as well as from the S.A. Hitler convinced President Hindenburg that the gory purge had saved the German Third Reich (Third Empire) from a plot.

Hindenburg's death in August 1934 allowed Hitler to combine the titles of chancellor and *Führer* ("leader"), which replaced that of "president," a title that smacked of a republic. The army agreed to take an oath of personal allegiance to "the executor of the whole people's will." Ninety percent of those voting in a plebiscite approved Hitler's assumption of both functions.

The Nazi program of "coordination" was applied to most aspects of civil society, such as organized groups and activities outside the family. The Nazis had already gradually taken over voluntary associations, such as professional associations and sports clubs. Depoliticized, closely monitored voluntary associations and churches could remain centers of local public life without threatening Nazi domination. The Nazis worked to convert schools into mouthpieces for Hitler's state, providing new textbooks with instructions for teachers as to what should be taught, including "racial theory" and "Teutonic prehistory." Instead of students fearing their teachers, as had often been the case in German schools, non-Nazi teachers now had reason to fear their students; members of the Hitler Youth organization were quick to report to Nazi Party members teachers who did not seem enthusiastic about Nazism. New university chairs in "racial hygiene," military history, and German prehistory reflected Nazi interests. Pictures of Hitler went up in every classroom and radios broadcast his speeches.

The Nazis brought hundreds of thousands of active Germans into carefully controlled Nazi organizations, the goal of each being to "reach toward Hitler"—that is, to share the racist, nationalist goals of the Führer. By 1936 the Hitler Youth included almost half of all German boys between ten and fourteen years of age; a League of German Girls also flourished. The Nazis reduced social life to its most basic component, the family. (At

Hitler paying homage to Hindenburg shortly before the latter's death.

the same time, the Nazis encouraged children to denounce their parents for being disloyal to the fatherland, and the party sponsored "Aryan breeding" programs outside the family.) Vicarious participation in Nazi ceremonies and rituals also helped augment a sense of national identity.

Hitler implemented the Nazi "leadership principle," which he defined as a "doctrine of conflict." He applied a strategy of "divide and rule" to the higher echelons of government, such as the three chancelleries that replaced the cabinet. He tolerated and even encouraged open competition between his most trusted subordinates and between branches of government. Those who enjoyed Hitler's confidence ruthlessly and aggressively carved out personal fiefdoms. Unlike Stalin, who watched over even the most minor details with obsessive care, the Führer provided little supervision to government agencies. Occasionally something would catch Hitler's attention and brief, frenzied activity would follow. But he missed meetings, worked irregular hours, and was often disorganized. Hitler valued personal loyalty far more than efficiency.

The "doctrine of conflict" adversely affected the economic goals Hitler set for the state. The army and the air force quarreled over resources, the S.S. and the police over jurisdiction. The Four-Year Plan launched in 1936 under Göring's direction illustrated the functioning of the Nazi state. Hitler wanted to stimulate economic development, above all in industries necessary for rearmament: steel, iron, and synthetic fuel and rubber. Göring spent much time warring with other branches of government. Furthermore, industrialists resisted state intervention in their businesses. The Four-Year Plan failed to achieve its lofty goals.

Hitler had to confront the daunting challenge of unemployment. Although he knew or cared very little about economics, Hitler correctly determined that the rapid rearmament of Germany would help create jobs. Food shortages remained severe until 1936, but public works projects helped reduce unemployment and inflation. Big industrial concerns prospered, particularly those manufacturing war materials. The German gross national product rose by 81 percent, in part because of state direction of the economy. Hitler bragged that he had wrought an economic miracle. Millions of Germans believed him. An ordinary German woman wrote in her diary, "One feels absolutely insignificant in the face of the greatness, the truthfulness and the openness of such a man."

More consumer goods, such as radios, reached the consumer market, contributing to a sense of optimism about material conditions of life. The Labor Front organized cut-rate Nazi vacations. Some families of modest means who had never had the opportunity to travel took cruises in the Baltic Sea or even in the Mediterranean Sea. Hitler named this program "Strength Through Joy," taking the idea from Mussolini's after-work program of recreational trips in Italy. However, production of Hitler's planned low-cost "Volkswagen," or "people's car," was postponed because factories were needed for military production.

Yet sectors of the German economy remained weak. German industry depended on imports of iron ore, copper, oil, rubber, and bauxite. Many Germans found that their share in the "national community" was small. And although Hitler liked to identify the German people with what he considered rural virtues—"blood and soil"—the number of small farms continued to decline. There was no marked return to the soil as Germany continued to urbanize.

Like Mussolini, the Führer preached that a woman's place was in the kitchen or in the delivery room. A Nazi book for children announced, "The German resurrection is a male event." The state offered attractive financial benefits to families with children, and the German birthrate continued to rise, bolstered by an improving economy. Just months after becoming chancellor, Hitler forced women to give up industrial jobs and excluded them from public service and teaching. Fewer women went on to university. Certain occupations were classified as "women's work," primarily those involving traditional textile or handicraft production or farm work. But, despite the slogan "Women at home," the reality in Nazi Germany, as in Mussolini's Italy, was increasingly otherwise. The campaign to remove women from paid employment ended in the late 1930s, as women were needed to replace men conscripted into the army. The number of women working in German industry rose by a third between 1933 and 1939.

Hitler and the Nazis did not rule by sheer terror alone. Hitler also sought and won overwhelming popular approval. After defeat in the Great War, humiliation by the Treaty of Versailles, and years of Weimar instability in which the Nazis and other right-wing groups played a major part, Germans applauded as he dismantled the treaty piece by piece. But most ordinary Germans also approved of police action undertaken by the well-organized apparatus of the Nazi state. Regular police units drawn from every walk of German life assisted. The Nazi state won approval with a harsh campaign against crime, which had increased during the Depression. Most ordinary Germans approved of and indeed many collaborated in the arrest and imprisonment of common criminals. The Gestapo and the "Kripo," or criminal police, who became ever more aggressive, also arrested people considered "work shy," or others like gays who did not seem to them to fit in. Doctors used sterilization as a form of punishment and social control, part of Nazi "racial hygiene." Germans looked the other way or were indifferent to the rounding up of political dissidents and Jews. A contemporary described a Gestapo office:

> Grimy corridors, offices furnished with Spartan simplicity, threats, kicks, troops chasing chained men up and down the reaches of the building, shouting, rows of girls and women standing with their noses and toes against the walls, overflowing ashtrays, portraits of Hitler and his aides, the smell of coffee, smartly dressed girls working at high speed

behind typewriters—girls seemingly indifferent to the squalor and agony about them . . . and Gestapo agents asleep on tables.

Moreover, thousands of Germans denounced neighbors to the Gestapo for being Jewish, Socialist, or Communist, and did so well aware of the consequences of their acts. Certainly by 1939, most Germans were fully aware of the existence of concentration camps. Indeed the Nazi government eagerly publicized the "trials" and sentences that sent people to them.

Some intellectuals and artists jumped on the Nazi bandwagon. Very few members—though the novelist Thomas Mann, who had moved from being an angry conservative to a supporter of the republic by 1922, was one—resigned from the prestigious Prussian Academy of Arts when called upon to pledge allegiance to Hitler. The philosopher Martin Heidegger (1889–1976) saluted the Führer as "guided by the inexorability of that spiritual mission that the destiny of the German people forcibly impresses upon its history." Hitler hauled out Heidegger on formal occasions to claim that Germany's finest scholars had become Nazis. In fact, some of the finest German minds were already leaving Germany.

The Nazis burned books that espoused ideas of which they disapproved. In May 1933 storm troopers coordinated the burning of books by Jews, Communists, Socialists, and other disapproved authors. In 1937, posters in the municipal library of Essen boasted that in the four years that had elapsed since the book burnings, there had been a "healthy" decline in books borrowed and in the use of the reading room.

Hitler railed against what he called "decadent" art and its new experimental forms, ordering many works removed from museums. During the Weimar period, Berlin, a city with 40 theaters and 120 newspapers, had become a center of daring and successful experimentation by artists, writers, and composers, as well as scholars. In 1919, the architect Walter Gropius (1883–1969) had begun a school that combined art and applied arts in the town of Weimar. The Bauhaus—"House of Building"—set the architectural and decorative style of Weimar, stressing simplicity and beauty, expressing function through form, combining art and craft. By using the most modern materials available in the quest for "total architecture," Gropius hoped to reconcile art and industry. The Bauhaus's modernism and the presence of foreign architects, artists, and designers made it suspect to Nazis. Hitler, the former aspiring artist, detested modernism. He closed the Bauhaus as a symbol of "cultural Bolshevism."

In 1937, the Nazis in Munich staged an "Exhibition of Degenerate Art," including expressionist and dadaist paintings, among other modernist works. A Great German Art Show opened at the same time, putting on view officially approved painting. While Stalin's preferred style of "socialist realism" emphasized work, Nazi art celebrated being German. Nazi artists offered sentimental portraits of German families tilling the land, blond

Adolf Hitler visiting the "Exhibition of Disgrace" in 1935, which anticipated the so-called "Exhibition of Degenerate Art" of 1937.

youths hiking in the Pomeranian forests, and square-jaw soldiers portrayed as medieval Teutonic knights.

In their attacks upon modernist composers, the Nazis reserved particular vehemence for the works of Jewish composers, while the late-nineteenth-century compositions of the anti-Semitic Richard Wagner delighted Hitler. The theater, too, suffered from censorship, as well as from the departure of a number of Germany's leading playwrights. Hitler himself preferred light plays, such as a rustic comedy that earned the Critic's Prize in Berlin in 1934, in which the leading character was a pig. Anti-modernism could be seen in Nazi attacks on the supposed hedonism of the "roaring twenties," which Nazis associated with licentiousness, homosexuality, neon lights, jazz, and modern dances. Nazis did not do the Charleston.

Joseph Goebbels (1897–1945), Hitler's minister of propaganda, orchestrated the cult of Hitler. The Führer commissioned the popular filmmaker Leni Riefenstahl (1902–2003) to produce *Triumph of the Will*. This imposing propaganda film, which depicts the carefully orchestrated Nuremberg rally of 1934 where 250,000 regimented, uniformed Germans with Nazi banners and flags saluted Hitler, contributed to the cult of the Führer. The Nazis encouraged the production of a number of virulently anti-Semitic films, above all *The Jew Suess* (1940), the story of an eighteenth-century

Jewish financier who betrays a German state and is executed, to the cheers of Nazi audiences.

Hitler's New Reich and the Jews

Hitler made anti-Semitism a cornerstone of Nazi ideology and state policy. In 1935, the Nuremberg Laws, which made the swastika the official symbol of Nazi Germany, deprived Jews (defined by having had at least one Jewish grandparent) of citizenship. Jews were forced to wear a yellow Star of David prominently on their clothing when they left their homes. In the quest for racial "purity," the laws also forbade marriage or sex between non-Jewish Germans and Jews. Signs in restaurants, movie houses, and parks warned that Jews were not allowed, such as one proclaiming "Jews enter this locality at their own peril!" Yet some Jewish businesses, including banks, at first continued to operate, if only because Hitler feared the economic consequences if they were closed. Some of these were "Aryanized" by removing Jewish owners and managers. By July 1938, only 9,000 of the 50,000 businesses owned by Jews were still open. Shortly thereafter, the German state forced Jewish families to list the value of what they owned and to turn over their assets to Gentile trustees, who could dispose of these estates as they wished. Decrees established a list of professions and occupations from which Jews were to be excluded.

When Hitler came to power, some Jews emigrated immediately, or made plans to do so. With Jews unable to teach in universities after early 1933 or to attend university as of 1937, many distinguished Jewish scholars and artists left for Britain or the United States, including the brilliant physicist Albert Einstein (1879–1955). More than 1,600 scholars and scientists had lost, resigned, or left their positions. Other intellectual exiles from Hitler's Germany were not Jewish, among them the poet Stefan George, the writer Thomas Mann, and the painter Max Beckmann. But one had to have some

Nazis post placards in a Jewish shop window. The notice reads "It is forbidden to buy from this Jewish shop."

place to go. The borders of Hungary and Yugoslavia were closed to refugees. One by one, countries that had accepted Jewish refugees refused to do so. In 1938, the French government greatly tightened restrictions on the admission of refugees. Britain made it harder for Jews to get in, or to go to Palestine, which Britain controlled. Switzerland, which had been known as a haven for political exiles, also in 1938 closed the door on Jews fleeing Germany or Austria. Moreover, the Swiss government suggested that German passport officials stamp "non-Aryan" on passports of Jews so that they could be easily identified and turned back at the frontier. The Swiss police hunted down refugees living in Switzerland whom they deemed illegal residents, putting them across the German border, or other frontiers.

On the evening of November 9, 1938, following the assassination of a German embassy official in Paris by a Polish Jew, S.S. and other Nazi activists launched planned attacks on specific Jewish businesses and homes throughout Germany. They destroyed stores, killed several hundred Jews, and beat up thousands of others. Thirty thousand Jews were imprisoned in camps. The terrifying night became known as *Kristallnacht,* because the sound of shattering glass windows resounded in German cities that night. Few Germans protested.

Hitler's Foreign Policy

Hitler had never concealed his goal of shattering the Treaty of Versailles. German foreign policy came to dominate European international affairs. Hitler planned to rearm Germany, and he demanded the return of the Saar Basin, whose rich mines the French held north of their border, and of German parts of Upper Silesia on the border of Poland, the remilitarization of the Rhineland, and the absorption of the Polish (or Danzig) Corridor, which divided Prussia from East Prussia. But Hitler's long-term goals, which were far greater, were inseparable from his megalomaniacal determination to expand Germany by armed conquest.

Hitler's foreign policy was predicated upon the German conquest of "living space" (*Lebensraum*) and his theory that the Aryan race was superior to any other and therefore had the right, indeed the obligation, to assert its will on the "inferior" Slav peoples. A week after becoming chancellor in January 1933, Hitler told German generals of his plans to rearm Germany, to conquer land for agricultural production, and to establish German settlements in Central and Eastern Europe and the Balkans. The Slavic peoples of the Soviet Union, Poland, and Czechoslovakia would serve the German "master race" as slaves.

Once Hitler came to power, he was less open about his previously stated goals because Germany was then vulnerable to invasion, but these goals did not change. Hitler had to move with particular caution to avoid confrontation with Britain and, particularly, France. For the moment, Poland and Czechoslovakia each had a stronger army than Germany. Hitler had to carry out his foreign policy with patience. He left in place the foreign minister and much of the old diplomatic corps, although he viewed them as weak and suspected their loyalty. Four months after coming to power, he declared that he had no intention of rearming Germany and that he wanted only peace. That October, in a typical switch, Hitler announced that Germany would walk out of the Geneva Disarmament Conference, which had begun the previous year, and that it would leave the League of Nations, to which it had been admitted in 1926. He insisted that Germany wanted peace and respect and would take only legal steps to "break the chains of Versailles."

In the meantime, Germany worked to extend its influence in Eastern Europe. During the Depression, as France pulled back credits, German officials signed a series of economic agreements with Eastern European states, bringing them into Germany's economic orbit and increasing their economic dependency. Hitler's policy of deficit spending—particularly to rebuild Germany's armed forces despite the Treaty of Versailles—was perceived in Eastern Europe as successful.

Hitler signed a nonaggression agreement with Poland in January 1934 (the Soviet Union had done the same two years earlier), while assuring his generals that he had no intention of respecting the agreement. The German-Polish pact was a blow to France's plans to maintain Germany's diplomatic isolation by a collective treaty system directed against Hitler. French military alliances with the Eastern European states of Poland, Czechoslovakia, Romania, and Yugoslavia would have left Germany surrounded by potential enemies, albeit relatively small ones. The Polish dictator Józef Pilsudski did not trust Hitler, but Pilsudski believed that he might be able to balance Poland's strategic position between Germany and the Soviet Union and could take advantage of a possible German attack on either Austria or Czechoslovakia to annex disputed territories. The Soviet Union, which had joined the League of Nations in 1934, signed a defense treaty with France a year later and another with Czechoslovakia soon after, which bound the Soviets to defend Czechoslovakia in case of a German attack, but only if France fulfilled its treaty obligations.

The Führer and the Duce

While France scurried to find allies, Germany for the moment had none. Hitler had long admired Benito Mussolini. Both had taken advantage of economic and social crisis to put themselves in a position of unchallenged authority. Both intended to overturn the Treaty of Versailles. Hitler's territorial ambitions in Eastern Europe did not conflict with Mussolini's goal of empire-building in the Balkans and North Africa. But because of possible conflicting interests, notably Hitler's long-range intention to annex Austria and Mussolini's claim of the Austrian Tyrol for Italy, some possible tension existed. Yet fascist Italy and Nazi Germany seemed natural allies, sharing an ideology as well as France as an enemy. The Duce had proclaimed in 1933, the year Hitler came to power, "Hitler's victory is also our victory."

Mussolini had reduced Albania, the small, impoverished nation across the Adriatic, to a virtual Italian protectorate, although it had almost no Italian population. In the South Tyrol, absorbed by Italy under the terms of the post-war settlement, Mussolini ordered a policy of Italianization, forbidding the use of the German and Slovene languages in schools. Somalia, the country at the horn of Africa that Italy had conquered before the war, turned into a military base from which new conquests could be launched. Italian troops burned villages and slaughtered their inhabitants. In Libya, Italian forces routinely ordered the use of mustard gas and public hangings to solidify their control.

Mussolini worked to increase international tensions in the hope of taking advantage of instability. The Duce had signed the Kellogg-Briand Pact in 1928, in which the major powers renounced war as an instrument of national policy, not because he believed in its principles, but because he wanted Britain and France to treat Italy as a great power. Meanwhile, Italy funneled secret arms to Germany and trained German pilots in violation of post-war treaties. In the Balkans, Italian agents provided financial support to right-wing terrorist groups, including ethnic Hungarians and Croats plotting against the Yugoslav government.

Hitler's plan to absorb Austria required Italian support, or at least neutrality, until Germany had been fully rearmed. But for the moment, Germany was still in no position to antagonize France. However, the German dictator took a calculated risk in 1934. Dictator Dollfuss shared much with the Nazis, but intended to maintain Austrian independence and had banned the Austrian Nazi Party, which was funded by German Nazis. He had also signed alliances with Italy and Hungary. Austrian Nazis, backed by Hitler, assassinated Dollfuss during their badly organized coup attempt. The steely Kurt von Schuschnigg (1897–1977) replaced Dollfuss as leader of an authoritarian government. Schuschnigg, like his predecessor, believed he could maintain right-wing rule in Austria without German help. The dual allegiances to Austrian independence and to an institutional role for the Catholic Church separated Austria's authoritarian regime from its German counterpart.

Hitler correctly assessed that it was unlikely that Britain, France, and Italy—Mussolini was absorbed by planning an invasion of Ethiopia in East Africa—would mount an effective, concerted response to blatant German moves to overthrow the Austrian government. Each government limited itself to a protest against German meddling in Austrian internal politics, asserting its interest in Austria's independence. The British government was convinced that conciliatory moves toward Germany might keep Hitler in line, particularly if, as a good many British conservatives believed, Hitler wanted no more than to be recognized as a power and to be able to defend Germany's borders. The French government did no more than express irritation, as it was confronting a fascist threat at home.

In 1935, Hitler's foreign policy entered a new and more aggressive phase. He defied the Versailles Treaty in March by announcing that Germany's army would be increased to half a million men, that military service would become compulsory, and that the German air force had already been rebuilt, despite the prohibition of the peace agreement. British, French, and Italian representatives met in Stresa, Italy, in April 1935 to discuss Germany's violation of the Treaty of Versailles—as did the League of Nations itself—and to reaffirm the Treaty of Locarno of 1925, in which the German government had joined Britain, France, and Italy in pledging to resolve future international disputes peacefully. Hitler then made the usual reassuring noises, stating that he would sign bilateral agreements with any of the powers (as opposed to the collective security agreements he had already helped shred), uphold the Treaty of Locarno, and recognize the territorial integrity of Austria.

Great Britain expressed wariness by signing a naval agreement with Germany in June 1935 that established a ratio of 100 to 35 between the two navies. This agreement, however, enraged the French government, which had not even been informed by Britain of the hasty negotiations that led to the agreement. France then signed a secret treaty with Italy, the goal of which was to assure Austrian independence.

In October 1935, Mussolini's armies invaded Ethiopia, where Italian forces had suffered humiliating defeat in 1896. Determined to expand Italy's fledgling empire, a quarter of a million Italian women, including the

Ethiopian soldiers use donkeys to carry machine guns to confront the Italian invasion, 1935.

queen, pawned their wedding rings (women who turned in their gold rings received in exchange tin ones blessed by the pope) to help raise money for the war of conquest. The Duce correctly assessed that Britain and France would do little more than denounce the invasion because they still desired Mussolini's support against Hitler. Realizing this, Hitler had encouraged Italy to attack Ethiopia.

Ethiopian Emperor Haile Selassie (1892–1975) appealed to the League of Nations for help for his country, which had been a member nation since 1923. The League imposed economic sanctions against Italy, but left them weak by excluding oil from the list of products affected, and it did not try to prevent passage of Italian ships through the Suez Canal on the way to Ethiopia. The British government made it clear that it considered the appeasement of Italy the only way to end the crisis and placed an embargo against the sale of arms to Ethiopia. U.S. President Franklin Roosevelt even offered Italy American loans in order to develop Ethiopia.

Italian troops took the Ethiopian capital of Addis Ababa in May 1936. Over 500,000 Ethiopians were killed in the one-sided fighting. Italy lost only 5,000 soldiers, a number Mussolini decried as so small that it seemed to cheapen his victory. On July 15, 1936, the League of Nations formally lifted all sanctions against Italy. The Stresa agreement, which had been made with the goal of containing Hitler, collapsed. The Duce now began referring to himself as the "invincible Duce."

Remilitarization and Rearmament

On March 7, 1936, German troops moved into the Rhineland, which had been declared by the Treaty of Versailles to be a demilitarized zone. Hitler had secretly promised his anxious generals that he would order German forces to pull back if the French army intervened. Whether or not an armed British and French response might have stopped Hitler at this point has long been debated.

German ambassadors in the European capitals then claimed that the move had been necessitated by the destruction of the Locarno agreements by France's pact with the Soviet Union. The German ambassador to Britain, Joachim von Ribbentrop (1893–1946, who had simply added the aristocratic "von" to his name), failed to browbeat the British into an alliance with Germany. France pushed the British government to react sharply against Hitler's brazen move, but would not act alone. In Germany, Hitler's prestige soared. He had delivered as promised, facing down the powers that had imposed the Treaty of Versailles and destroying the Locarno Treaty.

Hitler now speeded up the pace of German rearmament, particularly of the air force. By 1938, armament production absorbed 52 percent of state expenses and 17 percent of Germany's gross national product. Prodded by the Labour Party, British military expenses more than doubled between 1934 and 1937; however, the total amount was far less than what Germany spent

TABLE 25.2. DEFENSE EXPENDITURES OF THE GREAT POWERS, 1930–1938
(IN MILLIONS OF 1989 DOLLARS)

Year	Japan	Italy	Germany	U.S.S.R.	U.K.	France	U.S.
1930	218	266	162	772	512	498	699
1933	183	351	452	707	333	524	570
1934	292	455	709	3,479	540	707	803
1935	300	966	1,607	5,517	646	867	806
1936	313	1,149	2,332	2,933	892	995	932
1937	940	1,235	3,298	3,446	1,245	890	1,032
1938	1,740	746	7,415	5,429	1,863	919	1,131

Source: Paul Kennedy, *The Rise and Fall of the Great Powers* (New York: Vintage, 1989), p. 296.

at the same time (see Table 25.2). Germany also had the advantage of rearming with the most up-to-date war materials, including glistening fighter planes of steel and bombers with four engines that increased their range.

THE SOVIET UNION UNDER STALIN

In the meantime, under Joseph Stalin (1879–1953), the Soviet Union was transformed into a totalitarian Communist state. Stalin assured his dictatorship by purging dissident groups within the Soviet Leadership. The Left Opposition to Stalin was led by Leon Trotsky (1879–1940) and Gregory Zinoviev (1883–1936), the humorless but scrupulous curly-haired party secretary of Leningrad (Petrograd's name after Lenin's death) and a former ally of Stalin. The Left Opposition believed that the Soviet Union ought to support independent—that is, non-Communist—working-class organizations, and criticized Stalin for abandoning Communist internationalism. Stalin, in contrast, argued that the Bolsheviks first had to build "socialism in one country"—that is, the Soviet Union. Between 1925 and 1927, Stalin isolated leaders of the left by assigning their allies to inconsequential posts in distant places.

Against the backdrop of a severe shortage of grain that lasted two years, in 1927 the Left Opposition demanded an immediate accelerated industrialization in the state sector and worker mobilization against "bourgeois" bureaucrats. It feared the effects of Lenin's New Economic Policy (NEP), which it viewed as having been an unnecessary ideological compromise that risked bringing back capitalism (see Chapter 23). Wealthier peasant proprietors, the Left Opposition argued, could be forced to provide the surplus that would sustain gradual industrialization. If the state, which controlled heavy industries, kept the prices of manufactured goods high, state revenue would increase, permitting further industrial development. In

1927, the Central Committee, with Stalin completely in charge, voted to expel Trotsky and Zinoviev from the Communist Party and refused to publish Lenin's "Political Testament," which had suggested that Stalin be replaced as general secretary.

Five-Year Plans

Stalin believed that socialism could not be fully implemented until the Soviet Union had a stronger industrial base. Then an expanded proletariat would provide a larger base for Soviet Communism. After purging the Left Opposition, he then openly favored their plan of accelerated industrialization. This would be paid for by extracting more resources from the peasantry. In 1928 and 1929, Stalin resumed the forced requisitioning of "surpluses" and expropriated the land of wealthier peasants, the "kulaks." When this led to growing peasant opposition, he took the next step in 1930: the forced collectivization of agriculture—the elimination of private ownership of land and animals. The Five-Year Plan marked a complete abandonment of Lenin's New Economic Policy.

Nikolai Bukharin (1888–1938) objected to a policy of renewed requisitioning and immediate collectivization on the grounds that it would greatly undermine peasant support for the regime. The result would ultimately be to slow down rather than speed up industrialization. In 1928, he became the leader of the Right Opposition, which also disagreed with Stalin's complete abandonment of the principle of collective leadership, thus fortifying Stalin's personal authority. Stalin accused Bukharin of trying to surrender to "capitalist elements." By the end of 1930, Stalin had purged the Right Opposition from the party. With both the Left Opposition and the Right Opposition out of the way, the long dictatorship of Joseph Stalin really began. Bukharin was executed in 1938.

In formulating his Five-Year Plan, Stalin sought to take advantage of social tensions in Soviet society. He knew that workers believed that material progress was not coming fast enough and that they blamed peasants and smug bureaucrats. Stalin wanted to inspire workers to storm the "fortress" of remaining inequalities in Soviet society. He used the rhetoric of class struggle as a means of mobilizing effort, trying to turn workers against kulaks and "bourgeois" managers and technical specialists.

The first Five-Year Plan (1928–1933) led to a bloodbath in the countryside. Hundreds of thousands of peasants who refused to turn over their harvests, animals, or farms were killed. An officer in the secret police told a foreign journalist: "I am an old Bolshevik. I worked in the underground against the tsar and then I fought in the Civil War. Did I do all that in order that I should now surround villages with machine guns and order my men to fire indiscriminately into crowds of peasants?" Peasants, often led by women, resisted with determination and resourcefulness the establishment of collective farms, the redistribution of land, or the introduction of new

The deportation of prosperous peasants (kulaks) from a Russian village during land collectivization, 1930.

crop systems. In 1929, 30,000 fires were reported set in Russia. Peasants slaughtered livestock rather than allowing them to be taken by the collective farm. The number of horses fell from 36 million in 1929 to 15 million four years later, cattle from 67 million to 34 million.

Small plots were forcibly consolidated into collective farms. Peasants had to work a certain number of days each year for the collective farm; the state supplied machinery, seed, and clothing. The free market disappeared and the state set production quotas and prices. One of the primary goals of the collectivization of agriculture was to force peasants into industrial labor. During the first Five-Year Plan, the Soviet Union's industrial and urban populations doubled, as 9 million peasants were conscripted to work in factories.

In March 1930, Stalin signed an article in *Pravda* entitled "Dizzy with Success." He announced that his Five-Year Plan was succeeding beyond his wildest expectations and that the time had come for a pause. In fact, forced collectivization had catastrophically reduced Soviet agricultural production. Indeed, Stalin ordered officials to return expropriated animals to their owners. But he viewed this as a lull, not a change in theory.

When the Five-Year Plan ended in 1932 after four years and three months (in part because of the effects of peasant resistance), 62 percent of peasants now worked for the state on collective farms. Peasants were allowed to retain small private plots; the vegetables and fruits that they grew provided almost half of the produce reaching markets.

Overall, however, living conditions deteriorated in the Soviet Union during the Five-Year Plan. Shortages of fuel and machine parts became severe. Hundreds of thousands of peasants had been killed, and perhaps 2 million exiled to Siberia or other distant places under the sentence of hard labor. Around 7 million people died of hunger between 1930 and 1933, and 4 to 5 million people starved during 1932 and 1933, most in Ukraine. In Kazakhstan in Central Asia, about 2 million people (one-tenth of the population) died or were killed between 1926 and 1933.

The campaign for heavy industrialization was successful, but only if the human cost is conveniently forgotten. Despite inaccurate and sometimes misleading Soviet data, the state did meet some ambitious production targets in heavy industry (iron and steel), fuel production (oil and electricity), new industries (especially chemicals), and in the manufacture of tractors. While the Depression devastated Western economies, between 1929 and 1934 the Soviet economy may have had an annual growth rate of a remarkable 27 percent. These successes occurred despite inefficiency due to inadequate planning, chaotic reporting of figures (compounded by the mounting sense of urgency to report successes), and the replacement of many of the most able technicians (because of their social class) by dedicated but semiliterate workers or peasants who sometimes mistook mud for oil.

Giant show projects such as the Dnieper Dam and the new industrial city of Magnitogorsk in the Ural Mountains attracted international attention. Foreign visitors found many workers who seemed enthusiastic. Party officials selected "heroes of labor," praised for surpassing their production targets by record amounts. A certain Andrei Stakhanov, a Don Basin miner, was credited in August 1935 with cutting 102 tons of coal during a single shift. A "Stakhanovite" became the idealized Soviet worker, working as fast as he or she could, and ready to step forward to denounce "Trotskyite wreckers and saboteurs."

The second Five-Year Plan (1933–1937) relied less on the shrill rhetoric of class warfare, despite ongoing collectivization. By 1936, 93 percent of peasants labored on collective farms. Stalin relaxed the ideologically charged campaign against "experts" of bourgeois origins, and technocrats again appeared in factories. But the quality of Soviet life did not significantly improve. Centralized planning had its bizarre aspects: the sudden arrival of women's red stockings or of ketchup in stores, or of bathtubs, even if someone had forgotten to order the production of plugs for them. The promised "radiant" future always seemed to be far away.

In the meantime, Stalin reinforced his hold on power. Even with most consumer goods still wanting, 4.5 million radios in the Soviet Union broadcast Stalin's speeches in the 1930s. The grandson of a Soviet minister recalled, "Stalin was like a God for us. Somebody told me that Stalin could be the best surgeon. He could perform a brain operation better than anyone else, and I believed it." A poem from the 1930s entitled "There Is a Man in Moscow" reflects this bizarre, troubling adulation:

Who is that man who appears to the toilers,
Spreading happiness and joy all around?
It is Stalin, I shout, so the whole world will hear,
It is Stalin, our Leader and Friend.

Soviet Culture

Many artists and writers were originally enthusiastic about the Russian Revolution, and a spirit of utopianism survived into the early 1920s. The Communists wanted to build a unique culture based upon mass mobilization and commitment that would both reflect and accentuate the collectivization of life in the Soviet Union, helping forge consensus. The culture of utopianism would be defiantly proletarian and egalitarian.

In view of Stalin's determination that the Soviet Union rapidly industrialize, the machine was a common motif in Soviet imagery in the inter-war period. Soviet artists and writers believed that mechanization in the service of capitalists had further enslaved the masses but that technology could be potentially liberating. The state created art schools and provided assistance to struggling artists, hoping to enroll them in the service of the Revolution. In its first years, the Soviet state patronized futurists (see Chapter 20) as revolutionary artists who had embraced technological change and who would provide a new aesthetic for socialism in the construction of an ideal society. Soviet futurists issued a manifesto in which they promised to "re-examine the theory and practice of Leftist art, to free it from individualist distortions, and develop its Communist aspects." Artists collaborated with designers in producing models for standardized clothing and household items.

As the Soviet state subsumed most aspects of public life, the initial mini-explosion of cultural forms that had occurred during the first years of the Soviet state gave way to repressive orthodoxy. Rejecting traditional and avant-garde art as bourgeois escapism, Stalin believed that art and literature should assume a social function, depicting what he called "socialist realism." Stalin preferred monumental murals that presented smiling workers toiling for the state. Artists who did not conform stood accused of pandering to "bourgeois values," an increasingly dangerous denunciation. The Union of Communist Youth (*Komsomol*) sent out members to preach cultural uniformity, disrupting plays considered "bourgeois."

Stalin charmed and deceived many foreign statesmen and visitors, impressing them with the fact that millions of working-class children were now entering school for the first time. Some workers attended night classes, or even university. Women obtained training and positions in fields from which they previously had been excluded, such as medicine. Soviet guides whisked foreign visitors around on Moscow's new subway to see the Soviet capital's improved housing, water supply, and sewage facilities. "Potemkin village" was a series of gleaming facades that impressed visitors who did not realize that virtually nothing stood behind them. Although church and state had been officially separated in 1918, religious life went on as before, at least in rural areas, both in Orthodox regions and in the Islamic republics. Moreover, despite promoting atheism Stalin nonetheless discouraged unmarried couples from living together, banned abortion, and forbade homosexuality. Gradually in the 1930s, Stalin's early enthusiasm for equal opportunity for women waned; the state-approved image of the female as mother of committed Soviet children prevailed.

"Darkness at Noon": Stalin's Purges

By 1934, Stalin was no longer content merely to expel from the party those who did not share his views. He promulgated a state decree that expedited the punishment of those deemed to be "terrorists." As arrests mounted in number, executions replaced sentences of hard labor. The charges became more and more outrageous—accusations of secretly plotting to overthrow the state, of "wrecking" Soviet industries, of trying to restore capitalism, or of simply being "bourgeois" or the wife of an "enemy of the people." Lead-

The first Stalinist "show trial," 1930: an accused bureaucrat "confesses" to industrial sabotage.

ers of the Polish Communist Party were liquidated in Moscow in 1938 after having been invited there by Stalin.

The first of the great show trials—staged before audiences and cameras—took place in 1936, the last in March 1938, when Bukharin and the remainder of the Right Opposition faced judges who sometimes appeared to be more nervous than they. Those on trial were forced to sign confessions in court, where sympathetic foreign observers sometimes nodded in agreement to absurd accusations. Children—who could be executed at age twelve—were encouraged to denounce their parents for crimes against the state. At least 680,000 people were sentenced to death in 1937–1938 and probably about 1 million people were executed in the camps (in addition to those who died of harsh conditions).

The poet Osip Mandelstam (1889–1938) mocked Stalin with a poem that he read to friends in 1933. He noted the rumor about Stalin's origins in Ossetia, in the mountains of Georgia, and, as dictator, related the enormous weight of his words:

> We live, deaf to the land beneath us,
> Ten steps away no one hears our speeches,
> But where there's so much as half a conversation
> The Kremlin's mountaineer will get his mention
> His cockroach whiskers leer
> And his boot tops gleam.
> Around him a rabble of thin-necked leaders—
> Fawning half-men for him to play with.
> They whinny, purr or whine
> As he prates and points a finger,
> One by one forging his laws, to be flung,
> Like horseshoes at the head, the eye or the groin.
> And every killing is a treat
> For the broad-chested Ossete.

Mandelstam was arrested in 1934, sent to a camp for three years, and, after returning to Moscow, arrested again and sentenced to five years hard labor in another camp. There, in 1938, he died or was executed.

Estimates of the number of prisoners in labor camps, colonies, and prisons have ranged from about 1.5 million to 7 million. These included an elderly woman sentenced to camp terms for having said "if people prayed they would work better." Increasingly paranoid, Stalin's long arm reached far beyond the boundaries of the Soviet Union to force Communist parties in Spain, France, and other nations to purge those who disagreed with his policies. Stalin's agents caught up with Trotsky, who had gone into exile in 1929 and lived outside Mexico City, and stabbed him to death with an ice pick as he sat in a garden in August 1940.

The purge of the "national deviationists," accused of nationalist sentiments, for example in the Muslim lands of Central Asia, was an economic blow to the Soviet Union. It eliminated many engineers and other people with badly needed technical expertise. Furthermore, at a time when the rise of Hitler to power in Germany was increasing international tensions, the purge weakened the Soviet armed forces. Behind Stalin's move against military commanders was his fear that they might one day oppose his conduct of foreign policy. Among the 30,000 to 40,000 officers who perished, all 8 Soviet admirals were executed, as were 75 out of 80 members of the Supreme Military Council.

A journalist recalled that one of the most striking things about the Russian Revolution of 1917 "was the speed with which the masses, after the overthrow of tsarism, created new forms of organization," including soviets of workers and soldiers, factory committees, military organizations at the front, peasant soviets that supplemented township committees, and rural land committees. But once the Bolsheviks seized power on behalf of the working class and poor peasants, they never relinquished it. They destroyed these popular organizations that had embodied the aspirations of millions of people. The Russian Revolution, which had begun as a quest for economic and social justice by intellectuals, workers, middle-class and lower-middle-class radicals, peasants, and non-Russian nationalists, turned into the dictatorship of the Communist Party. Under the rule of Joseph Stalin, the Soviet Union took on some of the murderous characteristics of the fascist regimes its leaders so bitterly denounced. This was the tragedy of the Russian Revolution.

The Spanish Civil War

Spain became the battlefield of European ideologies during the bloody civil war that began in 1936. The world's attention turned to Spain for the first time since the time of Napoleon. Indeed, there was relatively little to distinguish the Spain of 1920 from that of more than a century earlier. The days of empire and glory had long since passed. With the exception of relatively industrialized Catalonia and the Basque provinces in the northwestern corner of the country, Spain remained an overwhelmingly agricultural society. Coalitions between the nobility, the Catholic Church, and the army determined political power in Madrid.

Social and Political Instability

The ineffectual King Alfonso XIII (ruled 1886–1931) confronted social and political problems that defied solution. Catalonian and Basque regional separatism challenged the Spanish government in Madrid. Chronic political and social instability helped push the army into the role of chief arbiter of political life. Labor strife, assassinations, street battles, and police violence became the order of the day in the early 1920s. Spain had declared a protectorate over northern Morocco in 1912 and used poison gas against

Moroccan insurgents who wanted independence. In 1921 Moroccans inflicted a shocking defeat on Spanish forces, costing the lives of 10,000 Spanish soldiers. This increased pressure from socialists and republicans on the monarchy.

In 1923, General Miguel Primo de Rivera (1870–1930) seized power with the support of the army and even the king. Four years later, espousing "nation, church and king," Primo de Rivera set out to "modernize" Spain, ordering the construction of dams, sewers, roads, and prisons. He became a familiar sight in the cafés and bars of Madrid, and such evenings occasionally were followed by gushing, incoherent bulletins to the Spanish people drafted on his return home. Primo de Rivera antagonized the left by promulgating a constitution in 1927 that left ministers no longer responsible to the Cortes and upset army officers (so numerous that they made up one-sixth of the army) by intervening in promotions. The weak Spanish economy eroded middle-class support for his regime. Primo de Rivera resigned in 1930.

The following year, Alfonso XIII left the country after elections returned an anti-monarchist majority to the Cortes. The army refused to save the monarchy, because most officers now hoped to impose authoritarian rule. The nobles, upon whose support the kings of Spain had for centuries depended, sat back and watched the monarchy fall.

A coalition of republicans and moderate Socialists established the Second Spanish Republic in 1931. The government of Manuel Azaña (1880–1940) enacted anticlerical measures, including the formal separation of church and state, imposed new taxes, passed labor reforms, and enacted land reform, including the outright expropriation of some of the largest estates. Strikes, land seizures by peasants, and attacks on churches and convents drove wealthy landowners and churchmen farther toward the anti-parliamentary right. The Spanish Republic could not count on the support of the unions, which wanted even more far-reaching social reforms, or of anarchists, who wanted the abolition of the state itself. Azaña fell from power in September 1933.

Thus began the republic's two "black years," marked by increasing social and political violence. The inclusion of the right in a more conservative republican government angered the left. During the "October Revolution" of 1934, leftists in Madrid, Catalan autonomists, and miners in the northern province of Asturias rose up, quickly setting up local "soviets" throughout their region. They held out for two weeks before being brutally crushed by Moroccan troops commanded by General Francisco Franco (1892–1975).

In 1935, Radicals, Socialists, Communists, and some anarchists formed a "Popular Front" in defense of the republic against the right. It barely won a majority in elections held at the beginning of the next year, and then quickly fell apart because of ideological differences amid high unemployment and political violence. The Falange, a small paramilitary fascist movement begun in 1933, further destabilized the republic, emulating the Italian fascist

MAP 25.2 THE SPANISH CIVIL WAR, 1936–1939 The growing domination of Spain by the nationalists; arrows show nationalist and republican loyalist attacks during the Spanish Civil War.

"black shirts." In response to a wave of violence against republicans, the government declared the Falange illegal and arrested its leader in March 1936.

A military insurrection against the republic began in Morocco on July 17, 1936. It was quickly followed by planned garrison uprisings in most of Spain's major cities (see Map 25.2). German and Italian planes carried insurgents to the Spanish mainland. Right-wing nationalist rebels overwhelmed loyalist troops and soon held the traditionally conservative regions of Castile, Galicia, and Navarre.

The fragility of the loyalist alliance compromised the loyalist defense of the Spanish Republic. In Madrid, socialist trade unions held the upper hand. In Catalonia and Andalusia, anarchist workers and peasants were a majority. They took the outbreak of the war as a signal to begin a social revolution, expropriating land, occupying factories, and establishing cooperatives. Workers' committees, holding power in some regions, unleashed terror against the upper classes. The Socialists now were in the awkward position of trying to rein in the social revolution for which they had originally called. Communists feared that an attempted social revolution from below would compromise the attempt to save the republic and, furthermore, that it might undercut support for their party. The Communist Party grew sixfold in less than a year, adopting the centralized, hierarchical structure upon which Stalin in Moscow insisted. It purged members who had joined the Workers' Party of Marxist Unification (POUM), which supported Trotsky against Stalin. The Communists withheld supplies and ammunition from anarchist and Socialist units.

Whereas the loyalists suffered the consequences of disunity, the nationalists benefited from increasing unity. General Franco, who believed that freemasons had undermined Catholic Spain, considered himself a warrior king struggling against infidels who deserved no mercy.

The Struggle between Loyalists and Nationalists

The Spanish Civil War was fought with a savagery unseen in Western Europe since the seventeenth-century wars of religion. At least 580,000 people, and probably many more, died as a result of the war. Of these, only about a sixth died on the battlefield. Ten thousand died in (largely nationalist) air raids on civilians, and thousands more died from disease and malnutrition. During the war, nationalists executed at least 200,000 loyalists, and about that same number died at the hands of the loyalist forces or from disease in prison. Throughout the first two months of the war, in areas controlled by the loyalists, social and political tensions exploded in violence and death. Members of the Falange and monarchists were taken from their cells in the Madrid prison and shot; in the province of Catalonia alone, more than 1,000 clergy and nuns perished. The nationalists made effective propaganda use of loyalist atrocities, real or imaginary—the pro-nationalist London *Daily Mail* proclaimed "Reds Crucify Nuns." The nationalists organized "fiestas of death" in bull rings, machine-gunning loyalists, including prominent intellectuals and Basque priests.

The Spanish Civil War polarized Europe because it pitted against each other the political extremes that had emerged in Europe since the Great War. For the political right, religion and social hierarchy were at stake in a pitched battle against socialism and communism, as well as anarchism. Those supporting the Spanish Republic saw the civil war as a struggle against international fascism. Foreign volunteers, including 20,000 Britons and Irish and many refugees from Nazi Germany, joined the loyalist forces. The volunteers of the Abraham Lincoln Brigade from the United States fought with idealism and determination—but with only occasional effectiveness. However, these "International Brigades" were largely responsible for the heroic defense of Madrid that began in November 1936. The writers who fought in the Spanish Civil War, virtually all on the loyalist side, produced some of the most remarkable literature about war written in the twentieth century, including the American novelist Ernest Hemingway's *For Whom the Bell Tolls* (1940). The British writer George Orwell's *Homage to Catalonia* (1938) memorably related an account of his service on the loyalist side and of the damaging divisions between the major political factions, above all, the role of the Communists.

The nationalists enjoyed a significant military advantage over the loyalists because their forces included the bulk of the Spanish armed forces. The loyalists lacked such necessities as reliable maps. Orwell recalled his amazement at being issued an 1896 model German Mauser rifle and at the difficulties of forging an able fighting force out of a motley crew of illiterate peasants, anarchist workers, shop clerks, and foreign volunteers, many of whom did not speak Spanish and for whom the only word known in common was "comrade."

The republican loyalists counted on receiving arms, munitions, and other supplies from the Western democracies. But the British government wanted to maintain peace at all costs, and many of its prominent political figures admired Franco. In France, Premier Léon Blum's Popular Front government hesitated to take any steps that would widen the Spanish conflict and further polarize his own country. Moreover, he did not want to alienate the British government, as he was counting on its assistance in any eventual war against Germany. Without tanks, airplanes, and other supplies from the Soviet Union, the Spanish Republic probably would have almost immediately collapsed in the face of the nationalist forces.

German and Italian assistance to the nationalists proved decisive. While Britain, France, and the United States abided by nonintervention agreements, Italy sent 100,000 soldiers to Spain. However, the loyalists easily defeated the ill-equipped Italian forces, which relied on Michelin tourist

Pablo Picasso's *Guernica* (1937), mourning a German and Italian air attack on the Basque village.

maps in a spring 1937 ground battle. The Italians fared somewhat better in the air, where they faced virtually no opposition. Mussolini's pilots helped destroy loyalist supply lines. Hitler used the Spanish Civil War as a military training ground, sending planes, guns, munitions, and other supplies through Portugal. German advisers trained nationalist pilots and military personnel. The pilots of the German Condor Legion flew bombing runs against loyalist forces, as well as against civilians. On April 26, 1937, German and Italian planes bombed and strafed the small town of Guernica, killing more than 100 residents. Within a month, the Spanish-born painter Pablo Picasso had immortalized the martyrdom of Guernica on his canvas depicting the horrors of modern warfare.

When the nationalists attacked Madrid at the end of August 1937, the Communist militant Dolores Ibarruri, known as "La Pasionaria" (1895–1989), rallied loyalists with her defiant shout, "They shall not pass!" However, in the north, the nationalists reached the Atlantic coast, cutting off the loyalist Basque region from France. The loyalists struggled along an imposing front that stretched from the Mediterranean south of Granada to the Pyrenees. When Franco's army reached the Mediterranean Sea, it isolated Catalonia from remaining loyalist territory. Barcelona fell in January 1939. Britain and France (where the Popular Front had fallen from power) quickly recognized the Franco regime. Republican refugees carried what they could through the mountains and snows of the Pyrenees to France. Those who fled into Portugal, where the republic had been overthrown in 1926, were returned to Spain by the dictatorship of Salazar to be killed or

(*Left*) Communist leader Dolores Ibarruri, "La Pasionaria." (*Right*) General Francisco Franco.

imprisoned. Bloody reprisals against loyalists in Spain began immediately, and 150,000 more Spaniards were executed.

Franco, now known as "Caudillo," or "leader"—like the Italian Duce and the German Führer—established authoritarian rule based on the support of the army, the Church, and wealthy landowners, three forces that had opposed the republic. But recognizing Spain's weakness, Franco did not pursue a policy of expansion that characterized Italian fascism or German National Socialism. The Catholic Church's institutional role in Franco's Spain or Salazar's Portugal would have been unthinkable in Nazi Germany, and was less significant in Italy.

CONCLUSION

The collapse of the political center in Europe in the aftermath of the Treaty of Versailles and the Depression helped create the Europe of dictatorships. When Germany invaded Poland on September 1, 1939, World War II began. In retrospect, given the deterioration of the political climate, the rise of dictatorships, and the violence of the inter-war period of economic, social, and political crisis in the Europe of extremes, one can view the entire period between 1914, when World War I began, and 1945, when World War II finally ended, as a war of thirty years.

26

WORLD WAR II

For the second time in just twenty-five years, a European conflict became a world war. It would be even more devastating than World War I, wreaking destruction on a global scale. Germany's invasion of Poland on September 1, 1939, like its invasion of Belgium in 1914, started a chain reaction that brought the world powers into the conflict. The Soviet Union occupied eastern Poland, Finland, and the Baltic states of Lithuania, Latvia, and Estonia. Japan joined Germany and Italy, and the United States entered the war on the side of Great Britain and the free French government exiled in London. Following Germany's invasion of the Soviet Union in June 1941, the Communist state became an ally of Britain and the United States.

The Second World War was the first in which civilian populations became systematic, strategic targets. Beginning with the invasion of Poland, Germany used genocide both as an instrument of war and as an end in itself. More than 6 million Jews perished in Europe during World War II, most in German death camps. The technology of warfare developed rapidly; existing weapons were perfected, and by the end of the war, the atomic bomb, a terrible new weapon, had taken a terrible toll on human life. When the war ended in 1945, Europe seemed to be entering an even more threatening era. Unlike at the end of World War I in 1918, few people imagined that World War II would be the "war to end all wars."

THE COMING OF WORLD WAR II

Determined to achieve his territorial goals and willing to go to war if necessary to do so, Adolph Hitler in 1936 allied with Italy and Japan. He sent German troops into Austria in 1938 and then Czechoslovakia a year later, believing that Great Britain and France would not resist, but prepared to go to war if they did so. Finally, Germany and the Soviet Union astonished the world in August 1939 by signing a mutual nonaggression pact. This cleared the way for Hitler to launch a murderous attack on Poland. That pact included a secret agreement by which Germany and the Soviet Union would divide Eastern Europe between them. Attempting to avoid war at all costs, Britain and France accepted the occupation of Austria and Czechoslovakia but drew the line at Poland. The Second World War began.

The Axis

Benito Mussolini had already signed a pact with Hitler in October 1936, forming what the Italian dictator called an "Axis." Hitler made clear that Germany's interests lay to the east; Mussolini could have the Mediterranean and a free hand in Yugoslavia, Albania, and Greece. Joint participation in support of the Spanish nationalists during the Spanish War (1936–1939; see Chapter 25) brought Nazi Germany and fascist Italy closer together. Mussolini accepted Austria's loss of independence in exchange for a closer relationship with Germany. Concluding that German military strength could further Italian aims, the Duce ordered his soldiers to goose-step like the Germans, claiming that it was the military stride of ancient Rome. This led to considerable embarrassment for the elderly King Victor Emmanuel III, who tried it but fell down. Mussolini also ordered his countrymen to stop shaking hands and take up the ancient Roman military salute of an outstretched arm at a 45-degree angle.

Racial theories had hitherto never played more than a minor part in Mussolini's rise to power or his daily bombast. The Duce, who had a Jewish mistress, had mocked Hitler's "delirium of race." Mussolini had at first enjoyed widespread support among Italian Jews—about one of every three had first joined the Fascist Party. But in 1938 Mussolini began a campaign against Italian Jews, who numbered no more than 50,000 in a country of 40 million people. These measures managed only to irritate many Italians in a country in which Jews seemed perfectly well assimilated.

Germany found another authoritarian partner in Japan. Over the last half of the nineteenth century following the Meiji Restoration of 1868, Japan had made itself an industrial and military power. In need of raw materials such as oil and rubber, the Japanese government sought to build an empire in Southeast Asia. By the late 1930s, the Japanese army had reached 1 million men, with reserves of twice that number. The Japanese air force had 2,000 fighter planes, including the new "Zero" fighter, as fast as any in the world. In 1931, Japan embarked on a piecemeal conquest of Manchuria at the expense of China. Since Japan has virtually no natural resources, its goal was to create a resource base, which would be necessary for fighting the total war that many young Japanese generals eagerly anticipated. A year later, the Japanese government created the client state of Manchukuo, declaring the last emperor of China, Henry Pu-Yi, to be its emperor.

Fearing that the Soviet Union might try to hinder its military expansion, Japan late in 1936 signed a formal friendship treaty with Germany, the "Anti-Comintern Pact" (anti–Communist International), hoping also to discourage possible British and American intervention in Asia. In 1937, Japa-

Prisoners of the war between China and Japan over the Japanese invasion of Manchuria, 1931.

nese forces began to conquer chunks of northern China to establish a buffer zone between Manchukuo and the Soviet Union. Japan then embarked on a major naval expansion program, exceeding both in number and size the limits stipulated by the Washington Naval Conference (1921–1922) to which Japan, among the other powers, had agreed. The United States was entrenched in isolationism and still suffering the Depression. Angered by Japanese aggression and Japan's alliance with Nazi Germany, Britain joined the United States in imposing an embargo on the sale of oil and other vital raw materials to Japan.

German Aggression and British and French Appeasement

In November 1937, Hitler unveiled to his generals plans to absorb Austria and Czechoslovakia, perhaps as early as the next year. Hitler's confidence derived partly from information he had received that Neville Chamberlain, the new Conservative British prime minister, who in a speech had once called Hitler's National Socialism "a great social experiment," might accept Germany's annexation of Austria and the Czech Sudetenland as inevitable. Chamberlain was concerned only that the annexation occur without strife. The British prime minister feared that if Britain went to war against Germany, Hitler's allies Italy and Japan would strike British imperial interests in the Middle and Far East—for example, in Egypt and Burma. Furthermore, he viewed German ambitions toward the German-speaking parts of Austria and Czechoslovakia, as well as toward the Polish Corridor, as in keeping with the principle of nationalism. He believed that Germany had been treated too harshly by the Treaty of Versailles.

Convinced that Britain would not act, Hitler bullied Austrian Chancellor Kurt von Schuschnigg to legalize the Austrian Nazi Party. When Schuschnigg announced that a plebiscite on the question of his nation's independence would be held, Hitler ordered German troops into Austria, justifying the invasion with the absurd claim that German citizens were being mistreated there and that Austria was plotting with Czechoslovakia against Germany. On March 12, 1938, most of the Austrian population greeted German troops not as conquerors, but as liberators. Hitler thus effected the unification (*Anschluss*) of Germany and Austria that had been specifically forbidden by the Versailles Peace Settlement. The Nazis arrested more than 70,000 people and frenzied Viennese crowds beat up Jews. Britain and France sent official protests, but the British government permitted the German Reichsbank to confiscate funds that the Austrian National Bank had deposited in the Bank of England. This provided the Nazis with valuable gold and foreign currency reserves.

Czechoslovakia was next on Hitler's list. During the summer of 1938, he orchestrated a campaign against the Czech government. At issue was the status of the 3 million Germans living in Czechoslovakia, most in Sudetenland. However, Hitler was also furious that some anti-Nazi Germans had found refuge in Prague. President Edvard Beneš (1884–1948), with Poland casting a covetous eye on the long-disputed coal-mining region of Teschen, now desperately sought reassurance from France and the Soviet Union. Both were obligated by separate treaties to defend Czechoslovakia against

Austrians salute Germany's annexation of Austria, March 1938.

attack. But the Soviets refused to act unless joined by France, and France refused to act without considerable British assistance, which Chamberlain had already ruled out. In any case, France could really only help its Eastern European allies by attacking Germany, which the French government viewed as out of the question. In May, German troops massed along the Czechoslovak border.

On September 15, 1938, Chamberlain flew to the Führer's mountain retreat in southern Germany. When Hitler informed him that he would risk world war to unite the Sudeten Germans to their fatherland, Chamberlain agreed to try to convince the French and Czech governments that Germany's absorption of the Sudetenland was the best hope for peace. Hitler promised Chamberlain that this would be the last territorial revision of the Treaty of Versailles that Germany would demand. On September 19, 1938, Britain and France virtually ordered the Prague government to cede to Germany territories where the 3 million ethnic Germans formed a majority. Chamberlain returned to Germany to see Hitler again on September 22. He asked only that the new borders of Czechoslovakia be protected by a joint agreement.

Faced with the kind of collective security agreement he loathed, Hitler now threatened that Germany would occupy the Sudetenland by October 1 and would recognize Polish and Hungarian claims on territory ceded to Czechoslovakia in 1918 (he was already encouraging Slovaks to push for autonomy). This would have dismembered Czechoslovakia for all practical purposes (see Map 26.1). The French government balked, demanding Hitler's original terms as presented to Chamberlain. Hitler then seemed to draw back, agreeing to meet with Mussolini, French Prime Minister Édouard Daladier, and Chamberlain to settle everything once and for all. In London, Chamberlain confronted mounting skepticism. The British government ordered preliminary measures for civil defense in case of war. Chamberlain tried to rally British public opinion with a speech on September 27: "How horrible, fantastic, incredible it is that we should be digging trenches and trying on gas masks here because of a quarrel in a faraway country between people of whom we know nothing. It seems still more impossible that a quarrel which has already been settled in principle should be the subject of war."

At the multilateral conference at Munich in September 1938, Hitler refused to allow representatives of the Soviet Union to attend. Czech officials were not even permitted to assist at the dismemberment of their own country. Chamberlain and Daladier agreed to immediate German occupation of the Sudetenland (the most industrialized part of the country), Poland's annexation of Teschen, and the transfer of parts of Slovakia to Hungary, all in exchange for Hitler's personal guarantee of the redrawn borders of the partitioned nation. Chamberlain stepped off the plane in London announcing to cheering crowds that he had brought his country "peace in our time."

MAP 26.1 GERMAN AND ITALIAN EXPANSION, 1935–1939   Aggression by Germany
and Italy against their neighbors.

In France, popular opinion did not want another war, and the military
expressed apprehension about taking on the refurbished and expanded
German armed forces. The French government felt abandoned by Britain,
and by neighboring Belgium, which three years earlier had abrogated its
1920 military agreement with France and proclaimed its neutrality. France,

Neville Chamberlain promises "peace in our time" after his return from Munich in September 1938.

which had completed a line of bunker-like fortifications—the Maginot Line—to the Belgian frontier and counted on Belgium's ability to defend against a German attack, was now more exposed to a German onslaught. The French government also feared that Hitler might convince Franco of Spain to join Germany in a war against republican France from the other side of the Pyrenees.

The appeasement of Hitler at Munich provided the German army with more time to prepare for the conquest of what remained of Czechoslovakia. Appeasement—the term would subsequently take on a negative sense—had already characterized both British and French foreign policy in dealing with Mussolini (as the Ethiopian invasion demonstrated). Appeasement as foreign policy was influenced by the sheer horror of the Great War and many Europeans' unwillingness to contemplate a new conflict. Appeasement did not mean peace at any price, but rather the belief that if Germany could be appeased on one or two demands, then Hitler would be satisfied, or so the reasoning went, and Europe would be safe from war. It was pure delusion.

On March 16, 1939, Hitler shattered the Munich agreements. German troops marched across the Czech border and occupied Prague. Again, as in the case of Austria, the British government helped Hitler out by allowing the transfer of 6 million pounds of Czech gold deposits from London banks to the German-occupied state. Germany strengthened its forces with the addition of the Czech air force and army, and it no longer had to maintain strong defenses on its southern border. Hitler's brazen move shocked Mussolini, who complained, "Each time Hitler occupies a country, he sends me a message." In April 1939, Italian troops invaded and annexed Albania. British factories began turning out fighter planes as quickly as possible.

Looking east, the euphoric Hitler now demanded that Lithuania relinquish the Baltic port of Memel, which had been given to Lithuania by the Treaty of Versailles. Lithuania did so. He then insisted that Poland relinquish the port of Gdańsk (Danzig) and international access to the Polish Corridor that had by virtue of the Treaty of Versailles separated East Prussia from the rest of Germany. As always, Hitler offered a concession that would prove empty as soon as it had served its purpose: this time it was support against the Soviet Union's claim to parts of Poland that bordered Ukraine.

The Polish government, which had been in a state of crisis since the death of Józef Pilsudski, its authoritarian ruler, in 1935, readied its military defenses. The British government, which had refused to consider any alliances with the small states of Central Europe, now hurriedly signed a pact with Poland on April 6, 1939, guaranteeing Polish independence and assistance in case of German aggression. On April 26, Chamberlain—even he had now lost his illusions—announced to the House of Commons that conscription of men twenty and twenty-one years of age would begin. France (which was now also committed to Poland by alliance) and Britain then signed pacts with Romania and Greece and offered military support to Turkey. Hitler probably hoped that rapid Polish capitulation in the face of a German invasion might present its Western allies with a *fait accompli* that could discourage a military response. But Hitler accepted the strong possibility that war would follow any German move against Poland, even though he knew that the German economy could not reach full capacity for war production until 1943.

Few statesmen in France or Great Britain still harbored any illusions about what was next. British public opinion rapidly turned against appeasement. Winston Churchill (1874–1965), one of the few British leaders who had been convinced since 1936 that war against Hitler was inevitable, called for an alliance with the Soviet Union against Germany. Discussions with Soviet diplomats dragged on, stumbling on the refusal of either Poland or Romania to accept Soviet troops on their territory, necessary to any effective defense against a German attack. Chamberlain then heard rumors that Stalin and Hitler were conducting diplomatic discussions, but laughed them off.

Undeterred by Britain's reaffirmation of its commitment to defend Polish independence, or by doubts expressed by some of his confidants in April 1939, Hitler ordered the German army to prepare for an invasion of Poland on the following September 1. He signed in May the "Pact of Steel," a formal military alliance with Italy. Mussolini, who called the pact "absolute dynamite," nonetheless thought that he could continue to play off Germany, Britain, and France against each other. He had believed Hitler when he said that he would not begin a war with Poland for several more years. But knowing that doctored statistics could not hide the fact that Italy was unprepared for war, and now tied by a formal alliance to Hitler, the Duce had painted his country into a corner.

The Unholy Alliance

Stalin himself no longer had doubts about Hitler's ultimate intentions toward the Soviet Union. But the Russian army needed time to prepare for war. Stalin had decimated the officer corps during the purges of the past three years. In the short run, Hitler wished to avoid war with the Soviet Union while he was fighting in Poland; in the longer run, anticipating war with the Western powers, he sought, like Bismarck in different circumstances before him, to avoid fighting a war on two fronts. Stalin did not trust the Western Allies to maintain their commitment to resist Hitler and did not think that even a Soviet pact with Britain and France would prevent Hitler from attacking Poland.

   In one of the most astonishing diplomatic turnarounds in history, Hitler announced on August 23, 1939, that Germany had signed the Molotov-Ribbentrop Nonaggression Pact with the Soviet Union, which was named for the two foreign ministers who negotiated it. The man Stalin had called "the bloody assassin of the workers" signed an agreement with the Communist leader Hitler had referred to as "the scum of the earth" and who dominated a state that Hitler planned to conquer. Hitler believed that a German pact with the Soviet Union would smash the will of Britain and France to defend Poland.

   Stalin had reasons not to trust Britain or France, which had not bothered to consult the Soviet Union while appeasing at Munich. Hitler and Stalin divided up eastern Central Europe into "spheres of influence." The German dictator assured Stalin that "in the event of a territorial and political rearrangement," the independent states of Latvia and Estonia, coveted by Russia, as well as Finland and eastern Poland, would be fair game for the Soviet Union. Stalin still assumed that the imperialist powers ultimately would destroy each other in a protracted war.

   In the meantime, most Germans seemed prepared to follow Hitler into a new war. A popular German magazine in April 1939 had cheerfully run the headline, "Gas Masks for German Children Now Ready."

THE WAR IN EUROPE BEGINS

The war for which Hitler had prepared for so long began with a rapid, brutal German attack on Poland. Stalin's Soviet Union then occupied eastern Poland. As Nazi troops overran Poland, the latter's Western allies, Great Britain and France, protested, but took no military action. Soviet troops soon invaded Finland, and German forces occupied Denmark and then

Norway. Hitler next turned his attention to the west, invading France, the Netherlands, and Belgium, and launching massive bombing attacks against Britain.

The German Invasion of Poland

On September 1, 1939, about 1.5 million German troops, led by an armored division, poured into Poland. Fighters and light bombers thundered overhead, carefully coordinating their attacks to protect the infantry. Britain and France responded two days later by declaring war on Germany.

Hitler wanted Polish resistance crushed quickly enough that Britain, and possibly France as well, would limit their reaction to a declaration of war. But he was prepared to fight the Western allies if necessary.

Poland had a large and well-trained army of more than 1 million soldiers. The German air force destroyed half of Poland's planes in the first attacks on its bases. Bombers battered Warsaw. Poland's frontier defenses collapsed before the onslaught of motorized columns of the German *Blitzkrieg* ("lightning war"). After moving east as German forces advanced, suffering heavy losses in the process, the Polish government moved to Paris on September 17. Warsaw fell ten days later. The German armies immediately implemented a policy of terror, killing prisoners of war, burning hundreds of towns and villages, and systematically massacring the Polish elite, while preparing the way for the settlement of the conquered lands by Germans.

German tanks move into Poland, September 1939.

From the east, Soviet armies invaded Poland on September 17. They did so with Hitler's blessing, under a secret agreement made between Stalin and Hitler as part of the Molotov-Ribbentrop Nonaggression Pact. Poland, partitioned three times late in the eighteenth century, was once again divided up. On Stalin's orders, more than 14,000 Polish officers and intellectuals were executed in the forest of Katyn about 200 miles southwest of Moscow. The Soviet dictator ordered the transfer of Poles in cattle wagons as "special settlers" to the eastern reaches of the Soviet Union.

The "Phony War"

As Hitler had hoped, Britain and France took no military action. Few people seemed willing to "die for Danzig (Gdańsk)," the Polish port Germany had lost by the Treaty of Versailles. British and French military experts, shocked by the speed of the German victory over Poland, overestimated the strength of Hitler's armies. An immediate French and British attack on Germany from the west might have been successful while the Germans were tied up in Poland, where the German army and air force had seriously depleted available munitions. Britain and France had more than twice as many divisions ready, and the German air force had few planes available to fight in the west. French troops made one brief, unopposed excursion fourteen miles into Germany, and then fell back. The British Royal Air Force flew over Germany, but dropped only leaflets calling for peace. Both the British and French governments believed that an attack on Germany would fail. They had been stunned by Hitler's pact with Stalin; unlike in World War I, it now appeared that Germany would only have to fight a war on one front.

Hitler confidently announced to his generals that he planned to order an invasion of France in the near future. The German army and air force were readied, while the French army dug in behind the supposedly impregnable fortifications of the Maginot Line, that line of bunkers stretching from Switzerland to the Belgian border (see Map 26.2).

The winter months that followed the Polish invasion became immediately known as the "phony war." Planned first for November and then for January, the German invasion of Western Europe was postponed until the spring of 1940. French troops stared into the rain, mist, and fog from their bunkers. Fearing German bombing attacks, the British government issued Londoners gas masks and imposed a nighttime blackout. In Rome, Mussolini had developed cold feet just before Hitler's invasion of Poland, because he knew that Italy lacked enough coal, oil, iron, and steel to wage a lengthy war. But he believed a German invasion of France inevitable. Mussolini announced that Italy's status would be one of "non-belligerence," a term he selected to avoid comparisons with the "neutrality" against which he had vociferously campaigned before Italy entered World War I in 1915.

MAP 26.2 THE GERMAN AND ITALIAN ADVANCE, 1939–1942   The opening of the war included advances by the Germans into Poland, the U.S.S.R., the Scandinavian countries, the Balkans, and North Africa. The Italians sent troops into Albania, and from there into Greece. The British unsuccessfully attempted to take a stand against the Germans in Norway, and British and French troops were evacuated from the continent at Dunkirk.

The War in the Frozen North

While the "phony war" continued in the west, fighting began in northern Europe. The Russian border with Finland, independent since the Russian Revolution, lay only fourteen miles from Leningrad. Stalin demanded that the Finnish government cede strategically important territories to the Soviets. When the Finnish government refused in November 1939, the Red

Army invaded. Badly outnumbered Finnish soldiers fought bravely in sub-zero temperatures, sometimes on skis, carrying light machine guns against Russian tanks and temporarily holding back the Soviet forces. Finland harbored no illusions about winning the "Winter War," but, like Poland, hoped to be saved by British and French diplomatic or military intervention. France now favored, at least in principle, armed intervention on behalf of Finland. So did Britain's Winston Churchill, who had angered his Conservative Party by opposing appeasement of Hitler at Munich. But Finnish resistance soon was broken. By the Peace of Moscow, signed March 12, 1940, the Soviet Union annexed about 10 percent of Finnish territory.

With the goal of stopping Swedish iron ore from being shipped to Germany, in April British ships mined the Norwegian harbor of Narvik, despite the objections of the government of Norway. On November 9 German troops occupied Denmark, which surrendered without a fight (see Map 26.2). German paratroopers landed at Oslo and other Norwegian port cities, followed by troops put ashore by ships. German soldiers repelled Allied troops, who arrived at the end of April with sketchy orders and inadequate weapons.

Prime Minister Chamberlain had assured the British House of Commons that Germany "had missed the bus" by waiting so long to attack in the west. But Germany's lightning occupation of Denmark and victory in Norway brought down the Chamberlain government. Churchill, who had been a member of Parliament on and off since 1900, became prime minister on May 10, 1940. The outspoken Churchill was an unpopular choice among even some Conservatives, who held an overwhelming majority in Parliament. Many remembered his impulsive attachment to far-fetched military operations during the First World War, which had led to the catastrophic defeat of British troops at Gallipoli in 1915. Even one of his trusted advisers said that Churchill had ten new ideas each day, but that nine of them were bad. Still, his resilience, determination, and dedication made Churchill an extraordinary wartime leader.

The Fall of France

German troops stared confidently across the Rhine River at their French opponents. The German army could simply sidestep the French Maginot Line, which stopped at the Belgian frontier. Germany enjoyed vast superiority over France in the air (France had only about 500 first-line fighter planes, Germany 4,000). Furthermore, the German army and air force were already well-practiced, having conquered Poland.

French soldiers had become demoralized by the winter months in the damp bunkers along the Maginot Line. The plan of the French high command to engage the enemy forces as they moved into the Low Countries was undermined by the Belgian and Dutch governments; both, hoping to remain neutral, had been unwilling to coordinate defense planning with the French army. The French generals lacked confidence in the strength of their forces and—at least some—in the Third Republic itself. French tanks were as good as those of Germany but lacked sufficient fuel and were dispersed among infantry divisions, instead of concentrated in tank divisions as in the German army. French communications networks along the front were inadequate. After eight months of "phony war," many people in France were uncertain as to why they might be once again fighting Germany.

Compounding serious military problems, the British and French governments were already sniping at each other. The French resented the fact that their ally sent a relatively small British Expeditionary Force to France; the British government seemed willing to defend France down to the last Frenchman. On the other hand, the French had irritated their British counterparts by opposing Allied bombing of Germany, fearing that the expected swift reprisals would strike them, not Britain.

On May 10, 1940, the "phony war" in the west suddenly ended. In a carefully rehearsed attack, German gliders landed troops who captured a massive Belgian fortress. Airborne divisions took the airport and central bridges of the Dutch port of Rotterdam; German bombers then destroyed ships, docks, and the heart of the old city, killing 40,000 people. The German assault on France began through the Ardennes Forest on the Belgian border; ten tank divisions pushed seventy miles into France. German planes, controlling the air, swept down on French troops and destroyed half the planes of the British Royal Air Force in three days. Mussolini, a portly vulture circling above the wounded French prey, declared war on France on May 10, but an Italian army managed to advance only about a hundred yards across the border toward Nice.

French commanders then foolishly sent most of their armored reserves into the Netherlands while German tanks, having reached the Meuse River in eastern France, now turned west and moved toward the English Channel. They were vulnerable to an Allied counterattack, but only a minor challenge by a tank column commanded by French General Charles de Gaulle (1890–1970) slowed the German drive to the Channel. Instead of attacking, British troops retreated from Belgium into France, heading toward the Channel. German columns reached the Channel on May 21, 1940, cutting the Allied forces in half. The Netherlands surrendered on May 15, Belgium on May 28. By now the roads of northern France were choked, not only with retreating British and French troops, but with Belgian and French refugees fleeing the battle zones, strafed by German planes.

France's defeat was now only a matter of time. British troops, joined by remnants of the French forces, managed to hold off the German army, making possible the evacuation of 340,000 British and French troops at the end of May and early June 1940 from Dunkirk by every available British vessel, including fishing trawlers and pleasure craft. The German army wheeled to confront the French troops still uselessly defending the Maginot Line. The French government left Paris for Bordeaux, as it had in 1870. The German

Hitler takes a triumphant stroll through Paris in June 1940.

army occupied the capital on June 14. On June 16, Marshal Philippe Pétain, hero of the Battle of Verdun in 1916, became premier. The next day, he asked Germany for an armistice. France and Britain had several months earlier agreed that neither ally would ask for an armistice without the approval of the other. The British government wanted the French armies to move to North Africa and continue the war from there. However, on June 22, the gleeful Hitler accepted the French surrender in a railway car in the spot where Germany had signed a similar document in November 1918. Hitler then set out to tour Paris. On July 3, the British navy sunk a battleship, a cruiser, and several destroyers of the French fleet as they lay in port at Mers el-Kébir in Algeria, killing 1,300 French sailors. The British command feared that the ships might fall into German hands.

The Battle of Britain

Britain would fight on. Addressing the House of Commons, Churchill declared, "I have nothing to offer but blood, toil, tears, and sweat. . . . You ask, what is our policy? I will say: it is to wage war, by sea, land, and air, with all our might and with all the strength that God can give us."

Hitler now considered whether an invasion of Britain could succeed. Germany held the French and Belgian Channel ports, a position it had never achieved during World War I. Furthermore, with Ireland having proclaimed its neutrality, the Royal Navy no longer had use of southern Irish ports.

Fearing a German attack, the British government interned German subjects, including some of the 50,000 Jewish refugees from Nazism. In some
places, officials took down road signs and place names, and shopkeepers
shredded local maps to disorient any German invading army. For an invasion of Britain to succeed, the German air force (the Luftwaffe) had to control the skies. The ensuing Battle of Britain, fought over the Channel and
above southern England, lasted four dramatic months, from the very end of
July through October 31, 1940, although most of the climactic duels in the
sky took place in August and September. The German bombing "blitz" of
London began on September 7. Londoners took to the subway stations and
underground air-raid shelters for protection. The British used radar, first
developed in 1935, to detect German attacks. Recently built British Spit-
fires and Hurricanes reached greater speeds than the German Messer-
schmitt fighters and could break through fighter escorts to get to the
cumbersome German bombers. Hitler ordered the bombing of key industries and aircraft factories in England even as British bombers appeared
over Berlin in August, demonstrating that Britain was far from defeated.

Britain lost 650 fighter planes, but factories were producing replace-
ments and new pilots were being trained. As German air losses mounted,
the Luftwaffe turned to less accurate night bombing to keep the British
fighters out of the air. At the end of September 1940, Hitler was forced to
abandon his plan to invade England. Churchill called the Battle of Britain
his country's "finest hour."

(*Left*) Evacuating children from London during the German bombing "blitz,"
1940. (*Right*) British Prime Minister Winston Churchill amid the rubble in
London, 1940.

A GLOBAL WAR

World War II rapidly spread to almost all corners of the globe. Total war absorbed national resources on an unprecedented scale, as factories began to turn out weapons, munitions, and war materiel. Governments assumed considerable control over economies, coordinating production, raising taxes, and imposing rationing. Scientists were put to work in the war effort.

In June 1941, Germany launched an air and ground attack on the Soviet Union. However, Hitler failed to reckon with determined Russian resistance, as well as with the harsh Russian winter. The largest invading army in history ground to a halt in the frozen snow. Finally, on December 7, 1941, Japanese planes carried out a surprise attack on the U.S. naval and air force base at Pearl Harbor, Hawaii. The raid inflicted great damage on the U.S. Pacific Fleet and brought the United States into what had become a global conflict fought on an unprecedented scale.

Total War

Britain was the first combatant in World War II to find itself engaged in a total war. As the war expanded, other states confronted similar challenges. German military planners counted on Hitler's confident assertion that the United States would stay out of the war and that Germany could bring the British to their knees. But the United States, where British resistance won sympathy and admiration, could help Britain in other ways. On December 29, 1940, President Franklin D. Roosevelt announced that the United States would be "the arsenal of democracy," despite official neutrality. Since direct loans might recall for many Americans the defaults by those countries in debt to the United States after World War I, Congress passed the Lend-Lease Act in March 1941. It authorized the president to lend destroyers, trucks, and other equipment, and to send food to Great Britain, which in exchange would lease naval bases in the Caribbean to the United States.

Unlike Germany, which had been preparing for war virtually since Hitler came to power, Britain had to start almost from scratch. The British government succeeded in rallying the king's subjects to wartime sacrifices. Because very few people had any doubts about the extent of the Nazi threat to Britain itself, military conscription at the beginning of the war was quickly accepted. Before the war began, the British armed forces comprised 500,000 people; at the end of the war, 5 million. Women took the places in industry vacated by departing troops, accounting for 80 percent of the increase in the labor force between 1939 and 1943. In 1939, 7,000 women worked in ordnance factories in Britain; in October 1944, there were 260,000.

The British War Cabinet imposed governmental controls on the economy and by 1942 had achieved a high degree of coordination in wartime production. The government imposed higher taxes, implemented rent control, established rationing, and called for voluntary restraints on wage raises.

Pants came without cuffs or zippers; a suspicious gray "utility loaf" replaced white bread. British farmers augmented agricultural production by increasing the amount of land under cultivation by a full third.

In October 1940, Churchill established a scientific advisory committee to put some of Britain's most eminent scientists to work designing more powerful and reliable weapons. One of the most significant breakthroughs of the war was not a technological innovation but the solving of the complex puzzle of a secret code. British intelligence officers, aided by mathematicians, deciphered communications between Hitler and his high command during the Battle of Britain. This subsequently allowed the Allies to know many German military moves in advance. British intelligence officers then broke the German communications code, facilitating, among other things, the identification of spies. By the end of 1943, the code breakers, some using the "Enigma" machine developed after World War I to decipher secret messages, were intercepting more than 90,000 messages a month. The British Psychological Warfare Division, along with their U.S. counterpart, also put the science of psychology into the service of modern warfare, waging radio and leaflet campaigns in an attempt to weaken the enemy's will to continue fighting.

Hitler's Allies

Hitler sought other allies in an attempt to win the war quickly. Seeking to discourage the United States, Japan's rival in the Pacific, from entering the war on the Allied side against Germany and Italy, the two Axis powers signed the Tripartite Pact with Japan in September 1940. Germany and Italy recognized Japan's interests in Asia, while Japan acknowledged those of Germany and Italy in Europe. The treaty specified that each power agreed to cooperate should any one of them be attacked by "a Power at present not involved in the European war or in the Chinese-Japanese conflict." Hitler then tried to convince Francisco Franco, whose victory in the Spanish Civil War Hitler had helped make possible, to join the war of the Axis powers against Britain. The German dictator envisioned a Spanish seizure of Gibraltar and German use of naval bases in the Spanish Canary Islands. The Spanish dictator pleaded the poverty of his country and, as if to emphasize the point, arrived at the meeting with Hitler hours late on a plodding train. After spending eight hours cajoling Franco, Hitler said, "I would prefer to have three or four teeth extracted rather than go through that again." Franco's Spain, however much ideologically in tune with Hitler's Germany, remained officially neutral.

In Romania, King Carol II was powerless in the face of his greedy neighbors, who were encouraged by Germany. He surrendered to Hungary a part of Transylvania that had been awarded to Romania by the Treaty of Versailles and that included a considerable Hungarian population. Stalin forced Romania to hand over to the Soviet Union northern Bukovina and Bessarabia, which had once been part of the Russian Empire. Bulgaria also helped itself to Romanian territory. As a result, the Romanian fascist Iron Guard rebelled and forced King Carol to abdicate in favor of his son Michael in September 1940.

Now convinced it was facing a long war, Germany hurried to secure a supply of raw materials by occupying Romania and its rich oil fields in October 1940. A right-wing general, Ion Antonescu (1882–1946), ran the country with the help of the Iron Guard, which served German interests and unleashed its fury against Romania's Jews and Communists. Both Romania and Hungary formally joined the Axis in November 1940.

From the beginning, it appeared that Italy's contributions to the German war effort would be minimal at best. Mussolini aimed to take as much territory in North Africa as possible before the British surrender upon which he counted. After having failed to launch air attacks, as Hitler had wanted, on British bases on the Mediterranean island of Malta, Mussolini invaded Egypt in September 1940, refusing a German offer to supply tanks because he wanted Italy to claim victory on its own. Unable to provide troops with air cover, Italian forces suffered a series of defeats at the hands of British forces.

Desperate for victory somewhere, on October 28, 1940, the Duce surprised Hitler—as well as his own generals—by ordering his army to invade Greece from Albania. Having paid large bribes to Greek generals and officials not to resist, Mussolini anticipated an easy victory. But a Greek patriot army drove the Italians back into Albania, where resistance movements made life difficult for Mussolini's troops. The Italian army took out its frustrations against the Croatian population of Dalmatia on the Adriatic coast. In the meantime, the British navy battered the Italian fleet.

Italy's imperial holdings in East Africa rapidly crumbled in the spring of 1941. A British and French force took Addis Ababa, Ethiopia's capital, in April. Hitler sent General Erwin Rommel (1891–1944), commander of a tank division, to North Africa to bail out the Italian troops. Mussolini vowed to continue the war "until the last Italian is killed."

The German Invasion of Russia

Hitler always intended to invade and defeat the Soviet Union, despite the Molotov-Ribbentrop Nonaggression Pact of August 1939. After occupying eastern Poland following the German invasion of Poland, Soviet troops had occupied the Baltic republics of Estonia, Latvia, and Lithuania during the summer of 1940, claiming that they had been illegitimately detached from Russia after World War I, when they had become independent. German interest in Finland and moves in Romania now made Soviet Foreign Minister Vyacheslav Molotov (1890–1986) anxious. The Soviets sought reassurance in a new pact, one that Mussolini would sign as well. Molotov went to Berlin. Assured personally by Hitler that Britain lay defeated,

Molotov replied, "Then whose bombers are those overhead, and why are we in this bomb shelter?"

Hitler intended "Operation Barbarossa," the invasion of Russia, to be a "quick campaign" of no more than ten weeks' duration. He hoped that Japan would attack Siberia, thereby forcing Stalin to divert troops there. Some German generals held the Russian army in such contempt that they ordered no serious assessment of Russia's existing or potential military strength. If the Finns on skis had been able to hold off Russian divisions with seemingly little more than snowballs, how could German fighters and tanks fail to break through with relative ease?

The opening of a Balkan front delayed Hitler's invasion of the Soviet Union, which had been planned for May 1941. Britain had sent forces to Greece following the Italian invasion, which made German bases in Yugoslavia even more crucial. An anti-German faction had overthrown the Yugoslav government in March and refused to join the Axis or to allow German troops into the country. Hitler ordered an invasion of Yugoslavia in April. German armies then pushed into Greece. As in World War I, Bulgaria in March cast its fate with Germany. Bulgarian troops occupied parts of Greek Macedonia and Thrace. The German army forced a British withdrawal from the Greek mainland to the Aegean island of Crete, which soon itself fell to German paratroopers. Greece was occupied by German, Italian, and Bulgarian troops. Five percent of the Greek population died of starvation, along with hundreds of thousands killed in the fighting or executed. By the end of May 1941, Hitler's armies held all of the Balkans.

Hitler could now concentrate on an invasion of the Soviet Union. Stalin, however, failed to heed warnings from Britain and the United States that Russia was Germany's next target. Believing these warnings, including some of his own army's military reports, to be part of a conspiracy to turn him against his German ally, Stalin ordered the execution of some of his intelligence officers.

On June 22, 1941, German planes, tanks, and more than 3 million troops attacked the Soviet Union. The German generals were convinced that the Soviet forces could be easily defeated. However, the Soviets had many more men, field artillery, tanks, and aircraft than Germany, and for the most part their weapons were of quality equal to or even superior to that of the Germans. But German forces quickly devastated Soviet defenses and communication and transportation networks. One army pushed toward Leningrad in July 1941, laying siege to the city. But Leningrad held. The battleship *Aurora,* which had served the Bolshevik cause in the Revolution of 1917, was pressed into service, its guns commandeered from a museum. A second German army captured more than 250,000 prisoners near Minsk (now in Belarus), 250 miles northeast of Warsaw; a third, finding support from anti-Russian Ukrainians, took Kiev in September 1941. Hitler rejected his generals' suggestion that the attack on Moscow be given priority. Instead, armored units were transferred to the northern army besieging Leningrad.

Peasants watching the effects of the German invasion of Ukraine, August 1941.

The German advance left Russian towns and villages in ruins, and hundreds of thousands of civilians dead. But despite enormous battlefield casualties, as well as half a million captured prisoners dying of hunger and cold in German camps, Russian resistance stiffened. News of Nazi atrocities helped rally virtually the entire population. German armies bogged down in the face of determined resistance around Smolensk. Soviet state-run factories were converted to wartime production, soon turning out great numbers of tanks of good quality. The United States, still officially neutral in the conflict, extended the Lend-Lease policy to the Soviet Union.

Their drive to victory stalled, despite having captured more than a million square miles of Soviet territory, the German troops, like Napoleon's armies in 1812, found that a frozen winter, the coldest in a century, followed the chilly Russian fall. "Hitler no more resembles Napoleon than a kitten resembles a lion," Stalin taunted. Oil for tanks and guns froze. So did soldiers. The German high command, so certain of a quick victory, had not bothered to provide them with warm clothing and blankets for temperatures reaching far below zero.

After ordering a halt in the push toward Moscow, Hitler, fearing the consequences of retreat on German morale, ignored the advice of his generals to pull back and await spring weather. Early in December 1941, a desperate German attack stalled twenty miles from Moscow. The German army never got closer. During the first year of the Russian campaign, German casualties reached 1.3 million, or 40 percent of the original invading force, the greatest losses of any single military operation in history.

Japan's Attack on the United States

Four years of aggression in Asia brought Japan to the point of confrontation with the United States. Since invading Manchuria in 1931 and proclaiming it the puppet state of Manchukuo a year later, Japan had sought to expand its influence and territory in the Pacific region. Southeast Asian oil was one Japanese target, particularly after the United States, Great Britain, and the Netherlands imposed an economic boycott following the Manchurian invasion. The Japanese quest for rubber, tin, and other raw materials threatened British economic interests in Burma and Malaya, as well as those of the Dutch in Java and of the United States in the Philippine Islands.

In 1937, Japan had joined the Anti-Comintern Pact that Germany and Italy had signed the previous year. Also in 1937, the Japanese army moved further into China and occupied the main ports, moves that the American government viewed with alarm. The Molotov-Ribbentrop Nonaggression Pact, signed between the Soviet Union and Germany in August 1939, had voided the Anti-Comintern Pact, as the Soviet Union was a Communist state. After Japanese troops entered Indochina, in September 1940, Japan concluded the Tripartite Pact with Germany and Italy, thus becoming part of the Axis. In an effort to stop the flow of Allied supplies to Chinese forces over the railway from Hanoi and a long dirt road from Burma, Japan had assumed a "protective" occupation of French Indochina in July 1941. A nonaggression

Japanese dive bombers preparing to take off from an aircraft carrier before attacking Pearl Harbor, December 7, 1941.

pact with the Soviet Union, signed in April 1941, two months before the German invasion of Russia, bolstered Japanese confidence that it could attack and inflict a stinging defeat on the United States and force the Americans to a negotiated settlement.

On Sunday morning, December 7, 1941, a Japanese force of fighters and dive-bombers surprised the American naval and air force base at Pearl Harbor, Hawaii. Three U.S. battleships were sunk, and five were severely damaged; ten other vessels were destroyed or disabled and 188 planes destroyed. The attack killed 2,403 naval and other military personnel, and more than 1,000 were wounded. However, three aircraft carriers were at sea and could still be readied to take on the Japanese fleet in the Pacific Ocean. Vast stocks of oil, too, survived. Japan quickly followed with successful invasions of Malaya, the Philippines, Singapore (where almost 60,000 British soldiers surrendered), and Pacific islands as far distant as the Aleutians near Alaska (see Map 26.3).

Because American intelligence officers had deciphered Japan's coded messages, President Roosevelt had known that Japan was planning to launch a war against the United States. Yet the attack on Pearl Harbor came as a surprise, in part because U.S. intelligence services were swamped with messages suggesting attacks at other locations. Calling December 7, 1941, "a day that will live in infamy," Roosevelt declared war on Japan.

Hitler, bound by treaty to Japan, then declared war against the United States. He believed that public opinion in the United States was against American involvement in another European war. In fact, he knew amazingly little about the United States.

Upon hearing the news of Pearl Harbor, Churchill exclaimed, "We have won the war!" The entry of the United States into the war against Germany provided, as in 1917, a crucial material advantage to the Allies. Despite its slow recovery from the Depression, which hit it harder than any other nation, the United States had become the largest industrial power in the world, producing more than the next six powers combined. American factories were quickly converted to military production. In response to wartime demand, industrial production in the United States doubled by the end of 1943, finally pulling the United States out of the Depression.

Despite the patronizing attitude of the self-assured British prime minister, a warm personal relationship gradually developed between Churchill and Roosevelt. Their rapport helped overcome the tension that had developed between the two powers because of the original unwillingness of the United States to join Britain in the war. The Japanese attack on Pearl Harbor ended U.S. isolationism. American citizens rallied to the war effort, particularly against the Japanese. "Remember Pearl Harbor!" struck a chord in the United States that "Remember Belgium" or "Remember France" could not have.

The fact that an Asian power had attacked the United States galled Americans, many of whom believed that Asians were inferior. Amid rumors

MAP 26.3 THE JAPANESE ADVANCE AND ALLIED COUNTEROFFENSIVE, 1941–1945   After launching a surprise attack against the U.S. naval and air force base at Pearl Harbor, Hawaii, the Japanese successfully invaded most of the Southeast Asian countries and many of the Pacific islands.

that Japanese citizens and Japanese Americans were preparing to carry out acts of sabotage in the United States, the U.S. government interned in "relocation centers" about 40,000 Japanese citizens residing in the United States and 70,000 Japanese Americans, most living on the West Coast. American citizens of German descent, in contrast, were not interned.

The first of several meetings between the British and American military chiefs of staff took place in Washington, D.C., in January 1942. The Allied commanders decided to give the European theater of war the highest priority. An immediate concentration of attacks against Japanese forces seemed less urgent. In any case, it would take considerable time to dislodge the Japanese from the Southeast Asian countries and Pacific islands they had conquered.

HITLER'S EUROPE

Whether or not each conquered state retained some autonomy, German policies were first directed at extracting useful raw materials needed to wage an extended war. The exact nature of the relationship between Germany and each occupied state varied from country to country. Yet in all of these states the Nazis carried out Hitler's policy of genocide against Jews and others belonging to what he considered to be inferior races, often aided by local collaborators.

In every country overrun by German troops, people could be found who were eager or willing to collaborate with the Nazis. These ranged from leaders willing to serve German interests to ordinary people whose political biases or hope for gain or even just survival led them to help the Nazis. Yet, in many countries, resistance movements bravely opposed the rule of the Nazis or their allies. The largest and most successful resistance was in mountainous Yugoslavia, where resisters were able to take on entire German divisions, and, to a lesser extent, in France, where groups of guerrilla fighters undertook hit-and-run attacks against the Germans and the collaborationist government. In Germany, resistance to Hitler and the Nazis barely existed, notwithstanding a courageous attempt by disenchanted army officers to assassinate Hitler in July 1944. To the end, most Germans remained loyal to the Führer, or at least could not or did not resist.

The Nazi "New European Order"

Hitler sought to exploit the economic resources of the countries his armies had conquered and to assure that no effective opposition could emerge in any of them. Germany annexed the disputed Polish territories it had claimed, including Poznan, Upper Silesia, and the Polish Corridor; Hitler considered them German in the first place. Direct German administration was extended to Ukraine and Belarus. Germans who lived in Poland,

MAP 26.4 HITLER'S EUROPE, 1942 Hitler's expansion to the east and west, showing the greatest extent of the German occupation of Europe.

Lithuania, or those parts of the Soviet Union that were behind German lines were "repatriated" to Germany, or settled in the newly conquered territories (see Map 26.4).

German policies were different in Poland and Russia, whose peoples Hitler considered to be racially inferior. Following the fall of Warsaw, Hitler had sent five special "action" squads to Poland with orders to wipe out the Polish upper class. All over the country, businessmen, political leaders, intellectuals, and teachers were executed or sent to extermination camps.

Norway and Denmark, deemed by Hitler to be sufficiently "Nordic" or "Aryan" to be "Germanized," were allowed relative autonomy. In Denmark, where the only elections in any country under a Nazi regime took place, the Danish Nazi Party won a paltry 2 percent of the vote. Hitler left Germany's central and southern European "independent" allies with some autonomy, depending on the extent to which they followed his wishes. Admiral Miklós Horthy ruled Hungary under increasingly close German supervision, particularly after Hitler learned that he tried to play both sides by getting in touch with the Allies in 1942. Slovakia, which had been denied independence by the Versailles settlements, had become autonomous when Germany marched into Czechoslovakia in 1938, splitting the country into two parts. Pro-German nationalist fascists held power in Slovakia. In wartime Romania, the fascist Ion Antonescu ruled. Hitler divided Yugoslavia into the states of Serbia, Montenegro, and Croatia. Placing Serbia under direct German administration, he put Croatia and Montenegro under the rule of an authoritarian leader informally responsible to Mussolini.

The Germans imposed crushing obligations on conquered lands, including enormous financial indemnities and exchange rates that strongly favored the German currency. Germans operated factories and shipping companies in occupied countries. In France, the Germans first took movable raw materials and equipment useful for war production. As the war went on, German demands became greater; the occupation authorities closely regulated the armament, aircraft, mining, and metal industries. Some French businesses made the best of the situation, eagerly working with German firms. A few quietly subverted German demands and expectations for cooperation.

The "Final Solution"

Hitler's obsessive racial theories had become official policy in Nazi Germany before the war (see Chapter 25). For the Nazis, the process of forging the "national community" meant the elimination of groups they considered to be "outsiders." They made a temporary exception of foreign laborers, upon whom the economy depended during the war. In 1939, Hitler had ordered the killing, often by injection, of Germans who were mentally deficient and handicapped. At least 70,000 mentally retarded people perished, including children, before public objections that the victims were German halted this practice in August 1941. In addition, the Nazis sterilized between

320,000 and 350,000 German "outcasts" between 1934 and 1945; these included people determined by Nazi doctors to manifest "hereditary simple-mindedness," alcoholism, homosexuality, chronic depression, schizophrenia, or those who were deemed "work shy." Hitler mandated experiments to determine how thousands of people could be killed "efficiently" in assembly-line fashion.

In 1939, Hitler told Heinrich Himmler (1900–1945), the leader of the S.S., to plan for the occupation of Poland and the Soviet Union. The short, stout Himmler was obsessed with the pagan Germans of prehistory, establishing several spurious academic institutes to study his crackpot theories. Himmler welcomed Hitler's order to "eliminate the harmful influence of such alien parts of the population." Hitler announced to the Reichstag on January 30, 1939, that the result of the anticipated war would be "the annihilation of the Jewish race in Europe," the "final solution."

Nazi plans to exterminate Jews took shape as German military defeats mounted in Russia. There the massacre of Russians had already begun. In January 1941, Himmler announced to S.S. leaders a change in policy. Hitler no longer wanted to transform Slavs into a slave labor force, but rather wanted to destroy at least 30 million of them. Germans eventually would occupy their lands. German troops and death squads executed Russian prisoners and civilians. Before the war ended, at least 3.3 million Soviet prisoners of war—of 5.7 million captured—were executed or died in German prisoner-of-war camps.

A Gestapo directive on July 17, 1941, ordered commanders of prison camps in the east to liquidate "all the Jews." In October 1941, the Nazis began to prepare for the Holocaust, the genocide of European Jews. Hermann Göring ordered Reinhard Heydrich (1904–1942), the chief of the secret police, to prepare "a total solution of the Jewish question." By the end of 1941, 1 million Jews had been massacred. Heydrich and other Nazi officials met in Wannsee, a Berlin suburb, in January 1942. There they drew up even more systematic plans for genocide.

The assembly-line-like murders of Jews began, first in mobile vans, using carbon monoxide gas, then in the extermination camp of Auschwitz-Birkenau near Krakow in southern Poland. By 1942, the Nazis had built other extermination camps, surrounded by barbed-wire, electrified fences, and watchtowers (see Map 26.5). Gallows stood in an open space near the prisoners' wooden huts. But most victims were exterminated in airtight gas chambers with Zyklon B gas, chosen because it killed with efficiency. The victims' eyeglasses, gold from their teeth, and all other valuables became the property of the Reich.

Inmates of the camps wore tattered striped uniforms, and they were identified by numbers tattooed on their arms. They were ordered to file past an officer, who selected those deemed "unfit" for hard labor, which at Auschwitz was about 70 to 75 percent. He sent them toward a building marked "shower" or "bath," and some were given, in the ultimate cynical

MAP 26.5 NAZI DEATH CAMPS   Sites of the death camps in Europe.

gesture, a small piece of soap. A recent, unknowing arrival at Auschwitz inquired of another prisoner as to the whereabouts of his friend. "'Was he sent to the left side?' . . . 'Yes,' I replied. 'Then you can see him there,' I was told. 'Where?' A hand pointed to the chimney a few hundred yards off, which was sending a column of flame up into the gray sky of Poland. It dissolved into a sinister cloud of smoke." Those people sent to the right— mostly the young in relatively good health—would continue to live until they dropped dead of fatigue or were subsequently sent to the left side in another "selection." Almost all children were killed right away, because they were too young to work as slave laborers in the I.G. Farben chemical factory near the camp. At Auschwitz, the daily death count reached as high as 15,000 victims. Overall, Hungarian Jews perished in the largest numbers, followed closely by Poles. One of the granddaughters of Alfred Dreyfus, the Jewish French army officer falsely accused of treason in the 1890s (see Chapter 18), perished there in 1944.

Jews being massacred in Lithuania, 1942.

The fascist states of Croatia and Romania, both Germany's allies, carried out the mass murder of Jews themselves. The Romanian government killed 300,000 Jews in the provinces that the Soviets had occupied in 1940, but few in what the Romanians considered the heartland of the country. In Lithuania, Ukraine, and, to a lesser extent, Poland, there were many cases of local populations massacring Jews.

Some people protected the Jews. A small French town took in Jewish children, producing identity cards for them that made them family members. In Marseille, Varian Fry, an American editor, journalist, and member of the American Refugee Committee, relentlessly planned escape routes, purchased tickets, and, where possible, obtained transit and other visas and found sponsors for about 1,000 Jews early in the war, including the painter Marc Chagall and the poet André Breton. A Warsaw woman rescued 2,500 children from the city's Jewish ghetto. In Amsterdam, Christians brought food and other supplies to a German Jewish family, hidden in a secret annex apartment in the father's office building for several years. In her resolutely cheerful diary, the young Anne Frank described her family's hiding place as "a paradise compared with how other Jews who are not in hiding must be living." It frightened her to think of her friends who had fallen into the clutches of "the cruelest brutes that walk the earth." Several months after her fourteenth birthday, Nazi soldiers discovered Frank's family. She and her family were deported to Auschwitz. Frank died in the death camp of Bergen-Belsen in the spring of 1945.

In Denmark, most of the Jewish population was saved in October 1943. When word came that the German occupying forces were preparing to

Dutch Jews on their way to the trains for transport from Amsterdam to a concentration camp.

deport Danish Jews, Danes ferried Jews across the straits to nearby neutral Sweden. There a courageous German cultural attaché had helped prepare the way. Perhaps fearing that mass deportations might spark Danish resistance, in this case the German authorities looked the other way. In Bulgaria, King Boris and his government, although allied with Nazi Germany, simply abandoned plans to deport the country's 50,000 Bulgarian Jews. (yet Bulgaria willingly handed over to the Nazis and thus to certain death Greek and Yugoslav Jews). In Hungary, Horthy resisted for three years German demands that the Jews of Hungary be sent to death camps. After German occupation in 1944, he ordered the deportations of Jews that had begun to be stopped. Yet Hungarian police killed tens of thousands of Jews in Hungary. In Croatia, where Italy had established an occupation zone, some Italian army officers protected Jews (and Serbs as well) from Croatian death squads. But when, in August 1942, Germany requested that the Italians turn the Croatian Jews over to the Nazis, Mussolini wrote "No objection" across the letter. Italian authorities had little interest in rounding up Italian Jews. They ignored German directives, or they could be bribed to look the other way. Some non-Jewish Romans contributed their jewelry to help raise a ransom demanded by the Germans from Jews under threat of deportation. Others helped Jews hide. They did so at great risk; German troops executed entire families of those who hid or even gave food to Jews.

Nazi doctors performed barbaric experiments on prisoners. These included experiments in the sterilization of Slavic women; measuring the pain a patient could survive when being operated on without anesthesia;

how long one could live in subfreezing temperatures; or whether prisoners would allow themselves to be killed if they thought their children might be spared. Gypsies were also Nazi targets, viewed as "biological outsiders" who were both "alien" by virtue of not being "Aryan" and "asocial," because they were nomadic. A half million gypsies perished. Communists, socialists, and repeat criminal offenders were also considered "asocial." Many of them perished as well. The Nazis persecuted homosexuals ruthlessly, identifying them in the death camps with pink stars.

One of the most haunting questions of World War II is at what point the leaders of the Allies and of neutral states actually learned that the Nazis were undertaking the extermination of an entire people. Rumors of mass exterminations had begun to reach Britain and the United States in 1942, although the details were not known. Even after confirmation provided by four young Jews who escaped from Auschwitz in the summer of 1942, and by information arriving via the Polish underground and diffused by the Polish government in London, many people—including even some leaders of the Jewish communities in Britain, Palestine, and the United States— refused to believe "the terrible secret." ("Who, after all, speaks today of the annihilation of the Armenians [by the Turks in 1915]?" Hitler exclaimed just before the war.) Articles in British, Swiss, and U.S. newspapers began to relate the mass killings of Jews. Pope Pius XII (pope 1939–1958), who had served as the Vatican's representative in Berlin before his election as pope and who issued no papal encyclicals condemning anti-Semitism, knew of the death camps by the end of 1943. Yet the pope did no more than offer reminders of the necessity of "justice and charity" in the world.

The U.S. and British governments had no official reactions to the terrifying news. A head of the British intelligence service claimed that Poles and Jews were exaggerating "in order to stoke us up." President Roosevelt certainly knew by the summer of 1942, but he rejected the idea of retaliatory bombing of German civilians. He believed that only a sustained military effort could defeat the Nazis. With Hitler's invasion of Russia having gone awry, it looked as though the tide was beginning to turn against Germany. The Allied governments feared that if too much publicity was given to the disappearance of hundreds of thousands of Jews—millions seemed simply too many to believe—it might generate calls to aid them directly. This, they worried, might undercut the united war effort. The Holocaust continued until the very end of the war; by then 6.2 million Jews had been murdered.

Collaboration

In Western Europe, the Nazis found leaders willing to follow German directives obediently and often enthusiastically. In Norway, Vidkun Quisling (1887–1945), organizer of a fascist party in the 1930s, became the puppet head of state in Norway, his name entering the dictionary as synonymous with traitor. In Belgium, principally Flanders, the Dutch-speaking part of the country, the German occupation gave the fascist leagues influence they had not had before the war. France had been divided by Germany in June 1940 into an occupied zone and a smaller southern zone that retained independence through collaboration with the Nazis. The free zone had its capital in the spa town of Vichy in central France, although in November 1942 German troops occupied all of France. The xenophobia and anti-Semitism of the right-wing French politicians and writers of the 1930s came to fruition in Vichy. Traditional conservatives dissatisfied with the Third Republic for religious and political reasons also lent their support to the Vichy regime.

The elderly Marshal Pétain served as the head of state of the Vichy government, which the United States officially recognized. He remained popular, at least until late 1942, because some people shared his anti-Marxism and anti-Semitism. He presented himself as having saved the French state from extinction at the hands of the German invaders.

But although Vichy may have temporarily saved the French state, Pétain and other collaborators sacrificed the French nation. In the "new order," "country, family, work" replaced "liberty, fraternity, equality" on French coins. Vichy proclaimed a "spiritual revival" against "decadence." Pétain dissolved the Chamber of Deputies and favored the Catholic Church by banning Masonic lodges and divorce. As in Mussolini's Italy, Vichy attempted to impose a structure of "corporatism" on the French economy and society, but with little success. These vertical economic structures were intended to replace unions, which, as in Germany and Italy, became illegal.

The Vichy *milice* (police) raiding a French farmhouse looking for *maquis* (resisters).

Vichy enacted restrictions on Jews similar to those in force in Germany. Beginning in October 1940, a series of laws forbade Jews from holding jobs in public service, education, or cultural affairs, or in professions such as medicine and law. A law in July 1941 sought "to eliminate all Jewish influence in the national economy"; the state appointed a trustee who could sell any property or liquidate any business owned by Jews.

These exclusions were only the beginning. French police cooperated with German soldiers after Hitler's May 1941 order to round up 3,600 Polish Jews in France. In December, the Vichy government proclaimed that it would collaborate with the Nazis with "acts, not words," and did just that. In July 1942, the French police seized 13,000 Jews, most of them foreign-born, in Paris, sending them to death camps in the east. Premier Pierre Laval (1883–1945) insisted that children be sent along with their parents. A Parisian woman later recalled, "I saw a train pass. In front, a car containing French police and German soldiers. Then came cattle cars, sealed. The thin arms of children clasped the grating. A hand waved outside like a leaf in a storm. When the train slowed down, voices cried, 'Mama!' And nothing answered except the squeaking of the springs of the train." Vichy France was the only territory in Europe in which local authorities deported Jews without the presence of German occupying forces, at least in the so-called free zone until November 1942. A militia of determined collaborators created in January 1943 continued to round up Jews, seeking to crush all resistance.

Resistance

Everyone in German-occupied territories knew the potential cost of resistance. In Czechoslovakia, the assassination in May 1942 of Reinhard Heydrich brought the destruction of the entire village of Lidice and most of its inhabitants. When partisans killed ten Germans in a Yugoslav town in October 1941, the Nazis retaliated by massacring 7,000 men, women, and children.

Yet people did resist. On April 19, 1943, the Jewish ghetto in Warsaw, from which already about 300,000 Jews had been sent to the death camps after German troops had concentrated Jews there from other places, rose up against the Nazis. They were crushed almost a month later with the loss of at least 12,000 lives. Thousands of those who had survived perished in the camps. Poland had what amounted to a secret underground state linked to the government in exile, many clandestine publications, and a "Home Army" about 300,000 strong, whose members fought with Allied troops in Europe and Africa, On August 1, 1944, the Warsaw Uprising began. After two months of intense fighting, German military strength again won out, with 200,000 Poles perishing in the fighting or executed afterwards.

Resistance movements were most effective where hills and mountains offered protection from German troops, as in central and southern France, Greece, and Yugoslavia. Active and effective resistance was least possible in the flatlands of Holland, western Belgium, Moravia, and northern France, areas in which it was difficult to hide and where there were heavy concentrations of German troops, and many collaborators as well. Wherever possible, the Allies dropped supplies to resistance groups. But only in Yugoslavia and, to some extent, France, did the resistance movements help bring about Germany's defeat.

In Yugoslavia, the tenacious Croatian Communist Josip Broz (1892–1980), who became known by his code name of Tito, formed the first army of partisans able to engage the Germans effectively in combat. Tito had served in the Austro-Hungarian army during World War I and was badly wounded and captured. Returning in 1920 to newly independent Yugoslavia, he became an active trade unionist and in 1923 joined the Yugoslav Communist Party. Tito spent six years in prison for his political activities. In 1937 he was named general secretary of the Communist Party.

Tito's partisans fought courageously against the collaborationist Yugoslav puppet states. The Croatian minister of education voiced the opinion that a third of the Serbs should be forced to convert, a third expelled from Croatia, and a third killed. Croatian forces killed 300,000 Serbs. The Cyrillic alphabet used by Serbs became illegal. When asked if he did not fear the punishment of God for what he had done, a fascist (Ustaša) guard retorted,

Marshal Tito (Josip Broz), pictured on the right, Communist head of the Yugoslav Resistance, with his wartime staff in the mountains of Yugoslavia, 1944.

"Don't talk to me about that. . . . For my past, present and future deeds I shall burn in hell, but at least I shall burn for Croatia." At the same time, members of the conservative Serb resistance (Chetniks), who remained loyal to the Yugoslav king, killed thousands of Croats and other non-Serbs.

Tito insisted on cooperation between Serb and Croat resisters, and maintained contacts with non-Communist groups. Protected by the rugged mountains of Croatia, Tito commanded 20,000 men by 1943. Despite being hounded by German, Italian, and Bulgarian troops, and both Croatian fascists and Serb Chetniks, he managed to carve out entire zones under his control. Late in the war, the British government ended support for the Chetniks and began to supply Tito's forces with heavy equipment. Yugoslav partisans tied up entire Italian and German divisions. Tito established local Communist committees to serve as governing authorities in each region liberated.

On June 18, 1940, General Charles de Gaulle, broadcasting from London, called on the French people to resist German rule. The next month, Churchill established an agency in London to provide material assistance to resistance groups. Churchill grudgingly respected de Gaulle for his uncompromising will to oppose the Nazis and the Vichy collaborators, but he also detested him personally. The same room could not hold the two domineering personalities. Roosevelt believed the towering Frenchman dangerously ambitious, a potential thorn in the Allied side. In December 1941, de Gaulle surprised the Allies by sending a small force to capture the French islands of Saint Pierre and Miquelon off the coast of Newfoundland, which were controlled by Vichy France.

Roosevelt believed that there was nothing to be gained from recognizing de Gaulle's London-based "Free French" movement as the legitimate French government. The U.S. government hoped that Vichy might be convinced to try to keep French North Africa out of German hands. The British and U.S. governments worried that recognizing de Gaulle's movement might alienate many people in France. In the meantime, Vichy propaganda repeatedly reminded the public that the British navy had sunk French ships in July 1940, with a huge loss of life.

Several resistance movements in France were united only by a hatred of Nazi occupation and Vichy collaboration. Communists, despite not officially turning against Vichy until Germany attacked the Soviet Union in June 1941, formed a well-organized and effective resistance force, building on pre-war organizational networks. Jean Moulin (1899–1943), a former departmental prefect during the Third Republic, led de Gaulle's Free French resistance in France. Moulin managed early in May 1943 to unify the resistance groups within the National Council of Resistance. He was betrayed by a collaborator and died under torture in July 1943 without revealing the names of others in the resistance network.

Resistance spread when the Germans in 1943 began to force France to provide workers for factories in Germany. Many of those refusing to go to

Germany fled into the hills and mountains of France. These resistance bands came to be called the *maquis,* a name for rugged brush in the south of France that could conceal them.

Better armed by airplane drops of guns, the *maquis* grew bolder. By 1944, they controlled some areas in southern France, at least at night, vulnerable only to the arrival of German military columns, diversions that the German army could by then ill afford. General Dwight Eisenhower (1890–1969), commander of Allied forces in the European theater of operations, later claimed that the resistance in France was the equivalent of fifteen military divisions.

Against Hitler in Germany

The vast majority of Germans remained loyal to their Führer, even as defeats mounted and Allied bombers frequently droned overhead and news of horrendous losses on the Russian front became known. Disgruntlement and bitter jokes were common, but they did not threaten the regime. Those who had never approved of Hitler retreated into family life and the daily struggle to get by. When wartime deprivation left people grumbling, Germans tended to blame Hitler's subordinates, not the Führer.

German resistance against Hitler was fragmented and ineffective. Courts sentenced 15,000 Germans to death for crimes against the state, under an expanded definition of capital crimes, which included listening to BBC radio broadcasts from London. Trade union and Communist groups, earlier smashed by the S.S., emerged again as economic conditions worsened in 1942 and 1943. Some students in Munich and Communists in Berlin bravely distributed anti-Nazi propaganda, but such courageous acts were not widespread. About 250,000 people in Germany were imprisoned or forced to emigrate because of their political opposition and at least 150,000 German Communists were executed. The active connivance of ordinary Germans aided the S.S. and Gestapo in rooting out potential sources of opposition. Even humane gestures toward Jews or foreign workers were dangerous. Here and there, young people responded to Nazism by adopting a counterculture of nonconformity, refusing to join the Hitler Youth, listening to American music deemed decadent by Hitler, and scrawling anti-Nazi graffiti on walls. The Nazis publicly hanged several sixteen-year-old boys for such actions.

The only serious plot against Hitler came among traditional conservatives within the army. On July 20, 1944, Colonel Claus von Stauffenberg (1907–1944) carried a bomb in his briefcase to a staff meeting with Hitler near the Russian front. Stauffenberg, who had been badly maimed in battle, was a conservative aristocrat appalled by the Nazi murder of Jews and Soviets and by what he considered Hitler's amateur management of the war. He hoped that Hitler's assassination would allow the army to impose its rule. He placed the bomb under the table beneath Hitler, who instinctively shoved the briefcase out of his way, moving it to the other side of a heavy table support.

The bomb exploded, wounding Hitler slightly. Those implicated in the plot were quickly arrested and slowly strangled by nooses of piano wire as they writhed on meat hooks. Movie cameras recorded their agonizing death for the later amusement of Hitler, his mistress, and friends. Hitler also ordered the execution of about 5,000 other Germans in positions of authority whose loyalty seemed suspect, including family members of conspirators. Thousands of Germans poured into the streets in major cities to celebrate their Führer's escape from death.

THE TIDE TURNS

By the end of 1942, the Germans were on the defensive on the high seas, in the Soviet Union, and in North Africa, where Italian forces were routed and German forces pushed back (see Map 26.6). The entry of the United States into the war in December 1941 helped turn the tide against Germany. American war supplies and then armed forces strengthened the Allied cause as they had in World War I. The German war machine was chaotically managed and German resources increasingly inadequate to fighting a war on so many fronts.

Hitler's invasion of Russia turned into a full-fledged military disaster, culminating in the crushing defeat and surrender of German forces at Stalingrad in February 1943. As Hitler's Balkan allies one by one pulled out of the war, the Allies launched an invasion of Italy from North Africa, forcing the king of Italy to agree to a secret armistice and pushing German troops to retreat to the north. On June 6, 1944, Western Allied forces launched a massive invasion of France, landing on the beaches of Normandy, and forcing the German army to pull back, fighting all the way. The Allies first reached the Rhine River in March 1945.

Now confident of victory over Hitler, the Big Three (Churchill, Roosevelt, and Stalin) began to plan for the end of the war. As the Soviet army began to push the Germans back across a broad front in July 1943, it became clear that when the war ended, the Red Army could control large parts of Eastern and Central Europe. This probability brought dissension to the Big Three, particularly as Churchill feared that the Red Army might never leave the Eastern European nations it liberated from German occupation.

Germany on the Defensive

With the majority of German men between the ages of eighteen and fifty in the army, Germany's war machine required more workers. By late 1941, there were already 4 million foreigners working in Germany, including prisoners of war (in violation of international agreements), and in May 1944, almost twice that number, the majority of whom were Soviet citizens. More German women now worked in the factories.

MAP 26.6 THE DEFEAT OF GERMANY, 1942–1945 Allied advances and Axis withdrawal up to the end of World War II.

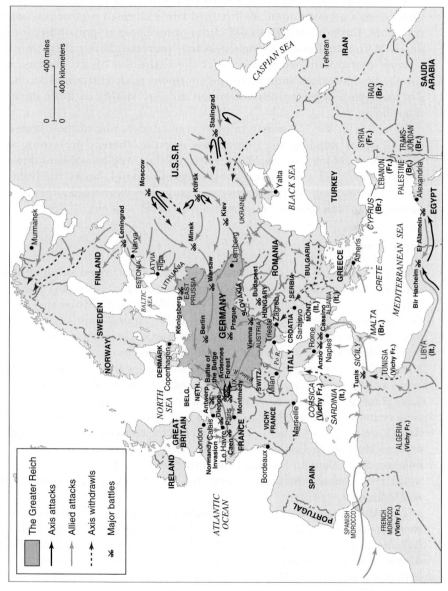

In the meantime, Germany's day-to-day operation of the war effort remained chaotic, as ministries, military branches, and Hitler's favored henchmen competed against each other. In the spring of 1942, Hitler named the architect Albert Speer to be minister of armaments production. Speer's organizational skill helped triple German production within two years. But not until 1944 did Hitler grant Speer responsibility for the needs of the air force, Göring's personal preserve. Hitler then awarded Göring "plenipotentiary powers" over the entire war effort. German war supplies remained inadequate to the enormous goals Hitler had set. Realists like Speer began to see a German military victory as difficult, even improbable.

As in World War I, German military commanders placed their hopes on closing Allied shipping lanes across the Atlantic, thereby preventing supplies from reaching Britain. Many American ships and crews went down in the icy Atlantic. However, most got through. German U-boats, the hunters, became the hunted. New submarine-detecting devices enabled airplanes and destroyers to sink German submarines with depth charges.

The War in North Africa

With the failure of the submarine campaign against Allied shipping, Germany now had to depend on its army's success on land. In North Africa, the German tank division commanded by Erwin Rommel, known as the "Desert Fox" because of his quick judgment and daring tactical improvisations, had forced British troops back from Libya into Egypt. Victories in the spring of 1942 at Bir Hacheim and Tobruk, where the Germans captured a garrison of 35,000 British troops, put Rommel only sixty miles from Alexandria. However, at the end of August 1942, the British tank force of General Bernard Montgomery (1887–1976) pushed back another Rommel offensive. Montgomery knew his enemy's plan of attack in advance through reports from British intelligence services. The Allied forces, enjoying superior strength and controlling the skies, then broke through the German and Italian defenses at El Alamein (in Egypt) in early November 1942. For the next ten weeks they pursued the German armored division across the desert all the way to Tunisia.

The Allies now faced major strategic decisions. Churchill wanted to strike at what he called the "soft underbelly" of the axis through Italy, the Balkans, and the Danube Basin after driving Hitler's armies from North Africa. This would leave British forces in an excellent position to protect British interests in the Middle East. Stalin, however, continued to insist on a major Allied attack against Germany in the west to force Hitler to divert resources from the Russian campaign. Stalin pointed out that the Red Army had borne the brunt of the war against Hitler, inflicting 90 percent of the losses the German armed forces had suffered in battle since June 1941. Churchill, however, feared that a direct confrontation with the

Free French troops attacking in the North African desert, 1942.

largest concentration of German troops might be disastrous and wanted to postpone a cross-Channel invasion of France as long as possible.

With the Axis reeling in North Africa and British troops now controlling Egypt and Libya, the Allied commanders now decided first to drive all German and Italian troops out of North Africa before contemplating an invasion of France from Britain. They had been sobered by a disastrous cross-Channel raid by Canadian troops against the French port of Dieppe in August 1942.

In November 1942, the Allies launched "Operation Torch." A British and American force commanded by American General Eisenhower landed on the coast of French Algeria and Morocco, easily overcoming Vichy French resistance. To his consternation, de Gaulle now learned that the Allies were negotiating with the Vichy commander in North Africa, Admiral Jean Darlan (1881–1942). Despite Pétain's order that Vichy forces in North Africa continue to oppose the Allied invasion, Darlan ordered his troops to accept a cease-fire after three days of fighting. Hitler used Darlan's capitulation in North Africa as an excuse in November 1942 for German forces to occupy the "free" zone of Vichy France. Little now remained of Vichy's illusion of independence. French naval commanders scuttled their own ships to prevent them from being used by the German navy.

The Allies named Darlan as "the head of the French state" in return for his promise that French troops in North Africa would now join the Allies. De Gaulle demanded that Britain and the United States recognize his

French Committee of National Liberation as France's legitimate government. But Churchill, an old imperialist, viewed with concern de Gaulle's pressing determination to maintain France's empire, in the context of the two powers' long-standing imperial rivalry. Churchill feared that if the British government recognized de Gaulle as the head of the French state, it would be committing itself to supporting a new France, the direction of which could not yet be seen. A French monarchist solved part of the Allied dilemma by assassinating Darlan. The Allies forced de Gaulle to share leadership of Free France with another general, a slap in the face that de Gaulle neither forgot nor forgave. After the defeat of a vigorous German counterattack, by the end of May 1943, no German or Italian troops remained in North Africa.

The Allies' strategic bombing campaign, the goal of which was to sap German morale as much as to hamper the production of planes and guns, began to take its toll in 1943. The American poet Randall Jarrell remembered, "In bombers named for girls, we burned / the cities we had learned about in school." The Royal Air Force could now strike at night with reasonable accuracy, and the ability to scramble German radar reduced losses. British bombers dumped tons of bombs during night raids over the industrial Ruhr Valley and major cities. Many American bombers were lost despite fighter escorts because the U.S. Air Force preferred daytime attacks, when pilots could more easily find their targets. However, the impact of the strategic bombing campaign on German wartime industrial production was far below Allied expectations.

Hitler's Russian Disaster

On the eastern front, Hitler's invasion of the Soviet Union turned into a military disaster. Defeats in Russia during the last months of 1942 and in 1943 sent the German invaders reeling. The Red Army was now receiving better and more plentiful supplies from the Allies through the icy northern port of Murmansk and from Iran in the south. By now Soviet factories were turning out a steady supply of tanks and trucks equipped to fight in the snow and ice. German tanks faced not only improved Soviet tanks but also handmade incendiary bombs consisting of bottles, gasoline, and cloth fuses known derisively as "Molotov cocktails," after the Soviet foreign minister, which had first been used by Finnish partisans against Soviet troops.

Improvements in the organization and discipline of the Red Army also made their mark. Stalin held back on the ideological indoctrination and murderous purges that had characterized the 1930s. The Soviet army that Hitler had once mocked, now larger and more effectively deployed than his own, wore down German forces.

In the north, Leningrad, first reached by German troops in July 1941, held on against a German siege that lasted 506 days, the longest in modern history. More than 300,000 Soviet troops were killed; more than a million Russian civilians starved to death. Hitler's printed invitations to celebrate

Leningrad's fall could never be sent out. Further defeats in the north made Germany's drive to the Soviet oil fields of the Caucasus Mountains, and the Donets Basin industrial region in the south, all the more critical. In the south, the Red Army slowed the German advance toward Stalingrad, a strategically located industrial city on the Volga River.

The battle of Stalingrad, which began in November 1942, was a great turning point in the European war. The Soviets had begun concentrating a huge force around the city, even as early German successes deluded Hitler into thinking Stalingrad's fall was inevitable. As Soviet troops held off the German assault in house-to-house fighting, Hitler confidently began to transfer some of his exhausted troops to the north. The Soviet army counter-attacked on November 19, trapping the weakened German armies as Soviet tanks moved easily across the frozen ground. From Berlin, Hitler ordered his troops to hold out until the last man. By the time German survivors surrendered on February 2, 1943, the German army had lost more than 300,000 soldiers.

Soviet troops fought their way into Leningrad. In July 1943, in a battle involving more than 9,000 tanks, the Red Army lost many times more men and tanks in a decisive battle in and around the city of Kursk, 500 miles south of Moscow. In the greatest tank battle ever fought, the Soviets managed to repel a massive German attack against an exposed Soviet line of defense and then pushed the Germans back, with a huge loss of life, a Pyrrhic victory. This further depleted the German armored divisions that had once seemed invincible. The Soviets were now battering the enemy on three fronts, even as Hitler was forced to divert troops to Italy and the

Red Army soldiers pick their way through the rubble of Stalingrad.

Devastation in Hamburg (*left*) and Stuttgart (*right*) after Allied bombing of Germany.

Balkans. The Red Army recaptured all of the Crimea in the south by May 1943, pushing the Germans back to Ukraine in the summer.

In February 1944, Soviet troops reached what had been the eastern Polish border before the German invasion. In the meantime, waves of British and American bombers continued to devastate German cities; over 40,000 people perished in attacks on Hamburg in July 1943, during which more than 9,000 tons of bombs rained down on the port city.

One by one, Germany's Balkan allies bailed out. Romanian troops had greatly aided the Nazi campaign in Odessa and the Crimea; Romanian oil and wheat had fueled the German war effort. Now, in March 1944, seeing the writing on the wall, the Romanian government approached the Allies, hoping to arrange a separate peace. In August, King Michael finally ended Ion Antonescu's military dictatorship, and the new Romanian government declared war on Germany.

Hitler intended Bulgaria to serve as a buffer against a possible Allied invasion from Turkey. Bulgaria enjoyed the most autonomy of any Nazi-held Eastern European state because it provided Germany with badly needed grain, permitted German military bases on its territory, and had declared war on Britain and the United States back in 1941. Hitler had allowed Bulgaria to annex Thrace from Greece (where Bulgarian forces had executed thousands of Greeks and banned the Greek language) and to take Greek and Yugoslav Macedonia. Now, as Germany's defeat appeared increasingly likely, the Bulgarian government brazenly announced its war against the Allies had ended. The Soviet Union declared war on Bulgaria in

September 1944. Following a popular insurrection, the Soviet Union controlled the resulting coalition government, as in the case of Romania. Soviet domination began to take shape.

The Allied Invasion of Italy

With North Africa and its airfields secure, the Allies decided to invade Sicily as a first step in an invasion of southern Italy. The plunging morale and material conditions of the Italian population, who had been promised an empire by Mussolini but had received only hardship, contributed to the Allied decision.

In July 1943, Palermo and Messina quickly fell to Allied troops. The fascist Grand Council asked King Victor Emmanuel III to end Mussolini's dictatorship. The king, eager to save his throne and fearing a complete German takeover, dismissed the stunned Mussolini as prime minister and ordered his arrest. The new government, while announcing that Italy would continue to fight alongside Germany, began secret negotiations with the Allies. When Hitler learned this in September 1943, he ordered his troops to occupy Italian airfields.

At a minimum, an Allied invasion of the Italian mainland would tie up considerable numbers of German troops and probably knock Italy completely out of the war. Romanian oil fields would be within reach of bombers taking off in Italy. The Italian resistance had gained momentum. Socialists, Catholic groups, and above all, Communists began to print clandestine newspapers and organize scattered attacks against fascists. The United States, still pushing for a full-scale landing in France, reluctantly agreed to the Italian invasion. In the meantime, the Italian king, fearing Hitler's wrath, reassured Germany of Italy's loyal participation in the war as an ally. However, the Italian government signed an armistice with the Allies on September 3, 1943. Victor Emmanuel naively hoped that Italy could make peace with both Germany and the Allies, and that his monarchy would survive the end of the war.

On the same day that the armistice was signed between Italy and the Allies, British and Canadian troops crossed the Strait of Messina, beginning the invasion of the Italian peninsula. The king and his family fled Rome with the new prime minister, leaving a million Italian soldiers with the choice of being interned by the Germans or deserting their units. Most deserted and 80,000 Allied prisoners of war escaped from camps in Italy.

The Allies set up a new government in the south, its members drawn from the resistance groups. In the meantime, on September 12, 1943, a daring German commando raid freed Mussolini from a mountaintop prison. In Berlin, Hitler proclaimed the Duce head of the "Italian Social Republic," a puppet regime. Mussolini ordered the execution of the members of the Grand Council who had opposed him and denounced the Italian people for having betrayed him.

The Germans slowly retreated behind one river after the next, with both sides taking large losses. The new front settled on a series of fortifications a hundred miles south of Rome, over which stood the old monastery of Monte Cassino. In January 1944, two Allied divisions landed behind the German lines at Anzio. Only in the spring, after terrible losses, were Allied troops able to break through the German defenses to free their armies still trapped near Anzio. The Allies took Rome on June 4, 1944. The German armies fell back to establish a new defensive perimeter south of the Po River between Pisa and Florence.

The Big Three

Soviet advances against German forces increasingly focused Western attention on the future of Central and Eastern Europe and the Balkans once Hitler's Germany had been defeated. At a meeting in Casablanca, Morocco, in January 1943, Churchill and Roosevelt had concerned themselves only with military strategy and not with the future of Europe. With Stalin absent, the British and American governments agreed to put off discussions of the territorial settlements that would follow Germany's defeat. Churchill and Stalin had already informally agreed to Soviet absorption of the Baltic states after the war. They did so despite the opposition of Roosevelt, who argued that Stalin had joined the war against the Nazis only after Hitler had attacked the Soviet Union.

Stalin's insistence that the United States and Britain open another front in the west by invading France in part stemmed from his fear that his allies wanted to see the Red Army slowed in its drive westward. As deliveries of Allied supplies to Russia through Murmansk trickled to a halt, Stalin seemed confirmed in his suspicions.

Meeting at Moscow in October 1943, the British, American, and Soviet foreign ministers reaffirmed an agreement that the Allies would accept nothing less than Germany's unconditional surrender. The Allies also reaffirmed their intention, originally stated in the Atlantic Charter of August 1941 signed by Roosevelt and Churchill, that a United Nations organization replace the ineffective, moribund League of Nations. But again they left open the thorny question of the political future of Central and Eastern Europe and the Balkans after the war.

Stalin finally met Churchill and Roosevelt in Teheran in November 1943. The leaders formulated harsh plans for post-war Germany. Stalin stated that the Soviet Union was not about to contemplate any change in its border with Poland as it existed in June 1941, the result of the Soviet invasion and absorption of much of eastern Poland in 1939. Yet, despite the occasional flurry of improvisational map-making—using knives, forks, and matchboxes on the tablecloths—the Big Three still left the essential specifics of the proposed outlines of post-war Europe for the future.

The D-Day Invasion of France

At Teheran, Stalin and Roosevelt convinced Churchill to accept a plan for the invasion of France. General Dwight Eisenhower coordinated the "D-Day" landing in France, "Operation Overlord." Born in a small town in Kansas, Eisenhower was a forthright man of integrity. Beneath his sparkling blue eyes, folksy manner, and smile lay shrewdness, cunning, and a remarkable ability for organization. The plan was for 150,000 troops to attack the English Channel beaches of Normandy in western France, followed in the next days and weeks by almost 500,000 more. About 4 million tons of support materiel would have to be landed as well. Floating caissons and old ships sunk off the coast would provide three makeshift harbors. In the meantime, German commanders believed that the most likely place for an all-out assault was near Calais to the north, which offered the closest crossing points from England.

The first hours of Operation Overlord would be crucial. The Allies needed to take and protect a beachhead that would allow the bulk of their troops to get ashore quickly. Planes would drop squadrons of parachutists behind German lines. Hitler had assigned Rommel to organize the German defense against the Allied invasion. Defenders would depend on the rapid arrival of armored units to back up the coastal batteries and infantry units trying to hold their positions against attacking Allied troops.

After a one-day postponement because of a gale, at dawn on the morning of June 6, 1944, Allied troops struggled ashore in shallow water from landing craft and established beachheads on the coast of Normandy. They confronted murderous fire from the cliffs above, taking heavy losses. But the landing succeeded, at least in part because the German air force was outnumbered by 20 to 1. As more men, tanks, trucks, and materiel came ashore, German troops gradually fell back. By the end of July 1944, despite fierce resistance, the Allies held most of Normandy. After seven weeks, the Allies had landed 1.3 million troops and sustained over 120,000 casualties. The Germans lost 500,000 men trying to defend Normandy. Hitler allowed Rommel, discovered to have known about the plot against the Führer's life, to escape execution by committing suicide.

On August 15, 1944, another Allied army landed on the French Mediterranean coast and moved up the Rhône Valley with little opposition. In the meantime, the main Allied army pushed from Normandy toward Paris. Encouraged by the proximity of Allied troops, on August 19, an uprising began in Paris. Because de Gaulle demanded that a French unit be the first to reach the capital, French forces reached Paris on August 22, 1944. In October the British government recognized de Gaulle's administration as the legitimate government of France.

German resistance stiffened at the Rhine River, and the first Allied attempts to cross into Germany failed. Hitler, whose moods varied between wild optimism and resigned depression, had aged rapidly through recurring

U.S. troops wading ashore at Utah Beach, Normandy, June 6, 1944 after the first bloody assault.

bouts with illness. Now, although Germany's collapse seemed imminent, he again seemed confident, telling Albert Speer in November 1944, "I haven't the slightest intention of surrendering. Besides, November has always been my lucky month." In December, Hitler ordered a massive counterattack in the hills and forests of the Ardennes in Belgium and Luxembourg, with the goal of pushing rapidly toward the Belgian river port of Antwerp. After retreating forty-five miles, the U.S. army pushed the Germans back in the Battle of the Bulge.

As the Nazi army retreated in northern Italy, the Red Army approached Germany from the east. On every front, Allied troops increasingly found that their enemies turned out to be boys and older men who had been rushed to the front with virtually no training. German cities burned, notably Dresden, which American planes fire-bombed early in 1945. About 50,000 residents of Berlin died in Allied air attacks. In 1993, about one unexploded World War II bomb was still being discovered every day in Berlin.

Hitler, expressing confidence that the Big Three alliance would break up, held out hope for Germany's newly developed weapons, in which he had earlier expressed no interest: the deadly V-1 jet-propelled "flying bomb" could strike targets from 3,000 feet at speeds of 470 miles per hour; the terrifying V-2 rocket could fly faster than the speed of sound. Launched from France, the first V-1 struck London on June 12, 1944, doing considerable damage. The first jet- and rocket-propelled fighter planes, the former reaching speeds of 500 miles per hour, arrived in time to join the Battle of the Bulge, but without significant effect. Many ordinary Germans, too, clung to the hope that such a new weapon would turn things around, or that the Western democracies would join Germany in a war against the Soviets. However, with defeat ever closer, Hitler accepted, even desired, the total destruction of Germany, considering it better than the shame of surrender.

ALLIED VICTORY

Romania and Bulgaria had surrendered in August and September 1944, respectively. With the Red Army in control of much of the Balkans, the question was not if Berlin would be taken, but when, and by whom. Though worried that the Soviets sought a preponderant role in Central Europe, as well as in Poland and the Balkans, Eisenhower was prepared to allow the Red Army the prestige of capturing Berlin. The much greater problem still remained: the future of Germany and Eastern Europe. As the Red Army moved closer to Berlin, the meetings of the Big Three in the waning months of the year proved exceptionally important for the future of Europe. Churchill and Stalin met in Moscow in October 1944 and worked out a rough division of post-war Western and Soviet interests in Central and Eastern Europe. By the time the Big Three came together at Yalta in Crimea in February 1945, German armies were falling back rapidly on every front and the Red Army was closing in on Berlin. The American army crossed the Rhine River on March 8, and on April 25, 1945, met up with Soviet troops at the Elbe River just sixty miles south of Berlin.

Victory in Europe

Churchill was determined to work out an informal agreement with the Soviets as to the respective spheres of influence in the Balkans when the war ended. In October 1944, he met with Stalin in Moscow. This time Roosevelt, who suspected Churchill of trying to maintain the British Empire at all costs, did not participate. Churchill later described the conference with Stalin: "I said, 'Let us settle about our affairs in the Balkans. How would it do for you to have ninety percent of the say in Romania, for us to have ninety percent of the say in Greece, and go fifty-fifty about Yugoslavia?'" After adding 75 percent for the Soviet Union in Bulgaria and fifty-fifty for Hungary, the British prime minister pushed the paper across to Stalin. "There was a slight pause. Then he took his blue pencil and made a large tick upon it, and passed it back to us. It was all settled in no more time than it takes to sit down."

When the Big Three met in the Soviet Black Sea resort of Yalta in February 1945, the Red Army had drawn within 100 miles of Berlin. Some soldiers in the Red Army enacted terrible revenge against the Germans, encouraged by Soviet propaganda that emphasized the necessity of humiliating the defeated German population, as well as by the impersonal nature of the war. Soviet soldiers, some of whom had come upon the ghastly death camps in Poland, gunned down German soldiers who had surrendered, and pillaged villages. Soviet soldiers sometimes systematically raped all German females who were more than about twelve years old. Hungarian and Romanian women also were attacked—in Hungary, Soviet soldiers entered a mental hospital, where they raped and killed. Soviet officers tried to bring the situation under control but incidents of rape occurred for several years in Germany after the Nazi defeat. For some Soviets the occupation seemed to represent a continuation of the war and the exacting of revenge.

Soviet military might in Eastern and Central Europe hung over Yalta, where the Allies considered the post-war fate of Germany. Churchill agreed to the post-war division of Germany into British, American, French, and Soviet zones of military occupation. The Soviet zone would be eastern Germany. In Eastern Europe, Communist Party members were working feverishly to expand Soviet influence. Stalin feared that his wartime allies might lead a post-war campaign against communism, which had been the case after World War I. He secretly agreed to Roosevelt's demand that the Soviet Union declare war on Japan three months after Germany's defeat, which the U.S. president believed would expedite Japan's defeat in Asia. But, in exchange, Stalin asked for and received Allied promises that the Soviet Union would control Outer Mongolia, the Kurile Islands, the southern half of Sakhalin Island, and its former naval base at Port Arthur.

Outlines of the Cold War began to take shape at Yalta. Stalin insisted that the new government of Poland be based on the provisional Polish Communist government (to which would be added representatives from the non-Communist Polish government, which had been functioning in London

Joseph Stalin, Franklin Roosevelt, Winston Churchill, and Vyacheslav Molotov at the Yalta Conference, 1945.

during the war). Churchill and Roosevelt also went along with Stalin's insistence that the Soviet Union keep the parts of eastern Poland that had been absorbed by the Soviet invasion in 1939. Poland's western frontier with Germany was to be left to a future conference, one that was never held. The Big Three all agreed that free elections would be held in Eastern Europe. Yet Stalin defied the Atlantic Charter of 1941, when the Allies had agreed that free elections would lead to democratic governments in the nations freed from German occupation, by setting up an unelected puppet government in Romania, as well as Poland.

At Yalta, the Allies remembered that the League of Nations had been doomed in its attempts to keep the peace by the nonparticipation of the then-isolationist United States and by the exclusion of the Soviet Union from the League. Roosevelt wanted to avoid committing the United States to an active role in post-war Europe. He counted instead on the United Nations to resolve future problems by facilitating collective security. In the meantime, with the Red Army occupying Eastern Europe, Stalin held all the cards. Eastern European peoples subsequently had reason to view Yalta as a betrayal and a victory for Stalin.

The awful world conflict moved toward an end. The Red Army launched a final attack on Berlin in April 1945. Italian partisans captured Mussolini near the Swiss frontier. They executed him and his mistress, hanging their bodies upside down at a gas station. Himmler, von Ribbentrop, and Göring

Soldiers from the Red Army hoist the Soviet flag over the German Reichstag in Berlin.

now agreed that Germany must end the war. As Soviet tanks drew near on the night of April 28–29, 1945, Hitler married his longtime mistress, Eva Braun, in the depths of a fortified bunker in central Berlin. Then they committed suicide on April 30 as the rumble of Russian tanks could be heard above. Joseph Goebbels poisoned his six children, shot his wife, and killed himself. Admiral Karl Dönitz, to whom Hitler had delegated authority, surrendered to the Allies on May 8, 1945. The Reich that Hitler had once bragged would last for a thousand years lay in ruins twelve years after its creation.

The Defeat of Japan

The German collapse in North Africa, Russia, and Eastern Europe now allowed the Allies to turn their attention more fully to the war in the Pacific. The sheer scope of Japanese military operations, spread from the Aleutian Islands southwest of Alaska to the South Pacific, put Japan on the defensive. Troops and supplies poured into the Pacific from the United States, which had speedily reconstituted its fleet after the Pearl Harbor disaster. Victory in the Battle of the Coral Sea (May 1942), which turned back Japanese ships carrying troops to the southern coast of New Guinea, protected Australia from possible invasion. A month later, the American fleet and torpedo bombers inflicted a major defeat on the Japanese navy at the Battle of Midway, an island almost a thousand miles northwest of Hawaii (see Map 26.3), sinking four Japanese aircraft carriers.

In August 1942, an American offensive had begun against Guadalcanal, one of the South Pacific Solomon Islands. Guadalcanal fell on February 8, 1943, the first of the Japanese wartime conquests to be recaptured. American assaults in New Guinea and far north in the Aleutian Islands also succeeded. General MacArthur's forces began driving the Japanese from New Guinea in January 1943, completing the task early in 1944. The Americans then adopted the strategy of driving Japanese forces from one island to another, "leapfrogging" through the Pacific. Gradually, the U.S. navy gained control of the seas, its submarines picking off Japanese supply ships. Hard-earned summer victories brought U.S. troops within 1,400 miles of Tokyo. In October 1944, MacArthur's forces attacked the Philippines, defeating the Japanese fleet and the demoralized Japanese troops. There, the Japanese first used kamikaze tactics, suicide missions flown by pilots who crashed their planes into American ships.

The American capture of the island of Iwo Jima on March 27, 1945, brought U.S. planes to within 700 miles of Japan. On Okinawa, the next stop, piles of bleached human bones could still be seen on the beaches a decade after the war's end. Saipan and Guam provided bases from which American long-range bombers could reach Japan. American "super fortress" bombers showered Japanese cities with incendiary bombs that turned wooden buildings into fiery death traps. One attack destroyed 40 percent of Tokyo within three hours. American forces prepared to invade the southern islands of Japan itself. With the American fleet off Okinawa confronting suicide missions by Japanese pilots, it was clear that such an invasion would cost many lives.

Meanwhile, the United States was readying a new weapon hitherto unimaginable. The development of the atomic bomb (and its more lethal successor, the hydrogen bomb, first tested by the U.S. in 1954) had its origins in theories developed by Albert Einstein (see Chapter 19). In 1938, a German scientist in Berlin had achieved nuclear fission, splitting the atom and releasing tremendous energy. This meant that if a means could be found to split the nucleus of the atom, setting off a nuclear chain reaction, a bomb of enormous destructive power could be built. During the first years of the war, British and American scientists had worked separately on the project. German scientists, too, were working in the same direction. In the United States, German scientists who had fled the Nazis first discovered that an isotope of uranium could set off the anticipated chain reaction. At the same time, Soviet scientists were frantically trying to come up with the atomic bomb, but they were several crucial years behind American scientists.

In 1945, nuclear theory became reality, and the United States exploded the first atomic bomb in a desert in New Mexico on July 16. President Harry Truman (1884–1972; Roosevelt had died in April 1945) learned of this the day before the opening of the Potsdam Conference in the Berlin suburb in July 1945. He informed Stalin of the new weapon the United States now had at its disposal. The Potsdam Proclamation of July 26, 1945, warned Japan that it risked "prompt and utter destruction" if it did not agree to unconditional surrender. When Japanese resistance continued, a U.S. plane dropped an atomic bomb on the Japanese port city of Hiroshima on August 6, 1945, engulfing the city in a mushroom cloud of fire and radiation that killed 80,000 people. The Soviet Union then declared war on Japan and Soviet troops moved into Manchuria. On August 9, a U.S. plane dropped a second atomic bomb that destroyed much of Nagasaki, killing 36,000 people in a storm of fire. Thousands more would die of radiation sickness in the days, months, and years to follow.

On September 2, 1945, Japanese representatives signed documents of unconditional surrender on the battleship *Missouri*. The Second World War was over. But a new and potentially even more dangerous atomic age had begun.

CONCLUSION

The first Soviet troops arriving at the Nazi death camps discovered nightmarish horrors. Technology harnessed to the task of genocide had created factories of death. They came upon piles of corpses and of children's shoes; and the few lucky survivors—the living dead—barefoot human skeletons fortunate enough to have been liberated before their turn to be exterminated

(*Left*) A mushroom cloud envelops Nagasaki after the U.S. Army's deployment of an atomic bomb. (*Right*) The destruction after the atomic blast at Hiroshima.

had come. The death camps became perhaps the most awful symbol of the total war that was World War II, during which 6.2 million Jews perished, including 2.7 million Polish Jews. At the end of the war, only about 40,000 to 50,000 Polish Jews had survived the Holocaust.

World War II brought mass military mobilization and mass death. At least 17 million people were killed in the fighting and another 20 million civilians perished, half in the Soviet Union, not including those who died in Stalin's gulags. About 30 million people in China perished in the war begun by Japan in Manchuria in 1937. Germany lost more than 6 million people, Japan 2 million, and Britain and France lost about 250,000 and 300,000 respectively. Part of the horror of the period is that we will never really know the full extent of human loss. Millions had been wounded, many crippled for life. Millions of survivors had been carried far from home. Husbands, wives, children, and other relatives were often lost forever. Europe became a continent of "displaced persons," as they were called.

The psychological damage to those who lived through night bombing in shelters, those who spent years waiting for definitive news about missing loved ones, or those who had somehow survived the death camps, cannot be calculated. Europe seemed haunted by the sad memories of last conversations and letters. One survivor recalled his determination to hold on against all odds "to tell the story, to bear witness; and that to survive, we must force ourselves to save at least the skeleton, the scaffolding, the form of civilization."

After World War II, in contrast to the end of World War I, there seemed little optimism that such a total war could not occur again. Two factors, in particular, contributed to this new feeling of angst. The first was the rising tension even before the war ended between the Soviet Union and the Western Allies. The second was the development of rockets, the jet plane, and above all, the atomic bomb, a terrifying weapon for a new age.

The cataclysmic experience of the Second World War weighed heavily on the social, political, and cultural climate of the post-war era. In every country, those who resisted Nazi rule played a major part in the reconstitution of their nations after the war. Politicians, intellectuals, and virtually everyone else would try to come to grips with what had happened to Europe, to assess blame, and to find hope. For the moment, however, for many, it seemed enough to have survived.

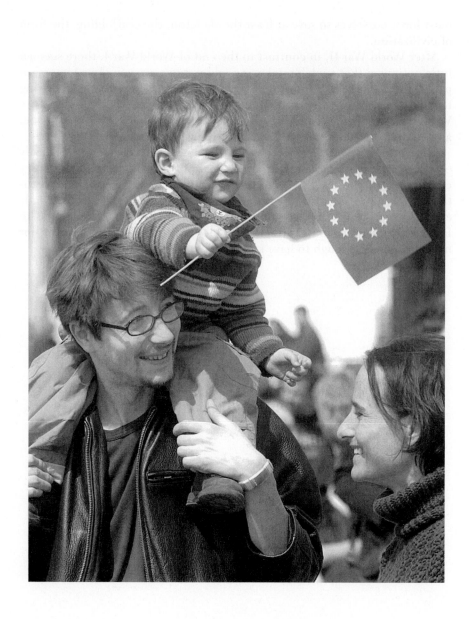

PART SEVEN

EUROPE IN THE POST-WAR ERA

Following the devastation of World War II, Europe rebuilt under the growing shadow of the Cold War between the Western powers, led by the United States, and the Soviet Union. The dawn of the nuclear age added to rising tensions. The Soviet Red Army, which had liberated Eastern Europe from the Nazis, became an occupying force. In Poland, Czechoslovakia, Bulgaria, and the other states of Eastern Europe, Soviet-backed Communists pushed other political parties aside until they held unchallenged authority in each state. They nationalized industries and undertook massive forced collectivization of agriculture. Germany, devastated by total defeat, was divided into a western zone, which became the German Federal Republic (West Germany), and an eastern zone, which became the Communist German Democratic Republic (East Germany). Berlin, lying within East Germany, remained divided between East and West, and quickly became a particular focus of Cold War rivalry. Soviet intervention in 1956 to crush a revolt against Communist rule in Hungary further strained relations between East and West. The Cuban Missile Crisis of 1962 brought the United States and the Soviet Union to the brink of nuclear war. The United Nations became a battleground for the Cold War (see Chapter 28). Yet it was an arena for verbal battles—hostile words and strident denunciations were better than war.

Signs of gnawing poverty were not hard to find in every country in the post-war period. Only half of the houses in France had running water, and only a third of those in Austria, Spain, and Italy. Providing decent housing became a goal of governments in most countries. However, Western Europe did slowly recover

from the ordeal of total war, and the relative peace and new prosperity engendered a "baby boom" (1946–1964), as in the United
States. More and more people lived in cities, with fewer working
the land, and a burgeoning culture of consumption took hold,
increasingly influenced by America. The status of and opportunities for women gradually improved. Women finally achieved the
right to vote in France and Italy. In Britain, the Labour government laid the foundations for the modern welfare state, with governments assuming increased responsibility for their citizens.
The welfare state emerged in part out of the experience of state
planning and social solidarity during World War II, as many
countries began wide-ranging social services to aid and protect
their people. Other Western states, too, increased the number of
social services provided by their governments, as did their Communist counterparts.

The period between 1950 and 1973 was a period of dynamic
economic growth in Western Europe. The number of people
working in manufacturing or the service sector increased dramatically, as the percentage of people working the land fell. Reflecting the wartime experience, economic and social planning played
an important part in the recovery of the European economy and
its rapid expansion.

In the post-war period, movements for independence in the
Asian and African colonies of the European powers led to rapid
decolonization and further loss of European authority. The age
of empire ended with decolonization. Britain granted independence to its former colonies. France, the Netherlands, Belgium,
and Portugal also lost their empires, but after nationalist insurrections and bloody fighting.

Political change in Europe came rapidly in the 1970s and
1980s. In Greece, Spain, and Portugal, repressive dictatorships
gave way to parliamentary regimes. Parties concerned with the
environment—the "Greens"—made sizable political inroads in
West Germany. But, at the same time, terrorism brought a new,
unsettling dimension to political life. Terrorist groups threatened
security in such areas as Northern Ireland and the Basque region
of Spain, where nationalists were demanding independence, and
in the Middle East, where militant Arab organizations opposed
the policies of Israel (which became independent in 1948)
toward the Palestinian people.

In the Soviet Union, following his rise to head of state in 1985,
Soviet leader Mikhail Gorbachev initiated a bold series of economic and political reforms, hoping to maintain communism by
eliminating its authoritarian nature, encouraging greater political
participation, and bringing economic prosperity. When move-

ments for reform arose in the countries of the Eastern European bloc, beginning in Poland and Hungary, Gorbachev made clear that the Soviet Union would not intervene. Communism collapsed in one Eastern European state after another in 1989. Throngs of East Germans pouring through the Berlin Wall in November 1989 symbolized the fall of communism in Eastern Europe. Germany became a unified state once again. The Soviet Union itself then broke apart, as one former Soviet republic after another declared independence. The Cold War ended, after having largely defined international relations since the end of World War II. The collapse of what has been called the Soviet Union's empire left the United States as the world's only superpower, with an informal empire of its own.

In the former Communist states, the challenges of achieving democratic rule with little or no democratic traditions or a successful market economy were daunting. The ethnic and religious complexity of these states compounded the difficulties. In the former Yugoslavia, a bloody civil war began in Bosnia in 1992. The war brought atrocities on a scale not seen since World War II, most of which were perpetuated by Serb forces against Muslims.

The post-war era also brought about European economic cooperation among Western states. European economic cooperation had begun in the years following World War II, with the founding of the Organization for European Economic Cooperation in 1948, the creation of the Common Market in 1959, and the European Community in 1967. The Treaty of Maastricht, signed in 1992 by the twelve members of the European Community, created the European Union, which had as a base a partnership between France and Germany. The single market that began for member states in 1993 led to the implementation of a common currency—the "euro"—in 2002 (although three states have retained their former currencies). Twenty-seven states are now members of the European Union. Romania and Bulgaria were admitted in 2007, with the candidacies of Croatia, Macedonia, and Turkey still pending.

The globalization of the world economy, reflecting remarkable improvements in transportation and communication, has brought the continents of the world closer together, facilitating the movement of people, ideas, and products across the globe. Migrants from Africa and Asia began to arrive in Europe in ever greater numbers, attracted by the possibility of jobs and a better life. Many fled political turmoil at home, arriving as political refugees or simply crossing borders without detection. Hundreds of thousands of immigrants from the Balkans also headed west. Periods of economic downturn have left immigrants unwanted by many in their adopted countries, which have been subject to xenophobia. Even as Europe now enjoys peace, the question of immigration remains a challenge, particularly in Western Europe. And so does the specter of increased terrorism across the globe, in the wake of the attacks in New York City and Washington, D.C., on September 11, 2001.

CHAPTER 27

REBUILDING DIVIDED EUROPE

The Second World War ended with little of the optimism that had followed the conclusion of the First World War. Winston Churchill, for one, was pessimistic: "What is Europe now? A rubble heap, a charnel house, a breeding ground of pestilence and hate." Four times more people had been killed in World War II (as a direct or indirect result of the fighting) than had died in World War I, which had been "the war to end all wars." As the smoke of war cleared, Europeans struggled to comprehend the devastation around them: flattened cities, crippled industry, and millions of refugees. The world soon learned that more than 6 million Jews had been exterminated by the Nazis. Countries that the German armies had occupied or that had been Nazi allies had to determine how to deal with collaborators, and they also faced the challenge of establishing democratic political institutions. In the meantime, intellectuals wrestled with the horrendous catastrophe that had occurred.

The shift from a wartime to a peacetime economy would pose a great challenge. The economies of the Western nations recovered from the war with remarkable speed and entered a period of spectacular economic growth. Economic growth came even as superpower competition between the United States and the Soviet Union made the other European powers less important in the world, as did the growing prodigious economic might of Japan and the rise of China as a great power.

The European population grew from 548 million in 1950 to 727 million in 2000. The post-war period brought a "baby boom." Life expectancy increased as people lived longer due to improvements in medicine and diet. Mechanization and commercialization augmented agricultural production. Because of what became known as a "Green Revolution," more and more rural people left the land for cities, which grew rapidly. Over the decades that followed, greater opportunities for women became available. At the same time, simultaneous revolutions in transportation, communications, and consumerism transformed the way Europeans lived.

In the Wake of Devastation

Putting Europe back together proved a daunting task. By the time World War II ended in 1945, as many as 60 million people had been killed as a result of the war. Although fewer people from France and Great Britain were killed in the Second World War than the First World War, death tolls in Central and Eastern Europe during the Second World War were almost beyond comprehension. In the Soviet Union, deaths due to the war can only be estimated at between 15 and 25 million people—even more, if one includes the millions who were victims of Joseph Stalin's purges. Moreover, 1,700 cities and towns and 70,000 villages were completely destroyed. About 6 million Germans died in Hitler's war. Poland lost 6 million people—a fifth of the population—including 3 million Jews, more than 90 percent of the Jewish population. Ten percent of the population of Yugoslavia had perished. Damage to property from air raids, ground warfare, and reprisals by retreating German forces was incalculable. German air raids in the first year of the war devastated sections of London and Coventry in Britain, Leningrad and Kiev in the Soviet Union, and the Dutch port of Rotterdam. The German army completely leveled Warsaw in retaliation for the 1944 uprising there. In turn, Allied bombing runs left Berlin, Dresden, and the industrial cities of the Rhineland in ruins, and key French industrial and port cities were severely damaged as well.

Only recently have historians become aware of the tragedies stemming from what would in the 1990s be known as "ethnic cleansing" during and immediately after the war. For example, between April 1943 and August 1947 in the territories that would become Communist Poland and the Soviet republic of Ukraine, about 100,000 civilian Poles and Ukrainians were killed and another 1.4 million were forced from their lands by the invading Red Army. During the period of Nazi and then Soviet occupation (for the second time, as the Soviets had occupied these territories during 1939–1941), first Ukrainians and then Poles themselves undertook "ethnic cleansing." Ukrainian nationalists killed Poles in Volhynia and Galicia in 1943, and the Poles committed atrocities when civil war between the two ethnic groups followed the liberation of Poland.

The Potsdam Conference

Decisions taken by the Allies toward the end of the war brought a radical restructuring of the national boundaries of Central and Eastern Europe. The restructuring was largely determined by the Soviet military advance. By the time of the German surrender in May 1945, the Red Army had occupied all of the states of Eastern Europe except Yugoslavia and Greece. In Germany, Soviet troops controlled what became the eastern zone; the British held the industrial Rhineland and Ruhr Basin, as well as much of the north; American and French armies held southern Germany; and the four powers divided Berlin.

At the Potsdam Conference of July 1945, Stalin, Churchill, and Truman considered the fate of defeated Germany. The defeat of Churchill's Conservative Party in the election that took place at the same time as the conference brought Clement Attlee (1883–1967) to Potsdam as British prime minister, leading one diplomat to conclude that the meeting of the "Big Three" had become a meeting of "the Big 2 and a half." The Allies had already decided to divide defeated Germany into a British, French, Russian, and American zone of occupation. They created a new border between Germany and Poland, which would be the Oder and Niesse Rivers. The port of Gdańsk was restored to Poland. The Allied leaders agreed that Germany should be reunified, despite the original opposition of de Gaulle, and that German populations living in Poland, Czechoslovakia, and Hungary should be forcibly resettled in Germany, as the new governments of those states demanded. The Four Power Allied Control Council (France had joined the Potsdam powers) planned a new, disarmed, and de-Nazified Germany.

The growing mistrust between the Western Allies and the Soviet Union affected the Potsdam Conference. Stalin's territorial demands included

Winston Churchill, Harry Truman, and Joseph Stalin at the Potsdam Conference in 1945.

strategically crucial parts of Turkey. The Western Allies refused, because such a move would have given the Soviet Union virtual control of the straits of Constantinople—which Russian tsars had sought since the eighteenth century. The Soviet Union had already occupied in 1940 the Baltic states of Estonia, Latvia, and Lithuania, a large chunk of East Prussia, and parts of Finland, Czechoslovakia, and Romania (Bessarabia and some of Bukovina). Poland, which lost much of its eastern territory to the Soviet Union, gained in the west at Germany's expense (see Map 27.1).

Other territorial adjustments came at the expense of Germany's wartime allies, such as Italy, from which Yugoslavia acquired a small border region. As the Allies dictated the new alignments, little attention was paid to the fact that the new borders, as after World War I, left various nationalities dissatisfied. Hungarians living in Transylvania did not want to be left within the redrawn borders of Romania; the many fewer Romanians who found themselves inside Hungary resented what they considered to be punishment for having been forced by the Nazis and their wartime dictators to fight on the side of Germany. Austria, which Hitler had annexed to his Reich in 1938, had its independence restored. Military occupation of Austria by the victorious World War II powers ended in 1955 with the withdrawal of Soviet troops in exchange for Austria's declaration of neutrality. In northern Europe, Finland retained its independence and the Soviet Union accepted Finnish neutrality.

As after the end of World War I, the Western Allies disagreed on the question of war reparations. The Soviet Union, which had suffered far more than Great Britain and the United States, demanded that Germany be forced to pay for the costs of the war. Specifically, Stalin wanted the equivalent of $20 billion in reparations, as well as German industrial equipment. The Soviet Union eventually received half the amount of money demanded (although in greatly inflated currency), as well as about 25 percent of industrial equipment from the German zones occupied by Britain, France, and the United States. In the meantime, Soviet trains and trucks began to haul German machinery and other industrial materials from the eastern zone back to Russia. By now fully suspicious of Soviet intentions in Eastern Europe, Truman eliminated the Soviet Union from the list of nations eligible for U.S. loans to help with rebuilding their economies.

The Western Allies concurred that the victors should negotiate peace treaties with Germany's former allies (Italy, Hungary, Romania, and Bulgaria), which were to be represented by "recognized democratic governments." But it was soon clear that the governments of the last three nations were anything but democratically elected.

The United Nations and Cold War Alliances

In November 1944, the Dumbarton Oaks Conference in Washington, D.C., planned the United Nations, which would replace the League of Nations.

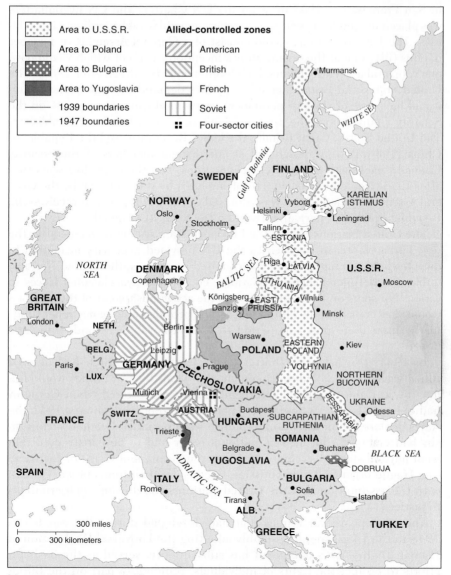

MAP 27.1 POST-WAR TERRITORIAL SETTLEMENTS Territorial changes as of 1947, including American, British, French, and Soviet zones in Germany, as well as boundaries of the Soviet Union, Poland, Bulgaria, and Yugoslavia after the war.

The League, which did not include the United States, Germany, Japan, or Italy as members, had stood by when Italy invaded Ethiopia and Germany re-occupied the Rhineland and then absorbed Czechoslovakia. Now, the Allies desired a system of international security that would protect the freedom and self-determination of member nations. An international conference in San Francisco in 1945 drew up the UN Charter. The UN headquarters was placed in New York, where a secretary-general would coordinate its activities. The United Nations would consist of a General Assembly of member nations (fifty-one at the organization's inception), each of which would have one vote, and a Security Council of eleven members (fifteen after 1965). The United States and Britain agreed to Stalin's demand that the Soviet Union would have one of the five permanent seats—and thus veto power—on the Security Council once the proposed United Nations had been established. The United States, Great Britain, the U.S.S.R., France, and the Republic of China (Taiwan) were designated as "permanent members of the Security Council," each with a veto over deliberations, and the other five seats (ten after 1965) would be filled on a revolving basis by states chosen by the General Assembly. When China was admitted to the UN in 1971, it received the Republic of China's permanent seat on the Security Council.

The United Nations helped the European state system reemerge after the war. Furthermore, in some cases the UN provided necessary mediation in disputes between nations. However limited its powers, the United Nations, unlike the defunct League of Nations, could send peacekeeping forces to various hot spots on the globe, although the accomplishments of these efforts would vary considerably. Moreover, the UN provided emergency relief funds in the immediate post-war period to Czechoslovakia, Poland, Italy, and Greece.

In 1941, the Atlantic Charter (see Chapter 26), which had defined Allied war aims, had led to agreement that trials for war crimes would follow the war, once national sovereignty had been restored when Germany had been defeated. At the Saint James Conference in January 1942 the Allies declared their intention to punish war criminals. Gradually, consensus had emerged that an international order had to be constructed that went beyond state sovereignty. In 1944, the Permanent Court of Justice in The Hague organized a commission to consider definitions of war crimes, with the assumption that the United Nations would bring such criminals to justice.

The concept of war crimes that had developed during the war led in 1948 to the UN General Assembly adopting the Universal Declaration of Human Rights. This document has subsequently served as the basis for efforts to protect the rights of individuals. Building in part on the Bill of Rights of the United States and the Declaration of the Rights of Man and of Citizen of the French Revolution, the Universal Declaration proclaimed civil and political rights; the right to a fair trial; the freedoms of assembly, belief, and speech; and the rights to education, an adequate standard of living, and to participation in cultural life. Moreover, slavery and torture were acknowledged as violations of human rights. The Genocide Convention of 1949 made genocide a crime under international law.

Besides joining the United Nations to mediate disputes, the states of Europe also hedged their bets by establishing military alliances, whereby they pledged to come to the defense of their allies in case any one of them was attacked. Thus, in March 1948, Great Britain, France, Belgium, the Netherlands, and Luxembourg signed the Pact of Brussels. It served as the military component of the subsequent Council of Europe to which most of the nations of Western Europe adhered. The United States joined members of the Pact of Brussels in the North Atlantic Treaty Organization (NATO) in 1949, which subsequently added Italy, Denmark, Norway, Iceland, Portugal, Canada, Greece, and Turkey (see Map 27.2). Directed against the Soviet Union, the treaty bound all of the member countries to defend jointly any of the signatories who were attacked, creating a unified command for a common army and placing NATO's headquarters in Paris. NATO became the cornerstone of the alliance between the United States and Western Europe.

Confronting Turmoil and Collaborators

Europe became a continent of "displaced persons" (DP's) as well as of widows and orphans. Now national minorities within newly redrawn boundaries were forced into boxcars and moved—displaced—to new locations so as to correspond more or less to newly drawn national frontiers. In all, there were about 50 million refugees in the immediate post-war period. Furthermore, millions of prisoners of war, such as Germans incarcerated in the Soviet Union, had to be repatriated. Germans living in Lithuania, which in 1940 had been incorporated against its will into the Soviet Union, were returned to Germany. In the spring of 1945, about 20 million people were on the move. In addition, tens of thousands of Germans were forcibly expelled from Czechoslovakia during the period from May to August of 1945 and during the organized transfers of January through November 1946. Thousands died during this hard time. In all, about 12 million Germans were forced to leave their homes. Almost 4 million returned to Germany, most arriving from the U.S.S.R. and Poland with virtually nothing. In Germany, one of every six persons was a refugee and 1.5 million Germans still lived in camps for displaced persons in 1947.

Although drab and carefully regulated along military lines by the American, British, and French occupiers, with barbed wire, the careful distribution of food and clothing, and curfews, DP camps brought some normalcy to the lives of their occupants, many of whom had been slave laborers for Germany, including Polish and Ukrainian Jews, as well as Jews from the Baltic states, and some fortunate survivors of the death camps.

Stalin repopulated East Prussia with about 1 million people hauled from Russia, Belarus, Ukraine, and even distant Kazakhstan. Poles whose homeland had become part of the Soviet Union now moved into western Poland. At the same time, almost 500,000 Ukrainians were forced by Poland to head eastward to the Soviet Union. Several hundred thousand Jews from Eastern Europe who had survived the Holocaust now headed west, some fleeing new pogroms in Poland in 1946. In all, about 7 million members of

MAP 27.2 EASTERN AND WESTERN BLOCS, 1955 NATO and the Warsaw Pact were the military alliances that defined the post-war world.

NATO countries

Warsaw Pact countries

Non-aligned Western countries

Non-aligned Communist country

U.S.A.
CANADA
ICELAND

ATLANTIC OCEAN

NORTH SEA

BALTIC SEA

IRELAND

GREAT BRITAIN

NETH.

BELG.

LUX.

FRANCE

SPAIN

PORTUGAL

MEDITERRANEAN SEA

NORWAY

SWEDEN

FINLAND

DENMARK

EAST GERMANY

WEST GERMANY

POLAND

CZECHOSLOVAKIA

AUSTRIA

SWITZ.

HUNGARY

ITALY

YUGOSLAVIA

ADRIATIC SEA

ALB.

ROMANIA

BULGARIA

GREECE

U.S.S.R.

BLACK SEA

TURKEY

400 miles

400 kilometers

Refugees waiting for food in a Displaced Persons Camp in Germany.

Eastern European ethnic groups faced resettlement. The result was a dramatic decrease in the percentage of ethnic minorities living in Poland, Czechoslovakia, and Romania, declining from 32 percent to 3 percent in the first case. Churches, synagogues, and even a few mosques were razed, depending on the location; towns and streets received new names to reflect the brutal transfer of ethnic minorities.

The punishment of those who had collaborated with the Nazis began as soon as the occupied territories were liberated (and, in some cases, had begun during the war itself). In France, resistance forces summarily executed (sometimes after quick trials) about 10,000 accused collaborators. Courts sentenced about 2,000 people to death (of whom about 800 were executed) and more than 40,000 to prison. Vichy Prime Minister Pierre Laval was executed. Marshal Philippe Pétain was found guilty of treason, but because of his age and stature as the "hero of Verdun" during the First World War, he was imprisoned on a small island off the western coast of France, where he died in 1951. Women who had slept with German soldiers had their heads shaved and were paraded through their towns in shame.

In countries that had been occupied by Hitler's armies, people struggled to determine degrees of guilt. In Belgium, courts prosecuted 634,000 people for their part in the German occupation—a staggering figure in a country of only 8 million people. In Norway, 55,000 members of the Norwegian Nazi Party were put on trial after the war, and although many drew jail terms, only 25 were executed. On the other hand, in Austria, where much

A French collaborator whose head has been shaved is paraded, with her baby, through a village near Cherbourg following liberation of the region by Allied troops, 1944.

of the population had seemed to welcome union with Hitler's Germany with frenzied enthusiasm, only 9,000 people were tried and only 35 collaborators executed. In Italy, where reprisals against Nazi collaborators at the war's end had been carried out with speed and efficiency (about 15,000 executions between 1943 and 1946), there were few trials of fascists after the war. This was in part because the Italian fascists had been, at least when compared to the Nazis, relatively mild in their treatment of their enemies. Furthermore, millions of people had joined fascist organizations or unions because they felt obliged to do so. In Eastern Europe, purges of former Nazi collaborators took on a high profile, such as in Yugoslavia, where Tito's victorious forces executed thousands of Serbs, Croats, and Slovenes who had collaborated, many of them murderously.

The most dramatic post-war trial occurred in Nuremberg in August 1945 when the Allies put twenty-four high-ranking German officials on trial before an international tribunal. The court found twenty-one of the defendants guilty of war crimes, and ten were executed. Hermann Göring committed suicide in his cell shortly before he was to be executed. Less spectacular trials of more minor Nazi figures went on in Germany for years.

Many war criminals, however, escaped or were let free after the war. Doctor Josef Mengele, who had carried out brutal experiments on living patients, including children, managed to escape to Paraguay. A good many Nazis found a warm welcome from right-wing dictatorships. The U.S. government facilitated the escape of a number of Nazi war criminals in exchange for information about Communists in Germany and elsewhere in Europe. Indeed, growing anti-communism put a brake on purges of wartime collaborators in Western Europe. Other war criminals managed to fade into the chaos of post-war Europe, some with new names and identities. Some did not even bother to change their names, and more than a few eventually served in the West German government. In 1959, Israeli agents in South America kidnapped Adolph Eichmann, who had participated in the murder of thousands of Jews. He was put on trial in Israel, where he was convicted and put to death. In the mid-1980s, a French court convicted Klaus Barbie, a Nazi war criminal who had fled after the war, sentencing him to life in prison. Maurice Papon, an official who had signed away the lives of hundreds of Jews during Vichy and then gone on to a successful career as an official in several French governments, was finally tried and convicted in 1998, proud to the end that his superiors thought well of his work as a bureaucrat. The justice meted out to Nazis and collaborators may have been imperfect, and sometimes came quite late, but it was better than no justice at all.

ECONOMIC RECOVERY AND PROSPERITY, THE WELFARE STATE, AND EUROPEAN ECONOMIC COOPERATION

The European economy lay in ruins. Bombing on both sides had been systematic, destroying with increasing accuracy the industrial structure of Europe. Sunken ships blocked port harbors. Almost all bridges over the major rivers had been destroyed. Only fragments of Europe's transportation and communication networks remained in service. In Britain, gold and silver reserves had sunk dramatically, and the government had been forced to take out large loans, initiating a long period of virtual British dependence on the United States, which provided the bulk of these funds. Non-military manufacturing had plunged during the war. The markets for British manufactured goods, which had all but disappeared during the war, could not be quickly reconstituted.

Agricultural production in every war zone had fallen by about half, leaving millions of people without enough to eat. Inflation was rampant; the value of European currencies plunged. As after World War I, the German currency became virtually worthless. German housewives picked through the rubble of bombed-out buildings looking for objects of value, combing forests for mushrooms and berries for their families to eat. The black market supplied many necessities.

However, the European economy revived with impressive, unanticipated speed (see Table 27.1). As a response to growing Communist influence, in March 1947 President Truman announced the "Truman Doctrine," which proclaimed "the policy of the United States to support free people who are resisting attempted subjugation by armed minorities or by outside pressures."

Table 27.1. Indices of Industrial Production, 1946–1950
(1938 = 100)

	1946	1947	1948	1949	1950
Belgium	91	106	120	129	139
Britain	106	114	128	137	148
France	79	95	111	122	125
Italy	75	93	99	105	119
Netherlands	74	94	113	126	137
W. Germany	29	34	51	75	90

Source: William I. Hitchcock, *The Struggle for Europe: The Turbulent History of a Divided Continent, 1945–2002* (New York: Doubleday, 2003), p. 135.

Because great economic turmoil had contributed to social and political instability between the world wars, the United States undertook a program of massive economic aid to Western Europe. Through the Marshall Plan, named after the American secretary of state, George Marshall, who devised it, the United States contributed $13 billion between 1948 and 1951 toward the rebuilding of the Western Allies' economies. The Marshall Plan was intended to help Western Europe resist communism—as the United States pressured the governments of France and Italy not to name Communists to key ministries—and to make Europe a powerful trading partner for American industry.

The Marshall Plan contributed to the revival of Western Europe. However, the European economic recovery was already well under way by the time the Marshall Plan began in 1948. Britain and France had already matched their industrial production of the pre-war period, and Italy, the Netherlands, and Belgium followed within a year. Moreover, the monies provided by the Marshall Plan amounted to only 6.5 percent of France's gross national product, 2.5 percent of that of Britain, and 5.3 percent of that of Italy. The Marshall Plan did assist Western European states to purchase raw materials, fuel, and machinery for industry. In Britain, about a third of the aid went to the purchase of food. Funds from the Marshall Plan also allowed Western European governments some margin to pay for the beginnings of social programs emerging with the construction of welfare states (see p. 1126). The United States offered loans and credits to a number of European countries, with an eye toward encouraging anti-communism, while having excluded the Soviet Union from the provisions of the Lend-Lease Act.

The difficult years in the immediate post-war period gave way to a period of considerable economic growth from 1950 to 1973. European economies benefited from the globalization of trade, the availability of a labor supply, and the use of oil instead of coal as the principal source of fuel for industrial growth. This rapid rise in the demand for oil dramatically increased the strategic importance of the Middle East. Natural gas, much of which was imported from the Soviet Union, offered another source of energy.

Economic growth followed a combination of state involvement in the economy and the liberalization of trade, creating mixed economies. The most successful mix seemed to be a combination of state planning, timely nationalizations (notably of railroads, coal, and steel), and encouragement of private industry. Nationalized railroads aided the process of rebuilding and expansion in West Germany, France, Belgium, and Britain. The Italian government owned almost 30 percent of Italian industry. In Italy, the role of the state in orchestrating industry, encouraged by Mussolini, survived the war. The Institute for Industrial Reconstruction, which had been founded in 1933, controlled an increasing number of enterprises. The National Agency for Hydrocarbons emerged as a veritable cartel in itself, drawing huge profits from a variety of activities, including construction, chemicals, and textile production. Government investment helped the emergence of the Italian steel industry, and a state-owned petroleum company provided industry with inexpensive fuel.

The British economy slowly revived following the war. Industrial production reached pre-war levels by 1946 and grew by a third by the end of the decade, despite increasingly obsolete factories and low rates of investment and savings. In France, the state assumed control of the largest banks, the Renault automobile plants (whose owner had collaborated with the Germans), natural resources (such as gas and coal), steel and electricity, and airlines. The brilliant French economist Jean Monnet (1888–1979) headed an Office of Planning, which encouraged and coordinated voluntary plans for modernizing business enterprises and agriculture, drawing on the capital and expertise of government technocrats. French industrial production in 1959 was twice that of 1938. Table 27.2 provides comparative rates of industrial productivity for the major nations of Europe, as well as for Japan and the United States. Italy also enjoyed a real boom. Real wages in Italy in 1954 were more than 50 percent higher than they had been before the war, as the Italian economy grew rapidly with the help of U.S. financial assistance. Smaller nations also thrived. Norway, Denmark, and Sweden all became more prosperous thanks largely to the development of fishing, agriculture, industry, and booming service sectors.

The Western Allies recognized that the economic recovery of West Germany was essential to achieving political stability in Central Europe and resisting communism. Aided by a stable political life, the German Federal Republic reformed its battered currency, the mark. Price controls and rationing ended. This helped restore confidence, which in turn helped fuel the economic resurgence. Black-marketeering gradually ceased as inflation and unemployment were brought under control.

An infusion of American aid—$1.5 billion between 1948 and 1952, primarily through the Marshall Plan—contributed to the rebuilding of key industries in West Germany, which contained most of the nation's natural

TABLE 27.2. INDEX OF INDUSTRIAL PRODUCTION

	1938	1948	1952	1959	1963	1967
United States	33	73	90	113	133	168
West Germany	53	27	61	107	137	158
France	52	55	70	101	129	155
Italy	43	44	64	112	166	212
Holland	47	53	72	110	141	182
Belgium	64	78	88	104	135	153
Britain	67	74	84	105	119	133
Austria	39	36	65	106	131	151
Spain				102	149	215
Sweden	52	74	81	106	140	176
Japan	58	22	50	120	212	347

Source: Walter Laqueur, *Europe Since Hitler* (New York: Penguin, 1982), p. 194.

resources. The German Federal Republic also had the advantage (one, to be sure, bought at horrific cost during the war) of starting from scratch and building new factories that utilized the most modern equipment. West Germany's other advantages included the presence of many engineers, a skilled labor force, and protection by the Western Allies—so it did not have to spend much for defense. The government of the German Federal Republic took a lesser role in economic planning, but imposed short-term tariffs and encouraged agricultural modernization. The influx of refugees from East Germany contributed to the remarkable growth of the West German economy. West Germany in the 1960s attracted streams of migrant workers from Spain, Italy, Greece, Yugoslavia, and above all, Turkey.

As a result of the German economic "miracle," West Germany's gross national product tripled between 1950 and 1964. West Germany's imports multiplied during the 1950s by four times and its exports by six times. German industrial production more than doubled between 1948 and 1951, and it increased by six times from 1948 to 1964. West Germany assumed pre-war Germany's role as a major producer of steel and machinery. The chemical industry, strong in Germany since the late nineteenth century, continued to develop. By 1960, the German Federal Republic was the world's second leading exporter of goods, including machinery, appliances, radios, chemicals, and automobiles, as Volkswagens now streamed off the assembly lines.

The continued concentration of industrial production in large companies characterized the post-war period. Western Europe entered the world of conglomerates. A single Belgian company controlled as much as 80 percent of Belgian bank deposits, 60 percent of insurance business, 40 percent of the iron and steel produced, 30 percent of coal, and 25 percent of electrical energy. This monopoly did not seem to slow the development of the Belgian economy, which expanded rapidly.

With the rapid development of the service sector of Western economies, the proliferation of white-collar jobs lifted the expectations, status, and income of hundreds of thousands of families. A more equitable distribution in taxation helped remove some of the tax burden from ordinary people. Still, in 1960, 5 percent of the British population owned about 75 percent of the nation's wealth.

Great economic disparities also remained between European nations. By the end of the 1960s, the German Federal Republic, Switzerland, and Sweden were the most prosperous European countries; Ireland, Portugal, Greece, and Spain were the poorest in Western Europe; and Romania and Albania were the poorest Communist states. In Table 27.2, Britain's relative decline clearly stands out.

Economic Cooperation

The post-war era also brought international economic cooperation among Western states. The Organization for European Economic Cooperation (OEEC) was founded in 1948 with seventeen member states, which the United States later joined. It was succeeded in 1961 by the Organization for Economic Cooperation and Development (OECD), which was expanded to include Australia, Canada, and New Zealand. The OEEC helped plan European economic reconstruction after World War II. Cooperation among the Western states also led to the creation in 1952 of the European Coal and Steel Community (ECSC). The inspiration of the French statesman Robert Schuman (1886–1963), the ECSC also reflected the influence of U.S. Secretary of State Dean Acheson and of French economist Jean Monnet. The ECSC, which overcame strenuous British opposition, coordinated production of French and German coal and steel in the interest of efficiency, but it also was intent on forging a new relationship that ultimately would place France and West Germany at the center of the new Europe. Despite inevitable problems stemming from sometimes competing interests, the ECSC first raised the possibility of serious European economic integration. Such economic cooperation between countries also contributed to economic growth in Western Europe.

The Treaty of Rome (1957) laid the groundwork for the European Atomic Energy Community and the European Economic Community (EEC, the European Common Market). The EEC began in 1958 with six member nations—France, Italy, the German Federal Republic, Belgium, Luxembourg, and the Netherlands. The EEC gradually eliminated trade barriers between member states in Western Europe, established common customs tariffs—thus reducing trade barriers and increasing trade between member states—and worked toward equalizing wages and social security arrangements among the member countries.

The Post-War Baby Boom

Following the war, a veritable "baby boom" occurred in Europe, as in the United States. Europe's population grew from 264 million in 1940 to 320 million by the early 1970s. The increase in the birthrate after the war more than made up for the loss of hundreds of thousands of emigrants to North America and Latin America, particularly from Italy. Europeans were also living longer, aided by improvements in diet and in medicine. The aging of the population presents major challenges for the twenty-first century. As the percentage of people no longer working rises, major strains on national budgets are a certainty because of increased costs for welfare and social security systems.

In the post-war period, increases in industrial and agricultural productivity, which opened up new jobs, encouraged families to have more children, as did government policies that aided families that had children. In France, where leaders had openly worried about the low birthrate, special incentives were offered to families that had more than two children. Medical advances (such as the virtual elimination of polio by the end of the 1950s) and an increase in the number of doctors further reduced infant mortality. The birthrate increased between 1950 and 1966 in every country in Western Europe, with Switzerland, the Netherlands, the German Federal Republic, and France leading the way. The Soviet Union and Poland, too, saw high annual natural increases. Nonetheless, because of virtually unchecked population growth in India, China, and other Third World nations, Europe's percentage of the world population fell to 16 percent in 1990.

The increase in the birthrate had far-reaching social and political implications. British, French, and German eighteen-year-olds received the right to vote in the early 1970s. Moreover, governments had to increase spending on education dramatically to prepare the young for jobs in an economy that was rapidly becoming more complex. The age until which school attendance was obligatory rose to fourteen or sixteen years old, depending on the country. Illiteracy became quite uncommon in Europe by the 1960s. As a result of the baby boom, more young people attended university. But despite the tripling of the number of university students in Britain, France, and Italy between 1938 and 1960, there was relatively little democratization of university enrollment, which remained the preserve of the upper classes. In 1967, fewer than 10 percent of French university students were the children of workers or peasants. In Great Britain, particularly, but also in the other countries of the West, working-class and farm families could not afford to send their children to university. Time away from earning a living represented an economic hardship. Still, in Eastern Europe and the Balkan countries, the number of students in higher education rose rapidly.

The Green Revolution

In the two decades that followed World War II, Western European agriculture was transformed by the "Green Revolution." Fewer farmers fed a much larger population. Large-scale, commercialized agriculture permitted most nations to produce most of the food consumed by their populations. Agricultural productivity rose by 30 percent between the end of the war and 1962. In the German Federal Republic, agricultural production increased by two-and-a-half times between 1950 and 1964.

There were several reasons for these changes in farming. First, mechanized agriculture was increasingly widespread, particularly use of the tractor. Second, fertilizers augmented farm yields in northern Europe, while pesticides—a mixed blessing because of the long-term ecological costs—prevented blight. Advances in types of seeds, animal husbandry (particularly artificial insemination), and irrigation also contributed to greater productivity. Third, the size of many farms increased as smaller and less productive plots were consolidated into larger units.

Government programs encouraged the cooperative use of tractors and provided agricultural information to farmers. In many countries, government assistance facilitated reforestation, electrification, irrigation projects, and road building that would have been beyond the means of private initiatives. Improvements in agriculture were spread unevenly across Europe. Agriculture became most efficient in Great Britain, the Netherlands, Belgium, West Germany, Denmark, and France. Agricultural surpluses helped some countries during the 1970s and 1980s become major exporters of food.

The continued commercialization of agriculture accentuated the exodus from the land to the rapidly growing cities of Europe. In Italy, the farming population fell from about 40 percent after the war to 24 percent in 1966. In Great Britain, the first European nation in which agriculture was substantially mechanized even before the war, less than 4 percent of the population worked the land by the early 1970s. Before World War I, about half the population of Europe worked in agriculture, a figure that included fishermen and foresters. In 1955, the percentage had fallen to about 24 percent, and it has continued to decline, although it remains higher in southern Europe. In every country, agriculture's share of the gross national product has fallen. At the same time, the increasing industrialization of agriculture and the use of synthetic fertilizers means that the old term "Green Revolution" in some ways no longer seems appropriate.

In the 1950s, Western European peasants started to join organizations to lobby for assistance and favorable tariffs. Peasants blocked traffic of capitals with tractors and farm animals to protest government policies. In France, wine producers have often attempted to block the arrival of cheaper products from Italy and Spain. Ironically, such protests have come at a time when peasants, because of the rural exodus in Western Europe, have lost most of their political voice.

Welfare States

The emergence of welfare states within the context of market capitalism was one of the most significant evolutions in the post-war period. State economic and military planning during World War II helped shape expectations of continued government assistance. In response to popular desire for social reforms, the British Parliament, spurred by the Labour Party, implemented new social benefits. These included the remarkable British National Health Service that began in 1948, funds for the unemployed, retirement pensions, and assistance for widows. It also enacted a series of bills nationalizing the Bank of England, airlines, railways, roads, canals, buses, London's subway, and the coal and steel industries. After the war, the shortage of homes was apparent and a quarter of all homes in Britain did not have their own lavatory. By 1951, a million new homes had been constructed in Britain. Economic growth and a low rate of unemployment made such programs, financed through taxation, easier than they would have been in a period of economic slowdown. The Conservatives, in power between 1951 and 1964, expanded the services of the British welfare state, even though Conservative policy had long been in principle against such strong government.

In other countries, too, the general appreciation of the sacrifices ordinary people had made during World War II led to a growing consensus that states should provide services to citizens. The welfare state also reflected the assumption that the monopoly of wealthy people over the economy had contributed to the rise of fascist movements in Europe between the wars.

Thus European states greatly expanded comprehensive welfare programs that provided social services for their citizens. "Welfare states" would provide cradle-to-grave social services. This was true in Western states, in which laissez-faire economic theory had long held the upper hand, as well as in Communist states, in which the role of centralized state economic planning was a major part of Communist ideology and practice. In many countries, social legislation provided government assistance to the sick and impoverished. Government insurance programs covered health care costs in Britain, Sweden, Denmark, France, Italy, and in the Soviet Union and other Communist states. Most countries in the West provided financial assistance to the unemployed; in Communist states, where there was not supposed to be any unemployment, menial jobs were found for almost everyone. In all, states expended four times more funds for social services in 1957 than in 1930. Progressive taxation helped raise funds to provide these services. In most European countries, education was made free, or fees were kept at modest rates. The prevalence of social programs in most European countries led to the characterization of welfare states as part of a "European" model of society, often contrasted with the United States. Between 1965 and 1981, the proportion of government expenditures in Britain that went to social welfare rose from 16 to 25 percent and in Sweden from 19 to 33 percent. Everywhere, the increase in government services added to the size of bureaucracies. Yet the advent of welfare states was predicated on economic growth. When economies do not grow, social-welfare costs become drains on national budgets. Great Britain, France, and Sweden would later find, for instance, that rising medical costs could outstrip the ability of government programs to pay for them.

POLITICS IN THE WEST IN THE POST-WAR ERA

With Germany, Italy, and Vichy France defeated, political continuity with pre-war governments could be found only in Britain among the major Western European powers. Yet, even in Britain, political change occurred as voters in the first post-war election turned against the Conservatives and brought the Labour Party to power in July 1945. Labour's victory was a repudiation of the Conservative government's pre-war economic policies and its inadequate reaction to Hitler's aggressive moves in Central Europe in the late 1930s. Clement Attlee (1883–1967), a hard-working but uninspiring man who lacked Churchill's charisma, became prime minister. Churchill allegedly remarked, "An empty cab pulled up to 10 Downing Street, and Attlee got out." Nonetheless, Attlee proved to be an effective leader.

Following the economic recovery after the war, Britain's share in international trade declined sharply during the 1950s, 1960s, and 1970s. West Germany and France passed Britain in most economic categories. Some conservatives blamed the welfare state and the strength of the unions for Britain's relative economic decline, arguing that both forced the government and private companies to pay higher wages. Yet British welfare costs were less than those of France, and British citizens paid proportionally fewer taxes than German or French citizens. Rather, the costs of maintaining the British Empire undercut the government's quest for austerity as it faced enormous trade deficits and debts to the United States. The Attlee government had to choose between financing domestic economic recovery and maintaining the British Empire. It chose the former (see Chapter 28).

Conservatives returned to power in Britain in 1951. Britain remained governed by an inter-connected elite of wealthy families—at one time during the government (1957–1963) of Conservative Prime Minister Harold Macmillan, thirty-five of his ministers, including seven members of his cabinet, were related to him by marriage. (Princess Margaret, sister of Queen Elizabeth, once suggested sarcastically that the traditional debutante balls no longer be held because "every little tart in London was getting in.") The Tories were committed to undoing the nationalizations undertaken by Labour after the war. But they found it difficult to privatize the iron and steel industries because they had become unprofitable and failed to attract private interest. Furthermore, the welfare system was generally popular. Labour

(*Left*) Winston Churchill giving his famous "V for Victory" sign. (*Right*) Charles de Gaulle returns to France after the German occupation and the Vichy years.

returned to power in 1964 with the support of the trade unions, and remained there until 1970.

In some ways, France emerged from World War II in better shape than it had from World War I. And although industrial cities and ports had been pounded by bombing raids—German in 1940 and Allied in the last years of the war—the systematic devastation that had taken place in northern and northeastern France during 1914–1918 had not been repeated, in part because the French armies had collapsed so rapidly in 1940.

In the eighteen months that followed his triumphant march down the Champs-Elysées to Paris's town hall in August 1944, Charles de Gaulle ruled virtually alone. In October 1945, the vast majority of French men and women voted against a return to the political institutions of the Third Republic, identified with France's defeat five years earlier. This referendum was the first election in which French women could vote after receiving the suffrage that year. In the subsequent elections for the Constituent Assembly, the Communist Party—whose contributions to the resistance had been essential—took the greatest percentage of seats. They were followed by the Popular Republican Movement (MRP), a new center-right party built on de Gaulle's reputation and Catholic support. However, frustrated that the new regime would have a weak executive authority, de Gaulle resigned from government in January 1946.

After voters overwhelmingly rejected the Constituent Assembly's proposed constitution in May, a second Constituent Assembly was then elected to write a new constitution. It was approved by a narrow majority of voters in October 1946. Like the Third Republic, the political institutions of the new Fourth Republic seemed conducive to governmental immobility and instability. Between 1946 and 1958, France had twenty-four different governments, most based on left-center coalitions of the MRP, the Socialists, and smaller parties. The president and the prime minister had influence, but little power. While de Gaulle cooled his heels in his village, awaiting a call for him to return to power, a new Gaullist party (the Rally of the French People, or RPF) became the opposition party of the right.

In Italy, a new regime had to be constructed after the war. The monarchy's passive capitulation to fascism had discredited King Victor Emmanuel III. In June 1946, more than half of those voting repudiated the monarchy, despite the abdication of the king in favor of his son and the pope's attempts to influence the election. Italy became a republic.

The new Italian constitution provided for the election of the president by the two houses of parliament, both of which were to be elected by popular vote, now including women for the first time. The president had little real authority. Many Italians feared a powerful centralized state, at least partially because it would seem a continuity of fascism, but also because it seemed antithetical to long-standing regional identities. Fearful of losing influence, the Church vigorously opposed state centralization.

The new Italy was to be built on values associated with the resistance, which had been active in the north. Some Italians now called this a "cleansing wind from the north." But the Italian south and Sicily had been liberated by the Allies with very little help from a resistance movement, which remained dominated not only by powerful landowners but also by the Mafia. Moreover, many fascist officials in the south retained their positions, weakening the republic's prestige.

The government of Italy remained rooted in the center-right. The Christian Democratic Party, a staunchly anti-Communist centrist force with close ties to the Catholic Church and powerful economic interests, controlled political life in post-war Italy, dispensing patronage and bribes. Like its counterparts in West Germany and France, the Italian Christian Democratic Party reflected the accommodation of most Catholics with democracy. At the same time, the Communist Party became the second-largest political party, claiming the allegiance of a quarter of the population. In the 1960s, Italian governments undertook modest social reforms, encouraged by the popular Pope John XXIII (pope 1958–1963). This pushed the Christian Democrats to form coalitions with the Socialists.

Political Realignments

Backed by the Soviet Union and its secret police, Communist governments took power in every Eastern European state in the post-war period. After first declaring support for the constitution of parliamentary democracies, calling for a union of "anti-fascist" political groups, and participating in elections, in each case Communist parties gradually eliminated competing parties, beginning with underground resistance organizations that had been created where possible during the war. Arguably only a mass base of Communist support existed in Yugoslavia. At the same time, Communist parties grew in strength in several Western European states. Communists dominated the major trade-union organizations in Italy and France; they entered post-war governments in Belgium and Denmark. Communist wartime resistance against Nazi Germany helped swell the prestige of Communist parties, even as their close identification with the Soviet Union began to engender suspicion among political elites. France, Italy, and the German Federal Republic had right-center governments in which Catholic parties played a major role.

Divided Germany

The Allies oversaw the development of the political institutions of what became the German Federal Republic. Until 1951, all legislation passed by the Federal Republic had to be approved by the Western Allies. They carried out a process of de-Nazification, beginning with education, but did not undertake any major social reforms. This meant that the powerful industrial cartels remained in place, despite the Allies' agreement to the contrary at Potsdam. The devastation of the German economy seemed to necessitate leaving what was left of Germany's industrial base intact. The constitution of the German Federal Republic stated that parties obtaining a minimum of 5 percent of the popular vote in an election could be represented in the Federal Parliament (the Bundestag). This kept small parties, principally those of the extreme right, out of the parliament. (During the Weimar Republic, many small parties had contributed to political instability.) The Federal Constitutional Court banned neo-Nazi parties, and the Communist Party was outlawed as well. The Allies insisted that the German president's powers be limited to avoid the unrestricted executive power that had existed in Hitler's Germany. The president was elected for a term of five years by a federal assembly consisting of all members of the Bundestag and about the same number of delegates from each state. The chancellor, appointed by the president, became the effective head of state. The states of the Federal Republic elected representatives to an upper house (Bundesrat). Because the upper house could block legislation, this electoral process, too, strengthened the decentralization of political power in West Germany.

Konrad Adenauer (1876–1967), the Catholic mayor of Cologne, served as chancellor of the German Federal Republic until 1963. His wartime opposition to the Nazis, hostility to the Soviets and to East Germany, and his social conservatism reassured the Allies. Yet at the same time, Adenauer handed out positions to former Nazis and bent over backward to help Germans who had endured Allied reprisals for their service to the Nazi cause. In West Germany, the Allied program of "de-Nazification," intended to remove all former Nazis from positions of power and influence, overall had relatively little impact. It proved impossible to purge millions of people from government, industry, and education. The Allies concluded that Germany could not do without tens of thousands of experienced doctors, teachers, and engineers. Moreover, it would be difficult to distinguish between different degrees of Nazi commitment and action. Supported by smaller parties on the right, the Christian Democratic Union Party held power from 1949 until 1969, with the Social Democratic Party the chief opposition party. Adenauer forged a close alliance with France intended to serve as a bulwark against the Soviet Union.

In the meantime, the Cold War hastened the acceptance by the Western powers of the German Federal Republic and its rearmament in the Western alliance. In 1950 the Federal Republic became a nonvoting member of the Council of Europe. Moreover, bolstered by economic recovery and the total discrediting of the extreme political right wing, the German Federal Republic achieved full sovereignty and diplomatic respectability, joining NATO in 1955.

West Berliners looking across the mined "death strip," intended to discourage East Berliners from attempting to cross into the western zone, before the construction of the Berlin Wall, 1961.

The Soviet-occupied eastern zone of Germany became in 1949 the German Democratic Republic (GDR, or the DDR, also commonly known as East Germany). Walter Ulbricht (1893–1973), who had spent the war years in the Soviet Union, returned to Berlin with the Red Army and became secretary of the Communist Party. He remained, for all practical purposes, head of state until his forced retirement in 1971.

The GDR took over the administration of the eastern zone in 1955 from the Soviets, although its government continued to follow Soviet instructions. The Communist Party controlled most facets of cultural life. Many writers and artists left for West Germany, although the talented playwright Bertolt Brecht (1898–1956) remained.

Eastern Europe under the Soviet Shadow

As the Red Army stood near, the states of Eastern Europe fell under the domination of Soviet-backed Communist parties. The Bulgarian Communist Party had about 14,000 members in late 1944 and 422,000 in 1946; that of Poland 20,000 in mid-1944 and 300,000 a year later. Moreover, the Soviet Union at first went along with the tide of Eastern European nationalism, supporting, for example, the annexation of Transylvania by Romania, at the expense of Hungary. During 1945–1946, coalition governments (in which Communists participated) took over large estates and distributed land to peasants, transferring about half of the land of Poland and a third of that of Hungary.

From the beginning, parties that had collaborated with the Nazis and other right-wing groups were excluded from power. The Communists eliminated coalition partners, as in Czechoslovakia and Hungary, including socialist and peasant agrarian parties, or absorbed them. Thus, coalition governments elected or otherwise constituted at the end of the war disappeared one by one until the Communists controlled each state. In Hungary in 1947, two years after the Communist Party had been roundly defeated in elections, the Communists ousted the Smallholders, or Peasant Party, which had won 57 percent of the vote. In neighboring Romania, King Michael was forced out in similar circumstances. Bulgarian Communists won a contested victory in a plebiscite that established a "People's Republic," which quickly became a single-party state. After the first election in post-war Poland, where no party had collaborated with the Germans, Communists gradually pushed aside the Socialists, who constituted the other major party. The Soviets completely destroyed the Polish People's Party in Poland, as they did the Smallholders Party in Hungary. Thereafter, Communist governments controlled the bureaucracies that increased in size with state management of the economy—above all, the police—and implemented strict censorship. In what were rapidly becoming Soviet "satellite" states, the Communists benefited from the fact that the Nazis had decimated the political elites of Eastern Europe and the Balkans during the war.

Czechoslovakia alone in Central and Eastern Europe and the Balkans had not become a dictatorship between the wars. In the first post-war elections there in May 1946, Communists won more than a third of the vote. Two non-Communists, Eduard Beneš (1884–1948) and Jan Masaryk (1886–1948), served as president and foreign minister, respectively, in a coalition government. But in 1948 the Communists seized power, shutting down other political parties. Masaryk died after he jumped—or was pushed—from his office window.

From Moscow, Stalin engineered purges that swept away even loyal party members in the Eastern European nations. Political arrests in Hungary have been estimated at 200,000, at 180,000 in Romania, and 80,000 in tiny Albania. Widely publicized trials (including those of popular Catholic prelates in Hungary and Czechoslovakia), prison sentences, labor camps, and many executions followed. In six years, the Communists in Hungary executed perhaps a thousand political opponents among the more than 1.3 million people hauled before tribunals (from a population of 9.5 million). Purges included not only fascists but many Social Democrats and even Communists thought to oppose Stalinism. Stalin also tightened Moscow's grip on the fourteen non-Russian republics in the Soviet Union, purging "bourgeois nationalists" in several of them.

The Soviet Union and Its Satellites in the Post-War Era

Rebuilding the Soviet economy after World War II was a monumental task. After the Soviet Union's decidedly Pyrrhic victory, those who had managed to flee the war zones returned to devastated cities. Successive years of harvest failure from 1946 to 1947 compounded the extreme suffering. The highly centralized planning of the fourth Five-Year Plan, which began in 1945, allowed the Soviets to concentrate on key industries like coal and steel. Soviet planners benefited from the commandeering of industrial capital goods from Germany and Eastern Europe. Large-scale industrial production exceeded pre-war levels in 1950 by a comfortable margin, although such results were only modestly reflected in the quality of life of Soviet citizens.

Once they recovered from being forced to contribute resources to Soviet economic growth and from buying Soviet products at inflated prices, the Communist states of Eastern Europe benefited from Soviet technological assistance. Yet they were prevented from importing technology from the West and had to export raw materials and manufactured goods to the Soviet Union at below market prices. In 1949, the Soviet Union and its Eastern European allies formed the Council of Mutual Economic Assistance, which sought to coordinate economic planning. Industrial production rose most rapidly in Eastern Europe in the German Democratic Republic and Czechoslovakia. Bulgaria, Romania, and Yugoslavia also developed manufacturing bases.

The economic development of the German Democratic Republic, however short on freedom, was at first impressive. Before Soviet occupation, the eastern zone of Germany had had a small industrial base, but this industrial infrastructure had suffered the Soviet extraction of raw materials and machinery. The collectivization of industrial production then proceeded rapidly, and by 1952 the state employed three of every four workers. Despite the loss of many skilled workers to the German Federal Republic, East Germany emerged with the strongest economy of the Soviet Union's Eastern bloc; only Hungary boasted a similar standard of living by the 1960s. Steel production and shipbuilding, particularly, expanded rapidly in the 1950s and 1960s, as the German Democratic Republic fulfilled its assigned role in the Soviet government's plan for economic development in the Communist states. Nonetheless, to many East Germans conditions of life seemed more attractive in West Germany. Hundreds of thousands of people voted with their feet and left for West Germany.

The planned economies of the Soviet Union and its Eastern European allies could count some accomplishments, although adequate attention to the desires of their citizens was not one of them. The Soviet gross national product, which had stood at 36 percent of that of the United States in 1957, rose to about 50 percent of that of its rival in 1962, and it edged closer in the subsequent two decades. Yet the Soviet economy remained haunted by daunting inefficiency. The housing shortage remained acute into the 1960s, and families still had long waits for better apartments.

While Stalin promoted economic growth in the Communist states of Eastern Europe, economic policies furthered a division of labor whereby some of the Soviet satellite states produced agricultural products and others manufactured particular goods. The Soviet Union used the Eastern European economies to further Soviet economic interests through unfavorable trade arrangements. One by one, beginning with Bulgaria and Czechoslovakia in 1949, the states of Eastern Europe launched five-year plans based on the Soviet model. However, consumer goods of all kinds were de-emphasized until the mid-1950s, sacrificed, as had been the case in the Soviet Union before the war, to the drive for heavy industrialization that gave birth to enormous plants that produced steel and iron.

The collectivization of agriculture began in earnest, but this at first sharply reduced productivity. Like peasants in the Soviet Union during the early 1930s, hundreds of thousands of peasants in Eastern Europe resisted by rebellion, arson, sabotage, and simply by dragging their feet. Yet gradually there were increases in productivity. By the mid-1960s, state farms accounted for more than 80 percent of the land in the German Democratic Republic, Bulgaria, Romania, and Czechoslovakia. In Poland, in sharp contrast, more than 85 percent of the land remained in private hands because the Polish Communist leadership feared open popular resistance to massive agricultural collectivization.

In Yugoslavia, Communist leader Tito refused to permit Soviet domination of his multinational country. In 1948, Tito broke with the Soviet Union. Over the next decades, Yugoslavia received millions of dollars in Western aid. The Yugoslav economy remained "mixed" in the sense that the private sector coexisted with state planning. Workers were permitted more self-administration through workers' councils or committees. In the 1950s, the collectivization of agriculture, which had begun after the war, was abandoned, with farmers retaking their old plots. Yugoslavia's economy improved, despite shortages and great inequalities among its six republics.

In the Soviet Union, Stalin had emerged from the war with his authority within the Communist Party unchallenged and with enormous prestige. But weakened by arteriosclerosis, Stalin's paranoia became virtually psychotic as he ordered more purges in the name of the Communist Party. The ruthless Lavrenty Beria (1899–1953), head of the omnipresent secret police, used a gold-plated phone to order arrests. Between 1948 and 1952, some prominent Jewish intellectuals and artists were tried and executed or simply disappeared, targeted because some were believed to have had contacts with the West. In 1953, Stalin died. Beria's subsequent arrest, trial, and execution signaled an end to the Stalinist period.

The Soviet Union entered a period of "collective leadership," a concept that had been abandoned during Stalin's personal dictatorship. Decisions were made by the fourteen members of the Presidium (a permanent executive committee) of the Communist Party, which included Georgy Malenkov (1902–1988), a pragmatist who had been trained as an engineer and who believed that Stalin's dictatorship had hampered the Soviet economy. Meanwhile, the coarse, rotund Nikita Khrushchev (1894–1971), the son of a miner in a family of peasants, advanced within the Communist Party. He was part of a "technocratic" faction, but he was also a successful party organizer. In 1955, Khrushchev, with support from within the Soviet bureaucracy, won the upper hand in his struggle with Malenkov for power. While maintaining an emphasis on heavy industry, Khrushchev also concentrated on planning and investing in Soviet agriculture, a sector that had never recovered from the effects of forced collectivization. He understood that the production of consumer goods would have to take a more prominent place in economic planning. The quality of life for most Soviet citizens began to improve gradually, although not as fast as that of highly placed Communist Party members, who sported cars and comfortable country houses.

The Soviet people were largely unaware of the power struggles fought in secrecy within the Kremlin. Like Western "sovietologists"—specialists who studied the Soviet Union—they could only chart the waxing and waning of party leaders' authority by their ranking or the omission of their names on official lists, or by their placement among the gray heads on the giant reviewing stand in Red Square during the annual May Day military parade.

In February 1956, Khrushchev denounced Stalin's "cult of personality" and his ruthless purges in an unpublished but widely cited speech delivered at the Twentieth Party Congress. Such direct criticism was unprecedented in the history of the Soviet Union. Khrushchev accepted the fact that different paths to socialism could exist in different countries. He allowed the national republics within the Soviet Union more authority over their own affairs and gave intellectuals and artists in the republics more freedom to develop non-Russian cultural interests. A brief relaxation of censorship permitted the publication of books that offered brutally frank critiques of the Stalin years.

However, the strict centralization of government and its domination by the Communist Party continued. The party's authority over the republics remained for the most part in the hands of ethnic Russians. The thaw in censorship soon ended. Censors banned *Doctor Zhivago* (completed in 1956 and translated in 1958) by Boris Pasternak (1890–1960). Published in Italy and winning the Nobel Prize for literature, it offered a nuanced picture of tsarist Russia and therefore implicitly stood as a criticism of the Soviet regime. Soviet artists and filmmakers, too, were reined in, although some remained daring and imaginative within the confines of official toleration.

As the Soviet Union's economic difficulties continued and the sixth Five-Year Plan floundered badly, Khrushchev blamed its failure on excessive centralization of planning and administration. His political rivals, however, blamed him. In 1957, Khrushchev ousted Malenkov, Vyacheslav Molotov, and the premier, Nikolai Bulganin (1895–1975), from key party positions.

CHANGING CONTOURS OF LIFE

Since World War II, the economic transformations in Europe have engendered several major social changes. Trade and technology led to an increasing interconnectedness and interdependence of global economies. The workforce changed as the percentage of population working the land fell sharply and more and more women began to work outside the home in careers that had traditionally been off-limits to them. Consumerism began to thrive, and goods that might have been considered luxury items just a few decades earlier became readily available.

Intellectual Currents in the Post-War Era

Outside of a sense of relief, there seemed little about which to be optimistic at the end of World War II. The British writer George Orwell summed up the general feeling when he wrote, "Since about 1930, the world had given no reason for optimism whatsoever. Nothing in sight except a welter of lies, cruelty, hatred, and ignorance." Unlike the period immediately following World War I, few people now believed that another total war was inconceivable. Many writers and artists seemed overwhelmed with pessimism, even hopelessness, in the face of the atomic age and the Cold War (see Chapter 28). Claiming "alienation" from the society they increasingly criticized, many Western intellectuals withdrew into introspection. However, for some, communism still seemed to offer a plan for the harmonious organization of society.

French existentialism became an influential cultural current during the first two decades following the war. The French philosopher Jean-Paul Sartre (1905–1980) believed that in the wake of the unparalleled destruction of World War II, the absurdity of life was the most basic discovery one could make. Denying the existence of God, existentialists like Sartre posited that life has no meaning. Their conclusion was that a person could only truly find any fulfillment while living "a suspended death" by becoming aware of his or her freedom to choose and to act. Sartre titled one of his plays *Huis clos* (*No Exit*), as he believed there was nothing beyond this life. Sartre's novels glorify the individual spirit seeking freedom, not through Enlightenment rationalism, but rather through a comprehension of life's irrationality. However, Sartre believed that violent revolution could free the individual from the human condition by allowing him or her to find truth by redefining reality. To this end, he joined the French Communist Party when the war was over. However, existentialism slowly lost its grip on French intellectual life, at least in part because of growing disillusionment with the Soviet Union among many leftist intellectuals.

The Algerian-born French writer Albert Camus (1913–1960) shared Sartre's view of mankind's tragic situation, but broke with Sartre in 1952 over the latter's enthusiasm for Stalin's Soviet Union. Camus's answer to the dark world of brutality reflected by the war (during which he participated in the resistance) and the frustrations of the post-war period was for the individual to search for meaning in life by choosing a path of action—even revolt—against absurdity, irrationality, and tyrannies of all kinds. The rebel should act, according to Camus, from a personal sense of responsibility and moral choice independent of belief in God or in a political system. Confronting the arrival of murderous disease in the Algerian city of Oran, Dr. Rieux, the central figure in Camus's *The Plague* (1947), does not believe in God or absolute standards of morality, but he nonetheless helps people respond to the epidemic.

The "theater of the absurd," which also reflected intellectuals' reaction to the horrors of the war, was centered in Paris from 1948 to about 1968. It offered highly unconventional and anti-rational plays. The Irish-born Samuel Beckett (1906–1989) and other playwrights sought to shock audiences with provocative themes and by stringing together seemingly unrelated events and dialogue to demonstrate that existence is without purpose—absurd. They rejected plots, conventional settings, and individual identities. Their clownish, mechanical characters are perpetual exiles alienated in a bizarre, nightmarish world that makes no sense. The lack of causality in these plays is a

A gathering of intellectuals after the war, including Jean-Paul Sartre (seated left), Albert Camus (seated center), Pablo Picasso (standing with arms folded), and Simone de Beauvoir (to the far right and standing next to some of Picasso's work).

commentary on life itself. Beckett's *Waiting for Godot* (begun in 1948 but not published in French until 1952 and in English two years later) tells a disconnected tale of two old derelicts, Vladimir and Estragon (although they call themselves by childish nicknames). They meet night after night in anticipation of the arrival of a certain Godot (perhaps intended to be a diminutive of God), though it is never clear what difference in their lives his arrival would ever make, if any. He never comes, so we never know.

Anti-Americanism emerged as a current among many European intellectuals in the post-war period. This reflected hostility to U.S. foreign and nuclear policy during the Cold War and fear of American domination of NATO. The U.S. placement of nuclear weapons in Western Europe, beginning in West Germany in 1955, generated both anti-nuclear organizations and protests. Intellectuals also criticized U.S. culture as reeking of vulgar materialism. There was an economic dimension to this struggle, as U.S. companies and products dramatically augmented their presence in Western Europe. None generated more controversy than Coca-Cola. During the early 1950s, the French government feared the competition that Coke could give the wine industry. Encouraged by the powerful wine lobby, the French government tried—ultimately without success—to keep Coke from the French market.

Yet Europe also continued to embrace some aspects of U.S. culture. World War II brought only a brief hiatus in the export to Europe of Hollywood films, which audiences flocked to see. American film stars became those of the continent (at the same time, some European actors and actresses, such as Richard Burton, Marlene Dietrich, Sophia Loren, Audrey Hepburn, and Elizabeth Taylor became stars in the United States). Yet Western European filmmakers made important contributions to cinema. While most American film producers emphasized light entertainment (such as westerns and war movies with special effects), Italy's Federico Fellini (*La Strada*, 1956, and *La Dolce Vita*, 1959) and Sweden's Ingmar Bergman (*The Seventh Seal*, 1956) turned out serious art films. French New Wave directors, including Jean-Luc Godard (*Breathless*, 1959) and François Truffaut (*400 Blows*, 1959), rebelled against traditional cinematographic techniques, using innovations such as jump cuts and disruptive editing to create a sense of dislocation. Their experimental films explored human relationships and often portrayed antiheroes. In contrast, the English producer and director Alfred Hitchcock (1899–1980) frightened and intrigued generations of audiences with riveting suspense films like *Psycho* (1960).

In France, some films took subjects from recent and sometimes painful history, notably Gilles Pontecorvo's *The Battle of Algiers* (1961), in which appeared some actual participants of the Algerian insurrection (see pp. 1169–1171), to which the film is sympathetic. Marcel Orphuls's documentary about collaboration and resistance in World War II France, *The Sorrow and the Pity* (1969), helped spur the rethinking of the extent of French collaboration with the Nazis during the Vichy years.

Intellectuals of the left were preoccupied by the possibilities of social liberation. Frantz Fanon (1925–1961), a black French social critic from Martinique, explored the revolutionary potential of the Third World, some of which were unaligned in the Cold War, in *The Wretched of the Earth* (1961). The French anthropologist Claude Lévi-Strauss (1908–) espoused cultural relativism, moving anthropology away from a Western-centered view of "peripheral" or "underdeveloped" regions with his work on Brazil and Southeast Asia. Lévi-Strauss's interest in how communities behave, too, led away from the emphasis on the individual that characterized both Freudianism and existentialism.

Intellectuals in the Soviet Union were stymied by the state. Writers, artists, and filmmakers confronted a state apparatus that made the costs of free expression so high that voluntary adherence to state-dictated norms followed. "Socialist realism" (art and literature of generally horrendous quality, intended to inspire the population by showing smiling Soviet citizens at work; see Chapter 25) was the only authorized form of artistic expression; the works of most Western artists were condemned as tools of capitalism. Art was intended to encourage devotion to and sacrifice for the state. Stalin gave official approval to the crackpot theories of the geneticist Trofim Lysenko (1898–1976), who insisted that knowledge or beliefs that were experienced by one generation could be genetically inherited. Stalin's particular interest in this theory was that it suggested that party members who learned official orthodoxy and experienced conformity in social behavior would pass on the same characteristics to their offspring.

Advances for Women

In the decades following World War II, the status of women gradually improved, although their situation varied across the continent. While women lost some skilled jobs to men returning from service after the war, economic expansion and the creation of more white-collar jobs provided new employment possibilities. Simone de Beauvoir's *The Second Sex* (1949) helped mobilize movements for the rights of women in the United States and, more slowly, in Europe. In Western countries, the important contribution of working women made it difficult to continue to deny half the population the right to vote. After the war, women received the suffrage in France, Italy, Belgium, and Portugal. Women probably were more equal in the countries of the Soviet bloc (where there were no free elections) in terms of employment opportunities, although in practice this often meant that they bore the dual burden of wage earning and domestic duties. In the Soviet Union and Sweden, women made up more than half of all employees, and more than a third in every European country. In Western Europe, more and more middle-class women began to work full-time. Beginning in 1977, French women no longer needed their husbands' permission to work. In Communist countries, women more easily entered the medical profession, but men dominated the state bureaucracies. Women were most successful in reaching rough equality in the Scandinavian countries, least so in the Mediterranean lands where traditional biases remained difficult to overcome.

At the same time, the number of female university students rose dramatically, and so did the number of women in the professions. Women received legal protection against job discrimination in England in the late 1960s, and in France the government created a Ministry for the Status of Women.

Feminism, reviving during the 1968 protests, helped the cause of women's rights. Gradually, the percentage of women serving in legislatures increased. Moreover, gays and lesbians gained more rights beginning in the 1970s, even if some countries retained laws permitting discrimination against them.

Catholicism in Modern Europe

Like the nations of Western Europe, the Catholic Church, for centuries a major force in European life, has been forced to confront pressure for change. Within the Catholic Church, a liberal current of thought and action developed in response to some of the social problems of modern life. "Worker priests" entered factories in the 1950s, trying to win back workers to the Church while supporting their demands for better working conditions, until the pope condemned the movement. The election in 1958 of the more liberal Pope John XXIII signaled a new direction, marked by the opening of dialogue with other religions. Pope John presided over a council (Vatican II) that undertook significant changes in Church practices, allowing the Mass to be said in local languages and appointing more cardinals from other places than Europe and North America, without altering dogma.

Pope John's successor Paul VI continued the move toward ecumenism, visiting Istanbul and Jerusalem to meet with leaders of the Eastern Orthodox churches. But several notable theologians who challenged Church doctrine drew the wrath of Rome. In 1978, Paul died, as did his successor, John Paul I, after only two months on the throne of Saint Peter. The puffs of white smoke rising from the Vatican chimney then announced the first non-Italian pope since the sixteenth century, the Polish-born Pope John Paul II (Karol Wojtyla, 1920–2005; succeeded by Benedict XVI). While remaining conservative on matters of faith and doctrine, the new pope traveled far and wide across the world, calling for social justice. He became a symbol of hope for millions of oppressed people. If the percentages of Catholics practicing their religion fell rapidly in France, Italy, and Spain, the Catholic Church retained particular allegiance in Poland, Croatia, Portugal, and Ireland. Yet even these solidly Catholic countries legalized divorce, despite ecclesiastical opposition.

An industrial chaplain speaks with a factory worker in Scotland, in an effort to liberalize the Catholic Church and bring it into modern life.

An Urban World

Europe rapidly urbanized following World War II. In the German industrial Rhineland, it became difficult to tell where one city ended and another began. Giant cities like London and Paris engulfed their surrounding regions. In Eastern Europe, the population living in cities increased from 37.5 million at the end of the 1940s to 58 million twenty years later.

The necessity of housing millions of new urban residents contributed to a uniformity of architectural style. Tall, drab, uniform towers filled with small apartments sprang up in and around major urban centers, providing adequate lodging, but not much more, in cramped quarters with thin walls. Commuting became a fact of urban life in much of Europe. By the 1980s, almost 20 percent of the French population resided in Paris and its surroundings. Of this 20 percent, only about 3 million lived in the City of Light itself, the rest inhabiting sprawling suburbs.

In the early 1960s, the Soviets began to build new suburbs and satellite towns to accommodate the population seeking to live in Moscow, which grew from 2 million in 1926 to more than 5 million in 1959. Leningrad's population increased from 1.7 million to 3.3 million during the same period.

Rapid urban growth, closely tied to the concentration of large-scale industries, posed problems of health and safety. Factories increasingly polluted the air of industrial regions. Moreover, the number of cars on the road increased from 5 million in 1948 to 44 million in 1965. The construction of new freeways and toll roads could not begin to keep up with the increase in traffic. The traffic jam in Europe began, as cities became increasingly clogged with automobiles, which also polluted the air. Nonetheless, projects of urban renewal enhanced the quality of life in cities and towns. West German, Belgian, French, and Dutch cities, among others, sported shining urban centers, with some streets reserved for beleaguered pedestrians tired of dodging onrushing cars and the aggressive chaos of honking horns.

Living Better

The transportation and communications revolutions made the world a much smaller place. With a gradual reduction in the workday and higher wages, families had more time and money for leisure. Travel became an essential part of life. Air travel gradually linked European cities to each other and to other continents. With the introduction of the passenger jet in the late 1950s, the airplane replaced the passenger ship for cross-Atlantic travel. The era of the shipboard romance was over.

The rapid rise of international tourism offers another example of economic globalization. Jumbo jets greatly increased the number of passengers who could be squeezed into a single plane, reducing the cost of tickets. The era of the charter flight began in the 1960s. Tourists from the United States and, beginning in the 1980s, from Japan, arrived in Europe in droves. North American, Asian, and African destinations became more common for Europeans.

The French and British governments collaborated on the development of the supersonic Concorde, which, in the late 1970s, began to fly a small number of extremely wealthy passengers from Paris and London to New York and Washington, D.C., in three hours and fifteen minutes, less than half the time of a regular jet. However, an aging fleet, a disastrous crash near a Paris airport, and years of financial losses ended supersonic travel by Concorde in 2003. Far more successful, the first high-speed trains (the TGVs) began service in France in 1981. They carry passengers in comfort at speeds well over 170 miles per hour. Other countries, too, developed fast trains. In 1994, the "Chunnel" opened, a thirty-mile tunnel linking France and Great Britain by trains running under the English Channel, putting London little more than two hours away from Paris and Brussels.

Beginning in the 1960s, millions of Europeans began to take to the road, above all in July and August, many heading toward the sunny beaches of southern Europe. Paid vacations became an expected part of the "good life." Tourism became essential to the economies of France, Spain, Italy, Portugal, and Greece.

American consumerism and popular culture found increasing favor in European societies. Supermarkets began to put many small grocery stores out of business. American words and terms crept into European languages. Tennis shoes and tee-shirts swept Europe, and so did American television shows. By the late 1970s, McDonald's had begun to dot European capitals and gradually smaller cities as well. In the 1980s, EuroDisney (now called Disneyland-Paris), opened its doors outside of Paris. One French theatrical director called it "a cultural Chernobyl" (referring to the nuclear accident in Ukraine in 1986). In the first decade of the new century, Starbuck's cafés began to arrive in Europe in increasing numbers.

Communications also underwent an amazing revolution in Europe as elsewhere. Household telephones became more common in the 1960s in most of Western Europe. Forty years later, cell phones had taken over, increasingly putting telephone booths out of business. (Reacting to the annoyance of people shouting into portable phones on trains and street corners and in restaurants, or while driving, one wag noted that he had had great faith in humanity until the arrival of the cell phone.) The cost of transatlantic phone calls fell rapidly with the advent of optical fiber in the 1980s. Then in the 1990s the computer revolution and the Internet put a world of information at the fingertips of Europeans, as well as people almost everywhere.

Television helped shape a mass consumer culture, catapulting entertainers to fame and making household names of politicians who could be heard instead of simply imagined. The first television sets had been viewed at the World's Fair in New York City in 1939. By the late 1960s, a majority of Western European households had a television, and by the mid-1970s, relatively

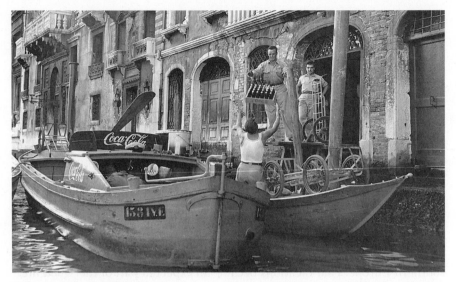

Delivering Coca-Cola in Venice.

few were without one. In the mid-1980s, the U.S.-based CNN network began to reach across the world. Just as television coverage of dramatic news events could be seen around the world, so sports took on an increasingly global dimension as well (above all, the World Cup and the Olympics, but also games of the National Basketball Association, with the globalization of that sport).

The era of television and radio ended the great age of the newspaper. During the first years after the war, Europeans read more—and arguably better—newspapers than ever before or since. As Europeans increasingly received their news and their entertainment from television and radio, however, newspapers merged and many folded. With the exception of the stately, serious dailies like *Le Monde* of Paris, the British *Manchester Guardian*, the German *Frankfurter Allgemeine*, and *La Stampa* of Milan, an increasing number of tabloid papers relied upon sensationalism, scandals, and the proclamation of juicy unsubstantiated rumor as truth to attract readers. In the Soviet Union, where the state was the only source of printed news, more than 7 million copies of *Pravda* were printed every day.

Credit cards and then personal computers transformed the way people make purchases. In the context of the ongoing revolution in communications, the advent of computer viruses demonstrated the extent to which the world has become increasingly interconnected. The apparent vulnerability of even the most sophisticated computer systems to knowledgeable hackers has led to fears for national security systems. In this way, too, Europe entered a new era.

Oil and the Global Economy

The Six-Day Arab-Israeli War of 1967 and the 1973 Yom Kippur War both resulted in easy Israeli victories over their Arab rivals. Israel now held all of Jerusalem, a holy city for Christians, Jews, and Arabs, and occupied the West Bank and the Gaza Strip. While the United States has almost always supported Israeli actions, the plight of the stateless Palestinian people has attracted the attention of Arab states, in particular. In 1973, following a short, unsuccessful war against Israel by its Arab neighbors, the oil-producing Arab states began an embargo of the supply of oil from the Middle East; it was undertaken by the Organization of Petroleum Exporting Countries (OPEC).

The Arab oil embargo led to a rapid rise in the price of oil and contributed to the high inflation that undermined Western economies for the rest of the 1970s. Dependency on oil led states to urge people to consume less gasoline (for example, by encouraging greater use of public transportation and, in the United States, by reducing speed limits). Britain and Norway each began to extract oil in the stormy North Sea. Some European countries, especially France, had already begun to develop nuclear installations to generate more energy.

The oil crisis helped bring an end to what had been a long period of relative prosperity and stability. The subsequent rising energy prices undermined

British motorists waiting for gasoline during the Arab oil embargo in 1973. The sign on the left indicates that French motorists are welcome to wait as well.

the ability of European states to support their extensive social services. The oil crisis also helped cause the economic recession that gripped Western Europe from the mid-1970s to the mid-1980s. Inflation, which had been at modest levels during the 1950s and 1960s but had been accentuated by the U.S. war in Vietnam, then began to soar. The oil embargo brought unemployment, which also strained European welfare budgets.

Conclusion

The end of World War II engendered two major changes that largely defined international politics for the next decades. First, the post-war division of Europe into zones of U.S. influence in the West and Soviet domination in the East brought a Cold War between the two superpowers, in which Western European states, Soviet Eastern European and Balkan satellites, and so-called Third World, or unaligned countries, most of them underdeveloped, became caught up. Second, sacrifices made by the colonies of the European great powers during the war—including military service and considerable loss of life—encouraged national liberation movements. These movements and the resistance they encountered from colonial powers led to a dramatic period of decolonization.

THE COLD WAR AND THE END OF EUROPEAN EMPIRES

The post-war period brought two major developments to Western Europe. Tensions between the Soviet Union and the Western Allies, which could be seen by the end of World War II, quickly degenerated into a "Cold War" that on several occasions threatened to become a hot one, and potentially even a nuclear war. Second, the end of the war accelerated movements for independence in the colonies of the imperial powers. During the first two decades following World War II, most of the colonies of the Western powers achieved independence, sometimes after protracted wars of independence. Decolonization brought the end of European overseas empires. It greatly expanded the number of sovereign states, particularly in Asia and Africa. The Cold War and the process of decolonization were linked, as the Western Powers and the Soviet Union and China both sought to make their influence predominant in emerging post-colonial states.

COLD WAR

In a speech in March 1946, Churchill lamented that "an iron curtain is drawn down upon their front. We do not know what is going on behind." As Europe counted its millions of dead, hot war gave way to the Cold War between East and West. The Red Army's drive into Central Europe in the waning months of the war had left part of Central Europe and Eastern Europe and the Balkans under Soviet domination. The division of Europe into two camps—Communist, dominated by the Soviet Union, and Western democracies, under the influence of the United States—was formalized by the creation of corresponding military alliances after the war. The

Cold War helped prevent any possible return to the relative isolationism that had characterized the United States during the inter-war period. The United States, now by far the wealthiest state in the world, had 450 military bases in 36 countries in 1955. At the same time, the Soviet Union rapidly added to its military arsenal, soon having the second largest navy in the world.

Germany became the first focal point for Cold War tensions. The failure of the Soviet, British, French, and U.S. foreign ministers to agree on the nature of a peace treaty with Germany in the spring of 1947 began the Cold War. That year Stalin, who had in 1943 officially announced the end of the Comintern, which had been established with the goal of fomenting world-wide revolution, inaugurated its successor organization, the Cominform. It was intended to consolidate Soviet authority in the states of Eastern Europe (see Chapter 27). This, too, accentuated tensions with the Western powers. In 1949, the Soviet-occupied eastern zone of Germany became the German Democratic Republic; the American, British, and French occupation zones became the German Federal Republic. The barbed wire and minefields that divided these zones reflected the ideological division between them. In the meantime, both the Soviet Union and the Western powers worked quickly to create intelligence agencies of great size to spy on the other.

Each international crisis between the Soviet Union and the United States took on great significance because scientists had developed bombs many

The U.S. airlift to Berlin, 1948–1949.

times more destructive than those that had leveled Hiroshima and Nagasaki. During the 1950s, children in the United States participated in mock air raid drills, putting their heads between their knees to practice bracing for the shock of a nuclear explosion, as if such a position would make the slightest difference in the case of a nuclear attack. The United States and the Soviet Union drew up plans to evacuate American and Soviet leaders into elaborate shelters from which they could order the launching of more missiles and bombs. Britain exploded its first atomic bomb in 1952, France in 1960. China, too, before long had "the bomb." In the 1970s, Israel, India, and Pakistan gained nuclear capability.

The Cold War focused on a series of crises that, drawing world attention, exacerbated tensions between the United States and the Soviet Union. The Soviet Union claimed that the Western Allies had unilaterally broken agreements reached at the Potsdam Conference. In July 1948, Soviet troops blocked trains and truck routes through the Soviet zone of occupation in East Germany to prevent supplies from reaching the Allied half of Berlin. The Allies began a massive airlift of supplies to West Berlin; at times, planes landed in Berlin every three minutes, bringing much-needed food, medicine, and other necessities. After secret negotiations, Stalin backed down, allowing trucks to roll through the German Democratic Republic beginning in 1949, the year of that state's creation. Berlin remained divided into eastern and western zones.

A Greek soldier stands guard during the Civil War in 1947.

In Greece, the departure of German troops led to a bloody civil war that lasted until 1949, pitting Greek Communists against an alliance of forces that supported the monarchy. The Soviet Union held to an agreement made with Churchill in 1944 not to intervene militarily, but it provided the Communists with considerable material assistance. The United States and Britain aided the monarchist forces, who finally prevailed in 1949 and then banned the Communist Party.

The Cold War soon reached Asia. Japan's defeat left China divided between the nationalist government of Chiang Kai-shek (1887–1975), which held the south, and the forces of the Communist leader Mao Zedong (1893–1976). In the civil war that followed, Mao's Communist forces gradually pushed the nationalist forces out of China. In full retreat by 1949, Chiang Kai-shek's army occupied the large island of Formosa (Taiwan). There Chiang established a government that claimed to represent all of China. On the mainland, Mao proclaimed the People's Republic of China. The Soviet Union quickly recognized the new, giant Communist state, while the United States recognized the nationalist government of Taiwan as China's legitimate government. In the atmosphere of the Cold War, the United States and its allies worried they would be facing a unified Communist front that included China.

People in Beijing welcome Chinese Communist forces, 1949. Note the portrait of Mao Zedong in the center.

The Korean War (1950–1953)

Adjoining China, Korea had a Communist "people's republic" in the north, supported by the Soviet Union, and in the south, a republic created under the patronage of the United States. In June 1950, North Korean troops, upon Stalin's go-ahead, invaded the southern zone. General Douglas MacArthur took command of the U.S. forces defending South Korea, backed by small contingents sent by other members of the United Nations, which had passed a resolution condemning the Communist invasion. For the first time—with the exception of events in Greece—Communist and non-Communist forces engaged in open warfare, a conflict fought with conventional weapons, but with nuclear bombs lurking in the background.

Although Chinese troops were aiding the northern side, U.S. forces pushed back the Communist forces in 1951. In any case, neither side wanted to see the war expand beyond Korea. The armistice signed in July 1953 left the division between North and South Korea almost the same as before the war, but at the cost of 3 million casualties (including 140,000 U.S. troops killed or wounded).

The Korean War heightened Cold War tensions in Europe. To the Allies, the war raised the outside possibility of a Soviet-led invasion of the German Federal Republic, similar to that launched by North Korean troops against South Korea. In the United States, the war contributed to a mood

U.S. marines file past a burning building in North Korea during the Korean War, 1950.

of anti-communism and fear of "the enemy within" that bordered on mass hysteria, orchestrated by Senator Joseph McCarthy. "McCarthyism" entered the dictionary as a term for political name-calling and persecution.

Stirrings in Eastern Europe

Following Stalin's death in 1953, East German workers complained loudly about high quotas, low wages, and food shortages. On June 17, 1953, Berlin workers rioted. East German troops, backed by Soviet tanks, ended the disturbances. A wave of repression followed. That year alone, more than 330,000 East Germans fled to the West.

The East German Communist government realized that state planning had to provide more consumer goods. Ideology alone could not generate commitment. The Soviet Union sent material assistance to the German Democratic Republic and let it write off most of the war reparations owed from the eastern zone. Despite inadequate housing, few automobiles, and occasional food shortages, more consumer goods gradually became available in the 1960s. Long rows of drab apartments sprang up near the Brandenburg Gate that divided East and West Berlin. State-sponsored clubs for children provided recreation, as well as ideological indoctrination. Through intensive training and programming—and, in some cases, steroids—East Germany began in the late 1960s to produce athletes of great accomplishment in international sporting events, particularly in swimming and track and field.

Khrushchev's denunciation of Stalin and the "thaw" in foreign and domestic policies had repercussions in Eastern Europe in 1956. That year the Communist government of Poland reined in the secret police and gave amnesty to thousands of political prisoners. However, strikes soon brought military repression. In October 1956, Wladyslaw Gomulka (1905–1982), a moderate imprisoned during the Stalin era, returned from oblivion to head the government by the Polish Politburo. A reformer, Gomulka purged Stalinists and reached accommodation with the enormously influential Polish Catholic Church. Furthermore, Gomulka halted the collectivization of agriculture. Independent peasants held three-quarters of the nation's arable land, a far greater percentage of privately held farms than in any other country in the Eastern bloc. However, Gomulka also reassured the Soviet Union that Poland had no intention of abandoning the Warsaw Pact or turning its back on socialism.

Soviet concessions to Yugoslavia and Poland encouraged a movement for reform in Hungary, where liberal Communists were already eager to turn their backs on Stalinism. Imre Nagy (c. 1895–1958), a liberal, had risen to become prime minister of Hungary. He had sought to move Hungarian manufacturing away from heavy industry in order to increase production of consumer goods. Nagy also tolerated peasant resistance to the implementation of agricultural collectivization. At the same time, workers' councils sprung up spontaneously, espousing reform. In 1955, Nagy's policies drew opposition from Communist hard-liners, and he was ousted from office. A profound movement for reform now took root in Hungary. Intellectuals and students held meetings to discuss possible paths to liberalization. A defiant response from the new prime minister led to a demonstration of 50,000 people on October 23, 1956. Protesters smashed a statue of Stalin. Police opened fire on a crowd trying to storm a radio station. Hungarian troops sent to rout the demonstrators refused to fire, in some cases joining those now protesting communism itself. That night, the Hungarian Communist leadership requested Soviet assistance but also named Nagy as prime minister in the hope of ending the demonstrations. Western radio broadcasts heard in Hungary hinted that outside help might be forthcoming, firming popular resolve. Nagy named a new coalition government that included liberal Communists. He began to negotiate with the Soviet government, but he made clear that he intended to end the one-party system by adding several non-Communists to his government. Furthermore, he called for Hungarian withdrawal from the Warsaw Pact and asked that Soviet troops be removed from his country.

To the Soviet government, Hungary's defection was unthinkable because it might spark similar movements in other Eastern European nations and even destabilize the republics of the Soviet Union. On November 4, Nagy announced that Hungary would withdraw from the Warsaw Pact. While the French, British, and U.S. governments were preoccupied with the Suez Canal crisis (see pp. 1164–1167), the Soviet government sent tanks and soldiers into Budapest and other major Hungarian cities to crush resistance. Nagy was tried and executed, along with about 2400 other people, perhaps many more. From 1956 through 1961, almost 400,000 people were found guilty of political crimes. More than 200,000 Hungarians fled to Western Europe and the United States. Soviet intervention ended hope that Stalin's death might bring about change in Eastern Europe and end the Cold War. János Kádár (1912–1989) became Hungary's new leader, backed by the Soviet army. Over the long run, Kádár skillfully liberalized the Communist regime, while remaining careful not to antagonize unnecessarily the Soviet Union with any ideological justification for his policies. He relaxed government control if the interests of the Communist Party were not at stake. Hungary's "goulash communism" included market-oriented, decentralized reforms and toleration of some degree of entrepreneurship and profit. The result was a higher standard of living than existed elsewhere in the Communist world.

With their hands full with Hungary, the Soviets were in no position to move aggressively against Poland. In any case, Gomulka was careful to give them no excuse for military action. He gradually rescinded some of the relatively liberal policies, including toleration of free artistic and political expression, and put workers' councils that had sprung up in 1956 under party control.

In Yugoslavia, despite its determined independence from the Soviet Union, open political opposition was not tolerated. One of the distinguished founders of post-war Yugoslavia, the Montenegrin intellectual Milovan Djilas (1911–1995), was expelled from the party in 1954 for having contended in his book *The New Class: An Analysis of the Communist System* (1961) that privileged party officials had become a ruling caste, with little in common with ordinary people.

In the meantime, in the Soviet Union the liberal agitation in Poland and the Hungarian Revolution in 1956 threatened Khrushchev's authority. Stalinists claimed that Khrushchev's attack on Stalin at the Twentieth Party Congress in 1956 was to blame for agitation in those countries. Furthermore, Soviet aid to stabilize its Eastern European client states undermined economic development at home. But, at the same time, the failure of the Western powers to intervene on behalf of Hungary—because they feared nuclear war with the Soviet Union—seemed to the Soviets to legitimize the division of Europe into spheres of influence dominated by the United States and the Soviet Union.

Soviet–U.S. Tensions

Khrushchev was responsible for a mild thaw in the Cold War. The Soviet leader claimed that "peaceful coexistence" was possible between the two political worlds. In 1955, Khrushchev met with U.S. President Dwight Eisenhower (1890–1969) in Geneva, the first of the "summit" meetings between the two great powers. At the Twentieth Party Congress the following year, Khrushchev rejected Stalin's contention that Communist and capitalist powers would inevitably go to war. Soviet foreign policy became less contentious and somewhat more flexible. Looking to the Third World for allies, the Soviet leader courted India, Egypt, and Syria, as well as a number of smaller states, winning their friendship with technical and material assistance. Soviet foreign policy was carried out with the aim of detaching countries from the direct influence of the United States.

In 1955, the Soviet Union and its Eastern European allies countered NATO, the defense organization of the Western powers, by signing the Warsaw Pact, which offered its members similar guarantees to those of NATO against attack. It formalized and internationalized the individual pacts of mutual defense that the Soviet Union had signed with its client states during or immediately following World War II. The Warsaw Pact provided a new justification for the stationing of Soviet troops in Poland, Hungary, Czechoslovakia, and East Germany.

Soviet armed intervention in Hungary in 1956 increased mutual suspicion between East and West, and rapid advances in Soviet military science further augmented the rivalry with the West. Bilateral negotiations between the Soviet Union and the United States to reduce their respective nuclear capabilities failed in 1955 and again in 1958. In 1957, the Soviets launched the first satellite (*Sputnik*) after developing an intercontinental ballistic missile (ICBM). Space exploration became part of the Cold War. The United States won the race to the moon, when American astronauts landed on the lunar surface in July 1969, an event seen by millions on television.

In May 1960, the Soviets shot down an American U-2 plane taking spy photographs from high over the Soviet Union. The Soviets demanded an apology for this violation of Soviet air space and received none. Khrushchev then refused to participate in a Geneva summit meeting (probably also because Soviet relations with China were rapidly deteriorating).

Again Cold War tensions centered on Germany. In 1958, the hot-tempered Khrushchev threatened to hand over to East German authorities the administration of all of Berlin, but backed down in the face of Allied intransigence. In the meantime, streams of East Germans—about 2.6 million people between 1950 and 1962—left for the West, most to the German Federal Republic. The exodus included many doctors and other trained specialists vital to East Germany. Yet between 1950 and 1964, about 500,000 West Germans moved to the East, some fleeing the persecution of Communists in the German Federal Republic, and others simply wanting to be with their families.

On August 17, 1961, Berliners awoke to find East German workers building a wall to divide the eastern sector from the western one. Ground floor windows that permitted escape from East to West were boarded up. Telephone lines leading to West Berlin were cut.

The Berlin Wall became a symbol of the Cold War. U.S. President John F. Kennedy visited Berlin later that summer to view the wall, proclaiming in a speech that he, too, was a "Berliner" (not realizing that a Berliner was also a popular name for a local pastry). Enforcement was brutal, although a subsequent relaxation of East German controls allowed Germans on both sides to visit their relatives. Guards checked car trunks and even the bottoms of cars looking for hidden passengers trying to escape. Western tourists climbed stairs to have a look at East German guards staring back from watchtowers behind barbed wire on the other side. Still, people tried to escape and many succeeded: they sprinted across no-man's-land, defying a hail of bullets, swam across rivers, flew small planes or homemade balloons into West Germany, dug tunnels, and hid in trucks and cars. Some did not make it: hundreds were killed attempting to escape.

Because of the threat of nuclear war, the Cuban Missile Crisis of 1962 was the world's most dangerous moment since the end of World War II. The island of Cuba, which had been a virtual protectorate of the United States since the Spanish-American War in 1898, became a Communist state in 1959 after Fidel Castro (1926–) led a guerrilla force that ousted the corrupt American protégé, Fulgencio Batista (1901–1973). Batista's supporters, with the help of the U.S. military, then launched an ill-conceived invasion of

(*Left*) The Berlin Wall goes up in 1961. (*Right*) U.S. President John F. Kennedy addresses West Berliners, 1961.

Cuba at the "Bay of Pigs" in 1961. It failed miserably. In October 1962, American aerial photographs revealed that Soviet missiles capable of being armed with nuclear warheads were stationed on the island of Cuba. The U.S. government demanded the removal of the missiles and threatened to destroy them if this demand was not met. Some knowledgeable advisers to President John F. Kennedy estimated the chances of the outbreak of a nuclear war at between one-third and one-half, dangerous odds indeed. Debates in the United Nations helped buy time while negotiations proceeded. The world breathed a collective sigh of relief as Khrushchev ordered the missiles removed.

Despite the fact that the United States and Soviet Union both signed a 1963 treaty banning nuclear tests, the arms race had accelerated. Soviet and American naval vessels and submarines closely monitored each other's movements. The Soviet secret police (KGB) and the American Central Intelligence Agency (CIA) spread their well-financed spy networks worldwide. Periodic spy scandals occurred in the West, most notably in Britain, where several prominent intellectuals turned out to have been spying for the Soviet Union. The growing number of colonies receiving their independence from Britain and France fostered increased competition between the two systems in Africa and Asia.

By the mid-1960s, the rivalry between the United States and the Soviet Union spread to Southeast Asia. In 1964, the United States officially became involved in the civil war in Vietnam. When President Lyndon B.

Johnson (1908–1973) announced that an American naval vessel had been attacked off the coast of Vietnam—which in fact never occurred—the American Congress passed the Tonkin Gulf Resolution against the North Vietnamese government. The United States committed more and more men and material in support of the South Vietnamese government against the North Vietnamese Communist troops of Ho Chi Minh and their allies, the Vietcong guerrillas fighting in the south. The Soviets backed the Communist forces. The costly American role in the civil war came under increasing opposition at home and in Europe,

Soviet leader Nikita Khrushchev and Cuban leader Fidel Castro meet in Moscow, 1963.

beginning with university students. The Vietnam War badly divided public opinion in the United States and strained U.S. relations with its allies.

Sino-Soviet Rivalry

The alliance between Mao's China and the Soviet Union, cemented by the Korean War, began to break apart. A common Communist ideology could not gloss over issues of power politics between the two giants. Not only did they share an immense frontier, but certain border regions—above all, Mongolia—had long been claimed by both states. Border clashes took place in 1969. In addition, growing Soviet influence in India threatened Chinese relations with the subcontinent. Khrushchev's turn away from Stalinism angered Mao, as did the Soviet leader's overtures for support among Asian political leaders. Khrushchev's policy of peaceful coexistence with the West—and particularly his visit to Washington, D.C., in 1959— irritated Mao, who used the perceived threat from the West as a means of pushing the Chinese to make more sacrifices to modernize the economy. In China, a "cult of personality" focused on Chairman Mao just as one in the Soviet Union had celebrated Stalin. Furthermore, attempts to modernize China's economy had been heavily influenced by Stalin's five-year plans, which had emphasized heavy industry. At the same time, China underwent rapid, ruthless collectivization of all industrial and agricultural production. Chinese economic growth made the Chinese less dependent on Soviet technical advisers and they were sent home.

The Chinese Communist government also grew increasingly uneasy about Russia's nuclear weapons. Mao believed Stalin's contention that war between capitalism and Communism was inevitable. He resented the unwillingness of the Soviets under Khrushchev, who had abandoned that particular tenet of Communist thought, to share their military secrets. In 1964, Mao accused the Soviet Union of itself being an "imperialist" power because it dominated the smaller states of Eastern Europe.

Chinese and Russian diplomats and advisers now competed as rivals for the ears of Third World leaders. The Chinese Communists received support from an unlikely place. Albania, the small, isolated, largely Muslim state squeezed between Yugoslavia and the Adriatic Sea, broke with the Soviet Union. The Soviet Union broke off diplomatic relations with Albania in 1961. This represented an embarrassing rejection of Soviet authority, particularly when put into the context of the ongoing Sino-Soviet split. However, Albanian Communist leader Enver Hoxha (1908–1985) then broke with the Chinese Communist leadership in 1978, criticizing China's improved relations with the United States.

The Brezhnev Era

Soviet economic stagnation and the humiliation of the Cuban Missile Crisis contributed to Khrushchev's sudden fall from power. Some military leaders had opposed Khrushchev's support of economic planning that emphasized consumer goods over heavy industry, although severe shortages still alienated many Soviet citizens. Old Stalinists surfaced again, resistant

Medium-range Soviet strategic missiles displayed in a military parade in Moscow on November 7, 1963, in a Soviet show of strength.

to any reform. Army commanders, wary of the Chinese situation, accused Khrushchev of having taken too great a risk by establishing missile sites in Cuba. In October 1964, Khrushchev returned to Moscow for a meeting called by his enemies only to find out that he was being retired into honorable obscurity.

Leonid Brezhnev (1906–1982), who had risen in the Communist Party with Khrushchev's assistance, became its general secretary. Brezhnev returned to Communist orthodoxy. He affirmed the authority and prestige of party bureaucrats and of the KGB, but he stopped well short of Stalinism. While building up Soviet military capability, the Soviet leader ordered an increase in the production of consumer goods. Nonetheless, centralized planning and agricultural collectivization remained the basis of the inefficient Soviet economy.

There was little talk of a "thaw" either inside or outside the Soviet Union during the Brezhnev era. Cynicism mounted within the Soviet Union, even among committed Communists who had long awaited the day when the corner would be turned and prosperity would arrive. That day never came.

Nuclear Weapons and Superpower Tensions

The phased U.S. withdrawal from Vietnam beginning in 1973 (followed two years later by the victory of the Communist North Vietnamese and their southern allies, the Vietcong) removed one thorny issue between the United States and the Soviet Union. Continued tension between the Soviet Union and China (accompanied by a concentration of Soviet forces along the disputed borders in Manchuria and Siberia) gradually eroded the old U.S. view of Communism as a monolithic force, engendering more realistic diplomatic assessments of international politics. Furthermore, both the United States and the Soviet Union faced daunting economic problems that partially shifted the focus of government to domestic concerns.

The period from 1969 to 1979 brought a period of détente between the Soviet Union and the United States, leading to serious negotiations between the two powers to reduce nuclear arms. In 1972, Soviet leader Leonid Brezhnev and U.S. President Richard Nixon (1913–1994) signed an arms-reduction agreement known as SALT I (Strategic Arms Limitation Talks), by which they agreed to maintain parity in nuclear offensive weapons systems. However, as military technology continued to advance rapidly, both sides began to defy the spirit of the agreement by developing new systems. Both the Soviet Union and the United States deployed new missiles in Europe. Nixon was forced to resign as U.S. president in 1974 because of the Watergate Affair: he had approved illegal operations against Democratic Party headquarters and then lied about what he knew. His successors sought to link further arms-reduction talks to issues of human rights in the Soviet Union. In 1979, U.S. President Jimmy Carter (1924–) and Brezhnev signed a new agreement, SALT II, by which the Soviets agreed to limit missile launchers and nuclear warheads and the United States agreed not to develop a new missile. Carter, however, had to withdraw the agreement from consideration by the Senate in January 1980 because of political opposition, primarily from conservatives who feared that the SALT II agreement would leave the Soviets with greater nuclear capability than that of the United States. As the number of nuclear weapons increased in Europe, anti-nuclear movements revived, particularly in Britain and Germany.

The Soviet invasion of Afghanistan in December 1979 put an end to détente. Soviet troops were sent in support of the pro-Soviet government, which was besieged by a variety of rebels, including Islamic fundamentalists, who received support from the United States. (One of the motives of the Soviet invasion of Afghanistan was to forestall fundamentalist movements in Soviet republics with sizable Muslim populations.) Reacting to the Soviet invasion, the United States limited grain sales to the Soviet Union and boycotted the Olympic Games in Moscow in 1980. The Soviet-American chill lasted into the mid-1980s.

DECOLONIZATION

The Second World War accelerated the independence movements that had developed after World War I. In the colonies in Africa, Asia, and Southeast Asia, the rise of nationalism led to movements demanding independence. Thus, beginning in the 1950s, European colonies became central actors in some of the dramas of international politics. The peacemakers at Versailles (particularly President Wilson) in 1919 had espoused nationalism as a principle for the territorial organization of states. But France and Britain, in particular, had been unwilling to grant freedom to their colonies, both viewing their empires as part of their national identities. During and after the war, the U.S. government had made clear its unwillingness to support the maintenance of the British and French colonial empires. The Soviet Union, too, was in principle against colonial empires, while, ironically, building something of an empire of its own by controlling states in Eastern Europe and the Balkans.

For his part, Winston Churchill had believed that if Britain was to remain a world power, it had to retain its empire, despite the opposition of Eisenhower to colonialism. "I have not become the king's first minister," Churchill thundered, "to preside over the liquidation of the British Empire." However, succeeding prime ministers realized that it would be better to grant colonies independence than to have to confront massive insurrections. With the economies of the Western European nations still suffering the effects of the war, the costs of resisting independence movements were high for the remaining imperial powers. Moreover, opposition to colonialism came not only from the colonized peoples but also from intellectuals, students, and political parties of the left at home.

The end of the colonial era reflected the relative decline of the European powers in international affairs. The sun finally set on the British Empire as its colonies became independent states. Britain and France left important traditions of government, culture, and language in Africa, Asia, and the Middle East (for example, French prestige in Lebanon). Britain's former colonies achieved independence peacefully for the most part. In contrast, France and Portugal battled to retain their colonies even in the face of popular insurgency. The Netherlands and Belgium both resisted nationalist movements briefly before recognizing the independence of their former colonies. In many colonies, educated and active groups stood ready to work for independence and, when that was achieved, to become leaders of new states. But during the 1960s and 1970s, the United States and the Soviet Union aggressively competed for influence in these young states. By 1980, more than half of the 154 members of the United Nations had been admitted to membership since 1956.

Decolonization in South and Southeast Asia

India, a densely populated, vastly complex subcontinent of many peoples, languages, cultures, and several major religions, was the largest colony in the world. Hindus formed the largest religion, but there were millions of Muslims as well, particularly in Bengal and Punjab in the north. Many Muslims wanted a partition of the subcontinent and the establishment of a Muslim state.

During the 1920s and 1930s, Indian nationalism developed among the Indian elite, some of whom had been educated in England (see Chapter 24). When World War II began, the British government asked the Congress Party, the largest Indian political organization, which included Sikhs and Muslims, for its support against the Japanese. The Hindu leaders of the Congress Party, Mahatmas Gandhi (1869–1948) and Jawaharlal Nehru (1889–1964), refused to offer unqualified support during the war, and the British government imprisoned them. In 1942, the British government promised them self-government following the war—and full status within the British Commonwealth—if India, which had provided thousands of soldiers for the fight (although Indian soldiers captured in Southeast Asia had joined the Japanese in 1943–1945), fully cooperated in the war against Japan. However, Nehru and Gandhi demanded complete independence for India. Gandhi, who dismissed the offer as "a post-dated check on a crashing bank," became a powerful symbol of Indian resolution to win independence by peaceful means. When he threatened a massive campaign of nonviolent resistance to British rule, the British government sent him to jail again. Political unrest swept through India following the war in 1945–1946.

Mahatmas Gandhi steps from a third-class train after Indian independence.

With the British Conservative Party out of government after the war, Labour Prime Minister Clement Attlee announced in 1946 that India would be granted full independence, which the Labour Party had long advocated. The last British viceroy, Lord Louis Mountbatten (1900–1979), oversaw the British departure in 1947. India became independent, but bitter fighting followed between Hindus and Muslims. The Muslim League, which represented Muslim interests, insisted on the creation of a separate Muslim nation; however, the Congress Party, dominated by Hindus, rejected this demand outright. Hindus and Muslims battled in much of India. Britain partitioned the Indian subcontinent: India would be largely Hindu, and Pakistan, which also obtained independence in 1947 and was divided into East Pakistan and West Pakistan on either side of India, would be Muslim. Since millions of Muslims lived in India and many Hindus lived in Pakistan, however, it proved impossible to draw state boundaries so that they exactly corresponded to ethnic and religious differences.

Fighting between Hindus and Muslims continued. Hindus drove millions of Muslims out of India. Many of them starved to death during forced marches to Pakistan. Likewise, about the same number of Hindus and Sikhs were expelled from Pakistan. A Hindu extremist assassinated Gandhi in 1948 because he had accepted the establishment of Pakistan.

India became the world's largest democracy (its population now is well over 1 billion people), but many daunting problems remained unsolved: poverty compounded by a phenomenally high birthrate, underdeveloped democratic institutions, and bitter religious rivalries. Pakistan faced similar challenges. The awkward division of Pakistan into East and West, separated by Hindu India, ended in 1971 when East Pakistan rebelled against

Pakistani authority. After Indian troops intervened against Pakistani forces, Bangladesh became an independent state, one of the poorest nations in the world. Meanwhile, the British government had also granted independence to other British colonies in Asia: the island of Ceylon (Sri Lanka) and Burma (Myanmar) in 1948, and Singapore in 1965.

In Southeast Asia, the end of Japanese occupation during World War II served as a catalyst for decolonization, leaving the way open for independence movements. The Japanese occupation had driven the British out of the Malay Peninsula and the Dutch colonists out of Indonesia. The states on the Malay Peninsula formed the Federation of Malaya after the war. Communists battled British troops off and on during the 1940s and 1950s, until Britain granted complete independence in 1957 to what became Malaysia in 1963. In Indonesia, the nationalist leader Sukarno (1901–1970) took advantage of the Dutch absence from the region to proclaim Indonesian independence. Negotiations arranged by the United Nations led the Netherlands to grant Indonesian independence in 1949. Sukarno called his government a "guided democracy," assuming the presidency for life in 1963. As the economy floundered, however, the Indonesian Communist Party grew in size. The Indonesian government accepted large sums of money from the Soviet Union and the United States. In 1965, Lieutenant General Suharto (1921–2008) seized power. Undertaking a bloody campaign of terror against Communists, he consolidated his dictatorship with the support of the armed forces. In 1998, riots in the capital of Jakarta led to his resignation.

Britain and the Middle East

British influence also declined in the Middle East. Growing dependence on oil as a source of energy made the Middle East increasingly important in international politics. Egypt had achieved independence after World War I. Britain still controlled Palestine as a Mandate. Zionists before World War I considered Palestine the promised land for Jews. In 1917, by the Balfour Declaration, the British government had supported the creation of a "national home for the Jewish people," with the understanding that "nothing shall be done which may prejudice the civil and religious rights of existing non-Jewish communities in Palestine." However, Palestine had an Arab majority. During the 1920s and 1930s, many Jews had emigrated there, hoping one day to construct a Jewish state. In the wake of World War II, they were joined by hundreds of thousands of Jews from Europe. For them, the Zionist revival and the creation of an independent Jewish state now seemed enormously more urgent, indeed becoming an important part of the collective identity of many Holocaust survivors. In 1947, the British government, already facing attacks from militant Jews committed to ending British occupation, asked the United Nations to resolve Palestine's future. In its first major international decision, the United Nations called for the division of Palestine into the Jewish state of Israel and an Arab state. That land intended for a new Arab state was incorporated into the neighboring states of Jordan and Egypt, as well as Israel. Israeli forces took over much of the British Mandate in 1948, achieving independence. Jerusalem, a holy city for Jews, Arabs, and Christians, was to remain temporarily under the control of the United Nations.

As in India, the policy of partition led to turmoil. Fighting between Palestinian Arabs and Jews began soon after the UN resolution. In May 1948, Arab forces from Egypt, Syria, Lebanon, and Jordan attacked the newly established state of Israel, but were defeated the following year. The victorious Israeli army expelled large numbers of Arabs from their lands, although about 150,000 Palestinian Arabs remained in Israel. At least 700,000 Palestinian refugees fled to Jordan, which had become independent in 1946. The seeds were sown for future conflicts. The Arab states refused to recognize the existence of Israel, as well as a separate Palestinian Arab identity. Palestinians retained some rights in Israel, such as being able to vote and to serve in the parliament. Yet those Palestinians remaining in Israel believed that they had been relegated to the status of second-class citizens, and they remained under military rule until 1965. After 1948, no new Arab towns were established in Israel, although the population of Palestinians increased five-fold, and until recently it remained Israeli policy that no land "redeemed" by Jews in Israel could be sold to non-Jews.

The Suez Canal Crisis

The Suez Canal had been the centerpiece of British interests and defenses in the Middle East since British troops first occupied Egypt in 1882. Although the British withdrawal from India in 1947 had somewhat reduced its strategic importance to Britain, about two-thirds of the oil from the Middle East on which Britain and Western Europe depended was transported through the canal. Egypt had been independent since 1922, but Britain maintained considerable influence there. Furthermore, the canal itself was owned by the British (more than 40 percent) and French governments, as well as by stockholders, primarily British.

In 1952, when Egyptian nationalist sentiment against Britain ran high (in part because the British government refused to allow Egypt to occupy Sudan), a group of young nationalist military officers overthrew Egyptian King Farouk in a bloodless coup. Gamal Abdel Nasser (1918–1970), the head of the new Egyptian government, emerged as one of the most influential figures in rising Pan-Arab nationalism. Nasser established Egyptian neutrality in the tug-of-war between East and West. He refused to sign a treaty with the United States, and he castigated Iran and Turkey for their pro-American policies.

As Egyptian nationalism mounted, the Egyptian government, which had renounced the Anglo-Egyptian alliance treaty of 1936, demanded British withdrawal from the narrow zone along the Suez Canal. In 1954, the Egypt-

(*Left*) A Russian cartoon salutes Nasser's seizure of the Suez Canal in July 1956. The banner reads "Shares of the Suez Canal Company Ltd." (*Right*) Sunken ships block the Suez Canal.

ian and British governments signed an agreement (vehemently opposed by some British Conservatives) by which British troops would begin a phased withdrawal that would be completed in June 1956. Britain would retain the right to send military forces back should the canal be attacked (presumably by the Soviet Union); the British and Egyptian governments would respect the freedom of navigation through the canal. Many Egyptians, particularly a radical organization, the Muslim Brotherhood, opposed this agreement, which seemed to maintain some degree of British control over the Suez Canal. They sought to end once and for all Egypt's semi-colonial status.

Egypt became a pawn in the struggle between the United States and the Soviet Union for the allegiance of non-aligned nations. Gradually, Nasser, who denounced the British and French role in the Middle East, turned toward the Soviet Union for economic and, in 1955, military support. He resented the United States for its close ties to Israel, which it had been quick to recognize in 1948, and spurned Britain's defensive pact with Turkey and Iraq (the Baghdad Pact, 1955). This pact was directed against the Soviet Union, which sought to increase its reach in the Middle East by capitalizing on considerable dissatisfaction among Arab nationalists with the role of the United States in the construction of a Middle East treaty association similar to NATO. The Soviet government signed an agreement with Egypt, promising to exchange weapons for Egyptian cotton. Egypt planned to construct the Aswan High Dam on the Upper Nile River, which Nasser believed would help modernize the Egyptian economy. The World Bank had agreed to finance the construction of the dam if Britain and the United States would contribute. But the U.S. government was increasingly suspicious of British goals. Indeed, the British government was planning Nasser's overthrow. On July 19, 1956, the United States suddenly withdrew its offer of a loan when it seemed that the Egyptian government would accept a Soviet offer to finance the dam's construction. On July 26, Nasser announced the nationalization of the Suez Canal, with the assurance, however, that shareholders would be compensated.

The British government, pushed by Conservatives who feared that Nasser would undermine British interests throughout the Middle East, decided on armed intervention. France, too, wanted Nasser out of power because of French interests in the canal. More than this, Nasser supported the Algerian National Liberation Front, which sought Algerian independence from France. The U.S. government sought to diffuse the crisis through negotiation.

The government of Israel, which was still technically at war with Egypt since 1948, was also concerned about emerging ties between Egypt and the Soviet Union. Moreover, the arrival of Soviet arms in Egypt raised fears of a possible Egyptian invasion of Israel. In October 1956, the British government came around to the French view that they should agree to an Israeli invasion of Egypt, which would provide both powers with an excuse to intervene militarily and occupy the Suez Canal Zone. (The U.S. government was kept unaware of these difficult negotiations.) Israel sent an invasion force into Egypt on October 29. The Egyptian army put up stiff resistance. A Franco-British ultimatum then demanded that Israeli and Egyptian forces both withdraw to ten miles from the canal. The Israeli government halted the military drive within Egypt. An Anglo-French force then occupied the Canal Zone after Nasser ordered the scuttling of ships to block the canal. On November 3, the General Assembly of the United Nations called for a cease-fire (supported by both the United States and the Soviet Union) and a day later authorized a peacekeeping force. On November 5, British and French troops parachuted into Port Said, followed by troops put ashore the next day. Britain agreed to accept the cease-fire. Pressure on both Israel and Egypt from the United States and the Soviet Union (which had reason to be pleased that the world's attention could be diverted from Hungary, where Russian tanks were crushing an anti-Communist revolt; see Chapter 29) brought an end to the Suez crisis. U.S. pressure proved decisive, particularly with Britain, as the U.S. government refused to support British sterling, and the currency fell dramatically in the face of fears of a cut-off of oil from the Middle East. British and French troops withdrew. The Suez Canal crisis had demonstrated that European Western powers could no longer impose their will on the Middle East. Thereafter, the process of decolonization proceeded rapidly.

In Britain, Prime Minister Sir Anthony Eden (1897–1977) suffered a nervous breakdown and resigned from office in January 1957. Conservative Harold Macmillan (1894–1986), who succeeded Eden as prime minister and who had been a proponent of the Suez action, then undertook what one of his colleagues called the "most spectacular retreat from Suez since the time of Moses." Following the salvaging of the forty ships that Egypt had sunk in the canal, the Suez Canal reopened in April 1957 under Egyptian control. British influence in the Middle East continued to decline. A year later, British ally King Faisal II was assassinated in Iraq. When the island of Cyprus gained its independence in 1960, Britain lost its last base in the Middle East.

French Decolonization

France, too, lost its colonial empire in the post-war era, but not without bloody struggles. The French had begun their conquest of North Africa in 1830, and in Southeast Asia had held modern-day Laos, Cambodia, and Vietnam since the 1880s. The French left Syria and Lebanon in 1946 by agreement with the United States and Britain. In 1947, French troops put down a massive insurrection in Madagascar, with an enormous loss of life. The island finally received its independence in 1960, one of fourteen former French colonies in Africa.

In Vietnam, Ho Chi Minh (Nguyen Tat Thanh or Nguyen Ai Quoc, or "the Patriot," 1890–1969) emerged as a Vietnamese Communist leader. His father was an official under the French who had resigned from his position because of his Vietnamese nationalism. Ho Chi Minh himself worked as a kitchen helper on a French passenger liner before becoming a Communist activist. In 1929 he founded the Indochinese Communist Party. Following condemnation to death by the French government, Ho was saved by the refusal of the British government in Hong Kong to turn him over to French authorities. Nonetheless, the British arrested him in 1931, and he remained in prison in Hong Kong for two years. During World War II, he led the Viet Minh, an organization of Vietnamese Communists.

During World War II, Vichy France had held Vietnam as a colony until Japanese forces took control in 1945. When Vietnam proclaimed its independence, France attempted to re-conquer its former colony. In November 1946, the French army attacked the port of Haiphong, killing 6,000 Vietnamese, and captured Hanoi, the Vietnamese capital. The French military restored the nominal authority of a playboy emperor, Bao Dai (1913–1997). Yet Vietnam remained a colony. War between Ho Chi Minh's Vietnamese army, which held most of the countryside, and the French continued. Ho, supported by the Chinese, prophesied, "You will kill ten of our men, but we will kill one of yours and you will end up by wearing yourselves out." The Korean War increased U.S. interest in the ongoing struggles in Vietnam, bringing U.S. military assistance to the French effort. In 1954, the French army suffered a crushing defeat at the hands of the Vietnamese at Dien Bien Phu. Pierre Mendès-France (1907–1982), the new Socialist premier, succeeded in extracting France from war in Vietnam (he would later prove less successful in encouraging the French to drink milk instead of wine, a more hopeless task). At the Geneva Convention that year, France agreed to the division of Vietnam into two states. North Vietnam became a Communist regime led by Ho Chi Minh; South Vietnam became a republic run by a succession of leaders who carried out U.S. policy in exchange for a free hand.

(*Left*) A Viet Minh fighter is taken prisoner by a French soldier in 1952. (*Right*) A French patrol in Vietnam in 1954.

The end of French colonialism was even more wrenching in North Africa. There were 1.2 million French citizens in Algeria, 300,000 in Morocco, and 200,000 in Tunisia. They were called *pieds noirs* ("black feet") because of the black boots worn by French soldiers. Morocco and Tunisia were French protectorates, although nominally ruled by a sultan and bey (sovereign), respectively. Algeria, in contrast, was directly administered as a colony by French officials. During the inter-war period, a small nationalist movement developed in Algeria. In 1945, French troops put down an uprising in Algeria at the cost of 40,000 Algerian lives. During the early 1950s, movements for national independence continued to develop in France's North African colonies.

The writer Albert Camus, born in Algeria, summed up the difficult choices for some French families who lived there; he said that if given the choice between justice and his mother, he would take his mother. Many of the French living in North Africa had become wealthy, successfully developing land taken from the Arab population over the past century. Others were of modest means, including café owners in Algiers, government functionaries, and farmers with small plots of land.

In 1954, the National Liberation Front (Front de Libération Nationale, the FLN) called for Algerian independence. An uprising for independence began just four months after the French defeat at Dien Bien Phu. Fearing that the movement might spread to Tunisia and Morocco (where, in fact, some fighting followed), the French government granted virtual independence to both states in 1956, despite the protests of French residents and the vigorous opposition of the French officer corps.

As guerrilla actions and bombings increased and losses mounted, many people in France began to accept Algerian independence as both inevitable and desirable. In February 1956, French residents in Algiers rioted against the government when French Premier Guy Mollet (1906–1975), who had at first been willing to negotiate with the FLN, came to introduce his newly appointed governor of Algeria. In October, the newly crowned king of Morocco met with leaders of the FLN, enraging the French right. Mollet, fearing the political consequences of the war, then ordered the kidnapping of Ahmed Ben Bella (1919–), a leader of the Algerians, and launched a repression in France of critics of the French Algerian policy. In November 1956, France joined Britain in the ill-fated Suez expedition in part because of French anger at Egyptian support for the Algerian insurrection. French troops undertook a brutal campaign that included torture against militants and civilians alike, culminating in "the battle of Algiers" fought in the Arab quarters of the Algerian capital. In France, the left increasingly demanded an end to the war; intellectuals, like the philosopher Jean-Paul Sartre and the novelist Camus, denounced the torture of Algerians by the French army. In the meantime, casualties mounted in the French army (which, unlike the French war in Vietnam, included conscripts). Throughout the Algerian war of independence, the FLN successfully played off Cold War rivalries, using mass communication and building support in Algerian communities abroad, while winning international support. Their campaign helped isolate France internationally.

After humiliating defeats at the hands of the German army in 1940 and by the Vietnamese at Dien Bien Phu in 1954, some French military officers

French riot police throw back stones, as well as tear gas bombs, at demonstrators in Algiers in 1960, during the Algerian war of independence.

saw the fight in Algeria as a last stand for their honor. Early in 1958, by which time French troops in Algeria numbered 500,000, French planes attacked FLN camps on the other side of the border with Tunisia. A new premier was rumored to be willing to negotiate with the insurgents. On May 13, 1958, a demonstration by French settlers in Algiers protesting against any compromise turned into a military-led insurrection against the French government. A "Committee of Public Safety" of rightists seized power, led by General Jacques Massu (1908–2002). On May 24, another right-wing group seized power in Corsica. A military coup d'état seemed possible on the mainland of France.

Charles de Gaulle, who had been waiting in self-imposed exile for something like this to happen, announced that he was ready to serve France again. Many politicians believed that de Gaulle alone could prevent chaos. On May 29, 1958, President René Coty appointed de Gaulle prime minister, a move approved by the National Assembly early in June. The general accepted on the condition that he could rule by emergency decree for six months and could then ask the nation to approve a new constitution. The right, which counted many army officers among its ranks, was delighted with de Gaulle's return to power, thinking that the general would never allow Algerian independence.

The new constitution greatly increased the authority of the president, whose term was set at seven years. Presidents under the Fifth French Republic would conduct foreign policy, appoint prime ministers, and dissolve the French parliament. In September 1958, 80 percent of French voters approved the new constitution.

But what about Algeria? De Gaulle went to Algiers and, in a remarkably noncommittal speech, told the settlers in June 1958, "I have understood you, I know what you have tried to do here." But he had already decided that the costs of continuing the war in Algeria were too great, too divisive. He removed the generals responsible for the coup in Algeria from their posts. For a man whose French nationalism underlay his political philosophy, it seemed an astonishing turnaround.

To some officers, de Gaulle's actions seemed an incredible betrayal, a stab in the back by a fellow military man. As the Dreyfus Affair had revealed in the 1890s and the Vichy years had confirmed, a right-wing anti-democratic tradition survived in the officer corps. Many officers now felt betrayed not only by de Gaulle but also by much of the population in France. They enjoyed some support among rightist parties. When de Gaulle recalled General Massu to Paris in January 1960, right-wing riots took place in Paris. In Algeria, *pieds noirs* began a general strike and put up barricades. De Gaulle rallied French public opinion to what had clearly become a policy of allowing Algerians to decide their own future.

Negotiations between Algerian leaders and de Gaulle's government began in the spring of 1961. In the meantime, a secret group within the army, the Secret Army Organization (OAS), had formed in January 1961, determined at all costs to keep Algeria French. In April it staged a coup d'état and held power in Algiers and in the city of Oran for three days, yet it did not win support of the entire army. Political parties of the left and center threw their support to de Gaulle. The general assumed emergency powers, this time for a year. The OAS twice tried to assassinate de Gaulle and once nearly succeeded, riddling his car with machine-gun fire. Members planted bombs in Algerian cities and in Paris to terrorize the civilian population. Given the chance to vote on their future, the Algerians opted for independence; in France, the vote for Algerian independence in July 1961 was 15 million to 5 million. On March 19, 1962, the Algerian War officially ended, with the French people overwhelmingly ratifying the peace terms. In July 1962, Algeria became independent. However, France contined to maintain considerable prestige in the Third World.

Decolonization in Sub-Saharan Africa

At the end of World War II, only Liberia, Ethiopia, and Egypt had achieved independence in Africa. Nationalist groups in Africa were less organized than had been their counterparts in India and Southeast Asia. But in the subsequent decades, British rule ended in one African colony after another. In 1957, Ghana (formerly the Gold Coast) became independent. Others soon followed, including Nigeria in 1960, Sierra Leone and Tanganyika in 1961, Uganda in 1962, and Kenya in 1963. Sixteen states in Africa became independent in 1960, including the Ivory Coast, Senegal, and Cameroon, all former French colonies (see Map 28.1).

British determination to hold onto its East African colony of Kenya—presented under the guise of the mission to "civilize" people that they considered inferior—was particularly bloody. In the late nineteenth century, British colonialists obtained huge estates in fertile central Kenya in what they called the "White Highlands." They were followed by other white settlers of more modest means. Livestock farming, coffee growing, and the production of cereals enriched many of them, as Kenya became known as a fitting home for privileged British gentry, a "colony for gentlemen." In 1914 almost 5,500 European settlers were in Kenya and, aided by a government campaign after World War II to encourage immigration there, in 1948 about 30,000 whites resided there (compared with an African population of 5.3 million and almost 100,000 Asians). By the early 1950s there were at least 40,000 Europeans. Many benefited from good land that could be purchased or leased for very little, government subsidies, and cheap African labor, working at wage rates set by the colonial government.

The Kikuyu people, who had lost enormous amounts of land to the settlers and been forced to work for and pay onerous taxes to the British, did not profit from the economic boom generated by World War II. The Kikuyu launched a campaign for self-determination. Jomo Kenyatta (1889–1978), who had studied in London, emerged as an effective, charismatic leader of

MAP 28.1 DECOLONIZATION The map shows movements for decolonization in Africa, Asia, and the Far East, giving the dates at which each of the colonies achieved independence.

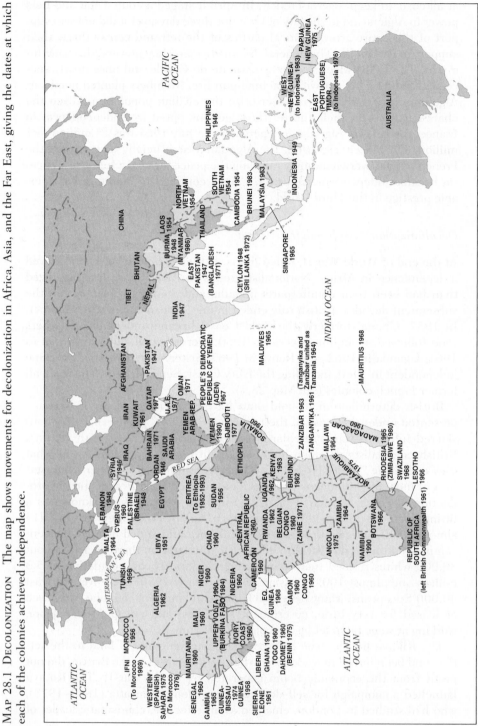

the Kenyan African Union, which by the early 1950s encompassed almost the entire Kikuyu population. What became known to the British as the "Mau Mau" rebellion (the origins of the term are mysterious but the rebels called themselves the "Land and Freedom Army") began in 1952, with violence directed at British settlers, thirty-two of whom were killed in the rebellion. Kenyatta's arrest, trial, conviction, and imprisonment for his role in the Mau Mau insurgency (despite no evidence) helped make him an international symbol of Kenyan resistance.

The British government declared a state of emergency and detained perhaps as many as 1.5 million people, virtually the entire Kikuyu population, in what amounted to a mass gulag. At the same time, the Mau Mau exacted bloody revenge against loyalist Kenyans with guerilla attacks. The British portrayed the struggle as one between civilization and savagery. British forces, including the Home Guard of white settlers recognized as part of the security forces in 1953, and indigenous loyalists killed tens of thousands of people, not counting thousands who perished in the detention camps or were shot when allegedly trying to escape. The counter-insurgency included terror, atrocious brutality, and widespread torture, most of which the British government succeeded in keeping secret. About 1,000 Kikuyu were hung after being convicted in British courts. British authorities enacted collective punishments against villagers who refused to cooperate with them, seizing livestock and closing down markets for months. The bloody struggle lasted until 1957, when British forces succeeded in breaking apart the Mau Mau armies.

Mau Mau soldiers training in Kenya, 1963.

However, the British government appeared in an increasingly bad light as word got out of the detention camps and conditions within them. In the meantime, Britain had accepted decolonization as inevitable. Prime Minister Harold Macmillan put together a "balance sheet of empire," which screamed out in red ink. He took the decision to end British colonial rule in Africa. Emergency rule ended and Kenyatta was freed in 1959. Majority rule followed. White settlers were allowed to sell their land under favorable conditions. Kenyatta's Kenya African National Union established a government after an overwhelming victory in elections in 1963. Britain granted Kenya independence later that year. Kenyatta earned his reputation as "the reconciler" and became president in 1964.

The Republic of South Africa left the British Commonwealth in 1961. With a white population of 21 percent in 1950 (and 68 percent African, 2 percent of mixed race, and 2 percent Asian), South Africa maintained a system of apartheid, an official policy of racial inequality and segregation implemented in 1948. It was supported by the white Afrikaner population of Dutch origin. In 1965 Rhodesia, which had been a self-governing colony, declared its independence from Britain. It did so, in part, so that its white minority would not have to share power with the black majority population. The British government then led a campaign of international economic sanctions against the white regime of its former colony. In 1980, Rhodesia was divided into the independent states of Zambia and Zimbabwe.

In the Belgian Congo in central West Africa, the Belgian government first tried to placate nationalists with concessions in the late 1950s and then to repress them following rioting in 1959. A year later, the Belgian government suddenly pulled out of its former colony (although the Congo's army retained Belgian officers), declaring the Congo independent. Civil war began between two nationalist leaders, a bloody conflict complicated by ethnic and tribal loyalties. Soldiers mutinied against their Belgian commanders and began to attack Europeans remaining in the Congo. The Congo's wealthiest province, Katanga, which has great mining resources such as cobalt, copper, and uranium, then declared its independence. At the request of the Congo's premier, the United Nations sent troops to restore order. After a year, the civil war ended. Katanga's secession lasted until 1963. Two years later, Colonel Mobutu Sese Seko (1930–1997) imposed military rule in Congo, which was known as Zaire between 1971 and 1997. After nationalizing his country's wealthy mines, Mobutu set about amassing enormous personal wealth.

Portugal's colonies were many times its size. It faced insurrections in its African colonies of Angola and Mozambique, which lie on the southwestern and southeastern coasts, respectively, beginning in 1961. Following years of bloody fighting, the new Portuguese government, which a year earlier had overthrown the dictatorship that had ruled Portugal for decades (see Chapter 29), recognized the independence of Angola and Mozambique. In both new states, horrendous civil war raged between left-wing and right-wing groups. In Angola, Cuban funds and soldiers helped the left-wing Popular

Movement, which emerged victorious. In Mozambique, too, the left won, despite assistance to the right by the South African government and a campaign of terror. Ordinary people suffered famine and slaughter.

Independence in many cases proved to be no panacea for the new African nations. Many post-colonial administrations proved unable or unwilling to provide a decent quality of life to their people. Some new states, like Angola and Mozambique, and more recently, Sudan, fell into bloody and debilitating civil wars. These conflicts were compounded by the multiplicity of ethnic groups, tribalism, and a lack of political experience—problems that still stand as major impediments to the construction of modern political systems in developing nations. Even with the departure of colonial governments, European companies still controlled valuable natural resources. Moreover, some African rulers have abused their power by enriching themselves at the expense of their people, while adopting, as in the case of Robert Mugabe (1924–) of Zimbabwe, anti-colonial rhetoric to justify their plunder. Appalling poverty and inadequate health care remain daunting challenges.

CONCLUSION

The end of European overseas empires was accompanied by significant political changes on the European continent as well. The late 1960s brought waves of student protest in many Western European countries and a movement for reform in Communist Czechoslovkia, which threatened Soviet orthodoxy before being crushed by Russian tanks. Dictatorships subsequently fell in Greece, Spain, and Portugal. And then, in a dramatic sequence of remarkable events, Communism collapsed in Central and Eastern Europe and the Balkans in 1989, followed by the break-up of the Soviet Union itself in 1991. Europe entered a new age.

CHAPTER 29

TRANSITIONS TO DEMOCRACY AND THE COLLAPSE OF COMMUNISM

After almost two decades of growing prosperity and relative political and social calm, domestic political conflict erupted in Europe—above all, in France—and the United States in 1968. The social, political, and cultural revolts that exploded that year seemed to pit young people, especially students, against those entrenched in power. Many "baby boomers" born after the war saw their revolt as one of an entire generation against its elders. They blamed them for a world that seemed unresponsive to demands for social justice and political change on behalf of the underprivileged and the oppressed. Many felt alienated (a word then much in vogue) from materialistic, industrial, bureaucratic society, and from the universities where they studied. Feminism, too, was a significant undercurrent during the protests of 1968, but it largely remained a movement of middle-class intellectuals and students.

Demonstrations and protest brought political reaction. The turmoil in France ended amid government repression and a conservative show of force. Demonstrations subsided elsewhere in Western Europe, although they continued in the United States against the war in Vietnam. In Western Europe, conservative or centrist parties dominated the governments of Britain, the German Federal Republic, and Italy for most of the 1970s and 1980s, while Socialists held power in France between 1981 and 1995. And, in southern Europe, democratic rule came to Portugal, Spain, and Greece.

A period of détente between the United States and the Soviet Union in the 1970s was followed by a chill that began as a result of Soviet intervention in Afghanistan in 1979. Then in 1989, dramatic change occurred in

Eastern Europe. Mikhail Gorbachev (1931–), the leader of the Soviet Union, had undertaken a dramatic series of reforms in the mid-1980s that liberalized the economy and political life in the Communist state. His bold moves encouraged further demands for reform and stimulated nationalist movements in the Soviet Union's republics. The impact was soon felt in Eastern Europe. As campaigns for liberalization revived in Poland and Hungary, it became clear that the Soviet leadership would not intervene to crush movements for reform, as Gorbachev indicated that he viewed reform in Eastern Europe as desirable.

Throughout Eastern Europe, one Communist government after another fell. These revolutions ranged from the "velvet revolution" in Czechoslovakia to the violent overthrow of Nicolae Ceaușescu in Romania, until there were no Communist regimes left in Eastern Europe (although in Bulgaria, Romania, and Albania, former Communists retained power). Overall, the fall of communism was achieved through a remarkably peaceful process of change. However, in 1989, Yugoslavia began to break apart in a cacophony of ethnic hatred generated by the very question that the polyglot state's creation after World War I could not resolve: the national question. In Bosnia, civil war raged. The Soviet Union itself collapsed in 1991. The U.S. official George Kennan's prediction in 1947 that the Soviet system "bears within it the seeds of its own decay" turned out to be correct.

Adulation of Mikhail Gorbachev in Stuttgart, West Germany, for his bold moves toward reform and liberalization in the Soviet Union.

Politics in a Changing Western World

During the late 1960s, a loosely connected movement for political and social change swept across university campuses in a number of Western countries. Youth increasingly trumpeted sexual freedom, aided by the availability of birth control (notably the pill, beginning in the 1960s and 1970s) and the legalization of abortion in some countries. Based largely but not exclusively in the surging generation of baby boomers born after World War II (in the United States, the student-age population increased from 16 million in 1960 to 26 million in 1970), the youth revolt challenged long-established hierarchies, party politics, and even consumerism. From Berkeley, California, to Paris, Berlin, and Amsterdam, students protested against American involvement in the Vietnamese civil war, where, despite government claims of a high-minded struggle against communism, the United States seemed to be supporting a corrupt political regime against determined nationalists, albeit Communists. In the United States, particularly, the movements of the 1960s were closely tied to the civil rights movement, as students protested against social injustice and racism. Long hair, sexual freedom, rock music, and marijuana seemed part of the idealistic youth rebellion against the state and capitalism. The British impact on popular culture was never greater than in the 1960s, when the Beatles, Mick Jagger and the Rolling Stones, and the Who, among other rock groups, became phenomenally popular across much of the globe. In France, student demonstrations, insurgency, and strikes shook the country, challenging the government of President Charles de Gaulle. Demonstrations also rocked Italy, West Germany, and other Western European countries.

Western European states began to turn away from U.S. foreign policy domination. De Gaulle, who believed that France had a special historic mission and never doubted for a moment the part he was to play in it, feared the domination of Europe and France by Britain and the United States. He insisted that France maintain an independent nuclear capability; the country's first nuclear bomb was tested in 1960. Moreover, ending decades of animosity, the close partnership between Germany and France formed the cornerstone of the new Europe. However, de Gaulle refused to cooperate with the other Western powers. In 1966, France left NATO's military command, forcing it to transfer its headquarters from Paris to Brussels. U.S. Army and Air Force bases in France were closed. De Gaulle angered the U.S. government by refusing to support its policies in Vietnam. He also outraged many Canadians during a state visit in 1967 by shouting, "Long live Free Quebec!" (Quebec, predominantly French-speaking, has had considerable sentiment for independence.) Although de Gaulle remained vehemently anti-Communist, he wanted France to provide leadership as a third force that stood between the Soviet Union and the United States.

Other European governments also no longer automatically accepted U.S. Cold War rhetoric, which had encouraged the arms race. They reasoned that if the two superpowers went to war, the battlefields (in conventional warfare) or the targets (in case of "limited" nuclear warfare) would be in Europe.

Student Protests Challenge Gaullist France

In the spring of 1968, demonstrators took to the streets of Paris, protesting the rigid, overcrowded, and under-funded French university system, which largely remained the preserve of the elite. Intellectual ferment was heightened by opposition to the war in Vietnam. In France, students rebelled against those in political power, inequality, and even modern technology, which seemed to them dehumanizing. Graffiti in the Latin Quarter (where students attended university) proclaimed, "Comrades, the Revolution is daily, it is a festival!"

Early in May 1968, a student radical was expelled from the University of Paris. In protest, students and some young faculty members occupied university buildings at the Sorbonne. After the police entered the university and began arresting students, the demonstrators fanned out and were joined by more students. Several students were killed and hundreds injured when police attacked hastily improvised barricades.

Unlike in the United States, where most workers found student demands too radical and many supported U.S. participation in the war in Vietnam, French workers took to the streets in support of the students. A general strike began on May 13 in protest against police brutality, the largest wave of French strikes since 1936. Strikers demanded raises, better working conditions, and rights of self-management. Union organizations and the Communist Party, which had considerable prestige among industrial workers, had little to do with the movement. The tail seemed to be wagging the dog. If anything, trade union and Communist leaders tried to bring the movement under their control in its first days. Gaullist Prime Minister Georges Pompidou (1911–1974) hurriedly returned from a state visit to Afghanistan to confront the growing crisis.

After a hurried flight to West Germany, presumably to assure himself of the loyalty of French army units stationed there, de Gaulle dissolved the National Assembly on May 30 and announced that new elections would be held on June 23. Gaullists organized counter-demonstrations in support of the government, capitalizing on the hostility of many middle-class citizens and peasants in traditionally conservative regions to the turmoil in Paris. The strike movement ebbed, in part because the government and many companies agreed to raise wages. This left the students standing alone.

After dismissing Pompidou as prime minister, de Gaulle won what amounted to a referendum on his rule. However, his towering presence seemed increasingly anachronistic. Speeches about national "grandeur" rang hollow as French influence in the world declined. De Gaulle's answer to a general crisis of confidence was to call for more "participation" in the

An outnumbered policeman during the massive protests in Paris in May 1968.

political process, as a way of expressing French "national ambition," which he believed was slipping away. "The French think of nothing but increasing their standard of living," he once complained. "Steak and French fries are fine. A family car is useful. But all that does not add up to national ambition." In 1969, the president announced another referendum, this one on local administrative reform. This seemed an unlikely issue for de Gaulle, who believed in an efficiently centralized state and cared little about regional liberties (he once asked rhetorically how one could govern a country with several hundred different kinds of cheese). De Gaulle lost what turned into a plebiscite on his government and retired from political life.

The contentious year 1968 also brought student demonstrations and riots to Italy and West Germany, where Berlin was the center of the student movement. The University of Rome had been built to accommodate 5,000 students but that year enrolled 60,000 students. Thousands of university graduates were frustrated because they could not find jobs. But Italian students found no support from workers, and the movement quickly collapsed.

Shifts in Western European Politics after 1968

During the 1970s, European domestic politics underwent a shift from the right to centrist governments. This change was apparent not only in the German Federal Republic and Britain (where Labour was in power from 1974 to 1979) but also in France. In Italy, the strikes of 1968 and 1969 generated further political instability, although the Christian Democrats, forming a series of center-left coalition governments, continued to dominate Italian politics. In West Germany, the Christian Democrats refused any negotiations of consequence with the German Democratic Republic or the Soviet Union. However, following waves of student protest, Social Democrats bucked the tide and came to power in 1969. They were helped by an alliance with the centrist Free Democrats, who abandoned their Christian Democrat allies. Willy Brandt (1913–1992), who had fled Nazi Germany and fought with the Norwegian resistance during the Second World War before becoming mayor of Berlin, took office as chancellor. In 1970, Brandt signed a nonaggression pact with the Soviet Union, paving the way for the development of trade between the two states. He signed the Treaty of Warsaw, which recognized the frontier between Poland and East Germany as redrawn after the war. While echoing his predecessors' commitment to NATO, Brandt improved relations with the German Democratic Republic, calling for an "opening toward the East." Millions of people were allowed to cross the wall to visit the other side, overwhelmingly most were West Germans allowed to visit East Berlin.

Brandt resigned in 1974 following the discovery that one of his aides was a spy for East Germany. Helmut Schmidt (1918–), a more conservative Social Democrat, became chancellor. Schmidt weathered political storms, but drew the wrath of environmentalists and anti-nuclear groups in 1979 when he asked the United States to station medium-range nuclear missiles on West German soil to counter similar Soviet missiles. Schmidt and centrist French President Valéry Giscard d'Estaing (1926– ; president 1974–1981) believed that Germany and France had to become the center of Western Europe. However, economic recession, rising unemployment, and Schmidt's refusal to reduce welfare payments led to the return to power in 1982 of the Christian Democrats. They were led by Helmut Kohl (1930–), who cut taxes and reduced government spending. However, in September 1998, elections swept the Social Democrat Gerhard Schröder into the chancellorship, based on a coalition between Social Democrats and the German ecological party, known as the Greens, replacing Kohl, who resigned two years later as chairman of the Christian Democratic Party in the wake of a financial scandal. In 2005, Angela Merkel (1954–), a Christian Democrat who had grown up in the Communist German Democratic Republic, became the first female chancellor of Germany.

In Britain, under the pressure of the oil crisis and following bitter mining strikes, the Conservative government fell in 1974. But the subsequent Labour governments of Harold Wilson (1916–1995) and James Callaghan (1912–2005) were buffeted by soaring inflation, which was exacerbated by a series of major union victories in prolonged strikes during the Callaghan government.

Upper- and middle-class Britons turned against Callaghan, claiming that the unions now held their country hostage. In 1979, Conservative leader

Margaret Thatcher (1925–), the daughter of a prosperous grocer from the English Midlands, became prime minister. She was the first woman to hold the position, although she vociferously repudiated feminism.

Thatcher was committed to putting into effect a tight monetary policy ("monetarism"). She promised to slash government expenses with cutbacks. Within three years, 1 million jobs in manufacturing had disappeared. The Conservative government eliminated some of the health and education measures Labour had implemented. "The Iron Lady" reduced inheritance and capital taxes and waged war against the trade unions. The government sold off some nationalized industries, notably the rail system, with disastrous results for service. Without government subsidies, many factories closed down and unemployment continued to rise. By 1983, Britain had 3 million unemployed workers (about 12 percent of the workforce). Cuts in housing subsidies left hundreds of thousands without adequate places to live. Thatcher had, after all, once advised Britons to "glory in inequality."

In May 1982, the military government of Argentina, seeking to reverse a decline in its popularity at home, invaded the Falkland Islands. Although the British occupied the sparsely populated Falklands, which lie about 300 miles from the coast of Argentina in the Atlantic Ocean, Argentina had claimed them since the nineteenth century. British forces easily recaptured the islands. The short war boosted the prime minister's standing at home. Furthermore, the British economy began to recover in the early 1980s and inflation slowed down. The Conservatives rolled to another impressive victory in the general elections of 1983 over the bitterly divided Labour Party. In 1985, she outlasted a long strike by coal miners. However, fearing the revival of the Labour Party, Conservative leaders unseated Thatcher in 1990, replacing her with the bland John Major (1943–), who became prime minister following elections two years later. Meanwhile, Tony Blair (1953–) moved the Labour Party toward the center—what he called "New Labour." Turning away from the class politics of the old Labour Party, "New Labour" reached out to liberals and even moderate conservatives. Blair emphasized a commitment to economic progress and to practical policies in place of shrill rhetoric. In sharp contrast to most Conservatives, Blair made clear that he believed Britain's future lay with Europe. The sweeping victory of "New Labour" in 1997 brought Blair to 10 Downing Street as prime minister, where he remained for ten years.

Blair's policies increasingly could have been confused with those of his Conservative rivals. In 2001, Blair's Labour Party swept to another easy victory in Britain, leaving Socialist or Social Democratic parties in power in nine of the fifteen member states of the European Union.

In the meantime, the death of Princess Diana (1961–1997) in a high-speed car crash in a Paris tunnel on August 31, 1997, plunged Britain into mourning. This was just the latest of a series of reverses for the British monarchy, including Diana's separation and then divorce from Prince

Charles in 1996. Despite the attachment of many people to the monarchy as an institution and the fascination with the royal family perpetuated by coverage in tabloid newspapers, to some British subjects, the monarchy seemed an expensive and irrelevant atavism. Yet, to fervent British royalists, Prince William (heir to the throne after his father, Charles) and his younger brother, Harry, offered hope for the future. Increasingly unpopular because of Britain's involvement in the Iraq War (see Chapter 30), Tony Blair resigned in 2007, succeeded by Gordon Brown, under whose leadership the Labor Party's popularity in Britain plunged to an all-time low.

In France, the economic slump that began with the oil crisis of 1973 and financial scandals undercut the presidency of the centrist Valéry Giscard d'Estaing, a technocrat committed to economic modernization. In 1981, the pragmatic Socialist François Mitterrand (1916–1996) won election as president. Social Democratic parties maintained power in Scandinavia. Andreas Papandreou (1919–1996), became Greece's first Socialist premier in 1981. Italy and Spain also had moderately left-wing governments. As in Britain, Socialist and other leftist governments in France and other countries governed with moderation, abandoning traditional agendas of the left in the interest of practical politics. In the meantime, the influence of unions declined along with the number of industrial workers. Abandoned factories in the German Ruhr region, northeastern France, northern England, and the Czech Republic stood as rusty symbols of an industrial world that was disappearing.

By nationalizing large corporations and more banks and initiating ambitious social reforms, French President Mitterrand confronted determined opposition from the business community. The French franc plunged on the international currency market; people of wealth began to remove their assets from France. A year after taking office, the Socialist government was forced to devalue the franc and freeze prices and wages. Pressure from the right mounted from the Gaullists and their ambitious leader, Jacques Chirac (1932–), the mayor of Paris. The inability of the Socialist government to revive the economy undercut its popularity.

In the 1986 elections for the Chamber of Deputies, the right triumphed, leading to an awkward period of government known as "cohabitation." Mitterrand selected a rightist premier, Chirac, with ministers drawn from the right and center. The new government sold off some nationalized banks and businesses and ended wage and price controls.

Given a slight majority in the elections for the National Assembly in 1988, Mitterrand appointed Socialist prime ministers, but the right swept into power in 1993. When his second term ended in 1995, Mitterrand had become the longest serving head of state in France since Napoleon III (emperor 1852–1870). Chirac was elected president in 1995. He began his presidency by authorizing the resumption of French nuclear testing in the South Pacific, leading to considerable international opposition, particularly in Australia, New Zealand, and Japan. Facing a high unemployment rate and a growing economic deficit, reductions in health, retirement, and other benefits followed. Strikes forced the government to make some concessions. In 1997, however, Chirac called elections a year early in hopes of receiving a sweeping mandate. Socialists dominated the elections, forcing Chirac to name the Socialist Lionel Jospin as prime minister, bringing another uncomfortable period of "cohabitation" with a conservative president and a Socialist prime minister.

In Italy, instability and corruption continued to characterize political life. Despite a general increase in prosperity, inflation and high unemployment left many Italians still dissatisfied with all political parties. The government of Bettino Craxi (1934–2000) from 1983 to 1986 was the longest and in many ways the most stable of the post-war period. Socialists replaced the Communists as Italy's second largest party, forcing the Christian Democrats to accept them as coalition partners in 1986. Craxi himself was convicted of corruption, however, and fled in 1993 to Tunisia. Giulio Andreotti (1919–), Christian Democrat prime minister on six different occasions, stood accused not only of corruption, but was eventually found guilty of arranging the murder of a journalist who had uncovered evidence of wrongdoing. More than 2,500 Italian politicians and businessmen were arrested for corruption over an eighteen-month period. Campaigns against the Mafia have been periodic (most energetically following the assassination in 1992 of a public prosecutor who had devoted himself to the difficult legal war against the Mafia). In the 1994 elections, conservative financier and media tycoon Silvio Berlusconi (1936–) became prime minister of Italy. His new right-wing party, Forza Italia, came out of the elections as Italy's most successful party, with two parties of the extreme right as allies, both denouncing the increase in the immigrant population: the Northern League, which campaigned on a program of independence for northern Italy, provocatively describing the south as a weight around the neck of the north, and the neo-fascist National Alliance. Cynicism and mistrust of politicians became even more prevalent in Italy.

In every Western country, a new political force began to be felt. "Green" parties, political groups of militant environmentalists angered by the deterioration of the environment, emerged in Western Europe during the 1980s. In the German Federal Republic, the Greens, Europe's largest environmental party, were alarmed by industrial pollution, which was slowly killing their country's forests. Environmental parties stridently opposed nuclear power, even before a deadly Soviet nuclear disaster at Chernobyl in Ukraine in 1986. Greens helped push for agreements that have led to some cleaning up of the Rhine River and Mediterranean beaches.

Finally, in almost all Western states, economic slumps have accentuated complaints that state-subsidized programs are too expensive. In Sweden and Denmark, Social Democratic parties were ousted after decades of rule by conservatives calling for sharp reductions in the tax rates that financed

A nuclear power plant dwarfs a more traditional source of power.

cradle-to-grave social programs. With the recession of the early 1990s reducing tax revenue, Western European governments reduced social benefits, such as unemployment payments.

The Transition to Democracy in Southern Europe

During the 1970s, three southern European dictatorships became democracies: Greece, Portugal, and Spain. Greece, the cradle of democracy, had been controlled by a series of right-wing governments since its civil war in the late 1940s. In 1967, military officers overthrew Greece's first post-war government of the left, ruthlessly crushed dissent, and imprisoned, and tortured political opponents. The military dictators planned to seize the island of Cyprus, which lies off the coast of Turkey and which both Greece and Turkey had claimed for centuries. Relations between Greece and Turkey had often been extremely tense. Now bitter disagreements over the form of a new constitution in Cyprus led to fighting between Greeks and Turks. The Greek Cypriot National Guard overthrew the government of Cyprus. At the same time, the Cypriot Turks defeated the Greeks and declared the northeastern, predominantly Turkish part of the island to be independent. Further fighting ended in a cease-fire. Meanwhile, in Greece, the power of the generals, who had not sent help to the Greek Cypriot insurgents, collapsed in 1974. Greece became a republic in which conservative and Socialist parties took turns in power.

In Portugal, authoritarian leaders, notably Antonio Salazar, dictator from 1932 to 1968, struggled inefficiently with economic backwardness. Thousands of Portuguese went abroad as seasonal workers each year or emigrated permanently to other countries in Western Europe or in the Western Hemisphere. At the same time, the dictatorship, determined to hold on to Portugal's African colonies at all costs, became entangled in a long, bitter war with nationalist rebels in its African colonies of first Angola, beginning in 1961, and then Mozambique, conflicts that Portugal could neither afford (at the annual cost of half the nation's budget) nor win (see Chapter 28). In April 1974, a group of liberal army officers overthrew the dictatorship. The Socialist Party emerged victorious in elections the following year and Angola and Mozambique became independent, lapsing into bloody civil wars. Despite another coup two years later by a group of officers, the Portuguese transition to democracy occurred without bloodshed. However, political turmoil forced the government to abandon a program of state nationalizations and some agricultural collectivization in 1976. That year, Mário Soares (1924–) took office as the first democratically elected prime minister in Portugal in fifty years, and he dominated Portuguese political life into the 1990s.

In Spain, General Francisco Franco survived as dictator long after his friends Hitler and Mussolini had gone to their graves. After World War II, the United States prevented the United Nations from imposing economic sanctions against Spain because of Franco's support of the Axis powers. Franco maintained Spain's authoritarian political structure. While repudiating secular values, he accepted economic modernization, with the help of the United States.

In the late 1960s, opposition to Franco's regime mounted in Catalonia and the Basque country, Spain's most industrial regions, each with an entrenched separatist movement. Franco struck hard against Basque and Catalan separatists; the Catalan language, for example, remained illegal in print. But Franco retained popularity in traditionally religious regions, such as Navarre and his native Galicia.

Franco agreed that Juan Carlos (1938–), the son of the heir to the throne before the civil war, would succeed him as head of state and that Spain would remain an authoritarian state. Within the Spanish government, however, many officials already believed political reform inevitable, even desirable. Socialist and Communist parties existed, although they were illegal. Government censorship itself became more lax in the 1970s.

Upon Franco's death, Juan Carlos became king in 1975. He accepted the transformation of Spain into a constitutional monarchy with a democratic political structure. Spain emerged from authoritarian rule and international isolation. Spectacular economic growth and increasing prosperity helped the centrist Adolfo Suarez (1932–) keep a series of governments afloat through skillful political negotiation, even without a parliamentary majority. The charismatic Felipe González and the Socialists swept Suarez aside in the 1980s. In 1996, José Maria Aznar became Spain's first conservative prime minister since the time of Franco.

RELIGIOUS AND ETHNIC CONFLICTS

Compared to the sixteenth, seventeenth, and eighteenth centuries, religious conflicts have diminished in modern Europe, with several notable exceptions. In Northern Ireland, the bitter centuries-old rivalry between Catholics and Protestants brought violence. Although the Catholic Republic of Ireland obtained independence in 1922, Northern Ireland is primarily Protestant (two-thirds of the population) and remains part of Britain. The Irish Republican Army (IRA), claiming to represent Ulster Catholics, struck at the British army and Protestants alike. Several weeks of disturbances in 1969 unleashed decades of violence, "the troubles" that took at least 3,500 lives. Secret Protestant paramilitary organizations, claiming that the British army inadequately protected Protestants, struck back against Catholics. Ian Paisley (1926–), a Protestant clergyman, heightened tension by speaking out provocatively against any compromise. On January 30, 1972—"Bloody Sunday"—British troops killed thirteen demonstrators in the Northern Irish town of Londonderry.

The economic crisis of the 1970s compounded Northern Ireland's problems, making Catholics even more disadvantaged compared to Protestants. The IRA, buying guns on the world weapons market with money stolen from banks or contributed by sympathetic Irish Americans, struck not only in Northern Ireland but also in England. Cease-fires in 1994 and 1996 could not still the violence that continued periodically, particularly during the

The aftermath of a bomb planted by the Irish Republican Army in Belfast, Northern Ireland, 1972.

period of the traditional Protestant summer marches. On April 10, 1998, Protestant and Catholic representatives signed the Belfast Agreement (or Good Friday Agreement), which provided for a National Assembly for Northern Ireland in which both religions would be represented. The people of Northern Ireland and of the Irish Republic overwhelmingly approved the Belfast Agreement. In December 1999, the British Parliament granted substantial power to the Northern Ireland Assembly, with a Catholic moderate as deputy first minister and David Trimble, a Protestant, as first minister. However, in February 2000, the British government suspended the Catholic and Protestant power-sharing government of Northern Ireland when the IRA refused to establish a timetable for the disarmament of its members.

The situation then began to improve dramatically. The IRA gradually abandoned the tactics of violence, and the Catholic political organization Sein Fein emerged as a force for conciliation. The expanding economy in Northern Ireland, as in the Republic, gave more people a stake in peace. Even Paisley now accepted compromise, becoming first minister of Northern Ireland in 2007.

Demands by ethnic minorities for independence surfaced in several countries. In Spain, Basque separatists (the ETA), sometimes hiding in the French Basque country, have moved across what they considered an arbitrary frontier to attack Spanish government, army, and police installations and to carry out assassinations. Popular support for the separatists in the Spanish Basque region waned in the 1980s, after the constitution of 1978 recognized "autonomous communities" within Spain. However, the violent ETA campaign has continued off and on. On the Mediterranean island of Corsica, violent groups opposed to French rule have planted bombs and carried out occasional assassinations, even as they feuded among themselves.

The Fall of Communism

In 1975, the leaders of European states gathered in Helsinki, Finland, to sign the Helsinki Accords, which concluded the first Conference on Security and Cooperation. All European states, with the exception of Albania, signed the accords, which recognized as valid the national borders drawn up after World War II. The thirty-five signatories also pledged to respect human rights and to cooperate in economic and scientific matters. To some critics, the Helsinki Accords seemed to recognize Soviet domination of Eastern Europe since the war. To other observers, they were a significant step forward because the heads of Communist states agreed in principle to respect human rights. The accords seemed a healthy pause in the renewed tension between East and West.

Hardly anyone at the time could have anticipated the fact that, fourteen years later, communism would collapse in Eastern Europe, bringing about an end to the Warsaw Pact two years later, or that the Soviet Union would

MAP 29.1 THE FALL OF COMMUNISM IN EASTERN EUROPE AND THE SOVIET UNION, 1989–1991 With the fall of communism came the reunification of Germany and the breakup of the Soviet Union.

Countries affected by boundary changes
- - - Old 1989 boundaries
- - - New 1993 boundaries

break up in 1991, leaving communism behind. However, the euphoria that arose from the realization that the Cold War had suddenly ended proved to be brief. New challenges and problems, among them those that had beset Europe for centuries, presented themselves. Decades of Communist rule had prevented the emergence of parliamentary political structures. Civic society in most Communist countries remained seriously undeveloped. Changing from planned economies with varying degrees of collectivization to free-market economies would prove extremely difficult. In Yugoslavia, ethnic conflicts exploded, and ethnic divisions also complicated the fall of communism in Romania, Hungary, Czechoslovakia, and Bulgaria.

Resistance to Soviet Domination

Calls for change echoed loudly in Communist Czechoslovakia in 1968. Intellectuals and writers accused the leadership of the Communist Party of clinging to Stalinism. The party leadership also acknowledged the need for change. In January 1968, party leaders named Alexander Dubček (1921–1992), a liberal Slovak, to be first secretary of the Communist Party, and thus head of state. During the "Prague Spring," Dubček tried to implement "socialism with a human face" by instituting reforms, but as he did so he glanced anxiously over his shoulder toward Leonid Brezhnev's Soviet Union. Crucial to these reforms was a democratization of decision making and greater freedom of expression. But, as in the case of Hungary in 1956, the Soviet leadership feared that, despite Dubček's assurances to the contrary, Czechoslovakia might attempt to move away from the Warsaw Pact. On August 21, 1968, Soviet tanks and troops moved rapidly across the border and rolled into Prague, ending the Prague Spring.

The Soviet invasion of Czechoslovakia initiated another chill in Soviet-Western relations. Moreover, the Communist parties of Italy and France denounced the invasion. In the mid-1970s, Western Communist leaders, particularly in Spain and Italy, began to call themselves "Euro-Communists." They stressed their independence—for example, by collaborating with Socialists and other left-wing parties. However, Euro-Communism proved unable to slow the decline in membership in the Communist parties of Western Europe.

Under the "Brezhnev Doctrine," the Soviet leadership tried to justify the invasion of Czechoslovakia and left open the possibility of future intervention in any of the satellite states of Eastern Europe. With the exception of Albania, which remained closed to virtually all foreign contact during the rigid dictatorship of Enver Hoxha, only Yugoslavia retained real independence. The Soviet invasion of Czechoslovakia disenchanted liberal Communists in Eastern European countries. Many no longer believed that communism could be reformed.

Opposition to Communist rule and Russian influence grew in all of the Eastern European states during the 1980s. The overwhelming economic

(*Left*) Communist leaders meet shortly before the Russian invasion of Czechoslovakia. Participants include Walter Ulbricht and Erich Honecker of East Germany (first two on the left), and Soviet Communist Party chief Leonid Brezhnev conferring with Premier Alexei Kosygin (on the right). (*Right*) Soviet armies occupy Prague, 1968.

failures of the Communist regimes grew ever more apparent. Television and radio carried images of the consumer culture of the more prosperous people in the West. In the meantime, Eastern European Communist states continued to borrow massively from the West, which merely patched over huge problems without bringing economic reform. Debt owed by Eastern European countries in hard currency rose from 6 billion dollars in 1971 to 66 billion dollars in 1980 and more than 95 billion dollars in 1988. Well-developed social services could not compensate for economic inefficiency and massive demoralization. Membership in the Communist Party declined, particularly among young people, while the age of the leadership increased dramatically.

Within the Soviet Bloc, resistance was most developed in Poland. In 1976 a variety of opposition groups unified, publishing underground books and newspapers and organizing strikes and demonstrations. Massive unrest led to strikes in Poland in 1970 and the organization of a Committee for the Defense of Workers. Edward Gierek (1913–2001), who had become head of the Polish United Workers' (Communist) Party in 1970, made some concessions while attempting to stimulate economic growth. However, despite massive foreign loans and credits, by 1976 Poland again had lapsed into economic stagnation, and another wave of strikes followed. In the meantime, the Catholic Church, which retained considerable influence (unlike in Czechoslovakia) helped mobilize opposition to the Communist government, particularly after the election in 1978 of Polish Pope John Paul II and his visit to his homeland in 1979. Strikes began in July 1980, and the following month Solidarity, a new illegal organization of trade unions, organized. Led by Lech Walesa (1943–), an electrician from Gdańsk, Solidarity put forward twenty-one demands for reform. Much more than a trade union, Solidarity's membership reached 10 million and came to represent opposition to communism. In the meantime, underground publishing had since the late 1970s emerged as a huge dissident industry undertaken by Polish intellectuals, who published more than 2,000 titles. In 1980, strikes and riots in protest of living conditions spread rapidly in industrial areas, particularly in the vast shipyards of Gdańsk. The Polish government agreed to tolerate the creation of new unions as long as they did not engage in political activity. Solidarity represented the first major challenge to the Communist system since the "Prague Spring" of 1968.

In September 1980, the Communist Central Committee responded to the ongoing crisis by forcing Gierek to resign as head of state. Two months later, the government officially recognized Solidarity's existence. However, accommodation between the government and the non-Communist trade unions did not last long, particularly after Solidarity members called for free elections. In December 1981, General Wojciech Jaruzelski (1923–), the new head of state, imposed martial law and replaced key Communist Party officials in government with military officers. He suspended Solidarity and put hundreds of leading dissidents under arrest, including Walesa. Troops brutally crushed strikes that broke out in response to the repression. In 1982, the government declared Solidarity illegal again. Although martial law ended a year later, the murder of a militant priest by policemen in 1984 generated enormous popular anger and protest.

In the meantime, East Germany, Bulgaria, and Czechoslovakia were the Eastern European nations that were most loyal to the Soviet Union. The German Democratic Republic's chief, Erich Honecker (1912–1994), who came to power in 1971, proved absolutely intransigent to reform. The Stasi, the East German secret police, employed 90,000 people and had about twice that number as informers. The Lutheran Church provided a center for some dissidents, organizing weekly "prayers for peace" in Leipzig. In Czechoslovakia, the state campaign against dissidents was more intense. In 1977, about 1,200 writers, philosophers, intellectuals, and musicians signed a protest against government limitation of freedoms in an attempt to force the government to respect the Helsinki human-rights convention it had signed. Despite the fact that this was anything but a revolutionary document (those who signed pledged not to engage in political activity), members of the "Charter 77" group suffered repression.

Gradual economic liberalization helped make Hungary the second (after the German Democratic Republic) most prosperous of the Eastern bloc countries. The gradual development of a market economy and a private agricultural sector helped stabilize the Communist regime, with the help of Soviet subsidies. In 1985 Hungary became the first Communist state to declare political pluralism to be an ideal. However, Hungary had no organized and tested opposition force such as Solidarity.

In sharp contrast, no liberalization of any kind took place in Romania. Nicolae Ceauşescu (1918–1989), head of the Romanian Communist Party, had brazenly adopted a position of relative independence, or "national communism," with respect to the Soviet Union, criticizing the Soviet invasion of Czechoslovakia, remaining neutral in the Sino-Soviet conflict, and refusing to participate in Warsaw Pact military maneuvers. Ceauşescu forged ahead with grandiose plans to generate industrial development. The results were disastrous. Romania became, after Albania, the poorest country in Europe while caught in the increasingly mad grip of Ceauşescu's "cult of personality." The dictator ordered 1,500 villages in Transylvania razed to the ground. These were largely in areas where many Hungarians resided, whom he targeted while trying to garner support from Romanians with nationalist appeals. He also ordered some of old Bucharest torn down to forge enormous boulevards that would lead to his reviewing stand.

The Gorbachev Era

In the Soviet Union, in the meantime, Leonid Brezhnev reinforced the powers of the oppressive Soviet bureaucracy and the prestige of the army and the KGB (the secret police). Reflecting the chill in relations with the United States, the Soviet Union, like its rival, poured more money into the manufacture of arms. After Brezhnev died in 1982, he was succeeded by Yuri Andropov (1914–1984), who, despite his long years in the KGB, was somewhat more liberal than Brezhnev. Andropov acknowledged that there was widespread inefficiency and corruption in Soviet economic planning and government. He called for greater popular participation in economic decision making and purged incompetent party hacks from important positions. Following Andropov's death in 1984, his successor, Konstantine Chernenko (1911–1985) was quite ill when he came to power, and both he and the Soviet state treaded water until his death the following year.

Mikhail Gorbachev (1931–) became general secretary of the Communist Party and thus head of the Soviet Union in 1985. Gorbachev had worked his way up in the party youth organization and studied law at the University of Moscow. Both his grandfathers had been arrested on false charges during the Stalin era. Gorbachev assumed responsibility for Soviet agriculture. Less instinctively xenophobic than other Soviet leaders, he was the first Soviet leader since Lenin to have a university degree. Relatively young, charming, flexible, and determined, Gorbachev was a master of Communist Party machinations.

Gorbachev began by exorcizing some ghosts from the Stalinist past. Like a number of optimistic party officials and intellectuals, Gorbachev believed that the Prague Spring could come to Moscow, but that the Communist Party should continue to dominate political life in the Soviet Union. He embraced a policy known in Russian as *glasnost*: openness in government combined with a greater degree of free expression. He put some liberals in positions of responsibility and ordered the relaxation of censorship. Artists and writers brought forth new work, including strident criticisms of the Soviet regime.

Gorbachev insisted that "we need a revolution of the mind." He espoused *perestroika*: a restructuring of the Soviet system to make it more efficient and responsive to the needs of Soviet citizens. The Soviet leader spoke openly about the failure of economic planning without sufficient material incentives for workers. Centralized state agricultural planning would have to be scrapped in favor of a free-market economy. He summarily cashiered some corrupt or incompetent local party officials and launched a full-fledged campaign against alcoholism, which had taken on epidemic proportions in the demoralized Soviet Union. But Gorbachev remained convinced that communism could be rescued by necessary reforms once the inefficiency and brutality of Stalinism had been completely eliminated. His model may well have been Lenin's implementation of the New Economic Policy in 1921 (see Chapter 23), which had revived the Soviet economy without sacrificing Communist authority.

In 1987, he reduced the role state corporations played in the Soviet economy, paving the way for increasing economic privatization. The state accepted private cooperatives and permitted state companies to sell their products on the open market (which encouraged luxury goods more than daily necessities). Furthermore, Gorbachev sought foreign investment in the Soviet Union. However, decades of economic inefficiency would clearly have to be overcome. Black marketeering remained a way of life for millions of people. The enormous costs of social programs weighed heavily on the sagging economy. The Communist countries of Eastern Europe, which had been exploited to economic advantage during the immediate post-war period, now represented an expensive drain on Soviet finances because of subsidy commitments and the cost of maintaining Soviet bases there.

In 1988, Gorbachev began to sponsor a series of remarkable political reforms. Dissidents within the Communist Party or even non-Communists could now be elected to the Congress of People's Deputies. He expressed determination to renew the "thaw" with the West that had ended during the Brezhnev era.

Three factors converged in the late 1980s to prepare the fall of communism and the end of the Soviet Union. First, nationalist movements gained momentum within the Soviet Union, particularly in the Baltic states of Lithuania, Latvia, and Estonia, and in Moldavia, Armenia, and Georgia, where in 1989 soldiers bludgeoned to death nineteen demonstrators demanding independence. Nationalists in Ukraine celebrated their culture by passing manuscripts written in Ukrainian from hand to hand. These movements, encouraged by the growing vulnerability of the Soviet state to a weak economy, were not placated by the belated toleration of greater cultural autonomy. In some of the republics, long-festering conflicts between nationalities began to surface violently, further undermining Soviet authority, for example, in Azerbaijan between Muslim Azerbaijanis and Christian Armenians.

Second, in 1989, a forceful democratic opposition emerged, led in Russia by the Nobel Prize–winning Russian physicist Andrey Sakharov (1921– 1989), who had helped develop the hydrogen bomb. Gorbachev's encouragement of participation in public life increased the ranks of Soviet citizens demanding reform. For many people, brutal tales of the Gulag became increasingly compelling, having been brought to light by works of the Russian writer Alexander Solzhenitsyn (1918–2008), first in his novel *A Day in the Life of Ivan Denisovitch* (1962) and then in *The Gulag Archipelago* (1973). Moreover, the campaign for human rights, led by Sakharov, discredited the regime, even if the Gulag itself no longer existed. The Helsinki Accords, signed by the Soviet Union as well as by the Western powers in 1975, encouraged dissidents. Increasingly, the Russian opposition reached a large audience through the circulation of handwritten, typed, or clandestinely printed manuscripts, as well as through the medium of Western radio broadcasts.

Third, the aggravation of the economic crisis beginning in 1988 increased the number of Soviet citizens convinced that a Communist government simply could not bring about a meaningful improvement in the quality of their lives. At the same time, television broadcasts from Finland day after day showed the advantages of a free-market economy. Gorbachev vacillated between free-market policies and traditional Communist state controls. The result was a further weakening of the economy, replete with shortages and undermined by enormous military spending.

Gorbachev determined that the Soviet Union could not afford to continue the arms race with the United States. He therefore moved to improve relations with the U.S. government. In the early 1980s, Soviet-U.S. relations had continued to sour dangerously. Following the U.S. ban on the export of oil and gas to the Soviet Union after the Soviet invasion of Afghanistan in 1979, the U.S. government had tried to prevent the Soviet Union from constructing a long pipeline that would bring Siberian natural gas to Central Europe by threatening sanctions against any state or company that assisted the endeavor. Then U.S. President Ronald Reagan (1911–2004) backed a plan to construct a space-based missile-defense shield, dubbed "Star Wars" (Strategic Defense Initiative), provoking an outcry by the Soviet Union and by some U.S. allies as well. In 1983, a Russian fighter shot down a South Korean passenger plane that had entered Soviet air space, killing 169 people, including Americans. The Soviet Union boycotted the 1984 Olympics, which were held in Los Angeles, as the United States had done four years earlier in Moscow.

Gorbachev now resumed arms-limitation negotiations with the United States, but he refused to sign an agreement because Reagan would not include the "Star Wars" experiments in the negotiations. Highly successful visits to Washington, D.C., and New York in 1987 gave the Soviet leader considerable global television exposure, leading to enormous personal popularity. That year the United States and the Soviet Union agreed to reduce the number of medium-range missiles, and two years later they signed another arms-control agreement. In 1988, the Soviet Union recalled troops from Afghanistan after nine years of bloody fighting against rebels there. For the first time in anyone's memory, government publications admitted the severe economic and social problems that troubled the Soviet Union. The Soviet Union began to allow Soviet Jews to emigrate abroad in greater numbers than ever before. In 1989, almost 70,000 Jews left, most for Israel or the United States.

In 1986, the most serious nuclear accident in history occurred in Ukraine, when a nuclear reactor exploded at Chernobyl, near Kiev, sending radioactive material pouring into the atmosphere. Thousands of people in the vicinity were killed or suffered grave illnesses. A nuclear cloud passed over Ukraine, Russia, and the Scandinavian states, among other countries. Following an initial official attempt to deny the seriousness of the disaster, Gorbachev discussed the situation with unexpected openness.

Early in 1989, some reform-minded government officials joined opposition leaders in Poland and Hungary in the belief that economic and political liberalization was urgent. Communist rule slowly floundered under the weight of economic decline and popular dissatisfaction. In Czechoslovakia, East Germany, Bulgaria, Romania, and Albania, Communist leaders sought desperately to hold on to power. The East German and Czech governments reverted to force in an attempt to halt popular movements for change.

A crucial factor made the outcome of this wave of demands for reform in Eastern Europe in 1989 different from those occurring earlier (in East Germany in 1953, Hungary in 1956, and Czechoslovakia in 1968): the Soviet government no longer was determined to preserve its empire. Indeed, the shout "Gorbi, Gorbi, Gorbi!" rang out from the ranks of Eastern European protesters. Even if the Communist leadership in Czechoslovakia, East Germany, and Romania, particularly, were determined to overwhelm dissent, Soviet tanks would no longer back them up. In a speech to the Council of Europe in Strasbourg in July 1989, Gorbachev made clear that he rejected the "Brezhnev Doctrine" that had brought Soviet intervention in Czechoslovakia in 1968. The Soviet leader called events in Eastern Europe "inspiring," adding, "What the Poles and Hungarians decide is their affair, but we will respect their decision whatever it is."

Transition to Parliamentary Government in Poland and Hungary

Poland became the first test case for the new Soviet relationship with its former satellites. Since its creation in 1980, the trade union organization Solidarity had virtually achieved the status of an unofficial opposition party. The Catholic Church remained a source of organized opposition to communism. But although these organizations exerted some pressure on the government, it was the continued pitiful performance of the economy that fatally undermined communism. In 1987, the government held a referendum, asking Poles to support price increases. When they were overwhelmingly voted down, the government imposed them anyway. Demonstrations and strikes followed, and renewed calls to legalize Solidarity were made, amid widespread shortages and a grotesquely inflated currency. The government could no longer meet the interest payments on its massive debt to Western banks. General Jaruzelski had no choice but to accept some reforms. In August 1988, the government invited Solidarity to negotiate. The opposition agreed to participate in exchange for government recognition of the legal status of Solidarity as the legitimate representative of Poles opposed to Communist rule. Negotiations between Solidarity representatives and the government in 1989 led to the creation of a senate and the position of president of Poland. In the first relatively free elections in Poland since the immediate post-war period, Solidarity candidates swept to victory in the Senate. In the lower chamber, negotiations had led to 65 percent of the seats being reserved for Communists and 35 percent for the candidates of Solidarity. Still, General Jaruzelski confidently believed he could orchestrate liberalization on his own terms.

Solidarity's candidates swept to victory. The extent of Communist humiliation was such that candidates supported by Solidarity (with the support of the Catholic Church) won all 161 of these parliamentary seats. Moreover, Communist candidates won only two of thirty-five seats in elections in which they ran unopposed. When the United Peasant Party began talks with Solidarity and left the government coalition, the Communist majority collapsed. The Communists could not put together a government acceptable to Solidarity. When parliament elected Solidarity leader Tadeusz Mazowiecki (1927–) Poland had the first non-Communist government in Eastern Europe since 1948, although Communists retained several important ministries. However, Solidarity leaders, still wary that popular momentum once again could lead to heavy-handed repression, supported the election by the Polish parliament of General Jaruzelski as president.

In 1990, the Communist era ended in Poland when the Polish Communist Party changed its name and espoused pluralist politics. In the wake of a split within Solidarity between the followers of Mazowiecki and those of Lech Walesa, the latter was elected president in December 1990. The Democratic Union, a party formed by Mazowiecki's followers within Solidarity, won the largest number of seats in the lower house and the senate. Economic reforms, aimed at introducing a full-fledged free-market economy, were slow to take effect, however. Poland began a long struggle for economic stability with mounting unemployment and a dramatically increased crime rate.

In Hungary, the Hungarian Democratic Forum and several smaller opposition groups began to emerge in 1988 out of café and living-room gatherings of longtime dissidents. Gorbachev's reforms in the Soviet Union

Border guards cut down the Hungarian "Iron Curtain."

greatly encouraged opposition groups. But with the economy floundering under declining productivity and rampaging inflation, liberal Communists ousted longtime leader János Kádár from power, intent on reforming Hungary. Opposition groups, with the memory of Soviet intervention in 1956 still looming large, hesitated to call the legitimacy of the Communist regime into question.

In the summer of 1989, the Hungarian opposition formed an "Opposition Round Table" and negotiated with the government. Candidates of the Democratic Forum won free elections. Faced with continuing popular mobilization, the Communist leadership decided to try to outbid the Hungarian liberals by initiating reforms. In May 1989, the government ordered the removal of barbed wire that defined the border with Austria. In June, the Communist Party itself admitted that the 1956 trial and execution of reform leaders had been illegal. The former premier Imre Nagy, who had been executed after the 1956 insurrection, was reburied with national honors. The Hungarian Communist Party changed its name to the Hungarian Socialist Party. It espoused democratic principles and encouraged the development of opposition parties, accepting a new constitution proclaimed later that year. The transition from communism to multiparty parliamentary rule in Hungary was therefore peaceful, with the Hungarian Democratic Forum leading a subsequent coalition government.

The Collapse of the Berlin Wall and of East German Communism

As pressure for change mounted in Poland and Hungary, East Germans fled the German Democratic Republic in record numbers. Many traveled to the German Federal Republic via Czechoslovakia and then Hungary, whose government in May 1989 had opened its border with Austria. About 150,000 East Germans reached the West during the first nine months of 1989. However, eschewing the reforms undertaken by Gorbachev in the Soviet Union, East German Communist leader Honecker in June 1989 praised the Chinese army and police for crushing the pro-democracy demonstrations in Beijing's Tiananmen Square. While other Communist governments negotiated with determined reformers, the East German leadership stood firm until it was too late. Honecker demanded that Hungary return fleeing East Germans to their country, as specified in an old treaty between the two Communist states. The Hungarian government refused to do so. When the East German government gave permission to East Germans on a train passing through Dresden and Leipzig to emigrate to West Germany, other East Germans frantically tried to climb aboard the train. About 1.5 million East Germans now applied for exit visas.

When Gorbachev visited East Berlin early in October 1989, demonstrators chanted his name, which had become synonymous with opposition to the East German regime. When demonstrations spread to other major cities, Honecker ordered the police to attack demonstrators, but Egon Krenz, responsible for state security, refused to do so. On October 18, 1989, Honecker, old, ill, and ignored, was forced out in favor of Krenz, more moderate, but no reformer. In Leipzig, anxious opposition leaders and fearful Communist officials had met and resolved that peace must be maintained at all costs.

On October 23, 1989, Soviet Foreign Minister Eduard Shevardnadze (1928–) declared that each country in Eastern Europe "has the right to an absolute, absolute freedom of choice." Such words further encouraged demonstrations and meetings in East Germany. On November 4, Krenz announced that East Germans were free to leave for West Germany via Czechoslovakia. A wholesale exodus began. On November 9, Krenz capitulated to the inevitable, announcing a sweeping change in government and promising to initiate legislation that would grant East Germans the right to travel where and when they wanted. He ordered that the Berlin Wall, which had divided East Berlin from West Berlin since August 1961, be torn down. Around 3 million East Germans (out of a population of 16 million) poured over the demolished wall, or crossed into West Germany at once-forbidden checkpoints. An East German poet remarked, "I must weep for joy that it happened so quickly and simply. And I must weep for wrath that it took so abysmally long."

When Egon Krenz announced that East Germans could travel where and when they wanted, people gathered at the Berlin Wall to forge openings with whatever tools they had.

Krenz still hoped that his promise to hold free elections would keep the Communists in power. But lacking popular support, Krenz's government fell on December 3 and was succeeded by a series of committees until elections were held in March 1990. Conservatives favoring German reunification (led by the equivalent of the West German Christian Democrats) won an easy victory over Social Democrats and the remnants of the (now renamed) Communist Party. A number of East German leaders already expressed eagerness for German reunification. Here, again, there would be no Russian opposition to what had seemed for decades to be unthinkable because of Russian fear that one day a united Germany might again threaten the peace. In the meantime, the German Democratic Republic began selling off state-owned companies and the West German mark became the currency of both Germanys. In September, Britain, France, and the United States, viewing reunification as inevitable, renounced their rights in Berlin. Unification took effect on October 3, 1990. In December, the first elections in the newly unified Germany returned the Christian Democrats to power. The former German Federal Republic would for years have to allocate a substantial part of its budget to modernize the former Communist state and to provide public services to new citizens (including unemployment benefits in the wake of the collapse of state-run industries). In 1999, Berlin again became the capital of Germany.

The "Velvet Revolution" in Czechoslovakia

In Czechoslovakia, where the Communist leadership resisted the forces for change as vehemently as their counterparts in East Germany, the regime was swept aside in ten days. As news arrived of the fall of the Berlin Wall, the number of determined dissidents rapidly swelled. Czechs and Slovaks alike signed petitions calling for reform. On November 17, 1989, students staged a demonstration in honor of a student executed by the Nazis fifty years earlier. But speakers quickly ignored the program censors had approved and began to call for academic freedom and respect for human rights. Then the crowd started to march toward the giant St. Wenceslas Square in the center of Prague. A squad of riot police moved in, throwing canisters of tear gas and beating students with clubs.

The next day, a crowd assembled on the spot where police had beaten protesters. Students called for a general strike to begin ten days later. As the demonstrations continued to grow, the minister of defense announced that the army was "ready to defend the achievements of socialism." Yet, without the support of the Soviet Union, the Czechoslovak Communist government took no steps to repress the movement for freedom. On November 19, 1989, the entire Politburo resigned. A group of leading dissidents formed the "Civic Forum," calling on the government to negotiate with them over four demands: the resignation of two Communist officials blamed for the police attack two days earlier, the establishment of a commission to investigate the police attack, the release of political prisoners, and the resignation of Communist leaders responsible for the Soviet invasion in 1968. Civic Forum was led by Václav Havel (1936–), a popular Czech playwright whose plays had been banned by the government but circulated in manuscript) and a veteran of "Charter 77." Havel had been imprisoned several times for dissent, once nearly dying from mistreatment.

On November 21, 1989, the elderly Alexander Dubček, the Slovak reformer who led the Communist Party of Czechoslovakia during the 1968 events, addressed a throng assembled in St. Wenceslas Square. The crowds, however, did not want any kind of socialism. Students went to factories in search of support from workers. Crowds poured into the streets almost every day, waving national flags and calling for freedom of speech, the release of political prisoners, and the end of communism. They lay wreaths on the spot where a Czech student burned himself to death in 1968 in protest of the Soviet invasion. On November 24, 1989, the Communist Central Committee narrowly voted against using the army to put an end to demonstrations. In Slovakia, intellectuals formed an organization called "Public Against Violence," the Slovak equivalent of the Czech Civic Forum.

The Communist government now had no choice but to negotiate with its opponents who demanded free elections. Yet, unlike Poland and Hungary, where political opposition was well developed within the constraints of the system, there were virtually no reform-minded Communists in

Czechoslovakia. From Moscow, Gorbachev advised the Czechoslovak leaders not to use force. Negotiations between the government and Havel and other representatives of Civic Forum began on November 26. That day, more than half of the top leadership within the party was purged. Two days later, Civic Forum demanded the formation of a new government.

The Communist-dominated Federal Assembly voted to end the party's domination of political life. On December 10, the first cabinet in Czechoslovakia since 1948 not dominated by Communists was sworn in. The general strike ended, and more than a third of the members of the Communist Party resigned during the first two weeks of December. The Federal Assembly unanimously elected Havel president of Czechoslovakia. What Havel called a "velvet revolution" had succeeded, led by writers, actors, and students. Free elections gave Civic Forum and its allies a majority of seats. Price controls ended. Havel quickly announced that Czechoslovakia "must return to Europe," suggesting that its future lay with the West.

The new government of Czechoslovakia immediately faced not only the problem of creating viable democratic institutions and establishing a market economy, but also of tensions between Czechs and Slovaks. Although the two peoples shared seventy years of common political history, much separated them. The Czech part of the state was more urban, prosperous, and Protestant than Slovakia, which was more rural and Catholic. Slovak nationalists, particularly on the right, called for the creation of an inde-

Václav Havel, leader of the Civic Forum and first president elected under free elections in Czechoslovakia after the fall of the Communists in 1989, reads the names of members of Czechoslovakia's first non-Communist government since 1948.

pendent Slovakia. On January 1, 1993, the "velvet divorce" took place: the Czech Republic and Slovakia became separate states.

Revolutions in Bulgaria, Romania, and Albania

Communist regimes also fell in Bulgaria, Romania, and Albania, the three Eastern European states without significant reform movements. In Bulgaria, long-suppressed unrest began to emerge in response to pressure for reform in other Eastern European countries. Todor Zhivkov (1911–1998), the first secretary of the Communist Party of Bulgaria since 1954 and the head of state since 1971, could boast a record of modest economic growth until the late 1970s. He also had orchestrated several cover-ups of the misdeeds of his family members (including the implication of his hard-drinking and -gambling son in the death of a television announcer). When a Bulgarian airliner crashed at the Sofia airport, killing most passengers, Zhivkov ordered that his jet leave at once for his Black Sea vacation, flying over the burning plane. Furthermore, the Bulgarian secret police had achieved international notoriety, blamed by some for an attempt to assassinate Pope John Paul II in Rome in 1981, as well as for a James Bond–like murder of a Bulgarian dissident killed by the deadly jab of a poison-tipped umbrella in London. The Bulgarian economy faltered badly in the late 1980s. Bulgarian exports (principally agricultural produce and light manufactured goods) had difficulty finding markets, particularly as the economic crisis deepened in the Soviet Union. Rural migrants poured into Sofia and other Bulgarian cities in search of work.

As the economy deteriorated, Zhivkov and the Communist leadership sought to displace popular anger in the direction of the country's large and rapidly growing Turkish minority. From time to time during the past several decades, the Turks had been the target of discriminatory government measures, including a law in 1984 requiring them to adopt Bulgarian names and forbidding the practice of Islam (the religion of most Turks). Just what the Bulgarian government hoped to achieve by such measures remains unclear (although this was hardly the first time in the often violent history of the region that an ethnic group had been targeted for discrimination in the hope of deflecting public opinion). After launching a harsh campaign against Turkish customs, Zhivkov's government encouraged the ethnic Turks to emigrate to Turkey, which further destabilized the Bulgarian economy. More than 300,000 of them left for Turkey within three months in 1989. Many soon returned, however, disappointed that conditions of life in Turkey seemed even worse than in Bulgaria.

With news of dramatic political changes occurring in the other Eastern European states, the Bulgarian Politburo surprised Zhivkov by suddenly demanding his resignation in November, the day after the Berlin Wall had fallen. The ease with which this was accomplished suggests that some party bureaucrats, army officers, and even members of the notorious government security force now believed change to be inevitable. The new government purged Stalinists and welcomed back Turks, contributing to a nationalist backlash among many Bulgarians. Zhivkov was tried for misuse of government funds and sentenced to prison.

In January 1990, the Communist monopoly on political power ended, and the Bulgarian Communist Party changed its name to the Bulgarian Socialist Party. However, in June, the former Communists, capitalizing on resurgent ethnic rivalries and fear of change in the countryside, won a majority of seats in the New National Assembly. A new constitution followed in October 1991. The Bulgarian Socialist Party and the Union of Democratic Forces remained the two largest parties, confronting a poor economy and the lack of foreign investment, although loans from the World Bank then helped stabilize the Bulgarian economy.

In Romania, the fall of the Ceauşescu clan and communism was anything but bloodless. Ceauşescu, who had enriched his family (at least thirty of whom held high office), vowed that reform would come to Romania "when pears grow on poplar trees." He awarded himself titles such as "Genius of the Carpathians" and the "Danube of Thought." His wife, Elena, fraudulently claimed to be a brilliant chemist, presenting papers at academic conferences that had been prepared by Romanian scientists, and then refusing to answer questions about them. On the occasion of a state visit to Britain, when the Queen of England for whatever reason knighted the Romanian leader, Ceauşescu and his wife virtually pillaged a suite at London's Buckingham Palace, carting away everything of value they could. In order to begin paying back $10 billion in foreign loans, Ceauşescu cut back food imports, increased food exports, rationed electricity, and banned the sale of contraceptives in the hope of increasing the Romanian population.

Ceauşescu's downfall began in 1989 in the Transylvanian town of Timisoara, where ethnic Hungarians resented second-class status. Ceauşescu had ordered the razing of 8,000 largely Hungarian villages and the relocation of their residents. Crowds rioted, smashing store windows and burning Ceauşescu's portraits. Romanians joined Hungarians in the protests. Army units refused to fire on demonstrators. The feared security forces (the Securitate, 180,000 strong) stepped in, shooting three army officers for disobeying orders and firing on crowds.

Discontent spread rapidly. As another cold Romanian winter approached along with the usual severe food and fuel shortages, Hungarian and Yugoslav television showed events rapidly transpiring in other Eastern European countries. Demonstrations now spread to other towns. In December, Ceauşescu called for a massive demonstration of support in Bucharest. Orchestrated cheers from the crowd soon became jeers, drowning out the dictator's pathetic speech blaming riots on Hungarian nationalists. From the safety of his palace, Ceauşescu ordered troops to fire on the crowds below. But most units refused to obey and, as a result, the minister of defense was executed on Ceauşescu's orders. The hated secret police eagerly fired on the assembled crowds, and tanks crushed protesters in a scene hauntingly reminiscent of Beijing's Tiananmen Square earlier that year. After soldiers battled the security forces outside the presidential palace, hundreds of bodies lay in the streets.

Several of the dictator's top officials now decided that Ceauşescu's days of iron rule were numbered. Ceauşescu and his wife left their stately residence on December 22, 1989, through secret tunnels,

A Romanian prays for countrymen executed on the orders of dictator Nicolae Ceauşescu in Timisoara, Romania.

and then commandeered a helicopter. They were captured and immediately charged with murder and embezzlement of government funds. On Christmas Day, they were tried by a hastily convoked tribunal—which, in fact, had no legal authority—and condemned to death. They were then taken behind the building and shot, their bloody bodies left lying stiffly in the snow for a worldwide television audience to see. More than 1,000 people died during the revolution that overthrew Ceauşescu and ended communism in Romania.

Communism was swept away even in Albania, which had remained largely isolated from change in Eastern Europe by sealed borders. In Europe's poorest country, where food shortages had generated sullen anger, the fall of Ceauşescu in December 1989 emboldened dissidents. As a crisis mounted, President Ramiz Alia (1925–) announced greater openness in the selection of government leaders and a larger role for workers in choosing managers. Agricultural cooperatives would be allowed to sell surplus produce. Alia then announced the right to travel abroad and the abrogation of the long-standing ban on "religious propaganda." A group of Albanian intellectuals demanded the end of the Communist monopoly on power and students went on strike. Like other Communist leaders, Alia believed that he could maintain control by placating Albanians with minor reforms.

Confronted by demonstrations that began in December 1990, Alia announced that henceforth the Communist Party would cease to be the only approved political party. The Democratic Party quickly constituted itself, and opposition newspapers began to publish, although the Communist Party of Labor retained control of radio and television. In February 1991, a crowd of 100,000 demonstrated in Tirana, pulling down a large statue of former strongman Hoxha, who had died in 1985. In early March, 20,000 Albanians tried to force their way onto boats departing for Italy. This event, which focused international attention on Albania, produced a

Communist backlash, particularly in the countryside, where Hoxha had been a cult figure. In elections, the Communists won 68 percent of the vote. Despite this victory, the handwriting was on the wall. In June 1991, the Communist government resigned. For the first time since 1944, a coalition government came to power. Elections in 1992 gave the Democratic Party a majority of the seats in the National Assembly, and Alia resigned as Albania's president. For the next decade, the Democratic Party and the Socialist Party battled it out against the background of economic hardship, the arrival of tens of thousands of refugees from Kosovo, political corruption and assassination, and the bizarre events of 1997 when a series of pyramid investment schemes collapsed on naive purchasers, leading to riots and a period of total chaos. Greek troops had to intervene to maintain peace. Despite some periods of relative political stability, Albania has changed very little in some ways: between 1991—the fall of Communism— and 2008, more than 9,000 people had been killed as a result of blood feuds between families.

The Collapse of the Soviet Union

As one by one the former Eastern European satellites of the Soviet Union abandoned communism, unhappiness with the system became more vocal within the Soviet Union itself. In March 1990, the Communist government voted to permit non-Communist parties in the Soviet Union, and created the office of president. State restrictions on religious practice ended. That month, the Congress of People's Deputies elected Mikhail Gorbachev president of the Soviet Union, a significant change, since previously the head of the Communist Party was the titular head of state.

Pressure for the breakup of the Soviet Union mounted from the republics. In Estonia, Latvia, and Lithuania, a human chain of more than 1 million people formed to support the independence of their nations. In June 1990, the Russian Republic declared that laws passed by its legislature could override those of the Soviet Union. The other republics followed suit with similar legislation. Gorbachev's attempt to enhance government decentralization fell short of what nationalists in the republics sought. In June 1990, Lithuania unilaterally declared its independence from the Soviet Union; Gorbachev responded by ordering an embargo on Soviet oil and gas shipped to the Baltic state.

Gorbachev still wanted to maintain a role for the Communist Party in the new era, and he wanted to ensure the existence of the Soviet Union itself. Moreover, he probably still believed that Soviet influence over its former satellites in Central and Eastern Europe could continue even after the fall of communism in those states. In 1990, he appointed several hard-line government officials and ordered a crackdown on nationalist movements in the Baltic states. This led to the dramatic resignation of Shevardnadze, the popular foreign minister.

In Russia, the charismatic, hard-drinking, impulsive Boris Yeltsin (1931–2007) had risen to positions of authority in the Communist Party as an efficient and honest administrator. Claiming that Gorbachev was not truly committed to reform, he challenged the latter's authority and the legitimacy of the Soviet state. As chair of the Supreme Soviet, the state's highest legislative body, he announced that henceforth Russia would be a sovereign, independent state. Yeltsin had no illusions about the survival of communism and had grave doubts that the Soviet Union itself would survive. He was willing to ally with the other republics against Gorbachev. When reactionary Communists attempted to unseat Yeltsin as chairman in the Russian Parliament, several hundred thousand Moscovites turned out to express their support for him.

Gorbachev now seemed to move away from reform, possibly encouraging right-wing officials within the Communist Party, army, and KGB, who believed their positions were threatened by a reduction in hostility with the United States. The hard-line group had begun putting pressure on Gorbachev in September 1990, and the army began mysterious maneuvers around Moscow.

In January 1991, Gorbachev may have approved an attempt to overthrow the democratically elected government of Lithuania, which began with an attack on a television installation in the capital of Vilnius. The clumsy plot, which involved army and KGB agents pretending they were a Lithuanian dissident group, failed miserably. A month later, in a referendum deemed by the Soviet government to be illegal, 90 percent of those voting in Lithuania expressed their support for independence, as did 77 percent of those voting in both Estonia and Latvia—the difference explained by the fact that more Russians lived in Estonia and Latvia.

In a nationally televised speech in February 1991, Yeltsin called for Gorbachev to resign. Gorbachev, in turn, ordered troops to surround the Kremlin in a show of force. However, Yeltsin had begun to undermine the army and security forces, where he had followers. Gorbachev's turn toward conservatives cost him supporters.

Gorbachev's conservative retrenchment proved short-lived. In April, he abandoned his commitment to preserving the Soviet Union at all costs and accepted the idea of autonomy for the republics. In June 1991, Yeltsin was elected

Atop a tank in front of the Russian Parliament building, Boris Yeltsin urges the Russian people to resist the coup d'état of August 1991.

president of the "Russian Federation," another sign of how quickly the Soviet Union was changing. The Communists now had little support in Russia, by far the Soviet Union's largest republic. Gorbachev announced a new Communist Party platform, which eliminated Marxism and Leninism in favor of "humane and democratic socialism." He then left for an August vacation in Crimea.

Intransigent Communists were now firmly convinced that Gorbachev's policies threatened the existence of the Soviet Union. In August 1991, hard-liners within the Communist Party, army, KGB, and some members of Gorbachev's own cabinet placed the Soviet leader under house arrest in his Crimean residence in an attempted coup d'état that looked more like a comic opera. Setting up an "Emergency Committee," the conspirators apparently hoped that they could convince or force Gorbachev to use his prestige against reform by declaring a state of emergency. Gorbachev agreed to do so, but only if such a move were approved "constitutionally" by the Supreme Soviet. The conspirators then publicly declared the president to be "incapacitated."

In Moscow, Yeltsin stood on a tank outside the Russian Parliament and encouraged resistance. The coup fell apart, its leaders having underestimated the strength of both Yeltsin's and Gorbachev's popular support. The Soviet army remained loyal to Gorbachev. Yeltsin mobilized people in Moscow by calling for resistance and the restoration of Gorbachev as the legitimate Soviet leader. This appeal to constitutionality revealed how much had changed in a very short time.

In August, Gorbachev returned to Moscow a hero, and again took a more reformist stance. Even as Gorbachev continued to defend the Communist Party before the Supreme Soviet, Yeltsin suspended the Communist Party and its newspaper *Pravda*. These bold moves amounted to the dismantling of communism in Russia.

The failed coup accelerated the collapse of the Soviet Union. Gorbachev appointed new people to key ministries. Some KGB officers were pensioned off, and television and radio were freed from the constraints of censorship. The Soviet government recognized the independence of the Baltic republics, just months after Gorbachev had insisted on retaining the structure of the Soviet Union. In late August 1991, the Supreme Soviet voted to put an end to the extraordinary powers previously accorded Gorbachev and to suspend the Communist Party in the entire Soviet Union. Yeltsin quickly moved to initiate a market economy in Russia.

One by one, the republics left the Soviet Union, where Russians had constituted only about half of the population. Moldavia, Uzbekistan, and Azerbaijan declared their independence. In December 1991, Ukraine followed, after 90 percent of the population voted to leave the Soviet Union. By the end of the year, thirteen of the fifteen Soviet republics had declared their independence. The Soviet Empire was no more. Yeltsin and the presidents of Belarus and Ukraine declared the Soviet Union dissolved. Gorbachev, too, acknowledged that the Soviet Union no longer existed. Symbolically, Leningrad again assumed its old name of Saint Petersburg. On December 25, 1991, Gorbachev resigned, closing one of the most remarkable political eras in modern European history.

The end of communism in Europe did not guarantee an easy transition to parliamentary democratic rule. The lack of democratic traditions, the economic turmoil, and the deep ethnic rivalries posed daunting challenges. Nowhere are the stakes higher for a peaceful transition to democracy than in Russia. The president of Ukraine put it this way: "When there's frost in Russia on Thursday, by Friday there's frost in Kiev." In 1993, Yeltsin declared a "special presidential regime," dissolving the legislature and overriding opposition to his reform program. Yeltsin insisted that the Russian presidency should have considerable authority, whereas the Congress of People's Deputies feared too much presidential power, remembering well the dictatorship of the Communist Party. In 1996, Yeltsin became the first democratically elected president of Russia. In ill health, his resignation at the end of 1999 led to the election of Vladimir Putin (1952–), a former KGB officer, as president of Russia. Putin provided some badly needed stability to Russia after considerable turmoil during the 1990s.

The Disintegration of Yugoslavia

The story of the disintegration of Yugoslavia most tragically illustrates the complexity of national identity, the impact of ethnic politics on the post-Communist era in Eastern Europe and the Balkans, and the challenges and hopes for the future. Marshal Josip Broz ("Tito"), a Croat, believed that communism in Yugoslavia could end ethnic rivalries and Serb domination. Yugoslavs lived in relative harmony, and following Tito's death in 1980, a collective presidency that rotated every year among the republics governed Yugoslavia. But tensions persisted between Serbs and Croats, the country's two largest ethnic groups. They shared a common spoken language (though Serbs use the Russian Cyrillic alphabet and Croats use the Latin alphabet). Yugoslavia's capital, Belgrade, was also that of Serbia. Serbs enjoyed disproportionate representation in the Communist state bureaucracy.

Regional disparities in economic development and prosperity compounded ethnic divisions. In the north, the republic of Slovenia, which was by far the most ethnically homogeneous of Yugoslavia's republics, enjoyed a standard of living not far below that of its neighbors, Austria and Italy. In the south, Macedonia and Bosnia remained backward and relatively impoverished. Within Bosnia, 85 percent of the population of the territory of Kosovo was Albanian and Muslim. Yet the minority Serbs—only about 10 percent of the population—viewed Kosovo as sacred Serb soil, because the Ottoman Turks had defeated them there in 1389 and Kosovo had become part of Serbia during the Balkan Wars (1912–1913). In the meantime, ethnic Albanians claimed the right to be the seventh Yugoslav republic.

In the mid-1980s, the Serb-run Yugoslav government launched a brutal repression of Albanians living in Kosovo, claiming that Albanian nationalism posed a threat to communism. In April 1987, Slobodan Milošević (1941–2006), the leader of the Serb Communist Party, provocatively told Serbs and Montenegrins that Kosovo was theirs and that they should remain at all costs.

Milošević turned the Communist Party and state apparatus into instruments serving Serb nationalist interests. He undertook what amounted to a military occupation of Kosovo, ending its administrative autonomy. In 1989, fighting broke out in Kosovo between ethnic Albanians and Serbs and Montenegrins, inflaming Serb nationalism.

Yugoslavia quickly disintegrated (see Map 29.2). The movement for political reform began in January 1990 in Slovenia. New parties formed in each of the six republics, including Serbia, where Communist leaders still opposed reform. Non-Communists won a majority of the parliamentary seats in Bosnia-Herzegovina, Croatia, Slovenia, and Macedonia. The Communist Party changed its name to the Socialist Party and won a majority in Milošević's Serbia and in Montenegro, Serbia's ally.

In December 1990, Slovenes voted overwhelmingly for independence. In Croatia, the nationalist Franjo Tudjman (1922–1999), won a clear electoral victory, accentuating tensions between Croatia and the Yugoslav state. Milošević loudly espoused the creation of a Greater Serbia that would include all territories populated by Serbs. In May 1991, Serbia prevented the succession of a Croat to the rotating presidency of Yugoslavia. In Slovenia, intervention by the Yugoslav army was met by determined resistance and was short-lived. But when Croatia declared independence from Yugoslavia in June 1991, as did Slovenia, violent conflicts between Croats and Serbs intensified. Serb militias, supported and armed by Yugoslav army units, began occupying large chunks of Croatia that had sizable Serb populations. Within several months they held about one-third of Croatian territory, driving Croats from their villages and killing thousands of people. From the heights above, Serbs shelled the walled Croatian city of Dubrovnik on the Adriatic coast, severely damaging one of Europe's most beautiful cities. Croatia became independent in January 1992, although parts of Croatia remained under Serb control.

Macedonia declared its independence in September 1991. In Bosnia-Herzegovina, ethnic rivalries also brought violence. The Yugoslav army occupied parts of Bosnia, allegedly to protect Serbs. In March 1992, a majority of Bosnian Muslims and ethnic Croats voted for the independence of Bosnia-Herzegovina. However, Bosnian Serbs refused to recognize the legality of the plebiscite. They declared their own independence. A bloody civil war broke out in Bosnia-Herzegovina. Bosnian Serbs carried out "ethnic cleansing," a term they invented. Serbs forced at least 170,000 non-

MAP 29.2 THE DISINTEGRATION OF YUGOSLAVIA, 1995   The fall of the Communists in Yugoslavia led to the breakup of the Yugoslav federation and to civil war between Croats, Serbs, and Bosnian Muslims. This map reflects the settlement reached in the Dayton Peace Accords, signed in November 1995.

Serbs from their homes and drove them away or imprisoned them. Bosnian Serb militias perpetuated atrocities against Bosnian Muslims, including rapes and mass executions. They massacred 8,000 men and boys in fields outside the town of Srebrenica. In the meantime, in predominantly Croat parts of Bosnia, Croats also carried out brutal measures against Muslims, some of whom reciprocated against Serbs and Croats.

Milošević, presiding over what remained of Yugoslavia (now including only Serbia and Montenegro), eliminated constitutional guarantees given by the old Yugoslav republic to the provinces of Kosovo and Vojvodina (a region of northern Serbia). Although Yugoslav armies withdrew, fearing international intervention, Bosnian Serb forces, supplied by the Yugoslav army, surrounded Sarajevo, the Bosnian capital, lobbing mortar and cannon shells from the heights above and killing civilians. In response to assistance given

(*Left*) A Kosovo Albanian refugee released from the custody of the Yugoslav army collapses. (*Right*). Yugoslav President Slobodan Milošević brandishes a mace, a gift from his supporters.

the Bosnian Serbs by Milošević's government, the United Nations placed an economic embargo on what was left of the Yugoslav state. However, the NATO alliance failed to act, thus allowing Serb nationalists to conquer more than 70 percent of Bosnia-Herzegovina. "Europe is dying in Sarajevo," warned a poster in Germany. To make things even worse, Croats and Muslims in Bosnia now began to fight each other.

The Bosnian conflict took a terrible toll, creating hundreds of thousands of refugees. Croatia also entered the conflict with an eye toward taking Bosnian territory that nationalists considered Croatian. Another full-scale Balkan war loomed.

Early in 1994, a cease-fire agreement took hold. Bosnian Muslim and Croatian leaders met in Washington, D.C., forming a Muslim-Croat Federation within Bosnia-Herzegovina. However, the Bosnian Serbs refused to respect either the cease-fire or an international plan for peace. The arrival of blue-helmeted UN peacekeepers in the first international attempt ever to stop ethnic cleansing at first made little difference. NATO launched air strikes against Serb targets in Bosnia. In August 1995, the Croats recaptured Krajina, contested territory bordering on Bosnia that Croatian Serbs had declared to be independent in 1991. Now tens of thousands of Serbs from Krajina took to the roads as refugees, heading toward Serb strongholds in Bosnia.

By the Dayton Peace Accords orchestrated in 1995 by the U.S. government, Bosnia was to be a single state that included a Bosnian-Croat federation and a Serb republic. This agreement would be supervised by a NATO peacekeeping force, including U.S. troops. However, Bosnian Serbs overran free zones that NATO forces had established to protect Bosnian Muslims. Mass murders perpetrated against Muslims in 1995 (including thousands in a so-called UN-protected safe zone) led to the indictment of Bosnian Serb leader Radovan Karadzić (1945–) by the International Criminal Tribunal, a UN tribunal that was established in The Hague (in the Netherlands) to judge those accused of crimes against humanity and genocide. (Karadzić was finally captured in Belgrade in 2008 and put on trial.) Europe's bloodiest conflict since World War II went on. Ethnic cleansing in Bosnia, overwhelmingly by Serbs, took more than 200,000 Bosnian lives, and by the end of the war about 2.1 million Bosnians were without homes.

In Kosovo, Albanians had formed the Kosovo Liberation Army with the goal of obtaining freedom from Yugoslavia. In 1998 and 1999, Milošević unleashed Serb forces against ethnic Albanians in Kosovo. A cease-fire arranged by the United States in October 1998 quickly collapsed and Milošević refused to allow NATO peacekeepers into the province. Serb troops began ethnic cleansing, killing thousands of Muslims, and drove 860,000 Albanians into Albania and Macedonia. When Serb forces did not withdraw from Kosovo, NATO forces in March 1999 began attacking military targets in Serbia from the air. The bombing campaign forced Serb forces to withdraw from Kosovo and to allow 50,000 NATO peacekeepers into Kosovo. They oversaw the return of about 720,000 ethnic Albanian refugees to Kosovo. In the meantime, 50,000 Serbs now fled possible reprisals.

Milošević's government in Yugoslavia collapsed in October 2000 in the face of mass demonstrations. The Serb leader was arrested six months later to face charges of crimes against humanity and genocide at the International Criminal Tribunal in The Hague. He died unrepentant in 2006 during his trial. In the meantime, the new Yugoslav government worked quickly to end the international isolation brought about by Milošević's policies. The United States and other states ended economic sanctions against Yugoslavia. In 2003, the remnants of Yugoslavia became Serbia-Montenegro, the only two of the six republics of Yugoslavia that remained together. The assassination in March 2003 of the prime minister of Serbia, Zoran Djindjic (1952–2003), who had been one of the forces behind the ouster of Milošević in 2000, attested to the continuing volatility of Serbia. In 2008, Kosovo proclaimed its outright independence from Serbia, a move that Serbia and Russia refused to recognize.

Challenges in the Post-Communist World

While the West breathed a sigh of relief after the collapse of communism in Europe, the existence of nuclear weapons in several of the former states of the Soviet Union became a considerable concern. The 1986 Chernobyl disaster clearly demonstrated the vulnerability of the rest of Europe to nuclear disasters. Ukraine's nuclear arsenal and its claim to the remnants of the Soviet Black Sea Fleet docked in Crimea raised tension between Russia and Ukraine. In 1992, Ukraine, Russia, Belarus, and Kazakhstan all agreed that nuclear weapons stored on their territory would either be destroyed or turned over to Russia. In 1996, nuclear warheads were shipped to Russia for destruction. However, the problem of preventing the theft and sale of nuclear materials, particularly to potential terrorists, remains one of the most important concerns for the future.

The end of communism has left other problems. The rapid industrialization in East Germany, Romania, and Czechoslovakia under communism left horrendous pollution from coal-burning furnaces and virtually unregulated factories. Acid rain destroyed forests, killed rivers, and compromised public health.

Suddenly freed from Soviet domination, the newly independent states faced the challenge of putting their own foreign relations on a firm footing. For many of the former Soviet republics, relations with Russia are complicated by centuries of animosity, nowhere more so than in Ukraine and Georgia. Soviet rule had favored Russian interests, and in the Baltic states, for example, brought the settlement of large Russian populations, as well as troops (250,000 Soviet troops were stationed in Soviet republics other than Russia at the time of the Soviet Union's dissolution).

Like the Soviet Union, the Eastern European Communist states were largely atomized societies of one-party rule without political infrastruc-

A factory in Poland polluting the atmosphere.

tures, traditions of political parties, civic cultures, or adequately developed voluntary associations. Only in Poland and Hungary had non-Communist political leadership gradually emerged in the 1980s, providing the basis for the emergence of party politics following the dismantling of one-party rule. In 1989, Civic Forum in Czechoslovakia served the same function, and in Hungary a series of right-center and left-center coalitions implemented far-reaching economic reforms. In some former Communist countries, the problem of creating political institutions in which basically only party members had experience in public life was daunting.

In the first free elections held in Eastern Europe since the late 1940s, two distinct trends were seen in the 1990s. Nationalist right-center parties emerged victorious in eastern Germany, Poland, and Hungary, where the parties of the left, including those formed by former Communists (some of them, to be sure, converted reformers), fared badly. In Poland, Solidarity was defeated in 1991 in the first free elections held since 1926, leading to the arrival in power of several center-right coalitions. On the other hand, in Bulgaria and Romania, former Communist parties (hurriedly renamed and claiming the mantle of reform) came out better than any other parties. They did particularly well in the countryside, where reform movements had been largely absent and Communist officials maintained considerable prestige, as they were identified with the modest increase in living standards that had occurred during the decades since the war. In late 1995, the Communist Party emerged as the biggest winner in the legislative elections in Russia. Six years after the fall of the Berlin Wall, Bulgaria, Hungary, Lithuania, and Poland, where Lech Walesa was turned out of office in 1995, were now led by former Communists. Many of them benefited from being familiar faces able to draw on old political networks and from protest votes from people exasperated by growing economic disparities.

The former Communist states moved to create modern economic systems based on private enterprise. Western economic advisers provided some of the expertise as the nationalized sector of Eastern European economies was drastically reduced. This process proved easier in the more northern countries than in the Balkans, where elected leaders in the 1990s tended toward authoritarian rule amid continuing corruption. With the exceptions of Poland and Hungary, economic privatization was not easy in post-Soviet Central and Eastern Europe and particularly in the Balkans. As in the former Soviet Union, weak economies and a relatively low standard of living continued to generate political instability. Policy changes came with numbing speed. The utilization of free-market "shock therapy," including the end of price controls on most consumer goods, at first brought economic chaos to Russia and Poland, where Communists were returned to power in 1993. In the region as a whole, industrial production fell by between 20 and 40 percent. Widespread unemployment and the sudden end of the massive welfare system under which entire populations had grown up left hardship, bewilderment, and anger. The distribution of state-owned property engendered problems. In Hungary, foreign conglomerates bought up property that had been held by the Communist state. Former owners of property collectivized by Communist regimes demanded their lands back. Yet, at the same time, in the former Soviet satellite states, the attraction of joining the European Union itself encouraged economic and political reform. In some countries, members of the former Communist elite managed to get hold of valuable assets. The end of authoritarian rule led to major increases in violent crime, above all in Russia and Bulgaria, where organized crime has become powerful as one unstable government has followed another (including, remarkably enough, the period of 2001–2005 when the man who had in 1946 briefly taken the title of "tsar" of Bulgaria became prime minister). Belarus remained a virtual dictatorship, a throwback to another time.

Foreign investment was far from adequate. In the short term, galloping inflation (up to 20 percent a month in Russia and 40 percent in Ukraine) engendered bitterness. Despite the fact that its Western creditors in March 1991 canceled half of the debts owed by Poland, the economic outlook in that country seemed bleak. The Russian economy virtually collapsed in the 1990s, and by the end of the decade about 30 percent of the population of Russia was classified as impoverished. With taxpayers simply not paying up, Russia barely avoided bankruptcy in 1998 by postponing paying off $43 billion in short-term loans. Romania, Bulgaria, and Albania, in particular, were confronted by the ravages of decades of Communist economic policies, leaving a ruinous emphasis on heavy industry, compounded by old technology, combined with an inefficient agricultural sector. However, in 1997, the new Romanian government undertook major economic reforms with the help of loans from the World Bank and the International Monetary Fund. These included the reduction of state subsidies to companies and the privatization of many state-run businesses.

Nation-states, which many liberals long assumed were necessary before constitutional rights and equality could be assured, have not always turned out to be liberal and tolerant. Even if bilateral treaties officially ended long-simmering disputes over some territorial boundaries, such as those between Germany and Poland, Hungary and Romania, and Hungary and Slovakia, tensions still remain between Turks and Bulgarians in Bulgaria, Hungarians and Romanians in Romania, Slovaks and Hungarians in Slovakia, and Albanians and Macedonians in Macedonia. In the Czech Republic, the Republican Party denounced in shrill nationalist tones Germans and, above all, the minority population of gypsies (Roma) until the party was dissolved in 2001. In Hungary and Romania, too, right-wing racism has focused on Roma, as well as Jews. The potential for ethnic violence in Russia and the other former Soviet republics also remained. Twenty-five million Russians lived in other republics within the Soviet Union at the time of the latter's disintegration, 17 million of whom were in Ukraine. It was telling that in Estonia, no sooner had Communist rule ended than new governments established language tests to determine who was a "real" Estonian. The newly independent Baltic republics established laws that classified Russians as foreigners. In Russia, the extreme right-wing Liberal Democratic Party won almost a quarter of the vote in parliamentary elections in 1993. Aggressive nationalism and xenophobia have become more in evidence in Russia. Azerbaijanis and Armenians battled in the Armenian enclave of Nagorno-Karabakh in the early 1990s. Since 1994, Russian troops have battled nationalist Muslim insurgents in Chechnya (which lies north of Georgia and west of the Caspian Sea). The revolt, which has taken the lives of thousands of civilians, has generated harsh Russian repression while generating terrorist attacks orchestrated by rebels inside Chechyna and inside Russia. The Russian government proposed greater Chechen autonomy, but not independence. Russian troops captured Grozny, the capital of the breakaway republic, in February 2000. Chechen rebels on several occasions took hundreds of hostages, many of whom were killed when Russian troops stormed a theater and a school. Russian troops responded with frequent brutality.

Elected to a second term in 2004, Putin oversaw a vigorous resurgence of Russian presence and assertiveness on the international scene. In Ukraine, tensions between those who wanted close relations with Russia and those who did not destabilized the government. The status of Crimea, which became part of Ukraine during the Soviet break-up, remains highly contentious because the Russian government still considers Crimea to be Russian and also because of the importance of Sebastopol as a Black Sea naval port. In 2007, Russia ended its participation in the Conventional Armed Forces in Europe Treaty, which had been signed in 1990 at the very end of the Cold War. In 2008, Putin's chosen successor, Dimitri Medvedev, was elected president. He quickly named Putin prime minister, leaving the latter's enormous influence in Russia virtually intact and keeping open the possibility that Putin might one day again be president.

Resurgent Russian nationalism was apparent in August 2008. Amid rising tensions between Georgia and separatists in two autonomous regions of the country, South Ossetia and Abkhazia, that were seeking to break away, Russian forces invaded, allegedly to protect the minorities, some of whom had been provided with Russian passports. The Russians pushed into Georgia itself before a cease-fire was signed. Russia declared that its troops would remain as "peacekeepers" in the contested zones. A sign of modern times, the offensive against Georgia included cybernet attacks intended to destabilize Georgian web sites. Russian actions drew virtually unanimous international condemnation, chilling relations, in particular, between Russia and the United States, which counted the pro-American Georgian government as an ally and had encouraged Georgian defiance. Russian military action and the subsequent official recognition of both enclaves as independent states reflected Russian anger at the recognition of the independence of Kosovo by the United States and other Western states, as well as Russian apprehension that Georgia, as well as Ukraine, both bordering states, might be invited to join NATO.

In January 2009, benefiting from considerable riches in energy, Russia seemed to flex its muscles by cutting off the supply of natural gas to Ukraine after a bitter dispute over prices. The shutdown had the immediate effect of leaving many countries in eastern and southern Europe without much heat during a very cold winter until the dispute was resolved.

Conclusion

The Western European nations failed to act effectively to resolve the Bosnian crisis, but the cooperation between states in the former Soviet bloc and the West is reassuring. Russia and the United States signed an arms treaty in 2002 and have cooperated in space ventures, notably a space station.

Freed from Communist rule, some of the Eastern European states lobbied to join NATO. In 1997, NATO announced that it would expand its membership to include eventually Poland, the Czech Republic, and Hungary, hoping that the adherence of former Communist states would help consolidate democracy. Furthermore, it was also announced that a Permanent Joint Council in Brussels would bring together NATO members and Russia to consider joint actions, including arms control and peacekeeping. This is a remarkable turnabout, as NATO, which now includes twenty-six nations, had been originally established with the goal of containing the Soviet Union. This, too, has been a sign of new times.

GLOBAL CHALLENGES: "FORTRESS EUROPE," EUROPEAN COOPERATION, AND THE UNCERTAINTIES OF A NEW AGE

∾

The remarkable increase in the movement of peoples from one part of the world to another has been a dramatic dimension of globalization. After centuries of sending millions of European emigrants to other continents, the trend was reversed. Beginning in the 1960s, Asians and Africans seeking a better life began to arrive in unprecedented numbers in Western Europe. Moreover, with the collapse of communism in Eastern Europe and the Balkans, tens of thousands of immigrants began arriving in Western Europe. Yet while immigrants have contributed enormously to the economies of many European states, their presence and the cultural differences they bring with them have generated xenophobia in many states and an increase in the political influence of nationalist parties of the extreme right. Immigration thus poses a challenge to the new Europe, raising difficult issues of identity and the very question of what it means to be European.

Globalization has brought other difficult challenges as well. For example, the financial crisis—indeed the near collapse of the financial sector—that began in 2008, the worst international economic crisis since the Great Depression, itself reflected dimensions of globalization. First, the rapid rise in the price of oil had immediate worldwide consequences. Then the subprime lending crisis, the result of irresponsible mortgage lending, was followed by the bankruptcy of several major financial giants and the propping up of others by national governments. In the United States, hundreds of thousands of houses were foreclosed upon when purchasers could not make payments. Overall, the prices of housing plunged. This had an immediate catastrophic impact on the world economy, and thus on ordinary people who have reason to fear for the safety of their money. Investments and retirement funds went up in smoke. The financial meltdown revealed the scale of global interconnectedness. As the world economy went into recession and economic growth slowed down in the United States and Europe, China and India—the world's two new booming economies—faced lower demand for their goods. In Europe, despite considerable economic integration provided by the European Union, the absence of comparable political integration made it difficult for the leading states to come up with effective comprehensive policies that cut across national boundaries.

The world economic crisis strained relations between member states. Some governments retreated from free trade policies in the context of a single European Union market by providing subsidies with the goal of protecting certain industries (for example, France aiding its automobile companies), raising the specter of protectionism. Tensions emerged between the states whose economies were doing relatively well and those like Spain, Ireland, and Greece who were suffering the most; and between the older member states, who feared an increased economic burden being placed on them, and those poorer Eastern European nations recently admitted to the European Union.

Europe has ceased to be the center of global political concern and conflict, a title that has arguably passed to the Middle East. Globalization has made Europe, like other parts of the world, vulnerable to the tensions linked to conflicts in the Middle East. Terrorist attacks have carried the struggles in that part of the world to Europe itself. Moreover, following the collapse of the Soviet Union, European unity and the traditional Western alliance have been challenged by the domination of the United States. Yet the European Union (EU) in the 1990s carried cooperation between European states to a level barely imaginable a decade or two before. Within the European Union, a single market led to the inauguration of a single currency—the "euro"—in 2002.

IMMIGRATION TO EUROPE

More than ever before, the world's population has been on the move. Millions of people have emigrated to Western Europe. Africans, Asians, Turks, and people from the Middle East have arrived, legally or illegally, in Western European countries. To be sure, immigration within Europe, particularly from the poorer countries of southern and eastern Europe, has also continued to be significant. The mass movement of people from the Third World, particularly from Africa and Asia, must be seen in the context of the rapid growth of the world's population. The population of Africa in 1950 was half that of Europe; by 1985, the two populations stood about even, and within several decades the population of Africa will probably be three times that of Europe. In some cases, it was newly independent colonies that sent immigrants to their former colonizers, as in the case of Indians and Pakistanis moving to Britain and of North Africans to France. Europe now has an estimated 18 million foreign workers.

Beginning in the late 1960s, foreign-born "guest workers" (as they are called in Germany) made up an increasing proportion of the workforce in every Western European state. Encouraged by European governments concerned about a labor shortage, they took up a variety of skilled but mostly unskilled work. The government of the German Federal Republic established recruiting offices in southern Europe and North Africa, hoping to encourage immigration. The number of foreigners living in Western Europe tripled in thirty years. In Switzerland, foreign workers make up about a quarter of the workforce. The ethnic composition varies from country to country. Turks have settled in Germany in great numbers because of the relative proximity and historically close ties between Turkey and Germany. Portuguese make up the largest non-French ethnic community in the Paris

North African immigrants captured by a patrol boat after trying to enter Spain illegally.

region, followed closely by Algerians, Moroccans, and Tunisians, and an increasing number of West Africans. In France, where the number of Muslim residents reached 5 million people, the number of mosques rose from 130 in 1976 to more than 1,000 twenty years later. The percentage of ethnic minorities living in Britain rose from 6 percent to 9 percent in the decade between 1991 and 2001. In the latter year, 1.5 million Muslims lived in England and Wales, representing more than 3 percent of the population. In 2007, 2 million of London's 7 million residents had been born outside of Britain.

Following the collapse of communism, the opening of Eastern European borders and the elimination of border controls between many Western European states increased the number of people trying to reach Western Europe. Kurds fled Iraq and Turkey for Europe, as North Africans left Algeria (ravaged by a bloody civil war following the army's seizure of power in 1992 and the rise of militant Islamic fundamentalist groups), Tunisia, and Morocco, trying to reach France via Spain, if they did not drown first. Between 1990 and 1993, 200,000 Albanians crossed the mountains to reach Greece. Thousands of others, desperately attempting to flee violence and economic ruin in their country, made the dangerous trip across the Adriatic Sea to Italy. Between 1980 and 1992, 15 million immigrants arrived in Western Europe. The number of people seeking asylum rose from about 65,000 in 1983 to over 500,000 in 1991—many from the ethnic conflict following the break-up of Yugoslavia, as well as from Romania and Turkey (see Table 30.1). By the early 1990s, at least 3 million clandestine immigrants were living in Western Europe, and probably many more.

In response, Western European governments have turned increasingly to new strategies and laws to try to reduce the number of immigrants, establishing tougher tests for claims of political asylum and sending illegal immigrants back to their countries. The percentage of asylum seekers whose cases are judged favorably by government authorities has been decreasing. With 7 percent of its population now made up of foreigners (60 percent of them non-European), France has turned away from its long-held belief that being born in that country was enough to become a French citizen; it now requires that children born in France to non-French parents must apply for citizenship between ages sixteen and twenty-one. The government has also made it more difficult for foreigners to acquire French citizenship through marriage. Yet massive migration to Europe will certainly continue. Referring to the smuggling of migrants into his country, the Austrian director of immigration put it memorably, "There are no distances any longer in this world. There are no islands."

Immigration became a politically explosive issue. When economic recession sharply reduced the number of available jobs, the political tide began to turn even more against foreign workers. The British government put laws restricting immigration (targeting nonwhite arrivals) in place in 1968 and 1971. In the former year, Enoch Powell, a Conservative MP, caused a

TABLE 30.1. FOREIGN-BORN POPULATION AND PERCENTAGE OF
TOTAL POPULATION, 1995

Country	Foreign-Born Population	Percentage
Austria	724,000	9
Belgium	910,000	9
Denmark	223,000	4.2
Finland	69,000	1.3
France	3.5 million	6.3
Germany	7.1 million	8.8
Ireland	96,000	2.7
Italy	991,000	1.7
Luxembourg	138,000	33.4
Spain	500,000	1.2
Switzerland	1.3 million	18.9
United Kingdom	2 million	3.4
United States	24.6 million	10

Source: *World Book, 1998* (Chicago: World Book, 1999), p. 245.

storm when he warned that unchecked immigration would swamp Britain. When the economic recession began in the mid-1970s, other European states began to enact more restrictive immigration policies. While many foreign-born workers, recruited as single young men before the economic recession, became permanent residents of the countries where they worked (and became citizens), they were joined by hundreds of thousands of undocumented clandestine workers.

Nations put into effect stricter border controls in an attempt to reduce illegal immigration. EU nations have continued to build on the Schengen Agreement (1985), which initiated the exchange of information about immigration, moving toward common policies of border policing to crack down on illegal immigration.

At the same time, the birthrates of many countries continued to decline. Early in the twenty-first century, fourteen countries are no longer reproducing their populations (with Italy and Spain leading the way, followed by Germany and Sweden); in other countries, population growth is zero, or not far above that. At the end of the twentieth century, economic uncertainty was closely related to the continued fall in the number of births. The birthrate now shows few signs of reversing the trend of decline. Many Western European countries will lose population without significant immigration, and their economies will continue to require the labor of immigrants, legal and otherwise.

Many Europeans felt themselves overwhelmed by immigrants. In 1987, foreign and minority prisoners accounted for one-third of those locked up in France, Belgium, and Switzerland. In the 1990s, riots by—but also against—immigrants (principally Indians, Pakistanis, Bangladeshis, and

West Indians) rocked several northern industrial cities and London. As in the inter-war years, economic weakness has encouraged hostility to those some consider to be outsiders, and a perceived lack of security against crime became a central focus of electoral campaigns. The severe recession of the early 1990s contributed to this dangerous situation, bringing high unemployment rates (in 1993 over 10 percent in the European Union). Polls have reflected popular fears (without any foundation) that the quality of education declines when too many immigrants and asylum seekers are present in the classroom. Many Europeans believe that immigrants abuse existing social welfare programs (indeed, they are more apt to draw disproportionately upon them), and that most of those asking for political asylum were fleeing economic hardship, not the political persecution that would make them eligible for refugee status. At the same time, the emigration of many educated people with special training deprives poor countries of much-needed talent.

Rising intolerance, racism, and xenophobia—hallmarks of the rise of fascism during the inter-war years—have become apparent in Europe, orchestrated by extreme right-wing nationalist parties and directed against foreign workers and their families. Brutal and even murderous attacks against foreigners proliferated in Germany, France, Britain, Belgium, and Russia, among other countries. Right-wing political parties, such as the National Front in Britain (founded in 1967) and the party of the same name in France (founded in 1972) adopted aggressive anti-immigrant stances. In Germany, the German People's Union denounced legal changes in 1999 that made it somewhat easier for longtime foreign-born residents to become citizens. Xenophobia has also been seen in such traditionally liberal, open-minded countries as Sweden and Denmark. In Belgium, the right-wing Vlams Belang (Flemish Interest) has made anti-immigration a central part of its appeal, while challenging Belgian unity. Russia has seen a spate of murderous attacks on foreigners, particularly those from Central Asia and Africa.

In France, Jean-Marie Le Pen (1982–) emerged as the leader of the far-right National Front. Le Pen, who had been accused of torture after a stint in the army in Algeria and who described the death camps as "a minor detail" of World War II, won as much as 17 percent of the vote as a candidate in three presidential elections. In 2007, Nicolas Sarkozy (1955–) was elected president of France by borrowing the anti-immigrant language of the National Front and appearing to make it respectable. In Austria, Jörg Haider (1950–2008), head of the Austrian Freedom Party, became prime minister after making immigration a central issue and allying with the conservative People's Party. In the Netherlands, long a haven of toleration for immigrants, Pim Fortuyn, a candidate for the post of prime minister, caused an uproar by stating that his country had been saturated by immigration and that there was no room left (he was assassinated in 2002). In

A prayer demonstration by Muslims to protest opposition to the construction of a mosque in Nice, France—an example of cultural tensions across a multicultural Europe.

Switzerland, too, a party of the extreme right made its mark, as the Swiss People's Party gained almost 25 percent of the votes in 1999. The Danish People's Party, the Norwegian Progress Party, and the Flemish Bloc in Belgium reflect the close association of extreme right-wing parties and anti-immigrant sentiments.

Indeed, acceptance of multiculturalism has been slow in coming. (In the United States, the very term "multiculturalism" in general has a positive sense, but in Germany it means "a disarray of cultures, in which each individual culture is stripped of its richness and uniqueness.") While some foreign workers have been assimilated in their countries of residence, many have not and have maintained the customs of their homelands while living in ethnic enclaves in their new countries. In the first years of the twenty-first century, more than 12 million Muslims lived in Western Europe. In Britain, France, and Germany, Muslims have been viewed with suspicion. Difficulties in learning the language of the new country of residence—as well as outright discrimination—have made it harder to find work. This has often put the younger generation of foreign workers, born in their countries of residence, in the uncomfortable position of being excluded from mainstream life where they reside and not wishing to return to their parents' country of origin, to which many feel no real connection. In France, when Muslim schoolgirls went to school wearing the traditional headscarf, they were expelled. A lengthy court process ensued until a new law reaffirmed the ban. In 2008, French authorities refused citizenship to a Muslim woman who made clear her strong religious beliefs. Riots in October and November 2005 in French suburbs reflected the isolation and alienation of North and West African Muslim minorities, particularly young people.

EUROPEAN COMMUNITY, EUROPEAN UNION

In the hope of enhancing economic cooperation and coordination, the European Community (EC) was created in 1967, when the European Atomic Energy Community, the European Coal and Steel Community (ECSC), and the European Economic Community (the EEC, or European Common Market) merged. The original members were Belgium, France, West Germany, Italy, Luxembourg, and the Netherlands (see Map 30.1). The government of Great Britain had first been disinclined to join the EC, fearing the flooding of its internal market by less expensive agricultural produce. Moreover, French president Charles de Gaulle had forcefully opposed Britain's membership. There were other reasons, as well, arguing against Britain seeking to join. The British government considered itself a great power, and this status seemed incompatible with membership in the EC. Moreover, Britain feared that the pound, once considered "as good as gold," might suffer. The government did not want to be necessarily constrained by policies favored by other European states. Many British subjects agreed with a Labour Party leader who warned that a "thousand years" of British history would be lost if the country joined the EC. However, British public opinion changed. Voters overwhelmingly approved their country's application for membership and Britain joined the EC in 1973. Edward Heath, a Conservative who believed that his nation's future lay with Europe, took Britain into the EC. However, Harold Wilson, Heath's Labour successor as prime minister, sought to renegotiate the terms of Britain's membership. Britain remained a hesitant, even skeptical member. The advent of staunchly Conservative and vigorously anti-European Margaret Thatcher as British prime minister in 1979 put her country's membership at risk, until an urgent EC meeting agreed to reduce British financial contributions.

In the meantime, the close relationship between France's president Valéry Giscard d'Estaing and West Germany's premier Helmut Schmidt lent stability to the EC. Denmark and Ireland had also joined the EC in 1973, followed by Greece in 1981, and Spain and Portugal in 1986.

The EC eliminated troublesome tariffs, aiding the most efficient producers, who were able to sell their products abroad easily. But it put smaller producers at a disadvantage. The Danish dairy industry profited greatly from sales of milk and cheese to other member countries, as did their French counterparts; but dairy farmers elsewhere often found that they could not compete with larger competitors. The problem of wine revealed the challenges posed by EC agricultural policy. New members Spain and Portugal produce great amounts of wine, threatening vintners producing inexpensive

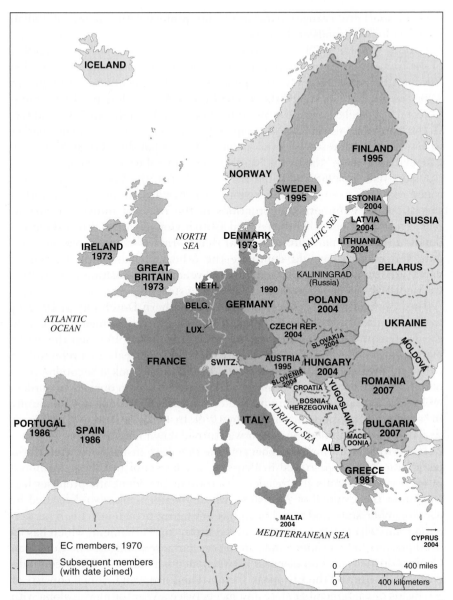

MAP 30.1 MEMBERS OF THE EUROPEAN COMMUNITY   The original six members of the European Community—France, West Germany, the Netherlands, Belgium, Luxembourg, and Italy—were later joined by twenty-one other countries.

wine in southern France. Wine producers protested the arrival of Italian wine by blocking roads at the frontier.

Jacques Delors (1925–), a former minister of finance, became president of the European Commission in 1985. Delors led the campaign for a unified Europe that could compete with Japanese and U.S. economic strength. In 1986, member states signed the Single Europe Act. Calling for the termination of all obstacles to the free movement of capital, goods, workers, and services, it pointed toward the anticipated establishment of a single market within member states. Moreover, Delors believed that the EC should include a "social dimension" that would protect the rights of ordinary people.

Delors had in 1988 indicated his hope that in the future a single currency could be used by member states, further accentuating trade within the EC while eliminating fluctuations in the value of individual currencies. From the outset, Thatcher and British Conservative "Euro-skeptics" opposed the plan, partially out of fear that Germany's then-booming economy and currency would dominate the other EC members. Thatcher's departure from office in 1990 did not end vehement opposition from British Conservatives to any thought of abandoning sterling.

The Treaty of Maastricht, signed in that southern Dutch city in 1992 by the twelve members of the European Community, transformed the EC into the European Union. The new name took effect in 1993 when the single market began operation. France barely approved the treaty in a referendum called by President Mitterrand in late 1992, and it took a second vote to obtain the same result in Denmark. The European Union opened all borders within the European Community and committed the European Community to "economic and monetary union" by 1999. In 1995, Austria, Norway, Sweden, and Finland joined, while Norway turned down membership.

The European Commission became the executive institution of the European Union. Headquartered in Brussels, it consists of members appointed by each member state. It is headed by a rotating president and proposes legislation to the Council of Ministers, whose members are also delegated by each member state and which also has a rotating presidency. Each participating state elects representatives to the European Parliament, which has its headquarters in Strasbourg and can reject a proposed budget. The European Court of Justice rules on disputes between member states and between individual plaintiffs and the European Union. The European Council consists of the heads of each member state and meets twice a year (or more), along with the president of the European Commission. The European Union even has a small army, established by virtue of the Amsterdam Treaty of 1999.

The European Union, comprising 370 million people in fifteen member states, now accounts for about 20 percent of the world's exports, more than that of the United States. One of the most daunting challenges of creating a single market has been to establish an effective agricultural policy that takes into consideration the tremendous variety of agricultural production within the member states. As part of the common agricultural policy, EU subsidies to farmers accounted for nearly half of the annual budget in 1995. Subsidies have protected member states by limiting the importation of products from outside the EU, but they also have generated overproduction, such that many farmers are paid not to produce, or for the surpluses they produce. Besides this, considerable European Union funds are diverted in the attempt to aid the continual development of the poorer member states, including Greece and Portugal, and disadvantaged regions within other countries, such as southern Italy and Sicily. For example, the admission of Poland requires sizeable subsidies for Polish agriculture, which in terms of efficiency lags considerably behind its Western counterparts, despite a booming economy in the first decade of the new century. In the meantime, the European Union maintains strict guidelines for agricultural producers (for example, on how cheese can be produced). An infusion of funds from the European Union has brought new roads and other benefits to new members. Beginning in December 2007 when borders were opened between nine new member states, one could travel from Estonia to Portugal without being stopped at any border, leaving some national authorities to worry whether such openness might aid illegal immigration and organized crime.

The problem of how the European Union can create a sense of legitimacy within the member states remains daunting. The institutions of the EU have to wrestle with the enormous challenge of creating a cultural

Irish farmers clog the streets of Dublin with their tractors to protest the reforms proposed by the Common Agricultural Policy of the European Union that would reduce their income.

"European" identity and "European" vision. This project is made even more difficult by over-bureaucratization, inefficiency, and corruption. Elections for the European Parliament cannot create European identity. Moreover, definitions of what it means to be European vary. People on the left who describe themselves as "European" tend to stress civic reasons for this identity, such as support for democratic political systems and the affirmation of social and human rights. Those on the political right are more apt to emphasize a common European cultural heritage.

Member states of the European Union are required to keep their budget deficits down to no more than 3 percent of gross domestic product. In 1998, the European Central Bank began operation, charged with managing the European Union currency, setting interest rates for the euro zone of eleven nations, and working to keep down inflation. The euro was launched as an accounting currency in 1999, but without the participation of Britain, Sweden, and Denmark, or of Greece, which failed to meet the financial criteria for monetary union that the EU had set for member states. The euro became the official currency in participating member states on January 1, 2002. A relatively smooth transition was made possible by considerable preparations, including effective publicity campaigns by governments, banks, and shopping centers, the conversion of machines accepting bills and coins, and assistance to the elderly, immigrants, and other groups. The euro soared in value, rapidly surpassing the U.S. dollar, weakened by the soaring U.S. trade deficit.

The European Union includes 27 member states and thus close to 500 million people. It has engendered not only feelings of ambivalence toward supranational economic and political organizations but also a nationalist response. Many ordinary people believe themselves disconnected from the workings of Brussels. Even some farmers who receive subsidies from the EU are unaware that they come from Brussels and not their own ministries of agriculture. In 2005, the European Union suffered a blow when votes in France and the Netherlands rejected approval of the proposed constitution, which had been promulgated the previous year. This led to the Treaty of Lisbon in December 2007. Its goal was to reform the original treaty that created the European Union by streamlining its administration by, for example, creating the position of president of the European Council. However, the rejection of the new treaty in a referendum in Ireland in June 2008 cast a new shadow over the functioning of the European Union.

Despite continuing operational challenges, however, new members can indeed look to the example of Ireland, whose economy has received a major boost from its EU membership, largely through the biotech revolution. High unemployment, low agricultural productivity, the necessity of institutional reform, and the great cost of becoming a member of the European Union, as well as the extremely limited democratic experience of some of the new members, poses challenges to new members and to the European Union itself. The economic gap between the wealthiest countries—Britain, France, and Germany—and the states of Central and Eastern Europe seeking the advantage of greater access to markets remains considerable. The possible admission of Turkey has generated great debate, in part because of some doubts that the country, which still bridges Europe and Asia, is really European. Successes of fundamentalist Islamic groups in elections in a country that is overwhelmingly Muslim but not militantly Islamic challenged the stridently secular basis of Turkey. In 2008, the country's highest court turned aside legislation inspired by the prime minister that would have allowed female students in state universities to wear head scarves, conforming to their Muslim religion.

Yet the number of citizens of countries within the European Union who describe themselves as feeling "European" has increased, despite continuing loyalty to nation-states based on ethnic identity and long-standing traditions of citizenship and a sense of shared values. However, the European Union has encouraged regionalism, assisting the revival of such languages as Catalan and Welsh in Spain and Britain, respectively. Such a process in the long run may help reduce ethnic tension and conflicts. Moreover, many Europeans hope that the European Union will guarantee the rights of individuals through its Charter of Fundamental Social Rights of Workers. Indeed, the EU allocates considerable funds to worldwide humanitarian causes.

The European Union has worked to protect member states by maintaining standards for the importation of agricultural and food products. For example, "mad cow" disease, which struck cattle in Britain in the 1990s and infected a few human beings with a degenerative disease of the brain, led not only to the slaughter of millions of animals in Britain but also to the European Union's ban on the import of British beef on the continent for thirty-two months. In 1997, the EU began labeling products made from genetically modified soybeans and corn. Such imports, principally from the United States, are more resistant to damage by insects, but the long-range effect of their consumption is still unknown. Environmental groups, as well as many scientists, strongly oppose their use.

OPPOSITION TO GLOBALIZATION

Globalization itself became the target of protests and demonstrations in the 1990s, for example at the gathering of leaders of the eight leading industrial powers—the G8 (the United States, Great Britain, France, Italy, Germany, Russia, Canada, and Japan). Giant companies and banks, multinational in their structure and interests, have enormous economic power. Huge sums can be sent, traded, or invested with the push of a button. Global finance has brought volatility to the world economy, accentuated by the enormous U.S. trade deficit. The sharp decline in the U.S. stock market that began in 2000 followed wild speculation on dot.com companies. International dependence on oil, too, has increased, with prices rising and falling, often in tune with international events. The dizzying rise in the price of oil in 2008 jolted world economies, contributing to rapid inflation.

To its critics, globalization could be identified with corporate greed and indifference to the fate of the poor of the Third World. A French farmer (who had spent part of his childhood in California), José Bové (1953–), became a symbol of protest when in 1999 he led an attack on a McDonald's in a southern French town, damaging the fast-food restaurant as a means of calling attention to globalization. Cases of corporate greed and deception—such as that of the giant Enron corporation in the United States, whose corporate officers had lied and deceived, then unloaded their shares before the fall, leaving employees with virtually nothing—cast a shadow over big multinational corporations. Demonstrations became riots during the meeting of the World Trade Organization in Seattle in 1999, and in Nice in 2000 during the European Union summit meetings. During the summer of 2001, protesters demonstrated and some battled police at the summit in Gothenburg (Sweden) and then in Genoa (Italy), the site of the G7 meeting, an informal association of the world's leading industrial nations.

Damage to the environment is itself linked to global interconnectedness. The oceans have become veritable highways for the shipment of oil in huge tankers, a good many of which are old and badly maintained. Periodic oil

The 1999 meeting of the World Trade Organization in Seattle, Washington, was greeted with protests against the negative effects of globalization.

spills have damaged coasts catastrophically, such as that off the Atlantic coast of Spain in 2003. The diffusion of nuclear power (to say nothing of the threat of nuclear weapons) presents great risks, for all the advantage in generating electricity. By the end of the twentieth century, nuclear reactors, many of them old, generated about one-third of Europe's electricity. France led the way in adopting nuclear technology to produce electricity and by the end of the twentieth century nuclear reactors produced 75 percent of it. Nuclear power generated 60 percent of Belgium's electricity and 45 percent of Sweden's. The horrendous explosion at Chernobyl in Ukraine in 1986 further mobilized opposition to nuclear power. And as the threat from international terrorism becomes more real, nuclear reactors stand as potentially inviting targets for terrorists intent on taking as many lives and causing as much damage as possible. The international organization Greenpeace has actively opposed potential threats to the environment by nuclear power.

Opposition to globalization has also centered on the profits Western-based companies earn by selling products produced at low wages in, for example, Southeast Asia. Caps or jerseys with logos from NBA basketball teams, brand-name tennis shoes, and T-shirts with the names of U.S. universities became part of popular culture around the globe. Some of the products that are sold for high prices in the West are produced by destitute people in Asia (or elsewhere) for pitiful wages.

Globalization has helped the spread of AIDS. The disease has ravaged Europe (although not nearly to the same extent as Africa, where it is now the number one killer) and increased the cost of health care. As of 2003, more than 60 million people worldwide have been infected by the HIV virus, at least a third of whom have died. Although many AIDS victims live longer than before, no cure has yet been found.

THE THREAT OF TERRORISM

During the 1970s and 1980s, small groups on the extreme left and right turned to political terrorism. Violence seemed to them the only means of destabilizing political elites in the hope of taking power. Some terrorist groups were militant nationalists seeking independence from what they considered foreign occupying powers. Such groups included factions within the Irish Republican Army committed to ending British rule in Northern Ireland, militant Basque separatists (the ETA) in Spain, and Kurdish rebels in Turkey.

Between 1969 and 1982, political terrorists killed more than 1,100 people, including the bombing by fascists of the railroad station of Bologna in 1980 in which 85 people died. In the early 1970s, left-wing extremists (organized into perhaps as many as 100 separate groups) launched deadly attacks. The Red Brigades, founded in 1970, kidnapped and killed former Italian Premier Aldo Moro in 1978. But by the early 1980s, Italian terrorism had ebbed, the campaigns at political destabilization having failed.

Italian politicians put aside their usual differences long enough to back a vigorous campaign that led to the arrest of militants. In the German Federal Republic, small groups of left-wing terrorists lashed out with bombings, bank robberies, kidnappings, assassinations, and even a plane hijacking. The most notorious of these groups, the Baader-Meinhof gang, had links to terrorist groups in France and other Western countries.

Indeed, terrorism has posed an increasing threat in Western Europe, as extremist political groups and Islamic fundamentalist groups launched attacks. Notorious attacks included the massacre of Israelis by Palestinian militants at the 1972 Olympic Games in Munich and the seizure of a cruise ship in 1985. A terrorist bomb in 1989, probably planned in Libya, blew up a U.S. passenger jet over Lockerbie, Scotland, killing all 259 people aboard. In 1995, an Algerian Islamic fundamentalist group claimed responsibility for placing deadly bombs on subways and underground trains in Paris.

On a day of horror, September 11, 2001, hijackers commandeered four U.S. jetliners shortly after they took off from several airports early that morning. Two were crashed into the World Trade Center in lower Manhattan in New York City and a third into the Pentagon outside Washington, D.C. The fourth airliner plunged to earth in eastern Pennsylvania. Nearly 3,000 people were killed, the vast majority perishing in the World Trade Center, both towers of which collapsed in a heap of rubble. A massive manhunt began for the Saudi Arabian–born Osama bin Laden (1957–), leader of the Al Qaeda ("The Base") movement, which claimed responsibility for the attacks. Many of its members had trained in Afghanistan, which was ruled by an Islamic fundamentalist militia called the Taliban. Late that fall, the United States launched massive air strikes against Taliban installations in Afghanistan, and troops on the ground searched the rugged mountains near the border with Pakistan. An interim government took power in Afghanistan, backed by U.S. forces, facing the chronic problems of tribalism and poverty. The Al Qaeda organization had spread almost worldwide, with cells in Germany, Italy, France, and Britain, as well as in Malaysia and the Philippines. European states supported and assisted the U.S. campaign to uproot the structure of the Al Qaeda network in their countries. International police cooperation led to the arrests of Al Qaeda members in Germany, France, Spain, Britain, and Italy, but the search for others continued.

Islamic fundamentalist groups based in the Middle East have been actively recruiting adherents in European states that have large concentrations of Muslims. In March 2004, terrorist bombs detonated on several commuter trains in Madrid, killing almost 200 people and injuring 1,800 others. In July 2005, suicide bombers who had grown up in Britain detonated explosives in subway cars and on a bus in London, killing 50 people and wounding many more.

One of the consequences of globalization has been the increased vulnerability of Europe, as well as the United States, to political struggles and

A security alert in London, July 2005, not long after the explosion of terrorist bombs in three subway trains and on a bus.

events occurring far away, and to the terrorism these events have generated. Terrorists detonated cars packed with bombs in front of U.S. embassies in Dar es Salaam, Tanzania, and Nairobi, Kenya, in the summer of 1998, killing 213 people and wounding more than 5,000 in the latter attack. Islamic fundamentalists were also responsible for terrorist attacks in Arab states where fundamentalists wanted to impose strict religious rule.

Islam is not the only religion in which aggressive fundamentalism has emerged. In Israel, Jewish extreme nationalist groups, in coalition with the Likud party, have helped shape Israeli hard-line policies toward Palestinian demands for an independent state. The Palestinian question divides public opinion in Europe. The Palestinian minority in Israel demands an independent Palestinian state. Groups of Palestinian militants have undertaken murderous attacks on Israelis. In a cycle of violence that has become tragically common, the Israeli government often responds by razing villages or by further restricting the rights of Palestinians. The assassination of Yitzhak Rabin by a right-wing Israeli in 1995 was a blow to peace in the Middle East, which in some ways hinges on the Palestinian situation. In 1996, the Palestinian leader Yasir Arafat struck from the Palestine Liberation Organization's charter the call for the destruction of Israel. However, the "peace process"—as U.S. officials refer to it optimistically—began to break down in 2000.

A United States Empire?

The collapse of the Soviet empire left the United States as the world's single superpower. The U.S. maintains what constitutes an informal empire, influenced by financial might and vast if over-extended armed forces, including more than 700 military bases abroad. Conservative, or "Neo-Con," exponents of exerting forceful U.S. domination operate under the principle that what seems good for the United States is good for the world. In the late 1990s, a more aggressive U.S. foreign policy increased fears in Europe about U.S. foreign unilateralism and a rush to use force. On a continent ravaged by two devastating world wars, this has not gone down well. The U.S. refused in 2001 to sign the Kyoto Protocol, an agreement that requires countries to reduce the harmful greenhouse gas emissions that have caused global warming. In 2002, the U.S. government announced that it would not accept the jurisdiction of a proposed new international court, which was being set up to try those accused of crimes against humanity. Five years later, the U.S. government announced its intention of placing a missile defense system in Poland and the Czech Republic intended, in principle, to defend against any attacks launched by Iran, which the U.S. accused of working to build nuclear weapons. Such a plan outraged Russia, which fears the presence of such a system in neighboring states.

European Responses to U.S. Policy

In the wake of the attacks of September 11, 2001, the administration of U.S. President George W. Bush turned its attention to Saddam Hussein (1937–2006), Iraq's dictator, arguing that he was continuing to produce and hide "weapons of mass destruction" and that he had links to Al Qaeda. Neither assertion was correct. While British Prime Minister Tony Blair (despite popular opposition to the war) and a number of other states actively supported the U.S. position, Germany, France, and Russia opposed the Bush administration's position. In the meantime, UN weapons inspectors found no "weapons of mass destruction." Moreover, the Iraqis began to destroy missiles whose range exceeded that permitted by the United Nations following the Gulf War of 1991, when U.S. troops drove Iraqi forces from Kuwait, which Saddam Hussein had invaded.

The United States and Britain launched an invasion of Iraq in March 2003, quickly defeating the Iraqi army. The United States set up military authority in Iraq, along with a British zone in the south, anticipating that it would eventually give way to some sort of democratic Iraqi government (assuming religious, ethnic, and other tensions could be overcome). However, no weapons of mass destruction were ever found. This left the impression in much of Europe that some of the U.S. and British intelligence documents used to reach the conclusion that the regime of Saddam Hussein posed an immediate threat to the region or to U.S. interests—thus justifying the invasion—had been exaggerated, misrepresented, or even simply fabricated. (Moreover, President Bush's rhetorical evocation of a "crusade" against terrorism called to mind the bloody campaigns by European Christians against Islam during the Middle Ages.)

The Iraq crisis threatened the prestige and effectiveness of the United Nations, because of the determination of the U.S. government to go it alone. The outpouring of European sympathy and goodwill toward the United States following the terrorist attacks in New York and Washington, D.C., dissipated. Iraq descended into chaos. Insurgents rose up (aided by arms shipped from Iran) against the occupying forces. Terrorist attacks—the war brought Al Qaeda into Iraq—became a daily occurrence and Iraq plunged into civil war. Probably about half a million Iraqis have perished since the U.S. invasion and more than 2 million are refugees.

The C.I.A. operated secret prisons and undertook illegal kidnappings in Europe, sending several suspects off to probable torture in their countries of origin. Images of prisoners mistreated by their U.S. captors in Abu Ghraib prison flashed across televisions and computer screens across the globe, along with reports of the C.I.A. torturing prisoners and Iraqi civilians being gunned down by private U.S. security contractors. At the U.S. prison at Guantanamo Bay in Cuba, prisoners were held year after year without knowing the charges against them and denied access to any kind of legal representation. The president's acceptance of interrogation techniques considered to be torture further sullied the United States's reputation. Even as the security situation improved in Iraq in late 2007 and in 2008, President George W. Bush no longer seemed to represent the high moral standard long projected by the United States. When asked in 2008 whether

British Royal Marine Commandos guarding Iraqi prisoners of war, 2003.

a new president could restore American credibility, the foreign minister of France spoke for many, if not most, Europeans when he said, "It will never be as it was before. . . . The magic is gone." However, the election of Barack Obama in 2008 was overwhelmingly greeted with a sense of optimism by most Europeans.

Conclusion

As Europe moves through the first decade of the twenty-first century, its influence over the rest of the world has been reduced. Yet Europeans now for the most part live in peace, a situation that seems likely to remain for the foreseeable future. Their quality of life has continued to improve, thanks to ongoing advances in medicine and the production of food. Europe still confronts the challenges of finding enough safe energy while protecting the environment. In 2007, leaders of the EU agreed to try to reduce emissions of carbon dioxide by 20 percent by 2020, by which date renewable energy sources such as wind and solar power are to make up one-fifth of energy consumed.

As in other regions, European economies must continually adapt to the challenges of globalization. Following the failure of Communist states in Europe, even China has embraced some aspects of a market economy, and China and India have become economic giants. High unemployment rates in Europe still suggest the vulnerability of many people to the vicissitudes of the market. Young people in particular are affected by unemployment. Confrontations between young people and the police in Athens, as well as in other cities, in December 2008 followed the shooting death of an adolescent by a policeman. Many students and other young men and women are disaffected, fearing they will not find jobs and that they will be the first generation in the post-war period to do worse economically than their parents. Finding an appropriate balance between the free market and state intervention remains essential. Determined protests against globalization reflect the fact that global interconnectedness has not benefited everyone; millions of desperately poor people in Asia and Africa, and on other continents as well, have been left behind.

Human rights around the world remains a European concern more than sixty years after the adoption of the Universal Declaration of Human Rights by the United Nations. Amnesty International has been a force for identifying countries in which human rights are not respected, as has Human Rights Watch. European states were among those that put enormous pressure on South Africa in the 1970s and early 1980s, as it defied the world by maintaining its now dismantled official system of racial apartheid. Genocide in the African nation of Rwanda in the 1990s, ethnic cleansing in Kosovo, starvation in Ethiopia, massacres in the Darfur region of Sudan, and the explosive situation in the Middle East have also been the focus of human-rights groups, as well as of European states. The European Union has made support of human rights one of its priorities.

Europeans have many reasons to be optimistic about the future. German unification was achieved peacefully. Two old enemies, Germany and France, stand as a stable center for the continent's future. Despite divisions over policy toward Iraq, NATO adapted to the fall of communism and expanded toward the east, as has the European Union. Signs of greater toleration can be found in Eastern Europe and the Balkans, as well. In 1997, for the first time, ethnic Hungarians living in Romania could use their own language in their dealings with government officials and in education. And in 2000 the Bulgarian government finally allowed the state television network to broadcast a weekly news program in Turkish. While in most of Europe, nationalist irredentist claims have largely subsided, ethnic and religious rivalries have by no means been eliminated.

The Cold War is no more, and in Europe there is seemingly little risk of a hot one, at least of European-wide dimensions. The European Union has brought a single market to much of Europe and will continue to expand, with the help of its single currency, the euro. This in itself has made the continent smaller, making it even easier for people to travel and giving them increasingly more in common. Moreover, arguably the most important success of the European Union has been to make war between member states unlikely. All this should carry Europe into an even more prosperous future, one that can be built on lasting peace.

Protest outside Parliament in London against alleged torture by U.S. forces in Iraq.

FURTHER READINGS

GENERAL

Feroz Ahmad, *The Making of Modern Turkey* (1993).

Benedict Anderson, *Imagined Communities: Reflections on the Origins and Spread of Nationalism* (1991).

Michael Anderson, *Approaches to the History of the Western Family, 1500–1914* (1980).

Philippe Ariès, *Centuries of Childhood: A Social History of Family Life* (1962).

Philippe Ariès and Georges Duby, eds., *A History of Private Life* (5 vols., 1987–1993).

Geoffrey Barraclough, *The Origins of Modern Germany* (1979).

Geoffrey Best, *War and Society in Revolutionary Europe, 1770–1870* (1982).

David Blackbourn, *The Long Nineteenth Century: A History of Germany, 1780–1918* (1997).

Jerome Blum, *The End of the Old Order in Rural Europe* (1978).

———, *Lord and Peasant in Russia from the Ninth to the Nineteenth Century* (1961).

Richard Bonney, *The European Dynastic States, 1494–1660* (1991).

John Bossy, *Christianity in the West, 1400–1700* (1985).

Fernand Braudel, *The Mediterranean World in the Age of Philip II* (1992).

Peter Brown, *The Rise of Western Christendom: Triumph and Diversity, A.D. 200–1000* (2003).

Peter Burke, *Popular Culture in Early Modern Europe* (1978).

Franco Cardini, *Europe and Islam* (2001).

S. G. Checkland, *British Public Policy, 1776–1939: An Economic, Social, and Political Perspective* (1985).

Carlo Cipolla, *Before the Industrial Revolution: European Society and Economy, 1000–1700* (1980).

Carlo Cipolla, ed., *The Fontana Economic History of Europe* (6 vols., 1976–1977).

Martin Clark, *Modern Italy, 1871–1982* (1984).

Eric Cochrane, *Italy, 1530–1630* (1988).

Linda Colley, *Captives: Britain, Empire, and the World, 1650–1800* (2002).

John Darwin, *After Tamerlane: The Global History of Empire since 1405* (2008).

David Brion Davis, *The Problem of Slavery in the Age of Revolution, 1770–1823* (1975).

A-1

Jan de Vries, *The Industrious Revolution: Consumer Behavior and the Household Economy, 1650 to the Present* (2008).

Georges Duby and Michelle Perrot, eds., *A History of Women in the West* (5 vols., 1992–1994).

Christopher Duggan, *A Concise History of Italy* (1994).

Richard Dunn, *The Age of Religious Wars, 1559–1715* (1979).

Elizabeth Eisenstein, *The Printing Revolution in Early Modern Europe* (1993).

Norbert Elias, *The Civilizing Process* (1994).

J. H. Elliott, *Empire of the Atlantic World* (2007).

Niall Ferguson, *Empire: How Britain Made the Modern World* (2003).

———, *Empire: The Rise and Demise of the British World Order and the Lessons for Global Power* (2002).

William Ferguson, *Scotland: 1689 to the Present* (1968).

Orlando Figes, *Natasha's Dance: A Cultural History of Russia* (2002).

R. F. Foster, *Modern Ireland, 1600–1972* (1988).

Peter Gay, *The Cultivation of Hatred: The Bourgeois Experience: Victoria to Freud, Vol. III* (1994).

———, *Education of the Senses: The Bourgeois Experience: Victoria to Freud, Vol. I* (1999).

———, *The Tender Passion: The Bourgeois Experience: Victoria to Freud, Vol. II* (1999).

Felix Gilbert and David Clay Large, *The End of the European Era, 1890 to the Present* (2002).

Robert Gildea, *Barricades and Borders: Europe, 1800–1914* (1987).

John Gillis, *Youth and History: Tradition and Change in European Age Relations, 1770 to the Present* (1981).

Mark Girouard, *Cities and People: A Social and Architectural History* (1985).

Jack Goldstone, *Revolution and Rebellion in the Early Modern World* (1991).

Avner Grief, *Institutions and the Path to the Modern Economy: Lessons from Medieval Trade* (2006).

E. J. Hobsbawm, *The Age of Extremes: The Short Twentieth Century, 1914–1991* (1994).

———, *The Age of Revolution, 1789–1848* (1962).

Paul Hohenberg and Lynn Lees, *The Making of Urban Europe, 1000–1950* (1985).

Geoffrey Hosking, *Russia and the Russians: A History* (2001).

Lindsey Hughes, *The Romanovs: Ruling Russia 1613–1917* (2008).

Charles Ingrao, *The Habsburg Monarchy, 1618–1815* (1994).

Barbara Jelavich, *History of the Balkans* (2 vols., 1983).

Henry Kamen, *European Society, 1500–1700* (1984).

John Keegan, *The Face of Battle* (1976).

———, *A History of Warfare* (1993).

Tom Kemp, *Industrialization in Nineteenth-Century Europe* (1985).

Paul Kennedy, *The Rise and Fall of the Great Powers* (1987).

Ben Kiernan, *Blood and Soil: A World History of Genocide and Extermination from Sparta to Darfur* (2007).

V. G. Kiernan, *European Empires from Conquest to Collapse, 1815–1960* (1982).

Tony Kushner and Katharine Knox, *Refugees in the Age of Genocide* (2001).

H. G. Koenigsberger, *Early Modern Europe, 1500–1789* (1987).

————, *The Habsburgs and Europe, 1516–1660* (1971).

E. H. Kossman, *The Low Countries, 1780–1940* (1978).

Andrew Lees and Lynn Hollen Lees, *Cities and the Making of Modern Europe, 1750–1914* (2007).

C. A. Macartney, *The Habsburg Empire, 1790–1918* (1969).

Roger Magraw, *France, 1815–1914: The Bourgeois Century* (1983).

Arno Mayer, *The Persistence of the Old Regime: Europe to the Great War* (1981).

Mary Jo Maynes, *Schooling in Western Europe: A Social History* (1985).

Mark Mazower, *The Balkans: A Short History* (2000).

Peter McPhee, *A Social History of France, 1780–1880* (2004).

John M. Merriman, *The Stones of Balazuc: A French Village in Time* (2002).

John Merriman and Jay Winter, eds., *Europe 1789 to 1914: Encyclopedia of the Age of Industry and Empire*, 5 vols. (2006).

————, *Europe since 1914: Encyclopedia of the Age of War and Reconstruction*, 5 vols. (2006).

Alec Reginald Meyers, *Parliaments and Estates in Europe to 1789* (1975).

Joel Mokyr, *The Gifts of Athena: Historical Origins of the Knowledge Economy* (2002).

————, *Twenty-Five Centuries of Technological Change: An Historical Survey* (1990).

P. K. O'Brien and C. Keyser, *Economic Growth in Britain and Europe, 1780–1914* (1978).

Geoffrey Parker, *The Military Revolution: Military Innovation and the Rise of the West, 1500–1800* (1988).

Pamela M. Pilbeam, *The Middle Classes in Europe, 1789–1914: France, Germany, Italy and Russia* (1990).

Leon Plantinga, *Romantic Music: A History of Musical Style in Nineteenth-Century Europe* (1984).

Kenneth Pomerantz, *Great Divergence: Europe, China, and the Making of the Modern World Economy* (2000).

Donald Quataert, *The Ottoman Empire, 1700–1922* (2007).

Colin Russell, *Science and Social Change in Britain and Europe, 1700–1900* (1983).

Peter Sahlins, *Boundaries: The Making of France and Spain in the Pyrenees* (1989).

Raffaella Sarti, *Europe at Home: Family and Material Culture 1500–1800* (2002).

Joan W. Scott, *Gender and the Politics of History* (1988).

Hugh Seton-Watson, *The Russian Empire, 1801–1917* (1967).

Stanford J. Shaw, *History of the Ottoman Empire and Modern Turkey* (2 vols., 1976–1977).

James Sheehan, *German History, 1770–1866* (1990).

————, *Where Have All the Soldiers Gone? The Transformation of Modern Europe* (2008).

Adrien Shubert, *A Social History of Modern Spain* (1990).

Yuri Slezkine, *Arctic Mirrors: Russia and the Small Peoples of the North* (1994).

Bonnie G. Smith, *Changing Lives: Women in European History since 1700* (1989).

Timothy Snyder, *The Reconstruction of Nations: Poland, Ukraine, Lithuania, Belarus, 1569–1999* (2003).

A. J. P. Taylor, *The Struggle for Mastery in Europe, 1848–1918* (1954).

Charles Tilly, *Coercion, Capital, and European States, AD 990–1990* (1990).
———, *The Contentious French: Four Centuries of Popular Struggle* (1986).
Richard Vinen, *A History in Fragments: Europe and the Twentieth Century* (2001).
Mack Walker, *German Home Towns: Community, State, and General Estate, 1648–1871* (1971).
Immanuel Wallerstein, *The Modern World System* (1974).
Piotr Wandycz, *The Price of Freedom: A History of East Central Europe from the Middle Ages to the Present* (1992).
Eric R. Wolf, *Europe and the People without History* (1983).
Isser Woloch, ed., *Revolution and the Meanings of Freedom in the Nineteenth Century* (1996).
Stuart Woolf, *A History of Italy, 1700–1860* (1986).
E. A. Wrigley, *Population and History* (1969).
Theodore Zeldin, *France, 1848–1945* (5 vols., 1978–1981).

CHAPTER 1. MEDIEVAL LEGACIES AND TRANSFORMING DISCOVERIES

Kenneth R. Andrews, *Trade, Plunder and Settlement: Maritime Enterprise and the Genesis of the British Empire, 1480–1630* (1984).
Robert Bartlett, *The Making of Europe: Conquest, Colonization and Cultural Change, 950–1350* (1993).
M. W. Beresford, *New Towns of the Middle Ages* (1988).
Marc Bloch, *Feudal Society* (2 vols., 1961).
Brenda Bolton, *The Medieval Reformation* (1983).
John Boswell, *Christianity, Social Tolerance, and Homosexuality: Gay People in Western Europe from the Beginning of the Christian Era to the Fourteenth Century* (1980).
———, *The Kindness of Strangers: The Abandonment of Children in Western Europe from Late Antiquity to the Renaissance* (1988).
Rosalind B. Brooke and Christopher Brooke, *Popular Religion in the Middle Ages* (1984).
Alfred W. Crosby, *Ecological Imperialism: The Biological Expansion of Europe, 900–1900* (1986).
R. O. Crummey, *The Formation of Muscovy, 1404–1613* (1987).
Natalie Zemon Davis, *Trichster Travels: A Sixteenth-Century Muslim Between Worlds* (2006).
Georges Duby, *Rural Economy and Country Life in the Medieval West* (1968).
Edith Ennen, *The Medieval Woman* (1989).
Robert Fossier, *Peasant Life in the Medieval West* (1988).
Paul Freedman, *Out of the East: Spices and the Medieval Imagination* (2008).
Bernard Hamilton, *Religion in the Medieval West* (1986).
Denys Hay, *Europe in the Fourteenth and Fifteenth Centuries* (1989).
———, *Europe, the Emergence of an Idea* (1968).
Norman Housley, *The Later Crusades, 1274–1580* (1992).
William C. Jordan, *Europe in the High Middle Ages* (2001).
Emmanuel Leroy Ladurie, *Montaillou: The Promised Land of Error* (1979).
Robert S. Lopez, *The Commercial Revolution of the Middle Ages, 950–1300* (1971).

Angus MacKay, *Society, Economy and Religion in Late Medieval Castile* (1987).
Richard Mackenney, *Sixteenth-Century Europe: Expansion and Conflict* (1993).
H. E. Mayer, *The Crusades* (1988).
Michel Mollat, *The Poor in the Middle Ages* (1986).
R. I. Moore, *The First European Revolution, c. 970–1215* (2000).
John H. Mundy, *Europe in the High Middle Ages, 1150–1309* (1991).
J. H. Parry, *The Age of Reconnaissance: Discovery, Exploration and Settlement, 1450–1650* (1981).
Fritz Rorig, *The Medieval Town* (1967).
Daniel Waley and Peter Denley, *Later Medieval Europe, 1250–1520* (2001).

Chapter 2. The Renaissance

William J. Bouwsma, *The Waning of the Renaissance, 1550–1640* (2002).
Judith Brown, *In the Shadow of Florence* (1982).
Eugene Brucker, *Renaissance Florence* (1983).
Peter Burke, *The Italian Renaissance: Culture and Society in Italy* (1987).
———, *Popular Culture in Renaissance Europe, 1450–1620* (1986).
Christopher S. Celenza, *The Lost Italian Renaissance: Humanists, Historians, and Latin's Legacy* (2004).
Carlo Ginzburg, *The Cheese and the Worms: The Cosmos of a Sixteenth-Century Miller* (1982).
———, *Night Battles* (1985).
Richard Goldthwaite, *The Building of Renaissance Florence* (1981).
Anthony Grafton and Lisa Jardine, *From Humanism to the Humanities: Education and the Liberal Arts in Fifteenth- and Sixteenth-Century Europe* (1986).
J. R. Hale, *Renaissance Europe* (1977).
———, *War and Society in Renaissance Europe, 1450–1620* (1986).
Denys Hay and John Law, *Italy in the Age of the Renaissance, 1380–1530* (1989).
Dale Kent, *The Rise of the Medici* (1979).
Margaret King, *Women in the Renaissance* (1991).
Lauro Martines, *April Blood: Florence and the Plot against the Medici* (2003).
———, *Power and Imagination: City-States in Renaissance Italy* (1988).
Garrett Mattingly, *Renaissance Diplomacy* (1988).
Margaret Meserve, *Empires of Islam in Renaissance Historical Thought* (2008).
John M. Najemy, *A History of Florence, 1200–1575* (2006).
J. G. A. Pocock, *The Machiavellian Moment: Florentine Political Thought and the Atlantic Republican Tradition* (1975).
John Stephens, *The Italian Renaissance: The Origins of Intellectual and Artistic Change before the Reformation* (1990).
Hugh Thomas, *The Conquest of Mexico* (1993).

Chapter 3. The Two Reformations

Cornelis Augustijn, *Erasmus: His Life, Works, and Influence* (1991).
Philip Benedict, *Christ's Churches Purely Reformed: A Social History of Calvinism* (2002).
William J. Bouwsma, *John Calvin: A Sixteenth-Century Portrait* (1987).
Euan Cameron, *The European Reformation* (1991).

Anwar Chejne, *Islam and the West: The Moriscos: A Cultural and Social History* (1983).

William A. Christian, Jr., *Local Religion in Sixteenth-Century Spain* (1981).

A. G. Dickens, *The English Reformation* (1989).

Carlos Eire, *From Madrid to Purgatory: The Art and Craft of Dying in Sixteenth-Century Spain* (1995).

———, *War against the Idol: The Reformation of Worship from Erasmus to Calvin* (1986).

Ronnie Po-Chia Hsia, *Social Discipline in the Reformation: Central Europe, 1550–1750* (1989).

———, *Society and Religion in Münster, 1535–1618* (1984).

Lisa Jardine, *Erasmus, Man of Letters: The Construction of Charisma in Print* (1993).

David Kirby, *Northern Europe in the Early Modern Period: The Baltic World, 1492–1772* (1990).

Sherrin Marshall, ed., *Women in Reformation and Counter-Reformation Europe: Public and Private Worlds* (1989).

Bernd Moeller, *Imperial Cities and the Reformation* (1982).

John W. O'Malley, *Trent and All That: Renaming Catholicism in the Early Modern Period* (2000).

Steven E. Ozment, *Flesh and Spirit: Private Life in Early Modern Germany* (1999).

———, *The Reformation in the Cities: The Appeal of Protestantism to Sixteenth-Century Germany and Switzerland* (1975).

———, *When Fathers Ruled: Family Life in Reformation Europe* (1983).

Eugene R. Rice, Jr., and Anthony Grafton, *The Foundations of Early Modern Europe, 1460–1559* (1994).

Thomas Robisheaux, *Rural Society and the Search for Order in Early Modern Germany* (1989).

John D. Roth and James M. Stayer, eds., *Companion to Anabaptism and Spiritualism, 1521–1700* (2007).

Robert W. Scribner, *For the Sake of Simple Folk: Popular Propaganda for the German Reformation* (1984).

Lewis Spitz, *The Protestant Reformation* (1987).

Keith Thomas, *Religion and the Decline of Magic* (1971).

Tessa Watt, *Cheap Print and Popular Piety, 1550–1640* (1991).

Merry E. Weisner, *Women and Gender in Early Modern Europe* (1993).

CHAPTER 4. THE WARS OF RELIGION

Susan Dwyer Amussen, *An Ordered Society: Gender and Class in Early Modern England* (1988).

Stuart Clarke, *Thinking with Demons: The Idea of Witchcraft in Early Modern Europe* (1997).

Natalie Zemon Davis, *The Gift in Sixteenth-Century France* (2000).

———, *The Return of Martin Guerre* (1983).

Eamon Duffy, *The Voices of Morebath: Reformation and Rebellion in an English Village* (2001).

J. H. Elliott, *Europe Divided, 1559–1598* (1968).

Bruce Gordon, *The Swiss Reformation* (2002).
Mark Greengrass, *France in the Age of Henry IV: The Struggle for Stability* (1995).
Brad S. Gregory, *Christian Martyrdom in Early Modern Europe* (1999).
R. J. Knecht, *Francis I* (1992).
———, *The French Civil Wars* (2000).
Geoffrey Parker, *Europe in Crisis, 1598–1648* (1979).
Geoffrey Parker, ed., *The Thirty Years' War* (1988).
N. M. Sutherland, *The Massacre of St. Bartholomew and the European Conflict, 1559–1572* (1973).

Chapter 5. The Rise of the Atlantic Economy: Spain and England

Ralph Davis, *The Rise of the Atlantic Economies* (1973).
Jan de Vries, *The Economy of Europe in an Age of Crisis, 1600–1750* (1978).
J. H. Elliott, *The Count-Duke of Olivares: The Statesman in an Age of Decline* (1987).
———, *Imperial Spain, 1469–1714* (1964).
———, *The Revolt of the Catalans: A Study in the Decline of Spain, 1598–1640* (1984).
G. R. Elton, *England under the Tudors* (1991).
Felipe Fernandez-Armesto, *The Spanish Armada: The Experience of War in 1588* (1989).
John Guy, *Tudor England* (1988).
Henry Kamen, *Empire: How Spain Became a World Power, 1492–1763* (2004).
John Lynch, *Spain, 1516–1598* (1994).
———, *Spain under the Habsburgs, 1516–1700* (2 vols., 1964–1969).
Colin Martin and Geoffrey Parker, *The Spanish Armada* (1988).
Geoffrey Parker, *The Grand Strategy of Philip II* (2000).
———, *Philip II* (1978).
Carla Rahn Philips, *Galleons for the King of Spain* (1986).
Penry Williams, *The Tudor Regime* (1979).
Joyce Youings, *Sixteenth-Century England* (1984).

Chapter 6. England and the Dutch Republic in the Seventeenth Century

Michael Braddick, *God's Fury, England's Fire: A New History of England's Civil Wars* (2008).
Harold J. Cook, *Masters of Exchange: Commerce, Medicine, and Science in the Dutch Golden Age* (2007).
Bruce R. Galloway, *The Union of England and Scotland, 1603–1608* (1986).
Pieter Geyl, *The Revolt of the Netherlands, 1555–1609* (1966).
Christopher Hill, *God's Englishman: Oliver Cromwell and the English Revolution* (1975).
———, *The World Turned Upside Down* (1972).
Derek Hirst, *Authority and Conflict: England, 1603–1658* (1986).
Ronald Hutton, *The British Republic, 1649–1660* (1990).

Jonathan I. Israel, *The Dutch Republic: Its Rise, Greatness, and Fall, 1477–1806* (1995).

J. R. Jones, *The Revolution of 1688 in England* (1972).

Anna Keay, *The Magnificent Monarch: Charles II and the Ceremonies of Power* (2008).

Mark Kishlansky, *A Monarchy Transformed: Britain, 1603–1714* (1996).

Mark Knights, *Representation and Misrepresentation in Later Stuart Britain: Partisanship and Political Culture* (2005).

Peter Laslett, *The World We Have Lost: England before the Industrial Age* (1983).

Brian P. Levack, *The Formation of the British State: England, Scotland, and the Union, 1603–1707* (1987).

John Morrill, *The Revolt of the Provinces: Conservatism and Revolution in the English Civil War, 1630–1650* (1980).

Geoffrey Parker, *The Army of Flanders and the Spanish Road, 1567–1659* (1972).

Steven C. Pincus, *1688: The First Modern Revolution* (2009).

Maarten Prak, *The Dutch Republic in the Seventeenth Century* (2005).

J. L. Price, *Culture and Society in the Dutch Republic during the Seventeenth Century* (1974).

Simon Schama, *An Embarrassment of Riches: An Interpretation of Dutch Culture in the Golden Age* (1988).

J. A. Sharpe, *Early Modern England: A Social History, 1550–1760* (1990).

Kevin Sharpe, *The Personal Rule of Charles I* (1995).

Lawrence Stone, *The Causes of the English Revolution, 1629–1642* (1990).

David Underdown, *Fire from Heaven: Life in an English Town in the Seventeenth Century* (1992).

———, *Revel, Riot, and Rebellion: Popular Politics and Culture in England, 1603–1660* (1985).

Keith Wrightson, *Earthly Necessities: Economic Lives in Early Modern Britain* (2000).

———, *English Society, 1550–1760* (1982).

Chapter 7. The Age of Absolutism, 1650–1720

Perry Anderson, *Lineages of the Absolutist State* (1974).

William Beik, *Absolutism and Society in Seventeenth-Century France: State Power and Provincial Aristocracy in Languedoc* (1985).

Joseph Bergin, *Cardinal Richelieu: Power and the Pursuit of Wealth* (1985).

Paul Bushkovitch, *Peter the Great* (2001).

James B. Collins, *The State in Early Modern France* (2001).

J. H. Elliott, *Richelieu and Olivares* (1984).

Richard J. Evans, *The Making of the Habsburg Empire, 1550–1770* (1979).

Pierre Goubert, *Louis XIV and Twenty Million Frenchmen* (1972).

Ragnhild Hatton, *Europe in the Age of Louis XIV* (1979).

Lindsey Hughes, *Russia in the Age of Peter the Great, 1682–1725* (1998).

Sharon Kettering, *French Society, 1589–1715* (2001).

Robert Mandrou, *Introduction to Modern France, 1500–1640* (1975).

Roland Mousnier, *Peasant Uprisings in Seventeenth-Century France, Russia, and China* (1970).

David Parker, *The Making of French Absolutism* (1983).

Theodore Rabb, *The Struggle for Stability in Early Modern Europe* (1975).
Orest Ranum, *The Fronde: A French Revolution* (1993).
———, *Paris in the Age of Absolutism* (2003).
John Stoye, *The Siege of Vienna: The Last Great Trial between Cross and Crescent* (2007).

CHAPTER 8. THE NEW PHILOSOPHY OF SCIENCE

Herbert Butterfield, *The Origins of Modern Science, 1300–1800* (1965).
John Fauvel, Raymond Flood, Michael Shortland, and Robin Wilson, eds., *Let Newton Be! A New Perspective on His Life and Works* (1988).
A. R. Hall, *The Revolution in Science, 1500–1750: The Formation of the Modern Scientific Attitude* (1983).
Margaret Jacobs, *The Cultural Meaning of the Scientific Revolution* (1988).
Hugh Kearney, *Science and Change, 1500–1700* (1971).
Alexandre Koyr, *The Formation of the Modern Scientific Attitude* (1983).
T. S. Kuhn, *The Structure of Scientific Revolution* (1989).
Robert K. Merton, *Science, Technology, and Society in Seventeenth-Century England* (1970).
Ingrid D. Rowland, *Giordino Bruno, Philosopher, Heretic* (2008).
Londa Schiebinger, *The Mind Has No Sex? Women and the Origins of Modern Science* (1990).
R. S. Westfall, *Never at Rest: A Biography of Isaac Newton* (1993).
B. H. G. Wormald, *Francis Bacon: History, Politics, and Science, 1561–1626* (1993).

CHAPTER 9. ENLIGHTENED THOUGHT AND THE REPUBLIC OF LETTERS

Keith Baker, *Inventing the French Revolution: Essays in the Political Culture of Eighteenth-Century France* (1990).
Roger Chartier, *The Cultural Origins of the French Revolution* (1991).
Maurice Cranston, *The Noble Savage: Jean-Jacques Rousseau, 1754–1762* (1991).
———, *Philosophers and Pamphleteers: Political Theorists of the Enlightenment* (1986).
Thomas E. Crow, *Painters and Public Life in Eighteenth-Century Paris* (1985).
Robert Darnton, *The Business of Enlightenment* (1979).
———, *The Great Cat Massacre* (1985).
———, *The Literary Underground of the Old Regime* (1985).
Peter Gay, *The Enlightenment: An Interpretation* (2 vols., 1966–1969).
———, *Voltaire's Politics: The Poet as Realist* (1988).
Dena Goodman, *The Republic of Letters: A Cultural History of the French Enlightenment* (1984).
Norman Hampson, *A Cultural History of the Enlightenment* (1969).
Carla Hesse, *The Other Enlightenment: How French Women Became Modern* (2001).
Darrin M. McMahon, *Enemies of the Enlightenment: Anti-Philosophes and the Birth of the French Far Right, 1778–1830* (1998).
J. M. McManners, *Death and Enlightenment: Changing Attitudes to Death among Christians and Unbelievers in Eighteenth-Century France* (1982).

Roy Porter and Mikulás Teich, eds., *The Enlightenment in National Context* (1981).

John Robertson, *The Case for the Enlightenment: Scotland and Naples, 1680–1760* (2005).

Franco Venturi, *Italy and the Enlightenment: Studies in a Cosmopolitan Century* (1972).

CHAPTER 10. EIGHTEENTH-CENTURY ECONOMIC AND SOCIAL CHANGE

M. S. Anderson, *Europe in the Eighteenth Century, 1713–1783* (1982).

C. A. Bayly, *Imperial Meridian: The British Empire and the World, 1780–1830* (1989).

David A. Bell, *The Cult of the Nation in France: Inventing Nationalism, 1680–1800* (2001).

Maxine Berg, *The Age of Manufacturers, 1700–1820: Industry, Innovation, and Work in Britain* (1985).

Peter Borsay, *The English Urban Renaissance: Culture and Society in the Provincial Town, 1660–1770* (1989).

Christopher Leslie Brown, *Moral Capital: The Foundations of British Abolitionism* (2008).

P. J. Corfield, *The Impact of English Towns, 1700–1800* (1982).

Douglas Hay, et al., *Albion's Fatal Tree: Crime and Punishment in Eighteenth-Century England* (1975).

Steven L. Kaplan, *Provisioning Paris: Merchants and Millers in the Grain and Flour Trade during the Eighteenth Century* (1984).

Emmanuel LeRoy Ladurie, *The Peasants of Languedoc* (1974).

Paul Langford, *A Polite and Commercial People: England, 1727–1783* (1989).

P. J. Marshall, *The Making and Unmaking of Empires: Britain, India, and America c. 1750–1783* (2005).

G. E. Mingay, *Land and Society in England, 1750–1980* (1994).

J. H. Parry, *Trade and Dominion: The European Overseas Empires in the Eighteenth Century* (1971).

Roy Porter, *English Society in the Eighteenth Century* (1986).

George Rudé, *Paris and London in the Eighteenth Century* (1971).

Bernard Semmel, *The Methodist Revolution* (1973).

Lawrence Stone, *The Family, Sex, and Marriage in England, 1500–1800* (1977).

E. P. Thompson, *Whigs and Hunters: The Origins of the Black Act* (1975).

Isser Woloch, *Eighteenth-Century Europe: Tradition and Progress, 1715–1789* (1982).

CHAPTER 11. EIGHTEENTH-CENTURY DYNASTIC RIVALRIES AND POLITICS

Paul Avrich, *Russian Rebels, 1600–1800* (1972).

Bernard Bailyn, *The Ideological Origins of the American Revolution* (1992).

C. B. A. Behrens, *The Ancien Régime* (1967).

———, *Society, Government, and the Enlightenment: The Experiences of Eighteenth-Century France and Prussia* (1985).

David Bell, *Lawyers and Citizens: The Making of a Political Elite in Old Regime France* (1994).

John Brewer, *Party Ideology and Popular Politics at the Accession of George III* (1976).

———, *The Sinews of Power: War, Money, and the English State, 1688–1783* (1989).

Linda Colley, *Britons: Forging the Nation, 1707–1837* (1992).

———, *In Defiance of Oligarchy: The Tory Party, 1714–1760* (1982).

———, *The Ordeal of Elizabeth Marsh: A Woman in World History* (2008).

Tim Harris, *Revolution: The Great Crisis of the British Monarchy, 1685–1729* (2006).

Olwen Hufton, *The Poor of Eighteenth-Century France, 1750–1789* (1974).

Maya Jasanoff, *Edge of Empire: Lives, Culture, and Conquest in the East, 1750–1850* (2005).

Isabel de Madariaga, *Catherine the Great: A Short History* (1990).

Sara Maza, *Private Lives and Public Affairs: The Causes Celebres of Prerevolutionary France* (1993).

Edmund Sears Morgan, *Benjamin Franklin* (2003).

———, *The Birth of the Republic, 1763–1789* (1977).

Daniel Roche, *The People of Paris* (1987).

Robert M. Schwartz, *Policing the Poor in Eighteenth-Century France* (1988).

Wayne Te Brake, *Regents and Rebels: The Revolutionary World of an Eighteenth-Century Dutch City* (1989).

Franco Venturi, *The End of the Old Regime in Europe, 1776–1789* (2 vols., 1991).

Ernst Wangermann, *The Austrian Achievement, 1700–1800* (1973).

CHAPTER 12. THE FRENCH REVOLUTION

Nigel Aston, *Religion and Revolution in France, 1780–1804* (2000).

Jean-Paul Bertaud, *The Army of the French Revolution: From Citizen-Soldiers to Instrument of Power* (1988).

T. C. W. Blanning, *The French Revolutionary Wars, 1787–1802* (1996).

Howard G. Brown, *Ending the French Revolution: Violence, Justice, and Repression from the Terror to Napoleon* (2006).

Richard Cobb, *The Police and the People: French Popular Protest, 1789–1820* (1972).

William Doyle, *Origins of the French Revolution* (1988).

Marianne Elliott, *Partners in Revolution: The United Irishmen and France* (1982).

Alan Forrest, *Conscripts and Deserters: The Army and French Society during the Revolution and Empire* (1989).

———, *The French Revolution and the Poor* (1981).

Francois Furet, *Interpreting the French Revolution* (1992).

David Garrioch, *The Making of Revolutionary Paris* (2002).

Dominique Godineau, *The Women of Paris and Their French Revolution* (1998).

Carla Hesse, *Publishing and Cultural Politics in Revolutionary Paris, 1789–1810* (1991).

Patrice Higonnet, *Sister Republics: The Origins of French and American Republicanism* (1988).

Lynn Hunt, *The Family Romance of the French Revolution* (1992).

———, *Politics, Culture, and Class in the French Revolution* (1984).

Peter Jones, *The Peasantry in the French Revolution* (1988).

Georges Lefebvre, *The Coming of the French Revolution* (1989).

Ted W. Margadant, *Urban Rivalries in the French Revolution* (1992).

Peter McPhee, *The French Revolution, 1789–1799* (2002).

Sarah E. Meltzer and Leslie W. Rabine, eds., *Rebel Daughters: Women and the French Revolution* (1989).

Mona Ozouf, *Festivals and the French Revolution* (1988).

R. R. Palmer, *The Age of the Democratic Revolution: A Political History of Europe and America, 1760–1800* (2 vols., 1959–1964).

———, *Twelve Who Ruled: The Year of the Terror in the French Revolution* (1989).

Jeremy D. Popkin, *Revolutionary News: The Press in France, 1789–1799* (1990).

George Rudé, *The Great Fear of 1789* (1973).

William H. Sewell, Jr., *A Rhetoric of Bourgeois Revolution: The Abbé Sieyès and "What is the Third Estate?"* (1994).

Donald Sutherland, *France, 1789–1815: Revolution and Counterrevolution* (1986).

Timothy Tackett, *Religion, Revolution, and Regional Culture in Eighteenth-Century France: The Ecclesiastical Oath of 1791* (1986).

———, *When the King Took Flight* (2003).

Charles Tilly, *The Vendée* (1964).

Isser Woloch, *The New Regime: Transformations of the French Civic Order, 1789–1820s* (1994).

CHAPTER 13. NAPOLEON AND EUROPE

David A. Bell, *The First Total War: Napoleon's Empire and the Birth of Warfare as We Know It* (2007).

Louis Bergeron, *France under Napoleon* (1981).

Michael Broers, *Europe under Napoleon* (1996).

———, *The Politics of Religion in Napoleonic Italy: The War against God, 1801–1814* (2002).

Philip Dwyer, *Napoleon: The Path to Power* (2007).

Steven Englund, *Napoleon: A Political Life* (2004).

Alan Forrest, *Napoleon's Men: The Soldiers of the Revolution and Empire* (2002).

Gunther Rothenberg, *The Art of Warfare in the Age of Napoleon* (1978).

Alan Schom, *One Hundred Days: Napoleon's Road to Waterloo* (1992).

Jakob Walter, *The Diary of a Napoleonic Foot Soldier* (1991).

Stuart Wolfe, *Napoleon's Integration of Europe* (1991).

D. G. Wright, *Napoleon and Europe* (1984).

CHAPTER 14. THE INDUSTRIAL REVOLUTION

Anna Clark, *The Struggle for the Breeches: Gender and the Making of the British Working Class* (1995).

Deborah Cohen, *Household Gods: The British and Their Possessions* (2006).
Leonore Davidoff and Catherine Hall, *Family Fortunes: Men and Women of the English Middle Class, 1780–1850* (1991).
James S. Donnelly, Jr., *The Great Irish Potato Famine* (2002).
Michel Foucault, *Madness and Civilization* (1973).
Colin Heywood, *Childhood in Nineteenth-Century France: Work, Health, and Education among the Classes Populaires* (1988).
E. J. Hobsbawm and George Rudé, *Captain Swing* (1975).
David J. V. Jones, *Rebecca's Children: A Study of Rural Society, Crime, and Protest* (1989).
Gareth Stedman Jones, *Languages of Class: Studies in English Working-Class History* (1983).
David Landes, *The Unbound Prometheus: Technological Change and Industrial Development in Western Europe from 1750 to the Present* (1976).
Lynn Hollen Lees, *Exiles of Erin: Irish Migrants to Victorian London* (1979).
David McLellan, *Karl Marx: His Life and Thought* (1977).
Joel Mokyr, *The Gift of Athena* (2003).
R. J. Morris, *Class, Sect and Party: The Making of the British Middle Class: Leeds, 1820–1850* (1990).
Claire Goldberg Moses, *French Feminism in the Nineteenth Century* (1984).
John Roach, *History of Secondary Education in England, 1800–1870* (1987).
William H. Sewell, Jr., *Work and Revolution in France: The Language of Labor from the Old Regime to 1848* (1980).
E. P. Thompson, *The Making of the English Working Class* (1963).
Louise A. Tilly and Joan W. Scott, *Women, Work, and Family* (1978).
Clive Trebilcock, *The Industrialization of the Continental Powers, 1780–1914* (1989).
Dror Wahrman, *Imagining the Middle Class: The Political Representation of Class in Britain, c. 1780–1840* (1995).
William Weber, *Music and the Middle Class: The Social Structure of Concert Life in London, Paris and Vienna* (1975).

CHAPTER 15. LIBERAL CHALLENGES TO RESTORATION EUROPE

Michael Brock, *Great Reform Act* (1973).
Clive H. Church, *1830 in Europe: Revolution and Political Change* (1983).
Gordon A. Craig, *The Triumph of Liberalism: Zurich in the Golden Age, 1830–1869* (1988).
Friedrich Engels, *The Condition of the Working Class in England* (1993).
Eric J. Evans, *Britain before the Reform Act: Politics and Society, 1815–1832* (1989).
Norman Gash, *Aristocracy and People: Britain, 1815–1865* (1979).
Hugh Honour, *Romanticism* (1979).
Clara M. Lovett, *The Democratic Movement in Italy, 1830–1876* (1982).
R. J. Morris, *Class, Sect and Party: The Making of the British Middle Class: Leeds, 1820–1850* (1990).
Harold Perkin, *The Origins of Modern English Society, 1780–1880* (1972).
Barbara Taylor, *Eve and the New Jerusalem: Socialism and Feminism in the Nineteenth Century* (1983).

Dror Wahrman, *Imagining the Middle Class: The Political Representation of Class in Britain, c. 1780–1840* (1995).

CHAPTER 16. THE REVOLUTIONS OF 1848

Maurice Agulhon, *The Republican Experiment, 1848–1852* (1983).
T. J. Clark, *The Absolute Bourgeois: Artists and Politics in France, 1848–1851* (1973).
István Deák, *The Lawful Revolution: Louis Kossuth and the Hungarians, 1848–1849* (1979).
Ted W. Margadant, *French Peasants in Revolt: The Insurrection of 1851* (1979).
Peter McPhee, *The Politics of Rural Life: Political Mobilization in the French Countryside, 1845–1852* (1992).
John M. Merriman, *The Agony of the Republic: The Repression of the Left in Revolutionary France, 1848–1851* (1978).
Jonathan Sperber, *The European Revolutions, 1848–1851* (1993).
———, *Rhineland Radicals: The Democratic Movement and the Revolution of 1848–1849* (1991).

CHAPTER 17. THE ERA OF NATIONAL UNIFICATION

David Blackbourn and Geoff Eley, *The Peculiarities of German History: Bourgeois Society and Politics in Nineteenth-Century German History* (1984).
István Deák, *Beyond Nationalism: A Social History of the Habsburg Officer Corps, 1848–1918* (1990).
Lothar Gall, *Bismarck: The White Revolutionary* (2 vols., 1986).
Lucy Riall, *Sicily and the Unification of Italy* (1998).
Denis Mack Smith, *Cavour* (1985).
———, *Cavour and Garibaldi, 1860: A Study of Political Conflict* (1985).
———, *Victor Emanuel, Cavour, and the Risorgimento* (1971).
Helmut Smith, *German Nationalism and Religious Conflict: Culture, Ideology, Politics, 1870–1914* (1995).

CHAPTER 18. THE DOMINANT POWERS IN THE AGE OF LIBERALISM: PARLIAMENTARY BRITAIN, REPUBLICAN FRANCE, AND TSARIST RUSSIA

Robert Anderson, *Education and Opportunity in Victorian Scotland* (1983).
Abraham Ascher, *The Revolution of 1905* (2 vols., 1992).
Jeffrey A. Auerbach, *The Great Exposition of 1851: A Nation on Display* (1999).
Edward Berenson, *The Trial of Madame Caillaux* (1992).
Victoria E. Bonnell, *Roots of Rebellion: Workers' Politics and Organizations in St. Petersburg and Moscow, 1900–1914* (1983).
Asa Briggs, *Victorian Cities* (1977).
———, *Victorian People* (1954).
Jeffrey Brooks, *When Russia Learned to Read: Literacy and Popular Literature, 1861–1917* (1985).
Michael Burns, *Dreyfus: A Family Affair, 1789–1945* (1992).

David Cannadine, *The Decline and Fall of the British Aristocracy* (1990).

G. Kitson Clark, *The Making of Victorian England* (1962).

H. J. Dyos and Michael Wolff, *The Victorian City: Images and Realities* (2 vols., 1983).

Catherine Evtuhov and Richard Stites, *A History of Russia: People, Legends, Events, Forces* (2004).

Michael Freeman, *Railways and the Victorian Imagination* (1999).

David M. Goldfrank, *The Origins of the Crimean War* (1994).

Sudhir Hazareesingh, *From Subject to Citizen: The Second Empire and the Emergence of Modern French Democracy* (1998).

E. J. Hobsbawm, *The Age of Capital, 1848–1875* (1976).

Steven L. Hoch, *Serfdom and Social Control in Russia: Petrovskoe, a Village in Tambov* (1986).

Michael Howard, *The Franco-Prussian War: The German Invasion of France, 1870–1871* (1981).

Paula Hyman, *From Dreyfus to Vichy: The Remaking of French Jewry, 1906–1939* (1979).

William Irvine, *The Boulanger Affair Reconsidered: Royalism, Boulangism, and the Origins of the Radical Right in France* (1989).

Gareth Stedman Jones, *Languages of Class: Studies in English Working Class History, 1832–1982* (1983).

James F. McMillan, *Napoleon III* (1991).

Roger Price, *The French Second Empire: An Anatomy of Political Power* (2001).

Norman Rich, *The Age of Nationalism and Reform, 1850–1890* (1970).

Séamas Ó Síocháin, *Roger Casement: Imperialist, Rebel, Revolutionary* (2008).

Alan Sked, *The Decline and Fall of the Habsburg Empire* (1989).

F. M. L. Thompson, *The Rise of Respectable Society, 1830–1900* (1986).

Robert Tombs, *The War against Paris, 1871* (1981).

Martha Vicinus, *Suffer and Be Still: Women in the Victorian Age* (1973).

Eugen Weber, *Peasants into Frenchmen: The Modernization of Rural France, 1870–1914* (1986).

G. M. Young, *Portrait of an Age: Victorian England* (1980).

Reginald E. Zelnick, *Labor and Society in Tsarist Russia: The Factory Workers of St. Petersburg, 1855–1870* (1971).

CHAPTER 19. RAPID INDUSTRIALIZATION AND ITS CHALLENGES, 1870–1914

Lenard Berlanstein, ed., *Rethinking Labor History* (1993).

David Blackbourn, *Margingen: Apparitions of the Virgin Mary in Bismarckian Germany* (1993).

Alain Corbin, *Women for Hire: Prostitution and Sexuality in France after 1850* (1990).

Michael Freeman, *Railways and the Victorian Imagination* (1999).

Nancy Green, *The Pletzl of Paris: Jewish Immigrant Workers in the Belle Époque* (1986).

Ruth Harris, *Lourdes: Body and Spirit in the Secular Age* (1999).

Stephen Heathorn, *For Home, Country, and Race: Constructing Gender, Class, and Englishness in the Elementary School, 1880–1914* (2000).

David P. Jordan, *Transforming Paris: The Life and Labors of Baron Haussmann* (1995).

Thomas A. Kselman, *Miracles and Prophecies in Nineteenth-Century France* (1983).

Thomas Laqueur, *Religion and Respectability: Sunday Schools and Working-Class Culture, 1780–1850* (1976).

William C. Lubenow, *Parliamentary Politics and the Home Rule Crisis* (1988).

John Lukacs, *Budapest, 1900: A Historical Portrait of a City and Its Culture* (1988).

Mary Jo Maynes, *Taking the Hard Road: Life Course in French and German Workers' Autobiographies in the Era of Industrialization* (1995).

Patricia M. Mazón, *Gender and the Modern Research University: The Admission of Women to German Higher Education, 1865–1914* (2003).

Patrick McDevitt, *May the Best Man Win: Sport, Masculinity, and Nationalism in Great Britain and the Empire, 1880–1935* (2004).

Michael B. Miller, *The Bon Marché: Bourgeois Culture and the Department Store, 1869–1920* (1981).

Alan S. Milward and S. B. Saul, *The Development of the Economies of Continental Europe, 1850–1914* (1977).

Leslie Moch, *Moving Europeans: Migration in Western Europe since 1650* (1993).

Donald Reid, *Paris Sewers and Sewermen: Realities and Representations* (1991).

Jonathan Schneer, *London, 1900: The Imperial Metropolis* (1999).

Bonnie G. Smith, *Ladies of the Leisure Class: The Bourgeoises of Northern France in the Nineteenth Century* (1982).

Gareth Stedman Jones, *Outcast London: A Study in the Relations between Classes in Victorian Society* (1992).

Judith R. Walkowitz, *City of Dreadful Delight* (1992).

———, *Prostitution and Victorian Society: Women, Class, and the State* (1983).

CHAPTER 20. POLITICAL AND CULTURAL RESPONSES TO A RAPIDLY CHANGING WORLD

Steven E. Aschheim, *The Nietzsche Legacy in Germany, 1890–1990* (1992).

Philipp Blom, *The Vertigo Years* (2008).

Peter Gay, *Freud: A Life for Our Time* (1988).

———, *Modernism: The Lure of Heresy, from Baudelaire to Beckett and Beyond* (2008).

Ruth Gay, *The Jews of Germany: A Historical Portrait* (1992).

Steven C. Hause and Anne R. Kenney, *Women's Suffrage and Social Politics in the French Third Republic* (1984).

James Joll, *The Anarchists* (1981).

John Merriman, *The Dynamite Club: How a Bombing in Fin-de-Siècle Paris Ignited the Age of Modern Terror* (2009).

———, *The Red City: Limoges and the French Nineteenth Century* (1991).

Peter G. Pulzer, *The Rise of Political Anti-Semitism in Germany and Austria* (1988).

Charles Rearick, *Pleasures of the Belle Époque* (1985).

Carl E. Schorske, *Fin-de-Siècle Vienna: Politics and Culture* (1980).

Roger Shattuck, *The Banquet Years: The Origins of the Avant-Garde in France 1885 to World War I* (1988).

Debora L. Silverman, *Art Nouveau in Fin-de-Siècle France: Politics, Psychology, and Style* (1989).

Mikulás Teich and Roy Porter, eds., *Fin-de-Siècle and Its Legacy* (1990).

Eugen Weber, *France, Fin-de-Siècle* (1986).

CHAPTER 21. THE AGE OF EUROPEAN IMPERIALISM

Imran Ali, *The Punjab under Imperialism* (1988).

W. Baumgart, *Imperialism: The Idea and Reality of British and French Colonial Expansion 1880–1914* (1982).

Henri Brunschwig, *French Colonialism, 1871–1914: Myths and Realities* (1966).

Antoinette Burton, *Burdens of History: British Feminists, Indian Women, and Imperial Culture, 1865–1915* (1994).

David Cannadine, *Ornamentalism: How the British Saw Their Empire* (2001).

Richard Drayton, *Nature's Government: Science, Imperial Britain and the "Improvement" of the World* (2000).

Adam Hochschild, *King Leopold's Ghost: A Story of Greed, Terror, and Heroism in Colonial Africa* (1998).

Alan Hodgart, *The Economics of European Imperialism* (1977).

Isabel V. Hull, *Absolute Destruction: Military Culture and the Practices of War in Imperial Germany* (2006).

Dane Kennedy, *Hill Stations and the British Raj* (1996).

———, *Islands of White: Settler Society and Culture in Kenya and South Rhodesia, 1890–1939* (1987).

Patricia M. E. Lorcin, *Imperial Identities: Stereotyping, Prejudice and Race in Colonial Algeria* (1995).

Timothy Mitchell, *Colonizing Egypt* (1988).

Bernard Porter, *The Lion's Share: A Short History of British Imperialism, 1850–1983* (1984).

Edward Said, *Orientalism* (1979).

Megan Vaughan, *Curing Their Ills: Colonial Power and African Illness* (1991).

Gwendolyn Wright, *The Politics of Design in French Colonial Urbanism* (1991).

CHAPTER 22. THE GREAT WAR

Stéphane Audoin-Rouzeau, *Men at War, 1914–1918: National Sentiment and Trench Journalism in France during the First World War* (1992).

Jean-Jacques Becker, *The Great War and the French People* (1985).

Margaret H. Darrow, *French Women and the First World War: War Stories of the Home Front* (2000).

Modris Eksteins, *Rites of Spring: The Great War and the Birth of the Modern Age* (1989).

Niall Ferguson, *The Pity of War: Explaining World War I* (1999).

Fritz Fischer, *Germany's Aims in The First World War* (1967).

Paul Fussel, *The Great War and Modern Memory* (1975).

Peter Gatrell, *A Whole Empire Walking: Refugees in Russia during World War I* (1999).

Martha Hanna, *Your Death Would Be Mine: Paul and Marie Pireaud in the Great War* (2006).

David G. Herrmann, *The Arming of Europe and the Making of the First World War* (1996).

Alistair Horne, *The Price of Glory: Verdun, 1916* (1963).

John Horne and Alan Kramer, *German Atrocities, 1914: A History of Denial* (2001).

Michael Howard, *The First World War* (2002).

Samuel Hynes, *A War Imagined: The First World War and English Culture* (1990).

James Joll, *The Origins of the First World War* (1992).

John Keegan, *The First World War* (1998).

George F. Kennan, *The Fateful Alliance: France, Russia, and the Coming of the First War* (1992).

Paul Kennedy, *The Rise of Anglo-German Antagonism, 1860–1914* (1980).

Alan Kramer, *Dynamic of Destruction: Culture and Mass Killing in the First World War* (2007).

Vejas G. Liulevicius, *War Land on the Eastern Front: Culture, National Identity and German Occupation in World War I* (2000).

Lyn Macdonald, *1915: The Death of Innocence* (1993).

———, *Somme* (1983).

Arthur Marwick, *The Deluge: British Society and the First World War* (1966).

———, *Women at War, 1914–1918* (1977).

Justin McCarthy, *The Ottoman People and the End of Empire* (2001).

Erich Maria Remarque, *All Quiet on the Western Front* (1929).

George Robb, *British Culture and the First World War* (2002).

Victor Rudenno, *Gallipoli: Attack from the Sea* (2008).

Gary Sheffield, *The Somme* (2003).

Kenneth Silver, *Esprit de Corps: Avant-Garde Art and the First World War in France* (1990).

Leonard V. Smith, *Between Mutiny and Obedience: The Case of the French Fifth Infantry Division during World War I* (1994).

Leonard V. Smith, Stéphane Audoin-Rouzeau, and Annette Becker, *France and the Great War* (2002).

Nigel Steel and Peter Hart, *Passchendaele: The Sacrificial Ground* (2000).

Norman Stone, *The Eastern Front, 1914–1917* (1998).

Mark Thompson, *The White War: Life and Death on the Italian Front, 1915–1919* (2008).

John W. Wheeler-Bennett, *Brest-Litovsk: The Forgotten Peace* (1971).

J. M. Winter, *The Great War and the British People* (1986).

———, *Sites of Memory, Sites of Mourning: The Great War in European Cultural History* (1995).

J. M. Winter and Jean-Louis Robert, *Capital Cities at War: Paris, London, Berlin, 1914–1919* (2 vols., 1997 and 2007).

CHAPTER 23. REVOLUTIONARY RUSSIA AND THE SOVIET UNION

Abraham Ascher, *The Revolution of 1905* (2 vols., 1992).

Paul Avrich, *Kronstadt, 1921* (1991).

Victoria E. Bonnell, *Roots of Rebellion: Workers' Politics and Organizations in St. Petersburg and Moscow, 1900–1914* (1983).

Orlando Figes, *Peasant Russia, Civil War* (1989).

——, *The Russian Revolution, 1917–1932* (1982).

Tsuyoshi Hasegawa, *The February Revolution: Petrograd, 1917* (1981).

Peter Holquist, *Making War, Forging Revolution: Russia's Continuum of Crisis, 1914–1921* (2002).

John L. H. Keep, *The Russian Revolution: A Study in Mass Mobilization* (1976).

Diane Koenker, *Moscow Workers and the 1917 Russian Revolution* (1982).

Stephen Kotkin, *Magnetic Mountain: Stalinism as a Civilization* (1995).

W. Bruce Lincoln, *Red Victory: A History of the Russian Civil War, 1918–1921* (1999).

Alexander Rabinowitch, *The Bolsheviks Come to Power: The Revolution of 1917 in Petrograd* (1978).

S. A. Smith, *Red Petrograd: Revolution in the Factories, 1917–1918* (1983).

Richard Stites, *Revolutionary Dreams: Utopian Vision and Experimental Life in the Russian Revolution* (1988).

CHAPTER 24. THE ELUSIVE SEARCH FOR STABILITY IN THE 1920s

Ivo Banac, *The National Question in Yugoslavia* (1985).

Manfred Franz Boemetie, Gerald D. Feldman, and Elizabeth Glaser, eds., *The Treaty of Versailles: A Reassessment after 75 Years* (1998).

Patrick Cohrs, *The Unfinished Peace after World War I: America, Britain, and the Stabilization of Europe, 1919–1932* (2008).

Victoria De Grazia, *How Fascism Ruled Women: Italy, 1922–1945* (1992).

Peter Gay, *My German Question: Growing Up in Nazi Berlin* (1998).

——, *Weimar Culture: The Outsider as Insider* (1968).

Robert Graves, *Goodbye to All That* (1960).

Robert Graves and Alan Hodge, *The Long Week-End: A Social History of Great Britain, 1918–1939* (1963).

Adrian Gregory, *A Silence of Memory: Armistice Day, 1919–1946* (1994).

Helmut Gruber, *Red Vienna: Experiments in Working-Class Culture, 1919–1934* (1991).

Pierre-Jakez Hélias, *The Horse of Pride: Life in a Breton Village* (1978).

Martin Kitchen, *Europe between the Wars: A Political History* (1988).

Richard F. Kuisel, *Capitalism and the State in Modern France* (1983).

Gregory M. Luebbert, *Liberalism, Fascism, or Social Democracy: Social Classes and the Political Origins of Regimes in Interwar Europe* (1991).

Charles Maier, *Recasting Bourgeois Europe: Stabilization in France, Germany, and Italy in the Decade after World War I* (1975).

Sally Marks, *The Illusion of Peace: Europe's International Relations, 1918–1933* (1976).

Walter A. McDougall, *France's Rhineland Diplomacy, 1914–1924* (1978).

Detlev J. K. Peukert, *The Weimar Republic* (1989).

Antony Polonsky, *Politics in Independent Poland 1921–1939: The Crisis of Constitutional Government* (1972).

Antoine Prost, *In the Wake of War: "Les Ancien Combattants" and French Society* (1992).

Joseph Rothschild, *East Central Europe between the Two World Wars* (1974).

Steven A. Schuker, *The End of French Predominance in Europe: The Financial Crisis of 1924 and the Adoption of the Dawes Plan* (1976).

Alan Sharp, *The Versailles Settlement: Peacemaking in Paris* (1991).

Daniel J. Sherman, *The Construction of Memory in Interwar France* (1999).

Dan P. Silverman, *Reconstructing Europe after the Great War* (1982).

Denis Mack Smith, *Italy and Its Monarchy* (1989).

A. J. P. Taylor, *English History, 1914–1945* (1965).

Mark Trachtenberg, *Reparation and World Politics* (1980).

Piotr Wandycz, *France and Her Eastern Allies, 1918–1925* (1985).

CHAPTER 25. THE EUROPE OF ECONOMIC DEPRESSION AND DICTATORSHIP

William Sheridan Allen, *The Nazi Seizure of Power: The Experience of a Single German Town, 1922–1945* (1984).

P. M. H. Bell, *The Origins of the Second World War* (1986).

Richard Bessel, ed., *Life in the Third Reich* (1987).

R. J. B. Bosworth, *The Italian Dictatorship: Problems and Perspectives in the Interpretation of Mussolini and Fascism* (1998).

Karl Dietrich Bracher, *The German Dictatorship: The Origins, Structure, and Effects of National Socialism* (1970).

Gerald Brenan, *The Spanish Labyrinth: An Account of the Social and Political Background of the Civil War* (2001).

Robert Conquest, *The Great Terror: A Reassessment* (1990).

Richard J. Evans, *The Coming of the Third Reich* (2003).

———, *The Third Reich in Power* (2005).

Orlando Figes, *The Whisperers: Private Life in Stalin's Russia* (2007).

Sheila Fitzpatrick, *Everyday Stalinism: Ordinary Life in Extraordinary Times: Soviet Russia in the 1930s* (1999).

Robert Gellately, *Backing Hitler: Consent and Coercion in Nazi Germany* (2001).

Geoffrey Hosking, *The First Socialist Society: A History of the Soviet Union from Within* (1993).

Gabriel Jackson, *The Spanish Republic and the Civil War, 1931–1939* (1974).

Julian Jackson, *The Popular Front in France: Defending Democracy, 1934–1938* (1988).

Eric A. Johnson, *Nazi Terror: The Gestapo, Jews, and Ordinary Germans* (1999).

Ian Kershaw, *Hitler* (2 vols., 1999–2000).

———, *The "Hitler Myth": Image and Reality in the Third Reich* (1991).

Charles Kindleberger, *The World in Depression, 1929–1939* (1986).

MacGregor Knox, *Common Destiny: Dictatorship, Foreign Policy and War in Fascist Italy and Nazi Germany* (2000).

Rudy Koshar, *Social Life, Local Politics, and Nazism: Marburg, 1880–1935* (1986).

David Clay Large, *Between Two Fires: Europe's Path in the 1930s* (1990).

George Mosse, *Fascist Revolution: Toward a General Theory of Fascism* (1999).

George Orwell, *Homage to Catalonia* (1980).

Detlev J. K. Peukert, *Inside Nazi Germany: Conformity, Opposition, and Racism in Everyday Life* (1987).

Anthony Read and David Fisher, *The Deadly Embrace: Hitler, Stalin and the Nazi-Soviet Pact, 1939–1941* (1989).

Joachim Remak, *The Origins of the Second World War* (1979).

Denis Mack Smith, *Mussolini: A Biography* (1983).

Robert Soucy, *Fascism in France: The First Wave, 1924–1933* (1986).

———, *Fascism in France: The Second Wave, 1933–1939* (1995).

Fritz Stern, *The Politics of Cultural Despair: A Study in the Use of the Germanic Ideology* (1974).

Hugh Thomas, *The Spanish Civil War* (2001).

Adam Tooze, *The Wages of Destruction: The Making and Unmaking of the Nazi Economy* (2006).

Henry A. Turner, Jr., *German Big Business and the Rise of Hitler* (1985).

———, *Hitler: Thirty Days to Power* (1996).

Gerhard L. Weinberg, *The Foreign Policy of Hitler's Germany: Diplomatic Revolution in Europe, 1933–1936* (1970).

———, *Starting World War II, 1937–1939* (1980).

Susan Zuccotti, *Under His Very Windows: The Vatican and the Holocaust* (2002).

CHAPTER 26. WORLD WAR II

Omer Bartov, *Hitler's Army: Soldiers, Nazis, and War in the Third Reich* (1992).

Anthony Beevor, *Stalingrad* (1998).

Marc Bloch, *Strange Defeat* (1968).

Norman Davies, *No Single Victory: World War II in Europe, 1939–1945* (2006).

Richard J. Evans, *The Third Reich at War, 1939–1945* (2008).

Sarah Farmer, *Martyred Village: Commemorating the 1944 Massacre at Oradour-sur-Glane* (1999).

Paul Fussell, *Wartime: Understanding and Behavior in the Second World War* (1989).

Robert Gellately, *Backing Hitler: Consent and Coercion in Nazi Germany* (2001).

Jan Tomasz Gross, *Neighbors: The Destruction of the Jewish Community in Jedwabne, Poland* (2001).

Raul Hilberg, *Perpetrators, Victims, Bystanders: The Jewish Catastrophe, 1933–1945* (1992).

Peter Hoffmann, *The History of the German Resistance, 1933–1945* (1977).

Julian Jackson, *France: The Dark Years, 1940–1944* (2002).

Eric T. Jennings, *Vichy in the Tropics: Pétain's National Revolution in Madagascar, Guadaloupe, and Indochina, 1940–1944* (2001).

H. R. Kedward, *In Search of the Maquis: Rural Resistance in Southern France, 1942–1944* (1993).

John Keegan, *The Second World War* (1989).

———, *Six Armies in Normandy* (1982).

Martin Kolinsky, *Britain's War in the Middle East: Strategy and Diplomacy, 1936–1942* (1999).

Walter Laqueur, *The Terrible Secret: Suppression of the Truth about Hitler's "Final Solution"* (1980).

David Clay Large, *And the World Closed Its Doors: One Family's Struggle to Escape the Holocaust* (2003).

Michael Marrus, *The Holocaust in History* (1988).

Arthur Marwick, *The Home Front: The British and the Second World War* (1977).

Ernest R. May, *Strange Victory: Hitler's Conquest of France* (2000).

Mark Mazower, *Hitler's Europe: How the Nazis Ruled Europe* (2008).

———, *Inside Hitler's Greece: The Experience of Occupation, 1941–1944* (1993).

Alan S. Milward, *War, Economy, and Society, 1939–1945* (1977).

Robert O. Paxton, *Vichy France: Old Guard and New Order, 1940–1944* (1972).

Robert O. Paxton and Michael R. Marrus, *Vichy France and the Jews* (1981).

Lyn Smith, *Remembering: Voices of the Holocaust* (2005).

Jonathan Steinberg, *The Axis and the Holocaust, 1941–1943* (1990).

John F. Sweets, *Choices in Vichy France* (1986).

Donald Cameron Watt, *How War Came* (1989).

Gerhard L. Weinberg, *A World at War: A Global History of World War II* (1994).

CHAPTER 27. REBUILDING DIVIDED EUROPE

Paul Ginsborg, *A History of Contemporary Italy: Society and Politics, 1943–1988* (1990).

Stanley Hoffmann, *Decline or Renewal? France since the Popular Front: Government and the People, 1936–1986* (1988).

Michael J. Hogan, *The Marshall Plan: America, Britain and the Reconstruction of Western Europe, 1947–1952* (1987).

George F. Kennan, *The Nuclear Delusion: Soviet-American Relations in the Atomic Age* (1983).

Paul Kennedy, *The Parliament of Man: The Past, Present, and Future of the United Nations* (2006).

Lothar Kettenacher, *Germany since 1945* (1997).

Richard Kuisel, *Seducing the French: The Dilemma of Americanization* (1993).

Bruce R. Kuniholm, *The Origins of the Cold War in the Near East: Great Power Conflict and Diplomacy in Iran, Turkey, and Greece* (1994).

Andrew Marr, *A History of Modern Britain* (2007).

Arthur Marwick, *British Society since 1945* (1982).

Vojtech Mastny, *Helsinki, Human Rights, and European Security* (1986).

Alan S. Milward, *The European Rescue of the Nation-State* (1992).

———, *The Reconstruction of Western Europe, 1945–1951* (1984).

Kenneth O. Morgan, *Labour in Power, 1945–1951* (1984).

———, *The People's Peace: British History, 1945–1990* (1991).

Norman M. Naimark, *A History of the Soviet Zone of Occupation, 1945–1949* (1995).

Robert A. Pollard, *Economic Security and the Origins of the Cold War* (1985).

Paul Preston, *Franco: A Biography* (1993).

Henry Rousso, *Vichy Syndrome: History and Memory in France since 1944* (1991).

Haig Simonian, *The Privileged Partnership: Franco-German Relations in the European Community, 1969–1984* (1985).

William Taubman, *Khrushchev: The Man and His Era* (2003).
Henry A. Turner, Jr., *Germany from Partition to Reunification* (1992).

CHAPTER 28. THE COLD WAR AND THE END OF EUROPEAN EMPIRES

David Anderson, *Histories of the Hanged: The Dirty War in Kenya and the End of Empire* (2005).
Franz Ansprenger, *The Dissolution of Colonial Empires* (1989).
P. J. Cain and A. G. Hopkins, *British Imperialism: Crisis and Deconstruction, 1914–1990* (1993).
Muriel Evelyn Chamberlain, *Decolonization: The Fall of the European Empires* (1985).
Matthew Connelly, *A Diplomatic Revolution: Algeria's Fight for Independence and the Origins of the Post–Cold War Era* (2002).
Jacques Dalloz, *The War in Indochina* (1990).
Caroline Elkins, *Imperial Reckoning: The Untold Story of Britain's Gulag in Kenya* (2005).
Prosser Gifford and William Roger Louis, eds., *Decolonization and African Independence: The Transfers of Power, 1960–1980* (1988).
John D. Hargeaves, *Decolonization in Africa* (1988).
Alistair Horne, *A Savage War of Peace: Algeria, 1954–1962* (1978).
Bruce R. Kuniholm, *The Origins of the Cold War in the Near East: Great Power Conflict and Diplomacy in Iran, Turkey, and Greece* (1994).
Robert J. Lieber, *Oil and the Middle East: Europe in the Energy Crisis* (1976).

CHAPTER 29. TRANSITIONS TO DEMOCRACY AND THE COLLAPSE OF COMMUNISM

Paul Arthur and Keith Jeffery, *Northern Ireland since 1968* (1988).
Timothy Garton Ash, *In Europe's Name: Germany and the Divided Continent* (1993).
———, *The Polish Revolution: Solidarity, 1980–1982* (1983).
Ivo Banac, *Eastern Europe in Revolution* (1992).
Corelli Barnett, *The Pride and the Fall: The Dream and Illusion of Britain as a Great Nation* (1987).
Serge Berstein, *The Republic of De Gaulle, 1958–1969* (1993).
George W. Breslauer, *Gorbachev and Yeltsin as Leaders* (2002).
David Caute, *The Year of Barricades: A Journey through 1968* (1989).
David Childs, *Britain since 1945* (2001).
Robert Darnton, *Berlin Journal: 1989–1990* (1991).
Karen Dawisha and Bruce Parrott, *Russia and the New States of Eurasia: The Politics of Upheaval* (1994).
Milovan Djilas, *Fall of the New Class: A History of Communism's Self-Destruction*, ed., Vasilije Kalezić (1998).
Milovan Djilas, *The New Class: An Analysis of the Communist System* (1957).
Paul Ginsborg, *Italy and Its Discontents: Family, Civil Society, State 1980–2001* (2001).
Václav Havel, *Art of the Impossible: Politics as Morality in Practice: Speeches and Writings, 1990–1996* (1997).

Václav Havel, et al., *Power of the Powerless: Citizens against the State in Central-Eastern Europe* (1985).

Robert O. Keohane, Joseph S. Nye, and Stanley Hoffmann, *Europe after the Cold War* (1993).

Stephen Kotkin, *Armageddon Averted: The Soviet Collapse, 1970–2000* (2001).

David Kynaston, *Austerity Britain, 1945–1951* (2008).

Walter Laqueur, *Europe since Hitler* (1983).

Carol Skalnick Leff, *The Czech and Slovak Republics: Nation versus State* (1997).

Paul Lendvai, *One Day That Shook the Communist World: The 1956 Hungarian Revolution and Its Legacy* (2008).

Anatol Lieven, *The Baltic Revolution: Estonia, Latvia, Lithuania and the Path to Independence* (1999).

Martin E. Malia, *The Soviet Tragedy: A History of Socialism in Russia, 1917–1991* (1993).

Kenneth Maxwell, *The Making of Portuguese Democracy* (1995).

Paul Preston, *Franco: A Biography* (1993).

———, *The Triumph of Democracy in Spain* (1986).

Peter Riddell, *The Thatcher Era and Its Legacy* (1991).

Joseph Rothschild and Nancy Wingfield, *Return to Diversity: A Political History of East Central Europe since World War II* (2006).

Alan Sked and Chris Cook, *Postwar Britain: A Political History* (1990).

Gale Stohes, *The Walls Came Tumbling Down* (1993).

Ronald Grigor Suny, *The Revenge of the Past: Nationalism, Revolution, and the Collapse of the Soviet Union* (1993).

George Weigel, *The Final Revolution: The Breaking of Communist Europe* (1991).

CHAPTER 30. GLOBAL CHALLENGES: "FORTRESS EUROPE," EUROPEAN COOPERATION, AND THE UNCERTAINTIES OF A NEW AGE

Martin Baldwin-Edwards and Martin A. Schain, eds., *The Politics of Immigration in Western Europe* (1994).

Rogers Brubaker, *Citizenship and Nationhood in France and Germany* (1992).

Desmond Dinan, *Ever Closer Union? An Introduction to the European Community* (1994).

François Gaspard, *A Small City in France* (1995).

Daniel Gros and Niels Thygesen, *European Monetary Integration* (1992).

Alec G. Hargraves, *Immigration, Race, and Ethnicity in Contemporary France* (1995).

Bernard Lewis, *Islam and the West* (1993).

Barbara Marshall, *The New Germany and Migration in Europe* (2000).

Jorgen Nielsen, *Muslims in Western Europe* (1992).

John Pinder, *The Building of the European Union* (1998).

Larry Siedentop, *Democracy in Europe* (2001).

Derek Urwin, *The Community of Europe: A History of European Integration since 1945* (1995).

John Wrench and John Solomos, eds., *Racism and Migration in Western Europe* (1993).

CREDITS

Frontispiece: The Art Archive/Corbis.

Part One (p. xxvi) National Gallery of London; **Part Two (p. 162)** © National Portrait Gallery, London; **Part Three (p. 284)** Lebrecht Music and Arts Photo Library/Alamy; **Part Four (p. 432)** Bildarchiv Preussischer Kulturbesitz, Berlin/Art Resource, NY; **Part Five (p. 644)** Private Collection/The Bridgeman Art Library; **Part Six (p. 860)** Bettmann/Corbis; **Part Seven (p. 1104)** AP Photo

Chapter 1: p. 4 (left) Staaliche Museen Preussicher Kulturbesitz; **p. 4 (right)** Ampliciones y Repoducciones MAS, Barcelona; **p. 9 (left)** Giraudon/Art Resource, NY; **p. 9 (middle)** Giraudon/Art Resource, NY; **p. 9 (right)** Giraudon/Art Resource, NY; **p. 12** Juniano Majo from De Majestate, Art Archive/Bibliothèque Nationale Paris/Dagli Orti; **p. 14** Erich Lessing / Art Resource, NY; **p. 15** Hans Wertinger, 1530, Germanisches Nationalmuseum, Nürnberg; **p. 17** Museum of Fine Arts, Houston, Texas, USA / Museum purchase with funds from The Brown Foundation, Inc. / The Bridgeman Art Library; **p. 22** Gerini Niccolo' di Pietro, Storie di S. Matteo (Banchieri) Scala/Art Resource, NY; **p. 23** Hulton-Deutsch Collection/Corbis; **p. 28** Mansell/Time & Life Pictures/Getty Images; **p. 31** Print Collection, Miriam and Ira D. Wallach Division of Art, Prints & Photographs, The New York Public Library, Astor, Lenox, and Tilden Foundations; **p. 36** Kobe Museum, Japan; **p. 39** Bettmann/Corbis

Chapter 2: p. 45 Scala/Art Resource, NY; **p. 47** Hulton Archive/Getty Images; **p. 52** Scala/Art Resource, NY; **p. 54** Palazzo Vecchio, Florence, Soprintendenza alle Gallerie, Florence; **p. 57** Oeffentliche Kuntstsammlung, Basel, Kunstmuseum, Inv. 311; **p. 60** Alinari/Art Resource, NY; **p. 64** Alinari/Art Resource, NY; **p. 65** Bildarchiv Preussischer Kulturbesitz / Art Resource, NY; **p. 67** Alinari Archives/Corbis; **p. 68** Alinari/Art Resource, NY; **p. 69** Alinari/Art Resource, NY; **p. 71** Nic Cleave Photography / Alamy; **p. 72** Alinari/Art Resource, NY; **p. 76** Gustavo Tomsich/Corbis; **p. 77** Scala/Art Resource, NY

Chapter 3: p. 81 (left) Scala/Art Resource, NY; **p. 81 (right)** woodcut from the series Passional Christi und Antichrist, Wittenberg, 1521; **p. 83** Blauel/Gnamm/Artothek; **p. 85** Lauros/Giraudon/Art Resource, NY; **p. 89** Archivo Iconografico, S.A./Corbis; **p. 93** Foto Marbug/Art Resource, NY; **p. 99** Kunstsammlungen der Veste, Coberg; **p. 104 (left)** Bettmann/Corbis; **p. 104 (right)** Illustration from Chronique de Stumpffen by Johan Stumf, Zurich, 1548; **p. 108 (left)** Bibliothèque Publique et Universitaire, Genève, Photograph by François Martin; **p. 108 (right)** Erich Lessing / Art Resource, NY; **p. 112 (left)** © National Portrait Gallery, London; **p. 112 (right)** Lauros-Giraudon/Art Resource, NY; **p. 113** Copyright The Frick Collection, New York; **p. 118** © Rijksmuseum-Stichting, Amsterdam; **p. 120** FotoMarburg/Art Resource, NY; **p. 123** Alinari/Art Resource, NY

Chapter 4: p. 128 Alinari/Art Resource, NY; **p. 130** Alinari/Art Resource, NY; **p. 133** Collection Musée Cantonal des Beaux-Arts, Lausanne, Switzerland; **p. 136** © cliché Bibliothèque Nationale de France, Paris; **p. 140** Réunion des Musées Nationaux/Art Resource, NY; **p. 142** The Art Archive / Musée Carnavalet Paris / Gianni Dagli Orti; **p. 145** Giraudon/Art Resource, NY; **p. 148** Bettmann/Corbis; **p. 153** Königliches Schlo , Kungl, Husgerlidekammaren, The Royal Collection, Stockholm; **p. 155** Fotomas Index

Deutsch Collection/Corbis; **p. 406** The Print Collector / Alamy; **p. 413 (left)** The Bridgeman Art Library; **p. 413 (right)** Stock Montage, Chicago; **p. 416** Courtesy of The New-York Historical Society, NYC; **p. 418** Réunion des Musées Nationaux/Art Resource, NY; **p. 422 (left)** Chateau de Versailles, France, The Bridgeman Art Library; **p. 422 (right)** Chateau de Versailles, France, The Bridgeman Art Gallery; **p. 426** Giraudon/Art Resource, NY

Chapter 12: p. 439 (left) Musée Carnavalet, Photographie Bulloz; **p. 439 (right)** Versailles Museum, Photographie Bulloz; **p. 443 (left)** Musée Carnavalet, Photographie Bulloz; **p. 443 (right)** Abbé Sieyès, Photographie Bulloz; **p. 444** Bibliothèque Nationale; **p. 446** Giraudon/Art Resource, NY; **p. 450** Giraudon/Art Resource, NY; **p. 454** Trustees of the British Museum; **p. 455** © cliché Bibliothèque Nationale de France, Paris; **p. 456** © cliché Bibliothèque Nationale de France, Paris; **p. 457 (left)** Classic Image / Alamy; **p. 457 (right)** Mansell/Time Life Pictures/Getty Images; **p. 459 (left)** Bridgeman-Giraudon / Art Resource, NY; **p. 459 (right)** Tate Gallery, London/Art Resource, NY; **p. 461** Photographie Bulloz; **p. 463** © cliché Bibliothèque Nationale de France, Paris; **p. 466** Photographie Bulloz; **p. 468** Hulton-Deutsch Collection/Corbis; **p. 472** © cliché Bibliothèque Nationale de France, Paris; **p. 475** The Trustees of the British Museum

Chapter 13: p. 480 Giraudon/Art Resource, NY; **p. 484** Bettmann/Corbis; **p. 487** Giraudon/Art Resource, NY; **p. 489** Stapleton Collection/Corbis; **p. 492** Patrick Lorette/Bridgeman Art Library; **p. 494** Alinari/Art Resource, NY; **p. 499** Print collection, The New York Public Library, Astor, Lenox, and Tilden Foundations; **p. 501** Alinari/Art Resource, NY; **p. 506** Bavarian Army Museum, Munich; **p. 507 (left)** National Gallery, London; **p. 507 (right)** Gianni Dagli Orti/Corbis; **p. 508** Warder Collection; **p. 510** Mary Evans Picture Library / Alamy

Chapter 14: p. 514 Lauros/Giraudon/Bridgeman Art Library; **p. 521** Mary Evans Picture Library; **p. 523** Collection David Artis; **p. 527** The Manchester Public Libraries; **p. 528** The Art Archive/Bibliothèque des Arts Décoratifs Paris/Dagli Orti; **p. 533** Martin Buhler/Oeffentliche Kunstsammlung, Basel; **p. 534** Osterreichische Galerie, Wien; **p. 536** Private Collection; **p. 539** Statens Museum fur Kunst, Copenhagen; **p. 540** Warder Collection; **p. 542** Courtesy Museum of Fine Arts, Boston; **p. 544** Graphische Sammlung Albertina; **p. 545** The Granger Collection, NY; **p. 548** British Library; **p. 552** Snark/Art Resource, NY; **p. 555** The Granger Collection, NY; **p. 557** Hulton Archive/Getty Images; **p. 558** Hulton Archive/Getty Images; **p. 562** © cliché Bibliothèque Nationale de France, Paris; **p. 565** Mary Evans Picture Library; **p. 567** Musée Carnavalet, Photographie Bulloz

Chapter 15: p. 570 Historisches Museen der Stadt Wien; **p. 572** Hulton Archive/Getty Images; **p. 578** Adoc-photos / Art Resource, NY; **p. 584** Giraudon/Art Resource, NY; **p. 585** Bettmann/Corbis; **p. 587** Private Collection/Archives Charmet/The Bridgeman Art Library; **p. 589** Ludwig Burger, Wartburg Festival, Staatsbibliothek, Berlin, Bildarchiv, Preussischer Kulturbesits; **p. 590** Giraudon/Art Resource, NY; **p. 592** INTERFOTO Pressebildagentur / Alamy; **p. 595** Art Resource, NY; **p. 597** Erich Lessing/Art Resource, NY; **p. 598** Versailles Museum, Photographie Bulloz; **p. 602** Archives Charmet/Bridgeman Art Library; **p. 606** Trustees of the British Museum; **p. 610** © Her Majesty Queen Elizabeth II/Royal Collection Enterprises Ltd.; **p. 611** Bettmann/Corbis

Chapter 16: p. 616 © Bibliothèque Nationale de France, Paris; **p. 618** Warder Collection; **p. 620** Bettmann/Corbis; **p. 622** Museen der Stadt Wien; **p. 625** Giuseppe Mazzini, Istituto Mazziniano, Genoa; **p. 627** The Art Archive / JFB; **p. 629** Fotomas Index; **p. 633** Nationalbibliothek, Wien; **p. 635** Mary Evans Picture Library/Alamy; **p. 637** Trustees of the British Museum; **p. 639** Roger-Viollet; **p. 641** Fotomas Index

Chapter 17: p. 651 (left) Bilderienst Süddeutscher Verlag, München; **p. 652 (right)** Roger-Viollet; **p. 654** Collection Bertarelli, Archivio Fotografico, Milan, Photo by Saporetti; **p. 656** Alinari/Art Resource, NY; **p. 662** Bettmann/Corbis; **p. 666** Ullstein Bilderienst; **p. 669** Lauros-Giraudon/Art Resource, NY; **p. 670** Trustees of the British Museum; **p. 671** Caricature of Bismark and Pope Leo XIII from Kladderadatsch, 1875, Staatsbibliothek, Berlin, Photo courtesy of Bildarchiv Preussischer Kilturbesitz; **p. 672** Bettmann/Corbis; **p. 676** Museen der Stadt Wien; **p. 678** Mary Evans Picture Library; **p. 681** © British Library

Chapter 18: p. 685 INTERFOTO Pressebildagentur / Alamy; p. 688 Fotomas Index; p. 692 (left) Hulton Archive/Getty Images; p. 692 (right) ©National Portrait Gallery, London; p. 694 (left) ©National Portrait Gallery, London; p. 694 (right) Warder Collection; p. 697 Barnaby's Picture Library; p. 702 (left) Hulton Archive/Getty Images; p. 702 (right) Hulton Archive/Getty Images; p. 707 Alexander Herzen, Sovphoto; p. 709 Warder Collection; p. 714 (left) Hulton-Deutsch Collection/Corbis; p. 714 (right) Bettmann/Corbis; p. 720 Hulton Archive/Getty Images; p. 722 Roger-Viollet; p. 724 Hulton-Deutsch Collection/Corbis; p. 727 (left) Corbis; p. 727 (right) Hulton Archive/Getty Images; p. 728 Bettmann/Corbis; p. 730 Erich Lessing, Art Resource, NY; p. 732 Photographie Bulloz; p. 733 The Print Collector / Alamy; p. 738 © cliché Bibliothèque Nationale de France, Paris; p. 739 (left) The Jewish Museum, NY; p. 739 (right) Alfred Dreyfus, Roger-Viollet

Chapter 19: p. 743 The Granger Collection, NY; p. 746 Musee d'Orsay, Paris, France / Giraudon / The Bridgeman Art Library; p. 748 © cliché Bibliothèque National de France, Paris; p. 754 © 1914 Ford Motor Co.; p. 755 Photoworld/FGP; p. 756 (left) Popperfoto/Getty Images; p. 756 (right) Cambridge University Library, Rutherford Collection, courtesy AIP Emilio Segrè Visual Archives; p. 757 The Hebrew University of Jerusalem; p. 761 Bettmann/Corbis; p. 764 Warder Collection; p. 765 Musee Toulouse-Lautrec, Albi, France, The Bridgeman Art Library; p. 767 (left) Mansell/Time Life Pictures/Getty Images; p. 767 (right) © cliche Bibliotheque Nationale, Paris; p. 768 Photographie Bulloz; p. 769 Archives Nationales, C.R.D.P. de Paris, © B.H.V.P.; p. 773 Hulton-Deutsch Collection/Corbis; p. 776 Hulton-Deutsch Collection/Corbis; p. 777 Bettmann/Corbis; p. 779 Bettmann/Corbis; p. 781 Hulton-Deutsch Collection/Corbis

Chapter 20: p. 786 Warder Collection; p. 789 Hulton-Deutsch Collection/Corbis; p. 794 (left) Photos12.com-Oasis; p. 794 (right) Houghton Library, Harvard University; p. 797 Mansell/Time Life Pictures/Getty Images; p. 799 Photos12.com-ARJ; p. 800 JThe Louvre, Paris, Gift of Mme. Pommery, photo courtesy of Musées Nationaux, Photographie Bulloz; p. 801 Lauros-Giraudon/Art Resource, NY; p. 803 Erich Lessing/Art Resource, NY; p. 804 Giraudon/Art Resource, NY; p. 806 Archives Charmet/Bridgeman Art Library; p. 807 Bettmann/Corbis; p. 809 Bettmann/Corbis; p. 811 Warder Collection; p. 814 © The Art Institute of Chicago, Helen Birch Bartlett; p. 815 (right) Ampliaciones y Reprocciones MAS, Barcelona; p. 815 (left) Cameraphoto Venezia/Art Resource, NY; p. 816 (left) © cliché Réunion des Musées Nationales, Paris; p. 816 (right) Museum of Modern Art, Lillie P. Bliss Bequest, © 1996 Museum of Modern Art, NY/ARS, NY

Chapter 21: p. 820 Illustrated London News Ltd/Mary Evans; p. 822 The Granger Collection, NY; p. 827 Hulton-Deutsch Collection/Corbis; p. 829 (left) Warder Collection; p. 829 (right) Warder Collection; p. 831 Mansell/Time Life Pictures/Getty Images; p. 834 (left) Corbis; p. 834 (right) Bettmann/Corbis; p. 837 Warder Collection; p. 838 (left) Victoria & Albert Museum/Art Resource, NY; p. 838 (right) Mansell/Time Life Pictures/Getty Images; p. 841 Bettmann/Corbis; p. 843 © British Library; p. 846 India Office Library; p. 849 Illustrated London News Ltd/Mary Evans; p. 853 © National Portrait Gallery, London; p. 856 Library of Congress, Prints and Photographs Division, Frank and Frances Carpenter Collection,

Chapter 22: p. 864 Snark / Art Resource, NY; p. 865 (left) Warder Collection; p. 865 (right) Hulton-Deutsch Collection/Corbis; p. 869 Mary Evans Picture Library; p. 873 INTERFOTO Pressebildagentur / Alamy; p. 877 The Granger Collection, NY; p. 881 Mansell/Time Life Pictures/Getty Images; p. 882 Bettmann/Corbis; p. 889 (left) Warder Collection; p. 889 (right) Hulton-Deutsch Collection/Corbis; p. 890 Imperial War Museum; p. 894 Imperial War Museum; p. 895 (left) Roger-Viollet; p. 895 (right) National Archives; p. 896 Warder Collection; p. 898 © Canadian War Museum. No. 19720028-006; p. 903 Hulton-Deutsch Collection/Corbis; p. 908 Hulton-Deutsch Collection/Corbis; p. 910 © Canadian War Museum. No. 19910238-758; p. 913 Ullstein Bilderdienst; p. 915 (left) © Canadian War Museum. No. 19810692-003; p. 915 (right) Hulton-Deutsch Collection/Corbis; p. 925 Photos12.com-Oasis

Chapter 23: p. 929 Popperfoto; p. 930 Warder Collection; p. 933 Bettmann/Corbis; p. 934 Alexander Meledin/Mary Evans Picture Library; p. 937 Sovfoto; p. 942 Warder Collection; p. 947 Warder Collection; p. 949 Bettmann/Corbis; p. 954 Photoworld/FPG

INDEX

Page numbers in *italics* refer to illustrations.